THE

# HISTORY

OF THE

# DISCOVERY AND SETTLEMENT

OF

# AMERICA.

BY WILLIAM ROBERTSON, D.D.,

PRINCIPAL OF THE UNIVERSITY AT EDINBURGH, ETC.

WITH AN ACCOUNT OF HIS LIFE AND WRITINGS.

TO WHICH ARE ADDED

QUESTIONS FOR THE EXAMINATION OF STUDENTS,

BY JOHN FROST, LL.D.

Complete in One Volume.

NEW YORK:

DERBY & JACKSON, 119 NASSAU STREET.

CINCINNATI:—H. W. DERBY.

1856.

THE

# LIFE OF DR. WM. ROBERTSON.

---

WILLIAM ROBERTSON, the eldest son of the Reverend William Robertson, was born on the 8th of September, 1721, at Borthwick, in the shire of Mid Lothian, of which parish his father was the minister. By the paternal line he descended from a respectable family in the county of Fife, a branch of that which, for many generations, possessed the estate of Struan, in Perthshire. His mother was the daughter of David Pitcairn, esq. of Dreghorn. He had one brother and six sisters; all of whom were well settled in life, and most of whom lived to an advanced age.

It was at the parochial school of Borthwick that Robertson received the initiatory part of his education; but as soon as he was sufficiently forward to enter on the study of the learned languages, he was removed to the school of Dalkeith. The latter seminary was then under the superintendence of Mr. Leslie, whose eminence as a teacher was such as to attract pupils from all parts of Scotland; and the father of Robertson was consequently induced to send him to Dalkeith rather than to the Scottish metropolis.

When the future historian was twelve years old, his father was transferred from Borthwick to one of the churches of Edinburgh. In the autumn of 1733 he joined his parents; and, in October, he was admitted into the college and university of the northern capital.

Whatever were his first attempts at composition, and it is probable they were many, nothing has been preserved to show how early he began to exercise his talents, or with what degree of rapidity those talents were expanded. It is certain, however, that in the pursuit of knowledge he displayed that ardour and perseverance without which nothing great will ever be accomplished. A strong proof of this is afforded by some of his early commonplace books, which bear the dates of 1735, 1736, and 1737. The motto, *vita sine literis mors est*, which he prefixed to these books, sufficiently indicates by what an honourable ambition and love of literature he was inspired at a very tender and generally thoughtless age. The boy of fourteen, who can cherish the feeling which is implied by this motto, gives promise that his manhood will reflect lustre on himself and on the country of his birth.

Among the men of eminence, by whose instructions he profited at the university, were sir John Pringle, afterwards president of the Royal Society, but then professor of moral philosophy; Maclaurin, justly celebrated for the extent of his mathematical skill and the purity of his style and Dr. Stevenson, the learned and indefatigable professor of logic. To the masterly prelections of the latter, especially to his illustrations of the poetics of Aristotle, and of Longinus on the Sublime, Robertson often declared that he considered himself to be more deeply indebted than to any circumstance in the course of his academical career. It was indeed not towards the abstract sciences that the bent of his genius was directed. To mathematical and mechanical speculations he seems to have been at least cold, perhaps averse. Neither was he remarkable for metaphysical acuteness. His delight was to trace and elucidate moral and religious truths, to apply the process of reasoning to subjects more immediately connected with the every-day business of existence, to search into the causes and effects of historical events, to expatiate amidst the perennial beauties of classic lore, and, by meditating on the great models of oratorical art, to render himself master of all the powerful resources of a ready and persuasive eloquence.

With respect to eloquence, the possession of it was in fact indispensable to one who, as in all probability was the case with Robertson, had determined to assume a prominent station among the pastors and leaders of the Scottish church. The mere knowledge of rules, however, or even a thorough acquaintance with the rich stores of ancient and modern oratory, will not suffice to form an orator. It is by use alone that facility of speech and promptitude of reply can be acquired. It is the collision of minds which strikes out the "thoughts that breathe, and words that burn." During the last years, therefore, of his residing at college, he joined with some of his contemporaries in establishing a society, the avowed purpose of which, as we are told by Mr. Stewart, was "to cultivate the study of elocution, and to prepare themselves, by the habits of extemporary discussion and debate, for conducting the business of popular assemblies."

Of the colleagues of Robertson in this society many ultimately rose, like himself, to high reputation. Among them were Cleghorn, subsequently professor of moral philosophy at Edinburgh, Dr. John Blair, who became a member of the Royal Society, and a prebendary of Westminster, and who gave to the public "The Chronology and History of the World," Wilkie, the author of the Epigoniad, a faulty poem, but above contempt, Home, the author of Douglas, and Dr. Erskine, who, in after life, was at once the coadjutor, rival, opponent, and friend of Robertson.

This society continued in existence, and, no doubt, was beneficial to its members, till it was broken up by a quarrel, which had its rise from a religious source, and which, consequently, was of more than common bitterness. In 1741 that extraordinary man Whitefield, who was then in the zenith of his fame, paid a visit to Scotland, and his preaching excited in that country a feeling equally as strong as it had excited in England. On the subject of his merit violent parties immediately sprang up, especially among the clergy. By the one side he was considered as a clerical wonder, a kind of apostle, from whose evangelical labours the happiest result might be expected; by the other side he was calumniated as an impostor, and a worthless private character, while some, in the excess of their holy zeal, did not scruple to stigmatize him, even from the pulpit, as "an agent of the devil." It was natural that this question should be debated by Robertson and his associates; and it was, perhaps, not less natural that it should be argued with so much heat and asperity as not only to cause the dissolution of the society, but even, it is said, to interrupt, for some time, the intercourse of the members as private individuals. Of those who entertained doubts with regard to the personal conduct of Whitefield, and the utility of his efforts, Robertson was one. From his acknowledged moderation and evenness of temper we may, however, infer that his hostility to the preacher was carried on in a liberal spirit, and that he did not think it either necessary or decorous to brand him as an agent of the prince of darkness.

To excel in his written style as much as in his oral was one object of his ambition. The practice of clothing in an English dress the standard works of the ancients has been often recommended, as conducive to the improvement of style; and he seems to have believed it to be so, for it was adopted by him. He carried it so far as to entertain serious thoughts of preparing for the press a version of Marcus Antoninus. His scheme was, however, frustrated by the appearance of an anonymous translation at Glasgow. "In making choice of this author," says Mr. Stewart, "he was probably not a little influenced by that partiality with which (among the writers of heathen moralists) he always regarded the remains of the stoical philosophy."

Having completed his academic course, and richly stored his mind, he quitted the university, and, in 1741, before he had quite attained the age of twenty, a license to preach the gospel was given to him by the presbytery of Dalkeith. This kind of license, which does not authorize to administer the sacraments or to undertake the cure of souls, is granted to laymen; and the person who receives it may be considered as being placed by it in a state of probation.

After the lapse of two years, from the period of his leaving the university, when he was yet little more than twenty-two, he was, in 1743, presented, by the Earl of Hopetoun, to the living of Gladsmuir. Of this preferment the yearly value was not more than one hundred pounds. Scanty, however, as were its emoluments, it was most opportunely bestowed. He had not long resided at Gladsmuir when an unexpected and melancholy event occurred, which put to the trial at once his firmness and his benevolence. His father and mother expired within a few hours of each other, leaving behind them a family of six daughters and one son, without the means of providing for their education and maintenance. On this occasion Robertson acted in a manner which bore irrefragable testimony to the goodness of his heart, and which was also, as Mr. Stewart justly observes, "strongly marked with that manly decision in his plans, and that persevering steadiness in their execution, which were the characteristic features of his mind." Regardless of the privations to which he must necessarily submit, and the interruption which his literary and other projects must experience, he received his father's family into his house at Gladsmuir, educated his sisters under his own roof, and retained them there till opportunities arose of settling them respectably in the world. His merit is enhanced by the circumstance of his fraternal affection having imposed on him a sacrifice far more painful than that of riches or fame. He was tenderly attached to his cousin Miss Mary Nesbit, daughter of the Reverend Mr. Nesbit, one of the ministers of Edinburgh, and his attachment was returned; but it was not till 1751, when his family had ceased to stand in need of his protecting care, that he thought himself at liberty to complete a union which had, for several years, been the object of his ardent wishes. It is pleasant to know that the wife whom he so tardily obtained was every way worthy of such a husband, and that he suffered no interruption of his domestic happiness.

While he was laudably occupied in promoting the welfare of his orphan relatives, the rebellion broke out in Scotland. "It afforded him," says Mr. Stewart, "an opportunity of evincing the sincerity of that zeal for the civil and religious liberties of his country, which he had imbibed with the first principles of his education; and which afterwards, at the distance of more than forty years, when he was called on to employ his eloquence in the national commemoration of the revolution, seemed to rekindle the fires of his youth. His situation as a country clergyman confined indeed his patriotic exertions within a narrow sphere; but even here his conduct was guided by a mind superior to the scene in which he acted. On one occasion (when the capital was in danger of falling into the hands of the rebels) the present state of public affairs appeared so critical that he thought himself justified in laying aside for a time the pacific habits of his profession, and in quitting his parochial residence at Gladsmuir to join the volunteers of Edinburgh. And when, at last, it was determined that the city should be surrendered, he was one of the small band who repaired to Haddington, and offered their services to the commander of His Majesty's forces."

With the exception of this one troubled interval he continued, for many years, in the tranquil performance of his pastoral duties. The hours of his leisure were devoted to literary researches and to laying the solid foundation of future eminence. It was his practice to rise early, and to read and write much before breakfast. The remainder of the day he devoted to the claims of his profession. As a minister of the gospel he was consci entious and active; not confining himself to the mere routine of his sacred office, but endeavouring by every means to extend the comforts and influence of religion. In the summer months it was customary for him, previous to the commencement of the church service, to assemble the youthful part of his flock for the purpose of explaining to them the doctrines of the catechism. By his zeal, his punctuality, and the suavity of his behaviour, he won the love of his parishioners; so that, in all their difficulties, it was to him that they resorted for consolation and for counsel. His pulpit eloquence was such as afforded delight to all classes of people; because, while it was adorned with those graces of style which are required to satisfy men of judgment and taste, it was rendered level to the comprehension of his humblest hearers, by the clearness of its argument and the perspicuity of its language.

The time at length arrived when the talents of Robertson were to be displayed on a more extensive and public scene of action, and he was to assume a leading share in the government of the Scottish church. He did not, however, come forward among his colleagues till he had attained the mature age of thirty, and had thoroughly prepared himself to sustain his new and important part with untiring vigour and a decisive effect. It was on the question of patronage that he first exerted his powers of eloquence in a deliberative assembly.

To enable the mere English reader to comprehend this subject, it may, perhaps, be proper to give some account of the constitution of the church of Scotland, and also of the right of patronage, out of which arose the contentions and heartburnings by which the church was disturbed for a considerable period.

The church of Scotland is ruled by a series of judicatories, rising by regular gradation from the kirk session, or parochial consistory, which is the lowest in order, to the general assembly, which is the highest. The kirk session is composed of the ministers and lay elders of parishes; a presbytery is formed of the ministers of contiguous parishes, with certain representatives from the kirk sessions; and a provincial synod is constituted by the union of a plurality of presbyteries. Crowning the whole is the general assembly. This body consists of three hundred and sixty-four members, of whom two hundred and two are ministers, and the remainder are laymen. Of this number two hundred and one ministers and eighty-nine lay elders are sent by the presbyteries; the royal boroughs elect sixty-seven laymen; the universities depute five persons, who may be either ecclesiastics or laymen; and the Scottish church of Campvere in Holland supplies two deputies, the one lay and the other clerical. The annual sittings of the assembly are limited to ten days; but whatever business it has left unsettled is transacted by a committee of the whole house (called the commission), which, in the course of the year, has four stated meetings. Among the lay members of the assembly are men of the highest consequence in the kingdom; lawyers, judges, and sometimes nobles

Though all the ministers in Scotland are on a perfect equality with each other, yet each individual and each judicatory is bound to yield a prompt obedience to the superintending authority, and each court must punctually lay the record of its proceedings before the tribunal which is next in rank above it; but the general assembly has the power of deciding without appeal, of enforcing, uncontrolled, its decrees, and, with the concurrence of a majority of the presbyteries, of enacting laws for the government of the Scottish church.

The history of clerical patronage in Scotland since the overthrow of catholicism, and of the struggles to which it has given rise, has been traced with so much clearness by Dr. Gleig that, though the passage is of some length, I shall give it in his own words. "The Reformation in Scotland," says he, "was irregular and tumultuous; and the great object of the powerful aristocracy of that kingdom seems to have been rather to get possession of the tithes, and the lands of the dignified clergy, than to purify the doctrine and reform the worship of the church. Of this Knox and the other reformed clergymen complained bitterly; and their complaints were extorted from them by their own sufferings. Never, I believe, were the established clergy of any Christian country reduced to such indigence as were those zealous and well meaning men, during the disastrous reign of queen Mary, and the minority of her son and successor; while the pittance that was promised to them, instead of being regularly paid, was often seized by the rapacity of the regents and the powerful barons who adhered to their cause, and the ministers left to depend for their subsistence on the generosity of the people.

"As nearly the whole of the ecclesiastical patronage of the kingdom had come into the possession of those barons, partly by inheritance from their ancestors, and partly with the church lands which, on the destruction of the monasteries, they had appropriated to themselves, it is not wonderful that, in an age when men were very apt to confound the illegal and mischievous conduct of him who exercised an undoubted right with the natural consequences of that right itself, strong prejudices were excited in the minds of the clergy and more serious part of the people against the law which vested in such sacrilegious robbers the right of presentation to parish churches. It is not indeed very accurately known by whom ministers were nominated to vacant churches for thirty years after the commencement of the Reformation, when there was hardly any settled government in the church or in the state. In some parishes they were probably called by the general voice of the people; in others, obtruded on them by the violence of the prevailing faction, to serve some political purpose of the day; and in others again appointed by the superintendent and his council: while in a few the legal patron may have exercised his right, without making any simoniacal contract with the presentee; which, however, there is reason to suspect was no uncommon practice.*

"Hitherto the government of the Protestant church of Scotland had fluctuated from one form to another, sometimes assuming the appearance of episcopacy under superintendents, and at other times being presbyterian in the strictest sense of the word. In the month of June, 1592, an act was passed, giving a legal sanction to the presbyterian form of government, and restoring the ancient law of patronage. By that act the patron of a vacant parish was authorized to present, to the presbytery comprehending that parish, a person properly qualified to be intrusted with the cure of souls; and the presbytery was enjoined, after subjecting the presentee to certain trials and examinations, of which its members were constituted the judges, 'to ordain and settle him as minister of the parish, provided no relevant objection should be stated to his life, doctrine, or qualifications.'

"Though we are assured by the highest authority† that this right of patronage, thus conferred by the fundamental charter of presbyterian government in Scotland, was early complained of as a grievance, it appears to have been regularly exercised until the era of the rebellion against Charles I. during the establishment as well of the presbyterian as of the episcopal church. It was indeed abolished by the usurping powers, which in 1649 established in its stead what was then called 'the gospel right of popular election;' but at the restoration it was re-established together with episcopacy, and was regularly exercised until the revolution, when epis

* The reader will derive much valuable information on this subject from Dr. Cook's "History of the Reformation in Scotland."

† Dr. Hill, Principal of St. Mary's College, in the University of St. Andrew's.

copacy was finally overthrown, and, by an act passed on the 26th of May, 'the presbyterian church, government, and discipline, by kirk sessions, presbyteries, provincial synods, and general assemblies, established in its stead. The act of James VI. in 1592 was 'revived and confirmed in every head thereof, except in that part of it relating to patronages,' which were utterly abolished, though nothing was substituted in their stead until the 19th of July immediately succeeding.

"It was then statuted and declared, to use the language of the act, 'that, in the vacancy of any particular church, and for supplying the same with a minister, the protestant heritors and elders are to name and propose the person to the whole congregation, to be either approven or disapproven by them; and if they disapprove, they are to give in their reasons, to the effect the affairs may be cognosced by the presbytery of the bounds; at whose judgment, and by whose determination, the calling and entry of every particular minister is to be ordered and concluded. In recompense of which rights of presentation the heritors of every parish were to pay to the patron six hundred merks (£33 6*s.* 8*d.* sterling), against a certain time, and under certain proportions.

"Whether this sum, which at that period was very considerable, was actually paid to the patrons of the several parishes, I know not; but if it was, or indeed whether it was or not, had it been the intention of the legislature to produce dissension in the country, it could not have devised any thing better calculated to effect its purpose than this mode of appointing ministers to vacant churches. The heritors or landholders, if the price was paid, would naturally contend for the uncontrolled exercise of the right which they, and they only, had purchased; but it is not by any means probable that at such a period they could often agree in their choice of a minister for a vacant parish. The elders, who were men of inferior rank and inferior education, would, by the envy of the low, when comparing themselves with the high, be prompted to thwart the wishes of their landlords, which the act of parliament enabled them to do effectully; and the consequence must have been that two or three candidates for every vacant church were at once proposed to the people of the parish for their approbation or disapprobation. The people might either give the preference to one of the candidates proposed, or reject them all, for reasons of which the members of the presbytery were constituted the judges; and as it appears that the presbytery generally took part with the people, a source of everlasting contention was thus established between the country gentlemen and the parochial clergy; an evil than which a greater cannot easily be conceived. For these, and other reasons, this ill digested law was repealed in the tenth year of the reign of queen Anne, and the right of patronage restored as in all other established churches.

"By many of the clergy, however, patronage seems to have been considered as an appendage of prelacy; though it has obviously no greater connexion with that form of ecclesiastical polity than with any other that is capable of being allied with the state; and, till after the year 1730, ministers continued to be settled in vacant parishes in the manner prescribed by the act of king William and queen Mary. 'Even then,' says Dr. Hill, 'the church courts, although they could not entirely disregard the law, continued, in many instances, to render it ineffectual, and by their authority sanctioned the prevailing prejudices of the people against it. They admitted, as an incontrovertible principle in presbyterian church government, that a presentee, although perfectly well qualified, and unexceptionable in his life and doctrine, was nevertheless inadmissible to his clerical office, till the concurrence of the people who were to be under his ministry had been regularly ascertained.' The form of expressing this concurrence was by the subscription of a paper termed 'a call;' to which many of the old ministers paid greater respect than to the deed of presentation by the patron of the church.

"To render the call good, however, the unanimous consent of the land holders, elders, and people, was not considered as necessary, nor indeed ever looked for. Nay, it appears that even a majority was not in all cases deemed indispensable; for the presbytery often admitted to his charge, and proceeded to ordain the presentee whose call, by whatever number of parishioners, appeared to them to afford a reasonable prospect of his becoming, by prudent conduct, a useful parish minister. On the other hand, presbyteries sometimes set aside the presentation altogether, when they were not satisfied with the call; and when the patron insisted on his right, and the presbytery continued inflexible, the general assembly was, in such cases, under the necessity either of compelling the members of the presbytery, by ecclesiastical censures, to do their duty, or of appointing a committee of its own body to relieve them from that duty, by ordaining the presentee, and inducting him into the vacant church. To compulsion recourse had seldom been had; and the consequence was that individuals openly claimed a right to disobey the injunctions of the assembly, whenever they conceived their disobedience justified by a principle of conscience.

"Such was the state of ecclesiastical discipline in Scotland when Mr. Robertson first took an active part in the debates of the general assembly; and he very justly thought that its tendency was to overturn the presbyterian establishment, and introduce in its stead a number of independent congregational churches. He therefore supported the law of patronage, not merely because it was part of the law of the land, but because he thought it the most expedient method of filling the vacant churches. It did not appear to him that the people at large are competent judges of those qualities which a minister should possess in order to be a useful teacher of the truth as it is in Jesus, or of the precepts of a sound morality. He more than suspected that if the candidates for churches were taught to consider their success in obtaining a settlement as depending on a popular election, many of them would be tempted to adopt a manner of preaching calculated rather to please the people than to promote their edification He thought that there is little danger to be apprehended from the abuse of the law of patronage; because the presentee must be chosen from among those whom the church had approved, and licensed as qualified for the office of a parish minister; because a presentee cannot be admitted to the benefice if any relevant objection to his life or doctrine be proved against him; and because, after ordination and admission, he is liable to be deposed for improper conduct, and the church declared vacant."

Whatever may be thought of the merits of the cause which Robertson espoused, it is impossible to doubt that he was a conscientious supporter of it. To undertake its defence some strength of nerve was, indeed, required. Success seemed, at the outset, to be scarcely within the verge of probability, and there was much danger of becoming unpopular. The result, nevertheless, gave ample proof of what may be accomplished by perseverance and talents. The first time that he came forward in the assembly was in May, 1751, when a debate arose on the conduct of a minister, who had disobeyed the sentence of a former assembly. Seizing this opportunity to enforce his principles of church discipline, Robertson, in a vigorous and eloquent speech, contended that if subordination were not rigidly maintained the presbyterian establishment would ultimately be overthrown, and, therefore, an exemplary punishment ought to be inflicted on the offending party. But, though he was heard with attention, his arguments produced so little present effect that, on the house being divided, he was left in a minority of no more than eleven against two hundred.

Though this decision was not calculated to encourage him, he determined to persist, and an occurrence very soon took place which enabled him to renew the contest. The presbytery of Dumferline having been guilty of disobedience, in refusing to admit a minister to the church of Inverkeithing, the commission of the assembly, which met in November, ordered them to cease from their opposition, and threatened, that, if they continued to be refractory, they should be subjected to a high censure Notwithstanding this, the presbytery again disobeyed the mandate of the superior court. Yet, instead of carrying its threat into effect, the commission came to a resolution that no censure should be inflicted.

Such a resolution as this, after the commission had gone so far as to resort to threats, was at least absurd. So fair an opening as this circumstance afforded was not neglected by Robertson. He accordingly drew up a protest, intituled, "Reasons of Dissent from the Judgment and Resolution of the Commission." This protest, which was signed by himself, Dr. Blair, Home, and a few other friends, is an able and closely reasoned production. It boldly declares the sentence of the commission to be inconsistent with the nature and first principles of society; charges the commission itself with having, by that sentence, gone beyond its powers, and betrayed the privileges and deserted the doctrines of the constitution; considers the impunity thus granted as encouraging and inviting contumacy, insists on the lawfulness and wisdom of ecclesiastical censures, and on the absolute necessity of preserving subordination and obedience in the church; and, finally, maintains that the exercise of no man's private judgment can justify him in disturbing all public order, that he who becomes a member of a church ought to conform to its decrees, or, "if he hath rashly joined himself, that he is bound, as an honest man and a good Christian, to withdraw, and to keep his conscience pure and undefiled."

When the assembly met, in 1752, the question was brought before it; and Robertson supported the principles of his protest with such cogency of argument, that he won over a majority to his side, and achieved a complete triumph. The judgment of the commission was reversed, Mr. Gillespie, one of the ministers of the presbytery of Dumferline, was deposed from his pastoral office, and ejected from his living, and three other individuals were suspended from their judicative capacity in the superior ecclesiastical courts. Gillespie, whose only crime was that of being absent on the day appointed for the induction of the presentee, was a pious and amiable man, and his deposition occasioned so much dissatisfaction, that it gave rise to a new sect of dissenters, afterwards known by the appellation of "the Presbytery of Relief;" a sect which still exists, and is of considerable magnitude.

From this time, though it was not till the year 1763 that he became its avowed leader, Robertson was, in fact, at the head of the assembly; which body, for the whole period of his ascendancy, he contrived to keep steady to his principles. In this task he was ably seconded by Dr. Drysdale, one of the ministers of Edinburgh. It was not, however, without many struggles that he retained his pre-eminence. Those which took place in 1765 and 1768 were peculiarly violent; motions having then been made, and vehemently contended for, to inquire into the causes of the rapid progress of secession from the established church; and, in order to counteract them to introduce a more popular mode of inducting the parochial ministers From what is mentioned by sir Henry Wellwood, in his "Memoirs of Dr. Erskine," it appears that the exertions of Robertson were kept continually on the stretch; and that for his victory he was partly indebted to cautious management, and to patience which nothing could tire. "During Dr. Robertson's time," says he, "the struggle with the people was perpetual; and the opposition to presentees so extremely pertinacious, as in a great measure to engross the business of the assemblies. The parties in the church were then more equally balanced than they have ever been since that period. The measures which were adopted, in the face of such perpetual opposition, it required no common talents to manage or defend; especially considering that the leaders in opposition were such men as Dr. Dick, Dr. Macqueen, Dr. Erskine, Mr. Stevenson of St. Madois, Mr. Freebairn of Dumbarton, Mr. Andrew Crosbie, &c. &c.; men of the first ability in the country, and some of them possessed of an eloquence for a popular assembly to which there was nothing superior in the church or in the state.

"Dr. Robertson's firmness was not easily shaken, but his caution and prudence never deserted him. He held it for a maxim, never wantonly to offend the prejudices of the people, and rather to endeavour to manage than directly to combat them. Some of the settlements in dispute were protracted for eight or ten years together; and though the general assemblies steadily pursued their system, and uniformly appointed the presentees to be inducted, their strongest sentences were not vindictive, and seldom went beyond the leading points to which they were directed."

In 1757 an event happened, which afforded to him an opportunity of manifesting the liberality of his spirit, and of exercising his influence over his colleagues, to moderate the vengeance which was threatened to be hurled on some of his brethren, for having been guilty of an act which was considered to be of the most profane nature The chief offender was his friend Home, who was then minister of Athelstaneford. The crime consisted in Home having not only produced the tragedy of Douglas, but having also had the temerity to be present at the acting of it in the Edinburgh theatre. With him were involved several of his clerical intimates, who, as much from a desire to share with him any odium or peril which might be incurred, as from a natural curiosity, had been induced to accompany him to the theatre on the first night of the performance. The storm which this circumstance raised among the Scottish clergy can, in the present age, hardly be imagined. It seemed as if they had witnessed nothing less than the abomination of desolation standing in the holy place. The presbytery of Edinburgh hastened to summon before its tribunal such of its members as had committed this heinous offence, and it likewise despatched circulars to the presbyteries in the vicinity, recommending rigorous measures against all clergymen who had desecrated themselves by appearing in the polluted region of the theatre. The alarm thus sounded awakened all the bigotry of the circumjacent presbyteries. That of Haddington, to which Home belonged, cited him and his friend Carlyle, of Inveresk, to answer for their misconduct. That of Glasgow had no criminals to chastise, but it was resolved not to remain silent, and, therefore, with a zeal which assuredly was not according to knowledge, it fulminated forth a series of resolutions on this appalling subject. It lamented "the melancholy but notorious fact, that one, who is a minister of the church of Scotland, did himself write and compose a play entitled the Tragedy of Douglas, and got it to be acted in the theatre at Edinburgh, and that he, with several other ministers of the church, were present, and some of them oftener than once, at the acting of the said play before a numerous audience;" it affirmed, in direct hostility to historical evidence, that stage plays had "been looked upon by the Christian church, in all ages, and of all different communions, as extremely prejudicial to religion and morality; and, as a natural consequence from this, it called on the general assembly to reprobate publicly "a practice unbecoming the character of clergymen, and of such pernicious tendency to the great interests of religion, industry, and virtue." The cry of the church was echoed from the press, angry disputants were arrayed on both sides, and a multitude of ephemeral pamphlets and pasquinades was rapidly produced.

Throughout the whole of the ecclesiastical proceedings, which on this occasion were instituted in the presbyteries and in the general assembly

Robertson exerted himself with more than common ardour and eloquence on behalf of his friends. Though, being restrained by a promise which he had given to his father, he had himself never been within the walls of a theatre, he did not hesitate to avow his belief that no culpability attached to the persons who were under prosecution. "The promise," said he, "which was exacted by the most indulgent of parents, I have hitherto religiously kept, and it is my intention to keep it till the day of my death. I am at the same time free to declare, that I perceive nothing sinful or inconsistent with the spirit of Christianity in writing a tragedy, which gives no encouragement to baseness or vice, and that I cannot concur in censuring my brethren for being present at the representation of such a tragedy, from which I was kept back by a promise, which, though sacred to me, is not obligatory on them."

Wholly to overcome the prevalent spirit of bigotry was more than Robertson could accomplish, but it is believed to have been at least greatly mitigated by his laudable efforts. To his persuasive eloquence is attributed, and no doubt justly, the comparative mildness of the sentence which was ultimately pronounced. A declaratory act was passed by the assembly, forbidding the clergy to visit the theatres, but not extending the prohibition to the writing of plays. The silence of the assembly on the latter head was at least one point gained in favour of liberal principles. As to the offending ministers, some of them were rebuked by the presbyteries to which they belonged, and one or two of them were suspended from their office for a few weeks. Home, however, being disgusted with the treatment which he had experienced, and having, perhaps, already been offered patronage in the British metropolis, resigned his living of Athelstaneford in June, 1757, and fixed his residence in London.

By the departure of Home, the Select Society, as it was called, lost one of its ablest members. This society was instituted at Edinburgh, in 1754, by Allan Ramsay, the painter, who was son to the poet of the same name. The object of it was philosophical and literary inquiry, and the improvement of the members in the art of speaking. It held its meetings in the Advocates' Library, and met regularly every Friday evening, during the sittings of the court of session. At the outset it consisted of only fifteen persons, of whom Robertson was one. It, however, soon acquired such high reputation, that its list of associates was swelled to more than a hundred and thirty names; among which were included those of the most eminent literary and political characters in the northern division of the kingdom. Of this number were Hume, Adam Smith, Wedderburn, afterwards Lord Chancellor, sir Gilbert Elliot, lord Elibank, lord Monboddo, lord Kames, lord Woodhouselee, Adam Furguson, Wilkie, Dr. Cullen, and many others less gifted perhaps, but still rising far above mediocrity of talent. This society flourished in full vigour for some years; and is said by professor Stewart, to have produced such debates as have not often been heard in modern assemblies; debates, where the dignity of the speakers was not lowered by the intrigues of policy, or the intemperance of faction; and where the most splendid talents that have ever adorned this country were roused to their best exertions, by the liberal and ennobling discussions of literature and philosophy." That such an assemblage of learning and genius must have done much towards diffusing through Scotland a taste for letters, there cannot be the shadow of a doubt. Robertson took an active part, and was one of its presidents. As a speaker, it was remarked of him, that "whereas most of the others in their previous discourses exhausted the subject so much that there was no room for debate, he gave only such brief but artful sketches, as served to suggest ideas, without leading to a decision."

By a few members of the society, a Review was attempted in 1755, the principal contributors to which were Blair, Smith, and Robertson. This undertaking was designed to form a record of the progress of Scottish literature, and, occasionally, to criticise such English and foreign works as might appear to be worthy of notice. After having published two numbers, which appeared in July and December, the reviewers were under the necessity of relinquishing their plan. The failure is said to have arisen from their having lashed, with just but caustic severity, "some miserable effusions of fanaticism, which it was their wish to banish from the church" Their attack upon this mischievous trash excited such a vehement party outcry, that they thought it prudent to discontinue labours which, while they must fail of being useful, could not fail to expose them to vulgar odium, and involve them in endless disputes. Time, the great worker of changes, has since produced a marvellous alteration. At a period less than half a century later, the most prejudice-scorning and pungent of all Reviews was established in the Scottish capital, and was received with enthusiasm!

The first separate literary production of Robertson, or at least the first known production, was also laid before the public in 1755. It is a sermon which he preached in that year before the Scotch society for propagating Christian knowledge. He chose for his subject, "The situation of the world at the time of Christ's appearance, and its connexion with the success of his religion." Though this discourse never rises into a strain of glowing eloquence, it is a dignified and argumentative composition, in a chaste and animated style. If it does not flash and dazzle, it at least shines with a steady lustre. Its merit, indeed, affords us ample cause to regret that, before his removal from Gladsmuir, he lost a volume of sermons, on which much care is said to have been bestowed. The sole specimen which remains of his talents as a preacher has passed through five editions, and has been translated into the German language by Mr. Edeling.

The time now came when the high character for learning and talent, which Robertson had acquired among his friends, was to be ratified by the public voice. He had long been sedulously engaged on the History of Scotland, the plan of which he is said to have formed soon after his settling at Gladsmuir. By his letters to Lord Hailes we are, in some measure, enabled to trace his progress. It appears that as early as 1753 he had commenced his labours, and that by the summer of 1757 he had advanced as far as the narrative of Gowrie's conspiracy. In the spring of 1758 he visited London, to concert measures for publishing; and the History, in two volumes, quarto, was given to the world on the first of February, 1759, about three months subsequent to the completion of it. While the last sheets were in the press, the author received, by diploma, the degree of Doctor of Divinity from the University of Edinburgh.

At the period when Dr. Robertson commenced his career, this country could boast of few historians, possessed of philosophic views and an elegant style. Rapin, who, besides, wrote in his native language, Carte, and others, could not aspire to a loftier title than that of annalists; and the recent production from the pen of Smollet, though displaying talent, was by far too imperfect to give him a place among eminent historical writers Hume alone had come near to the standard of excellence; and, after enduring a doubtful struggle, in the course of which his spirits were well nigh overpowered, had at length begun to enjoy the literary honours which he had so painfully acquired. For a considerable time past he had been occupied on the reigns of the Tudor race; and, as this subject is inseparably connected with Scottish history, Dr. Robertson was alarmed lest he himself should sustain injury from the volumes of his friend being published simultaneously with his own. The new candidate for fame endeavoured to induce Hume to proceed with some other portion of his narrative; and, having failed in this, he appears to have been desirous that he should at least be allowed to be the first to claim the notice of the public.

"I am (says Hume in a letter to him) nearly printed out, and shall be sure to send you a copy by the stage coach, or some other conveyance. I beg of you to make remarks as you go along. It would have been much better had we communicated before printing, which was always my desire and was most suitable to the friendship which always did, and I hope always will subsist between us. I speak this chiefly on my own account. For though I had the perusal of your sheets before I printed, I was not able to derive sufficient benefits from them, or indeed to make any alteration by their assistance. There still remain, I fear, many errors, of which you could have convinced me if we had canvassed the matter in conversation. Perhaps I might also have been sometimes no less fortunate with you." He adds, "Millar was proposing to publish me about March; but I shall communicate to him your desire, even though I think it entirely groundless, as you will likewise think after you have read my volume. He has very needlessly delayed your publication till the first week of February, at the desire of the Edinburgh booksellers, who could no way be affected by a publication in London. I was exceedingly sorry not to be able to comply with your desire, when you expressed your wish that I should not write this period. I could not write downward. For when you find occasion, by new discoveries, to correct your opinion with regard to facts which passed in queen Elizabeth's days; who, that has not the best opportunities of informing himself, could venture to relate any recent transactions? I must therefore have abandoned altogether this scheme of the English History, in which I had proceeded so far, if I had not acted as I did. You will see what light and force this history of the Tudors bestows on that of the Stewarts. Had I been prudent I should have begun with it."

The alarm which Dr. Robertson conceived from the rivalship of his friend was, however, groundless. His success was not, like that of Hume, the slow growth of years. It was complete and immediate. So rapid was the sale of the book, that, before a month had elapsed, his publisher informed him that it was necessary to set about preparing for a second edition. It was read and admired by a part of the royal family; and plausive and gratulatory letters were showered on him from all quarters. Warburton, Horace Walpole, Lord Mansfield, Lord Lyttelton, Dr. Douglas, Hurd, and many other men of eminence, all concurred in swelling the chorus of praise. Among the foremost to blazon his merits was his amicable rival, Hume, whose letters bear repeated testimony to the warmth of his friendship, and his noble freedom from the base dominion of envy. "I am diverting myself," says he, "with the notion of how much you will profit by the applause of my enemies in Scotland. Had you and I been such fools as to have given way to jealousy, to have entertained animosity and malignity against each other, and to have rent all our acquaintance into parties, what a noble amusement we should have exhibited to the blockheads, which now they are likely to be disappointed of! All the people whose friendship or judgment either of us value are friends to both, and will be pleased with the success of both, as we will be with that of each other. I declare to you I have not of a long time had a more sensible pleasure than the good reception of your History has given me within this fortnight." In another place, with a sportiveness not unusual in his correspondence, he exclaims, "But though I have given this character of your work to Monsieur Helvetius, I warn you that this is the last time that, either to Frenchman or Englishman, I shall ever speak the least good of it. A plague take you! Here I sat near the historical summit of Parnassus, immediately under Dr. Smollet; and you have the impudence to squeeze yourself by me, and place yourself directly under his feet. Do you imagine that this can be agreeable to me! And must not I be guilty of great simplicity to contribute my endeavours to your thrusting me out of my place in Paris as well as at London? But I give you warning that you will find the matter somewhat difficult, at least in the former city. A friend of mine, who is there, writes home to his father the strangest accounts on that head; which my modesty will not permit me to repeat, but which it allowed me very deliciously to swallow."

The hold which the History of Scotland thus suddenly acquired on the public mind it yet retains. Fourteen editions were published during the life-time of the author, and the editions since his decease have been still more numerous. It has undoubtedly established itself as a classical English production. For a while, indeed, the voice of criticism was mute; and the historian had only to enjoy the luxury of his triumph. But, at length, some of his opinions, particularly his belief of the guilt of Mary found opponents in the candid and well informed Tytler, the learned, acute, and eloquent Stuart, and the dogmatical Whitaker; the latter of whom, though master of talents, erudition, and forcible reasoning, almost rendered truth itself repulsive by the petulance and overbearingness of his manner, and the ruggedness of his style. Of his antagonists, however, the historian took not the slightest public notice, contenting himself with the silent correction of such passages in his work as his matured judgment had decided to be erroneous. In a letter to Gibbon he laconically notices Whitaker. "You will see," says he, "that I have got in Mr. Whitaker an adversary so bigoted and zealous, that though I have denied no article of faith, and am at least as orthodox as himself, yet he rails against me with all the asperity of theological hatred. I shall adhere to my fixed maxim of making no reply."

It was not merely a harvest of unproductive fame that was reaped by Dr. Robertson. He was no sooner known to the world than preferment was rapidly bestowed on him. In the autumn of 1758, while his work was in the hands of the printer, he was translated from Gladsmuir to one of the churches of the Scottish metropolis. I believe the church to which he was removed to have been that of the Old Gray Friars, in which, some years afterwards, his friend Dr. Erskine became his coadjutor. On the History issuing from the press, he was appointed chaplain of Stirling Castle, and, in 1761, one of his Majesty's chaplains in ordinary for Scotland. The dignity of Principal of the College of Edinburgh was conferred on him in 1762; and, two years subsequently to this, the office of Historiographer for Scotland, which, since the death of Crawfurd, in 1726, had been disused, was revived in his favour, with an annual stipend of two hundred pounds.

By the remuneration which he had received for his history, and the salaries which arose from his various appointments, Dr. Robertson was now in possession of an income far greater than had ever before been possessed by any Scotch presbyterian minister, and certainly not falling short of that which had been enjoyed by some bishops at the period when the church of Scotland was under episcopal government. A few of his indiscreet friends seem, however, to have thought that his talents were not adequately rewarded, and even that the clerical profession in the northern part of our island did not afford for them a sphere of action sufficiently extensive. The church of England held forth richer prospects to ambition and to mental endowments; and they were of opinion that, by transferring his services to that church, he might obtain a share in its highest dignities and emoluments. To this scheme allusions may be found in the letters which, about this time, were addressed to him by Dr. John Blair, Sir Gilbert Elliot, and Mr. Hume. But Dr. Robertson had a larger share of foresight and prudence than his advisers, and he rejected their dangerous though well intended counsel. It is, perhaps, more than doubtful whether, had it been executed, their plan would have produced the desired effect. This kind of transplanting has often been tried, but seldom, if ever, with any degree of success. The plant, vigorous on its native bed, languishes and is dwarfed on an alien soil. Dr. Robertson had now reached the mature age of forty-one; his opinions, his habits, his connexions, had all been formed with a reference to the circle in which he moved, and it was not probable that they could be suddenly bent with advantage in an opposite direction. In Scotland he had no competitors who could rise to a level with him; in England he would, perhaps, have had many; and he may be supposed to have thought with Cæsar, that it is better to be the first man in a village than the second at Rome. Nor was there any room in England for the exercise of that kind of eloquence in which he particularly excelled; the eloquence which is manifested in debate. By the force of his oratory he left far behind all his rivals and opponents, and wielded at will the general assembly of the Scottish church; but, since the convocation was shorn of its controversial and declamatory glories, since it was smitten with an incapacity of embarrassing the government, fostering theological rancour, and displaying the unseemly spectacle of Christian divines arrayed in worse than barbarian hostility to each other, there has not in this country existed any deliberative clerical body in which Dr. Robertson could have exerted those argumentative and rhetorical powers that, among his fellow ministers, obtained for him so entire an ascendancy. His preferment might also have stopped short of the point which his sanguine friends expected it to attain; and, whatever its degree, it would in all probability have been looked on with a jealous eye by many of his brethren on the south of the Tweed. There was, besides, another and still more powerful reason that must have influenced his decision. He had for nearly twenty years been a leading minister of the presbyterian establishment; and his now quitting it to enter into a prelatical church, which, as being deemed a scion from the hated stock of Rome, was still held in abomination by many of his countrymen, could scarcely have failed to be considered as an interested and base sacrifice of his principles and his character at the shrine of lucre and ambition. To be branded as a deserter by the zealots of the one institution, and by the envious of the other, was not a favourable auspice under which to commence his new career; and he therefore acted wisely, as well as honourably, in remaining a member of the Scottish church.

Having resolved to remain in Scotland, and to rely chiefly on his pen for the advancement of his fortune, Dr. Robertson had now to choose another theme on which his talents could be profitably employed. To the composition of history, in which he had met with such stimulating success, he wisely determined to adhere. It was, indeed, in that department that he was peculiarly qualified to excel, by his power of vivid description, and his happy delineation of character. His friends were consulted on this occasion; each had some favourite plan to suggest to him; and he seems to have been absolutely embarrassed by the affluence of subjects, many of which were worthy of his best exertions to illustrate and adorn them. If a ludicrous simile may be allowed, we may say that he found it no less difficult to fix his choice, than it was for Mr. Shandy to decide to what purpose he should apply the legacy which was left to him by his sister Dinah Dr. John Blair strenuously recommended to him to write a complete History of England, and assured him that Lord Chesterfield had declared his readiness to move, in the house of peers, for public encouragement to him, in case of his undertaking a work which might with justice be considered as being a national one. But from adopting this project, though it was one which he had early cherished, Dr. Robertson was deterred by his honourable unwillingness to interfere with his friend Hume, who was now putting the finishing hand to his great labour. Hume himself advised him to undertake a series of modern lives, in the manner of Plutarch. "You see," said he, "that in Plutarch the life of Cæsar may be read in half an hour

Were you to write the life of Henry the Fourth of France after that model, you might pillage all the pretty stories in Sully, and speak more of his mistresses than of his battles. In short, you might gather the flower of al modern history in this manner. The remarkable popes, the kings of Sweden, the great discoverers and conquerors of the New World, even the eminent men of letters might furnish you with matter, and the quick despatch of every different work would encourage you to begin a new one If one volume were successful, you might compose another at your leisure, and the field is inexhaustible. There are persons whom you might meet with in the corners of history, so to speak, who would be a subject of entertainment quite unexpected; and as long as you live, you might give and receive amusement by such a work." That so excellent an idea should not have been acted upon must be regretted by every one who is a lover of literature. By Horace Walpole two subjects, of no trivial interest, were pointed out. These were the History of Learning, and the History of the reigns of Nerva, Trajan, Adrian, and the two Antonines; the latter of which Walpole declared that he should be tempted to denominate the History of Humanity. Dr. Robertson himself seems, at one time, to have thought, though but transiently, of tracing the events which occurred in the age of Leo the Tenth. There is no reason to lament that he did not undertake this task, which was once meditated on by Warton, and has since been performed by a writer whom nature has largely gifted, and who possesses a profound knowledge of the records, arts, and language of Italy But the two plans which had the ascendancy in his mind, and between which he long hesitated, were the History of Greece, and the History of Charles the Fifth. At length, notwithstanding the objections which were urged by Hume and Horace Walpole, he made choice of the reign of Charles as the subject of his second attempt.

When he had for about a year been engaged, partly in those preliminary researches which are necessary to give value to a work like that on which he was occupied, and partly in composition, his progress was suddenly suspended, by the intervention of a personage of such elevated rank as to render it almost impossible for him to decline a compliance with that which was required from him. It has been seen, that he was early desirous to be the historian of his native island, and that friendship alone prevented him from being so. He was now informed that the wishes of the British sovereign were in unison with his own. In the latter part of July, 1761, he was written to on this head by lord Cathcart. "Lord Bute told me the king's thoughts as well as his own," said lord Cathcart, "with respect to your History of Scotland, and a wish his majesty had expressed to see a History of England by your pen. His lordship assured me, every source of information which government can command would be open to you, and that great, laborious, and extensive as the work must be, he would take care your encouragement should be proportioned to it. He seemed to be aware of some objections you once had, founded on the apprehension of clashing or interfering with Mr. David Hume, who is your friend. but as your performance and his will be upon plans so different from each other, and as *his* will, in point of time, have so much the start of yours, these objections did not seem to him such as, upon reflection, were likely to continue to have much weight with you. I must add, that though I did not think it right to inquire into lord Bute's intentions before I knew a little of your mind, it appeared to me plain, that they were higher than any views which can open to you in Scotland, and which, I believe, he would think inconsistent with the attention the other subject would necessarily require."

A proposition thus powerfully enforced it would, under any circumstances, have been difficult for Dr. Robertson to reject. But, in fact, the reasons which formerly influenced his conduct had ceased to exist. Hume had now completed his history, it was before the public, and its fate must be irrevocably decided before a line of the rival narrative could be com mitted to paper. Dr. Robertson was convinced of this, and therefore he did not hesitate to embrace the opportunity which was offered to him. "After the first publication of the History of Scotland, and the favourable reception it met with," said he in his answer to lord Cathcart, "I had both very tempting offers from booksellers, and very confident assurances of public encouragement, if I would undertake the History of England But as Mr. Hume, with whom, notwithstanding the contrariety of our sentiments both in religion and politics, I live in great friendship, was at that time in the middle of the subject, no consideration of interest or reputation would induce me to break in upon a field of which he had taken prior possession; and I determined that my interference with him should never be any obstruction to the sale or success of his work. Nor do I yet repent of my having resisted so many solicitations to alter this resolution. But the case I now think is entirely changed. His History will have been published several years before any work of mine on the same subject can appear; its first run will not be marred by any justling with me, and it will have taken that station in the literary system which belongs to it. This objection, therefore, which I thought, and still think, so weighty at that time, makes no impression on me at present, and I can now justify my undertaking the English History, to myself, to the world, and to him. Besides, our manner of viewing the same subject is so different or peculiar, that (as was the case in our last books) both may maintain their own rank, have their own partisans, and possess their own merit, without hurting each other."

To enable him to accomplish so arduous a labour, he considered it necessary, not only that he should be established in such a manner as would divest him of all anxiety as to pecuniary concerns, but that he should likewise have the power of devoting to study a larger portion of his time than it was now possible for him to allot to that purpose. "Were I to carve out my own fortune," said he, "I should wish to continue one of his majesty's chaplains for Scotland, but to resign my charge as a minister of Edinburgh, which engrosses more of my time than one who is a stranger to the many minute duties of that office can well imagine. I would wish to apply my whole time to literary pursuits, which is at present parcelled out among innumerable occupations. In order to enable me to make this resignation some appointment must be assigned me for life. What that should be, it neither becomes me, nor do I pretend to say. One thing, however I wish with some earnestness, that the thing might be executed soon, both as it will give me great vigour in my studies to have my future fortune ascertained in so honourable a manner, and because, by allowing me to apply myself wholly to my present work, it will enable me to finish it in a less time, and to begin so much sooner to my new task." But though he was desirous to obtain some appointment, in order that he might not be "reduced entirely to the profession of an author," he at the same moment, with becoming spirit, declared that he did not wish to derive any emolument from it before he could commence the particular task for which the appointment was to be given. The proposal that he should remove to London, he was averse from complying with, though he did not put a direct negative on it; and he could not consent to begin the History of Britain till he had completed that of Charles the Fifth.

This scheme, which seems to have been almost brought to maturity, was, nevertheless, dropped; but for what reason is unknown. Mr. Stewart is disposed to believe that the failure of it may in part be attributed to the resignation of lord Bute. It was certainly so much a favourite with Dr. Robertson that he long cherished it, and abandoned it with reluctance We may, perhaps, be allowed to smile, or to wonder, that a sovereign should have selected a writer confessedly of Whig principles to compose a History of England, in opposition to one produced by a friend of arbitrary power; and we may also be allowed to doubt, whether, as far as regarded its sentiments, such a work, written by a Whig under the auspices of a court, would have proved quite satisfactory either to the monarch or to the people. There might, at least, have been some danger that it would have justified the sarcasm which was uttered by Horace Walpole, on another occasion "You must know, sir," said Dr. Robertson to him, "that I look upon myself as a moderate Whig."—"Yes, doctor," replied Walpole, "I look on you as a *very* moderate Whig."

As soon as this negotiation was broken off, he bent all his exertions to the task which he had commenced. The public curiosity was highly excited, and it was long kept on the stretch before it was gratified In the summer of 1761, he stated that one third of the work was finished, and that two years more would be required to bring the whole to perfection. But there never yet was an author who did not deceive himself, and consequently deceive others, as to the period at which his labour would be completed. The stupid, the thoughtless, and the malignant (and there are many persons, not literary, though connected with literature, who belong to these classes) consider as intended for the purpose of deception the erroneous estimate which authors are thus apt to form. They either can not or will not be taught that, in spite of Dr. Johnson's bold assertion to the contrary, no man is at all hours capable of thinking deeply, or of clothing his thoughts in an attractive dress; that he who is dependent on his reputation for existence ought not to be compelled to hazard it by crude and slovenly efforts, the product of haste; that he who draws up a narrative from widely scattered, numerous, and conflicting documents must often, in painful research and in balancing evidence, spend more months than he had calculated on spending weeks; that the discovery of a single paper, the existence of which was previously unknown, may not only throw a new light upon a subject, but give to it an entirely new colour, and may compel a writer to modify, to arrange, and even to cancel, much that he had supposed to have received his last touches; and, therefore, that the delay which, as being a proof of literary indolence, is so frequently and so unfeelingly an object of censure, ought rather in many cases to be rewarded with praise, because it is a duty which an author conscientiously, and at his own cost, performs to society and to truth. Impediments of this kind no doubt retarded the progress of Dr. Robertson; to which must be added his multifarious avocations, as principal of the university, a minister of one of the churches of the Scottish metropolis, and an active member of the general assembly, in which body, as Mr. Stewart informs us, faction was running high at that epoch. The transactions relative to America he likewise found to be of too vast a magnitude, to allow of their being compressed into an episode. He was under the necessity of reserving them for a separate history; and this circumstance obliged him in some degree to make a change in his original plan. It is, there fore, not wonderful that the publication of his work was protracted six years beyond the time which he had himself assigned for it.

At length, early in 1769, appeared, in three volumes quarto, the History of Charles the Fifth. It had been perused, while in the press, by Hume, and probably by other friends, and had gained the warmest praise. "I got yesterday from Strahan," says Hume, in one of his letters, "about thirty sheets of your History, to be sent over to Suard, and last night and this morning have run them over with great avidity. I could not deny myself the satisfaction (which I hope also will not displease you) of expressing presently my extreme approbation of them. To say only they are very well written, is by far too faint an expression, and much inferior to the sentiments I feel: they are composed with nobleness, with dignity with elegance, and with judgment, to which there are few equals. They even excel, and I think in a sensible degree, your History of Scotland. I propose to myself great pleasure in being the only man in England, during some months, who will be in the situation of doing you justice, after which you may certainly expect that my voice will be drowned in that of the public."

Hume's anticipation was prophetic. Soon after the work had come out, he wrote to his friend, in the following unequivocal terms. "The success has answered my expectations, and I, who converse with the great, the fair, and the learned, have scarcely heard an opposite voice, or even whisper, to the general sentiments. Only I have heard that the Sanhedrim at Mrs. Macaulay's condemns you as little less a friend to government and monarchy than myself." Horace Walpole was almost equally laudatory; lord Lyttelton testified his admiration; and, as Hume had long before done, recommended to the historian to write, in the manner of Plutarch, the lives of eminent persons. Voltaire, also, paid a flattering tribute. "It is to you and to Mr. Hume," said he, "that it belongs to write history You are eloquent, learned, and impartial. I unite with Europe in esteeming you." Nor was the fame of the author confined to his native island. Through the intervention of the baron D'Holbach, M. Suard was induced to translate the work into French, while it was being printed in England, and his masterly translation is said to have established his own literary character, and to have been the means of his obtaining a seat in the French academy. The remuneration which the author himself received was magnificent; especially in an age when it was not customary to give a large sum of money for the purchase of copyright. It is affirmed to have been no less than four thousand five hundred pounds.

It is not to be imagined, however, that the History of Charles the Fifth could entirely escape the severity of criticism, which appears to be the common lot of all literary productions. By the Abbé Mably it was attacked in rude and contemptuous language; which, without having the power to injure the work, was disgraceful to the person who descended to use it. Gilbert Stuart likewise assailed it; but with more skill than the French critic, and with a vigour which was animated by personal resentment. That his acuteness detected many inaccuracies, it would be absurd to dispute; but no one can doubt that he pushed his censure farther than was consonant with justice, when he characterized Dr. Robertson as an author "whose total abstinence from all ideas and inventions of his own permitted him to carry an undivided attention to other men's thoughts and speculations." Walpole, too, in later life, asserted that the reading of Dr. Robertson was not extensive, that the Introduction to the History of Charles abounds with gross errors, and that in many instances he has mistaken exceptions for rules. The work, however, still maintains its station; and, even admitting all that truth or ingenious prejudice can urge against it, who is there who will now have the boldness to deny that it forms a splendid addition to our historical treasures?

After having completed this arduous undertaking, Dr. Robertson allowed himself some respite from literary toil; a respite which, in fact, was necessary for the preservation of his health. His mind was, however, too active to remain long unoccupied, and he hastened to resume the pen. As a sequel to the history of Charles, he had promised to give to the public a narrative of the Spanish discoveries, conquests, and proceedings in America. This plan he soon resolved to enlarge, so as to include in it the transactions of all the European colonizers of the American continent. To the origin and progress of the British empire in that quarter, it was originally his intention to devote an entire volume. Than the History of the New World it was impossible for him to have chosen a subject more fertile, more attractive, or better calculated for the display of his peculiar tal

There was "ample room and verge enough" for eloquence to expatiate in. The rapidly succeeding events which he was to describe were scarcely less marvellous than those of an oriental fiction; one of his heroes, the dauntless explorer of unknown oceans, will always excite the wonder, admiration, and pity of mankind; others, though villains, were at least villains of no common powers; and the characters, the customs, the manners, the scenery, every thing in short that was connected with the work, possessed throughout the charm of novelty, and, in many instances, that of the most picturesque and forcible contrast.

To the first part of his subject, that which relates to the discovery of the New World, and the conquests and policy of the Spaniards, eight years of studious toil were devoted by Dr. Robertson. At length, in the spring of 1777, he put forth, in two quartos, the result of his labours. The public again received him with enthusiasm, and his literary friends again pressed forward to congratulate and to praise him. Hume was no longer in existence; but his place was supplied by Gibbon, who testified his entire approbation of the volumes even before he had wholly perused them. "I have seen enough," said he, "to convince me that the present publication will support, and, if possible, extend the fame of the author; that the materials are collected with care, and arranged with skill; that the progress of discovery is displayed with learning and perspicuity; that the dangers, the achievements, and the views of the Spanish adventurers, are related with a temperate spirit; and that the most original, perhaps the most curious portion of human manners, is at length rescued from the hands of sophists and declaimers."

But, perhaps, of all the applause which was bestowed on Dr. Robertson, none was more gratifying than that which was given by Burke; a man eminent at once as a writer, an orator, and a statesman. "I am perfectly sensible," says he, "of the very flattering distinction I have received in your thinking me worthy of so noble a present as that of your History of America. I have, however, suffered my gratitude to lie under some suspicion, by delaying my acknowledgment of so great a favour. But my delay was only to render my obligation to you more complete, and my thanks, if possible, more merited. The close of the session brought a great deal of very troublesome though not important business on me at once. I could not go through your work at one breath at that time, though I have done it since. I am now enabled to thank you, not only for the honour you have done me, but for the great satisfaction, and the infinite variety and compass of instruction, I have received from your incomparable work. Every thing has been done which was so naturally to be expected from the author of the History of Scotland, and of the Age of Charles the Fifth. I believe few books have done more than this, towards clearing up dark points, correcting errors, and removing prejudices. You have too the rare secret of rekindling an interest on subjects that had so often been treated, and in which every thing which could feed a vital flame appeared to have been consumed. I am sure I read many parts of your History with that fresh concern and anxiety which attend those who are not previously apprized of the event. You have, besides, thrown quite a new light on the present state of the Spanish provinces, and furnished both materials and hints for a rational theory of what may be expected from them in future

"The part which I read with the greatest pleasure is the discussion on the manners and character of the inhabitants of the New World. I have always thought with you, that we possess at this time very great advantages towards the knowledge of human nature. We need no longer go to history to trace it in all its ages and periods. History, from its comparative youth, is but a poor instructer. When the Egyptians called the Greeks children in antiquities, we may well call them children; and so we may call all those nations which were able to trace the progress of society only within their own limits. But now the great map of mankind is unrolled at once, and there is no state or gradation of barbarism, and no mode of refinement, which we have not at the same moment under our view; the very different civility of Europe and of China; the barbarism of Persia and of Abyssinia; the erratic manners of Tartary and of Arabia; the savage state of North America and New Zealand. Indeed you have made a noble use of the advantages you have had. You have employed philosophy to judge on manners, and from manners you have drawn new resources for philosophy. I only think that in one or two points you have hardly done justice to the savage character."

The honours which were paid to him by foreigners were equally gratifying. The Royal Academy of History at Madrid unanimously elected him a member on the eighth of August, in 1777, "in testimony of their approbation of the industry and care with which he had applied to the study of Spanish History, and as a recompense for his merit in having contributed so much to illustrate and spread the knowledge of it in foreign countries." It likewise appointed one of its members to translate the History of America into the Spanish language, and considerable progress is believed to have been made in the translation. But the latter measure excited alarm in an absurd and decrepit government, which sought for safety in concealment rather than in a bold and liberal policy, and, like the silly bird, imagined that by hiding its own head it could escape from the view of its pursuers. The translation was, therefore, officially ordered to be suppressed, with the vain hope of keeping the world still in the dark, with respect to the nature of the Spanish American commerce, and of the system of colonial administration.

It was not from Spain alone that he received testimonies of respect. In 1781, the Academy of Sciences at Padua elected him one of its foreign members; and, in 1783, the same compliment was paid to him by the Imperial Academy of Sciences at St. Petersburgh. The empress Catharine also, who, numerous as were her faults, was a woman of a strong and enlightened intellect, also conferred on him a flattering distinction. She ordered his friend, Dr. Rogerson, to transmit to him, as a mark of her esteem, a gold snuff box, richly set with diamonds; observing at the same time, that a person whose labours had afforded her so much satisfaction merited some attention from her. So much, indeed, was she delighted with the works of the Scottish author, that she did not hesitate to assign to him the place of first model in historical composition, to express much admiration of the sagacity and discernment which he displayed in painting the human mind and character, and to declare that the History of Charles the Fifth was the constant companion of her journeys, and that she was never tired of perusing it, particularly the introductory volume.

As soon as enthusiasm had subsided, criticism began its labours in search of defects. It was objected to the author, that he had shown a disposition to palliate or to veil the enormities of the Spaniards, in their American conquests, and that he had shed an illusive lustre round the daring and intelligent but sanguinary and unprincipled Cortes. Even Professor Stewart, notwithstanding his honourable affection for the memory of his friend, shrinks from vindicating him on this score, and contents himself with opposing to the charge "those warm and enlightened sentiments of humanity which in general animate his writings." Unwilling to censure severely, and unable to exculpate, Bryan Edwards suggests, as an apology for Dr Robertson, that this is one of the cases in which the mind, shrinking from the contemplation of alleged horrors, wishes to resist conviction, and to relieve itself by incredulity. Dr. Gleig, however, the latest biographer of the historian, indignantly rejects this apology as absurd; and, more enterprising than his predecessors, partly labours to invalidate the accusation, by lessening the sum of Spanish cruelties, and partly to render it of no weight, by pleading that the writer probably considered the conquests of Mexico and Peru as means employed by Providence to accomplish the noblest and most beneficent purposes. That Dr. Robertson did really regard those conquests in such a light we may easily believe; since, in his sermon on the state of the world at the appearance of Christ, he manifests similar sentiments with respect to the measureless and unslumbering ambition of those universal robbers the Romans, whom he is pleased to style "the noblest people that ever entered on the stage of the world." But this defence is merely sophistical. Though we are not ignorant that a wise and benignant Providence educes good from evil, it is not the business of an historian to diminish the loathing which evil deeds ought to excite; nor does it appear that morality is likely to be much benefited, by teaching tyrants and murderers to imagine that, while they are giving the rein to their own furious and malignant passions, they are only performing their destined tasks as instruments of the Deity.

This was by no means all that was urged against the History of America. It is, in fact, not now attempted to be denied that, in many instances, Dr. Robertson was led astray by his partiality to the brilliant but fallacious theories of De Pauw and Buffon. Clavigero, in his History of Mexico, detected and somewhat harshly animadverted on several errors, a part of which were subsequently rectified. Bryan Edwards, too, pointed out some contradictions, and some erroneous statements. But the most severe censor is Mr. Southey, a man eminently well informed on ancient Spanish and American events. In his History of Brazil, after having described the mode of reckoning in use among the transatlantic tribes, he adds, "when Pauw reasoned upon the ignorance of the Americans in numbers, did he suppress this remarkable fact, or was he ignorant of it? The same question is applicable to Dr. Robertson, who, on this, and on many other subjects, in what he calls his History of America, is guilty of such omissions, and consequent misrepresentations, as to make it certain either that he had not read some of the most important documents to which he refers, or that he did not choose to notice the facts which he found there, because they were not in conformity to his own preconceived opinions. A remarkable example occurs respecting a circulating medium; when he mentions cocoanuts, which were used as money in Mexico, and says, 'this seems to be the utmost length which the Americans had advanced towards the discovery of any expedient for supplying the use of money.' Now, it is said by Cortes himself, that when he was about to make cannon, he had copper enough, but wanted tin; and having bought up all the plates and pots, which he could find among the soldiers, he began to inquire among the natives. He then found, that in the province of Tachco, little pieces of tin, like thin coin, were used for money, there and in other places. And this led him to a discovery of the mines from whence it was taken. The reputation of this author must rest upon his History of Scotland, if that can support it. His other works are grievously deficient."

Such are the defects which are attributed to Dr. Robertson's History On the other hand, it ought to be remembered, that many sources of knowledge, which were then hidden, have since become accessible, that no man is at all times exempted from the dominion of prejudice, that the most cautious vigilance may sink into a momentary slumber, and that to him who has achieved much, a tribute of gratitude is due, even though it may be discovered that he has left something undone. Were the History of the Spanish Conquests proved to be merely a fiction, it would nevertheless continue to be read, such attraction is there in the general elegance of the language, the skilful delineation of the characters, and the sustained interest and spirit of the narrative.

In the preface to this portion of his labours, he made known his intention to resume the subject at a future period; and he assigned the ferment which then agitated our North American colonies as a reason for suspending, at present, the execution of that part of his plan which related to British America. At the very beginning, in truth, of the contest with the colonies, he congratulated himself on his not having completed his narrative. "It is lucky," said he, in a letter to Mr. Strahan, "that my American History was not finished before this event. How many plausible theories that I should have been entitled to form, are contradicted by what has now happened." A fragment of this History, which, however, was carefully corrected by him, and which he preserved when he committed his manuscripts to the flames, was all that he subsequently wrote of the work; and this was published by his son to prevent it from falling into the hands of an editor who might make alterations and additions, and obtrude the whole on the public as the genuine composition of the author.

With respect to a separation between the mother country and the colonists, Dr. Robertson seems to have somewhat varied in his sentiments, and to have contemplated the probability of such an event with much more dislike in 1775 than he did in 1766. In the latter year, speaking of the repeal of the stamp act, he said, "I rejoice, from my love of the human species, that a million of men in America have some chance of running the same great career which other free people have held before them. I do not apprehend revolution or independence sooner than these must or should come. A very little skill and attention in the art of governing may preserve the supremacy of Britain as long as it ought to be preserved." But, in 1775, though he still acknowledged that the colonies must ultimately become independent, he was anxious that their liberation should be delayed till as distant a period as possible, and was clearly of opinion that they had as yet no right to throw off their allegiance. Nor was he sparing of his censure on the ministers for the want of policy and firmness, which he considered them to have displayed at the commencement of the quarrel. "I agree with you about the affairs of America," said he, in a letter, which was written in the autumn of 1775, "incapacity, or want of information, has led the people employed there to deceive the ministry. Trusting to them, they have been trifling for two years, when they should have been serious, until they have rendered a very simple piece of business extremely perplexed. They have permitted colonies, disjoined by nature and situation, to consolidate into a regular systematical confederacy; and when a few regiments stationed in each capital would have rendered it impossible for them to take arms, they have suffered them quietly to levy and train forces, as if they had not seen against whom they were prepared. But now we are fairly committed, and I do think it fortunate that the violence of the Americans has brought matters to a crisis too soon for themselves. From the beginning of the contest I have always asserted that independence was their object. The distinction between *taxation* and *regulation* is mere folly. There is not an argument against our right of taxation that does not conclude with tenfold force against our power of regulating their trade. They may profess or disclaim what they please, and hold the language that best suits their purpose; but, if they have any meaning, it must be that they should be free states, connected with us by blood, by habit, and by religion, but at liberty to buy and sell and trade where and with whom they please. This they will one day attain, but not just now, if there be any degree of political wisdom or vigour remaining. At the same time one cannot but regret that prosperous growing states should be checked in their career. As a lover of mankind, I bewail it; but as a subject of Great Britain, I must wish that their dependence on it should continue. If the wisdom of government can terminate the contest with honour instantly, that would be the most desirable issue This, however, I take to be *now* impossible; and I will venture to fore tell, that if our leaders do not at once exert the power of the British empire in its full force, the struggle will be long, dubious, and disgraceful We are past the hour of lenitives and half exertions. If the contest be protracted, the smallest interruption of the tranquillity that reigns in Europe, or even the appearance of it, may be fatal."

It must be owned, that language like this goes very far towards justifying the sarcasm of Horace Walpole, that the reverend historian was "a *very* moderate Whig." Perhaps, also, his belief that, at the outset, a few regiments in each capital would have sufficed to trample down the resistance of the Americans, may now appear difficult to be reconciled with a knowledge of military affairs, or of human nature. Yet we must, at the same time, remember that this erroneous idea was held by him in common with many other men of intellect, and that it was even brought forward in the British senate as an undeniable truth.

Though the American war precluded Dr. Robertson from bringing to a close his history of the British settlements, it is not easy to discover why he could not continue it to a certain point; or why, at least, he could not proceed with that part of his narrative which related to the colonization of Brazil, and the violent struggles between the Dutch and the Portuguese in that country—an extensive subject, and worthy of his pen, as it would have afforded him abundant opportunities for the display of his delineative talents. Our curiosity on this head is not satisfied by the reason which, as we have recently seen, he himself gave, in his preface and in his letter to Mr. Strahan. That reason, however, he repeated in a correspondence with his friend Mr. Waddilove, and it is now in vain to seek for a better. It is certain that a wish to retire from literary toil was not his motive; for, at the same moment that he postponed his History of America, he declared that it was "neither his inclination nor his interest to remain altogether idle." As a proof of his sincerity, he projected a History of Great Britain, from the revolution to the accession of the House of Hanover, and even began to collect the necessary documents. Notwithstanding this seems to have been, for a while, a favourite scheme, it was speedily relinquished; a circumstance which may justly be regretted. Hume then suggested the History of the Protestants in France. "The events," said he, 'are important in themselves, and intimately connected with the great revolutions of Europe: some of the boldest or most amiable characters of modern times, the admiral Coligny, Henry IV., &c. would be your peculiar heroes; the materials are copious, and authentic, and accessible; and the objects appear to stand at that just distance which excites curiosity without inspiring passion."

The hint given by Hume was, however, not adopted. About the year 1779 or 1780, Dr. Robertson seems, indeed, to have seriously resolved to write no more for the public, but to pursue his studies at leisure, and for his own amusement "His circumstances," says professor Stewart, "were independent: he was approaching to the age of sixty, with a constitution considerably impaired by a sedentary life; and a long application to the compositions he had prepared for the press had interfered with much of the gratification he might have enjoyed, if he had been at liberty to follow the impulse of his own taste and curiosity. Such a sacrifice must be more or less made by all who devote themselves to letters, whether with a view to emolument or to fame; nor would it perhaps be easy to make it, were it not for the prospect (seldom, alas! realized) of earning by their exertions, that learned and honourable leisure which he was so fortunate as to attain."

We must now contemplate Dr. Robertson in another point of view—that of his ecclesiastical and academical character; in which, no less than in his literary capacity, he occupied a prominent station. The eminence, however, which he had not attained without difficulty, he did not hold entirely without danger. In one instance he was near falling a victim to his spirit of liberality. In 1778, the British legislature relieved the English Roman catholics from some of the severest of the barbarous penalties to which they had been subjected nearly a century before. Encouraged by this event, the Scottish catholics determined to petition parliament to extend the benefit to themselves. To this measure Dr. Robertson was friendly, and he successfully exerted his influence, and that of his partisans, to procure the rejection of a remonstrance against it, which was brought forward in the general assembly. But on this occasion, as, unhappily, on too many others, bigotry and ignorance triumphed over sound policy and Christian charity. The trumpet of fanaticism was immediately sounded, and men of the most opposite principles and interests hurried to obey the call. Presbyterians, seceders, and even episcopalians, the latter of whom were themselves under the lash of penal statutes, all combined in the crusade against papistry. Pamphlets and speeches were lavished, to prove that the constitution in church and state must inevitably perish, if an iota of relief were granted to the faithless members of an idolatrous and sanguinary church. The Roman catholics were so terrified at the fury that was thus aroused, that the principal gentlemen among them informed the ministry that they would desist from appealing to parliament; and they endeavoured to calm the popular tempest, by publishing in the daily papers an account of their proceedings. But the enlightened mob of Edinburgh had sagely resolved that the catholics should not even dare to wish for the slightest participation in the privileges of British subjects, without being punished for their temerity. Accordingly, on the 2d of February, 1779, multitudes of the lowest classes, headed by disguised leaders, assembled in the Scottish capital, burnt the house of the popish bishop and two chapels: and, in their even-handed justice, were on the point of committing to the flames an episcopal chapel, when they were propitiated, by being told that an episcopal clergyman was the author of one of the ablest tracts which had been published against popery. As, however, they could not consent to remit their vengeance, but only to change its object, they turned their wrath upon those who had expressed opinions favourable to the claims of the catholics. Dr. Robertson was marked out as one of the most guilty, and nothing less than the destruction of his property and life was considered as sufficient to atone for his crime. Fortunately his friends had provided for his safety, and, when the self-appointed champions of religion reached his house, it was found to be defended by a military force, which they had not enough of courage to look in the face. As they had come only to destroy and to murder, they, of course, retreated, when they discovered that, to accomplish their purpose, it would also be necessary to fight. Dr. Robertson is said to have manifested great firmness and tranquillity during this trying scene.

In selecting Dr. Robertson as the person most worthy of suffering by their summary process of punishment without trial, the mob of Edinburgh acted with a more than mobbish share of injustice. Though desirous that the catholics should be released from their thraldom, he was not disposed to put any thing to the hazard for the furtherance of that object, and had already withdrawn his patronage from such obnoxious clients. He was not one of those who, as Goldsmith says of Burke, are "too fond of the *right* to pursue the *expedient*." With him prudence was a governing principle. When, therefore, he saw that his countrymen were adverse to the measure, he advised the ministry to forbear from lending their countenance to it. In an eloquent speech, delivered in the general assembly, he afterwards explained and vindicated the view which he originally took of the subject, and the manner in which he finally acted. The perusal of that which he urged, on the latter point, will not merely show what were his motives in this instance, but also afford some insight into his general character. How far his system of policy is consonant with dignity or wisdom, which, indeed, are inseparable, I shall not stop to inquire. It might, perhaps, not improperly, be objected to him, that he mistakes the voice of a blind infuriated multitude for the voice of the people; though it is impossible for any two things to be more different in their nature. It might be asked, too, why the fanatical prejudices of a Scottish mob were to be treated with more respect than the complaints of the American colonists why the one were to be indulged or complied with, while the other were to be silenced by "a few regiments stationed in each capital?" "As soon," says he, "as I perceived the extent and violence of the flame which the discussion of this subject had kindled in Scotland, my ideas concerning the expedience at this juncture of the measure in question, began to alter. For although I did think, and I do still believe, that if the protestants in this country had acquiesced in the repeal as quietly as our brethren in England and Ireland, a fatal blow would have been given to popery in the British dominions; I know, that in legislation, the sentiments and dispositions of the people, for whom laws are made, should be attended to with care. I remembered that one of the wisest men of antiquity declared, that he had framed for his fellow-citizens not the best laws, but the best laws which they could bear. I recollected with reverence, that the divine Legislator himself, accommodating his dispensations to the frailty of his subjects, had given the Israelites for a season *statutes which were not good*. Even the prejudices of the people are, in my opinion, respectable; and an indulgent legislator ought not unnecessarily to run counter to them. It appeared manifestly to be sound policy, in the present temper of the people, to sooth rather than to irritate them; and, however ill founded their apprehensions might be, some concession was now requisite in order to remove them."

This was, I believe, the last speech which he made in the General Assembly. While he was yet in the vigour of his faculties, and in the exercise of undiminished influence in that assembly, he came to a resolution to withdraw himself entirely from public business. It was in the year 1780, about the time when he ceased to be an historian, and when he was only fifty-nine, that he adopted this resolution. Several causes seem to have concurred in producing his retirement. It has been supposed by some, that he did not wish to remain on the scene till he was eclipsed by younger rivals; and it is known that he felt disgusted by the conduct of the violent men of his own party, who, though he had yielded many points to them against his better judgment, were nevertheless dissatisfied that he refused to resort to stronger measures than he deemed to be either right or prudent, and who, in consequence, tormented him with letters of remonstrance and reproach, which, as from their nature may easily be imagined, were written in a petulant and acrimonious style. In addition, there was one subject, which had long been a particular annoyance to him, and on which he had been more pertinaciously urged and fretted than on every other. This was a scheme for abolishing subscription to the Confession of Faith and Formula. Into this scheme, which he had avowed his determination to resist, whatever shape it might assume, many of his friends had zealously entered, and his patience was severely tried by their "beseeching or besieging" him with respect to so important an object. By his cautious and persuasive policy, he had for a considerable period prevented the controversy from being agitated in the assemblies; but he was of opinion that it would ultimately compel attention, and would give rise to vehement disputes; and it was this circumstance, as he himself confessed, that "at least confirmed his resolution to retire."

Having rendered triumphant a cause which, to say the least, had numerous enemies, it was hardly to be supposed that his character would not be aspersed by many of those who were mortified to witness his success.

Accordingly, the charge of having deserted the genuine principles of the Scottish church was often urged against him by some of his antagonists. Others, who had more of the zealot in their composition, did not stop here. These went so far as to accuse him of being indifferent to Christianity itself; and, in proof of this, they alleged his habits of intimacy with Hume, and his correspondence with Gibbon. It is difficult to say whether this stupid calumny ought to excite anger or contempt.

This, however, was the language of only malignant hearts, or little minds. By the great majority, even of those who were in opposition to him, full justice was done to his virtues, his talents, and the purity of his motives. Among those who, believing patronage to be a nuisance, were the most strenuous in contending with him, was Dr. Erskine, his college mate, and colleague in the ministry. That venerable and learned person always preserved for him a warm esteem, and, after the historian was no more, paid to his memory an animated and affectionate tribute from the pulpit. "His speeches in church courts," says Dr. Erskine, "were admired by those whom they did not convince, and acquired and preserved him an influence over a majority in them, which none before him enjoyed; though his measures were sometimes new, and warmly, and with great strength of argument, opposed, both from the press, and in the General Assembly. To this influence many causes contributed: his firm adherence to the principles of church policy, which he early adopted; his sagacity in forming plans; his steadiness in executing them; his quick discernment of whatever might hinder or promote his designs; his boldness in encountering difficulties; his presence of mind in improving every occasional advantage; the address with which, when he saw it necessary, he could make an honourable retreat; and his skill in stating a vote, and seizing the favourable moment for ending a debate and urging a decision. He guided and governed others, without seeming to assume any superiority over them; and fixed and strengthened his power, by often, in matters of form and expediency, preferring the opinions of those with whom he acted, to his own. In former times, hardly any rose up to speak in the General Assembly, till called upon by the *Moderator*, unless men advanced in years, of high rank, or of established characters. His example and influence encouraged young men of abilities to take their share of public business, and thus deprived *Moderators* of an engine for preventing causes being fairly and impartially discussed. The power of others, who formerly had in some measure guided ecclesiastical affairs, was derived from ministers of state, and expired with their fall. He remained unhurt amidst frequent changes of administration. Great men in office were always ready to countenance him, to co-operate with him, and to avail themselves of his aid. But he judged for himself, and scorned to be their slave, or to submit to receive their instructions. Hence, his influence, not confined to men of mercenary views, extended to many of a free and independent spirit, who supported, because they approved, his measures; which others, from the same independent spirit, thought it their duty steadily to oppose.

"Deliberate in forming his judgment, but, when formed, not easily moved to renounce it, he sometimes viewed the altered plans of others with too suspicious an eye. Hence, there were able and worthy men, of whom he expressed himself less favourably, and whose later appearances in church judicatories he censured as inconsistent with principles they had formerly professed: while they maintained, that the system of managing church affairs was changed, not their opinions or conduct. Still, however, keen and determined opposition to his schemes of ecclesiastical policy neither extinguished his esteem nor forfeited his friendly offices, when he saw opposition carried on without rancour, and when he believed that it originated from conscience and principle, not from personal animosity, or envy, or ambition."

Of his private character, Dr. Erskine adds, that "he enjoyed the bounties of Providence, without running into riot; was temperate without austerity; condescending and affable without meanness; and in expense neither sordid nor prodigal. He could feel an injury, and yet bridle his passion; was grave, not sullen; steady, not obstinate; friendly, not officious; prudent and cautious, not timid."

Than the triumph which the principles of Dr. Robertson obtained in the General Assembly nothing could be more complete; and it was the more flattering, inasmuch as it was consummated after he had ceased to take a part in the debates. It had, from the year 1736, been the custom, annually, for the Assembly to instruct the Commission, "to make due application to the king and parliament for redress of the grievance of patronage, in case a favourable opportunity for doing so should occur." So cautious was the policy of Dr. Robertson, that, although he had entirely subverted the very groundwork on which this instruction was raised, he never chose to move that it should be expunged. He knew that it was popular with the great body of the people, and, therefore, he did not think it expedient to risk the chance of dissension in the Assembly, by an unnecessary and idle attack upon this shadow of a shade. In the year 1784, however, it was omitted, without any struggle being made in its favour, and it has never since been renewed.

Whether the system established by him has contributed to the harmony and welfare of the Scottish church is a question which yet remains undecided. It is urged, by the friends of the system, that it has given peace to the church; that the General Assembly is no longer occupied with angry appeals and tumultuous disputes; that instead of there being, as formerly, a necessity to call in a military force, to protect the presbytery in the act of induction, ministers are now peaceably settled; and that the worst that ever happens is the secession of the discontented part of the parishioners, and the consequent erection of a separate place of worship, which they frequent only till their zeal cools, and then desert to rejoin the kirk. But, on the other hand, it is contended, that the peace is rather in appearance than in reality; that, though the people have ceased to appeal to the Assembly, their silence arises from disgust and weariness, and not from satisfaction; that, grown too wise to enter into a protracted and fruitless contest, they immediately set themselves to rear a seceding meeting house, which often carries off a large proportion of the parishioners; and that, by this quiet but continual increase of seceding meetings, the influence of the established church has been gradually weakened and contracted, a spirit of disunion has been spread, and a heavy additional burden has been imposed on property of every kind.

But, whatever doubt may exist on this point, there seems to be none with respect to another. It is generally acknowledged that Dr. Robertson conduced greatly to give a more dignified character to the proceedings of the General Assembly, to introduce an impartial exercise of the judicial authority of the church, and to diffuse the principles of tolerance among men who had hitherto prided themselves on their utter contempt of them. In such respect are his decisions held, that they still form a sort of common law in the church; and the time which elapsed between his being chosen Principal of the University and his withdrawing from public life, is distinguished by the name of Dr. Robertson's administration

It is in his capacity of Principal that he is next to be considered. In this important office he displayed his wonted activity and talent. He began the performance of his duties, as his predecessors had done, by delivering annually a Latin discourse before the University. Of these orations, the first, the object of which was to recommend the study of classical learning, was delivered on the third of February, 1763. It is said, among numerous other splendid passages, to have contained a beautiful panegyric on the stoical philosophy. In the following year, his discourse "consisted chiefly of moral and literary observations, adapted to the particular circumstances of youth," and the style is affirmed to be "uncommonly elegant and impressive, and possessed of all the distinguishing characteristics of his English compositions." In 1765 and 1766, he chose for his theme the comparative advantages of public and private education; a subject which he treated in a masterly manner. After 1766 these annual lectures ceased his time being too fully occupied to allow of the continuance of them.

But, though his lectures were of necessity discontinued, he never remitted in his attention even to the minutest duties of his office. He appears, indeed, to have felt a filial anxiety to omit nothing which could assist in giving lustre to the University at which his own talents had been cultivated. With very slender funds, he made large additions to the public library; he planned or reformed most of the literary and medical societies, which have raised Edinburgh to such eminence as a seminary of learning, and a focus of literature; and he contrived to preserve an uninterrupted harmony among the numerous members of the body which he superintended. "The good sense, temper, and address," says professor Stewart, "with which he presided for thirty years at our university meetings, were attended with effects no less essential to our prosperity; and are attested by a fact which is perhaps without a parallel in the annals of any other literary community, that during the whole of that period there did not occur a single question which was not terminated by a unanimous decision."

To his exertions Scotland is also chiefly indebted for its Royal Society, which received its charter of incorporation in March, 1763. The basis of this establishment was the Philosophical Society, the founder of which was the celebrated Maclaurin. In his zeal to give all possible lustre to the new institution, by drawing together men of every species of merit, Dr. Robertson seems, for once, to have acted with less than his usual liberality. An antiquarian society, at the head of which was the earl of Buchan, had, two years before, been formed in the Scottish metropolis; and this body also was desirous to obtain the royal charter. The application which it made to the crown was, however, eagerly opposed, in a "Memorial from the principal and professors of the University of Edinburgh." This memorial is signed by Dr. Robertson; but it is so feeble in composition as well as in reasoning, that it is difficult to believe it to have flowed from his pen. The argument on which it wholly relies is, that "narrow countries" cannot supply materials for more than one society; that Scotland is such a country; and, therefore, that it "ought not to form its literary plans upon the model of the more extensive kingdoms in Europe, but in imitation of those which are more circumscribed." To this hostile proceeding the antiquaries responded, in a long memorial, which was penned with much acuteness, and was naturally expressive of some degree of resentment. They were successful in the contest, and their charter was granted.

The labours of Dr. Robertson, as a writer, were closed by a work which entered largely into antiquarian investigation, as connected with history In 1791 he published a quarto volume, containing his "Historical Disquisition concerning the Knowledge which the Ancients had of India; and the Progress of Trade with that Country prior to the Discovery of the Passage to it by the Cape of Good Hope." An Appendix was dedicated to observations on the civil policy, the laws and judicial proceedings, the arts, the sciences, and the religious institutions of the Indians. This subject, which occupied him twelve months, was suggested to him by the perusal of major Rennell's Memoirs for illustrating his History of Hindostan, and was originally taken up with no other object than his own amusement and instruction. That it would become as popular as his other productions was, from its nature, not to be expected, but it obtained an honourable share of public approbation, and, though it has since been partly superseded by more elaborate inquiries, which, however, were grounded on more ample materials, it will always retain a certain degree of value, and will be considered as a proof of his industry, of his habits of research, and of the solidity of his judgment.

The latter years of Dr. Robertson's existence were passed in the well earned enjoyment of honourable leisure. But, though he ceased to write, he did not cease to be studious. Till the end of his life he is said to have risen early, and to have given up no part of his time to company before the hour of dinner. What he was in the moments of social ease has been so excellently described by professor Stewart, that his own words ought to be used. "A rich stock of miscellaneous information, acquired from books and from an extensive intercourse with the world, together with a perfect acquaintance at all times with the topics of the day, and the soundest sagacity and good sense applied to the occurrences of common life, rendered him the most instructive and agreeable of companions. He seldom aimed at art; but, with his intimate friends, he often indulged a sportive and fanciful species of humour. He delighted in good natured characteristical anecdotes of his acquaintance, and added powerfully to their effect by his own enjoyment in relating them. He was, in a remarkable degree, susceptible of the ludicrous; but on no occasion did he forget the dignity of his character, or the decorum of his profession; nor did he ever lose sight of that classical taste which adorned his compositions. His turn of expression was correct and pure; sometimes, perhaps, inclining more than is expected, in the carelessness of a social hour, to formal and artificial periods; but it was stamped with his own manner no less than his premeditated style: it was always the language of a superior and a cultivated mind, and it embellished every subject on which he spoke. In the company of strangers, he increased his exertions to amuse and to inform; and the splendid variety of his conversation was commonly the chief circumstance on which they dwelt in enumerating his talents; and yet, I must acknowledge, for my own part, that much as I always admired his powers when they were thus called forth, I enjoyed his society less than when I saw him in the circle of his intimates, or in the bosom of his family."

It is not one of the least amiable features of his character, that, though he was not forward to volunteer his advice, yet, when he was consulted by his young acquaintance, as was very often the case, "he entered into their concerns with the most lively interest, and seemed to have a pleasure and a pride in imparting to them all the lights of his experience and wisdom."

It was about the end of the year 1791 that the health of Dr. Robertson began to manifest indications of decline. Strong symptoms of jaundice next appeared, his constitution was sapped, and a lingering and fatal illness ensued. His spirits, however, remained unbroken. Till within a few months of his death, he persisted in officiating as a minister. When his decaying strength no longer allowed him to perform his clerical duties, he retired to Grange House, in the neighbourhood of Edinburgh, that he might have the advantage of more quiet, a pure air, and the sight of those rural and picturesque objects in which he had ever delighted. "While he was able to walk abroad," says Mr. Stewart, "he commonly passed a part of the day in a small garden, enjoying the simple gratifications it afforded with all his wonted relish. Some who now hear me will long remember, among the trivial yet interesting incidents which marked these last weeks of his memorable life, his daily visits to the fruit trees (which were then in blossom), and the smile with which he, more than once, contrasted the interest he took in their progress, with the event which was to happen before their maturity." It was while he was thus lingering on the verge of the grave, that he was visited by two gentlemen from New-York, who were extremely anxious for an interview with him. He rallied all his powers to entertain his guests, and to inspire in their minds a feeling of kindness towards the parent land of the late colonists; and, on their rising to take leave, he said to them, in accents at once dignified and pathetic, "When you go home, tell your countrymen that you saw the wreck of Dr. Robertson." In less than two months that wreck disappeared in the ocean of eternity. He expired, with the fortitude which became him, on the 11th of July, 1793, in the seventy-first year of his age, and the fiftieth of his ministry.

So much has been written by others, respecting the literary merit of Dr. Robertson, that on this point it is unnecessary, even would my con fined limits permit me, to enter into a lengthened discussion. His style has less of careless easy grace, but has more of equable dignity, than that of Hume; it does not display the masterly modulation, but it has none of the occasional obscurity and meretricious ornament, of that of Gibbon; it is well balanced, unstained by vulgarisms, more idiomatically English than might be expected from a native of Scotland, and is defective, perhaps, only in being too uniformly of an elevated tone. In arranging and linking together into one harmonious whole the scattered parts of his subject, he is eminently happy; and in delineating characters, manners, and scenery, in making vividly present to the mind that which he describes, he has few rivals, and no superiors. If all that has been urged against his works be admitted, and some of it cannot be denied, it may nevertheless safely be affirmed, that the balance heavily preponderates in his favour and that he will always continue to rank in the first class of modern historians.

# PREFACE.

In fulfilling the engagement which I had come under to the Public with respect to the History of America, it was my intention not to have published any part of the Work until the whole was completed. The present state of the British colonies has induced me to alter that resolution. While they are engaged in civil war with Great Britain, inquiries and speculations concerning their ancient forms of policy and laws, which exist no longer, cannot be interesting. The attention and expectation of mankind are now turned towards their future condition. In whatever manner this unhappy contest may terminate, a new order of things must arise in North America, and its affairs will assume another aspect. I wait with the solicitude of a good citizen, until the ferment subside, and regular government be re-established, and then I shall return to this part of my work, in which I had made some progress. That, together with the history of Portuguese America, and of the settlements made by the several nations of Europe in the West India Islands, will complete my plan.

The three volumes which I now publish contain an account of the discovery of the New World, and of the progress of the Spanish arms and colonies there. This is not only the most splendid portion of the American story, but so much detached, as by itself to form a perfect whole, remarkable for the unity of the subject. As the principles and maxims of the Spaniards in planting colonies, which have been adopted in some measure by every nation, are unfolded in this part of my work; it will serve as a proper introduction to the history of all the European establishments in America, and convey such information concerning this important article of policy, as may be deemed no less interesting than curious.

In describing the achievements and institutions of the Spaniards in the New World, I have departed in many instances, from the accounts of preceding historians, and have often related facts which seem to have been unknown to them. It is a duty I owe the Public to mention the sources from which I have derived such intelligence which justifies me either in placing transactions in a new light, or in forming any new opinion with respect to their causes and effects. This duty I perform with greater satisfaction, as it will afford an opportunity of expressing my gratitude to those benefactors who have honoured me with their countenance and aid in my researches.

As it was from Spain that I had to expect the most important information, with regard to this part of my work, I considered it as a very fortunate circumstance for me, when Lord Grantham, to whom I had the honour of being personally known, and with whose liberality of sentiment, and disposition to oblige, I was well acquainted, was appointed ambassador to the court of Madrid. Upon applying to him, I met with such a reception as satisfied me that his endeavours would be employed in the most proper manner, in order to obtain the gratification of my wishes; and I am perfectly sensible, that what progress I have made in my inquiries among the Spaniards, ought to be ascribed chiefly to their knowing how much his lordship interested himself in my success.

But did I owe nothing more to Lord Grantham than the advantages which I have derived from his attention in engaging Mr. Waddilove, the chaplain of his embassy, to take the conduct of my literary inquiries in Spain, the obligations I lie under to him would be very great. During five years that gentleman has carried on researches for my behoof, with such activity, perseverance, and knowledge of the subject, to which his attention was turned, as have filled me with no less astonishment than satisfaction. He procured for me the greater part of the Spanish books which I have consulted; and as many of them were printed early in the sixteenth century, and are become extremely rare, the collecting of these was such an occupation as alone required much time and assiduity. To his friendly attention I am indebted for copies of several valuable manuscripts, containing facts and details which I might have searched for in vain in works that have been made public. Encouraged by the inviting good will with which Mr. Waddilove conferred his favours, I transmitted to him a set of queries, with respect both to the customs and policy of the native Americans, and the nature of several institutions in the Spanish settlements, framed in such a manner that a Spaniard might answer them without disclosing any thing that was improper to be communicated to a foreigner. He translated these into Spanish, and obtained from various persons who had resided in most of the Spanish colonies, such replies as have afforded me much instruction.

Notwithstanding those peculiar advantages with which my inquiries were carried on in Spain, it is with regret I am obliged to add, that their success must be ascribed to the beneficence of individuals, not to any communication by public authority. By a singular arrangement of Philip II. the records of the Spanish monarchy are deposited in the *Archivo* of Simancas, near Valladolid, at the distance of a hundred and twenty miles from the seat of government and the supreme courts of justice. The papers relative to America, and chiefly to that early period of its history towards which my attention was directed, are so numerous, that they alone, according to one account, fill the largest apartment in the Archivo; and, according to another, they compose eight hundred and seventy-three large bundles. Conscious of possessing, in some degree, the industry which belongs to an historian, the prospect of such a treasure excited my most ardent curiosity. But the prospect of it is all that I have enjoyed. Spain, with an excess of caution, has uniformly thrown a veil over her transactions in America. From strangers they are concealed with peculiar solicitude. Even to her own subjects the Archivo of Simancas is not opened without a particular order from the crown; and, after obtaining that, papers cannot be copied without paying fees of office so exorbitant that the expense exceeds what it would be proper to bestow, when the gratification of literary curiosity is the only object. It is to be hoped, that the Spaniards will at last discover this system of concealment to be no less impolitic than illiberal. From what I have experienced in the course of my inquiries, I am satisfied, that upon a more minute scrutiny into their early operation in the New World, however reprehensible the actions of individuals may appear, the conduct of the nation will be placed in a more favourable light.

In other parts of Europe very different sentiments prevail. Having searched, without success, in Spain, for a letter of Cortes to Charles V., written soon after he landed in the Mexican Empire, which has not hitherto been published; it occurred to me, that as the Emperor was setting out for Germany at the time when the messengers from Cortes arrived in Europe, the letter with which they were intrusted might possibly be preserved in the Imperial library at Vienna. I communicated this idea to Sir Robert Murray Keith, with whom I have long had the honour to live in friendship, and I had soon the pleasure to learn, that upon his application her Imperial Majesty had been graciously pleased to issue an order, that not only a copy of that letter (if it were found), but of any other papers in the library which could throw light upon the History of America, should be transmitted to me. The letter from Cortes is not in the Imperial library; but an authentic copy, attested by a notary, of the letter written by the magistrates of the colony planted by him at Vera Cruz, which I have mentioned, p. 210, having been found, it was transcribed, and sent to me. As this letter is no less curious, and as little known as that which was the object of my inquiries, I have given some account, in its proper place, of what is most worthy of notice in it. Together with it, I received a copy of a letter from Cortes, containing a long account of his expedition to Honduras, with respect to which I did not think it necessary to enter into any particular detail; and likewise those curious Mexican paintings, which I have described, p. 321.

My inquiries at St. Petersburg were carried on with equal facility and success. In examining into the nearest communication between our continent and that of America, it became of consequence to obtain authentic information concerning the discoveries of the Russians in their navigation from Kamchatka towards the coast of America. Accurate relations of their first voyage, in 1741, have been published by Muller and Gmelin. Several foreign authors have entertained an opinion that the court of Russia studiously conceals the progress which has been made by more recent navigators, and suffers the Public to be amused with false accounts of their route. Such conduct appeared to me unsuitable to those liberal sentiments, and that patronage of science, for which the present sovereign of Russia is eminent; nor could I discern any political reason, that might render it improper to apply for information concerning the late attempts of the Russians to open a communication between Asia and America. My ingenious countryman, Dr. Rogerson, first physician to the Empress, presented my request to Her Imperial Majesty, who not only disclaimed any idea of concealment, but instantly ordered the journal of Captain Krenitzin, who conducted the only voyage of discovery made by public authority since the year 1741, to be translated, and his original chart to be copied for my use. By consulting them, I have been enabled to give a more accurate view of the progress and extent of the Russian discoveries than has hitherto been communicated to the Public.

From other quarters I have received information of great utility and importance. M. le Chevalier de Pinto, the minister from Portugal to the court of Great Britain, who commanded for several years at Matagrosso, a settlement of the Portuguese in the interior part of Brazil, where the Indians are numerous, and their original manners little altered by intercourse with Europeans, was pleased to send me very full answers to some queries concerning the character and institutions of the natives of America, which his polite reception of an application made to him in my name encouraged me to propose. These satisfied me, that he had contemplated with a discerning attention the curious objects which his situation presented to his view, and I have often followed him as one of my best instructed guides.

M. Suard, to whose elegant translation of the History of the Reign of Charles V., I owe the favourable reception of that work on the continent, procured me answers to the same queries from M. de Bougainville, who had opportunities of observing the Indians both of North and South America, and from M. Godin le Jeune, who resided fifteen years among Indians in Quito, and twenty years in Cayenne. The latter are more valuable from having been examined by M. de la Condamine, who, a few weeks before his death, made some short additions to them, which may be considered as the last effort of that attention to science which occupied a long life.

My inquiries were not confined to one region in America. Governor Hutchinson took the trouble of recommending the consideration of my queries to Mr. Hawley and Mr. Brainerd, two protestant missionaries employed among the Indians of the Five Nations, who favoured me with answers which discover a considerable knowledge of the people whose customs they describe. From William Smith, Esq. the ingenious historian of New York, I received some useful information. When I enter upon the History of our Colonies in North America, I shall have occasion to acknowledge how much I have been indebted to many other gentlemen of that country.

From the valuable Collection of Voyages made by Alexander Dalrymple, Esq., with whose attention to the History of Navigation and Discovery the Public is well acquainted, I have received some very rare books, particularly two large volumes of Memorials, partly manuscript and partly in print, which were presented to the court of Spain during the reigns of Philip III. and Philip IV. From these I have learned many curious particulars with respect to the interior state of the Spanish colonies, and the various schemes formed for their improvement. As this collection of Memorials formerly belonged to the Colbert Library, I have quoted them by that title.

All those books and manuscripts I have consulted with that attention which the respect due from an Author to the Public required; and by minute references to them, I have endeavoured to authenticate whatever I relate. The longer I reflect on the nature of historical composition, the more I am convinced that this scrupulous accuracy is necessary. The historian who records the events of his own time, is credited in proportion to the opinion which the Public entertains with respect to his means of information and his veracity. He who delineates the transactions of a remote period, has no title to claim assent, unless he produces evidence in proof of his assertions. Without this he may write an amusing tale, but cannot be said to have composed an authentic history. In those sentiments I have been confirmed by the opinion of an Author,* whom his industry, erudition, and discernment, have deservedly placed in a high rank among the most eminent historians of the age. Imboldened by a hint from him, I have published a catalogue of the Spanish books which I have consulted. This practice was frequent in the last century, and was considered as an evidence of laudable industry in an author; in the present, it may, perhaps, be deemed the effect of ostentation; but, as many of these books are unknown in Great Britain, I could not otherwise have referred to them as authorities, without encumbering the page with an insertion of their full titles. To any person who may choose to follow me in this path of inquiry, the catalogue must be very useful.

My readers will observe, that in mentioning sums of money, I have uniformly followed the Spanish method of computing by *pesos*. In America, the peso *fuerte*, or *duro*, is the only one known; and that is always meant when any sum imported from America is mentioned. The peso fuerte, as well as other coins, has varied in its numerary value; but I have been advised, without attending to such minute variations, to consider it as equal to four shillings and six-pence of our money. It is to be remembered, however, that, in the sixteenth century, the effective value of a peso, *i. e.* the quantity of labour which it represented, or of goods which it would purchase, was five or six times as much as at present.

N. B. Since this edition was put into the press, a History of Mexico, in two volumes in quarto, translated from the Italian of the Abbé D. Francesco Saverio Clavigero, has been published. From a person who is a native of New Spain, who has resided forty years in that country, and who is acquainted with the Mexican language, it was natural to expect much new information. Upon perusing his work, however, I find that it contains hardly any addition to the ancient History of the Mexican empire, as related by Acosta and Herrera, but what is derived from the improbable narratives and fanciful conjectures of Torquemada and Boturini. Having copied their splendid descriptions of the high state of civilization in the Mexican empire, M. Clavigero, in the abundance of his zeal for the honour of his native country, charges me with having mistaken some points, and with having misrepresented others, in the history of it. When an author is conscious of having exerted industry in research, and impartiality in decision, he may, without presumption, claim what praise is due to these qualities, and he cannot be insensible to any accusation that tends to weaken the force of his claim. A feeling of this kind has induced me to examine such strictures of M. Clavigero on my history of America as merited any attention, especially as these are made by one who seemed to possess the means of obtaining accurate information; and to show that the greater part of them is destitute of any just foundation. This I have done in notes upon the passages in my History which gave rise to his criticisms.

College of Edinburgh, *March* 1, 1788.

* Mr Gibbon

# CONTENTS.

A

# CATALOGUE

OF

# SPANISH BOOKS AND MANUSCRIPTS.

A CARETTE de Biscay, Relation des Voyages dans la Rivière de la Plata, et de là par Terre au Perou. Exst. Recueil de Thevenot. Part IV.

——— A Voyage up the River de la Plata, and thence by Land to Peru. 8vo. London, 1698.

Acosta (P. Jos. de) Historia Natural y Moral de las Indias. 4to. Madrid, 1590.

——— (Joseph de) Histoire Naturelle et Morale des Indes tant Orientales qu' Occidentales. 8vo. Paris, 1600.

———Novi Orbis Historia Naturalis et Moralis. Exst. in Collect. Theod. de Bry. Pars IX.

——— De Natura Novi Orbis, Libri duo, et de procuranda Indorum Salute, Libri sex. Salmant. 8vo. 1589.

——— (Christ.) Tratado de las Drogas y Medecinas, de las Indias Occidentales, con sus Plantas Dibuxadas al vivo. 4to. Burgos, 1578.

Acugna (P. Christoph.) Relation de la Revière des Amazones. 12mo. Tom. ii. Paris, 1682.

Acugna's Relation of the great River of the Amazons in South America. 8vo. London, 1698.

Alarchon (Fern.) Navigatione a Scoprere il Regno di sette Città. Ramusio iii. 363.

Albuquerque Coello (Duarté de) Memorial de Artes de la Guerra del Brasil. 4to. Mad. 1634.

Alcafarado (Franc.) An Historical Relation of the Discovery of the Isle of Madeira. 4to. Lond. 1675.

Alçedo y Herrera (D. Dionysio de) Aviso Historico-Politico-Geografico, con las Noticias mas particulares, del Peru, Tierra Firmé, Chili, y Nuevo Reyno de Granada. 4to. Mad. 1740.

Alçedo Compendi Historico de la Provincia y Puerto de Guayaquil. 4to. Mad. 1741.

——— Memorial sobre diferentes Puntos tocantes al estado de la real hazienda y del commercio, &c. en las Indias. fol.



Aldama y Guevara (D. Jos. Augustin de) Arde de la Lengua Mexicana. 12mo. Mexico, 1754.

Alvarado (Pedro de) Dos Relaciones a Hern. Cortes referiendole sus Expediciones y Conquistas en varias Provincias de N. Espagna. Exst. Barcia Historiad. Primit. tom. i.

——— Lettere due, &c. Exst. Ramus. iii. 296.

Aparicio y Leon (D. Lorenzo de) Discurso Historico-Politico del Hospital San Lazaro de Lima. 8vo. Lim. 1761.

Aranzeles Reales de los Ministros de la Real Audiencia de N. Espagna. fol. Mex. 1727.

Argensola (Bartolome Leonardo de) Conquista de las Islas Malucas. fol. Mad. 1609.

——— Anales de Aragon. fol. Saragoça, 1630.

Arguello (Eman.) Sentum Confessionis. 12mo. Mex. 1703.

Arriago (P. Pablo Jos. de) Extirpacian de la Idolatria de Peru. 4to. Lima, 1621.

Avendagno (Didac.) Thesaurus Indicus, ceu Generalis Instructor pro Regimine Conscientiæ, in ijs quæ ad Indias spectant. fol. 2 vols. Antwerp, 1660.

Aznar (D. Bern. Fran.) Discurso tocante a la real hazienda y administracion de ella. 4to.

Bandini (Angelo Maria) Vita é Lettere di Armerigo Vespucci. 4to. Firenze. 1745.

Barcia (D. And. Gonzal.) Historiadores Primitivos de las Indias Occidentales, fol. 3 vols. Mad. 1749.

Barco-Centinera (D. Martin de) Argentina y Conquista del Rio de la Plata: Poema. Exst. Barcia Historiad. Primit. iii.

Barros (Joao de) Decadas de Asia. fol. 4 vols. Lisboa, 1682.

Bellesteros (D. Thomas de) Ordenanzas del Peru. fol. 2 vols. Lima, 1685.

Beltran (P. F. Pedro) Arte de el Idioma Maya reducido a sucintas reglas, y Semilexicon. 4to. Mex. 1746.

Benzo (Hieron.) Novi Orbis Historiæ—De Bry America, Part IV, V, VI.

Betancurt y Figueroa (Don Luis) Derecho de las Inglesias Metropolitanas de las Indias. 4to. Mad. 1637.

Blanco (F. Matias Ruiz) Conversion de Piritu de Indios Cumanagotos y otros. 12mo. Mad. 1690.

Boturini Benaduci (Lorenzo) Idea de una nueva Historia general de la America Septentrional, fundada sobre material copiosa de Figuras, Symbolas, Caracteres, Cantares, y Manuscritos de Autores Indios. 4to. Mad. 1746.

Botello de Moraes y Vasconcellos (D. Francisco de) El Nuevo Mundo: Poema Heroyco. 4to. Barcelona, 1701.

Botero Benes (Juan) Description de Todas las Provincias, Reynos, y Ciudades del Mundo. 4to. Girona, 1748.

Brietius (Phil.) Paralela Geographiæ Veteris et Novæ. 4to. Paris, 1648.

Cabeza de Baca (Alvar. Nugnez) Relacion de los Naufragios. Exst. Barcia Hist. Prim. tom. i.

———— Examen Apologetico de la Historica Narration de los Naufragios. Exst. Barcia Hist. Prim. tom. i.

———— Commentarios de lo succedido duarante su gubierno del Rio de la Plata. Exst. ibid.

Cabo de Vacca, Relatione de. Exst. Ramus. iii. 310.

Cabota (Sebast.) Navigazione de. Exst. Ramus. ii. 211.

Cadamustus (Aloysius) Navigatio ad Terras incognitas. Exst. Nov. Orb. Grynæi, p. 1.

Calancha (F. Anton. de la) Cronica moralizada del Orden de San Augustin en el Peru. fol. Barcelona, 1638.

California—Diario Historico de los Viages de Mar y Tierra hechos en 1768, al Norte de California di orden del Marques de Croix Vi-rey de Nueva Espagna, &c. MS.

Calle (Juan Diaz de la) Memorial Informatorio de lo que a su Magestad Provien de la Nueva Espagna y Peru. 4to. 1645.

Campomanes (D. Pedro Rodrig.) Antiguedad Maritima de la Republica de Cartago, con en Periplo de su General Hannon traducido e illustrado. 4to. Mad. 1756.

———— Discurso sobre el fomento de la Industria popular. 8vo. Mad. 1774.

———— Discurso sobre la Educacion popular de los Artesanos. 8vo. 5 vol. Mad. 1775, &c.

Caracas—Real Cedula de Fundacion de la Real Compagnia Guipuscoana de Caracas. 12mo. Mad. 1765.

Caravantes (Fr. Lopez de) Relacion de las Provincias que tiene el Govierno del Peru, los Officios que en el se Provien, y la Hacienda que alli tiene su Magestad, lo que se Gasta de ella y le queda Libre, &c. &c. Dedicado al Marques de Santos Claros, Agno de 1611. MS.

Cardenas y Cano (Gabr.) Ensayo Chronologico para la Historia general de la Florida. fol. Mad. 1733.

Carranzana (D. Gonçales) A Geographical Description of the Coasts, &c. of the Spanish West Indies. 8vo. Lond. 1740.

Casas (Bart. de las) Brevissima Relacion de la Destruycion de las Indias. 4to. 1552.

———— (Bart. de las) Narratio Icon ibus illustrata per Theod. de Bry. 4to. Oppent. 1614.

———— (Bart. de las) An Account of the first Voyages and Discoveries of the Spaniards in America. 8vo. Lond. 1693.

Cassani (P. Joseph) Historia de la Provincia de Compagnia de Jesus del Nuevo Reyno de Granada. fol. Mad. 1741.

Castanheda (Fern. Lop. de) Historia do Descobrimento e Conquista de India pelos Portugueses. fol. 2 vol. Lisb. 1552.

Castellanos (Juan de) Primera y Secunda de las Elegias de Varones Illustres de Indias. 4to. 2 vol. Mad. 1589.

Castillo (Bernal Dias del) Historia Verdadera de la Conquista de Nueva Espagna. fol. Mad. 1632.

Castro, Figueroa y Salazar (D. Pedro de) Relacion di su ancimiento y servicios. 12mo.

Cavallero (D. Jos. Garcia) Brieve Cotejo y Valance de las Pesas y Medidas di varias Naciones, reducidas a las que Corren en Castilla. 4to. Mad. 1731.

Cepeda (D. Fern.) Relacion Universal del Sitio en que esta fundada la Ciudad de Mexico. fol. 1637.

Cieça de Leon (Pedro de) Chronica del Peru. fol. Seville. 1533.

Cisneros (Diego) Sitio, Naturaleza y Propriedades de la Ciudad de Mexico. 4to. Mexico. 1618.

Clemente (P. Claudio) Tablas Chro nologicas, en que contienen los Sucesos Ecclesiasticos y Seculares de Indias. 4to. Val. 1689.

Cogullado (P. Fr. Diego Lopez) Historia de Yucatan. fol. Mad. 1688.

Collecao dos Brives Pontificos e

Leyes Regias que Forao Expedidos v Publicadas desde o Anno 1741, sobre a la Liberdada das Pessoas bene e Commercio dos Indos de Bresil.

Colleccion General de la Providencias hasta aqui tomadas par el Gobierno sobre el Estragnimento, y Occupacion de Temporalidades de los Regulares de la Compagnia de Espagna, Indias, &c. Partes IV. 4to. Mad. 1767.

Colon (D. Fernando) La Historia del Almirante D. Christoval Colon. Exst. Barcia Hist. Prim. I. 1.

Columbus (Christ.) Navigatio qua multas Regiones hactenus incognitas invenit. Exst. Nov. Orb. Grynæi, p. 90.

——— (Ferd.) Life and Actions of his Father Admiral Christoph. Columbus. Exst. Churchill's Voyages, ii. 479.

Compagnia Real de Commercio para las Islas de Sto. Domingo Puerto-rico, y la Margarita. 12mo.

Compendio General de las Contribuciones y gattos que occasionan todos los effectos, frutos, caudales, &c. que trafican entre los reynos de Castilla y America. 4to.

Concilios Provinciales Primero y Segundo celebrados en la muy Noble y muy Leal Ciudad de Mexico en los Agnos de 1555 y 1565. fol. Mexico, 1769.

Concilium Mexicanum Provinciale tertium celebratum Mexici, anno 1585. fol. Mexici, 1770.

Continente Americano, Argonauta de las costas de Nueva Espagna y Tierra Firmé. 12mo.

Cordeyro (Antonio) Historia Insulana das Ilhas a Portugas sugeytas no Oceano Occidental. fol. Lisb. 1717.

Corita (Dr. Alonzo) Breve y sumaria Relacion de los Segnores, Manera, y Differencia de ellos, que havia en la Nueva Espagna, y otras Provincias sus Comarcanas, y de sus Leyes, Usos, y Costumbres, y de la Forma que tenian en Tributar sus Vasallos en Tiempo de su Gentilidad, &c. MS. 4to. pp. 307.

Coronada (Fr. Vasq. de) Sommario di due sue Lettere del Viaggio fatto del Fra. Marco da Nizza al sette Citta de Cevola. Exst. Ramusio iii. 354.

——— (Fr. Vasq. de) Relacion Viaggio alle sette Citta. Ramus. iii. 359.

Cortes (Hern.) Quattro Cartas dirigidas al Emperador Carlos V. en que ha Relacion de sus Conquistas en la Nueva Espagna. Exst. Barcia Hist. Prim. tom. i.

Cortessii (Ferd.) De Insulis nuper inventis Narrationes ad Car. V. fol. 1532.

Cortese (Fern.) Relacioni, &c. Exst. Ramusio ii. 225.

Cubero (D. Pedro) Peregrinacion del Mayor Parte del Mundo. Zaragoss. 4to. 1688.

Cumana, Govierno y Noticia de. fol. MS.

Davila Padilla (F. Aug.) Historia de la Fundacion y Discurso de Provincia de St. Jago de Mexico. fol. Bruss. 1625.

——— (Gil Gonzalez) Teatro Ecclesiastico de la Primitiva Iglesia de los Indias Occidentales. fol. 2 vols. 1649.

Documentos tocantes a la Persecucion, que los Regulares de la Compagnia suscitaron contra Don B. de Cardenas Obispo de Paraguay. 4to. Mad. 1768.

Echaveri (D. Bernardo Ibagnez de) El Reyno Jesuitico del Paraguay. Exst. tom. iv. Colleccion de Documentos. 4to. Mad. 1770.

Echave y Assu (D. Francisco de) La Estrella de Lima covertida en Sol sobre sur tres Coronas. fol. Amberes, 1688.

Eguiara El Egueren (D. J. Jos.) Bibliotheca Mexicana, sive Eruditorum Historia Virorum in America Boreali natorum, &c. tom. prim. fol. Mex. 1775. N. B. No more than one volume of this work has been published.

Ercilla y Zuniga (D. Alonzo de) La Araucana: Poema Eroico. fol. Mad. 1733.

——— 2 vols. 8vo. Mad. 1777.

Escalona (D. Gaspar de) Gazophylacium Regium Peruvicum. fol. Mad. 1775.

Faria y Sousa (Manuel de) Historia del Reyno de Portugal. fol. Amber. 1730.

Faria y Sousa, History of Portugal from the first Ages to the Revolution under John IV. 8vo. Lond. 1698.

Fernandez (Diego) Prima y secunda Parte de la Historia del Peru. fol. Sevill. 1571.

——— (P. Juan Patr.) Relacion Historial de las Missiones de los Indias que claman Chiquitos. 4to. Mad. 1726.

Feyjoo (Benit. Geron.) Espagnoles Americanos—Discurso VI. del. tom. iv. del Teatro Critico. Mad. 1769.

——— Solucion del gran Problema Historico sobre la Poblacion de la America—Discurso XV. del tom. v. de Teatro Critico.

——— (D. Miguel) Relacion Descriptiva de la Ciudad y Provincia Truxillo del Peru. fol. Mad. 1763.

Freyre (Ant.) Piratas de la America. 4to.

Frasso (D. Petro) De Regio Patronatu Indiarum. fol. 2 vols. Matriti, 1775.

Galvao (Antonio) Tratado dos Descobrimentos Antigos y Modernos. fol. Lisboa, 1731.

Galvano (Ant.) the Discoveries of the World from the first Original unto the Year 1555. Osborne's Collect. ii. 354.

Gamboa (D. Fran. Xavier de) Comentarios a los ordinanzas de Minas. fol. Mad. 1761.

Garcia (Gregorio) Historia Ecclesiastica y Seglar de la India Oriental y Occidental, y Predicacion de la Santa Evangelia en ella. 12mo. Baeca, 1626.

——— (Fr. Gregorio) Origen de los Indios del Nuevo Mundo. fol. Mad. 1729.

Gastelu (Ant. Velasquez) Arte de Lengua Mexicana. 4to. Puibla de los Angeles. 1716.

Gazeta de Mexico por los Annos 1728, 1729, 1730. 4to.

Girava (Hieronymo) Dos Libros de Cosmographia. Milan, 1556.

Godoy (Diego de) Relacion al H. Cortes, qua trata del Descubrimiento di diversas Ciudades, y Provincias, y Guerras que tuio con los Indios. Exst. Barcia Hist. Prim. tom. i.

——— Lettera a Cortese, &c. Exst. Ramusio iii. 300.

Gomara (Fr. Lopez de) La Historia general de las Indias. 12mo. Anv. 1554.

——— Historia general de las Indias. Exst. Barcia Hist. Prim. tom. ii.

——— (Fr. Lopez de) Chronica de la Nueva Espagna o Conquista de Mexico. Exst. Barcia Hist. Prim. tom. ii.

Guatemala—Razon puntual de los Successos mas memorabiles, y de los Estragos y dannos que ha padecido la Ciudad de Guatemala. fol. 1774.

Gumilla (P. Jos.) El Orinoco illustrado y defendido; Historia Natural, Civil, y Geographica de este Gran Rio, &c. 4to. 2 tom. Mad. 1745.

——— Histoire Naturelle, Civile, et Géographique de l'Orenoque. Traduite par M. Eidous. 12mo. tom. iii. Avig. 1758.

Gusman (Nugno de) Relacion scritta in Omitlan Provincia de Mechuacan della maggior Spagna nell 1530. Exst. Ramusio iii. 331.

Henis (P. Thadeus) Ephemerides Belli Guiaranici, ab Anno 1754. Exst. Colleccion general de Docum, tom. iv.

Hernandes (Fran.) Plantarum Animalium, et Mineralium Mexicanorum Historia. fol. Rom. 1651.

Herrera (Anton. de) Historia general de los Hechos de los Castellanos en las Islas y Tierra Firma de Mar Oceano. fol. 4 vols. Mad. 1601.

——— Historia General, &c. 4 vols Mad. 1730.

——— General History, &c. Translated by Stephens. 8vo. 6 vol. Lond. 1740.

——— Descriptio Indiæ Occidentalis. fol. Amst. 1622.

Huemez y Horcasitas (D. Juan Francisco de) Extracto de los Autos de Diligencias y reconocimientos de los rios, lagunas, vertientes, y desaguas de Mexico y su valle, &c. fol. Mex. 1748.

Jesuitas—Colleccion de las applicaciones que se van haciendo de los Cienes, Casas y Coligios que fueron de la Compagnia de Jesus, expatriados de estos Reales dominios. 4to. 2 vols. Lima, 1772 y 1773.

——— Colleccion General de Providencias hasta aqui tomadas por el Gobierno sobre el Estrannamiento y Occupacion de temporalidades, de los Regulares de la Compagnia de Espagna, Indias, e Islas Filipinas. 4to. Mad. 1767.

——— Retrato de los Jesuitas formado al natural. 4to. 2 vols. Mad. 1768.

——— Relacion Abbreviada da Republica que os Religiosos Jesuitas estabeleceraon. 12mo.

——— Idea del Origen, Gobierno, &c. de la Compagnia de Jesus. 8vo. Mad. 1768.

Lævinius (Apollonius) Libri V. de Peruviæ Invention. et rebus in eadem gestis. 12mo. Ant. 1567.

Leon (Fr. Ruiz de) Hernandia, Poema Heroyco de Conquista de Mexico. 4to. Mad. 1755.

——— (Ant. de) Epitome de la Bibliotheca Oriental y Occidental, Nautica y Geografica. fol. Mad. 1737.

Lima: A true Account of the Earthquake which happened there 28th of October, 1746. Translated from the Spanish. 8vo. London, 1748.

Lima Gozosa, Description de las fes tibas Demonstraciones, con que esta Ciudad celebrò la real Proclamacion de el Nombre Augusto del Catolico Monarcho D. Carlos III. Lim. 4to. 1760.

Llano Zapata (D. Jos. Euseb.) Preliminar al Tomo 1. de las Memorias Historico-Physicas, Critico-Apologeticas de la America Meridional. 8vo. Cadiz, 1759.

Lopez (D. Juan Luis) Discurso Historico Politico en defenso de la Jurisdicion Real. fol. 1685.

—— (Thom.) Atlas Geographico de la America Septentrional y Meridional. 12mo. Par. 1758.

Lorenzana (D. Fr. Ant.) Arzobispo de Mexico, ahora de Toledo, Historia de Nueva Espagna, escrita por su Esclarecido Conquistador Hernan. Cortes, Aumentada con otros Documentos y Notas. fol. Mex. 1770.

Lozano (P. Pedro) Description Chorographica, del Terretorios, Arboles, Animales del Gran Chaco, y de los Ritos y Costumbres de las innumerabiles Naciones que la habitan. 4to. Cordov. 1733.

—— Historia de la Compagnia de Jesus en la Provincia del Paraguay. fol. 2 vols. Mad. 1753.

Madriga (Pedro de) Description du Gouvernement du Pérou. Exst. Voyages qui ont servi à l'Etablissement de la Comp. des Indes, tom. ix. 105.

Mariana (P. Juan de) Discurso de les Enfermedades de la Compagnia de Jesus. 4to. Mad. 1658.

Martinez de la Puente (D. Jos.) Compendio de las Historias de los Descubrimientos, Conquistas, y Guerras de la India Oriental, y sus Islas, desde los Tiempos del Infante Don Enrique de Portugal su Inventor. 4to. Mad. 1681.

Martyr ab Angleria (Petr.) De Rebus Oceanicis et Novo Orbe Decades tres. 12mo. Colon. 1574.

———— De Insulis nuper inventis, et de Moribus Incolarum. Ibid. p. 329.

———— Opus Epistolarum. fol. Amst. 1670.

———— Il Sommario cavato della sua Historia del Nuevo Mundo. Ramusio iii. i.

Mata (D. Geron. Fern. de) Ideas politicas y morales. 12mo. Toledo, 1640.

Mechuacan—Relacion de las Ceremonias, Ritos, y Poblacion de los Indios de Mechuacan hecha al I. S. D. Ant. de Mendoza Vi-rey de Nueva Espagna. fol. MS.

Melendez (Fr. Juan) Tesoros Verdaderos de las Indias Historia de la Provincia de S. Juan Baptista del Peru, del Orden de Predicadores. fol. 3 vols. Rom. 1681.

Memorial Adjustado por D. A. Fern. de Heredia Gobernador de Nicaragua y Honduras. fol. 1753.

Memorial Adjustado contra los Officiales de Casa de Moneda a Mexico de el anno 1729. fol.

Mendoza (D. Ant. de) Lettera al Imperatore del Descoprimento della Terra Firma della N. Spagna verso Tramontano. Exst. Ramusio iii. 355.

——— (Juan Gonz. de) Historia del gran Reyno de China, con un Itinerario del Nuevo Mundo. 8vo. Rom. 1585.

Miguel (Vic. Jos.) Tablas de los Sucesos Ecclesiasticos en Africa, Indias Orientales y Occidentales. 4to. Val. 1689.

Miscellanea Economico-Politico, &c. fol. Pampl. 1749.

Molina (P. F. Anton.) Vocabulario Castellano y Mexicano. fol. 1571.

Monardes (El Dottor) Primera y Segunda y Tercera Parte de la Historia Medicinal, de las Cosas que se traen de nuestras Indias Occidentales, que sirven en Medicina. 4to. Sevilla, 1754.

Moncada (Sancho de) Restauracion Politica de Espagna, y de seos Publicos. 4to. Mad. 1746.

Morales (Ambrosio de) Coronica General de Espagna. fol. 4 vols. Alcala, 1574.

Moreno y Escaudon (D. Fran. Ant.) Descripcion y Estado del Virreynato de Santa Fé, Nuevo Reyno de Granada, &c. fol. MS.

Munoz (D. Antonio) Discurso sobre Economia politica. 8vo. Mad. 1769.

Nizza (F. Marco) Relatione del Viaggio fatta per Terra al Cevole, Regno di cette Città. Exst. Ramus. iii. 356.

Nodal—Relacion del Viage que hicieron los Capitanes Barth. y Gonz. de Nodal al descubrimiento del Estrecho que hoy es nombrado de Maire, y reconocimiento del de Magellanes. 4to. Mad.

Noticia Individual de los derechos segun lo reglado en ultimo proyecto de 1720. 4to. Barcelona, 1732.

Neuva Espagna—Historia de los Indios de Nueva Espagna dibidida en tres Partes. En la primera trata de los Ritos, Sacrificios y Idolatrias del Tiempo de su Gentilidad. En la segunda de su maravillosa Conversion a la Fé, y modo de celebrar las Fiestas de Neustra Santa Iglesia. En la tercera del Genio y Caracter de aquella Gente; y Figuras con que notaban sus Acontecimientos, con otras particularidades; y Noticias de las principales Ciudades an aquel Reyno. Escrita en el Agno 1541 por uno de los doce Religiosos Franciscos que primero passaron a entender en su Conversion. MS. fol. pp. 618.

Ogna (Pedro de) Arauco Domado. Poëma. 12mo. Mad. 1605.

Ordenanzas del Consejo real de las Indias. fol. Mad. 1681.

Ortega (D. Casimiro de) Refumen Historico del primer Viage hecho al rededor del Mundo. 4to. Mad. 1769.

Ossorio (Jerome) History of the Portuguese during the Reign of Emmanuel. 8vo. 2 vols. Lond. 1752.

Ossorius (Hieron.) De Rebus Emanuelis Lusitaniæ Regis. 8vo. Col. Agr. 1752.

Ovalle (Alonso) Historica Relacion del Reyno de Chili. fol. Rom. 1646.

——— An Historical Relation of the Kingdom of Chili. Exst. Churchill's Collect. iii. 1.

Oviedo y Bagnos (D. Jos.) Historia de la Conquista y Publicacion de Venezuela. fol. Mad. 1723.

——— Sommaria, &c. Exst. Ramusio iii. 44.

——— (Gonz. Fern. de) Relacion Sommaria de la Historia Natural de los Indias. Exst. Barcia Hist. Prim. tom. i.

——— Historia Generale et Naturale dell Indie Occidentale. Exst. Ramusio iii. 74.

——— Relatione della Navigatione per la grandissima Fiume Maragnon. Exst. Ramus. iii. 415.

Palacio (D. Raim. Mig.) Discurso Economico Politico. 4to. Mad. 1778.

Palafox y Mendoza (D. Juan) Virtudes del Indios, o Naturaliza y Costumbres de los Indios de N. Espagna. 4to.

——— Vie de Venerable Dom. Jean Palafox Evêque de l'Angelopolis. 12mo. Cologne, 1772.

Pegna (Juan Nugnez de la) Conquista y Antiguedades de las Islas de Gran Canaria. 4to. Mad. 1676.

Pegna Montenegro (D. Alonso de la) Itinerario para Parochos de Indios, en quo tratan les materias mas particulares, tocantes a ellos para se buen administracion. 4to. Amberes, 1754.

Penalosa y Mondragon (Fr. Benito de) Cinco Excellencias del Espagnol que des peublan a Espagna. 4to. Pampl. 1629

Peralta Barnuevo (D. Pedro de Lima fundada, o Conquista del Peru. Poëma Eroyco. 4to. Lima, 1732.

——— Calderon (D. Mathias de) El Apostol de las Indias y nueves gentes San Francisco Xavier de la Compagnia de Jesus Epitome de sus Apostolicos Hechos. 4to. Pampl. 1665.

Pereira de Berrido (Bernard.) Annales Historicos do Estado do Maranchao. fol. Lisboa, 1749.

Peru — Relatione d'un Capitano Spagnuolo del Descoprimento y Conquista del Peru. Exst. Ramus. iii. 371.

——— Relatione d'un Secretario de Franc. Pizarro della Conquista del Peru. Exst. Ramusio iii. 371.

——— Relacion del Peru. MS.

Pesquisa de los Oydores de Panama contra D. Jayme Mugnos, &c. por haverlos Commerciado illicitamente en tiempo de Guerra. fol. 1755.

Philipinas — Carta que escribe un Religioso antiguo de Philipinas, a un Amigo suyo en Espagna, que le pregunta el Naturel y Genio de los Indios Naturales de estas Islas. MS. 4to.

Piedrahita (Luc. Fern.) Historia general de las Conquistas del Nuevo Reyno de Granada. fol. Ambres.

Pinelo (Ant. de Leon) Epitome de la Bibliotheca Oriental y Occidental en que se contihen los Escritores de las Indias Orientales y Occidentales. fol. 2 vols. Mad. 1737.

Pinzonius socius Admirantis Columbi —Navigatio et Res per eum repertæ. Exst. Nov. Orb. Grynæi, p. 119.

Pizarro y Orellana (D. Fern.) Varones illustres del N. Mundo. fol. Mad. 1639.

Planctus Judorum Christianorum in America Peruntina. 12mo.

Puente (D. Jos. Martinez de la) Compendio de las Historias de los Descubrimientos de la India Oriental y sus Islas. 4to. Mad. 1681.

Quir (Ferd de) Terra Australis incognita; or a new Southern Discovery, containing a fifth part of the World, lately found out. 4to. Lond. 1617.

Ramusio (Giov. Battista) Racolto delle Navigationi e Viaggi. fol. 3 vols. Venet. 1588.

Real Compagnia Guipuzcoana de Caracas, Noticias historiales Practicas, de los Sucesos y Adelantamientos de esta Compagnia desde su Fundacion en 1728 hasta 1764. 4to. 1765.

Recopilacion de Leyes de los Reynos de las Indias. fol. 4 vols. Mad. 1756.

Reglamento y Aranceles Reales para el Commercio de Espagna a Indias.

Relatione d'un Gentilhuomo del Sig. Fern. Cortese della gran Città Temistatan, Mexico, et della altre cose delle Nova Spagna. Exst. Ramus. iii. 304.

Remesal (Fr. Ant.) Historia general de las Indias Occidentales y particular de la Governacion de Chiapa a Guatimala.

Ribadeneyra (De Diego Portichuelo) de Relacion del Viage desde qui salio de Lima, hasta que Illegò a Espagna.

Ribadeneyra y Barrientos (D. Ant. Joach.) Manuel Compendio de el Regio Patronato Indiano. fol. Mad. 1755.

Ribas (Andr. Perez de) Historia de los Triumphos de Nuestra Sta Fe, entre Gentes la mas Barbaras, en las Misiones de Nueva Espagna. Mad. 1645.

Riol (D. Santiago) Representacion a Philipe V. sobre el Estado actual de los Papeles universales de la Monarchia. MS.

Ripia (Juan de la) Practica de la Administracion y Cobranza de las rentas reales. fol. Mad. 1768.

Rocha Pitta (Sebastiano de) Historia de America Portougueza desde o Anno de 1500 du su Descobrimento ate o de 1724. fol. Lisboa, 1730.

Rodriguez (Manuel) Explicacion de la Bulla de la Santa Cruzada. 1589.

——— (P. Man.) El Maragnon y Amozonas Historia de los Descubrimientos, Entradas y Reducion de Naciones.

Roman (Hieron.) Republicas del Mundo. fol. 3 vols. Mad. 1595.

Roma y Rosell (De Franc.) Las segnales de la felicidad de Espagna y medios de hacerlas efficaces. Mad. 1768.

Rosende (P. Ant. Gonz. de) Vida del Juan de Palafox Arzobispo de Mexico.

Rubaclava (Don Jos. Gutierrez de) Tratado Historico-Politico y Legal de el Commercio de las Indias Occidentales.

Ruiz (P. Ant.) Conquista Espiritual hecha por los Religiosos de la Compagnia de Jesus, en las Provincias de la Paraguay, Uraguay, Parana y Tape.

Salazar de Mendoza (D. Pedro) Monarquia de Espagna, tom. i. ii. iii.

——— y Olarte (D. Ignacio) Historia de la Conquista de Mexico—Segunda parte. Cordov. 1743.

Salazar de Mendoza y Zevallos (D. Alonz. Ed. de) Constituciones y Ordenanzas antiguas Agnadidas y Modernas de la Real Universidad y estudio general ste San Marcos de la Ciudad de los Reyes del Peru. fol. En la Ciudad de los Reyes, 1735.

Sanchez (Ant. Ribero) Dissertation sur l'Origine de la Maladie Venerienne, dans laquelle on prouve qu'elle n'a point été portée de l'Amerique. 1765.

Sarmiento de Gamboa (Pedro de) Viage el Estrecho de Magellanes. 1768.

Santa Cruz (El Marq.) Commercio Suelto y en Companias General. 1732.

Sta. Domingo, Puerto Rico, y Margarita, Real Compagnia de Commercio.

Schemidel (Hulderico) Historia y Discubrimiento del Rio de la Plata y Paraguay. Exst. Barcia Hist. Prim. tom. iii.

Sebara da Sylva (Jos. de) Recueil Chronologique et Analytique de tout ce qu'a fait en Portugal la Société dite de Jésus, depuis son Entrée dans ce Royaume en 1540 jusqu'à son Expulsion 1759. 12mo. 3 vols. Lisb. 1769.

Segni (D. Diego Raymundo) Antiquario Noticiosa General de Espagna y sus Indios. 12mo. 1769.

Sepulveda (Genesius) Dialogus de justis Belli Causis, præsertim in Indos Novi Orbis. MS.

———(Jo. Genesius) Epist. Lib. VII.

Sepulveda de Regno, Libri III. 1570.

Seyxas y Lovero, (D. Fr.) Theatro Naval Hydrographico. 4to. 1648.

——— Descripcion Geographica y Derrotera de la Religion Austral Magellanica. 4to. Mad. 1690.

Simon (Pedro) Noticias Historiales de las Conquistas de Tierra Firme en las Indias Occidentales. Cuença, 1627

Solis (D. Ant. de) Historias de las Conquistas de Mexico. Mad. 1684.

—— History of the Conquest of Mexico.—Translated by Townshend. 1724

Solarzono y Pereyrra (Joan) Politica Indiana. fol. 2 vols. Mad. 1776.

—— De Indiarum Jure, sive de justa Indiarum Occidentalium Gubernatione.

—— Obras Varias posthumas. 1776.

Soto y Marne (P. Franc. de) Copia de la Relacion de Viage qui desde la Ciudad de Cadiz a la Cartagena de Indias hizo.

Spilbergen et Le Maire Speculum Orientalis Occidentalisque Navigationum.

Suarez de Figueroa (Chris.) Hechos de D. Garcia Hurtado de Mendoza.

Tanco (Luis Bezerra) Felicidad de Mexico en la admirable Aparicion de N. Signora di Guadalupe. Mad. 1745.

Tarragones (Hieron. Gir.) Dos Libros de Cosmographia. 4to. Milan, 1556.

Techo (F. Nichol. de), The History of the Provinces Paraguay, Tucuman, Rio de la Plata, &c. Exst. Churchill's Coll. vi. 3.

Torquemada (Juan de) Monarquia Indiana. fol. 3 vols. Mad. 1723.

Torres (Sim. Per. de) Viage del Mundo. Exst. Barcia Hist. Prim. iii.

—— (Franc. Caro de) Historia de las Ordenes Militares de Santiago, Calatrava y Alcantara, desde su Fundacion hasta el Rey D. Felipe II. Administrador perpetuo dellas. 1629.

Torribio (P. F. Jos.) Aparato para la Historia Natural Espagnala. fol. Mad. 1754.

—— Dissertacion Historico-Politica y en mucha parte Geographica de las Islas Philipinas. 12mo. Mad. 1753.

Totanes (F. Sebastian de) Manual Tagalog para auxilio de Provincia de las Philipinas. 4to. Samplai en las Philipinas. 1745.

Ulloa (D. Ant. de) Voyage Historique de l'Amerique Meridionale. 4to. 2 tom. Paris, 1752.

—— (D. Ant. de) Noticias Americanas, Entretenimientos Physicos-Historicos, sobre la America Meridional y la Septentrional Oriental. Mad. 1772.

—— (D. Bern. de) Restablecimiento de las Fabricas, Trafico, y Commercio maritimo de Espagna. Mad. 1740.

—— (Franc.) Navigatione per scoprire l'Isole delle Specierie fino all Mare detto Vermejo nel 1539. Exst. Ramus. iii. 339.

—— (D. Bernardo) Retablissement des Manufactures et du Commerce d'Espagne. 12mo. Amst. 1753.

Uztariz (D. Geron.) Theoria y Practica de Commercio y de Marina. fol. Mad. 1757.

—— The Theory and Practice of Commerce, and Maritime Affairs. 8vo. 2 vols. Lond. 1751.

Verages (D. Thom. Tamaio de) Restauracion de la Ciudad del Salvador y Baia de Todos Sanctos en la Provincia del Brasil. 4to. Mad. 1628.

Vargas Machuca (D. Bern. de) Milicia y Descripcion de las Indias. Mad. 1699.

Vega (Garcilasso de la) Histoire de la Conquête de la Floride. Traduite par Richelet. 12mo. 2 tom. Leyd. 1731.

—— Royal Commentaries of Peru, by Rycaut. fol. Lond. 1688.

Vega (L'Ynca Garcilasso de la) Histoires des Guerres Civiles des Espagnoles dans les Indes, par Baudoin. 1648.

Veitia Linage (Jos.) The Spanish Rule of Trade to the West Indies.

—— Declamacion Oratoria en Defensa de D. Jos. Fern. Veitia Linage.

Veitia Linage Norte de la Contratacion de las Indias Occidentales. fol. Sevill. 1672.

Venegas (Miguel), a Natural and Civil History of California. 8vo. 2 vols. Lond. 1759.

Verazzano (Giov.) Relatione delle Terra per lui scoperta nel 1524. Exst. Ramusio iii. p. 420.

Vesputius (Americus) Duæ Navigationes sub Auspiciis Ferdinandi, &c. Exst. de Bry America. Pars X.

—— Navigatio prima, secunda, tertia, quarta. Exst. Nov. Orb. Grynæi, p. 155.

Viage de Espagna. 12mo. 6 tom. Mad. 1776.

Victoria (Franc.) Relationes Theologicæ de Indis et de Jure Belli contra eos.

Viera y Clavijo (D. Jos.) Noticias de la Historia general de las Islas de Canaria.

Villalobos (D. Juan de) Manifesto sobre la introduccion de esclavos Negros en las Indias Occidentales. 4to. 1682.

Villagra (Gasp. de) Historia de Nueva Mexico, Poema. Alcala, 1610.

Villa Segnor y Sanchez (D. Jos. Ant.) Theatro Americano. Descripcion general de los Reynos y Provincias de la Nueva Espagna. 2 tom. Mex. 1746.

—— Res puesta sobre el precio de Azogue. 4to.

Vocabulario Brasiliano y Portugues. 4to. MS.

Ward (D. Bernardo) Proyecto Economico sobre la poblacion de Espagna, la agricultura en todos sus ramos, y de mas establecimientos de industria, comercio con nuestra marina, arreglo de nuestra intereses en America, libertad del comercio en Indias, &c. MS.

Xeres (Franc. de) Verdadera Relacion de la Conquista del Peru y Provincia de Cuzco, Embiada al Emperador Carlos V. Exst. Barcia Hist. Prim. tom. iii.

—— Relatione, &c. &c. Exst. Ramusio iii. 372.

Zarate (Aug. de) Historia del Descubrimiento y Conquista de la Provincia del Peru. Exst. Barcia Hist. Prim. tom. iii.

—— Histoire de la Découverte et de la Conquête du Perou Paris, 1742.

Zavala y Augnon (D. Miguel de) Representacion al Rey N. Segnor D. Philipe V. dirigida al mas seguro Aumento del Real Erario. 1732.

Zevallos (D. Pedro Ordognez de) Historia y Viage del Mundo. 1691.

THE

# HISTORY OF AMERICA.

---

BY WILLIAM ROBERTSON, D.D.

PRINCIPAL OF THE UNIVERSITY OF EDINBURGH, ETC. ETC.

THE

# HISTORY OF AMERICA.

## BOOK I.

The progress of men, in discovering and peopling the various parts of the earth, has been extremely slow. Several ages elapsed before they removed far from those mild and fertile regions in which they were originally placed by their Creator. The occasion of their first general dispersion is known; but we are unacquainted with the course of their migrations, or the time when they took possession of the different countries which they now inhabit. Neither history nor tradition furnishes such information concerning these remote events, as enables us to trace, with any certainty, the operations of the human race in the infancy of society.

We may conclude, however, that all the early migrations of mankind were made by land. The ocean which surrounds the habitable earth, as well as the various arms of the sea which separate one region from another, though destined to facilitate the communication between distant countries, seem, at first view, to be formed to check the progress of man, and to mark the bounds of that portion of the globe to which nature had confined him. It was long, we may believe, before men attempted to pass these formidable barriers, and became so skilful and adventurous as to commit themselves to the mercy of the winds and waves, or to quit their native shores in quest of remote and unknown regions.

Navigation and shipbuilding are arts so nice and complicated, that they require the ingenuity, as well as experience, of many successive ages to bring them to any degree of perfection. From the raft or canoe, which first served to carry a savage over the river that obstructed him in the chase, to the construction of a vessel capable of conveying a numerous crew with safety to a distant coast, the progress in improvement is immense. Many efforts would be made, many experiments would be tried, and much labour as well as invention would be employed, before men could accomplish this arduous and important undertaking. The rude and imperfect state in which navigation is still found among all nations which are not considerably civilized, corresponds with this account of its progress, and demonstrates that in early times the art was not so far improved as to enable men to undertake distant voyages, or to attempt remote discoveries.

As soon, however, as the art of navigation became known, a new species of correspondence among men took place. It is from this era that we must date the commencement of such an intercourse between nations as deserves the appellation of commerce. Men are, indeed, far advanced in improvement before commerce becomes an object of great importance to them. They must even have made some considerable progress towards civilization, before they acquire the idea of property, and ascertain it so perfectly as to be acquainted with the most simple of all contracts, that of exchanging by barter one rude commodity for another. But as soon as this important right is established, and every individual feels that he has an exclusive title to possess or to alienate whatever he has acquired by his own labour and dexterity, the wants and ingenuity of his nature suggest to him a new method of increasing his acquisitions and enjoyments, by disposing of what is superfluous in his own stores, in order to procure what is necessary or desirable in those of other men. Thus a commercial intercourse begins, and is carried on among the members of the same community. By degrees, they discover that neighbouring tribes possess what they themselves want, and enjoy comforts of which they wish to partake. In the same mode, and upon the same principles, that domestic traffic is carried on within the society, an external commerce is established with other tribes or nations. Their mutual interest and mutual wants render this intercourse desirable, and imperceptibly introduce the maxims and laws which facilitate its progress and render it secure. But no very extensive commerce can take place between contiguous provinces, whose soil and climate being nearly the same yield similar productions. Remote countries cannot convey their commodities, by land, to those places where on account of their rarity they are desired, and become valuable. It is to navigation that men are indebted for the power of transporting the superfluous stock of one part of the earth to supply the wants of another. The luxuries and blessings of a particular climate are no longer confined to itself alone, but the enjoyment of them is communicated to the most distant regions.

In proportion as the knowledge of the advantages derived from navigation and commerce continued to spread, the intercourse among nations extended. The ambition of conquest, or the necessity of procuring new settlements, were no longer the sole motives of visiting distant lands. The desire of gain became a new incentive to activity, roused adventurers, and sent them forth upon long voyages, in search of countries whose products or wants might increase that circulation which nourishes and gives vigour to commerce. Trade proved a great source of discovery: it opened unknown seas, it penetrated into new regions, and contributed more than any other cause to bring men acquainted with the situation, the nature, and commodities of the different parts of the globe. But even after a regular commerce was established in the world, after nations were considerably civilized, and the sciences and arts were cultivated with ardour and success, navigation continued to be so imperfect, that it can hardly be said to have advanced beyond the infancy of its improvement in the ancient world.

Among all the nations of antiquity, the structure of their vessels was extremely rude, and their method of working them very defective. They were unacquainted with several principles and operations in navigation, which are now considered as the first elements on which that science is founded. Though that property of the magnet by which it attracts iron was well known to the ancients, its more important and amazing virtue of pointing to the poles had entirely escaped their observation. Destitute of this faithful guide, which now conducts the pilot with so much certainty in the unbounded ocean, during the darkness of night, or when the heavens are covered with clouds, the ancients had no other method of regulating their course than by observing the sun and stars. Their navigation was of consequence uncertain and timid. They durst seldom quit sight of land, but crept along the coast, exposed to all the dangers, and retarded by all the obstructions, unavoidable in holding such an awkward course. An incredible length of time was requisite for performing voyages which are now finished in a short space. Even in the mildest climates, and in seas the least tempestuous, it was only during the summer months that the ancients ventured out of their harbours. The remainder of the year was lost in inactivity It would have been deemed most inconsiderate rashness to have braved the fury of the winds and waves during winter.*

While both the science and practice of navigation continued to be so defective, it was an undertaking of no small difficulty and danger to visit any remote region of the earth. Under every disadvantage, however, the active spirit of commerce exerted itself. The Egyptians, soon after the establishment of their monarchy, are said to have opened a trade between the Arabian Gulf, or Red Sea, and the western coast of the great Indian continent. The commodities which they imported from the East, were carried by land from the Arabian Gulf to the banks of the Nile, and conveyed down that river to the Mediterranean. But if the Egyptians in early times applied themselves to commerce, their attention to it was of short duration. The fertile soil and mild climate of Egypt produced the necessaries and comforts of life with such profusion, as rendered its inhabitants so independent of other countries, that it became an established maxim among that people, whose ideas and institutions differed in almost every point from those of other nations, to renounce all intercourse with foreigners. In consequence of this, they never went out of their own country; they held all seafaring persons in detestation, as impious and profane; and fortifying their own harbours, they denied strangers admittance into them.† It was in the decline of their power, and when their veneration for ancient maxims had greatly abated, that they again opened their ports, and resumed any communication with foreigners.

The character and situation of the Phenicians were as favourable to the spirit of commerce and discovery as those of the Egyptians were adverse to it. They had no distinguishing peculiarity in their manners and institutions; they were not addicted to any singular and unsocial form of superstition; they could mingle with other nations without scruple or reluctance The territory which they possessed was neither large nor fertile. Commerce was the only source from which they could derive opulence or power. Accordingly, the trade carried on by the Phenicians of Sidon and Tyre, was more extensive and enterprising than that of any state in the ancient world. The genius of the Phenicians, as well as the object of their policy and the spirit of their laws, were entirely commercial. They were a people of merchants, who aimed at the empire of the sea, and actually possessed it. Their ships not only frequented all the ports in the Mediterranean, but they were the first who ventured beyond the ancient boundaries of navigation, and, passing the Straits of Gades, visited the western coasts of Spain and Africa. In many of the places to which they resorted, they planted colonies, and communicated to the rude inhabitants some knowledge of their arts and improvements. While they extended their discoveries towards the north and the west, they did not neglect to penetrate into the more opulent and fertile regions of the south and east. Having rendered themselves masters of several commodious harbours towards the bottom of the Arabian Gulf, they, after the example of the Egyptians, established a regular intercourse with Arabia and the continent of India on the one hand, and with the eastern coast of Africa on the other. From these countries they imported many valuable commodities unknown to the rest of the world, and during a long period engrossed that lucrative branch of commerce without a rival. [1]

The vast wealth which the Phenicians acquired by monopolizing the trade carried on in the Red Sea, incited their neighbours the Jews, under the prosperous reigns of David and Solomon, to aim at being admitted to some share of it. This they obtained, partly by their conquest of Idumea, which stretches along the Red Sea, and partly by their alliance with Hi-

Vegitius de Re milit. lib. iv. † Diod. Sicul. lib. i. p. 78. ed. Wesselingii. Amst. 1756. Strabo, lib. xvii. p 1142. ed. Amst. 1707.

ram, king of Tyre Solomon fitted out fleets, which, under the direction of Phenician pilots, sailed from the Red Sea to Tarshish and Ophir. These, it is probable, were ports in India and Africa, which their conductors were accustomed to frequent, and from them the Jewish ships returned with such valuable cargoes as suddenly diffused wealth and splendour through the kingdom of Israel.* But the singular institutions of the Jews, the observance of which was enjoined by their divine Legislator, with an intention of preserving them a separate people, uninfected by idolatry, formed a national character, incapable of that open and liberal intercourse with strangers which commerce requires. Accordingly, this unsocial genius of the people, together with the disasters which befell the kingdom of Israel, prevented the commercial spirit which their monarchs laboured to introduce and to cherish, from spreading among them. The Jews cannot be numbered among the nations which contributed to improve navigation, or to extend discovery.

But though the instructions and example of the Phenicians were unable to mould the manners and temper of the Jews, in opposition to the tendency of their laws, they transmitted the commercial spirit with facility, and in full vigour, to their own descendants the Carthaginians. The commonwealth of Carthage applied to trade and naval affairs, with no less ardour, ingenuity, and success, than its parent state. Carthage early rivalled and soon surpassed Tyre in opulence and power, but seems not to have aimed at obtaining any share in the commerce with India. The Phenicians had engrossed this, and had such a command of the Red Sea as secured to them the exclusive possession of that lucrative branch of trade. The commercial activity of the Carthaginians was exerted in another direction. Without contending for the trade of the East with their mother country, they extended their navigation chiefly towards the west and north. Following the course which the Phenicians had opened, they passed the Straits of Gades, and pushing their discoveries far beyond those of the parent state, visited not only all the coasts of Spain, but those of Gaul, and penetrated at last into Britain. At the same time that they acquired knowledge of new countries in this part of the globe, they gradually carried their researches towards the south. They made considerable progress by land into the interior provinces of Africa, traded with some of them, and subjected others to their empire. They sailed along the western coast of that great continent almost to the tropic of Cancer, and planted several colonies, in order to civilize the natives and accustom them to commerce. They discovered the Fortunate Islands, now known by the name of the Canaries, the utmost boundary of ancient navigation in the western ocean.†

Nor was the progress of the Phenicians and Carthaginians in their knowledge of the globe, owing entirely to the desire of extending their trade from one country to another. Commerce was followed by its usual effects among both these people. It awakened curiosity, enlarged the ideas and desires of men, and incited them to bold enterprises. Voyages were undertaken, the sole object of which was to discover new countries, and to explore unknown seas. Such, during the prosperous age of the Carthaginian republic, were the famous navigations of Hanno and Himlico. Both their fleets were equipped by authority of the senate, and at public expense. Hanno was directed to steer towards the south, along the coast of Africa, and he seems to have advanced much nearer the equinoctial line than any former navigator.‡ Himlico had it in charge to proceed towards the north, and to examine the western coasts of the European continent.§ Of the same nature was the extraordinary navigation of the Phenicians

* Mémoire sur le Pays d'Ophir, par M. d'Anville, Mem. de l'Académ. des Inscript. &c. tom. xxx. 83. † Plinii Nat. Hist. lib. vi. c. 37. edit. in usum Delph. 4to. 1685. ‡ Plinii Nat. Hist. lib. v c 1. Hannonis Periplus ap. Geograph. minores, edit. Hudsoni, vol. i. p. 1. § Plinii Nat. Hist. lib. ii c 67. Festus Avienus apud Bochart. Geogr. Sacer. lib. i. c. 60. p. 652. Oper. vol. iii. L. Bat. 1707

round Africa. A Phenician fleet, we are told, fitted out by Necho king of Egypt, took its departure about six hundred and four years before the Christian era, from a port in the Red Sea, doubled the southern promontory of Africa, and after a voyage of three years returned by the Straits of Gades to the mouth of the Nile.* Eudoxus of Cyzicus is said to have held the same course, and to have accomplished the same arduous undertaking.†

These voyages, if performed in the manner which I have related, may justly be reckoned the greatest effort of navigation in the ancient world; and if we attend to the imperfect state of the art at that time, it is difficult to determine whether we should most admire the courage and sagacity with which the design was formed, or the conduct and good fortune with which it was executed. But unfortunately all the original and authentic accounts of the Phenician and Carthaginian voyages, whether undertaken by public authority or in prosecution of their private trade, have perished. The information which we receive concerning them from the Greek and Roman authors is not only obscure and inaccurate, but if we except a short narrative of Hanno's expedition, is of suspicious authority.[2] Whatever acquaintance with the remote regions of the earth the Phenicians or Carthaginians may have acquired, was concealed from the rest of mankind with a mercantile jealousy. Every thing relative to the course of their navigation was not only a mystery of trade, but a secret of state. Extraordinary facts are related concerning their solicitude to prevent other nations from penetrating into what they wished should remain undivulged.‡ Many of their discoveries seem, accordingly, to have been scarcely known beyond the precincts of their own states. The navigation round Africa, in particular, is recorded by the Greek and Roman writers rather as a strange amusing tale, which they did not comprehend or did not believe, than as a real transaction which enlarged their knowledge and influenced their opinions.[3] As neither the progress of the Phenician or Carthaginian discoveries, nor the extent of their navigation, were communicated to the rest of mankind, all memorials of their extraordinary skill in naval affairs seem, in a great measure, to have perished, when the maritime power of the former was annihilated by Alexander's conquest of Tyre, and the empire of the latter was overturned by the Roman arms.

Leaving, then, the obscure and pompous accounts of the Phenician and Carthaginian voyages to the curiosity and conjectures of antiquaries, history must rest satisfied with relating the progress of navigation and discovery among the Greeks and Romans, which, though less splendid, is better ascertained. It is evident that the Phenicians, who instructed the Greeks in many other useful sciences and arts, did not communicate to them that extensive knowledge of navigation which they themselves possessed; nor did the Romans imbibe that commercial spirit and ardour for discovery which distinguished their rivals the Carthaginians. Though Greece be almost encompassed by the sea, which formed many spacious bays and commodious harbours; though it be surrounded by a great number of fertile islands, yet, notwithstanding such a favourable situation, which seemed to invite that ingenious people to apply themselves to navigation, it was long before this art attained any degree of perfection among them. Their early voyages, the object of which was piracy rather than commerce, were so inconsiderable that the expedition of the Argonauts from the coast of Thessaly to the Euxine Sea, appeared such an amazing effort of skill and courage, as entitled the conductors of it to be ranked among the demigods, and exalted the vessel in which they sailed to a place among the heavenly constellations. Even at a later period, when the Greeks engaged in the famous enterprise against Troy, their knowledge in naval affairs seems not to have been much improved. According to the account of Homer, the only poet

* Herodot lib. iv. c. 42. † Plinii Nat. Hist. lib. ii c. 67. ‡ Strab. Geogr. lib. iii. p. 265. lib. xviii. 1154.

to whom history ventures to appeal, and who, by his scrupulous accuracy in describing the manners and arts of early ages, merits this distinction, the science of navigation at that time had hardly advanced beyond its rudest state. The Greeks in the heroic age seem to have been unacquainted with the use of iron, the most serviceable of all the metals, without which no considerable progress was ever made in the mechanical arts. Their vessels were of inconsiderable burden, and mostly without decks. They had only one mast, which was erected or taken down at pleasure. They were strangers to the use of anchors. All their operations in sailing were clumsy and unskilful. They turned their observations towards stars, which were improper for regulating their course, and their mode of observing them was inaccurate and fallacious. When they had finished a voyage they drew their paltry barks ashore, as savages do their canoes, and these remained on dry land until the season of returning to sea approached. It is not then in the early heroic ages of Greece that we can expect to observe the science of navigation, and the spirit of discovery, making any considerable progress. During that period of disorder and ignorance, a thousand causes concurred in restraining curiosity and enterprise within very narrow bounds.

But the Greeks advanced with rapidity to a state of greater civilization and refinement. Government, in its most liberal and perfect form, began to be established in their different communities; equal laws and regular police were gradually introduced; the sciences and arts which are useful or ornamental in life were carried to a high pitch of improvement; and several of the Grecian commonwealths applied to commerce with such ardour and success, that they were considered, in the ancient world, as maritime powers of the first rank. Even then, however, the naval victories of the Greeks must be ascribed rather to the native spirit of the people, and to that courage which the enjoyment of liberty inspires, than to any extraordinary progress in the science of navigation. In the Persian war, those exploits, which the genius of the Greek historians has rendered so famous, were performed by fleets composed chiefly of small vessels without decks;* the crews of which rushed forward with impetuous valour, but little art, to board those of the enemy. In the war of Peloponnesus, their ships seem still to have been of inconsiderable burden and force. The extent of their trade, how highly soever it may have been estimated in ancient times, was in proportion to this low condition of their marine. The maritime states of Greece hardly carried on any commerce beyond the limits of the Mediterranean sea. Their chief intercourse was with the colonies of their countrymen planted in the Lesser Asia, in Italy, and Sicily. They sometimes visited the ports of Egypt, of the southern provinces of Gaul, and of Thrace; or, passing through the Hellespont, they traded with the countries situated around the Euxine sea. Amazing instances occur of their ignorance, even of those countries which lay within the narrow precincts to which their navigation was confined. When the Greeks had assembled their combined fleet against Xerxes at Egina, they thought it unadvisable to sail to Samos, because they believed the distance between that island and Egina to be as great as the distance between Egina and the Pillars of Hercules.† They were either utterly unacquainted with all the parts of the globe beyond the Mediterranean sea, or what knowledge they had of them was founded on conjecture, or derived from the information of a few persons whom curiosity and the love of science had prompted to travel by land into the Upper Asia, or by sea into Egypt, the ancient seats of wisdom and arts. After all that the Greeks learned from them, they appear to have been ignorant of the most important facts on which an accurate and scientific knowledge of the globe is founded.

The expedition of Alexander the Great into the East considerably en-

* Thucyd. lib. i. c. 14.

† Herodot. lib viii. c. 132.

larged the sphere of navigation and of geographical knowledge among the Greeks. That extraordinary man, notwithstanding the violent passions which incited him at some times to the wildest actions and the most extravagant enterprises, possessed talents which fitted him, not only to conquer, but to govern the world. He was capable of framing those bold and original schemes of policy, which gave a new form to human affairs. The revolution in commerce, brought about by the force of his genius, is hardly inferior to that revolution in empire occasioned by the success of his arms. It is probable that the opposition and efforts of the republic of Tyre, which checked him so long in the career of his victories, gave Alexander an opportunity of observing the vast resources of a maritime power, and conveyed to him some idea of the immense wealth which the Tyrians derived from their commerce, especially that with the East Indies. As soon as he had accomplished the destruction of Tyre, and reduced Egypt to subjection, he formed the plan of rendering the empire which he proposed to establish, the centre of commerce as well as the seat of dominion. With this view he founded a great city, which he honoured with his own name, near one of the mouths of the river Nile, that by the Mediterranean sea, and the neighbourhood of the Arabian Gulf, it might command the trade both of the East and West.* This situation was chosen with such discernment, that Alexandria soon became the chief commercial city in the world. Not only during the subsistence of the Grecian empire in Egypt and in the East, but amidst all the successive revolutions in those countries from the time of the Ptolemies to the discovery of the navigation by the Cape of Good Hope, commerce, particularly that of the East Indies, continued to flow in the channel which the sagacity and foresight of Alexander had marked out for it.

His ambition was not satisfied with having opened to the Greeks a communication with India by sea; he aspired to the sovereignty of those regions which furnished the rest of mankind with so many precious commodities, and conducted his army thither by land. Enterprising, however, as he was, he may be said rather to have viewed than to have conquered that country. He did not, in his progress towards the East, advance beyond the banks of the rivers that fall into the Indus, which is now the western boundary of the vast continent of India. Amidst the wild exploits which distinguish this part of his history, he pursued measures that mark the superiority of his genius as well as the extent of his views. He had penetrated as far into India as to confirm his opinion of its commercial importance, and to perceive that immense wealth might be derived from intercourse with a country where the arts of elegance, having been more early cultivated, were arrived at greater perfection than in any other part of the earth.† Full of this idea, he resolved to examine the course of navigation from the mouth of the Indus to the bottom of the Persian Gulf; and, if it should be found practicable, to establish a regular communication between them. In order to effect this, he proposed to remove the cataracts, with which the jealousy of the Persians, and their aversion to correspondence with foreigners, had obstructed the entrance into the Euphrates;‡ to carry the commodities of the East up that river, and the Tigris, which unites with it, into the interior parts of his Asiatic dominions; while, by the way of the Arabian Gulf and the river Nile, they might be conveyed to Alexandria, and distributed to the rest of the world. Nearchus, an officer of eminent abilities, was intrusted with the command of the fleet fitted out for this expedition. He performed this voyage, which was deemed an enterprise so arduous and important, that Alexander reckoned it one of the most extraordinary events which distinguished his reign. Inconsiderable as it may now appear, it was at that

* Strab. Geogr. lib. xvii. p 1143. 1149. † Strab. Geogr. lib. xv. p. 1036. Q. Curtius, lib. xviii c. 9. ‡ Strab. Geogr. lib. xvi. p. 1075.

time an undertaking of no little merit and difficulty. In the prosecution of it, striking instances occur of the small progress which the Greeks had made in naval knowledge.[4] Having never sailed beyond the bounds of the Mediterranean, where the ebb and flow of the sea are hardly perceptible, when they first observed this phenomenon at the mouth of the Indus, it appeared to them a prodigy, by which the gods testified the displeasure of heaven against their enterprise.[5] During their whole course, they seem never to have lost sight of land, but followed the bearings of the coast so servilely, that they could not avail themselves of those periodical winds which facilitate navigation in the Indian ocean. Accordingly they spent no less than ten months in performing this voyage,* which, from the mouth of the Indus to that of the Persian Gulf, does not exceed twenty degrees. It is probable, that amidst the convulsions and frequent revolutions in the East, occasioned by the contests among the successors of Alexander, the navigation to India by the course which Nearchus had opened was discontinued. The Indian trade carried on at Alexandria, not only subsisted, but was so much extended, under the Grecian monarchs of Egypt, that it proved a great source of the wealth which distinguished their kingdom.

The progress which the Romans made in navigation and discovery, was still more inconsiderable than that of the Greeks. The genius of the Roman people, their military education, and the spirit of their laws, concurred in estranging them from commerce and naval affairs. It was the necessity of opposing a formidable rival, not the desire of extending trade, which first prompted them to aim at maritime power. Though they soon perceived, that in order to acquire the universal dominion after which they aspired, it was necessary to render themselves masters of the sea, they still considered the naval service as a subordinate station, and reserved for it such citizens as were not of a rank to be admitted into the legions.† In the history of the Roman republic, hardly one event occurs, that marks attention to navigation any further than it was instrumental towards conquest. When the Roman valour and discipline had subdued all the maritime states known in the ancient world; when Carthage, Greece, and Egypt had submitted to their power, the Romans did not imbibe the commercial spirit of the conquered nations. Among that people of soldiers, to have applied to trade would have been deemed a degradation to a Roman citizen. They abandoned the mechanical arts, commerce, and navigation, to slaves, to freedmen, to provincials, and to citizens of the lowest class. Even after the subversion of liberty, when the severity and haughtiness of ancient manners began to abate, commerce did not rise into high estimation among the Romans. The trade of Greece, Egypt, and the other conquered countries, continued to be carried on in its usual channels, after they were reduced into the form of Roman provinces. As Rome was the capital of the world, and the seat of government, all the wealth and valuable productions of the provinces flowed naturally thither. The Romans, satisfied with this, seem to have suffered commerce to remain almost entirely in the hands of the natives of the respective countries. The extent, however, of the Roman power, which reached over the greatest part of the known world, the vigilant inspection of the Roman magistrates, and the spirit of the Roman government, no less intelligent than active, gave such additional security to commerce as animated it with new vigour. The union among nations was never so entire, nor the intercourse so perfect, as within the bounds of this vast empire. Commerce, under the Roman dominion, was not obstructed by the jealousy of rival states, interrupted by frequent hostilities, or limited by partial restrictions. One superintending power moved and regulated the industry of mankind, and enjoyed the fruits of their joint efforts.

Navigation felt its influence, and improved under it. As soon as the

* Plin. Hist. Nat. lib. vi. c. 23.

† Polyb. lib v.

Romans acquired a taste for the luxuries of the East, the trade with India through Egypt was pushed with new vigour, and carried on to greater extent. By frequenting the Indian continent, navigators became acquainted with the periodical course of the winds, which, in the ocean that separates Africa from India, blow with little variation during one half of the year from the east, and during the other half blow with equal steadiness from the west. Encouraged by observing this, the pilots who sailed from Egypt to India abandoned their ancient slow and dangerous course along the coast, and, as soon as the western monsoon set in, took their departure from Ocelis, at the mouth of the Arabian Gulf, and stretched boldly across the ocean.* The uniform direction of the wind, supplying the place of the compass, and rendering the guidance of the stars less necessary, conducted them to the port of Musiris, on the western shore of the Indian continent. There they took on board their cargo, and, returning with the eastern monsoon, finished their voyage to the Arabian Gulf within the year. This part of India, now known by the name of the Malabar coast, seems to have been the utmost limit of ancient navigation in that quarter of the globe. What imperfect knowledge the ancients had of the immense countries which stretch beyond this towards the East, they received from a few adventurers who had visited them by land. Such excursions were neither frequent nor extensive, and it is probable that, while the Roman intercourse with India subsisted, no traveller ever penetrated further than to the banks of the Ganges.†[6] The fleets from Egypt which traded at Musiris were loaded it is true, with the spices and other rich commodities of the continent and islands of the further India; but these were brought to that port, which became the staple of the commerce between the east and west, by the Indians themselves in canoes hollowed out of one tree.‡ The Egyptian and Roman merchants, satisfied with acquiring those commodities in this manner, did not think it necessary to explore unknown seas, and venture upon a dangerous navigation, in quest of the countries which produced them. But though the discoveries of the Romans in India were so limited, their commerce there was such as will appear considerable, even to the present age, in which the Indian trade has been extended far beyond the practice or conception of any preceding period. We are informed by one author of credit,§ that the commerce with India drained the Roman empire every year of more than four hundred thousand pounds; and by another, that one hundred and twenty ships sailed annually from the Arabian Gulf to that country.‖

The discovery of this new method of sailing to India, is the most considerable improvement in navigation made during the continuance of the Roman power. But in ancient times, the knowledge of remote countries was acquired more frequently by land than by sea;[7] and the Romans, from their peculiar disinclination to naval affairs, may be said to have neglected totally the latter, though a more easy and expeditious method of discovery. The progress, however, of their victorious armies through a considerable portion of Europe, Asia, and Africa, contributed greatly to extend discovery by land, and gradually opened the navigation of new and unknown seas. Previous to the Roman conquests, the civilized nations of antiquity had little communication with those countries in Europe which now form its most opulent and powerful kingdoms. The interior parts of Spain and Gaul were imperfectly known. Britain, separated from the rest of the world, had never been visited, except by its neighbours the Gauls, and by a few Carthaginian merchants. The name of Germany had scarcely been heard of. Into all these countries the arms of the Romans penetrated. They entirely subdued Spain and Gaul; they conquered the greatest and most fertile part of Britain; they advanced into Germany, as far as the

* Plin. Nat. Hist. lib. vi. c. 23. † Strab. Geogr. lib. xv. p. 1006---1010. ‡ Plin. Nat. Hist lib. vi. c. 26. § Ibid. ‖ Strab. Geogr. lib. ii. p. 179.

banks of the river Elbe. In Africa, they acquired a considerable knowledge of the provinces, which stretched along the Mediterranean Sea, from Egypt westward to the Straits of Gades. In Asia, they not only subjected to their power most of the provinces which composed the Persian and the Macedonian empires, but after their victories over Mithridates and Tigranes, they seem to have made a more accurate survey of the countries contiguous to the Euxine and Caspian seas, and to have carried on a more extensive trade than that of the Greeks with the opulent and commercial nations then seated round the Euxine sea.

From this succinct survey of discovery and navigation, which I have traced from the earliest dawn of historical knowledge, to the full establishment of the Roman dominion, the progress of both appears to have been wonderfully slow. It seems neither adequate to what we might have expected from the activity and enterprise of the human mind, nor to what might have been performed by the power of the great empires which successively governed the world. If we reject accounts that are fabulous and obscure; if we adhere steadily to the light and information of authentic history, without substituting in its place the conjectures of fancy or the dreams of etymologists, we must conclude, that the knowledge which the ancients had acquired of the habitable globe was extremely confined. In Europe, the extensive provinces in the eastern part of Germany were little known to them. They were almost totally unacquainted with the vast countries which are now subject to the kings of Denmark, Sweden, Prussia, Poland, and the Russian empire. The more barren regions that stretch within the arctic circle, were quite unexplored. In Africa, their researches did not extend far beyond the provinces which border on the Mediterranean, and those situated on the western shore of the Arabian Gulf. In Asia, they were unacquainted, as I formerly observed, with all the fertile and opulent countries beyond the Ganges, which furnish the most valuable commodities that in modern times have been the great object of the European commerce with India; nor do they seem to have ever penetrated into those immense regions occupied by the wandering tribes, which they called by the general name of Sarmatians or Scythians, and which are now possessed by Tartars of various denominations, and by the Asiatic subjects of Russia.

But there is one opinion, that universally prevailed among the ancients, which conveys a more striking idea of the small progress they had made in the knowledge of the habitable globe than can be derived from any detail of their discoveries. They supposed the earth to be divided into five regions, which they distinguished by the name of Zones. Two of these, which were nearest the poles, they termed Frigid zones, and believed that the extreme cold which reigned perpetually there rendered them uninhabitable. Another, seated under the line, and extending on either side towards the tropics, they called the Torrid zone, and imagined it to be so burned up with unremitting heat, as to be equally destitute of inhabitants. On the two other zones, which occupied the remainder of the earth, they bestowed the appellation of Temperate, and taught that these, being the only regions in which life could subsist, were allotted to man for his habitation. This wild opinion was not a conceit of the uninformed vulgar, or a fanciful fiction of the poets, but a system adopted by the most enlightened philosophers, the most accurate historians and geographers in Greece and Rome. According to this theory, a vast portion of the habitable earth was pronounced to be unfit for sustaining the human species. Those fertile and populous regions within the torrid zone, which are now known not only to yield their own inhabitants the necessaries and comforts of life with most luxuriant profusion, but to communicate their superfluous stores to the rest of the world, were supposed to be the mansion of perpetual sterility and desolation. As all the parts of the globe with which the ancients were acquainted lay within the northern temperate zone, their opinion that the other temperate zone was filled with inhabitants, was founded on reasoning and conjecture, not on discovery. They even believed that, by the intolerable heat of the torrid zone such an insuperable barrier was placed between the two temperate regions of the earth as would prevent for ever any intercourse between their respective inhabitants. Thus, this extravagant theory not only proves that the ancients were unacquainted with the true state of the globe, but it tended to render their ignorance perpetual, by representing all attempts towards opening a communication with the remote regions of the earth, as utterly impracticable.[8]

But, however imperfect or inaccurate the geographical knowledge which he Greeks and Romans had acquired may appear, in respect of the present improved state of that science, their progress in discovery will seem considerable, and the extent to which they carried navigation and commerce must be reckoned great, when compared with the ignorance of early times. As long as the Roman Empire retained such vigour as to preserve its authority over the conquered nations, and to keep them united, it was an object of public policy, as well as of private curiosity, to examine and describe the countries which composed this great body. Even when the other sciences began to decline, geography, enriched with new observations, and receiving some accession from the experience of every age, and the reports of every traveller, continued to improve. It attained to the highest point of perfection and accuracy to which it ever arrived in the ancient world, by the industry and genius of Ptolemy the philosopher. He flourished in the second century of the Christian æra, and published a description of the terrestrial globe, more ample and exact than that of any of his predecessors.

But, soon after, violent convulsions began to shake the Roman state; the fatal ambition or caprice of Constantine, by changing the seat of government, divided and weakened its force; the barbarous nations, which Providence prepared as instruments to overturn the mighty fabric of the Roman power, began to assemble and to muster their armies on its frontier: the empire tottered to its fall. During this decline and old age of the Roman state, it was impossible that the sciences should go on improving. The efforts of genius were, at that period, as languid and feeble as those of government. From the time of Ptolemy, no considerable addition seems to have been made to geographical knowledge, nor did any important revolution happen in trade, excepting that Constantinople, by its advantageous situation, and the encouragement of the eastern emperors, became a commercial city of the first note.

At length, the clouds which had been so long gathering round the Roman empire burst into a storm. Barbarous nations rushed in from several quarters with irresistible impetuosity, and in the general wreck, occasioned by the inundation which overwhelmed Europe the arts, sciences, inventions, and discoveries of the Romans perished in a great measure, and disappeared.* All the various tribes which settled in the different provinces of the Roman empire were uncivilized, strangers to letters, destitute of arts, unacquainted with regular government, subordination, or laws. The manners and institutions of some of them were so rude as to be hardly compatible with a state of social union. Europe, when occupied by such inhabitants, may be said to have returned to a second infancy, and had to begin anew its career in improvement, science, and civility. The first effect of the settlement of those barbarous invaders was to dissolve the union by which the Roman power had cemented mankind together. They parcelled out Europe into many small and independent states, differing from each other in language and customs. No intercourse subsisted between the members of those divided and hostile communities. Accustomed to a simple mode

* Hist. of Charles V. vol. i.

of life, and averse to industry, they had few wants to supply, and few superfluities to dispose of. The names of *stranger* and *enemy* became once more words of the same import. Customs every where prevailed, and even laws were established, which rendered it disagreeable and dangerous to visit any foreign country.* Cities, in which alone an extensive commerce can be carried on, were few, inconsiderable, and destitute of those immunities which produce security or excite enterprise. The sciences, on which geography and navigation are founded, were little cultivated. The accounts of ancient improvements and discoveries, contained in the Greek and Roman authors, were neglected or misunderstood. The knowledge of remote regions was lost, their situation, their commodities, and almost their names, were unknown.

One circumstance prevented commercial intercourse with distant nations from ceasing altogether. Constantinople, though often threatened by the fierce invaders who spread desolation over the rest of Europe, was so fortunate as to escape their destructive rage. In that city the knowledge of ancient arts and discoveries was preserved; a taste for splendour and elegance subsisted; the productions and luxuries of foreign countries were in request; and commerce continued to flourish there when it was almost extinct in every other part of Europe. The citizens of Constantinople did not confine their trade to the islands of the Archipelago, or to the adjacent coasts of Asia; they took a wider range, and, following the course which the ancients had marked out, imported the commodities of the East Indies from Alexandria. When Egypt was torn from the Roman empire by the Arabians, the industry of the Greeks discovered a new channel by which the productions of India might be conveyed to Constantinople. They were carried up the Indus as far as that great river is navigable; thence they were transported by land to the banks of the river Oxus, and proceeded down its stream to the Caspian sea. There they entered the Volga, and, sailing up it, were carried by land to the Tanais, which conducted them into the Euxine sea, where vessels from Constantinople waited their arrival.† This extraordinary and tedious mode of conveyance merits attention, not only as a proof of the violent passion which the inhabitants of Constantinople had conceived for the luxuries of the East, and as a specimen of the ardour and ingenuity with which they carried on commerce; but because it demonstrates that, during the ignorance which reigned in the rest of Europe, an extensive knowledge of remote countries was still preserved in the capital of the Greek empire.

At the same time a gleam of light and knowledge broke in upon the East. The Arabians having contracted some relish for the sciences of the people whose empire they had contributed to overturn, translated the books of several of the Greek philosophers into their own language. One of the first was that valuable work of Ptolemy which I have already mentioned. The study of geography became, of consequence, an early object of attention to the Arabians. But that acute and ingenious people cultivated chiefly the speculative and scientific parts of geography. In order to ascertain the figure and dimensions of the terrestrial globe, they applied the principles of geometry, they had recourse to astronomical observations, they employed experiments and operations, which Europe in more enlightened times has been proud to adopt and to imitate. At that period, however, the fame of the improvements made by the Arabians did not reach Europe. The knowledge of their discoveries was reserved for ages capable of comprehending and of perfecting them.

By degrees the calamities and desolation brought upon the western provinces of the Roman empire by its barbarous conquerors were forgotten, and in some measure repaired. The rude tribes which settled there

* Hist of Charles V.

† Ramusio, vol. i. p. 372. F.

acquiring insensibly some idea of regular government, and some relish for the functions and comforts of civil life, Europe began to awake from its torpid and inactive state. The first symptoms of revival were discerned in Italy. The northern tribes which took possession of this country, made progress in improvement with greater rapidity than the people settled in other parts of Europe. Various causes, which it is not the object of this work to enumerate or explain, concurred in restoring liberty and independence to the cities of Italy.* The acquisition of these roused industry, and gave motion and vigour to all the active powers of the human mind. Foreign commerce revived, navigation was attended to and improved. Constantinople became the chief mart to which the Italians resorted. There they not only met with a favourable reception, but obtained such mercantile privileges as enabled them to carry on trade with great advantage. They were supplied both with the precious commodities of the East, and with many curious manufactures, the product of ancient arts and ingenuity which still subsisted among the Greeks. As the labour and expense of conveying the productions of India to Constantinople by that long and indirect course which I have described, rendered them extremely rare, and of an exorbitant price, the industry of the Italians discovered other methods of procuring them in greater abundance and at an easier rate. They sometimes purchased them in Aleppo, Tripoli, and other ports on the coast of Syria, to which they were brought by a route not unknown to the ancients They were conveyed from India by sea up the Persian Gulf, and, ascending the Euphrates and Tigris as far as Bagdat, were carried by land across the desert of Palmyra, and from thence to the towns on the Mediterranean. But, from the length of the journey, and the dangers to which the caravans were exposed, this proved always a tedious and often a precarious mode of conveyance. At length the Soldans of Egypt, having revived the commerce with India in its ancient channel, by the Arabian Gulf, the Italian merchants, notwithstanding the violent antipathy to each other with which Christians and the followers of Mahomet were then possessed, repaired to Alexandria, and enduring, from the love of gain, the insolence and exactions of the Mahometans, established a lucrative trade in that port. From that period the commercial spirit of Italy became active and enterprising. Venice, Genoa, Pisa, rose from inconsiderable towns to be populous and wealthy cities. Their naval power increased; their vessels frequented not only all the ports in the Mediterranean, but venturing sometimes beyond the Straits, visited the maritime towns of Spain, France, the Low Countries, and England; and by distributing their commodities over Europe, began to communicate to its various nations some taste for the valuable productions of the East, as well as some ideas of manufactures and arts, which were then unknown beyond the precincts of Italy.

While the cities of Italy were thus advancing in their career of improvement, an event happened, the most extraordinary, perhaps, in the history of mankind, which, instead of retarding the commercial progress of the Italians, rendered it more rapid. The martial spirit of the Europeans, heightened and inflamed by religious zeal, prompted them to attempt the deliverance of the Holy Land from the dominion of Infidels. Vast armies, composed of all the nations in Europe, marched towards Asia upon this wild enterprise. The Genoese, the Pisans, and Venetians, furnished the transports which carried them thither. They supplied them with provisions and military stores. Besides the immense sums which they received on this account, they obtained commercial privileges and establishments of great consequence in the settlements which the Crusaders made in Palestine, and in other provinces of Asia. From those sources prodigious wealth flowed into the cities which I have mentioned. This was accompanied with a propor-

* Hist. of Charles V.

tional increase of power; and, by the end of the Holy War, Venice in particular became a great maritime state, possessing an extensive commerce and ample territories.* Italy was not the only country in which the Crusades contributed to revive and diffuse such a spirit as prepared Europe for future discoveries. By their expeditions into Asia, the other European nations became well acquainted with remote regions, which formerly they knew only by name, or by the reports of ignorant and credulous pilgrims. They had an opportunity of observing the manners, the arts, and the accommodations of people more polished than themselves. This intercourse between the East and West subsisted almost two centuries. The adventurers who returned from Asia communicated to their countrymen the ideas which they had acquired, and the habits of life they had contracted by visiting more refined nations. The Europeans began to be sensible of wants with which they were formerly unacquainted: new desires were excited; and such a taste for the commodities and arts of other countries gradually spread among them, that they not only encouraged the resort of foreigners to their harbours, but began to perceive the advantage and necessity of applying to commerce themselves.†

This communication, which was opened between Europe and the western provinces of Asia, encouraged several persons to advance far beyond the countries in which the Crusaders carried on their operations, and to travel by land into the more remote and opulent regions of the East. The wild fanaticism, which seems at that period to have mingled in all the schemes of individuals, no less than in all the counsels of nations, first incited men to enter upon those long and dangerous peregrinations. They were afterwards undertaken from prospects of commercial advantage, or from motives of mere curiosity. Benjamin, a Jew of Tudela, in the kingdom of Navarre, possessed with a superstitious veneration for the law of Moses, and solicitous to visit his countrymen in the East, whom he hoped to find in such a state of power and opulence as might redound to the honour of his sect, set out from Spain, in the year 1160, and, travelling by land to Constantinople, proceeded through the countries to the north of the Euxine and Caspian seas, as far as Chinese Tartary. From thence he took his route towards the south, and after traversing various provinces of the further India, he embarked on the Indian Ocean, visited several of its islands, and returned at the end of thirteen years, by the way of Egypt, to Europe, with much information concerning a large district of the globe altogether unknown at that time to the western world.‡ The zeal of the head of the Christian church co-operated with the superstition of Benjamin the Jew in discovering the interior and remote provinces of Asia. All Christendom having been alarmed with the accounts of the rapid progress of the Tartar arms under Zengis Khan [1246], Innocent IV., who entertained most exalted ideas concerning the plenitude of his own power, and the submission due to his injunctions, sent Father John de Plano Carpini, at the head of a mission of Franciscan monks, and Father Ascolino, at the head of another of Dominicans, to enjoin Kayuk Khan, the grandson of Zengis, who was then at the head of the Tartar empire, to embrace the Christian faith, and to desist from desolating the earth by his arms. The haughty descendant of the greatest conqueror Asia had ever beheld, astonished at this strange mandate from an Italian priest, whose name and jurisdiction were alike unknown to him, received it with the contempt which it merited, though he dismissed the mendicants who delivered it with impunity. But, as they had penetrated into the country by different routes, and followed for some time the Tartar camps, which were always in motion, they had opportunity of visiting a great part of Asia. Carpini, who proceeded by the way of Poland

* Essai de l'Histoire du Commerce de Venise, p. 52, &c.

† Hist of Charles V.

‡ Bergeron, Recueil des Voyages, &c. tom i. p 1.

and Russia, travelled through its northern provinces as far as the extremities of Thibet. Ascolino, who seems to have landed somewhere in Syria, advanced through its southern provinces into the interior parts of Persia.*

Not long after [1253], St. Louis of France contributed further towards extending the knowledge which the Europeans had begun to acquire of those distant regions. Some designing impostor, who took advantage of the slender acquaintance of Christendom with the state and character of the Asiatic nations, having informed him that a powerful Khan of the Tartars had embraced the Christian faith, the monarch listened to the tale with pious credulity, and instantly resolved to send ambassadors to this illustrious convert, with a view of enticing him to attack their common enemy the Saracens in one quarter, while he fell upon them in another. As monks were the only persons in that age who possessed such a degree of knowledge as qualified them for a service of this kind, he employed in it Father Andrew, a Jacobine, who was followed by Father William de Rubruquis, a Franciscan. With respect to the progress of the former, there is no memorial extant. The journal of the latter has been published He was admitted into the presence of Mangu, the third Khan in succession from Zengis, and made a circuit through the interior parts of Asia, more extensive than that of any European who had hitherto explored them.†

To those travellers whom religious zeal sent forth to visit Asia, succeeded others who ventured into remote countries from the prospect of commercial advantage, or from motives of mere curiosity. The first and most eminent of these was Marco Polo, a Venetian of a noble family. Having engaged early in trade [1265], according to the custom of his country, his aspiring mind wished for a sphere of activity more extensive than was afforded to it by the established traffic carried on in those ports of Europe and Asia which the Venetians frequented. This prompted him to travel into unknown countries, in expectation of opening a commercial intercourse with them more suited to the sanguine ideas and hopes of a young adventurer.

As his father had already carried some European commodities to the court of the great Khan of the Tartars, and had disposed of them to advantage, he resorted thither. Under the protection of Kublay Khan, the most powerful of all the successors of Zengis, he continued his mercantile peregrinations in Asia upwards of twenty-six years; and during that time advanced towards the east, far beyond the utmost boundaries to which any European traveller had ever proceeded. Instead of following the course of Carpini and Rubruquis, along the vast unpeopled plains of Tartary, he passed through the chief trading cities in the more cultivated parts of Asia, and penetrated to Cambalu, or Peking, the capital of the great kingdom of Cathay, or China, subject at that time to the successors of Zengis. He made more than one voyage on the Indian ocean; he traded in many of the islands from which Europe had long received spiceries and other commodities which it held in high estimation, though unacquainted with the particular countries to which it was indebted for those precious productions: and he obtained information concerning several countries which he did not visit in person, particularly the island Zipangri, probably the same now known by the name of Japan.‡ On his return, he astonished his contemporaries with his descriptions of vast regions whose names had never been heard of in Europe, and with such pompous accounts of their fertility, their populousness, their opulence, the variety of their manufactures, and the extent of their trade, as rose far above the conception of an uninformed age

About half a century after Marco Polo [1322], Sir John Mandeville, an Englishman, encouraged by his example, visited most of the countries in the East which he had described, and, like him, published an account of

* Hakluyt, i. 21. Bergeron, tom. i. † Hakl. i. 71. Recueil des Voyages par Bergeron, tom 1.
‡ Viaggi di Marco Polo. Ramus. ii. 2. Bergeron. tom. ii.

them.* The narrations of those early travellers abound with many wild incoherent tales, concerning giants, enchanters, and monsters. But they were not from that circumstance less acceptable to an ignorant age, which delighted in what was marvellous. The wonders which they told, mostly on hearsay, filled the multitude with admiration. The facts which they related from their own observation attracted the attention of the more discerning. The former, which may be considered as the popular traditions and fables of the countries through which they had passed, were gradually disregarded as Europe advanced in knowledge. The latter, however incredible some of them may have appeared in their own time, have been confirmed by the observations of modern travellers. By means of both, however, the curiosity of mankind was excited with respect to the remote parts of the earth; their ideas were enlarged; and they were not only insensibly disposed to attempt new discoveries, but received such information as directed to that particular course in which these were afterwards carried on.

While this spirit was gradually forming in Europe, a fortunate discovery was made, which contributed more than all the efforts and ingenuity of preceding ages to improve and to extend navigation. That wonderful property of the magnet, by which it communicates such virtue to a needle or slender rod of iron as to point towards the poles of the earth, was observed. The use which might be made of this in directing navigation was immediately perceived. That valuable, but now familiar instrument, the *mariner's compass*, was constructed. When by means of it navigators found that, at all seasons and in every place, they could discover the north and south with so much ease and accuracy, it became no longer necessary to depend merely on the light of the stars and the observation of the sea-coast. They gradually abandoned their ancient timid and lingering course along the shore, ventured boldly into the ocean, and, relying on this new guide, could steer in the darkest night, and under the most cloudy sky, with a security and precision hitherto unknown. The compass may be said to have opened to man the dominion of the sea, and to have put him in full possession of the earth by enabling him to visit every part of it. Flavio Gioia, a citizen of Amalfi, a town of considerable trade in the kingdom of Naples, was the author of this great discovery, about the year one thousand three hundred and two. It hath been often the fate of those illustrious benefactors of mankind who have enriched science and improved the arts by their inventions, to derive more reputation than benefit from the happy efforts of their genius. But the lot of Gioia has been still more cruel; through the inattention or ignorance of contemporary historians, he has been defrauded even of the fame to which he had such a just title. We receive from them no information with respect to his profession, his character, the precise time when he made this important discovery, or the accidents and inquiries which led to it. The knowledge of this event, though productive of greater effects than any recorded in the annals of the human race, is transmitted to us without any of those circumstances which can gratify the curiosity that it naturally awakens.† But though the use of the compass might enable the Italians to perform the short voyages to which they were accustomed with greater security and expedition, its influence was not so sudden or extensive as immediately to render navigation adventurous, and to excite a spirit of discovery. Many causes combined in preventing this beneficial invention from producing its full effect instantaneously. Men relinquish ancient habits slowly and with reluctance. They are averse to new experiments, and venture upon them with timidity. The commercial jealousy of the Italians, it is probable, laboured to conceal the

* Voyages and Travels, by Sir John Mandeville.

† Collinas et Trombellus de Acus Nauticæ Inventore, Instit. Acad. Bonon. tom. ii. part iii. p. 372.

happy discovery of their countrymen from other nations. The art of steering by the compass with such skill and accuracy as to inspire a full confidence in its direction, was acquired gradually. Sailors unaccustomed to quit the sight of land, durst not launch out at once and commit themselves to unknown seas. Accordingly, near half a century elapsed from the time of Gioia's discovery, before navigators ventured into any seas which they had not been accustomed to frequent.

The first appearance of a bolder spirit may be dated from the voyages of the Spaniards to the Canary or Fortunate Islands. By what accident they were led to the discovery of those small isles, which lie near five hundred miles from the Spanish coast, and above a hundred and fifty miles from the coast of Africa, contemporary writers have not explained. But, about the middle of the fourteenth century, the people of all the different kingdoms into which Spain was then divided, were accustomed to make piratical excursions thither, in order to plunder the inhabitants, or to carry them off as slaves. Clement VI. in virtue of the right claimed by the Holy See to dispose of all countries possessed by infidels, erected those isles into a kingdom in the year one thousand three hundred and forty-four, and conferred it on Lewis de la Cerda descended from the royal family of Castile. But that unfortunate prince, destitute of power to assert his nominal title, having never visited the Canaries, John de Bethencourt, a Norman baron, obtained a grant of them from Henry III. of Castile.* Bethencourt, with the valour and good fortune which distinguished the adventurers of his country, attempted and effected the conquest; and the possession of the Canaries remained for some time in his family, as a fief held of the crown of Castile. Previous to this expedition of Bethencourt, his countrymen settled in Normandy are said to have visited the coast of Africa, and to have proceeded far to the south of the Canary Islands [1365]. But their voyages thither seem not to have been undertaken in consequence of any public or regular plan for extending navigation and attempting new discoveries. They were either excursions suggested by that roving piratical spirit which descended to the Normans from their ancestors, or the commercial enterprises of private merchants, which attracted so little notice that hardly any memorial of them is to be found in contemporary authors. In a general survey of the progress of discovery, it is sufficient to have mentioned this event; and leaving it among those of dubious existence, or of small importance, we may conclude, that though much additional information concerning the remote regions of the East had been received by travellers who visited them by land, navigation at the beginning of the fifteenth century had not advanced beyond the state to which it had attained before the downfal of the Roman empire.

At length the period arrived, when Providence decreed that men were to pass the limits within which they had been so long confined, and open to themselves a more ample field wherein to display their talents, their enterprise, and courage. The first considerable efforts towards this were not made by any of the more powerful states of Europe, or by those who had applied to navigation with the greatest assiduity and success. The glory of leading the way in this new career was reserved for Portugal, one of the smallest and least powerful of the European kingdoms. As the attempts of the Portuguese to acquire the knowledge of those parts of the globe with which mankind were then unacquainted, not only improved and extended the art of navigation, but roused such a spirit of curiosity and enterprise as led to the discovery of the New World, of which I propose to write the history, it is necessary to take a full view of the rise, the progress, and success of their various naval operations. It was in this school that the discoverer of America was trained; and unless we trace the steps by which

* Viera y Clavijo Notic. de la Histor. de Canaria, i. 268, &c. Glas. Hist. c. 1.

his instructors and guides advanced, it will be impossible to comprehend the circumstances which suggested the idea, or facilitated the execution, of his great design.

Various circumstances prompted the Portuguese to exert their activity in this new direction, and enabled them to accomplish undertakings apparently superior to the natural force of their monarchy. The kings of Portugal, having driven the Moors out of their dominions, had acquired power as well as glory, by the success of their arms against the infidels. By their victories over them, they had extended the royal authority beyond the narrow limits within which it was originally circumscribed in Portugal, as well as in other feudal kingdoms. They had the command of the national force, could rouse it to act with united vigour, and, after the expulsion of the Moors, could employ it without dread of interruption from any domestic enemy. By the perpetual hostilities carried on for several centuries against the Mahometans, the martial and adventurous spirit which distinguished all the European nations during the middle ages, was improved and heightened among the Portuguese. A fierce civil war towards the close of the fourteenth century, occasioned by a disputed succession, augmented the military ardour of the nation, and formed or called forth men of such active and daring genius as are fit for bold undertakings. The situation of the kingdom, bounded on every side by the dominions of a more powerful neighbour, did not afford free scope to the activity of the Portuguese by land, as the strength of their monarchy was no match for that of Castile. But Portugal was a maritime state, in which there were many commodious harbours; the people had begun to make some progress in the knowledge and practice of navigation, and the sea was open to them, presenting the only field of enterprise in which they could distinguish themselves.

Such was the state of Portugal, and such the disposition of the people, when John I. surnamed the Bastard, obtained secure possession of the crown by the peace concluded with Castile, in the year one thousand four hundred and eleven. He was a prince of great merit, who, by superior courage and abilities, had opened his way to a throne which of right did not belong to him. He instantly perceived that it would be impossible to preserve public order, or domestic tranquillity, without finding some employment for the restless spirit of his subjects. With this view he assembled a numerous fleet at Lisbon, composed of all the ships which he could fit out in his own kingdom, and of many hired from foreigners. This great armament was destined to attack the Moors settled on the coast of Barbary [1412.] While it was equipping, a few vessels were appointed to sail along the western shore of Africa bounded by the Atlantic ocean, and to discover the unknown countries situated there. From this inconsiderable attempt, we may date the commencement of that spirit of discovery which opened the barriers that had so long shut out mankind from the knowledge of one half of the terrestrial globe.

At the time when John sent forth these ships on this new voyage, the art of navigation was still very imperfect. Though Africa lay so near to Portugal, and the fertility of the countries already known on that continent invited men to explore it more fully, the Portuguese had never ventured to sail beyond Cape *Non.* That promontory, as its name imports, was hitherto considered as a boundary which could not be passed. But the nations of Europe had now acquired as much knowledge as emboldened them to disregard the prejudices and to correct the errors of their ancestors. The long reign of ignorance, the constant enemy of every curious inquiry and of every new undertaking, was approaching to its period. The light of science began to dawn. The works of the ancient Greeks and Romans began to be read with admiration and profit. The sciences cultivated by the Arabians were introduced into Europe by the Moors settled in Spain and Portugal, and by the Jews, who were very numerous in both these kingdoms. Geometry, astronomy, and geography, the sciences on which the art of navigation is founded, became objects of studious attention. The memory of the discoveries made by the ancients was revived, and the progress of their navigation and commerce began to be traced. Some of the causes which have obstructed the cultivation of science in Portugal, during this century and the last, did not exist, or did not operate in the same manner, in the fifteenth century; [9] and the Portuguese at that period seem to have kept pace with other nations on this side of the Alps in literary pursuits.

As the genius of the age favoured the execution of that new undertaking, to which the peculiar state of the country invited the Portuguese; it proved successful. The vessels sent on the discovery doubled that formidable Cape, which had terminated the progress of former navigators, and proceeded a hundred and sixty miles beyond it, to Cape Bojador. As its rocky cliffs, which stretched a considerable way into the Atlantic, appeared more dreadful than the promontory which they had passed, the Portuguese commanders durst not attempt to sail round it, but returned to Lisbon, more satisfied with having advanced so far, than ashamed of having ventured no further.

Inconsiderable as this voyage was, it increased the passion for discovery which began to arise in Portugal. The fortunate issue of the king's expedition against the Moors of Barbary added strength to that spirit in the nation, and pushed it on to new undertakings. In order to render these successful, it was necessary that they should be conducted by a person who possessed abilities capable of discerning what was attainable, who enjoyed leisure to form a regular system for prosecuting discovery, and who was animated with ardour that would persevere in spite of obstacles and repulses. Happily for Portugal, she found all those qualities in Henry Duke of Viseo, the fourth son of King John, by Philippa of Lancaster, sister of Henry IV. king of England. That prince, in his early youth, having accompanied his father in his expedition to Barbary, distinguished himself by many deeds of valour. To the martial spirit, which was the characteristic of every man of noble birth at that time, he added all the accomplishments of a more enlightened and polished age. He cultivated the arts and sciences, which were then unknown and despised by persons of his rank. He applied with peculiar fondness to the study of geography; and by the instruction of able masters, as well as by the accounts of travellers, he early acquired such knowledge of the habitable globe, as discovered the great probability of finding new and opulent countries, by sailing along the coast of Africa. Such an object was formed to awaken the enthusiasm and ardour of a youthful mind, and he espoused with the utmost zeal the patronage of a design which might prove as beneficial as it appeared to be splendid and honourable. In order that he might pursue this great scheme without interruption, he retired from court immediately after his return from Africa, and fixed his residence at Sagres, near Cape St. Vincent, where the prospect of the Atlantic ocean invited his thoughts continually towards his favourite project, and encouraged him to execute it. In this retreat he was attended by some of the most learned men in his country, who aided him in his researches. He applied for information to the Moors of Barbary, who were accustomed to travel by land into the interior provinces of Africa in quest of ivory, gold dust, and other rich commodities. He consulted the Jews settled in Portugal. By promises, rewards, and marks of respect, he allured into his service several persons, foreigners as well as Portuguese, who were eminent for their skill in navigation. In taking those preparatory steps, the great abilities of the prince were seconded by his private virtues. His integrity, his affability, his respect for religion, his zeal for the honour of his country, engaged persons of all ranks to applaud his design, and to favour the execution of it. His schemes were allowed, by the greater part of his countrymen, to proceed neither from ambition nor the desire of wealth, but to flow from the warm benevolence of a heart eager to promote the happiness of mankind, and which justly entitled him to assume a motto for his device, that described the quality by which he wished to be distinguished, *the talent of doing good.*

His first effort, as is usual at the commencement of any new undertaking, was extremely inconsiderable. He fitted out a single ship [1418], and giving the command of it to John Gonzales Zarco and Tristan Vaz, two gentlemen of his household, who voluntarily offered to conduct the enterprise, he instructed them to use their utmost efforts to double Cape Bojador, and thence to steer towards the south. They, according to the mode of navigation which still prevailed, held their course along the shore; and by following that direction, they must have encountered almost insuperable difficulties in attempting to pass Cape Bojador. But fortune came in aid to their want of skill, and prevented the voyage from being altogether fruitless. A sudden squall of wind arose, drove them out to sea, and when they expected every moment to perish, landed them on an unknown island, which from their happy escape they named *Porto Santo*. In the infancy of navigation, the discovery of this small island appeared a matter of such moment, that they instantly returned to Portugal with the good tidings, and were received by Henry with the applause and honour due to fortunate adventurers. This faint dawn of success filled a mind ardent in the pursuit of a favourite object, with such sanguine hopes as were sufficient incitements to proceed. Next year [1419] Henry sent out three ships under the same commanders, to whom he joined Bartholomew Perestrellow, in order to take possession of the island which they had discovered. When they began to settle in Porto Santo, they observed towards the south a fixed spot in the horizon like a small black cloud. By degrees, they were led to conjecture that it might be land; and steering towards it, they arrived at a considerable island, uninhabited and covered with wood, which on that account they called *Madeira.** As it was Henry's chief object to render his discoveries useful to his country, he immediately equipped a fleet to carry a colony of Portuguese to these islands [1420]. By his provident care, they were furnished not only with the seeds, plants, and domestic animals common in Europe; but, as he foresaw that the warmth of the climate and fertility of the soil would prove favourable to the rearing of other productions, he procured slips of the vine from the island of Cyprus, the rich wines of which were then in great request, and plants of the sugar-cane from Sicily, into which it had been lately introduced. These throve so prosperously in this new country, that the benefit of cultivating them was immediately perceived, and the sugar and wine of Madeira quickly became articles of some consequence in the commerce of Portugal.†

As soon as the advantages derived from this first settlement to the west of the European continent began to be felt, the spirit of discovery appeared less chimerical, and became more adventurous. By their voyages to Madeira, the Portuguese were gradually accustomed to a bolder navigation, and, instead of creeping servilely along the coast, ventured into the open sea. In consequence of taking this course, Gilianez, who commanded one of prince Henry's ships, doubled Cape Bojador [1433], the boundary of the Portuguese navigation upwards of twenty years, and which had hitherto been deemed unpassable. This successful voyage, which the ignorance of the age placed on a level with the most famous exploits recorded in history, opened a new sphere to navigation, as it discovered the vast continent of Africa, still washed by the Atlantic ocean, and stretching towards the south. Part of this was soon explored; the Portuguese ad-

* Historical Relation of the first Discovery of Madeira, translated from the Portuguese of Fran. Alcafarano, p. 15, &c.

† Lud. Guicciardini Descritt. de Paesi Bassi, p. 180, 181.

vanced within the tropics, and in the space of a few years they discovered the river Senegal, and all the coast extending from Cape Blanco to Cape de Verd.

Hitherto the Portuguese had been guided in their discoveries, or encouraged to attempt them, by the light and information which they received from the works of the ancient mathematicians and geographers. But when they began to enter the torrid zone, the notion which prevailed among the ancients, that the heat which reigned perpetually there was so excessive as to render it uninhabitable, deterred them, for some time, from proceeding. Their own observations, when they first ventured into this unknown and formidable region, tended to confirm the opinion of antiquity concerning the violent operation of the direct rays of the sun. As far as the river Senegal, the Portuguese had found the coast of Africa inhabited by people nearly resembling the Moors of Barbary. When they advanced to the south of that river, the human form seemed to put on a new appearance. They beheld men with skins black as ebony, with short curled hair, flat noses, thick lips, and all the peculiar features which are now known to distinguish the race of negroes. This surprising alteration they naturally attributed to the influence of heat, and if they should advance nearer to the line, they began to dread that its effects would be still more violent. Those dangers were exaggerated; and many other objections against attempting further discoveries were proposed by some of the grandees, who, from ignorance, from envy, or from that cold timid prudence which rejects whatever has the air of novelty or enterprise, had hitherto condemned all prince Henry's schemes. They represented, that it was altogether chimerical to expect any advantage from countries situated in that region which the wisdom and experience of antiquity had pronounced to be unfit for the habitation of men; that their forefathers, satisfied with cultivating the territory which Providence had allotted them, did not waste the strength of the kingdom by fruitless projects in quest of new settlements; that Portugal was already exhausted by the expense of attempts to discover lands which either did not exist, or which nature destined to remain unknown; and was drained of men, who might have been employed in undertakings attended with more certain success, and productive of greater benefit. But neither their appeal to the authority of the ancients, nor their reasonings concerning the interests of Portugal, made any impression upon the determined philosophic mind of prince Henry. The discoveries which he had already made, convinced him that the ancients had little more than a conjectural knowledge of the torrid zone. He was no less satisfied that the political arguments of his opponents, with respect to the interest of Portugal, were malevolent and ill founded. In those sentiments he was strenuously supported by his brother Pedro, who governed the kingdom as guardian of their nephew Alphonso V. who had succeeded to the throne during his minority [1438]; and, instead of slackening his efforts, Henry continued to pursue his discoveries with fresh ardour.

But in order to silence all the murmurs of opposition, he endeavoured to obtain the sanction of the highest authority in favour of his operations. With this view he applied to the Pope, and represented, in pompous terms, the pious and unwearied zeal with which he had exerted himself during twenty years, in discovering unknown countries, the wretched inhabitants of which were utter strangers to true religion, wandering in heathen darkness, or led astray by the delusions of Mahomet. He besought the holy father, to whom, as the vicar of Christ, all the kingdoms of the earth were subject, to confer on the crown of Portugal a right to all the countries possessed by infidels, which should be discovered by the industry of its subjects, and subdued by the force of its arms. He entreated him to enjoin all Christian powers, under the highest penalties, not to molest Portugal while engaged in this laudable enterprise, and to prohibit them from setting in any of the countries which the Portuguese should discover. He promised that, in all their expeditions, it should be the chief object of his countrymen to spread the knowledge of the Christian religion, to establish the authority of the Holy See, and to increase the flock of the universal pastor. As it was by improving with dexterity every favourable conjuncture for acquiring new powers, that the court of Rome had gradually extended its usurpations, Eugene IV., the Pontiff to whom this application was made, eagerly seized the opportunity which now presented itself. He instantly perceived that, by complying with prince Henry's request, he might exercise a prerogative no less flattering in its own nature than likely to prove beneficial in its consequences. A bull was accordingly issued, in which, after applauding in the strongest terms the past efforts of the Portuguese, and exhorting them to proceed in that laudable career on which they had entered, he granted them an exclusive right to all the countries which they should discover, from Cape Non to the continent of India.

Extravagant as this donation, comprehending such a large portion of the habitable globe, would now appear, even in Catholic countries, no person in the fifteenth century doubted that the Pope in the plentitude of his apostolic power, had a right to confer it. Prince Henry was soon sensible of the advantages which he derived from this transaction. His schemes were authorized and sanctified by the bull approving of them. The spirit of discovery was connected with zeal for religion, which in that age was a principle of such activity and vigour as to influence the conduct of nations. All Christian princes were deterred from intruding into those countries which the Portuguese had discovered, or from interrupting the progress of their navigation and conquests.[10]

The fame of the Portuguese voyages soon spread over Europe. Men long accustomed to circumscribe the activity and knowledge of the human mind within the limits to which they had been hitherto confined, were astonished to behold the sphere of navigation so suddenly enlarged, and a prospect opened of visiting regions of the globe the existence of which was unknown in former times. The learned and speculative reasoned and formed theories concerning those unexpected discoveries. The vulgar inquired and wondered; while enterprising adventurers crowded from every part of Europe, soliciting prince Henry to employ them in this honourable service. Many Venetians and Genoese, in particular, who were at that time superior to all other nations in the science of naval affairs, entered aboard the Portuguese ships, and acquired a more perfect and extensive knowledge of their profession in that new school of navigation. In emulation of these foreigners, the Portuguese exerted their own talents. The nation seconded the designs of the prince. Private merchants formed companies [1446], with a view to search for unknown countries. The Cape de Verd Islands, which lie off the promontory of that name, were discovered [1449], and soon after the isles called Azores. As the former of these are above three hundred miles from the African coast, and the latter nine hundred miles from any continent, it is evident by their venturing so boldly into the open seas, that the Portuguese had by this time improved greatly in the art of navigation.

While the passion for engaging in new undertakings was thus warm and active, it received an unfortunate check by the death of prince Henry [1463], whose superior knowledge had hitherto directed all the operations of the discoverers, and whose patronage had encouraged and protected them. But notwithstanding all the advantages which they derived from these, the Portuguese during his life did not advance in their utmost progress towards the south, within five degrees of the equinoctial line; and after their continued exertions for half a century [from 1412 to 1463], hardly fifteen hundred miles of the coast of Africa were discovered. To an age acquainted with the efforts of navigation in its state of maturity and improvement, those essays of its early years must necessarily appear feeble and unskilful. But inconsiderable as they may be deemed, they were sufficient to turn the curiosity of the European nations into a new channel, to excite an enterprising spirit, and to point the way to future discoveries.

Alphonso, who possessed the throne of Portugal at the time of prince Henry's death, was so much engaged in supporting his own pretensions to the crown of Castile, or in carrying on his expeditions against the Moors in Barbary, that, the force of his kingdom being exerted in other operations, he could not prosecute the discoveries in Africa with ardour. He committed the conduct of them to Fernando Gomez, a merchant in Lisbon, to whom he granted an exclusive right of commerce with all the countries of which prince Henry had taken possession. Under the restraint and oppression of a monopoly, the spirit of discovery languished. It ceased to be a national object, and became the concern of a private man more attentive to his own gain than to the glory of his country. Some progress, however, was made The Portuguese ventured at length [1471], to cross the line, and, to their astonishment, found that region of the torrid zone, which was supposed to be scorched with intolerable heat, to be not only habitable, but populous and fertile.

John II. who succeeded his father Alphonso [1481], possessed talents capable both of forming and executing great designs. As part of his revenues, while prince, had arisen from duties on the trade with the newly discovered countries, this naturally turned his attention towards them, and satisfied him with respect to their utility and importance. In proportion as his knowledge of these countries extended, the possession of them appeared to be of greater consequence. While the Portuguese proceeded along the coast of Africa, from Cape Non to the river of Senegal, they found all that extensive tract to be sandy, barren, and thinly inhabited by a wretched people professing the Mahometan religion, and subject to the vast empire of Morocco. But to the south of that river, the power and religion of the Mahometans were unknown. The country was divided into small independent principalities, the population was considerable, the soil fertile,* and the Portuguese soon discovered that it produced ivory, rich gums, gold, and other valuable commodities. By the acquisition of these, commerce was enlarged, and became more adventurous. Men, animated and rendered active by the certain prospect of gain, pursued discovery with greater eagerness than when they were excited only by curiosity and hope.

This spirit derived no small reinforcement of vigour from the countenance of such a monarch as John. Declaring himself the patron of every attempt towards discovery, he promoted it with all the ardour of his grand-uncle prince Henry, and with superior power. The effects of this were immediately felt. A powerful fleet was fitted out [1484], which after discovering the kingdoms of Benin and Congo, advanced above fifteen hundred miles beyond the line, and the Portuguese, for the first time, beheld a new heaven, and observed the stars of another hemisphere. John was not only solicitous to discover, but attentive to secure the possession of those countries. He built forts on the coast of Guinea; he sent out colonies to settle there; he established a commercial intercourse with the more powerful kingdoms; he endeavoured to render such as were feeble or divided tributary to the crown of Portugal. Some of the petty princes voluntarily acknowledged themselves his vassals. Others were compelled to do so by force of arms A regular and well digested system was formed with respect to this new object of policy, and, by firmly adhering to it, the Portuguese power and commerce in Africa were established upon a solid foundation.

By their constant intercourse with the people of Africa, the Portuguese gradually acquired some knowledge of those parts of that country which

* Navigatio Aloysii Cadamusti apud Novum Orbem Grynæi, p. 2. 18. Navigat. all Isola di San Tome per un Piloto Portug. Ramusio, i. 115

they had not visited. The information which they received from the natives, added to what they had observed in their own voyages, began to open prospects more extensive, and to suggest the idea of schemes more important than those which had hitherto allured and occupied them. They had detected the error of the ancients concerning the nature of the torrid zone. They found as they proceeded southwards, that the continent of Africa, instead of extending in breadth, according to the doctrine of Ptolemy,* at that time the oracle and guide of the learned in the science of geography, appeared sensibly to contract itself, and to bend towards the east. This induced them to give credit to the accounts of the ancient Phenician voyages round Africa, which had long been deemed fabulous, and led them to conceive hopes that, by following the same route, they might arrive at the East Indies, and engross that commerce which has been the source of wealth and power to every nation possessed of it. The comprehensive genius of prince Henry, as we may conjecture from the words of the Pope's bull, had early formed some idea of this navigation. But though his countrymen, at that period, were incapable of conceiving the extent of his views and schemes, all the Portuguese mathematicians and pilots now concurred in representing them as well founded and practicable. The king entered with warmth into their sentiments, and began to concert measures for this arduous and important voyage.

Before his preparations for this expedition were finished, accounts were transmitted from Africa, that various nations along the coast had mentioned a mighty kingdom situated on their continent, at a great distance towards the east, the king of which, according to their description, professed the Christian religion. The Portuguese monarch immediately concluded, that this must be the emperor of Abyssinia, to whom the Europeans, seduced by a mistake of Rubruquis, Marco Polo, and other travellers to the East, absurdly gave the name of Prester or Presbyter John; and, as he hoped to receive information and assistance from a Christian prince, in prosecuting a scheme that tended to propagate their common faith, he resolved to open, if possible, some intercourse with his court. With this view, he made choice of Pedro de Covillam and Alphonso de Payva, who were perfect masters of the Arabic language, and sent them into the East to search for the residence of this unknown potentate, and to make him proffers of friendship. They had in charge likewise to procure whatever intelligence the nations which they visited could supply, with respect to the trade of India, and the course of navigation to that continent.†

While John made this new attempt by land, to obtain some knowledge of the country which he wished so ardently to discover, he did not neglect the prosecution of this great design by sea. The conduct of a voyage for this purpose, the most arduous and important which the Portuguese had ever projected, was committed to Bartholomew Diaz [1486], an officer whose sagacity, experience, and fortitude rendered him equal to the undertaking. He stretched boldly towards the south, and proceeding beyond the utmost limits to which his countrymen had hitherto advanced, discovered near a thousand miles of new country. Neither the danger to which he was exposed, by a succession of violent tempests in unknown seas, and by the frequent mutinies of his crew, nor the calamities of famine which he suffered from losing his storeship, could deter him from prosecuting his enterprise. In recompense of his labours and perseverance, he at last descried that lofty promontory which bounds Africa to the south. But to descry it was all that he had in his power to accomplish. The violence of the winds, the shattered condition of his ships, and the turbulent spirit of the sailors, compelled him to return after a voyage of sixteen months, in which he discovered a far greater extent of country than any former navigator. Diaz had called the promontory which terminated his voyage *Cabo Tor*

* Vide Nov. Orbis Tabul. Geograph. secund. Ptolem. Amst. 1730. Asia vol. i. p. 26. Lafitau Decouv. de Port. i. 46.

† Faria y Sousa Port

*mentoso*, or the Stormy Cape; but the king, his master, as he now entertained no doubt of having found the long-desired route to India, gave it a name more inviting, and of better omen, *The Cape of Good Hope*.*

Those sanguine expectations of success were confirmed by the intelligence which John received over land, in consequence of his embassy to Abyssinia. Covillam and Payva, in obedience to their master's instructions, had repaired to Grand Cairo. From that city they travelled along with a caravan of Egyptian merchants, and, embarking on the Red Sea, arrived at Aden, in Arabia. There they separated; Payva sailed directly towards Abyssinia; Covillam embarked for the East Indies, and, having visited Calecut, Goa, and other cities on the Malabar coast, returned to Sofala, on the east side of Africa, and thence to Grand Cairo, which Payva and he had fixed upon as their place of rendezvous. Unfortunately the former was cruelly murdered in Abyssinia; but Covillam found at Cairo two Portuguese Jews, whom John, whose provident sagacity attended to every circumstance that could facilitate the execution of his schemes, had despatched after them, in order to receive a detail of their proceedings, and to communicate to them new instructions. By one of these Jews, Covillam transmitted to Portugal a journal of his travels by sea and land, his remarks upon the trade of India, together with exact maps of the coasts on which he had touched; and from what he himself had observed, as well as from the information of skilful seamen in different countries, he concluded, that, by sailing round Africa, a passage might be found to the East Indies.†

The happy coincidence of Covillam's opinion and report with the discoveries which Diaz had lately made, left hardly any shadow of doubt with respect to the possibility of sailing from Europe to India. But the vast length of the voyage, and the furious storms which Diaz had encountered near the Cape of Good Hope, alarmed and intimidated the Portuguese to such a degree, although by long experience they were now become adventurous and skilful mariners, that some time was requisite to prepare their minds for this dangerous and extraordinary voyage. The courage, however, and authority of the monarch gradually dispelled the vain fears of his subjects, or made it necessary to conceal them. As John thought himself now upon the eve of accomplishing that great design which had been the principal object of his reign, his earnestness in prosecuting it became so vehement, that it occupied his thoughts by day, and bereaved him of sleep through the night. While he was taking every precaution that his wisdom and experience could suggest, in order to ensure the success of the expedition, which was to decide concerning the fate of his favourite project, the fame of the vast discoveries which the Portuguese had already made, the reports concerning the extraordinary intelligence which they had received from the East, and the prospect of the voyage which they now meditated, drew the attention of all the European nations, and held them in suspense and expectation. By some, the maritime skill and navigations of the Portuguese were compared with those of the Phenicians and Carthaginians, and exalted above them. Others formed conjectures concerning the revolutions which the success of the Portuguese schemes might occasion in the course of trade, and the political state of Europe. The Venetians began to be disquieted with the apprehension of losing their Indian commerce, the monopoly of which was the chief source of their power as well as opulence, and the Portuguese already enjoyed in fancy the wealth of the East. But during this interval, which gave such scope to the various workings of curiosity, of hope, and of fear, an account was brought to Europe of an event no less extraordinary than unexpected, the discovery of a New World situated on the West; and the eyes and admiration of mankind turned immediately towards that great object.

* Faria y Sousa Port. Asia vol. i. p. 26. † Ibid. p. 27. Lafitau Decouv. i. p. 48.

# BOOK II.

Among the foreigners whom the fame of the discoveries made by the Portuguese had allured into their service, was Christopher Colon, or Columbus, a subject of the republic of Genoa. Neither the time nor place of his birth is known with certainty [11]; but he was descended of an honourable family, though reduced to indigence by various misfortunes. His ancestors having betaken themselves for subsistence to a seafaring life, Columbus discovered in his early youth the peculiar character and talents which mark out a man for that profession. His parents, instead of thwarting this original propensity of his mind, seem to have encouraged and confirmed it by the education which they gave him. After acquiring some knowledge of the Latin tongue, the only language in which science was taught at that time, he was instructed in geometry, cosmography, astronomy, and the art of drawing. To these he applied with such ardour and predilection, on account of their connexion with navigation, his favourite object, that he advanced with rapid proficiency in the study of them. Thus qualified, he went to sea at the age of fourteen [1461], and began his career on that element which conducted him to so much glory. His early voyages were to those ports in the Mediterranean which his countrymen the Genoese frequented. This being a sphere too narrow for his active mind, he made an excursion to the northern seas [1467], and visited the coast of Iceland, to which the English and other nations had begun to resort on account of its fishery. As navigation, in every direction, was now become enterprising, he proceeded beyond that island, the Thule of the ancients, and advanced several degrees within the polar circle. Having satisfied his curiosity, by a voyage which tended more to enlarge his knowledge of naval affairs than to improve his fortune, he entered into the service of a famous sea-captain of his own name and family. This man commanded a small squadron fitted out at his own expense, and by cruising sometimes against the Mahometans, sometimes against the Venetians, the rivals of his country in trade, had acquired both wealth and reputation. With him Columbus continued for several years, no less distinguished for his courage than for his experience as a sailor. At length, in an obstinate engagement off the coast of Portugal, with some Venetian caravals returning richly laden from the Low Countries, the vessel on board which he served took fire, together with one of the enemy's ships to which it was fast grappled. In this dreadful extremity his intrepidity and presence of mind did not forsake him. He threw himself into the sea, laid hold of a floating oar; and by the support of it, and his dexterity in swimming, he reached the shore, though above two leagues distant, and saved a life reserved for great undertakings.*

As soon as he recovered strength for the journey, he repaired to Lisbon, where many of his countrymen were settled. They soon conceived such a favourable opinion of his merit, as well as talents, that they warmly solicited him to remain in that kingdom, where his naval skill and experience could not fail of rendering him conspicuous. To every adventurer animated either with curiosity to visit new countries, or with ambition to distinguish himself, the Portuguese service was at that time extremely inviting. Columbus listened with a favourable ear to the advice of his friends, and, having gained the esteem of a Portuguese lady, whom he married, fixed his residence in Lisbon. This alliance, instead of detaching him from a seafaring life, contributed to enlarge the sphere of his naval knowledge, and to excite a

* Life of Columbus, c. v

desire of extending it still further. His wife was a daughter of Bartholomew Perestrello, one of the captains employed by prince Henry in his early navigations, and who, under his protection, had discovered and planted the islands of Porto Santo and Madeira. Columbus got possession of the journals and charts of this experienced navigator; and from them he learned the course which the Portuguese had held in making their discoveries, as well as the various circumstances which guided or encouraged them in their attempts. The study of these soothed and inflamed his favourite passion; and while he contemplated the maps, and read the descriptions of the new countries which Perestrello had seen, his impatience to visit them became irresistible. In order to indulge it, he made a voyage to Madeira, and continued during several years to trade with that island, with the Canaries, the Azores, the settlements in Guinea, and all the other places which the Portuguese had discovered on the continent of Africa.*

By the experience which Columbus acquired, during such a variety of voyages to almost every part of the globe with which at that time any intercourse was carried on by sea, he was now become one of the most skilful navigators in Europe. But, not satisfied with that praise, his ambition aimed at something more. The successful progress of the Portuguese navigators had awakened a spirit of curiosity and emulation, which set every man of science upon examining all the circumstances that led to the discoveries which they had made, or that afforded a prospect of succeeding in any new and bolder undertaking. The mind of Columbus, naturally inquisitive, capable of deep reflection, and turned to speculations of this kind, was so often employed in revolving the principles upon which the Portuguese had founded their schemes of discovery, and the mode on which they had carried them on, that he gradually began to form an idea of improving upon their plan, and of accomplishing discoveries which hitherto they had attempted in vain.

To find out a passage by sea to the East Indies, was the important object in view at that period. From the time that the Portuguese doubled Cape de Verd, this was the point at which they aimed in all their navigations, and in comparison with it all their discoveries in Africa appeared inconsiderable. The fertility and riches of India had been known for many ages: its spices and other valuable commodities were in high request throughout Europe, and the vast wealth of the Venetians, arising from their having engrossed this trade, had raised the envy of all nations. But how intent soever the Portuguese were upon discovering a new route to those desirable regions, they searched for it only by steering towards the south, in hopes of arriving at India by turning to the east after they had sailed round the further extremity of Africa. This course was still unknown, and even if discovered, was of such immense length, that a voyage from Europe to India must have appeared at that period an undertaking extremely arduous, and of very uncertain issue. More than half a century had been employed in advancing from Cape Non to the equator; a much longer space of time might elapse before the more extensive navigation from that to India could be accomplished. These reflections upon the uncertainty, the danger, and tediousness of the course which the Portuguese were pursuing, naturally led Columbus to consider whether a shorter and more direct passage to the East Indies might not be found out. After revolving long and seriously every circumstance suggested by his superior knowledge in the theory as well as the practice of navigation; after comparing attentively the observations of modern pilots with the hints and conjectures of ancient authors, he at last concluded, that by sailing directly towards the west, across the Atlantic ocean, new countries, which probably formed a part of the great continent of India, must infallibly be discovered.

* Life of Columbus, c. iv. v.

Principles and arguments of various kinds, and derived from different sources, induced him to adopt this opinion, seemingly as chimerical as it was new and extraordinary. The spherical figure of the earth was known, and its magnitude ascertained with some degree of accuracy. From this it was evident, that the continents of Europe, Asia, and Africa, as far as they were known at that time, formed but a small portion of the terraqueous globe. It was suitable to our ideas concerning the wisdom and beneficence of the Author of Nature, to believe that the vast space still unexplored was not covered entirely by a waste unprofitable ocean, but occupied by countries fit for the habitation of man. It appeared likewise extremely probable that the continent on this side of the globe was balanced by a proportional quantity of land in the other hemisphere. These conclusions concerning the existence of another continent, drawn from the figure and structure of the globe, were confirmed by the observations and conjectures of modern navigators. A Portuguese pilot, having stretched further to the west than was usual at that time, took up a piece of timber artificially carved floating upon the sea; and as it was driven towards him by a westerly wind, he concluded that it came from some unknown land situated in that quarter. Columbus's brother-in-law had found to the west of the Madeira isles, a piece of timber fashioned in the same manner, and brought by the same wind; and had seen likewise canes of an enormous size floating upon the waves, which resembled those described by Ptolemy as productions peculiar to the East Indies.* After a course of westerly winds, trees torn up by the roots were often driven upon the coasts of the Azores; and at one time, the dead bodies of two men with singular features, resembling neither the inhabitants of Europe nor of Africa, were cast ashore there.

As the force of this united evidence, arising from theoretical principles and practical observations, led Columbus to expect the discovery of new countries in the western ocean, other reasons induced him to believe that these must be connected with the continent of India. Though the ancients had hardly ever penetrated into India further than the banks of the Ganges, yet some Greek authors had ventured to describe the provinces beyond that river. As men are prone, and at liberty, to magnify what is remote or unknown, they represented them as regions of an immense extent. Ctesias affirmed that India was as large as all the rest of Asia. Onesicritus, whom Pliny the naturalist follows,† contended that it was equal to a third part of the habitable earth. Nearchus asserted, that it would take four months to march in a straight line from one extremity of India to the other.‡ The journal of Marco Polo, who had proceeded towards the East far beyond the limits to which any European had ever advanced, seemed to confirm these exaggerated accounts of the ancients. By his magnificent descriptions of the kingdoms of *Cathay* and *Cipango*, and of many other countries the names of which were unknown in Europe, India appeared to be a region of vast extent. From these accounts, which, however defective, were the most accurate that the people of Europe had received at that period with respect to the remote parts of the East, Columbus drew a just conclusion. He contended that, in proportion as the continent of India stretched out towards the East, it must, in consequence of the spherical figure of the earth, approach near to the islands which had lately been discovered to the west of Africa; that the distance from the one to the other was probably not very considerable; and that the most direct as well as shortest course to the remote regions of the East was to be found by sailing due west. [12] This notion concerning the vicinity of India to the western parts of our continent, was countenanced by some eminent writers among the ancients, the sanction of whose authority was necessary, in that age, to procure a favourable reception to any tenet. Aristotle thought it probable that the Columns of

* Lib. i. c. 17. † Nat. Hist. lib vi. c. 17. ‡ Strab. Geogr. lib. xv. p. 1011.

Hercules, or Straits of Gibraltar, were not far removed from the East Indies, and that there might be a communication by sea between them.* Seneca, in terms still more explicit, affirms, that with a fair wind one might sail from Spain to India in a few days.† The famous Atlantic island described by Plato, and supposed by many to be a real country, beyond which an unknown continent was situated, is represented by him as lying at no great distance from Spain. After weighing all these particulars, Columbus, in whose character the modesty and diffidence of true genius were united with the ardent enthusiasm of a projector, did not rest with such absolute assurance either upon his own arguments, or upon the authority of the ancients, as not to consult such of his contemporaries as were capable of comprehending the nature of the evidence which he produced in support of his opinion. As early as the year one thousand four hundred and seventy-four, he communicated his ideas concerning the probability of discovering new countries, by sailing westward, to Paul, a physician of Florence, eminent for his knowledge of cosmography, and who, from the learning as well as candour which he discovers in his reply, appears to have been well entitled to the confidence which Columbus placed in him. He warmly approved of the plan, suggested several facts in confirmation of it, and encouraged Columbus to persevere in an undertaking so laudable, and which must redound so much to the honour of his country and the benefit of Europe.‡

To a mind less capable of forming and of executing great designs than that of Columbus, all those reasonings and observations and authorities would have served only as the foundation of some plausible and fruitless theory, which might have furnished matter for ingenious discourse or fanciful conjecture. But with his sanguine and enterprising temper speculation led directly to action. Fully satisfied himself with respect to the truth of his system, he was impatient to bring it to the test of experiment, and to set out upon a voyage of discovery. The first step towards this was to secure the patronage of some of the considerable powers in Europe capable of undertaking such an enterprise. As long absence had not extinguished the affection which he bore to his native country, he wished that it should reap the fruits of his labours and invention. With this view, he laid his scheme before the senate of Genoa, and, making his country the first tender of his service, offered to sail under the banners of the republic in quest of the new regions which he expected to discover. But Columbus had resided for so many years in foreign parts, that his countrymen were unacquainted with his abilities and character; and, though a maritime people, were so little accustomed to distant voyages, that they could form no just idea of the principles on which he founded his hopes of success. They inconsiderately rejected his proposal, as the dream of a chimerical projector, and lost for ever the opportunity of restoring their commonwealth to its ancient splendour.§

Having performed what was due to his country, Columbus was so little discouraged by the repulse which he had received, that instead of relinquishing his undertaking he pursued it with fresh ardour. He made his next overture to John II. king of Portugal, in whose dominions he had been long established, and whom he considered on that account, as having the second claim to his service. Here every circumstance seemed to promise him a more favourable reception: he applied to a monarch of an enterprising genius, no incompetent judge in naval affairs, and proud of patronising every attempt to discover new countries. His subjects were the most experienced navigators in Europe, and the least apt to be intimidated either by the novelty or boldness of any maritime expedition. In Portugal, the professional skill of Columbus, as well as his personal good qualities, were thoroughly known. and as the former rendered it probable that his scheme was not

* Aristot. de Cœlo, lib. ii. c. 14. edit. Du Val. Par. 1629. vol. i. p. 472. † Senec. Quæst. Natur. lib. i. in proem. ‡ Life of Columbus. c. viii. § Herrera Hist. de las Indias Occid. dec. i. lib. i. c. vii.

altogether visionary, the latter exempted him from the suspicion of any sinister intention in proposing it. Accordingly, the king listened to him in the most gracious manner, and referred the consideration of his plan to Diego Ortiz, bishop of Ceuta, and two Jewish physicians, eminent cosmographers, whom he was accustomed to consult in matters of this kind. As in Genoa, ignorance had opposed and disappointed Columbus; in Lisbon, he had to combat with prejudice, an enemy no less formidable. The persons according to whose decision his scheme was to be adopted, or rejected, had been the chief directors of the Portuguese navigations, and had advised to search for a passage to India by steering a course directly opposite to that which Columbus recommended as shorter and more certain. They could not, therefore, approve of his proposal without submitting to the double mortification of condemning their own theory, and acknowledging his superior sagacity. After teasing him with captious questions, and starting innumerable objections, with a view of betraying him into such a particular explanation of his system as might draw from him a full discovery of its nature, they deferred passing a final judgment with respect to it. In the mean time they conspired to rob him of the honour and advantages which he expected from the success of his scheme, advising the king to despatch a vessel secretly, in order to attempt the proposed discovery by following exactly the course which Columbus seemed to point out. John, forgetting on this occasion the sentiments becoming a monarch, meanly adopted this perfidious counsel. But the pilot chosen to execute Columbus's plan had neither the genius nor the fortitude of its author. Contrary winds arose, no sight of approaching land appeared, his courage failed, and he returned to Lisbon, execrating the project as equally extravagant and dangerous.*

Upon discovering this dishonourable transaction, Columbus felt the indignation natural to an ingenuous mind, and in the warmth of his resentment determined to break off all intercourse with a nation capable of such flagrant treachery. He instantly quitted the kingdom, and landed in Spain towards the close of the year one thousand four hundred and eighty-four. As he was now at liberty to court the protection of any patron whom he could engage to approve of his plan, and to carry it into execution, he resolved to propose it in person to Ferdinand and Isabella, who at that time governed the united kingdoms of Castile and Aragon. But as he had already experienced the uncertain issue of application to kings and ministers, he took the precaution of sending into England his brother Bartholomew, to whom he had fully communicated his ideas, in order that he might negociate at the same time with Henry VII., who was reputed one of the most sagacious as well as opulent princes in Europe.

It was not without reason that Columbus entertained doubts and fears with respect to the reception of his proposals in the Spanish court. Spain was at that juncture engaged in a dangerous war with Granada, the last of the Moorish kingdoms in that country. The wary and suspicious temper of Ferdinand was not formed to relish bold or uncommon designs. Isabella, though more generous and enterprising, was under the influence of her husband in all her actions. The Spaniards had hitherto made no efforts to extend navigation beyond its ancient limits, and had beheld the amazing progress of discovery among their neighbours the Portuguese without one attempt to imitate or to rival them. The war with the Infidels afforded an ample field to the national activity and love of glory. Under circumstances so unfavourable, it was impossible for Columbus to make rapid progress with a nation naturally slow and dilatory in forming all its resolutions. His character, however, was admirably adapted to that of the people whose confidence and protection he solicited. He was grave, though courteous in his deportment; circumspect in his words and actions, irreproachable in his

* Life of Columbus, c. xi. Herrera, dec. i. lib. i. c. 7.

morals, and exemplary in his attention to all the duties and functions of religion. By qualities so respectable, he not only gained many private friends, but acquired such general esteem, that, notwithstanding the plainness of his appearance, suitable to the mediocrity of his fortune, he was not considered as a mere adventurer, to whom indigence had suggested a visionary project, but was received as a person to whose propositions serious attention was due.

Ferdinand and Isabella, though fully occupied by their operations against the Moors, paid so much regard to Columbus, as to remit the consideration of his plan to the queen's confessor, Ferdinand de Talavera. He consulted such of his countrymen as were supposed best qualified to decide with respect to a subject of this kind. But true science had hitherto made so little progress in Spain, that the pretended philosophers, selected to judge in a matter of such moment, did not comprehend the first principles upon which Columbus founded his conjectures and hopes. Some of them, from mistaken notions concerning the dimensions of the globe, contended that a voyage to those remote parts of the east which Columbus expected to discover, could not be performed in less than three years. Others concluded, that either he would find the ocean to be of infinite extent, according to the opinion of some ancient philosophers; or, if he should persist in steering towards the west beyond a certain point, that the convex figure of the globe would prevent his return, and that he must inevitably perish in the vain attempt to open a communication between the two opposite hemispheres which nature had for ever disjoined. Even without deigning to enter into any particular discussion, many rejected the scheme in general, upon the credit of a maxim, under which the ignorant and unenterprising shelter themselves in every age, "That it is presumptuous in any person, to suppose that he alone possesses knowledge superior to all the rest of mankind united." They maintained, that if there were really any such countries as Columbus pretended, they could not have remained so long concealed, nor would the wisdom and sagacity of former ages have left the glory of this invention to an obscure Genoese pilot.

It required all Columbus's patience and address to negotiate with men capable of advancing such strange propositions. He had to contend not only with the obstinacy of ignorance, but with what is still more intractable, the pride of false knowledge. After innumerable conferences, and wasting five years in fruitless endeavours to inform and to satisfy judges so little capable of deciding with propriety, Talavera at last made such an unfavourable report to Ferdinand and Isabella, as induced them to acquaint Columbus, that until the war with the Moors should be brought to a period it would be imprudent to engage in any new and extensive enterprise.

Whatever care was taken to soften the harshness of this declaration, Columbus considered it as a final rejection of his proposals. But, happily for mankind, that superiority of genius, which is capable of forming great and uncommon designs, is usually accompanied with an ardent enthusiasm, which can neither be cooled by delays nor damped by disappointment. Columbus was of this sanguine temper. Though he felt deeply the cruel blow given to his hopes, and retired immediately from a court where he had been amused so long with vain expectations, his confidence in the just ness of his own system did not diminish, and his impatience to demonstrate the truth of it by an actual experiment became greater than ever. Having courted the protection of sovereign states without success, he applied next to persons of inferior rank, and addressed successively the Dukes of Medina Sidonia and Medina Celi, who, though subjects, were possessed of power and opulence more than equal to the enterprise which he projected. His negotiations with them proved as fruitless as those in which he had been hitherto engaged; for these noblemen were either as little convinced by Columbus's arguments as their superiors, or they were afraid of alarming the jealousy and offending the pride of Ferdinand, by countenancing a scheme which he had rejected.*

Amid the painful sensations occasioned by such a succession of disappointments, Columbus had to sustain the additional distress of having received no accounts of his brother whom he had sent to the court of England. In his voyage to that country, Bartholomew had been so unfortunate as to fall into the hands of pirates, who having stripped him of every thing detained him a prisoner for several years. At length he made his escape, and arrived in London, but in such extreme indigence, that he was obliged to employ himself, during a considerable time in drawing and selling maps, in order to pick up as much money as would purchase a decent dress in which he might venture to appear at court. He then laid before the king the proposals with which he had been intrusted by his brother; and notwithstanding Henry's excessive caution and parsimony, which rendered him averse to new or extensive undertakings, he received Columbus's overtures with more approbation than any monarch to whom they had hitherto been presented.

Meanwhile, Columbus being unacquainted with his brother's fate, and having now no prospect of encouragement in Spain, resolved to visit the court of England in person, in hopes of meeting with a more favourable reception there. He had already made preparations for this purpose, and taken measures for the disposal of his children during his absence, when Juan Perez, the guardian of the monastery of Rabida, near Palos, in which they had been educated, earnestly solicited him to defer his journey for a short time. Perez was a man of considerable learning, and of some credit with queen Isabella, to whom he was known personally. He was warmly attached to Columbus, with whose abilities as well as integrity he had many opportunities of being acquainted. Prompted by curiosity or by friendship, he entered upon an accurate examination of his system, in conjunction with a physician settled in the neighbourhood, who was a considerable proficient in mathematical knowledge. This investigation satisfied them so thoroughly, with respect to the solidity of the principles on which Columbus founded his opinion, and the probability of success in executing the plan which he proposed, that Perez, in order to prevent his country from being deprived of the glory and benefit which must accrue to the patrons of such a grand enterprise, ventured to write to Isabella, conjuring her to consider the matter anew with the attention which it merited.

Moved by the representations of a person whom she respected, Isabella desired Perez to repair immediately to the village of Santa Fe, in which, on account of the siege of Granada, the court resided at that time, that she might confer with him upon this important subject. The first effect of their interview was a gracious invitation of Columbus back to court, accompanied with the present of a small sum to equip him for the journey. As there was now a certain prospect that the war with the Moors would speedily be brought to a happy issue by the reduction of Granada, which would leave the nation at liberty to engage in new undertakings; this, as well as the mark of royal favour, with which Columbus had been lately honoured, encouraged his friends to appear with greater confidence than formerly in support of his scheme. The chief of these, Alonso de Quintanilla, comptroller of the finances in Castile, and Luis de Santangel, receiver of the ecclesiastical revenues in Aragon, whose meritorious zeal in promoting this great design entitles their names to an honourable place in history, introduced Columbus to many persons of high rank, and interested them warmly in his behalf.

But it was not an easy matter to inspire Ferdinand with favourable sentiments. He still regarded Columbus's project as extravagant and chime-

* Life of Columb. c. 13 Herrera, dec. 1. lib. i. c. 7.

rical; and in order to render the efforts of his partisans ineffectual, he had the address to employ, in this new negotiation with him, some of the persons who had formerly pronounced his scheme to be impracticable. To their astonishment, Columbus appeared before them with the same confident hopes of success as formerly, and insisted upon the same high recompense. He proposed that a small fleet should be fitted out, under his command, to attempt the discovery, and demanded to be appointed hereditary admiral and viceroy of all the seas and lands which he should discover, and to have the tenths of the profits arising from them settled irrevocably upon himself and his descendants. At the same time, he offered to advance the eighth part of the sum necessary for accomplishing his design, on condition that he should be entitled to a proportional share of benefit from the adventure If the enterprise should totally miscarry, he made no stipulation for any reward or emolument whatever. Instead of viewing this conduct as the clearest evidence of his full persuasion with respect to the truth of his own system, or being struck with that magnanimity which, after so many delays and repulses, would stoop to nothing inferior to its original claims, the persons with whom Columbus treated began meanly to calculate the expense of the expedition, and the value of the reward which he demanded. The expense, moderate as it was, they represented to be too great for Spain in the present exhausted state of its finances. They contended that the honours and emoluments claimed by Columbus were exorbitant, even if he should perform the utmost of what he had promised; and if all his sanguine hopes should prove illusive, such vast concessions to an adventurer would be deemed not only inconsiderate, but ridiculous. In this imposing garb of caution and prudence, their opinion appeared so plausible, and was so warmly supported by Ferdinand, that Isabella declined giving any countenance to Columbus, and abruptly broke off the negotiation with him which she had begun.

This was more mortifying to Columbus than all the disappointments which he had hitherto met with. The invitation to court from Isabella, like an unexpected ray of light, had opened such prospects of success as encouraged him to hope that his labours were at an end; but now darkness and uncertainty returned, and his mind, firm as it was, could hardly support the shock of such an unforeseen reverse. He withdrew in deep anguish from court, with an intention of prosecuting his voyage to England as his last resource.

About that time Granada surrendered, and Ferdinand and Isabella, in triumphal pomp, took possession of a city [Jan. 2, 1492], the reduction of which extirpated a foreign power from the heart of their dominions, and rendered them masters of all the provinces extending from the bottom of the Pyrenees to the frontiers of Portugal. As the flow of spirits which accompanies success elevates the mind, and renders it enterprising, Quintanilla and Santangel, the vigilant and discerning patrons of Columbus, took advantage of this favourable situation, in order to make one effort more in behalf of their friend. They addressed themselves to Isabella; and after expressing some surprise, that she, who had always been the munificent patroness of generous undertakings, should hesitate so long to countenance the most splendid scheme that had ever been proposed to any monarch; they represented to her, that Columbus was a man of a sound understanding and virtuous character, well qualified, by his experience in navigation, as well as his knowledge of geometry, to form just ideas with respect to the structure of the globe and the situation of its various regions, that, by offering to risk his own life and fortune in the execution of his scheme, he gave the most satisfying evidence both of his integrity and hope of success; that the sum requisite for equipping such an armament as he demanded was inconsiderable, and the advantages which might accrue from his undertaking were immense; that he demanded no recompense for his invention and labour but what was to arise from the countries which he should discover; that, as it was worthy of her magnanimity to make this noble attempt to extend the sphere of human knowledge, and to open an intercourse with regions hitherto unknown, so it would afford the highest satisfaction to her piety and zeal, after re-establishing the Christian faith in those provinces of Spain from which it had been long banished, to discover a new world, to which she might communicate the light and blessings of divine truth; that if now she did not decide instantly, the opportunity would be irretrievably lost, that Columbus was on his way to foreign countries, where some prince, more fortunate or adventurous, would close with his proposals, and Spain would for ever bewail that fatal timidity which had excluded her from the glory and advantages that she had once in her power to have enjoyed.

These forcible arguments, urged by persons of such authority, and at a juncture so well chosen, produced the desired effect. They dispelled all Isabella's doubts and fears; she ordered Columbus to be instantly recalled, declared her resolution of employing him on his own terms, and, regretting the low estate of her finances, generously offered to pledge her own jewels in order to raise as much money as might be needed in making preparations for the voyage. Santangel, in a transport of gratitude, kissed the Queen's hand, and, in order to save her from having recourse to such a mortifying expedient for procuring money, engaged to advance immediately the sum that was requisite.*

Columbus had proceeded some leagues on his journey, when the messenger from Isabella overtook him. Upon receiving an account of the unexpected resolution in his favour, he returned directly to Santa Fe, though some remainder of diffidence still mingled itself with his joy. But the cordial reception which he met with from Isabella, together with the near prospect of setting out upon that voyage which had so long been the object of his thoughts and wishes, soon effaced the remembrance of all that he had suffered in Spain during eight tedious years of solicitation and suspense. The negotiation now went forward with facility and despatch, and a treaty or capitulation with Columbus was signed on the seventeenth of April, one thousand four hundred and ninety-two. The chief articles of it were:— 1. Ferdinand and Isabella, as sovereigns of the ocean, constituted Columbus their high admiral in all the seas, islands, and continents, which should be discovered by his industry; and stipulated that he and his heirs for ever should enjoy this office, with the same powers and prerogatives which belonged to the high admiral of Castile within the limits of his jurisdiction 2. They appointed Columbus their viceroy in all the islands and continents which he should discover; but if, for the better administration of affairs, it should hereafter be necessary to establish a separate governor in any of those countries, they authorized Columbus to name three persons of whom they would choose one for that office; and the dignity of viceroy, with all its immunities, was likewise to be hereditary in the family of Columbus. 3. They granted to Columbus and his heirs for ever, the tenth of the free profits accruing from the productions and commerce of the countries which he should discover. 4. They declared, that if any controversy or lawsuit shall arise with respect to any mercantile transaction in the countries which should be discovered, it should be determined by the sole authority of Columbus, or of judges to be appointed by him. 5. They permitted Columbus to advance one-eighth part of what should be expended in preparing for the expedition, and in carrying on commerce with the countries which he should discover, and entitled him, in return, to an eighth part of the profit.†

Though the name of Ferdinand appears conjoined with that of Isabella in this transaction, his distrust of Columbus was still so violent that he

* Herrera. dec. 1. lib. i. c. 8. † Life of Columbus, c. 15. Herrera, dec. 1. lib. i. c. 9

refused to take any part in the enterprise as king of Aragon. As the whole expense of the expedition was to be defrayed by the crown of Castile, Isabella reserved for her subjects of that kingdom an exclusive right to all the benefits which might redound from its success.

As soon as the treaty was signed, Isabella, by her attention and activity in forwarding the preparations for the voyage, endeavoured to make some reparation to Columbus for the time which he had lost in fruitless solicitation. By the twelfth of May, all that depended upon her was adjusted; and Columbus waited on the king and queen in order to receive their final instructions. Every thing respecting the destination and conduct of the voyage they committed implicitly to the disposal of his prudence. But that they might avoid giving any just cause of offence to the king of Portugal, they strictly enjoined him not to approach near to the Portuguese settlements on the coast of Guinea, or in any of the other countries to which the Portuguese claimed right as discoverers. Isabella had ordered the ships of which Columbus was to take the command to be fitted out in the port of Palos, a small maritime town in the province of Andalusia. As the guardian Juan Perez, to whom Columbus had already been so much indebted, resided in the neighbourhood of this place, he, by the influence of that good ecclesiastic, as well as by his own connection with the inhabitants, not only raised among them what he wanted of the sum that he was bound by treaty to advance, but engaged several of them to accompany him in the voyage. The chief of these associates were three brothers of the name of Pinzon, of considerable wealth, and of great experience in naval affairs, who were willing to hazard their lives and fortunes in the expedition.

But after all the efforts of Isabella and Columbus, the armament was not suitable either to the dignity of the nation by which it was equipped, or to the importance of the service for which it was destined. It consisted of three vessels. The largest, a ship of no considerable burden, was commanded by Columbus, as admiral, who gave it the name of *Santa Maria*, out of respect for the Blessed Virgin, whom he honoured with singular devotion. Of the second, called the *Pinta*, Marton Pinzon was captain, and his brother Francis pilot. The third, named the *Nigna*, was under the command of Vincent Yanez Pinzon. These two were light vessels hardly superior in burden or force to large boats. The squadron, if it merits that name, was victualled for twelve months, and had on board ninety men, mostly sailors, together with a few adventurers who followed the fortune of Columbus, and some gentlemen of Isabella's court, whom she appointed to accompany him. Though the expense of the undertaking was one of the circumstances which chiefly alarmed the court of Spain, and retarded so long the negotiation with Columbus, the sum employed in fitting out this squadron did not exceed four thousand pounds.

As the art of ship-building in the fifteenth century was extremely rude, and the bulk of vessels was accommodated to the short and easy voyages along the coast which they were accustomed to perform, it is a proof of the courage, as well as enterprising genius of Columbus, that he ventured, with a fleet so unfit for a distant navigation, to explore unknown seas, where he had no chart to guide him, no knowledge of the tides and currents, and no experience of the dangers to which he might be exposed. His eagerness to accomplish the great design which had so long engrossed his thoughts, made him overlook or disregard every circumstance that would have intimidated a mind less adventurous. He pushed forward the preparations with such ardour, and was seconded so effectually by the persons to whom Isabella committed the superintendence of this business, that every thing was soon in readiness for the voyage. But as Columbus was deeply impressed with sentiments of religion, he would not set out upon an expedition so arduous, and of which one great object was to extend the knowledge of the Christian faith, without imploring publicly the guidance and protection of Heaven. With this view, he, together with all the persons under his command, marched in solemn procession to the monastery of Rabida. After confessing their sins, and obtaining absolution, they received the holy sacrament from the hands of the guardian, who joined his prayers to theirs for the success of an enterprise which he had so zealously patronized.

Next morning, being Friday the third day of August, in the year one thousand four hundred and ninety-two, Columbus set sail, a little before sunrise, in presence of a vast crowd of spectators, who sent up their supplications to Heaven for the prosperous issue of the voyage, which they wished rather than expected. Columbus steered directly for the Canary Islands, and arrived there [Aug. 13] without any occurrence that would have deserved notice on any other occasion. But, in a voyage of such expectation and importance, every circumstance was the object of attention. The rudder of the Pinta broke loose the day after she left the harbour; and that accident alarmed the crew, no less superstitious than unskilful, as a certain omen of the unfortunate destiny of the expedition. Even in the short run to the Canaries, the ships were found to be so crazy and ill appointed, as to be very improper for a navigation which was expected to be both long and dangerous. Columbus refitted them, however, to the best of his power; and having supplied himself with fresh provisions, he took his departure from Gomera, one of the most westerly of the Canary Islands, on the sixth day of September.

Here the voyage of discovery may properly be said to begin; for Columbus, holding his course due west, left immediately the usual track of navigation, and stretched into unfrequented and unknown seas. The first day, as it was very calm, he made but little way; but on the second he lost sight of the Canaries; and many of the sailors, dejected already, and dismayed, when they contemplated the boldness of the undertaking, began to beat their breasts, and to shed tears, as if they were never more to behold land. Columbus comforted them with assurances of success, and the prospect of vast wealth in those opulent regions whither he was conducting them. This early discovery of the spirit of his followers taught Columbus that he must prepare to struggle not only with the unavoidable difficulties which might be expected from the nature of his undertaking, but with such as were likely to arise from the ignorance and timidity of the people under his command; and he perceived that the art of governing the minds of men would be no less requisite for accomplishing the discoveries which he had in view, than naval skill and undaunted courage. Happily for himself, and for the country by which he was employed, he joined to the ardent temper and inventive genius of a projector, virtues of another species, which are rarely united with them. He possessed a thorough knowledge of mankind, an insinuating address, a patient perseverance in executing any plan, the perfect government of his own passions, and the talent of acquiring an ascendant over those of other men. All these qualities, which formed him for command, were accompanied with that superior knowledge of his profession, which begets confidence in times of difficulty and danger. To unskilful Spanish sailors, accustomed only to coasting voyages in the Mediterranean, the maritime science of Columbus, the fruit of thirty years' experience, improved by an acquaintance with all the inventions of the Portuguese, appeared immense. As soon as they put to sea, he regulated every thing by his sole authority; he superintended the execution of every order; and allowing himself only a few hours for sleep, he was at all other times upon deck. As his course lay through seas which had not formerly been visited, the sounding line, or instruments for observation, were continually in his hands. After the example of the Portuguese discoverers, he attended to the motion of tides and currents, watched the flight of birds, the appear ance of fishes, of seaweeds, and of every thing that floated on the waves, and entered every occurrence, with a minute exactness, in the journal which he kept. As the length of the voyage could not fail of alarming sailors habituated only to short excursions, Columbus endeavoured to conceal from them the real progress which they made. With this view, though they run eighteen leagues on the second day after they left Gomera, he gave out that they had advanced only fifteen, and he uniformly employed the same artifice of reckoning short during the whole voyage. By the fourteenth of September the fleet was above two hundred leagues to the west of the Canary Isles, at a greater distance from land than any Spaniard had been before that time. There they were struck with an appearance no less astonishing than new They observed that the magnetic needle, in their compasses, did not point exactly to the polar star, but varied towards the west; and as they proceeded, this variation increased. This appearance, which is now familiar, though it still remains one of the mysteries of nature, into the cause of which the sagacity of man hath not been able to penetrate, filled the companions of Columbus with terror. They were now in a boundless and unknown ocean, far from the usual course of navigation; nature itself seemed to be altered, and the only guide which they had left was about to fail them. Columbus, with no less quickness than ingenuity, invented a reason for this appearance, which, though it did not satisfy himself, seemed so plausible to them, that it dispelled their fears, or silenced their murmurs.

He still continued to steer due west, nearly in the same latitude with the Canary Islands. In this course he came within the sphere of the trade wind, which blows invariably from east to west, between the tropics and a few degrees beyond them. He advanced before this steady gale with such uniform rapidity that it was seldom necessary to shift a sail. When about four hundred leagues to the west of the Canaries, he found the sea so covered with weeds, that it resembled a meadow of vast extent, and in some places they were so thick as to retard the motion of the vessels. This strange appearance occasioned new alarm and disquiet. The sailors imagined that they were now arrived at the utmost boundary of the navigable ocean; that these floating weeds would obstruct their further progress, and concealed dangerous rocks, or some large track of land, which had sunk, they knew not how, in that place. Columbus endeavoured to persuade them, that what had alarmed ought rather to have encouraged them, and was to be considered as a sign of approaching land. At the same time, a brisk gale arose, and carried them forward. Several birds were seen hovering about the ship [13], and directing their flight towards the west. The desponding crew resumed some degree of spirit, and began to entertain fresh hopes.

Upon the first of October they were, according to the admiral's reckoning, seven hundred and seventy leagues to the west of the Canaries; but lest his men should be intimidated by the prodigious length of the navigation, he gave out that they had proceeded only five hundred and eighty-four leagues, and fortunately, for Columbus, neither his own pilot, nor those of the other ships, had skill sufficient to correct this error, and discover the deceit. They had now been above three weeks at sea; they had proceeded far beyond what former navigators had attempted or deemed possible; all their prognostics of discovery, drawn from the flight of birds and other circumstances, had proved fallacious; the appearances of land, with which their own credulity or the artifice of their commander had from time to time flattered and amused them, had been altogether illusive, and their prospect of success seemed now to be as distant as ever. These reflections occurred often to men who had no other object or occupation than to reason and discourse concerning the intention and circumstances of their expedition They made impression at first upon the ignorant and timid, and, extending by degrees to such as were better informed or more resolute, the contagion spread at length from ship to ship. From secret whispers or murmurings, they proceeded to open cabals and public complaints. They taxed their sovereign with inconsiderate credulity, in paying such regard to the vain promises and rash conjectures of an indigent foreigner, as to hazard the lives of so many of her own subjects in prosecuting a chimerical scheme They affirmed that they had fully performed their duty, by venturing so far in an unknown and hopeless course, and could incur no blame for refusing to follow any longer a desperate adventurer to certain destruction. They contended, that it was necessary to think of returning to Spain, while their crazy vessels were still in a condition to keep the sea, but expressed their fears that the attempt would prove vain, as the wind, which had hitherto been so favourable to their course, must render it impossible to sail in an opposite direction. All agreed that Columbus should be compelled by force to adopt a measure on which their common safety depended. Some of the more audacious proposed, as the most expeditious and certain method of getting rid at once of his remonstrances, to throw him into the sea, being persuaded that, upon their return to Spain, the death of an unsuccessful projector would excite little concern, and be inquired into with no curiosity.

Columbus was fully sensible of his perilous situation. He had observed, with great uneasiness, the fatal operation of ignorance and of fear in producing disaffection among his crew, and saw, that it was now ready to burst out into open mutiny. He retained, however, perfect presence of mind. He affected to seem ignorant of their machinations. Notwithstanding the agitation and solicitude of his own mind, he appeared with a cheerful countenance, like a man satisfied with the progress he had made, and confident of success. Sometimes he employed all the arts of insinuation to soothe his men. Sometimes he endeavoured to work upon their ambition or avarice, by magnificent descriptions of the fame and wealth which they were about to acquire. On other occasions he assumed a tone of authority, and threatened them with vengeance from their sovereign, if, by their dastardly behaviour, they should defeat this noble effort to promote the glory of God, and to exalt the Spanish name above that of every other nation. Even with seditious sailors, the words of a man whom they had been accustomed to reverence, were weighty and persuasive, and not only restrained them from those violent excesses which they meditated, but prevailed with them to accompany their admiral for some time longer.

As they proceeded, the indications of approaching land seemed to be more certain, and excited hope in proportion. The birds began to appear in flocks, making towards the southwest. Columbus, in imitation of the Portuguese navigators, who had been guided, in several of their discoveries, by the motion of birds, altered his course from due west towards that quarter whither they pointed their flight. But, after holding on for several days in this new direction, without any better success than formerly, having seen no object, during thirty days, but the sea and the sky, the hopes of his companions subsided faster than they had risen; their fears revived with additional force; impatience, rage, and despair, appeared in every countenance. All sense of subordination was lost: the officers, who had hitherto concurred with Columbus in opinion, and supported his authority, now took part with the private men; they assembled tumultuously on the deck, expostulated with their commander, mingled threats with their expostulations, and required him instantly to tack about and to return to Europe. Columbus perceived that it would be of no avail to have recourse to any of his former arts, which, having been tried so often, had lost their effect; and that it was impossible to rekindle any zeal for the success of the expedition among men in whose breasts fear had extinguished every generous sentiment. He saw that it was no less vain to think of employing either gentle or severe measures to quell a mutiny so general and so violent. It was necessary, on all these accounts, to soothe passions which he could no longer command,

and to give way to a torrent too impetuous to be checked. He promised solemnly to his men that he would comply with their request, provided they would accompany him, and obey his command for three days longer, and if, during that time, land were not discovered, he would then abandon the enterprise, and direct his course towards Spain.*

Enraged as the sailors were, and impatient to turn their faces again towards their native country, this proposition did not appear to them unreasonable. Nor did Columbus hazard much in confining himself to a term so short. The presages of discovering land were now so numerous and promising, that he deemed them infallible. For some days the sounding line reached the bottom, and the soil which it brought up indicated land to be at no great distance. The flocks of birds increased, and were composed not only of seafowl, but of such land birds as could not be supposed to fly far from the shore. The crew of the Pinta observed a cane floating, which seemed to have been newly cut, and likewise a piece of timber artificially carved. The sailors aboard the Nigna took up the branch of a tree with red berries, perfectly fresh. The clouds around the setting sun assumed a new appearance; the air was more mild and warm, and during the night the wind became unequal and variable. From all these symptoms, Columbus was so confident of being near land, that on the evening of the eleventh of October, after public prayers for success, he ordered the sails to be furled, and the ships to lie to, keeping strict watch, lest they should be driven ashore in the night. During this interval of suspense and expectation, no man shut his eyes, all kept upon deck, gazing intently towards that quarter where they expected to discover the land, which had been so long the object of their wishes.

About two hours before midnight, Columbus, standing on the forecastle, observed a light at a distance, and privately pointed it out to Pedro Guttierez, a page of the Queen's wardrobe. Guttierez perceived it, and calling to Salcedo, comptroller of the fleet, all three saw it in motion, as if it were carried from place to place. A little after midnight the joyful sound of *land! land!* was heard from the Pinta, which kept always a head of the other ships. But, having been so often deceived by fallacious appearances, every man was now become slow of belief, and waited in all the anguish of uncertainty and impatience for the return of day. As soon as morning dawned [Oct. 12], all doubts and fears were dispelled. From every ship an island was seen about two leagues to the north, whose flat and verdant fields, well stored with wood, and watered with many rivulets, presented the aspect of a delightful country. The crew of the Pinta instantly began the *Te Deum*, as a hymn of thanksgiving to God, and were joined by those of the other ships, with tears of joy and transports of congratulation. This office of gratitude to Heaven was followed by an act of justice to their commander. They threw themselves at the feet of Columbus, with feelings of self-condemnation mingled with reverence. They implored him to pardon their ignorance, incredulity, and insolence, which had created him so much unnecessary disquiet, and had so often obstructed the prosecution of his well-concerted plan; and passing, in the warmth of their admiration, from one extreme to another, they now pronounced the man, whom they had so lately reviled and threatened, to be a person inspired by Heaven with sagacity and fortitude more than human, in order to accomplish a design so far beyond the ideas and conception of all former ages.

As soon as the sun arose, all their boats were manned and armed. They rowed towards the island with their colours displayed, with warlike music, and other martial pomp. As they approached the coast, they saw it covered with a multitude of people, whom the novelty of the spectacle had drawn together, whose attitudes and gestures expressed wonder and astonishment

* Oviedo, Hist. ap. Ramus, vol. iii. p. 81. E

at the strange objects which presented themselves to their view. Columbus was the first European who set foot in the New World which he had discovered. He landed in a rich dress, and with a naked sword in his hand. His men followed, and kneeling down, they all kissed the ground which they had so long desired to see. They next erected a crucifix, and prostrating themselves before it, returned thanks to God for conducting their voyage to such a happy issue. They then took solemn possession of the country, for the crown of Castile and Leon, with all the formalities which the Portuguese were accustomed to observe in acts of this kind, in their new discoveries.*

The Spaniards, while thus employed, were surrounded by many of the natives, who gazed in silent admiration upon actions which they could not comprehend, and of which they did not foresee the consequences. The dress of the Spaniards, the whiteness of their skins, their beards, their arms, appeared strange and surprising. The vast machines in which they had traversed the ocean, that seemed to move upon the waters with wings, and uttered a dreadful sound resembling thunder, accompanied with lightning and smoke, struck them with such terror, that they began to respect their new guests as a superior order of beings, and concluded that they were children of the Sun, who had descended to visit the earth.

The Europeans were hardly less amazed at the scene now before them. Every herb, and shrub, and tree, was different from those which flourished in Europe. The soil seemed to be rich, but bore few marks of cultivation. The climate, even to the Spaniards, felt warm, though extremely delightful. The inhabitants appeared in the simple innocence of nature, entirely naked. Their black hair, long and uncurled, floated upon their shoulders, or was bound in tresses around their heads. They had no beards, and every part of their bodies was perfectly smooth. Their complexion was of a dusky-copper colour, their features singular, rather than disagreeable, their aspect gentle and timid. Though not tall, they were well shaped and active. Their faces, and several parts of their body, were fantastically painted with glaring colours. They were shy at first through fear, but soon became familiar with the Spaniards, and with transports of joy received from them hawksbells, glass beads, or other baubles, in return for which they gave such provisions as they had, and some cotton yarn, the only commodity of value that they could produce. Towards evening, Columbus returned to his ship, accompanied by many of the islanders in their boats, which they called *canoes*, and though rudely formed out of the trunk of a single tree, they rowed them with surprising dexterity. Thus, in the first interview between the inhabitants of the old and new worlds, every thing was conducted amicably, and to their mutual satisfaction. The former, enlightened and ambitious, formed already vast ideas with respect to the advantages which they might derive from the regions that began to open to their view. The latter, simple and undiscerning, had no foresight of the calamities and desolation which were approaching their country.

Columbus, who now assumed the title and authority of admiral and viceroy, called the island which he had discovered *San Salvador*. It is better known by the name of *Guanahani*, which the natives gave to it, and is one of that large cluster of islands called the Lucaya or Bahama isles It is situated above three thousand miles to the west of Gomera; from which the squadron took its departure, and only four degrees to the south of it; so little had Columbus deviated from the westerly course, which he had chosen as the most proper.

Columbus employed the next day in visiting the coasts of the island; and from the universal poverty of the inhabitants, he perceived that this was not the rich country for which he sought. But, conformably to his theory

* Life of Columbus, c. 22, 23. Herrera, dec. 1. lib. i. c. 23.

concerning the discovery of those regions of Asia which stretched towards the east, he concluded that San Salvador was one of the isles which geographers described as situated in the great ocean adjacent to India.* Having observed that most of the people whom he had seen wore small plates of gold, by way of ornament, in their nostrils, he eagerly inquired where they got that precious metal. They pointed towards the south, and made him comprehend by signs, that gold abounded in countries situated in that quarter. Thither he immediately determined to direct his course, in full confidence of finding there those opulent regions which had been the object of his voyage, and would be a recompense for all his toils and dangers. He took along with him seven of the natives of San Salvador, that, by acquiring the Spanish language, they might serve as guides and interpreters; and those innocent people considered it as a mark of distinction when they were selected to accompany him.

He saw several islands, and touched at three of the largest, on which he bestowed the names of St. Mary of the Conception, Fernandina, and Isabella. But, as their soil, productions, and inhabitants nearly resembled those of San Salvador, he made no stay in any of them. He inquired every where for gold, and the signs that were uniformly made by way of answer, confirmed him in the opinion that it was brought from the south. He followed that course, and soon discovered a country which appeared very extensive, not perfectly level, like those which he had already visited, but so diversified with rising grounds, hills, rivers, woods, and plains, that he was uncertain whether it might prove an island, or part of the continent. The natives of San Salvador, whom he had on board, called it *Cuba;* Columbus gave it the name of Juana. He entered the mouth of a large river with his squadron, and all the inhabitants fled to the mountains as he approached the shore. But as he resolved to careen the ships in that place, he sent some Spaniards, together with one of the people of San Salvador, to view the interior part of the country. They, having advanced above sixty miles from the shore, reported, upon their return, that the soil was richer and more cultivated than any they had hitherto discovered; that, besides many scattered cottages, they had found one village, containing above a thousand inhabitants; that the people, though naked, seemed to be more intelligent than those of San Salvador, but had treated them with the same respectful attention, kissing their feet, and honouring them as sacred beings allied to heaven; that they had given them to eat a certain root, the taste of which resembled roasted chestnuts, and likewise a singular species of corn called *maize*, which, either when roasted whole or ground into meal, was abundantly palatable; that there seemed to be no four-footed animals in the country, but a species of dogs, which could not bark, and a creature resembling a rabbit, but of a much smaller size; that they had observed some ornaments of gold among the people, but of no great value.†

These messengers had prevailed with some of the natives to accompany them, who informed Columbus, that the gold of which they made their ornaments was found in *Cubanacan.* By this word they meant the middle or inland part of Cuba; but Columbus, being ignorant of their language, as well as unaccustomed to their pronunciation, and his thoughts running continually upon his own theory concerning the discovery of the East Indies, he was led, by the resemblance of sound, to suppose that they spoke of the great Khan, and imagined that the opulent kingdom of *Cathay*, described by Marco Polo, was not very remote. This induced him to employ some time in viewing the country. He visited almost every harbour, from Porto del Principe, on the north coast of Cuba, to the eastern extremity of the island: but, though delighted with the beauty of the scenes which every where presented themselves, and amazed at the luxuriant fertility of the

* Pet. Mart. epist. 135.

† Life of Columbus, c. 24—28. Herrera, dec. 1. lib. i. c. 14.

soil, both which, from their novelty, made a more lively impression upon his imagination [14], he did not find gold in such quantity as was sufficient to satisfy either the avarice of his followers, or the expectations of the court to which he was to return. The people of the country, as much astonished at his eagerness in quest of gold as the Europeans were at their ignorance and simplicity, pointed towards the east, where an island which they called *Hayti* was situated, in which that metal was more abundant than among them. Columbus ordered his squadron to bend its course thither; but Marton Alonso Pinzon, impatient to be the first who should take possession of the treasures which this country was supposed to contain, quitted his companions, regardless of all the admiral's signals to slacken sail until they should come up with him.

Columbus, retarded by contrary winds, did not reach Hayti till the sixth of December. He called the port where he first touched St. Nicholas, and the island itself Espagnola, in honour of the kingdom by which he was employed; and it is the only country, of those he had yet discovered, which has retained the name that he gave it. As he could neither meet with the Pinta, nor have any intercourse with the inhabitants, who fled in great consternation towards the woods, he soon quitted St. Nicholas, and, sailing along the northern coast of the island, he entered another harbour, which he called Conception. Here he was more fortunate; his people overtook a woman who was flying from them, and after treating her with great gentleness, dismissed her with a present of such toys as they knew were most valued in those regions. The description which she gave to her countrymen of the humanity and wonderful qualities of the strangers; their admiration of the trinkets, which she showed with exultation; and their eagerness to participate of the same favours; removed all their fears, and induced many of them to repair to the harbour. The strange objects which they beheld, and the baubles which Columbus bestowed upon them, amply gratified their curiosity and their wishes. They nearly resembled the people of Guanahani and Cuba. They were naked like them, ignorant and simple; and seemed to be equally unacquainted with all the arts which appear most necessary in polished societies; but they were gentle, credulous, and timid, to a degree which rendered it easy to acquire the ascendant over them, especially as their excessive admiration led them into the same error with the people of the other islands, in believing the Spaniards to be more than mortals, and descended immediately from heaven. They possessed gold in greater abundance than their neighbours, which they readily exchanged for bells, beads, or pins; and in this unequal traffic both parties were highly pleased, each considering themselves as gainers by the transaction. Here Columbus was visited by a prince or *cazique* of the country. He appeared with all the pomp known among a simple people, being carried in a sort of palanquin upon the shoulders of four men, and attended by many of his subjects, who served him with great respect. His deportment was grave and stately, very reserved towards his own people, but with Columbus and the Spaniards extremely courteous. He gave the admiral some thin plates of gold, and a girdle of curious workmanship, receiving in return presents of small value, but highly acceptable to him.*

Columbus, still intent on discovering the mines which yielded gold, continued to interrogate all the natives with whom he had any intercourse, concerning their situation. They concurred in pointing out a mountainous country, which they called *Cibao*, at some distance from the sea, and further towards the east. Struck with this sound, which appeared to him the same with *Cipango*, the name by which Marco Polo, and other travellers o the east, distinguished the island of Japan, he no longer doubted with respect to the vicinity of the countries which he had discovered to the remote parts

* Life of Columbus, c. 32. Herrera, dec. 1. lib. i. c. 15, &c.

of Asia; and, in full expectation of reaching soon those regions which had been the object of his voyage, he directed his course towards the east. He put into a commodious harbour, which he called St. Thomas, and found that district to be under the government of a powerful cazique, named *Guacanahari*, who, as he afterwards learned, was one of the five sovereigns among whom the whole island was divided. He immediately sent messengers to Columbus, who in his name delivered to him the present of a mask curiously fashioned with the ears, nose, and mouth of beaten gold, and invited him to the place of his residence, near the harbour now called Cape François, some leagues towards the east. Columbus despatched some of his officers to visit this prince, who, as he behaved himself with greater dignity, seemed to claim more attention. They returned with such favourable accounts both of the country and of the people, as made Columbus impatient for that interview with Guacanahari to which he had been invited.

He sailed for this purpose from St. Thomas, on the twenty-fourth of December, with a fair wind, and the sea perfectly calm; and as, amidst the multiplicity of his occupations, he had not shut his eyes for two days, he retired at midnight in order to take some repose, having committed the helm to the pilot, with strict injunctions not to quit it for a moment. The pilot, dreading no danger, carelessly left the helm to an unexperienced cabin boy, and the ship, carried away by a current, was dashed against a rock. The violence of the shock awakened Columbus. He ran up to the deck. There all was confusion and despair. He alone retained presence of mind. He ordered some of the sailors to take a boat, and carry out an anchor astern; but, instead of obeying, they made off towards the Nigna, which was about half a league distant. He then commanded the masts to be cut down, in order to lighten the ship; but all his endeavours were too late; the vessel opened near the keel, and filled so fast with water that its loss was inevitable. The smoothness of the sea, and the timely assistance of boats from the Nigna, enabled the crew to save their lives. As soon as the islanders heard of this disaster, they crowded to the shore, with their prince Guacanahari at their head. Instead of taking advantage of the distress in which they beheld the Spaniards, to attempt any thing to their detriment, they lamented their misfortune with tears of sincere condolence. Not satisfied with this unavailing expression of their sympathy, they put to sea a number of canoes, and, under the direction of the Spaniards, assisted in saving whatever could be got out of the wreck; and, by the united labour of so many hands, almost every thing of value was carried ashore. As fast as the goods were landed, Guacanahari in person took charge of them. By his orders they were all deposited in one place, and armed sentinels were posted, who kept the multitude at a distance, in order to prevent them not only from embezzling, but from inspecting too curiously what belonged to their guests. [15] Next morning this prince visited Columbus, who was now on board the Nigna, and endeavoured to console him for his loss, by offering all that he possessed to repair it.*

The condition of Columbus was such that he stood in need of consolation. He had hitherto procured no intelligence of the Pinta, and no longer doubted but that his treacherous associate had set sail for Europe, in order to have the merit of carrying the first tidings of the extraordinary discoveries which had been made, and to preoccupy so far the ear of their sovereign, as to rob him of the glory and reward to which he was justly entitled. There remained but one vessel, and that the smallest and most crazy of the squadron, to traverse such a vast ocean, and carry so many men back to Europe. Each of those circumstances was alarming, and filled the mind of Columbus with the utmost solicitude. The desire of overtaking Pinzon, and of effacing the unfavourable impressions which his misrepresentations might make in

* Herrera, dec. 1. lib. i. c. 18.

Spain, made it necessary to return thither without delay. The difficulty of taking such a number of persons on board the Nigna confirmed him in an opinion which the fertility of the country, and the gentle temper of the people, had already induced him to form. He resolved to leave a part of his crew in the island, that by residing there, they might learn the language of the natives, study their disposition, examine the nature of the country, search for mines, prepare for the commodious settlement of the colony with which he purposed to return, and thus secure and facilitate the acquisition of those advantages which he expected from his discoveries. When he mentioned this to his men, all approved of the design; and from impatience under the fatigue of a long voyage, from the levity natural to sailors, or from the hopes of amassing wealth in a country which afforded such promising specimens of its riches, many offered voluntarily to be among the number of those who should remain.

Nothing was now wanting towards the execution of this scheme, but to obtain the consent of Guacanahari; and his unsuspicious simplicity soon presented to the admiral a favourable opportunity of proposing it. Columbus having, in the best manner he could, by broken words and signs, expressed some curiosity to know the cause which had moved the islanders to fly with such precipitation upon the approach of his ships, the cazique informed him that the country was much infested by the incursions of certain people, whom he called *Carribeans*, who inhabited several islands to the south-east. These he described as a fierce and warlike race of men, who delighted in blood, and devoured the flesh of the prisoners who were so unhappy as to fall into their hands; and as the Spaniards at their first appearance were supposed to be Carribeans, whom the natives, however numerous, durst not face in battle, they had recourse to their usual method of securing their safety, by flying into the thickest and most impenetrable woods. Guacanahari, while speaking of those dreadful invaders, discovered such symptoms of terror, as well as such consciousness of the inability of his own people to resist them, as led Columbus to conclude that he would not be alarmed at the proposition of any scheme which afforded him the prospect of an additional security against their attacks. He instantly offered him the assistance of the Spaniards to repel his enemies: he engaged to take him and his people under the protection of the powerful monarch whom he served, and offered to leave in the island such a number of his men as should be sufficient, not only to defend the inhabitants from future incursions, but to avenge their past wrongs.

The credulous prince closed eagerly with the proposal, and thought himself already safe under the patronage of beings sprung from heaven, and superior in power to mortal men. The ground was marked out for a small fort, which Columbus called *Navidad*, because he had landed there on Christmas day. A deep ditch was drawn around it. The ramparts were fortified with pallisades, and the great guns, saved out of the admiral's ship, were planted upon them. In ten days the work was finished; that simple race of men labouring with inconsiderate assiduity in erecting this first monument of their own servitude. During this time, Columbus, by his caresses and liberality, laboured to increase the high opinion which the natives entertained of the Spaniards. But while he endeavoured to inspire them with confidence in their disposition to do good, he wished likewise to give them some striking idea of their power to punish and destroy such as were the objects of their indignation. With this view, in presence of a vast assembly, he drew up his men in order of battle, and made an ostentatious but innocent display of the sharpness of the Spanish swords, of the force of their spears, and the operation of their cross-bows. These rude people, strangers to the use of iron, and unacquainted with any hostile weapons but arrows of reed pointed with the bones of fishes, wooden swords, and javelins hardened in the fire, wondered and trembled. Before this surprise or fear had time to abate, he ordered the great guns to be fired. The sudden explosion struck them with such terror that they fell flat to the ground, covering their faces with their hands; and when they beheld the astonishing effect of the bullets among the trees, towards which the cannon had been pointed, they concluded that it was impossible to resist men, who had the command of such destructive instruments, and who came armed with thunder and lightning against their enemies.

After giving such impressions both of the beneficence and power of the Spaniards, as might have rendered it easy to preserve an ascendant over the minds of the natives, Columbus appointed thirty-eight of his people to remain in the island. He intrusted the command of these to Diego de Arado, a gentleman of Cordova, investing him with the same powers which he himself had received from Ferdinand and Isabella; and furnished him with every thing requisite for the subsistence or defence of this infant colony. He strictly enjoined them to maintain concord among themselves, to yield an unreserved obedience to their commander, to avoid giving offence to the natives by any violence or exaction, to cultivate the friendship of Guacanahari, but not to put themselves in his power by straggling in small parties, or marching too far from the fort. He promised to visit them soon with such a reinforcement of strength as might enable them to take full possession of the country, and to reap all the fruits of their discoveries. In the mean time he engaged to mention their names to the king and queen, and to place their merit and services in the most advantageous light.*

Having thus taken every precaution for the security of the colony, he left Navidad on the fourth of January, one thousand four hundred and ninety-three, and steering towards the east, discovered and gave names to most of the harbours on the northern coast of the island. On the sixth he descried the Pinta, and soon came up with her, after a separation of more than six weeks. Pinzon endeavoured to justify his conduct by pretending that he had been driven from his course by stress of weather, and prevented from returning by contrary winds. The admiral, though he still suspected his perfidious intentions, and knew well what he urged in his own defence to be frivolous as well as false, was so sensible that this was not a proper time for venturing upon any high strain of authority, and felt such satisfaction in this junction with his consort, which delivered him from many disquieting apprehensions, that, lame as Pinzon's apology was, he admitted of it without difficulty, and restored him to favour. During his absence from the admiral, Pinzon had visited several harbours in the island, had acquired some gold by trafficking with the natives, but had made no discovery of any importance.

From the condition of his ships, as well as the temper of his men, Columbus now found it necessary to hasten his return to Europe. The former having suffered much during a voyage of such an unusual length, were extremely leaky. The latter expressed the utmost impatience to revisit their native country, from which they had been so long absent, and where they had things so wonderful and unheard-of to relate. Accordingly, on the sixteenth of January, he directed his course towards the north-east, and soon lost sight of land. He had on board some of the natives, whom he had taken from the different islands which he discovered; and besides the gold, which was the chief object of research, he had collected specimens of all the productions which were likely to become subjects of commerce in the several countries, as well as many unknown birds, and other natural curiosities, which might attract the attention of the learned, or excite the wonder of the people. The voyage was prosperous to the fourteenth of February, and he had advanced near five hundred leagues across the Atlantic ocean, when the wind began to rise, and continued to blow with increasing

* Oviedo ap Ramusio, iii. p. 82. E. Herrera, dec. 1. lib. i. c. 20. Life of Columbus, c. 34.

rage, which terminated in a furious hurricane. Every thing that the naval skill and experience of Columbus could devise was employed in order to save the ships. But it was impossible to withstand the violence of the storm, and, as they were still far from any land, destruction seemed inevitable The sailors had recourse to prayers to Almighty God, to the invocation of saints, to vows, and charms, to every thing that religion dictates, or superstition suggests to the affrighted mind of man. No prospect of deliverance appearing, they abandoned themselves to despair, and expected every moment to be swallowed up in the waves. Besides the passions which naturally agitate and alarm the human mind in such awful situations, when certain death, in one of his most terrible forms, is before it, Columbus had to endure feelings of distress peculiar to himself. He dreaded that all knowledge of the amazing discoveries which he had made was now to perish; mankind were to be deprived of every benefit that might have been derived from the happy success of his schemes, and his own name would descend to posterity as that of a rash deluded adventurer, instead of being transmitted with the honour due to the author and conductor of the most noble enterprise that had ever been undertaken. These reflections extinguished all sense of his own personal danger. Less affected with the loss of life than solicitous to preserve the memory of what he had attempted and achieved, he retired to his cabin and wrote upon a parchment a short account of the voyage which he had made, of the course which he had taken, of the situation and riches of the countries which he had discovered, and of the colony that he had left there. Having wrapped up this in an oiled cloth, which he enclosed in a cake of wax, he put it into a cask carefully stopped up, and threw it into the sea, in hopes that some fortunate accident might preserve a deposit of so much importance to the world.*[16]

At length Providence interposed to save a life reserved for other services. The wind abated, the sea became calm, and on the evening of the fifteenth, Columbus and his companions discovered land; and though uncertain what it was, they made towards it. They soon knew it to be St. Mary, one of the Azores or western isles, subject to the crown of Portugal. There, after a violent contest with the governor, in which Columbus displayed no less spirit than prudence, he obtained a supply of fresh provisions, and whatever else he needed. One circumstance, however, greatly disquieted him. The Pinta, of which he had lost sight on the first day of the hurricane, did not appear; he dreaded for some time that she had foundered at sea, and that all her crew had perished; afterwards, his former suspicions recurred, and he became apprehensive that Pinzon had borne away for Spain, that he might reach it before him, and by giving the first account of his discoveries, might obtain some share of his fame.

In order to prevent this, he left the Azores as soon as the weather would permit [Feb. 24]. At no great distance from the coast of Spain, when near the end of his voyage, and seemingly beyond the reach of any disaster, another storm arose, little inferior to the former in violence; and after driving before it during two days and two nights, he was forced to take shelter in the river Tagus [March 4]. Upon application to the King of Portugal, he was allowed to come up to Lisbon; and, notwithstanding the envy which it was natural for the Portuguese to feel, when they beheld another nation entering upon that province of discovery which they had hitherto deemed peculiarly their own, and in its first essay not only rivalling but eclipsing their fame, Columbus was received with all the marks of distinction due to a man who had performed things so extraordinary and unexpected. The King admitted him into his presence, treated him with the highest respect, and listened to the account which he gave of his voyage

* Life of Columbus, c. 37. Herrera, dec. 1. lib. ii. c. 1, 2.

with admiration mingled with regret. While Columbus, on his part, enjoyed the satisfaction of describing the importance of his discoveries, and of being now able to prove the solidity of his schemes to those very persons, who, with an ignorance disgraceful to themselves, and fatal to their country, had lately rejected them as the projects of a visionary or designing adventurer.*

Columbus was so impatient to return to Spain, that he remained only five days in Lisbon. On the fifteenth of March he arrived in the port of Palos, seven months and eleven days from the time when he set out thence upon his voyage. As soon as the ship was discovered approaching the port, all the inhabitants of Palos ran eagerly to the shore, in order to welcome their relations and fellow-citizens, and to hear tidings of their voyage. When the prosperous issue of it was known, when they beheld the strange people, the unknown animals, and singular productions, brought from the countries which had been discovered, the effusion of joy was general and unbounded. The bells were rung, the cannon fired; Columbus was received at landing with royal honours, and all the people in solemn procession, accompanied him and his crew to the church, where they returned thanks to Heaven, which had so wonderfully conducted and crowned with success a voyage of greater length and of more importance than had been attempted in any former age. On the evening of the same day, he had the satisfaction of seeing the Pinta, which the violence of the tempest had driven far to the north, enter the harbour.

The first care of Columbus was to inform the King and Queen, who were then at Barcelona, of his arrival and success. Ferdinand and Isabella, no less astonished than delighted with this unexpected event, desired Columbus, in terms the most respectful and flattering, to repair immediately to court, that from his own mouth they might receive a full detail of his extraordinary services and discoveries. During his journey to Barcelona, the people crowded from the adjacent country, following him every where with admiration and applause. His entrance into the city was conducted, by order of Ferdinand and Isabella, with pomp suitable to the great event, which added such distinguishing lustre to their reign. The people whom he brought along with him from the countries which he had discovered, marched first, and by their singular complexion, the wild peculiarity of their features, and uncouth finery, appeared like men of another species. Next to them were carried the ornaments of gold, fashioned by the rude art of the natives, the grains of gold found in the mountains, and dust of the same metal gathered in the rivers. After these appeared the various commodities of the new discovered countries, together with their curious productions. Columbus himself closed the procession, and attracted the eyes of all the spectators, who gazed with admiration on the extraordinary man, whose superior sagacity and fortitude had conducted their countrymen, by a route concealed from past ages, to the knowledge of a new world. Ferdinand and Isabella received him clad in their royal robes, and seated upon a throne, under a magnificent canopy. When he approached, they stood up, and raising him as he kneeled to kiss their hands, commanded him to take his seat upon a chair prepared for him, and to give a circumstantial account of his voyage. He delivered it with a gravity and composure no less suitable to the disposition of the Spanish nation than to the dignity of the audience in which he spoke, and with that modest simplicity which characterizes men of superior minds, who, satisfied with having performed great actions, court not vain applause by an ostentatious display of their exploits. When he had finished his narration, the king and queen, kneeling down, offered up solemn thanks to Almighty God for the discovery of those new regions, from which they expected so many advantages to flow in upon

* Life of Columbus, c 40, 41. Herrera, dec. 1. lib. ii. c. 3

the kingdoms subject to their government. [17] Every mark of honour that gratitude or admiration could suggest was conferred upon Columbus. Letters patent were issued, confirming to him and to his heirs all the privileges contained in the capitulation concluded at Santa Fé ; his family was ennobled ; the king and queen, and after their example the courtiers, treated him on every occasion with all the ceremonious respect paid to persons of the highest rank. But what pleased him most, as it gratified his active mind, bent continually upon great objects, was an order to equip, without delay, an armament of such force as might enable him not only to take possession of the countries which he had already discovered, but to go in search of those more opulent regions which he still confidently expected to find.*

While preparations were making for this expedition, the fame of Columbus's successful voyage spread over Europe, and excited general attention. The multitude, struck with amazement when they heard that a new world had been found, could hardly believe an event so much above their conception. Men of science, capable of comprehending the nature, and of discerning the effects of this great discovery, received the account of it with admiration and joy. They spoke of his voyage with rapture, and congratulated one another upon their felicity in having lived in the period when, by this extraordinary event, the boundaries of human knowledge were so much extended, and such a new field of inquiry and observation opened, as would lead mankind to a perfect acquaintance with the structure and productions of the habitable globe.† [18] Various opinions and conjectures were formed concerning the new found countries, and what division of the earth they belonged to. Columbus adhered tenaciously to his original opinion, that they should be reckoned a part of those vast regions in Asia, comprehended under the general name of India. This sentiment was confirmed by the observations which he made concerning the productions of the countries he had discovered. Gold was known to abound in India, and he had met with such promising samples of it in the islands which he visited, as led him to believe that rich mines of it might be found. Cotton, another production of the East Indies, was common there. The pimento of the islands he imagined to be a species of the East Indian pepper. He mistook a root, somewhat resembling rhubarb, for that valuable drug, which was then supposed to be a plant peculiar to the East Indies.‡ The birds brought home by him were adorned with the same rich plumage which distinguishes those of India. The alligator of the one country appeared to be the same with the crocodile of the other. After weighing all these circumstances, not only the Spaniards, but the other nations of Europe, seem to have adopted the opinion of Columbus. The countries which he had discovered were considered as a part of India. In consequence of this notion, the name of Indies is given to them by Ferdinand and Isabella, in a ratification of their former agreement, which was granted to Columbus upon his return.§ Even after the error which gave rise to this opinion was detected, and the true position of the New World was ascertained, the name has remained, and the appellation of *West Indies* is given by all the people of Europe to the country, and that of *Indians* to its inhabitants.

The name by which Columbus distinguished the countries which he had discovered was so inviting, the specimens of their riches and fertility which he produced were so considerable, and the reports of his companions, delivered frequently with the exaggeration natural to travellers, so favourable, as to excite a wonderful spirit of enterprise among the Spaniards. Though little accustomed to naval expeditions, they were impatient to set out upon their voyage. Volunteers of every rank solicited to be employed. Allured by the inviting prospects which opened to their ambition and avarice,

* Life of Columbus, c. 42, 43. Herrera, dec. 1. lib. ii. c. 3. † 2 P. Mart. epist. 133, 134, 135.
‡ Herrera, dec. 1. lib. i. c. 20. Gomera Hist. c. 17. § Life of Columbus, c. 44

neither the length nor danger of the navigation intimidated them. Cautious as Ferdinand was, and averse to every thing new or adventurous, he seems to have catched the same spirit with his subjects. Under its influence, preparations for a second expedition were carried on with rapidity unusual in Spain, and to an extent that would be deemed not inconsiderable in the present age. The fleet consisted of seventeen ships, some of which were of good burden. It had on board fifteen hundred persons, among whom were many of noble families, who had served in honourable stations. The greater part of these, being destined to remain in the country, were furnished with every thing requisite for conquest or settlement, with all kinds of European domestic animals, with such seeds and plants as were most likely to thrive in the climate of the West Indies, with utensils and instruments of every sort, and with such artificers as might be most useful in an infant colony.*

But, formidable and well provided as this fleet was, Ferdinand and Isabella did not rest their title to the possession of the newly discovered countries upon its operations alone. The example of the Portuguese, as well as the superstition of the age, made it necessary to obtain from the Roman pontiff a grant of those territories which they wished to occupy. The Pope, as the vicar and representative of Jesus Christ, was supposed to have a right of dominion over all the kingdoms of the earth. Alexander VI., a pontiff infamous for every crime which disgraces humanity, filled the Papal throne at that time. As he was born Ferdinand's subject, and very solicitous to secure the protection of Spain, in order to facilitate the execution of his ambitious schemes in favour of his own family, he was extremely willing to gratify the Spanish monarchs. By an act of liberality which cost him nothing, and that served to establish the jurisdiction and pretensions of the Papal See, he granted in full right to Ferdinand and Isabella all the countries inhabited by Infidels, which they had discovered, or should discover; and, in virtue of that power which he derived from Jesus Christ, he conferred on the crown of Castile vast regions, to the possession of which he himself was so far from having any title, that he was unacquainted with their situation, and ignorant even of their existence. As it was necessary to prevent this grant from interfering with that formerly made to the crown of Portugal, he appointed that a line, supposed to be drawn from pole to pole, a hundred leagues to the westward of the Azores, should serve as a limit between them; and, in the plenitude of his power, bestowed all to the east of this imaginary line upon the Portuguese, and all to the west of it upon the Spaniards.† Zeal for propagating the Christian faith was the consideration employed by Ferdinand in soliciting this bull, and is mentioned by Alexander as his chief motive for issuing it. In order to manifest some concern for this laudable object, several friars, under the direction of Father Boyl, a Catalonian monk of great reputation, as apostolical vicar, were appointed to accompany Columbus, and to devote themselves to the instruction of the natives. The Indians, whom Columbus had brought along with him, having received some tincture of Christian knowledge, were baptized with much solemnity, the king himself, the prince his son, and the chief persons of his court, standing as their godfathers. Those first fruits of the New World have not been followed by such an increase as pious men wished, and had reason to expect.

Ferdinand and Isabella having thus acquired a title, which was then deemed completely valid, to extend their discoveries and to establish their dominion over such a considerable portion of the globe, nothing now retarded the departure of the fleet. Columbus was extremely impatient to revisit the colony which he had left, and to pursue that career of glory upon which

* Herrera, dec. 1. lib. ii. c. 5. Life of Columbus, c. 45. Torquemeda Mon. Ind. lib. xviii. c. 3.

† Herrera, dec. 1. lib. ii. c. 4.

he had entered. He set sail from the bay of Cadiz on the twenty-fifth of September, and touching again at the island of Gomera, he steered further towards the south than in his former voyage. By holding this course, he enjoyed more steadily the benefit of the regular winds, which reign within the tropics, and was carried towards a large cluster of islands, situated considerably to the east of those which he had already discovered. On the twenty-sixth day after his departure from Gomera [Nov. 2], he made land.* It was one of the Carribbee or Leeward Islands, to which he gave the name of Deseada, on account of the impatience of his crew to discover some part of the New World. After this he visited successively Dominica, Marigalante, Guadaloupe, Antigua, San Juan de Puerto Rico, and several other islands, scattered in his way as he advanced towards the north-west. All these he found to be inhabited by that fierce race of people whom Guacanahari had painted in such frightful colours. His descriptions appeared not to have been exaggerated. The Spaniards never attempted to land without meeting with such a reception as discovered the martial and daring spirit of the natives; and in their habitations were found relics of those horrid feasts which they had made upon the bodies of their enemies taken in war.

But as Columbus was eager to know the state of the colony which he had planted, and to supply it with the necessaries of which he supposed it to be in want, he made no stay in any of those islands, and proceeded directly to Hispaniola [Nov. 22].† When he arrived off Navidad, the station in which he had left the thirty-eight men under the command of Arada, he was astonished that none of them appeared, and expected every moment to see them running with transports of joy to welcome their countrymen. Full of solicitude about their safety, and foreboding in his mind what had befallen them, he rowed instantly to land. All the natives from whom he might have received information had fled. But the fort which he had built was entirely demolished, and the tattered garments, the broken arms and utensils scattered about it, left no room to doubt concerning the unhappy fate of the garrison.‡ While the Spaniards were shedding tears over those sad memorials of their fellow-citizens, a brother of the cazique Guacanahari arrived. From him Columbus received a particular detail of what had happened after his departure from the island. The familiar intercourse of the Indians with the Spaniards tended gradually to diminish the superstitious veneration with which their first appearance had inspired that simple people. By their own indiscretion and ill conduct, the Spaniards speedily effaced those favourable impressions, and soon convinced the natives, that they had all the wants, and weaknesses, and passions of men. As soon as the powerful restraint which the presence and authority of Columbus imposed was withdrawn, the garrison threw off all regard for the officer whom he had invested with command. Regardless of the prudent instructions which he had given them, every man became independent, and gratified his desires without control. The gold, the women, the provisions of the natives, were all the prey of those licentious oppressors They roamed in small parties over the island, extending their rapacity and insolence to every corner of it. Gentle and timid as the people were, those unprovoked injuries at length exhausted their patience, and roused their courage. The cazique of Cibao, whose country the Spaniards chiefly infested on account of the gold which it contained, surprised and cut off several of them, while they straggled in as perfect security as if their conduct had been altogether inoffensive. He then assembled his subjects, and surrounding the fort, set it on fire. Some of the Spaniards were killed in defending it; the rest perished in attempting to make their escape by crossing an arm of the sea. Guacanahari, whom all their exactions had

* Oviedo ap. Ramus. iii. 85. † P. Martyr, dec. p. 15. 18. Herrera, dec. 1. lib. ii. c. 7 Life of Columbus, c. 46. &c. ‡ Hist. de Cura de los Palacios. MS.

not alienated from the Spaniards, took arms in their behalf, and, in endeavouring to protect them, had received a wound, by which he was still confined.*

Though this account was far from removing the suspicions which the Spaniards entertained with respect to the fidelity of Guacanahari, Columbus perceived so clearly that this was not a proper juncture for inquiring into his conduct with scrupulous accuracy, that he rejected the advice of several of his officers, who urged him to seize the person of that Prince, and to revenge the death of their countrymen by attacking his subjects He represented to them the necessity of securing the friendship of some potentate of the country, in order to facilitate the settlement which they intended, and the danger of driving the natives to unite in some desperate attempt against them, by such an ill-timed and unavailing exercise of rigour. Instead of wasting his time in punishing past wrongs, he took precautions for preventing any future injury. With this view, he made choice of a situation more healthy and commodious than that of Navidad. He traced out the plan of a town in a large plain near a spacious bay, and obliging every person to put his hand to a work on which their common safety depended, the houses and ramparts were soon so far advanced, by their united labour, as to afford them shelter and security. This rising city, the first that the Europeans founded in the New World, he named Isabella, in honour of his patroness the Queen of Castile.†

In carrying on this necessary work, Columbus had not only to sustain all the hardships, and to encounter all the difficulties, to which infant colonies are exposed when they settle in an uncultivated country, but he had to contend with what was more insuperable, the laziness, the impatience, and mutinous disposition of his followers. By the enervating influence of a hot climate, the natural inactivity of the Spaniards seemed to increase. Many of them were gentlemen, unaccustomed to the fatigue of bodily labour, and all had engaged in the enterprise with the sanguine hopes excited by the splendid and exaggerated description of their countrymen who returned from the first voyage, or by the mistaken opinion of Columbus, that the country which he had discovered was either the Cipango of Marco Polo, or the Ophir,‡ from which Solomon imported those precious commodities which suddenly diffused such extraordinary riches through his kingdom. But when, instead of that golden harvest which they had expected to reap without toil or pains, the Spaniards saw that their prospect of wealth was remote as well as uncertain, and that it could not be attained but by the slow and persevering efforts of industry, the disappointment of those chimerical hopes occasioned such dejection of mind as bordered on despair, and led to general discontent. In vain did Columbus endeavour to revive their spirits by pointing out the fertility of the soil, and exhibiting the specimens of gold daily brought in from different parts of the island. They had not patience to wait for the gradual returns which the former might yield, and the latter they despised as scanty and inconsiderable. The spirit of disaffection spread, and a conspiracy was formed, which might have been fatal to Columbus and the colony. Happily he discovered it; and, seizing the ringleaders, punished some of them, sent others prisoners into Spain, whither he despatched twelve of the ships which had served as transports, with an earnest request for a reinforcement of men and a large supply of provisions.§

1494.] Meanwhile, in order to banish that idleness which, by allowing his people leisure to brood over their disappointment, nourished the spirit of discontent, Columbus planned several expeditions into the interior part of

* P. Martyr, dec. p. 22, &c. Herrera, dec. 1. lib. ii. c. 7. 9. Life of Columbus, c. 49, 50. † Life of Columbus, c. 51. Herrera, dec. 1. lib. ii. c. 10. ‡ P. Martyr, dec. p. 29. § Herrera, dec. 1. lib. ii. c. 10, 11.

the country. He sent a detachment, under the command of Alonzo de Ojeda, a vigilant and enterprising officer, to visit the district of Cibao, which was said to yield the greatest quantity of gold, and followed him in person with the main body of his troops. In this expedition he displayed all the pomp of military magnificence that he could exhibit, in order to strike the imagination of the natives. He marched with colours flying, with martial music, and with a small body of cavalry that paraded sometimes in the front and sometimes in the rear. As those were the first horses which appeared in the New World, they were objects of terror no less than of admiration to the Indians, who, having no tame animals themselves, were unacquainted with that vast accession of power which man hath acquired by subjecting them to his dominion. They supposed them to be rational creatures. They imagined that the horse and the rider formed one animal, with whose speed they were astonished, and whose impetuosity and strength they considered as irresistible. But while Columbus endeavoured to inspire the natives with a dread of his power, he did not neglect the arts of gaining their love and confidence. He adhered scrupulously to the principles of integrity and justice in all his transactions with them, and treated them, on every occasion, not only with humanity, but with indulgence. The district of Cibao answered the description given of it by the natives. It was mountainous and uncultivated, but in every river and brook gold was gathered either in dust or in grains, some of which were of considerable size. The Indians had never opened any mines in search of gold. To penetrate into the bowels of the earth, and to refine the rude ore, were operations too complicated and laborious for their talents and industry, and they had no such high value for gold as to put their ingenuity and invention upon the stretch in order to obtain it.* The small quantity of that precious metal which they possessed, was either picked up in the beds of the rivers, or washed from the mountains by the heavy rains that fall within the tropics. But from those indications, the Spaniards could no longer doubt that the country contained rich treasures in its bowels, of which they hoped soon to be masters.† In order to secure the command of this valuable province, Columbus erected a small fort, to which he gave the name of St. Thomas, by way of ridicule upon some of his incredulous followers, who would not believe that the country produced gold, until they saw it with their own eyes, and touched it with their hands.‡

The account of those promising appearances of wealth in the country of Cibao came very seasonably to comfort the desponding colony, which was affected with distresses of various kinds. The stock of provisions which had been brought from Europe was mostly consumed; what remained was so much corrupted by the heat and moisture of the climate as to be almost unfit for use; the natives cultivated so small a portion of ground, and with so little skill, that it hardly yielded what was sufficient for their own subsistence; the Spaniards at Isabella had hitherto neither time nor leisure to clear the soil, so as to reap any considerable fruits of their own industry. On all these accounts, they became afraid of perishing with hunger, and were reduced already to a scanty allowance. At the same time, the diseases predominant in the torrid zone, and which rage chiefly in those uncultivated countries where the hand of industry has not opened the woods, drained the marshes, and confined the rivers within a certain channel, began to spread among them. Alarmed at the violence and unusual symptoms of those maladies, they exclaimed against Columbus and his companions in the former voyage, who, by their splendid but deceitful descriptions of Hispaniola, had allured them to quit Spain for a barbarous uncultivated land, where they must either be cut off by famine, or die of unknown distempers.

* Oviedo, lib. ii. p. 90. A. † P. Martyr, dec p. 32. ‡ Herrera, dec. I. lib. ii. c. 12. Life of Columbus, c. 52.

Several of the officers and persons of note, instead of checking, joined in those seditious complaints. Father Boyl, the apostolical vicar, was one of the most turbulent and outrageous. It required all the authority and address of Columbus to re-establish subordination and tranquillity in the colony. Threats and promises were alternately employed for this purpose; but nothing contributed more to soothe the malecontents than the prospect of finding, in the mines of Cibao, such a rich store of treasure as would be a recompense for all their sufferings, and efface the memory of former disappointments.

When, by his unwearied endeavours, concord and order were so far restored that he could venture to leave the island, Columbus resolved to pursue his discoveries, that he might be able to ascertain whether those new countries with which he had opened a communication were connected with any region of the earth already known, or whether they were to be considered as a separate portion of the globe hitherto unvisited. He appointed his brother Don Diego, with the assistance of a council of officers, to govern the island in his absence; and gave the command of a body of soldiers to Don Pedro Margarita, with which he was to visit the different parts of the island, and endeavour to establish the authority of the Spaniards among the inhabitants. Having left them very particular instructions with respect to their conduct, he weighed anchor on the 24th of April, with one ship and two small barks under his command. During a tedious voyage of full five months, he had a trial of almost all the numerous hardships to which persons of his profession are exposed, without making any discovery of importance, except the island of Jamaica. As he ranged along the southern coast of Cuba [19], he was entangled in a labyrinth formed by an incredible number of small islands, to which he gave the name of the Queen's Garden. In this unknown course, among rocks and shelves, he was retarded by contrary winds, assaulted with furious storms, and alarmed with the terrible thunder and lightning which is often almost incessant between the tropics. At length his provisions fell short; his crew, exhausted with fatigue as well as hunger, murmured and threatened, and were ready to proceed to the most desperate extremities against him. Beset with danger in such various forms, he was obliged to keep continual watch, to observe every occurrence with his own eyes, to issue every order, and to superintend the execution of it. On no occasion was the extent of his skill and experience as a navigator so much tried. To these the squadron owed its safety. But this unremitted fatigue of body, and intense application of mind, overpowering his constitution, though naturally vigorous and robust, brought on a feverish disorder, which terminated in a lethargy, that deprived him of sense and memory, and had almost proved fatal to his life.*

But, on his return to Hispaniola [Sept. 27], the sudden emotion of joy which he felt upon meeting with his brother Bartholomew at Isabella, occasioned such a flow of spirits as contributed greatly to his recovery. It was now thirteen years since the two brothers, whom similarity of talents united in close friendship, had separated from each other, and during that long period there had been no intercourse between them. Bartholomew, after finishing his negotiation in the court of England, had set out for Spain by the way of France. At Paris he received an account of the extraordinary discoveries which his brother had made in his first voyage, and that he was then preparing to embark on a second expedition. Though this naturally induced him to pursue his journey with the utmost despatch, the admiral had sailed for Hispaniola before he reached Spain. Ferdinand and Isabella received him with the respect due to the nearest kinsman of a person whose merit and services rendered him so conspicuous; and as they knew what consolation his presence would afford to his brother, they persuaded him to

* Life of Columbus, c. 54, &c. Herrera, dec. 1. lib. ii. c. 13, 14 P. Martyr, dec. 1. p. 34, &c.

take the command of three ships, which they had appointed to carry provisions to the colony at Isabella.*

He could not have arrived at any juncture when Columbus stood more in need of a friend capable of assisting him with his counsels, or of dividing with him the cares and burdens of government. For although the provisions now brought from Europe afforded a temporary relief to the Spaniards from the calamities of famine, the supply was not in such quantity as to support them long, and the island did not hitherto yield what was sufficient for their sustenance. They were threatened with another danger, still more formidable than the return of scarcity, and which demanded more immediate attention. No sooner did Columbus leave the island on his voyage ot discovery, than the soldiers under Margarita, as if they had been set free from discipline and subordination, scorned all restraint. Instead of conforming to the prudent instructions of Columbus, they dispersed in straggling parties over the island, lived at discretion upon the natives, wasted their provisions, seized their women, and treated that inoffensive race with all th insolence of military oppression.†

As long as the Indians had any prospect that their sufferings might come to a period by the voluntary departure of the invaders, they submitted in silence, and dissembled their sorrow; but they now perceived that the yoke would be as permanent as it was intolerable. The Spaniards had built a town, and surrounded it with ramparts. They had erected forts in different places. They had enclosed and sown several fields. It was apparent that they came not to visit the country, but to settle in it. Though the number of those strangers was inconsiderable, the state of cultivation among these rude people was so imperfect, and in such exact proportion to their own consumption, that it was with difficulty they could afford subsistence to their new guests. Their own mode of life was so indolent and inactive, the warmth of the climate so enervating, the constitution of their bodies naturally so feeble, and so unaccustomed to the laborious exertions oi industry, that they were satisfied with a proportion of food amazingly small. A handful of maize, or a little of the insipid bread made of the cassada-root, was sufficient to support men whose strength and spirits were not exhausted by any vigorous efforts either of body or mind. The Spaniards, though the most abstemious of all the European nations, appeared to them excessively voracious. One Spaniard consumed as much as several Indians. This keenness of appetite surprised them so much, and seemed to be so insatiable, that they supposed the Spaniards had left their own country because it did not produce as much as was requisite to gratify their immoderate desire of food, and had come among them in quest of nourishment.‡ Self-preservation prompted them to wish for the departure of guests who wasted so fast their slender stock of provisions. The injuries which they suffered added to their impatience for this event. They had long expected that the Spaniards would retire of their own accord. They now perceived that, in order to avert the destruction with which they were threatened, either by the slow consumption of famine, or by the violence of their oppressors, it was necessary to assume courage, to attack those formidable invaders with united force, and drive them from the settlements of which they had violently taken possession.

Such were the sentiments which universally prevailed among the Indians, when Columbus returned to Isabella. Inflamed, by the unprovoked outrages of the Spaniards, with a degree of rage of which their gentle natures, formed to suffer and submit, seemed hardly susceptible, they waited only for a signal from their leaders to fall upon the colony. Some of the caziques had already surprised and cut off several stragglers. The dread of this impending danger united the Spaniards, and re-established the

* Herrera, dec. I. lib. ii. c. 15. † P. Martyr, dec. p. 47. ‡ Herrera, dec. I. lib. ii. c. 17

authority of Columbus, as they saw no prospect of safety but in committing themselves to his prudent guidance. It was now necessary to have recourse to arms, the employing of which against the Indians Columbus had hitherto avoided with the greatest solicitude. Unequal as the conflict may seem, between the naked inhabitants of the New World armed with clubs, sticks hardened in the fire, wooden swords, and arrows pointed with bones or flints, and troops accustomed to the discipline, and provided with the instruments of destruction known in the European art of war, the situation of the Spaniards was far from being exempt from danger. The vast superiority of the natives in number compensated many defects. A handful of men was about to encounter a whole nation. One adverse event, or even any unforeseen delay in determining the fate of the war, might prove fatal to the Spaniards Conscious that success depended on the vigour and rapidity of his operations, Columbus instantly assembled his forces. They were reduced to a very small number. Diseases, engendered by the warmth and humidity of the country, or occasioned by their own licentiousness, had raged among them with much violence; experience had not yet taught them the art either of curing these, or the precautions requisite for guarding against them, two-thirds of the original adventurers were dead, and many of those who survived were incapable of service.* The body which took the field [March 24, 1495] consisted only of two hundred foot, twenty horse, and twenty large dogs; and how strange soever it may seem to mention the last as composing part of a military force, they were not perhaps the least formidable and destructive of the whole, when employed against naked and timid Indians. All the caziques of the island, Guacanahari excepted, who retained an inviolable attachment to the Spaniards, were in arms to oppose Columbus, with forces amounting, if we may believe the Spanish historians, to a hundred thousand men. Instead of attempting to draw the Spaniards into the fastnesses of the woods and mountains, they were so imprudent as to take their station in the Vega Real, the most open plain in the country. Columbus did not allow them time to perceive their error, or to alter their position. He attacked them during the night, when undisciplined troops are least capable of acting with union and concert, and obtained an easy and bloodless victory. The consternation with which the Indians were filled by the noise and havoc made by the fire arms, by the impetuous force of the cavalry, and the fierce onset of the dogs was so great, that they threw down their weapons, and fled without attempting resistance. Many were slain; more were taken prisoners, and reduced to servitude [20]; and so thoroughly were the rest intimidated, that from that moment they abandoned themselves to despair, relinquishing all thoughts of contending with aggressors whom they deemed invincible.

Columbus employed several months in marching through the island, and in subjecting it to the Spanish government, without meeting with any opposition. He imposed a tribute upon all the inhabitants above the age of fourteen. Each person who lived in those districts where gold was found, was obliged to pay quarterly as much gold dust as filled a hawk's bell; from those in other parts of the country, twenty-five pounds of cotton were demanded. This was the first regular taxation of the Indians, and served as a precedent for exactions still more intolerable. Such an imposition was extremely contrary to those maxims which Columbus had hitherto inculcated with respect to the mode of treating them. But intrigues were carrying on in the court of Spain at this juncture, in order to undermine his power, and discredit his operations, which constrained him to depart from his own system of administration. Several unfavourable accounts of his conduct, as well as of the countries discovered by him, had been transmitted to Spain. Margarita and Father Boyl were now at court, and in order to justify their

* Life of Columbus, c. 61.

own conduct, or to gratify their resentment, watched with malevolent attention for every opportunity of spreading insinuations to his detriment. Many of the courtiers viewed his growing reputation and power with envious eyes. Fonseca, archdeacon of Seville, who was intrusted with the chief direction of Indian affairs, had conceived such an unfavourable opinion of Columbus, for some reason which the contemporary writers have not mentioned, that he listened with partiality to every invective against him. It was not easy for an unfriended stranger, unpractised in courtly arts, to counteract the machinations of so many enemies. Columbus saw that there was but one method of supporting his own credit, and of silencing all his adversaries. He must produce such a quantity of gold as would not only justify what he had reported with respect to the richness of the country, but encourage Ferdinand and Isabella to persevere in prosecuting his plans. The necessity of obtaining it forced him not only to impose this heavy tax upon the Indians, but to exact payment of it with extreme rigour; and may be pleaded in excuse for his deviating on this occasion from the mildness and humanity with which he uniformly treated that unhappy people.*

The labour, attention, and foresight which the Indians were obliged to employ in procuring the tribute demanded of them, appeared the most intolerable of all evils, to men accustomed to pass their days in a careless improvident indolence. They were incapable of such a regular and persevering exertion of industry, and felt it such a grievous restraint upon their liberty, that they had recourse to an expedient for obtaining deliverance from this yoke, which demonstrates the excess of their impatience and despair. They formed a scheme of starving those oppressors whom they durst not attempt to expel; and from the opinion which they entertained with respect to the voracious appetite of the Spaniards, they concluded the execution of it to be very practicable. With this view they suspended all the operations of agriculture; they sowed no maize, they pulled up the roots of the manioc or cassada which were planted, and, retiring to the most inaccessible parts of the mountains, left the uncultivated plains to their enemies. This desperate resolution produced in some degree the effects which they expected. The Spaniards were reduced to extreme want; but they received such seasonable supplies of provisions from Europe, and found so many resources in their own ingenuity and industry, that they suffered no great loss of men. The wretched Indians were the victims of their own ill-concerted policy. A great multitude of people, shut up in the mountainous or wooded part of the country, without any food but the spontaneous productions of the earth, soon felt the utmost distresses of famine. This brought on contagious diseases; and in the course of a few months more than a third part of the inhabitants of the island perished, after experiencing misery in all its various forms.†

But while Columbus was establishing the foundations of the Spanish grandeur in the New World, his enemies laboured with unwearied assiduity to deprive him of the glory and rewards which, by his services and sufferings, he was entitled to enjoy. The hardships unavoidable in a new settlement, the calamities occasioned by an unhealthy climate, the disasters attending a voyage in unknown seas, were all represented as the effects of his restless and inconsiderate ambition. His prudent attention to preserve discipline and subordination was denominated excess of rigour; the punishments which he inflicted upon the mutinous and disorderly were imputed to cruelty. These accusations gained such credit in a jealous court, that a commissioner was appointed to repair to Hispaniola, and to inspect into the conduct of Columbus. By the recommendation of his enemies, Aguado, a groom of the bedchamber, was the person to whom

* Herrera, dec. 1. lib. ii. c. 17.

† Herrera, dec. 1. lib. xi. c. 18. Life of Columbus, c. 61 Oviedo, lib. iii. p. 93. D. Benzon Hist. Novi Orbis, lib. i. c. 9. P. Martyr, dec. p. 48.

this important trust was committed. But in this choice they seem to have been more influenced by the obsequious attachment of the man to their interest, than by his capacity for the station. Puffed up with such sudden elevation, Aguado displayed, in the exercise of this office, all the frivolous self-importance, and acted with all the disgusting insolence which are natural to little minds, when raised to unexpected dignity, or employed in functions to which they are not equal. By listening with eagerness to every accusation against Columbus, and encouraging not only the malecontent Spaniards, but even the Indians, to produce their grievances, real or imaginary, he fomented the spirit of dissension in the island, without establishing any regulations of public utility, or that tended to redress the many wrongs, with the odium of which he wished to load the admiral's administration. As Columbus felt sensibly how humiliating his situation must be, if he should remain in the country while such a partial inspector observed his motions and controlled his jurisdiction, he took the resolution of returning to Spain, in order to lay a full account of all his transactions, particularly with respect to the points in dispute between him and his adversaries, before Ferdinand and Isabella, from whose justice and discernment he expected an equal and a favourable decision [1496]. He committed the administration of affairs, during his absence, to Don Bartholomew, his brother, with the title of Adelantado, or Lieutenant-Governor. By a choice less fortunate, and which proved the source of many calamities to the colony, he appointed Francis Roldan chief justice, with very extensive powers.*

In returning to Europe, Columbus held a course different from that which he had taken in his former voyage. He steered almost due east from Hispaniola, in the parallel of twenty-two degrees of latitude; as experience had not yet discovered the more certain and expeditious method of stretching to the north, in order to fall in with the south-west winds. By this ill advised choice, which, in the infancy of navigation between the New and Old Worlds, can hardly be imputed to the admiral as a defect in naval skill, he was exposed to infinite fatigue and danger, in a perpetual struggle with the trade winds, which blow without variation from the east between the tropics. Notwithstanding the almost insuperable difficulties of such a navigation, he persisted in his course with his usual patience and firmness, but made so little way that he was three months without seeing land. At length his provisions began to fail, the crew was reduced to the scanty allowance of six ounces of bread a day for each person. The admiral fared no better than the meanest sailor. But, even in this extreme distress, he retained the humanity which distinguishes his character, and refused to comply with the earnest solicitations of his crew, some of whom proposed to feed upon the Indian prisoners whom they were carrying over, and others insisted to throw them overboard, in order to lessen the consumption of their small stock. He represented that they were human beings, reduced by a common calamity to the same condition with themselves, and entitled to share an equal fate. His authority and remonstrances dissipated those wild ideas suggested by despair. Nor had they time to recur; as he came soon within sight of the coast of Spain, when all their fears and sufferings ended.†

Columbus appeared at court with the modest but determined confidence of a man conscious not only of integrity, but of having performed great services. Ferdinand and Isabella, ashamed of their own facility in lending too favourable an ear to frivolous or unfounded accusations, received him with such distinguished marks of respect as covered his enemies with shame. Their censures and calumnies were no more heard of at that juncture The gold, the pearls, the cotton, and other commodities of value

* Herrera, dec. 1. lib. ii. c. 18. lib. iii. c. 1. Columbus, c. 64.

† Herrera, dec. 1. lib. iii. c. 1. Life of

which Columbus produced, seemed fully to refute what the malecontents had propagated with respect to the poverty of the country. By reducing the Indians to obedience, and imposing a regular tax upon them, he had secured to Spain a large accession of new subjects, and the establishment of a revenue that promised to be considerable. By the mines which he had found out and examined, a source of wealth still more copious was opened. Great and unexpected as those advantages were, Columbus represented them only as preludes to future acquisitions, and as the earnest of more important discoveries, which he still meditated, and to which those he had already made would conduct him with ease and certainty.*

The attentive consideration of all these circumstances made such an impression, not only upon Isabella, who was flattered with the idea of being the patroness of all Columbus's enterprises, but even upon Ferdinand, who having originally expressed his disapprobation of his schemes, was still apt to doubt of their success, that they resolved to supply the colony of Hispaniola with every thing which could render it a permanent establishment, and to furnish Columbus with such a fleet, that he might proceed to search for those new countries of whose existence he seemed to be confident. The measures most proper for accomplishing both these designs were concerted with Columbus. Discovery had been the sole object of the first voyage to the New World; and though, in the second, settlement had been proposed, the precautions taken for that purpose had either been insufficient, or were rendered ineffectual by the mutinous spirit of the Spaniards, and the unforeseen calamities arising from various causes. Now a plan was to be formed of a regular colony, that might serve as a model in all future establishments. Every particular was considered with attention, and the whole arranged with a scrupulous accuracy. The precise number of adventurers who should be permitted to embark was fixed. They were to be of different ranks and professions, and the proportion of each was established according to their usefulness and the wants of the colony. A suitable number of women were to be chosen to accompany these new settlers. As it was the first object to raise provisions in a country where scarcity of food had been the occasion of so much distress, a considerable body of husbandmen was to be carried over. As the Spaniards had then no conception of deriving any benefit from those productions of the New World which have since yielded such large returns of wealth to Europe, but had formed magnificent ideas, and entertained sanguine hopes with respect to the riches contained in the mines which had been discovered, a band of workmen, skilled in the various arts employed in digging and refining the precious metals, was provided. All these emigrants were to receive pay and subsistence for some years, at the public expense.†

Thus far the regulations were prudent, and well adapted to the end in view. But as it was foreseen that few would engage voluntarily to settle in a country whose noxious climate had been fatal to so many of their countrymen, Columbus proposed to transport to Hispaniola such malefactors as had been convicted of crimes which, though capital, were of a less atrocious nature; and that for the future a certain proportion of the offenders usually sent to the galleys, should be condemned to labour in the mines which were to be opened. This advice, given without due reflection, was as inconsiderately adopted. The prisons of Spain were drained, in order to collect members for the intended colony; and the judges empowered to try criminals were instructed to recruit it by their future sentences. It was not, however, with such materials that the foundations of a society, destined to be permanent, should be laid. Industry, sobriety, patience, and mutual confidence, are indispensably requisite in an infant settlement, where purity of morals must contribute more towards establishing order than the operation

* Life of Columbus, c. 65. Herrera, dec. 1. lib. iii. c. 1.

† Herrera, dec. 1. lib. iii. c 2.

or authority of laws. But when such a mixture of what is corrupt is admitted into the original constitution of the political body, the vices of those unsound and incurable members will probably infect the whole, and must certainly be productive of violent and unhappy effects. This the Spaniards fatally experienced; and the other European nations having successively imitated the practice of Spain in this particular, pernicious consequences have followed in their settlements, which can be imputed to no other cause.*

Though Columbus obtained, with great facility and despatch, the royal approbation of every measure and regulation that he proposed, his endeavours to carry them into execution were so long retarded, as must have tired out the patience of any man less accustomed to encounter and to surmount difficulties. Those delays were occasioned partly by that tedious formality and spirit of procrastination, with which the Spaniards conduct business, and partly by the exhausted state of the treasury, which was drained by the expense of celebrating the marriage of Ferdinand and Isabella's only son with Margaret of Austria, and that of Joanna, their second daughter, with Philip Archduke of Austria ;† but must be chiefly imputed to the malicious arts of Columbus's enemies. Astonished at the reception which he met with upon his return, and overawed by his presence, they gave way, for some time, to a tide of favour too strong for them to oppose. Their enmity, however, was too inveterate to remain long inactive. They resumed their operations ; and by the assistance of Fonseca, the minister for Indian affairs, who was now promoted to the bishopric of Badajos, they threw in so many obstacles to protract the preparations for Columbus's expedition, that a year elapsed‡ before he could procure two ships to carry over a part of the supplies destined for the colony, and almost two years were spent before the small squadron was equipped, of which he himself was to take the command.§

1498.] This squadron consisted of six ships only, of no great burden, and but indifferently provided for a long or dangerous navigation. The voyage which he now meditated was in a course different from any he had under taken. As he was fully persuaded that the fertile regions of India lay to the south-west of those countries which he had discovered, he proposed, as the most certain method of finding out these, to stand directly south from the Canary or Cape de Verd islands, until he came under the equinoctial line, and then to stretch to the west before the favourable wind for such a course, which blows invariably between the tropics. With this idea he set sail [May 30], and touched first at the Canary, and then at the Cape de Verd islands [July 4]. From the former he despatched three of his ships with a supply of provisions for the colony in Hispaniola; with the other three, he continued his voyage towards the south. No remarkable occurrence happened until they arrived within five degrees of the line [July 19]. There they were becalmed, and at the same time the heat became so excessive that many of their wine casks burst, the liquors in others soured, and their provisions corrupted.‖ The Spaniards, who had never ventured so far to the south, were afraid that the ships would take fire, and began to apprehend the reality of what the ancients had taught concerning the destructive qualities of that torrid region of the globe. They were relieved, in some measure, from their fears by a seasonable fall of rain. This, however, though so heavy and unintermitting that the men could hardly keep the deck, did not greatly mitigate the intenseness of the heat. The admiral, who with his usual vigilance had in person directed every operation from the beginning of the voyage, was so much exhausted by

* Herrera, dec. 1. lib. iii. c. 2. Touron Hist. Gener. de l'Amerique, i. p. 51. † P. Martyr, epist. 168. ‡ Life of Columbus, c. 65. § Herrera, dec. 1. lib. iii. c. 9 ‖ P. Martyr, dec. p. 70.

fatigue and want of sleep, that it brought on a violent fit of the gout, accompanied with a fever. All these circumstances constrained him to yield to the importunities of his crew, and to alter his course to the north-west, in order to reach some of the Caribbee islands, where he might refit, and be supplied with provisions.

On the first of August, the man stationed in the round top surprised them with the joyful cry of *Land!* They stood toward it, and discovered a considerable island, which the admiral called Trinidad, a name it still retains. It lies on the coast of Guiana, near the mouth of the Orinoco. This, though a river only of the third or fourth magnitude in the New World, far surpasses any of the streams in our hemisphere. It rolls towards the ocean such a vast body of water, and rushes into it with such impetuous force, that when it meets the tide, which on that coast rises to an uncommon height, their collision occasions a swell and agitation of the waves no less surprising than formidable. In this conflict, the irresistible torrent of the river so far prevails, that it freshens the ocean many leagues with its flood.* Columbus, before he could conceive the danger, was entangled among those adverse currents and tempestuous waves, and it was with the utmost difficulty that he escaped through a narrow strait, which appeared so tremendous that he called it La Boca del Drago. As soon as the consternation which this occasioned permitted him to reflect upon the nature of an appearance so extraordinary, he discerned in it a source of comfort and hope. He justly concluded that such a vast body of water as this river contained, could not be supplied by any island, but must flow through a country of immense extent, and of consequence that he was now arrived at that continent which it had long been the object of his wishes to discover. Full of this idea, he stood to the west along the coast of those provinces which are now known by the names of Paria and Cumana. He landed in several places, and had some intercourse with the people, who resembled those of Hispaniola in their appearance and manner of life. They wore, as ornaments, small plates of gold, and pearls of considerable value, which they willingly exchanged for European toys. They seemed to possess a better understanding and greater courage than the inhabitants of the islands. The country produced four-footed animals of several kinds, as well as a great variety of fowls and fruits.† The admiral was so much delighted with its beauty and fertility, that, with the warm enthusiasm of a discoverer, he imagined it to be the Paradise described in Scripture, which the Almighty chose for the residence of man while he retained innocence that rendered him worthy of such a habitation.‡ [21] Thus Columbus had the glory not only of discovering to mankind the existence of a new World, but made considerable progress towards a perfect knowledge of it; and was the first man who conducted the Spaniards to that vast continent which has been the chief seat of their empire, and the source of their treasures in this quarter of the globe. The shattered condition of his ships, scarcity of provisions, his own infirmities, together with the impatience of his crew, prevented him from pursuing his discoveries any further, and made it necessary to bear away for Hispaniola. In his way thither he discovered the islands of Cubagua and Margarita, which afterwards became remarkable for their pearl-fishery. When he arrived at Hispaniola [Aug. 30], he was wasted to an extreme degree, with fatigue and sickness; but found the affairs of the colony in such a situation as afforded him no prospect of enjoying that repose of which he stood so much in need.

Many revolutions had happened in that country during his absence. His brother, the adelantado, in consequence of an advice which the admiral gave before his departure, had removed the colony from Isabella to a more

* Gumilla Hist. de l'Orenoque, tom. i. p. 14. † Herrera, dec. 1. lib. iii. c. 9—11. Life of Columbus, c. 66—73. ‡ Herrera, dec. 1. lib. iii. c. 12. Gomara, c. 84.

commodious station, on the opposite side of the island, and laid the foundation of St. Domingo,* which was long the most considerable European town in the New World, and the seat of the supreme courts in the Spanish dominions there. As soon as the Spaniards were established in this new settlement, the adelantado, that they might neither languish in inactivity, nor have leisure to form new cabals, marched into those parts of the island which his brother had not yet visited or reduced to obedience. As the people were unable to resist, they submitted every where to the tribute which he imposed. But they soon found the burden to be so intolerable that, overawed as they were by the superior power of their oppressors, they took arms against them. Those insurrections, however, were not formidable. A conflict with timid and naked Indians was neither dangerous nor of doubtful issue.

But while the adelantado was employed against them in the field, a mutiny of an aspect far more alarming broke out among the Spaniards. The ringleader of it was Francis Roldan, whom Columbus had placed in a station which required him to be the guardian of order and tranquillity in the colony. A turbulent and inconsiderate ambition precipitated him into this desperate measure, so unbecoming his rank. The arguments which he employed to seduce his countrymen were frivolous and ill founded. He accused Columbus and his two brothers of arrogance and severity; he pretended that they aimed at establishing an independent dominion in the country; he taxed them with an intention of cutting off part of the Spaniards by hunger and fatigue, that they might more easily reduce the remainder to subjection; he represented it as unworthy of Castilians, to remain the tame and passive slaves of these Genoese adventurers. As men have always a propensity to impute the hardships of which they feel the pressure to the misconduct of their rulers; as every nation views with a jealous eye the power and exaltation of foreigners, Roldan's insinuations made a deep impression on his countrymen. His character and rank added weight to them. A considerable number of the Spaniards made choice of him as their leader; and, taking arms against the adelantado and his brother, seized the king's magazine of provisions, and endeavoured to surprise the fort at St. Domingo. This was preserved by the vigilance and courage of Don Diego Columbus. The mutineers were obliged to retire to the province of Xaragua, where they continued not only to disclaim the adelantado's authority themselves, but excited the Indians to throw off the yoke.†

Such was the distracted state of the colony when Columbus landed at St. Domingo. He was astonished to find that the three ships which he had despatched from the Canaries were not yet arrived. By the unskilfulness of the pilots, and the violence of currents, they had been carried a hundred and sixty miles to the west of St. Domingo, and forced to take shelter in a harbour of the province of Xaragua, where Roldan and his seditious followers were cantoned. Roldan carefully concealed from the commanders of the ships his insurrection against the adelantado, and, employing his utmost address to gain their confidence, persuaded them to set on shore a considerable part of the new settlers whom they brought over, that they might proceed by land to St. Domingo. It required but few arguments to prevail with those men to espouse his cause. They were the refuse of the jails of Spain, to whom idleness, licentiousness, and deeds of violence were familiar; and they returned eagerly to a course of life nearly resembling that to which they had been accustomed. The commanders of the ships perceiving, when it was too late, their imprudence in disembarking so many of their men, stood away for St. Domingo, and got safe into the port a few

* P. Martyr, dec. p. 56.

† Herrera, dec. 1. lib. iii. c. 5—8. Life of Columbus, c. 74—77 Gomara, c. 23. P. Martyr, p. 78.

days after the admiral; but their stock of provisions was so wasted during a voyage of such long continuance that they brought little relief to the colony.*

By this junction with a band of such bold and desperate associates, Roldan became extremely formidable, and no less extravagant in his demands. Columbus, though filled with resentment at his ingratitude, and highly exasperated by the insolence of his followers, made no haste to take the field. He trembled at the thoughts of kindling the flames of a civil war, in which, whatever party prevailed, the power and strength of both must be so much wasted as might encourage the common enemy to unite and complete their destruction. At the same time, he observed, that the prejudices and passions which incited the rebels to take arms, had so far infected those who still adhered to him, that many of them were adverse, and all cold to the service. From such sentiments, with respect to the public interest, as well as from this view of his own situation, he chose to negotiate rather than to fight. By a seasonable proclamation, offering free pardon to such as should merit it by returning to their duty, he made impression upon some of the malecontents. By engaging to grant such as should desire it the liberty of returning to Spain, he allured all those unfortunate adventurers, who, from sickness and disappointment, were disgusted with the country. By promising to re-establish Roldan in his former office, he soothed his pride; and, by complying with most of his demands in behalf of his followers, he satisfied their avarice. Thus, gradually and without bloodshed, but after many tedious negotiations, he dissolved this dangerous combination, which threatened the colony with ruin; and restored the appearance of order, regular government, and tranquillity.†

In consequence of this agreement with the mutineers, lands were allotted them in different parts of the island, and the Indians settled in each district were appointed to cultivate a certain portion of ground for the use of those new masters [1499]. The performance of this work was substituted in place of the tribute formerly imposed; and how necessary soever such a regulation might be in a sickly and feeble colony, it introduced among the Spaniards the *Repartimientos*, or distributions of Indians established by them in all their settlements, which brought numberless calamities upon that unhappy people, and subjected them to the most grievous oppession.‡ This was not the only bad effect of the insurrection in Hispaniola; it prevented Columbus from prosecuting his discoveries on the continent, as self-preservation obliged him to keep near his person his brother the adelantado, and the sailors whom he intended to have employed in that service. As soon as his affairs would permit, he sent some of his ships to Spain with a journal of the voyage which he had made, a description of the new countries which he had discovered, a chart of the coast along which he had sailed, and specimens of the gold, the pearls, and other curious or valuable productions which he had acquired by trafficking with the natives. At the same time he transmitted an account of the insurrection in Hispaniola; he accused the mutineers not only of having thrown the colony into such violent convulsions as threatened its dissolution, but of having obstructed every attempt towards discovery and improvement, by their unprovoked rebellion against their superiors, and proposed several regulations for the better government of the island, as well as the extinction of that mutinous spirit, which, though suppressed at present, might soon burst out with additional rage. Roldan and his associates did not neglect to convey to Spain, by the same ships, an apology for their own conduct, together with their recriminations upon the admiral and his brothers. Unfortunately for the honour of

* Herrera, dec. 1. lib. iii. c. 12. Life of Columbus, c. 78, 79. † Herrera, dec. 1. lib. iii. c. 13, 14. Life of Columbus, c. 80. &c. ‡ Herrera, dec. 1. lib. iii. c. 14, &c.

Spain and the happiness of Columbus, the latter gained most credit in the court of Ferdinand and Isabella, and produced unexpected effects.*

But, previous to the relating of these, it is proper to take a view of some events, which merit attention, both on account of their own importance, and their connection with the history of the New World. While Columbus was engaged in his successive voyages to the west, the spirit of discovery did not languish in Portugal, the kingdom where it first acquired vigour and became enterprising. Self-condemnation and neglect were not the only sentiments to which the success of Columbus, and reflection upon their own imprudence in rejecting his proposals, gave rise among the Portuguese. They excited a general emulation to surpass his performances, and an ardent desire to make some reparation to their country for their own error. With this view, Emanuel, who inherited the enterprising genius of his predecessors, persisted in their grand scheme of opening a passage to the East Indies by the Cape of Good Hope, and soon after his accession to the throne equipped a squadron for that important voyage. He gave the command of it to Vasco de Gama, a man of noble birth, possessed of virtue, prudence, and courage, equal to the station. The squadron, like all those fitted out for discovery in the infancy of navigation, was extremely feeble, consisting only of three vessels, of neither burden nor force adequate to the service. As the Europeans were at that time little acquainted with the course of the trade-winds and periodical monsoons, which render navigation in the Atlantic ocean as well as in the sea that separates Africa from India, at some seasons easy, and at others not only dangerous but almost impracticable, the time chosen for Gama's departure was the most improper during the whole year. He set sail from Lisbon on the ninth of July, [1497], and, standing towards the south, had to struggle for four months with contrary winds before he could reach the Cape of Good Hope. Here their violence began to abate [Nov. 20]; and during an interval of calm weather, Gama doubled that formidable promontory, which had so long been the boundary of navigation, and directed his course towards the north-east, along the African coast. He touched at several ports; and after various adventures, which the Portuguese historians relate with high but just encomiums upon his conduct and intrepidity, he came to anchor before the city of Melinda. Throughout all the vast countries which extend along the coast of Africa, from the river Senegal to the confines of Zanguebar, the Portuguese had found a race of men rude and uncultivated, strangers to letters, to arts, and commerce, and differing from the inhabitants of Europe no less in their features and complexion than in their manners and institutions. As they advanced from this, they observed, to their inexpressible joy, that the human form gradually altered and improved; the Asiatic features began to predominate, marks of civilization appeared, letters were known, the Mahometan religion was established, and a commerce far from being inconsiderable was carried on. At that time several vessels from India were in the port of Melinda. Gama now pursued his voyage with almost absolute certainty of success, and, under the conduct of a Mahometan pilot, arrived at Calecut, upon the coast of Malabar, on the twenty-second of May, one thousand four hundred and ninety-eight. What he beheld of the wealth, the populousness, the cultivation, the industry, and arts of this highly civilized country, far surpassed any idea that he had formed, from the imperfect accounts which the Europeans had hitherto received of it. But as he possessed neither sufficient force to attempt a settlement, nor proper commodities with which he could carry on commerce of any consequence he hastened back to Portugal, with an account of his success in performing a voyage, the longest, as well as most difficult, that had ever been made since the first invention of navigation. He landed at Lisbon on the four

* Herrera, dec. 1. lib. iii. c. 14. Benzon. Hist. Nov. Orb. lib. i. c. 2.

teenth of September, one thousand four hundred and ninety-nine, two years two months and five days from the time he left that port.*

Thus, during the course of the fifteenth century, mankind made greater progress in exploring the state of the habitable globe, than in all the ages which had elapsed previous to that period. The spirit of discovery, feeble at first and cautious, moved within a very narrow sphere, and made its efforts with hesitation and timidity. Encouraged by success, it became adventurous, and boldly extended its operations. In the course of its progression, it continued to acquire vigour, and advanced at length with a rapidity and force which burst through all the limits within which ignorance and fear had hitherto circumscribed the activity of the human race. Almost fifty years were employed by the Portuguese in creeping along the coast of Africa from Cape Non to Cape de Verd, the latter of which lies only twelve degrees to the south of the former. In less than thirty years they ventured beyond the equinoctial line into another hemisphere, and penetrated to the southern extremity of Africa, at the distance of forty-nine degrees from Cape de Verd. During the last seven years of the century, a New World was discovered in the west, not inferior in extent to all the parts of the earth with which mankind were at that time acquainted. In the East, unknown seas and countries were found out, and a communication, long desired, but hitherto concealed, was opened between Europe and the opulent regions of India. In comparison with events so wonderful and unexpected, all that had hitherto been deemed great or splendid faded away and disappeared. Vast objects now presented themselves. The human mind, roused and interested by the prospect, engaged with ardour in pursuit of them, and exerted its active powers in a new direction.

This spirit of enterprise, though but newly awakened in Spain, began soon to operate extensively. All the attempts towards discovery made in that kingdom had hitherto been carried on by Columbus alone, and at the expense of the Sovereign. But now private adventurers, allured by the magnificent descriptions he gave of the regions which he had visited, as well as by the specimens of their wealth which he produced, offered to fit out squadrons at their own risk, and to go in quest of new countries. The Spanish court, whose scanty revenues were exhausted by the charge of its expeditions to the New World, which, though they opened alluring prospects of future benefit, yielded a very sparing return of present profit, was extremely willing to devolve the burden of discovery upon its subjects. It seized with joy an opportunity of rendering the avarice, the ingenuity, and efforts of projectors instrumental in promoting designs of certain advantage to the public, though of doubtful success with respect to themselves. One of the first propositions of this kind was made by Alonzo de Ojeda, a gallant and active officer, who had accompanied Columbus in his second voyage. His rank and character procured him such credit with the merchants of Seville, that they undertook to equip four ships, provided he could obtain the royal license, authorizing the voyage. The powerful patronage of the Bishop of Badajos easily secured success in a suit so agreeable to the court. Without consulting Columbus, or regarding the rights and jurisdiction which he had acquired by the capitulation in one thousand four hundred and ninety-two, Ojeda was permitted to set out for the New World. In order to direct his course, the bishop communicated to him the admiral's journal of his last voyage, and his charts of the countries which he had discovered. Ojeda struck out into no new path of navigation, but adhering servilely to the route which Columbus had taken, arrived on the coast of Paria [May]. He traded with the natives, and, standing to the west, proceeded as far as Cape de Vela, and ranged along a considerable extent of coast beyond that on which Columbus

* Ramusio, vol. i. 119. D.

had touched. Having thus ascertained the opinion of Columbus, that this country was a part of the continent, Ojeda returned by way of Hispaniola to Spain [October], with some reputation as a discoverer, but with little benefit to those who had raised the funds for the expedition.*

Amerigo Vespucci, a Florentine gentleman, accompanied Ojeda in this voyage. In what station he served is uncertain; but as he was an experienced sailor, and eminently skilled in all the sciences subservient to navigation, he seems to have acquired such authority among his companions, that they willingly allowed him to have a chief share in directing their operations during the voyage. Soon after his return, he transmitted an account of his adventures and discoveries to one of his countrymen; and labouring with the vanity of a traveller to magnify his own exploits, he had the address and confidence to frame his narrative so as to make it appear that he had the glory of having first discovered the continent in the New World. Amerigo's account was drawn up not only with art, but with some elegance. It contained an amusing history of his voyage, and judicious observations upon the natural productions, the inhabitants, and the customs of the countries which he had visited. As it was the first description of any part of the New World that was published, a performance so well calculated to gratify the passion of mankind for what is new and marvellous, circulated rapidly, and was read with admiration. The country of which Amerigo was supposed to be the discoverer, came gradually to be called by his name. The caprice of mankind, often as unaccountable as unjust, has perpetuated this error. By the universal consent of nations, America is the name bestowed on this new quarter of the globe. The bold pretensions of a fortunate impostor, have robbed the discoverer of the New World of a distinction which belonged to him. The name of Amerigo has supplanted that of Columbus; and mankind may regret an act of injustice, which, having received the sanction of time, it is now too late to redress. [22]

During the same year, another voyage of discovery was undertaken. Columbus not only introduced the spirit of naval enterprise into Spain, but all the first adventurers who distinguished themselves in this new career were formed by his instructions, and acquired in his voyages the skill and information which qualified them to imitate his example Alonso Nigno, who had served under the admiral in his last expedition, fitted out a single ship, in conjunction with Christopher Guerra, a merchant of Seville, and sailed to the coast of Paria. This voyage seems to have been conducted with greater attention to private emolument than to any general or national object. Nigno and Guerra made no discoveries of any importance; but they brought home such a return of gold and pearls as inflamed their countrymen with the desire of engaging in similar adventures.†

Soon after [Jan. 13, 1500], Vincent Yanez Pinzon, one of the admiral's companions in his first voyage, sailed from Palos with four ships. He stood boldly towards the south, and was the first Spaniard who ventured across the equinoctial line; but he seems to have landed on no part of the coast beyond the mouth of the Maragnon, or river of the Amazons. All these navigators adopted the erroneous theory of Columbus, and believed that the countries which they had discovered were part of the vast continent of India.‡

During the last year of the fifteenth century, that fertile district of America, on the confines of which Pinzon had stopped short, was more fully discovered. The successful voyage of Gama to the East Indies having encouraged the King of Portugal to fit out a fleet so powerful as not only to carry on trade but to attempt conquest, he gave the command of it to Pedro Alvarez Cabral. In order to avoid the coast of Africa, where he was

* Herrera, dec. 1. lib. iv. c. 1, 2, 3. † P. Martyr, dec. p. 87. Herrera, dec. 1. lib. iv. c. 5
‡ Herrera, dec. 1. lib. iv. c. 6. P. Martyr, dec. p. 95.

certain of meeting with variable breezes or frequent calms, which might retard his voyage, Cabral stood out to sea, and kept so far to the west, that, to his surprise, he found himself upon the shore of an unknown country, in the tenth degree beyond the line. He imagined at first that it was some island in the Atlantic ocean, hitherto unobserved; but, proceeding along its coast for several days, he was led gradually to believe, that a country so extensive formed a part of some great continent. This latter opinion was well founded. The country with which he fell in belongs to that province in South America now known by the name of Brasil. He landed; and having formed a very high idea of the fertility of the soil, and agreeableness of the climate, he took possession of it for the crown of Portugal, and despatched a ship to Lisbon with an account of this event, which appeared to be no less important than it was unexpected.* Columbus's discovery of the New World was the effort of an active genius enlightened by science, guided by experience, and acting upon a regular plan executed with no less courage than perseverance. But from this adventure of the Portuguese, it appears that chance might have accomplished that great design which it is now the pride of human reason to have formed and perfected. If the sagacity of Columbus had not conducted mankind to America, Cabral, by a fortunate accident, might have led them, a few years later, to the knowledge of that extensive continent.†

While the Spaniards and Portuguese, by those successive voyages, were daily acquiring more enlarged ideas of the extent and opulence of that quarter of the globe which Columbus had made known to them, he himself, far from enjoying the tranquillity and honours with which his services should have been recompensed, was struggling with every distress in which the envy and malevolence of the people under his command, or the ingratitude of the court which he served, could involve him. Though the pacification with Roldan broke the union and weakened the force of the mutineers, it did not extirpate the seeds of discord out of the island. Several of the malecontents continued in arms, refusing to submit to the admiral. He and his brothers were obliged to take the field alternately, in order to check their incursions, or to punish their crimes. The perpetual occupation and disquiet which this created, prevented him from giving due attention to the dangerous machinations of his enemies in the court of Spain. A good number of such as were most dissatisfied with his administration had embraced the opportunity of returning to Europe with the ships which he despatched from St. Domingo. The final disappointment of all their hopes inflamed the rage of these unfortunate adventurers against Columbus to the utmost pitch. Their poverty and distress, by exciting compassion, rendered their accusations credible, and their complaints interesting. They teased Ferdinand and Isabella incessantly with memorials, containing the detail of their own grievances, and the articles of their charge against Columbus. Whenever either the king or queen appeared in public, they surrounded them in a tumultuary manner, insisting with importunate clamours for the payment of the arrears due to them, and demanding vengeance upon the author of their sufferings. They insulted the admiral's sons wherever they met them, reproaching them as the offspring of the projector, whose fatal curiosity had discovered those pernicious regions which drained Spain of its wealth, and would prove the grave of its people. These avowed endeavours of the malecontents from America to ruin Columbus, were seconded by the secret but more dangerous insinuations of that party among the courtiers, which had always thwarted his schemes, and envied his success and credit.‡

Ferdinand was disposed to listen, not only with a willing but with a partial ear, to these accusations. Notwithstanding the flattering accounts which

* Herrera, dec. 1. lib. iv. c. 7. † Ibid dec. 1. lib. vii. c. 5. ‡ Life of Columbus, c. 85.

Columbus had given of the riches of America, the remittances from it had hitherto been so scanty that they fell far short of defraying the expense of the armaments fitted out. The glory of the discovery, together with the prospect of remote commercial advantages, was all that Spain had yet received in return for the efforts which she had made. But time had already diminished the first sensations of joy which the discovery of a New World occasioned, and fame alone was not an object to satisfy the cold interested mind of Ferdinand. The nature of commerce was then so little understood that, where immediate gain was not acquired, the hope of distant benefit, or of slow and moderate returns, was totally disregarded. Ferdinand considered Spain, on this account, as having lost by the enterprise of Columbus, and imputed it to his misconduct and incapacity for government, that a country abounding in gold had yielded nothing of value to its conquerors. Even Isabella, who from the favourable opinion which she entertained of Columbus had uniformly protected him, was shaken at length by the number and boldness of his accusers, and began to suspect that a disaffection so general must have been occasioned by real grievances which called for redress. The Bishop of Badajos, with his usual animosity against Columbus, encouraged these suspicions, and confirmed them.

As soon as the queen began to give way to the torrent of calumny, a resolution fatal to Columbus was taken. Francis de Bovadilla, a knight of Calatrava, was appointed to repair to Hispaniola, with full powers to inquire into the conduct of Columbus, and if he should find the charge of maladministration proved, to supersede him, and assume the government of the island. It was impossible to escape condemnation, when this preposterous commission made it the interest of the judge to pronounce the person whom he was sent to try, guilty. Though Columbus had now composed all the dissensions in the island; though he had brought both Spaniards and Indians to submit peaceably to his government; though he had made such effectual provision for working the mines, and cultivating the country, as would have secured a considerable revenue to the king, as well as large profits to individuals; Bovadilla, without deigning to attend to the nature or merit of those services, discovered from the moment that he landed in Hispaniola, a determined purpose of treating him as a criminal. He took possession of the admiral's house in St. Domingo, from which its master happened at that time to be absent, and seized his effects, as if his guilt had been already fully proved; he rendered himself master of the fort and of the King's stores by violence; he required all persons to acknowledge him as supreme governor; he set at liberty the prisoners confined by the admiral, and summoned him to appear before his tribunal, in order to answer for his conduct; transmitting to him, together with the summons, a copy of the royal mandate, by which Columbus was enjoined to yield implicit obedience to his commands.

Columbus, though deeply affected with the ingratitude and injustice of Ferdinand and Isabella, did not hesitate a moment about his own conduct. He submitted to the will of his sovereigns with a respectful silence, and repaired directly [October] to the court of that violent and partial judge whom they had authorized to try him. Bovadilla, without admitting him into his presence, ordered him instantly to be arrested, to be loaded with chains, and hurried on board a ship. Even under this humiliating reverse of fortune, the firmness of mind which distinguishes the character of Columbus did not forsake him. Conscious of his own integrity, and solacing himself with reflecting upon the great things which he had achieved, he endured this insult offered to his character, not only with composure but with dignity. Nor had he the consolation of sympathy to mitigate his sufferings. Bovadilla had already rendered himself so extremely popular, by granting various immunities to the colony, by liberal donations of Indians to all who applied for them, and by relaxing the reins of discipline and government, that the Spaniards, who were mostly adventurers, whom their indigence or crimes had compelled to abandon their native country, expressed the most indecent satisfaction with the disgrace and imprisonment of Columbus. They flattered themselves that now they should enjoy an uncontrolled liberty more suitable to their disposition and former habits of life. Among persons thus prepared to censure the proceedings, and to asperse the character of Columbus, Bovadilla collected materials for a charge against him. All accusations, the most improbable as well as inconsistent, were received. No informer, however infamous, was rejected. The result of this inquest, no less indecent than partial, he transmitted to Spain. At the same time he ordered Columbus, with his two brothers, to be carried thither in fetters; and, adding cruelty to insult, he confined them in different ships, and excluded them from the comfort of that friendly intercourse which might have soothed their common distress. But while the Spaniards in Hispaniola viewed the arbitrary and insolent proceedings of Bovadilla with a general approbation, which reflects dishonour upon their name and country, one man still retained a proper sense of the great actions which Columbus had performed, and was touched with the sentiments of veneration and pity due to his rank, his age, and his merit. Alonzo de Valejo, the captain of the vessel on board which the admiral was confined, as soon as he was clear of the island, approached his prisoner with great respect, and offered to release him from the fetters with which he was unjustly loaded. "No," replied Columbus with a generous indignation, "I wear these irons in consequence of an order from my sovereigns. They shall find me as obedient to this as to their other injunctions. By their command I have been confined, and their command alone shall set me at liberty."*

Nov. 23.] Fortunately, the voyage to Spain was extremely short As soon as Ferdinand and Isabella were informed that Columbus was brought home a prisoner and in chains, they perceived at once what universal astonishment this event must occasion, and what an impression to their disadvantage it must make. All Europe, they foresaw, would be filled with indignation at this ungenerous requital of a man who had performed actions worthy of the highest recompense, and would exclaim against the injustice of the nation, to which he had been such an eminent benefactor, as well as against the ingratitude of the princes whose reign he had rendered illustrious. Ashamed of their own conduct, and eager not only to make some reparation for this injury, but to efface the stain which it might fix upon their character, they instantly issued orders to set Columbus at liberty [Dec. 17], invited him to court, and remitted money to enable him to appear there in a manner suitable to his rank. When he entered the royal presence, Columbus threw himself at the feet of his sovereigns. He remained for some time silent; the various passions which agitated his mind suppressing his power of utterance. At length he recovered himself, and vindicated his conduct in a long discourse, producing the most satisfying proofs of his own integrity as well as good intention, and evidence, no less clear, of the malevolence of his enemies, who, not satisfied with having ruined his fortune, laboured to deprive him of what alone was now left, his honour and his fame. Ferdinand received him with decent civility, and Isabella with tenderness and respect. They both expressed their sorrow for what had happened, disavowed their knowledge of it, and joined in promising him protection and future favour. But though they instantly degraded Bovadilla, in order to remove from themselves any suspicion of having authorized his violent proceedings, they did not restore to Columbus his jurisdiction and privileges as viceroy of those countries which he had discovered. Though willing to appear the avengers of Columbus's wrongs, that illiberal jealousy which

* Life of Columbus, c. 86. Herrera, dec. 1. lib. iv. c. 8—11. Gomara Hist. c. 23. Oviedo, lib. iii. c. 6.

prompted them to invest Bovadilla with such authority, as put it in his power to treat the admiral with indignity, still subsisted. They were afraid to trust a man to whom they had been so highly indebted; and retaining him at court under various pretexts, they appointed Nicholas de Ovando, a knight of the military order of Alcantara, governor of Hispaniola.*

Columbus was deeply affected with this new injury, which came from hands that seemed to be employed in making reparation for his past sufferings. The sensibility with which great minds feel every thing that implies any suspicion of their integrity, or that wears the aspect of an affront, is exquisite. Columbus had experienced both from the Spaniards, and their ungenerous conduct exasperated him to such a degree that he could no longer conceal the sentiments which it excited. Wherever he went he carried about with him, as a memorial of their ingratitude, those fetters with which he had been loaded. They were constantly hung up in his chamber, and he gave orders, that when he died they should be buried in his grave.†

1501.] Meanwhile the spirit of discovery, notwithstanding the severe check which it had received by the ungenerous treatment of the man who first excited it in Spain, continued active and vigorous. [January.] Roderigo de Bastidas, a person of distinction, fitted out two ships in copartnery with John de la Cosa, who having served under the admiral in two of his voyages was deemed the most skilful pilot in Spain. They steered directly towards the continent, arrived on the coast of Paria, and, proceeding to the west, discovered all the coast of the province now known by the name of Tierra Firme, from Cape de Vela to the Gulf of Darien. Not long after Ojeda, with his former associate Amerigo Vespucci, set out upon a second voyage, and, being unacquainted with the destination of Bastidas, held the same course and touched at the same places. The voyage of Bastidas was prosperous and lucrative, that of Ojeda unfortunate. But both tended to increase the ardour of discovery; for in proportion as the Spaniards acquired a more extensive knowledge of the American continent, their idea of its opulence and fertility increased.‡

Before these adventurers returned from their voyages, a fleet was equipped, at the public expense, for carrying over Ovando, the new governor, to Hispaniola. His presence there was extremely requisite, in order to stop the inconsiderate career of Bovadilla, whose imprudent administration threatened the settlement with ruin. Conscious of the violence and iniquity of his proceedings against Columbus, he continued to make it his sole object to gain the favour and support of his countrymen, by accommodating himself to their passions and prejudices. With this view, he established regulations in every point the reverse of those which Columbus deemed essential to the prosperity of the colony. Instead of the severe discipline, necessary in order to habituate the dissolute and corrupted members of which the society was composed, to the restraints of law and subordination, he suffered them to enjoy such uncontrolled license as encouraged the wildest excesses. Instead of protecting the Indians, he gave a legal sanction to the oppression of that unhappy people. He took the exact number of such as survived their past calamities, divided them into distinct classes, distributed them in property among his adherents, and reduced all the people of the island to a state of complete servitude. As the avarice of the Spaniards was too rapacious and impatient to try any method of acquiring wealth but that of searching for gold, this servitude became as grievous as it was unjust. The Indians were driven in crowds to the mountains, and compelled to work in the mines, by masters who imposed their tasks without mercy or

* Herrera, dec. 1. lib. iv. c. 10—12. Life of Columbus, c. 87 p. 577.

† Life of Columbus, c. 86.

‡ Herrera, dec. 1. lib. iv. c. 11.

discretion. Labour so disproportioned to their strength and former habits of life, wasted that feeble race of men with such rapid consumption, as must have soon terminated in the utter extinction of the ancient inhabitants of the country.*

The necessity of applying a speedy remedy to those disorders hastened Ovando's departure. He had the command of the most respectable armament hitherto fitted out for the New World. It consisted of thirty-two ships, on board of which two thousand five hundred persons embarked with an intention of settling in the country. [1502.] Upon the arrival of the new governor with this powerful reinforcement to the colony, Bovadilla resigned his charge, and was commanded to return instantly to Spain, in order to answer for his conduct. Roldan and the other ringleaders of the mutineers, who had been most active in opposing Columbus, were required to leave the island at the same time. A proclamation was issued, declaring the natives to be free subjects of Spain, of whom no service was to be expected contrary to their own inclination, and without paying them an adequate price for their labour. With respect to the Spaniards themselves, various regulations were made, tending to suppress the licentious spirit which had been so fatal to the colony, and to establish that reverence for law and order on which society is founded, and to which it is indebted for its increase and stability. In order to limit the exorbitant gain which private persons were supposed to make by working the mines, an ordinance was published, directing all the gold to be brought to a public smelting-house, and declaring one half of it to be the property of the crown.†

While these steps were taking for securing the tranquillity and welfare of the colony which Columbus had planted, he himself was engaged in the unpleasant employment of soliciting the favour of an ungrateful court, and notwithstanding all his merit and services, he solicited in vain. He demanded, in terms of the original capitulation in one thousand four hundred and ninety-two, to be reinstated in his office of viceroy over the countries which he had discovered. By a strange fatality, the circumstance which he urged in support of his claim, determined a jealous monarch to reject it. The greatness of his discoveries, and the prospect of their increasing value, made Ferdinand consider the concessions in the capitulation as extravagant and impolitic. He was afraid of intrusting a subject with the exercise of a jurisdiction that now appeared to be so extremely extensive, and might grow to be no less formidable. He inspired Isabella with the same suspicions; and under various pretexts, equally frivolous and unjust, they eluded all Columbus's requisitions to perform that which a solemn compact bound them to accomplish. After attending the Court of Spain for near two years, as an humble suitor, he found it impossible to remove Ferdinand's prejudices and apprehensions; and perceived at length that he laboured in vain, when he urged a claim of justice or merit with an interested and unfeeling prince.

But even this ungenerous return did not discourage him from pursuing the great object which first called forth his inventive genius, and excited him to attempt discovery. To open a new passage to the East Indies was his original and favourite scheme. This still engrossed his thoughts; and either from his own observations in his voyage to Paria, or from some obscure hint of the natives, or from the accounts given by Bastidas and de la Cosa of their expedition, he conceived an opinion that beyond the continent of America there was a sea which extended to the East Indies, and hoped to find some strait or narrow neck of land, by which a communication might be opened with it and the part of the ocean already known. By a very fortunate conjecture, he supposed this strait or isthmus to be

* Herrera, dec. 1. lib. iv. c. 11, &c. Oviedo Hist. lib. iii. c. 6. p. 97. Benzon Hist. lib. i. c. 12. p. 51. † Solorzano Politica Indiana, lib. i. c. 12. Herrera, dec. 1. lib. iv. c. 12.

situated near the Gulf of Darien. Full of this idea, though he was now of an advanced age, worn out with fatigue, and broken with infirmities, he offered, with the alacrity of a youthful adventurer, to undertake a voyage which would ascertain this important point, and perfect the grand scheme which from the beginning he proposed to accomplish. Several circumstances concurred in disposing Ferdinand and Isabella to lend a favourable ear to this proposal. They were glad to have the pretext of any honourable employment for removing from court a man with whose demands they deemed it impolitic to comply, and whose services it was indecent to neglect. Though unwilling to reward Columbus, they were not insensible of his merit, and from their experience of his skill and conduct, had reason to give credit to his conjectures, and to confide in his success. To these considerations, a third must be added of still more powerful influence. About this time the Portuguese fleet, under Cabral, arrived from the Indies; and, by the richness of its cargo, gave the people of Europe a more perfect idea than they had hitherto been able to form, of the opulence and fertility of the East. The Portuguese had been more fortunate in their discoveries than the Spaniards. They had opened a communication with countries where industry, arts, and elegance flourished; and where commerce had been longer established, and carried to greater extent than in any region of the earth. Their first voyages thither yielded immediate as well as vast returns of profit, in commodities extremely precious and in great request. Lisbon became immediately the seat of commerce and wealth; while Spain had only the expectation of remote benefit, and of future gain, from the western world. Nothing, then, could be more acceptable to the Spaniards than Columbus's offer to conduct them to the East, by a route which he expected to be shorter, as well as less dangerous than that which the Portuguese had taken. Even Ferdinand was roused by such a prospect, and warmly approved of the undertaking.

But interesting as the object of this voyage was to the nation, Columbus could procure only four small barks, the largest of which did not exceed seventy tons in burden, for performing it. Accustomed to brave danger, and to engage in arduous undertakings with inadequate force, he did not hesitate to accept the command of this pitiful squadron. His brother Bartholomew, and his second son Ferdinand, the historian of his actions, accompanied him. He sailed from Cadiz on the ninth of May, and touched, as usual, at the Canary islands; from thence he proposed to have stood directly for the continent; but his largest vessel was so clumsy and unfit for service, as constrained him to bear away for Hispaniola, in hopes of exchanging her for some ship of the fleet that had carried out Ovando. When he arrived at St. Domingo [June 29], he found eighteen of these ships ready loaded, and on the point of departing for Spain. Columbus immediately acquainted the governor with the destination of his voyage, and the accident which had obliged him to alter his route. He requested permission to enter the harbour, not only that he might negotiate the exchange of his ship, but that he might take shelter during a violent hurricane, of which he discerned the approach from various prognostics which his experience and sagacity had taught him to observe. On that account, he advised him likewise to put off for some days the departure of the fleet bound for Spain. But Ovando refused his request, and despised his counsel. Under circumstances in which humanity would have afforded refuge to a stranger, Columbus was denied admittance into a country of which he had discovered the existence and acquired the possession. His salutary warning, which merited the greatest attention, was regarded as the dream of a visionary prophet, who arrogantly pretended to predict an event beyond the reach of human foresight. The fleet set sail for Spain. Next night the hurricane came on with dreadful impetuosity. Columbus, aware of the danger, took precautions against it, and saved his little squadron.

The fleet destined for Spain met with the fate which the rashness and obstinacy of its commanders deserved. Of eighteen ships two or three only escaped. In this general wreck perished Bovadilla, Roldan, and the greater part of those who had been the most active in persecuting Columbus, and oppressing the Indians. Together with themselves, all the wealth which they had acquired by their injustice and cruelty was swallowed up. It exceeded in value two hundred thousand *pesos;* an immense sum at that period, and sufficient not only to have screened them from any severe scrutiny into their conduct, but to have secured them a gracious reception in the Spanish court. Among the ships that escaped, one had on board all the effects of Columbus which had been recovered from the ruins of his fortune. Historians, struck with the exact discrimination of characters, as well as the just distribution of rewards and punishments, conspicuous in those events, universally attribute them to an immediate interposition of Divine Providence, in order to avenge the wrongs of an injured man, and to punish the oppressors of an innocent people. Upon the ignorant and superstitious race of men, who were witnesses of this occurrence, it made a different impression. From an opinion which vulgar admiration is apt to entertain with respect to persons who have distinguished themselves by their sagacity and inventions, they believed Columbus to be possessed of supernatural powers, and imagined that he had conjured up this dreadful storm by magical art and incantations in order to be avenged of his enemies.*

Columbus soon left Hispaniola [July 14], where he met with such an inhospitable reception, and stood towards the continent. After a tedious and dangerous voyage, he discovered Guanaia, an island not far distant from the coast of Honduras. There he had an interview with some inhabitants of the continent, who arrived in a large canoe. They appeared to be a people more civilized, and who had made greater progress in the knowledge of useful arts than any whom he had hitherto discovered. In return to the inquiries which the Spaniards made, with their usual eagerness, concerning the places where the Indians got the gold which they wore by way of ornament, they directed them to countries situated to the west, in which gold was found in such profusion that it was applied to the most common uses. Instead of steering in quest of a country so inviting, which would have conducted him along the coast of Yucatan to the rich Empire of Mexico, Columbus was so bent upon his favourite scheme of finding out the strait which he supposed to communicate with the Indian ocean, that he bore away to the east towards the gulf of Darien. In this navigation he discovered all the coast of the continent, from Cape Gracias a Dios to a harbour which, on account of its beauty and security, he called Porto Bello. He searched in vain for the imaginary strait, through which he expected to make his way into an unknown sea; and though he went on shore several times, and advanced into the country, he did not penetrate so far as to cross the narrow isthmus which separates the Gulf of Mexico from the great Southern ocean. He was so much delighted, however, with the fertility of the country, and conceived such an idea of its wealth from the specimens of gold produced by the natives, that he resolved to leave a small colony upon the river Belen, in the province of Veragua, under the command of his brother, and to return himself to Spain [1503], in order to procure what was requisite for rendering the establishment permanent. But the ungovernable spirit of the people under his command, deprived Columbus of the glory of planting the first colony on the continent of America Their insolence and rapaciousness provoked the natives to take arms; and as these were a more hardy and warlike race of men than the inhabitants of the islands, they cut off part of the Spaniards, and obliged the rest to abandon a station which was found to be untenable.†

* Oviedo, lib. iii. c. 7. 9. Herrera, dec. 1. lib. v. c. 1, 2. Life of Columbus, c. 88.

† Herrera dec 1. lib. v. c. 5, &c. Life of Columbus, c. 89, &c. Oviedo, lib iii c. 9

This repulse, the first that the Spaniards met with from any of the American nations, was not the only misfortune that befell Columbus: it was followed by a succession of all the disasters to which navigation is exposed Furious hurricanes, with violent storms of thunder and lightning, threatened his leaky vessels with destruction; while his discontented crew, exhausted with fatigue, and destitute of provisions, was unwilling or unable to execute his commands. One of his ships perished; he was obliged to abandon another, as unfit for service; and with the two which remained, he quitted that part of the continent, which, in his anguish, he named the Coast of Vexation,* and bore away for Hispaniola. New distresses awaited him in this voyage. He was driven back by a violent tempest from the coast of Cuba, his ships fell foul of one another, and were so much shattered by the shock that with the utmost difficulty they reached Jamaica [June 24], where he was obliged to run them aground, to prevent them from sinking. The measure of his calamities seemed now to be full. He was cast ashore upon an island at a considerable distance from the only settlement of the Spaniards in America. His ships were ruined beyond the possibility of being repaired. To convey an account of his situation to Hispaniola appeared impracticable; and without this it was in vain to expect relief. His genius, fertile in resources, and most vigorous in those perilous extremities when feeble minds abandon themselves to despair, discovered the only expedient which afforded any prospect of deliverance. He had recourse to the hospitable kindness of the natives, who, considering the Spaniards as beings of a superior nature, were eager, on every occasion, to minister to their wants. From them he obtained two of their canoes, each formed out of the trunk of a single tree hollowed with fire, and so misshapen and awkward as hardly to merit the name of boats. In these, which were fit only for creeping along the coast, or crossing from one side of a bay to another, Mendez, a Spaniard, and Fieschi, a Genoese, two gentlemen particularly attached to Columbus, gallantly offered to set out for Hispaniola, upon a voyage of above thirty leagues.† This they accomplished in ten days, after surmounting incredible dangers, and enduring such fatigues that several of the Indians who accompanied them sunk under it, and died. The attention paid to them by the governor of Hispaniola was neither such as their courage merited, nor the distress of the persons from whom they came required. Ovando, from a mean jealousy of Columbus, was afraid of allowing him to set foot in the island under his government. This ungenerous passion hardened his heart against every tender sentiment which reflection upon the services and misfortunes of that great man, or compassion for his own fellow-citizens, involved in the same calamities, must have excited. Mendez and Fieschi spent eight months in soliciting relief for their commander and associates, without any prospect of obtaining it.

During this period, various passions agitated the mind of Columbus and his companions in adversity. At first, the expectation of speedy deliverance, from the success of Mendez and Fieschi's voyage, cheered the spirits of the most desponding. After some time the most timorous began to suspect that they had miscarried in their daring attempt [1504]. At length, even the most sanguine concluded that they had perished. The ray of hope which had broke in upon them, made their condition appear now more dismal. Despair, heightened by disappointment, settled in every breast. Their last resource had failed, and nothing remained but the prospect of ending their miserable days among naked savages, far from their country and their friends. The seamen, in a transport of rage, rose in open mutiny, threatened the life ot Columbus, whom they reproached as the author of all their calamities, seized ten canoes, which they had purchased from the Indians, and, despising his remonstrances and entreaties, made off with

* La Costa de los Constrastes.

† Oviedo, lib. iii. c. 9.

them to a distant part of the island. At the same time the natives murmured at the long residence of the Spaniards in their country. As their industry was not greater than that of their neighbours in Hispaniola, like them they found the burden of supporting so many strangers to be altogether intolerable. They began to bring in provisions with reluctance, they furnished them with a sparing hand, and threatened to withdraw those supplies altogether. Such a resolution must have been quickly fatal to the Spaniards. Their safety depended upon the good will of the Indians; and unless they could revive the admiration and reverence with which that simple people had at first beheld them, destruction was unavoidable. Though the licentious proceedings of the mutineers had in a great measure effaced those impressions which had been so favourable to the Spaniards, the ingenuity of Columbus suggested a happy artifice, that not only restored but heightened the high opinion which the Indians had originally entertained of them. By his skill in astronomy, he knew that there was shortly to be a total eclipse of the moon. He assembled all the principal persons of the district around him on the day before it happened, and, after reproaching them for their fickleness in withdrawing their affection and assistance from men whom they had lately revered, he told them, that the Spaniards were servants of the Great Spirit who dwells in heaven, who made and governs the world; that he, offended at their refusing to support men who were the objects of his peculiar favour, was preparing to punish this crime with exemplary severity, and that very night the moon should withhold her light, and appear of a bloody hue, as a sign of the divine wrath and an emblem of the vengeance ready to fall upon them. To this marvellous prediction some of them listened with the careless indifference peculiar to the people of America; others, with the credulous astonishment natural to barbarians. But when the moon began gradually to be darkened, and at length appeared of a red colour, all were struck with terror. They ran with consternation to their houses, and returning instantly to Columbus loaded with provisions, threw them at his feet, conjuring him to intercede with the Great Spirit to avert the destruction with which they were threatened. Columbus, seeming to be moved by their entreaties, promised to comply with their desire. The eclipse went off, the moon recovered its splendour, and from that day the Spaniards were not only furnished profusely with provisions, but the natives, with superstitious attention, avoided every thing that could give them offence.*

During those transactions, the mutineers had made repeated attempts to pass over to Hispaniola in the canoes which they had seized. But, from their own misconduct or the violence of the winds and currents, their efforts were all unsuccessful. Enraged at this disappointment, they marched towards that part of the island where Columbus remained, threatening him with new insults and danger. While they were advancing, an event happened, more cruel and afflicting than any calamity which he dreaded from them. The governor of Hispaniola, whose mind was still filled with some dark suspicions of Columbus, sent a small bark to Jamaica, not to deliver his distressed countrymen, but to spy out their condition. Lest the sympathy of those whom he employed should afford them relief, contrary to his intention, he gave the command of this vessel to Escobar, an inveterate enemy of Columbus, who, adhering to his instructions with malignant accuracy, cast anchor at some distance from the island, approached the shore in a small boat, observed the wretched plight of the Spaniards, delivered a letter of empty compliments to the admiral, received his answer, and departed. When the Spaniards first descried the vessel standing towards the island, every heart exulted, as if the long expected hour of their deliverance had at length arrived; but when it disappeared so suddenly, they sunk into the

* Life of Columbus, c. 103. Herrera, dec. 1. lib. vi. c. 5, 6. Benzon, Hist. lib. i. c 14.

deepest dejection, and all their hopes died away. Columbus alone, though he felt most sensibly this wanton insult which Ovando added to his past neglect, retained such composure of mind as to be able to cheer his followers. He assured them that Mendez and Fieschi had reached Hispaniola in safety; that they would speedily procure ships to carry them off; but, as Escobar's vessel could not take them all on board, that he had refused to go with her, because he was determined never to abandon the faithful companions of his distress. Soothed with the expectation of speedy deliverance, and delighted with his apparent generosity in attending more to their preservation than to his own safety, their spirits revived, and he regained their confidence.*

Without this confidence he could not have resisted the mutineers, who were now at hand. All his endeavours to reclaim those desperate men had no effect but to increase their frenzy. Their demands became every day more extravagant, and their intentions more violent and bloody. The common safety rendered it necessary to oppose them with open force. Columbus, who had been long afflicted with the gout, could not take the field. His brother, the adelantado, marched against them [May 20]. They quickly met. The mutineers rejected with scorn terms of accommodation, which were once more offered them, and rushed on boldly to the attack. They fell not upon an enemy unprepared to receive them. In the first shock, several of their most daring leaders were slain. The adelantado, whose strength was equal to his courage, closed with their captain, wounded, disarmed, and took him prisoner.† At sight of this, the rest fled with a dastardly fear suitable to their former insolence. Soon after, they submitted in a body to Columbus, and bound themselves by the most solemn oaths to obey all his commands. Hardly was tranquillity re-established when the ships appeared, whose arrival Columbus had promised with great address, though he could foresee it with little certainty. With transports of joy the Spaniards quitted an island in which the unfeeling jealousy of Ovando had suffered them to languish above a year, exposed to misery in all its various forms.

When they arrived at St. Domingo [Aug. 13], the governor, with the mean artifice of a vulgar mind, that labours to atone for insolence by servility, fawned on the man whom he envied, and had attempted to ruin. He received Columbus with the most studied respect, lodged him in his own house, and distinguished him with every mark of honour. But amidst those overacted demonstrations of regard, he could not conceal the hatred and malignity latent in his heart. He set at liberty the captain of the mutineers, whom Columbus had brought over in chains to be tried for his crimes; and threatened such as had adhered to the admiral with proceeding to a judicial inquiry into their conduct. Columbus submitted in silence to what he could not redress; but discovered an extreme impatience to quit a country which was under the jurisdiction of a man who had treated him, on every occasion, with inhumanity and injustice. His preparations were soon finished, and he set sail for Spain with two ships [Sept. 12]. Disasters similar to those which had accompanied him through life continued to pursue him to the end of his career. One of his vessels being disabled, was soon forced back to St. Domingo; the other, shattered by violent storms, sailed several hundred leagues with jury-masts, and reached with difficulty the port of St Lucar [December].‡

There he received the account of an event the most fatal that could have befallen him, and which completed his misfortunes. This was the death of his patroness Queen Isabella [Nov. 9], in whose justice, humanity, and favour he confided as his last resource. None now remained to redress his wrongs, or to reward him for his services and sufferings, but Ferdinand, who

* Life of Columbus, c. 104. Herrera, dec. 1. lib. vi. c. 17. † Ibid. c. 107. Herrera, dec 1. lib. vi. c. 11. ‡ Ibid. c. 108. Herrera, dec. 1. lib. vi. c. 12.

had so long opposed and so often injured him. To solicit a prince thus prejudiced against him was an occupation no less irksome than hopeless. In this, however, was Columbus doomed to employ the close of his days. As soon as his health was in some degree re-established, he repaired to court; and though he was received there with civility barely decent, he plied Ferdinand with petition after petition, demanding the punishment of his oppressors, and the restitution of all the privileges bestowed upon him by the capitulation of one thousand four hundred and ninety-two. Ferdinand amused him with fair words and unmeaning promises. Instead of granting his claims, he proposed expedients in order to elude them, and spun out the affair with such apparent art, as plainly discovered his intention that it should never be terminated. The declining health of Columbus flattered Ferdinand with the hopes of being soon delivered from an importunate suitor, and encouraged him to persevere in this illiberal plan. Nor was he deceived in his expectations. Disgusted with the ingratitude of a monarch whom he had served with such fidelity and success, exhausted with the fatigues and hardships which he had endured, and broken with the infirmities which these had brought upon him, Columbus ended his life at Valladolid on the twentieth of May, one thousand five hundred and six in the fifty-ninth year of his age. He died with a composure of mind suitable to the magnanimity which distinguished his character, and with sentiments of piety becoming that supreme respect for religion which he manifested in every occurrence of his life.*

# BOOK III.

While Columbus was employed in his last voyage, several events worthy of notice happened in Hispaniola. The colony there, the parent and nurse of all the subsequent establishments of Spain in the New World, gradually acquired the form of a regular and prosperous society. The humane solicitude of Isabella to protect the Indians from oppression, and particularly the proclamation by which the Spaniards were prohibited to compel them to work, retarded, it is true, for some time the progress of improvement. The natives, who considered exemption from toil as extreme felicity, scorned every allurement and reward by which they were invited to labour. The Spaniards had not a sufficient number of hands either to work the mines or to cultivate the soil. Several of the first colonists who had been accustomed to the service of the Indians, quitted the island, when deprived of those instruments, without which they knew not how to carry on any operation. Many of the new settlers who came over with Ovando, were seized with the distempers peculiar to the climate, and in a short space above a thousand of them died. At the same time, the exacting one half of the product of the mines, as the royal share, was found to be a demand so exorbitant that no adventurers would engage to work them upon such terms. In order to save the colony from ruin, Ovando ventured to relax the rigour of the royal edicts [1505]. He made a new distribution of the Indians among the Spaniards, and compelled them to labour, for a stated time, in digging the mines, or in cultivating the ground; but in order to screen himself from the imputation of having subjected them again to servitude, he enjoined their masters to pay them a certain sum, as the price of their work. He

* Life of Columbus, c. 108. Herrera, dec. 1. lib. vi. c. 13, 14, 15.

reduced the royal share of the gold found in the mines from the half to the third part, and soon after lowered it to a fifth, at which it long remained. Notwithstanding Isabella's tender concern for the good treatment of the Indians, and Ferdinand's eagerness to improve the Royal revenue, Ovando persuaded the court to approve of both these regulations.*

But the Indians, after enjoying respite from oppression, though during a short interval, now felt the yoke of bondage to be so galling that they made several attempts to vindicate their own liberty. This the Spaniards considered as rebellion, and took arms in order to reduce them to subjection. When war is carried on between nations whose state of improvement is in any degree similar, the means of defence bear some proportion to those employed in the attack; and in this equal contest such efforts must be made, such talents are displayed, and such passions roused, as exhibit mankind to view in a situation no less striking than interesting. It is one of the noblest functions of history to observe and to delineate men at a juncture when their minds are most violently agitated, and all their powers and passions are called forth. Hence the operations of war, and the struggles between contending states, have been deemed by historians, ancient as well as modern, a capital and important article in the annals of human actions. But in a contest between naked savages, and one of the most warlike of the European nations, where science, courage, and discipline on one side, were opposed by ignorance, timidity, and disorder on the other, a particular detail of events would be as unpleasant as uninstructive. If the simplicity and innocence of the Indians had inspired the Spaniards with humanity, had softened the pride of superiority into compassion, and had induced them to improve the inhabitants of the New World, instead of oppressing them, some sudden acts of violence, like the too rigorous chastisements of impatient instructors, might have been related without horror. But, unfortunately, this consciousness of superiority operated in a different manner. The Spaniards were advanced so far beyond the natives of America in improvement of every kind, that they viewed them with contempt. They conceived the Americans to be animals of an inferior nature, who were not entitled to the rights and privileges of men. In peace they subjected them to servitude. In war they paid no regard to those laws which, by a tacit convention between contending nations, regulate hostility, and set some bounds to its rage. They considered them not as men fighting in defence of their liberty, but as slaves who had revolted against their masters. Their caziques, when taken, were condemned, like the leaders of banditti, to the most cruel and ignominious punishments; and all their subjects, without regarding the distinction of ranks established among them, were reduced to the same state of abject slavery. With such a spirit and sentiments were hostilities carried on against the cazique of Higuey, a province at the eastern extremity of the island. This war was occasioned by the perfidy of the Spaniards, in violating a treaty which they had made with the natives, and it was terminated by hanging up the cazique, who defended his people with bravery so far superior to that of his countrymen, as entitled him to a better fate.†

The conduct of Ovando, in another part of the island, was still more treacherous and crue The province anciently named Xaragua, which extends from the fertile plain where Leogane is now situated to the western extremity of the island, was subject to a female cazique, named Anacoana, highly respected by the natives. She, from that partial fondness with which the women of America were attached to the Europeans (the cause of which shall be afterwards explained), had always courted the friendship of the Spaniards, and loaded them with benefits. But some of the adherents of Roldan having settled in her country, were so much exasperated

* Herrera, dec. 1. lib. v c. 3

† Ibid. dec. 1. lib. vi. c. 9, 10.

at her endeavouring to restrain their excesses, that they accused her of having formed a plan to throw off the yoke, and to exterminate the Spaniards. Ovando, though he knew well what little credit was due to such profligate men, marched, without further inquiry, towards Xaragua, with three hundred foot and seventy horsemen. To prevent the Indians from taking alarm at this hostile appearance, he gave out that his sole intention was to visit Anacoana, to whom his countrymen had been so much indebted, in the most respectful manner, and to regulate with her the mode of levying the tribute payable to the king of Spain. Anacoana, in order to receive this illustrious guest with due honour, assembled the principal men in her dominions, to the number of three hundred; and advancing at the head of these, accompanied by a great crowd of persons of inferior rank, she welcomed Ovando with songs and dances, according to the mode of the country, and conducted him to the place of her residence. There he was feasted for some days, with all the kindness of simple hospitality, and amused with the games and spectacles usual among the Americans upon occasions of mirth and festivity. But amidst the security which this inspired, Ovando was meditating the destruction of his unsuspicious entertainer and her subjects; and the mean perfidy with which he executed this scheme, equalled his barbarity in forming it. Under colour of exhibiting to the Indians the parade of a European tournament, he advanced with his troops, in battle array, towards the house in which Anacoana and the chiefs who attended her were assembled. The infantry took possession of all the avenues which led to the village. The horsemen encompassed the house. These movements were the object of admiration, without any mixture of fear, until, upon a signal which had been concerted, the Spaniards suddenly drew their swords, and rushed upon the Indians, defenceless, and astonished at an act of treachery which exceeded the conception of undesigning men. In a moment Anacoana was secured. All her attendants were seized and bound. Fire was set to the house; and without examination or conviction, all these unhappy persons, the most illustrious in their own country, were consumed in the flames. Anacoana was reserved for a more ignominious fate. She was carried in chains to St. Domingo, and, after the formality of a trial before Spanish judges, she was condemned, upon the evidence of those very men who had betrayed her, to be publicly hanged.*

Overawed and humbled by this atrocious treatment of their princes and nobles, who were objects of their highest reverence, the people in all the provinces of Hispaniola submitted, without further resistance, to the Spanish yoke. Upon the death of Isabella all the regulations tending to mitigate the rigour of their servitude were forgotten. The small gratuity paid to them as the price of their labour was withdrawn, and at the same time the tasks imposed upon them were increased [1506]. Ovando, without any restraint, distributed Indians among his friends in the island. Ferdinand, to whom the Queen had left by will one half of the revenue arising from the settlements in the New World, conferred grants of a similar nature upon his courtiers, as the least expensive mode of rewarding their services. They farmed out the Indians, of whom they were rendered proprietors, to their countrymen settled in Hispaniola; and that wretched people, being compelled to labour in order to satisfy the rapacity of both, the exactions of their oppressors no longer knew any bounds. But, barbarous as their policy was, and fatal to the inhabitants of Hispaniola, it produced, for some time, very considerable effects. By calling forth the force of a whole nation, and exerting itself in one direction, the working of the mines was carried on with amazing rapidity and success. During several years the gold brought into the royal smelting houses in Hispaniola amounted annually to four hundred

* Oviedo, lib. iii. c. 12. Herrera, dec. 1. lib. vi. c. 4. Relacion de Destruyc. de las Indias por Bart. de las Casas, p. 8.

and sixty thousand pesos, above a hundred thousand pounds sterling; which, if we attend to the great change in the value of money since the beginning of the sixteenth century to the present times, must appear a considerable sum. Vast fortunes were created, of a sudden, by some. Others dissipated, in ostentatious profusion, what they acquired with facility. Dazzled by both, new adventurers crowded to America, with the most eager impatience, o share in those treasures which had enriched their countrymen; and, notwithstanding the mortality occasioned by the unhealthiness of the climate the colony continued to increase.*

Ovando governed the Spaniards with wisdom and justice not inferior to the rigour with which he treated the Indians. He established equal laws; and, by executing them with impartiality, accustomed the people of the colony to reverence them. He founded several new towns in different parts of the island, and allured inhabitants to them by the concession of various immunities. He endeavoured to turn the attention of the Spaniards to some branch of industry more useful than that of searching for gold in the mines. Some slips of the sugarcane having been brought from the Canary islands by way of experiment, they were found to thrive with such increase in the rich soil and warm climate to which they were transplanted, that the cultivation of them soon became an object of commerce. Extensive plantations were begun; sugarworks, which the Spaniards called *ingenios*, from the various machinery employed in them, were erected, and in a few years the manufacture of this commodity was the great occupation of the inhabitants of Hispaniola, and the most considerable source of their wealth.†

The prudent endeavours of Ovando, to promote the welfare of the colony, were powerfully seconded by Ferdinand. The large remittances which he received from the New World opened his eyes, at length, with respect to the importance of those discoveries, which he had hitherto affected to undervalue. Fortune, and his own address, having now extricated him out of those difficulties in which he had been involved by the death of his Queen [1507], and by his disputes with his son-in-law about the government of her dominions,‡ he had full leisure to turn his attention to the affairs of America. To his provident sagacity Spain is indebted for many of those regulations which gradually formed that system of profound but jealous policy, by which she governs her dominions in the New World. He erected a court distinguished by the title of *Casa de Contratacion*, or Board of Trade, composed of persons eminent for rank and abilities, to whom he committed the administration of American affairs. This board assembled regularly in Seville, and was invested with a distinct and extensive jurisdiction. He gave a regular form to ecclesiastical government in America, by nominating archbishops, bishops, deans, together with clergymen of subordinate ranks, to take charge of the Spaniards established there, as well as of the natives who should embrace the Christian faith, but notwithstanding the obsequious devotion of the Spanish court to the papal see, such was Ferdinand's solicitude to prevent any foreign power from claiming jurisdiction, or acquiring influence, in his new dominions, that he reserved to the crown of Spain the sole right of patronage to the benefices in America, and stipulated that no papal bull or mandate should be promulgated there until it was previously examined and approved of by his council. With the same spirit of jealousy, he prohibited any goods to be exported to America, or any person to settle there without a special license from that council.§

But, notwithstanding this attention to the police and welfare of the colony, a calamity impended which threatened its dissolution. The original inha-

* Herrera, dec. 1. lib. vi. c. 18, &c. † Oviedo, lib. iv. c. 8. ‡ History of the Reign of Charles V. p. 6, &c. § Herrera, dec. 1. lib. vi. c. 19 20

bitants, on whose labour the Spaniards in Hispaniola depended for their prosperity, and even their existence, wasted so fast that the extinction of the whole race seemed to be inevitable. When Columbus discovered Hispaniola, the number of its inhabitants was computed to be at least a million.* They were now reduced to sixty thousand in the space of fifteen years. This consumption of the human species, no less amazing than rapid, was the effect of several concurring causes. The natives of the American islands were of a more feeble constitution than the inhabitants of the other hemisphere. They could neither perform the same work nor endure the same fatigue with men whose organs were of a more vigorous conformation. The listless indolence in which they delighted to pass their days, as it was the effect of their debility, contributed likewise to increase it, and rendered them from habit, as well as constitution, incapable of hard labour. The food on which they subsisted afforded little nourishment, and they were accustomed to take it in small quantities, not sufficient to invigorate a languid frame, and render it equal to the efforts of active industry. The Spaniards, without attending to those peculiarities in the constitution of the Americans, imposed tasks upon them which, though not greater than Europeans might have performed with ease, were so disproportioned to their strength, that many sunk under the fatigue, and ended their wretched days. Others, prompted by impatience and despair, cut short their own lives with a violent hand. Famine, brought on by compelling such numbers to abandon the culture of their lands, in order to labour in the mines, proved fatal to many. Diseases of various kinds, some occasioned by the hardships to which they were exposed, and others by their intercourse with the Europeans, who communicated to them some of their peculiar maladies, completed the desolation of the island. The Spaniards, being thus deprived of the instruments which they were accustomed to employ, found it impossible to extend their improvements, or even to carry on the works which they had already begun [1508]. In order to provide an immediate remedy for an evil so alarming, Ovando proposed to transport the inhabitants of the Lucayo islands to Hispaniola, under pretence that they might be civilized with more facility, and instructed to greater advantage in the Christian religion, if they were united to the Spanish colony, and placed under the immediate inspection of the missionaries settled there. Ferdinand, deceived by this artifice, or willing to connive at an act of violence which policy represented as necessary, gave his assent to the proposal. Several vessels were fitted out for the Lucayos, the commanders of which informed the natives, with whose language they were now well acquainted, that they came from a delicious country, in which the departed ancestors of the Indians resided, by whom they were sent to invite their descendants to resort thither, to partake of the bliss enjoyed there by happy spirits. That simple people listened with wonder and credulity; and, fond of visiting their relations and friends in that happy region, followed the Spaniards with eagerness. By this artifice above forty thousand were decoyed into Hispaniola, to share in the sufferings which were the lot of the inhabitants of that island, and to mingle their groans and tears with those of that wretched race of men.†

The Spaniards had, for some time, carried on their operations in the mines of Hispaniola with such ardour as well as success, that these seemed to have engrossed their whole attention. The spirit of discovery languished; and, since the last voyage of Columbus, no enterprise of any moment had been undertaken. But as the decrease of the Indians rendered it impossible to acquire wealth in that island with the same rapidity as formerly, this urged some of the more adventurous Spaniards to search for new countries, where their avarice might be gratified with more facility.

* Herrera, dec. 1. lib. x. c. 12. † Ibid. lib. vii. c. 3. Oviedo, lib. iii. c. 6. Gomara Hist. c. 41.

Juan Ponce de Leon, who commanded under Ovando in the eastern district of Hispaniola, passed over to the island of St. Juan de Puerto Rico, which Columbus had discovered in his second voyage, and penetrated into the interior part of the country. As he found the soil to be fertile, and expected, from some symptoms, as well as from the information of the inhabitants, to discover mines of gold in the mountains, Ovando permitted him to attempt making a settlement in the island. This was easily effected by an officer eminent for conduct no less than for courage. In a few years Puerto Rico was subjected to the Spanish government, the natives were reduced to servitude; and being treated with the same inconsiderate rigour as their neighbours in Hispaniola, the race of original inhabitants, worn out with fatigue and sufferings, was soon exterminated.*

About the same time Juan Diaz de Solis, in conjunction with Vincent Yanez Pinzon, one of Columbus's original companions, made a voyage to the continent. They held the same course which Columbus had taken as far as the island of Guanaios; but, standing from thence to the west, they discovered a new and extensive province, afterwards known by the name of Yucatan, and proceeded a considerable way along the coast of that country.† Though nothing memorable occurred in this voyage, it deserves notice, because it led to discoveries of greater importance. For the same reason the voyage of Sebastian de Ocampo must be mentioned. By the command of Ovando he sailed round Cuba, and first discovered with certainty, that this country, which Columbus once supposed to be a part of the continent, was a large island.‡

This voyage round Cuba was one of the last occurrences under the administration of Ovando. Ever since the death of Columbus, his son, Don Diego, had been employed in soliciting Ferdinand to grant him the offices of viceroy and admiral in the New World, together with all the other immunities and profits which descended to him by inheritance, in consequence of the original capitulation with his father. But if these dignities and revenues appeared so considerable to Ferdinand, that, at the expense of being deemed unjust as well as ungrateful, he had wrested them from Columbus, it was not surprising that he should be unwilling to confer them on his son. Accordingly Don Diego wasted two years in incessant but fruitless importunity. Weary of this, he endeavoured at length to obtain by a legal sentence what he could not procure from the favour of an interested monarch. He commenced a suit against Ferdinand before the council which managed Indian affairs; and that court, with integrity which reflects honour upon its proceedings, decided against the king, and sustained Don Diego's claim of the viceroyalty, together with all the other privileges stipulated in the capitulation. Even after this decree Ferdinand's repugnance to put a subject in possession of such extensive rights might have thrown in new obstacles, if Don Diego had not taken a step which interested very powerful persons in the success of his claims. The sentence of the council of the Indies gave him a title to a rank so elevated, and a fortune so opulent, that he found no difficulty in concluding a marriage with Donna Maria, daughter of Don Ferdinand de Toledo, great commendator of Leon, and brother of the duke of Alva, a nobleman of the first rank, and nearly related to the king. The duke and his family espoused so warmly the cause of their new ally, that Ferdinand could not resist their solicitations [1509]. He recalled Ovando, and appointed Don Diego his successor, though even in conferring this favour he could not conceal his jealousy; for he allowed him to assume only the title of governor, not that of viceroy, which had been adjudged to belong to him.§

Don Diego quickly repaired to Hispaniola, attended by his brother, his uncles,

* Herrera, dec. 1. lib. vii. c. 1—4. Gomara Hist. c. 44. Relacion de B. de las Casas, p. 10.
† Ibid. dec. 1. lib. vi. c. 17. ‡ Ibid. lib. vii. c. 1. § Ibid. dec. 1. lib. vii. c. 4, &c.

his wife, whom the courtesy of the Spaniards honoured with the title of vicequeen, and a numerous retinue of persons of both sexes born of good families. He lived with a splendour and magnificence hitherto unknown in the New World; and the family of Columbus seemed now to enjoy the honours and rewards due to his inventive genius, of which he himself had been cruelly defrauded. The colony itself acquired new lustre by the accession of so many inhabitants, of a different rank and character from most of those who had hitherto migrated to America, and many of the most illustrious families in the Spanish settlements are descended from the persons who at that time accompanied Don Diego Columbus.*

No benefits accrued to the unhappy natives from this change of governors. Don Diego was not only authorized by a royal edict to continue the *repartimientos*, or distribution of Indians, but the particular number which he might grant to every person, according to his rank in the colony, was specified. He availed himself of that permission; and soon after he landed at St. Domingo, he divided such Indians as were still unappropriated, among his relations and attendants.†

The next care of the new governor was to comply with an instruction which he received from the king, about settling a colony in Cubagua, a small island which Columbus had discovered in his third voyage. Though this barren spot hardly yielded subsistence to its wretched inhabitants, such quantities of those oysters which produce pearls were found on its coast, that it did not long escape the inquisitive avarice of the Spaniards, and became a place of considerable resort. Large fortunes were acquired by the fishery of pearls, which was carried on with extraordinary ardour. The Indians, especially those from the Lucayo islands, were compelled to dive for them; and this dangerous and unhealthy employment was an additional calamity which contributed not a little to the extinction of that devoted race.‡

About this period, Juan Diaz de Solis and Pinzon set out, in conjunction, upon a second voyage. They stood directly south, towards the equinoctial line, which Pinzon had formerly crossed, and advanced as far as the fortieth degree of southern latitude. They were astonished to find that the continent of America stretched on their right hand through all this vast extent of ocean. They landed in different places, to take possession in name of their sovereign; but though the country appeared to be extremely fertile and inviting, their force was so small, having been fitted out rather for discovery than making settlements, that they left no colony behind them. Their voyage served, however, to give the Spaniards more exalted and adequate ideas with respect to the dimensions of this new quarter of the globe.§

Though it was about ten years since Columbus had discovered the main land of America, the Spaniards had hitherto made no settlement in any part of it. What had been so long neglected was now seriously attempted, and with considerable vigour; though the plan for this purpose was neither formed by the crown, nor executed at the expense of the nation, but carried on by the enterprising spirit of private adventurers. The scheme took its rise from Alonso de Ojeda, who had already made two voyages as a discoverer, by which he acquired considerable reputation, but no wealth. But his character for intrepidity and conduct easily procured him associates, who advanced the money requisite to defray the charges of the expedition. About the same time, Diego de Nicuessa, who had acquired a large fortune in Hispaniola, formed a similar design. Ferdinand encouraged both; and though he refused to advance the smallest sum, he was extremely liberal of titles and patents. He erected two governments on the continent, one extending from Cape de Vela to the Gulf of Darien, and the other from that to Cape Gracias a Dios. The former was given to Ojeda, the latter to Nicuessa.

* Oviedo. lib. iii. c. 1. † Recopilacion de Leyes, lib. vi. tit. 8 l. 1, 2. Herrera, dec. 1. lib. vii. c. 10. ‡ Herrera, dec. 1. lib. vii. c. 9. Gomara Hist. c. 78. § Ibid. dec. 1. lib. vii. c. 9.

Ojeda fitted out a ship and two brigantines, with three hundred men, Nicuessa, six vessels, with seven hundred and eighty men. They sailed about the same time from St. Domingo for their respective governments. In order to give their title to those countries some appearance of validity, several of the most eminent divines and lawyers in Spain were employed to prescribe the mode in which they should take possession of them.* There is not in the history of mankind any thing more singular or extravagant than the form which they devised for this purpose. They instructed those invaders, as soon as they landed on the continent, to declare to the natives the principal articles of the Christian faith; to acquaint them in particular, with the supreme jurisdiction of the Pope over all the kingdoms of the earth; to inform them of the grant which this holy pontiff had made of their country to the king of Spain; to require them to embrace the doctrines of that religion which the Spaniards made known to them; and to submit to the sovereign whose authority they proclaimed. If the natives refused to comply with this requisition, the terms of which must have been utterly incomprehensible to uninstructed Indians, then Ojeda and Nicuessa were authorized to attack them with fire and sword; to reduce them, their wives and children, to a state of servitude; and to compel them by force to recognise the jurisdiction of the church, and the authority of the monarch, to which they would not voluntarily subject themselves [23].

As the inhabitants of the continent could not at once yield assent to doctrines too refined for their uncultivated understandings, and explained to them by interpreters imperfectly acquainted with their language; as they did not conceive how a foreign priest, of whom they had never heard, could have any right to dispose of their country, or how an unknown prince should claim jurisdiction over them as his subjects; they fiercely opposed the new invaders of their territories. Ojeda and Nicuessa endeavoured to effect by force what they could not accomplish by persuasion. The contemporary writers enter into a very minute detail in relating their transactions; but as they made no discovery of importance, nor established any permanent settlement, their adventures are not entitled to any considerable place in the general history of a period where romantic valour, struggling with incredible hardships, distinguishes every effort of the Spanish arms. They found the natives in those countries of which they went to assume the government, to be of a character very different from that of their countrymen in the islands. They were free and warlike. Their arrows were dipped in a poison so noxious, that every wound was followed with certain death. In one encounter they slew above seventy of Ojeda's followers, and the Spaniards, for the first time, were taught to dread the inhabitants of the New World. Nicuessa was opposed by people equally resolute in defence of their possessions. Nothing could soften their ferocity. Though the Spaniards employed every art to soothe them, and to gain their confidence, they refused to hold any intercourse, or to exchange any friendly office, with men whose residence among them they considered as fatal to their liberty and independence [1510]. This implacable enmity of the natives, though it rendered an attempt to establish a settlement in their country extremely difficult as well as dangerous, might have been surmounted at length by the perseverance of the Spaniards, by the superiority of their arms, and their skill in the art of war. But every disaster which can be accumulated upon the unfortunate combined to complete their ruin. The loss of their ships by various accidents upon an unknown coast, the diseases peculiar to a climate the most noxious in all America, the want of provisions unavoidable in a country imperfectly cultivated, dissension among themselves, and the incessant hostilities of the natives, involved them in a succession of calamities, the bare recital of which strikes

* Herrera, dec. I. lib. vii. c. 15.

one with horror. Though they received two considerable reinforcements from Hispaniola, the greater part of those who had engaged in this unhappy expedition perished, in less than a year, in the most extreme misery. A few who survived settled as a feeble colony at Santa Maria el Antigua, on the Gulf of Darien, under the command of Vasco Nugnez de Balboa, who, in the most desperate exigencies, displayed such courage and conduct as first gained the confidence of his countrymen, and marked him out as their leader in more splendid and successful undertakings. Nor was he the only adventurer in this expedition who will appear with lustre in more important scenes. Francisco Pizarro was one of Ojeda's companions, and in this school of adversity acquired or improved the talents which fitted him for the extraordinary actions which he afterwards performed. Hernan Cortes, whose name became still more famous, had likewise engaged early in this enterprise, which roused all the active youth of Hispaniola to arms; but the good fortune that accompanied him in his subsequent adventures interposed to save him from the disasters to which his companions were exposed. He was taken ill at St. Domingo before the departure of the fleet, and detained there by a tedious indisposition.*

Notwithstanding the unfortunate issue of this expedition, the Spaniards were not deterred from engaging in new schemes of a similar nature. When wealth is acquired gradually by the persevering hand of industry, or accumulated by the slow operations of regular commerce, the means employed are so proportioned to the end attained, that there is nothing to strike the imagination, and little to urge on the active powers of the mind to uncommon efforts. But when large fortunes were created almost instantaneously; when gold and pearls were procured in exchange for baubles; when the countries which produced these rich commodities, defended only by naked savages, might be seized by the first bold invader; objects so singular and alluring roused a wonderful spirit of enterprise among the Spaniards, who rushed with ardour into this new path that was opened to wealth and distinction. While this spirit continued warm and vigorous, every attempt either towards discovery or conquest was applauded, and adventurers engaged in it with emulation. The passion for new undertakings, which characterizes the age of discovery in the latter part of the fifteenth and beginning of the sixteenth century, would alone have been sufficient to prevent the Spaniards from stopping short in their career. But circumstances peculiar to Hispaniola, at this juncture, concurred with it in extending their navigation and conquests. The rigorous treatment of the inhabitants of that island having almost extirpated the race, many of the Spanish planters, as I have already observed, finding it impossible to carry on their works with the same vigour and profit, were obliged to look out for settlements in some country where people were not yet wasted by oppression. Others, with the inconsiderate levity natural to men upon whom wealth pours in with a sudden flow, had squandered in thoughtless prodigality what they acquired with ease, and were driven by necessity to embark in the most desperate schemes, in order to retrieve their affairs. From all these causes, when Don Diego Columbus proposed [1511] to conquer the island of Cuba, and to establish a colony there, many persons of chief distinction in Hispaniola engaged with alacrity in the measure. He gave the command of the troops destined for that service to Diego Velasquez, one of his father's companions in his second voyage, and who, having been long settled in Hispaniola, had acquired an ample fortune, with such reputation for probity and prudence, that he seemed to be well qualified for conducting an expedition of importance. Three hundred men were deemed sufficient for the conquest of an island of above seven hundred miles in

* Herrera, dec. 1. lib. vii. c. 11, &c. Gomara Hist. c. 57, 58, 59. Benzon. Hist. lib. i. c. 19—23. P. Martyr, decad. p. 122.

length, and filled with inhabitants. But they were of the same unwarlike character with the people of Hispaniola. They were not only intimidated by the appearance of their new enemies, but unprepared to resist them. For though, from the time that the Spaniards took possession of the adjacent island, there was reason to expect a descent on their territories, none of the small communities into which Cuba was divided, had either made any provision for its own defence, or had formed any concert for their common safety. The only obstruction the Spaniards met with was from Hatuey, a cazique, who had fled from Hispaniola, and had taken possession of the eastern extremity of Cuba. He stood upon the defensive at their first landing, and endeavoured to drive them back to their ships. His feeble troops, however, were soon broken and dispersed; and he himself being taken prisoner, Velasquez, according to the barbarous maxim of the Spaniards, considered him as a slave who had taken arms against his master, and condemned him to the flames. When Hatuey was fastened to the stake, a Franciscan friar, labouring to convert him, promised him immediate admittance into the joys of heaven, if he would embrace the Christian faith. "Are there any Spaniards," says he, after some pause, "in that region of bliss which you describe?"—"Yes," replied the monk, "but only such as are worthy and good."—"The best of them," returned the indignant cazique, "have neither worth nor goodness: I will not go to a place where I may meet with one of that accursed race."* This dreadful example of vengeance struck the people of Cuba with such terror that they scarcely gave any opposition to the progress of their invaders; and Velasquez, without the loss of a man, annexed this extensive and fertile island to the Spanish monarchy.†

The facility with which this important conquest was completed served as an incitement to other undertakings. Juan Ponce de Leon, having acquired both fame and wealth by the reduction of Puerto Rico, was impatient to engage in some new enterprise. He fitted out three ships at his own expense, for a voyage of discovery [1512], and his reputation soon drew together a respectable body of followers. He directed his course towards the Lucayo islands; and after touching at several of them, as well as of the Bahama isles, he stood to the south-west, and discovered a country hitherto unknown to the Spaniards, which he called Florida, either because he fell in with it on Palm Sunday, or on account of its gay and beautiful appearance. He attempted to land in different places, but met with such vigorous opposition from the natives, who were fierce and warlike, as convinced him that an increase of force was requisite to effect a settlement. Satisfied with having opened a communication with a new country, of whose value and importance he conceived very sanguine hopes, he returned to Puerto Rico through the channel now known by the name of the Gulf of Florida.

It was not merely the passion of searching for new countries that prompted Ponce de Leon to undertake this voyage; he was influenced by one of those visionary ideas, which at that time often mingled with the spirit of discovery, and rendered it more active. A tradition prevailed among the natives of Puerto Rico, that in the isle of Bimini, one of the Lucayos, there was a fountain of such wonderful virtue as to renew the youth and recall the vigour of every person who bathed in its salutary waters. In hopes of finding this grand restorative, Ponce de Lēon and his followers ranged through the islands, searching with fruitless solicitude and labour for the fountain which was the chief object of their expedition. That a tale so fabulous should gain credit among simple and uninstructed Indians is not surprising. That it should make any impression upon an enlightened people appears in the present age altogether incredible. The fact, however, is

* B. de las Casas, p. 40. † Herrera, dec. 1. lib. ix. c. 2, 3, &c. Oviedo, lib. xvii c. 3. p. 170

certain; and the most authentic Spanish historians mention this extravagant sally of their credulous countrymen. The Spaniards at that period were engaged in a career of activity which gave a romantic turn to their imagination, and daily presented to them strange and marvellous objects. A New World was opened to their view. They visited islands and continents, of whose existence mankind in former ages had no conception. In those delightful countries nature seemed to assume another form: every tree and plant and animal was different from those of the ancient hemisphere. They seemed to be transported into enchanted ground; and after the wonders which they had seen, nothing, in the warmth and novelty of their admiration, appeared to them so extraordinary as to be beyond belief. If the rapid succession of new and striking scenes made such impression even upon the sound understanding of Columbus, that he boasted of having found the seat of Paradise, it will not appear strange that Ponce de Leon should dream of discovering the fountain of youth.*

Soon after the expedition to Florida, a discovery of much greater importance was made in another part of America. Balboa having been raised to the government of the small colony at Santa Maria in Darien, by the voluntary suffrage of his associates, was so extremely desirous to obtain from the crown a confirmation of their election, that he despatched one of his officers to Spain, in order to solicit a royal commission, which might invest him with a legal title to the supreme command. Conscious, however, that he could not expect success from the patronage of Ferdinand's ministers, with whom he was unconnected, or from negotiating in a court to the arts of which he was a stranger, he endeavoured to merit the dignity to which he aspired, and aimed at performing some signal service that would secure him the preference to every competitor. Full of this idea, he made frequent inroads into the adjacent country, subdued several of the caziques, and collected a considerable quantity of gold, which abounded more in that part of the continent than in the islands. In one of those excursions, the Spaniards contended with such eagerness about the division of some gold, that they were at the point of proceeding to acts of violence against one another. A young cazique who was present, astonished at the high value which they set upon a thing of which he did not discern the use, tumbled the gold out of the balance with indignation; and turning to the Spaniards, "Why do you quarrel (says he) about such a trifle? If you are so passionately fond of gold, as to abandon your own country, and to disturb the tranquillity of distant nations for its sake, I will conduct you to a region where the metal which seems to be the chief object of your admiration and desire is so common that the meanest utensils are formed of it." Transported with what they heard, Balboa and his companions inquired eagerly where this happy country lay, and how they might arrive at it. He informed them that at the distance of six suns, that is, of six days' journey, towards the south, they should discover another ocean, near to which this wealthy kingdom was situated; but if they intended to attack that powerful state, they must assemble forces far superior in number and strength to those with which they now appeared.†

This was the first information which the Spaniards received concerning the great southern ocean, or the opulent and extensive country known afterwards by the name of Peru. Balboa had now before him objects suited to his boundless ambition, and the enterprising ardour of his genius. He immediately concluded the ocean which the cazique mentioned, to be that for which Columbus had searched without success in this part of America, in hopes of opening a more direct communication with the East Indies; and he

* P. Martyr, decad. p. 202. Ensayo Chronol. para la Hist. de la Florida, par de Gab. Cardenas, p. 1. Oviedo, lib. xvi. c. 11. Herrera, dec. 1. lib. ix. c. 5. Hist. de la Conq. de la Florida, par Garc. de la Vega, lib. 1. c. 3

† Herrera, dec. 1. lib. ix. c, 2. Gomara, c. 60. P. Martyr dec p. 149.

jectured that the rich territory which had been described to him must be part of that vast and opulent region of the earth. Elated with the idea of performing what so great a man had attempted in vain, and eager to accomplish a discovery which he knew would be no less acceptable to the king than beneficial to his country, he was impatient until he could set out upon this enterprise, in comparison of which all his former exploits appeared inconsiderable. But previous arrangement and preparation were requisite to ensure success. He began with courting and securing the friendship of the neighbouring caziques. He sent some of his officers to Hispaniola with a large quantity of gold, as a proof of his past success, and an earnest of his future hopes. By a proper distribution of this, they secured the favour of the governor, and allured volunteers into the service. A considerable reinforcement from that island joined him, and he thought himself in a condition to attempt the discovery.

The isthmus of Darien is not above sixty miles in breadth; but this neck of land which binds together the continents of North and South America, is strengthened by a chain of lofty mountains stretching through its whole extent, which render it a barrier of solidity sufficient to resist the impulse of two opposite oceans. The mountains are covered with forests almost inaccessible. The valleys in that moist climate where it rains during two-thirds of the year, are marshy, and so frequently overflowed that the inhabitants find it necessary, in many places, to build their houses upon trees, in order to be elevated at some distance from the damp soil, and the odious reptiles engendered in the putrid waters.* Large rivers rush down with an impetuous current from the high grounds. In a region thinly inhabited by wandering savages, the hand of industry had done nothing to mitigate or correct those natural disadvantages. To march across this unexplored country with no other guides but Indians, whose fidelity could be little trusted, was, on all those accounts, the boldest enterprise on which the Spaniards had hitherto ventured in the New World. But the intrepidity of Balboa was such as distinguished him among his countrymen, at a period when every adventurer was conspicuous for daring courage [1513]. Nor was bravery his only merit; he was prudent in conduct, generous, affable, and possessed of those popular talents which, in the most desperate undertakings, inspire confidence and secure attachment. Even after the junction of the volunteers from Hispaniola, he was able to muster only a hundred and ninety men for his expedition. But they were hardy veterans, inured to the climate of America, and ready to follow him through every danger. A thousand Indians attended them to carry their provisions; and, to complete their warlike array, they took with them several of those fierce dogs, which were no less formidable than destructive to their naked enemies.

Balboa set out upon this important expedition on the first of September, about the time that the periodical rains began to abate. He proceeded by sea, and without any difficulty, to the territories of a cazique whose friendship he had gained; but no sooner did he begin to advance into the interior part of the country, than he was retarded by every obstacle, which he had reason to apprehend, from the nature of the territory, or the disposition of its inhabitants. Some of the caziques, at his approach, fled to the mountains with all their people, and carried off or destroyed whatever could afford subsistence to his troops. Others collected their subjects, in order to oppose his progress; and he quickly perceived what an arduous undertaking it was to conduct such a body of men through hostile nations, across swamps, and rivers, and woods, which had never been passed but by straggling Indians. But by sharing in every hardship with the meanest soldier, by appearing the foremost to meet every danger, by promising confidently to his troops the enjoyment of honour and riches superior to

* P. Martyr, dec. p. 158.

what had been attained by the most successful of their countrymen, he inspired them with such enthusiastic resolution, that they followed him without murmuring. When they had penetrated a good way into the mountains, a powerful cazique appeared in a narrow pass, with a numerous body of his subjects, to obstruct their progress. But men who had surmounted so many obstacles, despised the opposition of such feeble enemies They attacked them with impetuosity, and, having dispersed them with much ease and great slaughter, continued their march. Though their guides had represented the breadth of the isthmus to be only a journey of six days, they had already spent twenty-five in forcing their way through the woods and mountains. Many of them were ready to sink under such uninterrupted fatigue in that sultry climate, several were taken ill of the dysentery and other diseases frequent in that country, and all became impatient to reach the period of their labours and sufferings. At length the Indians assured them, that from the top of the next mountain they should discover the ocean which was the object of their wishes. When, with infinite toil, they had climbed up the greater part of that steep ascent, Balboa commanded his men to halt, and advanced alone to the summit, that he might be the first who should enjoy a spectacle which he had so long desired. As soon as he beheld the South Sea stretching in endless prospect below him, he fell on his knees, and, lifting up his hands to heaven, returned thanks to God, who had conducted him to a discovery so beneficial to his country, and so honourable to himself. His followers, observing his transports of joy, rushed forward to join in his wonder, exultation, and gratitude. They held on their course to the shore with great alacrity, when Balboa, advancing up to the middle in the waves with his buckler and sword, took possession of that ocean in the name of the king his master, and vowed to defend it with these arms, against all his enemies.*

That part of the great Pacific or Southern Ocean which Balboa first discovered, still retains the name of the Gulf of St. Michael, which he gave to it, and is situated to the east of Panama. From several of the petty princes, who governed in the districts adjacent to that gulf, he extorted provisions and gold by force of arms. Others sent them to him voluntarily. To these acceptable presents, some of the caziques added a considerable quantity of pearls; and he learned from them, with much satisfaction, that pearl oysters abounded in the sea which he had newly discovered.

Together with the acquisition of this wealth, which served to soothe and encourage his followers, he received accounts which confirmed his sanguine hopes of future and more extensive benefits from the expedition. All the people on the coast of the South Sea concurred in informing him that there was a mighty and opulent kingdom situated at a considerable distance towards the south-east, the inhabitants of which had tame animals to carry their burdens. In order to give the Spaniards an idea of these, they drew upon the sand the figure of the llamas or sheep, afterwards found in Peru, which the Peruvians had taught to perform such services as they described. As the llama in its form nearly resembles a camel, a beast of burden deemed peculiar to Asia, this circumstance, in conjunction with the discovery of the pearls, another noted production of that country, tended to confirm the Spaniards in their mistaken theory with respect to the vicinity of the New World to the East Indies.†

But though the information which Balboa received from the people on the coast, as well as his own conjectures and hopes, rendered him extremely impatient to visit this unknown country, his prudence restrained him from

* Herrera, dec. 1. lib. x. c. 1, &c. Gomara, c. 62, &c. P. Martyr, dec. p. 205, &c. † Ibid. dec. 1. lib. x. c. 2.

attempting to invade it with a handful of men exhausted by fatigue and weakened by diseases. [24] He determined to lead back his followers, at present, to their settlement of Santa Maria in Darien, and to return next season with a force more adequate to such an arduous enterprise. In order to acquire a more extensive knowledge of the isthmus, he marched back by a different route, which he found to be no less dangerous and difficult than that which he had formerly taken. But to men elated with success, and animated with hope, nothing is insurmountable. Balboa returned to Santa Maria [1514], from which he had been absent four months, with greater glory and more treasure than the Spaniards had acquired in any expedition in the New World. None of Balboa's officers distinguished themselves more in this service than Francisco Pizarro, or assisted with greater courage and ardour in opening a communication with those countries in which he was destined to act soon a more illustrious part.*

Balboa's first care was to send information to Spain of the important discovery which he had made: and to demand a reinforcement of a thousand men, in order to attempt the conquest of that opulent country concerning which he had received such inviting intelligence. The first account of the discovery of the New World hardly occasioned greater joy than the unexpected tidings that a passage was at last found to the great southern ocean. The communication with the East Indies, by a course to the westward of the line of demarcation drawn by the Pope, seemed now to be certain. The vast wealth which flowed into Portugal, from its settlements and conquests in that country, excited the envy and called forth the emulation of other states. Ferdinand hoped now to come in for a share in this lucrative commerce, and, in his eagerness to obtain it, was willing to make an effort beyond what Balboa required. But even in this exertion, his jealous policy, as well as the fatal antipathy of Fonseca, now Bishop of Burgos, to every man of merit who distinguished himself in the New World, was conspicuous. Notwithstanding Balboa's recent services, which marked him out as the most proper person to finish that great undertaking which he had begun, Ferdinand was so ungenerous as to overlook these, and to appoint Pedrarias Davila governor of Darien. He gave him the command of fifteen stout vessels and twelve hundred soldiers. These were fitted out at the public expense, with a liberality which Ferdinand had never displayed in any former armament destined for the New World; and such was the ardour of the Spanish gentlemen to follow a leader who was about to conduct them to a country where, as fame reported, they had only to throw their nets into the sea and draw out gold,† that fifteen hundred embarked on board the fleet, and, if they had not been restrained, a much greater number would have engaged in the service.‡

Pedrarias reached the Gulf of Darien without any remarkable accident, and immediately sent some of his principal officers ashore to inform Balboa of his arrival, with the king's commission to be governor of the colony. To their astonishment, they found Balboa, of whose great exploits they had heard so much, and of whose opulence they had formed such high ideas, clad in a canvass jacket, and wearing coarse hempen sandals used only by the meanest peasants, employed, together with some Indians, in thatching his own hut with reeds. Even in this simple garb, which corresponded so ill with the expectations and wishes of his new guests, Balboa received them with dignity. The fame of his discoveries had drawn so many adventurers from the islands, that he could now muster four hundred and fifty men. At the head of those daring veterans, he was more than a match for the forces which Pedrarias brought with him. But, though his troops murmured loudly at the injustice of the king in superseding their commander,

* Herrera, dec. 1. lib. x. c. 3—6. Gomara, c. 64. P. Martyr, dec. p. 229, &c. † Ibid. c. 14.
‡ Ibid. c. 6, 7. P. Martyr, dec. p. 177. 296.

and complained that strangers would now reap the fruits of their toil and success, Balboa submitted with implicit obedience to the will of his sovereign, and received Pedrarias with all the deference due to his character.*

Notwithstanding this moderation, to which Pedrarias owed the peaceable possession of his government, he appointed a judicial inquiry to be made into Balboa's conduct, while under the command of Nicuessa, and imposed a considerable fine upon him, on account of the irregularities of which he had then been guilty. Balboa felt sensibly the mortification of being subjected to trial and to punishment in a place where he had so lately occupied the first station. Pedrarias could not conceal his jealousy of his superior merit; so that the resentment of the one and the envy of the other gave rise to dissensions extremely detrimental to the colony. It was threatened with a calamity still more fatal. Pedrarias had landed in Darien at a most unlucky time of the year [July], about the middle of the rainy season, in that part of the torrid zone where the clouds pour down such torrents as are unknown in more temperate climates.† The village of Santa Maria was seated in a rich plain, environed with marshes and woods. The constitution of Europeans was unable to withstand the pestilential influence of such a situation, in a climate naturally so noxious, and at a season so peculiarly unhealthy. A violent and destructive malady carried off many of the soldiers who accompanied Pedrarias. An extreme scarcity of provision augmented this distress, as it rendered it impossible to find proper refreshment for the sick, or the necessary sustenance for the healthy.‡ In the space of a month, above six hundred persons perished in the utmost misery. Dejection and despair spread through the colony. Many principal persons solicited their dismission, and were glad to relinquish all their hopes of wealth, in order to escape from that pernicious region. Pedrarias endeavoured to divert those who remained from brooding over their misfortunes, by finding them employment. With this view, he sent several detachments into the interior parts of the country, to levy gold among the natives, and to search for the mines in which it was produced. Those rapacious adventurers, more attentive to present gain than to the means of facilitating their future progress, plundered without distinction wherever they marched. Regardless of the alliances which Balboa had made with several of the caziques, they stripped them of every thing valuable, and treated them, as well as their subjects, with the utmost insolence and cruelty. By their tyranny and exactions, which Pedrarias, either from want of authority or inclination, did not restrain, all the country from the Gulf of Darien to the lake of Nicaragua was desolated, and the Spaniards were inconsiderately deprived of the advantages which they might have derived from the friendship of the natives, in extending their conquests to the South Sea. Balboa, who saw with concern that such ill-judged proceedings retarded the execution of his favourite scheme, sent violent remonstrances to Spain against the imprudent government of Pedrarias, who had ruined a happy and flourishing colony. Pedrarias, on the other hand, accused him of having deceived the King, by magnifying his own exploits, as well as by a false representation of the opulence and value of the country.§

Ferdinand became sensible at length of his imprudence in superseding the most active and experienced officer he had in the New World, and, by way of compensation to Balboa, appointed him *Adelantado*, or Lieutenant-Governor of the countries upon the South Sea, with very extensive privileges and authority. At the same time he enjoined Pedrarias to support Balboa in all his operations, and to consult with him concerning every measure which he himself pursued. [1515] But to effect such a sudden

* Herrera, dec. 1. lib. x. c. 13, 14. † Richard, Hist. Naturelle de l'Air, tom. 1, p. 204.

‡ Herrera, dec. 1. lib. x. c. 14. P. Martyr, decad. p. 272. § Ibid. dec. 1. lib. x. c. 15. dec. 2. c. 1, &c. Gomara, c. 66. P. Martyr, dec. 3. c. 10. Relacion de B. de las Casas, p. 12.

transition from inveterate enmity to perfect confidence, exceeded Ferdinand's power. Pedrarias continued to treat his rival with neglect; and Balboa's fortune being exhausted by the payment of his fine, and other exactions of Pedrarias, he could not make suitable preparations for taking possession of his new government. At length, by the interposition and exhortations of the Bishop of Darien, they were brought to a reconciliation; and, in order to cement this union more firmly, Pedrarias agreed to give his daughter in marriage to Balboa. [1516.] The first effect of their concord was, that Balboa was permitted to make several small incursions into the country. These he conducted with such prudence, as added to the reputation which he had already acquired. Many adventurers resorted to him, and, with the countenance and aid of Pedrarias, he began to prepare for his expedition to the South Sea. In order to accomplish this, it was necessary to build vessels capable of conveying his troops to those provinces which he purposed to invade. [1517.] After surmounting many obstacles, and enduring a variety of those hardships which were the portion of the conquerors of America, he at length finished four small brigantines. In these, with three hundred chosen men, a force superior to that with which Pizarro afterwards undertook the same expedition, he was ready to sail towards Peru, when he received an unexpected message from Pedrarias.* As his reconciliation with Balboa had never been cordial, the progress which his son-in-law was making revived his ancient enmity, and added to its rancour. He dreaded the prosperity and elevation of a man whom he had injured so deeply. He suspected that success would encourage him to aim at independence upon his jurisdiction; and so violently did the passions of hatred, fear, and jealousy operate upon his mind, that, in order to gratify his vengeance, he scrupled not to defeat an enterprise of the greatest moment to his country. Under pretexts which were false, but plausible, he desired Balboa to postpone his voyage for a short time, and to repair to Acla, in order that he might have an interview with him. Balboa, with the unsuspicious confidence of a man conscious of no crime, instantly obeyed the summons; but as soon as he entered the place, he was arrested by order of Pedrarias, whose impatience to satiate his revenge did not suffer him to languish long in confinement. Judges were immediately appointed to proceed to his trial. An accusation of disloyalty to the king, and of an intention to revolt against the governor was preferred against him. Sentence of death was pronounced; and though the judges who passed it, seconded by the whole colony, interceded warmly for his pardon, Pedrarias continued inexorable; and the Spaniards beheld, with astonishment and sorrow, the public execution of a man whom they universally deemed more capable than any one who had borne command in America, of forming and accomplishing great designs.† Upon his death, the expedition which he had planned was relinquished. Pedrarias, notwithstanding the violence and injustice of his proceedings, was not only screened from punishment by the powerful patronage of the Bishop of Burgos and other courtiers, but continued in power. Soon after he obtained permission to remove the colony from its unwholesome station of Santa Maria to Panama, on the opposite side of the isthmus; and though it did not gain much in point of healthfulness by the change, the commodious situation of this new settlement contributed greatly to facilitate the subsequent conquests of the Spaniards in the extensive countries situated upon the Southern Ocean.‡

During these transactions in Darien [1515], the history of which it was proper to carry on in an uninterrupted tenour, several important events occurred with respect to the discovery, the conquest, and government of other provinces in the New World. Ferdinand was so intent upon opening

* Herrera, dec. 2. lib. i. c. 3. lib. ii. c. 11. 13. 21. † Ibid. dec. 2. lib. ii. c. 21, 22. ‡ Ibid. lib iv. c. 1.

a communication with the Molucca or Spice Islands by the west, that in the year one thousand five hundred and fifteen he fitted out two ships at his own expense, in order to attempt such a voyage, and gave the command of them to Juan Diaz de Solis, who was deemed one of the most skilful navigators in Spain. He stood along the coast of South America, and on the first of January, one thousand five hundred and sixteen, entered a river which he called Janeiro, where an extensive commerce is now carried on. From thence he proceeded to a spacious bay, which he supposed to be the entrance into a strait that communicated with the Indian Ocean; but, upon advancing further, he found it to be the mouth of Rio de Plata, one of the vast rivers by which the southern continent of America is watered. In endeavouring to make a descent in this country, De Solis and several of his crew were slain by the natives, who, in sight of the ships, cut their bodies in pieces, roasted and devoured them. Discouraged with the loss of their commander, and terrified at this shocking spectacle, the surviving Spaniards set sail for Europe, without aiming at any further discovery.* Though this attempt proved abortive, it was not without benefit. It turned the attention of ingenious men to this course of navigation, and prepared the way for a more fortunate voyage, by which, a few years posterior to this period, the great design that Ferdinand had in view was accomplished.

Though the Spaniards were thus actively employed in extending their discoveries and settlements in America, they still considered Hispaniola as their principal colony, and the seat of government. Don Diego Columbus wanted neither inclination nor abilities to have rendered the members of this colony, who were most immediately under his jurisdiction, prosperous and happy. But he was circumscribed in all his operations by the suspicious policy of Ferdinand, who on every occasion, and under pretexts the most frivolous, retrenched his privileges, and encouraged the treasurer, the judges, and other subordinate officers to counteract his measures, and to dispute his authority. The most valuable prerogative which the governor possessed was that of distributing Indians among the Spaniards settled in the island. The rigorous servitude of those unhappy men having been but little mitigated by all the regulations in their favour, the power of parcelling out such necessary instruments of labour at pleasure, secured to the governor great influence in the colony. In order to strip him of this, Ferdinand created a new office, with the power of distributing the Indians, and bestowed it upon Rodrigo Albuquerque, a relation of Zapata, his confidential minister Mortified with the injustice as well as indignity of this invasion upon his rights, in a point so essential, Don Diego could no longer remain in a place where his power and consequence were almost annihilated. He repaired to Spain with the vain hopes of obtaining redress.† Albuquerque entered upon his office with all the rapacity of an indigent adventurer impatient to amass wealth. He began with taking the exact number of Indians in the island, and found that from sixty thousand, who in the year one thousand five hundred and eight survived after all their sufferings, they were now reduced to fourteen thousand. These he threw into separate divisions or lots, and bestowed them upon such as were willing to purchase them at the highest price. By this arbitrary distribution several of the natives were removed from their original habitations, many were taken from their ancient masters, and all of them subjected to heavier burdens, and to more intolerable labour, in order to reimburse their new proprietors.—Those additional calamities completed the misery, and hastened on the extinction of this wretched and innocent race of men.‡

The violence of these proceedings, together with the fatal consequences which attended them, not only excited complaints among such as thought

* Herrera, dec. 2. lib. i c. 7. P. Martyr, dec. p. 317.

† Ibid. dec 1 lib. ix. c. 5. lib x. c. 12.

‡ Ibid. dec. 1. lib. x c. 12.

themselves aggrieved, but touched the hearts of all who retained any sentiments of humanity. From the time that ecclesiastics were sent as instructors into America, they perceived that the rigour with which their countrymen treated the natives, rendered their ministry altogether fruitless. The missionaries, in conformity to the mild spirit of that religion which they were employed to publish, early remonstrated against the maxims of the planters with respect to the Americans, and condemned the *repartimientos*, or *distributions*, by which they were given up as slaves to their conquerors, as no less contrary to natural justice and the precepts of Christianity than to sound policy. The Dominicans, to whom the instruction of the Americans was originally committed, were most vehement in testifying against the *repartimientos*. In the year one thousand five hundred and eleven, Montesino, one of their most eminent preachers, inveighed against this practice, in the great church of St. Domingo, with all the impetuosity of popular eloquence. Don Diego Columbus, the principal officers of the colony, and all the laymen who had been his hearers, complained of the monk to his superiors; but they, instead of condemning, applauded his doctrine as equally pious and seasonable. The Franciscans, influenced by the spirit of opposition and rivalship which subsists between the two orders, discovered some inclination to take part with the laity, and to espouse the defence of the *repartimientos*. But as they could not with decency give their avowed approbation to a system of oppression so repugnant to the spirit of religion, they endeavoured to palliate what they could not justify, and alleged, in excuse for the conduct of their countrymen, that it was impossible to carry on any improvement in the colony, unless the Spaniards possessed such dominion over the natives that they could compel them to labour.*

The Dominicans, regardless of such political and interested considerations, would not relax in any degree the rigour of their sentiments, and even refused to absolve, or admit to the sacrament, such of their countrymen as continued to hold the natives in servitude.† Both parties applied to the king for his decision in a matter of such importance. Ferdinand empowered a committee of his privy council, assisted by some of the most eminent civilians and divines in Spain, to hear the deputies sent from Hispaniola in support of their respective opinions. After a long discussion, the speculative point in controversy was determined in favour of the Dominicans, the Indians were declared to be a free people entitled to all the natural rights of men; but notwithstanding this decision, the *repartimientos* were continued upon their ancient footing.‡ As this determination admitted the principle upon which the Dominicans founded their opinion, they renewed their efforts to obtain relief for the Indians with additional boldness and zeal. At length, in order to quiet the colony, which was alarmed by their remonstrances and censures, Ferdinand issued a decree of his privy council [1513], declaring, that after mature consideration of the Apostolic Bull, and other titles by which the crown of Castile claimed a right to its possessions in the New World, the servitude of the Indians was warranted both by the laws of God and of man; that unless they were subjected to the dominion of the Spaniards, and compelled to reside under their inspection, it would be impossible to reclaim them from idolatry, or to instruct them in the principles of the Christian faith; that no further scruple ought to be entertained concerning the lawfulness of the *repartimientos*, as the king and council were willing to take the charge of that upon their own consciences; and that therefore the Dominicans and monks of other religious orders should abstain for the future from those invectives which, from an excess of charitable but ill-informed zeal, they had uttered against that practice.§

That his intention of adhering to this decree might be fully understood,

* Herrera, dec. 1. lib. viii. c. 11. Oviedo, lib. iii. c. 6. p. 97. † Oviedo, lib. iii. c. 6. p. 97.
‡ Herrera, dec. 1. lib. viii. c. 12. lib. ix. c. 5 § Ibid. dec. 1. lib. ix. c. 14.

Ferdinand conferred new grants of Indians upon several of his courtiers [25]. But, in order that he might not seem altogether inattentive to the rights of humanity, he published an edict, in which he endeavoured to provide for the mild treatment of the Indians under the yoke to which he subjected them; he regulated the nature of the work which they should be required to perform; he prescribed the mode in which they should be clothed and fed, and gave directions with respect to their instructions in the principles of Christianity.*

But the Dominicans, who from their experience of what was past judged concerning the future, soon perceived the inefficacy of those provisions, and foretold, that as long as it was the interest of individuals to treat the Indians with rigour, no public regulations could render their servitude mild or tolerable. They considered it as vain, to waste their own time and strength in attempting to communicate the sublime truths of religion to men whose spirits were broken and their faculties impaired by oppression. Some ot them in despair, requested the permission of their superiors to remove to the continent, and to pursue the object of their mission among such of the natives as were not hitherto corrupted by the example of the Spaniards, or alienated by their cruelty from the Christian faith. Such as remained in Hispaniola continued to remonstrate, with decent firmness, against the servitude of the Indians.†

The violent operations of Albuquerque, the new distributor of Indians, revived the zeal of the Dominicans against the *repartimientos*, and called forth an advocate for that oppressed people, who possessed all the courage, the talents, and activity requisite in supporting such a desperate cause. This was Bartholomew de las Casas, a native of Seville, and one of the clergymen sent out with Columbus in his second voyage to Hispaniola, in order to settle in that island. He early adopted the opinion prevalent among ecclesiastics, with respect to the unlawfulness of reducing the natives to servitude; and that he might demonstrate the sincerity of his conviction, he relinquished all the Indians who had fallen to his own share in the division of the inhabitants among their conquerors, declaring that he should ever bewail his own misfortune and guilt, in having exercised for a moment this impious dominion over his fellow-creatures.‡ From that time he became the avowed patron of the Indians; and by his bold interpositions in their behalf, as well as by the respect due to his abilities and character, he had often the merit of setting some bounds to the excesses of his countrymen. He did not fail to remonstrate warmly against the proceedings of Albuquerque; and though he soon found that attention to his own interest rendered this rapacious officer deaf to admonition, he did not abandon the wretched people whose cause he had espoused. He instantly set out for Spain, with the most sanguine hopes of opening the eyes and softening the heart of Ferdinand, by that striking picture of the oppression of his new subjects which he would exhibit to his view.§

He easily obtained admittance to the King, whom he found in a declining state of health. With much freedom, and no less eloquence, he represented to him all the fatal effects of the *repartimientos* in the New World, boldly charging him with the guilt of having authorized this impious measure, which had brought misery and destruction upon a numerous and innocent race of men, whom Providence had placed under his protection. Ferdinand, whose mind as well as body was much enfeebled by his distemper, was greatly alarmed at this charge of impiety, which at another juncture he would have despised. He listened with deep compunction to the discourse of Las Casas, and promised to take into serious consideration

* Herrera, dec. 1. lib. ix. c. 14. † Id. ibid. Touron. Histoire Générale de l'Amérique, tom. i p. 252. ‡ Fr. Aug. Davila Padilla Hist. de la Fundacion de la Provincia de St. Jago de Mexico, p. 303, 304. Herrera, dec. 1. lib. x. c. 12. § Herrera, dec. 1. lib. x. c. 12. Dec. 2. lib. i. c. 11. Davila Padilla Hist. p. 304.

the means of redressing the evil of which he complained. But death prevented him from executing his resolution. Charles of Austria, to whom all his crowns devolved, resided at that time in his paternal dominions in the Low Countries. Las Casas, with his usual ardour, prepared immediately to set out for Flanders, in order to occupy the ear of the young monarch, when Cardinal Ximenes, who, as regent, assumed the reins of government in Castile, commanded him to desist from the journey, and engaged to hear his complaints in person.

He accordingly weighed the matter with attention equal to its importance; and as his impetuous mind delighted in schemes bold and uncommon, he soon fixed upon a plan which astonished the ministers trained up under the formal and cautious administration of Ferdinand. Without regarding either the rights of Don Diego Columbus, or the regulations established by the late King, he resolved to send three persons to America as superintendents of all the colonies there, with authority, after examining all circumstances on the spot, to decide finally with respect to the point in question. It was a matter of deliberation and delicacy to choose men qualified for such an important station. As all the laymen settled in America, or who had been consulted in the administration of that department, had given their opinion that the Spaniards could not keep possession of their new settlements, unless they were allowed to retain their dominion over the Indians, he saw that he could not rely on their impartiality, and determined to commit the trust to ecclesiastics. As the Dominicans and Franciscans had already espoused opposite sides in the controversy, he, from the same principle of impartiality, excluded both these fraternities from the commission. He confined his choice to the monks of St. Jerome, a small but respectable order in Spain. With the assistance of their general, and in concert with Las Casas, he soon pitched upon three persons whom he deemed equal to the charge. To them he joined Zuazo, a private lawyer of distinguished probity, with unbounded power to regulate all judicial proceedings in the colonies. Las Casas was appointed to accompany them, with the title of protector of the Indians.*

To vest such extraordinary powers, as might at once overturn the system of government established in the New World, in four persons, who, from their humble condition in life, were little entitled to possess this high authority, appeared to Zapata, and other ministers of the late king, a measure so wild and dangerous, that they refused to issue the despatches necessary for carrying it into execution. But Ximenes was not of a temper patiently to brook opposition to any of his schemes. He sent for the refractory ministers, and addressed them in such a tone that in the utmost consternation they obeyed his orders.† The superintendents, with their associate Zuazo and Las Casas, sailed for St. Domingo. Upon their arrival, the first act of their authority was to set at liberty all the Indians who had been granted to the Spanish courtiers, or to any person not residing in America. This, together with the information which had been received from Spain concerning the object of the commission, spread a general alarm. The colonists concluded that they were to be deprived at once of the hands with which they carried on their labour, and that, of consequence, ruin was unavoidable. But the fathers of St. Jerome proceeded with such caution and prudence as soon dissipated all their fears. They discovered, in every step of their conduct, a knowledge of the world, and of affairs, which is seldom acquired in a cloister; and displayed a moderation as well as gentleness still more rare among persons trained up in the solitude and austerity of a monastic life. Their ears were open to information from every quarter; they compared the different accounts which they received; and, after a mature consideration of the whole, they were fully satisfied that the state of the colony rendered it impossible to adopt the plan proposed by Las Casas,

* Herrera, dec. 2. lib. ii. c. 3. † Ibid. dec. 2. lib. ii. c. 6.

and recommended by the Cardinal. They plainly perceived that the Spaniards settled in America were so few in number, that they could neither work the mines which had been opened, nor cultivate the country; that they depended for effecting both upon the labour of the natives, and, if deprived of it, they must instantly relinquish their conquests, or give up all the advantages which they derived from them; that no allurement was so powerful as to surmount the natural aversion of the Indians to any laborious effort, and that nothing but the authority of a master could compel them to work; and if they were not kept constantly under the eye and discipline of a superior, so great was their natural listlessness and indifference, that they would neither attend to religious instruction, nor observe those rites of Christianity which they had been already taught. Upon all those accounts, the superintendents found it necessary to tolerate the *repartimientos*, and to suffer the Indians to remain under subjection to their Spanish masters. They used their utmost endeavours, however, to prevent the fatal effects of this establishment, and to secure to the Indians the consolation of the best treatment compatible with a state of servitude. For this purpose, they revived former regulations, they prescribed new ones, they neglected no circumstance that tended to mitigate the rigour of the yoke; and by their authority, their example, and their exhortations, they laboured to inspire their countrymen with sentiments of equity and gentleness towards the unhappy people upon whose industry they depended. Zuazo, in his department, seconded the endeavours of the superintendents. He reformed the courts of justice in such a manner as to render their decisions equitable as well as expeditious, and introduced various regulations which greatly improved the interior policy of the colony. The satisfaction which his conduct and that of the superintendents gave was now universal among the Spaniards settled in the New World; and all admired the boldness of Ximenes in having departed from the ordinary path of business in forming his plan, as well as his sagacity in pitching upon persons whose wisdom, moderation, and disinterestedness rendered them worthy of this high trust.*

Las Casas alone was dissatisfied. The prudential consideration which influenced the superintendents made no impression upon him. He regarded their idea of accommodating their conduct to the state of the colony, as the maxim of an unhallowed timid policy, which tolerated what was unjust because it was beneficial. He contended that the Indians were by nature free, and, as their protector, he required the superintendents not to bereave them of the common privilege of humanity. They received his most virulent remonstrances without emotion, but adhered firmly to their own system. The Spanish planters did not bear with him so patiently, and were ready to tear him in pieces for insisting in a requisition so odious to them. Las Casas, in order to screen himself from their rage, found it necessary to take shelter in a convent; and perceiving that all his efforts in America were fruitless, he soon set out for Europe, with a fixed resolution not to abandon the protection of a people whom he deemed to be cruelly oppressed.†

Had Ximenes retained that vigour of mind with which he usually applied to business, Las Casas must have met with no very gracious reception upon his return to Spain. But he found the Cardinal languishing under a mortal distemper, and preparing to resign his authority to the young king, who was daily expected from the Low Countries. Charles arrived, took possession of the government, and, by the death of Ximenes, lost a minister whose abilities and integrity entitled him to direct his affairs. Many of the Flemish nobility had accompanied their sovereign to Spain. From that warm predilection to his countrymen, which was natural at his age, he consulted them with respect to all the transactions in his new kingdom; and they, with

* Herrera, dec. 2. lib. ii. c. 15. Remesal, Hist. Gener. lib. ii. c. 14, 15, 16 † Ibid. dec. 2 lib. ii. c 16.

an indiscreet eagerness, intruded themselves into every business, and seized almost every department of administration.* The direction of American affairs was an object too alluring to escape their attention. Las Casas observed their growing influence; and though projectors are usually too sanguine to conduct their schemes with much dexterity, he possessed a bustling, indefatigable activity, which sometimes accomplishes its purposes with greater success than the most exquisite discernment and address. He courted the Flemish ministers with assiduity. He represented to them the absurdity of all the maxims hitherto adopted with respect to the government of America, particularly during the administration of Ferdinand, and pointed out the defects of those arrangements which Ximenes had introduced. The memory of Ferdinand was odious to the Flemings. The superior virtues and abilities of Ximenes had long been the object of their envy. They fondly wished to have a plausible pretext for condemning the measures both of the monarch and of the minister, and of reflecting some discredit on their political wisdom. The friends of Don Diego Columbus, as well as the Spanish courtiers who had been dissatisfied with the Cardinal's administration, joined Las Casas in censuring the scheme of sending superintendents to America. This union of so many interests and passions was irresistible; and in consequence of it the fathers of St. Jerome, together with their associate Zuazo, were recalled. Roderigo de Figueroa, a lawyer of some eminence, was appointed chief judge of the island, and received instructions, in compliance with the request of Las Casas, to examine once more, with the utmost attention, the point in controversy between him and the people of the colony, with respect to the treatment of the natives; and in the mean time to do every thing in his power to alleviate their sufferings, and prevent the extinction of the race.†

This was all that the zeal of Las Casas could procure at that juncture in favour of the Indians. The impossibility of carrying on any improvements in America, unless the Spanish planters could command the labour of the natives, was an insuperable objection to his plan of treating them as free subjects. In order to provide some remedy for this, without which he found it was in vain to mention his scheme, Las Casas proposed to purchase a sufficient number of negroes from the Portuguese settlements on the coast of Africa, and to transport them to America, in order that they might be employed as slaves in working the mines and cultivating the ground. One of the first advantages which the Portuguese had derived from their discoveries in Africa arose from the trade in slaves. Various circumstances concurred in reviving this odious commerce, which had been long abolished in Europe, and which is no less repugnant to the feelings of humanity than to the principles of religion. As early as the year one thousand five hundred and three, a few negro slaves had been sent into the New World.‡ In the year one thousand five hundred and eleven, Ferdinand permitted the importation of them in greater numbers.§ They were found to be a more robust and hardy race than the natives of America. They were more capable of enduring fatigue, more patient under servitude, and the labour of one negro was computed to be equal to that of four Indians.|| Cardinal Ximenes, however, when solicited to encourage this commerce, peremptorily rejected the proposition, because he perceived the iniquity of reducing one race of men to slavery, while he was consulting about the means of restoring liberty to another.¶ But Las Casas, from the inconsistency natural to men who hurry with headlong impetuosity towards a favourite point, was incapable of making this distinction. While he contended earnestly for the liberty of the people born in one quarter of the globe, he laboured to enslave the

* History of Charles V. † Herrera, dec. 2. lib. ii. c. 16. 19. 21. lib. iii. c. 7, 8. ‡ Ibid. dec. 1. lib. v. c. 12. § Ibid. lib. viii. c. 9. || Ibid. lib. ix. c. 5. ¶ Ibid. dec. 2. lib. ii. c. 8.

inhabitants of another region; and in the warmth of his zeal to save the Americans from the yoke, pronounced it to be lawful and expedient to impose one still heavier upon the Africans. Unfortunately for the latter, Las Casas's plan was adopted. Charles granted a patent to one of his Flemish favourites, containing an exclusive right of importing four thousand negroes into America. The favourite sold his patent to some Genoese merchants for twenty-five thousand ducats, and they were the first who brought into a regular form that commerce for slaves between Africa and America, which has since been carried on to such an amazing extent.*

But the Genoese merchants [1518], conducting their operations, at first, with the rapacity of monopolists, demanded such a high price for negroes, that the number imported into Hispaniola made no great change upon the state of the colony. Las Casas, whose zeal was no less inventive than indefatigable, had recourse to another expedient for the relief of the Indians He observed, that most of the persons who had settled hitherto in America, were sailors and soldiers employed in the discovery or conquest of the country; the younger sons of noble families, allured by the prospect of acquiring sudden wealth; or desperate adventurers, whom their indigence or crimes forced to abandon their native land. Instead of such men, who were dissolute, rapacious, and incapable of that sober persevering industry which is requisite in forming new colonies, he proposed to supply the settlements in Hispaniola and other parts of the New World with a sufficient number of labourers and husbandmen, who should be allured by suitable premiums to remove thither. These, as they were accustomed to fatigue, would be able to perform the work to which the Indians, from the feebleness of their constitution, were unequal, and might soon become useful and opulent citizens. But though Hispaniola stood much in need of a recruit of inhabitants, having been visited at this time with the small-pox, which swept off almost all the natives who had survived their long continued oppression; and though Las Casas had the countenance of the Flemish ministers, this scheme was defeated by the bishop of Burgos, who thwarted all his projects.†

Las Casas now despaired of procuring any relief for the Indians in those places where the Spaniards were already settled. The evil was become so inveterate there as not to admit of a cure. But such discoveries were daily making in the continent as gave a high idea both of its extent and populousness. In all those vast regions there was but one feeble colony planted; and except a small spot on the isthmus of Darien, the natives still occupied the whole country. This opened a new and more ample field for the humanity and zeal of Las Casas, who flattered himself that he might prevent a pernicious system from being introduced there, though he had failed of success in his attempts to overturn it where it was already established. Full of this idea, he applied for a grant of the unoccupied country stretching along the seacoast from the Gulf of Paria to the western frontier of that province now known by the name of Santa Martha. He proposed to settle there with a colony composed of husbandmen, labourers, and ecclesiastics. He engaged in the space of two years to civilize ten thousand of the natives, and to instruct them so thoroughly in the arts of social life, that from the fruits of their industry an annual revenue of fifteen thousand ducats should arise to the king. In ten years he expected that his improvements would be so far advanced as to yield annually sixty thousand ducats. He stipulated, that no soldier or sailor should ever be permitted to settle in this district; and that no Spaniard whatever should enter it without his permission. He even projected to clothe the people whom he took along with him in some distinguishing garb, which did not resemble the Spanish dress, that they might appear to the natives to be a different race of men

* Herrera dec. 1. lib. ii. c. 20. † Ibid. dec. 2. lib. ii. c. 21.

from those who had brought so many calamities upon their country.* From this scheme, of which I have traced only the great lines, it is manifest that Las Casas had formed ideas concerning the method of treating the Indians, similar to those by which the Jesuits afterwards carried on their great operations in another part of the same continent. He supposed that the Europeans, by availing themselves of that ascendant which they possessed in consequence of their superior progress in science and improvement, might gradually form the minds of the Americans to relish those comforts of which they were destitute, might train them to the arts of civil life, and render them capable of its functions.

But to the bishop of Burgos, and the council of the Indies, this project appeared not only chimerical, but dangerous in a high degree. They deemed the faculties of the Americans to be naturally so limited, and their indolence so excessive, that every attempt to instruct or to improve them would be fruitless. They contended, that it would be extremely imprudent to give the command of a country extending above a thousand miles along the coast to a fanciful presumptuous enthusiast, a stranger to the affairs of the world, and unacquainted with the arts of government. Las Casas, far from being discouraged with a repulse, which he had reason to expect, had recourse once more to the Flemish favourites, who zealously patronized his scheme merely because it had been rejected by the Spanish ministers. They prevailed with their master, who had lately been raised to the Imperial dignity, to refer the consideration of this measure to a select number of his privy counsellors; and Las Casas having excepted against the members of the council of the Indies, as partial and interested, they were all excluded. The decision of men chosen by recommendation of the Flemings was perfectly conformable to their sentiments. They warmly approved of Las Casas's plan, and gave orders for carrying it into execution, but restricted the territory allotted him to three hundred miles along the coast of Cumana; allowing him, however, to extend it as far as he pleased towards the interior part of the country.†

This determination did not pass uncensured. Almost every person who had been in the West Indies exclaimed against it, and supported their opinion so confidently, and with such plausible reasons, as made it advisable to pause and to review the subject more deliberately. Charles himself, though accustomed, at this early period of his life, to adopt the sentiments of his ministers with such submissive deference as did not promise that decisive vigour of mind which distinguished his riper years, could not help suspecting that the eagerness with which the Flemings took part in every affair relating to America flowed from some improper motive, and began to discover an inclination to examine in person into the state of the question concerning the character of the Americans, and the proper manner of treating them. An opportunity of making this inquiry with great advantage soon occurred [June 20]. Quevedo, the bishop of Darien, who had accompanied Pedrarias to the continent in the year one thousand five hundred and thirteen, happened to land at Barcelona, where the court then resided. It was quickly known that his sentiments concerning the talents and disposition of the Indians differed from those of Las Casas: and Charles naturally concluded that by confronting two respectable persons, who, during their residence in America, had full leisure to observe the manners of the people whom they pretended to describe, he might be able to discover which of them had formed his opinion with the greatest discernment and accuracy.

A day for this solemn audience was appointed. The emperor appeared with extraordinary pomp, and took his seat on a throne in the great hall of

* Herrera, dec. 2. lib. iv. c. 2.

† Gomara Hist. Gener. c. 77 Herrera, dec. 2. lib. iv c. 3. Oviedo, lib. xix. c. 5.

the palace. His principal courtiers attended. Don Diego Columbus, admiral of the Indies, was summoned to be present. The bishop of Darien was called upon first to deliver his opinion. He, in a short discourse, lamented the fatal desolation of America by the extinction of so many of its inhabitants; he acknowledged that this must be imputed, in some degree, to the extensive rigour and inconsiderate proceedings of the Spaniards; but declared that all the people of the New World whom he had seen, either in the continent or in the islands, appeared to him to be a race of men marked out, by the inferiority of their talents, for servitude, and whom it would be impossible to instruct or improve, unless they were kept under the continual inspection of a master. Las Casas, at greater length and with more fervour, defended his own system. He rejected with indignation the idea that any race of men was born to servitude as irreligious and inhuman. He asserted that the faculties of the Americans were not naturally despicable, but unimproved; that they were capable of receiving instruction in the principles of religion, as well as of acquiring the industry and arts which would qualify them for the various offices of social life; that the mildness and timidity of their nature rendered them so submissive and docile, that they might be led and formed with a gentle hand. He professed that his intentions in proposing the scheme now under consideration were pure and disinterested; and though from the accomplishment of his designs inestimable benefits would result to the crown of Castile, he never had claimed, nor ever would receive, any recompense on that account.

Charles, after hearing both, and consulting with his ministers, did not think himself sufficiently informed to establish any general arrangement with respect to the state of the Indians; but as he had perfect confidence in the integrity of Las Casas, and as even the bishop of Darien admitted his scheme to be of such importance that a trial should be made of its effects, he issued a patent [1522], granting him the district of Cumana formerly mentioned, with full power to establish a colony there according to his own plan.*

Las Casas pushed on the preparations for his voyage with his usual ardour. But, either from his own inexperience in the conduct of affairs, or from the secret opposition of the Spanish nobility, who universally dreaded the success of an institution that might rob them of the industrious and useful hands which cultivated their estates, his progress in engaging husbandmen and labourers was extremely slow, and he could not prevail on more than two hundred to accompany him to Cumana.

Nothing, however, could damp his zeal. With this slender train, hardly sufficient to take possession of such a large territory, and altogether unequal to any effectual attempt towards civilizing its inhabitants, he set sail. The first place at which he touched was the island of Puerto Rico. There he received an account of a new obstacle to the execution of his scheme, more insuperable than any he had hitherto encountered. When he left America, in the year one thousand five hundred and sixteen, the Spaniards had little intercourse with any part of the continent except the countries adjacent to the Gulf of Darien. But as every species of internal industry began to stagnate in Hispaniola, when, by the rapid decrease of the natives, the Spaniards were deprived of those hands with which they had hitherto carried on their operations, this prompted them to try various expedients for supplying that loss. Considerable numbers of negroes were imported; but, on account of their exorbitant price, many of the planters could not afford to purchase them. In order to procure slaves at an easier rate, some of the Spaniards in Hispaniola fitted out vessels to cruise along the coast

* Herrera, dec. 2. lib. iv. c. 3, 4, 5. Argensola Annales d'Aragon, 74. 97. Remisal Hist. Gener. lib. ii. c. 19, 20.

of the continent. In places where they found themselves inferior in strength, they traded with the natives, and gave European toys in exchange for the plates of gold worn by them as ornaments; but, wherever they could surprise or overpower the Indians, they carried them off by force, and sold them as slaves.* In those predatory excursions such atrocious acts of violence and cruelty had been committed, that the Spanish name was held in detestation all over the continent. Whenever any ships appeared, the inhabitants either fled to the woods, or rushed down to the shore in arms to repel those hated disturbers of their tranquillity. They forced some parties of the Spaniards to retreat with precipitation; they cut off others; and in the violence of their resentment against the whole nation, they murdered two Dominican missionaries, whose zeal had prompted them to settle in the province of Cumana.† This outrage against persons revered for their sanctity excited such indignation among the people of Hispaniola, who, notwithstanding all their licentious and cruel proceedings, were possessed with a wonderful zeal for religion, and a superstitious respect for its ministers, that they determined to inflict exemplary punishment, not only upon the perpetrators of that crime, but upon the whole race. With this view, they gave the command of five ships and three hundred men to Diego Ocampo, with orders to lay waste the country of Cumana with fire and sword, and to transport all the inhabitants as slaves to Hispaniola. This armament Las Casas found at Puerto Rico, in its way to the continent; and as Ocampo refused to defer his voyage, he immediately perceived that it would be impossible to attempt the execution of his pacific plan in a country destined to be the seat of war and desolation.‡

In order to provide against the effects of this unfortunate incident, he set sail directly for St. Domingo [April 12], leaving his followers cantoned out among the planters in Puerto Rico. From many concurring causes, the reception which Las Casas met with in Hispaniola was very unfavourable. In his negotiations for the relief of the Indians, he had censured the conduct of his countrymen settled there with such honest severity as rendered him universally odious to them. They considered their own ruin as the inevitable consequence of his success. They were now elated with hope of receiving a large recruit of slaves from Cumana, which must be relinquished if Las Casas were assisted in settling his projected colony there. Figueroa, in consequence of the instructions which he had received in Spain, had made an experiment concerning the capacity of the Indians, that was represented as decisive against the system of Las Casas. He collected in Hispaniola a good number of the natives, and settled them in two villages, leaving them at perfect liberty, and with the uncontrolled direction of their own actions. But that people, accustomed to a mode of life extremely different from that which takes place wherever civilization has made any considerable progress, were incapable of assuming new habits at once. Dejected with their own misfortunes as well as those of their country, they exerted so little industry in cultivating the ground, appeared so devoid of solicitude or foresight in providing for their own wants, and were such strangers to arrangement in conducting their affairs, that the Spaniards pronounced them incapable of being formed to live like men in social life, and considered them as children, who should be kept under the perpetual tutelage of persons superior to themselves in wisdom and sagacity.§

Notwithstanding all those circumstances, which alienated the persons in Hispaniola to whom Las Casas applied from himself and from his measures, he, by his activity and perseverance, by some concessions and many threats, obtained at length a small body of troops to protect him

* Herrera, dec. 3. lib. ii. c. 3. † Oviedo, Hist. lib. xix. p. 3 ‡ Herrera, dec. 2. lib. ix. c. 8, 9. § Ibid. dec. 2. lib. x c. 5.

and his colony at their first landing. But upon his return to Puerto Rico, he found that the diseases of the climate had been fatal to several of his people; and that others having got employment in that island, refused to follow him. With the handful that remained, he set sail and landed in Cumana. Ocampo had executed his commission in that province with such barbarous rage, having massacred many of the inhabitants, sent others in chains to Hispaniola, and forced the rest to fly for shelter to the woods, that the people of a small colony, which he had planted at a place which he named *Toledo*, were ready to perish for want in a desolated country There, however, Las Casas was obliged to fix his residence, though deserted both by the troops appointed to protect him, and by those under the command of Ocampo, who foresaw and dreaded the calamities to which he must be exposed in that wretched station. He made the best provision in his power for the safety and subsistence of his followers, but as his utmost efforts availed little towards securing either the one or the other, he returned to Hispaniola, in order to solicit more effectual aid for the preservation of men who, from confidence in him, had ventured into a post of so much danger. Soon after his departure, the natives, having discovered the feeble and defenceless state of the Spaniards, assembled secretly, attacked them with the fury natural to men exasperated by many injuries, cut off a good number, and compelled the rest to fly in the utmost consternation to the island of Cubagua. The small colony settled there on account of the pearl fishery, catching the panic with which their countrymen had been seized, abandoned the island, and not a Spaniard remained in any part of the continent, or adjacent islands, from the Gulf of Paria to the borders of Darien. Astonished at such a succession of disasters, Las Casas was ashamed to show his face after this fatal termination of all his splendid schemes. He shut himself up in the convent of the Dominicans at St. Domingo, and soon after assumed the habit of that order.*

Though the expulsion of the colony from Cumana happened in the year one thousand five hundred and twenty-one, I have chosen to trace the progress of Las Casas's negotiations from their first rise to their final issue without interruption. His system was the object of long and attentive discussion; and though his efforts in behalf of the oppressed Americans, partly from his own rashness and imprudence, and partly from the malevolent opposition of his adversaries, were not attended with that success which he promised with too sanguine confidence, great praise is due to his humane activity, which gave rise to various regulations that were of some benefit to that unhappy people. I return now to the history of the Spanish discoveries as they occur in the order of time.†

Diego Velasquez, who conquered Cuba in the year one thousand five hundred and eleven, still retained the government of that island, as the deputy of Don Diego Columbus, though he seldom acknowledged his superior, and aimed at rendering his own authority altogether independent.‡ Under his prudent administration, Cuba became one of the most flourishing of the Spanish settlements. The fame of this allured thither many persons from the other colonies, in hopes of finding either some permanent establishment or some employment for their activity. As Cuba lay to the west of all the islands occupied by the Spaniards, and as the ocean which stretches beyond it towards that quarter had not hitherto been explored, these circumstances naturally invited the inhabitants to attempt new discoveries. An expedition for this purpose, in which activity and resolution might conduct to sudden wealth, was more suited to the genius of the age than the patient industry requisite in clearing ground and manufacturing sugar. Instigated

* Herrera, dec. 2. lib. x. c. 5. dec. 3. lib. ii. c. 3, 4, 5. Oviedo, Hist. lib. xix. c. 5. Gomara, c. 77. Davila Padilla, lib. i. c. 97. Remisal Hist. Gen. lib xi. c. 22, 23. † Herrera. dec. 2. lib. x. c 5. p 329 ‡ Ibid. lib. ii. c. 19.

by this spirit, several officers, who had served under Pedrarias in Darien, entered into an association to undertake a voyage of discovery. They persuaded Franscisco Hernandez Cordova, an opulent planter in Cuba, and a man of distinguished courage, to join with them in the adventure, and chose him to be their commander. Velasquez not only approved of the design, but assisted in carrying it on. As the veterans from Darien were extremely indigent, he and Cordova advanced money for purchasing three small vessels, and furnished them with every thing requisite either for traffic or for war. A hundred and ten men embarked on board of them, and sailed from St. Jago de Cuba, on the eighth of February, one thousand five hundred and seventeen. By the advice of their chief pilot, Antonio Alaminos, who had served under the first admiral Columbus, they stood directly west, relying on the opinion of that great navigator, who uniformly maintained that a westerly course would lead to the most important discoveries.

On the twenty-first day after their departure from St. Jago, they saw land, which proved to be *Cape Catoche*, the eastern point of that large peninsula projecting from the continent of America, which still retains its original name of *Yucatan*. As they approached the shore, five canoes came off full of people decently clad in cotton garments; an astonishing spectacle to the Spaniards, who had found every other part of America possessed by naked savages. Cordova endeavoured by small presents to gain the good will of these people. They, though amazed at the strange objects now presented for the first time to their view, invited the Spaniards to visit their habitations, with an appearance of cordiality. They landed accordingly, and as they advanced into the country, they observed with new wonder some large houses built with stone. But they soon found that, if the people of Yucatan had made progress in improvement beyond their countrymen, they were likewise more artful and warlike. For though the cazique had received Cordova with many tokens of friendship, he had posted a considerable body of his subjects in ambush behind a thicket, who, upon a signal given by him, rushed out and attacked the Spaniards with great boldness, and some degree of martial order. At the first flight of their arrows, fifteen of the Spaniards were wounded; but the Indians were struck with such terror by the sudden explosion of the fire arms, and so surprised at the execution done by them, by the cross bows, and by the other weapons of their new enemies, that they fled precipitately. Cordova quitted a country where he had met with such a fierce reception, carrying off two prisoners, together with the ornaments of a small temple which he plundered in his retreat.

He continued his course towards the west, without losing sight of the coast, and on the sixteenth day arrived at Campeachy. There the natives received them more hospitably; but the Spaniards were much surprised, that on all the extensive coast along which they had sailed, and which they imagined to be a large island, they had not observed any river [26]. As their water had began to fail, they advanced, in hopes of finding a supply; and at length they discovered the mouth of a river at Potonchan, some leagues beyond Campeachy.

Cordova landed all his troops, in order to protect the sailors while employed in filling the casks; but notwithstanding this precaution, the natives rushed down upon them with such fury and in such numbers, that forty seven of the Spaniards were killed upon the spot, and one man only of the whole body escaped unhurt. Their commander, though wounded in twelve different places, directed the retreat with presence of mind equal to the courage with which he had led them on in the engagement, and with much difficulty they regained their ships. After this fatal repulse, nothing remained but to hasten back to Cuba with their shattered forces. In their passage thither they suffered the most exquisite distress for want of water, that men, wounded and sickly, shut up in small vessels, and exposed to the heat of the torrid zone, can be supposed to endure. Some of them, sinking under these calamities, died by the way; Cordova, their commander, expired soon after they landed in Cuba.*

Notwithstanding the disastrous conclusion of this expedition, it contributed rather to animate than to damp a spirit of enterprise among the Spaniards. They had discovered an extensive country, situated at no great distance from Cuba, fertile in appearance, and possessed by a people far superior in improvement to any hitherto known in America. Though they had carried on little commercial intercourse with the natives, they had brought off some ornaments of gold, not considerable in value, but of singular fabric. These circumstances, related with the exaggeration natural to men desirous of heightening the merit of their own exploits, were more than sufficient to excite romantic hopes and expectations. Great numbers offered to engage in a new expedition. Velasquez, solicitous to distinguish himself by some service so meritorious as might entitle him to claim the government of Cuba independent of the admiral, not only encouraged their ardour, but at his own expense fitted out four ships for the voyage. Two hundred and forty volunteers, among whom were several persons of rank and fortune, embarked in this enterprise. The command of it was given to Juan de Grijalva, a young man of known merit and courage, with instructions to observe attentively the nature of the countries which he should discover, to barter for gold, and, if circumstances were inviting, to settle a colony in some proper station. He sailed from St. Jago de Cuba on the eighth of April, one thousand five hundred and eighteen. The pilot, Alaminos, held the same course as in the former voyage; but the violence of the currents carrying the ships to the south, the first land which they made was the island of *Cozumel*, to the east of Yucatan. As all the inhabitants fled to the woods and mountains at the approach of the Spaniards, they made no long stay there, and without any remarkable occurrence they reached Potonchan on the opposite side of the peninsula. The desire of avenging their countrymen, who had been slain there, concurred with their ideas of good policy, in prompting them to land, that they might chastise the Indians of that district with such exemplary rigour as would strike terror into all the people round them. But though they disembarked all their troops, and carried ashore some field pieces, the Indians fought with such courage, that the Spaniards gained the victory with difficulty, and were confirmed in their opinion that the inhabitants of this country would prove more formidable enemies than any they had met with in other parts of America. From Potonchan they continued their voyage towards the west, keeping as near as possible to the shore, and casting anchor every evening, from dread of the dangerous accidents to which they might be exposed in an unknown sea. During the day their eyes were turned continually towards land, with a mixture of surprise and wonder at the beauty of the country, as well as the novelty of the objects which they beheld. Many villages were scattered along the coast, in which they could distinguish houses of stone that appeared white and lofty at a distance. In the warmth of their admiration, they fancied these to be cities adorned with towers and pinnacles; and one of the soldiers happening to remark that this country resembled Spain in appearance, Grijalva, with universal applause, called it *New Spain*, the name which still distinguishes this extensive and opulent province of the Spanish empire in America [27]. They landed in a river which the natives called *Tabasco* [June 9]; and the fame of their

* Herrera, dec. 3. lib. ii. c. 17, 18. Hist. Verdadera de la Conquista de la Nueva Espana por Bernal Diaz del Castillo, cap. 1—7. Oviedo, lib. xvii. c. 3. Gomara, c. 52. P. Martyr de Insulis nuper inventis p. 329.

victory at Potonchan having reached this place, the cazique not only received them amicably, but bestowed presents upon them of such value, as confirmed the high ideas which the Spaniards had formed with respect to the wealth and fertility of the country. These ideas were raised still higher by what occurred at the place where they next touched. This was considerably to the west of Tabasco, in the province since known by the name of Guaxaca. There they were received with the respect paid to superior beings. The people perfumed them, as they landed, with incense of gum copal, and presented to them as offerings the choicest delicacies of their country. They were extremely fond of trading with their new visitants, and in six days the Spaniards obtained ornaments of gold of curious workmanship, to the value of fifteen thousand pesos, in exchange for European toys of small price. The two prisoners whom Cordova had brought from Yucatan, had hitherto served as interpreters; but as they did not understand the language of this country, the Spaniards learned from the natives by signs, that they were subjects of a great monarch called Montezuma, whose dominions extended over that and many other provinces Leaving this place, with which he had so much reason to be pleased, Grijalva continued his course towards the west. He landed on a small island [June 19], which he named the Isle of Sacrifices, because there the Spaniards beheld, for the first time, the horrid spectacle of human victims, which the barbarous superstition of the natives offered to their gods. He touched at another small island, which he called St. Juan de Ulua. From this place he despatched Pedro de Alvarado, one of his officers, to Velasquez, with a full account of the important discoveries which he had made, and with all the treasure that he acquired by trafficking with the natives. After the departure of Alvarado, he himself, with the remaining vessels, proceeded along the coast as far as the river Panuco, the country still appearing to be well peopled, fertile, and opulent.

Several of Grijalva's officers contended that it was not enough to have discovered those delightful regions, or to have performed, at their different landing-places, the empty ceremony of taking possession of them for the crown of Castile, and that their glory was incomplete, unless they planted a colony in some proper station, which might not only secure the Spanish nation a footing in the country, but, with the reinforcements which they were certain of receiving, might gradually subject the whole to the dominion of their sovereign. But the squadron had now been above five months at sea; the greatest part of their provisions was exhausted, and what remained of their stores so much corrupted by the heat of the climate, as to be almost unfit for use; they had lost some men by death; others were sickly; the country was crowded with people who seemed to be intelligent as well as brave; and they were under the government of one powerful monarch, who could bring them to act against their invaders with united force. To plant a colony under so many circumstances of disadvantage, appeared a scheme too perilous to be attempted. Grijalva, though possessed both of ambition and courage, was destitute of the superior talents capable of forming or executing such a great plan. He judged it more prudent to return to Cuba, having fulfilled the purpose of his voyage, and accomplished all that the armament which he commanded enabled him to perform. He returned to St. Jago de Cuba, on the twenty-sixth of October, from which he had taken his departure about six months before.*

This was the longest as well as the most successful voyage which the Spaniards had hitherto made in the New World. They had discovered that Yucatan was not an island as they had supposed, but part of the great

* Herrera, dec. 11, lib. iii. c. 1, 2. 9, 10. Bernal Diaz, c. 8. 17. Oviedo Hist. lib. xvii. c. 9. 20 Gomara, c. 49

continent of America. From Potonchan they had pursued their course for many hundred miles along a coast formerly unexplored, stretching at first towards the west, and then turning to the north; all the country which they had discovered appeared to be no less valuable than extensive. As soon as Alvarado reached Cuba, Velasquez, transported with success so far beyond his most sanguine expectations, immediately despatched a person of confidence to carry this important intelligence to Spain, to exhibit the rich productions of the countries which had been discovered by his means, and to solicit such an increase of authority as might enable and encourage him to attempt the conquest of them. Without waiting for the return of his messenger, or for the arrival of Grijalva, of whom he was become so jealous or distrustful that he was resolved no longer to employ him, he began to prepare such a powerful armament as might prove equal to an enterprise of so much danger and importance.

But as the expedition upon which Velasquez was now intent terminated in conquests of greater moment than what the Spaniards had hitherto achieved, and led them to the knowledge of a people, who, if compared with those tribes of America with whom they were hitherto acquainted, may be considered as highly civilized; it is proper to pause before we proceed to the history of events extremely different from those which we have already related, in order to take a view of the state of the New World when first discovered, and to contemplate the policy and manners of the rude uncultivated tribes that occupied all the parts of it with which the Spaniards were at this time acquainted.

# BOOK IV.

Twenty-six years had elasped since Columbus had conducted the people of Europe to the New World. During that period the Spaniards had made great progress in exploring its various regions. They had visited all the islands scattered in different clusters through that part of the ocean which flows in between North and South America. They had sailed along the eastern coast of the continent from the river De la Plata to the bottom of the Mexican Gulf, and had found that it stretched without interruption through this vast portion of the globe. They had discovered the great Southern Ocean, which opened new prospects in that quarter. They had acquired some knowledge of the coast of Florida, which led them to observe the continent as it extended in an opposite direction; and though they pushed their discoveries no further towards the North, other nations had visited those parts which they neglected. The English, in a voyage the motives and success of which shall be related in another part of this History, had sailed along the coast of America from Labrador to the confines of Florida; and the Portuguese, in quest of a shorter passage to the East Indies, had ventured into the northern seas, and viewed the same regions.* Thus, at the period where I have chosen to take a view of the state of the New World, its extent was known almost from its northern extremity to thirty-five degrees south of the equator. The countries which stretch from thence to the southern boundary of America, the great empire of Peru, and the interior state of the extensive dominions subject to the sovereigns of Mexico, were still undiseovered.

* Horrera, dec. 1. lib. vi c. 16

When we contemplate the New World, the first circumstance that strikes us is its immense extent. It was not a small portion of the earth, so inconsiderable that it might have escaped the observation or research of former ages, which Columbus discovered. He made known a new hemisphere, larger than either Europe, or Asia, or Africa, the three noted divisions of the ancient continent, and not much inferior in dimensions to a third part of the habitable globe.

America is remarkable, not only for its magnitude, but for its position. It stretches from the northern polar circle to a high southern latitude, above fifteen hundred miles beyond the furthest extremity of the old continent on that side of the line. A country of such extent passes through all the climates capable of becoming the habitation of man, and fit for yielding the various productions peculiar either to the temperate or to the torrid regions of the earth.

Next to the extent of the New World, the grandeur of the objects which it presents to view is most apt to strike the eye of an observer. Nature seems here to have carried on her operations upon a larger scale and with a bolder hand, and to have distinguished the features of this country by a peculiar magnificence. The mountains in America are much superior in height to those in the other divisions of the globe. Even the plain of Quito, which may be considered as the base of the Andes, is elevated further above the sea than the top of the Pyrenees. This stupendous ridge of the Andes, no less remarkable for extent than elevation, rises in different places more than one-third above the Peak of Teneriffe, the highest land in the ancient hemisphere. The Andes may literally be said to hide their heads in the clouds; the storms often roll, and the thunder bursts below their summits, which, though exposed to the rays of the sun in the centre of the torrid zone, are covered with everlasting snows [28].

From these lofty mountains descend rivers, proportionably large, with which the streams in the ancient continent are not to be compared, either for length of course, or the vast body of water which they roll towards the ocean. The Maragnon, the Orinoco, the Plata in South America, the Mississippi and St. Laurence in North America, flow in such spacious channels, that long before they feel the influence of the tide, they resemble arms of the sea rather than rivers of fresh water [29].

The lakes of the New World are no less conspicuous for grandeur than its mountains and rivers. There is nothing in other parts of the globe which resembles the prodigious chain of lakes in North America. They may properly be termed inland seas of fresh water; and even those of the second or third class in magnitude are of larger circuit (the Caspian Sea excepted) than the greatest lake of the ancient continent.

The New World is of a form extremely favourable to commercial intercourse. When a continent is formed, like Africa, of one vast solid mass, unbroken by arms of the sea penetrating into its interior parts, with few large rivers, and those at a considerable distance from each other, the greater part of it seems destined to remain for ever uncivilized, and to be debarred from any active or enlarged communication with the rest of mankind. When, like Europe, a continent is opened by inlets of the ocean of great extent, such as the Mediterranean and Baltic; or when, like Asia, its coasts is broken by deep bays advancing far into the country, such as the Black Sea, the Gulfs of Arabia, of Persia, of Bengal, of Siam, and of Leotang; when the surrounding seas are filled with large and fertile islands, and the continent itself watered with a variety of navigable rivers, those regions may be said to possess whatever can facilitate the progress of their inhabitants in commerce and improvement. In all these respects America may bear a comparison with the other quarters of the globe. The Gulf of Mexico, which flows in between North and South America, may be considered as a Mediterranean sea, which opens a maritime commerce with all the fertile countries by which it is encircled. The islands scattered in it are inferior only to those in the Indian Archipelago, in number, in magnitude, and in value. As we stretch along the northern division of the American hemisphere, the Bay of Chesapeak presents a spacious inlet, which conducts the navigator far into the interior parts of provinces no less fertile than extensive; and if ever the progress of culture and population shall mitigate the extreme rigour of the climate in the more northern districts of America, Hudson's Bay may become as subservient to commercial intercourse in that quarter of the globe, as the Baltic is in Europe. The other great portion of the New World is encompassed on every side by the sea, except one narrow neck which separates the Atlantic from the Pacific Ocean; and though it be not opened by spacious bays or arms of the sea, its interior parts are rendered accessible by a number of large rivers, fed by so many auxiliary streams, flowing in such various directions, that almost without any aid from the hand of industry and art, an inland navigation may be carried on through all the provinces from the river De la Plata to the Gulf of Paria. Nor is this bounty of nature confined to the southern division of America; its northern continent abounds no less in rivers which are navigable almost to their sources, and by its immense chain of lakes provision is made for an inland communication, more extensive and commodious than in any quarter of the globe. The countries stretching from the Gulf of Darien on one side, to that of California on the other, which form the chain that binds the two parts of the American continent together, are not destitute of peculiar advantages. Their coast on one side is washed by the Atlantic Ocean, on the other by the Pacific. Some of their rivers flow into the former, some into the latter, and secure to them all the commercial benefits that may result from a communication with both.

But what most distinguishes America from other parts of the earth is the peculiar temperature of its climate, and the different laws to which it is subject with respect to the distribution of heat and cold. We cannot determine with precision the portion of heat felt in any part of the globe, merely by measuring its distance from the equator. The climate of a country is affected, in some degree, by its elevation above the sea, by the extent of continent, by the nature of the soil, the height of adjacent mountains, and many other circumstances. The influence of these, however, is from various causes less considerable in the greater part of the ancient continent; and from knowing the position of any country there, we can pronounce with greater certainty what will be the warmth of its climate, and the nature of its productions.

The maxims which are founded upon observation of our hemisphere will not apply to the other. In the New World, cold predominates. The rigour of the frigid zone extends over half of those regions which should be temperate by their position. Countries where the grape and the fig should ripen, are buried under snow one half of the year; and lands situated in the same parallel with the most fertile and best cultivated provinces in Europe, are chilled with perpetual frosts, which almost destroy the power of vegetation [30]. As we advance to those parts of America which lie in the same parallel with provinces of Asia and Africa, blessed with a uniform enjoyment of such genial warmth as is most friendly to life and to vegetation, the dominion of cold continues to be felt, and winter reigns, though during a short period, with extreme severity. If we proceed along the American continent into the torrid zone, we shall find the cold prevalent in the New World extending itself also to this region of the globe, and mitigating the excess of its fervour. While the negro on the coast of Africa is scorched with unremitting heat, the inhabitant of Peru breathes an air equally mild and temperate, and is perpetually shaded under a canopy of gray clouds, which intercepts the fierce beams of the sun, without obstructing his friendly influence.* Along the eastern coast of America, the climate, though more similar to that of the torrid zone in other parts of the earth, is nevertheless considerably milder than in those countries of Asia and Africa which lie in the same latitude. If from the southern tropic we continue our progress to the extremity of the American continent, we meet with frozen seas, and countries horrid, barren, and scarcely habitable for cold, much sooner than in the north.†

Various causes combine in rendering the climate of America so extremely different from that of the ancient continent. Though the utmost extent of America towards the north be not yet discovered, we know that it advances much nearer to the pole than either Europe or Asia. Both these have large seas to the north, which are open during part of the year; and even when covered with ice, the wind that blows over them is less intensely cold than that which blows over land in the same high latitudes. But in America the land stretches from the river St. Laurence towards the pole, and spreads out immensely to the west. A chain of enormous mountains covered with snow and ice, runs through all this dreary region. The wind, in passing over such an extent of high and frozen land, becomes so impregnated with cold, that it acquires a piercing keenness, which it retains in its progress through warmer climates, and it is not entirely mitigated until it reach the Gulf of Mexico. Over all the continent of North America, a north-westerly wind and excessive cold are synonymous terms. Even in the most sultry weather, the moment that the wind veers to that quarter, its penetrating influence is felt in a transition from heat to cold no less violent than sudden. To this powerful cause we may ascribe the extraordinary dominion of cold, and its violent inroads into the southern provinces, in that part of the globe.‡

Other causes, no less remarkable, diminish the active power of heat in those parts of the American continent which lie between the tropics. In all that portion of the globe, the wind blows in an invariable direction from east to west. As this wind holds its course across the ancient continent, it arrives at the countries which stretch along the western shores of Africa, inflamed with all the fiery particles which it hath collected from the sultry plains of Asia, and the burning sands in the African deserts. The coast of Africa is, accordingly, the region of the earth which feels the most fervent heat, and is exposed to the unmitigated ardour of the torrid zone But this same wind, which brings such an accession of warmth to the countries lying between the river of Senegal and Cafraria, traverses the Atlantic Ocean before it reaches the American shore. It is cooled in its passage over this vast body of water, and is felt as a refreshing gale along the coast of Brazil [31], and Guiana, rendering these countries, though among the warmest in America, temperate, when compared with those which lie opposite to them in Africa [32]. As this wind advances in its course across America, it meets with immense plains covered with impenetrable forests, or occupied by large rivers, marshes, and stagnating waters, where it can recover no considerable degree of heat. At length it arrives at the Andes, which run from north to south through the whole continent. In passing over their elevated and frozen summits, it is so thoroughly cooled, that the greater part of the countries beyond them hardly feel the ardour to which they seem exposed by their situation.§ In the other provinces of America, from Tierra Ferme westward to the Mexican empire, the heat of the climate is tempered, in some places, by the elevation of the land above the sea, in others, by their extraordinary

* Voyage de Ulloa, tom. i. p. 453. Anson's Voyage, p.184.

† Anson's Voyage, p. 74; and Voyage de Quiros, chez. Hist. Gen. des Voyages, tom. xiv. p. 83. Richard Hist. Natur. de l'Air, ii. 305, &c.

‡ Charlevoix Hist. de Nouv. Fr. iii. 165. Hist. Généralé des Voyages, tom. xv 215, &c.

§ Acosta Hist. Novi Orbis, lib. ii. c. 11. Buffon Hist. Naturelle, &c. tom. ii. 512, &c. ix. 107, &c. Osborn's Collect. of Voyages, ii. p. 868.

humidity, and in all, by the enormous mountains scattered over this tract The islands of America in the torrid zone are either small or mountainous, and are fanned alternately by refreshing sea and land breezes.

The causes of the extraordinary cold towards the southern limits of America, and in the seas beyond it, cannot be ascertained in a manner equally satisfying. It was long supposed that a vast continent, distinguished by the name of *Terra Australis Incognita*, lay between the southern extremity of America and the Antarctic pole. The same principles which account for the extraordinary degree of cold in the northern regions of America, were employed in order to explain that which is felt at Cape Horn and the adjacent countries. The immense extent of the southern continent, and the large rivers which it poured into the ocean, were mentioned and admitted by philosophers as causes sufficient to occasion the unusual sensation of cold, and the still more uncommon appearances of frozen seas in that region of the globe. But the imaginary continent to which such influence was ascribed, having been searched for in vain, and the space which it was supposed to occupy having been found to be an open sea, new conjectures must be formed with respect to the causes of a temperature of climate, so extremely different from that which we experience in countries removed at the same distance from the opposite pole [33].

After contemplating those permanent and characteristic qualities of the American continent, which arise from the peculiarity of its situation, and the disposition of its parts, the next object that merits attention is its condition when first discovered, as far as that depended upon the industry and operations of man. The effects of human ingenuity and labour are more extensive and considerable than even our own vanity is apt at first to imagine. When we survey the face of the habitable globe, no small part of that fertility and beauty which we ascribe to the hand of nature, is the work of man. His efforts, when continued through a succession of ages, change the appearance and improve the qualities of the earth. As a great part of the ancient continent has long been occupied by nations far advanced in arts and industry, our eye is accustomed to view the earth in that form which it assumes when rendered fit to be the residence of a numerous race of men, and to supply them with nourishment.

But in the New World, the state of mankind was ruder, and the aspect of nature extremely different. Throughout all its vast regions, there were only two monarchies remarkable for extent of territory, or distinguished by any progress in improvement. The rest of this continent was possessed by small independent tribes, destitute of arts and industry, and neither capable to correct the defects nor desirous to meliorate the condition of hat part of the earth allotted to them for their habitation. Countries occupied by such people were almost in the same state as if they had been without inhabitants. Immense forests covered a great part of the uncultivated earth ; and as the hand of industry had not taught the rivers to run in a proper channel, or drained off the stagnating water, many of the most fertile plains were overflowed with inundations, or converted into marshes. In the southern provinces, where the warmth of the sun, the moisture of the climate, and the fertility of the soil, combine in calling forth the most vigorous powers of vegetation, the woods are so choked with its rank luxuriance as to be almost impervious, and the surface of the ground is hid from the eye under a thick covering of shrubs and herbs and weeds. In this state of wild unassisted nature, a great part of the large provinces in South America, which extend from the bottom of the Andes to the sea, still remain. The European colonies have cleared and cultivated a few spots along the coast ; but the original race of inhabitants, as rude and indolent as ever, have done nothing to open or improve a country possessing almost every advantage of situation and climate. As we advance towards the northern provinces of America, nature continues to wear the same uncultivated aspect, and, in proportion as the rigour of the climate increases, appears more desolate and horrid. There the forests, though not encumbered with the same exuberance of vegetation, are of immense extent; prodigious marshes overspread the plains, and few marks appear of human activity in any attempt to cultivate or embellish the earth. No wonder that the colonies sent from Europe were astonished at their first entrance into the New World. It appeared to them waste, solitary, and uninviting. When the English began to settle in America, they termed the countries of which they took possession, *The Wilderness*. Nothing but their eager expectation of finding mines of gold could have induced the Spaniards to penetrate through the woods and marshes of America, where at every step they observed the extreme difference between the uncultivated face of nature, and that which it acquires under the forming hand of industry and art [34].

The labour and operations of man not only improve and embellish the earth, but render it more wholesome and friendly to life. When any region lies neglected and destitute of cultivation, the air stagnates in the woods; putrid exhalations arise from the waters; the surface of the earth, loaded with rank vegetation, feels not the purifying influence of the sun or of the wind; the malignity of the distempers natural to the climate increases, and new maladies no less noxious are engendered. Accordingly, all the provinces of America, when first discovered, were found to be remarkably unhealthy. This the Spaniards experienced in every expedition into the New World, whether destined for conquest or settlement. Though by the natural constitution of their bodies, their habitual temperance, and the persevering vigour of their minds, they were as much formed as any people in Europe for active service in a sultry climate, they felt severely the fatal and pernicious qualities of those uncultivated regions through which they marched, or where they endeavoured to plant colonies. Great numbers were cut off by the unknown and violent diseases with which they were infected. Such as survived the destructive rage of those maladies, were not exempted from the noxious influence of the climate. They returned to Europe, according to the description of the early Spanish historians, feeble, emaciated, with languid looks, and complexions of such a sickly yellow colour as indicated the unwholesome temperature of the countries where they had resided.*

The uncultivated state of the New World affected not only the temperature of the air, but the qualities of its productions. The principle of life seems to have been less active and vigorous there than in the ancient continent. Notwithstanding the vast extent of America, and the variety of its climates, the different species of animals peculiar to it are much fewer in proportion than those of the other hemisphere. In the islands there were only four kinds of quadrupeds known, the largest of which did not exceed the size of a rabbit. On the continent, the variety was greater; and though the individuals of each kind could not fail of multiplying exceedingly when almost unmolested by men, who were neither so numerous, nor so united in society, as to be formidable enemies to the animal creation, the number of distinct species must still be considered as extremely small. Of two hundred different kinds of animals spread over the face of the earth, only about one-third existed in America at the time of its discovery.† Nature was not only less prolific in the New World, but she appears likewise to have been less vigorous in her productions. The animals originally belonging to this quarter of the globe appear to be of an inferior race, neither so robust nor so fierce as those of the other continent. America gives birth to no creature of such bulk as

* Gomara Hist. c. 20. 22. Oviedo Hist. lib. ii. c. 13. lib. v. c. 10. P. Martyr, Epist. 545. Decad. p. 176. † Buffon Hist. Naturelle, tom. ix. p. 86.

to be compared with the elephant or rhinoceros, or that equals the lion and tiger in strength and ferocity [35]. The *Tapyr* of Brazil, the largest quadruped of the ravenous tribe in the New World, is not larger than a calf of six months old. The *Puma* and *Jaguar*, its fiercest beasts of prey, which Europeans have inaccurately denominated lions and tigers, possess neither the undaunted courage of the former, nor the ravenous cruelty of the latter.* They are inactive and timid, hardly formidable to man, and often turn their backs upon the least appearance of resistance.† The same qualities in the climate of America which stinted the growth, and enfeebled the spirit, of its native animals, have proved pernicious to such as have migrated into it voluntarily from the other continent, or have been transported thither by the Europeans.‡ The bears, the wolves, the deer of America, are not equal in size to those of the Old World.§ Most of the domestic animals, with which the Europeans have stored the provinces wherein they settled, have degenerated with respect either to bulk or quality, in a country whose temperature and soil seem to be less favourable to the strength and perfection of the animal creation [36].

The same causes which checked the growth and the vigour of the more noble animals, were friendly to the propagation and increase of reptiles and insects. Though this is not peculiar to the New World, and those odious tribes, nourished by heat, moisture, and corruption, infest every part of the torrid zone; they multiply faster, perhaps, in America, and grow to a more monstrous bulk. As this country is on the whole less cultivated and less peopled than the other quarters of the earth, the active principle of life wastes its force in productions of this inferior form. The air is often darkened with clouds of insects, and the ground covered with shocking and noxious reptiles. The country around Porto Bello swarms with toads in such multitudes as hide the surface of the earth. At Guayaquil, snakes and vipers are hardly less numerous. Carthagena is infested with numerous flocks of bats, which annoy not only the cattle but the inhabitants.‖ In the islands, legions of ants have at different times consumed every vegetable production [37], and left the earth entirely bare as if it had been burned with fire. The damp forests and rank soil of the countries on the banks of the Orinoco and Maragnon teem with almost every offensive and poisonous creature which the power of a sultry sun can quicken into life.¶

The birds of the New World are not distinguished by qualities so conspicuous and characteristical as those which we have observed in its quadrupeds. Birds are more independent of man, and less affected by the changes which his industry and labour make upon the state of the earth. They have a greater propensity to migrate from one country to another, and can gratify this instinct of their nature without difficulty or danger. Hence the number of birds common to both continents is much greater than that of quadrupeds; and even such as are peculiar to America nearly resemble those with which mankind were acquainted in similar regions of the ancient hemisphere. The American birds of the torrid zone, like those of the same climate in Asia and Africa, are decked in plumage which dazzles the eye with the beauty of its colours; but nature, satisfied with clothing them in this gay dress, has denied most of them that melody of sound and variety of notes which catch and delight the ear. The birds of the temperate climates there, in the same manner as in our continent, are less

* Buffon Hist. Natur. tom. ix. p. 87. Maregravii Hist. Nat. Brazil, p. 229. † Buffon Hist. Natur. ix. 13. 203. Acosta Hist. lib. iv. c. 34. Pisonis Hist. p. 6. Herrera, dec. 4. lib. iv. c. 1. lib. x. c. 13. ‡ Churchill, v. p. 691. Ovalle Relat. of Chili, Church. iii. p. 10. Somario de Oviedo, c. 14—22. Voyage du Des Marchais, iii. 299. § Buffon Hist. Natur. ix. 103. Kalm's Travels i. 102. Biet. voy. de France Equinox. p. 339. ‖ Voyage de Ulloa, tom. i. p. 89. Ib. p 147. Herrera, dec. 11. lib. iii. c. 3. 19. ¶ Voyage de Condamine, p. 167. Gumilla, iii. 120, &c. Hist. Gener. des Voyages, xiv. 317. Dumont Mémoires sur la Louisiane, i. 108. Somario de Oviedo, c. 52—62.

splendid in their appearance; but, in compensation for that defect, they have voices of greater compass, and more melodious. In some districts of America, the unwholesome temperature of the air seems to be unfavourable even to this part of the creation. The number of birds is less than in other countries, and the traveller is struck with the amazing solitude and silence of its forests.* It is remarkable, however, that America, where the quadrupeds are so dwarfish and dastardly, should produce the *Condor* which is entitled to pre-eminence over all the flying tribe, in bulk, in strength, and in courage.†

The soil in a continent so extensive as America must, of course, be extremely various. In each of its provinces we find some distinguishing peculiarities, the description of which belongs to those who write their particular history. In general we may observe, that the moisture and cold, which predominate so remarkably in all parts of America, must have great influence upon the nature of its soil; countries lying in the same parallel with those regions which never feel the extreme rigour of winter in the ancient continent, are frozen over in America during a great part of the year. Chilled by this intense cold, the ground never acquires warmth sufficient to ripen the fruits which are found in the corresponding parts of the other continent. If we wish to rear in America the productions which abound in any particular district of the ancient world, we must advance several degrees nearer to the line than in the other hemisphere, as it requires such an increase of heat to counterbalance the natural frigidity of the soil and climate [38]. At the Cape of Good Hope, several of the plants and fruits peculiar to the countries within the tropics are cultivated with success; whereas, at St. Augustine in Florida, and Charles Town in South Carolina, though considerably nearer the line, they cannot be brought to thrive with equal certainty [39]. But, if allowance be made for this diversity in the degree of heat, the soil of America is naturally as rich and fertile as in any part of the earth. As the country was thinly inhabited, and by a people of little industry, who had none of the domestic animals which civilized nations rear in such vast numbers, the earth was not exhausted by their consumption. The vegetable productions, to which the fertility of the soil gave birth, often remained untouched, and, being suffered to corrupt on its surface, returned with increase into its bosom.‡ As trees and plants derive a great part of their nourishment from air and water; if they were not destroyed by man and other animals, they would render to the earth more, perhaps, than they take from it, and feed rather than impoverish it. Thus the unoccupied soil of America may have gone on enriching for many ages. The vast number as well as enormous size of the trees in America, indicate the extraordinary vigour of the soil in its native state. When the Europeans first began to cultivate the New World, they were astonished at the luxuriant power of vegetation in its virgin mould; and in several places the ingenuity of the planter is still employed in diminishing and wasting its superfluous fertility, in order to bring it down to a state fit for profitable culture§ [40].

Having thus surveyed the state of the New World at the time of its discovery, and considered the peculiar features and qualities which distinguish and characterize it, the next inquiry that merits attention is, How was America peopled? By what course did mankind migrate from the one continent to the other? And in what quarter is it most probable that a communication was opened between them?

We know, with infallible certainty, that all the human race spring from

* Bouguer Voy. au Perou, 17. Chanvalon Voyage à la Martinique, p. 96. Warren's Descript. Surinam. Osborn's Collect. ii. 924. Lettres Edif. xxiv. p. 339. Charlev. Hist. de la Nouv. France, iii. 155. † Voyage de Ulloa, i. 363. Voyage de Condamine, 175. Buffon Hist. Nat. xvi. 184. Voyage du Des Marchais, iii. 320. ‡ Buffon, Hist. Natur. i. 242. Kalm, i. 151. § Charlevoix, Hist de Nouv. Fran. iii. 405. Voyage du Des Marchais, iii. 229. Lery ap. de Bry. part iii. p. 174.

the same source, and that the descendants of one man, under the protection, as well as in obedience to the command of Heaven, multiplied and replenished the earth. But neither the annals nor the traditions of nations reach back to those remote ages, in which they took possession of the different countries where they are now settled. We cannot trace the branches of this first family, or point out with certainty the time and manner in which they divided and spread over the face of the globe Even among the most enlightened people, the period of authentic history is extremely short; and every thing prior to that is fabulous or obscure. It is not surprising, then, that the unlettered inhabitants of America, who have no solicitude about futurity, and little curiosity concerning what is passed, should be altogether unacquainted with their own original. The people on the two opposite coasts of America, who occupy those countries in America which approach nearest to the ancient continent are so remarkably rude, that it is altogether vain to search among them for such information as might discover the place from whence they came, or the ancestors of whom they are descended.* Whatever light has been thrown on this subject is derived not from the natives of America, but from the inquisitive genius of their conquerors.

When the people of Europe unexpectedly discovered a New World, removed at a vast distance from every part of the ancient continent which was then known, and filled with inhabitants whose appearance and manners differed remarkably from the rest of the human species, the question concerning their original became naturally an object of curiosity and attention. The theories and speculations of ingenious men with respect to this subject, would fill many volumes; but are often so wild and chimerical, that I should offer an insult to the understanding of my readers, if I attempted either minutely to enumerate or to refute them. Some have presumptuously imagined, that the people of America were not the offspring of the same common parent with the rest of mankind, but that they formed a separate race of men, distinguishable by peculiar features in the constitution of their bodies, as well as in the characteristic qualities of their minds. Others contend, that they are descended from some remnant of the antediluvian inhabitants of the earth, who survived the deluge which swept away the greatest part of the human species in the days of Noah; and preposterously suppose rude, uncivilized tribes, scattered over an uncultivated continent, to be the most ancient race of people on the earth. There is hardly any nation from the north to the south pole, to which some antiquary, in the extravagance of conjecture, has not ascribed the honour of peopling America. The Jews, the Canaanites, the Phœnicians, the Carthaginians, the Greeks, the Scythians, in ancient times, are supposed to have settled in this western world. The Chinese, the Swedes, the Norwegians, the Welsh, the Spaniards, are said to have sent colonies thither in later ages, at different periods and on various occasions. Zealous advocates stand forth to support the respective claims of those people; and though they rest upon no better foundation than the casual resemblance of some customs, or the supposed affinity between a few words in their different languages, much erudition and more zeal have been employed, to little purpose, in defence of the opposite systems. Those regions of conjecture and controversy belong not to the historian. His is a more limited province, confined by what is established by certain or highly probable evidence. Beyond this I shall not venture, in offering a few observations which may contribute to throw some light upon this curious and much agitated question

1. There are authors who have endeavoured by mere conjecture to account for the peopling of America. Some have supposed that it was

* Vinegas's Hist. of California, i. 60

originally united to the ancient continent, and disjoined from it by the shock of an earthquake, or the irruption of a deluge. Others have imagined, that some vessel being forced from its course by the violence of a westerly wind, might be driven by accident towards the American coast, and have given a beginning to population in that desolate continent.* But with respect to all those systems, it is in vain either to reason or inquire, because it is impossible to come to any decision. Such events as they suppose are barely possible, and may have happened. That they ever did happen, we have no evidence, either from the clear testimony of history, or from the obscure intimations of tradition.

2. Nothing can be more frivolous or uncertain than the attempts to discover the original of the Americans merely by tracing the resemblance between their manners and those of any particular people in the ancient continent. If we suppose two tribes, though placed in the most remote regions of the globe, to live in a climate nearly of the same temperature, to be in the same state of society, and to resemble each other in the degree of their improvement, they must feel the same wants, and exert the same endeavours to supply them. The same objects will allure, the same passions will animate them, and the same ideas and sentiments will arise in their minds. The character and occupations of the hunter in America must be little different from those of an Asiatic who depends for subsistence on the chase. A tribe of savages on the banks of the Danube must nearly resemble one upon the plains washed by the Mississippi. Instead then of presuming from this similarity, that there is any affinity between them, we should only conclude that the disposition and manners of men are formed by their situation, and arise from the state of society in which they live. The moment that begins to vary, the character of a people must change. In proportion as it advances in improvement, their manners refine. their powers and talents are called forth. In every part of the earth, the progress of man hath been nearly the same; and we can trace him in his career from the rude simplicity of savage life, until he attains the industry, the arts, and the elegance of polished society. There is nothing wonderful, then, in the similitude between the Americans and the barbarous nations of our continent. Had Lafitau, Garcia, and many other authors attended to this, they would not have perplexed a subject, which they pretend to illustrate, by their fruitless endeavours to establish an affinity between various races of people, in the old and new continents, upon no other evidence than such a resemblance in their manners as necessarily arises from the similarity of their condition. There are, it is true, among every people, some customs which, as they do not flow from any natural want or desire peculiar to their situation, may be denominated usages of arbitrary institution. If between two nations settled in remote parts of the earth, a perfect agreement with respect to any of these should be discovered, one might be led to suspect that they were connected by some affinity. If, for example, a nation were found in America that consecrated the seventh day to religious worship and rest, we might justly suppose that it had derived its knowledge of this usage, which is of arbitrary institution, from the Jews. But, if it were discovered that another nation celebrated the first appearance of every new moon with extraordinary demonstrations of joy, we should not be entitled to conclude that the observation of this monthly festival was borrowed from the Jews, but ought to consider it merely as the expression of that joy which is natural to man on the return of the planet which guides and cheers him in the night. The instances of customs merely arbitrary, common to the inhabitants of both hemispheres, are, indeed, so few and so equivocal, that no theory concerning the population of the New World ought to be founded upon them.

* Parson's Remains of Japhet, p. 240. Ancient Univers. Hist. vol. xx. p. 164. P. Feyjoo Teatro Critico, tom. v. p. 304, &c. Acosta Hist. Moral. Novi Orbis, lib. i. 16. c. 19.

3. The theories which have been formed with respect to the original of the Americans, from observation of their religious rites and practices, are no less fanciful and destitute of solid foundation. When the religious opinions of any people are neither the result of rational inquiry, nor derived from the instructions of revelation, they must needs be wild and extravagant. Barbarous nations are incapable of the former, and have not been blessed with the advantages arising from the latter. Still, however, the human mind, even where its operations appear most wild and capricious, holds a course so regular, that in every age and country the dominion of particular passions will be attended with similar effects. The savage of Europe or America, when filled with superstitious dread of invisible beings, or with inquisitive solicitude to penetrate into the events of futurity, trembles alike with fear, or glows with impatience. He has recourse to rites and practices of the same kind, in order to avert the vengeance which he supposes to be impending over him, or to divine the secret which is the object of his curiosity. Accordingly, the ritual of superstition in one continent seems, in many particulars, to be a transcript of that established in the other, and both authorize similar institutions, sometimes so frivolous as to excite pity, sometimes so bloody and barbarous as to create horror. But without supposing any consanguinity between such distant nations, or imagining that their religious ceremonies were conveyed by tradition from the one to the other, we may ascribe this uniformity, which in many instances seems very amazing, to the natural operation of superstition and enthusiasm upon the weakness of the human mind.

4. We may lay it down as a certain principle in this inquiry, that America was not peopled by any nation of the ancient continent which had made considerable progress in civilization. The inhabitants of the New World were in a state of society so extremely rude as to be unacquainted with those arts which are the first essays of human ingenuity in its advance towards improvement. Even the most cultivated nations of America were strangers to many of those simple inventions which were almost coeval with society in other parts of the world, and were known in the earliest periods of civil life with which we have any acquaintance. From this it is manifest, that the tribes which originally migrated to America, came off from nations which must have been no less barbarous than their posterity, at the time when they were first discovered by the Europeans. For, although the elegant or refined arts may decline or perish, amidst the violent shocks of those revolutions and disasters to which nations are exposed, the necessary arts of life, when once they have been introduced among any people, are never lost. None of the vicissitudes in human affairs affect these, and they continue to be practised as long as the race of men exists. If ever the use of iron had been known to the savages of America, or to their progenitors; if ever they had employed a plough, a loom, or a forge, the utility of those inventions would have preserved them, and it is impossible that they should have been abandoned or forgotten. We may conclude, then, that the Americans sprung from some people, who were themselves in such an early and unimproved stage of society, as to be unacquainted with all those necessary arts, which continued to be unknown among their posterity when first visited by the Spaniards.

5. It appears no less evident that America was not peopled by any colony from the more southern nations of the ancient continent. None of the rude tribes settled in that part of our hemisphere can be supposed to have visited a country so remote. They possessed neither enterprise, nor ingenuity, nor power that could prompt them to undertake, or enable them to perform such a distant voyage. That the more civilized nations in Asia or Africa are not the progenitors of the Americans, is manifest not only from the observations which I have already made concerning their ignorance of the most simple and necessary arts, but from an additional circumstance

Whenever any people have experienced the advantages which men enjoy by their dominion over the inferior animals, they can neither subsist without the nourishment which these afford, nor carry on any considerable operation independent of their ministry and labour. Accordingly, the first care of the Spaniards, when they settled in America, was to stock it with all the domestic animals of Europe; and if, prior to them, the Tyrians, the Carthaginians, the Chinese, or any other polished people, had taken possession of that continent, we should have found there the animals peculiar to those regions of the globe where they were originally seated. In all America, however, there is not one animal, tame or wild, which properly belongs to the warm or even the more temperate countries of the ancient continent. The camel, the dromedary, the horse, the cow, were as much unknown in America as the elephant or the lion. From which it is obvious, that the people who first settled in the western world did not issue from the countries where those animals abound, and where men, from having been long accustomed to their aid, would naturally consider it not only as beneficial, but as indispensably necessary to the improvement, and even the preservation of civil society.

6. From considering the animals with which America is stored, we may conclude that the nearest point of contact between the old and new continents is towards the northern extremity of both, and that there the communication was opened, and the intercourse carried on between them. All the extensive countries in America which lie within the tropics, or approach near to them, are filled with indigenous animals of various kinds, entirely different from those in the corresponding regions of the ancient continent. But the northern provinces of the New World abound with many of the wild animals which are common in such parts of our hemisphere as lie in a similar situation. The bear, the wolf, the fox, the hare, the deer, the roebuck, the elk, and several other species, frequent the forests of North America, no less than those in the north of Europe and Asia.* It seems to be evident, then, that the two continents approach each other in this quarter, and are either united, or so nearly adjacent that these animals might pass from the one to the other.

7. The actual vicinity of the two continents is so clearly established by modern discoveries, that the chief difficulty with respect to the peopling of America is removed. While those immense regions which stretch eastward from the river Oby to the sea of Kamchatka were unknown or imperfectly explored, the north-east extremities of our hemisphere were supposed to be so far distant from any part of the New World, that it was not easy to conceive how any communication should have been carried on between them. But the Russians, having subjected the western part of Siberia to their empire, gradually extended their knowledge of that vast country, by advancing towards the east into unknown provinces. These were discovered by hunters in their excursions after game, or by soldiers employed in levying the taxes; and the court of Moscow estimated the importance of those countries, only by the small addition which they made to its revenue. At length Peter the Great ascended the Russian throne. His enlightened, comprehensive mind, intent upon every circumstance that could aggrandize his empire, or render his reign illustrious, discerned consequences of those discoveries which had escaped the observation of his ignorant predecessors. He perceived that in proportion as the regions of Asia extended towards the east, they must approach nearer to America; that the communication between the two continents, which had long been searched for in vain, would probably be found in this quarter; and that by opening it, some part of the wealth and commerce of the western world might be made to flow into his dominions by a new channel. Such an object suited

* Buffon, Hist. Nat. ix. p. 97, &c.

a genius that delighted in grand schemes. Peter drew up instructions with his own hand for prosecuting this design, and gave orders for carrying it into execution.*

His successors adopted his ideas and pursued his plan. The officers whom the Russian court employed in this service had to struggle with so many difficulties, that their progress was extremely slow. Encouraged by some faint traditions among the people of Siberia, concerning a successful voyage in the year one thousand six hundred and forty-eight, round the north-east promontory of Asia, they attempted to follow the same course. Vessels were fitted out, with this view, at different times, from the rivers Lena and Kolyma; but in a frozen ocean, which nature seems not to have destined for navigation, they were exposed to many disasters, without being able to accomplish their purpose. No vessel fitted out by the Russian court ever doubled this formidable Cape [41]; we are indebted for what is known of those extreme regions of Asia, to the discoveries made in excursions by land. In all those provinces an opinion prevails, that there are countries of great extent and fertility which lie at no considerable distance from their own coasts. These the Russians imagined to be part of America; and several circumstances concurred not only in confirming them in this belief, but in persuading them that some portion of that continent could not be very remote. Trees of various kinds unknown in those naked regions of Asia, are driven upon the coast by an easterly wind. By the same wind, floating ice is brought thither in a few days; flights of birds arrive annually from the same quarter; and a tradition obtains among the inhabitants, of an intercourse formerly carried on with some countries situated to the east.

After weighing all these particulars, and comparing the position of the countries in Asia which had been discovered, with such parts in the north-west of America as were already known, the Russian court formed a plan, which would have hardly occurred to a nation less accustomed to engage in arduous undertakings, and to contend with great difficulties. Orders were issued to build two vessels at the small village of Ochotz, situated on the sea of Kamchatka, to sail on a voyage of discovery. Though that dreary uncultivated region furnished nothing that could be of use in constructing them, but some larch trees: though not only the iron, the cordage, the sails, and all the numerous articles requisite for their equipment, but the provisions for victualling them were to be carried through the immense deserts of Siberia, down rivers of difficult navigation, and along roads almost impassable, the mandate of the sovereign, and the perseverance of the people, at last surmounted every obstacle. Two vessels were finished, and, under the command of the Captains Behring and Tschirikow, sailed from Kamchatka, in quest of the New World in a quarter where it had never been approached. They shaped their course towards the east; and though a storm soon separated the vessels, which never rejoined, and many disasters befell them, the expectations from the voyage were not altogether frustrated. Each of the commanders discovered land, which to them appeared to be part of the American continent; and, according to their observation, it seems to be situated within a few degrees of the north-west coast of California. Each set some of his people ashore: but in one place the inhabitants fled as the Russians approached; in another, they carried off those who landed, and destroyed their boats. The violence of the weather, and the distress of their crews, obliged both captains to quit this inhospitable coast. In their return they touched at several islands which stretch in a chain from east to west between the country which they had discovered and the coast of Asia. They had some intercourse with the natives, who seemed to them to resemble the North Americans They

* Muller, Voyages et Découvertes par les Russes, tom. i. p. 4, 5. 141.

presented to the Russians the *calumet*, or pipe of peace, which is a symbol of friendship universal among the people of North America, and a usage of arbitrary institution peculiar to them.

Though the islands of this New Archipelago have been frequented since that time by the Russian hunters, the court of St. Petersburgh, during a period of more than forty years, seems to have relinquished every thought of prosecuting discoveries in that quarter. But in the year one thousand seven hundred and sixty-eight it was unexpectedly resumed. The sovereign who had been lately seated on the throne of Peter the Great, possessed the genius and talents of her illustrious predecessor. During the operations of the most arduous and extensive war in which the Russian empire was ever engaged, she formed schemes and executed undertakings, to which more limited abilities would have been incapable of attending but amidst the leisure of pacific times. A new voyage of discovery from the eastern extremity of Asia was planned, and Captain Krenitzin and Lieutenant Levasheff were appointed to command the two vessels fitted out for that purpose. In their voyage outward they held nearly the same course with the former navigators, they touched at the same islands, observed their situation and productions more carefully, and discovered several new islands with which Behring and Tschirikow had not fallen in. Though they did not proceed so far to the east as to revisit the country which Behring and Tschirikow supposed to be part of the American continent, yet, by returning in a course considerably to the north of theirs, they corrected some capital mistakes into which their predecessors had fallen, and have contributed to facilitate the progress of future navigators in those seas [42].

Thus the possibility of a communication between the continents in this quarter rests no longer upon mere conjecture, but is established by undoubted evidence.* Some tribe, or some families of wandering Tartars, from the restless spirit peculiar to their race, might migrate to the nearest islands, and, rude as their knowledge of navigation was, might, by passing from one to the other, reach at length the coast of America, and give a beginning to population in that continent. The distance between the Marian or Ladrone islands and the nearest land in Asia, is greater than that between the part of America which the Russians discovered, and the coast of Kamchatka; and yet the inhabitants of those islands are manifestly of Asiatic extract. If, notwithstanding their remote situation, we admit that the Marian islands were peopled from our continent, distance alone is no reason why we should hesitate about admitting that the Americans may derive their original from the same source. It is probable, that future navigators in those seas, by steering further to the north, may find that the continent of America approaches still nearer to Asia. According to the information of the barbarous people who inhabit the country about the north-east promontory of Asia, there lies, off the coast, a small island, to which they sail in less than a day. From that they can descry a large continent which, according to their description, is covered with forests, and possessed by people whose language they do not understand.† By them they are supplied with the skins of martens, an animal unknown in the northern parts of Siberia, and which is never found but in countries abounding with trees. If we could rely on this account, we might conclude that the American continent is separated from ours only by a narrow strait, and all the difficulties with respect to the communication between them would vanish. What could be offered only as a conjecture, when this History was first published, is now known to be certain. The near approach of the two continents to each other has been discovered and traced in a voyage undertaken upon principles so pure and so liberal, and conducted with so much professional skill, as reflect lustre

* Muller's Voyages, tom. i. p. 248, &c. 267. 276. † Ibid. tom. i. p. 166.

upon the reign of the sovereign by whom it was planned, and do honour to the officers intrusted with the execution of it [43].

It is likewise evident from recent discoveries, that an intercourse between our continent and America might be carried on with no less facility from the north-west extremities of Europe. As early as the ninth century [A. D. 830], the Norwegians discovered Greenland, and planted colonies there. The communication with that country, after a long interruption, was renewed in the last century. Some Lutheran and Moravian missionaries, prompted by zeal for propagating the Christian faith, have ventured to settle in this frozen and uncultivated region.* To them we are indebted for much curious information with respect to its nature and inhabitants. We learn that the north-west coast of Greenland is separated from America by a very narrow strait; that, at the bottom of the bay into which this strait conducts, it is highly probable that they are united;† that the inhabitants of the two countries have some intercourse with one another; that the Esquimaux of America perfectly resemble the Greenlanders in their aspect, dress, and mode of living; that some sailors who had acquired the knowledge of a few words in the Greenlandish language, reported that these were understood by the Esquimaux; that, at length [A. D. 1764], a Moravian missionary, well acquainted with the language of Greenland, having visited the country of the Esquimaux, found, to his astonishment, that they spoke the same language with the Greenlanders; that they were in every respect the same people, and he was accordingly received and entertained by them as a friend and a brother.‡

By these decisive facts, not only the consanguinity of the Esquimaux and Greenlanders is established, but the possibility of peopling America from the north of Europe is demonstrated. If the Norwegians, in a barbarous age, when science had not begun to dawn in the north of Europe, possessed such naval skill as to open a communication with Greenland, their ancestors, as much addicted to roving by sea, as the Tartars are to wandering by land, might, at some more remote period, accomplish the same voyage, and settle a colony there, whose descendants might, in progress of time, migrate into America. But if, instead of venturing to sail directly from their own coast to Greenland, we suppose that the Norwegians held a more cautious course, and advanced from Shetland to the Feroe islands, and from them to Iceland, in all which they had planted colonies; their progress may have been so gradual, that this navigation cannot be considered as either longer or more hazardous than those voyages which that hardy and enterprising race of men is known to have performed in every age.

8. Though it be possible that America may have received its first inhabitants from our continent, either by the north-west of Europe or the north-east of Asia, there seems to be good reason for supposing that the progenitors of all the American nations from Cape Horn to the southern confines of Labrador, migrated from the latter rather than the former. The Esquimaux are the only people in America, who in their aspect or character bear any resemblance to the northern Europeans. They are manifestly a race of men distinct from all the nations of the American continent, in language, in disposition, and in habits of life. Their original, then, may warrantably be traced up to that source which I have pointed out. But among all the other inhabitants of America, there is such a striking similitude in the form of their bodies and the qualities of their minds, that, notwithstanding the diversities occasioned by the influences of climate, or unequal progress in improvement, we must pronounce them to be descended from one source. There may be a variety in the shades, but we can every where trace the same original colour. Each tribe has something peculiar which distinguishes

* Crantz' Hist. of Greenl. i. 242. 244. Prevot, Hist. Gén. des Voyages, tom. xv. 152, note (96).
† Eggede, p. 2, 3. ‡ Crantz' Hist. of Greenl. p. 261, 262.

t, but in all of them we discern certain features common to the whole race. It is remarkable, that in every peculiarity, whether in their persons or dispositions, which characterize the Americans, they have some resemblance to the rude tribes scattered over the north-east of Asia, but almost none to the nations settled in the northern extremities of Europe. We may, therefore, refer them to the former origin, and conclude that their Asiatic progenitors, having settled in those parts of America where the Russians have discovered the proximity of the two continents, spread gradually over its various regions. This account of the progress of population in America coincides with the traditions of the Mexicans concerning their own origin, which, imperfect as they are, were preserved with more accuracy, and merit greater credit, than those of any people in the New World. According to them, their ancestors came from a remote country situated to the north-west of Mexico. The Mexicans point out their various stations as they advanced from this into the interior provinces, and it is precisely the same route which they must have held if they had been emigrants from Asia. The Mexicans, in describing the appearance of their progenitors, their manners and habits of life at that period, exactly delineate those of the rude Tartars from whom I suppose them to have sprung.*

Thus have I finished a Disquisition which has been deemed of so much importance that it would have been improper to omit it in writing the history of America. I have ventured to inquire, but without presuming to decide. Satisfied with offering conjectures, I pretend not to establish any system. When an investigation is, from its nature, so intricate and obscure, that it is impossible to arrive at conclusions which are certain, there may be some merit in pointing out such as are probable.†

The condition and character of the American nations, at the time when they became known to the Europeans, deserve more attentive consideration than the inquiry concerning their original. The latter is merely an object of curiosity; the former is one of the most important as well as instructive researches which can occupy the philosopher or historian. In order to complete the history of the human mind, and attain to a perfect knowledge of its nature and operations, we must contemplate man in all those various situations wherein he has been placed. We must follow him in his progress through the different stages of society, as he gradually advances from the infant state of civil life towards its maturity and decline. We must observe, at each period, how the faculties of his understanding unfold; we must attend to the efforts of his active powers, watch the various movements of desire and affection, as they rise in his breast, and mark whither they tend, and with what ardour they are exerted. The philosophers and historians of ancient Greece and Rome, our guides in this as well as every other disquisition, had only a limited view of this subject, as they had hardly any opportunity of surveying man in his rudest and most early state. In all those regions of the earth with which they were well acquainted, civil society had made considerable advances, and nations had finished a good part of their career before they began to observe them. The Scythians and Germans, the rudest people of whom any ancient author has transmitted to us an authentic account, possessed flocks and herds, had acquired property of various kinds, and, when compared with mankind in their primitive state, may be reckoned to have attained to a great degree of civilization.

But the discovery of the New World enlarged the sphere of contemplation, and presented nations to our view, in stages of their progress, much less advanced than those wherein they have been observed in our continent. In America, man appears under the rudest form in which we

* Acosta, Hist. Nat. et Mor. lib. vii. c. 2, &c. Garcia, Origen de los Indios, lib. v. c. 3. Torquemada Monar Ind. lib. i. c. 2, &c. Boturini Benaduci Idea de una Hist. de la Amer. Septentr. sect. xvii. p. 127. † Mémoires sur la Louisiane, par Dumont, tom. 1. p. 119.

can conceive him to subsist. We behold communities just beginning to unite, and may examine the sentiments and actions of human beings in the infancy of social life, while they feel but imperfectly the force of its ties, and have scarcely relinquished their native liberty. That state of primeval simplicity, which was known in our continent only by the fanciful description of poets, really existed in the other. The greater part of its inhabitants were strangers to industry and labour, ignorant of arts, imperfectly acquainted with the nature of property, and enjoying almost without restriction or control the blessings which flowed spontaneously from the bounty of nature. There were only two nations in this vast continent which had emerged from this rude state, and had made any considerable progress in acquiring the ideas, and adopting the institutions, which belong to polished societies Their government and manners will fall naturally under our review in relating the discovery and conquest of the Mexican and Peruvian empires; and we shall have there an opportunity of contemplating the Americans in the state of highest improvement to which they ever attained.

At present, our attention and researches shall be turned to the small independent tribes which occupied every other part of America. Among these, though with some diversity in their character, their manners, and institutions, the state of society was nearly similar, and so extremely rude, that the denomination of *savage* may be applied to them all. In a general history of America, it would be highly improper to describe the condition of each petty community, or to investigate every minute circumstance which contributes to form the character of its members. Such an inquiry would lead to details of immeasurable and tiresome extent. The qualities belonging to the people of all the different tribes have such a near resemblance, that they may be painted with the same features. Where any circumstances seem to constitute a diversity in their character and manners worthy of attention, it will be sufficient to point these out as they occur, and to inquire into the cause of such peculiarities.

It is extremely difficult to procure satisfying and authentic information concerning nations while they remain uncivilized. To discover their true character under this rude form, and to select the features by which they are distinguished, requires an observer possessed of no less impartiality than discernment. For, in every stage of society, the faculties, the sentiments, and desires of men are so accommodated to their own state, that they become standards of excellence to themselves, they affix the idea of perfection and happiness to those attainments which resemble their own, and, wherever the objects and enjoyments to which they have been accustomed are wanting, confidently pronounce a people to be barbarous and miserable. Hence the mutual contempt with which the members of communities, unequal in their degrees of improvement, regard each other. Polished nations, conscious of the advantages which they derive from their knowledge and arts, are apt to view rude nations with peculiar scorn, and, in the pride of superiority, will hardly allow either their occupations, their feelings, or their pleasures, to be worthy of men. It has seldom been the lot of communities, in their early and unpolished state, to fall under the observation of persons endowed with force of mind superior to vulgar prejudices, and capable of contemplating man, under whatever aspect he appears, with a candid and discerning eye.

The Spaniards, who first visited America, and who had opportunity of beholding its various tribes while entire and unsubdued, and before any change had been made in their ideas or manners by intercourse with a race of men much advanced beyond them in improvement, were far from possessing the qualities requisite for observing the striking spectacle presented to their view. Neither the age in which they lived, nor the nation to which they belonged, had made such progress in true science, as inspires enlarged and liberal sentiments. The conquerors of the New World were mostly illiterate adventurers, destitute of all the ideas which should have directed them in contemplating objects so extremely different from those with which they were acquainted. Surrounded continually with danger or struggling with hardships, they had little leisure, and less capacity, for any speculative inquiry. Eager to take possession of a country of such extent and opulence, and happy in finding it occupied by inhabitants so incapable to defend it, they hastily pronounced them to be a wretched order of men, formed merely for servitude; and were more employed in computing the profits of their labour, than in inquiring into the operations of their minds, or the reasons of their customs and institutions. The persons who penetrated at subsequent periods into the interior provinces, to which the knowledge and devastations of the first conquerors did not reach, were generally of a similar character; brave and enterprising in a high degree, but so uninformed as to be little qualified either for observing or describing what they beheld.

Not only the incapacity but the prejudices of the Spaniards rendered their accounts of the people of America extremely defective. Soon after they planted colonies in their new conquests, a difference in opinion arose with respect to the treatment of the natives. One party, solicitous to render their servitude perpetual, represented them as a brutish, obstinate race, incapable either of acquiring religious knowledge, or of being trained to the functions of social life. The other, full of pious concern for their conversion, contended that, though rude and ignorant, they were gentle, affectionate, docile, and by proper instructions and regulations might be formed gradually into good Christians and useful citizens. This controversy, as I have already related, was carried on with all the warmth which is natural, when attention to interest on the one hand, and religious zeal on the other, animate the disputants. Most of the laity espoused the former opinion; all the ecclesiastics were advocates for the latter; and we shall uniformly find that, accordingly as an author belonged to either of these parties, he is apt to magnify the virtues or aggravate the defects of the Americans far beyond truth. Those repugnant accounts increase the difficulty of attaining a perfect knowledge of their character, and render it necessary to peruse all the descriptions of them by Spanish writers with distrust, and to receive their information with some grains of allowance.

Almost two centuries elapsed after the discovery of America, before the manners of its inhabitants attracted, in any considerable degree, the attention of philosophers. At length they discovered that the contemplation of the condition and character of the Americans, in their original state, tended to complete our knowledge of the human species; might enable us to fill up a considerable chasm in the history of its progress; and lead to speculations no less curious than important. They entered upon this new field of study with great ardour; but, instead of throwing light upon the subject, they have contributed in some degree to involve it in additional obscurity. Too impatient to inquire, they hastened to decide; and began to erect systems, when they should have been searching for facts on which to establish their foundations. Struck with the appearance of degeneracy in the human species throughout the New World, and astonished at beholding a vast continent occupied by a naked, feeble, and ignorant race of men, some authors, of great name, have maintained that this part of the globe had but lately emerged from the sea, and become fit for the residence of man; that every thing in it bore marks of a recent original; and that its inhabitants, lately called into existence, and still at the beginning of their career, were unworthy to be compared with the people of a more ancient and improved continent.* Others have imagined, that, under the influence of an unkindly climate, which checks and enervates

* M. de Buffon Hist. Nat. iii. 484, &c. ix. 103. 114.

the principle of life, man never attained in America the perfection which belongs to his nature, but remained an animal of an inferior order, defective in the vigour of his bodily frame, and destitute of sensibility, as well as of force, in the operations of his mind.* In opposition to both these, other philosophers have supposed that man arrives at his highest dignity and excellence long before he reaches a state of refinement; and, in the rude simplicity of savage life, displays an elevation of sentiment, an independence of mind, and a warmth of attachment, for which it is vain to search among the members of polished societies.† They seem to consider that as the most perfect state of man which is the least civilized. They describe the manners of the rude Americans with such rapture, as if they proposed them for models to the rest of the species. These contradictory theories have been proposed with equal confidence, and uncommon powers of genius and eloquence have been exerted, in order to clothe them with an appearance of truth.

As all those circumstances concur in rendering an inquiry into the state of the rude nations in America intricate and obscure, it is necessary to carry it on with caution. When guided in our researches by the intelligent observations of the few philosophers who have visited this part of the globe, we may venture to decide. When obliged to have recourse to the superficial remarks of vulgar travellers, of sailors, traders, buccaneers, and missionaries, we must often pause, and, comparing detached facts, endeavour to discover what they wanted sagacity to observe. Without indulging conjecture, or betraying a propensity to either system, we must study with equal care to avoid the extremes of extravagant admiration, or of supercilious contempt for those manners which we describe.

In order to conduct this inquiry with greater accuracy, it should be rendered as simple as possible. Man existed as an individual before he became the member of a community; and the qualities which belong to him under his former capacity should be known, before we proceed to examine those which arise from the latter relation. This is peculiarly necessary in investigating the manners of rude nations. Their political union is so incomplete, their civil institutions and regulations so few, so simple, and of such slender authority, that men in this state ought to be viewed rather as independent agents, than as members of a regular society. The character of a savage results almost entirely from his sentiments or feelings as an individual, and is but little influenced by his imperfect subjection to government and order. I shall conduct my researches concerning the manners of the Americans in this natural order, proceeding gradually from what is simple to what is more complicated.

I shall consider, I. The bodily constitution of the Americans in those regions now under review. II. The qualities of their minds. III. Their domestic state. IV. Their political state and institutions. V. Their system of war, and public security. VI. The arts with which they were acquainted. VII. Their religious ideas and institutions. VIII. Such singular detached customs as are not reducible to any of the former heads. IX. I shall conclude with a general review and estimate of their virtues and defects.

I. The bodily constitution of the Americans.—The human body is less affected by climate than that of any other animal. Some animals are confined to a particular region of the globe, and cannot exist beyond it; others, though they may be brought to bear the injuries of a climate foreign to them, cease to multiply when carried out of that district which nature destined to be their mansion. Even such as seem capable of being naturalized in various climates feel the effect of every remove from their proper station, and gradually dwindle and degenerate from the vigour and

* M de P. Recherches Philos. sur les Améric. passim. † M. Rousseau.

perfection peculiar to their species. Man is the only living creature whose frame is at once so hardy and so flexible, that he can spread over the whole earth, become the inhabitant of every region, and thrive and multiply under every climate. Subject, however, to the general law of Nature, the human body is not entirely exempt from the operation of climate; and when exposed to the extremes either of heat or cold, its size or vigour diminishes.

The first appearance of the inhabitants of the New World filled the discoverers with such astonishment that they were apt to imagine them a race of men different from those of the other hemisphere. Their complexion is of a reddish brown, nearly resembling the colour of copper.* The hair of their heads is always black, long, coarse, and uncurled. They have no beard, and every part of their body is perfectly smooth. Their persons are of a full size, extremely straight, and well proportioned [44]. Their features are regular, though often distorted by absurd endeavours to improve the beauty of their natural form, or to render their aspect more dreadful to their enemies. In the islands, where four-footed animals were both few and small, and the earth yielded her productions almost spontaneously, the constitution of the natives, neither braced by the active exercises of the chase, nor invigorated by the labour of cultivation, was extremely feeble and languid. On the continent, where the forests abound with game of various kinds, and the chief occupation of many tribes was to pursue it, the human frame acquired greater firmness. Still, however, the Americans were more remarkable for agility than strength. They resembled beasts of prey, rather than animals formed for labour [45]. They were not only averse to toil, but incapable of it; and when roused by force from their native indolence, and compelled to work, they sunk under tasks which the people of the other continent would have performed with ease.† This feebleness of constitution was universal among the inhabitants of those regions in America which we are surveying, and may be considered as characteristic of the species there.‡

The beardless countenance and smooth skin of the American seems to indicate a defect of vigour, occasioned by some vice in his frame. He is destitute of one sign of manhood and of strength. This peculiarity, by which the inhabitants of the New World are distinguished from the people of all other nations, cannot be attributed, as some travellers have supposed, to their mode of subsistence.§ For though the food of many Americans be extremely insipid, as they are altogether unacquainted with the use of salt, rude tribes in other parts of the earth have subsisted on aliments equally simple, without this mark of degradation, or any apparent symptom of a diminution in their vigour.

As the external form of the Americans leads us to suspect that there is some natural debility in their frame, the smallness of their appetite for food has been mentioned by many authors as a confirmation of this suspicion. The quantity of food which men consume varies according to the temperature of the climate in which they live, the degree of activity which they exert, and the natural vigour of their constitutions. Under the enervating heat of the torrid zone, and when men pass their days in indolence and ease, they require less nourishment than the active inhabitants of temperate or cold countries. But neither the warmth of their climate, nor their extreme laziness, will account for the uncommon defect of appetite among the Americans. The Spaniards were astonished with observing this, not only in the islands, but in several parts of the continent. The constitutional temperance of the natives far exceeded, in their opinion,

* Oviedo Somario p. 46. D. Life of Columbus, c. 24. † Oviedo Som. p. 51. C: Voy. de Correal, ii. 138. Wafer's Description, p. 131. ‡ B. Las Casas Brev. Relac. p. 4. Torquem. Monar. i. 580. Oviedo Somario, p. 41. Histor. lib. iii. c. 6. Herrera, dec. i. lib. xi. c. 5. Simon, p. 41. § Charlev. Hist. de. Nouv: Fr. iii. 310.

the abstinence of the most mortified hermits:* while, on the other hand, the appetite of the Spaniards appeared to the Americans insatiably voracious; and they affirmed, that one Spaniard devoured more food in a day than was sufficient for ten Americans.†

A proof of some feebleness in their frame, still more striking, is the insensibility of the Americans to the charms of beauty, and the power of love. That passion which was destined to perpetuate life, to be the bond of social union, and the source of tenderness and joy, is the most ardent in the human breast. Though the perils and hardships of the savage state, though excessive fatigue on some occasions, and the difficulty at all times of procuring subsistence, may seem to be adverse to this passion, and to have a tendency to abate its vigour, yet the rudest nations in every other part of the globe seem to feel its influence more powerfully than the inhabitants of the New World. The negro glows with all the warmth of desire natural to his climate; and the most uncultivated Asiatics discover that sensibility, which, from their situation on the globe, we should expect them to have felt. But the Americans are, in an amazing degree, strangers to the force of this first instinct of nature. In every part of the New World the natives treat their women with coldness and indifference. They are neither the objects of that tender attachment which takes place in civilized society, nor of that ardent desire conspicuous among rude nations. Even in climates where this passion usually acquires its greatest vigour, the savage of America views his female with disdain, as an animal of a less noble species. He is at no pains to win her favour by the assiduity of courtship, and still less solicitous to preserve it by indulgence and gentleness.‡ Missionaries themselves, notwithstanding the austerity of monastic ideas, cannot refrain from expressing their astonishment at the dispassionate coldness of the American young men in their intercourse with the other sex.§ Nor is this reserve to be ascribed to any opinion which they entertain with respect to the merit of female chastity. That is an idea too refined for a savage, and suggested by a delicacy of sentiment and affection to which he is a stranger.

But in inquiries concerning either the bodily or mental qualities of particular races of men, there is not a more common or more seducing error, than that of ascribing to a single cause, those characteristic peculiarities which are the effect of the combined operation of many causes. The climate and soil of America differ in so many respects from those of the other hemisphere, and this difference is so obvious and striking, that philosophers of great eminence have laid hold on this as sufficient to account for what is peculiar in the constitution of its inhabitants. They rest on physical causes alone, and consider the feeble frame and languid desire of the Americans, as consequences of the temperament of that portion of the globe which they occupy. But the influences of political and moral causes ought not to have been overlooked. These operate with no less effect than that on which many philosophers rest as a full explanation of the singular appearances which have been mentioned. Wherever the state of society is such as to create many wants and desires, which cannot be satisfied without regular exertions of industry, the body accustomed to labour becomes robust and patient of fatigue. In a more simple state, where the demands of men are so few and so moderate that they may be gratified, almost without any effort, by the spontaneous productions of nature, the powers of the body are not called forth, nor can they attain their proper strength. The natives of Chili and of North America, the two

* Ramusio, iii. 304. F. 306. A. Simon Conquista, &c. p. 39. Hakluyt, iii. 468. 508. † Herrera, dec. 1. lib. ii. c. 16. ‡ Hennepin Mœurs des Sauvages, 32, &c. Rochefort Hist. des Isles Antilles, p. 461. Voyage de Correal, ii. 141. Ramusio, iii. 309. F. Lozano Descr. del Gran Chaco, 71. Falkner's Descr. of Patagon, p. 125. Lettere di P. Cataneo ap. Muratori Il Christian. Felice, i. 305. § Chanvalon, p. 51. Lettr. Edif. tom. xxiv. 318. Tertre, ii. 377. Venegas, i. 81. Ribas Hist. de los Triumf. p. 11.

temperate regions in the New World, who live by hunting, may be deemed an active and vigorous race, when compared with the inhabitants of the isles, or of those parts of the continent where hardly any labour is requisite to procure subsistence. The exertions of a hunter are not, however, so regular, or so continued, as those of persons employed in the culture of the earth, or in the various arts of civilized life; and though his agility may be greater than theirs, his strength is on the whole inferior. If another direction were given to the active powers of man in the New World, and his force augmented by exercise, he might acquire a degree of vigour which he does not in his present state possess. The truth of this is confirmed by experience. Wherever the Americans have been gradually accustomed to hard labour, their constitutions become robust, and they have been found capable of performing such tasks, as seemed not only to exceed the powers of such a feeble frame as has been deemed peculiar to their country, but to equal any effort of the natives either of Africa or of Europe [46].

The same reasoning will apply to what has been observed concerning their slender demand for food. As a proof that this should be ascribed as much to their extreme indolence, and often total want of occupation, as to any thing peculiar in the physical structure of their bodies, it has been observed, that in those districts where the people of America are obliged to exert any unusual effort of activity, in order to procure subsistence, or wherever they are employed in severe labour, their appetite is not inferior to that of other men, and in some places, it has struck observers as remarkably voracious.*

The operation of political and moral causes is still more conspicuous in modifying the degree of attachment between the sexes. In a state of high civilization, this passion, inflamed by restraint, refined by delicacy, and cherished by fashion, occupies and engrosses the heart. It is no longer a simple instinct of nature; sentiment heightens the ardour of desire, and the most tender emotions of which our frame is susceptible soothe and agitate the soul. This description, however, applies only to those, who, by their situation, are exempted from the cares and labours of life. Among persons of inferior order, who are doomed by their condition to incessant toil, the dominion of this passion is less violent; their solicitude to procure subsistence, and to provide for the first demand of nature, leaves little leisure for attending to its second call. But if the nature of the intercourse between the sexes varies so much in persons of different rank in polished societies, the condition of man while he remains uncivilized must occasion a variation still more apparent. We may well suppose, that amidst the hardships, the dangers, and the simplicity of domestic life, where subsistence is always precarious and often scanty, where men are almost continually engaged in the pursuit of their enemies, or in guarding against their attacks, and where neither dress nor reserve are employed as arts of female allurement, that the attention of the Americans to their women would be extremely feeble, without imputing this solely to any physical defect or degradation in their frame.

It is accordingly observed, that in those countries of America where, from the fertility of the soil, the mildness of the climate, or some further advances which the natives have made in improvement, the means of subsistence are more abundant, and the hardships of savage life are less severely felt, the animal passion of the sexes becomes more ardent. Striking examples of this occur among some tribes seated on the banks of great rivers well stored with food, among others who are masters of hunting grounds abounding so much with game, that they have a regular and plentiful supply of nourishment with little labour. The superior degree

* Gumilla, ii. 12. 70. 247. Lafitau, i. 515. Ovalle Church. ii. 81. Muratori, i. 295.

of security and affluence which those tribes enjoy is followed by their natural effects. The passions implanted in the human frame by the hand of nature acquire additional force; new tastes and desires are formed; the women, as they are more valued and admired, become more attentive to dress and ornament; the men beginning to feel how much of their own happiness depends upon them, no longer disdain the arts of winning their favour and affection. The intercourse of the sexes becomes very different from that which takes place among their ruder countrymen; and as hardly any restraint is imposed on the gratification of desire, either by religion or laws or decency, the dissolution of their manners is excessive.*

Notwithstanding the feeble make of the Americans, hardly any of them are deformed, or mutilated, or defective in any of their senses. All travellers have been struck with this circumstance, and have celebrated the uniform symmetry and perfection of their external figure. Some authors search for the cause of this appearance in their physical condition. As the parents are not exhausted or over fatigued with hard labour, they suppose that their children are born vigorous and sound. They imagine that, in the liberty of savage life, the human body, naked and unconfined from its earliest age, preserves its natural form; and that all its limbs and members acquire a juster proportion than when fettered with artificial restraints, which stint its growth and distort its shape.† Something, without doubt, may be ascribed to the operation of these causes; but the true reasons of this apparent advantage, which is common to all savage nations, lie deeper, and are closely interwoven with the nature and genius of that state. The infancy of man is so long and so helpless, that it is extremely difficult to rear children among rude nations. Their means of subsistence are not only scanty, but precarious. Such as live by hunting must range over extensive countries, and shift often from place to place. The care of children, as well as every other laborious task, is devolved upon the women. The distresses and hardships of the savage life, which are often such as can hardly be supported by persons in full vigour, must be fatal to those of more tender age. Afraid of undertaking a task so laborious, and of such long duration, as that of rearing their offspring, the women, in some parts of America, procure frequent abortions by the use of certain herbs, and extinguish the first sparks of that life which they are unable to cherish.‡ Sensible that only stout and well formed children have force of constitution to struggle through such a hard infancy, other nations abandon and destroy such of their progeny as appear feeble or defective, as unworthy of attention.§ Even when they endeavour to rear all their children without distinction, so great a proportion of the whole number perishes under the rigorous treatment which must be their lot in the savage state, that few of those who laboured under any original frailty attain the age of manhood.‖ Thus in polished societies, where the means of subsistence are secured with certainty, and acquired with ease; where the talents of the mind are often of more importance than the powers of the body; children are preserved notwithstanding their defects or deformity, and grow up to be useful citizens. In rude nations, such persons are either cut off as soon as they are born, or, becoming a burden to themselves and to the community, cannot long protract their lives. But in those provinces of the New World, where, by the establishment of the Europeans, more regular provision has been made for the subsistence of its inhabitants, and they are restrained from laying violent hands on their children, the Americans are so far from being eminent for any superior perfection in their form, that one should rather suspect some peculiar imbecility in the race, from the

* Biet. 389. Charlev. iii. 423. Dumont. Mém. sur Louisiane, i. 155.

† Piso, p. 6.

‡ Ellis's Voyage to Hudson's Bay, 198. Herrera, dec. 7. lib. ix. c. 4.

§ Gumilla Hist. ii. 234. Techo's Hist. of Paraguay, &c. Churchill's Collect. vi. 108.

‖ Creuxii. Hist. Canad, p. 57

extraordinary number of individuals who are deformed, dwarfish, mutilated, blind, or deaf.*

How feeble soever the constitution of the Americans may be, it is remarkable that there is less variety in the human form throughout the New World than in the ancient continent. When Columbus and the other discoverers first visited the different countries of America which lie within the torrid zone, they naturally expected to find people of the same complexion with those in the corresponding regions of the other hemisphere. To their amazement, however, they discovered that America contained no negroes;† and the cause of this singular appearance became as much the object of curiosity as the fact itself was of wonder. In what part or membrane of the body that humour resides which tinges the complexion of the negro with a deep black, it is the business of anatomists to inquire and describe. The powerful operation of heat appears manifestly to be the cause which produces this striking variety in the human species. All Europe, a great part of Asia, and the temperate countries of Africa, are inhabited by men of a white complexion. All the torrid zone in Africa, some of the warmer regions adjacent to it, and several countries in Asia, are filled with people of a deep black colour. If we survey the nations of our continent, making our progress from cold and temperate countries towards those parts which are exposed to the influence of vehement and unremitting heat, we shall find that the extreme whiteness of their skin soon begins to diminish; that its colour deepens gradually as we advance; and, after passing through all the successive gradations of shade, terminates in a uniform unvarying black. But in America, where the agency of heat is checked and abated by various causes, which I have already explained, the climate seems to be destitute of that force which produces such wonderful effects on the human frame. The colour of the natives of the torrid zone in America is hardly of a deeper hue than that of the people in the more temperate parts of their continent. Accurate observers, who had an opportunity of viewing the Americans in very different climates, and in provinces far removed from each other, have been struck with the amazing similarity of their figure and aspect [47].

But though the hand of nature has deviated so little from one standard in fashioning the human form in America, the creation of fancy hath been various and extravagant. The same fables that were current in the ancient continent, have been revived with respect to the New World, and America too has been peopled with human beings of monstrous and fantastic appearance. The inhabitants of certain provinces were described to be pigmies of three feet high; those of others to be giants of an enormous size. Some travellers published accounts of people with only one eye; others pretended to have discovered men without heads, whose eyes and mouths were planted in their breasts. The variety of Nature in her productions is indeed so great, that it is presumptuous to set bounds to her fertility, and to reject indiscriminately every relation that does not perfectly accord with our own limited observation and experience. But the other extreme, of yielding a hasty assent on the slighest evidence to whatever has the appearance of being strange and marvellous, is still more unbecoming a philosophical inquirer; as, in every period, men are more apt to be betrayed into error by their weakness in believing too much, than by their arrogance in believing too little. In proportion as science extends, and nature is examined with a discerning eye, the wonders which amused ages of ignorance disappear. The tales of credulous travellers concerning America are forgotten; the monsters which they describe have been searched for in vain; and those provinces where they pretend to have

* Voy. de Ulloa, i. 232.

† P. Martyr, dec. p. 71.

found inhabitants of singular forms, are now known to be possessed by a people nowise different from the other Americans.

Though those relations may, without discussion, be rejected as fabulous, there are other accounts of varieties in the human species in some parts of the New World, which rest upon better evidence, and merit more attentive examination. This variety has been particularly observed in three different districts. The first of these is situated in the isthmus of Darien, near the centre of America. Lionel Wafer, a traveller possessed of more curiosity and intelligence than we should have expected to find in an associate of Buccaneers, discovered there a race of men few in number, but of a singular make. They are of low stature, according to his description, of a feeble frame, incapable of enduring fatigue. Their colour is a dead milk white; not resembling that of fair people among the Europeans, but without any tincture of a blush or sanguine complexion. Their skin is covered with a fine hairy down of a chalky white; the hair of their heads, their eyebrows, and eye-lashes, are of the same hue. Their eyes are of a singular form, and so weak that they can hardly bear the light of the sun; but they see clearly by moonlight, and are most active and gay in the night.* No race similar to this has been discovered in any other part of America. Cortes, indeed, found some persons exactly resembling the white people of Darien among the rare and monstrous animals which Montezuma had collected.† But as the power of the Mexican empire extended to the provinces bordering on the isthmus of Darien, they were probably brought thence. Singular as the appearance of those people may be, they cannot be considered as constituting a distinct species. Among the negroes of Africa, as well as the natives of the Indian islands, nature sometimes produces a small number of individuals, with all the characteristic features and qualities of the white people of Darien. The former are called *Albinos* by the Portuguese, the latter *Kackerlakes* by the Dutch. In Darien the parents of those *Whites* are of the same colour with the other natives of the country; and this observation applies equally to the anomalous progeny of the Negroes and Indians. The same mother who produces some children of a colour that does not belong to the race, brings forth the rest with a complexion peculiar to her country.‡ One conclusion may then be formed with respect to the people described by Wafer, the *Albinos* and the *Kackerlakes;* they are a degenerated breed, not a separate class of men; and from some disease or defect of their parents, the peculiar colour and debility which mark their degradation are transmitted to them. As a decisive proof of this, it has been observed, that neither the white people of Darien, nor the Albinos of Africa, propagate their race: their children are of the colour and temperament peculiar to the natives of their respective countries§ [48].

The second district that is occupied by inhabitants differing in appearance from the other people of America, is situated in a high northern latitude, extending from the coast of Labrador towards the pole, as far as the country is habitable. The people scattered over those dreary regions are known to the Europeans by the name of *Esquimaux*. They themselves, with that idea of their own superiority, which consoles the rudest and most wretched nations, assume the name of *Keralit* or *Men*. They are of a middle size, and robust, with heads of a disproportioned bulk, and feet as remarkably small. Their complexion though swarthy, by being continually exposed to the rigour of a cold climate, inclines to the European white rather than to the copper colour of America, and the men have beards which are sometimes bushy and long.|| From these marks of

* Wafer's Descript. of Isth. ap. Dampier, iii. p. 346. † Cortes ap. Ramus. iii. p. 241. E. ‡ Margrav. Hist. Rer. Nat. Bras. lib. viii. c. 4. § Wafer, p. 348. Demanet Hist. de l'Afrique, ii. 234. Recherch. Philos. sur les Amer. ii. 1, &c. || Ellis Voy. to Huds. Bay, p. 131. 139. De la Potherie, tom. 1. p. 79. Wales Journ. of a Voy. to Churchill River, Phil. Trans. vol lx 109.

distinction, as well as from one still less equivocal, the affinity of their language to that of the Greenlanders, which I have already mentioned, we may conclude, with some degree of confidence, that the Esquimaux are a race different from the rest of the Americans.

We cannot decide with equal certainty concerning the inhabitants of the third district, situated at the southern extremity of America. These are the famous *Patagonians*, who, during two centuries and a half, have afforded a subject of controversy to the learned, and an object of wonder to the vulgar. They are supposed to be one of the wandering tribes which occupy the vast but least known region of America, which extends from the river de la Plata to the Straits of Magellan. Their proper station is in that part of the interior country which lies on the banks of the river Negro; but, in the hunting season, they often roam as far as the straits which separate Tierra del Fuego from the main land. The first accounts of this people were brought to Europe by the companions of Magellan,* who described them as a gigantic race, above eight feet high, and of strength in proportion to their enormous size. Among several tribes of animals, a disparity in bulk as considerable may be observed. Some large breeds of horses and dogs exceed the more diminutive races in stature and strength, as far as the Patagonian is supposed to rise above the usual standard of the human body. But animals attain the highest perfection of their species only in mild climates, or where they find the most nutritive food in greatest abundance. It is not then in the uncultivated waste of the Magellanic regions, and among a tribe of improvident savages, that we should expect to find man possessing the highest honours of his race, and distinguished by a superiority of size and vigour, far beyond what he has reached in any other part of the earth. The most explicit and unexceptionable evidence is requisite, in order to establish a fact repugnant to those general principles and laws, which seem to affect the human frame in every other instance, and to decide with respect to its nature and qualities. Such evidence has not hitherto been produced. Though several persons, to whose testimony great respect is due, have visited this part of America since the time of Magellan, and have had interviews with the natives; though some have affirmed, that such as they saw were of gigantic stature, and others have formed the same conclusion from measuring their footsteps, or from viewing the skeletons of their dead; yet their accounts vary from each other in so many essential points, and are mingled with so many circumstances manifestly false or fabulous, as detract much from their credit. On the other hand, some navigators, and those among the most eminent of their order for discernment and accuracy, have asserted that the natives of Patagonia, with whom they had intercourse, though stout and well made, are not of such extraordinary size as to be distinguished from the rest of the human species [49]. The existence of this gigantic race of men seems, then, to be one of those points in natural history, with respect to which a cautious inquirer will hesitate, and will choose to suspend his assent until more complete evidence shall decide whether he ought to admit a fact, seemingly inconsistent with what reason and experience have discovered concerning the structure and condition of man, in all the various situations in which he has been observed.

In order to form a complete idea with respect to the constitution of the inhabitants of this and the other hemisphere, we should attend not only to the make and vigour of their bodies, but consider what degree of health they enjoy, and to what period of longevity they usually arrive. In the simplicity of the savage state, when man is not oppressed with labour, or enervated by luxury, or disquieted with care, we are apt to imagine that his life will flow on almost untroubled by disease or suffering, until his

* Falkner's Description of Patagonia, p. 102.

days be terminated in extreme old age by the gradual decays of nature We find, accordingly, among the Americans, as well as among other rude people, persons whose decrepit and shrivelled form seems to indicate an extraordinary length of life. But as most of them are unacquainted with the art of numbering, and all of them as forgetful of what is past, as they are improvident of what is to come, it is impossible to ascertain their age with any degree of precision.* It is evident that the period of their longevity must vary considerably, according to the diversity of climates, and their different modes of subsistence. They seem, however, to be every where exempt from many of the distempers which afflict polished nations. None of the maladies, which are the immediate offspring of luxury, ever visited them; and they have no names in their languages by which to distinguish this numerous train of adventitious evils.

But whatever be the situation in which man is placed, he is born to suffer; and his diseases in the savage state, though fewer in number, are, like those of the animals whom he nearly resembles in his mode of life, more violent and more fatal. If luxury engenders and nourishes distempers of one species, the rigour and distresses of savage life bring on those of another. As men in this state are wonderfully improvident, and their means of subsistence precarious, they often pass from extreme want to exuberant plenty, according to the vicissitudes of fortune in the chase, or in consequence of the various degrees of abundance with which the earth affords to them its productions in different seasons. Their inconsiderate gluttony in the one situation, and their severe abstinence in the other, are equally pernicious. For though the human constitution may be accustomed by habit, like that of animals of prey, to tolerate long famine, and then to gorge voraciously, it is not a little affected by such sudden and violent transitions. The strength and vigour of savages are at some seasons impaired by what they suffer from a scarcity of food; at others they are afflicted with disorders arising from indigestion and a superfluity of gross aliment. These are so common, that they may be considered as the unavoidable consequence of their mode of subsisting, and cut off considerable numbers in the prime of life. They are likewise extremely subject to consumptions, to pleuritic, asthmatic, and paralytic disorders,† brought on by the immoderate hardships and fatigue which they endure in hunting and in war; or owing to the inclemency of the seasons to which they are continually exposed. In the savage state, hardships and fatigue violently assault the constitution. In polished societies, intemperance undermines it. It is not easy to determine which of them operates with most fatal effect, or tends most to abridge human life. The influence of the former is certainly most extensive. The pernicious consequences of luxury reach only a few members in any community; the distresses of savage life are felt by all. As far as I can judge, after very minute inquiry, the general period of human life is shorter among savages than in well regulated and industrious societies.

One dreadful malady, the severest scourge with which, in this life, offended Heaven chastens the indulgence of criminal desire, seems to have been peculiar to the Americans. By communicating it to their conquerors, they have not only amply avenged their own wrongs, but, by adding this calamity to those which formerly imbittered human life, they have, perhaps, more than counterbalanced all the benefits which Europe has derived from the discovery of the New World. This distemper, from the country in which it first raged, or from the people by whom it was supposed to have been spread over Europe, has been sometimes called the Neapolitan, and sometimes the French disease. At its first appearance, the infection was

* Ulloa Notic. Americ. 323. Bancroft Nat. Hist. of Guiana, 334. † Charlev. N. Fr. iii. 364. Lafitau, ii. 360. De la Potherie, ii. 37.

so malignant, its symptoms so violent, its operation so rapid and fatal, as to baffle all the efforts of medical skill. Astonishment and terror accompanied this unknown affliction in its progress, and men began to dread the extinction of the human race by such a cruel visitation. Experience, and the ingenuity of physicians, gradually discovered remedies of such virtue as to cure or to mitigate the evil. During the course of two centuries and a half, its virulence seems to have abated considerably. At length, in the same manner with the leprosy, which raged in Eorope for some centuries, it may waste its force and disappear; and in some happier age, this western infection, like that from the east, may be known only by description [50].

II. After considering what appears to be peculiar in the bodily constitution of the Americans, our attention is naturally turned towards the powers and qualities of their minds. As the individual advances from the ignorance and imbecility of the infant state to vigour and maturity of understanding, something similar to this may be observed in the progress of the species. With respect to it, too, there is a period of infancy, during which several powers of the mind are not unfolded, and all are feeble and defective in their operation. In the early ages of society, while the condition of man is simple and rude, this reason is but little exercised, and his desires move within a very narrow sphere. Hence arise two remarkable characteristics of the human mind in this state. Its intellectual powers are extremely limited; its emotions and efforts are few and languid. Both these distinctions are conspicuous among the rudest and most unimproved of the American tribes, and constitute a striking part of their description.

What, among polished nations, is called speculative reasoning or research, is altogether unknown in the rude state of society, and never becomes the occupation or amusement of the human faculties, until man be so far improved as to have secured, with certainty, the means of subsistence, as well as the possession of leisure and tranquillity. The thoughts and attention of a savage are confined within the small circle of objects immediately conducive to his preservation or enjoyment. Every thing beyond that escapes his observation, or is perfectly indifferent to him. Like a mere animal, what is before his eyes interests and affects him; what is out of sight, or at a distance, makes little impression.* There are several people in America whose limited understandings seem not to be capable of forming an arrangement for futurity; neither their solicitude nor their foresight extends so far. They follow blindly the impulse of the appetite which they feel, but are entirely regardless of distant consequences, and even of those removed in the least degree from immediate apprehension. While they highly prize such things as serve for present use, or minister to present enjoyment, they set no value upon those which are not the object of some immediate want.† When, on the approach of the evening, a Caribbee feels himself disposed to go to rest, no consideration will tempt him to sell his hammock. But, in the morning, when he is sallying out to the business or pastime of the day, he will part with it for the slightest toy that catches his fancy.‡ At the close of winter, while the impression of what he has suffered from the rigour of the climate is fresh in the mind of the North American, he sets himself with vigour to prepare materials for erecting a comfortable hut to protect him against the inclemency of the succeeding season; but, as soon as the weather becomes mild, he forgets what is past, abandons his work, and never thinks of it more until the return of cold compels him, when too late, to resume it.§

If in concerns the most interesting, and seemingly the most simple, the

* Ullo Noticias Americ. 222. † Venegas Hist. of Calif. i. 66. Supp. Church. Coll. v. 693 Borde Descr. des Caraibes, p. 16. Ellis Voy. 194. ‡ Labat Voyages, ii. 114, 115. Tertre, ii. 385. § Adair's Hist. of Amer. Indians, 417

reason of man, while rude and destitute of culture, differs so little from the thoughtless levity of children, or the improvident instinct of animals, its exertions in other directions cannot be very considerable. The objects towards which reason turns, and the disquisitions in which it engages, must depend upon the state in which man is placed, and are suggested by his necessities and desires. Disquisitions, which appear the most necessary and important to men in one state of society, never occur to those in another. Among civilized nations, arithmetic, or the art of numbering, is deemed an essential and elementary science: and in our continent, the invention and use of it reaches back to a period so remote as is beyond the knowledge of history. But among savages, who have no property to estimate, no hoarded treasures to count, no variety of objects or multiplicity of ideas to enumerate, arithmetic is a superfluous and useless art. Accordingly, among some tribes in America it seems to be quite unknown. There are many who cannot reckon further than three; and have no denomination to distinguish any number above it.* Several can proceed as far as ten, others to twenty. When they would convey an idea of any number beyond these, they point to the hair of their head, intimating that it is equal to them, or with wonder declare it to be so great that it cannot be reckoned.† Not only the Americans, but all nations while extremely rude, seem to be unacquainted with the art of computation.‡ As soon, however, as they acquire such acquaintance or connexion with a variety of objects, that there is frequent occasion to combine or divide them, their knowledge of numbers increases, so that the state of this art among any people may be considered as one standard by which to estimate the degree of their improvement. The Iroquoise, in North America, as they are much more civilized than the rude inhabitants of Brazil, Paraguay, or Guiana, have likewise made greater advances in this respect; though even their arithmetic does not extend beyond a thousand, as in their petty transactions they have no occasion for any higher number.§ The Cherokee, a less considerable nation on the same continent, can reckon only as far as a hundred, and to that extent have names for the several numbers; the smaller tribes in their neighbourhood can rise no higher than ten‖ [51].

In other respects, the exercise of the understanding among rude nations is still more limited. The first ideas of every human being must be such as he receives by the senses. But in the mind of man, while in the savage state, there seem to be hardly any ideas but what enter by this avenue. The objects around him are presented to his eye. Such as may be subservient to his use, or can gratify any of his appetites, attract his notice; he views the rest without curiosity or attention. Satisfied with considering them under that simple mode in which they appear to him, as separate and detached, he neither combines them so as to form general classes, nor contemplates their qualities apart from the subject in which they inhere, nor bestows a thought upon the operations of his own mind concerning them. Thus he is unacquainted with all the ideas which have been denominated *universal*, or *abstract*, or *of reflection*. The range of his understanding must, of course, be very confined, and his reasoning powers be employed merely on what is sensible. This is so remarkably the case with the ruder nations of America, that their languages (as we shall afterwards find) have not a word to express any thing but what is material or corporeal. *Time, space, substance*, and a thousand terms, which represent abstract and universal ideas, are altogether unknown to them.¶ A naked savage, cowering over the fire in his miserable cabin, or stretched under a few

* Condam. p. 67. Stadius ap. de Bry, ix. 128. Lery, ibid. 251. Biet. 362. Lettr. Edif. 23. 314. † Dumont Louis. i. 187. Herrera, dec. 1. lib. iii. c. 3. Biet. 396. Borde, 6. ‡ This is the case with the Greenlanders, Crantz, i. 225, and with Kamchatkadales, M. l'Abbé Chappé, iii. 17. § Charlev. Nouv Franc. iii. 402. ‖ Adair's Hist. of Amer. Indians, 77. ¶ Condam. p. 54.

branches which afford him a temporary shelter, has as little inclination as capacity for useless speculation. His thoughts extend not beyond what relates to animal life; and when they are not directed towards some of its concerns, his mind is totally inactive. In situations where no extraordinary effort either of ingenuity or labour is requisite, in order to satisfy the simple demands of nature, the powers of the mind are so seldom roused to any exertion, that the rational faculties continue almost dormant and unexercised. The numerous tribes scattered over the rich plains of South America, the inhabitants of some of the islands, and of several fertile regions on the continent, come under this description. Their vacant countenance, their staring unexpressive eye, their listless inattention, and total ignorance of subjects which seemed to be the first which should occupy the thoughts of rational beings, made such impression upon the Spaniards, when they first beheld those rude people, that they considered them as animals of an inferior order, and could not believe that they belonged to the human species.* It required the authority of a papal bull to counteract this opinion, and to convince them that the Americans were capable of the functions and entitled to the privileges of humanity.† Since that time, persons more enlightened and impartial than the discoverers or conquerors of America, have had an opportunity of contemplating the most savage of its inhabitants, and they have been astonished and humbled with observing how nearly man in this condition approaches to the brute creation. But in severer climates, where subsistence cannot be procured with the same ease, where men must unite more closely, and act with greater concert, necessity calls forth their talents and sharpens their invention, so that the intellectual powers are more exercised and improved. The North American tribes, and the natives of Chili, who inhabit the temperate regions in the two great districts of America, are people of cultivated and enlarged understandings, when viewed in comparison with some of those seated in the islands, or on the banks of the Maragnon and Orinoco. Their occupations are more various, their system of policy, as well as of war, more complex, their arts more numerous. But even among them the intellectual powers are extremely limited in their operations, and, unless when turned directly to those objects which interest a savage, are held in no estimation. Both the North Americans and Chilese, when not engaged in some of the functions belonging to a warrior or hunter, loiter away their time in thoughtless indolence, unacquainted with any other subject worthy of their attention, or capable of occupying their minds.‡ If even among them reason is so much circumscribed in its exertions, and never arrives, in its highest attainments, at the knowledge of those general principles and maxims which serve as the foundation of science, we may conclude that the intellectual powers of man in the savage state are destitute of their proper object, and cannot acquire any considerable degree of vigour and enlargement.

From the same causes, the active efforts of the mind are few, and on most occasions languid. If we examine into the motives which rouse men to activity in civilized life, and prompt them to persevere in fatiguing exertions of their ingenuity or strength, we shall find that they arise chiefly from acquired wants and appetites. These are numerous and importunate; they keep the mind in perpetual agitation, and, in order to gratify them, invention must be always on the stretch, and industry must be incessantly employed. But the desires of simple nature are few, and where a favourable climate yields almost spontaneously what suffices to gratify them, they scarcely stir the soul, or excite any violent emotion. Hence the people of several tribes in America waste their life in a listless indolence. To be free from occupation, seems to be all the enjoyment

* Herrera, dec. 2. lib. ii. c. 15 † Torquem. Mon Ind iii. 198. ‡ Lafitau, ii. 2.

towards which they aspire. They will continue whole days stretched out in their hammocks, or seated on the earth in perfect idleness, without changing their posture, or raising their eyes from the ground, or uttering a single word.*

Such is their aversion to labour that neither the hope of future good nor the apprehension of future evil can surmount it. They appear equally indifferent to both, discovering little solicitude, and taking no precautions to avoid the one or to secure the other. The cravings of hunger may rouse them; but as they devour, with little distinction, whatever will appease its instinctive demands, the exertions which these occasion are of short duration. Destitute of ardour, as well as variety of desire, they feel not the force of those powerful springs which give vigour to the movements of the mind, and urge the patient hand of industry to persevere in its efforts. Man, in some parts of America, appears in a form so rude that we can discover no effects of his activity, and the principle of understanding, which should direct it, seems hardly to be unfolded Like the other animals, he has no fixed residence; he has erected no habitation to shelter him from the inclemency of the weather; he has taken no measures for securing certain subsistence; he neither sows nor reaps; but roams about as led in search of the plants and fruits which the earth brings forth in succession; and in quest of the game which he kills in the forest, or of the fish which he catches in the rivers.

This description, however, applies only to some tribes. Man cannot continue long in this state of feeble and uninformed infancy. He was made for industry and action, and the powers of his nature, as well as the necessity of his condition, urge him to fulfil his destiny. Accordingly, among most of the American nations, especially those seated in rigorous climates, some efforts are employed, and some previous precautions are taken, for securing subsistence. The career of regular industry is begun, and the laborious arm has made the first essays of its power. Still, however, the improvident and slothful genius of the savage state predominates. Even among those more improved tribes, labour is deemed ignominious and degrading. It is only to work of a certain kind that a man will deign to put his hand. The greater part is devolved entirely upon the women. One-half of the community remains inactive, while the other is oppressed with the multitude and variety of its occupations. Thus their industry is partial, and the foresight which regulates it is no less limited. A remarkable instance of this occurs in the chief arrangement with respect to their manner of living. They depend for their subsistence, during one part of the year, on fishing; during another, on hunting; during a third, on the produce of their agriculture. Though experience has taught them to foresee the return of those various seasons, and to make some provision for the respective exigencies of each, they either want sagacity to proportion this provision to their consumption, or are so incapable of any command over their appetites, that, from their inconsiderate waste, they often feel the calamities of famine as severely as the rudest of the savage tribes. What they suffer one year does not augment their industry, or render them more provident to prevent similar distresses.† This inconsiderate thoughtlessness about futurity, the effect of ignorance and the cause of sloth, accompanies and characterizes man in every stage of savage life;‡ and, by a capricious singularity in his operations, he is then least solicitous about supplying his wants, when the means of satisfying them are most precarious, and procured with the greatest difficulty [52].

III. After viewing the bodily constitution of the Americans, and con-

* Bouguer Voy. au Pérou, 102. Borde, 15 † Charlev. N. Fr. iii. 338. Lettr. Edif. 23. 298. Descript. of N. France, Osborn's Collect. ii. 880. De la Potherie, ii. 63. ‡ Bancroft's Nat. Hist. of Guiana, 326. 333.

templating the powers of their minds, we are led, in the natural order of inquiry, to consider them as united together in society. Hitherto our researches have been confined to the operations of understanding respecting themselves as individuals; now they will extend to the degree of their sensibility and affection towards their species.

The domestic state is the first and most simple form of human association. The union of the sexes among different animals is of longer or shorter duration in proportion to the ease or difficulty of rearing their offspring. Among those tribes where the season of infancy is short, and the young soon acquire vigour or agility, no permanent union is formed. Nature commits the care of training up the offspring to the mother alone, and her tenderness, without any other assistance, is equal to the task. But where the state of infancy is long and helpless, and the joint assiduity of both parents is requisite in tending their feeble progeny, there a more intimate connexion takes place, and continues until the purpose of nature be accomplished, and the new race grow up to full maturity. As the infancy of man is more feeble and helpless than that of any other animal, and he is dependent during a much longer period on the care and foresight of his parents, the union between husband and wife came early to be considered not only as a solemn but as a permanent contract. A general state of promiscuous intercourse between the sexes never existed but in the imagination of poets. In the infancy of society, when men, destitute of arts and industry, lead a hard precarious life, the rearing of their progeny demands the attention and efforts of both parents; and if their union had not been formed and continued with this view, the race could not have been preserved. Accordingly in America, even among the rudest tribes, a regular union between husband and wife was universal, and the rights of marriage were understood and recognised. In those districts where subsistence was scanty, and the difficulty of maintaining a family was great, the man confined himself to one wife. In warmer and more fertile provinces, the facility of procuring food concurred with the influence of climate in inducing the inhabitants to increase the number of their wives.* In some countries the marriage-union subsisted during life; in others, the impatience of the Americans under restraint of any species, together with their natural levity and caprice, prompted them to dissolve it on very slight pretexts, and often without assigning any cause.†

But in whatever light the Americans considered the obligation of this contract, either as perpetual or only as temporary, the condition of women was equally humiliating and miserable. Whether man has been improved by the progress of arts and civilization in society, is a question which, in the wantonness of disputation, has been agitated among philosophers. That women are indebted to the refinements of polished manners, for a happy change in their state, is a point which can admit of no doubt. To despise and to degrade the female sex is a characteristic of the savage state in every part of the globe. Man, proud of excelling in strength and in courage, the chief marks of pre-eminence among rude people, treats woman, as an inferior, with disdain. The Americans, perhaps from that coldness and insensibility which has been considered as peculiar to their constitution, add neglect and harshness to contempt. The most intelligent travellers have been struck with this inattention of the Americans to their women. It is not, as I have already observed, by a studied display of tenderness and attachment that the American endeavours to gain the heart of the woman whom he wishes to marry. Marriage itself, instead of being a union of affection and interests between equals, becomes among them the unnatural conjunction of a master with his slave. It is the observation of

* Lettr. Edif. 23. 318. Lafitau Mœurs, i. 554. Lery ap. de Bry, iii. 234. Journal de Grillet et Bechamel, p. 88. † Lafitau, i. 580. Joutel Journ. Histor. 345. Lozano Desc. del Gran Chaco, 70. Hennepin Mœurs des Sauvages, p. 30. 33.

an author whose opinions are deservedly of great weight, that wherever wives are purchased their condition is extremely depressed.* They become the property and the slaves of those who buy them. In whatever part of the globe this custom prevails, the observation holds. In countries where refinement has made some progress, women when purchased are excluded from society, shut up in sequestered apartments, and kept under the vigilant guard of their masters. In ruder nations they are degraded to the meanest functions. Among many people of America the marriage contract is properly a purchase. The man buys his wife of her parents. Though unacquainted with the use of money, or with such commercial transactions as take place in more improved society, he knows how to give an equivalent for any object which he desires to possess. In some places, the suitor devotes his service for a certain time to the parents of the maid whom he courts; in others he hunts for them occasionally, or assists in cultivating their fields and forming their canoes; in others, he offers presents of such things as are deemed most valuable on account of their usefulness or rarity.† In return for these he receives his wife; and this circumstance, added to the low estimation of women among savages, leads him to consider her as a female servant whom he has purchased, and whom he has a title to treat as an inferior. In all unpolished nations, it is true, the functions in domestic economy which fall naturally to the share of women are so many, that they are subjected to hard labour, and must bear more than their full portion of the common burden. But in America their condition is so peculiarly grievous, and their depression so complete, that servitude is a name too mild to describe their wretched state. A wife among most tribes is no better than a beast of burden, destined to every office of labour and fatigue. While the men loiter out the day in sloth, or spend it in amusement, the women are condemned to incessant toil. Tasks are imposed upon them without pity, and services are received without complacence or gratitude.‡ Every circumstance reminds women of this mortifying inferiority. They must approach their lords with reverence; they must regard them as more exalted beings, and are not permitted to eat in their presence.§ There are districts in America where this dominion is so grievous, and so sensibly felt, that some women, in a wild emotion of maternal tenderness, have destroyed their female children in their infancy, in order to deliver them from that intolerable bondage to which they knew they were doomed.|| Thus the first institution of social life is perverted. That state of domestic union towards which nature leads the human species, in order to soften the heart to gentleness and humanity, is rendered so unequal as to establish a cruel distinction between the sexes, which forms the one to be harsh and unfeeling, and humbles the other to servility and subjection.

It is owing, perhaps, in some measure, to this state of depression, that women in rude nations are far from being prolific.¶ The vigour of their constitution is exhausted by excessive fatigue, and the wants and distresses of savage life are so numerous as to force them to take various precautions in order to prevent too rapid an increase of their progeny. Among wandering tribes, or such as depend chiefly upon hunting for subsistence, the mother cannot attempt to rear a second child until the first has attained such a degree of vigour as to be in some measure independent of her care From this motive, it is the universal practice of the American women to suckle their children during several years;** and, as they seldom marry early, the period of their fertility is over before they can finish the long

* Sketches of Hist. of Man, i. 184. † Lafitau Mœurs, &c. i. 560, &c. Charlev. iii. 285, &c. Herrera, dec. 4. lib. iv. c. 7. Dumont, ii. 156. ‡ Tertre, ii. 382. Borde Relat. des Mœurs des Caraibes, p. 21. Biet. 357. Condamine, p. 110. Fermin. i. 79. § Gumilla, i. 153. Barrere, 164. Labat, Voy. ii. 78. Chanvalon, 51. Tertre, ii. 300. || Gumilla, ii. 233. 238. Herrera, dec. 7. lib. ix. c. iv. ¶ Lafitau, i. 590. Charlevoix, iii. 304. ** Herrera, dec. 6. lib. i. c. 4

but necessary attendance upon two or three children.* Among some of the least polished tribes, whose industry and foresight do not extend so far as to make any regular provision for their own subsistence, it is a maxim not to burden themselves with rearing more than two children;† and no such numerous families as are frequent in civilized societies are to be found among men in the savage state.‡ When twins are born, one of them commonly is abandoned, because the mother is not equal to the task of rearing both§ [53]. When a mother dies while she is nursing a child, all hope of preserving its life fails, and it is buried together with her in the same grave.‖ As the parents are frequently exposed to want by their own improvident indolence, the difficulty of sustaining their children becomes so great that it is not uncommon to abandon or destroy them.¶ Thus their experience of the difficulty of training up an infant to maturity, amidst the hardships of savage life, often stifles the voice of nature among the Americans, and suppresses the strong emotions of parental tenderness.

But though necessity compels the inhabitants of America thus to set bounds to the increase of their families, they are not deficient in affection and attachment to their offspring. They feel the power of this instinct in its full force, and as long as their progeny continue feeble and helpless, no people exceed them in tenderness and care.** But in rude nations the dependence of children upon their parents is of shorter continuance than in polished societies. When men must be trained to the various functions of civil life by previous discipline and education, when the knowledge of abstruse sciences must be taught, and dexterity in intricate arts must be acquired, before a young man is prepared to begin his career of action, the attentive feelings of a parent are not confined to the years of infancy, but extend to what is more remote, the establishment of his child in the world. Even then his solicitude does not terminate. His protection may still be requisite, and his wisdom and experience still prove useful guides. Thus a permanent connection is formed; parental tenderness is exercised, and filial respect returned, throughout the whole course of life. But in the simplicity of the savage state the affection of parents, like the instinctive fondness of animals, ceases almost entirely as soon as their offspring attain maturity. Little instruction fits them for that mode of life to which they are destined. The parents, as if their duty were accomplished, when they have conducted their children through the helpless years of infancy, leave them afterwards at entire liberty. Even in their tender age, they seldom advise or admonish, they never chide or chastise them. They suffer them to be absolute masters of their own actions.†† In an American hut, a father, a mother, and their posterity, live together like persons assembled by accident, without seeming to feel the obligation of the duties mutually arising from this connection.‡‡ As filial love is not cherished by the continuance of attention or good offices, the recollection of benefits received in early infancy is too faint to excite it. Conscious of their own liberty, and impatient of restraint, the youth of America are accustomed to act as if they were totally independent. Their parents are not objects of greater regard than other persons. They treat them always with neglect, and often with such harshness and insolence as to fill those who have been witnesses of their conduct with horror.§§ Thus the ideas which seem to be natural to man in his savage state, as they result necessarily from his circumstances and condition in that period of his progress,

* Charlev. iii. 303. Dumont, Mém. sur Louisiane, ii. 270. Deny's Hist. Natur. de l'Amérique, &c. ii. 365. Charlev. Hist. de Parag. ii. 422. † Techo's Account of Paraguay, &c. Church. Collect. vi. 108. Lett. Edif. xxxiv. 200. Lozano Descr. 92. ‡ Maccleur's Journal, 63. § Lett. Edif. x. 200. ‖ Charlev. iii. 368. Lett. Ediff. x. 200. P. Melch. Hernandez Memor. de Cheriqui. Colbert. Collect. Orig. Pap. i. ¶ Venega's Hist. of Californ. i. 82. ** Gumilla, i 211. Biet. 390. †† Charlev. iii. 272. Biet. 390. Gumilla, i. 212. Lafitau, i. 602. Creuxii Hist Canad. p. 71. Fernandez, Relac. Hist. de los Chequit. 33. ‡‡ Charlev. Hist. N. Fr. iii. 273. §§ Gumilla, i. 212. Tertre, ii. 376. Charlev. Hist. de N. France, iii. 309. Charlev. Hist. de Parag. i. 115. Lozano Descript. del Gran. Chaco, p. 68. 100, 101. Fernand. Relac. Histor. de los Chequit. 426.

affect the two capital relations in domestic life. They render the union between husband and wife unequal. They shorten the duration and weaken the force of the connection between parents and children.

IV. From the domestic state of the Americans, the transition to the consideration of their civil government and political institutions is natural. In every inquiry concerning the operations of men when united together in society, the first object of attention should be their mode of subsistence. Accordingly as that varies, their laws and policy must be different. The institution suited to the ideas and exigencies of tribes which subsist chiefly by fishing or hunting, and which have as yet acquired but an imperfect conception of any species of property, will be much more simple than those which must take place when the earth is cultivated with regular industry; and a right of property, not only in its productions, but in the soil itself, is completely ascertained.

All the people of America, now under review, belong to the former class. But though they may all be comprehended under the general denomination of savage, the advances which they had made in the art of procuring to themselves a certain and plentiful subsistence were very unequal. On the extensive plains of South America man appears in one of the rudest states in which he has been ever observed, or perhaps can exist. Several tribes depend entirely upon the bounty of nature for subsistence. They discover no solicitude, they employ little foresight, they scarcely exert any industry to secure what is necessary for their support. The *Topayers*, of Brazil, the *Guaxeros*, of Tierra Firme, the *Caiguas*, the *Moxos*, and several other people of Paraguay, are unacquainted with every species of cultivation. They neither sow nor plant. Even the culture of the manioc, of which cassada bread is made, is an art too intricate for their ingenuity, or too fatiguing to their indolence. The roots which the earth produces spontaneously; the fruits, the berries, and the seeds which they gather in the woods; together with lizards and other reptiles, which multiply amazingly with the heat of the climate in a fat soil moistened by frequent rains, supply them with food during some part of the year.* At other times they subsist by fishing; and nature seems to have indulged the laziness of the South American tribes by the liberality with which she ministers in this way to their wants. The vast rivers of that region in America abound with an infinite variety of the most delicate fish. The lakes and marshes formed by the annual overflowing of the waters are filled with all the different species, where they remain shut up, as in natural reservoirs, for the use of the inhabitants. They swarm in such shoals, that in some places they are catched without art or industry [54]. In others, the natives have discovered a method of infecting the water with the juice of certain plants, by which the fish are so intoxicated that they float on the surface and are taken with the hand [55]. Some tribes have ingenuity enough to preserve them without salt, by drying or smoking them upon hurdles over a slow fire.† The prolific quality of the rivers in South America induces many of the natives to resort to their banks, and to depend almost entirely for nourishment on what their waters supply with such profusion.‡ In this part of the globe hunting seems not to have been the first employment of men, or the first effort of their invention and labour to obtain food. They were fishers before they became hunters; and as the occupations of the former do not call for equal exertions of activity or talents with those of the latter, people in that state appear to possess neither the same degree of enterprise nor of ingenuity. The

* Nieuhoff. Hist. of Brazil. Church. Coll. ii. 134. Simon Conquista de Tierra Firmè, p. 166. Techo, Account of Paraguay, &c. Church. vi. 78. Lettr. Edif. 23. 384. 10. 190. Lozano, Descrip. del. Gran Chaco, p. 81. Ribas Histor. de los Triumfos, &c. p. 7. † Condam. 159. Gumilla, ii. 37. Lettr. Edif. 14. 199. 23. 328. Acugna, Relat. de la Riv. des Amas. 138. ‡ Barrere Relat. de Fr. Equin. p. 155

petty nations adjacent to the Maragnon and Orinoco are manifestly the most inactive and least intelligent of all the Americans.

None but tribes contiguous to great rivers can sustain themselves in this manner. The greater part of the American nations, dispersed over the forests with which their country is covered, do not procure subsistence with the same facility. For although these forests, especially in the southern continent of America, are stored plentifully with game,* considerable efforts of activity and ingenuity are requisite in pursuit of it. Necessity incited the natives to the one, and taught them the other. Hunting became their principal occupation; and as it called forth strenuous exertions of courage, of force, and of invention, it was deemed no less honourable than necessary. This occupation was peculiar to the men. They were trained to it from their earliest youth. A bold and dexterous hunter ranked next in fame to the distinguished warrior, and an alliance with the former is often courted in preference to one with the latter.† Hardly any device, which the ingenuity of man has discovered for ensnaring or destroying wild animals, was unknown to the Americans. While engaged in this favourite exercise, they shake off the indolence peculiar to their nature, the latent powers and vigour of their minds are roused, and they become active, persevering, and indefatigable. Their sagacity in finding their prey and their address in killing it are equal. Their reason and their senses being constantly directed towards this one object, the former displays such fertility of invention and the latter acquire such a degree of acuteness as appear almost incredible They discern the footsteps of a wild beast, which escape every other eye, and can follow them with certainty through the pathless forest. If they attack their game openly, their arrow seldom errs from the mark:‡ if they endeavour to circumvent it by art, it is almost impossible to avoid their toils. Among several tribes, their young men were not permitted to marry until they had given such proofs of their skill in hunting as put it beyond doubt that they were capable of providing for a family. Their ingenuity, always on the stretch, and sharpened by emulation as well as necessity, has struck out many inventions which greatly facilitate success in the chase. The most singular of these is the discovery of a poison, in which they dip the arrows employed in hunting. The slightest wound with those envenomed shafts is mortal. If they only pierce the skin, the blood fixes and congeals in a moment, and the strongest animal falls motionless to the ground. Nor does this poison, notwithstanding its violence and subtlety, infect the flesh of the animal which it kills. That may be eaten with perfect safety, and retain its native relish and qualities. All the nations situated upon the banks of the Maragnon and Orinoco are acquainted with this composition, the chief ingredient in which is the juice extracted from the root of the *curare*, a species of withe.§ In other parts of America they employ the juice of the *manchenille* for the same purpose, and it operates with no less fatal activity. To people possessed of those secrets the bow is a more destructive weapon than the musket, and, in their skilful hands, does great execution among the birds and beasts which abound in the forests of America

But the life of a hunter gradually leads man to a state more advanced. The chase, even where prey is abundant, and the dexterity of the hunter much improved, affords but an uncertain maintenance, and at some seasons it must be suspended altogether. If a savage trusts to his bow alone for food, he and his family will be often reduced to extreme distress [56] Hardly any region of the earth furnishes man spontaneously with what his wants require. In the mildest climates, and most fertile soils, his own

* P. Martyr, Decad. p. 324. Gumilla, ii. 4, &c. Acugna, i. 156. † Charlev. Histoire de la N. France, iii. 115. ‡ Biet. Voy. de France Equin. 357. Davies's Discov. of the River of Amaz. Purchas, iv. p. 1287. § Gumilla, ii. 1. &c Condam. 208. Recherch. Philos. ii 239 ncroft's Nat. Hist. of Guiana, 281, &c.

industry and foresight must be exerted in some degree to secure a regular supply of food. Their experience of this surmounts the abhorrence of labour natural to savage nations, and compels them to have recourse to culture, as subsidiary to hunting. In particular situations, some small tribes may subsist by fishing, independent of any production of the earth raised by their own industry. But throughout all America, we scarcely meet with any nation of hunters which does not practise some species of cultivation.

The agriculture of the Americans, however, is neither extensive nor laborious. As game and fish are their principal food, all they aim at by cultivation is to supply any occasional defect of these. In the southern continent of America, the natives confined their industry to rearing a few plants, which, in a rich soil and warm climate, were easily trained to maturity. The chief of these is *maize*, well known in Europe by the name of Turkey or Indian wheat, a grain extremely prolific, of simple culture, agreeable to the taste, and affording a strong hearty nourishment. The second is the *manioc*, which grows to the size of a large shrub or small tree, and produces roots somewhat resembling parsnips. After carefully squeezing out the juice, these roots are grated down to a fine powder, and formed into thin cakes called *cassada* bread, which, though insipid to the taste, proves no contemptible food.* As the juice of the manioc is a deadly poison, some authors have celebrated the ingenuity of the Americans in converting a noxious plant into wholesome nourishment. But it should rather be considered as one of the desperate expedients for procuring subsistence, to which necessity reduces rude nations; or, perhaps, men were led to the use of it by a progress in which there is nothing marvellous. One species of manioc is altogether free of any poisonous quality, and may be eaten without any preparation but that of roasting it in the embers. This, it is probable, was first used by the Americans as food; and, necessity having gradually taught them the art of separating its pernicious juice from the other species, they have by experience found it to be more prolific as well as more nourishing† [57]. The third is the *plantain*, which, though it rises to the height of a tree, is of such quick growth, that in less than a year it rewards the industry of the cultivator with its fruit. This, when roasted, supplies the place of bread, and is both palatable and nourishing [58]. The fourth is the *potatoe*, whose culture and qualities are too well known to need any description. The fifth is *pimento*, a small tree yielding a strong aromatic spice. The Americans, who, like other inhabitants of warm climates, delight in whatever is hot and of poignant flavour, deem this seasoning a necessary of life, and mingle it copiously with every kind of food they take.‡

Such are the various productions, which were the chief object of culture among the hunting tribes on the continent of America; and with a moderate exertion of active and provident industry these might have yielded a full supply to the wants of a numerous people. But men, accustomed to the free and vagrant life of hunters, are incapable of regular application to labour, and consider agriculture as a secondary and inferior occupation. Accordingly, the provision for subsistence, arising from cultivation, was so limited and scanty among the Americans, that, upon any accidental failure of their usual success in hunting, they were often reduced to extreme distress.

In the islands, the mode of subsisting was considerably different. None of the large animals which abound on the continent were known there. Only four species of quadrupeds, besides a kind of small dumb dog,

* Sloane Hist. of Jam. Introd. p. 18. Labat, i. 394. Acosta, Hist. Ind. Occid. Natur. lib. iv. c. 17. Ulloa, i. 62. Aublet, Mem. sur le Magnioc. Hist. des Plantes, tom. ii. p. 65, &c. † Martyr, Decad. 301. Labat, i. 411. Gumilla, iii. 192. Machucha Milic. Indiana, 164. ‡ Gumilla, iii. 171. Acosta, lib. iv. c. 20.

existed in the islands, the biggest of which did not exceed the size of a rabbit.* To hunt such a diminutive prey was an occupation which required no effort either of activity or courage. The chief employment of a hunter in the isles was to kill birds, which on the continent are deemed ignoble game, and left chiefly to the pursuit of boys.† This want of animals, as well as their peculiar situation, led the islanders to depend principally upon fishing for their subsistence.‡ Their rivers, and the sea with which they are surrounded, supplied them with this species of food. At some particular seasons, turtle, crabs, and other shellfish abounded in such numbers that the natives could support themselves with a facility in which their indolence delighted.§ At other times, they ate lizards and various reptiles of odious forms.|| To fishing the inhabitants of the islands added some degree of agriculture. Maize [59], manioc, and other plants were cultivated in the same manner as on the continent. But all the fruits of their industry, together with what their soil and climate produced spontaneously, afforded them but a scanty maintenance. Though their demands for food were very sparing, they hardly raised what was sufficient for their own consumption. If a few Spaniards settled in any district, such a small addition of supernumerary mouths soon exhausted their scanty stores, and brought on a famine.

Two circumstances, common to all the savage nations of America, concurred with those which I have already mentioned, not only in rendering their agriculture imperfect, but in circumscribing their power in all their operations. They had no tame animals; and they were unacquainted with the useful metals.

In other parts of the globe, man, in his rudest state, appears as lord of the creation, giving law to various tribes of animals, which he has tamed and reduced to subjection. The Tartar follows his prey on the horse which he has reared; or tends his numerous herds, which furnish him both with food and clothing: the Arab has rendered the camel docile, and avails himself of its persevering strength: the Laplander has formed the reindeer to be subservient to his will; and even the people of Kamchatka have trained their dogs to labour. This command over the inferior creatures is one of the noblest prerogatives of man, and among the greatest efforts of his wisdom and power. Without this his dominion is incomplete. He is a monarch who has no subjects, a master without servants, and must perform every operation by the strength of his own arm. Such was the condition of all the rude nations in America. Their reason was so little improved, or their union so incomplete, that they seem not to have been conscious of the superiority of their nature, and suffered all the animal creation to retain its liberty, without establishing their own authority over any one species. Most of the animals, indeed, which have been rendered domestic in our continent, do not exist in the New World; but those peculiar to it are neither so fierce nor so formidable as to have exempted them from servitude. There are some animals of the same species on both continents. But the rein-deer, which has been tamed and broken to the yoke in the one hemisphere, runs wild in the other. The *bison* of America is manifestly of the same species with the horned cattle of the other hemisphere.¶ The latter, even among the rudest nations in our continent, have been rendered domestic; and, in consequence of his dominion over them, man can accomplish works of labour with greater facility, and has made a great addition to his means of subsistence. The inhabitants of many regions of the New World, where the bison abounds, might have derived the same advantages from it. It is not of a nature so indocile, but that it might have been trained to be as subservient to man

* Oviedo, lib. xii. in proém. † Ribas Hist. de los Triumph. p. 13. De la Potherie, ii. 33. iii. 20. ‡ Oviedo, lib. xiii. c. 1. Gomara, Hist. Gener. c. 28. § Gomara, Hist. Gener. c 9 Labat, ii. 221, &c. || Oviedo, lib. xiii c 3 ¶ Buffon. artic. *Bison*.

as our cattle.* But a savage, in that uncultivated state wherein the Americans were discovered, is the enemy of the other animals, not their superior. He wastes and destroys, but knows not how to multiply or to govern them.†

This, perhaps, is the most notable distinction between the inhabitants of the Ancient and New Worlds, and a high pre-eminence of civilized men above such as continue rude. The greatest operations of man in changing and improving the face of nature, as well as his most considerable efforts in cultivating the earth, are accomplished by means of the aid which he receives from the animals that he has tamed, and employs in labour. It is by their strength that he subdues the stubborn soil, and converts the desert or marsh into a fruitful field. But man, in his civilized state, is so accustomed to the service of the domestic animals, that he seldom reflects upon the vast benefits which he derives from it. If we were to suppose him, even when most improved, to be deprived of their useful ministry, his empire over nature must in some measure cease, and he would remain a feeble animal, at a loss how to subsist, and incapable of attempting such arduous undertakings as their assistance enables him to execute with ease.

It is a doubtful point, whether the dominion of man over the animal creation, or his acquiring the useful metals, has contributed most to extend his power. The era of this important discovery is unknown, and in our hemisphere very remote. It is only by tradition, or by digging up some rude instruments of our forefathers, that we learn that mankind were originally unacquainted with the use of metals, and endeavoured to supply the want of them by employing flints, shells, bones, and other hard substances, for the same purposes which metals serve among polished nations. Nature completes the formation of some metals. Gold, silver, and copper, are found in their perfect state in the clefts of rocks, in the sides of mountains, or the channels of rivers. These were accordingly the metals first known, and first applied to use. But iron, the most serviceable of all, and to which man is most indebted, is never discovered in its perfect form; its gross and stubborn ore must feel twice the force of fire, and go through two laborious processes, before it becomes fit for use. Man was long acquainted with the other metals before he acquired the art of fabricating iron, or attained such ingenuity as to perfect an invention, to which he is indebted for those instruments wherewith he subdues the earth, and commands all its inhabitants. But in this, as well as in many other respects, the inferiority of the Americans was conspicuous. All the savage tribes, scattered over the continent and islands, were totally unacquainted with the metals which their soil produces in great abundance, if we except some trifling quantity of gold, which they picked up in the torrents that descended from their mountains, and formed into ornaments. Their devices to supply this want of the serviceable metals were extremely rude and awkward. The most simple operation was to them an undertaking of immense difficulty and labour. To fell a tree with no other instruments than hatchets of stone, was employment for a month.‡ To form a canoe into shape, and to hollow it, consumed years; and it frequently began to rot before they were able to finish it.§ Their operations in agriculture were equally slow and defective. In a country covered with woods of the hardest timber, the clearing of a small field destined for culture required the united efforts of a tribe, and was a work of much time and great toil. This was the business of the men, and their indolence was satisfied with performing it in a very slovenly manner. The labour of cultivation was left to the women, who, after digging, or rather stirring the

* Nouv. Découverte par Hennepin, p. 192. Kalm, i. 207. † Buffon Hist. Nat. ix. 85. Hist. Philos. et Polit. des Etablissem. des Europ. dans les deux Indes, vi. 364 ‡ Gumilla, iii 196. § Bordê Relat. des Caraibes, p. 22.

field, with wooden mattocks, and stakes hardened in the fire, sowed or planted it; but they were more indebted for the increase to the fertility of the soil than to their own rude industry.*

Agriculture, even when the strength of man is seconded by that of the animals which he has subjected to the yoke, and his power augmented by the use of the various instruments with which the discovery of metals has furnished him, is still a work of great labour; and it is with the sweat of his brow that he renders the earth fertile. It is not wonderful, then, that people destitute of both these advantages should have made so little progress in cultivation, that they must be considered as depending for subsistence on fishing and hunting, rather than on the fruits of their own labour.

From this description of the mode of subsisting among the rude American tribes, the form and genius of their political institutions may be deduced, and we are enabled to trace various circumstances of distinction between them and more civilized nations.

1. They were divided into small independent communities. While hunting is the chief source of subsistence, a vast extent of territory is requisite for supporting a small number of people. In proportion as men multiply and unite, the wild animals on which they depend for food diminish, or fly at a greater distance from the haunts of their enemy. The increase of a society in this state is limited by its own nature, and the members of it must either disperse, like the game which they pursue, or fall upon some better method of procuring food than by hunting. Beasts of prey are by nature solitary and unsocial, they go not forth to the chase in herds, but delight in those recesses of the forest where they can roam and destroy undisturbed. A nation of hunters resembles them both in occupation and in genius. They cannot form into large communities, because it would be impossible to find subsistence; and they must drive to a distance every rival who may encroach on those domains, which they consider as their own. This was the state of all the American tribes; the numbers in each were inconsiderable, though scattered over countries of great extent; they were far removed from one another, and engaged in perpetual hostilities or rivalship.† In America, the word *nation* is not of the same import as in other parts of the globe. It is applied to small societies, not exceeding, perhaps, two or three hundred persons, but occupying provinces, greater than some kingdoms in Europe. The country of Guiana, though of larger extent than the kingdom of France, and divided among a greater number of nations, did not contain above twenty-five thousand inhabitants.‡ In the provinces which border on the Orinoco, one may travel several hundred miles in different directions, without finding a single hut, or observing the footsteps of a human creature.§ In North America, where the climate is more rigorous, and the soil less fertile, the desolation is still greater. There, journeys of some hundred leagues have been made through uninhabited plains and forests‖ [60]. As long as hunting continues to be the chief employment of man, to which he trusts for subsistence, he can hardly be said to have occupied the earth [61].

2. Nations which depend upon hunting are in a great measure strangers to the idea of property. As the animals on which the hunter feeds are not bred under his inspection, nor nourished by his care, he can claim no right to them while they run wild in the forest. Where game is so plentiful that it may be catched with little trouble, men never dream of appropriating what is of small value, or of easy acquisition. Where it is so rare, that the labour or danger of the chase requires the united efforts of a tribe, or village, what is killed is a common stock belonging equally to all, who, by their

* Gumilla, iii. 166, &c. Lettr. Edif. xii. 10. † Lozano Descrip. del Gran Chaco, 59. 62. Fernandez Relac. Hist. de los Chequit. 162. ‡ Voyages de Marchais, iv. 353. § Gumilla, ii. 101. ‖ M. Fabry, quoted by Buffon, iii. 448. Lafitau, ii. 179. Bossu, Travels through Louisiana, i. 111.

skill or their courage, have contributed to the success of the excursion The forest or hunting-grounds are deemed the property of the tribe, from which it has a title to exclude every rival nation. But no individual arrogates a right to any district of these in preference to his fellow-citizens They belong alike to all; and thither, as to a general and undivided store, all repair in quest of sustenance. The same principles by which they regulate their chief occupation extend to that which is subordinate. Even agriculture has not introduced among them a complete idea of property. As the men hunt, the women labour together, and after they have shared the toils of the seed time, they enjoy the harvest in common.* Among some tribes, the increase of their cultivated lands is deposited in a public granary, and divided among them at stated times, according to their wants† [62] Among others, though they lay up separate stores, they do not acquire such an exclusive right of property, that they can enjoy superfluity while those around them suffer want.‡ Thus the distinctions arising from the inequality of possessions are unknown. The terms rich or poor enter not into their language; and being strangers to property, they are unacquainted with what is the great object of laws and policy, as well as the chief motive which induced mankind to establish the various arrangements of regular government.§

3. People in this state retain a high sense of equality and independence. Wherever the idea of property is not established, there can be no distinction among men but what arises from personal qualities. These can be conspicuous only on such occasions as call them forth into exertion. In times of danger, or in affairs of intricacy, the wisdom and experience of age are consulted, and prescribe the measures which ought to be pursued. When a tribe of savages takes the field against the enemies of their country, the warrior of most approved courage leads the youth to the combat.‖ If they go forth in a body to the chase, the most expert and adventurous hunter is foremost, and directs their motions. But during seasons of tranquillity and inaction, when there is no occasion to display those talents, all pre-eminence ceases. Every circumstance indicates that all the members of the community are on a level. They are clothed in the same simple garb. They feed on the same plain fare. Their houses and furniture are exactly similar. No distinction can arise from the inequality of possessions. Whatever forms dependence on one part, or constitutes superiority on the other, is unknown. All are freemen, all feel themselves to be such, and assert with firmness the rights which belong to that condition.¶ This sentiment of independence is imprinted so deeply in their nature that no change of condition can eradicate it, and bend their minds to servitude. Accustomed to be absolute masters of their own conduct, they disdain to execute the orders of another; and having never known control, they will not submit to correction. [63] Many of the Americans, when they found that they were treated as slaves by the Spaniards, died of grief; many destroyed themselves in despair.**

4. Among people in this state, government can assume little authority, and the sense of civil subordination must remain very imperfect. While the idea of property is unknown, or incompletely conceived; while the spontaneous productions of the earth, as well as the fruits of industry, are considered as belonging to the public stock, there can hardly be any such subject of difference or discussion among the members of the same community, as will require the hand of authority to interpose in order to adjust it. Where the right of separate and exclusive possession is not introduced, the

* Dr. Furguson's Essay, 125. † Gumilla, i. 265. Brickell, Hist. of N. Carol. 327. ‡ Deny's Hist. Natur. ii. 392, 393. § P. Martyr, Decad. p. 45. Veneg. Hist. of Californ. i 66. Lery, Navig. in Brazil, c. 17. ‖ Acosta Hist. lib. vi. c. 19. Stadius Hist. Brazil, lib. ii. c. 13. De Bry, iii. p. 110. Biet, 361. ¶ Labat, vi. 124. Brickell. Hist. of Carol. 310. ** Oviedo, lib. iii. c. 6. p. 97. Vega Conquist. de la Florida, i. 30. ii. 416. Labat, ii. 138. Benzo. Hist. Nov. Orb. lib. iv. c. 25.

great object of law and jurisdiction does not exist. When the members of a tribe are called into the field, either to invade the territories of their enemies, or to repel their attacks; when they are engaged together in the toil and dangers of the chase, they then perceive that they are part of a political body. They are conscious of their own connexion with the companions in conjunction with whom they act; and they follow and reverence such as excel in conduct and valour. But during the intervals between such common efforts they seem scarcely to feel the ties of political union* [64]. No visible form of government is established. The names of *magistrate* and *subject* are not in use. Every one seems to enjoy his natural independence almost entire. If a scheme of public utility be proposed, the members of the community are left at liberty to choose whether they will or will not assist in carrying it into execution. No statute imposes any service as a duty, no compulsory laws oblige them to perform it. All their resolutions are voluntary, and flow from the impulse of their own minds.† The first step towards establishing a public jurisdiction has not been taken in those rude societies. The right of revenge is left in private hands.‡ If violence is committed, or blood is shed, the community does not assume the power either of inflicting or of moderating the punishment. It belongs to the family and friends of the person injured or slain to avenge the wrong, or to accept of the reparation offered by the aggressor. If the elders interpose, it is to advise, not to decide, and it is seldom their counsels are listened to; for, as it is deemed pusillanimous to suffer an offender to escape with impunity, resentment is implacable and everlasting.§ The object of government among savages is rather foreign than domestic. They do not aim at maintaining interior order and police by public regulations, or the exertions of any permanent authority, but labour to preserve such union among the members of their tribe, that they may watch the motions of their enemies, and act against them with concert and vigour.

Such was the form of political order established among the greater part of the American nations. In this state were almost all the tribes spread over the provinces extending eastward of the Mississippi, from the mouth of the St. Lawrence to the confines of Florida. In a similar condition were the people of Brazil, the inhabitants of Chili, several tribes in Paragua and Guiana, and in the countries which stretch from the mouth of the Orinoco to the peninsula of Yucatan. Among such an infinite number of petty associations, there may be peculiarities which constitute a distinction, and mark the various degrees of their civilization and improvement. But an attempt to trace and enumerate these would be vain, as they have not been observed by persons capable of discerning the minute and delicate circumstances which serve to discriminate nations resembling one another in their general character and features. The description which I have given of the political institutions that took place among those rude tribes in America, concerning which we have received most complete information, will apply, with little variation, to every people, both in its northern and southern division, who have advanced no further in civilization than to add some slender degree of agriculture to fishing and hunting.

Imperfect as those institutions may appear, several tribes were not so far advanced in their political progress. Among all those petty nations which trusted for subsistence entirely to fishing and hunting without any species of cultivation, the union was so incomplete, and their sense of mutual dependence so feeble, that hardly any appearance of government or order can be discerned in their proceedings. Their wants are few, their objects of pursuit simple, they form into separate tribes, and act together, from

* Lozano Descr. del Gran. Chaco, 93. Melendez Teforos Verdaderos, ii. 23. † Charlev. Hist. N. France. iii. 266 268. ‡ Herrera, dec. 8. lib. iv. c. 8. § Charlev. Hist. N. France, iii. 271, 272. Lafit. i. 486. Cassini, Hist. de Nuovo Reyno de Granada, 226.

instinct, habit, or conveniency, rather than from any formal concert and association. To this class belong the Californians, several of the small nations in the extensive country of Paragua, some of the people on the banks of the Orinoco, and on the river St. Magdalene, in the new kingdom of Granada.*

But though among these last mentioned tribes there was hardly any shadow of regular government, and even among those which first described its authority is slender and confined within narrow bounds there were, however, some places in America where government was carried far beyond the degree of perfection which seems natural to rude nations. In surveying the political operations of man, either in his savage or civilized state, we discover singular and eccentric institutions, which start as it were from their station, and fly off so wide, that we labour in vain to bring them within the general laws of any system, or to account for them by those principles which influence other communities in a similar situation. Some instances of this occur among those people of America whom I have included under the common denomination of savage. These are so curious and important that I shall describe them, and attempt to explain their origin.

In the New World, as well as in other parts of the globe, cold or temperate countries appear to be the favourite seat of freedom and independence. There the mind, like the body, is firm and vigorous. There men, conscious of their own dignity, and capable of the greatest efforts in asserting it, aspire to independence, and their stubborn spirits stoop with reluctance to the yoke of servitude. In warmer climates, by whose influence the whole frame is so much enervated that present pleasure is the supreme felicity, and mere repose is enjoyment, men acquiesce, almost without a struggle, in the dominion of a superior. Accordingly, if we proceed from north to south along the continent of America, we shall find the power of those vested with authority gradually increasing, and the spirit of the people becoming more tame and passive. In Florida, the authority of the sachems, caziques, or chiefs, was not only permanent, but hereditary. They were distinguished by peculiar ornaments, they enjoyed prerogatives of various kinds, and were treated by their subjects with that reverence which people accustomed to subjection pay to a master.†

Among the Natchez, a powerful tribe now extinct, formerly situated on the banks of the Mississippi, a difference of rank took place, with which the northern tribes were altogether unacquainted. Some families were reputed noble, and enjoyed hereditary dignity. The body of the people was considered as vile, and formed only for subjection. This distinction was marked by appellations which intimated the high elevation of the one state, and the ignominious depression of the other. The former were called *Respectable;* the latter, the *Stinkards.* The great Chief, in whom the supreme authority was vested, is reputed to be a being of superior nature, the brother of the sun, the sole object of their worship. They approach this great Chief with religious veneration, and honour him as the representative of their deity. His will is a law, to which all submit with implicit obedience. The lives of his subjects are so absolutely at his disposal, that if any one has incurred his displeasure, the offender comes with profound humility and offers him his head. Nor does the dominion of the Chiefs end with their lives; their principal officers, their favourite wives, together with many domestics of inferior rank, are sacrificed at their tombs, that they may be attended in the next world by the same persons who served them in this; and such is the reverence in which they are held,

* Venegas, i. 68. Lettr. Edif. ii. 176. Techo Hist. of Parag. Churchill, vi. 78. Hist. Gen. des Voyages, xiv. 74. † Cardenas y Cano Ensayo Chronol. à la Hist. de Florida, p. 46. Le Moyne de Morgues Icones Floridæ, ap. de Bry, p. 1 4, &c. Charlev. Hist. N. France, iii 467, 468

that those victims welcome death with exultation, deeming it a recompense of their fidelity and a mark of distinction to be selected to accompany their deceased master.* Thus a perfect despotism, with its full train of superstition, arrogance, and cruelty, is established among the Natchez, and, by a singular fatality, that people has tasted of the worst calamities incident to polished nations, though they themselves are not far advanced beyond the tribes around them in civility and improvement. In Hispaniola, Cuba, and the larger islands, their caziques or chiefs possessed extensive power. The dignity was transmitted by hereditary right from father to son. Its honours and prerogatives were considerable. Their subjects paid great respect to the caziques, and executed their orders without hesitation or reserve.† They were distinguished by peculiar ornaments, and in order to preserve or augment the veneration of the people, they had the address to call in the aid of superstition to uphold their authority. They delivered their mandates as the oracles of heaven, and pretended to possess the power of regulating the seasons, and of dispensing rain or sunshine, according as their subjects stood in need of them.

In some parts of the southern continent, the power of the caziques seems to have been as extensive as in the isles. In Bogota, which is now a province of the new kingdom of Granada, there was settled a nation more considerable in number, and more improved in the various arts of life, than any in America, except the Mexicans and Peruvians. The people of Bogota subsisted chiefly by agriculture. The idea of property was introduced among them, and its rights, secured by laws, handed down by tradition, and observed with great care.‡ They lived in towns which may be termed large when compared with those in other parts of America. They were clothed in a decent manner, and their houses may be termed commodious when compared with those of the small tribes around them. The effects of this uncommon civilization were conspicuous. Government had assumed a regular form. A jurisdiction was established, which took cognizance of different crimes, and punished them with rigour. A distinction of ranks was known; their chief, to whom the Spaniards gave the title of monarch, and who merited that name on account of his splendour as well as power, reigned with absolute authority. He was attended by officers of various conditions; he never appeared in public without a numerous retinue; he was carried in a sort of palanquin with much pomp, and harbingers went before him to sweep the road and strew it with flowers. This uncommon pomp was supported by presents or taxes received from his subjects, to whom their prince was such an object of veneration that none of them presumed to look him directly in the face, or ever approached him but with an averted countenance.§ There were other tribes on the same continent, among which, though far less advanced than the people of Bogota in their progress towards refinement, the freedom and independence natural to man in his savage state was much abridged, and their caziques had assumed extensive authority.

It is not easy to point out the circumstances, or to discover the causes which contributed to introduce and establish among each of those people a form of government so different from that of the tribes around them, and so repugnant to the genius of rude nations. If the persons who had an opportunity of observing them in their original state had been more attentive and more discerning, we might have received information from the conquerors sufficient to guide us in this inquiry. If the transactions of people unacquainted with the use of letters were not involved in impenetrable obscurity, we might have derived some information from this

* Dumont Memoir. Hist. sur Louisiane, i, 175. Charlev. Hist. N. France, iii. 419, &c. Lettr. Edif. 20. 106. 111. † Herrera, dec. 1. lib. i. c. 16. lib. iii. c. 44. p. 88. Life of Columbus, ch. 32. ‡ Piedrahita Hist. de las Conquist. del Reyno de Granada, p. 46. § Herrera, dec. 6. lib. i c 2 lib v. c. 56. Piedrahita, c. 5. p. 25, &c. Gomara, Hist. c. 72.

domestic source. But as nothing satisfactory can be gathered either from the accounts of the Spaniards, or from their own traditions, we must have recourse to conjectures in order to explain the irregular appearances in the political state of the people whom I have mentioned. As all those tribes which had lost their native liberty and independence were seated in the torrid zone, or in countries approaching to it, the climate may be supposed to have had some influence in forming their minds to that servitude which seems to be the destiny of man in those regions of the globe. But though the influence of climate, more powerful than that of any other natural cause, is not to be overlooked, that alone cannot be admitted as a solution of the point in question. The operations of men are so complex that we must not attribute the form which they assume to the force of a single principle or cause. Although despotism be confined in America to the torrid zone, and to the warm regions bordering upon it, I have already observed that these countries contain various tribes, some of which possess a high degree of freedom, and others are altogether unacquainted with the restraints of government. The indolence and timidity peculiar to the inhabitants of the islands, render them so incapable of the sentiments or efforts necessary for maintaining independence, that there is no occasion to search for any other cause of their tame submission to the will of a superior. The subjection of the Natchez, and of the people of Bogota, seems to have been the consequence of a difference in their state from that of the other Americans. They were settled nations, residing constantly in one place. Hunting was not the chief occupation of the former, and the latter seem hardly to have trusted to it for any part of their subsistence. Both had made such progress in agriculture and arts that the idea of property was introduced in some degree in the one community, and fully established in the other. Among people in this state, avarice and ambition have acquired objects, and have begun to exert their power ; views of interest allure the selfish ; the desire of pre-eminence excites the enterprising ; dominion is courted by both ; and passions unknown to man in his savage state prompt the interested and ambitious to encroach on the rights of their fellow-citizens. Motives, with which rude nations are equally unacquainted, induce the people to submit tamely to the usurped authority of their superiors. But even among nations in this state, the spirit of subjects could not have been rendered so obsequious, or the power of rulers so unbounded, without the intervention of superstition. By its fatal influence the human mind, in every stage of its progress, is depressed, and its native vigour and independence subdued. Whoever can acquire the direction of this formidable engine, is secure of dominion over his species. Unfortunately for the people whose institutions are the subject of inquiry, this power was in the hands of their chiefs. The caziques of the isles could put what responses they pleased into the mouths of their *Cemis* or gods; and it was by their interposition, and in their name, that they imposed any tribute or burden on their people.* The same power and prerogative was exercised by the great chief of the Natchez, as the principal minister as well as the representative of the Sun, their deity. The respect which the people of Bogota paid to their monarchs was likewise inspired by religion, and the heir apparent of the kingdom was educated in the inner most recess of their principal temple, under such austere discipline, and with such peculiar rites, as tended to fill his subjects with high sentiments concerning the sanctity of his character and the dignity of his station.† Thus superstition, which in the rudest period of society, is either altogether unknown, or wastes its force in childish unmeaning practices, had acquired such an ascendant over those people of America, who had made some little progress towards refinement, that it became the chief instrument of bending

* Herrera, dec. 1. lib. iii. c. 3. † Piedrahita, p. 27

their minds to an untimely servitude, and subjected them, in the beginning of their political career, to a despotism hardly less rigorous than that which awaits nations in the last stage of their corruption and decline.

V. After examining the political institutions of the rude nations in America, the next object of attention is their art of war, or their provision for public security and defence. The small tribes dispersed over America are not only independent and unconnected, but engaged in perpetual hostilities with one another.* Though mostly strangers to the idea of separate property, vested in any individual, the rudest of the American nations are well acquainted with the rights of each community to its own domains. This right they hold to be perfect and exclusive, entitling the possessor to oppose the encroachment of neighbouring tribes. As it is of the utmost consequence to prevent them from destroying or disturbing the game in their hunting grounds, they guard this national property with a jealous attention. But as their territories are extensive, and the boundaries of them not exactly ascertained, innumerable subjects of dispute arise, which seldom terminate without bloodshed. Even in this simple and primitive state of society, interest is a source of discord, and often prompts savage tribes to take arms in order to repel or punish such as encroach on the forests or plains to which they trust for subsistence.

But interest is not either the most frequent or the most powerful motive of the incessant hostilities among rude nations. These must be imputed to the passion of revenge, which rages with such violence in the breast of savages, that eagerness to gratify it may be considered as the distinguishing characteristic of men in their uncivilized state. Circumstances of powerful influence, both in the interior government of rude tribes, and in their external operations against foreign enemies, concur in cherishing and adding strength to a passion fatal to the general tranquillity. When the right of redressing his own wrongs is left in the hands of every individual, injuries are felt with exquisite sensibility, and vengeance exercised with unrelenting rancour. No time can obliterate the memory of an offence, and it is seldom that it can be expiated but by the blood of the offender. In carrying on their public wars, savage nations are influenced by the same ideas, and animated with the same spirit, as in prosecuting private vengeance. In small communities, every man is touched with the injury or affront offered to the body of which he is a member, as if it were a personal attack upon his own honour or safety. The desire of revenge is communicated from breast to breast, and soon kindles into rage. As feeble societies can take the field only in small parties, each warrior is conscious of the importance of his own arm, and feels that to it is committed a considerable portion of the public vengeance. War, which between extensive kingdoms is carried on with little animosity, is prosecuted by small tribes with all the rancour of a private quarrel. The resentment of nations is as implacable as that of individuals. It may be dissembled or suppressed, but is never extinguished; and often, when least expected or dreaded, it bursts out with redoubled fury.† When polished nations have obtained the glory of victory, or have acquired an addition of territory, they may terminate a war with honour. But savages are not satisfied until they extirpate the community which is the object of their hatred. They fight, not to conquer, but to destroy. If they engage in hostilities, it is with a resolution never to see the face of the enemy in peace, but to prosecute the quarrel with immortal enmity.‡ The desire of vengeance is the first and almost the only principle which a savage instils into the minds of his children.§ This grows up

* Ribas Hist. de los Triumph. p. 9.

† Boucher Hist. Nat. de N. France, p. 93. Charlev. Hist. de N. France, iii. 215. 251. Lery ap. de Bry, iii. 204. Creux. Hist. Canad. p. 72. Lozano Descr. del Gran Chaco, 25. Hennep. Mœurs des Sauv. 40.

‡ Charlev. Hist. N. Fr. iii. 251. Colden. i. 108. ii. 126. Barrere, p. 170. 173.

§ Charlev. Hist. N. Fr. iii. 326. Lery ap. de Bry, iii. 236. Lozano Hist. de Parag. i. 144.

with him as he advances in life; and as his attention is directed to few objects, it requires a degree of force unknown among men whose passions are dissipated and weakened by the variety of their occupations and pursuits. The desire of vengeance, which takes possession of the heart of savages, resembles the instinctive rage of an animal rather than the passion of a man. It turns, with undiscerning fury, even against inanimate objects. If hurt accidentally by a stone, they often seize it in a transport of anger, and endeavour to wreak their vengeance upon it.* If struck with an arrow in a battle, they will tear it from the wound, break and bite it with their teeth, and dash it on the ground.† With respect to their enemies the rage of vengeance knows no bounds. When under the dominion of this passion, man becomes the most cruel of all animals. He neither pities, nor forgives, nor spares.

The force of this passion is so well understood by the Americans themselves, that they always apply to it in order to excite their people to take arms. If the elders of any tribe attempt to rouse their youth from sloth, if a chief wishes to allure a band of warriors to follow him in invading an enemy's country, the most persuasive topics of their martial eloquence are drawn from revenge. "The bones of our countrymen," say they, "lie uncovered; their bloody bed has not been washed clean. Their spirits cry against us; they must be appeased. Let us go and devour the people by whom they were slain. Sit no longer inactive upon your mats; lift the hatchet, console the spirits of the dead, and tell them that they shall be avenged."‡

Animated with such exhortations, the youth snatch their arms in a transport of fury, raise the song of war, and burn with impatience to imbrue their hands in the blood of their enemies. Private chiefs often assemble small parties and invade a hostile tribe without consulting the rulers of the community. A single warrior, prompted by caprice or revenge, will take the field alone, and march several hundred miles to surprise and cut off a straggling enemy [65]. The exploits of a noted warrior, in such solitary excursions, often form the chief part in the history of an American campaign [66]; and their elders connive at such irregular sallies, as they tend to cherish a martial spirit, and accustom their people to enterprise and danger.§ But when a war is national, and undertaken by public authority, the deliberations are formal and slow. The elders assemble, they deliver their opinions in solemn speeches, they weigh with maturity the nature of the enterprise, and balance its beneficial or disadvantageous consequences with no inconsiderable portion of political discernment or sagacity. Their priests and soothsayers are consulted, and sometimes they ask the advice even of their women.‖ If the determination be for war, they prepare for it with much ceremony. A leader offers to conduct the expedition, and is accepted. But no man is constrained to follow him; the resolution of the community to commence hostilities imposes no obligation upon any member to take part in the war. Each individual is still master of his own conduct, and his engagement in the service is perfectly voluntary.¶

The maxims by which they regulate their military operations, though extremely different from those which take place among more civilized and populous nations, are well suited to their own political state, and the nature of the country in which they act. They never take the field in numerous bodies, as it would require a greater effort of foresight and industry than is usual among savages, to provide for their subsistence during a march of some hundred miles through dreary forests, or during a long voyage upon their lakes and rivers. Their armies are not encumbered with baggage or

* Lery ap. de Bry, iii. 190 † Ibid. iii. 208. Herrera, dec. i. lib. vi. c. 8. ‡ Charlev Hist. N. Fr. iii. 216, 217. Lery ap. de Bry, iii. 204. § Bossu, i. 140. Lery ap. de Bry, 215. Hennepin Mœurs des Sauv. 41. Lafitau, ii. 169. ‖ Charlev. Hist. N. Fr. 215. 268. Biet. 367 380. ¶ Charlev. Hist. N. Fr. 217, 218.

military stores. Each warrior, besides his arms, carries a mat and a small bag of pounded maize, and with these is completely equipped for any service. While at a distance from the enemy's frontier, they disperse through the woods, and support themselves with the game which they kill, or the fish which they catch. As they approach nearer to the territories of the nation which they intend to attack, they collect their troops, and advance with greater caution. Even in their hottest and most active wars they proceed wholly by stratagem and ambuscade. They place not their glory in attacking their enemies with open force. To surprise and destroy is the greatest merit of a commander, and the highest pride of his followers. War and hunting are their only occupations, and they conduct both with the same spirit and the same arts. They follow the track of their enemies through the forest. They endeavour to discover their haunts, they lurk in some thicket near to these, and, with the patience of a sportsman lying in wait for game, will continue in their station day after day until they can rush upon their prey when most secure, and least able to resist them. If they meet no straggling party of the enemy, they advance towards their villages, but with such solicitude to conceal their own approach, that they often creep on their hands and feet through the woods, and paint their skins of the same colour with the withered leaves, in order to avoid detection.* If so fortunate as to remain unobserved, they set on fire the enemies' huts in the dead of night, and massacre the inhabitants as they fly naked and defenceless from the flames. If they hope to effect a retreat without being pursued, they carry off some prisoners, whom they reserve for a more dreadful fate. But if, notwithstanding all their address and precautions, they find that their motions are discovered, that the enemy has taken the alarm, and is prepared to oppose them, they usually deem it most prudent to retire. They regard it as extreme folly to meet an enemy who is on his guard, upon equal terms, or to give battle in an open field. The most distinguished success is a disgrace to a leader if it has been purchased with any considerable loss of his followers [67], and they never boast of a victory if stained with the blood of their own countrymen.† To fall in battle, instead of being reckoned an honourable death, is a misfortune which subjects the memory of a warrior to the imputation of rashness or imprudence‡ [68].

This system of war was universal in America; and the small uncivilized tribes, dispersed through all its different regions and climates, display more craft than boldness in carrying on their hostilities. Struck with this conduct, so opposite to the ideas and maxims of Europeans, several authors contend that it flows from a feeble and dastardly spirit peculiar to the Americans, which is incapable of any generous or manly exertion.§ But when we reflect that many of these tribes, on occasions which call for extraordinary efforts, not only defend themselves with obstinate resolution, but attack their enemies with the most daring courage, and that they possess fortitude of mind superior to the sense of danger or the fear of death, we must ascribe their habitual caution to some other cause than constitutional timidity.‖ The number of men in each tribe is so small, the difficulty of rearing new members amidst the hardships and dangers of savage life is so great, that the life of a citizen is extremely precious, and the preservation of it becomes a capital object in their policy. Had the point of honour been the same among the feeble American tribes as among the powerful nations of Europe, had they been taught to court fame or victory in contempt of danger and death, they must have been ruined by maxims so ill adapted to their condition. But wherever their com-

* Charlev. Hist. N. Fr. iii. 237, 238. Hennep. Mœurs des Sauv. p. 59

† Charlev. Hist. N. Fr. iii. 238. 307. Biet, 381. Lafitau Mœurs des Sauv. ii. 248.

‡ Charlev. iii. 376.

§ Recherches Philos. sur les Améric. i. 115. Voyage de March. iv. 410

‖ Lafitau Mœurs des Sauv. ii. 248, 249. Charlev. N. Fr. iii. 307.

munities are more populous, so that they can act with considerable force, and can sustain the loss of several of their members without being sensibly weakened, the military operations of the Americans more nearly resemble those of other nations. The Brazilians, as well as the tribes situated upon the banks of the river De la Plata, often take the field in such numerous bodies as deserve the name of armies.* They defy their enemies to the combat, engage in regular battles, and maintain the conflict with that desperate ferocity which is natural to men who, having no idea of war but that of exterminating their enemies, never give or take quarter [69]. In the powerful empires of Mexico and Peru, great armies were assembled, frequent battles were fought, and the theory as well as practice of war were different from what took place in those petty societies which assume the name of nations.

But though vigilance and attention are the qualities chiefly requisite where the object of war is to deceive and to surprise; and though the Americans, when acting singly, display an amazing degree of address in concealing their own motions, and discovering those of an enemy, yet it is remarkable that, when they take the field in parties, they can seldom be brought to observe the precautions most essential to their own security. Such is the difficulty of accustoming savages to subordination, or to act in concert; such is their impatience under restraint, and such their caprice and presumption, that it is rarely they can be brought to conform themselves to the counsels and directions of their leaders. They never station sentinels around the place where they rest at night, and after marching some hundred miles to surprise an enemy, are often surprised themselves, and cut off, while sunk in as profound sleep as if they were not within reach of danger.†

If, notwithstanding this negligence and security, which often frustrate their most artful schemes, they catch the enemy unprepared, they rush upon them with the utmost ferocity, and tearing off the scalps of all those who fall victims to their rage [70], they carry home those strange trophies in triumph. These they preserve as monuments, not only of their own prowess, but of the vengeance which their arm has inflicted upon the people who were objects of public resentment.‡ They are still more solicitous to seize prisoners. During their retreat, if they hope to effect it unmolested, the prisoners are commonly exempt from any insult, and treated with some degree of humanity, though guarded with the most strict attention.

But after this temporary suspension, the rage of the conquerors rekindles with new fury. As soon as they approach their own frontier, some of their number are despatched to inform their countrymen with respect to the success of the expedition. Then the prisoners begin to feel the wretchedness of their condition. The women of the village, together with the youth who have not attained to the age of bearing arms, assemble, and forming themselves into two lines, through which the prisoners must pass, beat and bruise them with sticks or stones in a cruel manner.§ After this first gratification of their rage against their enemies, follow lamentations for the loss of such of their own countrymen as have fallen in the service, accompanied with words and actions which seem to express the utmost anguish and grief. But in a moment, upon a signal given, their tears cease; they pass, with a sudden and unaccountable transition, from the depths of sorrow to the transports of joy; and begin to celebrate their victory with all the wild exultation of a barbarous triumph.‖ The fate of the prisoners remains still undecided. The old men deliberate concerning it. Some are destined to be tortured to death, in order to satiate

* Fabri Veriss. Descrip. Indiæ ap. de Bry, vii. p. 42. † Charlev. N. Fr. iii. 236, 237. Lettr. Edif. xvii. 308. xx. 130. Lafit. Mœurs, 247. Lahontan, ii. 176. ‡ Lafitau Mœurs, ii. 256 § Lahontan, ii. 184. ‖ Charlev. Hist. N. Fr. iii. 241. Lafitau Mœurs, ii. 264.

the revenge of the conquerors; some to replace the members which the community has lost in that or former wars. They who are reserved for this milder fate, are led to the huts of those whose friends have been killed. The women meet them at the door, and if they receive them, their sufferings are at an end. They are adopted into the family, and, according to their phrase, are seated upon the mat of the deceased. They assume his name, they hold the same rank, and are treated thenceforward with all the tenderness due to a father, a brother, a husband, or a friend. But, if either from caprice or an unrelenting desire of revenge, the women of any family refuse to accept of the prisoner who is offered to them, his doom is fixed. No power can then save him from torture and death.

While their lot is in suspense, the prisoners themselves appear altogether unconcerned about what may befall them. They talk, they eat, they sleep, as if they were perfectly at ease, and no danger impending. When the fatal sentence is intimated to them, they receive it with an unaltered countenance, raise their death song, and prepare to suffer like men. Their conquerors assemble as to a solemn festival, resolved to put the fortitude of the captive to the utmost proof. A scene ensues, the bare description of which is enough to chill the heart with horror, wherever men have been accustomed, by milder institutions, to respect their species, and to melt into tenderness at the sight of human sufferings. The prisoners are tied naked to a stake, but so as to be at liberty to move round it. All who are present, men, women, and children, rush upon them like furies. Every species of torture is applied that the rancour of revenge can invent. Some burn their limbs with redhot irons, some mangle their bodies with knives, others tear their flesh from their bones, pluck out their nails by the roots, and rend and twist their sinews. They vie with one another in refinements of torture. Nothing sets bounds to their rage but the dread of abridging the duration of their vengeance by hastening the death of the sufferers; and such is their cruel ingenuity in tormenting, that, by avoiding industriously to hurt any vital part, they often prolong this scene of anguish for several days. In spite of all that they suffer, the victims continue to chant their death song with a firm voice, they boast of their own exploits, they insult their tormentors for their want of skill in avenging their friends and relations, they warn them of the vengeance which awaits them on account of what they are now doing, and excite their ferocity by the most provoking reproaches and threats. To display undaunted fortitude, in such dreadful situations, is the noblest triumph of a warrior. To avoid the trial by a voluntary death, or to shrink under it, is deemed infamous and cowardly. If any one betray symptoms of timidity, his tormentors often despatch him at once with contempt, as unworthy of being treated like a man.* Animated with those ideas, they endure without a groan what it seems almost impossible that human nature should sustain. They appear to be not only insensible of pain, but to court it. "Forbear," said an aged chief of the Iroquois, when his insults had provoked one of his tormentors to wound him with a knife, "forbear these stabs of your knife, and rather let me die by fire, that those dogs, your allies, from beyond the sea, may learn by my example to suffer like men."† This magnanimity, of which there are frequent instances among the American warriors, instead of exciting admiration, or calling forth sympathy, exasperates the fierce spirits of their torturers to fresh acts of cruelty.‡ Weary, at length of contending with men whose constancy of mind they cannot vanquish, some chief, in a rage, puts a period to their sufferings, by despatching them with his dagger or club.§

* De la Potherie, ii. 237. iii. 48. † Colden, Hist. of Five Nations, i 200. ‡ Voyages de Lahont, i. 236. § Charlev. Hist. N. Fr. iii. 243, &c. 385. Lafitau Mœurs, ii. 265. Creuxij Hist. Canad. p. 73. Hennep. Mœurs des Sauv. p. 64, &c. Lahont, i 233, &c. Tertre, ii. 405. De la Potherie, ii. 22 &c.

This barbarous scene is often succeeded by one no less shocking. As it is impossible to appease the fell spirit of revenge which rages in the heart of a savage, this frequently prompts the Americans to devour those unhappy persons who have been the victims of their cruelty. In the ancient world, tradition has preserved the memory of barbarous nations of cannibals, who fed on human flesh. But in every part of the New World there were people to whom this custom was familiar. It prevailed in the southern continent,* in several of the islands,† and in various districts of North America.‡ Even in those parts where circumstances with which we are unacquainted had in a great measure abolished this practice, it seems formerly to have been so well known that it is incorporated into the idiom of their language. Among the Iroquois, the phrase by which they express their resolution of making war against an enemy is, "Let us go and eat that nation." If they solicit the aid of a neighbouring tribe, they invite it "to eat broth made of the flesh of their enemies"§ [71]. Nor was the practice peculiar to rude unpolished tribes; the principle from which they took rise is so deeply rooted in the minds of the Americans, that it subsisted in Mexico, one of the civilized empires in the New World, and relics of it may be discovered among the more mild inhabitants of Peru. It was not scarcity of food, as some authors imagine, and the importunate cravings of hunger, which forced the Americans to those horrid repasts on their fellow-creatures. Human flesh was never used as common food in any country, and the various relations concerning people who reckoned it among the stated means of subsistence, flow from the credulity and mistakes of travellers. The rancour of revenge first prompted men to this barbarous action.‖ The fiercest tribes devoured none but prisoners taken in war, or such as they regarded as enemies [72]. Women and children who were not the objects of enmity, if not cut off in the fury of their first inroad into a hostile country, seldom suffered by the deliberate effects of their revenge.¶

The people of South America gratify their revenge in a manner some what different, but with no less unrelenting rancour. Their prisoners, after meeting at their first entrance with the same rough reception as among the North Americans,** are not only exempt from injury, but treated with the greatest kindness. They are feasted and caressed, and some beautiful young women are appointed to attend and solace them. It is not easy to account for this part of their conduct, unless we impute it to a refinement in cruelty. For, while they seem studious to attach the captives to life, by supplying them with every enjoyment that can render it agreeable, their doom is irrevocably fixed. On a day appointed the victorious tribe assembles, the prisoner is brought forth with great solemnity, he views the preparations for the sacrifice with as much indifference as if he himself were not the victim, and meeting his fate with undaunted firmness, is despatched with a single blow. The moment he falls, the women seize the body and dress it for the feast. They besmear their children with the blood, in order to kindle in their bosoms a hatred of their enemies, which is never extinguished, and all join in feeding upon the flesh with amazing greediness and exultation.†† To devour the body of a slaughtered enemy they deem the most complete and exquisite gratification of revenge. Wherever this practice prevails, captives never escape death, but they are not tortured with the same cruelty as among tribes which are less accustomed to such horrid feasts [73].

* Stadius ap. de Bry, iii. 123. Lery, ibid. 210. Biet, 384. Lettr. Edif. xxiii. 341. Piso, 8. Condam, 84. 97. Ribas, Hist. de los Triumph. 473. † Life of Columb. 529 Mart. Dec. p. 18. Tertre, ii. 405. ‡ Dumont. Mem. i. 254. Charlev. Hist. N. France, i. 259. ii. 14. iii. 21. De la Potherie, iii. 50. § Charlev. Hist. N. Fr. iii. 208, 209. Lettr. Edif. xxiii. p. 277. De la Potherie, ii. 298. ‖ Biet, 383. Blanco, Conversion de Piritu, p. 28. Bancroft, Nat. Hist. of Guiana, p. 259, &c. ¶ Biet, 382. Bandini, Vita di Americo, 84. Tertre, 405 Fermin. Descrip. de Surin. i. 54. ** Stadius ap. de Bry iii. 40 123. †† Stadius ap. de Bry, iii. 128, &c. Lery ap. de Bry, iii. 210.

As the constancy of every American warrior may be put to such severe proof, the great object of military education and discipline in the New World is to form the mind to sustain it. When nations carry on war with open force, defy their enemies to the combat, and vanquish them by the superiority of their skill or courage, soldiers are trained to be active, vigorous, and enterprising. But in America, where the genius and maxims of war are extremely different, passive fortitude is the quality in highest estimation. Accordingly, it is early the study of the Americans to acquire sentiments and habits which will enable them to behave like men when their resolution shall be put to the proof. As the youth of other nations exercise themselves in feats of activity and force, those of America vie with one another in exhibitions of their patience under sufferings. They harden their nerves by those voluntary trials, and gradually accustom themselves to endure the sharpest pain without complaining. A boy and girl will bind their naked arms together, and place a burning coal between them, in order to try who first discovers such impatience as to shake it off.* All the trials customary in America, when a youth is admitted into the class of warriors, or when a warrior is promoted to the dignity of captain or chief, are accommodated to this idea of manliness. They are not displays of valour, but of patience; they are not exhibitions of their ability to offend, but of their capacity to suffer. Among the tribes on the banks of the Orinoco, if a warrior aspires to the rank of captain, his probation begins with a long fast, more rigid than any ever observed by the most abstemious hermit. At the close of this the chiefs assemble, each gives him three lashes with a large whip, applied so vigorously that his body is almost flayed, and if he betrays the least symptoms of impatience or even sensibility, he is disgraced for ever, and rejected as unworthy of the honour to which he aspires. After some interval, the constancy of the candidate is proved by a more excruciating trial. He is laid in a hammoc with his hands bound fast, and an innumerable multitude of venomous ants, whose bite occasions exquisite pain, and produces a violent inflammation, are thrown upon him. The judges of his merit stand around the hammoc, and, while these cruel insects fasten upon the most sensible parts of his body, a sigh, a groan, an involuntary motion, expressive of what he suffers, would exclude him for ever from the rank of captain. Even after this evidence of his fortitude, it is not deemed to be completely ascertained, but must stand another test more dreadful than any he has hitherto undergone. He is again suspended in his hammoc, and covered with leaves of the palmetto. A fire of stinking herbs is kindled underneath, so as he may feel its heat and be involved in its smoke. Though scorched and almost suffocated, he must continue to endure with the same patien insensibility. Many perish in this rude essay of their firmness and courage, but such as go through it with applause, receive the ensigns of their new dignity with much solemnity, and are ever after regarded as leaders of approved resolution, whose behaviour in the most trying situations will do honour to their country.† In North America the previous trial of a warrior is neither so formal nor so severe. Though even there, before a youth is permitted to bear arms, his patience and fortitude are proved by blows, by fire, and by insults more intolerable to a haughty spirit than both.‡

The amazing steadiness with which the Americans endure the most exquisite torments, has induced some authors to suppose that, from the peculiar feebleness of their frame, their sensibility is not so acute as that of other people; as women, and persons of a relaxed habit, are observed o be less affected with pain than robust men, whose nerves are more firmly braced. But the constitution of the Americans is not so different

* Charlev. Hist. N. Fr. iii. 307. † Gumilla, ii. 286, &c. Biet, 376, &c. ‡ Charlev. Hist. N. Fr. iii. 219.

in its texture from that of the rest of the human species, as to account for this diversity in their behaviour. It flows from a principle of honour, instilled early and cultivated with such care, as to inspire man in his rudest state with an heroic magnanimity, to which philosophy hath endeavoured in vain to form him, when more highly improved and polished. This invincible constancy he has been taught to consider as the chief distinction of a man, and the highest attainment of a warrior. The ideas which influence his conduct, and the passions which take possession of his heart, are few. They operate of course with more decisive effect than when the mind is crowded with a multiplicity of objects, or distracted by the variety of its pursuits; and when every motive that acts with any force in forming the sentiments of a savage, prompts him to suffer with dignity, he will bear what might seem to be impossible for human patience to sustain. But wherever the fortitude of the Americans is not roused to exertion by their ideas of honour, their feelings of pain are the same with those of the rest of mankind [74]. Nor is that patience under sufferings for which the Americans have been so justly celebrated, a universal attainment. The constancy of many of the victims is overcome by the agonies of torture. Their weakness and lamentations complete the triumph of their enemies, and reflect disgrace upon their own country.*

The perpetual hostilities carried on among the American tribes are productive of very fatal effects. Even in seasons of public tranquillity, their imperfect industry does not supply them with any superfluous store of provisions; but when the irruption of an enemy desolates their cultivated lands, or disturbs them in their hunting excursions, such a calamity reduces a community, naturally unprovident and destitute of resources, to extreme want. All the people of the district that is invaded are frequently forced to take refuge in woods and mountains, which can afford them little subsistence, and where many of them perish. Notwithstanding their excessive caution in conducting their military operations, and the solicitude of every leader to preserve the lives of his followers, as the rude tribes in America seldom enjoy any interval of peace, the loss of men among them is considerable in proportion to the degree of population. Thus famine and the sword combine in thinning their numbers. All their communities are feeble, and nothing now remains of several nations which were once considerable, but the name.†

Sensible of this continual decay, there are tribes which endeavour to recruit their national force when exhausted, by adopting prisoners taken in war, and by this expedient prevent their total extinction. The practice, however, is not universally received. Resentment operates more powerfully among savages than considerations of policy. Far the greater part of their captives was anciently sacrificed to their vengeance, and it is only since their numbers began to decline fast, that they have generally adopted milder maxims. But such as they do naturalize renounce for ever their native tribe, and assume the manners as well as passions of the people by whom they are adopted‡ so entirely, that they often join them in expeditions against their own countrymen. Such a sudden transition, and so repugnant to one of the most powerful instincts implanted by nature, would be deemed strange among many people; but among the members of small communities, where national enmity is violent and deep rooted, it has the appearance of being still more unaccountable. It seems, however, to result naturally from the principles upon which war is carried on in America. When nations aim at exterminating their enemies, no exchange of prisoners can ever take place. From the moment one is made a prisoner, his country and his friends consider him as dead [75]. He has incurred indelible

* Charlev. Hist. N. Fr. iii. 248. 385. De la Potherie, iii. 48. † Charlev. Hist. N. Fr. iii. 202, 203. 429 Gumilla, ii. 227, &c. ‡ Charlev. Hist. N. Fr. iii. 245, &c. Lafit. ii. 308.

disgrace by suffering himself to be surprised or to be taken by an enemy; and were he to return home, after such a stain upon his honour, his nearest relations would not receive or even acknowledge that they knew him.* Some tribes were still more rigid, and if a prisoner returned, the infamy which he had brought on his country was expiated, by putting him instantly to death.† As the unfortunate captive is thus an outcast from his own country, and the ties which bound him to it are irreparably broken, he feels less reluctance in forming a new connexion with people, who, as an evidence of their friendly sentiments, not only deliver him from a cruel death, but offer to admit him to all the rights of a fellow-citizen. The perfect similarity of manners among savage nations facilitates and completes the union, and induces a captive to transfer not only his allegiance, but his affection to the community into the bosom of which he is received.

But though war be the chief occupation of men in their rude state, and to excel in it their highest distinction and pride, their inferiority is always manifest when they engage in competition with polished nations. Destitute of that foresight which discerns and provides for remote events, strangers to the union and mutual confidence requisite in forming any extensive plan of operations, and incapable of the subordination no less requisite in carrying such plans into execution, savage nations may astonish a disciplined enemy by their valour, but seldom prove formidable to him by their conduct; and whenever the contest is of long continuance, must yield to superior art [76]. The empires of Peru and Mexico, though their progress in civilization, when measured by the European or Asiatic standards, was inconsiderable, acquired such an ascendency over the rude tribes around them, that they subjected most of them with great facility to their power. When the people of Europe overran the various provinces of America, this superiority was still more conspicuous. Neither the courage nor number of the natives could repel a handful of invaders. The alienation and enmity, prevalent among barbarians, prevented them from uniting in any common scheme of defence, and while each tribe fought separately, all were subdued.

VI. The arts of rude nations unacquainted with the use of metals, hardly merit any attention on their own account, but are worthy of some notice, as far as they serve to display the genius and manners of man in this stage of his progress. The first distress a savage must feel, will arise from the manner in which his body is affected by the heat, or cold, or moisture of the climate under which he lives; and his first care will be to provide some covering for his own defence. In the warmer, and more mild climates of America, none of the rude tribes were clothed. To most of them nature had not even suggested any idea of impropriety in being altogether uncovered.‡ As under a mild climate there was little need of any defence from the injuries of the air, and their extreme indolence shunned every species of labour to which it was not urged by absolute necessity, all the inhabitants of the isles, and a considerable part of the people on the continent, remained in this state of naked simplicity. Others were satisfied with some slight covering, such as decency required. But though naked, they were not unadorned. They dressed their hair in many different forms. They fastened bits of gold, or shells, or shining stones, in their ears, their noses, and cheeks.§ They stained their skins with a great variety of figures; and they spent much time, and submitted to great pain, in ornamenting their persons in this fantastic manner. Vanity, however, which finds endless occupation for ingenuity and invention in nations where dress has become a complex and intricate art, is circumscribed within so

* Lahont, ii. 185, 186. † Herrera, dec. 3. lib. iv. c. 16. p. 173. ‡ Lery Navigat. ap. de Bry, iii. p. 164. Life of Columbus, c. 24. Venegas Hist. of Californ. p. 70. § Lery ap. de Bry, iii. p. 165. Lettr. Edifiantes, xx. p. 223.

narrow bounds, and confined to so few articles among naked savages, that they are not satisfied with those simple decorations, and have a wonderful propensity to alter the natural form of their bodies, in order to render it (as they imagine) more perfect and beautiful. This practice was universal among the rudest of the American tribes. Their operations for that purpose begin as soon as an infant is born. By compressing the bones of the skull, while still soft and flexible, some flatten the crown of their heads; some squeeze them into the shape of a cone; others mould them as much as possible into a square figure;* and they often endanger the lives of their posterity by their violent and absurd efforts to derange the plan of nature, or to improve upon her designs. But in all their attempts either to adorn or to new model their persons, it seems to have been less the object of the Americans to please, or to appear beautiful, than to give an air of dignity and terror to their aspect. Their attention to dress had more reference to war than to gallantry. The difference in rank and estimation between the two sexes was so great, as seems to have extinguished, in some measure, their solicitude to appear mutually amiable. The man deemed it beneath him to adorn his person, for the sake of one on whom he was accustomed to look down as a slave. It was when the warrior had in view to enter the council of his nation, or to take the field against its enemies, that he assumed his choicest ornaments, and decked his person with the nicest care.† The decorations of the women were few and simple; whatever was precious or splendid was reserved for the men. In several tribes the women were obliged to spend a considerable part of their time every day in adorning and painting their husbands, and could bestow little attention upon ornamenting themselves. Among a race of men so haughty as to despise, or so cold as to neglect them, the women naturally became careless and slovenly, and the love of finery and show, which had been deemed their favourite passion, was confined chiefly to the other sex.‡ To deck his person was the distinction of a warrior, as well as one of his most serious occupations [77]. In one part of their dress, which at first sight appears the most singular and capricious, the Americans have discovered considerable sagacity in providing against the chief inconveniences of their climate, which is often sultry and moist to excess. All the different tribes, which remain unclothed, are accustomed to anoint and rub their bodies with the grease of animals, with viscous gums, and with oils of different kinds. By this they check that profuse perspiration, which in the torrid zone wastes the vigour of the frame, and abridges the period of human life. By this, too, they provide a defence against the extreme moisture during the rainy season [78]. They likewise, at certain seasons, temper paint of different colours with those unctuous substances, and bedaub themselves plentifully with that composition. Sheathed with this impenetrable varnish, their skins are not only protected from the penetrating heat of the sun, but as all the innumerable tribes of insects have an antipathy to the smell or taste of that mixture, they are delivered from their teasing persecution, which amidst forests and marshes, especially in the warmer regions, would have been altogether intolerable in a state of perfect nakedness.§

The next object to dress that will engage the attention of a savage, is to prepare some habitation which may afford him shelter by day, and a retreat at night. Whatever is connected with his ideas of personal dignity, whatever bears any reference to his military character, the savage warrior deems an object of importance. Whatever relates only to peaceable and inactive

* Oviedo Hist. lib. iii. c. 5. Ulloa, i. 329. Voyage de Labat, ii. 72. Charlevoix, iii. 323. Gumilla, i. 197, &c. Acugna Relat. de la Riv. des Amaz. ii. 83. Lawson's Voyage to Carolina, p. 33.

† Wafer's Voyage, p. 142. Lery ap. de Bry, iii. 167. Charlev. Hist. N. Fran. iii. 216. 222.

‡ Charlev. Hist. de la Nouv. France, iii. 278. 327. Lafitau, ii. 53. Kalm's Voyage, iii. 273. Lery ap. de Bry, iii. 169, 170. Purch. Pilgr. iv. 1287. Ribas Hist. de los Triumph, &c. 472

§ Labat, ii. 73. Gumilla, i. 190. 202. Bancroft Nat. Hist. of Guiana, 81. 280.

life, he views with indifference. Hence, though finically attentive to dress, he is little solicitous about the elegance or disposition of his habitation Savage nations, far from that state of improvement, in which the mode of living is considered as a mark of distinction, and unacquainted with those wants, which require a variety of accommodation, regulate the construction of their houses according to their limited ideas of necessity. Some of the American tribes were so extremely rude, and had advanced so little beyond the primæval simplicity of nature, that they had no houses at all. During the day, they take shelter from the scorching rays of the sun under thick trees; at night they form a shed with their branches and leaves [79]. In the rainy season they retire into coves, formed by the hand of Nature, or hollowed out by their own industry.* Others, who have no fixed abode, and roam through the forest in quest of game, sojourn in temporary huts, which they erect with little labour, and abandon without any concern. The inhabitants of those vast plains, which are deluged by the overflowing of rivers during the heavy rains that fall periodically between the tropics, raise houses upon piles fastened in the ground, or place them among the boughs of trees, and are thus safe amidst that wide extended inundation which surrounds them.† Such were the first essays of the rudest Americans towards providing themselves with habitations. But even among tribes which are more improved, and whose residence is become altogether fixed, the structure of their houses is extremely mean and simple. They are wretched huts, sometimes of an oblong and sometimes of a circular form, intended merely for shelter, with no view to elegance, and little attention to conveniency. The doors are so low that it is necessary to bend or to creep on the hands and feet in order to enter them. They are without windows, and have a large hole in the middle of the root, to convey out the smoke. To follow travellers in other minute circumstances of their descriptions, is not only beneath the dignity of history, but would be foreign to the object of my researches. One circumstance merits attention, as it is singular, and illustrates the character of the people. Some of their houses are so large as to contain accommodation for fourscore or a hundred persons. These are built for the reception of different families, which dwell together under the same roof [80], and often around a common fire, without separate apartments, or any kind of screen or partition between the spaces which they respectively occupy. As soon as men have acquired distinct ideas of property; or when they are so much attached to their females, as to watch them with care and jealousy; families of course divide and settle in separate houses, where they can secure and guard whatever they wish to preserve. This singular mode of habitation, among several people of America, may therefore be considered not only as the effect of their imperfect notions concerning property, but as a proof of inattention, and indifference towards their women. If they had not been accustomed to perfect equality, such an arrangement could not have taken place. If their sensibility had been apt to have taken alarm, they would not have trusted the virtue of their women amidst the temptations and opportunities of such a promiscuous intercourse. At the same time, the perpetual concord, which reigns in habitations where so many families are crowded together, is surprising, and affords a striking evidence that they must be people of either a very gentle, or of a very phlegmatic temper, who in such a situation, are unacquainted with animosity, brawling, and discord.‡

After making some provision for his dress and habitation, a savage

* Lettres Edif. v. 273. Venegas Hist. of Califor. i. 76. Lozano, Descrip. del Gran. Chaco, p. 55. Lettres Edif. ii. 176. Gumilla, i. 383. Bancroft, Nat. Hist. of Guiana, 277.

† Gumilla, i. 225. Herrera, dec. 1, lib. ix. c. 6. Oviedo Somar. p. 53. C.

‡ Journ. de Grillet et Bechamel dans la Goyane, p. 65. Lafitau Mœurs, ii. 4. Torquem. Monarq. i, 247. Journal Hist. de Joutel, 217. Lery Hist. Brazil, ap. de Bry, iii. 238. Lozano Descr. del Gran. Chaco, 67.

will perceive the necessity of preparing proper arms with which to assault or repel an enemy. This, accordingly, has early exercised the ingenuity and invention of all rude nations. The first offensive weapons were doubtless such as chance presented, and the first efforts of art to improve upon these, were extremely awkward and simple. Clubs made of some heavy wood, stakes hardened in the fire, lances whose heads were armed with flint or the bones of some animal, are weapons known to the rudest nations. All these, however, are of use only in close encounter. But men wished to annoy their enemies while at a distance, and the bow and arrow is the most early invention for this purpose. This weapon is in the hands of people whose advances in improvement are extremely inconsiderable, and is familiar to the inhabitants of every quarter of the globe. It is remarkable, however, that some tribes in America were so destitute of art and ingenuity, that they had not attained to the discovery of this simple invention,* and seem to have been unacquainted with the use of any missile weapon. The sling, though in its construction not more complex than the bow, and among many nations of equal antiquity, was little known to the people of North America,† or the islands, but appears to have been used by a few tribes in the southern continent‡ [81]. The people, in some provinces of Chili, and those of Patagonia, towards the southern extremity of America, use a weapon peculiar to themselves. They fasten stones, about the size of a fist, to each end of a leather thong of eight feet in length, and swing these round their heads, throw them with such dexterity, that they seldom miss the object at which they aim.§

Among people who had hardly any occupation but war or hunting, the chief exertions of their invention [82], as well as industry, were naturally directed towards these objects. With respect to every thing else, their wants and desires were so limited, that their invention was not upon the stretch. As their food and habitations are perfectly simple, their domestic utensils are few and rude. Some of the southern tribes had discovered the art of forming vessels of earthen ware, and baking them in the sun, so as they could endure the fire. In North America, they hollowed a piece of hard wood in the form of a kettle, and filling it with water, brought it to boil, by putting red-hot stones into it [83]. These vessels they used in preparing part of their provisions; and this may be considered as a step towards refinement and luxury; for men in their rudest state were not acquainted with any method of dressing their victuals but by roasting them on the fire; and among several tribes in America, this is the only species of cookery yet known.|| But the masterpiece of art, among the savages of America, is the construction of the canoes. An Esquimaux, shut up in his boat of whalebone, covered with the skins of seals, can brave that stormy ocean on which the barrenness of his country compels him to depend for the chief part of his subsistence.¶ The people of Canada venture upon their rivers and lakes in boats made of the bark of trees, and so light that two men can carry them, wherever shallows or cataracts obstruct the navigation [84]. In these frail vessels they undertake and accomplish long voyages.** The inhabitants of the isles and of the southern continent form their canoes by hollowing the trunk of a large tree, with infinite labour; and though in appearance they are extremely awkward and unwieldy, they paddle and steer them with such dexterity, that Europeans, well acquainted with all the improvements in the science of navigation, have been astonished at the rapidity of their motion, and the quickness of their evolutions. Their *pirogues*, or war boats, are so large as to carry forty or fifty men; their canoes, employed in fishing and in short voyages are less capa-

* Piedrahita Conq. del Nuevo Reyno, ix. 12. † Nauf. de Alv. Nun. Cabeca de Vaca, c. x. p. 12. ‡ Piedrah. p. 16. § Ovalle's Relation of Chili. Church. Collect. iii. 82. Falkner's Descript. of Patagon. p. 130. || Charlev. Hist. N. Fr. iii. 332. ¶ Ellis Voy. 133. ** Lafitau Mœurs, &c. ii. 213.

cious.* The form as well as materials of all these various kinds of vessels, is well adapted to the service for which they are destined; and the more minutely they are examined, the mechanism of their structure, as well as neatness of their fabric, will appear the more surprising.

But, in every attempt towards industry among the Americans, one striking quality in their character is conspicuous. They apply to work without ardour, carry it on with little activity, and, like children, are easily diverted from it. Even in operations which seem the most interesting, and where the most powerful motives urge them to vigorous exertions, they labour with a languid listlessness. Their work advances under their hand with such slowness, that an eyewitness compares it to the imperceptible progress of vegetation.† They will spend so many years in forming a canoe, that it often begins to rot with age before they finish it. They will suffer one part of a roof to decay and perish, before they complete the other.‡ The slightest manual operation consumes an amazing length of time, and what in polished nations would hardly be an effort of industry, is among savages an arduous undertaking. This slowness of the Americans in executing works of every kind may be imputed to various causes. Among savages, who do not depend for subsistence upon the efforts of regular industry, time is of so little importance that they set no value upon it; and provided they can finish a design, they never regard how long they are employed about it. The tools which they employ are so awkward and defective that every work in which they engage must necessarily be tedious. The hand of the most industrious and skilful artist, were it furnished with no better instrument than a stone hatchet, a shell, or the bone of some animal, would find it difficult to perfect the most simple work. It is by length of labour that he must endeavour to supply his defect of power. But above all, the cold phlegmatic temper peculiar to the Americans, renders their operations languid. It is almost impossible to rouse them from that habitual indolence to which they are sunk; and unless when engaged in war or in hunting, they seem incapable of exerting any vigorous effort. Their ardour of application is not so great as to call forth that inventive spirit which suggests expedients for facilitating and abridging labour. They will return to a task day after day, but all their methods of executing it are tedious and operose [85]. Even since the Europeans have communicated to them the knowledge of their instruments, and taught them to imitate their arts, the peculiar genius of the Americans is conspicuous in every attempt they make. They may be patient and assiduous in labour, they can copy with a servile and minute accuracy, but discover little invention and no talents for despatch. In spite of instruction and example, the spirit of the race predominates; their motions are naturally tardy, and it is in vain to urge them to quicken their pace. Among the Spaniards in America, *the work of an Indian* is a phrase by which they describe any thing, in the execution of which an immense time has been employed and much labour wasted.§

VII. No circumstance respecting rude nations has been the object of greater curiosity than their religious tenets and rites; and none, perhaps, has been so imperfectly understood, or represented with so little fidelity. Priests and missionaries are the persons who have had the best opportunities of carrying on this inquiry among the most uncivilized of the American tribes. Their minds, engrossed by the doctrines of their own religion, and habituated to its institutions, are apt to discover something which resembles those objects of their veneration, in the opinions and rites of every people. Whatever they contemplate they view through one medium, and draw and accommodate it to their own system. They study to reconcile the

* Labat, Voyages, ii. 91, &c. 131. † Gumilla, ii. 297. ‡ Borde Relat. des Caraibes, p. 22. § Voyages de Ulloa, i. 335. Lettr. Edif. &c. xv. 348.

institutions which fall under their observation to their own creed, not to explain them according to the rude notions of the people themselves. They ascribe to them ideas which they are incapable of forming, and suppose them to be acquainted with principles and facts, which it is impossible that they should know. Hence, some missionaries have been induced to believe, that even among the most barbarous nations in America, they had discovered traces, no less distinct than amazing, of their acquaintance with the sublime mysteries and peculiar institutions of Christianity. From their own interpretation of certain expressions and ceremonies, they have concluded that these people had some knowledge of the doctrine of the Trinity, of the incarnation of the Son of God, of his expiatory sacrifice, of the virtue of the cross, and of the efficacy of the sacraments.* In such unintelligent and credulous guides we can place little confidence.

But even when we make our choice of conductors with the greatest care, we must not follow them with implicit faith. An inquiry into the religious notions of rude nations is involved in peculiar intricacies, and we must often pause in order to separate the facts which our informers relate from the reasonings with which they are accompanied, or the theories which they build upon them. Several pious writers, more attentive to the importance of the subject than to the condition of the people whose sentiments they were endeavouring to discover, have bestowed much unprofitable labour in researches of this nature [86].

There are two fundamental doctrines, upon which the whole system of religion, as far as it can be discovered by the light of nature, is established. The one respects the being of a God, the other the immortality of the soul. To discover the ideas of the uncultivated nations under our review, with regard to those important points, is not only an object of curiosity, but may afford instruction. To these two articles I shall confine my researches, leaving subordinate opinions, and the detail of local superstitions, to more minute inquirers. Whoever has had any opportunity of examining into the religious opinions of persons in the inferior ranks of life, even in the most enlightened and civilized nations, will find that their system of belief is derived from instruction, not discovered by inquiry. That numerous part of the human species, whose lot is labour, whose principal and almost sole occupation is to secure subsistence, views the arrangement and operations of nature with little reflection, and has neither leisure nor capacity for entering into that path of refined and intricate speculation which conducts to the knowledge of the principles of natural religion. In the early and most rude periods of savage life, such disquisitions are altogether unknown. When the intellectual powers are just beginning to unfold, and their first feeble exertions are directed towards a few objects of primary necessity and use; when the faculties of the mind are so limited as not to have formed abstract or general ideas; when language is so barren as to be destitute of names to distinguish any thing that is not perceived by some of the senses; it is preposterous to expect that man should be capable of tracing with accuracy the relation between cause and effect; or to suppose that he should rise from the contemplation of the one to the knowledge of the other, and form just conceptions of a Deity, as the Creator and Governor of the universe. The idea of creation is so familiar, wherever the mind is enlarged by science and illuminated with revelation, that we seldom reflect how profound and abstruse this idea is, or consider what progress man must have made in observation and research, before he could arrive at any knowledge of this elementary principle in religion. Accordingly, several tribes have been discovered in America, which have no idea whatever of a Supreme Being, and no rites of religious worship. Inattentive to that

* Venegas, i. 88. 92. Torquemada, ii. 445. Garcia Origen. 122. Herrera, dec. 4. lib. ix. c. 7. dec. 5. lib. iv. c. 7.

magnificent spectacle of beauty and order presented to their view, unaccustomed to reflect either upon what they themselves are, or to inquire who is the author of their existence, men, in their savage state, pass their days like the animals around them, without knowledge or veneration of any superior power. Some rude tribes have not in their language any name for the Deity, nor have the most accurate observers been able to discover any practice or institution which seemed to imply that they recognised his authority, or were solicitous to obtain his favour* [87]. It is however only among men in the most uncultivated state of nature, and while their intellectual faculties are so feeble and limited as hardly to elevate them above the irrational creation, that we discover this total insensibility to the impressions of any invisible power.

But the human mind, formed for religion, soon opens to the reception of ideas, which are destined, when corrected and refined, to be the great source of consolation amidst the calamities of life. Among some of the American tribes, still in the infancy of improvement, we discern apprehensions of some invisible and powerful beings. These apprehensions are originally indistinct and perplexed, and seem to be suggested rather by the dread of impending evils than to flow from gratitude for blessings received. While nature holds on her course with uniform and undisturbed regularity, men enjoy the benefits resulting from it, without inquiring concerning its cause. But every deviation from this regular course rouses and astonishes them. When they behold events to which they are not accustomed, they search for the reasons of them with eager curiosity. Their understanding is unable to penetrate into these; but imagination, a more forward and ardent faculty of the mind, decides without hesitation. It ascribes the extraordinary occurrences in nature to the influence of invisible beings, and supposes that the thunder, the hurricane, and the earthquake are effects of their interposition. Some such confused notion of spiritual or invisible power, superintending over those natural calamities which frequently desolate the earth, and terrify its inhabitants, may be traced among many rude nations [88]. But besides this, the disasters and dangers of savage life are so many, and men often find themselves in situations so formidable, that the mind, sensible of its own weakness, has no resource but in the guidance and protection of wisdom and power superior to what is human. Dejected with calamities which oppress him, and exposed to dangers which he cannot repel, the savage no longer relies upon himself; he feels his own impotence, and sees no prospect of being extricated, but by the interposition of some unseen arm. Hence, in all unenlightened nations, the first rites or practices which bear any resemblance to acts of religion, have it for their object to avert evils which men suffer or dread. The *Manitous* or *Okkis* of the North Americans were amulets or charms, which they imagined to be of such virtue as to preserve the persons who reposed confidence in them from any disastrous event, or they were considered as tutelary spirits, whose aid they might implore in circumstances of distress.† The *Cemis* of the islanders were reputed by them to be the authors of every calamity that afflicts the human race; they were represented under the most frightful forms, and religious homage was paid to them with no other view than to appease these furious deities.‡ Even among those tribes whose religious system was more enlarged, and who had formed some conception of benevolent beings, which delighted in conferring benefits, as well as of malicious powers prone to inflict evil; superstition still appears

* Biet, 539. Lery ap. de Bry, iii. 221. Nieuhoff. Church. Coll. ii. 132. Lettr. Edif. 2. 177. Id. 12, 13. Venegas, i. 87. Lozano Descr. del Gran Chaco, 59. Fernand. Mission. de Chequit. 39. Gumilla, ii. 156. Rochefort Hist. des Antilles, p. 468. Margrave Hist. in Append. de Chiliensibus, 286. Ulloa, Notic. Amer. 335, &c. Barrere, 218, 219. Harcourt Voy. to Guiana, Purch. Pilgr. iv p. 1273. Account of Brazil, by a Portuguese. Ibid. p. 1289. Jones's Journal, p. 59. † Charlev N. Fr. iii 343. &c. Creuxii Hist. Canab. p. 82, &c. ‡ Oviedo. lib. iii. c. 1. p. 111. P. Martyr, decad. p. 102, &c.

as the offspring of fear, and all its efforts were employed to avert calamities. They were persuaded that their good deities, prompted by the beneficence of their nature, would bestow every blessing in their power, without solicitation or acknowledgment; and their only anxiety was to soothe and deprecate the wrath of the powers whom they regarded as the enemies of mankind.*

Such were the imperfect conceptions of the greater part of the Americans with respect to the interposition of invisible agents, and such, almost universally, was the mean and illiberal object of their superstitions. Were we to trace back the ideas of other nations to that rude state in which history first presents them to our view, we should discover a surprising resemblance in their tenets and practices; and should be convinced, that in similar circumstances, the faculties of the human mind hold nearly the same course in their progress, and arrive at almost the same conclusions. The impressions of fear are conspicuous in all the systems of superstition formed in this situation. The most exalted notions of men rise no higher than to a perplexed apprehension of certain beings, whose power, though supernatural, is limited as well as partial.

But, among other tribes, which have been longer united, or have made greater progress in improvement, we discern some feeble pointing towards more just and adequate conceptions of the power that presides in nature. They seem to perceive that there must be some universal cause to whom all things are indebted for their being. If we may judge by some of their expressions, they appear to acknowledge a divine power to be the maker of the world, and the disposer of all events. They denominate him the *Great Spirit*.† But these ideas are faint and confused, and when they attempt to explain them, it is manifest that among them the word *spirit* has a meaning very different from that in which we employ it, and that they have no conception of any deity but what is corporeal. They believe their gods to be of the human form, though of a nature more excellent than man, and retail such wild incoherent fables concerning their functions and operations, as are altogether unworthy of a place in history. Even among these tribes, there is no established form of public worship; there are no temples erected in honour of their deities; and no ministers peculiarly consecrated to their service. They have the knowledge, however, of several superstitious ceremonies and practices handed down to them by tradition, and to these they have recourse with a childish credulity, when roused by any emergence from their usual insensibility, and excited to acknowledge the power, and to implore the protection of superior beings.‡

The tribe of the Natchez, and the people of Bogota, had advanced beyond the other uncultivated nations of America in their ideas of religion, as well as in their political institutions; and it is no less difficult to explain the cause of this distinction than of that which we have already considered. The Sun was the chief object of religious worship among the Natchez. In their temples, which were constructed with some magnificence, and decorated with various ornaments, according to their mode of architecture, they preserved a perpetual fire, as the purest emblem of their divinity. Ministers were appointed to watch and feed this sacred flame. The first function of the great chief of the nation, every morning, was an act of obeisance to the Sun; and festivals returned at stated seasons, which were celebrated by the whole community with solemn but unbloody rites.§ This is the most refined species of superstition known in America, and perhaps one of the most natural as well as most seducing. The Sun is the apparent source of the joy, fertility, and life, diffused through nature; and

* Tertre, ii. 365. Borde, p. 14. State of Virginia, by a Native, book iii. p. 32, 33. Dumont, i. 165. Bancroft Nat. Hist. of Guiana, 309. † Charlev. N. Fr. iii. 343. Sagard, Voy. du Pays des Hurons, 226. ‡ Charlev. N. Fr. iii. 345. Colden, i. 17. § Dumont, i. 158, &c. Charlev N. Fr. iii. 417, &c. 429. Lafitau, i. 167.

while the human mind, in its earlier essays towards inquiry, contemplates and admires his universal and animating energy, its admiration is apt to stop short at what is visible, without reaching to the unseen cause; and pays that adoration to the most glorious and beneficial work of God, which is due only to him who formed it. As fire is the purest and most active of the elements, and in some of its qualities and effects resembles the Sun, it was, not improperly, chosen to be the emblem of his powerful operation. The ancient Persians, a people far superior, in every respect, to that rude tribe whose rites I am describing, founded their religious system on similar principles, and established a form of public worship, less gross and exceptionable than that of any people destitute of guidance from revelation. This surprising coincidence in sentiment between two nations, in such different states of improvement, is one of the many singular and unaccountable circumstances which occur in the history of human affairs.

Among the people of Bogota, the Sun and Moon were, likewise, the chief objects of veneration. Their system of religion was more regular and complete, though less pure, than that of the Natchez. They had temples, altars, priests, sacrifices, and that long train of ceremonies, which superstition introduces wherever she has fully established her dominion over the minds of men. But the rites of their worship were cruel and bloody. They offered human victims to their deities, and many of their practices nearly resembled the barbarous institutions of the Mexicans, the genius of which we shall have an opportunity of considering more attentively in its proper place.*

With respect to the other great doctrine of religion, concerning the immortality of the soul, the sentiments of the Americans were more united: the human mind, even when least improved and invigorated by culture, shrinks from the thoughts of annihilation, and looks forward with hope and expectation to a state of future existence. This sentiment, resulting from a secret consciousness of its own dignity, from an instinctive longing after immortality, is universal, and may be deemed natural. Upon this are founded the most exalted hopes of man in his highest state of improvement; nor has nature withheld from him this soothing consolation, in the most early and rude period of his progress. We can trace this opinion from one extremity of America to the other, in some regions more faint and obscure, in others more perfectly developed, but nowhere unknown. The most uncivilized of its savage tribes do not apprehend death as the extinction of being. All entertain hopes of a future and more happy state, where they shall be for ever exempt from the calamities which imbitter human life in its present condition. This future state they conceive to be a delightful country, blessed with perpetual spring, whose forests abound with game, whose rivers swarm with fish, where famine is never felt, and uninterrupted plenty shall be enjoyed without labour or toil. But as men, in forming their first imperfect ideas concerning the invisible world, suppose that there they shall continue to feel the same desires, and to be engaged in the same occupations, as in the present world; they naturally ascribe eminence and distinction, in that state, to the same qualities and talents which are here the object of their esteem. The Americans, accordingly, allotted the highest place, in their country of spirits, to the skilful hunter, to the adventurous and successful warrior, and to such as had tortured the greatest number of captives, and devoured their flesh.† These notions were so prevalent that they gave rise to a universal custom, which is at once the strongest evidence that the Americans believe in a future state, and the best illustration of what they expect there. As they imagine, that departed spirits begin their career anew in the world whither they are gone, that their friends may not enter upon it defenceless and unprovided,

* Piedrahita, Conq. del N. Reyno, p. 17. Herrera, dec. 6. lib. v. c. 6.

† Lery ap. de Bry, iii, 222. Charlev. N. Fr. iii. 351, &c. De la Potherie, ii. 45, &c. iii. 5.

they bury together with the bodies of the dead their bow, their arrows, and other weapons used in hunting or war; they deposit in their tombs the skins or stuffs of which they make garments, Indian corn, manioc, venison, domestic utensils, and whatever is reckoned among the necessaries in their simple mode of life.* In some provinces, upon the decease of a cazique or chief, a certain number of his wives, of his favourites, and of his slaves, were put to death, and interred together with him, that he might appear with the same dignity in his future station, and be waited upon by the same attendants.† This persuasion is so deep rooted that many of the deceased person's retainers offer themselves as voluntary victims, and court the privilege of accompanying their departed master, as a high distinction. It has been found difficult, on some occasions, to set bounds to this enthusiasm of affectionate duty, and to reduce the train of a favourite leader to such a number as the tribe could afford to spare [89].

Among the Americans, as well as other uncivilized nations, many of the rites and observances which bear some resemblance to acts of religion, have no connection with devotion, but proceed from a fond desire of prying into futurity. The human mind is most apt to feel and to discover this vain curiosity, when its own powers are most feeble and uninformed. Astonished with occurrences of which it is unable to comprehend the cause, it naturally fancies that there is something mysterious and wonderful in their origin. Alarmed at events of which it cannot discern the issue or the consequences, it has recourse to other means of discovering them than the exercise of its own sagacity. Wherever superstition is so established as to form a regular system, this desire of penetrating into the secrets of futurity is connected with it. Divination becomes a religious act. Priests, as the ministers of heaven, pretend to deliver its oracles to men. They are the only soothsayers, augurs, and magicians, who profess the sacred and important art of disclosing what is hid from other eyes.

But, among rude nations, who pay no veneration to any superintending power, and who have no established rites or ministers of religion, their curiosity, to discover what is future and unknown, is cherished by a different principle, and derives strength from another alliance. As the diseases of men, in the savage state, are (as has been already observed) like those of the animal creation, few, but extremely violent, their impatience under what they suffer, and solicitude for the recovery of health, soon inspired them with extraordinary reverence for such as pretended to understand the nature of their maladies, and to be possessed of knowledge sufficient to preserve or deliver them from their sudden and fatal effects. These ignorant pretenders, however, were such utter strangers to the structure of the human frame, as to be equally unacquainted with the causes of its disorders, and the manner in which they will terminate. Superstition, mingled frequently with some portion of craft, supplied what they wanted in science. They imputed the origin of diseases to supernatural influence, and prescribed or performed a variety of mysterious rites, which they gave out to be of such efficacy as to remove the most dangerous and inveterate maladies. The credulity and love of the marvellous, natural to uninformed men, favoured the deception, and prepared them to be the dupes of those impostors. Among savages, their first physicians are a kind of conjurers or wizards, who boast that they know what is past, and can foretell what is to come. Incantations, sorcery, and mummeries of diverse kinds, no less strange than frivolous, are the means which they employ to expel the imaginary causes of malignity;‡ and, relying upon

* Chronica de Cieca de Leon, c. 28. Sagard, 288. Creux. Hist. Canad. p. 91. Rochefort. Hist. des Antiles, 568. Biet, 391. De la Potherie, ii. 44. iii. 8. Blanco Convers. de Piritu, p. 35.
† Dumont Louisiane, i. 208, &c. Oviedo, lib. v. c. 3. Gomara Hist. Gen. c. 28. P. Mart. decad. 304. Charlev. N. Fr. iii. 421. Herrera, dec. 1. lib. iii. c. 3. P. Melchior Hernandez Memor. de Cheriqui. Coll. Orig. Papers, i. Chron. de Cieca de Leon, c. 33.
‡ P. Melch. Hernandez Memorial de Cheriqui. Collect. Orig. Pap. i.

the efficacy of these, they predict with confidence what will be the fate of their deluded patients. Thus superstition, in its earliest form, flowed from the solicitude of man to be delivered from present distress, not from his dread of evils awaiting him in a future life, and was originally ingrafted on medicine, not on religion. One of the first and most intelligent historians of America, was struck with this alliance between the art of divination and that of physic, among the people of Hispaniola.* But this was not peculiar to them. The *Alexis*, the *Piayas*, the *Autmoins*, or whatever was the distinguishing name of their diviners and charmers in other parts of America, were all the physicians of their respective tribes, in the same manner as the *Bubitos* of Hispaniola. As their function led them to apply to the human mind when enfeebled by sickness, and as they found it, in that season of dejection, prone to be alarmed with imaginary fears, or amused with vain hopes, they easily induced it to rely with implicit confidence on the virtue of their spells, and the certainty of their predictions.†

Whenever men acknowledge the reality of supernatural power and discernment in one instance, they have a propensity to admit it in others. The Americans did not long suppose the efficacy of conjuration to be confined to one subject. They had recourse to it in every situation of danger or distress. When the events of war were peculiarly disastrous, when they met with unforeseen disappointment in hunting, when inundations or drought threatened their crops with destruction, they called upon their conjurors to begin their incantations, in order to discover the causes of those calamities, or to foretell what would be their issue.‡ Their confidence in this delusive art gradually increased, and manifested itself in all the occurrences of life. When involved in any difficulty, or about to enter upon any transaction of moment, every individual regularly consulted the sorcerer, and depended upon his instructions to extricate him from the former, as well as to direct his conduct in the latter. Even among the rudest tribes in America, superstition appears in this form, and divination is an art in high esteem. Long before man had acquired such knowledge of a deity as inspires reverence, and leads to adoration, we observe him stretching out a presumptuous hand to draw aside that veil with which Providence kindly conceals its purposes from human knowledge; and we find him labouring with fruitless anxiety to penetrate into the mysteries of the divine administration. To discern and to worship a superintending power is an evidence of the enlargement and maturity of the human understanding; a vain desire of prying into futurity is the error of its infancy, and a proof of its weakness.

From this weakness proceeded likewise the faith of the Americans in dreams, their observation of omens, their attention to the chirping of birds, and the cries of animals, all which they suppose to be indications of future events; and if any one of these prognostics is deemed unfavourable, they instantly abandon the pursuit of those measures on which they are most eagerly bent.§

VIII. But if we would form a complete idea of the uncultivated nations of America, we must not pass unobserved some singular customs, which, though universal and characteristic, could not be reduced, with propriety, to any of the articles into which I have divided my inquiry concerning their manners.

Among savages, in every part of the globe, the love of dancing is a favourite passion. As, during a great part of their time, they languish in

* Oviedo, lib. v. c. 1. † Herrera, dec. 1. lib. iii. c. 4. Osborne Coll. ii. 860. Dumont, I. 169, &c. Charlev. N. Fr. iii. 361. 364, &c. Lawson, N. Carrol. 214. Ribas, Triumf. p. 17. Biet, 386. De la Potherie, ii. 35, &c. ‡ Charlev. N. Fr. iii. 3. Dumont, i. 173. Fernand. Relac. de los Chequit. p. 40. Lozano, 84. Margrave, 279. § Charlev. N. Fr. iii. 262. 353. Stadius ap de Bry, iii. 120. Creuxj. Hist. Canad 84. Techo Hist. of Parag. Church. Coll. vi. 37. De la Potherie, iii. 6.

a state of inactivity and indolence, without any occupation to rouse or interest them, they delight universally in a pastime which calls forth the active powers of their nature into exercise. The Spaniards, when they first visited America, were astonished at the fondness of the natives for dancing, and beheld with wonder a people, cold and unanimated in most of their other pursuits, kindle into life, and exert themselves with ardour, as often as this favourite amusement recurred. Among them, indeed, dancing ought not to be denominated an amusement. It is a serious and important occupation which mingles in every occurrence of public or private life. If any intercourse be necessary between two American tribes, the ambassadors of the one approach in a solemn dance, and present the calumet or emblem of peace; the sachems of the other receive it with the same ceremony.* If war is denounced against an enemy, it is by a dance expressive of the resentment which they feel, and of the vengeance which they meditate.† If the wrath of their gods is to be appeased, or their bene ficence to be celebrated; if they rejoice at the birth of a child, or mourn the death of a friend,‡ they have dances appropriated to each of these situations, and suited to the different sentiments with which they are then animated. If a person is indisposed, a dance is prescribed as the most effectual means of restoring him to health; and if he himself cannot endure the fatigue of such an exercise, the physician or conjuror performs it in his name, as if the virtue of his activity could be transferred to his patient.§

All their dances are imitations of some action; and though the music by which they are regulated is extremely simple, and tiresome to the ear by its dull monotony, some of their dances appear wonderfully expressive and animated. The war dance is, perhaps, the most striking. It is the representation of a complete American campaign. The departure of the warriors from their village, their march into the enemy's country, the caution with which they encamp, the address with which they station some of their party in ambush, the manner of surprising the enemy, the noise and ferocity of the combat, the scalping of those who are slain, the seizing of prisoners, the triumphant return of the conquerors, and the torture of the victims, are successively exhibited. The performers enter with such enthusiastic ardour into their several parts; their gestures, their countenance, their voice, are so wild and so well adapted to their various situations, that Europeans can hardly believe it to be a mimic scene, or view it without emotions of fear and horror.‖

But however expressive some of the American dances may be, there is one circumstance in them remarkable, and connected with the character of the race. The songs, the dances, the amusements of other nations, expressive of the sentiments which animate their hearts, are often adapted to display or excite that sensbility which mutually attaches the sexes. Among some people, such is the ardour of this passion, that love is almost the sole object of festivity and joy; and as rude nations are strangers to delicacy, and unaccustomed to disguise any emotion of their minds, their dances are often extremely wanton and indecent. Such is the *Calenda*, of which the natives of Africa are so passionately fond;¶ and such the feats of the dancing girls which the Asiatics contemplate with so much avidity of desire. But among the Americans, more cold and indifferent to their females, from causes which I have already explained, the passion of love mingles but little with their festivals and pastimes. Their songs and

* De la Potherie Hist. ii. 17, &c. Charlev. N. Fr. iii. 211. 297. La Hontan, i. 100 137. Hennepin Decou. 146, &c. † Charlev. N. Fr. iii. 298. Lafitau, i. 523. ‡ Joutel, 343. Gomara Hist. Gen. c. 196. § Denys Hist. Nat. 189. Brickell, 372. De la Potherie, ii. 36. ‖ De la Potherie, ii. 116. Charlev. N. F. iii. 297. Lafitau, i. 523. ¶ Adanson Voyage to Senegal, iii. 287. Labat, Voyages, iv. 463. Sloane Hist. Nat. of Jam. Introd. p. 48. Fermin Descript. de Surin, i. 139.

dances are mostly solemn and martial; they are connected with some of the serious and important affairs of life;* and, having no relation to love or gallantry, are seldom common to the two sexes, but executed by the men and women apart† [90]. If, on some occasions, the women are permitted to join in the festival, the character of the entertainment is still the same, and no movement or gesture is expressive of attachment, or encourages familiarity.‡

An immoderate love of play, especially at games of hazard, which seems to be natural to all people unaccustomed to the occupations of regular industry, is likewise universal among the Americans. The same causes, which so often prompt persons in civilized life, who are at their ease, to have recourse to this pastime, render it the delight of the savage. The former are independent of labour, the latter do not feel the necessity of it; and as both are unemployed, they run with transport to whatever is interesting enough to stir and to agitate their minds. Hence the Americans, who at other times are so indifferent, so phlegmatic, so silent, and animated with so few desires, as soon as they engage in play become rapacious, impatient, noisy, and almost frantic with eagerness. Their furs, their domestic untensils, their clothes, their arms, are staked at the gaming table, and when all is lost, high as their sense of independence is, in a wild emotion of despair or of hope, they will often risk their personal liberty upon a single cast.§ Among several tribes, such gaming parties frequently recur, and become their most acceptable entertainment at every great festival. Superstition, which is apt to take hold of those passions which are most vigorous, frequently lends its aid to confirm and strengthen this favourite inclination. Their conjurors are accustomed to prescribe a solemn match at play as one of the most efficacious methods of appeasing their gods, or of restoring the sick to health.‖

From causes similar to those which render them fond of play, the Americans are extremely addicted to drunkenness. It seems to have been one of the first exertions of human ingenuity to discover some composition of an intoxicating quality; and there is hardly any nation so rude, or so destitute of invention, as not to have succeeded in this fatal research. The most barbarous of the American tribes have been so unfortunate as to attain this art; and even those which are so deficient in knowledge, as to be unacquainted with the method of giving an inebriating strength to liquors by fermentation, can accomplish the same end by other means. The people of the islands of North America, and of California, used, for this purpose, the smoke of tobacco, drawn up with a certain instrument into the nostrils, the fumes of which ascending to the brain, they felt all the transports and phrensy of intoxication¶ [91]. In almost every other part of the New World, the natives possessed the art of extracting an intoxicating liquor from maize or the manioc root, the same substances which they convert into bread. The operation by which they effect this nearly resembles the common one of brewing, but with this difference, that, in place of yeast, they use a nauseous infusion of a certain quantity of maize or manioc chewed by their women. The saliva excites a vigorous fermentation, and in a few days the liquor becomes fit for drinking. It is not disagreeable to the taste, and, when swallowed in large quantities, is of an intoxicating quality.** This is the general beverage of the Americans, which they distinguish by various names, and for which they feel such a violent and insatiable desire as it is not easy either to conceive or

* Descript. of N. France. Osborne Coll. ii. 883. Charlev. N. Fr. iii. 84. † Wafer's Account of Isthmus, &c. 169. Lery ap. de Bry, iii. 177. Lozano Hist. de Parag. i. 149. Herrera, dec. 2. lib. vii. c. 8. dec. 4. lib. x. c. 4. ‡ Barrere, Fr. Equin. p. 191. § Charlev. N. Fr. iii. 261 318. Lafitau, ii. 338. &c. Ribas Triumf. 13. Brickell, 335. ‖ Charlev. N. Fr. iii. 262 ¶ Oviedo Hist. ap. Ramus, iii. 113. Venegas, i. 68. Naufrag. de Cabeca de Vaca, cap. 26. ** Stadius ap. de Bry, iii. 111. Lery, ibid. 175.

describe. Among polished nations, where a succession of various functions and amusements keeps the mind in continual occupation, the desire for strong drink is regulated in a great measure by the climate, and increases or diminishes according to the variations of its temperature. In warm regions, the delicate and sensible frame of the inhabitants does not require the stimulation of fermented liquors. In colder countries, the constitution of the natives, more robust and more sluggish, stands in need of generous liquors to quicken and animate it. But among savages, the desire of something that is of power to intoxicate is in every situation the same. All the people of America, if we except some small tribes near the Straits of Magellan, whether natives of the torrid zone, or inhabitants of its more temperate regions, or placed by a harder fate in the severe climates towards its northern or southern extremity, appear to be equally under the dominion of this appetite.* Such a similarity of taste, among people in such different situations, must be ascribed to the influence of some moral cause, and cannot be considered as the effect of any physical or constitutional want. While engaged in war or in the chase, the savage is often in the most interesting situations, and all the powers of his nature are roused to the most vigorous exertions. But those animating scenes are succeeded by long intervals of repose, during which the warrior meets with nothing that he deems of sufficient dignity or importance to merit his attention. He languishes and mopes in this season of indolence. The posture of his body is an emblem of the state of his mind. In one climate, cowering over the fire in his cabin; in another, stretched under the shade of some tree, he dozes away his time in sleep, or in an unthinking joyless inactivity not far removed from it. As strong liquors awake him from this torpid state, give a brisker motion to his spirits, and enliven him more thoroughly than either dancing or gaming, his love of them is excessive. A savage, when not engaged in action, is a pensive melancholy animal; but as soon as he tastes, or has a prospect of tasting, the intoxicating draught, he becomes gay and frolicsome.† Whatever be the occasion or pretexts on which the Americans assemble, the meeting always terminates in a debauch. Many of their festivals have no other object, and they welcome the return of them with transports of joy. As they are not accustomed to restrain any appetite, they set no bounds to this. The riot often continues without intermission several days; and whatever may be the fatal effects of their excess, they never cease from drinking as long as one drop of liquor remains. The persons of greatest eminence, the most distinguished warriors, and the chiefs most renowned for their wisdom, have no greater command of themselves than the most obscure members of the community. Their eagerness for present enjoyment renders them blind to its fatal consequences; and those very men, who in other situations seem to possess a force of mind more than human, are in this instance inferior to children, in foresight as well as consideration, and mere slaves of brutal appetite.‡ When their passions, naturally strong, are heightened and inflamed by drink, they are guilty of the most enormous outrages, and the festivity seldom concludes without deeds of violence or bloodshed.§

But, amidst this wild debauch, there is one circumstance remarkable the women, in most of the American tribes, are not permitted to partake of it [92]. Their province is to prepare the liquor, to serve it about to the guests, and to take care of their husbands and friends when their reason is overpowered. This exclusion of the women from an enjoyment so highly valued by savages, may be justly considered as a mark of their inferiority, and as an additional evidence of that contempt with which they were

* Gumilla, i. 257. Lozano Descrip. del Gran. Chaco, 56. 103. Ribas, 8. Ulloa, i. 249. 337. Marchais, iv. 436. Fernandez Mission. de las Chequit. 35. Barrere, p. 203. Blanco Convers. de Piritu, 31. † Melendez Tesóres Verdad. iii. 369. ‡ Ribas, 9. Ulloa, i 338. § Lettr. Edif. ii. 178. Torquemada Mond. Ind. i. 339.

treated in the New World. The people of North America, when first discovered, were not acquainted with any intoxicating drink; but as the Europeans early found it their interest to supply them with spirituous liquors, drunkenness soon became as universal among them as among their countrymen to the south; and their women, having acquired this new taste, indulge it with as little decency and moderation as the men.*

It were endless to enumerate all the detached customs which have excited the wonder of travellers in America; but I cannot omit one seemingly as singular as any that has been mentioned. When their parents and other relations become old, or labour under any distemper which their slender knowledge of the healing art cannot remove, the Americans cut short their days with a violent hand, in order to be relieved from the burden of supporting and tending them. This practice prevailed among the ruder tribes in every part of the continent, from Hudson's Bay to the river De la Plata; and however shocking it may be to those sentiments of tenderness and attachment, which, in civilized life, we are apt to consider as congenial with our frame, the condition of man in the savage state leads and reconciles him to it. The same hardships and difficulty of procuring subsistence, which deter savages, in some cases, from rearing their children, prompt them to destroy the aged and infirm. The declining state of the one is as helpless as the infancy of the other. The former are no less unable than the latter to perform the functions that belong to a warrior or hunter, or to endure those various distresses in which savages are so often involved by their own want of foresight and industry. Their relations feel this; and, incapable of attending to the wants or weaknesses of others, their impatience under an additional burden prompts them to extinguish that life which they find it difficult to sustain. This is not regarded as a deed of cruelty, but as an act of mercy. An American, broken with years and infirmities, conscious that he can no longer depend on the aid of those around him, places himself contentedly in his grave; and it is by the hands of his children or nearest relations that the thong is pulled, or the blow inflicted, which releases him for ever from the sorrows of life.†

IX. After contemplating the rude American tribes in such various lights; after taking a view of their customs and manners from so many different stations, nothing remains but to form a general estimate of their character compared with that of more polished nations. A human being, as he comes originally from the hand of nature, is every where the same. At his first appearance in the state of infancy, whether it be among the rudest savages or in the most civilized nation, we can discern no quality which marks any distinction or superiority. The capacity of improvement seems to be the same; and the talents he may afterwards acquire, as well as the virtues he may be rendered capable of exercising, depend, in a great measure, upon the state of society in which he is placed. To this state his mind naturally accommodates itself, and from it receives discipline and culture. In proportion to the wants which it accustoms a human being to feel, and the functions in which these engage him, his intellectual powers are called forth. According to the connexions which it establishes between him and the rest of his species, the affections of his heart are exerted. It is only by attending to this great principle that we can discover what is the character of man in every different period of his progress.

If we apply it to savage life, and measure the attainments of the human mind in that state by this standard, we shall find, according to an observation which I have already made, that the intellectual powers of man must be extremely limited in their operations. They are confined

* Hutchinson Hist. of Massachus. 469. Lafitau, ii. 125. Sagard, 146.

† Cassani Histor de N. Reyno de Gran. p. 300. Piso, p. 6. Ellis Voy. 191. Gumilla, i. 333.

within the narrow sphere of what he deems necessary for supplying his own wants. Whatever has not some relation to these neither attracts his attention, nor is the object of his inquiries. But however narrow the bounds may be within which the knowledge of a savage is circumscribed, he possesses thoroughly that small portion which he has attained. It was not communicated to him by formal instruction; he does not attend to it as a matter of mere speculation and curiosity; it is the result of his own observation, the fruit of his own experience, and accommodated to his condition and exigencies. While employed in the active occupations of war or of hunting, he often finds himself in difficult and perilous situations, from which the efforts of his own sagacity must extricate him. He is frequently engaged in measures, where every step depends upon his own ability to decide, where he must rely solely upon his own penetration to discern the dangers to which he is exposed, and upon his own wisdom in providing against them. In consequence of this, he feels the knowledge which he possesses, and the efforts which he makes, and either in deliberation or action rests on himself alone.

As the talents of individuals are exercised and improved by such exertions, much political wisdom is said to be displayed in conducting the affairs of their small communities. The council of old men in an American tribe, deliberating upon its interests, and determining with respect to peace or war, has been compared to the senate in more polished republics. The proceedings of the former, we are told, are often no less formal and sagacious than those of the latter. Great political wisdom is exhibited in pondering the various measures proposed, and in balancing their probable advantages against the evils of which they may be productive. Much address and eloquence are employed by the leaders, who aspire at acquiring such confidence with their countrymen as to have an ascendant in those assemblies.* But, among savage tribes, the field for displaying political talents cannot be extensive. Where the idea of private property is incomplete, and no criminal jurisdiction is established, there is hardly any function of internal government to exercise. Where there is no commerce, and scarcely any intercourse among separate tribes; where enmity is implacable, and hostilities are carried on almost without intermission; there will be few points of public concern to adjust with their neighbours; and that department of their affairs which may be denominated foreign, cannot be so intricate as to require much refined policy in conducting it. Where individuals are so thoughtless and improvident as seldom to take effectual precautions for self-preservation, it is vain to expect that public measures and deliberations will be regulated by the contemplation of remote events. It is the genius of savages to act from the impulse of present passion. They have neither foresight nor temper to form complicated arrangements with respect to their future conduct. The consultations of the Americans, indeed, are so frequent, and their negotiations are so many [93], and so long protracted, as to give their proceedings an extraordinary aspect of wisdom. But this is not owing so much to the depth of their schemes, as to the coldness and phlegm of their temper, which render them slow in determining.† If we except the celebrated league, that united the Five Nations in Canada, into a federal republic, which shall be considered in its proper place, we can discern few such traces of political wisdom, among the rude American tribes, as discover any great degree of foresight or extent of intellectual abilities. Even among them, we shall find public measures more frequently directed by the impetuous ferocity of their youth, than regulated by the experience and wisdom of their old men.

As the condition of man in the savage state is unfavourable to the

* Charlev. Hist. N. Fr. iii. 269, &c. † Ibid. iii. 271.

progress of the understanding, it has a tendency likewise, in some respects, to check the exercise of affection, and to render the heart contracted. The strongest feeling in the mind of a savage is a sense of his own independence. He has sacrificed so small a portion of his natural liberty by becoming a member of society, that he remains, in a great degree, the sole master of his own actions.* He often takes his resolutions alone, without consulting or feeling any connection with the persons around him. In many of his operations he stands as much detached from the rest of his species as if he had formed no union with them. Conscious how little he depends upon other men, he is apt to view them with a careless indifference. Even the force of his mind contributes to increase this unconcern; and as he looks not beyond himself in deliberating with respect to the part which he should act, his solicitude about the consequences of it seldom extends further. He pursues his own career, and indulges his own fancy, without inquiring or regarding whether what he does be agreeable or offensive to others, whether they may derive benefit or receive hurt from it. Hence the ungovernable caprice of savages, their impatience under any species of restraint, their inability to suppress or moderate any inclination, the scorn or neglect with which they receive advice, their high estimation of themselves, and their contempt of other men. Among them, the pride of independence produces almost the same effects with interestedness in a more advanced state of society; it refers every thing to a man himself, it leads him to be indifferent about the manner in which his actions may affect other men, and renders the gratification of his own wishes the measure and end of conduct.

To the same cause may be imputed the hardness of heart and insensibility remarkable in all savage nations Their minds, roused only by strong emotions, are little susceptible of gentle, delicate, or tender affections.† Their union is so incomplete that each individual acts as if he retained all his natural rights entire and undiminished. If a favour is conferred upon him, or any beneficial service is performed on his account, he receives it with much satisfaction, because it contributes to his enjoyment; but this sentiment extends not beyond himself, it excites no sense of obligation, he neither feels gratitude, nor thinks of making any return‡ [94]. Even among persons the most closely connected, the exchange of those good offices which strengthen attachment, mollify the heart, and sweeten the intercourse of life, is not frequent. The high ideas of independence among the Americans nourish a sullen reserve, which keeps them at a distance from each other. The nearest relations are mutually afraid to make any demand, or to solicit any service,§ lest it should be considered by the other as imposing a burden, or laying a restraint upon his will.

I have already remarked the influence of this hard unfeeling temper upon domestic life, with respect to the connection between husband and wife, as well as that between parents and children. Its effects are no less conspicuous, in the performance of those mutual offices of tenderness which the infirmities of our nature frequently exact. Among some tribes, when any of their number are seized with any violent disease, they are generally abandoned by all around them, who, careless of their recovery, fly in the utmost consternation from the supposed danger of infection.‖ But even where they are not thus deserted, the cold indifference with which they are attended can afford them little consolation. No look of sympathy, no soothing expressions, no officious services, contribute to alleviate the distress of the sufferers, or to make them forget what they endure.¶ Their nearest relations will often refuse to submit to the smallest inconveniency, or to part with the least trifle, however much it may tend

* Fernandez Mission. de los Chequit. 33. † Charlev. Hist. N. Fr. iii. 309. ‡ Oviedo, Hist lib. xvi. c. 2. § De la Potherie, iii. 28. ‖ Lettre de P. Cataneo ap. Muratori Christian. i. 30. Tertre, ii, 410. Lozano, 100. Herrera, dec. 4. lib. viii. c. 5. dec. 5. lib. iv. c. 2. Falkner's Descript. of Patagonia, 98 ¶ Gumilla, i. 329 Lozano, 100.

to their accommodation or relief.* So little is the breast of a savage susceptible of those sentiments which prompt men to that feeling attention which mitigates the calamities of human life, that, in some provinces of America, the Spaniards have found it necessary to enforce the common duties of humanity by positive laws, and to oblige husbands and wives, parents and children, under severe penalties, to take care of each other during their sickness.† The same harshness of temper is still more conspicuous in their treatment of the animal creation. Prior to their intercourse with the people of Europe, the North Americans had some tame dogs, which accompanied them in their hunting excursions, and served them with all the ardour and fidelity peculiar to the species. But, instead of that fond attachment which the hunter naturally feels towards those useful companions of his toils, they requite their services with neglect, seldom feed, and never caress them.‡ In other provinces the Americans have become acquainted with the domestic animals of Europe, and availed themselves of their service; but it is universally observed that they always treat them harshly,§ and never employ any method either for breaking or managing them, but force and cruelty. In every part of the deportment of man in his savage state, whether towards his equals of the human species, or towards the animals below him, we recognise the same character, and trace the operations of a mind intent on its own gratifications, and regulated by its own caprice, with little attention or sensibility to the sentiments and feelings of the beings around him.

After explaining how unfavourable the savage state is to the cultivation of the understanding, and to the improvement of the heart, I should not have thought it necessary to mention what may be deemed its lesser defects, if the character of nations, as well as of individuals, were not often more distinctly marked by circumstances apparently trivial than by those of greater moment. A savage frequently placed in situations of danger and distress, depending on himself alone, and wrapped up in his own thoughts and schemes, is a serious melancholy animal. His attention to others is small. The range of his own ideas is narrow. Hence that taciturnity which is so disgusting to men accustomed to the open intercourse of social conversation. When they are not engaged in action, the Americans often sit whole days in one posture, without opening their lips.‖ When they go forth to war, or to the chase, they usually march in a line at some distance from one another, and without exchanging a word. The same profound silence is observed when they row together in a canoe.¶ It is only when they are animated by intoxicating liquors, or roused by the jollity of the festival and dance, that they become gay and conversible.

To the same causes may be imputed the refined cunning with which they form and execute their schemes. Men who are not habituated to a liberal communication of their own sentiments and wishes, are apt to be so distrustful as to place little confidence in others, and to have recourse to an insidious craft in accomplishing their own puposes. In civilized life, those persons who by their situations have but a few objects of pursuit on which their minds incessantly dwell, are most remarkable for low artifice in carrying on their little projects. Among savages, whose views are equally confined, and their attention no less persevering, those circumstances must operate still more powerfully, and gradually accustom them to a disingenuous subtlety in all their transactions. The force of this is increased by habits which they acquire in carrying on the two most interesting operations wherein they are engaged. With them war is a system of craft, in which they trust for success to stratagem more than to open force, and have their

* Gargia Origen, &c. 90. Herrera, dec. 4. lib. viii. c. 5 † Cogarludo Hist. de Yucathan, p. 300.
‡ Charlev. N. Fr. iii. 119. 337. § Ulloa Notic. American. 312 ‖ Voyage de Bouguer, 102
¶ Charlev. iii. 340.

invention continually on the stretch to circumvent and surprise their enemies. As hunters, it is their constant object to ensnare in order that they may destroy. Accordingly, art and cunning have been universally observed as distinguishing characteristics of all savages. The people of the rude tribes of America are remarkable for their artifice and duplicity. Impenetrably secrect in forming their measures, they pursue them with a patient undeviating attention, and there is no refinement of dissimulation which they cannot employ, in order to ensure success. The natives of Peru were engaged above thirty years, in concerting the plan of that insurrection which took place under the vice-royalty of the Marquis de Villa Garcia; and though it was communicated to a great number of persons, in all different ranks, no indication of it ever transpired during that long period; no man betrayed his trust, or, by an unguarded look, or rash word, gave rise to any suspicion of what was intended.* The dissimulation and craft of individuals is no less remarkable than that of nations. When set upon deceiving, they wrap themselves up so artificially, that it is impossible to penetrate into their intentions, or to detect their designs.†

But if there be defects or vices peculiar to the savage state, there are likewise virtues which it inspires, and good qualities, to the exercise of which it is friendly. The bonds of society sit so loose upon the members of the more rude American tribes, that they hardly feel any restraint. Hence the spirit of independence, which is the pride of a savage, and which he considers as the unalienable prerogative of man. Incapable of control, and disdaining to acknowledge any superior, his mind, though limited in its powers, and erring in many of its pursuits, acquires such elevation by the consciousness of its own freedom, that he acts on some occasions with astonishing force, and perseverance, and dignity.

As independence nourishes this high spirit among savages, the perpetual wars in which they are engaged call it forth into action. Such long intervals of tranquillity as are frequent in polished societies are unknown in the savage state. Their enmities, as I have observed, are implacable and immortal. The valour of the young men is never allowed to rust in inaction. The hatchet is always in the hand, either for attack or defence. Even in their hunting excursions, they must be on their guard against surprise from the hostile tribes by which they are surrounded. Accustomed to continual alarms, they grow familiar with danger; courage becomes an habitual virtue, resulting naturally from their situation, and strengthened by constant exertions. The mode of displaying fortitude may not be the same in small and rude communities, as in more powerful and civilized states. Their system of war, and standard of valour may be formed upon different principles; but in no situation does the human mind rise more superior to the sense of danger, or the dread of death, than in its most simple and uncultivated state.

Another virtue remarkable among savages, is attachment to the community of which they are members. From the nature of their political union, one might expect this tie to be extremely feeble. But there are circumstances which render the influence, even of their loose mode of association, very powerful. The American tribes are small; combined against their neighbours, in prosecution of ancient enmities, or in avenging recent injuries, their interests and operations are neither numerous nor complex. These are objects which the uncultivated understanding of a savage can comprehend. His heart is capable of forming connections which are so little diffused. He assents with warmth to public measures, dictated by passions similar to those which direct his own conduct. Hence the ardour with which individuals undertake the most perilous service, when the commu-

* Voyage de Ulloa, ii. 309.

† Gumilla, i. 162. Charlev.

nity deems it necessary. Hence their fierce and deep rooted antipathy to the public enemies. Hence their zeal for the honour of their tribe, and that love of their country, which prompts them to brave danger that it may triumph, and to endure the most exquisite torments, without a groan, that it may not be disgraced.

Thus, in every situation where a human being can be placed, even in the most unfavourable, there are virtues which peculiarly belong to it; there are affections which it calls forth; there is a species of happiness which it yields. Nature, with the most beneficent intention, conciliates and forms the mind to its condition; the ideas and wishes of man extend not beyond that state of society to which he is habituated. What it presents as objects of contemplation or enjoyment, fills and satisfies his mind, and he can hardly conceive any other mode of life to be pleasant, or even tolerable. The Tartar, accustomed to roam over extensive plains, and to subsist on the product of his herds, imprecates upon his enemy, as the greatest of all curses, that he may be condemned to reside in one place, and to be nourished with the top of a weed. The rude Americans, fond of their own pursuits, and satisfied with their own lot, are equally unable to comprehend the intention or utility of the various accommodations, which, in more polished society are deemed essential to the comfort of life. Far from complaining of their own situation, or viewing that of men in a more improved state with admiration or envy, they regard themselves as the standard of excellence, as beings the best entitled, as well as the most perfectly qualified, to enjoy real happiness. Unaccustomed to any restraint upon their will or their actions, they behold with amazement the inequality of rank, and the subordination which takes place in civilized life, and consider the voluntary submission of one man to another as a renunciation no less base than unaccountable, of the first distinction of humanity. Void of foresight, as well as free from care themselves, and delighted with that state of indolent security, they wonder at the anxious precautions, the unceasing industry, and complicated arrangements of Europeans, in guarding against distant evils, or providing for future wants; and they often exclaim against their preposterous folly, in thus multiplying the troubles and increasing the labour of life.* This preference of their own manners is conspicuous on every occasion. Even the names, by which the various nations wish to be distinguished, are assumed from this idea of their own pre-eminence. The appellation which the Iroquois give to themselves is *the chief of men.*† *Caraibe*, the original name of the fierce inhabitants of the Windward Islands, signifies *the warlike people.*‡ The Cherokees, from an idea of their own superiority, call the Europeans *Nothings*, or *the accursed race*, and assume to themselves the name of *the beloved people.*§ The same principle regulated the notions of the other Americans concerning the Europeans; for although at first they were filled with astonishment at their arts, and with dread of their power, they soon came to abate their estimation of men whose maxims of life were so different from their own. Hence they called them the froth of the sea, men without father or mother. They supposed, that either they had no country of their own, and therefore invaded that which belonged to others;|| or that, being destitute of the necessaries of life at home, they were obliged to roam over the ocean, in order to rob such as were more amply provided.

Men thus satisfied with their condition are far from any inclination to relinquish their own habits, or to adopt those of civilized life. The transition is too violent to be suddenly made. Even where endeavours have been used to wean a savage from his own customs, and to render the accommodations of polished society familiar to him; even where he has been

* Charlev. N. Fr. iii. 338. Lahontan, ii. 97. † Colden, i. 3. ‡ Rochefort Hist. des Antilles, 455. § Adair Hist. Amer. Indians, p. 32. || Benzon. Hist. Novi Orbis, lib. iii. c 21.

allowed to taste of those pleasures, and has been honoured with those distinctions, which are the chief objects of our desire, he droops and languishes under the restraint of laws and forms, he seizes the first opportunity of breaking loose from them, and returns with transport to the forest or the wild, where he can enjoy a careless and uncontrolled freedom.*

Thus I have finished a laborious delineation of the character and manners of the uncivilized tribes scattered over the vast continent of America. In this, I aspire not at rivalling the great masters who have painted and adorned savage life, either in boldness of design, or in the glow and beauty of their colouring. I am satisfied with the more humble merit of having persisted with patient industry, in viewing my subject in many various lights, and collecting from the most accurate observers such detached, and often minute features, as might enable me to exhibit a portrait that resembles the original.

Before I close this part of my work, one observation more is necessary, in order to justify the conclusions which I have formed, or to prevent the mistakes into which such as examine them may fall. In contemplating the inhabitants of a country so widely extended as America, great attention should be paid to the diversity of climates under which they are placed. The influence of this I have pointed out with respect to several important particulars which have been the object of research; but even where it has not been mentioned, it ought not to be overlooked. The provinces of America are of such different temperament, that this alone is sufficient to constitute a distinction between their inhabitants. In every part of the earth where man exists, the power of climate operates, with decisive influence, upon his condition and character. In those countries which approach near to the extremes of heat or cold, this influence is so conspicuous as to strike every eye. Whether we consider man merely as an animal, or as being endowed with rational powers which fit him for activity and speculation, we shall find that he has uniformly attained the greatest perfection of which his nature is capable, in the temperate regions of the globe. There his constitution is most vigorous, his organs most acute, and his form most beautiful. There, too, he possesses a superior extent of capacity, greater fertility of imagination, more enterprising courage, and a sensibility of heart which gives birth to desires, not only ardent, but persevering. In this favourite situation he has displayed the utmost efforts of his genius, in literature, in policy, in commerce, in war, and in all the arts which improve or embellish life.†

This powerful operation of climate is felt most sensibly by rude nations, and produces greater effects than in societies more improved. The talents of civilized men are continually exerted in rendering their own condition more comfortable; and by their ingenuity and inventions, they can in a great measure supply the defects, and guard against the inconveniences of any climate. But the improvident savage is affected by every circumstance peculiar to his situation. He takes no precaution either to mitigate or to improve it. Like a plant or an animal, he is formed by the climate under which he is placed, and feels the full force of its influence.

In surveying the rude nations of America, this natural distinction between the inhabitants of the temperate and torrid zones is very remarkable. They may, accordingly, be divided into two great classes. The one comprehends all the North Americans from the river St. Laurence to the Gulf of Mexico, together with the people of Chili, and a few small tribes towards the extremity of the southern continent. To the other belong all the inhabitants of the islands, and those settled in the various provinces which extend from the isthmus of Darien almost to the southern confines

* Charlev. N. Fr. iii. 322.

† Dr. Ferguson's Essay on the Hist. of Civil Society, art iii. ch. 1.

of Brasil, along the east side of the Andes. In the former, which comprehends all the regions of the temperate zone that in America are inhabited, the human species appears manifestly to be more perfect. The natives are more robust, more active, more intelligent, and more courageous. They possess, in the most eminent degree, that force of mind, and love of independence, which I have pointed out as the chief virtues of man in his savage state. They have defended their liberty with persevering fortitude against the Europeans, who subdued the other rude nations of America with the greatest ease. The natives of the temperate zone are the only people in the New World who are indebted for their freedom to their own valour. The North Americans, though long encompassed by three formidable European powers, still retain part of their original possessions, and continue to exist as independent nations. The people of Chili, though early invaded, still maintain a gallant contest with the Spaniards, and have set bounds to their encroachments; whereas, in the warmer regions, men are more feeble in their frame, less vigorous in the efforts of their minds, of a gentle but dastardly spirit, more enslaved by pleasure, and more sunk in indolence. Accordingly, it is in the torrid zone that the Europeans have most completely established their dominion over America; the most fertile and desirable provinces in it are subjected to their yoke; and if several tribes there still enjoy independence, it is either because they have never been attacked by an enemy already satiated with conquest, and possessed of larger territories than he was able to occupy, or because they have been saved from oppression by their remote and inaccessible situation.

Conspicuous as this distinction may appear between the inhabitants of those different regions, it is not, however, universal. Moral and political causes, as I have formerly observed, affect the disposition and character of individuals, as well as nations, still more powerfully than the influence of climate. There are, accordingly, some tribes, in various parts of the torrid zone, possessed of courage, high spirit, and the love of independence, in a degree hardly inferior to the natives of more temperate climates. We are too little acquainted with the history of those people, to be able to trace the several circumstances in their progress and condition, to which they are indebted for this remarkable pre-eminence. The fact, nevertheless, is certain. As early as the first voyage of Columbus, he received information that several of the islands were inhabited by the *Caribbees*, a fierce race of men, nowise resembling their feeble and timid neighbours. In his second expedition to the New World, he found this information to be just, and was himself a witness of their intrepid valour* [95]. The same character they have maintained invariably in all subsequent contests with the people of Europe;† and even in our own times we have seen them make a gallant stand in defence of the last territory which the rapacity of the invaders had left in their possession [96]. Some nations in Brasil were no less eminent for vigour of mind and bravery in war.‡ The people of the isthmus of Darien boldly met the Spaniards in the field, and frequently repelled those formidable invaders.§ Other instances might be produced. It is not by attending to any single cause or principle, how powerful and extensive soever its influence may appear, that we can explain the actions, or account for the character of men. Even the law of climate, more universal, perhaps, in its operation than any that affects the human species, cannot be applied, in judging of their conduct, without many exceptions.

* Life of Columbus, c. 47, 48. † Rochefort Hist. des Antilles, 531 ‡ Lery ap. de Bry, iii. 207, &c. § Herrera, dec. 1. lib. x. c. 15, &c. dec. 2. passim.

# BOOK V.

WHEN Grijalva [1518.] returned to Cuba, he found the armament destined to attempt the conquest of that rich country which he had discovered almost complete. Not only ambition, but avarice, had urged Velasquez to hasten his preparations; and having such a prospect of gratifying both, he had advanced considerable sums out of his private fortune towards defraying the expenses of the expedition. At the same time, he exerted his influence as governor, in engaging the most distinguished persons in the colony to undertake the service [97]. At a time when the spirit of the Spanish nation was adventurous to excess, a number of soldiers, eager to embark in any daring enterprise, soon appeared. But it was not so easy to find a person qualified to take the command in an expedition of so much importance; and the character of Velasquez, who had the right of nomination, greatly increased the difficulty of the choice. Though of most aspiring ambition, and not destitute of talents for government, he possessed neither such courage, nor such vigour and activity of mind, as to undertake in person the conduct of the armament which he was preparing. In this embarrassing situation, he formed the chimerical scheme, not only of achieving great exploits by a deputy, but of securing to himself the glory of conquests which were to be made by another. In the execution of this plan, he fondly aimed at reconciling contradictions. He was solicitous to choose a commander of intrepid resolution, and of superior abilities, because he knew these to be requisite in order to ensure success; but, at the same time, from the jealousy natural to little minds, he wished this person to be of a spirit so tame and obsequious as to be entirely dependent on his will. But when he came to apply those ideas in forming an opinion concerning the several officers who occurred to his thoughts as worthy of being intrusted with the command, he soon perceived that it was impossible to find such incompatible qualities united in one character. Such as were distinguished for courage and talents were too high spirited to be passive instruments in his hands. Those who appeared more gentle and tractable were destitute of capacity, and unequal to the charge. This augmented his perplexity and his fears. He deliberated long and with much solicitude, and was still wavering in his choice when Amador de Lares, the royal treasurer in Cuba, and Andres Duero, his own secretary, the two persons in whom he chiefly confided, were encouraged by this irresolution to propose a new candidate; and they supported their recommendation with such assiduity and address, that, no less fatally for Velasquez than happily for their country, it proved successful.*

The man whom they pointed out to him was Fernando Cortes. He was born at Medellin, a small town in Estremadura, in the year one thousand four hundred and eighty-five, and descended from a family of noble blood, but of very moderate fortune. Being originally destined by his parents to the study of law, as the most likely method of bettering his condition, he was sent early to the university of Salamanca, where he imbibed some tincture of learning. But he was soon disgusted with an academic life, which did not suit his ardent and restless genius, and retired to Medellin, where he gave himself up entirely to active sports and martial exercises At this period of life he was so impetuous, so overbearing, and so dissipated, that his father was glad to comply with his inclination, and sent him abroad as an adventurer in arms. There were in that age two conspicuous theatres, on which such of the Spanish youth as courted military glory

* B. Diaz, c. 19. Gomara Cron. c. 7. Herrera, dec. 2. lib. iii. c. 11.

might display their valour; one in Italy, under the command of the Great Captain; the other in the New World. Cortes preferred the former, but was prevented by indisposition from embarking with a reinforcement of troops sent to Naples. Upon this disappointment he turned his views towards America, whither he was allured by the prospect of the advantages which he might derive from the patronage of Ovando [98], the governor of Hispaniola, who was his kinsman. When he landed at St. Domingo, in one thousand five hundred and four, his reception was such as equalled his most sanguine hopes, and he was employed by the Governor in several honourable and lucrative stations. These, however, did not satisfy his ambition; and, in the year one thousand five hundred and eleven, he obtained permission to accompany Diego Velasquez in his expedition to Cuba. In this service he distinguished himself so much, that, notwithstanding some violent contests with Velasquez, occasioned by trivial events unworthy of remembrance, he was at length taken into favour, and received an ample concession of lands and of Indians, the recompense usually bestowed upon adventurers in the New World.*

Though Cortes had not hitherto acted in high command, he had displayed such qualities in several scenes of difficulty and danger, as raised universal expectation, and turned the eyes of his countrymen towards him as one capable of performing great things. The turbulence of youth, as soon as he found objects and occupations suited to the ardour of his mind, gradually subsided and settled into a habit of regular indefatigable activity. The impetuosity of his temper, when he came to act with his equals, insensibly abated, by being kept under restraint, and mellowed into a cordial soldierly frankness. These qualities were accompanied with calm prudence in concerting his schemes, with persevering vigour in executing them, and with, what is peculiar to superior genius, the art of gaining the confidence and governing the minds of men. To all which were added the inferior accomplishments that strike the vulgar, and command their respect; a graceful person, a winning aspect, extraordinary address in martial exercises, and a constitution of such vigour as to be capable of enduring any fatigue.

As soon as Cortes was mentioned to Velasquez by his two confidants, he flattered himself that he had at length found what he had hitherto sought in vain, a man with talents for command, but not an object for jealousy. Neither the rank nor the fortune of Cortes, as he imagined, was such that he could aspire at independence. He had reason to believe that by his own readiness to bury ancient animosities in oblivion, as well as his liberality in conferring several recent favours, he had already gained the good will of Cortes, and hoped, by this new and unexpected mark of confidence, that he might attach him for ever to his interest.

Cortes, receiving his commission [Oct. 23], with the warmest expressions of respect and gratitude to the governor, immediately erected his standard before his own house, appeared in a military dress, and assumed all the ensigns of his new dignity. His utmost influence and activity were exerted in persuading many of his friends to engage in the service, and in urging forward the preparations for the voyage. All his own funds, together with what money he could raise by mortgaging his lands and Indians, were expended in purchasing military stores and provisions, or in supplying the wants of such of his officers as were unable to equip themselves in a manner suited to their rank [99]. Inoffensive and even laudable as this conduct was, his disappointed competitors were malicious enough to give it a turn to his disadvantage. They represented him as aiming already, with little disguise, at establishing an independent authority over his troops, and endeavouring to secure their respect or love by his ostentatious and inter

* Gomara Cron. c. 1, 2, 3.

ested liberality. They reminded Velasquez of his former dissensions with the man in whom he now reposed so much confidence, and foretold that Cortes would be more apt to avail himself of the power which the governor was inconsiderately putting in his hands, to avenge past injuries than to requite recent obligations. These insinuations made such impression upon the suspicious mind of Velasquez, that Cortes soon observed some symptoms of a growing alienation and distrust in his behaviour, and was advised by Lares and Duero to hasten his departure before these should become so confirmed as to break out with open violence. Fully sensible of this danger, he urged forward his preparations with such rapidity that he set sail from St. Jago de Cuba on the eighteenth of November. Velasquez accompanying him to the shore, and taking leave of him with an appearance of perfect friendship and confidence, though he had secretly given it in charge to some of Cortes' officers, to keep a watchful eye upon every part of their commander's conduct.*

Cortes proceeded to Trinidad, a small settlement on the same side of the island, where he was joined by several adventurers, and received a supply of provisions and military stores, of which his stock was still very incomplete. He had hardly left St. Jago, when the jealousy which had been working in the breast of Velasquez grew so violent that it was impossible to suppress it. The armament was no longer under his own eye and direction; and he felt that as his power over it ceased, that of Cortes would become more absolute. Imagination now aggravated every circumstance which had formerly excited suspicion: the rivals of Cortes industriously threw in reflections which increased his fear; and with no less art than malice they called superstition to their aid, employing the predictions of an astrologer in order to complete the alarm. All these, by their united operation, produced the desired effect. Velasquez repented bitterly of his own imprudence, in having committed a trust of so much importance to a person whose fidelity appeared so doubtful, and hastily despatched instructions to Trinidad, empowering Verdugo, the chief magistrate there, to deprive Cortes of his commission. But Cortes had already made such progress in gaining the esteem and confidence of his troops, that, finding officers as well as soldiers equally zealous to support his authority, he soothed or intimidated Verdugo, and was permitted to depart from Trinidad without molestation.

From Trinidad Cortes sailed for the Havana, in order to raise more soldiers, and to complete the victualling of his fleet. There several persons of distinction entered into the service, and engaged to supply what provisions were still wanting; but as it was necessary to allow them some time for performing what they had promised, Velasquez, sensible that he ought no longer to rely on a man of whom he had so openly discovered his distrust, availed himself of the interval which this unavoidable delay afforded, in order to make one attempt more to wrest the command out of the hands of Cortes. He loudly complained of Verdugo's conduct, accusing him either of childish facility, or of manifest treachery, in suffering Cortes to escape from Trinidad. Anxious to guard against a second disappointment, he sent a person of confidence to the Havana, with peremptory injunctions to Pedro Barba, his lieutenant-governor in that colony, instantly o arrest Cortes, to send him prisoner to St. Jago under a strong guard, and o countermand the sailing of the armament until he should receive further orders. He wrote likewise to the principal officers, requiring them to assist Barba in executing what he had given him in charge. But before the arrival of this messenger, a Franciscan friar of St. Jago had secretly conveyed an account of this interesting transaction to Bartholomew de Olmedo, a monk of the same order, who acted as chaplain to the expedition.

* Gomara, Cron. c. 7. B. Diaz, c. 20.

Cortes, forewarned of the danger, had time to take precautions for his own safety. His first step was to find some pretext for removing from the Havana Diego de Ordaz, an officer of great merit, but in whom, on account of his known attachment to Velasquez, he could not confide in this trying and delicate juncture. He gave him the command of a vessel destined tc take on board some provisions in a small harbour beyond Cape Antonio, and thus made sure of his absence without seeming to suspect his fidelity. When he was gone, Cortes no longer concealed the intentions of Velasquez from his troops; and as officers and soldiers were equally impatient to set out on an expedition, in preparing for which most of them had expended all their fortunes, they expressed their astonishment and indignation at that illiberal jealousy to which the governor was about to sacrifice, not only the honour of their general, but all their sanguine hopes of glory and wealth. With one voice they entreated that he would not abandon the important station to which he had such a good title. They conjured him not to deprive them of a leader whom they followed with such well founded confidence, and offered to sned the ɪast drop of their blood in maintaining his authority. Cortes was easily induced to comply with what he himself so ardently desired. He swore that he would never desert soldiers who had given him such a signal proof of their attachment, and promised instantly to conduct them to that rich country which had been so long the object of their thoughts and wishes. This declaration was received with transports of military applause, accompanied with threats and imprecations against all who should presume to call in question the jurisdiction of their general, or to obstruct the execution of his designs.

Every thing was now ready for their departure; but though this expedition was fitted out by the united effort of the Spanish power in Cuba; though every settlement had contributed its quota of men and provisions; though the governor had laid out considerable sums, and each adventurer had exhausted his stock, or strained his credit, the poverty of the preparations was such as must astonish the present age, and bore, indeed, no resemblance to an armament destined for the conquest of a great empire. The fleet consisted of eleven vessels; the largest of a hundred tons, which was dignified by the name of Admiral; three of seventy or eighty tons, and the rest small open barks. On board of these were six hundred and seventeen men; of which five hundred and eight belonged to the land service, and a hundred and nine were seamen or artificers. The soldiers were divided into eleven companies, according to the number of the ships; to each of which Cortes appointed a captain, and committed to him the command of the vessel while at sea, and of the men when on shore [100]. As the use of fire arms among the nations of Europe was hitherto confined to a few battalions of regularly disciplined infantry, only thirteen soldiers were armed with muskets, thirty-two were cross-bow men, and the rest had swords and spears. Instead of the usual defensive armour, which must have been cumbersome in a hot climate, the soldiers wore jackets quilted with cotton, which experience had taught the Spaniards to be a sufficient protection against the weapons of the Americans. They had only sixteen horses, ten small field pieces, and four falconets.*

With this slender and ill provided train did Cortes set sail [Feb. 10, 1519], to make war upon a monarch whose dominions were more extensive than all the kingdoms subject to the Spanish crown. As religious enthusiasm always mingled with the spirit of adventure in the New World, and, by a combination still more strange, united with avarice, in prompting the Spaniards to all their enterprises, a large cross was displayed in their standards, with this inscription, *Let us follow the cross, for under this sign we shall conquer.*

* B. Diaz, c. 19.

So powerfully were Cortes and his followers animated with both these passions, that no less eager to plunder the opulent country whither they were bound, than zealous to propagate the Christian faith among its inhabitants, they set out, not with the solicitude natural to men going upon dangerous services, but with that confidence which arises from security of success, and certainty of the divine protection.

As Cortes had determined to touch at every place where Grijalva had visited, he steered directly towards the island of Cozumel; there he had the good fortune to redeem Jerome de Aguilar, a Spaniard, who had been eight years a prisoner among the Indians. This man was perfectly acquainted with a dialect of their language understood through a large extent of country, and possessing besides a considerable share of prudence and sagacity, proved extremely useful as an interpreter. From Cozumel, Cortes proceeded to the river of Tabasco [March 4], in hopes of a reception as friendly as Grijalva had met with there, and of finding gold in the same abundance; but the disposition of the natives, from some unknown cause, was totally changed. After repeated endeavours to conciliate their good will, he was constrained to have recourse to violence. Though the forces of the enemy were numerous, and advanced with extraordinary courage, they were routed with great slaughter in several successive actions The loss which they had sustained, and still more the astonishment and terror excited by the destructive effect of the fire arms, and the dreadful appearance of the horses, humbled their fierce spirits, and induced them to sue for peace. They acknowledged the King of Castile as their sovereign, and granted Cortes a supply of provisions with a present of cotton garments, some gold, and twenty female slaves [101].

Cortes continued his course to the westward, keeping as near the shore as possible, in order to observe the country; but could discover no proper place for landing until he arrived at St. Juan de Ulua.* As he entered this harbour [April 2], a large canoe full of people, among whom were two who seemed to be persons of distinction, approached his ship with signs of peace and amity. They came on board without fear or distrust, and addressed him in a most respectful manner, but in a language altogether unknown to Aguilar. Cortes was in the utmost perplexity and distress at an event of which he instantly foresaw the consequences, and already felt the hesitation and uncertainty with which he should carry on the great schemes which he meditated, if, in his transactions with the natives, he must depend entirely upon such an imperfect, ambiguous, and conjectural mode of communication as the use of signs. But he did not remain long in his embarrassing situation; a fortunate accident extricated him when his own sagacity could have contributed little towards his relief. One of the female slaves, whom he had received from the cazique of Tabasco, happened to be present at the first interview between Cortes and his new guests. She perceived his distress, as well as the confusion of Aguilar; and, as she perfectly understood the Mexican language, she explained what they had said in the Yucatan tongue, with which Aguilar was acquainted. This woman, known afterwards by the name of Donna Marina, and who makes a conspicuous figure in the history of the New World, where great revolutions were brought about by small causes and inconsiderable instruments, was born in one of the provinces of the Mexican Empire. Having been sold as a slave in the early part of her life, after a variety of adventures she fell into the hands of the Tabascans, and had resided long enough among them to acquire their language without losing the use of her own. Though it was both tedious and troublesome to converse by the intervention of two different interpreters, Cortes was so highly pleased with having discovered this method of carrying on some

* B. Diaz, c. 31—36. Gomara Cron. c. 18—23. Herrera, dec. 2. lib. iv. c. 11, &c.

intercourse with the people of a country into which he was determined to penetrate, that in the transports of his joy he considered it as a visible interposition of Providence in his favour.*

He now learned that the two persons whom he had received on board of his ship were deputies from Teutile and Pilpatoe, two officers intrusted with the government of that province by a great monarch whom they called Montezuma; and that they were sent to inquire what his intentions were in visiting their coast, and to offer him what assistance he might need, in order to continue his voyage. Cortes, struck with the appearance of those people, as well as the tenor of the message, assured them, in respectful terms, that he approached their country with most friendly sentiments, and came to propose matters of great importance to the welfare of their prince and his kingdom, which he would unfold more fully, in person, to the governor and the general. Next morning, without waiting for any answer, he landed his troops, his horses, and artillery; and, having chosen proper ground, began to erect huts for his men, and to fortify his camp. The natives, instead of opposing the entrance of those fatal guests into their country, assisted them in all their operations with an alacrity of which they had ere long good reason to repent.

Next day Teutile and Pilpatoe entered the Spanish camp with a numerous retinue; and Cortes, considering them as the ministers of a great monarch entitled to a degree of attention very different from that which the Spaniards were accustomed to pay the petty caziques with whom they had intercourse in the isles, received them with much formal ceremony. He informed them, that he came as ambassador from Don Carlos of Austria, King of Castile, the greatest monarch of the East, and was intrusted with propositions of such moment, that he could impart them to none but the Emperor Montezuma himself, and therefore required them to conduct him, without loss of time, into the presence of their master. The Mexican officers could not conceal their uneasiness at a request which they knew would be disagreeable, and which they foresaw might prove extremely embarrassing to their sovereign, whose mind had been filled with many disquieting apprehensions ever since the former appearance of the Spaniards on his coasts. But before they attempted to dissuade Cortes from insisting on his demand, they endeavoured to conciliate his good will by entreating him to accept of certain presents, which, as humble slaves of Montezuma, they laid at his feet. They were introduced with great parade, and consisted of fine cotton cloth, of plumes of various colours, and of ornaments of gold and silver to a considerable value; the workmanship of which appeared to be as curious as the materials were rich. The display of these produced an effect very different from what the Mexicans intended Instead of satisfying, it increased the avidity of the Spaniards, and rendered them so eager and impatient to become masters of a country which abounded with such precious productions, that Cortes could hardly listen with patience to the arguments which Pilpatoe and Teutile employed to dissuade him from visiting the capital, and in a haughty determined tone he insisted on his demand of being admitted to a personal audience of their sovereign. During this interview, some painters, in the train of the Mexican chiefs, had been diligently employed in delineating, upon white cotton cloths, figures of the ships, the horses, the artillery, the soldiers, and whatever else attracted their eyes as singular. When Cortes observed this, and was informed that these pictures were to be sent to Montezuma, in order to convey to him a more lively idea of the strange and wonderful objects now presented to their view than any words could communicate, he resolved to render the representation still more animating and interesting, by exhibiting such a spectacle as might give both them and their

* B. Diaz, c. 37, 38, 39. Gomara Cron. c. 25, 26. Herrera, dec. 2. lib. v. c. 4.

monarch an awful impression of the extraordinary prowess of his followers, and the irresistible force of their arms. The trumpets, by his order, sounded an alarm; the troops, in a moment, formed in order of battle, the infantry performed such martial exercises as were best suited to display the effect of their different weapons; the horse, in various evolutions, gave a specimen of their agility and strength; the artillery, pointed towards the thick woods which surrounded the camp, were fired, and made dreadful havoc among the trees. The Mexicans looked on with that silent amazement which is natural when the mind is struck with objects which are both awful and above its comprehension. But, at the explosion of the cannon, many of them fled, some fell to the ground, and all were so much confounded at the sight of men whose power so nearly resembled that of the gods, that Cortes found it difficult to compose and reassure them. The painters had now many new objects on which to exercise their art, and they put their fancy on the stretch in order to invent figures and symbols to represent the extraordinary things which they had seen.

Messengers were immediately despatched to Montezuma with those pictures, and a full account of every thing that had passed since the arrival of the Spaniards, and by them Cortes sent a present of some European curiosities to Montezuma, which, though of no great value, he believed would be acceptable on account of their novelty. The Mexican monarchs, in order to obtain early information of every occurrence in all the corners of their extensive empire, had introduced a refinement in police unknown at that time in Europe. They had couriers posted at proper stations along the principal roads; and as these were trained to agility by a regular education, and relieved one another at moderate distances, they conveyed intelligence with surprising rapidity. Though the capital in which Montezuma resided was above a hundred and eighty miles from St. Juan de Ulua, Cortes's presents were carried thither, and an answer to his demands was received in a few days. The same officers who had hitherto treated with the Spaniards were employed to deliver this answer; but as they knew how repugnant the determination of their master was to all the schemes and wishes of the Spanish commander, they would not venture to make it known until they had previously endeavoured to soothe and mollify him. For this purpose they renewed their negotiation, by introducing a train of a hundred Indians loaded with presents sent to him by Montezuma. The magnificence of these was such as became a great monarch, and far exceeded any idea which the Spaniards had hitherto formed of his wealth. They were placed on mats spread on the ground in such order as showed them to the greatest advantage. Cortes and his officers viewed with admiration the various manufactures of the country; cotton stuffs so fine, and of such delicate texture as to resemble silk; pictures of animals, trees, and other natural objects, formed with feathers of different colours, disposed and mingled with such skill and elegance as to rival the works of the pencil in truth and beauty of imitation. But what chiefly attracted their eyes were two large plates of a circular form, one of massive gold representing the sun, the other of silver, an emblem of the moon [102]. These were accompanied with bracelets, collars, rings, and other trinkets of gold; and that nothing might be wanted which could give the Spaniards a complete idea of what the country afforded, with some boxes filled with pearls, precious stones, and grains of gold unwrought, as they had been found in the mines or rivers. Cortes received all these with an appearance of profound veneration for the monarch by whom they were bestowed. But when the Mexicans, presuming upon this, informed him that their master, though he had desired him to accept of what he had sent as a token of regard for that monarch whom Cortes represented, would not give his consent that foreign troops should approach nearer to his capital, or even allow them to continue longer in his dominions, the Spanish general declared, in a manner more resolute and peremptory than formerly, that he must insist on his first demand, as he could not without dishonour, return to his own country, until he was admitted into the presence of the prince whom he was appointed to visit in the name of his sovereign. The Mexicans, astonished at seeing any man dare to oppose that will which they were accustomed to consider as supreme and irresistible, yet afraid of precipitating their country into an open rupture with such formidable enemies, prevailed with Cortes to promise that he would not remove from his present camp until the return of a messenger whom they sent to Montezuma for further instructions.*

The firmness with which Cortes adhered to his original proposal should naturally have brought the negotiation between him and Montezuma to a speedy issue, as it seemed to leave the Mexican monarch no choice, but either to receive him with confidence as a friend, or to oppose him openly as an enemy. The latter was what might have been expected from a haughty prince in possession of extensive power. The Mexican empire at this period was at a pitch of grandeur to whicn no society ever attained in so short a period. Though it had subsisted, according to their own traditions, only a hundred and thirty years, its dominion extended from the North to the South Sea, over territories stretching, with some small interruption, above five hundred leagues from east to west, and more than two hundred from north to south, comprehending provinces not inferior in fertility, population, and opulence, to any in the torrid zone. The people were warlike and enterprising; the authority of the monarch unbounded, and his revenues considerable. If, with the forces which might have been suddenly assembled in such an empire, Montezuma had fallen upon the Spaniards while encamped on a barren unhealthy coast, unsupported by any ally, without a place of retreat, and destitute of provisions, it seems to be impossible, even with all the advantages of their superior discipline and arms, that they could have stood the shock, and they must either have perished in such an unequal contest, or have abandoned the enterprise.

As the power of Montezuma enabled him to take this spirited part, his own dispositions were such as seemed naturally to prompt him to it. Of all the princes who had swayed the Mexican sceptre, he was the most haughty, the most violent, and the most impatient of control. His subjects looked up to him with awe, and his enemies with terror. The former he governed with unexampled rigour; but they were impressed with such an opinion of his capacity as commanded their respect; and, by many victories over the latter, he had spread far the dread of his arms, and had added several considerable provinces to his dominions. But though his talents might be suited to the transactions of a state so imperfectly polished as the Mexican empire, and sufficient to conduct them while in their accustomed course, they were altogether inadequate to a conjuncture so extraordinary, and did not qualify him either to judge with the discernment or to act with the decision requisite in such trying emergence.

From the moment that the Spaniards appeared on his coast, he discovered symptoms of timidity and embarrassment. Instead of taking such resolutions as the consciousness of his own power, or the memory of his former exploits, might have inspired, he deliberated with an anxiety and hesitation which did not escape the notice of his meanest courtiers. The perplexity and discomposure of Montezuma's mind upon this occasion, as well as the general dismay of his subjects, were not owing wholly to the impression which the Spaniards had made by the novelty of their appearance and the terror of their arms. Its origin may be traced up to a more remote source. There was an opinion, if we may believe the earliest and most authentic Spanish historians, almost universal among the Americans,

* B. Diaz, c. 39 Gomara Cron. c. 27 Herrera, dec. 2 lib v. c. 5, 6

that some dreadful calamity was impending over their heads, from a race of formidable invaders, who should come from regions towards the rising sun, to overrun and desolate their country. Whether this disquieting apprehension flowed from the memory of some natural calamity which had afflicted that part of the globe, and impressed the minds of the inhabitants with superstitious fears and forebodings, or whether it was an imagination accidentally suggested by the astonishment which the first sight of a new race of men occasioned, it is impossible to determine. But as the Mexicans were more prone to superstition than any people in the New World, they were more deeply affected by the appearance of the Spaniards, whom their credulity instantly represented as the instrument destined to bring about this fatal revolution which they dreaded. Under those circumstances it ceases to be incredible that a handful of adventurers should alarm the monarch of a great empire, and all his subjects.*

Notwithstanding the influence of this impression, when the messenger arrived from the Spanish camp with an account that the leader of the strangers, adhering to his original demand, refused to obey the order enjoining him to leave the country, Montezuma assumed some degree of resolution; and in a transport of rage natural to a fierce prince unaccustomed to meet with any opposition to his will, he threatened to sacrifice those presumptuous men to his gods. But his doubts and fears quickly returned; and instead of issuing orders to carry his threats into execution, he again called his ministers to confer and offer their advice. Feeble and temporising measures will always be the result when men assemble to deliberate in a situation where they ought to act. The Mexican counsellors took no effectual measure for expelling such troublesome intruders, and were satisfied with issuing a more positive injunction, requiring them to leave the country; but this they preposterously accompanied with a present of such value as proved a fresh inducement to remain there.

Meanwhile, the Spaniards were not without solicitude, or a variety of sentiments, in deliberating concerning their own future conduct. From what they had already seen, many of them formed such extravagant ideas concerning the opulence of the country, that, despising danger or hardships when they had in view treasures which appeared to be inexhaustible, they were eager to attempt the conquest. Others, estimating the power of the Mexican empire by its wealth, and enumerating the various proofs which had occurred of its being under a well regulated administration, contended, that it would be an act of the wildest frenzy to attack such a state with a small body of men, in want of provisions, unconnected with any ally, and already enfeebled by the diseases peculiar to the climate, and the loss of several of their number.† Cortes secretly applauded the advocates for bold measures, and cherished their romantic hopes, as such ideas corresponded with his own, and favoured the execution of the schemes which he had formed. From the time that the suspicions of Velasquez broke out with open violence in the attempts to deprive him of the command, Cortes saw the necessity of dissolving a connection which would obstruct and embarrass all his operations, and watched for a proper opportunity of coming to a final rupture with him. Having this in view, he had laboured by every art to secure the esteem and affection of his soldiers. With his abilities for command, it was easy to gain their esteem and his followers were quickly satisfied that they might rely, with perfect confidence, on the conduct and courage of their leader. Nor was it more difficult to acquire their affection. Among adventurers nearly of the same rank, and serving at their own expense, the dignity of command did not elevate a general above mingling with those who acted under him. Cortes

* Cortes Relatione Seconda, ap. Ramus, iii. 234, 235. Herrera, dec. 2. lib. iii. c. 1. lib. v. c. 11. lib. vii. c. 6. Gomara Cron. c. 66. 92. 144. † B. Diaz, c. 40.

availed himself of this freedom of intercourse to insinuate himself into their favour, and by his affable manners, by well timed acts of liberality to some, by inspiring all with vast hopes, and by allowing them to trade privately with the natives [103], he attached the greater part of his soldiers so firmly to himself, that they almost forgot that the armament had been fitted out by the authority and at the expense of another.

During these intrigues, Teutile arrived with the present from Montezuma, and, together with it, delivered the ultimate order of that monarch to depart instantly out of his dominions; and when Cortes, instead of complying, renewed his request of an audience, the Mexican turned from him abruptly, and quitted the camp with looks and gestures which strongly expressed his surprise and resentment. Next morning, none of the natives, who used to frequent the camp in great numbers in order to barter with the soldiers, and to bring in provisions, appeared. All friendly correspondence seemed now to be at an end, and it was expected every moment that hostilities would commence. This, though an event that might have been foreseen, occasioned a sudden consternation among the Spaniards, which emboldened the adherents of Velasquez not only to murmur and cabal against their general, but to appoint one of their number to remonstrate openly against his imprudence in attempting the conquest of a mighty empire with such inadequate force, and to urge the necessity of returning to Cuba, in order to refit the fleet and augment the army. Diego de Ordaz, one of his principal officers, whom the malecontents charged with this commission, delivered it with a soldierly freedom and bluntness, assuring Cortes that he spoke the sentiments of the whole army. He listened to this remonstrance without any appearance of emotion; and as he well knew the temper and wishes of his soldiers, and foresaw how they would receive a proposition fatal at once to all the splendid hopes and schemes which they had been forming with such complacency, he carried his dissimulation so far as to seem to relinquish his own measures in compliance with the request of Ordaz, and issued orders that the army should be in readiness next day to re-embark for Cuba. As soon as this was known, the disappointed adventurers exclaimed and threatened; the emissaries of Cortes, mingling with them, inflamed their rage; the ferment became general; the whole camp was almost in open mutiny; all demanding with eagerness to see their commander. Cortes was not slow in appearing; when, with one voice, officers and soldiers expressed their astonishment and indignation at the orders which they had received. It was unworthy, they cried, of the Castilian courage to be daunted at the first aspect of danger, and infamous to fly before any enemy appeared. For their parts, they were determined not to relinquish an enterprise that had hitherto been successful, and which tended so visibly to spread the knowledge of true religion, and to advance the glory and interest of their country. Happy under his command, they would follow him with alacrity through every danger in quest of those settlements and treasures which he had so long held out to their view; but if he chose rather to return to Cuba, and tamely give up all his hopes of distinction and opulence to an envious rival, they would instantly choose another general to conduct them in that path of glory which he had not spirit to enter.

Cortes, delighted with their ardour, took no offence at the boldness with which it was uttered. The sentiments were what he himself had inspired, and the warmth of expression satisfied him that his followers had imbibed them thoroughly. He affected, however, to be surprised at what he heard, declaring that his orders to prepare for embarking were issued from a persuasion that this was agreeable to his troops; that, from deference to what he had been informed was their inclination, he had sacrificed his own private opinion, which was firmly bent on establishing immediately a settlement on the sea coast, and then on endeavouring to penetrate into the interior part of the country; that now he was convinced of his error; and as he perceived that they were animated with the generous spirit which breathed in every true Spaniard, he would resume, with fresh ardour, his original plan of operation, and doubted not to conduct them, in the career of victory, to such independent fortunes as their valour merited. Upon this declaration, shouts of applause testified the excess of their joy. The measure seemed to be taken with unanimous consent; such as secretly condemned it being obliged to join in the acclamations, partly to conceal their disaffection from their general, and partly to avoid the imputation of cowardice from their fellow-soldiers.*

Without allowing his men time to cool or to reflect, Cortes set about carrying his design into execution. In order to give a beginning to a colony, he assembled the principal persons in his army, and by their suffrage elected a council and magistrates, in whom the government was to be vested. As men naturally transplant the institutions and forms of the mother country into their new settlements, this was framed upon the model of a Spanish corporation. The magistrates were distinguished by the same names and ensigns of office, and were to exercise a similar jurisdiction. All the persons chosen were most firmly devoted to Cortes, and the instrument of their election was framed in the king's name, without any mention of their dependence on Velasquez. The two principles of avarice and enthusiasm, which prompted the Spaniards to all their enterprises in the New World, seem to have concurred in suggesting the name which Cortes bestowed on his infant settlement. He called it, *The Rich Town of the True Cross.*†

The first meeting of the new council was distinguished by a transaction of great moment. As soon as it assembled, Cortes applied for leave to enter; and approaching with many marks of profound respect, which added dignity to the tribunal, and set an example of reverence for its authority, he began a long harangue, in which, with much art, and in terms extremely flattering to persons just entering upon their new function, he observed, that as the supreme jurisdiction over the colony which they had planted was now vested in this court, he considered them as clothed with the authority and representing the person of their sovereign; that accordingly he would communicate to them what he deemed essential to the public safety, with the same dutiful fidelity as if he were addressing his royal master; that the security of a colony settled in a great empire, whose sovereign had already discovered his hostile intentions, depended upon arms, and the efficacy of these upon the subordination and discipline preserved among the troops; that his right to command was derived from a commission granted by the governor of Cuba; and as that had been long since revoked, the lawfulness of his jurisdiction might well be questioned; that he might be thought to act upon a defective or even a dubious title; nor could they trust an army which might dispute the powers of its general, at a juncture when it ought implicitly to obey his orders; that, moved by these considerations, he now resigned all his authority to them, that they, having both right to choose, and power to confer full jurisdiction, might appoint one in the king's name to command the army in its future operations; and as for his own part, such was his zeal for the service in which they were engaged, that he would most cheerfully take up a pike with the same hand that laid down the general's truncheon, and convince his fellow-soldiers, that though accustomed to command, he had not forgotten how to obey. Having finished his discourse, he laid the commission from Velasquez upon the table, and, after kissing his truncheon, delivered it to the chief magistrate, and withdrew.

The deliberations of the council were not long, as Cortes had concerted this important measure with his confidants, and had prepared the other

* B. Diaz, c. 40, 41, 42. Herrera, dec. 2. lib. v. c. 6. 7. † Villa Rica de la Vera Cruz.

members with great address for the part which he wished them to take His resignation was accepted; and as the uninterrupted tenor of their prosperity under his conduct afforded the most satisfying evidence of his abilities for command, they, by their unanimous suffrage, elected him chief justice of the colony, and captain-general of its army, and appointed his commission to be made out in the king's name, with most ample powers, which were to continue in force until the royal pleasure should be further known. That this deed might not be deemed the machination of a junto, the council called together the troops, and acquainted them with what had been resolved. The soldiers, with eager applause, ratified the choice which the council had made; the air resounded with the name of Cortes, and all vowed to shed their blood in support of his authority.

Cortes, having now brought his intrigues to the desired issue, and shaken off his mortifying dependence on the governor of Cuba, accepted of the commission, which vested in him supreme jurisdiction, civil as well as military, over the colony, with many professions of respect to the council and gratitude to the army. Together with this new command, he assumed greater dignity, and began to exercise more extensive powers. Formerly he had felt himself to be only the deputy of a subject; now he acted as the representative of his sovereign. The adherents of Velasquez, fully aware of what would be the effect of this change in the situation of Cortes, could no longer continue silent and passive spectators of his actions. They exclaimed openly against the proceedings of the council as illegal, and against those of the army as mutinous. Cortes, instantly perceiving the necessity of giving a timely check to such seditious discourse by some vigorous measure, arrested Ordaz, Escudero, and Velasquez de Leon, the ringleaders of this faction, and sent them prisoners aboard the fleet, loaded with chains. Their dependants, astonished and overawed, remained quiet; and Cortes, more desirous to reclaim than to punish his prisoners, who were officers of great merit, courted their friendship with such assiduity and address, that the reconciliation was perfectly cordial; and on the most trying occasions, neither their connection with the governor of Cuba, nor the memory of the indignity with which they had been treated, tempted them to swerve from an inviolable attachment to his interest.* In this, as well as his other negotiations at this critical conjuncture, which decided with respect to his future fame and fortune, Cortes owed much of his success to the Mexican gold, which he distributed with a liberal hand both among his friends and his opponents.†

Cortes, having thus rendered the union between himself and his army indissoluble, by engaging it to join him in disclaiming any dependence on the governor of Cuba, and in repeated acts of disobedience to his authority, thought he now might venture to quit the camp in which he had hitherto remained, and advance into the country. To this he was encouraged by an event no less fortunate than seasonable. Some Indians having approached his camp in a mysterious manner, were introduced into his presence. He found that they were sent with a proffer of friendship from the cazique of Zempoalla, a considerable town at no great distance; and from their answers to a variety of questions which he put to them, according to his usual practice in every interview with the people of the country, he gathered, that their master, though subject to the Mexican empire, was impatient of the yoke, and filled with such dread and hatred of Montezuma, that nothing could be more acceptable to him than any prospect of deliverance from the oppression under which he groaned. On hearing this, a ray of light and hope broke in upon the mind of Cortes. He saw that the great empire which he intended to attack was neither perfectly united, nor its sovereign universally beloved. He concluded, that the

* B. Diaz, c. 42, 43. Gomara Cron. c. 30, 31. Herrera, dec. 2. lib. v. c. 7. † B. Diaz. c. 44.

causes of disaffection could not be confined to one province, but that in other corners there must be malecontents, so weary of subjection, or so desirous of change, as to be ready to follow the standard of any protector. Full of those ideas, on which he began to form a scheme that time and more perfect information concerning the state of the country enabled him to mature, he gave a most gracious reception to the Zempoallans, and promised soon to visit their cazique.*

In order to perform this promise, it was not necessary to vary the route which he had already fixed for his march. Some officers, whom he had employed to survey the coast, having discovered a village named Quiabislan, about forty miles to the northward, which, both on account of the fertility of the soil and commodiousness of the harbour, seemed to be a more proper station for a settlement than that where he was encamped, Cortes determined to remove thither. Zempoalla lay in his way, where the cazique received him in the manner which he had reason to expect; with gifts and caresses, like a man solicitous to gain his good will; with respect approaching almost to adoration, like one who looked up to him as a deliverer. From him he learned many particulars with respect to the character of Montezuma, and the circumstances which rendered his dominion odious. He was a tyrant, as the cazique told him with tears, haughty, cruel, and suspicious; who treated his own subjects with arrogance, ruined the conquered provinces by excessive exactions, and often tore their sons and daughters from them by violence; the former to be offered as victims to his gods; the latter to be reserved as concubines for himself or favourites Cortes, in reply to him, artfully insinuated, that one great object of the Spaniards in visiting a country so remote from their own, was to redress grievances, and to relieve the oppressed; and having encouraged him to hope for this interposition in due time, he continued his march to Quiabislan.

The spot which his officers had recommended as a proper situation appeared to him to be so well chosen, that he immediately marked out ground for a town. The houses to be erected were only huts; but these were to be surrounded with fortifications of sufficient strength to resist the assaults of an Indian army. As the finishing of those fortifications was essential to the existence of a colony, and of no less importance in prosecuting the designs which the leader and his followers meditated, both in order to secure a place of retreat, and to preserve their communication with the sea, every man in the army, officers as well as soldiers, put his hand to the work, Cortes himself setting them an example of activity and perseverance in labour. The Indians of Zempoalla and Quiabislan lent their aid; and this petty station, the parent of so many mighty settlements, was soon in a state of defence.†

While engaged in this necessary work, Cortes had several interviews with the caziques of Zempoalla and Quiabislan; and availing himself of their wonder and astonishment at the new objects which they daily beheld, he gradually inspired them with such a high opinion of the Spaniards, as beings of a superior order, and irresistible in arms, that, relying on their protection, they ventured to insult the Mexican power, at the very name of which they were accustomed to tremble. Some of Montezuma's officers having appeared to levy the usual tribute, and to demand a certain number of human victims, as an expiation for their guilt in presuming to hold intercourse with those strangers whom the emperor had commanded to leave his dominions; instead of obeying the order, the caziques made them prisoners, treated them with great indignity, and as their superstition was no less barbarous than that of the Mexicans, they prepared to sacri-

* B. Diaz. c. 41. Gomara Cron. c. 28. Herrera, dec. 2. lib. v. c. 8, 9.

† B. Diaz, c. 45, 46. 48. Gomara Cron. c. 32, 33. 37.

fice them to their gods. From this last danger they were delivered by the interposition of Cortes, who manifested the utmost horror at the mention of such a deed. The two caziques having now been pushed to an act of such open rebellion, as left them no hope of safety but in attaching themselves inviolably to the Spaniards, they soon completed their union with them, by formally acknowledging themselves to be vassals of the same monarch. Their example was followed by the Totonaques, a fierce people who inhabited the mountainous part of the country. They willingly subjected themselves to the crown of Castile, and offered to accompany Cortes, with all their forces, in his march towards Mexico.*

Cortes had now been above three months in New Spain; and though this period had not been distinguished by martial exploits, every moment had been employed in operations which, though less splendid, were more important. By his address in conducting his intrigues with his own army, as well as his sagacity in carrying on his negotiations with the natives, he had already laid the foundations of his future success. But whatever confidence he might place in the plan which he had formed, he could not but perceive, that as his title to command was derived from a doubtful authority, he held it by a precarious tenure. The injuries which Velasquez had received were such as would naturally prompt him to apply for redress to their common sovereign; and such a representation, he foresaw, might be given of his conduct that, he had reason to apprehend, not only that he might be degraded from his present rank, but subjected to punishment. Before he began his march, it was necessary to take the most effectual precautions against this impending danger. With this view he persuaded the magistrates of the colony at Vera Cruz to address a letter to the king, the chief object of which was to justify their own conduct in establishing a colony independent on the jurisdiction of Velasquez. In order to accomplish this, they endeavoured to detract from his merit in fitting out the two former armaments under Cordova and Grijalva, affirming that these had been equipped by the adventurers who engaged in the expeditions, and not by the governor. They contended that the sole object of Velasquez was to trade or barter with the natives, not to attempt the conquest of New Spain, or to settle a colony there. They asserted that Cortes and the officers who served under him had defrayed the greater part of the expense of fitting out the armament. On this account, they humbly requested their sovereign to ratify what they had done in his name, and to confirm Cortes in the supreme command by his royal commission. That Charles might be induced to grant more readily what they demanded, they gave him a pompous description of the country which they had discovered; of its riches, the number of its inhabitants, their civilization and arts; they related the progress which they had already made in annexing some parts of the country situated on the sea coast to the crown of Castile: and mentioned the schemes which they had formed, as well as the hopes which they entertained, of reducing the whole to subjection.† Cortes himself wrote in a similar strain; and as he knew that the Spanish court, accustomed to the exaggerated representations of every new country by its discoverers, would give little credit to their splendid accounts of New Spain, if these were not accompanied with such a specimen of what it contained as would excite a high idea of its opulence, he

* B. Diaz, c. 47. Gomara Cron. 35, 36. Herrera, dec. 2. lib. v. c. 9, 10, 11.

† In this letter it is asserted, that though a considerable number of Spaniards have been wounded in their various encounters with the people of Tobasco, not one of them died, and all had recovered in a very short time. This seems to confirm what I observe in p. 214, concerning the imperfection of the offensive weapons used by the Americans. In this letter, the human sacrifices offered by the Mexicans to their deities are described minutely, and with great horror; some of the Spaniards, it is said, had been eye-witnesses of those barbarous rites. To the letter is subjoined a catalogue and description of the presents sent to the emperor. That published by Gomara, Cron. c. 29, seems to have been copied from it. Pet. Martyr describes many of the articles in his treatise, 'De Insulis nuper inventis,' p. 354, &c.

solicited his soldiers to relinquish what they might claim as their part of the treasures which had hitherto been collected, in order that the whole might be sent to the king. Such was the ascendant which he had acquired over their minds, and such their own romantic expectations of future wealth, that an army of indigent and rapacious adventurers was capable of this generous effort, and offered to their sovereign the richest present that had hitherto been transmitted from the New World [104]. Portocarrero and Montejo, the chief magistrates of the colony, were appointed to carry this present to Castile, with express orders not to touch at Cuba in their passage thither.*

While a vessel was preparing for their departure an unexpected event occasioned a general alarm. Some soldiers and sailors, secretly attached to Velasquez, or intimidated at the prospect of the dangers unavoidable in attempting to penetrate into the heart of a great empire with such unequal force, formed the design of seizing one of the brigantines, and making their escape to Cuba, in order to give the governor such intelligence as might enable him to intercept the ship which was to carry the treasure and despatches to Spain. This conspiracy, though formed by persons of low rank, was conducted with profound secrecy; but at the moment when every thing was ready for execution, they were betrayed by one of their associates.

Though the good fortune of Cortes interposed so seasonably on this occasion, the detection of this conspiracy filled his mind with most disquieting apprehensions, and prompted him to execute a scheme which he had long revolved. He perceived that the spirit of disaffection still lurked among his troops; that though hitherto checked by the uniform success of his schemes, or suppressed by the hand of authority, various events might occur which would encourage and call it forth. He observed, that many of his men, weary of the fatigue of service, longed to revisit their settlements in Cuba; and that upon any appearance of extraordinary danger or any reverse of fortune, it would be impossible to restrain them from returning thither. He was sensible that his forces, already too feeble, could bear no diminution, and that a very small defection of his followers would oblige him to abandon the enterprise. After ruminating often, and with much solicitude, upon those particulars, he saw no hope of success but in cutting off all possibility of retreat, and in reducing his men to the necessity of adopting the same resolution with which he himself was animated, either to conquer or to perish. With this view he determined to destroy his fleet; but as he durst not venture to execute such a bold resolution by his single authority, he laboured to bring his soldiers to adopt his ideas with respect to the propriety of this measure. His address in accomplishing this was not inferior to the arduous occasion in which it was employed. He persuaded some that the ships had suffered so much by having been long at sea, as to be altogether unfit for service; to others he pointed out what a seasonable reinforcement of strength they would derive from the junction of a hundred men, now unprofitably employed as sailors; and to all he represented the necessity of fixing their eyes and wishes upon what was before them, without allowing the idea of a retreat once to enter their thoughts. With universal consent the ships were drawn ashore, and after stripping them of their sails, rigging, iron works, and whatever else might be of use, they were broke in pieces. Thus, from an effort of magnanimity, to which there is nothing parallel in history, five hundred men voluntarily consented to be shut up in a hostile country, filled with powerful and unknown nations; and, having precluded every means of escape, left themselves without any resource but their own valour and perseverance.†

* B Diaz, c. 54. Gomara, Cron. c. 40

† Relat. di Cortes. Ramus. iii. 225. B. Diaz. c. 57, 58. Herrera, dec. 2. lib. v. c. 14.

Nothing now retarded Cortes; the alacrity of his troops and the disposition of his allies were equally favourable. All the advantages, however, derived from the latter, though procured by much assiduity and address, were well nigh lost in a moment, by an indiscreet sally of religious zeal, which on many occasions precipitated Cortes into actions inconsistent with the prudence that distinguishes his character. Though hitherto he had neither time nor opportunity to explain to the natives the errors of their own superstition, or to instruct them in the principles of the Christian faith, he commanded his soldiers to overturn the altars and to destroy the idols in the chief temple of Zempoalla, and in their place to erect a crucifix and an image of the Virgin Mary. The people beheld this with astonishment and horror; the priests excited them to arms: but such was the authority of Cortes, and so great the ascendant which the Spaniards had acquired, that the commotion was appeased without bloodshed, and concord perfectly re-established.*

Cortes began his march from Zempoalla, on the sixteenth of August, with five hundred men, fifteen horse, and six field pieces. The rest of his troops, consisting chiefly of such as from age or infirmity were less fit for active service, he left as a garrison in Villa Rica, under the command of Escalante, an officer of merit, and warmly attached to his interest. The cazique of Zempoalla supplied him with provisions, and with two hundred of those Indians called *Tamemes,* whose office, in a country where tame animals were unknown, was to carry burdens, and to perform all servile labour. They were a great relief to the Spanish soldiers, who hitherto had been obliged not only to carry their own baggage, but to drag along the artillery by main force. He offered likewise a considerable body of his troops, but Cortes was satisfied with four hundred; taking care, however, to choose persons of such note as might prove hostages for the fidelity of their master. Nothing memorable happened in his progress, until he arrived on the confines of Tlascala. The inhabitants of that province, a warlike people, were implacable enemies of the Mexicans, and had been united in an ancient alliance with the caziques of Zempoalla. Though less civilized than the subjects of Montezuma, they were advanced in improvement far beyond the rude nations of America whose manners we have described. They had made considerable progress in agriculture; they dwelt in large towns; they were not strangers to some species of commerce; and in the imperfect accounts of their institutions and laws, transmitted to us by the early Spanish writers, we discern traces both of distributive justice and of criminal jurisdiction in their interior police. But still, as the degree of their civilization was incomplete, and as they depended for subsistence not on agriculture alone, but trusted for it in a great measure to hunting, they retained many of the qualities natural to men in this state. Like them they were fierce and revengeful; like them, too, they were high spirited and independent. In consequence of the former, they were involved in perpetual hostilities, and had but a slender and occasional intercourse with neighbouring states. The latter inspired them with such detestation of servitude, that they not only refused to stoop to a foreign yoke, and maintain an obstinate and successful contest in defence of their liberty against the superior power of the Mexican empire, but they guarded with equal solicitude against domestic tyranny; and disdaining to acknowledge any master, they lived under the mild and limited jurisdiction of a council elected by their several tribes.

Cortes, though he had received information concerning the martial character of this people, flattered himself that his professions of delivering the oppressed from the tyranny of Montezuma, their inveterate enmity to the Mexicans, and the example of their ancient allies the Zempoallans,

* B. Diaz, c. 41, 42. Herrera, dec. 2. lib. v. c. 3, 4.

might induce the Tlascalans to grant him a friendly reception. In order to dispose them to this, four Zempoallans of great eminence were sent ambassadors, to request in his name, and in that of their cazique, that they would permit the Spaniards to pass through the territories of the republic in their way to Mexico. But instead of the favourable answer which was expected, the Tlascalans seized the ambassadors, and, without any regard to their public character, made preparations for sacrificing them to their gods. At the same time they assembled their troops, in order to oppose those unknown invaders if they should attempt to make their passage good by force of arms. Various motives concurred in precipitating the Tlascalans into this resolution. A fierce people, shut up within its own narrow precincts, and little accustomed to any intercourse with foreigners, is apt to consider every stranger as an enemy, and is easily excited to arms. They concluded, from Cortes's proposal of visiting Montezuma in his capital, that, notwithstanding all his professions, he courted the friendship of a monarch whom they both hated and feared The imprudent zeal of Cortes in violating the temples in Zempoalla, filled the Tlascalans with horror; and as they were no less attached to their superstition than the other nations of New Spain, they were impatient to avenge their injured gods, and to acquire the merit of offering up to them as victims, those impious men who had dared to profane their altars; they contemned the small number of the Spaniards, as they had not yet measured their own strength with that of these new enemies, and had no idea of the superiority which they derived from their arms and discipline.

Cortes, after waiting some days, in vain, for the return of his ambassadors, advanced [Aug. 30,] into the Tlascalan territories. As the resolutions of people who delight in war are executed with no less promptitude than they are formed, he found troops in the field ready to oppose him. They attacked him with great intrepidity, and, in the first encounter, wounded some of the Spaniards, and killed two horses; a loss, in their situation, of great moment, because it was irreparable. From this specimen of their courage, Cortes saw the necessity of proceeding with caution. His army marched in close order; he chose the stations where he halted, with attention, and fortified every camp with extraordinary care. During fourteen days he was exposed to almost uninterrupted assaults, the Tlascalans advancing with numerous armies, and renewing the attack in various forms, with a degree of valour and perseverance to which the Spaniards had seen nothing parallel in the New World. The Spanish historians describe those successive battles with great pomp, and enter into a minute detail of particulars, mingling many exaggerated and incredible circumstances [105] with such as are real and marvellous. But no power of words can render the recital of a combat interesting, where there is no equality of danger; and when the narrative closes with an account of thousands slain on the one side, while not a single person falls on the other, the most laboured descriptions of the previous disposition of the troops, or of the various vicissitudes in the engagement, command no attention.

There are some circumstances, however, in this war, which are memorable, and merit notice, as they throw light upon the character both of the people of New Spain, and of their conquerors. Though the Tlascalans brought into the field such numerous armies as appear sufficient to have overwhelmed the Spaniards, they were never able to make any impression upon their small battalion. Singular as this may seem, it is not inexplicable. The Tlascalans, though addicted to war, were like all unpolished nations, strangers to military order and discipline, and lost in a great measure the advantage which they might have derived from their numbers, and the impetuosity of their attack, by their constant solicitude to carry off the dead and wounded. This point of honour, founded on a sentiment of tenderness natural to the human mind, and strengthened by anxiety to preserve the bodies of their countrymen from being devoured by their enemies, was universal among the people of New Spain. Attention to this pious office occupied them even during the heat of combat,* broke their union, and diminished the force of the impression which they might have made by a joint effort.

Not only was their superiority in number of little avail, but the imperfection of their military weapons rendered their valour in a great measure inoffensive. After three battles, and many skirmishes and assaults, not one Spaniard was killed in the field. Arrows and spears, headed with flint or the bones of fishes, stakes hardened in the fire, and wooden swords, though destructive weapons among naked Indians, were easily turned aside by the Spanish bucklers, and could hardly penetrate the *escaupiles,* or quilted jackets, which the soldiers wore. The Tlascalans advanced boldly to the charge, and often fought hand to hand. Many of the Spaniards were wounded, though all slightly, which cannot be imputed to any want of courage or strength in their enemies, but to the defect of the arms with which they assailed them.

Notwithstanding the fury with which the Tlascalans attacked the Spaniards, they seemed to have conducted their hostilities with some degree of barbarous generosity. They gave the Spaniards warning of their hostile intentions; and as they knew that their invaders wanted provisions, and imagined, perhaps, like the other Americans, that they had left their own country because it did not afford them subsistence, they sent to their camp a large supply of poultry and maize, desiring them to eat plentifully, because they scorned to attack an enemy enfeebled by hunger, and it would be an affront to their gods to offer them famished victims, as well as disagreeable to themselves to feed on such emaciated prey.†

When they were taught by the first encounter with their new enemies, that it was not easy to execute this threat; when they perceived, in the subsequent engagements, that notwithstanding all the efforts of their own valour, of which they had a very high opinion, not one of the Spaniards was slain or taken, they began to conceive them to be a superior order of beings, against whom human power could not avail. In this extremity, they had recourse to their priests, requiring them to reveal the mysterious causes of such extraordinary events, and to declare what new means they should employ in order to repulse those formidable invaders. The priests, after many sacrifices and incantations, delivered this response: That these strangers were the offspring of the sun, procreated by his animating energy in the regions of the east; that, by day, while cherished with the influence of his parental beams, they were invincible; but by night, when his reviving heat was withdrawn, their vigour declined and faded like the herbs in the field, and they dwindled down into mortal men.‡ Theories less plausible have gained credit with more enlightened nations, and have influenced their conduct. In consequence of this, the Tlascalans, with the implicit confidence of men who fancy themselves to be under the guidance of Heaven, acted in contradiction to one of their most established maxims in war, and ventured to attack the enemy, with a strong body, in the night time, in hopes of destroying them when enfeebled and surprised. But Cortes had greater vigilance and discernment than to be deceived by the rude stratagems of an Indian army. The sentinels at his outposts, observing some extraordinary movement among the Tlascalans, gave the alarm. In a moment the troops were under arms, and sallying out, dispersed the party with great slaughter, without allowing it to approach the camp. The Tlascalans convinced by sad experience that their priests had deluded them, and satisfied that they attempted in vain either to deceive or to vanquish their enemies, their fierceness abated, and they began to incline seriously to peace.

* B. Diaz, c. 65. † Herrera, dec 2. lib. vi. c. 6. Gomara Cron. c. 47. ‡ B. Diaz, c. 66

They were at a loss, however, in what manner to address the strangers, what idea to form of their character, and whether to consider them as beings of a gentle or of a malevolent nature. There were circumstances in their conduct which seemed to favour each opinion. On the one hand, as the Spaniards constantly dismissed the prisoners whom they took, not only without injury, but often with presents of European toys, and renewed their offers of peace after every victory; this lenity amazed people, who according to the exterminating system of war known in America, were accustomed to sacrifice and devour without mercy all the captives taken in battle, and disposed them to entertain favourable sentiments of the humanity of their new enemies. But, on the other hand, as Cortes had seized fifty of their countrymen who brought provisions to his camp, and supposing them to be spies, had cut off their hands;* this bloody spectacle, added to the terror occasioned by the fire-arms and horses, filled them with dreadful impressions of the ferocity of their invaders [106]. This uncertainty was apparent in the mode of addressing the Spaniards. "If," said they, "you are divinities of a cruel and savage nature, we present to you five slaves, that you may drink their blood and eat their flesh. If you are mild deities, accept an offering of incense and variegated plumes. If you are men, here is meat, and bread, and fruit to nourish you.† The peace, which both parties now desired with equal ardour, was soon concluded. The Tlascalans yielded themselves as vassals to the crown of Castile, and engaged to assist Cortes in all his future operations. He took the republic under his protection, and promised to defend their persons and possessions from injury or violence.

This treaty was concluded at a seasonable juncture for the Spaniards. The fatigue of service among a small body of men, surrounded by such a multitude of enemies, was incredible. Half the army was on duty every night, and even they whose turn it was to rest, slept always upon their arms, that they might be ready to run to their posts on a moment's warning. Many of them were wounded; a good number, and among these Cortes himself, laboured under the distempers prevalent in hot climates, and several had died since they set out from Vera Cruz. Notwithstanding the supplies which they received from the Tlascalans, they were often in want of provisions, and so destitute of the necessaries most requisite in dangerous service, that they had no salve to dress their wounds, but what was composed with the fat of the Indians whom they had slain.‡ Worn out with such intolerable toil and hardships, many of the soldiers began to murmur, and when they reflected on the multitude and boldness of their enemies, more were ready to despair. It required the utmost exertion of Cortes's authority and address to check this spirit of despondency in its progress, and to reanimate his followers with their wonted sense of their own superiority over the enemies with whom they had to contend.§ The submission of the Tlascalans, and their own triumphant entry into the capital city, where they were received with the reverence paid to beings of a superior order, banished at once from the minds of the Spaniards all memory of past sufferings, dispelled every anxious thought with respect to their future operations, and fully satisfied them that there was not now any power in America able to withstand their arms.||

Cortes remained twenty days in Tlascala, in order to allow his troops a short interval of repose after such hard service. During that time he was employed in transactions and inquiries of great moment with respect to his future schemes. In his daily conferences with the Tlascalan chiefs, he received information concerning every particular relative to the state of the Mexican empire, or to the qualities of its sovereign,

* Cortes Relat. Ramus. iii. 228. C. Gomara Cron. c. 48. † B. Diaz, c. 70. Gomara Cron c. 47. Herrera, dec. 2. lib. vi. c. 7. ‡ B. Diaz, c. 62. 65. § Cortes Relat. Ramus. iii. 229 B Diaz, c. 69. Gomara Cron. c. 51. || Cortes Relat. Ramus. iii. 230. B. Diaz, c. 72.

which could be of use in regulating his conduct, whether he should be obliged to act as a friend or as an ememy. As he found that the antipathy of his new allies to the Mexican nation was no less implacable than had been represented, and perceived what benefit he might derive from the aid of such powerful confederates, he employed all his powers of insinuation in order to gain their confidence. Nor was any extraordinary exertion of these necessary. The Tlascalans, with the levity of mind natural to unpolished men, were, of their own accord, disposed to run from the extreme of hatred to that of fondness. Every thing in the appearance and conduct of their guests was to them matter of wonder [107]. They gazed with admiration at whatever the Spaniards did, and, fancying them to be of heavenly origin, were eager not only to comply with their demands, but to anticipate their wishes. They offered, accordingly, to accompany Cortes in his march to Mexico, with all the forces of the republic, under the command of their most experienced captains.

But, after bestowing so much pains on cementing this union, all the beneficial fruits of it were on the point of being lost by a new effusion of that intemperate religious zeal with which Cortes was animated no less than the other adventurers of the age. They all considered themselves as instruments employed by Heaven to propagate the Christian faith, and the less they were qualified, either by their knowledge or morals, for such a function, they were more eager to discharge it. The profound veneration of the Tlascalans for the Spaniards having encouraged Cortes to explain to some of their chiefs the doctrines of the Christian religion, and to insist that they should abandon their own superstitions, and embrace the faith of their new friends, they, according to an idea universal among barbarous nations, readily acknowledged the truth and excellence of what he taught; but contended, that the *Teules* of Tlascala were divinities no less than the God in whom the Spaniards believed; and as that Being was entitled to the homage of Europeans, so they were bound to revere the same powers which their ancestors had worshipped. Cortes continued, nevertheless, to urge his demand in a tone of authority, mingling threats with his arguments, until the Tlascalans could bear it no longer, and conjured him never to mention this again, lest the gods should avenge on their heads the guilt of having listened to such a proposition. Cortes, astonished and enraged at their obstinacy, prepared to execute by force what he could not accomplish by persuasion, and was going to overturn their altars and cast down their idols with the same violent hand as at Zempoalla, if Father Bartholomew de Olmedo, chaplain to the expedition, had not checked his inconsiderate impetuosity. He represented the imprudence of such an attempt in a large city newly reconciled, and filled with people no less superstitious than warlike; he declared, that the proceeding at Zempoalla had always appeared to him precipitate and unjust; that religion was not to be propagated by the sword, or infidels to be converted by violence; that other weapons were to be employed in this ministry; patient instruction must enlighten the understanding, and pious example captivate the heart, before men could be induced to abandon error, and embrace the truth.* Amidst scenes where a narrow minded bigotry appears in such close union with oppression and cruelty, sentiments so liberal and humane soothe the mind with unexpected pleasure; and at a time when the rights of conscience were little understood in the Christian world, and the idea of toleration unknown, one is astonished to find a Spanish monk of the sixteenth century among the first advocates against persecution, and in behalf of religious liberty. The remonstrances of an ecclesiastic, no less respectable for wisdom than virtue, had their proper weight with Cortes. He left the Tlascalans in the undisturbed exercise of their own rites, requiring only that

* B. Diaz, c. 77. p. 54. c. 83. p. 61.

they should desist from their horrid practice of offering human victims in sacrifice.

Cortes, as soon as his troops were fit for service, resolved to continue his march towards Mexico, notwithstanding the earnest dissuasives of the Tlascalans, who represented his destruction as unavoidable if he put himself in the power of a prince so faithless and cruel as Montezuma. As he was accompanied by six thousand Tlascalans, he had now the command of forces which resembled a regular army. They directed their course towards Cholula [Oct. 13]; Montezuma, who had at length consented to admit the Spaniards into his presence, having informed Cortes that he had given orders for his friendly reception there. Cholula was a considerable town, and though only five leagues distant from Tlascala, was formerly an independent state, but had been lately subjected to the Mexican empire. This was considered by all the people of New Spain as a holy place, the sanctuary and chief seat of their gods, to which pilgrims resorted from every province, and a greater number of human victims were offered in its principal temple than even in that of Mexico.* Montezuma seems to have invited the Spaniards thither, either from some superstitious hope that the gods would not suffer this sacred mansion to be defiled, without pouring down their wrath upon those impious strangers, who ventured to insult their power in the place of its peculiar residence; or from a belief that he himself might there attempt to cut them off with more certain success, under the immediate protection of his divinities.

Cortes had been warned by the Tlascalans, before he set out on his march, to keep a watchful eye over the Cholulans. He himself, though received into the town with much seeming respect and cordiality, observed several circumstances in their conduct which excited suspicion. Two of the Tlascalans, who were encamped at some distance from the town, as the Cholulans refused to admit their ancient enemies within its precincts, having found means to enter in disguise, acquainted Cortes that they observed the women and children of the principal citizens retiring in great hurry every night; and that six children had been sacrificed in the chief temple, a rite which indicated the execution of some warlike enterprise to be approaching. At the same time, Marina the interpreter received information from an Indian woman of distinction, whose confidence she had gained, that the destruction of her friends was concerted; that a body of Mexican troops lay concealed near the town; that some of the streets were barricaded, and in others, pits or deep trenches were dug, and slightly covered over, as traps into which the horses might fall; that stones or missive weapons were collected on the tops of the temples, with which to overwhelm the infantry; that the fatal hour was now at hand, and their ruin unavoidable. Cortes, alarmed at this concurring evidence, secretly arrested three of the chief priests, and extorted from them a confession, that confirmed the intelligence which he had received. As not a moment was to be lost, he instantly resolved to prevent his enemies, and to inflict on them such dreadful vengeance as might strike Montezuma and his subjects with terror. For this purpose, the Spaniards and Zempoallans were drawn up in a large court, which had been allotted for their quarters near the centre of the town; the Tlascalans had orders to advance; the magistrates and several of the chief citizens were sent for, under various pretexts, and seized. On a signal given, the troops rushed out and fell upon the multitude, destitute of leaders, and so much astonished, that the weapons dropping from their hands, they stood motionless, and incapable of defence. While the Spaniards pressed them in front, the Tlascalans attacked them in the rear. The streets were filled with bloodshed and death. The temples, which afforded a retreat to the priests and some of the leading men, were set on fire,

* Torquemada Monar. Ind. i. 281, 282. ii. 291. Gomara Cron. c. 61. Herrera, dec. 2. lib vii. c. 2

and they perished in the flames. This scene of horror continued two days, during which, the wretched inhabitants suffered all that the destructive rage of the Spaniards, or the implacable revenge of their Indian allies, could inflict. At length the carnage ceased, after the slaughter of six thousand Cholulans, without the loss of a single Spaniard. Cortes then released the magistrates, and, reproaching them bitterly for their intended treachery, declared, that as justice was now appeased, he forgave the offence, but required them to recall the citizens who had fled, and re-establish order in the town. Such was the ascendant which the Spaniards had acquired over this superstitious race of men, and so deeply were they impressed with an opinion of their superior discernment, as well as power, that, in obedience to this command, the city was in a few days filled again with people, who, amidst the ruins of their sacred buildings, yielded respectful service to men whose hands were stained with the blood of their relations and fellow-citizens* [108].

From Cholula, Cortes advanced directly towards Mexico [Oct. 29], which was only twenty leagues distant. In every place through which he passed, he was received as a person possessed of sufficient power to deliver the empire from the oppression under which it groaned; and the caziques or governors communicated to him all the grievances which they felt under the tyrannical government of Montezuma, with that unreserved confidence which men naturally repose in superior beings. When Cortes first observed the seeds of discontent in the remote provinces of the empire, hope dawned upon his mind; but when he now discovered such symptoms of alienation from their monarch near the seat of government, he concluded that the vital parts of the constitution were affected, and conceived the most sanguine expectations of overturning a state whose natural strength was thus divided and impaired. While those reflections encouraged the general to persist in his arduous undertaking, the soldiers were no less animated by observations more obvious to their capacity. In descending from the mountains of Chalco, across which the road lay, the vast plain of Mexico opened gradually to their view. When they first beheld this prospect, one of the most striking and beautiful on the face of the earth; when they observed fertile and cultivated fields stretching further than the eye could reach; when they saw a lake resembling the sea in extent, encompassed with large towns, and discovered the capital city rising upon an island in the middle, adorned with its temples and turrets; the scene so far exceeded their imagination, that some believed the fanciful descriptions of romance were realized, and that its enchanted palaces and gilded domes were presented to their sight; others could hardly persuade themselves that this wonderful spectacle was any thing more than a dream [109]. As they advanced, their doubts were removed, but their amazement increased. They were now fully satisfied that the country was rich beyond any conception which they had formed of it, and flattered themselves that at length they should obtain an ample recompense for all their services and sufferings.

Hitherto they had met with no enemy to oppose their progress, though several circumstances occurred which led them to suspect that some design was formed to surprise and cut them off. Many messengers arrived successively from Montezuma, permitting them one day to advance, requiring them on the next to retire, as his hopes or fears alternately prevailed; and so wonderful was this infatuation, which seems to be unaccountable on any supposition but that of a superstitious dread of the Spaniards, as beings of a superior nature, that Cortes was almost at the gates of the capital, before the monarch had determined whether to receive him as a friend, or to oppose him as an enemy. But as no sign of open hostility appeared, the Spaniards, without regarding the fluctuations of Montezuma's sentiments,

* Cortes Relat. Ramus. iii. 231. B. Diaz, c. 83. Gomara Cron. c. 64. Herrera, dec. 2. lib. vii. c. 1, 2.

continued their march along the causeway which led to Mexico through the lake, with great circumspection and the strictest discipline, though without seeming to suspect the prince whom they were about to visit.

When they drew near the city, about a thousand persons, who appeared to be of distinction, came forth to meet them, adorned with plumes and clad in mantles of fine cotton. Each of these in his order passed by Cortes, and saluted him according to the mode deemed most respectful and submissive in their country They announced the approach of Montezuma himself, and soon after his harbingers came in sight. There appeared first two hundred persons in a uniform dress, with large plumes of feathers, alike in fashion, marching two and two, in deep silence, barefooted, with their eyes fixed on the ground. These were followed by a company of higher rank, in their most showy apparel, in the midst of whom was Montezuma, in a chair or litter richly ornamented with gold, and feathers of various colours. Four of his principal favourites carried him on their shoulders, others supported a canopy of curious workmanship over his head. Before him marched three officers with rods of gold in their hands, which they lifted up on high at certain intervals, and at that signal all the people bowed their heads and hid their faces, as unworthy to look on so great a monarch. When he drew near, Cortes dismounted, advancing towards him with officious haste, and in a respectful posture. At the same time Montezuma alighted from his chair, and, leaning on the arms of two of his near relations, approached with a slow and stately pace, his attendants covering the streets with cotton cloths, that he might not touch the ground. Cortes accosted him with profound reverence, after the European fashion. He returned the salutation, according to the mode of his country, by touching the earth with his hand, and then kissing it. This ceremony, the customary expression of veneration from inferiors towards those who were above them in rank, appeared such amazing condescension in a proud monarch, who scarcely deigned to consider the rest of mankind as of the same species with himself, that all his subjects firmly believed those persons, before whom he humbled himself in this manner, to be something more than human. Accordingly, as they marched through the crowd, the Spaniards frequently, and with much satisfaction, heard themselves denominated *Teules*, or divinities. Nothing material passed in this first interview. Montezuma conducted Cortes to the quarters which he had prepared for his reception, and immediately took leave of him, with a politeness not unworthy of a court more refined. "You are now," says he, "with your brothers, in your own house; refresh yourselves after your fatigue, and be happy until I return."* The place allotted to the Spaniards for their lodging, was a house built by the father of Montezuma. It was surrounded by a stone wall, with towers at proper distances, which served for defence as well as for ornament, and its apartments and courts were so large as to accommodate both the Spaniards and their Indian allies. The first care of Cortes was to take precautions for his security, by planting the artillery so as to command the different avenues which led to it, by appointing a large division of his troops to be always on guard, and by posting sentinels at proper stations, with injunctions to observe the same vigilant discipline as if they were within sight of an enemy's camp.

In the evening, Montezuma returned to visit his guests with the same pomp as in their first interview, and brought presents of such value, not only to Cortes and to his officers, but even to the private men, as proved the liberality of the monarch to be suitable to the opulence of his kingdom. A long conference ensued, in which Cortes learned what was the opinion of Montezuma with respect to the Spaniards. It was an established tra-

* Cortes Relat. Ram iii. 232—235. B. Diaz, c. 83—88. Gomara Cron. c. 64, 65. Herrera, dec 2. lib. vii. c. 3, 4, 5.

dition, he told him, among the Mexicans, that their ancestors came originally from a remote region, and conquered the provinces now subject to his dominion; that after they were settled there, the great captain who conducted this colony returned to his own country, promising that at some future period his descendants should visit them, assume the government, and reform their constitution and laws; that from what he had heard and seen of Cortes and his followers, he was convinced that they were the very persons whose appearance the Mexican traditions and prophecies taught them to expect; that accordingly he had received them, not as strangers, but as relations of the same blood and parentage, and desired that they might consider themselves as masters in his dominions, for both himself and his subjects should be ready to comply with their will, and even to prevent their wishes. Cortes made a reply in his usual style, with respect to the dignity and power of his sovereign, and his intention of sending him into that country; artfully endeavouring so to frame his discourse, that it might coincide as much as possible with the idea which Montezuma had formed concerning the origin of the Spaniards. Next morning, Cortes and some of his principal attendants were admitted to a public audience of the emperor. The three subsequent days were employed in viewing the city; the appearance of which, so far superior in the order of its buildings and the number of its inhabitants to any place the Spaniards had beheld in America, and yet so little resembling the structure of a European city, filled them with surprise and admiration.

Mexico, or *Tenuchtitlan*, as it was anciently called by the natives, is situated in a large plain, evironed by mountains of such height that, though within the torrid zone, the temperature of its climate is mild and healthful. All the moisture which descends from the high grounds, is collected in several lakes, the two largest of which, of about ninety miles in circuit, communicate with each other. The waters of the one are fresh, those of the other brackish. On the banks of the latter, and on some small islands adjoining to them, the capital of Montezuma's empire was built. The access to the city was by artificial causeways or streets formed of stones and earth, about thirty feet in breadth. As the waters of the lake during the rainy season overflowed the flat country, these causeways were of considerable length. That of Tacuba, on the west, extended a mile and a half; that of Tepeaca, on the north-west, three miles; that of Cuoyacan, towards the south, six miles. On the east* there was no causeway, and the city could be approached only by canoes.† In each of these causeways were openings at proper intervals, through which the waters flowed, and over these beams of timber were laid, which being covered with earth, the causeway or street had every where a uniform appearance. As the approaches to the city were singular, its construction was remarkable. Not only the temples of their gods, but the houses belonging to the monarch, and to persons of distinction, were of such dimensions, that, in comparison with any other buildings which hitherto had been discovered in America, they might be termed magnificent. The habitations of the common people were mean, resembling the huts of other Indians. But they were all placed in a regular manner, on the banks of the canals which passed through the city, in some of its districts, or on the sides of the streets which intersected it in other quarters. In several places were large openings or squares, one of which, allotted for the great market, is said to have been so spacious, that forty or fifty thousand persons carried on traffic there. In this city,

* I am indebted to M. Clavigero for correcting an error of importance in my description of Mexico. From the east, where Tezeuco was situated, there was no causeway, as I have observed, and yet by some inattention on my part, or on that of the printer, in all the former editions one of the causeways was said to lead to Tezeuco. M. Clavigero's measurement of the length of these causeways differs somewhat from that which I have adopted from F. Torribio Clavig. ii. p. 72.

† F. Torribio MS.

the pride of the New World, and the noblest monument of the industry and art of man, while unacquainted with the use of iron, and destitute of aid from any domestic animal, the Spaniards, who are most moderate in their computations, reckon that there were at least sixty thousand inhabitants.*

But how much soever the novelty of those objects might amuse or astonish the Spaniards, they felt the utmost solicitude with respect to their own situation. From a concurrence of circumstances, no less unexpected than favourable to their progress, they had been allowed to penetrate into the heart of a powerful kingdom, and were now lodged in its capital without having once met with open opposition from its monarch. The Tlascalans, however, had earnestly dissuaded them from placing such confidence in Montezuma, as to enter a city of such peculiar situation as Mexico, where that prince would have them at mercy, shut up as it were in a snare, from which it was impossible to escape. They assured them that the Mexican priests had, in the name of the gods, counselled their sovereign to admit the Spaniards into the capital, that he might cut them off there at one blow with perfect security.† They now perceived too plainly, that the apprehensions of their allies were not destitute of foundation; that, by breaking the bridges placed at certain intervals on the causeways, or by destroying part of the causeways themselves, their retreat would be rendered impracticable, and they must remain cooped up in the centre of a hostile city, surrounded by multitudes sufficient to overwhelm them, and without a possibility of receiving aid from their allies. Montezuma had, indeed, received them with distinguished respect. But ought they to reckon upon this as real, or to consider it as feigned? Even if it were sincere, could they promise on its continuance? Their safety depended upon the will of a monarch in whose attachment they had no reason to confide; and an order flowing from his caprice, or a word uttered by him in passion, might decide irrevocably concerning their fate.‡

These reflections, so obvious as to occur to the meanest soldier, did not escape the vigilant sagacity of their general. Before he set out from Cholula, Cortes had received advice from Villa Rica,§ that Qualpopoca, one of the Mexican generals on the frontiers, having assembled an army in order to attack some of the people whom the Spaniards had encouraged to throw off the Mexican yoke, Escalante had marched out with part of the garrison to support his allies; that an engagement had ensued, in which, though the Spaniards were victorious, Escalante, with seven of his men, had been mortally wounded, his horse killed, and one Spaniard had been surrounded by the enemy and taken alive; that the head of this unfortunate captive, after being carried in triumph to different cities, in order to convince the people that their invaders were not immortal, had been sent to Mexico.‖ Cortes, though alarmed with this intelligence, as an indication of Montezuma's hostile intentions, had continued his march. But as soon as he entered Mexico he became sensible, that, from an excess of confidence in the superior valour and discipline of his troops, as well as from the disadvantage of having nothing to guide him in an unknown country, but the defective intelligence which he had received from people with whom his mode of communication was very imperfect, he had pushed forward into a situation where it was difficult to continue, and from which it was dangerous to retire. Disgrace, and perhaps ruin, was the certain consequence of attempting the latter. The success of his enterprise depended upon supporting the high opinion which the people of New Spain had formed with respect to the irresistible power of his arms. Upon

* Cortes Relat. Ram. iii. 239. D. Relat. della gran Citta de Mexico, par un Gentelhuomo del Cortese. Ram. ibid. 304. E. Herrera, dec. 2. lib. vii. c. 14, &c. † B. Diaz, c. 85, 86. ‡ Ibid. c. 94. § Cortes Relat. Ram. iii. 235. C. ‖ B. Diaz, c. 93, 94. Herrera, dec. 2. lib. viii. c. 1.

the first symptom of timidity on his part, their veneration would cease, and Montezuma, whom fear alone restrained at present, would let loose upon him the whole force of his empire. At the same time, he knew that the countenance of his own sovereign was to be obtained only by a series of victories, and that nothing but the merit of extraordinary success could screen his conduct from the censure of irregularity. From all these considerations, it was necessary to maintain his station, and to extricate himself out of the difficulties in which one bold step had involved him, by venturing upon another still bolder. The situation was trying, but his mind was equal to it; and after revolving the matter with deep attention, he fixed upon a plan no less extraordinary than daring. He determined to seize Montezuma in his palace, and to carry him as a prisoner to the Spanish quarters. From the superstitious veneration of the Mexicans for the person of their monarch, as well as their implicit submission to his will, he hoped, by having Montezuma in his power, to acquire the supreme direction of their affairs; or, at least, with such a sacred pledge in his hands, he made no doubt of being secure from any effort of their violence.

This he immediately proposed to his officers. The timid startled at a measure so audacious, and raised objections. The more intelligent and resolute, conscious that it was the only resource in which there appeared any prospect of safety, warmly approved of it, and brought over their companions so cordially to the same opinion, that it was agreed instantly to make the attempt. At his usual hour of visiting Montezuma, Cortes went to the palace, accompanied by Alvarado, Sandoval, Lugo, Velasquez de Leon, and Davila, five of his principal officers, and as many trusty soldiers. Thirty chosen men followed, not in regular order, but sauntering at some distance, as if they had no object but curiosity; small parties were posted at proper intervals, in all the streets leading from the Spanish quarters to the court; and the remainder of his troops, with the Tlascalan allies, were under arms ready to sally out on the first alarm. Cortes and his attendants were admitted without suspicion; the Mexicans retiring, as usual, out of respect. He addressed the monarch in a tone very different from that which he had employed in former conferences, reproaching him bitterly as the author of the violent assault made upon the Spaniards by one of his officers, and demanded public reparation for the loss which they had sustained by the death of some of their campanions, as well as for the insult offered to the great prince whose servants they were. Montezuma, confounded at this unexpected accusation, and changing colour, either from consciousness of guilt, or from feeling the indignity with which he was treated, asserted his own innocence with great earnestness, and, as a proof of it, gave orders instantly to bring Qualpopoca and his accomplices prisoners to Mexico. Cortes replied with seeming complaisance, that a declaration so respectable left no doubt remaining in his own mind, but that something more was requisite to satisfy his followers, who would never be convinced that Montezuma did not harbour hostile intentions against them, unless, as an evidence of his confidence and attachment, he removed from his own palace, and took up his residence in the Spanish quarters, where he should be served and honoured as became a great monarch. The first mention of so strange a proposal bereaved Montezuma of speech, and almost of motion. At length indignation gave him utterance, and he haughtily answered, "That persons of his rank were not accustomed voluntarily to give up themselves as prisoners; and were he mean enough to do so, his subjects would not permit such an affront to be offered to their sovereign." Cortes, unwilling to employ force, endeavoured alternately to soothe and to intimidate him. The altercation became warm; and having continued above three hours, Velasquez de Leon, an impetuous and gallant young man, exclaimed with impatience, "Why waste more time in vain? Let us either seize him instantly, or stab him to the heart." The threatening voice and fierce gestures with which these words were uttered, struck Montezuma. The Spaniards, he was sensible, had now proceeded so far, as left him no hope that they would recede. His own danger was imminent, the necessity unavoidable. He saw both, and, abandoning himself to his fate, complied with their request.

His officers were called. He communicated to them his resolution Though astonished and afflicted, they presumed not to question the will of their master, but carried him in silent pomp, all bathed in tears, to the Spanish quarters. When it was known that the strangers were conveying away the Emperor, the people broke out into the wildest transports of grief and rage, threatening the Spaniards with immediate destruction, as the punishment justly due to their impious audacity. But as soon as Montezuma appeared, with a seeming gayety of countenance, and waved his hand, the tumult was hushed; and upon his declaring it to be of his own choice that he went to reside for some time among his new friends, the multitude, taught to revere every intimation of their sovereign's pleasure, quietly dispersed.*

Thus was a powerful prince seized by a few strangers in the midst of his capital, at noonday, and carried off as a prisoner, without opposition or bloodshed. History contains nothing parallel to this event, either with respect to the temerity of the attempt, or the success of the execution; and were not all the circumstances of this extraordinary transaction authenticated by the most unquestionable evidence, they would appear so wild and extravagant as to go far beyond the bounds of that probability which must be preserved even in fictitious narrations.

Montezuma was received in the Spanish quarters with all the ceremonious respect which Cortes had promised. He was attended by his own domestics, and served with his usual state. His principal officers had free access to him, and he carried on every function of government as if he had been at perfect liberty. The Spaniards, however, watched him with the scrupulous vigilance which was natural in guarding such an important prize [110], endeavouring at the same time to sooth and reconcile him to his situation by every external demonstration of regard and attachment. But from captive princes, the hour of humiliation and suffering is never far distant. Qualpopoca, his son, and five of the principal officers who served under him, were brought prisoners to the capital [Dec. 4], in consequence of the orders which Montezuma had issued. The Emperor gave them up to Cortes, that he might inquire into the nature of their crime, and determine their punishment. They were formally tried by a Spanish court martial; and though they had acted no other part than what became loyal subjects and brave men, in obeying the orders of their lawful sovereign, and in opposing the invaders of their country, they were condemned to be burnt alive. The execution of such atrocious deeds is seldom long suspended. The unhappy victims were instantly led forth. The pile on which they were laid was composed of the weapons collected in the royal magazine for the public defence. An innumerable multitude of Mexicans beheld, in silent astonishment, the double insult offered to the majesty of their empire, an officer of distinction committed to the flames by the authority of strangers for having done what he owed in duty to his natural sovereign; and the arms provided by the foresight of their ancestors for avenging public wrongs, consumed before their eyes.

But these were not the most shocking indignities which the Mexicans had to bear. The Spaniards, convinced that Qualpopoca would not have ventured to attack Escalante without orders from his master, were not

* Diaz, c. 95. Gomara Cron. c. 83. Cortes Relat. Ram. iii. p 235, 236. Herrera, dec. 2. lib. viii. c. 2, 3.

satisfied with inflicting vengeance on the instrument employed in committing that crime while the author of it escaped with impunity. Just before Qualpopoca was led out to suffer, Cortes entered the apartment of Montezuma, followed by some of his officers, and a soldier, carrying a pair of fetters; and approaching the monarch with a stern countenance told him, that as the persons who were now to undergo the punishment which they merited, had charged him as the cause of the outrage committed, it was necessary that he likewise should make atonement for that guilt; then turning away abruptly, without waiting for a reply, commanded the soldier to clap the fetters on his legs. The orders were instantly executed. The disconsolate monarch, trained up with an idea that his person was sacred and inviolable, and considering this profanation of it as the prelude of immediate death, broke out into loud lamentations and complaints. His attendants, speechless with horror, fell at his feet, bathing them with their tears; and, bearing up the fetters in their hands, endeavoured with officious tenderness to lighten their pressure. Nor did their grief and despondency abate, until Cortes returned from the execution, and with a cheerful countenance ordered the fetters to be taken off. As Montezuma's spirits had sunk with unmanly dejection, they now rose into indecent joy; and with an unbecoming transition, he passed at once from the anguish of despair to transports of gratitude and expressions of fondness towards his deliverer.

In those transactions, as represented by the Spanish historians, we search in vain for the qualities which distinguish other parts of Cortes's conduct. To usurp a jurisdiction which could not belong to a stranger, who assumed no higher character than that of an ambassador from a foreign prince, and, under colour of it, to inflict a capital punishment on men whose conduct entitled them to esteem, appears an act of barbarous cruelty. To put the monarch of a great kingdom in irons, and, after such ignominious treatment, suddenly to release him, seems to be a display of power no less inconsiderate than wanton. According to the common relation, no account can be given either of the one action or the other, but that Cortes, intoxicated with success, and presuming on the ascendant which he had acquired over the minds of the Mexicans, thought nothing too bold for him to undertake, or too dangerous to execute. But, in one view, these proceedings, however repugnant to justice and humanity, may have flowed from that artful policy which regulated every part of Cortes's behaviour towards the Mexicans. They had conceived the Spaniards to be an order of beings superior to men. It was of the utmost consequence to cherish this illusion, and to keep up the veneration which it inspired. Cortes wished that shedding the blood of a Spaniard should be deemed the most heinous of all crimes; and nothing appeared better calculated to establish this opinion than to condemn the first Mexicans who had ventured to commit it to a cruel death, and to oblige their monarch himself to submit to a mortifying indignity as an expiation for being accessary to a deed so atrocious [111]

1520.] The rigour with which Cortes punished the unhappy persons who first presumed to lay violent hands upon his followers, seems accordingly to have made all the impression that he desired. The spirit of Montezuma was not only overawed but subdued. During six months that Cortes remained in Mexico, the monarch continued in the Spanish quarters with an appearance of as entire satisfaction and tranquillity as if he had resided there not from constraint, but through choice. His ministers and officers attended him as usual. He took cognisance of all affairs; every order was issued in his name. The external aspect of government appearing the same, and all its ancient forms being scrupulously observed, the people were so little sensible of any change, that they obeyed the mandates of their monarch with the same submissive reverence as ever. Such was the dread which both Montezuma and his subjects had of the Spaniards, or such the veneration in which they held them, that no attempt was made to deliver their sovereign from confinement; and though Cortes, relying on this ascendant which he had acquired over their minds, permitted him not only to visit his temples, but to make hunting excursions beyond the lake, a guard of a few Spaniards carried with it such a terror as to intimidate the multitude, and secure the captive monarch.*

Thus, by the fortunate temerity of Cortes in seizing Montezuma, the Spaniards at once secured to themselves more extensive authority in the Mexican Empire than it was possible to have acquired in a long course of time by open force; and they exercised more absolute sway in the name of another, than they could have done in their own. The arts of polished nations, in subjecting such as are less improved, have been nearly the same in every period. The system of screening a foreign usurpation, under the sanction of authority derived from the natural rulers of a country, the device of employing the magistrates and forms already established as instruments to introduce a new dominion, of which we are apt to boast as sublime refinements in policy peculiar to the present age, were inventions of a more early period, and had been tried with success in the West long before they were practised in the East.

Cortes availed himself to the utmost of the powers which he possessed by being able to act in the name of Montezuma. He sent some Spaniards, whom he judged best qualified for such commissions, into different parts of the empire, accompanied by persons of distinction, whom Montezuma appointed to attend them, both as guides and protectors. They visited most of the provinces, viewed their soil and productions, surveyed with particular care the districts which yielded gold or silver, pitched upon several places as proper stations for future colonies, and endeavoured to prepare the minds of the people for submitting to the Spanish yoke. While they were thus employed, Cortes, in the name and by the authority of Montezuma, degraded some of the principal officers in the empire, whose abilities or independent spirit excited his jealousy, and substituted in their place persons less capable or more obsequious.

One thing still was wanting to complete his security. He wished to have such command of the lake as might ensure a retreat if, either from levity or disgust, the Mexicans should take arms against him, and break down the bridges or causeways. This, too, his own address, and the facility of Montezuma, enabled him to accomplish. Having frequently entertained his prisoner with pompous accounts of the European marine and art of navigation, he awakened his curiosity to see those moving palaces which made their way through the water without oars. Under pretext of gratifying this desire, Cortes persuaded Montezuma to appoint some of his subjects to fetch part of the naval stores which the Spaniards had deposited at Vera Cruz to Mexico, and to employ others in cutting down and preparing timber. With their assistance, the Spanish carpenters soon completed two brigantines, which afforded a frivolous amusement to the monarch, and were considered by Cortes as a certain resource if he should be obliged to retire.

Encouraged by so many instances of the monarch's tame submission to his will, Cortes ventured to put it to a proof still more trying. He urged Montezuma to acknowledge himself a vassal of the king of Castile, to hold his crown of him as superior, and to subject his dominions to the payment of an annual tribute. With this requisition, the last and most humbling that can be made to one possessed of sovereign authority, Montezuma was so obsequious as to comply. He called together the chief men of his empire, and in a solemn harangue, reminding them of the traditions and prophecies which led them to expect the arrival of a people

* Cortes Relat. p. 236. E. B. Diaz, c. 97, 98, 99.

sprung from the same stock with themselves, in order to take possession of the supreme power, he declared his belief that the Spaniards were this promised race; that therefore he recognised the right of their monarch to govern the Mexican empire; that he would lay his crown at his feet, and obey him as a tributary. While uttering these words, Montezuma discovered how deeply he was affected in making such a sacrifice. Tears and groans frequently interrupted his discourse. Overawed and broken as his spirit was, it still retained such a sense of dignity as to feel that pang which pierces the heart of princes when constrained to resign independent power. The first mention of such a resolution struck the assembly dumb with astonishment. This was followed by a sudden murmur of sorrow, mingled with indignation, which indicated some violent irruption of rage to be near at hand. This Cortes foresaw, and seasonably interposed to prevent it by declaring that his master had no intention to deprive Montezuma of the royal dignity, or to make any innovation upon the constitution and laws of the Mexican empire. This assurance, added to their dread of the Spanish power and to the authority of their monarch's example, extorted a reluctant consent from the assembly [112]. The act of submission and homage was executed with all the formalities which the Spaniards were pleased to prescribe.*

Montezuma, at the desire of Cortes, accompanied this profession of fealty and homage with a magnificent present to his new sovereign; and after his example his subjects brought in very liberal contributions The Spaniards now collected all the treasures which had been either voluntarily bestowed upon them at different times by Montezuma, or had been extorted from his people under various pretexts; and having melted the gold and silver, the value of these, without including jewels and ornaments of various kinds, which were preserved on account of their curious workmanship, amounted to six hundred thousand *pesos*. The soldiers were impatient to have it divided, and Cortes complied with their desire. A fifth of the whole was first set apart as the tax due to the king. Another fifth was allotted to Cortes as commander in chief. The sums advanced by Velasquez, by Cortes, and by some of the officers, towards defraying the expense of fitting out the armament, were then deducted. The remainder was divided among the army, including the garrison of Vera Cruz, in proportion to their different ranks. After so many defalcations, the share of a private man did not exceed a hundred pesos. This sum fell so far below their sanguine expectations, that some soldiers rejected it with scorn, and others murmured so loudly at this cruel disappointment of their hopes, that it required all the address of Cortes, and no small exertion of his liberality, to appease them. The complaints of the army were not altogether destitute of foundation. As the crown had contributed nothing towards the equipment or success of the armament, it was not without regret that the soldiers beheld it sweep away so great a proportion of the treasure purchased by their blood and toil. What fell to the share of the general appeared, according to the ideas of wealth in the sixteenth century, an enormous sum. Some of Cortes's favourites had secretly appropriated to their own use several ornaments of gold, which neither paid the royal fifth, nor were brought into account as part of the common stock. It was, however, so manifestly the interest of Cortes at this period to make a large remittance to the king, that it is highly probable those concealments were not of great consequence.

The total sum amassed by the Spaniards bears no proportion to the ideas which might be formed, either by reflecting on the descriptions given by historians of the ancient splendour of Mexico, or by considering the productions of its mines in modern times. But among the ancient Mexi-

* Cortes Relat. 238. D. B. Diaz, c 101 Gomara Cron. c. 92. Herrera, dec. 2, lib. x. c. 4

cans, gold and silver were not the standards by which the worth of other commodities was estimated; and destitute of the artificial value derived from this circumstance, were no further in request than as they furnished materials for ornaments and trinkets. These were either consecrated to the gods in their temples, or were worn as marks of distinction by their princes and some of their most eminent chiefs. As the consumption of the precious metals was inconsiderable, the demand for them was not such as o put either the ingenuity or industry of the Mexicans on the stretch in order to augment their store. They were altogether unacquainted with the art of working the rich mines with which their country abounded. What gold they had was gathered in the beds of rivers, native, and ripened into a pure metallic state.* The utmost effort of their labour in search of it was to wash the earth carried down by torrents from the mountains, and to pick out the grains of gold which subsided; and even this simple operation, according to the report of the persons whom Cortes appointed to survey the provinces where there was a prospect of finding mines, they performed very unskilfully.† From all those causes, the whole mass of gold in possession of the Mexicans was not great. As silver is rarely found pure, and the Mexican art was too rude to conduct the process for refining it in a proper manner, the quantity of this metal was still less considerable.‡ Thus, though the Spaniards had exerted all the power which they possessed in Mexico, and often with indecent rapacity, in order to gratify their predominant passion, and though Montezuma had fondly exhausted his treasures, in hopes of satiating their thirst for gold, the product of both, which probably included a great part of the bullion in the empire, did not rise in value above what has been mentioned [113].

But however pliant Montezuma might be in other matters, with respect to one point he was inflexible. Though Cortes often urged him, with the importunate zeal of a missionary, to renounce his false gods, and to embrace the Christian faith, he always rejected the proposition with horror. Superstition, among the Mexicans, was formed into such a regular and complete system, that its institutions naturally took fast hold of the mind; and while the rude tribes in other parts of America were easily induced to relinquish a few notions and rites, so loose and arbitrary as hardly to merit the name of a public religion, the Mexicans adhered tenaciously to their mode of worship, which, however barbarous, was accompanied with such order and solemnity as to render it an object of the highest veneration. Cortes, finding all his attempts ineffectual to shake the constancy of Montezuma, was so much enraged at his obstinacy, that in a transport of zeal he led out his soldiers to throw down the idols in the grand temple by force. But the priests taking arms in defence of their altars, and the people crowding with great ardour to support them, Cortes's prudence overruled his zeal, and induced him to desist from his rash attempt, after dislodging the idols from one of the shrines, and placing in their stead an image of the Virgin Mary [114].

From that moment the Mexicans, who had permitted the imprisonment of their sovereign, and suffered the exactions of strangers without a struggle, began to meditate how they might expel or destroy the Spaniards, and thought themselves called upon to avenge their insulted deities. The priests and leading men held frequent consultations with Montezuma for this purpose. But as it might prove fatal to the captive monarch to attempt either the one or the other by violence, he was willing to try more gentle means. Having called Cortes into his presence, he observed, that now, as all the purposes of his embassy were fully accomplished, the gods had declared their will, and the people signified their desire, that he and his followers should instantly depart out of the empire. With this he re-

* Cortes Relat. p. 236. F. B Diaz, c. 102, 103. Gomara Cron c. 90. † B. Diaz, c. 103.
‡ Herrera, dec. 2. lib. ix. c. 4.

quired them to comply, or unavoidable destruction would fall suddenly on their heads. The tenour of this unexpected requisition, as well as the determined tone in which it was uttered, left Cortes no room to doubt, that it was the result of some deep scheme concerted between Montezuma and his subjects. He quickly perceived that he might derive more advantage from a seeming compliance with the monarch's inclinations, than from an ill-timed attempt to change or to oppose it; and replied, with great composure, that he had already begun to prepare for returning to his own country; but as he had destroyed the vessels in which he arrived, some time was requisite for building other ships. This appeared reasonable. A number of Mexicans were sent to Vera Cruz to cut down timber, and some Spanish carpenters were appointed to superintend the work. Cortes flattered himself that during this interval he might either find means to avert the threatened danger, or receive such reinforcements as would enable him to despise it.

Almost nine months were elapsed since Portocarrero and Montejo had sailed with his despatches to Spain; and he daily expected their return with a confirmation of his authority from the King. Without this, his condition was insecure and precarious; and after all the great things which he had done, it might be his doom to bear the name and suffer the punishment of a traitor. Rapid and extensive as his progress had been, he could not hope to complete the reduction of a great empire with so small a body of men, which by this time diseases of various kinds considerably thinned; nor could he apply for recruits to the Spanish settlements in the islands, until he received the royal approbation of his proceedings.

While he remained in this cruel situation, anxious about what was past, uncertain with respect to the future, and, by the late declaration of Montezuma, oppressed with a new addition of cares, a Mexican courier arrived with an account of some ships having appeared on the coast. Cortes, with fond credulity, imagining that his messengers were returned from Spain, and that the completion of all his wishes and hopes was at hand, imparted the glad tidings to his companions, who received them with transports of mutual gratulation. Their joy was not of long continuance. A courier from Sandoval, whom Cortes had appointed to succeed Escalante in command at Vera Cruz, brought certain information that the armament was fitted out by Velasquez, governor of Cuba, and, instead of bringing the aid which they expected, threatened them with immediate destruction.

The motives which prompted Velasquez to this violent measure are obvious. From the circumstances of Cortes' departure, it was impossible not to suspect his intention of throwing off all dependence upon him. His neglecting to transmit any account of his operations to Cuba, strengthened this suspicion, which was at last confirmed beyond doubt by the indiscretion of the officers whom Cortes sent to Spain. They, from some motive which is not clearly explained by the contemporary historians, touched at the island of Cuba, contrary to the peremptory orders of their general.* By this means Velasquez not only learned that Cortes and his followers, after formally renouncing all connection with him, had established an independent colony in New Spain, and were soliciting the King to confirm their proceedings by his authority; but he obtained particular information concerning the opulence of the country, the valuable presents which Cortes had received, and the inviting prospects of success that opened to his view. Every passion which can agitate an ambitious mind; shame, at having been so grossly overreached; indignation, at being betrayed by the man whom he had selected as the object of his favour and confidence; grief, for having wasted his fortune to aggrandize an enemy; and despair of recovering so fair an opportunity of establishing

* B. Diaz, c. 54, 55. Herrera, dec. 2. lib. v. c. 14 Gomara Cron. c. 96.

his fame and extending his power, now raged in the bosom of Velasquez. All these, with united force, excited him to make an extraordinary effort in order to be avenged on the author of his wrongs, and to wrest from him his usurped authority and conquests. Nor did he want the appearance of a good title to justify such an attempt. The agent whom he sent to Spain with an account of Grijalva's voyage, had met with a most favourable reception; and from the specimens which he produced, such high expectations were formed concerning the opulence of New Spain, that Velasquez was authorized to prosecute the discovery of the country, and appointed governor of it during life, with more extensive power and privileges than had been granted to any adventurer from the time of Columbus.* Elated by this distinguishing mark of favour, and warranted to consider Cortes not only as intruding upon his jurisdiction, but as disobedient to the royal mandate, he determined to vindicate his own rights, and the honour of his sovereign by force of arms [115]. His ardour in carrying on his preparations was such as might have been expected from the violence of the passions with which he was animated; and in a short time an armament was completed, consisting of eighteen ships which had on board fourscore horsemen, eight hundred foot soldiers, of which eighty were musketeers, and a hundred and twenty cross-bow men, together with a train of twelve pieces of cannon. As Velasquez's experience of the fatal consequence of committing to another what he ought to have executed himself, had not rendered him more enterprising, he vested the command of this formidable body, which, in the infancy of the Spanish power in America, merits the appellation of an army, in Pamphilo de Narvaez, with instructions to seize Cortes and his principal officers, to send them prisoners to him, and then to complete the discovery and conquest of the country in his name.

After a prosperous voyage, Narvaez landed his men without opposition near St. Juan de Ulua [April]. Three soldiers, whom Cortes had sent to search for mines in that district, immediately joined him. By this accident he not only received information concerning the progress and situation of Cortes, but, as these soldiers had made some progress in the knowledge of the Mexican language, he acquired interpreters, by whose means he was enabled to hold some intercourse with the people of the country. But, according to the low cunning of deserters, they framed their intelligence with more attention to what they thought would be agreeable than to what they knew to be true; and represented the situation of Cortes to be so desperate, and the disaffection of his followers to be so general, as increased the natural confidence and presumption of Narvaez. His first operation, however, might have taught him not to rely on their partial accounts. Having sent to summon the governor of Vera Cruz to surrender, Guevara, a priest whom he employed in that service, made the requisition with such insolence, that Sandoval, an officer of high spirit, and zealously attached to Cortes, instead of complying with his demands, seized him and his attendants, and sent them in chains to Mexico.

Cortes received them not like enemies, but as friends, and, condemning the severity of Sandoval, set them immediately at liberty. By this well timed clemency, seconded by caresses and presents, he gained their confidence, and drew from them such particulars concerning the force and intentions of Narvaez, as gave him a view of the impending danger in its full extent. He had not to contend now with half naked Indians, no match for him in war, and still more inferior in the arts of policy, but to take the field against an army in courage and martial discipline equal to his own, in number far superior, acting under the sanction of royal authority, and commanded by an officer of known bravery. He was informed that Narvaez, more solicitous to gratify the resentment of Velasquez than

* Herrera, dec 2. lib. iii. c. 11.

attentive to the honour or interest of his country, had begun his intercourse with the natives, by representing him and his followers as fugitives and outlaws, guilty of rebellion against their own sovereign, and of injustice in invading the Mexican empire; and had declared that his chief object in visiting the country was to punish the Spaniards who had committed these crimes, and to rescue the Mexicans from oppression. He soon perceived that the same unfavourable representations of his character and actions had been conveyed to Montezuma, and that Narvaez had found means to assure him, that as the conduct of those who kept him under restraint was highly displeasing to the King his master, he had it in charge not only to rescue an injured monarch from confinement, but to reinstate him in the possession of his ancient power and independence. Animated with this prospect of being set free from subjection to strangers, the Mexicans in several provinces began openly to revolt from Cortes, and to regard Narvaez as a deliverer no less able than willing to save them. Montezuma himself kept up a secret intercourse with the new commander, and seemed to court him as a person superior in power and dignity to those Spaniards whom he had hitherto revered as the first of men [116].

Such were the various aspects of danger and difficulty which presented themselves to the view of Cortes. No situation can be conceived more trying to the capacity and firmness of a general, or where the choice of the plan which ought to be adopted was more difficult. If he should wait the approach of Narvaez in Mexico, destruction seemed to be unavoidable; for, while the Spaniards pressed him from without, the inhabitants, whose turbulent spirit he could hardly restrain with all his authority and attention, would eagerly lay hold on such a favourable opportunity of avenging all their wrongs. If he should abandon the capital, set the captive monarch at liberty, and march out to meet the enemy, he must at once forego the fruits of all his toils and victories, and relinquish advantages which could not be recovered without extraordinary efforts and infinite danger. If, instead of employing force, he should have recourse to conciliating measures, and attempt an accommodation with Narvaez; the natural haughtiness of that officer, augmented by consciousness of his present superiority, forbade him to cherish any sanguine hope of success. After revolving every scheme with deep attention, Cortes fixed upon that which in execution was most hazardous, but, if successful, would prove most beneficial to himself and to his country; and with the decisive intrepidity suited to desperate situations, determined to make one bold effort for victory under every disadvantage, rather than sacrifice his own conquests and the Spanish interests in Mexico.

But though he foresaw that the contest must be terminated finally by arms, it would have been not only indecent but criminal to have marched against his countrymen, without attempting to adjust matters by an amicable negotiation. In this service he employed Olmedo, his chaplain, to whose character the function was well suited, and who possessed, besides, such prudence and address as qualified him to carry on the secret intrigues in which Cortes placed his chief confidence. Narvaez rejected with scorn every scheme of accommodation that Olmedo proposed, and was with difficulty restrained from laying violent hands on him and his attendants. He met, however, with a more favourable reception among the followers of Narvaez, to many of whom he delivered letters, either from Cortes or his officers, their ancient friends and companions. Cortes artfully accompanied these with presents of rings, chains of gold, and other trinkets of value, which inspired those needy adventurers with high ideas of the wealth that he had acquired, and with envy of their good fortune who were engaged in his service. Some, from hopes of becoming sharers in those rich spoils, declared for an immediate accommodation with Cortes. Others, from public spirit, laboured to prevent a civil war, which, whatever party should prevail, must shake, and perhaps subvert the Spanish power in a country where it was so imperfectly established. Narvaez disregarded both, and by a public proclamation denounced Cortes and his adherents rebels and enemies to their country. Cortes, it is probable, was not much surprised at the untractable arrogance of Narvaez; and after having given such a proof of his own pacific disposition as might justify his recourse to other means, he determined to advance towards an enemy whom he had laboured in vain to appease.

He left a hundred and fifty men in the capital [May], under the command of Pedro de Alvarado, an officer of distinguished courage, for whom the Mexicans had conceived a singular degree of respect. To the custody of this slender garrison he committed a great city, with all the wealth he had amassed, and, what was of still greater importance, the person of the imprisoned monarch. His utmost art was employed in concealing from Montezuma the real cause of his march. He laboured to persuade him, that the strangers who had lately arrived were his friends and fellow-subjects; and that, after a short interview with them, they would depart together, and return to their own country. The captive prince, unable to comprehend the designs of the Spaniard, or to reconcile what he now heard with the declarations of Narvaez, and afraid to discover any symptom of suspicion or distrust of Cortes, promised to remain quietly in the Spanish quarters, and to cultivate the same friendship with Alvarado which he had uniformly maintained with him Cortes, with seeming confidence in this promise, but relying principally upon the injunctions which he had given Alvarado to guard his prisoner with the most scrupulous vigilance, set out from Mexico.

His strength, even after it was reinforced by the junction of Sandoval and the garrison of Vera Cruz, did not exceed two hundred and fifty men. As he hoped for success chiefly from the rapidity of his motions, his troops were not encumbered either with baggage or artillery. But as he dreaded extremely the impression which the enemy might make with their cavalry, he had provided against this danger with the foresight and sagacity which distinguish a great commander. Having observed that the Indians in the province of Chinantla used spears of extraordinary length and force, he armed his soldiers with these, and accustomed them to that deep and compact arrangement which the use of this formidable weapon, the best perhaps that was ever invented for defence, enabled them to assume.

With this small but firm battalion, Cortes advanced towards Zempoalla, of which Narvaez had taken possession. During his march, he made repeated attempts towards some accommodation with his opponent. But Narvaez requiring that Cortes and his followers should instantly recognise his title to be governor of New Spain, in virtue of the powers which he derived from Velasquez; and Cortes refusing to submit to any authority which was not founded on a commission from the Emperor himself, under whose immediate protection he and his adherents had placed their infant colony; all these attempts proved fruitless. The intercourse, however, which this occasioned between the two parties, proved of no small advantage to Cortes, as it afforded him an opportunity of gaining some of Narvaez's officers by liberal presents, of softening others by a semblance of moderation, and of dazzling all by the appearance of wealth among his troops, most of his soldiers having converted their share of the Mexican gold into chains, bracelets, and other ornaments, which they displayed with military ostentation. Narvaez and a little junto of his creatures excepted, all the army leaned towards an accommodation with their countrymen. This discovery of their inclination irritated his violent temper almost to madness. In a transport of rage, he set a price upon the head of Cortes, and of his principal officers; and having learned that he was now advanced within a league of Zempoalla with his small body of men, he considered this as an insult which merited immediate chastisement, and marched out with all his troops to offer him battle.

But Cortes was a leader of greater abilities and experience than, on equal ground, to fight an enemy so far superior in number, and so much better appointed. Having taken his station on the opposite bank of the river de Canoas, where he knew that he could not be attacked, he beheld the approach of the enemy without concern, and disregarded this vain bravade. It was then the beginning of the wet season,* and the rain had poured down, during a great part of the day, with a violence peculiar to the torrid zone. The followers of Narvaez, unaccustomed to the hardships of military service, murmured so much at being thus fruitlessly exposed, that, from their unsoldierlike impatience, as well as his own contempt of his adversary, their general permitted them to retire to Zempoalla. The very circumstance which induced them to quit the field, encouraged Cortes to form a scheme by which he hoped at once to terminate the war. He observed that his hardy veterans, though standing under the torrents which continued to fall, without a single tent or any shelter whatsoever to cover them, were so far from repining at hardships which were become familiar to them, that they were still fresh and alert for service. He foresaw that the enemy would naturally give themselves up to repose after their fatigue, and that, judging of the conduct of others by their own effeminacy, they would deem themselves perfectly secure at a season so unfit for action. He resolved, therefore, to fall upon them in the dead of night, when the surprise and terror of this unexpected attack might more than compensate the inferiority of his numbers. His soldiers, sensible that no resource remained but in some desperate effort of courage, approved of the measure with such warmth, that Cortes, in a military oration which he addressed to them before they began their march, was more solicitous to temper than to inflame their ardour. He divided them into three parties. At the head of the first he placed Sandoval; intrusting this gallant officer with the most dangerous and important service, that of seizing the enemy's artillery, which was planted before the principal tower of the temple where Narvaez had fixed his head-quarters. Christoval de Olid commanded the second, with orders to assault the tower, and lay hold on the general. Cortes himself conducted the third and smallest division, which was to act as a body of reserve, and to support the other two as there should be occasion. Having passed the river de Canoas, which was much swelled with the rains, not without difficulty, the water reaching almost to their chins, they advanced in profound silence, without beat of drum, or sound of any warlike instrument; each man armed with his sword, his dagger, and his Chinantlan spear. Narvaez, remiss in proportion to his security, had posted only two sentinels to watch the motions of an enemy whom he had such good cause to dread. One of these was seized by the advanced guard of Cortes's troops; the other made his escape, and, hurrying to the town with all the precipitation of fear and zeal, gave such timely notice of the enemy's approach, that there was full leisure to have prepared for their reception. But, through the arrogance and infatuation of Narvaez, this important interval was lost. He imputed this alarm to the cowardice of the sentinel, and treated with derision the idea of being attacked by forces so unequal to his own. The shouts of Cortes's soldiers, rushing on to the assault, convinced him at last that the danger which he despised was real. The rapidity with which they advanced was such that only one cannon could be fired before Sandoval's party closed with the enemy, drove them from their guns, and began to force their way up the steps of the tower. Narvaez, no less brave in action than presumptuous in conduct, armed himself in haste, and by his

* Hakluyt, vol. iii. 467. De Laet Descr. Ind. Occid. 221.

voice and example animated his men to the combat. Olid advanced to sustain his companions; and Cortes himself rushing to the front, conducted and added new vigour to the attack. The compact order in which this small body pressed on, and the impenetrable front which they presented with their long spears, bore down all opposition before it. They had now reached the gate, and were struggling to burst it open, when a soldier having set fire to the reeds with which the tower was covered, compelled Narvaez to sally out. In the first encounter he was wounded in the eye with the spear, and, falling to the ground, was dragged down the steps, and in a moment clapped in fetters. The cry of victory resounded among the troops of Cortes. Those who had sallied out with their leader now maintained the conflict feebly, and began to surrender. Among the remainder of his soldiers, stationed in two smaller towers of the temple, terror and confusion prevailed. The darkness was so great, that they could not distinguish between their friends and foes. Their own artillery was pointed against them. Wherever they turned their eyes, they beheld lights gleaming through the obscurity of the night, which, though proceeding only from a variety of shining insects that abound in moist and sultry climates, their affrighted imaginations represented as numerous bands of musketeers advancing with kindled matches to the attack. After a short resistance, the soldiers compelled their officers to capitulate, and before morning all laid down their arms, and submitted quietly to their conquerors.

This complete victory proved more acceptable, as it was gained almost without bloodshed, only two soldiers being killed on the side of Cortes, and two officers, with fifteen private men of the adverse faction. Cortes treated the vanquished not like enemies, but as countrymen and friends, and offered either to send them back directly to Cuba, or to take them into his service, as partners in his fortune, on equal terms with his own soldiers. This latter proposition, seconded by a seasonable distribution of some presents from Cortes, and liberal promises of more, opened prospects so agreeable to the romantic expectations which had invited them to engage in this service, that all, a few partisans of Narvaez excepted, closed with it, and vied with each other in professions of fidelity and attachment to a general, whose recent success had given them such a striking proof of his abilities for command. Thus, by a series of events no less fortunate than uncommon, Cortes not only escaped from perdition which seemed inevitable, but, when he had least reason to expect it, was placed at the head of a thousand Spaniards, ready to follow wherever he should lead them. Whoever reflects upon the facility with which this victory was obtained, or considers with what sudden and unanimous transition the followers of Narvaez ranged themselves under the standard of his rival, will be apt to ascribe both events as much to the intrigues as to the arms of Cortes, and cannot but suspect that the ruin of Narvaez was occasioned no less by the treachery of his own followers, than by the valour of the enemy.*

But in one point the prudent conduct and good fortune of Cortes were equally conspicuous. If, by the rapidity of his operations after he began his march, he had not brought matters to such a speedy issue, even this decisive victory would have come too late to have saved his companions whom he left in Mexico. A few days after the discomfiture of Narvaez, a courier arrived with an account that the Mexicans had taken arms, and, having seized and destroyed the two brigantines which Cortes had built in order to secure the command of the lake, and attacked the Spaniards in their quarters, had killed several of them, and wounded more, had reduced to ashes their magazine of provisions, and carried on hostilities with such fury, that though Alvarado and his men defended themselves

* Cortes Relat. 242. D. B. Diaz, c. 110—125. Herrera, dec. 2. lib. ix. c. 18, &c. Gomara Cron. c. 97, &c.

with undaunted resolution, they must either be soon cut off by famine, or sink under the multitude of their enemies. This revolt was excited by motives which rendered it still more alarming. On the departure of Cortes for Zempoalla, the Mexicans flattered themselves that the long-expected opportunity of restoring their sovereign to liberty, and of vindicating their country from the odious dominion of strangers, was at length arrived; that while the forces of their oppressors were divided, and the arms of one party turned against the other, they might triumph with greater facility over both. Consultations were held, and schemes formed with this intention. The Spaniards in Mexico, conscious of their own feebleness, suspected and dreaded those machinations. Alvarado, though a gallant officer, possessed neither that extent of capacity nor dignity of manners, by which Cortes had acquired such an ascendant over the minds of the Mexicans, as never allowed them to form a just estimate of his weakness or of their own strength. Alvarado knew no mode of supporting his authority but force. Instead of employing address to disconcert the plans or to soothe the spirits of the Mexicans, he waited the return of one of their solemn festivals. When the principal persons in the empire were dancing, according to custom, in the court of the great temple, he seized all the avenues which led to it; and allured partly by the rich ornaments which they wore in honour of their gods, and partly by the facility of cutting off at once the authors of that conspiracy which he dreaded, he fell upon them, unarmed and unsuspicious of any danger, and massacred a great number, none escaping but such as made their way over the battlements of the temple. An action so cruel and treacherous filled not only the city, but the whole empire with indignation and rage. All called aloud for vengeance; and regardless of the safety of their monarch, whose life was at the mercy of the Spaniards, or of their own danger in assaulting an enemy who had been so long the object of their terror, they committed all those acts of violence of which Cortes received an account.

To him the danger appeared so imminent as to admit neither of deliberation nor delay. He set out instantly with all his forces, and returned from Zempoalla with no less rapidity than he had advanced thither. At Tlascala he was joined by two thousand chosen warriors. On entering the Mexican territories, he found that disaffection to the Spaniards was not confined to the capital. The principal inhabitants had deserted the towns through which he passed; no person of note appearing to meet him with the usual respect; no provision was made for the subsistence of his troops; and though he was permitted to advance without opposition, the solitude and silence which reigned in every place, and the horror with which the people avoided all intercourse with him, discovered a deep-rooted antipathy that excited the most just alarm. But implacable as the enmity of the Mexicans was, they were so unacquainted with the science of war, that they knew not how to take the proper measures either for their own safety or the destruction of the Spaniards. Uninstructed by their former error in admitting a formidable enemy into their capital, instead of breaking down the causeways and bridges, by which they might have enclosed Alvarado and his party, and have effectually stopped the career of Cortes, they again suffered him to march into the city [June 24] without molestation, and to take quiet possession of his ancient station.

The transports of joy with which Alvarado and his soldiers received their companions cannot be expressed. Both parties were so much elated, the one with their seasonable deliverance, and the other with the great exploits which they had achieved, that this intoxication of success seems to have reached Cortes himself; and he behaved on this occasion neither with his usual sagacity nor attention. He not only neglected to visit Montezuma, but embittered the insult by expressions full of contempt for that unfortunate prince and his people. The forces of which he had now the command appeared to him so irresistible that he might assume a higher tone, and lay aside the mask of moderation under which he had hitherto concealed his designs. Some Mexicans, who understood the Spanish language, heard the contemptuous words which Cortes uttered, and, reporting them to their countrymen, kindled their rage anew. They were now convinced that the intentions of the general were equally bloody with those of Alvarado, and that his original purpose in visiting their country had not been, as he pretended, to court the alliance of their sovereign, but to attempt the conquest of his dominions. They resumed their arms with the additional fury which this discovery inspired, attacked a considerable body of Spaniards who were marching towards the great square in which the public market was held, and compelled them to retire with some loss. Emboldened by this success, and delighted to find that their oppressors were not invincible, they advanced the next day with extraordinary martial pomp to assault the Spaniards in their quarters. Their number was formidable, and their undaunted courage still more so. Though the artillery pointed against their numerous battalions, crowded together in narrow streets, swept off multitudes at every discharge ; though every blow of the Spanish weapons fell with mortal effect upon their naked bodies, the impetuosity of the assault did not abate. Fresh men rushed forward to occupy the places of the slain, and, meeting with the same fate, were succeeded by others no less intrepid and eager for vengeance The utmost efforts of Cortes's abilities and experience, seconded by the disciplined valour of his troops, were hardly sufficient to defend the fortifications that surrounded the post where the Spaniards were stationed, into which the enemy were more than once on the point of forcing their way.

Cortes beheld with wonder the implacable ferocity of a people who seemed at first to submit tamely to the yoke, and had continued so long passive under it. The soldiers of Narvaez, who fondly imagined that they followed Cortes to share in the spoils of a conquered empire, were astonished to find that they were involved in a dangerous war with an enemy whose vigour was still unbroken, and loudly execrated their own weakness in giving such easy credit to the delusive promises of their new leader.* But surprise and complaints were of no avail. Some immediate and extraordinary effort was requisite to extricate themselves out of their present situation. As soon as the approach of evening induced the Mexicans to retire in compliance with their national custom of ceasing from hostilities with the setting sun, Cortes began to prepare for a sally, next day, with such a considerable force as might either drive the enemy out of the city, or compel them to listen to terms of accommodation.

He conducted in person the troops destined for this important service. Every invention known in the European art of war, as well as every precaution suggested by his long acquaintance with the Indian mode of fighting were employed to ensure success. But he found an enemy prepared and determined to oppose him. The force of the Mexicans was greatly augmented by fresh troops, which poured in continually from the country, and their animosity was in no degree abated. They were led by their nobles, inflamed by the exhortations of their priests, and fought in defence of their temples and families, under the eye of their gods, and in presence of their wives and children. Notwithstanding their numbers, and enthusiastic contempt of danger and death, wherever the Spaniards could close with them, the superiority of their discipline and arms obliged the Mexicans to give way. But in narrow streets, and where many of the bridges of communication were broken down, the Spaniards could seldom come to a fair rencounter with the enemy, and, as they advanced, were exposed to showers of arrows and stones from the tops of houses. After a day of

* B. Diaz, c. 126.

incessant exertion, though vast numbers of the Mexicans fell, and part of the city was burnt, the Spaniards weary with the slaughter, and harassed by multitudes which successively relieved each other, were obliged at length to retire, with the mortification of having accomplished nothing so decisive as to compensate the unusual calamity of having twelve soldiers killed, and above sixty wounded. Another sally, made with greater force, was not more effectual, and in it the general himself was wounded in the hand.

Cortes now perceived, too late, the fatal error into which he had been betrayed by his own contempt of the Mexicans, and was satisfied that he could neither maintain his present station in the centre of a hostile city, nor retire from it without the most imminent danger. One resource still remained, to try what effect the interposition of Montezuma might have to soothe or overawe his subjects. When the Mexicans approached next morning to renew the assault, that unfortunate prince, at the mercy of the Spaniards, and reduced to the sad necessity of becoming the instrument of his own disgrace, and of the slavery of his people [117], advanced to the battlements in his royal robes, and with all the pomp in which he used to appear on solemn occasions. At sight of their sovereign, whom they had long been accustomed to honour, and almost to revere as a god, the weapons dropped from their hands, every tongue was silent, all bowed their heads, and many prostrated themselves on the ground. Montezuma addressed them with every argument that could mitigate their rage, or persuade them to cease from hostilities. When he ended his discourse, a sullen murmur of disapprobation ran through the ranks; to this succeeded reproaches and threats; and the fury of the multitude rising in a moment above every restraint of decency or respect, flights of arrows and volleys of stones poured in so violently upon the ramparts, that before the Spanish soldiers, appointed to cover Montezuma with their bucklers, had time to lift them in his defence, two arrows wounded the unhappy monarch, and the blow of a stone on his temple struck him to the ground. On seeing him fall, the Mexicans were so much astonished, that with a transition not uncommon in popular tumults, they passed in a moment from one extreme to the other, remorse succeeded to insult, and they fled with horror, as if the vengeance of heaven were pursuing the crime which they committed. The Spaniards without molestation carried Montezuma to his apartments, and Cortes hastened thither to console him under his misfortune. But the unhappy monarch now perceived how low he was sunk; and the haughty spirit which seemed to have been so long extinct, returning, he scorned to survive this last humiliation, and to protract an ignominious life, not only as the prisoner and tool of his enemies, but as the object of contempt or detestation among his subjects. In a transport of rage he tore the bandages from his wounds, and refused, with such obstinacy, to take any nourishment, that he soon ended his wretched days, rejecting with disdain all the solicitations of the Spaniards to embrace the Christian faith.

Upon the death of Montezuma, Cortes, having lost all hope of bringing the Mexicans to an accommodation, saw no prospect of safety but in attempting a retreat, and began to prepare for it. But a sudden motion of the Mexicans engaged him in new conflicts. They took possession of a high tower in the great temple which overlooked the Spanish quarters, and placing there a garrison of their principal warriors, not a Spaniard could stir without being exposed to their missile weapons. From this post it was necessary to dislodge them at any risk; and Juan de Escobar, with a numerous detachment of chosen soldiers, was ordered to make the attack. But Escobar, though a gallant officer, and at the head of troops accustomed to conquer, and who now fought under the eyes of their countrymen, was thrice repulsed. Cortes, sensible that not only the reputation but the safety of his army depended on the success of this assault, ordered a buckler to be tied to his arm, as he could not manage it with his wounded hand, and rushed with his drawn sword into the thickest of the combatants. Encouraged by the presence of their general, the Spaniards returned to the charge with such vigour, that they gradually forced their way up the steps, and drove the Mexicans to the platform at the top of the tower. There a dreadful carnage began; when two young Mexicans of high rank, observing Cortes as he animated his soldiers by his voice and example, resolved to sacrifice their own lives in order to cut off the author of all the calamities which desolated their country. They approached him in a suppliant posture, as if they had intended to lay down their arms, and seizing him in a moment, hurried him towards the battlements, over which they threw themselves headlong, in hopes of dragging him along to be dashed in pieces by the same fall. But Cortes, by his strength and agility, broke loose from their grasp, and the gallant youths perished in this generous though unsuccessful attempt to save their country.* As soon as the Spaniards became masters of the tower, they set fire to it, and, without farther molestation, continued the preparations for their retreat.

This became the more necessary, as the Mexicans were so much astonished at the last effort of the Spanish valour, that they began to change their whole system of hostility, and, instead of incessant attacks, endeavoured, by barricading the streets and breaking down the causeways, to cut off the communication of the Spaniards with the continent, and thus to starve an enemy whom they could not subdue. The first point to be determined by Cortes and his followers, was, whether they should march out openly in the face of day, when they could discern every danger, and see how to regulate their own motions, as well as how to resist the assaults of the enemy; or, whether they should endeavour to retire secretly in the night? The latter was preferred, partly from hopes that their national superstition would restrain the Mexicans from venturing to attack them in the night, and partly from their own fond belief in the predictions of a private soldier, who having acquired universal credit by a smattering of learning, and his pretensions to astrology, boldly assured his countrymen of success, if they made their retreat in this manner. They began to move, towards midnight, in three divisions. Sandoval led the van; Pedro Alvarado and Velasquez de Leon had the conduct of the rear; and Cortes commanded in the centre, where he placed the prisoners, among whom were a son and two daughters of Montezuma, together with several Mexicans of distinction, the artillery, the baggage, and a portable bridge of timber intended to be laid over the breaches in the causeway. They marched in profound silence along the causeway which led to Tacuba, because it was shorter than any of the rest, and, lying most remote from the road towards Tlascala and the sea-coast, had been left more entire by the Mexicans. They reached the first breach in it without molestation, hoping that their retreat was undiscovered.

But the Mexicans, unperceived, had not only watched all their motions with attention, but had made proper dispositions for a most formidable attack. While the Spaniards were intent upon placing their bridge in the breach, and occupied in conducting their horses and artillery along it, they were suddenly alarmed with a tremendous sound of warlike instruments, and a general shout from an innumerable multitude of enemies; the lake was covered with canoes; flights of arrows and showers of stones poured in upon them from every quarter; the Mexicans rushing forward to the

* M. Clavigero has censured me with asperity for relating this gallant action of the two Mexicans, and for supposing that there were battlements round the temple of Mexico. I related the attempt to destroy Cortes on the authority of Her. dec. 2. lib. x. c. 9. and of Torquemado, lib. iv. c. 69. I followed them likewise in supposing the uppermost platform of the temple to be encompassed by a battlement or rail.

charge with fearless impetuosity, as if they hoped in that moment to be avenged for all their wrongs. Unfortunately the wooden bridge, by the weight of the artillery, was wedged so fast into the stones and mud, that it was impossible to remove it. Dismayed at this accident, the Spaniards advanced with precipitation towards the second breach. The Mexicans hemmed them in on every side; and though they defended themselves with their usual courage, yet crowded together as they were on a narrow causeway, their discipline and military skill were of little avail, nor did the obscurity of the night permit them to derive great advantage from their fire-arms, or the superiority of their other weapons. All Mexico was now in arms; and so eager were the people on the destruction of their oppressors, that they who were not near enough to annoy them in person, impatient of the delay, pressed forward with such ardour as drove on their countrymen in the front with irresistible violence. Fresh warriors instantly filled the place of such as fell. The Spaniards, weary with slaughter, and unable to sustain the weight of the torrent that poured in upon them, began to give way. In a moment the confusion was universal; horse and foot, officers and soldiers, friends and enemies, were mingled together; and while all fought, and many fell, they could hardly distinguish from what hand the blow came.

Cortes, with about a hundred foot soldiers and a few horse, forced his way over the two remaining breaches in the causeway, the bodies of the dead serving to fill up the chasms, and reached the main land. Having formed them as soon as they arrived, he returned with such as were yet capable of service to assist his friends in their retreat, and to encourage them, by his presence and example, to persevere in the efforts requisite to effect it. He met with part of his soldiers who had broke through the enemy, but found many more overwhelmed by the multitude of their aggressors, or perishing in the lake; and heard the piteous lamentations of others, whom the Mexicans, having taken alive, were carrying off in triumph to be sacrificed to the god of war. Before day, all who had escaped assembled at Tacuba. But when the morning dawned, and discovered to the view of Cortes his shattered battalion reduced to less than half its number, the survivors dejected, and most of them covered with wounds, the thoughts of what they had suffered, and the remembrance of so many faithful friends and gallant followers who had fallen in that night of sorrow,* pierced his soul with such anguish, that while he was forming their ranks, and issuing some necessary orders, his soldiers observed the tears trickling from his eyes, and remarked with much satisfaction, that while attentive to the duties of a general, he was not insensible to the feelings of a man.

In this fatal retreat many officers of distinction perished [118], and among these Velasquez de Leon, who having forsaken the party of his kinsman, the governor of Cuba, to follow the fortune of his companions, was, on that account, as well as for his superior merit, respected by them as the second person in the army. All the artillery, ammunition, and baggage, were lost; the greater part of the horses, and above two thousand Tlascalans, were killed, and only a very small portion of the treasure which they had amassed was saved. This, which had been always their chief object, proved a great cause of their calamity; for many of the soldiers having so overloaded themselves with bars of gold as rendered them unfit for action, and retarded their flight, fell ignominiously, the victims of their own inconsiderate avarice. Amidst so many disasters, it was some consolation to find that Aguilar and Marina, whose function as interpreters was of such essential importance, had made their escape.†

The first care of Cortes was to find some shelter for his wearied troops;

* *Noche triste* is the name by which it is still distinguished in New Spain. † Cortes Relat. p. 248 B. Diaz c. 128. Gomara Cron. c. 109. Herrera, dec. 2. lib. x. c. 11, 12.

tor, as the Mexicans infested them on every side, and the people of Tacuba began to take arms, he could not continue in his present station. He directed his march towards the rising ground, and, having fortunately discovered a temple situated on an eminence, took possession of it. There he found not only the shelter for which he wished, but, what was no less wanted, some provisions to refresh his men; and though the enemy did not intermit their attacks throughout the day, they were with less difficulty prevented from making any impression. During this time Cortes was engaged in deep consultation with his officers, concerning the route which they ought to take in their retreat. They were now on the west side of the lake. Tlascala, the only place where they could hope for a friendly reception, lay about sixty-four miles to the east of Mexico;* so that they were obliged to go round the north end of the lake before they could fall into the road which led thither. A Tlascalan soldier undertook to be their guide, and conducted them through a country in some places marshy, in others mountainous, in all ill cultivated and thinly peopled. They marched for six days with little respite, and under continual alarms, numerous bodies of the Mexicans hovering around them, sometimes harassing them at a distance with their missile weapons, and sometimes attacking them closely in front, in rear, in flank, with great boldness, as they now knew that they were not invincible. Nor were the fatigue and danger of those incessant conflicts the worst evils to which they were exposed. As the barren country through which they passed afforded hardly any provisions, they were reduced to feed on berries, roots, and the stalks of green maize; and at the very time that famine was depressing their spirits and wasting their strength, their situation required the most vigorous and unremitting exertions of courage and activity. Amidst those complicated distresses, one circumstance supported and animated the Spaniards. Their commander sustained this sad reverse of fortune with unshaken magnanimity. His presence of mind never forsook him; his sagacity foresaw every event, and his vigilance provided for it. He was foremost in every danger, and endured every hardship with cheerfulness. The difficulties with which he was surrounded seemed to call forth new talents; and his soldiers, though despairing themselves, continued to follow him with increasing confidence in his abilities.

On the sixth day they arrived near to Otumba, not far from the road between Mexico and Tlascala. Early next morning they began to advance towards it, flying parties of the enemy still hanging on their rear; and, amidst the insults with which they accompanied their hostilities, Marina remarked that they often exclaimed with exultation, "Go on, robbers; go to the place where you shall quickly meet the vengeance due to your crimes." The meaning of this threat the Spaniards did not comprehend, until they reached the summit of an eminence before them. There a spacious valley opened to their view, covered with a vast army, extending as far as the eye could reach. The Mexicans, while with one body of their troops they harassed the Spaniards in their retreat, had assembled their principal force on the other side of the lake; and marching along the road which led directly to Tlascala, posted it in the plain of Otumba, through which they knew Cortes must pass. At the sight of this incredible multitude, which they could survey at once from the rising ground, the Spaniards were astonished, and even the boldest began to despair. But Cortes, without allowing leisure for their fears to acquire strength by reflection, after warning them briefly that no alternative now remained but to conquer or to die, led them instantly to the charge. The Mexicans waited their approach with unusual fortitude. Such, however, was the superiority of the Spanish discipline and arms, that the impression of this small body

* Villa Segnor Teatro Americanos, lib. ii. c. 11.

was irresistible; and whichever way its force was directed, it penetrated and dispersed the most numerous battalions. But while these gave way in one quarter, new combatants advanced from another, and the Spaniards, though successful in every attack, were ready to sink under those repeated efforts, without seeing any end of their toil, or any hope of victory. At that time Cortes observed the great standard of the empire, which was carried before the Mexican general, advancing; and fortunately recollecting to have heard, that on the fate of it depended the event of every battle, he assembled a few of his bravest officers, whose horses were still capable of service, and, placing himself at their head, pushed forward towards the standard with an impetuosity which bore down every thing before it. A chosen body of nobles, who guarded the standard, made some resistance, but were soon broken. Cortes, with a stroke of his lance, wounded the Mexican general, and threw him on the ground. One of the Spanish officers, alighting, put an end to his life, and laid hold of the imperial standard. The moment that their leader fell, and the standard, towards which all directed their eyes, disappeared, a universal panic struck the Mexicans; and, as if the bond which held them together had been dissolved, every ensign was lowered, each soldier threw away his weapons, and all fled with precipitation to the mountains. The Spaniards unable to pursue them far, returned to collect the spoils of the field, which were so valuable as to be some compensation for the wealth which they had lost in Mexico; for in the enemy's army were most of their principal warriors dressed out in their richest ornaments as if they had been marching to assured victory. Next day [July 8], to their great joy, they entered the Tlascalan territories.*

But amidst their satisfaction in having got beyond the precincts of a hostile country, they could not look forward without solicitude, as they were still uncertain what reception they might meet with from allies to whom they returned in a condition very different from that in which they had lately set out from their dominions. Happily for them, the enmity of the Tlascalans to the Mexican name was so inveterate, their desire to avenge the death of their countrymen so vehement, and the ascendant which Cortes had acquired over the chiefs of the republic so complete, that, far from entertaining a thought of taking any advantage of the distressed situation in which they beheld the Spaniards, they received them with a tenderness and cordiality which quickly dissipated all their suspicions.

Some interval of tranquillity and indulgence was now absolutely necessary; not only that the Spaniards might give attention to the cure of their wounds, which had been too long neglected, but in order to recruit their strength, exhausted by such a long succession of fatigue and hardships. During this, Cortes learned that he and his companions were not the only Spaniards who had felt the effects of the Mexican enmity. A considerable detachment which was marching from Zempoalla towards the capital, had been cut off by the people of Tepeaca. A smaller party, returning from Tlascala to Vera Cruz, with the share of the Mexican gold allotted to the garrison, had been surprised and destroyed in the mountains. At a juncture when the life of every Spaniard was of importance, such losses were deeply felt. The schemes which Cortes was meditating rendered them peculiarly afflictive to him. While his enemies, and even many of his own followers, considered the disasters which had befallen him as fatal to the progress of his arms, and imagined that nothing now remained but speedily to abandon a country which he had invaded with unequal force, his mind, as eminent for perseverance as for enterprise, was still bent on accomplishing his original purpose, of subjecting the Mexican empire to the crown of Castile. Severe and unexpected as the check was which he had received, it did not

* Cortes Relat. p. 219 B Diaz, c. 128. Gomara Cron. c. 110 Herrera, dec. 2. lib. x. c. 12, 13

appear to him a sufficient reason for relinquishing the conquests which he had already made, or against resuming his operations with better hopes of success. The colony at Vera Cruz was not only safe, but had remained unmolested. The people of Zempoalla and the adjacent districts had discovered no symptoms of defection. The Tlascalans continued faithful to their alliance. On their martial spirit, easily roused to arms, and inflamed with implacable hatred of the Mexicans, Cortes depended for powerful aid. He had still the command of a body of Spaniards, equal in number to that with which he had opened his way into the centre of the empire, and had taken possession of the capital; so that with the benefit of greater experience, as well as more perfect knowledge of the country, he did not despair of quickly recovering all that he had been deprived of by untoward events.

Full of this idea, he courted the Tlascalan chiefs with such attention, and distributed among them so liberally the rich spoils of Otumba, that he was secure of obtaining whatever he should require of the republic. He drew a small supply of ammunition and two or three fieldpieces from his stores at Vera Cruz. He despatched an officer of confidence with four ships of Narvaez's fleet to Hispaniola and Jamaica, to engage adventurers, and to purchase horses, gunpowder, and other military stores. As he knew that it would be vain to attempt the reduction of Mexico, unless he could secure the command of the lake, he gave orders to prepare in the mountains of Tlascala, materials for building twelve brigantines, so as they might be carried thither in pieces ready to be put together, and launched when he stood in need of their service.*

But while, with provident attention, he was taking those necessary steps towards the execution of his measures, an obstacle arose in a quarter where 't was least expected, but most formidable. The spirit of discontent and mutiny broke out in his own army. Many of Narvaez's followers were planters rather than soldiers, and had accompanied him to New Spain with sanguine hopes of obtaining settlements, but with little inclination to engage in the hardships and dangers of war. As the same motives had induced them to enter into their new engagements with Cortes, they no sooner became acquainted with the nature of the service, than they bitterly repented of their choice. Such of them as had the good fortune to survive the perilous adventures in which their own imprudence had involved them, happy in having made their escape, trembled at the thoughts of being exposed a second time to similar calamities. As soon as they discovered the intention of Cortes, they began secretly to murmur and cabal, and, waxing gradually more audacious, they, in a body, offered a remonstrance to their general against the imprudence of attacking a powerful empire with his shattered forces, and formally required him to lead them back directly to Cuba. Though Cortes, long practised in the arts of command, employed arguments, entreaties, and presents to convince or to soothe them; though his own soldiers, animated with the spirit of their leader, warmly seconded his endeavours; he found their fears too violent and deep rooted to be removed, and the utmost he could effect was to prevail with them to defer their departure for some time, on a promise that he would, at a more proper juncture, dismiss such as should desire it.

That the malecontents might have no leisure to brood over the causes of their disaffection, he resolved instantly to call forth his troops into action. He proposed to chastise the people of Tepeaca for the outrage which they had committed; and as the detachment which they had cut off happened to be composed mostly of soldiers who had served under Narvaez, their companions, from the desire of vengeance, engaged the more willingly in this war. He took the command in person, [August] accompanied by a

* Cortes Relat. p. 253. E. Gomara Cron. c 117

numerous body of Tlascalans, and in the space of a few weeks, after various encounters, with great slaughter of the Tepeacans, reduced that province to subjection. During several months, while he waited for the supplies of men and ammunition which he expected, and was carrying on his preparations for constructing the brigantines, he kept his troops constantly employed in various expeditions against the adjacent provinces, all of which were conducted with a uniform tenour of success. By these, his men became again accustomed to victory, and resumed their wonted sense of superiority; the Mexican power was weakened; the Tlascalan warriors acquired the habit of acting in conjunction with the Spaniards; and the chiefs of the republic delighted to see their country enriched with the spoils of all the people around them; and astonished every day with fresh discoveries of the irresistible prowess of their allies, they declined no effort requisite to support them.

All those preparatory arrangements, however, though the most prudent and efficacious which the situation of Cortes allowed him to make, would have been of little avail without a reinforcement of Spanish soldiers. Of this he was so deeply sensible, that it was the chief object of his thoughts and wishes; and yet his only prospect of obtaining it from the return of the officer whom he had sent to the isles to solicit aid, was both distant and uncertain. But what neither his own sagacity nor power could have procured, he owed to a series of fortunate and unforeseen incidents. The governor of Cuba, to whom the success of Narvaez appeared an event of infallible certainty, having sent two small ships after him with new instructions, and a supply of men and military stores, the officer whom Cortes had appointed to command on the coast, artfully decoyed them into the harbour of Vera Cruz, seized the vessels, and easily persuaded the soldiers to follow the standard of a more able leader than him whom they were destined to join.* Soon after, three ships of more considerable force came into the harbour separately. These belonged to an armament fitted out by Francisco de Garay, governor of Jamaica, who, being possessed with the rage of discovery and conquest which animated every Spaniard settled in America, had long aimed at intruding into some district of New Spain, and dividing with Cortes the glory and gain of annexing that empire to the crown of Castile. They unadvisedly made their attempt on the northern provinces, where the country was poor, and the people fierce and warlike; and after a cruel succession of disasters, famine compelled them to venture into Vera Cruz, and cast themselves upon the mercy of their countrymen [Oct. 28]. Their fidelity was not proof against the splendid hopes and promises which had seduced other adventurers; and, as if the spirit of revolt had been contagious in New Spain, they likewise abandoned the master whom they were bound to serve, and enlisted under Cortes.† Nor was it America alone that furnished such unexpected aid; a ship arrived from Spain, freighted by some private merchants with military stores, in hopes of a profitable market in a country, the fame of whose opulence began to spread over Europe. Cortes eagerly purchased a cargo which to him was invaluable, and the crew, following the general example, joined him at Tlascala.‡

From those various quarters, the army of Cortes was augmented with a hundred and eighty men, and twenty horses, a reinforcement too inconsiderable to produce any consequence which would have entitled it to have been mentioned in the history of other parts of the globe. But in that of America, where great revolutions were brought about by causes which seemed to bear no proportion to their effects, such small events rise into importance, because they were sufficient to decide with respect to the fate of

* B. Diaz, c. 131. † Cortes Relat. 253 F. B. Diaz, c. 133. ‡ Cortes Relat. 253. F. B. Diaz, c. 136.

kingdoms. Nor is it the least remarkable instance of the singular felicity conspicuous in many passages of Cortes's story, that the two persons chiefly instrumental in furnishing him with those seasonable supplies, should be an avowed enemy who aimed at his destruction, and an envious rival who wished to supplant him.

The first effect of the junction with his new followers was to enable him to dismiss such of Narvaez's soldiers as remained with reluctance in his service. After their departure, he still mustered five hundred and fifty infantry, of which fourscore were armed with muskets or crossbows, forty horsemen, and a train of nine field-pieces.* At the head of these, accompanied by ten thousand Tlascalans and other friendly Indians, Cortes began his march towards Mexico, on the twenty-eighth of December, six months after his disastrous retreat from that city.†

Nor did he advance to attack an enemy unprepared to receive him. Upon the death of Montezuma, the Mexican chiefs, in whom the right of electing the emperor was vested, had instantly raised his brother Quetlavaca to the throne. His avowed and inveterate enmity to the Spaniards would have been sufficient to gain their suffrages, although he had been less distinguished for courage and capacity. He had an immediate opportunity of showing that he was worthy of their choice, by conducting in person those fierce attacks which compelled the Spaniards to abandon his capital; and as soon as their retreat afforded him any respite from action, he took measures for preventing their return to Mexico, with prudence equal to the spirit which he had displayed in driving them out of it. As from the vicinity of Tlascala, he could not be unacquainted with the motions and intentions of Cortes, he observed the storm that was gathering, and began early to provide against it. He repaired what the Spaniards had ruined in the city, and strengthened it with such new fortifications as the skill of his subjects was capable of erecting. Besides filling his magazines with the usual weapons of war, he gave directions to make long spears headed with the swords and daggers taken from the Spaniards, in order to annoy the cavalry. He summoned the people in every province of the empire to take arms against their oppressors, and as an encouragement to exert themselves with vigour, he promised them exemption from all the taxes which his predecessors had imposed.‡ But what he laboured with the greatest earnestness was, to deprive the Spaniards of the advantages which they derived from the friendship of the Tlascalans, by endeavouring to persuade that people to renounce all connexion with men who were not only avowed enemies of the gods whom they worshipped, but who would not fail to subject them at last to the same yoke which they were now inconsiderately lending their aid to impose upon others. These representations, no less striking than well founded, were urged so forcibly by his ambassadors, that it required all the address of Cortes to prevent their making a dangerous impression.§

But while Quetlavaca was arranging his plan of defence, with a degree of foresight uncommon in an American, his days were cut short by the small-pox. This distemper, which raged at that time in New Spain with fatal malignity, was unknown in that quarter of the globe until it was introduced by the Europeans, and may be reckoned among the greatest calamities brought upon them by their invaders. In his stead the Mexicans raised to the throne Guatimozin, nephew and son-in-law of Montezuma, a young man of such high reputation for abilities and valour, that in this dangerous crisis, his countrymen, with one voice, called him to the supreme command.‖

* Cortes Relat. 255. E. 254. A. B. Diaz, c. 140.
† Relat. 256. A. B. Diaz, c. 137.
‡ Cortes Relat. p. 253. E.
§ B. Diaz, c. 129. Herrera, dec. 2. lib. x. c. 14. 19.
‖ B. Diaz, c. 130

1521.] As soon as Cortes entered the enemies territories, he discovered various preparations to obstruct his progress. But his troops forced their way with little difficulty, and took possession of Tezeuco, the second city of the empire, situated on the banks of the lake about twenty miles from Mexico.* Here he determined to establish his head-quarters, as the most proper station for launching his brigantines, as well as for making his approaches to the capital. In order to render his residence there more secure, he deposed the cazique, or chief, who was at the head of that community, under pretext of some defect in his title, and substituted in his place a person whom a faction of the nobles pointed out as the right heir of that dignity. Attached to him by this benefit, the cazique and his adherents served the Spaniards with inviolable fidelity.†

As the preparations for constructing the brigantines advanced slowly under the unskilful hands of soldiers and Indians, whom Cortes was obliged to employ in assisting three or four carpenters who happened fortunately to be in his service; and as he had not yet received the reinforcement which he expected from Hispaniola, he was not in a condition to turn his arms directly against the capital. To have attacked at this period, a city so populous, so well prepared for defence, and in a situation of such peculiar strength, must have exposed his troops to inevitable destruction. Three months elapsed before the materials for the brigantines were finished, and before he heard any thing with respect to the success of the officer whom he had sent to Hispaniola. This, however, was not a season of inaction to Cortes. He attacked successively several of the towns situated around the lake; and though all the Mexican power was exerted to obstruct his operations, he either compelled them to submit to the Spanish crown, or reduced them to ruins. The inhabitants of other towns he endeavoured to conciliate by more gentle means; and though he could not hold any intercourse with them but by the intervention of interpreters, yet, under all the disadvantages of that tedious and imperfect mode of communication he had acquired such thorough knowledge of the state of the country, as well as of the dispositions of the people, that he conducted his negotiations and intrigues with astonishing dexterity and success. Most of the cities adjacent to Mexico were originally the capitals of small independent states· and some of them having been but lately annexed to the Mexican empire, still retained the remembrance of their ancient liberty, and bore with impatience the rigorous yoke of their new masters. Cortes, having early observed symptoms of their disaffection, availed himself of this knowledge to gain their confidence and friendship. By offering with confidence to deliver them from the odious dominion of the Mexicans, and by liberal promises of more indulgent treatment if they would unite with him against their oppressors, he prevailed on the people of several considerable districts, not only to acknowledge the King of Castile as their sovereign, but to supply the Spanish camp with provisions, and to strengthen his army with auxiliary troops. Guatimozin, on the first appearance of defection among his subjects, exerted himself with vigour to prevent or to punish their revolt; but, in spite of his efforts, the spirit continued to spread. The Spaniards gradually acquired new allies, and with deep concern he beheld Cortes arming against his empire those very hands which ought to have been active in its defence, and ready to advance against the capital at the head of a numerous body of his own subjects.‡

While, by those various methods, Cortes was gradually circumscribing the Mexican power in such a manner that his prospect of overturning it seemed neither to be uncertain nor remote, all his schemes were well nigh

* Villa Senor Theatro Americano, i. 156. † Cortes Relat. 256, &c. B. Diaz, c. 137. Gomara Cron. c. 121. Herrera, dec. 3. c. 1. ‡ Cortes Relat. 256—260. B. Diaz, c. 137—140 Gomara Cron. c. 122, 123. Herrera, dec. 3. lib. i. c. 1, 2.

defeated by a conspiracy no less unexpected than dangerous. The soldiers of Narvaez had never united perfectly with the original companions of Cortes, nor did they enter into his measures with the same cordial zeal. Upon every occasion that required any extraordinary effort of courage or of patience, their spirits were apt to sink; and now, on a near view of what they had to encounter, in attempting to reduce a city so inaccessible as Mexico, and defended by a numerous army, the resolution even of those among them who had adhered to Cortes when he was deserted by their associates, began to fail. Their fears led them to presumptuous and unsoldierlike discussions concerning the propriety of their general's measures, and the improbability of their success. From these they proceeded to censure and invectives, and at last began to deliberate how they might provide for their own safety, of which they deemed their commander to be totally negligent. Antonio Villefagna, a private soldier, but bold, intriguing, and strongly attached to Velasquez, artfully fomented this growing spirit of disaffection. His quarters became the rendezvous of the malecontents, where, after many consultations, they could discover no method of checking Cortes in his career, but by assassinating him and his most considerable officers, and conferring the command upon some person who would relinquish his wild plans, and adopt measures more consistent with the general security. Despair inspired them with courage. The hour for perpetrating the crime, the persons whom they destined as victims, the officers to succeed them in command, were all named: and the conspirators signed an association, by which tney bound themselves with most solemn oaths to mutual fidelity. But on the evening before the appointed day, one of Cortes's ancient followers, who had been seduced into the conspiracy, touched with compunction at the imminent danger of a man whom he had long been accustomed to revere, or struck with horror at his own treachery, went privately to his general, and revealed to him all that he knew. Cortes, though deeply alarmed, discerned at once what conduct was proper in a situation so critical. He repaired instantly to Villefagna's quarters, accompanied by some of his most trusty officers. The astonishment and confusion of the man at this unexpected visit anticipated the confession of his guilt. Cortes, while his attendants seized the traitor, snatched from his bosom a paper, containing the association, signed by the conspirators. Impatient to know how far the infection extended, he retired to read it, and found there names which filled him with surprise and sorrow. But aware how dangerous a strict scrutiny might prove at such a juncture, he confined his judicial inquiries to Villefagna alone. As the proofs of his guilt were manifest, he was condemned after a short trial, and next morning he was seen hanging before the door of the house in which he had lodged. Cortes called his troops together, and having explained to them the atrocious purpose of the conspirators, as well as the justice of the punishment inflicted on Villefagna, he added, with an appearance of satisfaction, that he was entirely ignorant with respect to all the circumstances of this dark transaction, as the traitor, when arrested, had suddenly torn and swallowed a paper which probably contained an account of it, and under the severest tortures possessed such constancy as to conceal the names of his accomplices. This artful declaration restored tranquillity to many a breast that was throbbing, while he spoke, with consciousness of guilt and dread of detection; and by this prudent moderation, Cortes had the advantage of having discovered, and of being able to observe such of his followers as were disaffected; while they, flattering themselves that their past crime was unknown, endeavoured to avert any suspicion of it by redoubling their activity and zeal in his service.*

Cortes did not allow them leisure to ruminate on what had happened;

* Cortes Relat. 283. C. B. Diaz, c. 146. Herrera, dec 3. lib. i. c. 1

and as the most effectual means of preventing the return of a mutinous spirit, he determined to call forth his troops immediately to action. Fortunately, a proper occasion for this occurred without his seeming to court it. He received intelligence that the materials for building the brigantines were at length completely finished, and waited only for a body of Spaniards to conduct them to Tezeuco. The command of this convoy, consisting of two hundred foot soldiers, fifteen horsemen, and two field-pieces, he gave to Sandoval, who, by the vigilance, activity, and courage which he manifested on every occasion, was growing daily in his confidence, and in the estimation of his fellow-soldiers. The service was no less singular than important; the beams, the planks, the masts, the cordage, the sails, the ironwork, and all the infinite variety of articles requisite for the construction of thirteen brigantines, were to be carried sixty miles over land, through a mountainous country, by people who were unacquainted with the ministry of domestic animals, or the aid of machines to facilitate any work of labour. The Tlascalans furnished eight thousand *Tamenes*, an inferior order of men destined for servile tasks, to carry the materials on their shoulders, and appointed fifteen thousand warriors to accompany and defend them. Sandoval made the disposition for their progress with great propriety, placing the *Tamenes* in the centre, one body of warriors in the front, another in the rear, with considerable parties to cover the flanks. To each of these he joined some Spaniards, not only to assist them in danger, but to accustom them to regularity and subordination. A body so numerous, and so much encumbered, advanced leisurely but in excellent order; and in some places, where it was confined by the woods or mountains, the line of march extended above six miles. Parties of Mexicans frequently appeared hovering around them on the high grounds; but perceiving no prospect of success in attacking an enemy continually on his guard, and prepared to receive them, they did not venture to molest him; and Sandoval had the glory of conducting safely to Tezeuco, a convoy on which all the future operations of his countrymen depended.*

This was followed by another event of no less moment. Four ships arrived at Vera Cruz from Hispaniola, with two hundred soldiers, eighty horses, two battering cannon, and a considerable supply of ammunition and arms.† Elevated with observing that all his preparatory schemes, either for recruiting his own army, or impairing the force of the enemy, had now produced their full effect, Cortes, impatient to begin the siege in form, hastened the launching of the brigantines. To facilitate this, he had employed a vast number of Indians for two months, in deepening the small rivulet which runs by Tezeuco into the lake, and in forming it into a canal near two miles in length [119]; and though the Mexicans, aware of his intentions, as well as of the danger which threatened them, endeavoured frequently to interrupt the labourers, or to burn the brigantines, the work was at last completed.‡ On the twenty-eighth of April, all the Spanish troops, together with the auxiliary Indians, were drawn up on the banks of the canal; and with extraordinary military pomp, rendered more solemn by the celebration of the most sacred rites of religion, the brigantines were launched. As they fell down the canal in order, Father Olmedo blessed them, and gave each its name. Every eye followed them with wonder and hope, until they entered the lake, when they hoisted their sails and bore away before the wind. A general shout of joy was raised; all admiring that bold inventive genius, which, by means so extraordinary that their success almost exceeded belief, had acquired the command of a fleet, without the aid of which Mexico would have continued to set the Spanish power and arms at defiance.§

* Cortes Relat. 260. C. E. B. Diaz, c. 140. † Cortes Relat. 259. F. 262. D. Gomara Cron. c. 129. ‡ B. Diaz, c. 140. § Cortes Relat. 266. Herrera, dec. 3. lib. 1. c. 5. Gomara Cron. c. 129

Cortes determined to attack the city from three different quarters; from Tepeaca on the north side of the lake, from Tacuba on the west, and from Cuyocan towards the south. Those towns were situated on the principal causeways which led to the capital, and intended for their defence. He appointed Sandoval to command in the first, Pedro de Alvarado in the second, and Christoval de Olid in the third; allotting to each a numerous body of Indian auxiliaries, together with an equal division of Spaniards, who, by the junction of the troops from Hispaniola, amounting now to eighty-six horsemen, and eight hundred and eighteen foot soldiers; of whom one hundred and eighteen were armed with muskets or crossbows. The train of artillery consisted of three battering cannon, and fifteen field-pieces.* He reserved for himself, as the station of greatest importance and danger, the conduct of the brigantines, each armed with one of his small cannon, and manned with twenty-five Spaniards.

As Alvarado and Olid proceeded towards the posts assigned them [May 10], they broke down the aqueducts which the ingenuity of the Mexicans had erected for conveying water into the capital, and, by the distress to which this reduced the inhabitants, gave a beginning to the calamities which they were destined to suffer.† Alvarado and Olid found the towns of which they were ordered to take possession deserted by their inhabitants, who had fled for safety to the capital, where Guatimozin had collected the chief force of his empire, as there alone he could hope to make a successful stand against the formidable enemies who were approaching to assault him.

The first effort of the Mexicans was to destroy the fleet of brigantines, the fatal effects of whose operations they foresaw and dreaded. Though the brigantines, after all the labour and merit of Cortes in forming them, were of inconsiderable bulk, rudely constructed, and manned chiefly with landsmen hardly possessed of skill enough to conduct them, they must have been objects of terror to a people unacquainted with any navigation but that of their lake, and possessed of no vessel larger than a canoe. Necessity, however, urged Guatimozin to hazard the attack; and hoping to supply by numbers what he wanted in force, he assembled such a multitude of canoes as covered the face of the lake. They rowed on boldly to the charge, while the brigantines, retarded by a dead calm, could scarcely advance to meet them. But as the enemy drew near, a breeze suddenly sprung up; in a moment the sails were spread, the brigantines, with the utmost ease, broke through their feeble opponents, overset many canoes, and dissipated the whole armament with such slaughter, as convinced the Mexicans, that the progress of the Europeans in knowledge and arts rendered their superiority greater on this new element than they had hitherto found it by land.‡

From that time Cortes remained master of the lake, and the brigantines not only preserved a communication between the Spaniards in their different stations, though at considerable distance from each other, but were employed to cover the causeways on each side, and keep off the canoes when they attempted to annoy the troops as they advanced towards the city. Cortes formed the brigantines in three divisions, appointing one to cover each of the stations from which an attack was to be carried on against the city, with orders to second the operations of the officer who commanded there. From all the three stations he pushed on the attack against the city with equal vigour; but in a manner so very different from the conduct of sieges in regular war, that he himself seems afraid it would appear no less improper than singular to persons unacquainted with his situation.§ Each morning his troops assaulted the barricades which the enemy had erected on the causeways, forced their way over the trenches which they

* Cortes Relat 266. C. † Cortes Relat. 267. B. B. Diaz, c. 150. Herrera, dec. 3. lib. 1. c. 13.
‡ Cortes Relat. 267. C. B. Diaz, c. 150. Gomara Cron. c. 131. Herrera, dec. 3. lib. 1. c. 17
§ Cortes Relat. 270. F.

had dug, and through the canals where the bridges were broken down, and endeavoured to penetrate into the heart of the city, in hopes of obtaining some decisive advantage which might force the enemy to surrender, and terminate the war at once; but when the obstinate valour of the Mexicans rendered the efforts of the day ineffectual, the Spaniards retired in the evening to their former quarters Thus their toil and danger were in some measure continually renewed; the Mexicans repairing in the night what the Spaniards had destroyed through the day, and recovering the posts from which they had driven them. But necessity prescribed this slow and untoward mode of operation. The number of his troops were so small that Cortes durst not, with a handful of men, attempt to make a lodgment in a city where he might be surrounded and annoyed by such a multitude of enemies. The remembrance of what he had already suffered by the ill judged confidence with which he had ventured into such a dangerous situation, was still fresh in his mind. The Spaniards, exhausted with fatigue, were unable to guard the various posts which they daily gained; and though their camp was filled with Indian auxiliaries, they durst not devolve this charge upon them, because they were so little accustomed to discipline, that no confidence could be placed in their vigilance. Besides this, Cortes was extremely solicitous to preserve the city as much as possible from being destroyed, both because he destined it to be the capital of his conquests, and wished that it might remain as a monument of his glory. From all these considerations, he adhered obstinately, for a month after the siege was opened, to the system which he had adopted. The Mexicans, in their own defence, displayed valour which was hardly inferior to that with which the Spaniards attacked them. On land, on water, by night and by day, one furious conflict succeeded to another. Several Spaniards were killed, more wounded, and all were ready to sink under the toils of unintermitting service, which were rendered more intolerable by the injuries of the season, the periodical rains being now set in with their usual violence.*

Astonished and disconcerted with the length and difficulties of the siege, Cortes determined to make one great effort to get possession of the city, before he relinquished the plan which he had hitherto followed, and had recourse to any other mode of attack. With this view he sent instructions to Alvarado and Sandoval to advance with their divisions to a general assault, and took the command in person [July 3] of that posted on the causeway of Cuyocan. Animated by his presence, and the expectation of some decisive event, the Spaniards pushed forward with irresistible impetuosity. They broke through one barricade after another, forced their way over the ditches and canals, and, having entered the city, gained ground incessantly in spite of the multitude and ferocity of their opponents. Cortes, though delighted with the rapidity of his progress, did not forget that he might still find it necessary to retreat; and, in order to secure it, appointed Julien de Alderete, a captain of chief note in the troops which he had received from Hispaniola, to fill up the canals and gaps in the causeway as the main body advanced. That officer, deeming it inglorious to be thus employed, while his companions were in the heat of action and the career of victory, neglected the important charge committed to him, and hurried on, inconsiderately, to mingle with the combatants. The Mexicans, whose military attention and skill were daily improving, no sooner observed this than they carried an account of it to their monarch.

Guatimozin instantly discerned the consequence of the error which the Spaniards had committed, and, with admirable presence of mind, prepared to take advantage of it. He commanded the troops posted in the front to slacken their efforts, in order to allure the Spaniards to push forward, while

* B Diaz, c. 151.

he despatched a large body of chosen warriors through different streets, some by land, and others by water, towards the great breach in the causeway which had been left open. On a signal which he gave, the priests in the principal temple struck the great drum consecrated to the god of war. No sooner did the Mexicans hear its doleful solemn sound, calculated to inspire them with contempt of death, and enthusiastic ardour, than they rushed upon the enemy with frantic rage. The Spaniards, unable to resist men urged on no less by religious fury than hope of success, began to re tire, at first leisurely, and with a good countenance; but as the enemy pressed on, and their own impatience to escape increased, the terror and confusion became so general, that when they arrived at the gap in the causeway, Spaniards and Tlascalans, horsemen and infantry, plunged in promiscuously, while the Mexicans rushed upon them fiercely from every side, their light canoes carrying them through shoals which the brigantines could not approach. In vain did Cortes attempt to stop and rally his flying troops; fear rendered them regardless of his entreaties or commands. Finding all his endeavours to renew the combat fruitless, his next care was to save some of those who had thrown themselves into the water; but while thus employed, with more attention to their situation than to his own, six Mexican captains suddenly laid hold of him, and were hurrying him off in triumph; and though two of his officers rescued him at the expense of their own lives, he received several dangerous wounds before he could break loose. Above sixty Spaniards perished in the rout; and what rendered the disaster more afflicting, forty of these fell alive into the hands of an enemy never known to show mercy to a captive.*

The approach of night, though it delivered the dejected Spaniards from the attacks of the enemy, ushered in what was hardly less grievous, the noise of their barbarous triumph, and of the horrid festival with which they celebrated their victory. Every quarter of the city was illuminated; the great temple shone with such peculiar splendour, that the Spaniards could plainly see the people in motion, and the priests busy in hastening the preparations for the death of the prisoners. Through the gloom, they fancied that they discerned their companions by the whiteness of their skins, as they were stript naked, and compelled to dance before the image of the god to whom they were to be offered. They heard the shrieks of those who were sacrificed, and thought that they could distinguish each unhappy victim by the well known sound of his voice. Imagination added to what they really saw or heard, and augmented its horror. The most unfeeling melted into tears of compassion, and the stoutest heart trembled at the dreadful spectacle which they beheld [120].

Cortes, who, besides all that he felt in common with his soldiers, was oppressed with the additional load of anxious reflections natural to a general on such an unexpected calamity, could not, like them, relieve his mind by giving vent to its anguish. He was obliged to assume an air of tranquillity, in order to revive the spirit and hopes of his followers. The juncture, indeed, required an extraordinary exertion of fortitude. The Mexicans, elated with their victory, sallied out next morning to attack him in his quarters. But they did not rely on the efforts of their own arms alone They sent the heads of Spaniards whom they had sacrificed to the leading men in the adjacent provinces, and assured them that the god of war, appeased by the blood of their invaders, which had been shed so plentifully on his altars, had declared with an audible voice, that in eight days time those hated enemies should be finally destroyed, and peace and prosperity re-established in the empire.

A prediction uttered with such confidence, and in terms so void of ambiguity, gained universal credit among a people prone to superstition,

* Cortes Relat. p. 273. B. Diaz, c. 152. Gomara Cron. c. 138. Herrera, dec. 3. lib. i. c. 23.

The zeal of the provinces, which had already declared against the Spaniards, augmented; and several which had hitherto remained inactive, took arms, with enthusiastic ardour, to execute the decree of the gods. The Indian auxiliaries who had joined Cortes, accustomed to venerate the same deities with the Mexicans, and to receive the responses of their priests with the same implicit faith, abandoned the Spaniards as a race of men devoted to certain destruction. Even the fidelity of the Tlascalans was shaken, and the Spanish troops were left almost alone in their stations. Cortes, finding that he attempted in vain to dispel the superstitious fears of his confederates by argument, took advantage, from the imprudence of those who had framed the prophecy in fixing its accomplishment so near at hand, to give a striking demonstration of its falsity. He suspended all military operations, during the period marked out by the oracle. Under cover of the brigantines, which kept the enemy at a distance, his troops lay in safety, and the fatal term expired without any disaster.*

Many of his allies, ashamed of their own credulity, returned to their station. Other tribes, judging that the gods, who had now deceived the Mexicans, had decreed finally to withdraw their protection from them, joined his standard; and such was the levity of a simple people, moved by every slight impression, that in a short time after such a general defection of his confederates, Cortes saw himself, if we may believe his own account, at the head of a hundred and fifty thousand Indians. Even with such a numerous army, he found it necessary to adopt a new and more wary system of operation. Instead of renewing his attempts to become master of the city at once, by such bold but dangerous efforts of valour as he had already tried, he made his advances gradually, and with every possible precaution against exposing his men to any calamity similar to that which they still bewailed. As the Spaniards pushed forward, the Indians regularly repaired the causeways behind them. As soon as they got possession of any part of the town, the houses were instantly levelled with the ground. Day by day, the Mexicans, forced to retire as their enemies gained ground, were hemmed in within more narrow limits. Guatimozin, though unable to stop the career of the enemy, continued to defend his capital with obstinate resolution, and disputed every inch of ground. The Spaniards not only varied their mode of attack, but, by orders of Cortes, changed the weapons with which they fought. They were again armed with the long Chinantlan spears which they had employed with such success against Narvaez; and, by the firm array in which this enabled them to range themselves, they repelled, with little danger, the loose assault of the Mexicans: incredible numbers of them fell in the conflicts which they renewed every day.† While war wasted without, famine began to consume them within the city. The Spanish brigantines having the entire command of the lake, rendered it almost impossible to convey to the besieged any supply of provisions by water. The immense number of his Indian auxiliaries enabled Cortes to shut up the avenues to the city by land. The stores which Guatimozin had laid up were exhausted by the multitudes which had crowded into the capital to defend their sovereign and the temples of their gods. Not only the people, but persons of the highest rank, felt the utmost distresses of famine. What they suffered brought on infectious and mortal distempers, the last calamity that visits besieged cities, and which filled up the measure of their woes.‡

But, under the pressure of so many and such various evils, the spirit of Guatimozin remained firm and unsubdued. He rejected with scorn every overture of peace from Cortes; and, disdaining the idea of submitting to the oppressors of his country, determined not to survive its ruin. The Spaniards continued their progress. At length all the three divisions

* B. Diaz, c. 153. Gomara Cron. c. 138. † Cortes Relat. p. 275. C. 276. F. B. Diaz, c. 153. ‡ Cortes Relat. 276. E. 277 F. B. Diaz 155 Gomara Cron. c. 141.

penetrated into the great square in the centre of the city, and made a secure lodgment there [July 27]. Three-fourths of the city were now reduced and laid in ruins. The remaining quarter was so closely pressed, that it could not long withstand assailants, who attacked it from their new station with superior advantage, and more assured expectation of success. The Mexican nobles, solicitous to save the life of a monarch whom they revered, prevailed on Guatimozin to retire from a place where resistance was now vain, that he might rouse the more distant provinces of the empire to arms, and maintain there a more successful struggle with the public enemy. In order to facilitate the execution of this measure, they endeavoured to amuse Cortes with overtures of submission, that, while his attention was employed in adjusting the articles of pacification, Guatimozin might escape unperceived. But they made this attempt upon a leader of greater sagacity and discernment than to be deceived by their arts. Cortes, suspecting their intention, and aware of what moment it was to defeat it, appointed Sandoval, the officer on whose vigilance he could most perfectly rely, to take the command of the brigantines, with strict injunctions to watch every motion of the enemy. Sandoval, attentive to the charge, observing some large canoes crowded with people rowing across the lake with extraordinary rapidity, instantly gave the signal to chase. Garcia Holguin, who commanded the swiftest sailing brigantine, soon overtook them, and was preparing to fire on the foremost canoe, which seemed to carry some person whom all the rest followed and obeyed. At once the rowers dropped their oars, and all on board, throwing down their arms, conjured him with cries and tears to forbear, as the emperor was there. Holguin eagerly seized his prize; and Guatimozin, with a dignified composure, gave himself up into his hands, requesting only that no insult might be offered to the empress or his children. When conducted to Cortes, he appeared neither with the sullen fierceness of a barbarian, nor with the dejection of a supplicant. "I have done," said he, addressing himself to the Spanish general, "what became a monarch. I have defended my people to the last extremity. Nothing now remains but to die. Take this dagger," laying his hand on one which Cortes wore, "plant it in my breast, and put an end to a life which can no longer be of use."*

As soon as the fate of their sovereign was known, the resistance of the Mexicans ceased; and Cortes took possession of that small part of the capital which yet remained undestroyed [Aug. 13]. Thus terminated the siege of Mexico, the most memorable event in the conquest of America. It continued seventy-five days, hardly one of which passed without some extraordinary effort of one party in the attack, or of the other in the defence of a city, on the fate of which both knew that the fortune of the empire depended. As the struggle here was more obstinate, it was likewise more equal than any between the inhabitants of the Old and New Worlds. The great abilities of Guatimozin, the number of his troops, the peculiar situation of his capital, so far counterbalanced the superiority of the Spaniards in arms and discipline, that they must have relinquished the enterprise if they had trusted for success to themselves alone. But Mexico was overturned by the jealousy of neighbours who dreaded its power, and by the revolt of subjects impatient to shake off its yoke. By their effectual aid, Cortes was enabled to accomplish what, without such support, he would hardly have ventured to attempt. How much soever this account of the reduction of Mexico may detract, on the one hand, from the marvellous relations of some Spanish writers, by ascribing that to simple and obvious causes which they attribute to the romantic valour of their countrymen, it adds, on the other, to the merit and abilities of Cortes, who, under every disadvantage, acquired such an ascendant over

* Cortes Relat. 279. B. Diaz, c. 156. Gomara Cron. c. 142. Herrera, dec. 3. lib. i. c. 7.

unknown nations, as to render them instruments towards carrying his schemes into execution [121].

The exultation of the Spaniards, on accomplishing this arducus enterprise, was at first excessive. But this was quickly damped by the cruel disappointment of those sanguine hopes which had animated them amidst so many hardships and dangers Instead of the inexhaustible wealth which they expected from becoming masters of Montezuma's treasures, and the ornaments of so many temples, their rapaciousness could only collect an inconsiderable booty amidst ruins and desolation.* Guatimozin, aware of his impending fate, had ordered what remained of the riches amassed by his ancestors, to be thrown into the lake. The Indian auxiliaries, while the Spaniards were engaged in conflict with the enemy, had carried off the most valuable part of the spoil. The sum to be divided among the conquerors was so small that many of them disdained to accept of the pittance which fell to their share, and all murmured and exclaimed; some against Cortes and his confidants, whom they suspected of having secretly appropriated to their own use a large portion of the riches which should have been brought into the common stock; others, against Guatimozin, whom they accused of obstinacy in refusing to discover the place where he had hidden his treasure.

Arguments, entreaties, and promises were employed in order to soothe them, but with so little effect, that Cortes, from solicitude to check this growing spirit of discontent, gave way to a deed which stains the glory of all his great actions. Without regarding the former dignity of Guatimozin, or feeling any reverence for those virtues which he had displayed, he subjected the unhappy monarch, together with his chief favourite, to torture, in order to force from them a discovery of the royal treasures, which it was supposed they had concealed. Guatimozin bore whatever the refined cruelty of his tormentors could inflict, with the invincible fortitude of an American warrior. His fellow-sufferer, overcome by the violence of the anguish, turned a dejected eye towards his master, which seemed to implore his permission to reveal all that he knew. But the high spirited prince, darting on him a look of authority mingled with scorn, checked his weakness by asking, "Am I now reposing on a bed of flowers?" Overawed by the reproach, the favourite persevered in his dutiful silence, and expired. Cortes, ashamed of a scene so horrid, rescued the royal victim from the hands of his torturers, and prolonged a life reserved for new indignities and sufferings.†

The fate of the capital, as both parties had foreseen, decided that of the empire. The provinces submitted one after another to the conquerors. Small detachments of Spaniards marching through them without interruption, penetrated in different quarters to the great Southern Ocean, which, according to the ideas of Columbus, they imagined would open a short as well as easy passage to the East Indies, and secure to the crown of Castile all the envied wealth of those fertile regions;‡ and the active mind of Cortes began already to form schemes for attempting this important discovery.§

He did not know, that during the progress of his victorious arms in Mexico, the very scheme, of which he began to form some idea, had been undertaken and accomplished. As this is one of the most splendid events in the history of the Spanish discoveries, and has been productive of effects peculiarly interesting to those extensive provinces which Cortes had now subjected to the crown of Castile, the account of its rise and progress merits a particular detail.

* The gold and silver according to Cortes, amounted only to 120,000 pesos. Relat. 280. A. a sum much inferior to that which the Spaniards had formerly divided in Mexico. † B. Diaz, c. 157 Gomara Cron. c. 146. Herrera, dec. 3. lib. ii. c. 8. Torquem, Mon. Ind. i. 574. ‡ Cortes Relat. 280. D. &c. B. Diaz, c. 157. § Herrera, dec. 3. lib. ii. c. 17. Gomara Cron. c. 149.

Ferdinand Magalhaens, or Magellan, a Portuguese gentleman of honourable birth, having served several years in the East Indies, with distinguished valour, under the famous Albuquerque, demanded the recompense which he thought due to his services, with the boldness natural to a high spirited soldier. But as his general would not grant his suit, and he expected greater justice from his sovereign, whom he knew to be a good judge and a generous rewarder of merit, he quitted India abruptly, and returned to Lisbon. In order to induce Emanuel to listen more favourably to his claim, he not only stated his past services, but offered to add to them by conducting his countrymen to the Molucca or Spice Islands, by holding a westerly course; which he contended would be both shorter and less hazardous than that which the Portuguese now followed by the Cape of Good Hope, through the immense extent of the Eastern Ocean. This was the original and favourite project of Columbus, and Magellan founded his hopes of success on the ideas of that great navigator, confirmed by many observations, the result of his own naval experience, as well as that of his countrymen in their intercourse with the East. But though the Portuguese monarchs had the merit of having first awakened and encouraged the spirit of discovery in that age, it was their destiny, in the course of a few years, to reject two grand schemes for this purpose, the execution of which would have been attended with a great accession of glory to themselves, and of power to their kingdom. In consequence of some ill founded prejudice against Magellan, or of some dark intrigue which contemporary historians have not explained, Emanuel would neither bestow the recompense which he claimed, nor approve of the scheme which he proposed; and dismissed him with a disdainful coldness intolerable to a man conscious of what he deserved, and animated with the sanguine hopes of success peculiar to those who are capable of forming or of conducting new and great undertakings. In a transport of resentment [1517], Magellan formally renounced his allegiance to an ungrateful master, and fled to the court of Castile, where he expected that his talents would be more justly estimated. He endeavoured to recommend himself by offering to execute, under the patronage of Spain, that scheme which he had laid before the court of Portugal, the accomplishment of which, he knew, would wound the monarch against whom he was exasperated in the most tender part. In order to establish the justness of his theory, he produced the same arguments which he had employed at Lisbon; acknowledging, at the same time, that the undertaking was both arduous and expensive, as it could not be attempted but with a squadron of considerable force, and victualled for at least two years. Fortunately, he applied to a minister who was not apt to be deterred, either by the boldness of a design, or the expense of carrying it into execution. Cardinal Ximenes, who at that time directed the affairs of Spain, discerning at once what an increase of wealth and glory would accrue to his country by the success of Magellan's proposal, listened to it with a most favourable ear. Charles V., on his arrival in his Spanish dominions, entered into the measure with no less ardour, and orders were issued for equipping a proper squadron at the public charge, of which the command was given to Magellan, whom the King honoured with the habit of St. Jago and the title of Captain general.*

On the tenth of August, one thousand five hundred and nineteen, Magellan sailed from Seville with five ships, which, according to the ideas of the age, were deemed to be of considerable force, though the burden of the largest did not exceed one hundred and twenty tons. The crews of the whole amounted to two hundred and thirty-four men, among whom were some of the most skilful pilots in Spain, and several Portuguese

* Herrera, dec. 2. lib. ii. c. 19. lib. iv. c. 9. Gomara Hist. c, 91. Dalrymple's Collect. of Voyages to the South Pacific Ocean, vol. i. p. 1, &c.

sailors, in whose experience, as more extensive, Magellan placed still greater confidence. After touching at the Canaries, he stood directly south towards the equinoctial line along the coast of America, but was so long retarded by tedious calms, and spent so much time in searching every bay and inlet for that communication with the Southern Ocean which he wished to discover, that he did not reach the river De la Plata till the twelfth of January [1520]. That spacious opening through which its vast body of water pours into the Atlantic allured him to enter; but after sailing up it for some days, he concluded from the shallowness of the stream and the freshness of the water, that the wished-for strait was not situated there, and continued his course towards the south. On the thirty-first of March he arrived in the Port of St. Julian, about forty-eight degrees south of the line, where he resolved to winter. In this uncomfortable station he lost one of his squadron; and the Spaniards suffered so much from the excessive rigour of the climate, that the crews of three of his ships, headed by their officers, rose in open mutiny, and insisted on relinquishing the visionary project of a desperate adventurer, and returning directly to Spain. This dangerous insurrection Magellan suppressed, by an effort of courage no less prompt than intrepid, and inflicted exemplary punishment on the ringleaders. With the remainder of his followers, overawed but not reconciled to his scheme, he continued his voyage towards the south, and at length discovered, near the fifty-third degree of latitude, the mouth of a strait, into which he entered, notwithstanding the murmurs and remonstrances of the people under his command. After sailing twenty days in that winding dangerous channel, to which he gave his own name, and where one of his ships deserted him, the great Southern Ocean opened to his view, and with tears of joy he returned thanks to Heaven for having thus far crowned his endeavours with success.*

But he was still at a greater distance than he imagined from the object of his wishes. He sailed during three months and twenty days in a uniform direction towards the north-west, without discovering land. In this voyage, the longest that had ever been made in the unbounded ocean, he suffered incredible distress. His stock of provisions was almost exhausted, the water became putrid, the men were reduced to the shortest allowance with which it was possible to sustain life, and the scurvy, the most dreadful of all the maladies with which seafaring people are inflicted, began to spread among the crew. One circumstance alone afforded them some consolation; they enjoyed an uninterrupted course of fair weather, with such favourable winds that Magellan bestowed on that ocean the name of *Pacific*, which it still retains. When reduced to such extremity that they must have sunk under their sufferings, they fell in with a cluster of small but fertile islands [March 6], which afforded them refreshments in such abundance, that their health was soon re-established. From these isles, which he called *De los Ladrones*, he proceeded on his voyage, and soon made a more important discovery of the islands now known by the name of the *Philippines*. In one of these he got into an unfortunate quarrel with the natives, who attacked him with a numerous body of troops well armed; and while he fought at the head of his men with his usual valour, he fell [April 26] by the hands of those barbarians, together with several of his principal officers.

The expedition was prosecuted under other commanders. After visiting many of the smaller isles scattered in the eastern part of the Indian ocean, they touched at the great island of Borneo [Nov. 8], and at length landed in Tidore, one of the Moluccas, to the astonishment of the Portuguese, who could not comprehend how the Spaniards, by holding a westerly

* Herrera, dec. 2. lib. iv. c. 10. lib. ix. c. 10, &c. Gomara Hist. c. 92. Pigafetta Viaggio ap. Ramus. ii. p. 352, &c.

course, had arrived at that sequestered seat of their most valuable commerce, which they themselves had discovered by sailing in an opposite direction. There, and in the adjacent isles, the Spaniards found a people acquainted with the benefits of extensive trade, and willing to open an intercourse with a new nation. They took in a cargo of the precious spices, which are the distinguished production of these islands; and with that, as well as with specimens of the rich commodities yielded by the other countries which they had visited, the *Victory*, which, of the two ships that remained of the squadron, was most fit for a long voyage, set sail for Europe [Jan. 1522], under the command of Juan Sebastian del Cano. He followed the course of the Portuguese, by the Cape of Good Hope, and after many disasters and sufferings he arrived at St. Lucar on the seventh of September, one thousand five hundred and twenty-two, having sailed round the globe in the space of three years and twenty-eight days.*

Though an untimely fate deprived Magellan of the satisfaction of accomplishing this great undertaking, his contemporaries, just to his memory and talents, ascribed to him not only the honour of having formed the plan, but of having surmounted almost every obstacle, to the completion of it; and in the present age his name is still ranked among the highest in the roll of eminent and successful navigators. The naval glory of Spain now eclipsed that of every other nation; and by a singular felicity she had the merit, in the course of a few years, of discovering a new continent almost as large as that part of the earth which was formerly known, and of ascertaining by experience the form and extent of the whole of the terraqueous globe.

The Spaniards were not satisfied with the glory of having first encompassed the earth; they expected to derive great commercial advantages from this new and boldest effort of their maritime skill. The men of science among them contended, that the Spice Islands, and several of the richest countries in the East, were so situated as to belong of right to the crown of Castile, in consequence of the partitions made by Alexander VI. The merchants, without attending to this discussion, engaged eagerly in that lucrative and alluring commerce, which was now open to them. The Portuguese, alarmed at the intrusion of such formidable rivals, remonstrated and negotiated in Europe, while in Asia they obstructed the trade of the Spaniards by force of arms. Charles V., not sufficiently instructed with respect to the importance of this valuable branch of commerce, or distracted by the multiplicity of his schemes and operations, did not afford his subjects proper protection. At last, the low state of his finances, exhausted by the efforts of his arms in every part of Europe, together with the dread of adding a new war with Portugal to those in which he was already engaged, induced him to make over his claim of the Moluccas to the Portuguese for three hundred and fifty thousand ducats. He reserved, however, to the crown of Castile the right of reviving its pretensions on repayment of that sum; but other objects engrossed his attention and that of his successors; and Spain was finally excluded from a branch of commerce in which it was engaging with sanguine expectations of profit.†

Though the trade with the Moluccas was relinquished, the voyage of Magellan was followed by commercial effects of great moment to Spain. Philip II., in the year one thousand five hundred and sixty-four, reduced those islands which he discovered in the Eastern ocean to subjection, and established settlements there; between which and the kingdom of New Spain a regular intercourse, the nature of which shall be explained in its proper place, is still carried on. I return now to the transactions in New Spain.

* Herrera, dec. 3. lib. i. c. 3. 9. lib. iv. c. 1. Gomara Cron. c. 93, &c. Pigafetta ap. Ramus. ii. p. 361, &c. † Herrera, dec. 3. lib. iii. c. 5 &c. dec. 4. lib. v. c 7, &c.

At the time that Cortes was acquiring such extensive territories for his native country, and preparing the way for future conquests, it was his singular fate not only to be destitute of any commission or authority from the sovereign whom he was serving with such successful zeal, but to be regarded as an undutiful and seditious subject. By the influence of Fonseca, Bishop of Burgos, his conduct in assuming the government of New Spain was declared to be an irregular usurpation, in contempt of the royal authority; and Christoval de Tapia received a commission, empowering him to supersede Cortes, to seize his person, to confiscate his effects, to make a strict scrutiny into his proceedings, and to transmit the result of all the inquiries carried on in New Spain to the Council of the Indies, of which the Bishop of Burgos was president. A few weeks after the reduction of Mexico, Tapia landed at Vera Cruz with the royal mandate to strip its conqueror of his power, and treat him as a criminal. But Fonseca had chosen a very improper instrument to wreak his vengeance on Cortes. Tapia had neither the reputation nor the talents that suited the high command to which he was appointed. Cortes, while he publicly expressed the most respectful veneration for the emperor's authority, secretly took measures to defeat the effect of his commission; and having involved Tapia and his followers in a multiplicity of negotiations and conferences, in which he sometimes had recourse to threats, but more frequently employed bribes and promises, he at length prevailed upon that weak man to abandon a province which he was unworthy of governing.*

But notwithstanding the fortunate dexterity with which he had eluded this danger, Cortes was so sensible of the precarious tenure by which he held his power, that he despatched deputies to Spain [May 15], with a pompous account of the success of his arms, with further specimens of the productions of the country, and with rich presents to the emperor, as the earnest of future contributions from his new conquests; requesting, in recompense for all his services, the approbation of his proceedings, and that he might be intrusted with the government of those dominions, which his conduct and the valour of his followers had added to the crown of Castile. The juncture in which his deputies reached the court was favourable. The internal commotions in Spain, which had disquieted the beginning of Charles's reign, were just appeased.† The ministers had leisure to turn their attention towards foreign affairs. The account of Cortes's victories filled his countrymen with admiration. The extent and value of his conquests became the object of vast and interesting hopes. Whatever stain he might have contracted, by the irregularity of the steps which he took in order to attain power, was so fully effaced by the splendour and merit of the great actions which this had enabled him to perform, that every heart revolted at the thought of inflicting any censure on a man whose services entitled him to the highest marks of distinction. The public voice declared warmly in favour of his pretensions; and Charles, arriving in Spain about this time, adopted the sentiments of his subjects with a youthful ardour. Notwithstanding the claims of Velasquez, and the partial representations of the Bishop of Burgos, the emperor appointed Cortes captain general and governor of New Spain, judging that no person was so capable of maintaining the royal authority, or of establishing good order both among his Spanish and Indian subjects, as the victorious leader whom the former had long been accustomed to obey, and the latter had been taught to fear and to respect.‡

Even before his jurisdiction received this legal sanction, Cortes ventured to exercise all the powers of a governor, and, by various arrangements,

* Herrera, dec. 3. lib. iii. c. 16. 3. dec. 4. c. 1. Cort. Relat. 281. E. B. Diaz. c. 158. † Hist. of Charles V. b. iii. ‡ Herrera, dec. 3. lib. iv. c 3. Gomara Cron. c. 164, 165. B. Diaz 167, 168

endeavoured to render his conquest a secure and beneficial acquisition to his country. He determined to establish the seat of government in its ancient station, and to raise Mexico again from its ruins; and having conceived high ideas concerning the future grandeur of the state of which he was laying the foundation, he began to rebuild its capital on a plan which hath gradually formed the most magnificent city in the New World. At the same time, he employed skilful persons to search for mines, in different parts of the country, and opened some which were found to be richer than any which the Spaniards had hitherto discovered in America. He detached his principal officers into the remote provinces, and encouraged them to settle there, not only by bestowing upon them large tracts of land, but by granting them the same dominion over the Indians, and the same right to their service, which the Spaniards had assumed in the islands.

It was not, however, without difficulty that the Mexican empire could be entirely reduced into the form of a Spanish colony. Enraged and rendered desperate by oppression, the natives often forgot the superiority of their enemies, and ran to arms in defence of their liberties. In every contest, however, the European valour and discipline prevailed. But fatally for the honour of their country, the Spaniards sullied the glory redounding from these repeated victories by their mode of treating the vanquished people. After taking Guatimozin, and becoming masters of his capital, they supposed that the king of Castile entered on possession of all the rights of the captive monarch, and affected to consider every effort of the Mexicans to assert their own independence, as the rebellion of vassals against their sovereign, or the mutiny of slaves against their master. Under the sanction of those ill founded maxims, they violated every right that should be held sacred between hostile nations. After each insurrection, they reduced the common people, in the provinces which they subdued, to the most humiliating of all conditions, that of personal servitude. Their chiefs, supposed to be more criminal, were punished with greater severity, and put to death in the most ignominious or the most excruciating mode that the insolence or the cruelty of their conquerors could devise. In almost every district of the Mexican empire, the progress of the Spanish arms is marked with blood, and with deeds so atrocious as disgrace the enterprising valour that conducted them to success. In the country of Panuco, sixty caziques or leaders, and four hundred nobles, were burned at one time. Nor was this shocking barbarity perpetrated in any sudden sally of rage, or by a commander of inferior note. It was the act of Sandoval, an officer whose name is entitled to the second rank in the annals of New Spain, and executed after a solemn consultation with Cortes; and to complete the horror of the scene, the children and relations of the wretched victims were assembled, and compelled to be spectators of their dying agonies.* It seems hardly possible to exceed in horror this dreadful example of severity; but it was followed by another, which affected the Mexicans still more sensibly, as it gave them a most feeling proof of their own degradation, and of the small regard which their haughty masters retained for the ancient dignity and splendour of their state. On a slight suspicion, confirmed by very imperfect evidence, that Guatimozin had formed a scheme to shake off the yoke, and to excite his former subjects to take arms, Cortes, without the formality of a trial, ordered the unhappy monarch, together with the caziques of Tezeuco and Tacuba, the two persons of greatest eminence in the empire, to be hanged; and the Mexicans, with astonishment and horror, beheld this disgraceful punishment inflicted upon persons to whom they were accustomed to look up with reverence hardly inferior to that which they paid to the gods themselves† [122]. The example of Cortes and his principal officers encou

* Cortes Relat. 291. C. Gomara Cron. c. 155. Herrera, dec. 3. lib. viii. c. 9.

† Gomara Cron. c. 170. B. Diaz, c. 177.

raged and justified persons of subordinate rank to venture upon committing greater excesses. Nuno de Guzman, in particular, stained an illustrious name by deeds of peculiar enormity and rigour, in various expeditions which he conducted.*

One circumstance, however, saved the Mexicans from further consumption, perhaps from as complete as that which had depopulated the islands. The first conquerors did not attempt to search for the precious metals in the bowels of the earth. They were neither sufficiently wealthy to carry on the expensive works which are requisite for opening those deep recesses where nature has concealed the veins of gold and silver, nor sufficiently skilful to perform the ingenious operations by which those precious metals are separated from their respective ores. They were satisfied with the more simple method, practised by the Indians, of washing the earth carried down rivers and torrents from the mountains, and collecting the grains of native metal deposited there. The rich mines of New Spain, which have poured forth their treasures with such profusion on every quarter of the globe, were not discovered for several years after the conquest.† By that time [1552, &c.], a more orderly government and police were introduced into the colony; experience, derived from former errors, had suggested many useful and humane regulations for the protection and preservation of the Indians; and though it then became necessary to increase the number of those employed in the mines, and they were engaged in a species of labour more pernicious to the human constitution, they suffered less hardship or diminution than from the ill judged, but less extensive, schemes of the first conquerors.

While it was the lot of the Indians to suffer, their new masters seemed not to have derived any considerable wealth from their ill conducted researches. According to the usual fate of first settlers in new colonies, it was their lot to encounter danger and to struggle with difficulties; the fruits of their victories and toils were reserved for times of tranquillity, and reaped by successors of great industry, but of inferior merit. The early historians of America abound with accounts of the sufferings and of the poverty of its conquerors.‡ In New Spain, their condition was rendered more grievous by a peculiar arrangement. When Charles V. advanced Cortes to the government of that country, he at the same time appointed certain commissioners to receive and administer the royal revenue there, with independent jurisdiction.§ These men, chosen from inferior stations in various departments of public business at Madrid, were so much elevated with their promotion, that they thought they were called to act a part of the first consequence. But being accustomed to the minute formalities of office, and having contracted the narrow ideas suited to the sphere in which they had hitherto moved, they were astonished on arriving in Mexico [1524], at the high authority which Cortes exercised, and could not conceive that the mode of administration, in a country recently subdued and settled, must be different from what took place in one where tranquillity and regular government had been long established. In their letters, they represented Cortes as an ambitious tyrant, who, having usurped a jurisdiction superior to law, aspired at independence, and, by his exorbitant wealth and extensive influence, might accomplish those disloyal schemes which he apparently meditated.|| These insinuations made such deep impression upon the Spanish ministers, most of whom had been formed to business under the jealous and rigid administration of Ferdinand, that, unmindful of all Cortes's past services, and regardless of what he was then suffering in conducting that extraordinary expedition, in which he advanced from the lake of Mexico to the western extremities of Hon-

* Herrera, dec. 4 and 5. passim. † Ibid. dec. 8. lib. x. c. 21. ‡ Cortes Relat. 283. F. B Diaz, c. 209. § Herrera, dec. 3. lib. iv. c. 3. || Ibid. dec. 3. lib. v. c 14.

duras [123], they infused the same suspicions into the minds of their master, and prevailed on him to order a solemn inquest to be made into his conduct [1525], with powers to the licentiate Ponce de Leon, intrusted with that commission, to seize his person, if he should find that expedient, and send him prisoner to Spain.*

The sudden death of Ponce de Leon, a few days after his arrival in New Spain, prevented the execution of this commission. But as the object of his appointment was known, the mind of Cortes was deeply wounded with this unexpected return for services which far exceeded whatever any subject of Spain had rendered to his sovereign. He endeavoured, however, to maintain his station, and to recover the confidence of the court. But every person in office, who had arrived from Spain since the conquest, was a spy upon his conduct, and with malicious ingenuity gave an unfavourable representation of all his actions. The apprehensions of Charles and his ministers increased. A new commission of inquiry was issued [1528], with more extensive powers, and various precautions were taken in order to prevent or to punish him, if he should be so presumptuous as to attempt what was inconsistent with the fidelity of a subject.† Cortes beheld the approaching crisis of his fortune with all the violent emotions natural to a haughty mind conscious of high desert, and receiving unworthy treatment. But though some of his desperate followers urged him to assert his own rights against his ungrateful country, and with a bold hand to seize that power which the courtiers meanly accused him of coveting,‡ he retained such self-command, or was actuated with such sentiments of loyalty, as to reject their dangerous counsels, and to choose the only course in which he could secure his own dignity, without departing from his duty. He resolved not to expose himself to the ignominy of a trial in that country which had been the scene of his triumphs; but, without waiting for the arrival of his judges, to repair directly to Castile, and commit himself and his cause to the justice and generosity of his sovereign.§

Cortes appeared in his native country with the splendour that suited the conqueror of a mighty kingdom. He brought with him a great part of his wealth, many jewels and ornaments of great value, several curious productions of the country [124], and was attended by some Mexicans of the first rank, as well as by the most considerable of his own officers. His arrival in Spain removed at once every suspicion and fear that had been entertained with respect to his intentions. The emperor, having now nothing to apprehend from the designs of Cortes, received him like a person whom consciousness of his own innocence had brought into the presence of his master, and who was entitled, by the eminence of his services, to the highest marks of distinction and respect. The order of St. Jago, the title of Marquis del Valle de Guaxaca, the grant of an ample territory in New Spain, were successively bestowed upon him; and as his manners were correct and elegant, although he had passed the greater part of his life among rough adventurers, the emperor admitted him to the same familiar intercourse with himself, that was enjoyed by noblemen of the first rank.||

But, amidst those external proofs of regard, symptoms of remaining distrust appeared. Though Cortes earnestly solicited to be reinstated in the government of New Spain, Charles, too sagacious to commit such an important charge to a man whom he had once suspected, peremptorily refused to invest him again with powers which he might find it impossible to control. Cortes, though dignified with new titles, returned to Mexico [1530], with diminished authority. The military department, with powers to attempt new discoveries, was left in his hands; but the supreme direction of civil affairs was placed in a board called *The Audience of*

* Herrera, dec. 3. lib. viii. c. 14, 15. † Ibid. dec. 3. lib. viii. c. 15. dec. 4. lib. ii. c. 1. lib. iv. c. 9, 10. B. Diaz, c. 172. 196. Gomara Cron. c. 166. ‡ B. Diaz, c. 194. § Herrera, dec 3. lib. iv. c. 8. || Ibid. dec. 3 lib iv. c. 1. lib. vi. c. 4. B. Diaz, c. 196. Gomara Cron. c. 192.

*New Spain.* At a subsequent period, when, upon the increase of the colony, the exertion of authority more united and extensive became necessary, Antonio de Mendoza, a nobleman of high rank, was sent thither as *Viceroy*, to take the government into his hands.

This division of power in New Spain proved, as was unavoidable, the source of perpetual dissension, which imbittered the life of Cortes, and thwarted all his schemes. As he had now no opportunity to display his active talents but in attempting new discoveries, he formed various schemes for that purpose, all of which bear impressions of a genius that delighted in what was bold and splendid. He early entertained an idea, that, either by steering through the Gulf of Florida along the east coast of North America, some strait would be found that communicated with the western ocean; or that, by examining the isthmus of Darien, some passage would be discovered between the North and South Seas.* But having been disappointed in his expectations with respect to both, he now confined his views to such voyages of discovery as he could make from the ports of New Spain in the South Sea. There he fitted out successively several small squadrons, which either perished in the attempt, or returned without making any discovery of moment. Cortes, weary of intrusting the conduct of his operations to others, took the command of a new armament in person [1536]; and, after enduring incredible hardships, and encountering dangers of every species, he discovered the large peninsula of California, and surveyed the greater part of the gulf which separates it from New Spain. The discovery of a country of such extent would have reflected credit on a common adventurer; but it could add little new honour to the name of Cortes, and was far from satisfying the sanguine expectations which he had formed.† Disgusted with ill success, to which he had not been accustomed, and weary of contesting with adversaries to whom he considered it as a disgrace to be opposed, he once more sought for redress in his native country [1540].

But his reception there was very different from that which gratitude, and even decency, ought to have secured for him. The merit of his ancient exploits was already, in a great measure, forgotten or eclipsed by the fame of recent and more valuable conquests in another quarter of America. No service of moment was now expected from a man of declining years, and who began to be unfortunate. The emperor behaved to him with cold civility; his ministers treated him sometimes with neglect, sometimes with insolence. His grievances received no redress; his claims were urged without effect; and after several years spent in fruitless application to ministers and judges, an occupation the most irksome and mortifying to a man of high spirit, who had moved in a sphere where he was more accustomed to command than to solicit, Cortes ended his days on the second of December, one thousand five hundred and forty-seven, in the sixty-second year of his age. His fate was the same with that of all the persons who distinguished themselves in the discovery or conquest of the New World. Envied by his contemporaries, and ill requited by the court which he served, he has been admired and celebrated by succeeding ages Which has formed the most just estimate of his character, an impartial consideration of his actions must determine.

* Cortes Relat. Ram. iii. 294. B. † Herrera, dec. 5. lib. viii. c. 9, 10. dec. 8. lib. vi. c. 14. Vonegas Hist. of Californ. i. 125. Lorenziana Hist. p. 322, &c.

# BOOK VI.

1523.] FROM the time that Nugnez de Balboa discovered the great Southern Ocean, and received the first obscure hints concerning the opulent countries with which it might open a communication, the wishes and schemes of every enterprising person in the colonies of Darien and Panama were turned towards the wealth of those unknown regions. In an age when the spirit of adventure was so ardent and vigorous, that large fortunes were wasted, and the most alarming dangers braved, in pursuit of discoveries merely possible, the faintest ray of hope was followed with an eager expectation, and the slightest information was sufficient to inspire such perfect confidence as conducted men to the most arduous undertakings [125].

Accordingly, several armaments were fitted out in order to explore and take possession of the countries to the east of Panama, but under the conduct of leaders whose talents and resources were unequal to the attempt.* As the excursions of those adventurers did not extend beyond the limits of the province to which the Spaniards have given the name of Tierra Firme, a mountainous region covered with woods, thinly inhabited, and extremely unhealthy, they returned with dismal accounts concerning the distresses to which they had been exposed, and the unpromising aspect of the places which they had visited. Damped by these tidings, the rage for discovery in that direction abated; and it became the general opinion that Balboa had founded visionary hopes, on the tale of an ignorant Indian, ill understood, or calculated to deceive.

1524.] But there were three persons settled in Panama, on whom the circumstances which deterred others made so little impression, that, at the very moment when all considered Balboa's expectations of discovering a rich country, by steering towards the east, as chimerical, they resolved to attempt the execution of his scheme. The names of those extraordinary men were Francisco Pizarro, Diego de Almagro, and Hernando Luque Pizarro was the natural son of a gentleman of an honourable family by a very low woman, and, according to the cruel fate which often attends the offspring of unlawful love, had been so totally neglected in his youth by the author of his birth, that he seems to have destined him never to rise beyond the condition of his mother. In consequence of this ungenerous idea, he set him, when bordering on manhood, to keep hogs. But the aspiring mind of young Pizarro disdaining that ignoble occupation, he abruptly abandoned his charge, enlisted as a soldier, and after serving some years in Italy, embarked for America, which, by opening such a boundless range to active talents, allured every adventurer whose fortune was not equal to his ambitious thoughts. There Pizarro early distinguished himself. With a temper of mind no less daring than the constitution of his body was robust, he was foremost in every danger, patient under the greatest hardships, and unsubdued by any fatigue. Though so illiterate that he could not even read, he was soon considered as a man formed to command. Every operation committed to his conduct proved successful, as, by a happy but rare conjunction, he united perseverance with ardour, and was as cautious in executing as he was bold in forming his plans. By engaging early in active life, without any resource but his own talents and industry, and by depending on himself alone in his struggles to emerge from obscurity, he acquired such a thorough knowledge of affairs, and of

* Calancha Coronica, p. 100

men, that he was fitted to assume a superior part in conducting the former, and in governing the latter.*

Almagro had as little to boast of his descent as Pizarro. The one was a bastard, the other a foundling. Bred, like his companion, in the camp, he yielded not to him in any of the soldierly qualities of intrepid valour, indefatigable activity, or insurmountable constancy in enduring the hardships inseparable from military service in the New World. But in Almagro these virtues were accompanied with the openness, generosity, and candour, natural to men whose profession is arms; in Pizarro, they were united with the address, the craft, and the dissimulation of a politician, with the art of concealing his own purposes, and with sagacity to penetrate into those of other men.

Hernando de Luque was an ecclesiastic, who acted both as priest and schoolmaster at Panama, and, by means which the contemporary writers have not described, had amassed riches that inspired him with thoughts of rising to greater eminence.

Such were the men destined to overturn one of the most extensive empires on the face of the earth. Their confederacy for this purpose was authorized by Pedrarias, the governor of Panama. Each engaged to employ his whole fortune in the adventure. Pizarro, the least wealthy of the three, as he could not throw so large a sum as his associates into the common stock, engaged to take the department of greatest fatigue and danger, and to command in person the armament which was to go first upon discovery. Almagro offered to conduct the supplies of provisions and reinforcements of troops, of which Pizarro might stand in need. Luque was to remain at Panama to negotiate with the governor, and superintend whatever was carrying on for the general interest. As the spirit of enthusiasm uniformly accompanied that of adventure in the New World, and by that strange union both acquired an increase of force, this confederacy, formed by ambition and avarice, was confirmed by the most solemn act of religion. Luque celebrated mass, divided a consecrated host into three, and, reserving one part to himself, gave the other two to his associates, of which they partook; and thus, in the name of the Prince of Peace, ratified a contract of which plunder and bloodshed were the objects.†

The attempt was begun with a force more suited to the humble condition of the three associates than to the greatness of the enterprise in which they were engaged. Pizarro set sail from Panama [Nov. 14], with a single vessel of small burden and a hundred and twelve men. But in that age, so little were the Spanish acquainted with the peculiarities of the climate in America, that the time which Pizarro chose for his departure was the most improper in the whole year; the periodical winds, which were then set in, being directly adverse to the course which he proposed to steer.‡ After beating about for seventy days, with much danger and incessant fatigue, Pizarro's progress towards the south-east was not greater than what a skilful navigator will now make in as many hours. He touched at several places on the coast of Tierra Firme, but found every where the same uninviting country which former adventurers had described; the low grounds converted into swamps by an overflowing of rivers; the higher, covered with impervious woods; few inhabitants, and those fierce and hostile. Famine, fatigue, frequent rencounters with the natives, and, above all, the distempers of a moist, sultry climate, combined in wasting his slender band of followers. [1525.] The undaunted resolution of their leader continued, however, for some time, to sustain their spirits, although no sign had yet appeared of discovering those golden regions to which he

* Herrera, dec. 1 & 2. passim, dec. 4. lib. vi. c. 107. Gomara Hist. c. 144. Zarate, lib. iv. c. 9

† Herrera, dec. 3. lib. vi. c. 13. Zarate, lib. i. c. 1.

‡ Ibid. dec. 4. lib. ii c. 8. Xerez, p. 179.

had promised to conduct them. At length he was obliged to abandon that inhospitable coast, and retire to Chuchama, opposite to the pearl islands, where he hoped to receive a supply of provisions and troops from Panama.

But Almagro, having sailed from that port with seventy men, stood directly towards that part of the continent where he hoped to meet with his associates. Not finding him there, he landed his soldiers, who, in searching for their companions, underwent the same distresses, and were exposed to the same dangers, which had driven them out of the country. Repulsed at length by the Indians in a sharp conflict, in which their leader lost one of his eyes by the wound of an arrow, they likewise were compelled to re-embark. Chance led them to the place of Pizarro's retreat, where they found some consolation in recounting to each other their adventures, and comparing their sufferings. As Almagro had advanced as far as the river St. Juan [June 24], in the province of Popayan, where both the country and inhabitants appeared with a more promising aspect, that dawn of better fortune was sufficient to determine such sanguine projectors not to abandon their scheme, notwithstanding all that they had suffered in prosecuting it* [126].

1526.] Almagro repaired to Panama in hopes of recruiting their shattered troops. But what he and Pizarro had suffered gave his countrymen such an unfavourable idea of the service, that it was with difficulty he could levy fourscore men.† Feeble as this reinforcement was, Almagro took the command of it, and, having joined Pizarro, they did not hesitate about resuming their operations. After a long series of disasters and disappointments, not inferior to those which they had already experienced, part of the armament reached the Bay of St. Matthew, on the coast of Quito, and landing at Tacamez, to the south of the river of Emeraulds, they beheld a country more champaign and fertile than any they had yet discovered in the Southern Ocean, the natives clad in garments of woollen or cotton stuff, and adorned with several trinkets of gold and silver.

But notwithstanding those favourable appearances, magnified beyond the truth, both by the vanity of the persons who brought the report from Tacamez, and by the fond imagination of those who listened to them, Pizarro and Almagro durst not venture to invade a country so populous with a handful of men enfeebled by fatigue and diseases. They retired to the small island of Gallo, where Pizarro remained with part of the troops, and his associate returned to Panama, in hopes of bringing such a reinforcement as might enable them to take possession of the opulent territories whose existence seemed to be no longer doubtful.‡

But some of the adventurers, less enterprising, or less hardy, than their leaders, having secretly conveyed lamentable accounts of their sufferings and losses to their friends at Panama, Almagro met with an unfavourable reception from Pedro de los Rios, who had succeeded Pedrarias in the government of that settlement. After weighing the matter with that cold economical prudence which appears the first of all virtues to persons whose limited faculties are incapable of conceiving or executing great designs, he concluded an expedition, attended with such certain waste of men, to be so detrimental to an infant and feeble colony, that he not only prohibited the raising of new levies, but despatched a vessel to bring home Pizarro and his companions from the island of Gallo. Almagro and Luque, though deeply affected with those measures, which they could not prevent, and durst not oppose, found means of communicating their sentiments privately to Pizarro, and exhorted him not to relinquish an enterprise that was the foundation of all their hopes, and the only means of re-establishing their reputation and fortune, which were both on the decline. Pizarro's mind,

* Herrera, dec. 3. lib. viii. c. 11, 12.

† Zarate, lib. i. c. 1.

‡ Xerez, 181. Herrera, dec. 3. lib. viii. c. 13.

bent with inflexible obstinacy on all its purposes, needed no incentive to persist in the scheme. He peremptorily refused to obey the governor of Panama's orders, and employed all his address and eloquence in persuading his men not to abandon him. But the incredible calamities to which they had been exposed were still so recent in their memories, and the thoughts of revisiting their families and friends, after a long absence, rushed with such joy into their minds, that when Pizarro drew a line upon the sand with his sword, permitting such as wished to return home to pass over it, only thirteen of all the daring veterans in his service had resolution to remain with their commander.*

This small but determined band, whose names the Spanish historians record with deserved praise, as the persons to whose persevering fortitude their country is indebted for the most valuable of all its American possessions, fixed their residence in the island of Gorgona. This, as it was further removed from the coast than Gallo, and uninhabited, they considered as a more secure retreat, where, unmolested, they might wait for supplies from Panama, which they trusted that the activity of their associates would be able to procure. Almagro and Luque were not inattentive or cold solicitors, and their incessant importunity was seconded by the general voice of the colony, which exclaimed loudly against the infamy of exposing brave men, engaged in the public service, and chargeable with no error but what flowed from an excess of zeal and courage, to perish like the most odious criminals in a desert island. Overcome by those entreaties and expostulations, the governor at last consented to send a small vessel to their relief. But that he might not seem to encourage Pizarro to any new enterprise, he would not permit one landman to embark on board of it.

By this time, Pizarro and his companions had remained five months in an island infamous for the most unhealthy climate in that region of America [127]. During all this period, their eyes were turned towards Panama, in hopes of succour from their countrymen; but worn out at length with fruitless expectations, and dispirited with suffering hardships of which they saw no end, they, in despair, came to a resolution of committing themselves to the ocean on a float, rather than continue in that detestable abode. But, on the arrival of the vessel from Panama, they were transported with such joy that all their sufferings were forgotten. Their hopes revived; and, with a rapid transition not unnatural among men accustomed by their mode of life to sudden vicissitudes of fortune, high confidence succeeding to extreme dejection, Pizarro easily induced not only his own followers, but the crew of the vessel from Panama, to resume his former scheme with fresh ardour. Instead of returning to Panama, they stood towards the south-east, and, more fortunate in this than in any of their past efforts, they, on the twentieth day after their departure from Gorgona, discovered the coast of Peru. After touching at several villages near the shore, which they found to be nowise inviting, they landed at Tumbez, a place of some note about three degrees south of the line, distinguished for its stately temple, and a palace of the *Incas* or sovereigns of the country.† There the Spaniards feasted their eyes with the first view of the opulence and civilization of the Peruvian empire. They beheld a country fully peopled, and cultivated with an appearance of regular industry; the natives decently clothed, and possessed of ingenuity so far surpassing the other inhabitants of the New World as to have the use of tame domestic animals. But what chiefly attracted their notice was such a show of gold and silver, not only in the ornaments of their persons and temples, but in several vessels and utensils for common use, formed of those precious metals, as left no room to doubt that they abounded with profusion in the country. Pizarro and his companions

* Herrera, dec. 3. lib. x. c 2, 3. Zarate, lib. i. c. 2. Xerez, 181. Gomara Hist c. 109.

† Calancha, p. 103

seemed now to have attained to the completion of their most sanguine hopes, and fancied that all their wishes and dreams of rich domains, and inexhaustible treasures, would soon be realized.

But with the slender force then under his command, Pizarro could only view the rich country of which he hoped hereafter to obtain possession. He ranged, however, for some time along the coast, maintaining every where a peaceable intercourse with the natives, no less astonished at their new visitants than the Spaniards were with the uniform appearance of opulence and cultivation which they beheld. [1527.] Having explored the country as far as requisite to ascertain the importance of the discovery, Pizarro procured from the inhabitants some of their *Llamas* or tame cattle, to which the Spaniards gave the name of sheep, some vessels of gold and silver, as well as some specimens of their other works of ingenuity, and two young men, whom he proposed to instruct in the Castilian language, that they might serve as interpreters in the expedition which he meditated. With these he arrived at Panama, towards the close of the third year from the time of his departure thence.* No adventurer of the age suffered hardships or encountered dangers which equal those to which he was exposed during this long period. The patience with which he endured the one, and the fortitude with which he surmounted the other, exceed whatever is recorded in the history of the New World, where so many romantic displays of those virtues occur.

1528.] Neither the splendid relation that Pizarro gave of the incredible opulence of the country which he had discovered, nor his bitter complaints on account of that unreasonable recall of his forces, which had put it out of his power to attempt making any settlement there, could move the governor of Panama to swerve from his former plan of conduct. He still contended, that the colony was not in a condition to invade such a mighty empire, and refused to authorize an expedition which he foresaw would be so alluring that it might ruin the province in which he presided, by an effort beyond its strength. His coldness, however, did not in any degree abate the ardour of the three associates; but they perceived that they could not carry their scheme into execution without the countenance of superior authority, and must solicit their sovereign to grant that permission which they could not extort from his delegate. With this view, after adjusting among themselves that Pizarro should claim the station of governor, Almagro that of lieutenant-governor, and Luque the dignity of bishop in the country which they proposed to conquer, they sent Pizarro as their agent to Spain, though their fortunes were now so much exhausted by the repeated efforts which they had made, that they found some difficulty in borrowing the small sum requisite towards equipping him for the voyage.†

Pizarro lost no time in repairing to court; and new as the scene might be to him, he appeared before the emperor with the unembarrassed dignity of a man conscious of what his services merited; and he conducted his negotiations with an insinuating dexterity of address, which could not have been expected either from his education or former habits of life. His feeling description of his own sufferings, and his pompous account of the country which he had discovered, confirmed by the specimens of its productions which he exhibited, made such an impression both on Charles and his ministers, that they not only approved of the intended expedition, but seemed to be interested in the success of its leader. Presuming on those dispositions in his favour, Pizarro paid little attention to the interest of his associates. As the pretensions of Luque did not interfere with his own, he obtained for him the ecclesiastical dignity to which he aspired. For Almagro he claimed only the command of the fortress which should be erected

* Herrera, dec. 3. lib. x. c. 3—6. dec. 4. lib. ii. c. 7, 8. Vega, 2. lib. i. c. 10—14. Zarate, lib. i. c 2. Benzo Hist. Novi Orbis, lib. iii. c. 1. † Herrera, dec. 4. lib. iii. c. 1. Vega, 2 lib. i. c. 14.

at Tumbez. To himself he secured whatever his boundless ambition could desire. He was appointed [July 26], governor, captain-general, and adelantado of all the country which he had discovered, and hoped to conquer, with supreme authority, civil as well as military; and with full right to all the privileges and emoluments usually granted to adventurers in the New World. His jurisdiction was declared to extend two hundred leagues along the coast to the south of the river St. Jago; to be independent of the governor of Panama; and he had power to nominate all the officers who were to serve under him. In return for those concessions, which cost the court of Spain nothing, as the enjoyment of them depended upon the success of Pizarro's own efforts, he engaged to raise two hundred and fifty men, and to provide the ships, arms, and warlike stores requisite towards subjecting to the crown of Castile the country of which the government was allotted him.

1529.] Inconsiderable as the body of men was which Pizarro had undertaken to raise, his funds and credit were so low that he could hardly complete half the number; and after obtaining his patents from the crown, he was obliged to steal privately out of the port of Seville, in order to elude the scrutiny of the officers, who had it in charge to examine whether he had fulfilled the stipulations in his contract.* Before his departure, however, he received some supply of money from Cortes, who having returned to Spain about this time, was willing to contribute his aid towards enabling an ancient companion, with whose talents and courage he was well acquainted, to begin a career of glory similar to that which he himselt had finished.†

He landed at Nombre de Dios, and marched across the isthmus to Panama, accompanied by his three brothers Ferdinand, Juan, and Gonzalo, of whom the first was born in lawful wedlock, the two latter, like himself, were of illegitimate birth, and by Francisco de Alcantara, his mother's brother. They were all in the prime of life, and of such abilities and courage as fitted them to take a distinguished part in his subsequent transactions.

1530.] On his arrival at Panama, Pizarro found Almagro so much exasperated at the manner in which he had conducted his negotiation, that he not only refused to act any longer in concert with a man by whose perfidy he had been excluded from the power and honours to which he had a just claim, but laboured to form a new association, in order to thwart or to rival his former confederate in his discoveries. Pizarro, however, had more wisdom and address than to suffer a rupture so fatal to all his schemes, to become irreparable. By offering voluntarily to relinquish the office of adelantado, and promising to concur in soliciting that title, with an independent government for Almagro, he gradually mitigated the rage of an open-hearted soldier, which had been violent, but was not implacable. Luque, highly satisfied with having been successful in all his own pretensions, cordially seconded Pizarro's endeavours. A reconciliation was effected, and the confederacy renewed on its original terms, that the enterprise should be carried on at the common expense of the associates, and the profits accruing from it should be equally divided among them.‡

Even after their reunion, and the utmost efforts of their interest, three small vessels, with a hundred and eighty soldiers, thirty-six of whom were horsemen, composed the armament which they were able to fit out. But the astonishing progress of the Spaniards in America had inspired them with such ideas of their own superiority, that Pizarro did not hesitate to sail with this contemptible force, [Feb. 1531] to invade a great empire. Almagro was left at Panama, as formerly, to follow him with what rein-

* Herrera, dec. 4. lib. vii. c. 9. † Ibid. lib. vii. c. 10. ‡ Ibid. dec. 4. lib. vii. c. 9. Zarat lib. i. c. 3. Vega, 2. lib. i. c. 14.

forcement of men he should be able to muster. As the season for embarking was properly chosen, and the course of navigation between Panama and Peru was now better known, Pizarro completed the voyage in thirteen days; though by the force of the winds and currents he was carried above a hundred leagues to the north of Tumbez, the place of his destination, and obliged to land his troops in the bay of Saint Matthew. Without losing a moment, he began to advance towards the south, taking care, however, not to depart far from the seashore, both that he might easily effect a junction with the supplies which he expected from Panama, and secure a retreat in case of any disaster, by keeping as near as possible to his ships. But as the country in several parts on the coast of Peru is barren, unhealthful, and thinly peopled; as the Spaniards had to pass all the rivers near their mouth, where the body of water is greatest; and as the imprudence of Pizarro, in attacking the natives when he should have studied to gain their confidence, had forced them to abandon their habitations; famine, fatigue, and diseases of various kinds brought upon him and his followers, calamities hardly inferior to those which they had endured in their former expedition. What they now experienced corresponded so ill with the alluring description of the country given by Pizarro, that many began to reproach him, and every soldier must have become cold to the service, if even in this unfertile region of Peru, they had not met with some appearances of wealth and cultivation, which seemed to justify the report of their leader. At length they reached the province of Coaque [April 14]; and having surprised the principal settlement of the natives, they seized their vessels and ornaments of gold and silver, to the amount of thirty thousand pesos, with other booty of such value as dispelled all their doubts, and inspired the most desponding with sanguine hopes.*

Pizarro himself was so much delighted with this rich spoil, which he considered as the first fruits of a land abounding with treasure, that he instantly despatched one of his ships to Panama with a large remittance to Almagro; and another to Nicaragua with a considerable sum to several persons of influence in that province, in hopes of alluring adventurers by this early display of the wealth which he had acquired. Meanwhile, he continued his march along the coast, and disdaining to employ any means of reducing the natives but force, he attacked them with such violence in their scattered habitations, as compelled them either to retire into the interior country, or to submit to his yoke. This sudden appearance of invaders, whose aspect and manners were so strange, and whose power seemed to be so irresistible, made the same dreadful impression as in other parts of America. Pizarro hardly met with resistance until he attacked the island of Puna in the bay of Guayaquil. As that was better peopled than the country through which he had passed, and its inhabitants fiercer and less civilized than those of the continent, they defended themselves with such obstinate valour, that Pizarro spent six months in reducing them to subjection. From Puna he proceeded to Tumbez, where the distempers which raged among his men compelled him to remain for three months.†

While he was thus employed, he began to reap advantage from his attention to spread the fame of his first success to Coaque. Two different detachments arrived from Nicaragua [1532], which, though neither exceeded thirty men, he considered as a reinforcement of great consequence to his feeble band, especially as the one was under the command of Sebastian Benalcazar, and the other of Hernando Soto, officers not inferior in merit and reputation to any who had served in America. From Tumbez he proceeded to the river Piura [May 16], and in an advantageous station near the mouth of it he established the first Spanish colony in Peru; to which he gave the name of St. Michael.

* Herrera, dec. 4. lib. vii. c. 9. lib. ii. c. 1. Xerez, 182.

† P. Sancho ap Ramus. iii. p. 371. F Herrera, dec. 4. lib. vii. c. 18. lib. ix. c. 1. Zarate, lib. ii. c. 2, 3. Xerez, p. 182, &c.

As Pizarro continued to advance towards the centre of the Peruvian empire, he gradually received more full information concerning its extent and policy, as well as the situation of its affairs at that juncture. Without some knowledge of these, he could not have conducted his operations with propriety; and without a suitable attention to them, it is impossible to account for the progress which the Spaniards had already made, or to unfold the causes of their subsequent success.

At the time when the Spaniards invaded Peru, the dominions of its sovereigns extended in length, from north to south, above fifteen hundred miles along the Pacific Ocean. Its breadth, from east to west, was much less considerable; being uniformly bounded by the vast ridge of the Andes, stretching from its one extremity to the other. Peru, like the rest of the New World, was originally possessed by small independent tribes, differing from each other in manners, and in their forms of rude policy. All, however, were so little civilized, that, if the traditions concerning their mode of life, preserved among their descendants, deserve credit, they must be classed among the most unimproved savages of America. Strangers to every species of cultivation or regular industry, without any fixed residence, and unacquainted with those sentiments and obligations which form the first bonds of social union, they are said to have roamed about naked in the forests, with which the country was then covered, more like wild beasts than like men. After they had struggled for several ages with the hardships and calamities which are inevitable in such a state, and when no circumstance seemed to indicate the approach of any uncommon effort towards improvement, we are told that there appeared, on the banks of the lake Titiaca, a man and woman of majestic form, clothed in decent garments. They declared themselves to be children of the Sun, sent by their beneficent parent, who beheld with pity the miseries of the human race, to instruct and to reclaim them. At their persuasion, enforced by reverence for the divinity in whose name they were supposed to speak, several of the dispersed savages united together, and, receiving their commands as heavenly injunctions, followed them to Cuzco, where they settled, and began to lay the foundations of a city.

Manco Capac and Mama Ocollo, for such were the names of those extraordinary personages, having thus collected some wandering tribes, formed that social union which, by multiplying the desires and uniting the efforts of the human species, excites industry and leads to improvement. Manco Capac instructed the men in agriculture, and other useful arts. Mama Ocollo taught the women to spin and to weave. By the labour of the one sex, subsistence became less precarious; by that of the other, life was rendered more comfortable. After securing the objects of first necessity in an infant state, by providing food, raiment, and habitations for the rude people of whom he took charge, Manco Capac turned his attention towards introducing such laws and policy as might perpetuate their happiness. By his institutions, which shall be more particularly explained hereafter, the various relations in private life were established, and the duties resulting from them prescribed with such propriety, as gradually formed a barbarous people to decency of manners. In public administration, the functions of persons in authority were so precisely defined, and the subordination of those under their jurisdiction maintained with such a steady hand, that the society in which he presided soon assumed the aspect of a regular and well governed state.

Thus, according to the Indian tradition, was founded the empire of the *Incas* or *Lords* of Peru. At first its extent was small. The territory of Manco Capac did not reach above eight leagues from Cuzco. But within its narrow precincts he exercised absolute and uncontrolled authority. His successors, as their dominions extended, arrogated a similar jurisdiction over the new subjects which they acquired; the despotism of Asia was not more complete. The Incas were not only obeyed as monarchs, but revered as divinities. Their blood was held to be sacred, and, by prohibiting intermarriages with the people, was never contaminated by mixing with that of any other race. The family, thus separated from the rest of the nation, was distinguished by peculiarities in dress and ornaments, which it was unlawful for others to assume. The monarch himself appeared with ensigns of royalty reserved for him alone; and received from his subjects marks of obsequious homage and respect which approached almost to adoration.

But, among the Peruvians, this unbounded power of their monarch seems to have been uniformly accompanied with attention to the good o their subjects. It was not the rage of conquest, if we may believe the accounts of their countrymen, that prompted the Incas to extend their dominions, but the desire of diffusing the blessings of civilization, and the knowledge of the arts which they possessed, among the barbarous people whom they reduced. During a succession of twelve monarchs, it is said that not one deviated from this beneficent character.*

When the Spaniards first visited the coast of Peru, in the year one thousand five hundred and twenty-six, Huana Capac, the twelfth monarch from the founder of the state, was seated on the throne. He is represented as a prince distinguished not only for the pacific virtues peculiar to the race, but eminent for his martial talents. By his victorious arms the kingdom of Quito was subjected, a conquest of such extent and importance as almost doubled the power of the Peruvian empire. He was fond of residing in the capital of that valuable province which he had added to his dominions; and notwithstanding the ancient and fundamental law of the monarchy against polluting the royal blood by any foreign alliance, he married the daughter of the vanquished monarch of Quito. She bore him a son named Atahualpa, whom, on his death at Quito, which seems to have happened about the year one thousand five hundred and twenty-nine, he appointed his successor in that kingdom, leaving the rest of his dominions to Huascar, his eldest son by another of the royal race. Greatly as the Peruvians revered the memory of a monarch who had reigned with greater reputation and splendour than any of his predecessors, the destination of Huana Capac concerning the succession appeared so repugnant to a maxim coeval with the empire, and founded on authority deemed sacred, that it was no sooner known at Cuzco than it excited general disgust. Encouraged by those sentiments of his subjects, Huascar required his brother to renounce the government of Quito, and to acknowledge him as his lawful superior. But it had been the first care of Atahualpa to gain a large body of troops which had accompanied his father to Quito. These were the flower of the Peruvian warriors, to whose valour Huana Capac had been indebted for all his victories. Relying on their support, Atahualpa first eluded his brother's demand, and then marched against him in hostile array.

Thus the ambition of two young men, the title of the one founded on ancient usage, and that of the other asserted by the veteran troops, involved Peru in a civil war, a calamity to which, under a succession of virtuous princes, it had hitherto been a stranger. In such a contest the issue was obvious. The force of arms triumphed over the authority of laws Atahualpa remained victorious, and made a cruel use of his victory. Conscious of the defect in his own title to the crown, he attempted to exterminate the royal race, by putting to death all the children of the Sun descended from Manco Capac, whom he could seize either by force or stratagem. From a political motive, the life of his unfortunate rival Huascar, who had been taken prisoner in a battle which decided the fate

* Cieca de Leon, Chron. c. 44, Herrera, dec. 3. lib. x. c. 4. dec. 5. lib. iii. c. 17.

of the empire, was prolonged for some time, that by issuing orders in his name, the usurper might more easily establish his own authority.*

When Pizarro landed in the bay of St. Matthew, this civil war raged between the two brothers in its greatest fury. Had he made any hostile attempt in his former visit to Peru, in the year one thousand five hundred and twenty-seven, he must then have encountered the force of a powerful state, united under a monarch possessed of capacity as well as courage, and unembarrassed with any care that could divert him from opposing his progress. But at this time, the two competitors, though they received early accounts of the arrival and violent proceedings of the Spaniards, were so intent upon the operations of a war which they deemed more interesting, that they paid no attention to the motions of an enemy, too inconsiderable in number to excite any great alarm, and to whom it would be easy, as they imagined, to give a check when more at leisure.

By this fortunate coincidence of events, whereof Pizarro could have no foresight, and of which, from his defective mode of intercourse with the people of the country, he remained long ignorant, he was permitted to carry on his operations unmolested, and advanced to the centre of a great empire before one effort of its power was exerted to stop his career. During their progress, the Spaniards had acquired some imperfect knowledge of this struggle between the two contending factions. The first complete information with respect to it they received from messengers whom Huascar sent to Pizarro, in order to solicit his aid against Atahualpa, whom he represented as a rebel and a usurper.† Pizarro perceived at once the importance of this intelligence, and foresaw so clearly all the advantages which might be derived from this divided state of the kingdom which he had invaded, that without waiting for the reinforcement which he expected from Panama, he determined to push forward, while intestine discord put it out of the power of the Peruvians to attack him with their whole force, and while, by taking part, as circumstances should incline him, with one of the competitors, he might be enabled with greater ease to crush both. Enterprising as the Spaniards of that age were in all their operations against Americans, and distinguished as Pizarro was among his countrymen for daring courage, we can hardly suppose that, after having proceeded hitherto slowly, and with much caution, he would have changed at once his system of operation, and have ventured upon a measure so hazardous, without some new motive or prospect to justify it.

As he was obliged to divide his troops, in order to leave a garrison in St. Michael, sufficient to defend a station of equal importance as a place of retreat in case of any disaster, and as a port for receiving any supplies which should come from Panama, he began his march with a very slender and ill-accoutred train of followers. They consisted of sixty-two horsemen [128], and a hundred and two foot soldiers, of whom twenty were armed with cross bows, and three with muskets. He directed his course towards Caxamalca, a small town at the distance of twelve days' march from St. Michael, where Atahualpa was encamped with a considerable body of troops. Before he had proceeded far, an officer despatched by the Inca met him with a valuable present from that prince, accompanied with a proffer of his alliance, and assurances of a friendly reception at Caxamalca. Pizarro, according to the usual artifice of his countrymen in America, pretended to come as the ambassador of a very powerful monarch, and declaring that he was now advancing with an intention to offer Atahualpa his aid against those enemies who disputed his title to the throne.‡

As the object of the Spaniards in entering their country was altogether

* Zarate, lib. i. c. 15. Vega, 1. lib. ix. c. 12. and 32—40. Herrera, dec. 5. lib. i. c. 2. lib. iii. c. 17.
† Zarate, lib. ii. c. 3. ‡ Herrera, dec. 5. lib. i. c. 3. Xerez, p. 189

incomprehensible to the Peruvians, they had formed various conjectures concerning it without being able to decide whether they should consider their new guests as beings of a superior nature, who had visited them from some beneficent motive, or as formidable avengers of their crimes, and enemies to their repose and liberty. The continual professions of the Spaniards, that they came to enlighten them with the knowledge of truth, and lead them in the way of happiness, favoured the former opinion; the outrages which they committed, their rapaciousness and cruelty, were awful confirmations of the latter. While in this state of uncertainty, Pizarro's declaration of his pacific intentions so far removed all the Inca's fears that he determined to give him a friendly reception. In consequence of this resolution, the Spaniards were allowed to march in tranquillity across the sandy desert between St. Michael and Motupe, where the most feeble effort of an enemy, added to the unavoidable distresses which they suffered in passing through that comfortless region, must have proved fatal to them [129]. From Motupe they advanced towards the mountains which encompassed the low country of Peru, and passed through a defile so narrow and inaccessible, that a few men might have defended it against a numerous army. But here likewise, from the same inconsiderate credulity of the Inca, the Spaniards met with no opposition, and took quiet possession of a fort erected for the security of that important station. As they now approached near to Caxamalca, Atahualpa renewed his professions of friendship; and, as an evidence of their sincerity, sent them presents of greater value than the former.

On entering Caxamalca, Pizarro took possession of a large court, on one side of which was a house which the Spanish historians call a palace of the Inca, and on the other a temple of the Sun, the whole surrounded with a strong rampart or wall of earth. When he had posted his troops in this advantageous station, he despatched his brother Ferdinand and Hernando Soto to the camp of Atahualpa, which was about a league distant from the town. He instructed them to confirm the declaration which he had formerly made of his pacific disposition, and to desire an interview with the Inca, that he might explain more fully the intention of the Spaniards in visiting his country. They were treated with all the respectful hospitality usual among the Peruvians in the reception of their most cordial friends, and Atahualpa promised to visit the Spanish commander next day in his quarters. The decent deportment of the Peruvian monarch, the order of his court, and the reverence with which his subjects approached his person and obeyed his commands, astonished those Spaniards who had never met in America with any thing more dignified than the petty cazique of a barbarous tribe. But their eyes were still powerfully attracted by the vast profusion of wealth which they observed in the Inca's camp. The rich ornaments worn by him and his attendants, the vessels of gold and silver in which the repast offered to them was served up, the multitude of utensils of every kind formed of those precious metals, opened prospects far exceeding any idea of opulence that a European of the sixteenth century could form.

On their return to Caxamalca, while their minds were yet warm with admiration and desire of the wealth which they had beheld, they gave such a description of it to their countrymen as confirmed Pizarro in a resolution which he had already taken. From his own observation of American manners during his long service in the New World, as well as from the advantages which Cortes had derived from seizing Montezuma, he knew of what consequence it was to have the Inca in his power. For this purpose, he formed a plan as daring as it was perfidious. Notwithstanding the character that he had assumed of an ambassador from a powerful monarch, who courted an alliance with the Inca, and in violation of the repeated offers which he had made to him of his own friendship and assistance, he determined to avail himself of the unsuspicious simplicity with which Atahualpa relied on his professions, and to seize the person of the Inca during the interview to which he had invited him. He prepared for the execution of his scheme with the same deliberate arrangement, and with as little compunction as if it had reflected no disgrace on himself or his country. He divided his cavalry into three small squadrons, under the command of his brother Ferdinand, Soto, and Benalcazar; his infantry were formed in one body, except twenty of most tried courage, whom he kept near his own person to support him in the dangerous service, which he reserved for himself; the artillery, consisting of two fieldpieces,* and the cross bowmen, were placed opposite to the avenue by which Atahualpa was to approach. All were commanded to keep within the square, and not to move until the signal for action was given.

Early in the morning [Nov. 16] the Peruvian camp was all in motion. But as Atahualpa was solicitous to appear with the greatest splendour and magnificence in his first interview with the strangers, the preparations for this were so tedious that the day was far advanced before he began his march. Even then, lest the order of the procession should be deranged, he moved so slowly, that the Spaniards became impatient, and apprehensive that some suspicion of their intention might be the cause of this delay. In order to remove this, Pizarro despatched one of his officers with fresh assurances of his friendly disposition. At length the Inca approached. First of all appeared four hundred men, in a uniform dress, as harbingers to clear the way before him. He himself, sitting on a throne or couch adorned with plumes of various colours, and almost covered with plates of gold and silver enriched with precious stones, was carried on the shoulders of his principal attendants. Behind him came some chief officers of his court, carried in the same manner. Several bands of singers and dancers accompanied this cavalcade; and the whole plain was covered with troops, amounting to more than thirty thousand men.

As the Inca drew near the Spanish quarters, Father Vincent Valverde, chaplain to the expedition, advanced with a crucifix in one hand, and a breviary in the other, and in a long discourse explained to him the doctrine of the creation, the fall of Adam, the incarnation, the sufferings and resurrection of Jesus Christ, the appointment of St. Peter as God's vicegerent on earth, the transmission of his apostolic power by succession to the Popes, the donation made to the King of Castile by Pope Alexander of all the regions of the New World. In consequence of all this, he required Atahualpa to embrace the Christian faith, to acknowledge the supreme jurisdiction of the Pope, and to submit to the King of Castile as his lawful sovereign; promising, if he complied instantly with this requisition, that the Castilian monarch would protect his dominions, and permit him to continue in the exercise of his royal authority; but if he should impiously refuse to obey this summons, he denounced war against him in his master's name, and threatened him with the most dreadful effects of his vengeance.

This strange harangue, unfolding deep mysteries, and alluding to unknown facts, of which no power of eloquence could have conveyed at once a distinct idea to an American, was so lamely translated by an unskilful interpreter, little acquainted with the idiom of the Spanish tongue, and incapable of expressing himself with propriety in the language of the Inca, that its general tenour was altogether incomprehensible to Atahualpa. Some parts in it, of more obvious meaning, filled him with astonishment and indignation. His reply, however, was temperate. He began with observing, that he was lord of the dominions over which he reigned by hereditary succession; and added, that he could not conceive how a foreign priest should pretend to dispose of territories which did not belong to him; that

* Xerez, p. 194

if such a preposterous grant had been made, he, who was the rightful possessor, refused to confirm it; that he had no inclination to renounce the religious institutions established by his ancestors; nor would he forsake the service of the Sun, the immortal divinity whom he and his people revered, in order to worship the God of the Spaniards, who was subject to death; that with respect to other matters contained in his discourse, as he had never heard of them before, and did not now understand their meaning, he desired to know where the priest had learned things so extraordi nary. "In this book," answered Valverde, reaching out to him his breviary. The Inca opened it eagerly, and, turning over the leaves, lifted it to his ear: "This," says he, "is silent; it tells me nothing;" and threw it with disdain to the ground. The enraged monk, running towards his countrymen, cried out, "To arms, Christians, to arms; the word of God is insulted; avenge this profanation on those impious dogs" [130].

Pizarro, who, during this long conference, had with difficulty restrained his soldiers, eager to seize the rich spoils of which they had now so near a view, immediately gave the signal of assault. At once the martial music struck up, the cannon and muskets began to fire, the horse sallied out fiercely to the charge, the infantry rushed on sword in hand. The Peruvians, astonished at the suddenness of an attack which they did not expect, and dismayed with the destructive effect of the firearms, and the irresistible impression of the cavalry, fled with universal consternation on every side, without attempting either to annoy the enemy, or to defend themselves. Pizarro, at the head of his chosen band, advanced directly towards the Inca; and though his nobles crowded around him with officious zeal, and fell in numbers at his feet, while they vied one with another in sacrificing their own lives, that they might cover the sacred person of their sovereign, the Spaniards soon penetrated to the royal seat; and Pizarro, seizing the Inca by the arm, dragged him to the ground, and carried him as a prisoner to his quarters. The fate of the monarch increased the precipitate flight of his followers. The Spaniards pursued them towards every quarter, and with deliberate and unrelenting barbarity continued to slaughter wretched fugitives, who never once offered to resist. The carnage did not cease until the close of day. Above four thousand Peruvians were killed. Not a single Spaniard fell, nor was one wounded but Pizarro himself, whose hand was slightly hurt by one of his own soldiers, while struggling eagerly to lay hold on the Inca [131].

The plunder of the field was rich beyond any idea which the Spaniards had yet formed concerning the wealth of Peru; and they were so transported with the value of the acquisition, as well as the greatness of their success, that they passed the night in the extravagant exultation natural to indigent adventurers on such an extraordinary change of fortune.

At first the captive monarch could hardly believe a calamity which he so little expected to be real. But he soon felt all the misery of his fate, and the dejection into which he sunk was in proportion to the height of grandeur from which he had fallen. Pizarro, afraid of losing all the advantages which he hoped to derive from the possession of such a prisoner, laboured to console him with professions of kindness and respect, that corresponded ill with his actions. By residing among the Spaniards, the Inca quickly discovered their ruling passion, which indeed they were nowise solicitous to conceal, and, by applying to that, made an attempt to recover his liberty. He offered as a ransom what astonished the Spaniards, even after all they now knew concerning the opulence of his kingdom. The apartment in which he was confined was twenty-two feet in length and sixteen in breadth; he undertook to fill it with vessels of gold as high as he could reach. Pizarro closed eagerly with this tempting proposal, and a line was drawn upon the walls of the chamber, to mark the stipulated height to which the treasure was to rise.

Atahualpa, transported with having obtained some prospect of liberty took measures instantly for fulfilling his part of the agreement, by sending messengers to Cuzco, Quito, and other places, where gold had been amassed in largest quantities, either for adorning the temples of the gods, or the houses of the Inca, to bring what was necessary for completing his ransom directly to Caxamalca. Though Atahualpa was now in the custody of his enemies, yet so much were the Peruvians accustomed to respect every mandate issued by their sovereign, that his orders were executed with the greatest alacrity. Soothed with hopes of recovering his liberty by this means, the subjects of the Inca were afraid of endangering his life by forming any other scheme for his relief; and though the force of the empire was still entire, no preparations were made, and no army assembled to avenge their own wrongs or those of their monarch.* The Spaniards remained in Caxamalca tranquil and unmolested. Small detachments of their number marched into remote provinces of the empire, and, instead of meeting with any opposition, were every where received with marks of the most submissive respect [132].

Inconsiderable as those parties were, and desirous as Pizarro might be to obtain some knowledge of the interior state of the country, he could not have ventured upon any diminution of his main body, if he had not about this time [December], received an account of Almagro's having landed at St. Michael with such a reinforcement as would almost double the number of his followers.† The arrival of this long expected succour was not more agreeable to the Spaniards than alarming to the Inca. He saw the power of his enemies increase; and as he knew neither the source whence they derived their supplies, nor the means by which they were conveyed to Peru, he could not foresee to what a height the inundation that poured in upon his dominions might rise [1533]. While disquieted with such apprehensions, he learned that some Spaniards, in their way to Cuzco, had visited his brother Huascar in the place where he kept him confined, and that the captive prince had represented to them the justice of his own cause, and, as an inducement to espouse it, had promised them a quantity of treasure greatly beyond that which Atahualpa had engaged to pay for his ransom. If the Spaniards should listen to this proposal, Atahualpa perceived his own destruction to be inevitable; and suspecting that their insatiable thirst for gold would tempt them to lend a favourable ear to it, he determined to sacrifice his brother's life that he might save his own; and his orders for this purpose were executed, like all his other commands, with scrupulous punctuality.‡

Meanwhile, Indians daily arrived at Caxamalca from different parts of the kingdom, loaded with treasure. A great part of the stipulated quantity was now amassed, and Atahualpa assured the Spaniards that the only thing which prevented the whole from being brought in, was the remoteness of the provinces where it was deposited. But such vast piles of gold presented continually to the view of needy soldiers, had so inflamed their avarice, that it was impossible any longer to restrain their impatience to obtain possession of this rich booty. Orders were given for melting down the whole, except some pieces of curious fabric reserved as a present for the emperor. After setting apart the fifth due to the crown, and a hundred thousand pesos as a donative to the soldiers which arrived with Almagro, there remained one million five hundred and twenty-eight thousand five hundred pesos to Pizarro and his followers. The festival of St. James [July 25], the patron saint of Spain, was the day chosen for the partition of this enormous sum, and the manner of conducting it strongly marks the strange alliance of fanaticism with avarice, which I have more than once

* Xerez, 205. † Ibid. 204. Herrera, dec. 5. lib. iii. c. 1, 2. ‡ Zarate, lib. ii. c. 6 Gomara, Hist. c. 115. Herrera, dec. 5. lib. iii. c. 2.

had occasion to point out as a striking feature in the character of the conquerors of the New World. Though assembled to divide the spoils of an innocent people, procured by deceit, extortion, and cruelty, the transaction began with a solemn invocation of the name of God,* as if they could have expected the guidance of heaven in distributing those wages of iniquity. In this division above eight thousand pesos, at that time not inferior in effective value to as many pounds sterling in the present century, fell to the share of each horseman, and half that sum to each foot soldier. Pizarro himself, and his officers, received dividends in proportion to the dignity of their rank.

There is no example in history of such a sudden acquisition of wealth by military service, nor was ever a sum so great divided among so small a number of soldiers. Many of them having received a recompense for their services far beyond their most sanguine hopes, were so impatient to retire from fatigue and danger, in order to spend the remainder of their days in their native country in ease and opulence, that they demanded their discharge with clamorous importunity. Pizarro, sensible that from such men he could expect neither enterprise in action nor fortitude in suffering, and persuaded that wherever they went the display of their riches would allure adventurers, less opulent but more hardy, to his standard, granted their suit without reluctance, and permitted above sixty of them to accompany his brother Ferdinand, whom he sent to Spain with an account of his success, and the present destined for the emperor.†

The Spaniards having divided among them the treasure amassed for the Inca's ransom, he insisted with them to fulfil their promise of setting him at liberty. But nothing was further from Pizarro's thoughts. During his long service in the New World, he had imbibed those ideas and maxims of his fellow-soldiers, which led them to consider its inhabitants as an inferior race, neither worthy of the name, nor entitled to the rights of men. In his compact with Atahualpa, he had no other object than to amuse his captive with such a prospect of recovering his liberty, as might induce him to lend all the aid of his authority towards collecting the wealth of his kingdom. Having now accomplished this, he no longer regarded his plighted faith; and at the very time when the credulous prince hoped to be replaced on his throne, he had secretly resolved to bereave him of life. Many circumstances seem to have concurred in prompting him to this action, the most criminal and atrocious that stains the Spanish name, amidst all the deeds of violence committed in carrying on the conquests of the New World.

Though Pizarro had seized the Inca in imitation of Cortes's conduct towards the Mexican monarch, he did not possess talents for carrying on the same artful plan of policy. Destitute of the temper and address requisite for gaining the confidence of his prisoner, he never reaped all the advantages which might have been derived from being master of his person and authority. Atahualpa was, indeed, a prince of greater abilities and discernment than Montezuma, and seems to have penetrated more thoroughly into the character and intentions of the Spaniards. Mutual suspicion and distrust accordingly took place between them. The strict attention with which it was necessary to guard a captive of such importance, greatly increased the fatigue of military duty. The utility of keeping him appeared inconsiderable; and Pizarro felt him as an encumbrance, from which he wished to be delivered.‡

Almagro and his followers had made a demand of an equal share in the Inca's ransom; and though Pizarro had bestowed upon the private men the large gratuity which I have mentioned, and endeavoured to soothe their leader by presents of great value, they still continued dissatisfied. They were apprehensive, that as long as Atahualpa remained a prisoner

* Herrera, dec. 5. lib. iii. c. 3.

† Ibid. dec. 5. lib. iii. c. 4. Vega, p. 2. lib i. c. 38.

‡ Herrera, dec. 5. lib. iii. c. 4.

Pizarro's soldiers would apply whatever treasure should be acquired, to make up what was wanting of the quantity stipulated for his ransom, and under that pretext exclude them from any part of it. They insisted eagerly on putting the Inca to death, that all the adventurers in Peru might thereafter be on an equal footing.*

Pizarro himself began to be alarmed with accounts of forces assembling in the remote provinces of the empire, and suspected Atahualpa of having issued orders for that purpose. These fears and suspicions were artfully increased by Philippillo, one of the Indians, whom Pizarro had carried off from Tumbez in the year one thousand five hundred and twenty-seven, and whom he employed as an interpreter. The function which he performed admitting this man to familiar intercourse with the captive monarch, he presumed, notwithstanding the meanness of his birth, to raise his affections to a Coya, or descendant of the Sun, one of Atahualpa's wives; and seeing no prospect of gratifying that passion during the life of the monarch, he endeavoured to fill the ears of the Spaniards with such accounts of the Inca's secret designs and preparations, as might awaken their jealousy, and excite them to cut him off.

While Almagro and his followers openly demanded the life of the Inca, and Philippillo laboured to ruin him by private machinations, that unhappy prince inadvertently contributed to hasten his own fate. During his confinement he had attached himself with peculiar affection to Ferdinand Pizarro and Hernando Soto; who, as they were persons of birth and education superior to the rough adventurers with whom they served, were accustomed to behave with more decency and attention to the captive monarch. Soothed with this respect from persons of such high rank, he delighted in their society. But in the presence of the governor he was always uneasy and overawed. This dread soon came to be mingled with contempt. Among all the European arts, what he admired most was that of reading and writing; and he long deliberated with himself, whether he should regard it as a natural or acquired talent. In order to determine this, he desired one of the soldiers, who guarded him, to write the name of God on the nail of his thumb. This he showed successively to several Spaniards, asking its meaning; and to his amazement, they all, without hesitation, returned the same answer. At length Pizarro entered; and, on presenting it to him, he blushed, and with some confusion was obliged to acknowledge his ignorance. From that moment Atahualpa considered him as a mean person less instructed than his own soldiers; and he had not address enough to conceal the sentiments with which this discovery inspired him. To be the object of a barbarian's scorn, not only mortified the pride of Pizarro, but excited such resentment in his breast, as added force to all the other considerations which prompted him to put the Inca to death.†

But in order to give some colour of justice to this violent action, and that he himself might be exempted from standing singly responsible for the commission of it, Pizarro resolved to try the Inca with all the formalities observed in the criminal courts of Spain. Pizarro himself, and Almagro, with two assistants, were appointed judges, with full power to acquit or to condemn; an attorney-general was named to carry on the prosecution in the king's name; counsellors were chosen to assist the prisoner in his defence; and clerks were ordained to record the proceedings of court. Before this strange tribunal, a charge was exhibited still more amazing. It consisted of various articles; that Atahualpa, though a bastard, had dispossessed the rightful owner of the throne, and usurped the regal power; that he had put his brother and lawful sovereign to death; that he was an idolater, and had not only permitted but commanded the offering of human

* Zarate, lib. ii. c. 7. Vega, p. 2. lib. i. c. 7. Herrera, dec. 5. lib. iii. c. 4.

† Herrera, dec. 5. lib. iii. c. 4. Vega, p. 11. lib. i. c. 38.

sacrifices; that he had a great number of concubines; that since his imprisonment he had wasted and embezzled the royal treasures, which now belonged of right to the conquerors; that he had incited his subjects to take arms against the Spaniards. On these heads of accusation, some of which are so ludicrous, others so absurd, that the effrontery of Pizarro, in making them the foundation of a serious procedure, is not less surprising than his injustice, did this strange court go on to try the sovereign of a great empire, over whom it had no jurisdiction. With respect to each of the articles, witnesses were examined; but as they delivered their evidence in their native tongue, Philippillo had it in his power to give their words whatever turn best suited his malevolent intentions. To judges pre-determined in their opinion, this evidence appeared sufficient. They pronounced Atahualpa guilty, and condemned him to be burnt alive. Friar Valverde prostituted the authority of his sacred function to confirm this sentence, and by his signature warranted it to be just. Astonished at his fate, Atahualpa endeavoured to avert it by tears, by promises, and by entreaties that he might be sent to Spain, where a monarch would be the arbiter of his lot. But pity never touched the unfeeling heart of Pizarro. He ordered him to be led instantly to execution; and what added to the bitterness of his last moments, the same monk who had just ratified his doom, offered to console and attempted to convert him. The most powerful argument Valverde employed to prevail with him to embrace the Christian faith, was a promise of mitigation in his punishment. The dread of a cruel death extorted from the trembling victim a desire of receiving baptism. The ceremony was performed; and Atahualpa, instead of being burnt, was strangled at the stake.*

Happily for the credit of the Spanish nation, even among the profligate adventurers which it sent forth to conquer and desolate the New World, there were persons who retained some tincture of the Castilian generosity and honour. Though, before the trial of Atahualpa, Ferdinand Pizarro had set out for Spain, and Soto was sent on a separate command at a distance from Caxamalca, this odious transaction was not carried on without censure and opposition. Several officers, and among those some of the greatest reputation and most respectable families in the service, not only remonstrated but protested against this measure of their general, as disgraceful to their country, as repugnant to every maxim of equity, as a violation of public faith, and a usurpation of jurisdiction over an independent monarch, to which they had no title. But their laudable endeavours were vain. Numbers, and the opinion of such as held every thing to be lawful which they deemed advantageous, prevailed. History, however, records even the unsuccessful exertions of virtue with applause; and the Spanish writers, in relating events where the valour of their nation is more conspicuous than its humanity, have not failed to preserve the names of those who made this laudable effort to save their country from the infamy of having perpetrated such a crime.†

On the death of Atahualpa, Pizarro invested one of his sons with the ensigns of royalty, hoping that a young man without experience might prove a more passive instrument in his hands than an ambitious monarch, who had been accustomed to independent command. The people of Cuzco, and the adjacent country, acknowledged Manco Capac, a brother of Huascar, as Inca.‡ But neither possessed the authority which belonged to a sovereign of Peru. The violent convulsions into which the empire had been thrown, first by the civil war between the two brothers, and then by the invasion of the Spaniards, had not only deranged the order of the Peruvian government, but almost dissolved its frame. When they beheld

* Zarate, lib. ii. c. 7. Xerez, p. 233. Vega, p. 11. lib. i. c 36, 37. Gomara Hist. c. 117. Herrera, dec. 3. lib. iii. c. 4.

† Vega, p. 11. lib. i. c. 37. Xerez, i. 235. Herrera, dec. 5. lib. iii. c. 5.

‡ Vega, p. 11. lib. ii. c 7.

their monarch a captive in the power of strangers, and at last suffering an ignominious death, the people in several provinces, as if they had been set free from every restraint of law and decency, broke out into the most licentious excesses.* So many descendants of the Sun, after being treated with the utmost indignity, had been cut off by Atahualpa, that not only their influence in the state diminished with their number, but the accustomed reverence for that sacred race sensibly decreased. In consequence of this state of things, ambitious men in different parts of the empire aspired to independent authority, and usurped jurisdiction to which they had no title. The general who commanded for Atahualpa in Quito, seized the brother and children of his master, put them to a cruel death, and, disclaiming any connection with either Inca, endeavoured to establish a separate kingdom for himself.†

The Spaniards with pleasure beheld the spirit of discord diffusing itself, and the vigour of government relaxing among the Peruvians. They considered those disorders as symptoms of a state hastening towards its dissolution. Pizarro no longer hesitated to advance towards Cuzco, and he had received such considerable reinforcements, that he could venture, with little danger, to penetrate so far into the interior part of the country. The account of the wealth acquired at Caxamalca operated as he had foreseen. No sooner did his brother Ferdinand, with the officers and soldiers to whom he had given their discharge after the partition of the Inca's ransom, arrive at Panama, and display their riches in the view of their astonished countrymen, than fame spread the account with such exaggeration through all the Spanish settlements on the South Sea, that the governors of Guatimala, Panama, and Nicaragua, could hardly restrain the people under their jurisdiction, from abandoning their possessions, and crowding to that inexhaustible source of wealth which seemed to be opened in Peru.‡ In spite of every check and regulation, such numbers resorted thither, that Pizarro began his march at the head of five hundred men, after leaving a considerable garrison in St. Michael, under the command of Benalcazar. The Peruvians had assembled some large bodies of troops to oppose his progress. Several fierce encounters happened. But they terminated like all the actions in America; a few Spaniards were killed or wounded; the natives were put to flight with incredible slaughter. At length Pizarro forced his way to Cuzco, and took quiet possession of that capital. The riches found there, even after all that the natives had carried off and concealed, either from a superstitious veneration for the ornaments of their temples, or out of hatred to their rapacious conquerors, exceed in value what had been received as Atahualpa's ransom. But as the Spaniards were now accustomed to the wealth of the country, and it came to be parcelled out among a great number of adventurers, this dividend did not excite the same surprise, either from novelty, or the largeness of the sum that fell to the share of each individual [133].

During the march to Cuzco, that son of Atahualpa whom Pizarro treated as Inca, died; and as the Spaniards substituted no person in his place, the title of Manco Capac seems to have been universally recognised.§

While his fellow-soldiers were thus employed, Benalcazar, governor of St. Michael, an able and enterprising officer, was ashamed of remaining inactive, and impatient to have his name distinguished among the discoverers and conquerors of the New World. The seasonable arrival of a fresh body of recruits from Panama and Nicaragua put it in his power to gratify this passion. Leaving a sufficient force to protect the infant settlement intrusted to his care, he placed himself at the head of the rest, and set out to attempt the reduction of Quito, where, according to the report of

* Herrera, dec. 5. lib. ii. c. 12. lib. iii. c. 5. † Zarate, lib. ii. c. 8. Vega, p. 11. lib. ii. c. 3, 4. ‡ Gomara Hist. c. 125. Vega, p. 11. lib. ii. c. 1. Herrera, dec. 5. lib. iii. c. 5. § Herrera, dec. 5. lib. v. c. 2.

the natives, Atahualpa had left the greatest part of his treasure. Notwithstanding the distance of that city from St. Michael, the difficulty of marching through a mountainous country covered with woods, and the frequent and fierce attacks of the best troops in Peru commanded by a skilful leader, the valour, good conduct, and perseverance of Benalcazar surmounted every obstacle, and he entered Quito with his victorious troops. But they met with a cruel mortification there. The natives now acquainted to their sorrow with the predominant passion of their invaders, and knowing how to disappoint it, had carried off all those treasures, the prospect of which had prompted them to undertake this arduous expedition, and had supported them under all the dangers and hardships wherewith they had to struggle in carrying it on.*

Benalcazar was not the only Spanish leader who attacked the kingdom of Quito. The fame of its riches attracted a more powerful enemy. Pedro de Alvarado, who had distinguished himself so eminently in the conquest of Mexico, having obtained the government of Guatimala as a recompense for his valour, soon became disgusted with a life of uniform tranquillity, and longed to be again engaged in the bustle of military service. The glory and wealth acquired by the conquerors of Peru heightened this passion, and gave it a determined direction. Believing, or pretending to believe, that the kingdom of Quito did not lie within the limits of the province allotted to Pizarro, he resolved to invade it. The high reputation of the commander allured volunteers from every quarter. He embarked with five hundred men, of whom above two hundred were of such distinction as to serve on horseback. He landed at Puerto Viejo, and without sufficient knowledge of the country, or proper guides to conduct him, attempted to march directly to Quito, by following the course of the river Guayoquil, and crossing the ridge of the Andes towards its head. But in this route, one of the most impracticable in all America, his troops endured such fatigue in forcing their way through forests and marshes on the low grounds, and suffered so much from excessive cold when they began to ascend the mountains, that before they reached the plain of Quito, a fifth part of the men and half their horses died, and the rest were so much dispirited and worn out, as to be almost unfit for service [134]. There they met with a body, not of Indians, but of Spaniards, drawn in hostile array against them. Pizarro having received an account of Alvarado's armament, had detached Almagro with some troops to oppose this formidable invader of his jurisdiction; and these were joined by Benalcazar and his victorious party. Alvarado, though surprised at the sight of enemies whom he did not expect, advanced boldly to the charge. But, by the interposition of some moderate men in each party, an amicable accommodation took place; and the fatal period when Spaniards suspended their conquests to imbrue their hands in the blood of their countrymen, was postponed a few years. Alvarado engaged to return to his goverment, upon Almagro's paying him a hundred thousand pesos to defray the expense of his armament. Most of his followers remained in the country; and an expedition, which threatened Pizarro and his colony with ruin, contributed to augment its strength †

1534.] By this time Ferdinand Pizarro had landed in Spain. The immense quantities of gold and silver which he imported [135] filled the kingdom with no less astonishment than they had excited in Panama and the adjacent provinces. Pizarro was received by the emperor with the attention due to the bearer of a present so rich as to exceed any idea which the Spaniards had formed concerning the value of their acquisitions in America,

* Zarate, lib. ii. c. 9. Vega, p. 11. lib. ii. c. 9. Herrera, dec. 5. lib. iv. c. 11, 12. lib. v. c. 2, 3 lib. vi. c. 3.

† Zarate, lib. ii. c. 10—13. Vega, p. 11. lib. ii. c. 1, 2. 9, &c. Gomara Hist. c. 126, &c. Remesa. Hist. Guatimal. lib. iii. c. 6. Herrera, dec. 5. lib. vi. c, 1, 2. 7, 8.

even after they had been ten years masters of Mexico. In recompense of his brother's services, his authority was confirmed with new powers and privileges, and the addition of seventy leagues, extending along the coast, to the southward of the territory granted in his former patent. Almagro received the honours which he had so long desired. The title of Adelantado, or governor, was conferred upon him, with jurisdiction over two hundred leagues of country, stretching beyond the southern limits of the province allotted to Pizarro. Ferdinand himself did not go unrewarded. He was admitted into the military order of St. Jago, a distinction always acceptable to a Spanish gentleman, and soon set out on his return to Peru, accompanied by many persons of higher rank than had yet served in that country.*

Some account of his negotiations reached Peru before he arrived there himself. Almagro no sooner learned that he had obtained the royal grant of an independent government, than pretending that Cuzco, the imperial residence of the Incas, lay within its boundaries, he attempted to render himself master of that important station. Juan and Gonzalez Pizarro prepared to oppose him. Each of the contending parties was supported by powerful adherents, and the dispute was on the point of being terminated by the sword, when Francis Pizarro arrived in the capital. The reconciliation between him and Almagro had never been cordial. The treachery of Pizarro in engrossing to himself all the honours and emoluments, which ought to have been divided with his associate, was always present in both their thoughts. The former, conscious of his own perfidy, did not expect forgiveness; the latter feeling, that he had been deceived, was impatient to be avenged; and though avarice and ambition had induced them not only to dissemble their sentiments, but even to act in concert while in pursuit of wealth and power, no sooner did they obtain possession of these, than the same passions which had formed this temporary union, gave rise to jealousy and discord. To each of them was attached a small band of interested dependants, who, with the malicious art peculiar to such men, heightened their suspicions, and magnified every appearance of offence. But with all those seeds of enmity in their minds, and thus assiduously cherished, each was so thoroughly acquainted with the abilities and courage of his rival, that they equally dreaded the consequences of an open rupture. The fortunate arrival of Pizarro at Cuzco, and the address mingled with firmness which he manifested in his expostulations with Almagro and his partisans, averted that evil for the present. A new reconciliation took place; the chief article of which was, that Almagro should attempt the conquest of Chili; and if he did not find in that province an establishment adequate to his merit and expectations, Pizarro, by way of indemnification, should yield up to him a part of Peru. This new agreement, though confirmed [June 12] with the same sacred solemnities as their first contract, was observed with as little fidelity.†

Soon after he concluded this important transaction, Pizarro marched back to the countries on the seacoast; and as he now enjoyed an interval of tranquillity undisturbed by any enemy, either Spaniard or Indian, he applied himself with that persevering ardour, which distinguishes his character, to introduce a form of regular government into the extensive provinces subject to his authority. Though ill qualified by his education to enter into any disquisition concerning the principles of civil policy, and little accustomed by his former habits of life to attend to its arrangements, his natural sagacity supplied the want both of science and experience. He distributed the country into various districts; he appointed proper magistrates to preside in each; and established regulations concerning the ad-

* Zarate, lib. iii. c. 3. Vega, p. 11. lib. ii. c. 19. Herrera, dec. 5. lib. vi. c. 13. † Zarate, lib. ii. c. 13. Vega, p. 11. lib. ii. c. 19. Benzo, lib. iii. c. 6. Herrera, dec. 5. lib. vii. c. 8

ministration of justice, the collection of the royal revenue, the working of the mines, and the treatment of the Indians, extremely simple, but well calculated to promote the public prosperity. But though, for the present, he adapted his plan to the infant state of his colony, his aspiring mind looked forward to its future grandeur. He considered himself as laying the foundation of a great empire, and deliberated long, and with much solicitude, in what place he should fix the seat of government. Cuzco, the imperial city of the Incas, was situated in a corner of the empire, above four hundred miles from the sea, and much further from Quito, a province of whose value he had formed a high idea. No other settlement of the Peruvians was so considerable as to merit the name of a town, or to allure the Spaniards to fix their residence in it. But in marching through the country, Pizarro had been struck with the beauty and fertility of the valley of Rimac, one of the most extensive and best cultivated in Peru. There, on the banks of a small river of the same name with the vale which it waters and enriches, at the distance of six miles from Callao, the most commodious harbour in the Pacific Ocean, he founded a city which he destined to be the capital of his government [Jan. 18, 1535]. He gave it the name of Ciudad de los Reyes, either from the circumstance of having laid the first stone at that season when the church celebrates the festival of the Three Kings, or, as is more probable, in honour of Juana and Charles, the joint sovereigns of Castile. This name it still retains among the Spaniards, in all legal and formal deeds; but it is better known to foreigners by that of *Lima*, a corruption of the ancient appellation of the valley in which it is situated. Under his inspection, the buildings advanced with such rapidity, that it soon assumed the form of a city, which, by a magnificent palace that he erected for himself, and by the stately houses built by several of his officers, gave, even in its infancy, some indication of its subsequent grandeur.*

In consequence of what had been agreed with Pizarro, Almagro began his march towards Chili; and as he possessed in an eminent degree the virtues most admired by soldiers, boundless liberality and fearless courage, his standard was followed by five hundred and seventy men, the greatest body of Europeans that had hitherto been assembled in Peru. From impatience to finish the expedition, or from that contempt of hardship and danger acquired by all the Spaniards who had served long in America, Almagro, instead of advancing along the level country on the coast, chose to march across the mountains by a route that was shorter indeed, but almost impracticable. In this attempt his troops were exposed to every calamity which men can suffer, from fatigue, from famine, and from the rigour of the climate in those elevated regions of the torrid zone, where the degree of cold is hardly inferior to what is felt within the polar circle. Many of them perished; and the survivors, when they descended into the fertile plains of Chili, had new difficulties to encounter. They found there a race of men very different from the people of Peru, intrepid, hardy, independent, and in their bodily constitution, as well as vigour of spirit, nearly resembling the warlike tribes in North America. Though filled with wonder at the first appearance of the Spaniards, and still more astonished at the operations of their cavalry and the effects of their fire-arms, the Chilese soon recovered so far from their surprise, as not only to defend themselves with obstinacy, but to attack their new enemies with more determined fierceness than any American nation had hitherto discovered. The Spaniards, however, continued to penetrate into the country, and collected some considerable quantities of gold; but were so far from thinking of making any settlement amidst such formidable neighbours, that, in spite of all the experience and valour of their leader, the final issue

* Herrera, dec. 5. lib. vi. c. 12. lib. vii. c. 13. Calancho, Coronica, lib. i. c. 37. Barneuvo, Lima fundata, ii. 294.

of the expedition still remained extremely dubious, when they were recalled from it by an unexpected revolution at Peru.* The causes of this important event I shall endeavour to trace to their source.

So many adventurers had flocked to Peru from every Spanish colony in America, and all with such high expectations of accumulating independent fortunes at once, that, to men possessed with notions so extravagant, any mention of acquiring wealth gradually, and by schemes of patient industry, would have been not only a disappointment, but an insult. In order to find occupation for men who could not with safety be allowed to remain inactive, Pizarro encouraged some of the most distinguished officers who had lately joined him, to invade different provinces of the empire, which the Spaniards had not hitherto visited. Several large bodies were formed for this purpose; and about the time that Almagro set out for Chili, they marched into remote districts of the country. No sooner did Manco Capac, the Inca, observe the inconsiderate security of the Spaniards in thus dispersing their troops, and that only a handful of soldiers remained in Cuzco, under Juan and Gonzalez Pizarro, than he thought that the happy period was at length come for vindicating his own rights, for avenging the wrongs of his country, and extirpating its oppressors. Though strictly watched by the Spaniards who allowed him to reside in the palace of his ancestors at Cuzco, he found means of communicating his scheme to the persons who were to be intrusted with the execution of it. Among people accustomed to revere their sovereign as a divinity, every hint of his will carries the authority of a command; and they themselves were now convinced, by the daily increase in the number of their invaders, that the fond hopes which they had long entertained of their voluntary departure were altogether vain. All perceived that a vigorous effort of the whole nation was requisite to expel them, and the preparations for it were carried on with the secrecy and silence peculiar to Americans.

After some unsuccessful attempts of the Inca to make his escape, Ferdinand Pizarro happening to arrive at that time in Cuzco [1536], he obtained permission from him to attend a great festival which was to be celebrated a few leagues from the capital. Under pretext of that solemnity, the great men of the empire were assembled. As soon as the Inca joined them, the standard of war was erected; and in a short time all the fighting men, from the confines of Quito to the frontier of Chili, were in arms. Many Spaniards, living securely on the settlements allotted them, were massacred. Several detachments, as they marched carelessly through a country which seemed to be tamely submissive to their dominion, were cut off to a man. An army amounting (if we may believe the Spanish writers) to two hundred thousand men, attacked Cuzco, which the three brothers endeavoured to defend with only one hundred and seventy Spaniards. Another formidable body invested Lima, and kept the governor closely shut up. There was no longer any communication between the two cities; the numerous forces of the Peruvians spreading over the country, intercepted every messenger; and as the parties in Cuzco and Lima were equally unacquainted with the fate of their countrymen, each boded the worst concerning the other, and imagined that they themselves were the only persons who had survived the general extinction of the Spanish name in Peru.†

It was at Cuzco, where the Inca commanded in person, that the Peruvians made their chief efforts. During nine months they carried on the siege with incessant ardour, and in various forms; and though they displayed not the same undaunted ferocity as the Mexican warriors, they conducted some of their operations in a manner which discovered greater sagacity, and a genius more susceptible of improvement in the military

* Zarate, lib. iii. c. 1. Gomara Hist. c. 131. Vega, p. 2. lib. ii. c. 20. Ovale Hist. de Chile, lib. iv. c. 15, &c. Herrera, dec. 5. lib. vi. c. 9. lib. x. c. 1, &c. † Vega, p. 11, lib. ii. c. 28. Zarate, lib. iii. c. 3. Cieca de Leon, c. 82. Gomara Hist. c. 135. Herrera, dec. 5. lib. viii. c. 5.

art. They not only observed the advantages which the Spaniards derived from their discipline and their weapons, but they endeavoured to imitate the former, and turned the latter against them. They armed a considerable body of their bravest warriors with the swords, the spears, and bucklers, which they had taken from the Spanish soldiers whom they had cut off in different parts of the country. These they endeavoured to marshal in that regular compact order, to which experience had taught them that the Spaniards were indebted for their irresistible force in action. Some appeared in the field with Spanish muskets, and had acquired skill and resolution enough to use them. A few of the boldest, among whom was the Inca himself, were mounted on the horses which they had taken, and advanced briskly to the charge like Spanish cavaliers, with their lances in the rest. It was more by their numbers, however, than by those imperfect essays to imitate European arts and to employ European arms, that the Peruvians annoyed the Spaniards [136]. In spite of the valour, heightened by despair, with which the three brothers defended Cuzco, Manco Capac recovered possession of one-half of his capital; and in their various efforts to drive him out of it, the Spaniards lost Juan Pizarro, the best beloved of all the brothers, together with some other persons of note. Worn out with the fatigue of incessant duty, distressed with want of provisions, and despairing of being able any longer to resist an enemy whose numbers daily increased, the soldiers became impatient to abandon Cuzco, in hopes either of joining their countrymen, if any of them yet survived, or of forcing their way to the sea, and finding some means of escaping from a country which had been so fatal to the Spanish name.* While they were brooding over those desponding thoughts, which their officers laboured in vain to dispel, Almagro appeared suddenly in the neighbourhood of Cuzco.

The accounts transmitted to Almagro concerning the general insurrection of the Peruvians, were such as would have induced him, without hesitation, to relinquish the conquest of Chili, and hasten to the aid of his countrymen. But in this resolution he was confirmed by a motive less generous, but more interesting. By the same messenger who brought him intelligence of the Inca's revolt, he received the royal patent creating him governor of Chili, and defining the limits of his jurisdiction. Upon considering the tenor of it, he deemed it manifest beyond contradiction, that Cuzco lay within the boundaries of his government, and he was equally solicitous to prevent the Peruvians from recovering possession of their capital, and to wrest it out of the hands of the Pizarros. From impatience to accomplish both, he ventured to return by a new route; and in marching through the sandy plains on the coast, he suffered from heat and drought, calamities of a new species hardly inferior to those in which he had been involved by cold and famine on the summits of the Andes.

1537.] His arrival at Cuzco was in a critical moment. The Spaniards and Peruvians fixed their eyes upon him with equal solicitude. The former, as he did not study to conceal his pretensions, were at a loss whether to welcome him as a deliverer, or to take precautions against him as an enemy. The latter, knowing the points in contest between him and his countrymen, flattered themselves that they had more to hope than to dread from his operations. Almagro himself, unacquainted with the detail of the events which had happened in his absence, and solicitous to learn the precise posture of affairs, advanced towards the capital slowly, and with great circumspection. Various negotiations with both parties were set on foot. The Inca conducted them on his part with much address At first he endeavoured to gain the friendship of Almagro; and after many fruitless overtures, despairing of any cordial union with a Spaniard, he

* Herrera, dec. 5. lib. viii. c. 4.

attacked him by surprise with a numerous body of chosen troops. But the Spanish discipline and valour maintained their wonted superiority. The Peruvians were repulsed with such slaughter that a great part of their army dispersed, and Almagro proceeded to the gates of Cuzco without interruption.

The Pizarros, as they had no longer to make head against the Peruvians, directed all their attention towards their new enemy, and took measures to obstruct his entry into the capital. Prudence, however, restrained both parties for some time from turning their arms against one another, while surrounded by common enemies, who would rejoice in the mutual slaughter. Different schemes of accommodation were proposed. Each endeavoured to deceive the other, or to corrupt his followers. The generous, open, affable temper of Almagro gained many adherents of the Pizarros, who were disgusted with their harsh, domineering manners. Encouraged by this defection, he advanced towards the city by night, surprised the sentinels, or was admitted by them, and, investing the house where the two brothers resided, compelled them, after an obstinate defence, to surrender at discretion. Almagro's claim of jurisdiction over Cuzco was universally acknowledged, and a form of administration established in his name.*

Two or three persons only were killed in this first act of civil hostility; but it was soon followed by scenes more bloody. Francisco Pizarro having dispersed the Peruvians who had invested Lima, and received some considerable reinforcements from Hispaniola and Nicaragua, ordered five hundred men, under the command of Alonzo de Alvarado, to march to Cuzco, in hopes of relieving his brothers, if they and their garrison were not already cut off by the Peruvians. This body, which at that period of the Spanish power in America must be deemed a considerable force, advanced near to the capital before they knew that they had any enemy more formidable than Indians to encounter. It was with astonishment that they beheld their countrymen posted on the banks of the river Abancay to oppose their progress. Almagro, however, wished rather to gain than to conquer them, and by bribes and promises, endeavoured to seduce their leader. The fidelity of Alvarado remained unshaken; but his talents for war were not equal to his virtue. Almagro amused him with various movements, of which he did not comprehend the meaning, while a large detachment of chosen soldiers passed the river by night [July 12], fell upon his camp by surprise, broke his troops before they had time to form, and took him prisoner, together with his principal officers.†

By the sudden rout of this body, the contest between the two rivals must have been decided, if Almagro had known as well how to improve as how to gain a victory. Rodrigo Orgognez, an officer of great abilities, who having served under the Constable Bourbon, when he led the imperial army to Rome, had been accustomed to bold and decisive measures, advised him instantly to issue orders for putting to death Ferdinand and Gonzalo Pizarros, Alvarado, and a few other persons whom he could not hope to gain, and to march directly with his victorious troops to Lima, before the governor had time to prepare for his defence. But Almagro, though he discerned at once the utility of the counsel, and though he had courage to have carried it into execution, suffered himself to be influenced by sentiments unlike those of a soldier of fortune grown old in service, and by scruples which suited not the chief of a party who had drawn his sword in civil war. Feelings of humanity restrained him from shedding the blood of his opponents; and the dread of being deemed a rebel deterred him from entering a province which the King had allotted to another. Though

* Zarate, lib. iii. c. 4. Vega, p. 11. lib. ii. c. 29. 31. Gomara Hist. c. 134. Herrera, dec. 6. lib. ii. c. 1—5. † Zarate, lib. iii. c. 6. Gom. Hist. c. 138. Vega, p. 11. lib. ii. c. 32. 34. Herrera, dec. 6. lib. ii. c. 9.

he knew that arms must terminate the dispute between him and Pizarro, and resolved not to shun that mode of decision; yet, with a timid delicacy, preposterous at such a juncture, he was so solicitous that his rival should be considered as the aggressor, that he marched quietly back to Cuzco, to wait his approach.*

Pizarro was still unacquainted with all the interesting events which had happened near Cuzco. Accounts of Almagro's return, of the loss of the capital, of the death of one brother, of the imprisonment of the other two, and of the defeat of Alvarado, were brought to him at once. Such a tide of misfortunes almost overwhelmed a spirit which had continued firm and erect under the rudest shocks of adversity. But the necessity of attending to his own safety, as well as the desire of revenge, preserved him from sinking under it. He took measures for both with his wonted sagacity. As he had the command of the seacoast, and expected considerable supplies both of men and military stores, it was no less his interest to gain time, and to avoid action, than it was that of Almagro to precipitate operations, and bring the contest to a speedy issue. He had recourse to arts which he had formerly practised with success; and Almagro was again weak enough to suffer himself to be amused with a prospect of terminating their differences by some amicable accommodation. By varying his overtures, and shifting his ground as often as it suited his purpose, sometimes seeming to yield to every thing which his rival could desire, and then retracting all that he had granted, Pizarro dexterously protracted the negotiation to such a length, that, though every day was precious to Almagro, several months elapsed without coming to any final agreement. While the attention of Almagro, and of the officers with whom he consulted, was occupied in detecting and eluding the fraudulent intentions of the governor, Gonzalo Pizarro and Alvarado found means to corrupt the soldiers to whose custody they were committed, and not only made their escape themselves, but persuaded sixty of the men who formerly guarded them to accompany their flight.† Fortune having thus delivered one of his brothers, the governor scrupled not at one act of perfidy more to procure the release of the other. He proposed that every point in controversy between Almagro and himself should be submitted to the decision of their sovereign; that until his award was known, each should retain undisturbed possession of whatever part of the country he now occupied; that Ferdinand Pizarro should be set at liberty, and return instantly to Spain, together with the officers whom Almagro purposed to send thither to represent the justice of his claims. Obvious as the design of Pizarro was in those propositions, and familiar as his artifices might now have been to his opponent, Almagro, with a credulity approaching to infatuation, relied on his sincerity, and concluded an agreement on these terms.‡

The moment that Ferdinand Pizarro recovered his liberty, the governor, no longer fettered in his operations by anxiety about his brother's life, threw off every disguise which his concern for it had obliged him to assume The treaty was forgotten; pacific and conciliating measures were no more mentioned; it was in the field he openly declared, and not in the cabinet, —by arms and not by negotiation,—that it must now be determined who should be master of Peru. The rapidity of his preparations suited such a decisive resolution. Seven hundred men were soon ready to march towards Cuzco. The command of these was given to his two brothers, in whom he could perfectly confide for the execution of his most violent schemes, as they were urged on, not only by the enmity flowing from the rivalship between their family and Almagro, but animated with the desire of vengeance, excited by recollection of their own recent disgrace and sufferings.

* Herrera, dec. 6. lib. ii. c. 10, 11. † Zarate, lib. iii. c. 8. Herrera, dec. 6. lib. ii. c. 14.
‡ Herrera, dec. 6. lib. iii. c. 9. Zarate, lib. iii. c. 9. Gomara Hist. c. 140. Vega, p. 11. lib. ii. c. 35

After an unsuccessful attempt to cross the mountains in the direct road between Lima and Cuzco, they marched towards the south along the coast as far as Nasca, and then turning to the left, penetrated through the defiles in that branch of the Andes which lay between them and the capital. Almagro, instead of hearkening to some of his officers, who advised him to attempt the defence of those difficult passes, waited the approach of the enemy in the plain of Cuzco. Two reasons seem to have induced him to take this resolution. His followers amounted hardly to five hundred, and he was afraid of weakening such a feeble body by sending any detachment towards the mountains. His cavalry far exceeded that of the adverse party, both in number and discipline, and it was only in an open country that he could avail himself of that advantage.

The Pizarros advanced without any obstruction, but what arose from the nature of the desert and horrid regions through which they marched. As soon as they reached the plain, both factions were equally impatient to bring this long protracted contest to an issue. Though countrymen and friends, the subjects of the same sovereign, and each with the royal standard displayed; and though they beheld the mountains that surrounded the plain in which they were drawn up, covered with a vast multitude of Indians assembled to enjoy the spectacle of their mutual carnage, and prepared to attack whatever party remained master of the field; so fell and implacable was the rancour which had taken possession of every breast, that not one pacific counsel, not a single overture towards accommodation proceeded from either side. Unfortunately for Almagro, he was so worn out with the fatigues of service, to which his advanced age was unequal, that, at this crisis of his fate, he could not exert his wonted activity, and he was obliged to commit the leading his troops to Orgognez, who, though an officer of great merit, did not possess the same ascendant either over the spirit or affections of the soldiers, as the chief whom they had long been accustomed to follow and revere.

The conflict was fierce, and maintained by each party with equal courage [April 26]. On the side of Almagro were more veteran soldiers, and a larger proportion of cavalry; but these were counterbalanced by Pizarro's superiority in numbers, and by two companies of well disciplined musketeers, which, on receiving an account of the insurrection of the Indians, the emperor had sent from Spain.* As the use of fire-arms was not frequent among the adventurers in America,† hastily equipped for service, at their own expense, this small band of soldiers regularly trained and armed, was a novelty in Peru, and decided the fate of the day. Wherever it advanced, the weight of a heavy and well sustained fire bore down horse and foot before it; and Orgognez, while he endeavoured to rally and animate his troops, having received a dangerous wound, the route became general. The barbarity of the conquerors stained the glory which they acquired by this complete victory. The violence of civil rage hurried on some to slaughter their countrymen with indiscriminate cruelty; the meanness of private revenge instigated others to single out individuals as the objects of their vengeance. Orgognez and several officers of distinction were massacred in cold blood; above a hundred and forty soldiers fell in the field; a large proportion, where the number of combatants was few, and the heat of the contest soon over. Almagro, though so feeble that he could not bear the motion of a horse, had insisted on being carried in a litter to an eminence which overlooked the field of battle. From thence, in the utmost agitation of mind, he viewed the various movements of both parties, and at last beheld the total defeat of his own troops, with all the passionate indignation of a veteran leader long accustomed tc

* Herrera, dec. 6, lib. iii. c. 8.

† Zarate, lib. iii. c. 8.

victory. He endeavoured to save himself by flight, but was taken prisoner, and guarded with the strictest vigilance.*

The Indians, instead of executing the resolution which they had formed, retired quietly after the battle was over; and in the history of the New World, there is not a more striking instance of the wonderful ascendant which the Spaniards had acquired over its inhabitants, than that, after seeing one of the contending parties ruined and dispersed, and the other weakened and fatigued, they had not courage to fall upon their enemies, when fortune presented an opportunity of attacking them with such advantage.†

Cuzco was pillaged by the victorious troops, who found there a considerable booty, consisting partly of the gleanings of the Indian treasures, and partly of the wealth amassed by their antagonists from the spoils of Peru and Chili. But so far did this, and whatever the bounty of their leader could add to it, fall below the high ideas of the recompense which they conceived to be due to their merit, that Ferdinand Pizarro, unable to gratify such extravagant expectations, had recouse to the same expedient which his brother had employed on a similar occasion, and endeavoured to find occupation for this turbulent assuming spirit, in order to prevent it from breaking out into open mutiny. With this view, he encouraged his most active officers to attempt the discovery and reduction of various provinces which had not hitherto submitted to the Spaniards. To every standard erected by the leaders who undertook any of those new expeditions, volunteers resorted with the ardour and hope peculiar to the age. Several of Almagro's soldiers joined them, and thus Pizarro had the satisfaction of being delivered both from the importunity of his discontented friends, and the dread of his ancient enemies.‡

Almagro himself remained for several months in custody, under all the anguish of suspense. For although his doom was determined by the Pizarros from the moment that he fell into their hands, prudence constrained them to defer gratifying their vengeance, until the soldiers who had served under him, as well as several of their own followers in whom they could not perfectly confide, had left Cuzco. As soon as they set out upon their different expeditions, Almagro was impeached of treason, formally tried, and condemned to die. The sentence astonished him; and though he had often braved death with undaunted spirit in the field, its approach under this ignominious form appalled him so much, that he had recourse to abject supplications unworthy of his former fame. He besought the Pizarros to remember the ancient friendship between their brother and him, and how much he had contributed to the prosperity of their family; he reminded them of the humanity with which, in opposition to the repeated remonstrances of his own most attached friends, he had spared their lives when he had them in his power; he conjured them to pity his age and infirmities, and to suffer him to pass the wretched remainder of his days in bewailing his crimes, and in making his peace with Heaven. The entreaties, says a Spanish historian, of a man so much beloved touched many an unfeeling heart, and drew tears from many a stern eye. But the brothers remained inflexible. As soon as Almagro knew his fate to be inevitable, he met it with the dignity and fortitude of a veteran. He was strangled in prison, and afterwards publicly beheaded. He suffered in the seventy-fifth year of his age, and left one son by an Indian woman of Panama, whom, though at that time a prisoner in Lima, he named as successor to his government, pursuant to a power which the emperor had granted him.§

* Zarate, lib. iii. c. 11, 12. Vega, p. 11. lib. ii. c. 36—38. Herrera, dec. 6. lib. iii. c. 10—12. lib. iv. c. 1—6.
† Zarate, lib. iii. c. 11. Vega, p. 11. lib. ii. c. 38.
‡ Zarate, lib. iii. c. 12. Gomara Hist. c. 141. Herrera, dec. 6. lib. iv. c. 7.
§ Zarate, lib. iii. c. 12. Gomara Hist. c 141 Vega, p. 11. lib. ii. c. 39. Herrera, dec. 6. lib. iv. c 9. lib. v. c. 1.

1539.] As, during the civil dissensions in Peru, all intercourse with Spain was suspended, the detail of the extraordinary transactions there did not soon reach the court. Unfortunately for the victorious faction, the first intelligence was brought thither by some of Almagro's officers, who left the country upon the ruin of their cause; and they related what had happened, with every circumstance, unfavourable to Pizarro and his brothers. Their ambition, their breach of the most solemn engagements, their violence and cruelty, were painted with all the malignity and exaggeration of party hatred. Ferdinand Pizarro, who arrived soon after, and appeared in court with extraordinary splendour, endeavoured to efface the impression which their accusations had made, and to justify his brother and himself by representing Almagro as the aggressor. The emperor and his ministers, though they could not pronounce which of the contending factions was most criminal, clearly discerned the fatal tendency of their dissensions. It was obvious, that while the leaders, intrusted with the conduct of two infant colonies, employed the arms which should have been turned against the common enemy, in destroying one another, all attention to the public good must cease, and there was reason to dread that the Indians might improve the advantage which the disunion of the Spaniards presented to them, and extirpate both the victors and vanquished. But the evil was more apparent than the remedy. Where the information which had been received was so defective and suspicious, and the scene of action so remote, it was almost impossible to chalk out the line of conduct that ought to be followed; and before any plan that should be approved of in Spain could be carried into execution, the situation of the parties, and the circumstances of affairs, might alter so entirely as to render its effects extremely pernicious.

Nothing therefore remained, but to send a person to Peru, vested with extensive and discretionary power, who, after viewing deliberately the posture of affairs with his own eyes, and inquiring upon the spot into the conduct of the different leaders, should be authorized to establish the government in that form which he deemed most conducive to the interest of the parent state, and the welfare of the colony. The man selected for this important charge was Christoval Vaca de Castro, a judge in the court of royal audience at Valladolid; and his abilities, integrity, and firmness justified the choice. His instructions, though ample, were not such as to fetter him in his operations. According to the different aspect of affairs, he had power to take upon him different characters. If he found the governor still alive, he was to assume only the title of judge, to maintain the appearance of acting in concert with him, and to guard against giving any just cause of offence to a man who had merited so highly of his country. But if Pizarro were dead, he was intrusted with a commission that he might then produce, by which he was appointed his successor in the government of Peru. This attention to Pizarro, however, seems to have flowed rather from dread of his power than from any approbation of his measures; for, at the very time that the court seemed so solicitous not to irritate him, his brother Ferdinand was arrested at Madrid, and confined to a prison, where he remained above twenty years.*

1540.] While Vaca de Castro was preparing for his voyage, events of great moment happened in Peru. The governor, considering himself, upon the death of Almagro, as the unrivalled possessor of that vast empire, proceeded to parcel out its territories among the conquerors; and had this division been made with any degree of impartiality, the extent of country which he had to bestow was sufficient to have gratified his friends, and to have gained his enemies. But Pizarro conducted this transaction, not with the equity and candour of a judge attentive to discover and to reward

* Gomara Hist. c. 142. Vega, p. 11. lib. ii. c. 40. Herrera, dec. 6. lib. viii. c 10, 11. lib. x. c 1

ment, but with the illiberal spirit of a party leader. Large districts, in parts of the country most cultivated and populous, were set apart as his own property, or granted to his brothers, his adherents, and favourites. To others, lots less valuable and inviting were assigned. The followers of Almagro, amongst whom were many of the original adventurers to whose valour and perseverance Pizarro was indebted for his success, were totally excluded from any portion in those lands, towards the acquisition of which they had contributed so largely. As the vanity of every individual set an immoderate value upon his own services, and the idea of each concerning the recompense due to them rose gradually to a more exorbitant height in proportion as their conquests extended, all who were disappointed in their expectations exclaimed loudly against the rapaciousness and partiality of the governor. The partisans of Almagro murmured in secret, and meditated revenge.*

Rapid as the progress of the Spaniards in South America had been since Pizarro landed in Peru, their avidity of dominion was not yet satisfied. The officers to whom Ferdinand Pizarro gave the command of different detachments, penetrated into several new provinces; and though some of them were exposed to great hardships in the cold and barren regions of the Andes, and others suffered distress not inferior amidst the woods and marshes of the plains, they made discoveries and conquests which not only extended their knowledge of the country, but added considerably to the territories of Spain and the New World. Pedro de Valdivia reassumed Almagro's scheme of invading Chili, and notwithstanding the fortitude of the natives in defending their possessions, made such progress in the conquest of the country, that he founded the city of St. Jago, and gave a beginning to the establishment of the Spanish dominion in that province.† But of all the enterprises undertaken about this period, that of Gonzalo Pizarro was the most remarkable. The governor, who seems to have resolved that no person in Peru should possess any station of distinguished eminence or authority but those of his own family, had deprived Benalcazar, the conqueror of Quito, of his command in that kingdom, and appointed his brother Gonzalo to take the government of it. He instructed him to attempt the discovery and conquest of the country to the east of the Andes, which, according to the information of the Indians, abounded with cinnamon and other valuable spices. Gonzalo, not inferior to any of his brothers in courage, and no less ambitious of acquiring distinction, eagerly engaged in this difficult service. He set out from Quito at the head of three hundred and forty soldiers, near one half of whom were horsemen; with four thousand Indians to carry their provisions. In forcing their way through the defiles, or over the ridges of the Andes, excess of cold and fatigue, to neither of which they were accustomed, proved fatal to the greater part of their wretched attendants. The Spaniards, though more robust, and inured to a variety of climates, suffered considerably, and lost some men: but when they descended into the low country, their distress increased. During two months it rained incessantly, without any interval of fair weather long enough to dry their clothes.‡ The immense plains upon which they were now entering, either altogether without inhabitants, or occupied by the rudest and least industrious tribes in the New World, yielded little subsistence. They could not advance a step but as they cut a road through woods, or made it through marshes. Such incessant toil, and continual scarcity of food, seem more than sufficient to have exhausted and dispirited any troops. But the fortitude and perseverance of the Spaniards in the sixteenth century were insuperable. Allured by frequent but false accounts of rich countries before them, they persisted in struggling on, until they reached

* Vega, p. II. lib. iii. c. 2. Herrera, dec. 6. lib. viii. c. 5. † Zarate, lib. iii. c. 13. Ovalle, lib. ii. c. 1, &c. ‡ Zarate, lib. iv. c. 2.

the banks of the Coca or Napo, one of the large rivers whose waters pour into the Maragnon, and contribute to its grandeur. There, with infinite labour, they built a bark, which they expected would prove of great utility in conveying them over rivers, in procuring provisions, and in exploring the country. This was manned with fifty soldiers, under the command of Francis Orellana, the officer next in rank to Pizarro. The stream carried them down with such rapidity, that they were soon far ahead of their countrymen, who followed slowly and with difficulty by land.

At this distance from his commander, Orellana, a young man of an aspiring mind, began to fancy himself independent; and transported with the predominant passion of the age, he formed the scheme of distinguishing himself as a discoverer, by following the course of the Maragnon until it joined the ocean, and by surveying the vast regions through which it flows. This scheme of Orellana's was as bold as it was treacherous. For, if he be chargeable with the guilt of having violated his duty to his commander, and with having abandoned his fellow soldiers in a pathless desert, where they had hardly any hopes of success, or even of safety, but what were founded on the service which they expected from the bark; his crime is in some measure balanced by the glory of having ventured upon a navigation of near two thousand leagues, through unknown nations, in a vessel hastily constructed, with green timber, and by very unskilful hands, without provisions, without a compass, or a pilot. But his courage and alacrity supplied every defect. Committing himself fearlessly to the guidance of the stream, the Napo bore him along to the south, until he reached the great channel of the Maragnon. Turning with it towards the coast, he held on his course in that direction. He made frequent descents on both sides of the river, sometimes seizing by force of arms the provisions of the fierce savages seated on its banks; and sometimes procuring a supply of food by a friendly intercourse with more gentle tribes. After a long series of dangers, which he encountered with amazing fortitude, and of distresses which he supported with no less magnanimity, he reached the ocean [137], where new perils awaited him. These he likewise surmounted, and got safely to the Spanish settlement in the island of Cubagua; from thence he sailed to Spain. The vanity natural to travellers who visit regions unknown to the rest of mankind, and the art of an adventurer solicitous to magnify his own merit, concurred in prompting him to mingle an extraordinary proportion of the marvellous in the narrative of his voyage. He pretended to have discovered nations so rich that the roofs of their temples were covered with plates of gold; and described a republic of women so warlike and powerful, as to have extended their dominion over a considerable tract of the fertile plains which he had visited. Extravagant as those tales were, they gave rise to an opinion, that a region abounding with gold, distinguished by the name of *El Dorada*, and a community of Amazons, were to be found in this part of the world; and such is the propensity of mankind to believe what is wonderful, that it has been slowly and with difficulty that reason and observation have exploded those fables. The voyage, however, even when stripped of every romantic embellishment, deserves to be recorded not only as one of the most memorable occurrences in that adventurous age, but as the first event which led to any certain knowledge of the extensive countries that stretch eastward from the Andes to the ocean.*

No words can describe the consternation of Pizarro, when he did not find the bark at the confluence of the Napo and Maragnon, where he had ordered Orellana to wait for him. He would not allow himself to suspect that a man, whom he had intrusted with such an important command, could be so base and so unfeeling as to desert him at such a juncture. But imputing his absence from the place of rendezvous to some unknown

* Zarate, lib. iv. c. 4. Gomara Hist. c. 86. Vega, p. 11. lib. iii. c. 4. Herrera, dec. 6. lib. xi. c. 2—5. Rodriguez el Maragnon y Amazonas, lib. i. c. 3.

accident, he advanced above fifty leagues along the banks of the Maragnon, expecting every moment to see the bark appear with a supply of provisions [1541]. At length he came up with an officer whom Orellana had left to perish in the desert, because he had the courage to remonstrate against his perfidy. From him he learned the extent of Orellana's crime, and his followers perceived at once their own desperate situation, when deprived of their only resource. The spirit of the stoutest hearted veteran sunk within him, and all demanded to be led back instantly. Pizarro, though he assumed an appearance of tranquillity, did not oppose their inclination. But he was now twelve hundred miles from Quito; and in that long march the Spaniards encountered hardships greater than those which they had endured in their progress outward, without the alluring hopes which then soothed and animated them under their sufferings. Hunger compelled them to feed on roots and berries, to eat all their dogs and horses, to devour the most loathsome reptiles, and even to gnaw the leather of their saddles and swordbelts. Four thousand Indians, and two hundred and ten Spaniards, perished in this wild disastrous expedition, which continued near two years; and as fifty men were aboard the bark with Orellana, only fourscore got back to Quito. These were naked like savages, and so emaciated with famine, or worn out with fatigue, that they had more the appearance of spectres than of men.*

But, instead of returning to enjoy the repose which his condition required, Pizarro, on entering Quito, received accounts of a fatal event that threatened calamities more dreadful to him than those through which he had passed. From the time that his brother made that partial division of his conquests which has been mentioned, the adherents of Almagro, considering themselves as proscribed by the party in power, no longer entertained any hope of bettering their condition. Great numbers in despair resorted to Lima, where the house of young Almagro was always open to them, and the slender portion of his father's fortune, which the governor allowed him to enjoy, was spent in affording them subsistence. The warm attachment with which every person who had served under the elder Almagro devoted himself to his interests, was quickly transferred to his son, who was now grown up to the age of manhood, and possessed all the qualities which captivate the affections of soldiers. Of a graceful appearance, dexterous at all martial exercises, bold, open, generous, he seemed to be formed for command; and as his father, conscious of his own inferiority from the total want of education, had been extremely attentive to have him instructed in every science becoming a gentleman; the accomplishments which he had acquired heightened the respect of his followers, as they gave him distinction and eminence among illiterate adventurers. In this young man the Almagrians found a point of union which they wanted, and, looking up to him as their head, were ready to undertake any thing for his advancement. Nor was affection for Almagro their only incitement; they were urged on by their own distresses. Many of them, destitute of common necessaries [138], and weary of loitering away life, a burden to their chief, or to such of their associates as had saved some remnant of their fortune from pillage and confiscation, longed impatiently for an occasion to exert their activity and courage, and began to deliberate how they might be avenged on the author of all their misery. Their frequent cabals did not pass unobserved; and the governor was warned to be on his guard against men who meditated some desperate deed, and had resolution to execute it. But either from the native intrepidity of his mind, or from contempt of persons whose poverty seemed to render their machinations of little consequence, he disregarded the admonitions of his friends. "Be in no pain," said he carelessly, "about my life; it is per-

* Zarate, lib. iv. c. 2—5. Vega, p. 11. lib. iii. c. 3, 4, 5. 14. Herrera, dec. 6. lib. viii. c. 7, 8. lib. ix. c. 2—5 dec. 7. lib. iii c. 14. Pizar. Varones Illust. 349, &c.

fectly safe, as long as every man in Peru knows that I can in a moment cut off any head which dares to harbour a thought against it." This security gave the Almagrians full leisure to digest and ripen every part of their scheme; and Juan de Herrada, an officer of great abilities, who had the charge of Almagro's education, took the direction of their consultations with all the zeal which this connection inspired, and with all the authority which the ascendant that he was known to have over the mind of his pupil gave him.

On Sunday the twenty-sixth of June, at mid-day, the season of tranquillity and repose in all sultry climates, Herrada, at the head of eighteen of the most determined conspirators, sallied out of Almagro's house, in complete armour; and, drawing their swords, as they advanced hastily towards the governor's palace, cried out, "Long live the King, but let the tyrant die!" Their associates, warned of their motions by a signal, were in arms at different stations ready to support them. Though Pizarro was usually surrounded by such a numerous train of attendants as suited the magnificence of the most opulent subject of the age in which he lived; yet as he was just risen from table, and most of his domestics had retired to their own apartments, the conspirators passed through the two outer courts of the palace unobserved. They were at the bottom of the staircase before a page in waiting could give the alarm to his master, who was conversing with a few friends in a large hall. The governor, whose steady mind no form of danger could appal, starting up, called for arms, and commanded Francisco de Chaves to make fast the door. But that officer, who did not retain so much presence of mind as to obey this prudent order, running to the top of the staircase, wildly asked the conspirators what they meant, and whither they were going? Instead of answering, they stabbed him to the heart, and burst into the hall. Some of the persons who were there threw themselves from the windows; others attempted to fly; and a few drawing their swords followed their leader into an inner apartment. The conspirators, animated with having the object of their vengeance now in view, rushed forward after them. Pizarro, with no other arms than his sword and buckler, defended the entry; and, supported by his half brother Alcantara, and his little knot of friends, he maintained the unequal contest with intrepidity worthy of his past exploits, and with the vigour of a youthful combatant. "Courage," cried he, "companions! we are yet enow to make those traitors repent of their audacity." But the armour of the conspirators protected them, while every thrust they made took effect. Alcantara fell dead at his brother's feet his other defenders were mortally wounded. The governor, so weary that he could hardly wield his sword, and no longer able to parry the many weapons furiously aimed at him, received a deadly thrust full in his throat, sunk to the ground, and expired.

As soon as he was slain, the assassins ran out into the streets, and, waving their bloody swords, proclaimed the death of the tyrant. Above two hundred of their associates having joined them, they conducted young Almagro in solemn procession through the city, and, assembling the magistrates and principal citizens, compelled them to acknowledge him as lawful successor to his father in his government. The palace of Pizarro, together with the houses of several of his adherents, was pillaged by the soldiers, who had the satisfaction at once of being avenged on their enemies, and of enriching themselves by the spoils of those through whose hands al the wealth of Peru had passed.*

The boldness and success of the conspiracy, as well as the name and popular qualities of Almagro, drew many soldiers to his standard. Every adventurer of desperate fortune, all who were dissatisfied with Pizarro

* Zarate, lib. iv. c. 6—8. Gomara Hist. c. 144, 145. Vega, p. 11. lib. iii. c. 5—7. Herrera, dec 6 lib. x. c. 4—7. Pizarro Var. Illust. p. 183.

(and from the rapaciousness of his government in the latter years of his life the number of malecontents was considerable), declared without hesitation in favour of Almagro, and he was soon at the head of eight hundred of the most gallant veterans in Peru. As his youth and inexperience disqualified him from taking the command of them himself, he appointed Herrada to act as general. But though Almagro speedily collected such a respectable force, the acquiescence in his government was far from being general. Pizarro had left many friends to whom his memory was dear; the barbarous assassination of a man to whom his country was so highly indebted, filled every impartial person with horror. The ignominious birth of Almagro, as well as the doubtful title on which he founded his pretensions, led others to consider him as a usurper. The officers who commanded in some provinces refused to recognise his authority until it was confirmed by the emperor. In others, particularly at Cuzco, the royal standard was erected, and preparations were begun in order to revenge the murder of their ancient leader.

Those seeds of discord, which could not have lain long dormant, acquired great vigour and activity when the arrival of Vaca de Castro was known. After a long and disastrous voyage, he was driven by stress of weather into a small harbour in the province of Popayan; and proceeding from thence by land, after a journey no less tedious than difficult, he reached Quito. In his way he received accounts of Pizarro's death, and of the events which followed upon it. He immediately produced the royal commission appointing him governor of Peru, with the same privileges and authority; and his jurisdiction was acknowledged without hesitation by Benalcazar, adelantado or lieutenant-general for the emperor in Popayan, and by Pedro de Puelles, who, in the absence of Gonzalo Pizarro, had the command of the troops left in Quito. Vaca de Castro not only assumed the supreme authority, but showed that he possessed the talents which the exercise of it at that juncture required. By his influence and address he soon assembled such a body of troops, as not only to set him above all fear of being exposed to any insult from the adverse party, but enabled him to advance from Quito with the dignity which became his character. By despatching persons of confidence to the different settlements in Peru with a formal notification of his arrival and of his commission, he communicated to his countrymen the royal pleasure with respect to the government of the country. By private emissaries, he excited such officers as had discovered their disapprobation of Almagro's proceedings, to manifest their duty to their sovereign by supporting the person honoured with his commission. Those measures were productive of great effects. Encouraged by the approach of the new governor, or prepared by his machinations, the loyal were confirmed in their principles, and avowed them with greater boldness; the timid ventured to declare their sentiments; the neutral and wavering, finding it necessary to choose a side, began to lean to that which now appeared to be the safest as well as the most just.*

Almagro observed the rapid progress of this spirit of disaffection to his cause; and in order to give an effectual check to it before the arrival of Vaca de Castro, he set out at the head of his troops for Cuzco [1542], where the most considerable body of opponents had erected the royal standard, under the command of Pedro Alvarez Holguin. During his march thither, Herrada, the skilful guide of his youth and of his counsels, died; and from that time his measures were conspicuous for their violence, but concerted with little sagacity, and executed with no address. Holguin, who, with forces far inferior to those of the opposite party, was descend-

* Benzon, lib. iii. c. 9. Zarate, lib. iv. c. 11. Gomara, c. 146, 147 Herrera, dec. 6. lib. x. c. 1. 2, 3. 7, &c.

ing towards the coast at the very time that Almagro was on his way to Cuzco, deceived his inexperienced adversary by a very simple stratagem, avoided an engagement, and effected a junction with Alvarado, an officer of note, who had been the first to declare against Almagro as a usurper.

Soon after, Vaca de Castro entered their camp with the troops which he brought from Quito; and erecting the royal standard before his own tent, he declared that, as governor, he would discharge in person all the functions of general of their combined forces. Though formed by the tenor of his past life to the habits of a sedentary and pacific profession, he at once assumed the activity and discovered the decision of an officer long accustomed to command. Knowing his strength to be now far superior to that of the enemy, he was impatient to terminate the contest by a battle. Nor did the followers of Almagro, who had no hopes of obtaining a pardon for a crime so atrocious as the murder of the governor, decline that mode of decision. They met at Chupaz [Sept. 16], about two hundred miles from Cuzco, and fought with all the fierce animosity inspired by the violence of civil rage, the rancour of private enmity, the eagerness of revenge, and the last efforts of despair. Victory, after remaining long doubtful, declared at last for Vaco de Castro. The superior number of his troops, his own intrepidity, and the martial talents of Francisco de Carvajal, a veteran officer formed under the great captain in the wars of Italy, and who on that day laid the foundation of his future fame in Peru, triumphed over the bravery of his opponents, though led on by young Almagro with a gallant spirit worthy of a better cause, and deserving another fate. The carnage was great in proportion to the number of the combatants. Many of the vanquished, especially such as were conscious that they might be charged with being accessary to the assassination of Pizarro, rushing on the swords of the enemy, chose to fall like soldiers rather than wait an ignominious doom. Of fourteen hundred men, the total amount of combatants on both sides, five hundred lay dead on the field, and the number of the wounded was still greater.*

If the military talents displayed by Vaca de Castro, both in the council and in the field, surprised the adventurers in Peru, they were still more astonished at his conduct after the victory. As he was by nature a rigid dispenser of justice, and persuaded that it required examples of extraordinary severity to restrain the licentious spirit of soldiers so far removed from the seat of government, he proceeded directly to try his prisoners as rebels. Forty were condemned to suffer the death of traitors, others were banished from Peru. Their leader, who made his escape from the battle, being betrayed by some of his officers, was publicly beheaded in Cuzco; and in him the name of Almagro, and the spirit of the party, was extinct.†

During those violent convulsions in Peru, the emperor and his ministers were intently employed in preparing regulations, by which they hoped not only to re-establish tranquillity there, but to introduce a more perfect system of internal policy into all their settlements in the New World. It is manifest from all the events recorded in the history of America, that, rapid and extensive as the Spanish conquests there had been, they were not carried on by any regular exertion of the national force, but by the occasional efforts of private adventurers. After fitting out a few of the first armaments for discovering new regions, the court of Spain, during the busy reigns of Ferdinand and Charles V., the former the most intriguing prince of the age, and the latter the most ambitious, was encumbered with such a multiplicity of schemes, and involved in war with so many nations of Europe, that he had not leisure to attend to distant and less interesting

* Zarate, lib. iv. c. 12—19. Gomara, c. 148. Vega, p. 11 lib. iii. c. 11—18. Herrera, dec. 7. lib. i. c. 1, 2, 3. lib. iii. c. 1—11.

† Zarate, lib. iv. c. 21. Gomara, c. 150. Herrera, dec. 7. lib. iii. c 12. lib. vi. c. 1.

objects. The care of prosecuting discovery, or of attempting conquest, was abandoned to individuals; and with such ardour did men push forward in this new career, on which novelty, the spirit of adventure, avarice, ambition, and the hope of meriting heaven, prompted them with combined influence to enter, that in less than half a century almost the whole of that extensive empire which Spain now possesses in the New World, was subjected to its dominion. As the Spanish court contributed nothing towards the various expeditions undertaken in America, it was not entitled to claim much from their success. The sovereignty of the conquered provinces, with the fifth of the gold and silver, was reserved for the crown; every thing else was seized by the associates in each expedition as their own right. The plunder of the countries which they invaded served to indemnify them for what they had expended in equipping themselves for the service, and the conquered territory was divided among them, according to rules which custom had introduced, as permanent establishments which their successful valour merited. In the infancy of those settlements, when their extent as well as their value was unknown, many irregularities escaped observation, and it was found necessary to connive at many excesses. The conquered people were frequently pillaged with destructive rapacity, and their country parcelled out among its new masters in exorbitant shares, far exceeding the highest recompense due to their services. The rude conquerors of America, incapable of forming their establishments upon any general or extensive plan of policy, attentive only to private interest, unwilling to forego present gain from the prospect of remote or public benefit, seem to have had no object but to amass sudden wealth, without regarding what might be the consequences of the means by which they acquired it. But when time at length discovered to the Spanish court the importance of its American possessions, the necessity of new-modelling their whole frame became obvious, and in place of the maxims and practices prevalent among military adventurers, it was found requisite to substitute the institutions of regular government.

One evil in particular called for an immediate remedy. The conquerors of Mexico and Peru imitated the fatal example of their countrymen settled in the islands, and employed themselves in searching for gold and silver with the same inconsiderate eagerness. Similar effects followed. The natives employed in this labour by masters, who in imposing tasks had no regard either to what they felt or to what they were able to perform, pined away and perished so fast, that there was reason to apprehend that Spain, instead of possessing countries peopled to such a degree as to be susceptible of progressive improvement, would soon remain proprietor only of a vast uninhabited desert.

The emperor and his ministers were so sensible of this, and so solicitous to prevent the extinction of the Indian race, which threatened to render their acquisitions of no value, that from time to time various laws, which I have mentioned, had been made for securing to that unhappy people more gentle and equitable treatment. But the distance of America from the seat of empire, the feebleness of government in the new colonies, the avarice and audacity of soldiers unaccustomed to restraint, prevented these salutary regulations from operating with any considerable influence. The evil continued to grow, and at this time the emperor found an interval of leisure from the affairs of Europe to take it into attentive consideration. He consulted not only with his ministers and the members of the council of the Indies, but called upon several persons who had resided long in the New World to aid them with the result of their experience and observation. Fortunately for the people of America, among these was Bartholomew de las Casas, who happened to be then at Madrid on a mission from a Chapter of his order at Chiapa.* Though since the miscarriage of his

* Remesal Hist. de Chiapa, p. 146.

former schemes for the relief of the Indians, he had continued shut up in his cloister, or occupied in religious functions, his zeal in behalf of the former objects of his pity was so far from abating, that, from an increased knowledge of their sufferings, its ardour had augmented. He seized eagerly this opportunity of reviving his favourite maxims concerning the treatment of the Indians. With the moving eloquence natural to a man on whose mind the scenes which he had beheld had made a deep impression, he described the irreparable waste of the human species in the New World, the Indian race almost totally swept away in the islands in less than fifty years, and hastening to extinction on the continent with the same rapid decay. With the decisive tone of one strongly prepossessed with the truth of his own system, he imputed all this to a single cause, to the exactions and cruelty of his countrymen, and contended that nothing could prevent the depopulation of America, but the declaring of its natives to be freemen, and treating them as subjects, not as slaves. Nor did he confide for the success of this proposal in the powers of his oratory alone. In order to enforce them, he composed his famous treatise concerning the destruction of America,* in which he relates, with many horrid circumstances, but with apparent marks of exaggerated description, the devastation of every province which had been visited by the Spaniards.

The emperor was deeply afflicted with the recital of so many actions shocking to humanity. But as his views extended far beyond those of Las Casas, he perceived that relieving the Indians from oppression was but one step towards rendering his possessions in the New World a valuable acquisition, and would be of little avail, unless he could circumscribe the power and usurpations of his own subjects there. The conquerors of America, however great their merit had been towards their country, were mostly persons of such mean birth, and of such an abject rank in society, as gave no distinction in the eye of a monarch. The exorbitant wealth with which some of them returned, gave umbrage to an age not accustomed to see men in inferior condition elevated above their level, and rising to emulate or to surpass the ancient nobility in splendour. The territories which their leaders had appropriated to themselves were of such enormous extent [139], that, if the country should ever be improved in proportion to the fertility of the soil, they must grow too wealthy and too powerful for subjects. It appeared to Charles that this abuse required a remedy no less than the other, and that the regulations concerning both must be enforced by a mode of government more vigorous than had yet been introduced into America.

With this view he framed a body of laws, containing many salutary appointments with respect to the constitution and powers of the supreme council of the Indies; concerning the station and jurisdiction of the royal audiences in different parts of America; the administration of justice; the order of government, both ecclesiastical and civil. These were approved of by all ranks of men. But together with them were issued the following regulations, which excited universal alarm, and occasioned the most violent convulsions. "That as the *repartimientos* or shares of land seized by several persons appeared to be excessive, the royal audiences are empowered to reduce them to a moderate extent: That upon the death of any conqueror or planter, the lands and Indians granted to him shall not descend to his widow or children, but return to the crown: That the Indians shall henceforth be exempt from personal service, and shall not be compelled to carry the baggage of travellers, to labour in the mines, or to dive in the pearl fisheries: That the stated tribute due by them to their superior shall be ascertained, and they shall be paid as servants for any work they voluntarily perform: That all persons who are or have been in public offices, all ecclesiastics of every denomination, all hospitals and monasteries, shall be deprived of the lands and Indians allotted to them, and these be annexed

* Remesal, p. 192. 199.

to the crown: That every person in Peru, who had any criminal concern in the contest between Pizarro and Almagro should forfeit his lands and Indians."*

All the Spanish ministers who had hitherto been intrusted with the direction of American affairs, and who were best acquainted with the state of the country, remonstrated against those regulations as ruinous to their infant colonies. They represented, that the number of Spaniards who had hitherto emigrated to the New World was so extremely small, that nothing could be expected from any effort of theirs towards improving the vast regions over which they were scattered; that the success of every scheme for this purpose must depend upon the ministry and service of the Indians, whose native indolence and aversion to labour, no prospect of benefit or promise of reward could surmount; that the moment the right of imposing a task, and exacting the performance of it, was taken from their masters, every work of industry must cease, and all the sources from which wealth began to pour in upon Spain must be stopped for ever. But Charles, tenacious at all times of his own opinions, and so much impressed at present with the view of the disorders which reigned in America, that he was willing to hazard the application even of a dangerous remedy, persisted in his resolution of publishing the laws. That they might be carried into execution with greater vigour and authority, he authorized Francisco Tello de Sandoval to repair to Mexico as *Visitador*, or superintendent of that country, and to co-operate with Antonio de Mendoza, the viceroy, in enforcing them. He appointed Blasco Nugnez Vela to be governor of Peru, with the title of viceroy; and in order to strengthen his administration, he established a court of royal audience in Lima [1543], in which four lawyers of eminence were to preside as judges.†

The viceroy and superintendent sailed at the same time; and an account of the laws which they were to enforce reached America before them. The entry of Sandoval into Mexico was viewed as the prelude of general ruin. The unlimited grant of liberty to the Indians affected every Spaniard in America without distinction, and there was hardly one who might not on some pretext be included under the other regulations, and suffer by them. But the colony in New Spain had now been so long accustomed to the restraints of law and authority under the steady and prudent administration of Mendoza, that, how much soever the spirit of the new statutes was detested and dreaded, no attempt was made to obstruct the publication of them by any act of violence unbecoming subjects. The magistrates and principal inhabitants, however, presented dutiful addresses to the viceroy and superintendent, representing the fatal consequences of enforcing them. Happily for them Mendoza, by long residence in the country, was so thoroughly acquainted with its state, that he knew what was for its interest as well as what it could bear; and Sandoval, though new in office, displayed a degree of moderation seldom possessed by persons just entering upon the exercise of power. They engaged to suspend, for some time, the execution of what was offensive in the new laws, and not only consented that a deputation of citizens should be sent to Europe to lay before the emperor the apprehensions of his subjects in New Spain with respect to their tendency and effects, but they concurred with them in supporting their sentiments. Charles, moved by the opinion of men whose abilities and integrity entitled them to decide concerning what fell immediately under their own view, granted such a relaxation of the rigour of the laws as re-established the colony in its former tranquillity.‡

In Peru the storm gathered with an aspect still more fierce and threaten-

* Herrera, dec. 7. lib. vi. c. 4. Fernandez Hist. lib. i. c. 1, 2. † Zarate, lib. iii. c. 24. Gomara. c. 151. Vega, p. 2. lib. iii. c. 20. ‡ Fernandez Hist. lib. i. c. 3, 4, 5. Vega, p. 11. lib. iii. c. 21, 22. Herrera, dec. 7. lib. v. c. 7. lib. vii. c. 14, 15. Torquem. Mond. Ind. lib. v. c. 13

ing, and was not so soon dispelled. The conquerors of Peru, of a rank much inferior to those who had subjected Mexico to the Spanish crown, further removed from the inspection of the parent state, and intoxicated with the sudden acquisition of wealth, carried on all their operations with greater license and irregularity than any body of adventurers in the New World. Amidst the general subversion of law and order, occasioned by two successive civil wars, when each individual was at liberty to decide for himself, without any guide but his own interest or passions, this turbulent spirit rose above all sense of subordination. To men thus corrupted by anarchy, the introduction of regular government, the power of a viceroy, and the authority of a respectable court of judicature, would of themselves have appeared formidable restraints, to which they would have submitted with reluctance. But they revolted with indignation against the idea of complying with laws, by which they were to be stripped at once of all they had earned so hardly during many years of service and suffering. As the account of the new laws spread successively through the different settlements, the inhabitants ran together, the women in tears, and the men exclaiming against the injustice and ingratitude of their sovereign in depriving them, unheard and unconvicted, of their possessions. "Is this," cried they, "the recompense due to persons, who, without public aid, at their own expense, and by their own valour, have subjected to the crown of Castile territories of such immense extent and opulence? Are these the rewards bestowed for having endured unparalleled distress, for having encountered every species of danger in the service of their country? Whose merit is so great, whose conduct has been so irreproachable, that he may not be condemned by some penal clause in regulations, conceived in terms as loose and comprehensive, as if it had been intended that all should be entangled in their snare? Every Spaniard of note in Peru has held some public office, and all, without distinction, have been constrained to take an active part in the contest between the two rival chiefs. Were the former to be robbed of their property because they had done their duty? Were the latter to be punished on account of what they could not avoid? Shall the conquerors of this great empire, instead of receiving marks of distinction, be deprived of the natural consolation of providing for their widows and children, and leave them to depend for subsistence on the scanty supply they can extort from unfeeling courtiers?* We are not able now," continued they, "to explore unknown regions in quest of more secure settlements; our constitutions debilitated with age, and our bodies covered with wounds, are no longer fit for active service; but still we possess vigour sufficient to assert our just rights, and we will not tamely suffer them to be wrested from us."†

By discourses of this sort, uttered with vehemence, and listened to with universal approbation, their passions were inflamed to such a pitch that they were prepared for the most violent measures; and began to hold consultations in different places, how they might oppose the entrance of the viceroy and judges, and prevent not only the execution but the promulgation of the new laws. From this, however, they were diverted by the address of Vaca de Castro, who flattered them with hopes, that, as soon as the viceroy and judges should arrive, and had leisure to examine their petitions and remonstrances, they would concur with them in endeavouring to procure some mitigation in the rigour of laws which had been framed without due attention either to the state of the country, or to the sentiments of the people. A greater degree of accommodation to these, and even some concessions on the part of government, were now become requisite to compose the present ferment, and to soothe the colonists into sub-

* Herrera, dec. 7. lib. vii. c. 14, 15.

† Gomara, c. 152. Herrera, dec. 7. lib. vi. c. 10, 11. Vega. p. 11. lib. iii. c. 20. 22. lib. iv. c. 3, 4.

mission, by inspiring them with confidence in their superiors. But without profound discernment, conciliating manners, and flexibility of temper, such a plan could not be carried on. The viceroy possessed none of these. Of all the qualities that fit men for high command, he was endowed only with integrity and courage; the former harsh and uncomplying, the latter bordering so frequently on rashness or obstinacy, that, in his situation, they were defects rather than virtues. From the moment that he landed at Tumbez [March 4], Nugnez Vela seems to have considered himself merely as an executive officer, without any discretionary power; and, regardless of whatever he observed or heard concerning the state of the country, he adhered to the letter of the regulations with unrelenting rigour. In all the towns through which he passed, the natives were declared to be free, every person in public office was deprived of his lands and servants; and as an example of obedience to others, he would not suffer a single Indian to be employed in carrying his own baggage in his march towards Lima. Amazement and consternation went before him as he approached; and so little solicitous was he to prevent these from augmenting, that, on entering the capital, he openly avowed that he came to obey the orders of his sovereign, not to dispense with his laws. This harsh declaration was accompanied with what rendered it still more intolerable, haughtiness in deportment, a tone of arrogance and decision in discourse, and an insolence of office grievous to men little accustomed to hold civil authority in high respect. Every attempt to procure a suspension or mitigation of the new laws, the viceroy considered as flowing from a spirit of disaffection that tended to rebellion. Several persons of rank were confined, and some put to death, without any form of trial. Vaca de Castro was arrested; and notwithstanding the dignity of his former rank, and his merit, in having prevented a general insurrection in the colony, he was loaded with chains, and shut up in the common jail.*

But however general the indignation was against such proceedings, it is probable the hand of authority would have been strong enough to suppress it, or to prevent it bursting out with open violence, if the malecontents had not been provided with a leader of credit and eminence to unite and to direct their efforts. From the time that the purport of the new regulations was known in Peru, every Spaniard there turned his eyes towards Gonzalo Pizarro, as the only person able to avert the ruin with which they threatened the colony. From all quarters, letters and addresses were sent to him, conjuring him to stand forth as their common protector, and offering to support him in the attempt with their lives and fortunes. Gonzalo, though inferior in talents to his other brothers, was equally ambitious, and of courage no less daring. The behaviour of an ungrateful court towards his brothers and himself dwelt continually on his mind. Ferdinand a state prisoner in Europe, the children of the governor in custody of the viceroy, and sent aboard his fleet, himself reduced to the condition of a private citizen in a country for the discovery and conquest of which Spain was indebted to his family—these thoughts prompted him to seek for vengeance, and to assert the rights of his family, of which he now considered himself as the guardian and the heir. But as no Spaniard can easily surmount that veneration for his sovereign which seems to be interwoven in his frame, the idea of marching in arms against the royal standard filled him with horror. He hesitated long, and was still unresolved, when the violence of the viceroy, the universal call of his countrymen, and the certainty of becoming soon a victim himself to the severity of the new laws, moved him to quit his residence at Chuquisaca de la Plata, and repair to Cuzco. All the inhabitants went out to meet him, and received him with transports of

* Zarate, lib. iv. c. 23, 24, 25. Gomara, c. 153—155. Vega, p. II. lib. iv c. 4, 5. Fernandez, lib. i c. 6—10.

oy as the deliverer of the colony. In the fervour of their zeal, they elected him procurator-general of the Spanish nation in Peru, to solicit the repeal of the late regulations. They empowered him to lay their remonstrances before the royal audience in Lima, and, upon pretext of danger from the Indians, authorized him to march thither in arms [1544]. Under sanction of this nomination Pizarro took possession of the royal treasure, appointed officers, levied soldiers, seized a large train of artillery which Vaca de Castro had deposited in Gumanga, and set out for Lima as if he had been advancing against a public enemy. Disaffection having now assumed a regular form, and being united under a chief of such distinguished name, many persons of note resorted to his standard; and a considerable part of the troops, raised by the viceroy to oppose his progress, deserted to him in a body.*

Before Pizarro reached Lima, a revolution had happened there, which encouraged him to proceed with almost certainty of success. The violence of the viceroy's administration was not more formidable to the Spaniards of Peru than his overbearing haughtiness was odious to his associates, the judges of the royal audience. During their voyage from Spain, some symptoms of coldness between the viceroy and them began to appear.† But as soon as they entered upon the exercise of their respective offices, both parties were so much exasperated by frequent contests, arising from interference of jurisdiction and contrariety of opinion, that their mutual disgust soon grew into open enmity. The judges thwarted the viceroy in every measure, set at liberty prisoners whom he had confined, justified the malecontents, and applauded their remonstrances. At a time when both departments of government should have united against the approaching enemy, they were contending with each other for superiority. The judges at length prevailed. The viceroy, universally odious, and abandoned even by his own guards, was seized in his palace [Sept. 18], and carried to a desert island on the coast, to be kept there until he could be sent home to Spain.

The judges, in consequence of this, having assumed the supreme direction of affairs into their own hands, issued a proclamation suspending the execution of the obnoxious laws, and sent a message to Pizarro, requiring him, as they had already granted whatever he could request, to dismiss his troops, and to repair to Lima with fifteen or twenty attendants. They could hardly expect that a man so daring and ambitious would tamely comply with this requisition. It was made, probably, with no such intention, but only to throw a decent veil over their own conduct; for Cepeda, the president of the court of audience, a pragmatical and aspiring lawyer, seems to have held a secret correspondence with Pizarro, and had already formed the plan, which he afterwards executed, of devoting himself to his service. The imprisonment of the viceroy, the usurpation of the judges, together with the universal confusion and anarchy consequent upon events so singular and unexpected, opened new and vast prospects to Pizarro. He now beheld the supreme power within his reach. Nor did he want courage to push on towards the object which fortune presented to his view. Carvajal, the prompter of his resolutions, and guide of all his actions, had long fixed his eye upon it as the only end at which Pizarro ought to aim. Instead of the inferior function of procurator for the Spanish settlements in Peru, he openly demanded to be governor and captain-general of the whole province, and required the court of audience to grant him a commission to that effect. At the head of twelve hundred men, within a mile of Lima, where there was neither leader nor army to oppose him, such a request carried with it the authority of a command. But the

* Zarate, lib. v. c. 1. Gomara, c. 156, 157. Vega, p. II. lib. iv. c. 4—12. Fernandez, lib. i. c. 12—17. Herrera, dec. 7. lib. vii. c. 18, &c. lib. viii. c. 1—5. † Gomara, c. 171.

judges, either from unwillingness to relinquish power, or from a desire of preserving some attention to appearances, hesitated, or seemed to hesitate, about complying with what he demanded. Carvajal, impatient of delay, and impetuous in all his operations, marched into the city by night, seized several officers of distinction obnoxious to Pizarro, and hanged them without the formality of a trial. Next morning the court of audience issued a commission in the emperor's name, appointing Pizarro governor of Peru, with full powers, civil as well as military, and he entered the town that day with extraordinary pomp, to take possession of his new dignity.*

Oct. 28.] But amidst the disorder and turbulence which accompanied this total dissolution of the frame of government, the minds of men, set loose from the ordinary restraints of law and authority, acted with such capricious irregularity, that events no less extraordinary than unexpected followed in a rapid succession. Pizarro had scarcely begun to exercise the new powers with which he was invested, when he beheld formidable enemies rise up to oppose him. The viceroy having been put on board a vessel by the judges of the audience, in order that he might be carried to Spain under custody of Juan Alvarez one of their own number; as soon as they were out at sea, Alvarez, either touched with remorse, or moved by fear, kneeled down to his prisoner, declared him from that moment to be free, and that he himself, and every person in the ship, would obey him as the legal representative of their sovereign. Nugnez Vela ordered the pilot of the vessel to shape his course towards Tumbez, and as soon as he landed there, erected the royal standard, and resumed his functions of viceroy. Several persons of note, to whom the contagion of the seditious spirit which reigned at Cuzco and Lima had not reached, instantly avowed their resolution to support his authority.† The violence of Pizarro's government, who observed every individual with the jealousy natural to usurpers, and who punished every appearance of disaffection with unforgiving severity, soon augmented the number of the viceroy's adherents, as it forced some leading men in the colony to fly to him for refuge. While he was gathering such strength at Tumbez, that his forces began to assume the appearance of what was considered as an army in America, Diego Centeno, a bold and active officer, exasperated by the cruelty and oppression of Pizarro's lieutenant-governor in the province of Charcas, formed a conspiracy against his life, cut him off, and declared for the viceroy.‡

1545.] Pizarro, though alarmed with those appearances of hostility in the opposite extremes of the empire, was not disconcerted. He prepared to assert the authority, to which he had attained, with the spirit and conduct of an officer accustomed to command, and marched directly against the viceroy as the enemy who was nearest as well as most formidable. As he was master of the public revenues in Peru, and most of the military men were attached to his family, his troops were so numerous, that the viceroy, unable to face them, retreated towards Quito. Pizarro followed him; and in that long march, through a wild, mountainous country, suffered hardships, and encountered difficulties, which no troops but those accustomed to serve in America could have endured or surmounted [140]. The viceroy had scarcely reached Quito, when the vanguard of Pizarro's forces appeared, led by Carvajal, who, though near fourscore, was as hardy and active as any young soldier under his command. Nugnez Vela instantly abandoned a town incapable of defence, and, with a rapidity more resembling a flight than a retreat, marched into the province of Popayan. Pizarro continued to pursue; but, finding it impossible to overtake him, returned to Quito. From thence he despatched Carvajal to oppose

* Zarate, lib. v. c. 8—10. Vega, p. 11. lib. iv. c. 13—19. Gomara, c. 159—163. Fernandez, lib. i. c. 18—25. Herrera, dec. 7. lib. viii. c. 10—20.

† Zarate, lib. v. c. 9. Gomara, c. 165. Fernandez, lib. i. c. 23. Herrera, dec. 7. lib. viii. c. 15.

‡ Zarate, lib. v. c. 18. Gomara, c. 160. Herrera, dec. 7. lib. ix. c. 27.

Centeno, who was growing formidable in the southern provinces of the empire, and he himself remained there to make head against the viceroy.*

By his own activity, and the assistance of Benalcazar, Nugnez Vela soon assembled four hundred men in Popayan. As he retained, amidst all his disasters, the same elevation of mind, and the same high sense of his own dignity, he rejected with disdain the advice of some of his followers who urged him to make overtures of accommodation to Pizarro, declaring that it was only by the sword that a contest with rebels could be decided. With this intention he marched back to Quito [1546]. Pizarro, relying on the superior number, and still more on the discipline and valour of his troops, advanced resolutely to meet him [Jan. 18]. The battle was fierce and bloody, both parties fighting like men who knew that the possession of a great empire, the fate of their leaders, and their own future fortune, depended upon the issue of that day. But Pizarro's veterans pushed forward with such regular and well directed force, that they soon began to make impression on their enemies. The viceroy, by extraordinary exertions, in which the abilities of a commander and the courage of a soldier were equally displayed, held victory for some time in suspense. At length he fell, pierced with many wounds; and the route of his followers became general. They were hotly pursued. His head was cut off, and placed on the public gibbet in Quito, which Pizarro entered in triumph. The troops assembled by Centeno were dispersed soon after by Carvajal, and he himself compelled to fly to the mountains, where he remained for several months concealed in a cave. Every person in Peru, from the frontiers of Popayan to those of Chili, submitted to Pizarro; and by his fleet, under Pedro de Hinojosa, he had not only the unrivalled command of the South Sea, but had taken possession of Panama, and placed a garrison in Nombre de Dios, on the opposite side of the isthmus, which rendered him master of the only avenue of communication between Spain and Peru, that was used at that period.†

After this decisive victory, Pizarro and his followers remained for some time at Quito; and during the first transports of their exultation, they ran into every excess of licentious indulgence, with the riotous spirit usual among low adventurers upon extraordinary success. But amidst this dissipation, their chief and his confidants were obliged to turn their thoughts sometimes to what was serious, and deliberated with much solicitude concerning the part that he ought now to take. Carvajal, no less bold and decisive in council than in the field, had from the beginning warned Pizarro, that in the career on which he was entering, it was vain to think of holding a middle course; that he must either boldly aim at all, or attempt nothing. From the time that Pizarro obtained possession of the government of Peru, he inculcated the same maxim with greater earnestness. Upon receiving an account of the victory at Quito, he remonstrated with him in a tone still more peremptory. "You have usurped," said he, in a letter written to Pizarro on that occasion, "the supreme power in this country, in contempt of the emperor's commission to the viceroy. You have marched in hostile array against the royal standard; you have attacked the representative of your sovereign in the field, have defeated him, and cut off his head. Think not that ever a monarch will forgive such insults on his dignity, or that any reconciliation with him can be cordial or sincere. Depend no longer on the precarious favour of another. Assume yourself the sovereignty over a country to the dominion of which your family has a title founded on the rights both of discovery and conquest. It is in your power to attach every Spaniard in Peru of any consequence inviolably to

* Zarate, lib. v. c. 15, 16—24. Gomara, c. 167. Vega, p. 11. lib. iv. c. 25—28. Fernandez, lib i. c. 34. 40. Herrera, dec. 7. lib. viii. c. 16. 20—27.

† Zarate, lib. v. c. 31, 32. Gomara, c. 170. Vega, p. 11. lib. iv. c. 33, 34. Fernandez, lib. i. c. 51—54. Herrera, dec. 7. lib. x. c. 12. 19—22. dec 8. lib. i. c. 1—3. Benzo, lib. iii. c. 12.

your interest, by liberal grants of lands and of Indians, or by instituting ranks of nobility, and creating titles of honour similar to those which are courted with so much eagerness in Europe. By establishing orders of knighthood, with privileges and distinctions resembling those in Spain, you may bestow a gratification upon the officers in your service, suited to the ideas of military men. Nor is it to your countrymen only that you ought to attend; endeavour to gain the natives. By marrying the Coya or daughter of the Sun next in succession to the crown, you will induce the Indians, out of veneration for the blood of their ancient princes, to unite with the Spaniards in support of your authority.—Thus, at the head of the ancient inhabitants of Peru, as well as of the new settlers there, you may set at defiance the power of Spain, and repel with ease any feeble force which it can send at such a distance." Cepeda, the lawyer, who was now Pizarro's confidential counsellor, warmly seconded Carvajal's exhortations, and employed whatever learning he possessed in demonstrating, that all the founders of great monarchies had been raised to pre-eminence, not by the antiquity of their lineage, or the validity of their rights, but by their own aspiring valour and personal merit.*

Pizarro listened attentively to both, and could not conceal the satisfaction with which he contemplated the object that they presented to his view. But, happily for the tranquillity of the world, few men possess that superior strength of mind, and extent of abilities, which are capable of forming and executing such daring schemes, as cannot be accomplished without overturning the established order of society, and violating those maxims of duty which men are accustomed to hold sacred. The mediocrity of Pizarro's talents circumscribed his ambition within more narrow limits. Instead of aspiring at independent power, he confined his views to the obtaining from the court of Spain a confirmation of the authority which he now possessed; and for that purpose he sent an officer of distinction thither, to give such a representation of his conduct, and of the state of the country, as might induce the emperor and his ministers, either from inclination or from necessity, to continue him in his present station.

While Pizarro was deliberating with respect to the part which he should take, consultations were held in Spain, with no less solicitude, concerning the measures which ought to be pursued in order to re-establish the emperor's authority in Peru. Though unacquainted with the last excesses of outrage to which the malecontents had proceeded in that country, the court had received an account of the insurrection against the viceroy, of his imprisonment, and the usurpation of the government by Pizarro. A revolution so alarming called for an immediate interposition of the emperor's abilities and authority. But as he was fully occupied at that time in Germany, in conducting the war against the famous league of Smalkalde, one of the most interesting and arduous enterprises in his reign, the care of providing a remedy for the disorders in Peru devolved upon his son Philip, and the counsellors whom Charles had appointed to assist him in the government of Spain during his absence. At first view, the actions of Pizarro and his adherents appeared so repugnant to the duty of subjects towards their sovereign, that the greater part of the ministers insisted on declaring them instantly to be guilty of rebellion, and on proceeding to punish them with exemplary rigour. But when the fervour of their zeal and indignation began to abate, innumerable obstacles to the execution of this measure presented themselves. The veteran bands of infantry, the strength and glory of the Spanish armies, were then employed in Germany. Spain, exhausted of men and money by a long series of wars, in which she had been involved by the restless ambition of two successive monarchs, could not easily equip an armament of sufficient force to reduce

* Vega, p. 11. lib. iv. c. 40. Fernandez, lib. i. c. 34 lib. ii. c. 1 49. Herrera, dec. 8. lib. ii. c. 10

Pizarro. To transport any respectable body of troops to a country so remote as Peru, appeared almost impossible. While Pizarro continued master of the South Sea, the direct route by Nombre de Dios and Panama was impracticable. An attempt to march to Quito by land through the new kingdom of Granada, and the province of Popayan, across regions of prodigious extent, desolate, unhealthy, or inhabited by fierce and hostile tribes, would be attended with insurmountable danger and hardships. The passage to the South Sea by the Straits of Magellan was so tedious, so uncertain, and so little known in that age, that no confidence could be placed in any effort carried on in a course of navigation so remote and precarious. Nothing then remained but to relinquish the system which the ardour of their loyalty had first suggested, and to attempt by lenient measures what could not be effected by force. It was manifest from Pizarro's solicitude to represent his conduct in a favourable light to the emperor, that notwithstanding the excesses of which he had been guilty, he still retained sentiments of veneration for his sovereign. By a proper application to these, together with some such concessions as should discover a spirit of moderation and forbearance in government, there was still room to hope that he might be yet reclaimed, or the ideas of loyalty natural to Spaniards might so far revive among his followers, that they would no longer lend their aid to uphold his usurped authority.

The success, however, of this negotiation, no less delicate than it was important, depended entirely on the abilities and address of the person to whom it should be committed. After weighing with much attention the comparative merit of various persons, the Spanish ministers fixed with unanimity of choice upon Pedro de la Gasca, a priest in no higher station than that of counsellor to the Inquisition. Though in no public office, he had been occasionally employed by government in affairs of trust and consequence, and had conducted them with no less skill than success; displaying a gentle and insinuating temper, accompanied with much firmness; probity, superior to any feeling of private interest; and a cautious circumspection in concerting measures, followed by such vigour in executing them as is rarely found in alliance with the other. These qualities marked him out for the function to which he was destined. The emperor, to whom Gasca was not unknown, warmly approved of the choice, and communicated it to him in a letter containing expressions of good will and confidence, no less honourable to the prince who wrote, than to the subject who received it. Gasca, notwithstanding his advanced age and feeble constitution, and though, from the apprehensions natural to a man, who, during the course of his life, had never been out of his own country, he dreaded the effects of a long voyage, and of an unhealthy climate,* did not hesitate a moment about complying with the will of his sovereign. But as a proof that it was from this principle alone he acted, he refused a bishopric which was offered to him in order that he might appear in Peru with a more dignified character; he would accept of no higher title than that of President of the Court of Audience in Lima; and declared that he would receive no salary on account of his discharging the duties of that office. All he required was, that the expense of supporting his family should be defrayed by the public; and as he was to go like a minister of peace with his gown and breviary, and without any retinue but a few domestics, this would not load the revenue with any enormous burden.†

But while he discovered such disinterested moderation with respect to whatever related personally to himself, he demanded his official powers in a very different tone. He insisted, as he was to be employed in a country so remote from the seat of government, where he could not have recourse to his sovereign for new instructions on every emergence; and as the whole

* Fernandez, lib. ii. c. 17.

† Zarate, lib. vi. c. 6. Gomara, c. 174. Fernandez, lib. ii. c. 14—16. Vega, p. 11. lib. v. c. 1. Herrera, dec. 8. lib. i. c. 4, &c.

success of his negotiations must depend upon the confidence which the people with whom he had to treat could place in the extent of his powers, that he ought to be invested with unlimited authority; that his jurisdiction must reach to all persons and to all causes; that he must be empowered to pardon, to punish, or to reward, as circumstances and the behaviour of different men might require; that in case of resistance from the malecontents, he might be authorized to reduce them to obedience by force of arms, to levy troops for that purpose, and to call for assistance from the governors of all the Spanish settlements in America. These powers, though manifestly conducive to the great objects of his mission, appeared to the Spanish ministers to be inalienable prerogatives of royalty, which ought not to be delegated to a subject, and they refused to grant them. But the emperor's views were more enlarged. As, from the nature of his employment, Gasca must be intrusted with discretionary power in several points, and all his efforts might prove ineffectual if he was circumscribed in any one particular, Charles scrupled not to invest him with authority to the full extent that he demanded. Highly satisfied with this fresh proof of his master's confidence, Gasca hastened his departure, and, without either money or troops, set out to quell a formidable rebellion.*

On his arrival at Nombre de Dios [July 27], he found Herman Mexia, an officer of note posted there, by order of Pizarro, with a considerable body of men, to oppose the landing of any hostile forces. But Gasca appeared in such pacific guise, with a train so little formidable, and with a title of no such dignity as to excite terror, that he was received with much respect. From Nombre de Dios he advanced to Panama, and met with a similar reception from Hinojosa, whom Pizarro had intrusted with the government of that town, and the command of his fleet stationed there. In both places he held the same language, declaring that he was sent by their sovereign as a messenger of peace, not as a minister of vengeance; that he came to redress all their grievances, to revoke the laws which had excited alarm, to pardon past offences, and to re-establish order and justice in the government of Peru. His mild deportment, the simplicity of his manners, the sanctity of his profession, and a winning appearance of candour, gained credit to his declarations. The veneration due to a person clothed with legal authority, and acting in virtue of a royal commission, began to revive among men accustomed for some time to nothing more respectable than a usurped jurisdiction. Hinojosa, Mexia, and several other officers of distinction, to each of whom Gasca applied separately, were gained over to his interest, and waited only for some decent occasion of declaring openly in his favour.†

This the violence of Pizarro soon afforded them. As soon as he heard of Gasca's arrival at Panama, though he received, at the same time, an account of the nature of his commission, and was informed of his offers not only to render every Spaniard in Peru easy concerning what was past, by an act of general oblivion, but secure with respect to the future, by repealing the obnoxious laws; instead of accepting with gratitude his sovereign's gracious concessions, he was so much exasperated on finding that he was not to be continued in his station as governor of the country, that he instantly resolved to oppose the president's entry into Peru, and to prevent his exercising any jurisdiction there. To this desperate resolution he added another highly preposterous. He sent a new deputation to Spain to justify this conduct, and to insist, in name of all the communities in Peru, for a confirmation of the government to himself during life, as the only means of preserving tranquillity there. The persons intrusted with this strange commission, intimated the intention of Pizarro to the president, and required him, in his name, to depart from Panama and return to Spain.

* Fernandez, lib. ii. c. 16—18. † Ibid. lib. ii. c. 21 &c. Zarate, lib. vi. c. 6, 7. Gomara, c. 175. Vega, p. 11. lib. v. c. 3

They carried likewise secret instructions to Hinojosa, directing him to offer Gasca a present of fifty thousand pesos, if he would comply voluntarily with what was demanded of him; and if he should continue obstinate, to cut him off, either by assassination or poison.*

Many circumstances concurred in pushing on Pizarro to those wild measures. Having been once accustomed to supreme command, he could not bear the thoughts of descending to a private station. Conscious of his own demerit, he suspected that the emperor studied only to deceive him, and would never pardon the outrages which he had committed. His chief confidants, no less guilty, entertained the same apprehensions. The approach of Gasca without any military force excited no terror. There were now above six thousand Spaniards settled in Peru;† and at the head of these he doubted not to maintain his own independence, if the court of Spain should refuse to grant what he required. But he knew not that a spirit of defection had already begun to spread among those whom he trusted most. Hinojosa, amazed at Pizarro's precipitate resolution of setting himself in opposition to the emperor's commission, and disdaining to be his instrument in perpetrating the odious crimes pointed out in his secret instructions, publicly recognised the title of the president to the supreme authority in Peru. The officers under his command did the same. Such was the contagious influence of the example, that it reached even the deputies who had been sent from Peru; and at the time when Pizarro expected to hear either of Gasca's return to Spain, or of his death, he received an account of his being master of the fleet, of Panama, and of the troops stationed there.

1547.] Irritated almost to madness by events so unexpected, he openly prepared for war; and in order to give some colour of justice to his arms, he appointed the court of audience in Lima to proceed to the trial of Gasca, for the crimes of having seized his ships, seduced his officers, and prevented his deputies from proceeding in their voyage to Spain. Cepeda, though acting as a judge in virtue of the royal commission, did not scruple to prostitute the dignity of his function by finding Gasca guilty of treason, and condemning him to death on that account.‡ Wild and even ridiculous as this proceeding was, it imposed on the low illiterate adventurers, with whom Peru was filled, by the semblance of a legal sanction warranting Pizarro to carry on hostilities against a convicted traitor. Soldiers accordingly resorted from every quarter to his standard, and he was soon at the head of a thousand men, the best equipped that had ever taken the field in Peru.

Gasca, on his part, perceiving that force must be employed in order to accomplish the purpose of his mission, was no less assiduous in collecting troops from Nicaragua, Carthagena, and other settlements on the continent; and with such success, that he was soon in a condition to detach a squadron of his fleet, with a considerable body of soldiers, to the coast of Peru [April]. Their appearance excited a dreadful alarm: and though they did not attempt for some time to make any descent, they did more effectual service by setting ashore in different places persons who dispersed copies of the act of general indemnity, and the revocation of the late edicts; and who made known every where the pacific intentions, as well as mild temper, of the president. The effect of spreading this information was wonderful. All who were dissatisfied with Pizarro's violent administration, all who retained any sentiments of fidelity to their sovereign, began to meditate revolt. Some openly deserted a cause which they now deemed to be unjust. Centeno, leaving the cave in which he lay concealed.

* Zarate, lib. vi. c. 8. Fernandez, lib. ii. c. 33, 34. Herrera, dec. 8. lib. ii. c. 9, 10. † Herrera, dec. 8. lib. iii. c. 1. ‡ Fernandez, lib. ii. c. 55. Vega, p. 11. lib. v. c. 7. Herrera, dec. 8 lib iii. c. 6

assembled about fifty of his former adherents, and with this feeble half-armed band advanced boldly to Cuzco. By a sudden attack in the night-time, in which he displayed no less military skill than valour, he rendered himself master of that capital, though defended by a garrison of five hundred men. Most of these having ranged themselves under his banners, he had soon the command of a respectable body of troops.*

Pizarro, though astonished at beholding one enemy approaching by sea, and another by land, at a time when he trusted to the union of all Peru in his favour, was of a spirit more undaunted, and more accustomed to the vicissitudes of fortune, than to be disconcerted or appalled. As the danger from Centeno's operations was the most urgent, he instantly set out to oppose him. Having provided horses for all his soldiers, he marched with amazing rapidity. But every morning he found his force diminished, by numbers who had left him during the night; and though he became suspicious to excess, and punished without mercy all whom he suspected, the rage of desertion was too violent to be checked. Before he got within sight of the enemy at Huarina, near the lake of Titiaca, he could not muster more than four hundred soldiers. But these he justly considered as men of tried attachment, on whom he might depend. They were indeed the boldest and most desperate of his followers, conscious, like himself, of crimes for which they could hardly expect forgiveness, and without any hope but in the success of their arms. With these he did not hesitate to attack Centeno's troops [Oct. 20], though double to his own in number. The royalists did not decline the combat. It was the most obstinate and bloody that had hitherto been fought in Peru. At length the intrepid valour of Pizarro, and the superiority of Carvajal's military talents, triumphed over numbers, and obtained a complete victory. The booty was immense [141], and the treatment of the vanquished cruel. By this signal success the reputation of Pizarro was re-established; and being now deemed invincible in the field, his army increased daily in number.†

But events happened in other parts of Peru, which more than counterbalanced the splendid victory at Huarina. Pizarro had scarcely left Lima, when the citizens, weary of his oppressive dominion, erected the royal standard, and Aldana, with a detachment of soldiers from the fleet, took possession of the town. About the same time,‡ Gasca landed at Tumbez with five hundred men. Encouraged by his presence, every settlement in the low country declared for the king. The situation of the two parties was now perfectly reversed; Cuzco and the adjacent provinces were possessed by Pizarro; all the rest of the empire, from Quito southward, acknowledged the jurisdiction of the president. As his numbers augmented fast, Gasca advanced into the interior part of the country. His behaviour still continued to be gentle and unassuming; he expressed, on every occasion, his ardent wish of terminating the contest without bloodshed. More solicitous to reclaim than to punish, he upbraided no man for past offences, but received them as a father receives penitent children returning to a sense of their duty. Though desirous of peace, he did not slacken his preparations for war. He appointed the general rendezvous of his troops in the fertile valley of Xauxa, on the road to Cuzco.§ There he remained for some months, not only that he might have time to make another attempt towards an accommodation with Pizarro, but that he might train his new soldiers to the use of arms, and accustom them to the discipline of a camp, before he led them against a body of victorious veterans. Pizarro, intoxicated with the success which

* Zarate, lib. vi. c. 13—16. Gomara, c. 180, 181. Fernandez, lib. ii. c. 28. 64, &c. † Zarate, lib. vii. c. 2, 3. Gomara, c. 181. Vega, p. 11. lib. v. c. 18, &c. Fernandez, lib. ii. c. 79. Herrera, dec. 8. lib. iv. c. 1, 2. ‡ Zarate, lib. vi. c. 17. § Ibid. lib. vii. c. 9. Fernandez, lib ii. c. 77. 82

had hitherto accompanied his arms, and elated with having again near a thousand men under his command, refused to listen to any terms, although Cepeda, together with several of his officers, and even Carvajal himself [142], gave it as their advice, to close with the president's offer of a general indemnity, and the revocation of the obnoxious laws.* Gasca, having tried in vain every expedient to avoid imbruing his hands in the blood of his countrymen, began to move towards Cuzco [Dec. 29] at the head of sixteen hundred men.

Pizarro, confident of victory, suffered the royalists to pass all the rivers which lie between Guamanga and Cuzco without opposition [1548], and to advance within four leagues of that capital, flattering himself that a defeat in such a situation as rendered escape impracticable would at once terminate the war. He then marched out to meet the enemy, and Carvajal chose his ground, and made the disposition of the troops with the discerning eye and profound knowledge in the art of war conspicuous in all his operations. As the two armies moved forward slowly to the charge [April 9], the appearance of each was singular. In that of Pizarro, composed of men enriched with the spoils of the most opulent country in America, every officer, and almost all the private men, were clothed in stuffs of silk, or brocade, embroidered with gold and silver; and their horses, their arms, their standards, were adorned with all the pride of military pomp.† That of Gasca, though not so splendid, exhibited what was no less striking. He himself, accompanied by the archbishop of Lima, the bishops of Quito and Cuzco, and a great number of ecclesiastics, marching along the lines, blessing the men, and encouraging them to a resolute discharge of their duty.

When both armies were just ready to engage, Cepeda set spurs to his horse, galloped off, and surrendered himself to the president. Garcilasso de la Vega, and other officers of note, followed his example. The revolt of persons in such high rank struck all with amazement. The mutual confidence on which the union and strength of armies depend, ceased at once. Distrust and consternation spread from rank to rank. Some silently slipped away, others threw down their arms, the greatest number went over to the royalists. Pizarro, Carvajal, and some leaders, employed authority, threats, and entreaties, to stop them, but in vain. In less than half an hour, a body of men, which might have decided the fate of the Peruvian empire, was totally dispersed. Pizarro, seeing all irretrievably lost, cried out in amazement to a few officers who still faithfully adhered to him, "What remains for us to do?"—"Let us rush," replied one of them, "upon the enemy's firmest battalion, and die like Romans." Dejected with such a reverse of fortune, he had not spirit to follow this soldierly counsel, and with a tameness disgraceful to his former fame he surrendered to one of Gasca's officers. Carvajal, endeavouring to escape, was overtaken and seized.

Gasca, happy in this bloodless victory, did not stain it with cruelty. Pizarro, Carvajal, and a small number of the most distinguished or notorious offenders, were punished capitally. Pizarro was beheaded the day after he surrendered. He submitted to his fate with a composed dignity, and seemed desirous to atone by repentance for the crimes which he had committed. The end of Carvajal was suitable to his life. On his trial he offered no defence. When the sentence adjudging him to be hanged was pronounced, he carelessly replied, "One can die but once." During the interval between the sentence and execution, he discovered no sign either of remorse for the past, or of solicitude about the future; scoffing at all who visited him, in his usual sarcastic vein of mirth, with the same quickness of repartee and gross pleasantry as at any other period of his

* Zarate, lib. vii. c. 6 Vega, p. 11. lib. v c. 27. Zarate, lib. vi. c. 11.

life. Cepeda, more criminal than either, ought to have shared the same fate, but the merit of having deserted his associates at such a critical moment, and with such decisive effect, saved him from immediate punishment. He was sent, however, as a prisoner to Spain, and died in confinement.*

In the minute details which the contemporary historians have given of the civil dissensions that raged in Peru, with little interruption, during ten years, many circumstances occur so striking, and which indicate such an uncommon state of manners as to merit particular attention.

Though the Spaniards who first invaded Peru were of the lowest order in society, and the greater part of those who afterwards joined them were persons of desperate fortune, yet in all the bodies of troops brought into the field by the different leaders who contended for superiority, not one man acted as a hired soldier, that follows his standard for pay. Every adventurer in Peru considered himself as a conqueror, entitled by his services, to an establishment in that country which had been acquired by his valour. In the contests between the rival chiefs, each chose his side as he was directed by his own judgment or affections. He joined his commander as a companion of his fortunes, and disdained to degrade himself by receiving the wages of a mercenary. It was to their sword, not to pre-eminence in office, or nobility of birth, that most of the leaders whom they followed were indebted for their elevation; and each of their adherents hoped, by the same means, to open a way for himself to the possession of power and wealth.†

But though the troops in Peru served without any regular pay, they were raised at immense expense. Among men accustomed to divide the spoils of an opulent country, the desire of obtaining wealth acquired incredible force. The ardour of pursuit augmented in proportion to the hope of success. Where all were intent on the same object, and under the dominion of the same passion, there was but one mode of gaining men, or of securing their attachment. Officers of name and influence, besides the promise of future establishments, received in hand large gratuities from the chief with whom they engaged. Gonzalo Pizarro, in order to raise a thousand men, advanced five hundred thousand pesos.‡ Gasca expended in levying the troops which he led against Pizarro nine hundred thousand pesos.§ The distribution of property, bestowed as the reward of services, was still more exorbitant. Cepeda, as the recompense of his perfidy and address, in persuading the court of royal audience to give the sanction of its authority to the usurped jurisdiction of Pizarro, received a grant of lands which yielded an annual income of a hundred and fifty thousand pesos.|| Hinojosa, who by his early defection from Pizarro, and surrender of the fleet to Gasca, decided the fate of Peru, obtained a district of country affording two hundred thousand pesos of yearly value.¶ While such rewards were dealt out to the principal officers, with more than royal munificence, proportional shares were conferred upon those of inferior rank.

Such a rapid change of fortune produced its natural effects. It gave birth to new wants and new desires. Veterans, long accustomed to hardship and toil, acquired of a sudden a taste for profuse and inconsiderate dissipation, and indulged in all the excesses of military licentiousness. The riot of low debauchery occupied some; a relish for expensive luxuries spread among others.** The meanest soldier in Peru would have thought himself degraded by marching on foot; and at a time when the prices of horses in that country were exorbitant, each insisted on being furnished with one before he would take the field. But though less patient under the fatigue and hardships of service, they were ready to face danger and

* Zarate, lib. vii. c. 6, 7, 8. Gomara, c. 185, 186. Vega, p. 11. lib. v. c. 30, &c. Fernandez, lib. ii. c. 86, &c. Herrera, dec. 8. lib. iv. c. 14, &c. † Vega, p. 11. lib. iv. c. 38. 41. ‡ Fernandez, lib. ii. c. 54. § Zarate, lib. vii. c. 10. Herrera, dec. 8. lib. v. c. 7. || Gomara, c. 164. ¶ Vega, p. 11. lib. vi. c. 3. ** Herrera, dec. 5. lib. ii. c. 3. dec. 8. lib. viii. c. 10.

death with as much intrepidity as ever; and animated by the hope of new rewards, they never failed, on the day of battle, to display all their ancient valour.

Together with their courage, they retained all the ferocity by which they were originally distinguished. Civil discord never raged with a more fell spirit than among the Spaniards in Peru. To all the passions which usually envenom contests among countrymen, avarice was added, and rendered their enmity more rancorous. Eagerness to seize the valuable forfeitures, expected upon the death of every opponent, shut the door against mercy. To be wealthy was of itself sufficient to expose a man to accusation, or to subject him to punishment. On the slightest suspicions, Pizarro condemned many of the most opulent inhabitants in Peru to death. Carvajal, without searching for any pretext to justify his cruelty, cut off many more. The number of those who suffered by the hands of the executioner was not much inferior to what fell in the field [143]; and the greater part was condemned without the formality of any legal trial.

The violence with which the contending parties treated their opponents was not accompanied with its usual attendants, attachment and fidelity to those with whom they acted. The ties of honour, which ought to be held sacred among soldiers, and the principle of integrity, interwoven as thoroughly in the Spanish character as in that of any nation, seem to have been equally forgotten. Even regard for decency, and the sense of shame, were totally lost. During their dissensions, there was hardly a Spaniard in Peru who did not abandon the party which he had originally espoused, betray the associates with whom he had united, and violate the engagements under which he had come. The viceroy Nugnez Vela was ruined by the treachery of Cepeda and the other judges of the royal audience, who were bound by the duties of their function to have supported his authority. The chief advisers and companions of Gonzalo Pizarro's revolt were the first to forsake him, and submit to his enemies. His fleet was given up to Gasca by the man whom he had singled out among his officers to intrust with that important command. On the day that was to decide his fate, an army of veterans, in sight of the enemy, threw down their arms without striking a blow, and deserted a leader who had often conducted them to victory. Instances of such general and avowed contempt of the principles and obligations which attach man to man, and bind them together in social union, rarely occur in history. It is only where men are far removed from the seat of government, where the restraints of law and order are little felt, where the prospect of gain is unbounded, and where immense wealth may cover the crimes by which it is acquired, that we can find any parallel to the levity, the rapaciousness, the perfidy, and corruption prevalent among the Spaniards in Peru.

On the death of Pizarro, the malecontents in every corner of Peru laid down their arms, and tranquillity seemed to be perfectly re-established. But two very interesting objects still remained to occupy the president's attention. The one was to find immediately such employment for a multitude of turbulent and daring adventurers with which the country was filled, as might prevent them from exciting new commotions. The other, to bestow proper gratifications upon those to whose loyalty and valour he had been indebted for his success. The former of these was in some measure accomplished, by appointing Pedro de Valdivia to prosecute the conquest of Chili; and by empowering Diego Centeno to undertake the discovery of the vast regions bordering on the river De la Plata. The reputation of those leaders, together with the hopes of acquiring wealth, and of rising to consequence in some unexplored country, alluring many of the most indigent and desperate soldiers to follow their standards, drained off no inconsiderable portion of that mutinous spirit which Gasca dreaded.

The latter was an affair of greater difficulty and to be adjusted with a more attentive and delicate hand. The *repartimientos*, or allotments of lands and Indians which fell to be distributed, in consequence of the death or forfeiture of the former possessors, exceeded two millions of pesos of yearly rent.* Gasca, when now absolute master of this immense property, retained the same disinterested sentiments which he had originally professed, and refused to reserve the smallest portion of it for himself. But the number of claimants was great; and whilst the vanity or avarice of every individual fixed the value of his own services, and estimated the recompense which he thought due to him, the pretensions of each were so extravagant that it was impossible to satisfy all. Gasca listened to them one by one, with the most patient attention; and that he might have leisure to weigh the comparative merit of their several claims with accuracy, he retired, with the archbishop of Lima and a single secretary, to a village twelve leagues from Cuzco. There he spent several days in allotting to each a district of lands and number of Indians, in proportion to his idea of their past services and future importance. But that he might get beyond the reach of the fierce storm of clamour and rage, which he foresaw would burst out on the publication of his decree, notwithstanding the impartial equity with which he had framed it, he set out for Lima, leaving the instrument of partition sealed up, with orders not to open it for some days after his departure.

The indignation excited by publishing the decree of partition [Aug. 24] was not less than Gasca had expected. Vanity, avarice, emulation, envy, shame, rage, and all the other passions which most vehemently agitate the minds of men when both their honour and their interest are deeply affected, conspired in adding to its violence. It broke out with all the fury of military insolence. Calumny, threats, and curses, were poured out openly upon the president. He was accused of ingratitude, of partiality, and of injustice. Among soldiers prompt to action, such seditious discourse would have been soon followed by deeds no less violent, and they already began to turn their eyes towards some discontented leaders, expecting them to stand forth in redress of their wrongs. By some vigorous interpositions of government, a timely check was given to this mutinous spirit, and the danger of another civil war was averted for the present.†

1549.] Gasca, however, perceiving that the flame was suppressed, rather than extinguished, laboured with the utmost assiduity to soothe the malecontents, by bestowing large gratuities on some, by promising *repartimientos*, when they fell vacant, to others, and by caressing and flattering all. But that the public security might rest on a foundation more stable than their good affection, he endeavoured to strengthen the hands of his successors in office, by re-establishing the regular administration of justice in every part of the empire. He introduced order and simplicity into the mode of collecting the royal revenue. He issued regulations concerning the treatment of the Indians, well calculated to protect them from oppression, and to provide for their instruction in the principles of religion, without depriving the Spaniards of the benefit accruing from their labour. Having now accomplished every object of his mission, Gasca, longing to return again to a private station, committed the government of Peru to the court of audience, and set out for Spain [Feb. 1, 1550]. As, during the anarchy and turbulence of the four last years, there had been no remittance made of the royal revenue, he carried with him thirteen hundred thousand pesos of public money, which the economy and order of his administration enabled him to save, after paying all the expenses of the war.

He was received in his native country with universal admiration of his

* Vega, p. 11. lib. vi. c. 4. † Zarate, lib. vii. c. 9. Gomara, c. 187. Vega, p. 11. lib. vii. c. 1, &c. Fernandez, p. 11. lib. I. c. 1, &c. Herrera, dec. 8. lib. iv. c. 17, &c.

abilities and of his virtue. Both were, indeed, highly conspicuous. Without army, or fleet, or public funds; with a train so simple, that only three thousand ducats were expended in equipping him,* he set out to oppose a formidable rebellion. By his address and talents he supplied all those defects, and seemed to create instruments for executing his designs. He acquired such a naval force as gave him the command of the sea. He raised a body of men able to cope with the veteran bands which gave law to Peru. He vanquished their leader, on whose arms victory had hitherto attended, and in place of anarchy and usurpation, he established the government of laws, and the authority of the rightful sovereign. But the praise bestowed on his abilities was exceeded by that which his virtue merited. After residing in a country where wealth presented allurements which had seduced every person who had hitherto possessed power there, he returned from that trying station with integrity not only untainted but unsuspected. After distributing among his countrymen possessions of greater extent and value than had ever been in the disposal of a subject in any age or nation, he himself remained in his original state of poverty; and at the very time when he brought such a large recruit to the royal treasury, he was obliged to apply by petition for a small sum to discharge some petty debts which he had contracted during the course of his service.† Charles was not insensible to such disinterested merit. Gasca was received by him with the most distinguishing marks of esteem; and being promoted to the bishopric of Palencia, he passed the remainder of his days in the tranquillity of retirement, respected by his country, honoured by his sovereign, and beloved by all.

Notwithstanding all Gasca's wise regulations, the tranquillity of Peru was not of long continuance. In a country where the authority of government had been almost forgotten during the long prevalence of anarchy and misrule, where there were disappointed leaders ripe for revolt, and seditious soldiers ready to follow them, it was not difficult to raise combustion. Several successive insurrections desolated the country for some years. But as those, though fierce, were only transient storms, excited rather by the ambition and turbulence of particular men, than by general or public motives, the detail of them is not the object of this history. These commotions in Peru, like every thing of extreme violence either in the natural or political body, were not of long duration; and by carrying off the corrupted humours which had given rise to the disorders, they contributed in the end to strengthen the society which at first they threatened to destroy. During their fierce contests, several of the first invaders of Peru, and many of those licentious adventurers whom the fame of their success had allured thither, fell by each other's hands. Each of the parties, as they alternately prevailed in the struggle, gradually cleared the country of a number of turbulent spirits, by executing, proscribing, or banishing their opponents. Men less enterprising, less desperate, and more accustomed to move in the path of sober and peaceable industry, settled in Peru; and the royal authority was gradually established as firmly there as in other Spanish colonies.

* Fernandez, lib. ii. c. 18. † MS. penes me.

# BOOK VII.

As the conquest of the two great empires of Mexico and Peru forms the most splendid and interesting period in the history of America, a view of their political institutions, and a description of their national manners, will exhibit the human species to the contemplation of intelligent observers in a very singular stage of its progress. [144]

When compared with other parts of the New World, Mexico and Peru may be considered as polished states. Instead of small, independent, hostile tribes, struggling for subsistence amidst woods and marshes, strangers to industry and arts, unacquainted with subordination, and almost without the appearance of regular government, we find countries of great extent subjected to the dominion of one sovereign, the inhabitants collected together in cities, the wisdom and foresight of rulers employed in providing for the maintenance and security of the people, the empire of laws in some measure established, the authority of religion recognised, many of the arts essential to life brought to some degree of maturity, and the dawn of such as are ornamental beginning to appear.

But if the comparison be made with the people of the ancient continent, the inferiority of America in improvement will be conspicuous, and neither the Mexicans nor Peruvians will be entitled to rank with those nations which merit the name of civilized. The people of both the great empires in America, like the rude tribes around them, were totally unacquainted with the useful metals, and the progress which they had made in extending their dominion over the animal creation was inconsiderable. The Mexicans had gone no further than to tame and rear turkeys, ducks, a species of small dogs, and rabbits.* By this feeble essay of ingenuity, the means of subsistence were rendered somewhat more plentiful and secure than when men depend solely on hunting; but they had no idea of attempting to subdue the more robust animals, or of deriving any aid from their ministry in carrying on works of labour. The Peruvians seem to have neglected the inferior animals, and had not rendered any of them domestic except the duck; but they were more fortunate in taming the Llama, an animal peculiar to their country, of a form which bears some resemblance to a deer, and some to a camel, and is of a size somewhat larger than a sheep. Under the protection of man, this species multiplied greatly. Its wool furnished the Peruvians with clothing, its flesh with food. It was even employed as a beast of burden, and carried a moderate load with much patience and docility.† It was never used for draught; and the breed being confined to the mountainous country, its service, if we may judge by incidents which occur in the early Spanish writers, was not very extensive among the Peruvians in their original state.

In tracing the line by which nations proceed towards civilization, the discovery of the useful metals, and the acquisition of dominion over the animal creation, have been marked as steps of capital importance in their progress. In our continent, long after men had attained both, society continued in that state which is denominated barbarous. Even with all that command over nature which these confer, many ages elapse before industry becomes so regular as to render subsistence secure, before the arts which supply the wants and furnish the accommodations of life are brought to any considerable degree of perfection, and before any idea is conceived of various institutions requisite in a well ordered society. The Mexicans

* Herrera, dec. II. lib. vii. c. 12. † Vega, p. 1. lib. viii. c. 16. Zarate, lib. 1. c. 14.

and Peruvians, without knowledge of the useful metals, or the aid of domestic animals, laboured under disadvantages which must have greatly retarded their progress, and in their highest state of improvement their power was so limited, and their operations so feeble, that they can hardly be considered as having advanced beyond the infancy of civil life.

After this general observation concerning the most singular and distinguishing circumstance in the state of both the great empires in America, I shall endeavour to give such a view of the constitution of the interior police of each as may enable us to ascertain their place in the political scale, to allot them their proper station between the rude tribes in the New World, and the polished states of the ancient, and to determine how far they had risen above the former, as well as how much they fell below the latter.

Mexico was first subjected to the Spanish crown. But our acquaintance with its laws and manners is not, from that circumstance, more complete. What I have remarked concerning the defective and inaccurate information on which we must rely with respect to the condition and customs of the savage tribes in America, may be applied likewise to our knowledge of the Mexican empire. Cortes, and the rapacious adventurers who accompanied him, had not leisure or capacity to enrich either civil or natural history with new observations. They undertook their expedition in quest of one object, and seemed hardly to have turned their eyes towards any other. Or, if during some short interval of tranquillity, when the occupations of war ceased, and the ardour of plunder was suspended, the institutions and manners of the people whom they invaded, drew their attention, the inquiries of illiterate soldiers were conducted with so little sagacity and precision, that the accounts given by them of the policy and order established in the Mexican monarchy are superficial, confused, and inexplicable. It is rather from incidents which they relate occasionally, than from their own deductions and remarks, that we are enabled to form some idea of the genius and manners of that people. The obscurity in which the ignorance of its conquerors involved the annals of Mexico, was augmented by the superstition of those who succeeded them. As the memory of past events was preserved among the Mexicans by figures painted on skins, on cotton cloth, on a kind of pasteboard, or on the bark of trees, the early missionaries, unable to comprehend their meaning, and struck with their uncouth forms, conceived them to be monuments of idolatry, which ought to be destroyed in order to facilitate the conversion of the Indians. In obedience to an edict issued by Juan de Zummaraga, a Franciscan monk, the first bishop of Mexico, as many records of the ancient Mexican story as could be collected were committed to the flames. In consequence of this fanatical zeal of the monks who first visited New Spain (which their successors soon began to lament), whatever knowledge of remote events such rude monuments contained was almost entirely lost, and no information remained concerning the ancient revolutions and policy of the empire, but what was derived from tradition, or from some fragments of their historical paintings that escaped the barbarous researches of Zummaraga.* From the experience of all nations it is manifest, that the memory of past transactions can neither be long preserved, nor be transmitted with any fidelity, by tradition. The Mexican paintings which are supposed to have served as annals of their empire, are few in number, and of ambiguous meaning. Thus, amidst the uncertainty of the former, and the obscurity of the latter, we must glean what intelligence can be collected from the scanty materials scattered in the Spanish writers.†

* Acosta, lib. vi. c. 7. Torquem. Proem. lib ii. lib. iii. c. 6. lib. xiv. c 6.

† In the first edition, I observed that in consequence of the destruction of the ancient Mexican paintings, occasioned by the zeal of Zummaraga, whatever knowledge they might have conveyed was *entirely* lost. Every candid reader must have perceived that the expression was inaccurate;

According to the account of the Mexicans themselves, their empire was not of long duration. Their country, as they relate, was originally possessed, rather than peopled, by small independent tribes, whose mode of life and manners resembled those of the rudest savages which we have described. But about a period corresponding to the beginning of the tenth century in the Christian era, several tribes moved in successive migrations from unknown regions towards the north and north-west, and settled in different provinces of *Anahuac*, the ancient name of New Spain. These, more civilized than the original inhabitants, began to form them to the arts of social life. At length, towards the commencement of the thirteenth century, the Mexicans, a people more polished than any of the former, advanced from the border of the Californian gulf, and took possession of the plains adjacent to the great lake near the centre of the country. After residing there about fifty years, they founded a town, since distinguished by the name of *Mexico*, which, from humble beginnings, soon grew to be the most considerable city in the New World. The Mexicans, long after they were established in their new possessions, continued, like other martial tribes in America, unacquainted with regal dominion, and were governed in peace, and conducted in war, by such as were entitled to pre-eminence by their wisdom or their valour. But among them, as in other states whose power and territories become extensive, the supreme authority centred at last in a single person; and when the Spaniards under Cortes invaded the country, Montezuma was the ninth monarch in order who had swayed the Mexican sceptre, not by hereditary right, but by election.

Such is the traditional tale of the Mexicans concerning the progress of their own empire. According to this, its duration was very short. From the first migration of their parent tribe, they can reckon little more than three hundred years. From the establishment of monarchical government, not above a hundred and thirty years according to one account,* or a hundred and ninety-seven according to another computation,† had elapsed. If, on one hand, we suppose the Mexican state to have been of higher antiquity, and to have subsisted during such a length of time as the Spanish accounts of its civilization would naturally lead us to conclude, it is difficult to conceive how, among a people who possessed the art of record-

as in a few lines afterwards I mention some ancient paintings to be still extant. M. Clavigero, not satisfied with laying hold of this inaccuracy, which I corrected in the subsequent editions, labours to render it more glaring by the manner in which he quotes the remaining part of the sentence. He reprehends with great asperity the account which I gave of the scanty materials for writing the ancient history of Mexico. Vol. I. Account of Writers, p. xxvi. Vol. II. 380. My words, however, are almost the same with those of Torquemada, who seems to have been better acquainted with the ancient monuments of the Mexicans than any Spanish author whose works I have seen. Lib. xiv. c. 6. M. Clavigero himself gives a description of the destruction of ancient paintings in almost the same terms I have used; and mentions as an additional reason of there being so small a number of ancient paintings known to the Spaniards, that the natives have become so solicitous to preserve and conceal them, that it is "difficult, if not impossible, to make them part with one of them." Vol. I. 407. II. 194. No point can be more ascertained than that few of the Mexican historical paintings have been preserved. Though several Spaniards have carried on inquiries into the antiquities of the Mexican empire, no engravings from Mexican paintings have been communicated to the public, except those by Purchas, Gemelli Carreri, and Lorenzana. It affords me some satisfaction, that in the course of my researches I have discovered two collections of Mexican paintings which were unknown to former inquirers. The cut which I published is an exact copy of the original, and gives no high idea of the progress which the Mexicans had made in the art of painting. I cannot conjecture what could induce M. Clavigero to express some dissatisfaction with me for having published it without the same colours it has in the original painting, p. xxix. He might have recollected, that neither Purchas, nor Gemelli Carreri, nor Lorenzana, thought it necessary to colour the prints which they have published, and they have never been censured on that account. He may rest assured, that though the colours in the paintings in the Imperial Library are remarkably bright, they are laid on without art, and without "any of that regard to light and shade, or the rules of perspective," which M. Clavigero requires. Vol. II. 378. If the public express any desire to have the seven paintings still in my possession engraved, I am ready to communicate them. The print published by Gemelli Carreri, of the route of the ancient Mexicans when they travelled towards the lake on which they built the capital of their empire, (Churchill, Vol. IV. p. 481.) is the most finished monument of art brought from the New World, and yet a very slight inspection of it will satisfy every one, that the annals of a nation conveyed in this manner must be very meagre and imperfect.

* Acost. Hist. lib. vii. c. 8, &c. † Purchas Pilgr. iii. p. 1068, &c.

ing events by pictures, and who considered it as an essential part of their national education, to teach their children to repeat the historical songs which celebrated the exploits of their ancestors,* the knowledge of past transactions should be so slender and limited. If, on the other hand, we adopt their own system with respect to the antiquities of their nation, it is no less difficult to account either for that improved state of society, or for the extensive dominion to which their empire had attained when first visited by the Spaniards. The infancy of nations is so long, and, even when every circumstance is favourable to their progress, they advance so slowly towards any maturity of strength or policy, that the recent origin of the Mexicans seems to be a strong presumption of some exaggeration in the splendid descriptions which have been given of their government and manners.

But it is not by theory or conjectures that history decides with regard to the state or character of nations. It produces facts as the foundation of every judgment which it ventures to pronounce. In collecting those which must regulate our opinion in the present inquiry, some occur that suggest an idea of considerable progress in civilization in the Mexican empire, and others which seem to indicate that it had advanced but little beyond the savage tribes around it. Both shall be exhibited to the view of the reader, that, from comparing them, he may determine on which side the evidence preponderates.

In the Mexican empire, the right of private property was perfectly understood, and established in its full extent. Among several savage tribes, we have seen, that the idea of a title to the separate and exclusive possession of any object was hardly known; and that among all it was extremely limited and ill defined. But in Mexico, where agriculture and industry had made some progress, the distinction between property in land and property in goods had taken place. Both might be transferred from one person to another by sale or barter; both might descend by inheritance. Every person who could be denominated a freeman had property in land. This, however, they held by various tenures. Some possessed it in full right, and it descended to their heirs. The title of others to their lands was derived from the office or dignity which they enjoyed; and when deprived of the latter, they lost possession of the former. Both these modes of occupying land were deemed noble, and peculiar to citizens of the highest class. The tenure by which the great body of the people held their property, was very different. In every district a certain quantity of land was measured out in proportion to the number of families. This was cultivated by the joint labour of the whole; its produce was deposited in a common storehouse, and divided among them according to their respective exigencies. The members of the *Calpullee*, or associations, could not alienate their share of the common estate; it was an indivisible permanent property, destined for the support of their families.† In consequence of this distribution of the territory of the state, every man had an interest in its welfare, and the happiness of the individual was connected with the public security.

Another striking circumstance, which distinguishes the Mexican empire from those nations in America we have already described, is the number and greatness of its cities. While society continues in a rude state, the wants of men are so few, and they stand so little in need of mutual assistance, that their inducements to crowd together are extremely feeble. Their industry at the same time is so imperfect, that it cannot secure subsistence for any considerable number of families settled in one spot. They live dispersed, at this period, from choice, as well as from necessity, or at the utmost assemble in small hamlets on the banks of the river

* Herrera, dec. 3. lib. ii. c. 18. † Herrera, dec. 3. lib. iv. c. 15. Torquem. Mon. Ind. lib. xiv c. 7. Corita MS.

which supplies them with food, or on the border of some plain left open by nature, or cleared by their own labour. The Spaniards, accustomed to this mode of habitation among all the savage tribes with which they were hitherto acquainted, were astonished, on entering New Spain, to find the natives residing in towns of such extent as resembled those of Europe. In the first fervour of their admiration, they compared Zempoalla, though a town only of the second or third size, to the cities of greatest note in their own country. When, afterwards, they visited in succession Tlascala, Cholula, Tacuba, Tezeuco, and Mexico itself, their amazement increased so much, that it led them to convey ideas of their magnitude and populousness bordering on what is incredible. Even when there is leisure for observation, and no interest that leads to deceive, conjectural estimates of the number of people in cities are extremely loose, and usually much exaggerated. It is not surprising, then, that Cortes and his companions, little accustomed to such computations, and powerfully tempted to magnify, in order to exalt the merit of their own discoveries and conquests, should have been betrayed into this common error, and have raised their descriptions considerably above truth. For this reason, some considerable abatement ought to be made from their calculations of the number of inhabitants in the Mexican cities, and we may fix the standard of their population much lower than they have done; but still they will appear to be cities of such consequence as are not to be found but among people who have made some considerable progress in the arts of social life [145]. From their accounts, we can hardly suppose Mexico, the capital of the empire, to have contained fewer than sixty thousand inhabitants.

The separation of professions among the Mexicans is a symptom of improvement no less remarkable. Arts, in the early ages of society, are so few and so simple, that each man is sufficiently master of them all, to gratify every demand of his own limited desires. The savage can form his bow, point his arrows, rear his hut, and hollow his canoe, without calling in the aid of any hand more skilful than his own. Time must have augmented the wants of men, and ripened their ingenuity, before the productions of art became so complicated in their structure, or so curious in their fabric, that a particular course of education was requisite towards forming the artificer to expertness in contrivance and workmanship. In proportion as refinement spreads, the distinction of professions increases, and they branch out into more numerous and minute subdivisions. Among the Mexicans, this separation of the arts necessary in life had taken place to a considerable extent. The functions of the mason, the weaver, the goldsmith, the painter, and of several other crafts, were carried on by different persons. Each was regularly instructed in his calling. To it alone his industry was confined, and by assiduous application to one object, together with the persevering patience peculiar to Americans, their artisans attained to a degree of neatness and perfection in work, far beyond what could have been expected from the rude tools which they employed. Their various productions were brought into commerce; and by the exchange of them in the stated markets held in the cities, not only were their mutual wants supplied,* in such orderly intercourse as characterizes an improved state of society, but their industry was daily rendered persevering and inventive.

The distinction of ranks established in the Mexican empire, is the next circumstance that merits attention. In surveying the savage tribes of America, we observed, that consciousness of equality, and impatience of subordination, are sentiments natural to man in the infancy of civil life. During peace, the authority of a superior is hardly felt among them, and even in

* Cortes Relat. ap. Ramus, iii. 239, &c. Gom. Cron. c. 79. Torquem. lib. xiii. c. 34. Herrera, dec. 2. lib. vii. c. 15, &c.

war it is but little acknowledged. Strangers to the idea of property, the difference in condition resulting from the inequality of it is unknown. Birth or titles confer no pre-eminence; it is only by personal merit and accom plishments that distinction can be acquired. The form of society was very different among the Mexicans. The great body of the people was in a most humiliating state. A considerable number, known by the name of *Mayeques*, nearly resembled in condition those peasants who, under various denominations, were considered, during the prevalence of the feudal system, as instruments of labour attached to the soil. The *Mayeques* could not change their place of residence without permission of the superior on whom they depended. They were conveyed, together with the lands on which they were settled, from one proprietor to another; and were bound to cultivate the ground, and to perform several kinds of servile work.* Others were reduced to the lowest form of subjection, that of domestic servitude, and felt the utmost rigour of that wretched state. Their condition was held to be so vile, and their lives deemed of so little value, that a person who killed one of these slaves was not subjected to any punishment.† Even those considered as freemen were treated by their haughty lords as beings of an inferior species. The nobles, possessed of ample territories, were divided into various classes, to each of which peculiar titles of honour belonged. Some of these titles, like their lands, descended from father to son in perpetual succession. Others were annexed to particular offices, or conferred during life as marks of personal distinction.‡ The monarch, exalted above all, enjoyed extensive power and supreme dignity. Thus the distinction of ranks was completely established, in a line of regular subordination, reaching from the highest to the lowest member of the community. Each of these knew what he could claim, and what he owed. The people, who were not allowed to wear a dress of the same fashion, or to dwell in houses of a form similar to those of the nobles, accosted them with the most submissive reverence. In the presence of their sovereign, they durst not lift their eyes from the ground, or look him in the face.§ The nobles themselves, when admitted to an audience of their sovereign, entered barefooted, in mean garments, and, as his slaves, paid him homage approaching to adoration. This respect, due from inferiors to those above them in rank, was prescribed with such ceremonious accuracy, that it incorporated with the language, and influenced its genius and idiom. The Mexican tongue abounded in expressions of reverence and courtesy. The style and appellations used in the intercourse between equals would have been so unbecoming in the mouth of one in a lower sphere, when he accosted a person in higher rank, as to be deemed an insult [146]. It is only in societies, which time and the institution of regular government have moulded into form, that we find such an orderly arrangement of men into different ranks, and such nice attention paid to their various rights.

The spirit of the Mexicans, thus familiarized and bended to subordina tion, was prepared for submitting to monarchical government. But the description of their policy and laws, by the Spaniards who overturned them, are so inaccurate and contradictory, that it is difficult to delineate the form of their constitution with any precision. Sometimes they represent the monarchs of Mexico as absolute, deciding according to their pleasure with respect to every operation of the state. On other occasions, we discover the traces of established customs and laws, framed in order to circumscribe the power of the crown, and we meet with rights and privileges of the nobles which seemed to be opposed as barriers against its encroachments. This appearance of inconsistency has arisen from inatten-

* Herrera, dec 3. lib. iv. c. 17. Corita MS. † Herrera, dec. 3. lib. iv. c. 7. ‡ Ibid c. 15. Corita MS. § Herrera, dec. 3. lib ii c. 14.

tion to the innovations of Montezuma upon the Mexican policy. His aspiring ambition subverted the original system of government, and introduced a pure despotism. He disregarded the ancient laws, violated the privileges held most sacred, and reduced his subjects of every order to the level of slaves.* The chiefs, or nobles of the first rank, submitted to the yoke with such reluctance that, from impatience to shake it off, and hope of recovering their rights, many of them courted the protection of Cortes, and joined a foreign power against their domestic oppressor.† It is not then under the dominion of Montezuma, but under the government of his predecessors, that we can discover what was the original form and genius of Mexican policy. From the foundation of the monarchy to the election of Montezuma, it seems to have subsisted with little variation. That body of citizens, which may be distinguished by the name of nobility, formed the chief and most respectable order in the state. They were of various ranks, as has been already observed, and their honours were acquired and transmitted in different manners. Their number seems to have been great. According to an author accustomed to examine with attention what he relates, there were in the Mexican empire thirty of this order, each of whom had in his territories about a hundred thousand people; and subordinate to these, there were about three thousand nobles of a lower class.‡ The territories belonging to the chiefs of Tezeuco and Tacuba were hardly inferior in extent to those of the Mexican monarch.§ Each of these possessed complete territorial jurisdiction, and levied taxes from their own vassals. But all followed the standard of Mexico in war, serving with a number of men in proportion to their domain, and most of them paid tribute to its monarch as their superior lord.

In tracing those great lines of the Mexican constitution, an image of feudal policy, in its most rigid form, rises to view, and we discern its three distinguishing characteristics, a nobility possessing almost independent authority, a people depressed into the lowest state of subjection, and a king intrusted with the executive power of the state. Its spirit and principles seem to have operated in the New World in the same manner as in the ancient. The jurisdiction of the crown was extremely limited. All real and effective authority was retained by the Mexican nobles in their own hands, and the shadow of it only left to the king. Jealous to excess of their own rights, they guarded with the most vigilant anxiety against the encroachments of their sovereigns. By a fundamental law of the empire, it was provided that the king should not determine concerning any point of general importance without the approbation of a council composed of the prime nobility.‖ Unless he obtained their consent, he could not engage the nation in war, nor could he dispose of the most considerable branch of the public revenue at pleasure; it was appropriated to certain purposes from which it could not be diverted by the regal authority alone.¶ In order to secure full effect to those constitutional restraints, the Mexican nobles did not permit their crown to descend by inheritance, but disposed of it by election. The right of election seems to have been originally vested in the whole body of nobility, but was afterwards committed to six electors, of whom the chiefs of Tezeuco and Tacuba were always two. From respect for the family of their monarchs, the choice fell generally upon some person sprung from it. But as the activity and valour of their prince were of greater moment to a people perpetually engaged in war, than a strict adherence to the order of birth, collaterals of mature age or of distinguished merit were often preferred to those who were nearer the throne in direct descent.** To this maxim in their

* Herrera, dec. 3. lib. ii. c 14. Torquem. lib. ii. c. 69. † Herrera, dec. 2. lib. v. c. 10, 11. Torquem. lib. iv. c. 49. ‡ Herrera, dec. 2. lib. viii. c. 12. § Torquem. lib. ii. c. 57. Corita MS. ‖ Herrera, dec. 3. lib. ii. c. 19 lib. iv. c. 16. Corita MS. ¶ Herrera, dec. 3. lib. iv. c. 17. ** Acosta, lib. vi. c. 24. Herrera, dec. 3. lib. ii. c. 13. Corita MS.

policy, the Mexicans appear to be indebted for such a succession of able and warlike princes, as raised their empire in a short period to that extraordinary height of power which it had attained when Cortes landed in New Spain.

While the jurisdiction of the Mexican monarch continued to be limited, it is probable that it was exercised with little ostentation. But as their authority became more extensive, the splendour of their government augmented. It was in this last state that the Spaniards beheld it; and struck with the appearance of Montezuma's court, they describe its pomp at great length, and with much admiration. The number of his attendants, the order, the silence, and the reverence with which they served him; the extent of his royal mansion, the variety of its apartments allotted to different officers, and the ostentation with which his grandeur was displayed, whenever he permitted his subjects to behold him, seem to resemble the magnificence of the ancient monarchies in Asia, rather than the simplicity of the infant states in the New World.

But it was not in the mere parade of royalty that the Mexican potentates exhibited their power; they manifested it more beneficially in the order and regularity with which they conducted the internal administration and police of their dominions. Complete jurisdiction, civil as well as criminal, over its own immediate vassals, was vested in the crown. Judges were appointed for each department; and if we may rely on the account which the Spanish writers give of the maxims and laws upon which they founded their decisions with respect to the distribution of property and the punishment of crimes, justice was administered in the Mexican empire with a degree of order and equity resembling what takes place in societies highly civilized.

Their attention in providing for the support of government was not less sagacious. Taxes were laid upon land, upon the acquisitions of industry, and upon commodities of every kind exposed to sale in the public markets. These duties were considerable, but not arbitrary or unequal. They were imposed according to established rules, and each knew what share of the common burden he had to bear. As the use of money was unknown, all the taxes were paid in kind; and thus not only the natural productions of all the different provinces in the empire, but every species of manufacture, and every work of ingenuity and art, were collected in the public storehouses. From those the emperor supplied his numerous train of attendants in peace, and his armies during war, with food, with clothes, and ornaments. People of inferior condition, neither possessing land nor engaged in commerce, were bound to the performance of various services. By their stated labour the crown lands were cultivated, public works were carried on, and the various houses belonging to the emperor were built and kept in repair* [147].

The improved state of government among the Mexicans is conspicuous, not only in points essential to the being of a well-ordered society, but in several regulations of inferior consequence with respect to police. The institution which I have already mentioned, of public couriers, stationed at proper intervals, to convey intelligence from one part of the empire to the other, was a refinement in police not introduced into any kingdom of Europe at that period. The structure of the capital city in a lake, with artificial dykes, and causeways of great length, which served as avenues to it from different quarters, erected in the water, with no less ingenuity than labour, seems to be an idea that could not have occurred to any but a civilized people. The same observation may be applied to the structure of the aqueducts, or conduits, by which they conveyed a stream of fresh water from a considerable distance, into the city, along one of the

* Herrera, dec. 2. lib. vii. c. 13 dec. 3. lib. iv c. 16, 17.

causeways [148]. The appointment of a number of persons to clean the streets, to light them by fires kindled in different places, and to patrol as watchmen during the night,* discovers a degree of attention which even polished nations are late in acquiring.

The progress of the Mexicans in various arts is considered as the most decisive proof of their superior refinement. Cortes and the early Spanish authors describe this with rapture, and maintain, that the most celebrated European artists could not surpass or even equal them in ingenuity and neatness of workmanship. They represented men, animals, and other objects, by such a disposition of various coloured feathers, as is said to have produced all the effects of light and shade, and to have imitated nature with truth and delicacy. Their ornaments of gold and silver have been described to be of a fabric no less curious. But in forming any idea, from general descriptions, concerning the state of arts among nations imperfectly polished, we are extremely ready to err. In examining the works of people whose advances in improvement are nearly the same with our own, we view them with a critical and often with a jealous eye. Whereas, when conscious of our own superiority, we survey the arts of nations comparatively rude, we are astonished at works executed by them under such manifest disadvantages, and, in the warmth of our admiration, are apt to represent them as productions more finished than they really are. To the influence of this illusion, without supposing any intention to deceive, we may impute the exaggeration of some Spanish authors, in their accounts of the Mexican arts.

It is not from those descriptions, but from considering such specimens of their arts as are still preserved, that we must decide concerning their degree of merit. As the ship in which Cortes sent to Charles V. the most curious productions of the Mexican artisans, which were collected by the Spaniards when they first pillaged the empire, was taken by a French corsair,† the remains of their ingenuity are less numerous than those of the Peruvians. Whether any of their works with feathers, in imitation of painting, be still extant in Spain, I have not learned; but many of their ornaments in gold and silver, as well as various utensils employed in common life, are deposited in the magnificent cabinet of natural and artificial productions lately opened by the king of Spain; and I am informed by persons on whose judgment and taste I can rely, that these boasted efforts of their art are uncouth representations of common objects, or very coarse images of the human and some other forms, destitute of grace and propriety [149]. The justness of these observations is confirmed by inspecting the wooden prints and copper plates of their paintings, which have been published by various authors. In them every figure of men, of quadrupeds, or birds, as well as every representation of inanimated nature, is extremely rude and awkward.‡

* Herrera, dec. 2. lib. viii. c. 4. Torribio MS. † Relat. de Cort. Ramus, iii. 294. F.

‡ As a specimen of the spirit and style in which M. Clavigero makes his strictures upon my History of America, I shall publish his remarks upon this passage. "Thus far Robertson; to whom we answer, first, That there is no reason to believe that those rude works were really Mexican: secondly, That neither do we know whether those persons in whose judgment he confides, may be persons fit to merit our faith, because we have observed that Robertson trusts frequently to the testimony of Gage, Correal, Ibagnez, and other such authors, who are entirely undeserving of credit: thirdly, It is more probable that the arms of copper, believed by those intelligent judges to be certainly Oriental, are really Mexican." Vol. II. 391.—When an author, not entirely destitute of integrity or discernment, and who has some solicitude about his own character, asserts that he received his information concerning any particular point from persons "on whose judgment and taste he can rely;" a very slender degree of candour, one should think, might induce the reader to believe that he does not endeavour to impose upon the public by an appeal to testimony altogether unworthy of credit. My information concerning the Mexican works of art, deposited in the king of Spain's cabinet, was received from the late Lord Grantham, ambassador extraordinary from the court of London to that of Madrid, and from Mr. Archdeacon Waddilove, chaplain to the embassy; and it was upon their authority that I pronounced the coat of armour, mentioned in the note, to be of Oriental fabric. As they were both at Madrid in their public character, when the first edition of the History of America was published, I thought it improper at that time to mention their names. Did their decision concerning a matter of taste, or their testimony concerning a point of fact, stand in need of confirmation, I might produce the evidence of an intelligent traveller, who, in describing

The hardest Egyptian style, stiff and imperfect as it was, is more elegant. The scrawls of children delineate objects almost as accurately.

But however low the Mexican paintings may be ranked, when viewed merely as works of art, a very different station belongs to them when considered as the records of their country, as historical monuments of its policy and transactions; and they become curious as well as interesting objects of attention. The noblest and most beneficial invention of which human ingenuity can boast, is that of writing. But the first essays of this art, which hath contributed more than all others to the improvement of the species, were very rude, and it advanced towards perfection slowly, and by a gradual progression. When the warrior, eager for fame, wished to transmit some knowledge of his exploits to succeeding ages; when the gratitude of a people to their sovereign prompted them to hand down an account of his beneficent deeds to posterity; the first method of accomplishing this, which seems to have occurred to them, was to delineate, in the best manner they could, figures representing the action, of which they were solicitous to preserve the memory. Of this, which has very properly been called *picture writing*,* we find traces among some of the most savage tribes of America. When a leader returns from the field, he strips a tree of its bark, and with red paint scratches upon it some uncouth figures which represent the order of his march, the number of his followers, the enemy whom he attacked, the scalps and captives which he brought home. To those simple annals he trusts for renown, and soothes himself with hope that by their means he shall receive praise from the warriors of future times.†

Compared with those awkward essays of their savage countrymen, the paintings of the Mexicans may be considered as works of composition and design. They were not acquainted, it is true, with any other method of recording transactions than that of delineating the objects which they wished to represent. But they could exhibit a more complex series of events in progressive order, and describe, by a proper disposition of figures, the occurrences of a king's reign from his accession to his death; the progress of an infant's education from its birth until it attain to the years of maturity; the different recompenses and marks of distinction conferred upon warriors, in proportion to the exploits which they had performed. Some singular specimens of this picture writing have been preserved, which are justly considered as the most curious monuments of art brought from the New World. The most valuable of these was published by Purchas in sixty-six plates. It is divided into three parts. The first contains the history of the Mexican empire under its ten monarchs. The second is a tribute roll, representing what each conquered town paid into the royal treasury. The third is a code of their institutions, domestic, political, and military. Another specimen of Mexican painting has been published in thirty-two plates, by the present archbishop of Toledo. To both is annexed a full explanation of what the figures were intended to represent, which was obtained by the Spaniards from Indians well acquainted with their own arts. The style of painting in all these is the same. They

the royal cabinet of Madrid, takes notice that it contains "specimens of Mexican and Peruvian utensils, vases, &c. in earthenware, wretched both in taste and execution." Dillon's Travels through Spain, p. 77. As Gage composed his Survey of New Spain with all the zeal and acrimony of a new convert, I have paid little regard to his testimony with respect to points relating to religion. But as he resided in several provinces in New Spain, which travellers seldom visit, and as he seems to have observed their manners and laws with an intelligent eye, I have availed myself of his information with respect to matters where religious opinion could have little influence. Correal I have seldom quoted, and never rested upon his evidence alone. The station in which Ibagnez was employed in America, as well as the credit given to his veracity, by printing his Regno Jesuitico among the large collection of documents published (as I believe by authority) at Madrid, A. D. 1767, justifies me for appealing to his authority.

* Divine Legat. of Moses, iii. 73. † Sir W. Johnson, Philos. Transact. vol. lxiii. p. 143 Mém. de la Hontan, ii. 191. Lafitau Mœurs de Sauv. ii. 43.

epresent *things*, not *words*. They exhibit images to the eye, not ideas to he understanding. They may therefore be considered as the earliest and nost imperfect essay of men in their progress towards discovering the art of writing. The defects in this mode of recording transactions must have been early felt. To paint every occurrence was from its nature a very tedious operation; and as affairs became more complicated, and events multiplied in any society, its annals must have swelled to an enormous bulk. Besides this, no objects could be delineated but those of sense; the conceptions of the mind had no corporeal form; and as long as picture writing could not convey an idea of these, it must have been a very imperfect art. The necessity of improving it must have roused and sharpened invention; and the human mind, holding the same course in the New World as in the Old, might have advanced by the same successive steps, first, from an actual picture to the plain hieroglyphic; next to the allegorical symbol; then to the arbitrary character; until, at length, an alphabet of letters was discovered, capable of expressing all the various combinations of sound employed in speech. In the paintings of the Mexicans we accordingly perceive that this progress was begun among them. Upon an attentive inspection of the plates, which I have mentioned, we may observe some approach to the plain or simple hieroglyphic, where some principal part or circumstance in the subject is made to stand for the whole. In the annals of their kings, published by Purchas, the towns conquered by each are uniformly represented in the same manner by a rude delineation of a house; but in order to point out the particular towns which submitted to their victorious arms, peculiar emblems, sometimes natural objects, and sometimes artificial figures, are employed. In the tribute-roll published by the Archbishop of Toledo, the house which was properly the picture of the town, is omitted, and the emblem alone is employed to represent it. The Mexicans seem even to have made some advances beyond this, towards the use of the more figurative and fanciful hieroglyphic. In order to describe a monarch who had enlarged his dominions by force of arms, they painted a target ornamented with darts, and placed it between him and those towns which he subdued. But it is only in one instance, the notation of numbers, that we discern any attempt to exhibit ideas which had no corporeal form. The Mexican painters had invented artificial marks, or *signs of convention*, for this purpose. By means of these, they computed the years of their kings' reigns, as well as the amount of tribute to be paid into the royal treasury. The figure of a circle represented unit; and in small numbers, the computation was made by repeating it. Larger numbers were expressed by a peculiar mark; and they had such as denoted all integral numbers, from twenty to eight thousand. The short duration of their empire prevented the Mexicans from advancing further in that long course which conducts men from the labour of delineating real objects, to the simplicity and ease of alphabetic writing. Their records, notwithstanding some dawn of such ideas as might have led to a more perfect style, can be considered as little more than a species of picture-writing, so far improved as to mark their superiority over the savage tribes of America; but still so defective as to prove that they had not proceeded far beyond the first stage in that progress which must be completed before any people can be ranked among polished nations [150].

Their mode of computing time may be considered as a more decisive evidence of their progress in improvement. They divided their year into eighteen months, consisting of twenty days; amounting in all to three hundred and sixty. But as they observed that the course of the sun was not completed in that time, they added five days to the year. These, which were properly intercalary days, they termed *supernumerary* or *waste;* and as they did not belong to any month, no work was done, and no sacred rite performed on them; they were devoted wholly to festivity and pastime.* This near approach to philosophical accuracy is a remarkable proof, that the Mexicans had bestowed some attention upon inquiries and speculations to which men in a very rude state never turn their thoughts.†

Such are the most striking particulars in the manners and policy of the Mexicans, which exhibit them to view as a people considerably refined. But from other circumstances, one is apt to suspect that their character, and many of their institutions, did not differ greatly from those of the other inhabitants of America.

Like the rude tribes around them, the Mexicans were incessantly engaged in war, and the motives which prompted them to hostility seem to have been the same. They fought in order to gratify their vengeance by shedding the blood of their enemies. In battle they were chiefly intent on taking prisoners; and it was by the number of these that they estimated the glory of victory. No captive was ever ransomed or spared. All were sacrificed without mercy, and their flesh devoured with the same barbarous joy as among the fiercest savages. On some occasions it arose to even wilder excesses. Their principal warriors covered themselves with the skins of the unhappy victims, and danced about the streets, boasting of their own valour, and exulting over their enemies.‡ Even in their civil institutions we discover traces of that barbarous disposition which their system of war inspired. The four chief counsellors of the empire were distinguished by titles, which could have been assumed only by a people who delighted in blood [151]. This ferocity of character prevailed among all the nations of New Spain. The Tlascalans, the people of Mechoacan, and other states at enmity with the Mexicans, delighted equally in war, and treated their prisoners with the same cruelty. In proportion as mankind combine in social union, and live under the influence of equal laws and regular policy, their manners soften, sentiments of humanity arise, and the rights of the species come to be understood. The fierceness of war abates, and even while engaged in hostility, men remember what they owe one to another. The savage fights to destroy, the citizen to conquer. The former neither pities nor spares, the latter has acquired sensibility which tempers his rage. To this sensibility the Mexicans seem to have been perfect strangers; and among them war was carried on with so much of its original barbarity, that we cannot but suspect their degree of civilization to have been very imperfect.

Their funeral rites were not less bloody than those of the most savage tribes. On the death of any distinguished personage, especially of the emperor, a certain number of his attendants were chosen to accompany him to the other world; and those unfortunate victims were put to death without mercy, and buried in the same tomb.§

Though their agriculture was more extensive than that of the roving tribes who trusted chiefly to their bow for food, it seems not to have supplied them with such subsistence as men require when engaged in efforts of active industry. The Spaniards appear not to have been struck with any superiority of the Mexicans over the other people of America in bodily vigour. Both, according to their observation, were of such a feeble frame as to be unable to endure fatigue, and the strength of one Spaniard exceeded that of several Indians. This they imputed to their scanty diet, on poor fare, sufficient to preserve life, but not to give firmness to their constitution. Such a remark could hardly have been made with respect to any people furnished plentifully with the necessaries of life. The diffi-

* Acosta, lib vi. c. 2.

† The Mexican mode of computing time, and every other particular relating to their chronology, have been considerably elucidated by M. Clavigero, vol. i. 288; vol. ii. 225, &c. The observations and theories of the Mexicans concerning those subjects discover a greater progress in speculative science than we find among any people in the New World.

‡ Herrera, dec. 3. lib. ii. c. 15. Gom. Cron. c. 217.

§ Herrera. dec. 3. lib. ii. c. 18. Gom. Cron. c. 202.

culty which Cortes found in procuring subsistence for his small body of soldiers, who were often constrained to live on the spontaneous productions of the earth, seems to confirm the remark of the Spanish writers, and gives no high idea of the state of cultivation in the Mexican empire.*

A practice that was universal in New Spain appears to favour this opinion. The Mexican women gave suck to their children for several years, and during that time they did not cohabit with their husbands.† This precaution against a burdensome increase of progeny, though necessary, as I have already observed, among savages, who from the hardships of their condition, and the precariousness of their subsistence, find it impossible to rear a numerous family, can hardly be supposed to have continued among a people who lived at ease and in abundance.

The vast extent of the Mexican empire, which has been considered, and with justice, as the most decisive proof of a considerable progress in regular government and police, is one of those facts in the history of the New World which seems to have been admitted without due examination or sufficient evidence. The Spanish historians, in order to magnify the valour of their countrymen, are accustomed to represent the dominion of Montezuma as stretching over all the provinces of New Spain from the Northern to the Southern Ocean. But a great part of the mountainous country was possessed by the *Otomies*, a fierce uncivilized people, who seem to have been the residue of the original inhabitants. The provinces towards the north and west of Mexico, were occupied by the *Chichemecas*, and other tribes of hunters. None of these recognised the Mexican monarch as their superior. Even in the interior and more level country, there were several cities and provinces which had never submitted to the Mexican yoke. Tlascala, though only twenty-one leagues from the capital of the empire, was an independent and hostile republic. Cholula, though still nearer, had been subjected only a short time before the arrival of the Spaniards. Tepeaca, at the distance of thirty leagues from Mexico, seems to have been a separate state, governed by its own laws.‡ Mechoacan, the frontier of which extended within forty leagues of Mexico, was a powerful kingdom, remarkable for its implacable enmity to the Mexican name.§ By these hostile powers the Mexican empire was circumscribed on every quarter, and the high ideas which we are apt to form of it from the description of the Spanish historians, should be considerably moderated.

In consequence of this independence of several states in New Spain upon the Mexican empire, there was not any considerable intercourse between its various provinces. Even in the interior country not far distant from the capital, there seems to have been no roads to facilitate the communication of one district with another; and when the Spaniards first attempted to penetrate into its several provinces, they had to open their way through forests and marshes.‖ Cortes, in his adventurous march from Mexico to Honduras, in 1525, met with obstructions, and endured hardships little inferior to those with which he must have struggled in the most uncivilized regions of America. In some places he could hardly force a passage through impervious woods, and plains overflowed with water. In others he found so little cultivation, that his troops were frequently in danger of perishing by famine. Such facts correspond ill with the pompous description which the Spanish writers give of Mexican police and industry, and convey an idea of a country nearly similar to that possessed by the Indian tribes in North America. Here and there a trading or a war path, as they are called in North America, led from one settlement to another;¶ but generally there appeared no sign of any established communication, few marks of industry, and fewer monuments of art.

* Relat. ap. Ramus, iii. 306. A. Herrera, dec. 3. lib. iv. c. 17. dec. 2. lib. vi. c. 16. † Gom. Cron. c. 208. Herrera, dec. 3. lib. iv. c. 16. ‡ Herrera, dec. 3. lib. x. c. 15. 21. B. Diaz, c. 130. § Herrera, dec. 3. lib. ii. c. 10. ‖ B. Diaz, c. 166. 176. ¶ Herrera, dec. 3. lib. vii c 8.

A proof of this imperfection in their commercial intercourse no less striking is their want of money, or some universal standard by which to estimate the value of commodities. The discovery of this is among the steps of greatest consequence in the progress of nations. Until it has been made, all their transactions must be so awkward, so operose, and so limited, that we may boldly pronounce that they have advanced but a little way in their career. The invention of such a commercial standard is of such high antiquity in our hemisphere, and rises so far beyond the era of authentic history, as to appear almost coeval with the existence of society. The precious metals seem to have been early employed for this purpose; and from their permanent value, their divisibility, and many other qualities, they are better adapted to serve as a common standard than any other substance of which nature has given us the command. But in the New World, where these metals abound most, this use of them was not known. The exigencies of rude tribes, or of monarchies imperfectly civilized, did not call for it. All their commercial intercourse was carried on by barter, and their ignorance of any common standard by which to facilitate that exchange of commodities which contributes so much towards the comfort of life, may be justly mentioned as an evidence of the infant state of their policy. But even in the New World the inconvenience of wanting some general instrument of commerce began to be felt, and some efforts were making towards supplying that defect. The Mexicans, among whom the number and greatness of their cities gave rise to a more extended commerce than in any other part of America, had begun to employ a common standard of value, which rendered smaller transactions much more easy. As chocolate was the favourite drink of persons in every rank of life, the nuts or almonds of cacao, of which it is composed, were of such universal consumption, that, in their stated markets, these were willingly received in return for commodities of small price. Thus they came to be considered as the instrument of commerce, and the value of what one wished to dispose of was estimated by the number of nuts of the cacao, which he might expect in exchange for it. This seems to be the utmost length which the Americans had advanced towards the discovery of any expedient for supplying the use of money. And if the want of it is to be held, on one hand, as a proof of their barbarity, this expedient for supplying that want should be admitted, on the other, as an evidence no less satisfying of some progress which the Mexicans had made in refinement and civilization beyond the savage tribes around them.

In such a rude state were many of the Mexican provinces when first visited by their conquerors. Even their cities, extensive and populous as they were, seem more fit to be the habitation of men just emerging from barbarity, than the residence of a polished people. The description of Tlascala nearly resembles that of an Indian village. A number of low straggling huts, scattered about irregularly, according to the caprice of each proprietor, built with turf and stone, and thatched with reeds, without any light but what they received by a door, so low that it could not be entered upright.* In Mexico, though, from the peculiarity of its situation, the disposition of the houses was more orderly, the structure of the greater part was equally mean. Nor does the fabric of their temples, and other public edifices, appear to have been such as entitled them to the high praise bestowed upon them by many Spanish authors. As far as one can gather from their obscure and inaccurate descriptions, the great temple of Mexico, the most famous in New Spain, which has been represented as a magnificent building, raised to such a height, that the ascent to it was by a flight of a hundred and fourteen steps, was a solid mass of earth of a square form, faced partly with stone. Its base on each side extended

* Herrera, dec. 2. lib. vi. c. 12.

ninety feet; and decreasing gradually as it advanced in height, it terminated in a quadrangle of about thirty feet, where were placed a shrine of the deity, and two altars on which the victims were sacrificed.* All the other celebrated temples of New Spain exactly resembled that of Mexico [152]. Such structures convey no high idea of progress in art and ingenuity; and one can hardly conceive that a form more rude and simple could have occurred to a nation in its first efforts towards erecting any great work.

Greater skill and ingenuity were displayed, if we may believe the Spanish historians, in the houses of the emperor, and in those of the principal nobility. There, some elegance of design was visible, and a commodious arrangement of the apartments was attended to. But if buildings corresponding to such descriptions had ever existed in the Mexican cities, it is probable that some remains of them would still be visible. From the manner in which Cortes conducted the siege of Mexico, we can indeed easily account for the total destruction of whatever had any appearance of splendour in that capital. But as only two centuries and a half have elapsed since the conquest of New Spain, it seems altogether incredible that in a period so short, every vestige of this boasted elegance and grandeur should have disappeared; and that in the other cities, particularly in those which did not suffer by the destructive hand of the conquerors, there are any ruins which can be considered as monuments of their ancient magnificence.

Even in a village of the rudest Indians, there are buildings of greater extent and elevation than common dwelling houses. Such as are destined for holding the council of the tribe, and in which all assemble on occasions of public festivity, may be called stately edifices, when compared with the rest. As among the Mexicans the distinction of ranks was established, and property was unequally divided, the number of distinguished structures in their towns would of course be greater than in other parts of America. But these seem not to have been either so solid or magnificent as to merit the pompous epithets which some Spanish authors employ in describing them. It is probable that, though more ornamented, and built on a larger scale, they were erected with the same slight materials which the Indians employed in their common buildings [153], and Time, in a space much less than two hundred and fifty years, may have swept away all remains of them [154].

From this enumeration of facts, it seems, upon the whole, to be evident, that the state of society in Mexico was considerably advanced beyond that of the savage tribes which we have delineated. But it is no less manifest that, with respect to many particulars, the Spanish accounts of their progress appear to be highly embellished. There is not a more frequent or a more fertile source of deception in describing the manners and arts of savage nations, or of such as are imperfectly civilized, than that of applying to them the names and phrases appropriated to the institutions and refinements of polished life. When the leader of a small tribe, or the head of a rude community, is dignified with the name of King or Emperor, the place of his residence can receive no other name but that of his palace; and whatever his attendants may be, they must be called his court Under such appellations they acquire, in our estimation, an importance and dignity which does not belong to them. The illusion spreads; and giving a false colour to every part of the narrative, the imagination is so much carried away with the resemblance, that it becomes difficult to discern objects as they really are. The Spaniards, when they first touched on the Mexican coast, were so much struck with the appearance of attainments in policy and in the arts of life, far superior to those of the rude

* Herrera, dec. 2. lib. vii. c. 17.

tribes with which they were hitherto acquainted, that they fancied they had at length discovered a civilized people in the New World. This comparison between the people of Mexico and their uncultivated neighbours, they appear to have kept constantly in view; and observing with admiration many things which marked the pre-eminence of the former, they employ, in describing their imperfect policy and infant arts, such terms as are applicable to the institutions of men far beyond them in improvement. Both these circumstances concur in detracting from the credit due to the descriptions of Mexican manners by the early Spanish writers. By drawing a parallel between them and those of people so much less civilized, they raised their own ideas too high. By their mode of describing them, they conveyed ideas to others no less exalted above truth. Later writers have adopted the style of the original historians, and improved upon it. The colours with which De Solis delineates the character and describes the actions of Montezuma, the splendour of his court, the laws and policy of his empire, are the same that he must have employed in exhibiting to view the monarch and institutions of a highly polished people.

But though we may admit, that the warm imagination of the Spanish writers has added some embellishment to their descriptions, this will not justify the decisive and peremptory tone with which several authors pronounce all their accounts of the Mexican power, policy, and laws, to be the fictions of men who wished to deceive, or who delighted in the marvellous. There are few historical facts that can be ascertained by evidence more unexceptionable, than may be produced in support of the material articles in the description of the Mexican constitution and manners. Eye-witnesses relate what they beheld. Men who had resided among the Mexicans, both before and after the conquest, describe institutions and customs which were familiar to them. Persons of professions so different that objects must have presented themselves to their view under every various aspect; soldiers, priests, and lawyers, all concur in their testimony. Had Cortes ventured to impose upon his sovereign, by exhibiting to him a picture of imaginary manners, there wanted not enemies and rivals who were qualified to detect his deceit, and who would have rejoiced in exposing it. But according to the just remark of an author, whose ingenuity has illustrated, and whose eloquence has adorned, the history of America,* this supposition is in itself as improbable as the attempt would have been audacious. Who, among the destroyers of this great empire, was so enlightened by science, or so attentive to the progress and operations of men in social life, as to frame a fictitious system of policy so well combined and so consistent, as that which they delineate in their accounts of the Mexican government? Where could they have borrowed the idea of many institutions in legislation and police, to which, at that period, there was nothing parallel in the nations with which they were acquainted? There was not, at the beginning of the sixteenth century, a regular establishment of posts for conveying intelligence to the sovereign of any kingdom in Europe. The same observation will apply to what the Spaniards relate with respect to the structure of the city of Mexico, the regulations concerning its police, and various laws established for the administration of justice, or securing the happiness of the community. Whoever is accustomed to contemplate the progress of nations will often, at very early stages of it, discover a premature and unexpected dawn of those ideas which gave rise to institutions that are the pride and ornament of its most advanced period. Even in a state as imperfectly polished as the Mexican empire, the happy genius of some sagacious observer, excited or aided by circumstances unknown to us, may have introduced institutions which are seldom found but in societies highly refined. But it is almost

* M. l'Abbe Raynal Hist. philos. et polit. &c. iii. 127.

impossible that the illiterate conquerors of the New World should have formed in any one instance a conception of customs and laws beyond the standard of improvement in their own age and country. Or if Cortes had been capable of this, what inducement had those by whom he was superseded to continue the deception? Why should Corita, or Motolinea, or Acosta, have amused their sovereign or their fellow-citizens with a tale purely fabulous?

In one particular, however, the guides whom we must follow have represented the Mexicans to be more barbarous, perhaps, than they really were. Their religious tenets and the rites of their worship are described by them as wild and cruel in an extreme degree. Religion, which occupies no considerable place in the thoughts of a savage, whose conceptions of any superior power are obscure, and his sacred rites few as well as simple, was formed, among the Mexicans, into a regular system, with its complete train of priests, temples, victims, and festivals. This, of itself, is a clear proof that the state of the Mexicans was very different from that of the ruder American tribes. But from the extravagance of their religious notions, or the barbarity of their rites, no conclusion can be drawn with certainty concerning the degree of their civilization. For nations, long after their ideas begin to enlarge, and their manners to refine, adhere to systems of superstition founded on the crude conceptions of early ages. From the genius of the Mexican religion we may, however, form a most just conclusion with respect to its influence upon the character of the people. The aspect of superstition in Mexico was gloomy and atrocious. Its divinities were clothed with terror, and delighted in vengeance. They were exhibited to the people under detestable forms, which created horror. The figures of serpents, of tigers, and of other destructive animals, decorated their temples. Fear was the only principle that inspired their votaries. Fasts, mortifications, and penances, all rigid, and many of them excruciating to an extreme degree, were the means employed to appease the wrath of their gods, and the Mexicans never approached their altars without sprinkling them with blood drawn from their own bodies. But, of all offerings, human sacrifices were deemed the most acceptable. This religious belief mingling with the implacable spirit of vengeance, and adding new force to it, every captive taken in war was brought to the temple, was devoted as a victim to the deity, and sacrificed with rites no less solemn than cruel* [155]. The heart and head were the portion consecrated to the gods; the warrior, by whose prowess the prisoner had been seized, carried off the body to feast upon it with his friends. Under the impression of ideas so dreary and terrible, and accustomed daily to scenes of bloodshed rendered awful by religion, the heart of man must harden and be steeled to every sentiment of humanity. The spirit of the Mexicans was accordingly unfeeling; and the genius of their religion so far counterbalanced the influence of policy and arts, that notwithstanding their progress in both, their manners, instead of softening, became more fierce. To what circumstances it was owing that superstition assumed such a dreadful form among the Mexicans, we have not sufficient knowledge of their history to determine. But its influence is visible, and produced an effect that is singular in the history of the human species. The manners of the people in the New World, who had made the greatest progress in the arts of policy, were, in several respects, the most ferocious, and the barbarity of some of their customs exceeded even those of the savage state.

The empire of Peru boasts of a higher antiquity than that of Mexico. According to the traditionary accounts collected by the Spaniards, it had subsisted four hundred years, under twelve successive monarchs. But the

* Cort. Relat. ap Ramus. iii. 240, &c. B. Diaz, c. 82. Acosta, lib. v. c. 13, &c Herrera, dec. 3. lib. ii. c. 15, &c. Gomara Chron. c. 80, &c.

knowledge of their ancient story, which the Peruvians could communicate to their conquerors, must have been both imperfect and uncertain [156] Like the other American nations, they were totally unacquainted with the art of writing, and destitute of the only means by which the memory of past transactions can be preserved with any degree of accuracy. Even among people to whom the use of letters is known, the era where the authenticity of history commences is much posterior to the introduction of writing. That noble invention continued every where to be long subservient to the common business and wants of life, before it was employed in recording events, with a view of conveying information from one age to another. But in no country did ever tradition alone carry down historical knowledge, in any full continued stream, during a period of half the length that the monarchy of Peru is said to have subsisted.

The *Quipos*, or knots on cords of different colours, which are celebrated by authors fond of the marvellous, as if they had been regular annals of the empire, imperfectly supplied the place of writing. According to the obscure description of them by Acosta,* which Garcilasso de la Vega has adopted with little variation and no improvement, the quipos seem to have been a device for rendering calculation more expeditious and accurate. By the various colours different objects were denoted, and by each knot a distinct number. Thus an account was taken, and a kind of register kept, of the inhabitants in each province, or of the several productions collected there for public use. But as by these knots, however varied or combined, no moral or abstract idea, no operation or quality of the mind could be represented, they contributed little towards preserving the memory of ancient events and institutions. By the Mexican paintings and symbols, rude as they were, more knowledge of remote transactions seems to have been conveyed than the Peruvians could derive from their boasted quipos. Had the latter been even of more extensive use, and better adapted to supply the place of written records, they perished so generally, together with other monuments of Peruvian ingenuity, in the wreck occasioned by the Spanish conquest, and the civil wars subsequent to it, that no accession of light or knowledge comes from them. All the zeal of Garcilasso de la Vega, for the honour of that race of monarchs from whom he descended, all the industry of his researches, and the superior advantages with which he carried them on, opened no source of information unknown to the Spanish authors who wrote before him. In his *Royal Commentaries*, he confines himself to illustrate what they had related concerning the antiquities and institutions of Peru;† and his illustrations, like their accounts, are derived entirely from the traditionary tales current among his countrymen.

Very little credit then is due to the minute details which have been given of the exploits, the battles, the conquests, and private character of the early Peruvian monarchs. We can rest upon nothing in their story as authentic, but a few facts so interwoven in the system of their religion and policy, as preserved the memory of them from being lost; and upon the description of such customs and institutions as continued in force at the time of the conquest, and fell under the immediate observation of the Spaniards. By attending carefully to these, and endeavouring to separate them from what appears to be fabulous or of doubtful authority, I have laboured to form an idea of the Peruvian government and manners.

The people of Peru, as I have already observed,‡ had not advanced beyond the rudest form of savage life, when Manco Capac, and his consort Mama Ocollo, appeared to instruct and to civilize them. Who these extraordinary personages were, whether they imported their system of legislation and knowledge of arts from some country more improved, or, if natives of Peru, how they acquired ideas so far superior to those of the

* Hist. lib. vi c. 8. † Lib. i. c. 10. ‡ Book vi

people whom they addressed, are circumstances with respect to which the Peruvian tradition conveys no information. Manco Capac and his consort, taking advantage of the propensity in the Peruvians to superstition, and particularly of their veneration for the Sun, pretended to be children of that glorious luminary, and to deliver their instructions in his name, and by authority from him. The multitude listened and believed. What reformation in policy and manners the Peruvians ascribe to those founders of their empire, and how, from the precepts of the Inca and his consort, their ancestors gradually acquired some knowledge of those arts, and some relish for that industry, which render subsistence secure and life comfortable, hath been formerly related. Those blessings were originally confined within narrow precincts; but in process of time, the successors of Manco Capac extended their dominion over all the regions that stretch to the west of the Andes from Chili to Quito, establishing in every province their peculiar policy and religious institutions.

The most singular and striking circumstance in the Peruvian government is the influence of religion upon its genius and laws. Religious ideas make such a feeble impression on the mind of a savage, that their effect upon his sentiments and manners is hardly perceptible. Among the Mexicans, religion, reduced into a regular system, and holding a considerable place in their public institutions, operated with conspicuous efficacy in forming the peculiar character of that people. But in Peru, the whole system of policy was founded on religion. The Inca appeared not only as a legislator, but as the messenger of Heaven. His precepts were received not merely as the injunctions of a superior, but as the mandates of the Deity. His race was to be held sacred; and in order to preserve it distinct, without being polluted by any mixture of less noble blood, the sons of Manco Capac married their own sisters, and no person was ever admitted to the throne who could not claim it by such a pure descent. To those *Children of the Sun*, for that was the appellation bestowed upon all the offspring of the first Inca, the people looked up with the reverence due to beings of a superior order. They were deemed to be under the immediate protection of the deity from whom they issued, and by him every order of the reigning Inca was supposed to be dictated.

From those ideas two consequences resulted. The authority of the Inca was unlimited and absolute in the most extensive meaning of the words. Whenever the decrees of a prince are considered as the commands of the Divinity, it is not only an act of rebellion, but of impiety, to dispute or oppose his will. Obedience becomes a duty of religion; and as it would be profane to control a monarch who is believed to be under the guidance of Heaven, and presumptuous to advise him, nothing remains but to submit with implicit respect. This must necessarily be the effect of every government established on pretensions of intercourse with superior powers. Such accordingly was the blind submission which the Peruvians yielded to their sovereigns. The persons of highest rank and greatest power in their dominions acknowledged them to be of a more exalted nature; and in testimony of this, when admitted into their presence, they entered with a burden upon their shoulders, as an emblem of their servitude, and willingness to bear whatever the Inca was pleased to impose. Among their subjects, force was not requisite to second their commands. Every officer intrusted with the execution of them was revered, and, according to the account* of an intelligent observer of Peruvian manners, he might proceed alone from one extremity of the empire to another without meeting opposition; for, on producing a fringe from the royal *borla*, an ornament of the head peculiar to the reigning Inca, the lives and fortunes of the people were at his disposal.

* Zarate, lib. i. c. 13.

Another consequence of establishing government in Peru on the foundation of religion was, that all crimes were punished capitally. They were not considered as transgressions of human laws, but as insults offered to the Deity. Each, without any distinction between such as were slight and such as were atrocious, called for vengeance, and could be expiated only by the blood of the offender. Consonantly to the same ideas, punishment followed the trespass with inevitable certainty, because an offence against Heaven was deemed such a high enormity as could not be pardoned.* Among a people of corrupted morals, maxims of jurisprudence so severe and unrelenting, by rendering men ferocious and desperate, would be more apt to multiply crimes than to restrain them. But the Peruvians, of simple manners and unsuspicious faith, were held in such awe by this rigid discipline, that the number of offenders was extremely small Veneration for monarchs enlightened and directed, as they believed, by the divinity whom they adored, prompted them to their duty; the dread of punishment, which they were taught to consider as unavoidable vengeance inflicted by offended Heaven, withheld them from evil.

The system of superstition, on which the Incas ingrafted their pretensions to such high authority, was of a genius very different from that established among the Mexicans. Manco Capac turned the veneration of his followers entirely towards natural objects. The Sun, as the great source of light, of joy, and fertility in the creation, attracted their principal homage. The Moon and Stars, as co-operating with him, were entitled to secondary honours. Wherever the propensity in the human mind to acknowledge and to adore some superior power takes this direction, and is employed in contemplating the order and beneficence that really exists in nature, the spirit of superstition is mild. Wherever imaginary beings, created by the fancy and the fears of men, are supposed to preside in nature, and become the objects of worship, superstition always assumes a more severe and atrocious form. Of the latter we have an example among the Mexicans, of the former among the people of Peru. The Peruvians had not, indeed, made such progress in observation or inquiry, as to have attained just conceptions of the Deity; nor was there in their language any proper name or appellation of the Supreme Power, which intimated that they had formed any idea of him as the Creator and Governor of the world.†

But by directing their veneration to that glorious luminary, which, by its universal and vivifying energy, is the best emblem of Divine beneficence, the rites and observances which they deemed acceptable to him were innocent and humane. They offered to the Sun a part of those productions which his genial warmth had called forth from the bosom of the earth, and reared to maturity. They sacrificed, as an oblation of gratitude, some of the animals which were indebted to his influence for nourishment. They presented to him choice specimens of those works of ingenuity which his light had guided the hand of man in forming. But the Incas never stained his altars with human blood, nor could they conceive that their beneficent father, the Sun, would be delighted with such horrid victims [157]. Thus the Peruvians, unacquainted with those barbarous rites which extinguish sensibility, and suppress the feelings of nature at the sight of human sufferings, were formed by the spirit of the superstition which they had adopted, to a national character more gentle than that of any people in America.

The influence of this superstition operated in the same manner upon their civil institutions, and tended to correct in them whatever was adverse to gentleness of character. The dominion of the Incas, though the most absolute of all despotisms, was mitigated by its alliance with religion. The

* Vega, lib. ii. c. 6. † Acosta, lib. v. c. 3.

mind was not humbled and depressed by the idea of a forced subjection to the will of a superior; obedience, paid to one who was believed to be clothed with Divine authority, was willingly yielded, and implied no degradation. The sovereign, conscious that the submissive reverence of his people flowed from their belief of his heavenly descent, was continually reminded of a distinction which prompted him to imitate that beneficent power which he was supposed to represent. In consequence of those impressions, there hardly occurs in the traditional history of Peru, any instance of rebellion against the reigning prince, and among twelve successive monarchs there was not one tyrant.

Even the wars in which the Incas engaged were carried on with a spirit very different from that of other American nations. They fought not, like savages, to destroy and to exterminate; or, like the Mexicans, to glut blood-thirsty divinities with human sacrifices. They conquered, in order to reclaim and civilize the vanquished, and to diffuse the knowledge of their own institutions and arts. Prisoners seem not to have been exposed to the insults and tortures which were their lot in every other part of the New World. The Incas took the people whom they subdued under their protection, and admitted them to a participation of all the advantages enjoyed by their original subjects. This practice, so repugnant to American ferocity, and resembling the humanity of the most polished nations, must be ascribed, like other peculiarities which we have observed in the Peruvian manners, to the genius of their religion. The Incas, considering the homage paid to any other object than to the heavenly powers which they adored as impious, were fond of gaining proselytes to their favourite system. The idols of every conquered province were carried in triumph to the great temple at Cuzco,* and placed there as trophies of the superior power of the divinity who was the protector of their empire. The people were treated with lenity, and instructed in the religious tenets of their new masters,† that the conqueror might have the glory of having added to the number of the votaries of his father the Sun.

The state of property in Peru was no less singular than that of religion, and contributed, likewise, towards giving a mild turn of character to the people. All the lands capable of cultivation were divided into three shares. One was consecrated to the Sun, and the product of it was applied to the erection of temples, and furnishing what was requisite towards celebrating the public rites of religion. The second belonged to the Inca, and was set apart as the provision made by the community for the support of government. The third and largest share was reserved for the maintenance of the people, among whom it was parcelled out. Neither individuals, however, nor communities had a right of exclusive property in the portion set apart for their use. They possessed it only for a year, at the expiration of which a new division was made in proportion to the rank, the number, and exigencies of each family. All those lands were cultivated by the joint industry of the community. The people summoned by a proper officer, repaired in a body to the fields, and performed their common task, while songs and musical instruments cheered them to their labour.‡ By this singular distribution of territory, as well as by the mode of cultivating it, the idea of a common interest, and of mutual subserviency, was continually inculcated. Each individual felt his connexion with those around him, and knew that he depended on their friendly aid for what increase he was to reap. A state thus constituted may be considered as one great family, in which the union of the members was so complete, and the exchange of good offices so perceptible, as to create stronger attachment, and to bind man to man in closer intercourse than subsisted under any form of society

* Herrera, dec. 5. lib. iv. c. 4. Vega, lib. v. c. 12. † Herrera, dec. 5. lib. iv. c. 8. ‡ Ib. c. 2. Vega, lib. v. c. 5.

established in America. From this resulted gentle manners and mild virtues unknown in the savage state, and with which the Mexicans were little acquainted.

But, though the institutions of the Incas were so framed as to strengthen the bonds of affection among their subjects, there was great inequality in their condition. The distinction of ranks was fully established in Peru. A great body of the inhabitants, under the denomination of *Yanaconas*, were held in a state of servitude. Their garb and houses were of a form different from those of freemen. Like the *Tamenes* of Mexico, they were employed in carrying burdens, and in performing every other work of drudgery.* Next to them, in rank, were such of the people as were free, but distinguished by no official or hereditary honours. Above them were raised those whom the Spaniards call *Orejones*, from the ornaments worn in their ears. They formed what may be denominated the order of nobles, and in peace as well as war held every office of power or trust.† And the head of all were the children of the Sun, who, by their high descent and peculiar privileges, were as much exalted above the Orejones, as these were elevated above the people.

Such a form of society, from the union of its members, as well as from the distinction in their ranks, was favourable to progress in the arts. But the Spaniards, having been acquainted with the improved state of various arts in Mexico several years before they discovered Peru, were not so much struck with what they observed in the latter country, and describe the appearances of ingenuity there with less warmth of admiration. The Peruvians, nevertheless, had advanced far beyond the Mexicans, both in the necessary arts of life, and in such as have some title to the name of elegant.

In Peru, agriculture, the art of primary necessity in social life, was more extensive, and carried on with greater skill than in any part of America. The Spaniards, in their progress through the country, were so fully supplied with provisions of every kind, that in the relation of their adventures we meet with few of those dismal scenes of distress occasioned by famine, in which the conquerors of Mexico were so often involved. The quantity of soil under cultivation was not left to the discretion of individuals, but regulated by public authority in proportion to the exigencies of the community. Even the calamity of an unfruitful season was but little felt; for the product of the lands consecrated to the Sun, as well as those set apart for the Incas, being deposited in the *Tambos*, or public storehouses, it remained there as a stated provision for times of scarcity.‡ As the extent of cultivation was determined with such provident attention to the demands of the state, the invention and industry of the Peruvians were called forth to extraordinary exertions, by certain defects peculiar to their climate and soil. All the vast rivers that flow from the Andes take their course eastward to the Atlantic Ocean. Peru is watered only by some streams which rush down from the mountains like torrents. A great part of the low country is sandy and barren, and never refreshed with rain. In order to render such an unpromising region fertile, the ingenuity of the Peruvians had recourse to various expedients. By means of artificial canals, conducted with much patience and considerable art from the torrents that poured across their country, they conveyed a regular supply of moisture to their fields§ [158]. They enriched the soil by manuring it with the dung of sea fowls, of which they found an inexhaustible store on all the islands scattered along the coasts.‖ In describing the customs of any nation thoroughly civilized, such practices would hardly draw attention, or be mentioned as in any degree

* Herrera, dec. 5. lib. iii. c. 4. lib. x. c. 8. † Ib. lib. iv. c. 1. ‡ Zarate, lib. i. c. 14. Vega, lib i. c. 8. § Zarate, lib. i. c. 4 Vega, lib. v. c. 1 & 24 ‖ Acosta, lib. iv. c. 37. Vega, lib. v. c. 3

remarkable; but in the history of the improvident race of men in the New World, they are entitled to notice as singular proofs of industry and of art. The use of the plough, indeed, was unknown to the Peruvians. They turned up the earth with a kind of mattock of hard wood.* Nor was this labour deemed so degrading as to be devolved wholly upon the women. Both sexes joined in performing this necessary work. Even the children of the Sun set an example of industry, by cultivating a field near Cuzco with their own hands, and they dignified this function by denominating it their triumph over the earth.†

The superior ingenuity of the Peruvians is obvious, likewise, in the construction of their houses and public buildings. In the extensive plains which stretch along the Pacific Ocean, where the sky is perpetually serene, and the climate mild, their houses were very properly of a fabric extremely slight. But in the higher regions, where rain falls, where the vicissitude of seasons is known, and their rigour felt, houses were constructed with greater solidity. They were generally of a square form, the walls about eight feet high, built with bricks hardened in the sun, without any windows, and the door low and straight. Simple as these structures were, and rude as the materials may seem to be of which they were formed, they were so durable that many of them still subsist in different parts of Peru, long after every monument that might have conveyed to us any idea of the domestic state of the other American nations has vanished from the face of the earth. But it was in the temples consecrated to the Sun, and in the buildings destined for the residence of their monarchs, that the Peruvians displayed the utmost extent of their art and contrivance. The descriptions of them by such of the Spanish writers as had an opportunity of contemplating them, while in some measure entire, might have appeared highly exaggerated, if the ruins which still remain did not vouch the truth of their relations. These ruins of sacred or royal buildings are found in every province of the empire, and by their frequency demonstrate that they are monuments of a powerful people, who must have subsisted, during a period of some extent, in a state of no inconsiderable improvement. They appear to have been edifices various in their dimensions: some of a moderate size, many of immense extent, all remarkable for solidity, and resembling each other in the style of architecture. The temple of Pachacamac, together with a palace of the Inca, and a fortress, were so connected together as to form one great structure above half a league in circuit. In this prodigious pile, the same singular taste in building is conspicuous as in other works of the Peruvians. As they were unacquainted with the use of the pulley, and other mechanical powers, and could not elevate the large stones and bricks which they employed in building to any considerable height, the walls of this edifice, in which they seem to have made their greatest effort towards magnificence, did not rise above twelve feet from the ground. Though they had not discovered the use of mortar or of any other cement in building, the bricks or stones were joined with so much nicety, that the seams can hardly be discerned [159]. The apartments, as far as the distribution of them can be traced in the ruins, were ill disposed, and afforded little accommodation. There was not a single window in any part of the building; and as no light could enter but by the door, all the apartments of largest dimensions must either have been perfectly dark, or illuminated by some other means. But with all these, and many other imperfections that might be mentioned in their art of building, the works of the Peruvians which still remain must be considered as stupendous efforts of a people unacquainted with the use of iron, and convey to us a high idea of the power possessed by their ancient monarchs

These, however, were not the noblest or most useful works of the Incas The two great roads from Cuzco to Quito, extending in an uninterrupted

* Zarate, lib. i. c. 8 † Vega, lib. v. c. 2.

stretch above fifteen hundred miles, are entitled to still higher praise. The one was conducted through the interior and mountainous country, the other through the plains on the sea coast. From the language of admiration in which some of the early writers express their astonishment when they first viewed those roads, and from the more pompous description of later writers, who labour to support some favourite theory concerning America, one might be led to compare this work of the Incas to the famous military ways which remain as monuments of the Roman power; but in a country where there was no tame animal except the llama, which was never used for draught, and but little as a beast of burden, where the high roads were seldom trod by any but a human foot, no great degree of labour or art was requisite in forming them. The Peruvian roads were only fifteen feet in breadth,* and in many places so slightly formed, that time has effaced every vestige of the course in which they ran. In the low country, little more seems to have been done than to plant trees or to fix posts at certain intervals, in order to mark the proper route to travellers. To open a path through the mountainous country was a more arduous task. Eminences were levelled, and hollows filled up, and for the preservation of the road it was fenced with a bank of turf. At proper distances, Tambos, or storehouses, were erected for the accommodation of the Inca and his attendants, in their progress through his dominions. From the manner in which the road was originally formed in this higher and more impervious region, it has proved more durable; and though, from the inattention of the Spaniards to every object but that of working their mines, nothing has been done towards keeping it in repair, its course may still be traced.† Such was the celebrated road of the Incas; and even from this description, divested of every circumstance of manifest exaggeration or of suspicious aspect, it must be considered as a striking proof of an extraordinary progress in improvement and policy. To the savage tribes of America, the idea of facilitating communication with places at a distance had never occurred. To the Mexicans it was hardly known. Even in the most civilized countries in Europe, men had advanced far in refinement, before it became a regular object of national police to form such roads as render intercourse commodious. It was a capital object of Roman policy to open a communication with all the provinces of their extensive empire by means of those roads which are justly considered as one of the noblest monuments both of their wisdom and their power. But during the long reign of barbarism, the Roman roads were neglected or destroyed; and at the time when the Spaniards entered Peru, no kingdom in Europe could boast of any work of public utility that could be compared with the great roads formed by the Incas.

The formation of those roads introduced another improvement in Peru equally unknown over all the rest of America. In its course from south to north, the road of the Incas was intersected by all the torrents which roll from the Andes towards the Western Ocean. From the rapidity of their course, as well as from the frequency and violence of their inundation, these were not fordable. Some expedient, however, was to be found for passing them. The Peruvians from their unacquaintance with the use of arches, and their inability to work in wood, could not construct bridges either of stone or timber. But necessity, the parent of invention, suggested a device which supplied that defect. They formed cables of great strength, by twisting together some of the pliable withs, or osiers, with which their country abounds; six of these cables they stretched across the stream parallel to one another, and made them fast on each side. These they bound firmly together by interweaving smaller ropes so close as to

* Cieca, c. 60. † Xerez, p. 189. 191. Zarate, lib. i. c. 13, 14. Vega, lib. ix. c. 13. Bourguer Voyage, p. 105. Ulloa Entretenemientos, p. 365.

form a compact piece of net-work, which being covered with branches of trees and earth, they passed along it with tolerable security [160]. Proper persons were appointed to attend at each bridge, to keep it in repair, and to assist passengers.* In the level country, where the rivers became deep and broad and still, they are passed in *balzas*, or floats; in the construction, as well as navigation of which the ingenuity of the Peruvians appears to be far superior to that of any people in America. These had advanced no further in naval skill than the use of the paddle or oar; the Peruvians ventured to raise a mast, and spread a sail, by means of which their balzas not only went nimbly before the wind, but could veer and tack with great celerity.†

Nor were the ingenuity and art of the Peruvians confined solely to objects of essential utility. They had made some progress in arts, which may be called elegant. They possessed the precious metals in greater abundance than any people of America. They obtained gold in the same manner with the Mexicans, by searching in the channels of rivers, or washing the earth in which particles of it were contained. But in order to procure silver, they exerted no inconsiderable degree of skill and invention. They had not, indeed, attained the art of sinking a shaft into the bowels of the earth, and penetrating to the riches concealed there; but they hollowed deep caverns on the banks of rivers and the sides of mountains, and emptied such veins as did not dip suddenly beyond their reach. In other places, where the vein lay near the surface, they dug pits to such a depth, that the person who worked below could throw out the ore, or hand it up in baskets.‡ They had discovered the art of smelting and refining this, either by the simple application of fire, or, where the ore was more stubborn or impregnated with foreign substances, by placing it in small ovens or furnaces, on high grounds, so artificially constructed that the draught of air performed the function of a bellows, an engine with which they were totally unacquainted. By this simple device, the purer ores were smelted with facility, and the quantity of silver in Peru was so considerable, that many of the utensils employed in the functions of common life were made of it.§ Several of those vessels and trinkets are said to have merited no small degree of estimation, on account of the neatness of the workmanship, as well as the intrinsic value of the materials. But as the conquerors of America were well acquainted with the latter, but had scarcely any conception of the former, most of the silver vessels and trinkets were melted down, and rated according to the weight and fineness of the metal in the division of the spoil.

In other works of mere curiosity or ornament, their ingenuity has been highly celebrated. Many specimens of those have been dug out of the *Guacas*, or mounds of earth, with which the Peruvians covered the bodies of the dead. Among these are mirrors of various dimensions, of hard shining stones highly polished; vessels of earthen ware of different forms; hatchets, and other instruments, some destined for war, and others for labour. Some were of flint, some of copper, hardened to such a degree by an unknown process, as to supply the place of iron on several occasions. Had the use of those tools, formed of copper, been general, the progress of the Peruvians in the arts might have been such as to emulate that of more cultivated nations. But either the metal was so rare, or the operation by which it was hardened so tedious, that their instruments of copper were few, and so extremely small, that they seem to have been employed only in slighter works. But even to such a circumscribed use of this imperfect metal, the Peruvians were indebted for their superiority to the

* Sancho ap. Ram. iii. 376. B. Zarate, lib. i. c. 14. Vega, lib. iii. c. 7, 8. Herrera, dec. 5. lib iv. c. 3, 4. † Ulloa Voy. i. 167, &c. ‡ Ramusio, iii. 414. A. § Acosta, lib. iv. c. 4, 5. Vega, p. 1. lib. viii. c 25. Ulloa Entreten. 258.

other people of America in various arts.* The same observation, however, may be applied to them, which I formerly made with respect to the arts of the Mexicans. From several specimens of Peruvian utensils and ornaments, which are deposited in the royal cabinet of Madrid, and from some preserved in different collections in other parts of Europe, I have reason to believe that the workmanship is more to be admired on account of the rude tools with which it was executed, than on account of its intrinsic neatness and elegance; and that the Peruvians, though the most improved of all the Americans, were not advanced beyond the infancy of arts.

But notwithstanding so many particulars, which seemed to indicate a high degree of improvement in Peru, other circumstances occur that suggest the idea of a society still in the first stages of its transition from barbarism to civilization. In all the dominions of the Incas, Cuzco was the only place that had the appearance, or was entitled to the name, of a city. Every where else the people lived mostly in detached habitations, dispersed over the country, or, at the utmost, settled together in small villages.† But until men are brought to assemble in numerous bodies, and incorporated in such close union as to enjoy frequent intercourse, and to feel mutual dependence, they never imbibe perfectly the spirit, or assume the manners of social life. In a country of immense extent, with only one city, the progress of manners, and the improvement either of the necessary or more refined arts, must have been so slow, and carried on under such disadvantages, that it is more surprising the Peruvians should have advanced so far in refinement, than that they did not proceed further.

In consequence of this state of imperfect union, the separation of professions in Peru was not so complete as among the Mexicans. The less closely men associate, the more simple are their manners, and the fewer their wants. The crafts of common and most necessary use in life do not, in such a state, become so complex or difficult as to render it requisite that men should be trained to them by any particular course of education. All the arts, accordingly, which were of daily and indispensable utility, were exercised by every Peruvian indiscriminately. None but the artists employed in works of mere curiosity, or ornament, constituted a separate order of men, or were distinguished from other citizens.‡

From the want of cities in Peru, another consequence followed. There was little commercial intercourse among the inhabitants of that great empire. The activity of commerce is coeval with the foundation of cities; and from the moment that the members of any community settle in considerable numbers in one place, its operations become vigorous. The citizen must depend for subsistence on the labour of those who cultivate the ground. They, in return, must receive some equivalent. Thus mutual intercourse is established, and the productions of art are regularly exchanged for the fruits of agriculture. In the towns of the Mexican empire, stated markets were held, and whatever could supply any want or desire of man was an object of commerce. But in Peru, from the singular mode of dividing property, and the manner in which the people were settled, there was hardly any species of commerce carried on between different provinces,§ and the community was less acquainted with that active intercourse, which is at once a bond of union and an incentive to improvement.

But the unwarlike spirit of the Peruvians was the most remarkable as well as the most fatal defect in their character.‖ The greater part of the rude nations of America opposed their invaders with undaunted ferocity, though with little conduct or success. The Mexicans maintained the struggle in defence of their liberties, with such persevering fortitude, that

* Ulloa, Voy. tom. i. 381, &c. Id. Entreten. p. 369, &c. † Zarate, lib. i. c. 9. Herrera, dec. 5. lib. vi. c. 4. ‡ Acosta, lib. vi. c. 15. Vega, lib. v. c. 9. Herrera, dec. 5. lib. iv. c. 4. § Vega lib. vi. c. 8. ‖ Xerez, 190. Sancho, ap. Ram. iii. 372. Herrera, dec. 5. lib. i. c. 3.

it was with difficulty the Spaniards triumphed over them. Peru was subdued at once, and almost without resistance; and the most favourable opportunities of regaining their freedom, and of crushing their oppressors, were lost through the timidity of the people. Though the traditional history of the Peruvians represents all the Incas as warlike princes, frequently at the head of armies, which they led to victory and conquest, few symptoms of such a martial spirit appear in any of their operations subsequent to the invasion of the Spaniards. The influence, perhaps, of those institutions which rendered their manners gentle, gave their minds this unmanly softness; perhaps the constant serenity and mildness of the climate may have enervated the vigour of their frame; perhaps some principles in their government, unknown to us, was the occasion of this political debility. Whatever may have been the cause, the fact is certain; and there is not an instance in history of any people so little advanced in refinement, so totally destitute of military enterprise. This character had descended to their posterity. The Indians of Peru are now more tame and depressed than any people of America. Their feeble spirits, relaxed in lifeless inaction, seem hardly capable of any bold or manly exertion.

But, besides those capital defects in the political state of Peru, some detached circumstances and facts occur in the Spanish writers, which discover a considerable remainder of barbarity in their manners. A cruel custom, that prevailed in some of the most savage tribes, subsisted among the Peruvians. On the death of the Incas, and of other eminent persons, a considerable number of their attendants were put to death, and interred around their Guacas, that they might appear in the next world with their former dignity, and be served with the same respect. On the death of Huana-Capac, the most powerful of their monarchs, above a thousand vcitims were doomed to accompany him to the tomb.* In one particular their manners appear to have been more barbarous than those of most rude tribes. Though acquainted with the use of fire in preparing maize and other vegetables for food, they devoured both flesh and fish perfectly raw, and astonished the Spaniards with a practice repugnant to the ideas of all civilized people.†

But though Mexico and Peru are the possessions of Spain in the New World, which, on account both of their ancient and present state, have attracted the greatest attention; her other dominions there are far from being inconsiderable either in extent or value. The greater part of them was reduced to subjection during the first part of the sixteenth century, by private adventurers, who fitted out their small armaments either in Hispaniola or in Old Spain: and were we to follow each leader in his progress, we should discover the same daring courage, the same persevering ardour, the same rapacious desire for wealth, and the same capacity for enduring and surmounting every thing in order to attain it, which distinguished the operations of the Spaniards in their greater American conquests. But, instead of entering into a detail, which, from their similarity of the transactions, would appear almost a repetition of what has been already related, I shall satisfy myself with such a view of those provinces of the Spanish empire in America, which have not hitherto been mentioned, as may convey to my readers an adequate idea of its greatness, fertility, and opulence.

I begin with the countries contiguous to the two great monarchies o. whose history and institutions I have given some account, and shall then briefly describe the other districts of Spanish America. The jurisdiction of the viceroy of New Spain extends over several provinces which were not subject to the dominion of the Mexicans. The countries of Cinaloa and Sonora that stretch along the east side of the Vermilion Sea, or Gulf

* Acosta, lib. v. c. 7. † Xerez, p. 190. Sancho, Ram. iii. 372. C Herrera, dec. 5. lib i. c. 3.

of California, as well as the immense kingdoms of New Navarre, and New Mexico, which bend towards the west and north, did not acknowledge the sovereignty of Montezuma, or his predecessors. These regions, not inferior in magnitude to all the Mexican empire, are reduced some to a greater, others to a less degree of subjection to the Spanish yoke. They extend through the most delightful part of the temperate zone; their soil is, in general, remarkably fertile; and all their productions, whether animal or vegetable, are most perfect in their kind. They have all a communication either with the Pacific Ocean, or with the Gulf of Mexico, and are watered by rivers which not only enrich them, but may become subservient to commerce. The number of Spaniards settled in those vast countries is indeed extremely small. They may be said to have subdued rather than to have occupied them. But if the population in their ancient establishments in America shall continue to increase, they may gradually spread over those provinces, of which, however inviting, they have not hitherto been able to take full possession.

One circumstance may contribute to the speedy population of some districts. Very rich mines both of gold and silver have been discovered in many of the regions which I have mentioned. Wherever these are opened, and worked with success, a multitude of people resort. In order to supply them with the necessaries of life, cultivation must be increased, artisans of various kinds must assemble, and industry as well as wealth will be gradually diffused. Many examples of this have occurred in different parts of America, since they fell under the dominion of the Spaniards. Populous villages and large towns have suddenly arisen amidst uninhabitable wilds and mountains; and the working of mines, though far from being the most proper object towards which the attention of an infant society should be turned, may become the means both of promoting useful activity, and of augmenting the number of people. A recent and singular instance of this has happened, which, as it is but little known in Europe, and may be productive of great effects, merits attention. The Spaniards settled in the provinces of Cinaloa and Sonora had been long disturbed by the depredations of some fierce tribes of Indians. In the year 1765, the incursions of those savages became so frequent and so destructive, that the Spanish inhabitants, in despair, applied to the Marquis de Croix, viceroy of Mexico, for such a body of troops as might enable them to drive those formidable invaders from their places of retreat in the mountains. But the treasury of Mexico was so much exhausted by the large sums drawn from it, in order to support the late war against Great Britain, that the viceroy could afford them no aid. The respect due to his virtues accomplished what his official power could not effect. He prevailed with the merchants of New Spain to advance about two hundred thousand pesos for defraying the expenses of the expedition. The war was conducted by an officer of abilities; and after being protracted for three years, chiefly by the difficulty of pursuing the fugitives over mountains, and through defiles which were almost impassable, it terminated, in the year 1771, in the final submission of the tribes which had been so long the object of terror to the two provinces. In the course of this service, the Spaniards marched through countries into which they seem not to have penetrated before that time, and discovered mines of such value as was astonishing even to men acquainted with the riches contained in the mountains of the New World. At Cineguilla, in the province of Sonora, they entered a plain of fourteen leagues in extent, in which, at the depth of only sixteen inches, they found gold in grains of such a size, that some of them weighed nine marks, and in such quantities, that in a short time, with a few labourers, they collected a thousand marks of gold in grains, even without taking time to wash the earth that had been dug, which appeared to be so rich, that persons of skill computed that it might yield what would be equal in value to a million of pesos. Before the end of the year 1771, above two thousand persons were settled in Cineguilla, under the government of proper magistrates, and the inspection of several ecclesiastics. As several other mines, not inferior in richness to that of Cineguilla, have been discovered, both in Sonora and Cinaloa [161], it is probable that these neglected and thinly inhabited provinces may soon become as populous and valuable as any part of the Spanish empire of America.

The peninsula of California, on the other side of the Vermilion Sea, seems to have been less known to the ancient Mexicans than the provinces which I have mentioned. It was discovered by Cortes in the year* 1536. During a long period it continued to be so little frequented, that even its form was unknown, and in most charts it was represented as an island, not as a peninsula [162]. Though the climate of this country, if we may judge from its situation, must be very desirable, the Spaniards have made small progress in peopling it. Towards the close of the last century, the Jesuits, who had great merit in exploring this neglected province, and in civilizing its rude inhabitants, imperceptibly acquired a dominion over it as complete as that which they possessed in their missions in Paraguay, and they laboured to introduce into it the same policy, and to govern the natives by the same maxims. In order to prevent the court of Spain from conceiving any jealousy of their designs and operations, they seem studiously to have depreciated the country, by representing the climate as so disagreeable and unwholesome, and the soil as so barren, that nothing but a zealous desire of converting the natives could have induced them to settle there.† Several public spirited citizens endeavoured to undeceive their sovereigns, and to give them a better view of California; but in vain. At length, on the expulsion of the Jesuits from the Spanish dominions, the court of Madrid, as prone at that juncture to suspect the purity of the Order's intentions, as formerly to confide in them with implicit trust, appointed Don Joseph Galvez, whose abilities have since raised him to the high rank of minister for the Indies, to visit that peninsula. His account of the country was favourable; he found the pearl fishery on its coast to be valuable, and he discovered mines of gold of a very promising appearance.‡ From its vicinity to Cinaloa and Sonora, it is probable that, if the population of these provinces shall increase in the manner which I have supposed, California may, by degrees, receive from them such a recruit of inhabitants, as to be no longer reckoned among the desolate and useless districts of the Spanish empire.

On the east of Mexico, Yucatan and Honduras are comprehended in the government of New Spain, though anciently they can hardly be said to have formed a part of the Mexican empire. These large provinces, stretching from the bay of Campeachy beyond Cape Gracias a Dios, do not, like the other territories of Spain in the New World, derive their value either from the fertility of their soil, or the richness of their mines; but they produce in greater abundance than any part of America, the logwood tree, which, in dying some colours, is so far preferable to any other material, that the consumption of it in Europe is considerable, and it has become an article in commerce of great value. During a long period, no European nation intruded upon the Spaniards in those provinces, or attempted to obtain any share in this branch of trade. But after the conquest of Jamaica by the English, it soon appeared that a formidable rival was now seated in the neighbourhood of the Spanish territories. One of the first objects which tempted the English settled in that island, was the great profit arising from the logwood trade, and the facility of wresting some portion of it from the Spaniards. Some adventurers from Jamaica

* Book v † Venegas, Hist. of California, i. 26. ‡ Lorenzano, 349, 350.

made the first attempt at Cape Catoche, the south-east promontory of Yucatan, and by cutting logwood there carried on a gainful traffic. When most of the trees near the coast in that place were felled, they removed to the island of Trist, in the bay of Campeachy, and in later times their principal station has been in the bay of Honduras. The Spaniards, alarmed at this encroachment, endeavoured by negotiation, remonstrances, and open force, to prevent the English from obtaining any footing on that part of the American continent. But after struggling against it for more than a century, the disasters of the last war extorted from the court of Madrid a reluctant consent to tolerate this settlement of foreigners in the heart of its territories.* The pain which this humbling concession occasioned seems to have prompted the Spaniards to devise a method of rendering it of little consequence, more effectual than all the efforts of negotiation or violence. The logwood produced on the west coast of Yucatan, where the soil is drier, is in quality far superior to that which grows on the marshy grounds where the English are settled. By encouraging the cutting of this, and permitting the importation of it into Spain without paying any duty,† such vigour has been given to this branch of commerce, and the logwood which the English bring to market has sunk so much in value, that their trade to the bay of Honduras has gradually declined [163] since it obtained a legal sanction; and, it is probable, will soon be finally abandoned. In that event, Yucatan and Honduras will become possessions of considerable importance to Spain.

Still further east than Honduras lie the two provinces of Costa Rica and Veragua, which likewise belong to the viceroyalty of New Spain; but both have been so much neglected by the Spaniards, and are apparently of such small value, that they merit no particular attention.

The most important province depending on the viceroyalty of Peru is Chili. The Incas had established their dominion in some of its northern districts; but in the greater part of the country, its gallant and high spirited inhabitants maintained their independence. The Spaniards, allured by the fame of its opulence, early attempted the conquest of it under Diego Almagro; and after his death Pedro de Valdivia resumed the design. Both met with fierce opposition. The former relinquished the enterprise in the manner which I have mentioned.‡ The latter, after having given many displays both of courage and military skill, was cut off, together with a considerable body of troops under his command. Francisco de Villagra, Valdivia's lieutenant, by his spirited conduct checked the natives in their career, and saved the remainder of the Spaniards from destruction. By degrees, all the champaign country along the coast was subjected to the Spanish dominion. The mountainous country is still possessed by the Puelches, Araucos, and other tribes of its original inhabitants, formidable neighbours to the Spaniards; with whom, during the course of two centuries, they have been obliged to maintain an almost perpetual hostility, suspended only by a few intervals of insecure peace.

That part of Chili, then, which may properly be deemed a Spanish province, is a narrow district, extended along the coast from the desert of Atacamas to the island of Chiloe, above nine hundred miles. Its climate is the most delicious in the New World, and is hardly equalled by that of any region on the face of the earth. Though bordering on the Torrid Zone, it never feels the extremity of heat, being screened on the east by the Andes, and refreshed from the west by cooling sea breezes. The temperature of the air is so mild and equable, that the Spaniards give it the preference to that of the southern provinces in their native country. The fertility of the soil corresponds with the benignity of the climate, and is wonderfully accommodated to European productions. The most valuable

* Treaty of Paris, Art. xviii. † Real Cedula, Campomanes, iii. 145. ‡ Book vi.

of these, corn, wine, and oil, abound in Chili as if they had been native to the country. All the fruits imported from Europe attained to full maturity there. The animals of our hemisphere not only multiply, but improve in this delightful region. The horned cattle are of larger size than those of Spain. Its breed of horses surpasses, both in beauty and spirit, the famous Andalusian race, from which they sprung. Nor has nature exhausted her bounty on the surface of the earth; she has stored its bowels with riches. Valuable mines of gold, of silver, of copper, and of lead, have been discovered in various parts of it.

A country distinguished by so many blessings, we may be apt to conclude, would early become a favourite station of the Spaniards, and must have been cultivated with peculiar predilection and care. Instead of this, a great part of it remains unoccupied. In all this extent of country, there are not above eighty thousand white inhabitants, and about three times that number of Negroes and people of a mixed race. The most fertile soil in America lies uncultivated, and some of its most promising mines remain unwrought. Strange as this neglect of the Spaniards to avail themselves of advantages which seemed to court their acceptance may appear, the causes of it can be traced. The only intercourse of Spain with its colonies in the South Sea was carried on during two centuries by the annual fleet to Porto Bello. All the produce of these colonies was shipped in the ports of Callao or Arica in Peru, for Panama, and carried from thence across the isthmus. All the commodities which they received from the mother countries were conveyed from Panama to the same harbours. Thus both the exports and imports of Chili passed through the hands of merchants settled in Peru. These had of course a profit on each; and in both transactions the Chilese felt their own subordination; and having no direct intercourse with the parent state, they depended upon another province for the disposal of their productions, as well as for the supply of their wants. Under such discouragements, population could not increase, and industry was destitute of one chief incitement. But now that Spain, from motives which I shall mention hereafter, has adopted a new system, and carries on her commerce with the colonies in the South Sea by ships which go round Cape Horn, a direct intercourse is opened between Chili and the mother country. The gold, the silver, and the other commodities of the province, will be exchanged in its wn harbours for the manufactures of Europe. Chili may speedily rise into that importance among the Spanish settlements to which it is entitled by its natural advantages. It may become the granary of Peru, and the other provinces along the Pacific Ocean. It may supply them with wine, with cattle, with horses, with hemp, and many other articles for which they now depend upon Europe. Though the new system has been established only a few years, those effects of it begin already to be observed.* If it shall be adhered to with any steadiness for half a century, one may venture to foretell that population, industry, and opulence will advance in this province with rapid progress

To the east of the Andes, the provinces of Tucuman and Rio de la Plata border on Chili, and like it were dependent on the viceroyalty of Peru. These regions of immense extent stretch in length from north to south above thirteen hundred miles, and in breadth more than a thousand. This country, which is larger than most European kingdoms, naturally forms itself into two great divisions, one on the north and the other on the south of Rio de la Plata. The former comprehends Paraguay, the famous missions of the Jesuits, and several other districts. But as disputes have long subsisted between the courts of Spain and Portugal, concerning its boundaries, which, it is probable, will be soon finally ascertained, either amicably or by the decision of the sword, I choose to reserve my account

* Campomanes, ii. 157.

of this northern division, until I enter upon the history of Portuguese America, with which it is intimately connected; and in relating it, I shall be able, from authentic materials supplied both by Spain and Portugal, to give a full and accurate description of the operations and views of the Jesuits, in rearing that singular fabric of policy in America, which has drawn so much attention, and has been so imperfectly understood. The latter division of the province contains the governments of Tucuman and Buenos Ayres, and to these I shall at present confine my observations.

The Spaniards entered this part of America by the river De la Plata, and though a succession of cruel disasters befell them in their early attempts to establish their dominion in it, they were encouraged to persist in the design, at first by the hopes of discovering mines in the interior country, and afterwards by the necessity of occupying it, in order to prevent any other nation from settling there, and penetrating by this route into their rich possessions in Peru. But except at Buenos Ayres, they have made no settlement of any consequence in all the vast space which I have mentioned. There are indeed, scattered over it, a few places on which they have bestowed the name of towns, and to which they have endeavoured to add some dignity, by erecting them into bishoprics; but they are no better than paltry villages, each with two or three hundred inhabitants One circumstance, however, which was not originally foreseen, has contributed to render this district, though thinly peopled, of considerable importance. The province of Tucuman, together with the country to the south of the Plata, instead of being covered with wood like other parts of America, forms one extensive open plain, almost without a tree. The soil is a deep fertile mould, watered by many streams descending from the Andes, and clothed in perpetual verdure. In this rich pasturage, the horses and cattle imported by the Spaniards from Europe have multiplied to a degree which almost exceeds belief. This has enabled the inhabitants not only to open a lucrative trade with Peru, by supplying it with cattle, horses, and mules, but to carry on a commerce no less beneficial, by the exportation of hides to Europe. From both, the colony has derived great advantages. But its commodious situation for carrying on contraband trade has been the chief source of its prosperity. While the court of Madrid adhered to its ancient system, with respect to its communication with America, the river De la Plata lay so much out of the course of Spanish navigation, that interlopers, almost without any risk of being either observed or obstructed, could pour in European manufactures in such quantities, that they not only supplied the wants of the colony, but were conveyed into all the eastern districts of Peru. When the Portuguese in Brazil extended their settlements to the banks of Rio de la Plata, a new channel was opened, by which prohibited commodities flowed into the Spanish territories with still more facility, and in greater abundance. This illegal traffic, however detrimental to the parent state, contributed to the increase of the settlement which had the immediate benefit of it, and Buenos Ayres became gradually a populous and opulent town. What may be the effect of the alteration lately made in the government of this colony, the nature ot which shall be described in the subsequent Book, cannot hitherto be known.

All the other territories of Spain in the New World, the islands excepted, of whose discovery and reduction I have formerly given an account, are comprehended under two great divisions; the former denominated the kingdom of Tierra Firme, the provinces of which stretch along the Atlantic, from the eastern frontier of New Spain to the mouth of the Orinoco; the latter, the New Kingdom of Granada, situated in the interior country. With a short view of these I shall close this part of my work.

To the east of Veragua, the last province subject to the viceroy of Mexico, lies the isthmus of Darien. Though it was in this part of the continent that the Spaniards first began to plant colonies, they have made nc considerable progress in peopling it. As the country is extremely mountainous, deluged with rain during a good part of the year, remarkably unhealthful, and contains no mines of great value, the Spaniards would probably have abandoned it altogether, if they had not been allured to continue by the excellence of the harbour of Porto Bello on the one sea, and that of Panama on the other. These have been called the keys to the communication between the north and south sea, between Spain and her most valuable colonies. In consequence of this advantage, Panama has become a considerable and thriving town. The peculiar noxiousness of its climate has prevented Porto Bello from increasing in the same proportion. As the intercourse with the settlements in the Pacific Ocean is now carried on by another channel, it is probable that both Porto Bello and Panama will decline, when no longer nourished and enriched by that commerce to which they were indebted for their prosperity, and even their existence.

The provinces of Carthagena and Santa Martha stretch to the eastward of the isthmus of Darien. The country still continues mountainous, but its valleys begin to expand, are well watered, and extremely fertile. Pedro de Heredia subjected this part of America to the crown of Spain about the year 1532. It is thinly peopled, and of course ill cultivated. It produces, however, a variety of valuable drugs, and some precious stones, particularly emeralds. But its chief importance is derived from the harbour of Carthagena, the safest and best fortified of any in the American dominions of Spain. In a situation so favourable, commerce soon began to flourish. As early as the year 1544, it seems to have been a town of some note. But when Carthagena was chosen as the port in which the galeons should first begin to trade on their arrival from Europe, and to which they were directed to return, in order to prepare for their voyage homeward, the commerce of its inhabitants were so much favoured by this arrangement, that it soon became one of the most populous, opulent, and beautiful cities in America. There is, however, reason to apprehend that it has reached its highest point of exaltation, and that it will be so far affected by the change in the Spanish system of trade with America, which has withdrawn from it the desirable visits of the galeons, as to feel at least a temporary decline. But the wealth now collected there will soon find or create employment for itself, and may be turned with advantage into some new channel. Its harbour is so safe, and so conveniently situated for receiving commodities from Europe, its merchants have been so long accustomed to convey these into all the adjacent provinces, that it is probable they will still retain this branch of trade, and Carthagena continue to be a city of great importance.

The province contiguous to Santa Martha on the east, was first visited by Alonso de Ojeda, in the year 1499;* and the Spaniards, on their landing there, having observed some huts in an Indian village, built upon piles, in order to raise them above the stagnated water which covered the plain, were led to bestow upon it the name of Venezuela, or little Venice, by their usual propensity to find a resemblance between what they discovered in America, and the objects which were familiar to them in Europe. They made some attempts to settle there, but with little success. The final reduction of the province was accomplished by means very different from those to which Spain was indebted for its other acquisitions in the New World. The ambition of Charles V. often engaged him in operations of such variety and extent, that his revenues were not sufficient to defray the expense of carrying them into execution. Among other expedients for supplying the deficiency of his funds, he had borrowed large sums from the Velsers of Augsburg, the most opulent merchants at that time in Europe. By way of retribution for these, or in hopes, perhaps, of obtaining a new loan, he bestowed upon them the province of Venezuela, to be held as an

* Book ii. p. 48.

hereditary fief from the crown of Castile, on condition that within a limited time they should render themselves masters of the country, and establish a colony there. Under the direction of such persons, it might have been expected that a settlement would have been established on maxims very different from those of the Spaniards, and better calculated to encourage such useful industry, as mercantile proprietors might have known to be the most certain source of prosperity and opulence. But unfortunately they committed the execution of their plan to some of those soldiers of fortune with which Germany abounded in the sixteenth century. These adventurers, impatient to amass riches, that they might speedily abandon a station which they soon discovered to be very uncomfortable, instead of planting a colony in order to cultivate and improve the country, wandered from district to district in search of mines, plundering the natives with unfeeling rapacity, or oppressing them by the imposition of intolerable tasks In the course of a few years, their avarice and exactions, in comparison with which those of the Spaniards were moderate, desolated the province so completely, that it could hardly afford them subsistence, and the Velsers relinquished a property from which the inconsiderate conduct of their agents left them no hope of ever deriving any advantage.* When the wretched remainder of the Germans deserted Venezuela, the Spaniards again took possession of it; but notwithstanding many natural advantages, it is one of their most languishing and unproductive settlements.

The provinces of Caraccas and Cumana are the last of the Spanish territories on this coast; but in relating the origin and operations of the mercantile company in which an exclusive right of trade with them has been vested, I shall hereafter have occasion to consider their state and productions.

The New Kingdom of Granada is entirely an inland country of great extent. This important addition was made to the dominions of Spain about the year 1536, by Sebastian de Benalcazar and Gonzalo Ximenes de Quesada, two of the bravest and most accomplished officers employed in the conquest of America. The former, who commanded at that time in Quito, attacked it from the south; the latter made his invasion from Santa Martha on the north. As the original inhabitants of this region were further advanced in improvement than any people in America but the Mexicans and Peruvians,† they defended themselves with great resolution and good conduct. The abilities and perseverance of Benalcazar and Quesada surmounted all opposition, though not without encountering many dangers, and reduced the country into the form of a Spanish province.

The New Kingdom of Granada is so far elevated above the level of the sea that though it approaches almost to the equator, the climate is remarkably temperate. The fertility of its valleys is not inferior to that of the richest districts in America, and its higher grounds yield gold and precious stones of various kinds. It is not by digging into the bowels of the earth that this gold is found; it is mingled with the soil near the surface, and separated from it by repeated washing with water. This operation is carried on wholly by Negro slaves; for though the chill subterranean air has been discovered, by experience, to be so fatal to them, that they cannot be employed with advantage in the deep silver mines, they are more capable of performing the other species of labour than Indians As the natives in the New Kingdom of Granada are exempt from that service, which has wasted their race so rapidly in other parts of America, the country is still remarkably populous. Some districts yield gold with a profusion no less wonderful than that in the vale of Cineguilla, which I have formerly mentioned, and it is often found in large *petitas*, or grains, which manifest the abundance in which it is produced. On a rising ground near

* Civedo y Bagnos Hist. de Venezuela, p. 11, &c. † Book iv. p. 111, &c.

Pamplona, single labourers have collected in a day what was equal in value to a thousand pesos.* A late governor of Santa Fe brought with him to Spain a lump of pure gold, estimated to be worth seven hundred and forty pounds sterling. This, which is perhaps the largest and finest specimen ever found in the New World, is now deposited in the royal cabinet of Madrid. But without founding any calculation on what is rare and extraordinary, the value of the gold usually collected in this country, particularly in the provinces of Popayan and Choco, is of considerable amount. Its towns are populous and flourishing. The number of inhabitants in almost every part of the country daily increases. Cultivation and industry of various kinds begin to be encouraged, and to prosper. A considerable trade is carried on with Carthagena, the produce of the mines, and other commodities, being conveyed down the great river of St. Magdalene to that city. On another quarter, the New Kingdom of Granada has a communication with the Atlantic by the river Orinoco; but the country which stretches along its banks towards the east, is little known, and imperfectly occupied by the Spaniards.

# BOOK VIII.

After tracing the progress of the Spaniards in their discoveries and conquests during more than half a century, I have conducted them to that period when their authority was established over almost all the vast regions in the New World still subject to their dominion. The effect of their settlements upon the countries of which they took possession, the maxims which they adopted in forming their new colonies, the interior structure and policy of these, together with the influence of their progressive improvement upon the parent state, and upon the commercial intercourse of nations, are the objects to which we now turn our attention.

The first visible consequence of the establishments made by the Spaniards in America, was the diminution of the ancient inhabitants, to a degree equally astonishing and deplorable. I have already, on different occasions, mentioned the disastrous influence under which the connection of the Americans with the people of our hemisphere commenced, both in the islands and in several parts of the continent, and have touched upon various causes of their rapid consumption. Wherever the inhabitants of America had resolution to take arms in defence of their liberty and rights, many perished in the unequal contest, and were cut off by their fierce invaders. But the greatest desolation followed after the sword was sheathed, and the conquerors were settled in tranquillity. It was in the islands, and in those provinces of the continent which stretch from the Gulf of Trinidad to the confines of Mexico, that the fatal effects of the Spanish dominion were first and most sensibly felt. All these were occupied either by wandering tribes of hunters, or by such as had made but small progress in cultivation and industry. When they were compelled by their new masters to take up a fixed residence, and to apply to regular labour; when tasks were imposed upon them disproportioned to their strength, and were enacted with unrelenting severity, they possessed not vigour either of mind or of body to sustain this unusual load of oppression. Dejection and despair drove many to end their lives by violence. Fatigue and famine destroyed more. In

* Piedrahita Hist. del N. Reyno, p. 481. MS. penes me.

all those extensive regions, the original race of inhabitants wasted away; in some it was totally extinguished. In Mexico, where a powerful and martial people distinguished their opposition to the Spaniards by efforts of courage worthy of a better fate, great numbers fell in the field; and there, as well as in Peru, still greater numbers perished under the hardships of attending the Spanish armies in their various expeditions and civil wars, worn out with the incessant toil of carrying their baggage, provisions, and military stores.

But neither the rage nor cruelty of the Spaniards was so destructive to the people of Mexico and Peru, as the inconsiderate policy with which they established their new settlements. The former were temporary calamities, fatal to individuals: the latter was a permanent evil, which, with gradual consumption, wasted the nation. When the provinces of Mexico and Peru were divided among the conquerors, each was eager to obtain a district from which he might expect an instantaneous recompense for all his services. Soldiers, accustomed to the carelessness and dissipation of a military life, had neither industry to carry on any plan of regular cultivation, nor patience to wait for its slow but certain returns. Instead of settling in the valleys occupied by the natives, where the fertility of the soil would have amply rewarded the diligence of the planter, they chose to fix their stations in some of the mountainous regions, frequent both in New Spain and in Peru. To search for mines of gold and silver was the chief object of their activity. The prospects which this opens, and the alluring hopes which it continually presents, correspond wonderfully with the spirit of enterprise and adventure that animated the first emigrants to America in every part of their conduct. In order to push forward those favourite projects, so many hands were wanted, that the service of the natives became indispensably requisite. They were accordingly compelled to abandon their ancient habitations in the plains, and driven in crowds to the mountains. This sudden transition from the sultry climate of the valleys to the chill penetrating air peculiar to high lands in the torrid zone; exorbitant labour, scanty or unwholesome nourishment, and the despondency occasioned by a species of oppression to which they were not accustomed, and of which they saw no end, affected them nearly as much as their less industrious countrymen in the islands. They sunk under the united pressure of those calamities, and melted away with almost equal rapidity.* In consequence of this, together with the introduction of the smallpox, a malady unknown in America, and extremely fatal to the natives,† the number of people both in New Spain and Peru was so much reduced, that in a few years the accounts of their ancient population appeared almost incredible.‡

Such are the most considerable events and causes which, by their combined operation, contributed to depopulate America. Without attending to these, many authors, astonished at the suddenness of the desolation, have ascribed this unexampled event to a system of policy no less profound than atrocious. The Spaniards, as they pretend, conscious of their own inability to occupy the vast regions which they had discovered, and foreseeing the impossibility of maintaining their authority over a people infinitely superior to themselves in number, in order to preserve the possession of America, resolved to exterminate the inhabitants, and, by converting a great part of the country into a desert, endeavoured to secure their own dominion over it [165]. But nations seldom extend their views to objects so remote, or lay their plans so deep; and for the honour of humanity we may observe, that no nation ever deliberately formed such an execrable scheme. The Spanish monarchs, far from acting upon any such system of

* Torquemada, i. 613. † B. Diaz, c. 124. Herrera, dec. 2. lib. x. c. 4. Ulloa Entreten 206
‡ Torquem, 615. 642, 643 [164].

destruction, were uniformly solicitous for the preservation of their new subjects. With Isabella, zeal for propagating the Christian faith, together with the desire of communicating the knowledge of truth, and the consolations of religion, to people destitute of spiritual light, were more than ostensible motives for encouraging Columbus to attempt his discoveries. Upon his success, she endeavoured to fulfil her pious purpose, and manifested the most tender concern to secure not only religious instruction, but mild treatment, to that inoffensive race of men subjected to her crown [166]. Her successors adopted the same ideas; and, on many occasions, which I have mentioned, their authority was interposed, in the most vigorous exertions, to protect the people of America from the oppression of their Spanish subjects. Their regulations for this purpose were numerous, and often repeated. They were framed with wisdom, and dictated by humanity. After their possessions in the New World became so extensive as might have excited some apprehensions of difficulty in retaining their dominion over them, the spirit of their regulations was as mild as when their settlements were confined to the islands alone. Their solicitude to protect the Indians seems rather to have augmented as their acquisitions increased: and from ardour to accomplish this, they enacted, and endeavoured to enforce the execution of laws, which excited a formidable rebellion in one of their colonies, and spread alarm and disaffection through all the rest. But the avarice of individuals was too violent to be controlled by the authority of laws. Rapacious and daring adventurers, far removed from the seat of government, little accustomed to the restraints of military discipline while in service, and still less disposed to respect the feeble jurisdiction of civil power in an infant colony, despised or eluded every regulation that set bounds to their exactions and tyranny. The parent state, with persevering attention, issued edicts to prevent the oppression of the Indians; the colonists, regardless of these, or trusting to their distance for impunity, continued to consider and treat them as slaves. The governors themselves, and other officers employed in the colonies, several of whom were as indigent and rapacious as the adventurers over whom they presided, were too apt to adopt their contemptuous ideas of the conquered people; and, instead of checking, encouraged or connived at their excesses. The desolation of the New World should not then be charged on the court of Spain, or be considered as the effect of any system of policy adopted there. It ought to be imputed wholly to the indigent and often unprincipled adventurers, whose fortune it was to be the conquerors and first planters of America, who, by measures no less inconsiderate than unjust, counteracted the edicts of their sovereign, and have brought disgrace upon their country.

With still greater injustice have many authors represented the intolerating spirit of the Roman Catholic religion, as the cause of exterminating the Americans, and have accused the Spanish ecclesiastics of animating their countrymen to the slaughter of that innocent people, as idolaters and enemies of God. But the first missionaries who visited America, though weak and illiterate, were pious men. They early espoused the defence of the natives, and vindicated their character from the aspersions of their conquerors, who, describing them as incapable of being formed to the offices of civil life, or of comprehending the doctrines of religion, contended, that they were a subordinate race of men, on whom the hand of nature had set the mark of servitude. From the accounts which I have given of the humane and persevering zeal of the Spanish missionaries, in protecting the helpless flock committed to their charge, they appear in a light which reflects lustre upon their function. They were ministers o. peace, who endeavoured to wrest the rod from the hands of oppressors. To their powerful interposition the Americans were indebted for every regulation tending to mitigate the rigour of their fate. The clergy in the

Spanish settlements, regular as well as secular, are still considered by the Indians as their natural guardians, to whom they have recourse under the hardships and exactions to which they are too often exposed [167].

But, notwithstanding the rapid depopulation of America, a very considerable number of the native race still remains both in Mexico and Peru, especially in those parts which were not exposed to the first fury of the Spanish arms, or desolated by the first efforts of their industry, still more ruinous. In Guatimala, Chiapa, Nicaragua, and the other delightful provinces of the Mexican empire, which stretch along the South Sea, the race of Indians is still numerous. Their settlements in some places are so populous as to merit the name of cities [168]. In the three audiences into which New Spain is divided, there are at least two millions of Indians; a pitiful remnant, indeed, of its ancient population, but such as still forms a body of people superior in number to that of all the other inhabitants of this extensive country [169]. In Peru several districts, particularly in the kingdom of Quito, are occupied almost entirely by Indians. In other provinces they are mingled with the Spaniards, and in many of their settlements are almost the only persons who practise the mechanic arts, and fill most of the inferior stations in society. As the inhabitants both of Mexico and Peru were accustomed to a fixed residence, and to a certain degree of regular industry, less violence was requisite in bringing them to some conformity with the European modes of civil life. But wherever the Spaniards settled among the savage tribes of America, their attempts to incorporate with them have been always fruitless, and often fatal to the natives. Impatient of restraint, and disdaining labour as a mark of servility, they either abandoned their original seats, and sought for independence in mountains and forests inaccessible to their oppressors, or perished when reduced to a state repugnant to their ancient ideas and habits. In the districts adjacent to Carthagena, to Panama, and to Buenos Ayres, the desolation is more general than even in those parts of Mexico and Peru of which the Spaniards have taken most full possession.

But the establishments of the Spaniards in the New World, though fatal to its ancient inhabitants, were made a ta period when that monarchy was capable of forming them to best advantage. By the union of all its petty kingdoms, Spain was become a powerful state, equal to so great an undertaking. Its monarchs, having extended their prerogatives far beyond the limits which once circumscribed the regal power in every kingdom of Europe, were hardly subject to control, either in concerting or in executing their measures. In every wide-extended empire, the form of government must be simple, and the sovereign authority such, that its resolutions may be taken with promptitude, and may pervade the whole with sufficient force. Such was the power of the Spanish monarchs when they were called to deliberate concerning the mode of establishing their dominions over the most remote provinces which had ever been subjected to any European state. In this deliberation, they felt themselves under no constitutional restraint, and that, as independent masters of their own resolves, they might issue the edicts requisite for modelling the government of the new colonies, by a mere act of prerogative.

This early interposition of the Spanish crown, in order to regulate the policy and trade of its colonies, is a peculiarity which distinguishes their progress from that of the colonies of any other European nation. When the Portuguese, the English, and French took possession of the regions in America which they now occupy, the advantages which these promised to yield were so remote and uncertain, that their colonies were suffered to struggle through a hard infancy, almost without guidance or protection from the parent state. But gold and silver, the first productions of the Spanish settlements in the New World, were more alluring, and immediately attracted the attention of their monarchs. Though they had contributed little to the discovery, and almost nothing to the conquest of the New World, they instantly assumed the function of its legislators; and having acquired a species of dominion formerly unknown, they formed a plan for exercising it, to which nothing similar occurs in the history of human affairs.

The fundamental maxim of the Spanish jurisprudence, with respect to America, is to consider what has been acquired there as vested in the crown, rather than in the state. By the bull of Alexander VI., on which, as its great charter, Spain founded its right, all the regions that had been or should be discovered were bestowed as a free gift upon Ferdinand and Isabella. They and their successors were uniformly held to be the universal proprietors of the vast territories which the arms of their subjects conquered in the New World. From them all grants of land there flowed, and to them they finally returned. The leaders who conducted the various expeditions, the governors who presided over the different colonies, the officers of justice, and the ministers of religion, were all appointed by their authority, and removable at their pleasure. The people who composed infant settlements were entitled to no privileges independent of the sovereign, or that served as a barrier against the power of the crown. It is true, that when towns were built, and formed into bodies corporate, the citizens were permitted to elect their own magistrates, who governed them by laws which the community enacted. Even in the most despotic states, this feeble spark of liberty is not extinguished. But in the cities of Spanish America, this jurisdiction is merely municipal, and is confined to the regulation of their own interior commerce and police. In whatever relates to public government, and the general interest, the will of the sovereign is law. No political power originates from the people. All centres in the crown, and in the officers of its nomination.

When the conquests of the Spaniards in America were completed, their monarchs, in forming the plan of internal policy for their new dominions, divided them into two immense governments, one subject to the viceroy of New Spain, the other to the viceroy of Peru. The jurisdiction of the former extended over all the provinces belonging to Spain in the northern division of the American continent. Under that of the latter, was comprehended whatever she possessed in South America. This arrangement, which, from the beginning, was attended with many inconveniences, became intolerable when the remote provinces of each viceroyalty began to improve in industry and population. The people complained of their subjection to a superior, whose place of residence was so distant, or so inaccessible, as almost excluded them from any intercourse with the seat of government. The authority of the viceroy over districts so far removed from his own eye and observation, was unavoidably both feeble and ill directed. As a remedy for those evils, a third viceroyalty has been established in the present century, at Santa Fe de Bogota, the capital of the new kingdom of Granada, the jurisdiction of which extends over the whole kingdom of Tierra Firme and the province of Quito.* Those viceroys not only represent the person of their sovereign, but possess his regal prerogatives within the precincts of their own governments in their utmost extent. Like him, they exercise supreme authority in every department of government, civil, military, and criminal. They have the sole right of nominating the persons who hold many offices of the highest importance, and the occasional privilege of supplying those which, when they become vacant by death, are in the royal gift, until the successor appointed by the king shall arrive. The external pomp of their government is suited to its real dignity and power. Their courts are formed upon the model of that at Madrid, with horse and foot guards, a household

* Voy. de Ulloa, i. 23. 255

regularly established, numerous attendants, and ensigns of command, displaying such magnificence as hardly retains the appearance of delegated authority.*

But as the viceroys cannot discharge in person the functions of a supreme magistrate in every part of their extensive jurisdiction, they are aided in their government by officers and tribunals similar to those in Spain. The conduct of civil affairs in the various provinces and districts, into which the Spanish dominions in America are divided, is committed to magistrates of various orders and denominations; some appointed by the king, others by the viceroy, but all subject to the command of the latter, and amenable to his jurisdiction. The administration of justice is vested in tribunals, known by the name of *Audiences*, and formed upon the model of the court of Chancery in Spain. These are eleven in number, and dispense justice to as many districts into which the Spanish dominions in America are divided [170]. The number of judges in the Court of Audience is various, according to the extent and importance of their jurisdiction. The station is no less honourable than lucrative, and is commonly filled by persons of such abilities and merit as render this tribunal extremely respectable. Both civil and criminal causes come under their cognizance, and for each peculiar judges are set apart. Though it is only in the most despotic governments that the sovereign exercises in person the formidable prerogative of administering justice to his subjects, and, in absolving or condemning, consults no law but what is deposited in his own breast; though, in all the monarchies of Europe, judicial authority is committed to magistrates, whose decisions are regulated by known laws and established forms; the Spanish viceroys have often attempted to intrude themselves into the seat of justice, and, with an ambition which their distance from the control of a superior rendered bold, have aspired at a power which their master does not venture to assume. In order to check a usurpation which must have annihilated justice and security in the Spanish colonies, by subjecting the lives and property of all to the will of a single man, the viceroys have been prohibited in the most explicit terms, by repeated laws, from interfering in the judicial proceedings of the Courts of Audience, or from delivering an opinion, or giving a voice, with respect to any point litigated before them.† In some particular cases, in which any question of civil right is involved, even the political regulations of the viceroy may be brought under the review of the Court of Audience, which in those instances may be deemed an intermediate power placed between him and the people, as a constitutional barrier to circumscribe his jurisdiction. But as legal restraints on a person who represents the sovereign, and is clothed with his authority, are little suited to the genius of Spanish policy; the hesitation and reserve with which it confers this power on the Courts of Audience are remarkable. They may advise, they may remonstrate; but, in the event of a direct collision between their opinion and the will of the viceroy, what he determines must be carried into execution, and nothing remains for them, but to lay the matter before the king and the Council of the Indies.‡ But to be entitled to remonstrate, and inform against a person before whom all others must be silent, and tamely submit to his decrees, is a privilege which adds dignity to the Courts of Audience. This is further augmented by another circumstance. Upon the death of a viceroy, without any provision of a successor by the king, the supreme power is vested in the Court of Audience resident in the capital of the viceroyalty; and the senior judge, assisted by his brethren, exercises all the functions of the viceroy while the office continues vacant.§ In matters which come under

* Ulloa, Voy. i. 432. Gage, 61. † Recop. lib. ii. tit. xv. l. 35. 38. 44. lib. iii. tit. iii. l. 36, 37.
‡ Solorz. de Jure Ind. lib. iv. c. 3. n. 40, 41. Recop. lib. ii. tit. xv. l. 36. lib. iii. tit. iii. l. 34. lib v tit ix. l. 1. § Recop. lib. ii. tit. xv l. 57 &c.

the cognizance of the Audiences, in the course of their ordinary jurisdiction, as courts of justice, their sentences are final in every litigation concerning property of less value than six thousand pesos; but when the subject in dispute exceeds that sum, their decisions are subject to review, and may be carried by appeal before the royal Council of the Indies.*

In this council, one of the most considerable in the monarchy for dignity and power, is vested the supreme government of all the Spanish dominions in America. It was first established by Ferdinand in the year 1511, and brought into a more perfect form by Charles V. in the year 1524. Its jurisdiction extends to every department, ecclesiastical, civil, military, and commercial. All laws and ordinances relative to the government and police of the colonies originate there, and must be approved of by two-thirds of the members before they are issued in the name of the king. All the offices, of which the nomination is reserved to the crown, are conferred in this council. To it each person employed in America, from the viceroy downwards, is accountable. It reviews their conduct, rewards their services, and inflicts the punishments due to their malversations.† Before it is laid whatever intelligence, either public or secret, is received from America; and every scheme of improving the administration, the police, or the commerce of the colonies, is submitted to its consideration. From the first institution of the Council of the Indies, it has been the constant object of the Catholic monarchs to maintain its authority, and to make such additions from time to time, both to its power and its splendour, as might render it formidable to all their subjects in the New World. Whatever degree of public order and virtue still remains in that country, where so many circumstances conspire to relax the former, and to corrupt the latter, may be ascribed in a great measure to the wise regulations and vigilant inspection of this respectable tribunal.‡

As the king is supposed to be always present in his Council of the Indies, its meetings are held in the place where he resides. Another tribunal has been instituted in order to regulate such commercial affairs, as required the immediate and personal inspection of those appointed to superintend them. This is called *Casa de la Contratacion*, or the house of trade, and was established in Seville, the port to which commerce with the New World was confined, as early as the year 1501. It may be considered both as a board of trade, and as a court of judicature. In the former capacity, it takes cognizance of whatever relates to the intercourse of Spain with America, it regulates what commodities should be exported thither, and has the inspection of such as are received in return. It decides concerning the departure of the fleets for the West Indies, the freight and burden of the ships, their equipment and destination. In the latter capacity, it judges with respect to every question, civil, commercial, or criminal, arising in consequence of the transactions of Spain with America; and in both these departments its decisions are exempted from the review of any court but that of the Council of the Indies.§

Such is the great outline of that system of government which Spain has established in her American colonies. To enumerate the various subordinate boards and officers employed in the administration of justice, in collecting the public revenue, and in regulating the interior police of the country; to describe their different functions, and to inquire into the mode and effect of their operations; would prove a detail no less intricate than minute and uninteresting.

The first object of the Spanish monarchs was to secure the productions of the colonies to the parent state, by an absolute prohibition of any intercourse with foreign nations. They took possession of America by right

* Recop. lib. v. tit xiii. l. 1, &c. † Ibid. lib. ii. tit. ii. l. 1, 2, &c. ‡ Solorz. de Jure Ind. lib. iv. c. 12. § Recop. lib. ix. tit. i. Veitia Norte de la Contratacion, lib. i. 1.

of conquest, and conscious not only of the feebleness of their infant settlements, but aware of the difficulty in establishing their dominions over regions so extensive, or in retaining so many reluctant nations under the yoke, they dreaded the intrusion of strangers; they even shunned their inspection, and endeavoured to keep them at a distance from their coasts. This spirit of jealousy and exclusion, which at first was natural, and perhaps necessary, augmented as their possessions in America extended, and the value of them came to be more fully understood. In consequence of it, a system of colonising was introduced, to which there had hitherto been nothing similar among mankind. In the ancient world, it was not uncommon to send forth colonies. But they were of two kinds only. They were either migrations, which served to disburden a state of its superfluous subjects, when they multiplied too fast for the territory which they occupied; or they were military detachments, stationed as garrisons in a conquered province. The colonies of some Greek republics, and the swarms of northern barbarians which settled in different parts of Europe, were of the first species. The Roman colonies were of the second. In the former, the connection with the mother country quickly ceased, and they became independent states. In the latter, as the disjunction was not complete, the dependence continued. In their American settlements, the Spanish monarchs took what was peculiar to each, and studied to unite them. By sending colonies to regions so remote, by establishing in each a form of inferior policy and administration, under distinct governors, and with peculiar laws, they disjoined them from the mother country. By retaining in their own hands the rights of legislation, as well as that of imposing taxes, together with the power of nominating the persons who filled every department of executive government, civil or military, they secured their dependence upon the parent state. Happily for Spain, the situation of her colonies was such as rendered it possible to reduce this new idea into practice. Almost all the countries which she had discovered and occupied, lay within the tropics. The productions of that large portion of the globe are different from those of Europe, even in its most southern provinces. The qualities of the climate and of the soil naturally turn the industry of such as settle there into new channels. When the Spaniards first took possession of their dominions in America, the precious metals which they yielded were the only object that attracted their attention. Even when their efforts began to take a better direction, they employed themselves almost wholly in rearing such peculiar productions of the climate as, from their rarity or value, were of chief demand in the mother country. Allured by vast prospects of immediate wealth, they disdained to waste their industry on what was less lucrative, but of superior moment. In order to render it impossible to correct this error, and to prevent them from making any efforts in industry which might interfere with those of the mother country, the establishment of several species of manufactures, and even the culture of the vine or olive, are prohibited in the Spanish colonies [171], under severe penalties.* They must trust entirely to the mother country for the objects of primary necessity. Their clothes, their furniture, their instruments of labour, their luxuries, and even a considerable part of the provisions which they consume, were imported from Spain. During a great part of the sixteenth century, Spain, possessing an extensive commerce and flourishing manufactures, could supply with ease the growing demands of her colonies from her own stores. The produce of their mines and plantations was given in exchange for these. But all that the colonies received, as well as all that they gave, was conveyed in Spanish bottoms No vessel belonging to the colonies was ever permitted to carry the commodities of America to Europe. Even the commercial intercourse of one

* B Ulloa Retab. des Manuf. &c. p. 206

colony with another was either absolutely prohibited, or limited by many jealous restrictions. All that America yields flows into the ports of Spain; all that it consumes must issue from them. No foreigner can enter its colonies without express permission; no vessel of any foreign nation is received into their harbours; and the pains of death, with confiscation of moveables, are denounced against every inhabitant who presumes to trade with them.* Thus the colonies are kept in a state of perpetual pupilage; and by the introduction of this commercial dependence, a refinement in policy of which Spain set the first example to European nations, the supremacy of the parent state hath been maintained over remote colonies during two centuries and a half.

Such are the capital maxims to which the Spanish monarchs seem to have attended in forming their new settlements in America. But they could not plant with the same rapidity that they had destroyed; and from many concurring causes, their progress has been extremely slow in filling up the immense void which their devastations had occasioned. As soon as the rage for discovery and adventure began to abate, the Spaniards opened their eyes to dangers and distresses which at first they did not perceive, or had despised. The numerous hardships with which the members of infant colonies have to struggle, the diseases of unwholesome climates fatal to the constitution of Europeans; the difficulty of bringing a country covered with forests into culture; the want of hands necessary for labour in some provinces, and the slow reward of industry in all, unless where the accidental discovery of mines enriched a few fortunate adventurers, were evils universally felt and magnified. Discouraged by the view of these, the spirit of migration was so much damped, that sixty years after the discovery of the New World, the number of Spaniards in all its provinces is computed not to have exceeded fifteen thousand [172].

The mode in which property was distributed in the Spanish colonies, and the regulations established with respect to the transmission of it, whether by descent or by sale, were extremely unfavourable to population. In order to promote a rapid increase of people in any new settlement, property in land ought to be divided into small shares, and the alienation of it should be rendered extremely easy.† But the rapaciousness of the Spanish conquerors of the New World paid no regard to this fundamental maxim of policy; and, as they possessed power which enabled them to gratify the utmost extravagance of their wishes, many seized districts of great extent, and held them as *encomiendas*. By degrees they obtained the privilege of converting a part of these into *Mayorasgos*, a species of fief, introduced into the Spanish system of feudal jurisprudence,‡ which can neither be divided nor alienated. Thus a great portion of landed property under this rigid form of entail, is withheld from circulation, and descends from father to son unimproved, and of little value either to the proprietor or to the community. In the account which I have given of the reduction of Peru, various examples occur of enormous tracts of country occupied by some of the conquerors.§ The excesses in other provinces were similar; for, as the value of the lands which the Spaniards acquired was originally estimated according to the number of Indians which lived upon them, America was in general so thinly peopled, that only districts of great extent could afford such a number of labourers as might be employed in the mines with any prospect of considerable gain. The pernicious effects of those radical errors in the distribution and nature of property in the Spanish settlements are felt through every department of industry, and may be considered as one great cause of a progress in population so much slower than that which has taken place in better constituted colonies [173].

* Recopil lib. ix. tit. xxvii. l. 1. 4. 7, &c. † Dr. Smith's Inquiry, ii. 166. ‡ Recop. lib. iv. tit. iii. l. 24. § Book vi.

To this we may add, that the support of the enormous and expensive fabric of their ecclesiastical establishment has been a burden on the Spanish colonies, which has greatly retarded the progress of population and industry. The payment of tithes is a heavy tax on industry: and if the exaction of them be not regulated and circumscribed by the wisdom of the civil magistrate, it becomes intolerable and ruinous. But, instead of any restraint on the claims of ecclesiastics, the inconsiderate zeal of the Spanish legislators admitted them into America in their full extent, and at once imposed on their infant colonies a burden which is in no slight degree oppressive to society, even in its most improved state. As early as the year 1501, the payment of tithes in the colonies was enjoined, and the mode of it regulated by law. Every article of primary necessity, towards which the attention of new settlers must naturally be turned, is subjected to that grievous exaction.* Nor were the demands of the clergy confined to articles of simple and easy culture. Its more artificial and operose productions, such as sugar, indigo, and cochineal, were soon declared to be titheable;† and thus the industry of the planter was taxed in every stage of its progress, from its rudest essay to its highest improvement. To the weight of this legal imposition, the bigotry of the American Spaniards has made many voluntary additions. From their fond delight in the external pomp and parade of religion, and from superstitious reverence for ecclesiastics of every denomination, they have bestowed profuse donatives on churches and monasteries, and have unprofitably wasted a large proportion of that wealth, which might have nourished and given vigour to productive labour in growing colonies.

But so fertile and inviting are the regions of America, which the Spaniards have occupied, that, notwithstanding all the circumstances which have checked and retarded population, it has gradually increased, and filled the colonies of Spain with citizens of various orders. Among these, the Spaniards who arrive from Europe, distinguished by the name of *Chapetones*, are the first in rank and power. From the jealous attention of the Spanish court to secure the dependence of the colonies on the parent state, all departments of consequence are filled by persons sent from Europe; and in order to prevent any of dubious fidelity from being employed, each must bring proof of a clear descent from a family of *Old Christians*, untainted with any mixture of Jewish or Mahometan blood, and never disgraced by any censure of the Inquisition.‡ In such pure hands power is deemed to be safely lodged, and almost every function, from the viceroyalty downwards, is committed to them alone. Every person, who, by his birth or residence in America, may be suspected of any attachment or interest adverse to the mother country, is the object of distrust to such a degree, as amounts nearly to an exclusion from all offices of confidence or authority [174]. By this conspicuous predilection of the court, the Chapetones are raised to such pre-eminence in America, that they look down with disdain on every other order of men.

The character and state of the *Creoles*, or descendants of Europeans settled in America, the second class of subjects in the Spanish colonies, have enabled the Chapetones to acquire other advantages, hardly less considerable than those which they derived from the partial favour of government. Though some of the Creolian race are descended from the conquerors of the New World; though others can trace up their pedigree to the noblest families in Spain; though many are possessed of ample fortunes; yet, by the enervating influence of a sultry climate, by the rigour of a jealous government, and by their despair of attaining that distinction to which mankind naturally aspire, the vigour of their minds is so entirely broken,

* Recop. lib. i. tit. xiv. l. 2. † Recop. lib. i. tit. xiv. l. 3, 4. ‡ Recop. lib. ix. tit. xxvi. l. 15, 16.

that a great part of them waste life in luxurious indulgences, mingled with an illiberal superstition still more debasing.

Languid and unenterprising, the operations of an active extended commerce would be to them so cumbersome and oppressive, that in almost every part of America they decline engaging in it. The interior traffic of every colony, as well as any trade which is permitted with the neighbouring provinces, and with Spain itself, is carried on chiefly by the Chapetones;* who, as the recompense of their industry, amass immense wealth, while the Creoles, sunk in sloth, are satisfied with the revenues of their paternal estates.

From this stated competition for power and wealth between those two orders of citizens, and the various passions excited by a rivalship so interesting, their hatred is violent and implacable. On every occasion, symptoms of this aversion break out, and the common appellations which each bestows on the other are as contemptuous as those which flow from the most deep-rooted national antipathy.† The court of Spain, from a refinement of distrustful policy, cherishes those seeds of discord, and foments this mutual jealousy, which not only prevents the two most powerful classes of its subjects in the New World from combining against the parent state, but prompts each, with the most vigilant zeal, to observe the motions and to counteract the schemes of the other.

The third class of inhabitants in the Spanish colonies is a mixed race, the offspring either of a European and a Negro, or of a European and Indian, the former called *Mulattoes*, the latter *Mestizos*. As the court of Spain, solicitous to incorporate its new vassals with its ancient subjects, early encouraged the Spaniards settled in America to marry the natives of that country, several alliances of this kind were formed in their infant colonies.‡ But it has been more owing to licentious indulgence, than to compliance with this injunction of their sovereigns, that this mixed breed has multiplied so greatly as to constitute a considerable part of the population in all the Spanish settlements. The several stages of descent in this race, and the gradual variations of shade until the African black or the copper colour of America brighten into a European complexion, are accurately marked by the Spaniards, and each distinguished by a peculiar name. Those of the first and second generations are considered and treated as mere Indians and Negroes; but in the third descent, the characteristic hue of the former disappears; and in the fifth, the deeper tint of the latter is so entirely effaced, that they can no longer be distinguished from Europeans, and become entitled to all their privileges.§ It is chiefly by this mixed race, whose frame is remarkably robust and hardy, that the mechanic arts are carried on in the Spanish settlements, and other active functions in society are discharged, which the two higher classes of citizens, from pride, or from indolence, disdain to exercise.||

The Negroes hold the fourth rank among the inhabitants of the Spanish colonies. The introduction of that unhappy part of the human species into America, together with their services and sufferings there, shall be fully explained in another place; here they are mentioned chiefly in order to point out a peculiarity in their situation under the Spanish dominion. In several of their settlements, particularly in New Spain, Negroes are mostly employed in domestic service. They form a principal part in the train of luxury, and are cherished and caressed by their superiors, to whose vanity and pleasures they are equally subservient. Their dress and appearance are hardly less splendid than that of their masters, whose manners they imitate, and whose passions they imbibe.¶ Elevated by this distinction,

* Voy. de Ulloa, i. 27. 251. Voy. de Frezier, 227. † Gage's Survey, p. 9. Frezier, 226. ‡ Recopil. lib. vi. tit. i. l. 2. Herrera, dec. 1. lib. v. c. 12. dec. 3. lib vii. c. 2. § Voy. de Ulloa, i p. 27. || Ibid. i. 29. Voyage de Bouguer, p. 104. Melendez, Tesoros Verdaderos, i. 354. ¶ Gage, p. 56. Voy. de Ulloa, i. 451.

they have assumed such a tone of superiority over the Indians, and treat them with such insolence and scorn, that the antipathy between the two races has become implacable. Even in Peru, where Negroes seem to be more numerous, and are employed in field work as well as domestic service, they maintain their ascendant over the Indians, and the mutual hatred of one to the other subsists with equal violence. The laws have industriously fomented this aversion, to which accident gave rise, and, by most rigorous injunctions, have endeavoured to prevent every intercourse that might form a bond of union between the two races. Thus, by an artful policy, the Spaniards derive strength from that circumstance in population which is the weakness of other European colonies, and have secured, as associates and defenders, those very persons who elsewhere are objects of jealousy and terror.*

The Indians form the last and most depressed order of men in the country which belonged to their ancestors. I have already traced the progress of the Spanish ideas with respect to the condition and treatment of that people; and have mentioned the most important of their more early regulations, concerning a matter of so much consequence in the administration of their new dominions. But since the period to which I have brought down the history of America, the information and experience acquired during two centuries have enabled the court of Spain to make such improvements in this part of its American system, that a short view of the present condition of the Indians may prove both curious and interesting.

By the famous regulations of Charles V. in 1542, which have been so often mentioned, the high pretensions of the conquerors of the New World, who considered its inhabitants as slaves to whose service they had acquired a full right of property, were finally abrogated. From that period, the Indians have been reputed freemen, and entitled to the privileges of subjects. When admitted into this rank, it was deemed just that they should contribute towards the support and improvement of the society which had adopted them as members. But as no considerable benefit could be expected from the voluntary efforts of men unacquainted with regular industry, and averse to labour, the court of Spain found it necessary to fix and secure, by proper regulations, what it thought reasonable to exact from them. With this view, an annual tax was imposed upon every male, from the age of eighteen to fifty; and at the same time the nature as well as the extent of the services, which they might be required to perform, was ascertained with precision. This tribute varies in different provinces; but if we take that paid in New Spain as a medium, its annual amount is nearly four shillings a head; no exorbitant sum in countries where, as at the source of wealth, the value of money is extremely low† [175]. The right of levying this tribute likewise varies. In America, every Indian is either an immediate vassal of the crown, or depends upon some subject to whom the district in which he resides has been granted for a limited time, under the denomination of an *encomienda.* In the former case, about three-fourths of the tax is paid into the royal treasury; in the latter, the same proportion of it belongs to the holder of the grant. When Spain first took possession of America, the greater part of it was parcelled out among its conquerors, or those who first settled there, and but a small portion reserved for the crown. As those grants, which were made for two lives only,‡ reverted successively to the sovereign, he had it in his power either to diffuse his favours by grants to new proprietors, or to augment his own revenue by valuable annexations [176]. Of these, the latter has been frequently chosen; the number of Indians now depending immediately on

* Recopil. lib. vii. tit. v. l. 7 Herrera, dec. 8. lib. vii. c. 12. Frezier, 244. † Recopil. lib. vi. tit. v. l. 42. Hakluyt, vol. iii. p. 461. ‡ Recopil. lib. vi. tit. viii. l. 48. Solorz. de Ind. Jure lib. ii. c 16

the crown is much greater than in the first stage after the conquest, and this branch of the royal revenue continues to extend.

The benefit arising from the services of the Indians accrues either to the crown, or to the holder of the *encomienda*, according to the same rule observed in the payment of tribute. Those services, however, which can now be legally exacted, are very different from the tasks originally imposed upon the Indians. The nature of the work which they must perform is defined, and an equitable recompense is granted for their labour. The stated services demanded of the Indians may be divided into two branches They are either employed in works of primary necessity, without which society cannot subsist comfortably, or are compelled to labour in the mines, from which the Spanish colonies derive their chief value and importance. In consequence of the former, they are obliged to assist in the culture of maize, and other grain of necessary consumption; in tending cattle; in erecting edifices of public utility; in building bridges; and in forming high roads;* but they cannot be constrained to labour in raising vines, olives, and sugar-canes, or any species of cultivation which has for its object the gratification of luxury or commercial profit.† In consequence of the latter, the Indians are compelled to undertake the more unpleasant task of extracting ore from the bowels of the earth, and of refining it by successive processes, no less unwholesome than operose [177].

The mode of exacting both these services is the same, and is under regulations framed with a view of rendering it as little oppressive as possible to the Indians. They are called out successively in divisions, termed *Mitas*, and no person can be compelled to go but in his turn. In Peru, the number called out must not exceed the seventh part of the inhabitants in any district.‡ In New Spain, where the Indians are more numerous, it is fixed at four in the hundred.§ During what time the labour of such Indians as are employed in agriculture continues, I have not been able to learn [178]. But in Peru, each *mita*, or division, destined for the mines, remains there six months; and while engaged in this service, a labourer never receives less than two shillings a day, and often earns more than double that sum.‖ No Indian, residing at a greater distance than thirty miles from a mine, is included in the mita, or division employed working it;¶ nor are the inhabitants of the low country exposed now to certain destruction, as they were at first when under the dominion of the conquerors, by compelling them to remove from that warm climate to the cold elevated regions where minerals abound** [179].

The Indians who live in the principal towns are entirely subject to the Spanish laws and magistrates; but in their own villages they are governed by caziques, some of whom are the descendants of their ancient lords, others are named by the Spanish viceroys. These regulate the petty affairs of the people under them, according to maxims of justice transmitted to them by tradition from their ancestors. To the Indians this jurisdiction, lodged in such friendly hands, affords some consolation; and so little formidable is this dignity to their new masters, that they often allow it to descend by hereditary right.†† For the further relief of men so much exposed to oppression, the Spanish court has appointed an officer in every district with the title of Protector of the Indians. It is his function, as the name implies, to assert the rights of the Indians; to appear as their defender in the courts of justice; and, by the interposition of his authority, to set bounds to the encroachments and exactions of his countrymen.‡‡ A certain portion of the reserved fourth of the annual tribute is destined for the salary of the

* Recop lib. vi. tit xiii l. 19. Solorz. de Ind. Jure, ii. lib. i. c. 6, 7. 9. † Recop. lib. vi. tit. xiii. l. 8. Solorz. lib. i. c. 7. No. 41, &c. ‡ Recop. lib. vi. tit. xii. l. 21. § Ibid. lib. vi. l. 22. ‖ Ulloa Entreten. 265, 266. ¶ Recop. lib. vi tit. xii. l. 3. ** Ibid. lib. vi. tit. xii. l. 29, tit. l. l. 13. †† Solorz. de Jure Ind. lib. i. c. 26. Recopil. lib. vi. tit. vii. ‡‡ Solorz. lib. i. c. 17. p. 201. Recop. lib. vi. tit. vi.

caziques and protectors; another is applied to the maintenance of the clergy employed in the instruction of the Indians.* Another part seems to be appropriated for the benefit of the Indians themselves, and is applied for the payment of their tribute in years of famine, or when a particular district is affected by any extraordinary local calamity.† Besides this, provision is made by various laws, that hospitals shall be founded in every new settlement for the reception of Indians.‡ Such hospitals have accordingly been erected, both for the indigent and infirm, in Lima, in Cuzco, and in Mexico, where the Indians are treated with tenderness and humanity.§

Such are the leading principles in the jurisprudence and policy by which the Indians are now governed in the provinces belonging to Spain. In those regulations of the Spanish monarchs, we discover no traces of that cruel system of extermination, which they have been charged with adopting; and if we admit that the necessity of securing subsistence for their colonies, or the advantages derived from working the mines, give them a right to avail themselves of the labour of the Indians, we must allow, that the attention with which they regulate and recompense that labour is provident and sagacious. In no code of laws is greater solicitude displayed, or precautions multiplied with more prudent concern, for the preservation, the security, and the happiness of the subject, than we discover in the collection of the Spanish laws for the Indies. But those latter regulations, like the more early edicts which have been already mentioned, have too often proved ineffectual remedies against the evils which they were intended to prevent. In every age, if the same causes continue to operate, the same effects must follow. From the immense distance between the power intrusted with the execution of laws, and that by whose authority they are enacted, the vigour even of the most absolute government must relax, and the dread of a superior, too remote to observe with accuracy or to punish with despatch, must insensibly abate. Notwithstanding the numerous injunctions of the Spanish monarch, the Indians still suffer, on many occasions, both from the avarice of individuals, and from the exactions of the magistrates who ought to have protected them; unreasonable tasks are imposed; the term of their labour is prolonged beyond the period fixed by law, and they groan under many of the insults and wrongs which are the lot of a dependent people [180]. From some information on which I can depend, such oppression abounds more in Peru than in any other colony. But it is not general. According to the accounts even of those authors who are most disposed to exaggerate the sufferings of the Indians, they, in several provinces, enjoy not only ease but affluence; they possess large farms; they are masters of numerous herds and flocks; and, by the knowledge which they have acquired of European arts and industry, are supplied not only with the necessaries but with many luxuries of life.‖

After explaining the form of civil government in the Spanish colonies, and the state of the various orders of persons subject to it, the peculiarities in their ecclesiastical constitution merit consideration. Notwithstanding the superstitious veneration with which the Spaniards are devoted to the Holy See, the vigilant and jealous policy of Ferdinand early prompted him to take precautions against the introduction of the Papal dominion in America. With this view, he solicited Alexander VI. for a grant to the crown of the tithes in all the newly-discovered countries,¶ which he obtained on condition of his making provision for the religious instruction of the natives. Soon after Julius II. conferred on him and his successors, the right of patronage, and the absolute disposal of all ecclesiastical benefices there.**

* Recop. lib. vi. tit. v. l. 30. tit. xvi. l. 12—15. † Ibid. lib. vi. tit. iv. l. 13. ‡ Ibid. lib. i. tit. iv. l. 1, &c. § Voy. de Ulloa, i. 439. 509. Churchill, iv. 496. ‖ Gage's Survey, p. 85. 90. 104, 110, &c. ¶ Bulla Alex. VI. A.D. 1501, ap. Solorz. de Jure Ind. ii. p. 498. ** Bulla Julii II 1508, ap. Solorz. de Jure Ind. ii. 509.

But these Pontiffs, unacquainted with the value of what he demanded, bestowed these donations with an inconsiderate liberality, which their successors have often lamented, and wished to recall. In consequence of those grants, the Spanish monarchs have become in effect the heads of the American church. In them the administration of its revenues is vested. Their nomination of persons to supply vacant benefices is instantly confirmed by the Pope. Thus, in all Spanish America, authority of every species centres in the crown. There no collision is known between spiritual and temporal jurisdiction. The King is the only superior, his name alone is heard of, and no dependence upon any foreign power has been introduced. Papal bulls cannot be admitted into America, nor are they of any force there until they have been previously examined and approved of by the royal council of the Indies;* and if any bull should be surreptitiously introduced and circulated in America without obtaining that approbation, ecclesiastics are required not only to prevent it from taking effect, but to seize all the copies of it, and transmit them to the council of the Indies.† To this limitation of the Papal jurisdiction, equally singular, whether we consider the age and nation in which it was devised, or the jealous attention with which Ferdinand and his successors have studied to maintain it in full force,‡ Spain is indebted, in a great measure, for the uniform tranquillity which has reigned in her American dominions.

The hierarchy is established in America in the same form as in Spain, with its full train of archbishops, bishops, deans, and other dignitaries. The inferior clergy are divided into three classes, under the denomination of *Curas*, *Doctrineros*, and *Missioneros*. The first are parish priests in those parts of the country where the Spaniards have settled. The second have the charge of such districts as are inhabited by Indians subjected to the Spanish government, and living under its protection. The third are employed in instructing and converting those fiercer tribes which disdain submission to the Spanish yoke, and live in remote or inaccessible regions to which the Spanish arms have not penetrated. So numerous are the ecclesiastics of all those various orders, and such the profuse liberality with which many of them are endowed, that the revenues of the church in America are immense. The Romish superstition appears with its utmost pomp in the New World. Churches and convents there are magnificent, and richly adorned; and on high festivals, the display of gold and silver, and precious stones, is such as exceeds the conception of a European.§ An ecclesiastical establishment so splendid and extensive is unfavourable, as has been formerly observed, to the progress of rising colonies; but in countries where riches abound, and the people are so delighted with parade that religion must assume it in order to attract their veneration, this propensity to ostentation has been indulged, and becomes less pernicious.

The early institution of monasteries in the Spanish colonies, and the inconsiderate zeal in multiplying them, have been attended with consequences more fatal. In every new settlement, the first object should be to encourage population, and to incite every citizen to contribute towards augmenting the number and strength of the community. During the youth and vigour of society, while there is room to spread, and sustenance is procured with facility, mankind increase with amazing rapidity. But the Spaniards had hardly taken possession of America, when, with a most preposterous policy, they began to erect convents, where persons of both sexes were shut up, under a vow to defeat the purpose of nature, and to counteract the first of her laws. Influenced by a misguided piety, which ascribes transcendent merit to a state of celibacy, or allured by the prospect

* Recopil. lib. i. tit. ix. l. 2. and Autas del Consejo de las Indias, clxi. † Recop. lib. i. tit. vii l. 55. ‡ Id. lib. i. tit. vii. l. 55. passim. § Voy. de Ulloa, i. 430.

of that listless ease which in sultry climates is deemed supreme felicity, numbers crowded into those mansions of sloth and superstition, and are lost to society. As none but persons of Spanish extract are admitted into the monasteries of the New World, the evil is more sensibly felt, and every monk or nun may be considered as an active person withdrawn from civil life. The impropriety of such foundations in any situation where the extent of territory requires additional hands to improve it, is so obvious, that some Catholic states have expressly prohibited any person in their colonies from taking the monastic vows.* Even the Spanish monarchs, on some occasions, seem to have been alarmed with the spreading of a spirit so adverse to the increase and prosperity of their colonies, that they have endeavoured to check it.† But the Spaniards in America, more thoroughly under the influence of superstition than their countrymen in Europe, and directed by ecclesiastics more bigoted and illiterate, have conceived such a high opinion of monastic sanctity, that no regulations can restrain their zeal; and, by the excess of their ill judged bounty, religious houses have multiplied to a degree no less amazing than pernicious to society [181].

In viewing the state of colonies, where not only the number but influence of ecclesiastics is so great, the character of this powerful body is an object that merits particular attention. A considerable part of the secular clergy in Mexico and Peru are natives of Spain. As persons long accustomed, by their education, to the retirement and indolence of academic life are more incapable of active enterprise, and less disposed to strike into new paths than any order of men, the ecclesiastical adventurers by whom the American church is recruited, are commonly such as, from merit or rank in life, have little prospect of success in their own country. Accordingly, the secular priests in the New World are still less distinguished than their brethren in Spain for literary accomplishments of any species; and though, by the ample provision which has been made for the American church, many of its members enjoy the ease and independence which are favourable to the cultivation of science, the body of secular clergy has hardly, during two centuries and a half, produced one author whose works convey such useful information, or possess such a degree of merit, as to be ranked among those which attract the attention of enlightened nations. But the greatest part of the ecclesiastics in the Spanish settlements are regulars. On the discovery of America, a new field opened to the pious zeal of the monastic orders; and, with a becoming alacrity, they immediately sent forth missionaries to labour in it. The first attempt to instruct and convert the Americans was made by monks; and as soon as the conquest of any province was completed, and its ecclesiastical establishment began to assume some form, the Popes permitted the missionaries of the four mendicant orders, as a reward for their services, to accept of parochial charges in America, to perform all spiritual functions, and to receive the tithes and other emoluments of the benefice, without depending on the jurisdiction of the bishop of the diocess, or being subject to his censures. In consequence of this, a new career of usefulness, as well as new objects of ambition, presented themselves. Whenever a call is made for a fresh supply of missionaries, men of the most ardent and aspiring minds, impatient under the restraint of a cloister, weary of its insipid uniformity, and fatigued with the irksome repetition of its frivolous functions, offer their service with eagerness, and repair to the New World in quest of liberty and distinction. Nor do they pursue distinction without success The highest ecclesiastical honours, as well as the most lucrative preferments in Mexico and Peru, are often in the hands of regulars; and it is chiefly to

* Voy. de Ulloa, ii. 124. † Herrera, dec. v. lib. ix. c. 1, 2. Recop. lib. i. tit. iii. l. 1, 2. tit. iv. c. ii. Solorz. lib. iii. c. 23.

the monastic orders that the Americans are indebted for any portion of science which is cultivated among them. They are almost the only Spanish ecclesiastics from whom we have received any accounts either of the civil or natural history of the various provinces in America. Some of them, though deeply tinged with the indelible superstition of their profession, have published books which give a favourable idea of their abilities. The natural and moral history of the New World, by the Jesuit Acosta, contains more accurate observations, perhaps, and more sound science, than are to be found in any description of remote countries published in the sixteenth century.

But the same disgust with monastic life, to which America is indebted for some instructers of worth and abilities, filled it with others of a very different character. The giddy, the profligate, the avaricious, to whom the poverty and rigid discipline of a convent are intolerable, consider a mission to America as a release from mortification and bondage. There they soon obtain some parochial charge; and far removed, by their situation, from the inspection of their monastic superiors, and exempt, by their character, from the jurisdiction of their diocesan,* they are hardly subjected to any control. According to the testimony of the most zealous catholics, many of the regular clergy in the Spanish settlements are not only destitute of the virtues becoming their profession, but regardless of that external decorum and respect for the opinion of mankind, which preserve a semblance of worth where the reality is wanting. Secure of impunity, some regulars, in contempt of their vow of poverty, engage openly in commerce, and are so rapaciously eager in amassing wealth, that they become the most grievous oppressors of the Indians whom it was their duty to have protected. Others, with no less flagrant violation of their vow of chastity, indulge with little disguise in the most dissolute licentiousness [182].

Various schemes have been proposed for redressing enormities so manifest and so offensive. Several persons, no less eminent for piety than discernment, have contended, that the regulars, in conformity to the canons of the church, ought to be confined within the walls of their cloisters, and should no longer be permitted to encroach on the functions of the secular clergy. Some public-spirited magistrates, from conviction of its being necessary to deprive the regulars of a privilege bestowed at first with good intention, but of which time and experience had discovered the pernicious effects, openly countenanced the secular clergy in their attempts to assert their own rights. The prince D'Esquilache, viceroy of Peru under Philip III., took measures so decisive and effectual for circumscribing the regulars within their proper sphere as struck them with general consternation [183]. They had recourse to their usual arts. They alarmed the superstitious, by representing the proceedings of the viceroy as innovations fatal to religion. They employed all the refinements of intrigue in order to gain persons in power; and seconded by the powerful influence of the Jesuits, who claimed and enjoyed all the privileges which belonged to the Mendicant orders in America, they made a deep impression on a bigoted prince and a weak ministry. The ancient practice was tolerated. The abuses which it occasioned continued to increase, and the corruption of monks, exempt from the restraints of discipline, and the inspection of any superior, became a disgrace to religion. At last, as the veneration of the Spaniards for the monastic orders began to abate, and the power of the Jesuits was on the decline, Ferdinand VI. ventured to apply the only effectual remedy, by issuing an edict [June 23, 1757], prohibiting regulars of every denomination from taking the charge of any parish with the cure of souls; and declaring that on the demise of the present incumbents,

* Avendano Thes. Indic. ii. 253.

none but secular priests, subject to the jurisdiction of their diocesans, shall be presented to vacant benefices.* If this regulation is carried into execution with steadiness in any degree proportional to the wisdom with which it is framed, a very considerable reformation may take place in the ecclesiastical state of Spanish America, and the secular clergy may gradually become a respectable body of men. The deportment of many ecclesiastics, even at present, seems to be decent and exemplary; otherwise we can hardly suppose that they would be held in such high estimation, and possess such a wonderful ascendant over the minds of their countrymen throughout all the Spanish settlements.

But whatever merit the Spanish ecclesiastics in America may possess, the success of their endeavours in communicating the knowledge of true religion to the Indians, has been more imperfect than might have been expected, either from the degree of their zeal, or from the dominion which they had acquired over that people. For this, various reasons may be assigned. The first missionaries, in their ardour to make proselytes, admitted the people of America into the Christian church without previous instruction in the doctrines of religion, and even before they themselves had acquired such knowledge in the Indian language, as to be able to explain to the natives the mysteries of faith, or the precepts of duty. Resting upon a subtle distinction in scholastic theology, between that degree of assent which is founded on a complete knowledge and conviction of duty, and that which may be yielded when both these are imperfect, they adopted this strange practice, no less inconsistent with the spirit of a religion which addresses itself to the understanding of men, than repugnant to the dictates of reason. As soon as any body of people overawed by dread of the Spanish power, moved by the example of their own chiefs, incited by levity, or yielding from mere ignorance, expressed the slightest desire of embracing the religion of their conquerors, they were instantly baptized. While this rage of conversion continued, a single clergyman baptized in one day above five thousand Mexicans, and did not desist until he was so exhausted by fatigue that he was unable to lift his hands.† In the course of a few years after the reduction of the Mexican empire, the sacrament of baptism was administered to more than four millions.‡ Proselytes adopted with such inconsiderate haste, and who were neither instructed in the nature of the tenets to which it was supposed they had given assent, nor taught the absurdity of those which they were required to relinquish, retained their veneration for their ancient superstitions in full force, or mingled an attachment to its doctrine and rites with that slender knowledge of Christianity which they had acquired. These sentiments the new converts transmitted to their posterity, into whose minds they have sunk so deep, that the Spanish ecclesiastics, with all their industry, have not been able to eradicate them. The religious institutions of their ancestors, are still remembered and held in honour by many of the Indians, both in Mexico and Peru; and whenever they think themselves out of reach of inspection by the Spaniards, they assemble and celebrate their idolatrous rites.§

But this is not the most unsurmountable obstacle to the progress of Christianity among the Indians. The powers of their uncultivated understandings are so limited, their observations and reflections reach so little beyond the mere objects of sense, that they seem hardly to have the capacity of forming abstract ideas, and possess not language to express them. To such men the sublime and spiritual doctrines of Christianity must be, in a great measure, incomprehensible. The numerous and splendid ceremonies of the Popish

* Real Cedula MS. penes me.

† P. Torribio, MS. Torquem. Mond. Ind. lib. xvi. c. 6.

‡ Torribio, MS. Torquem. lib. xvi. c. 8.

§ Voy. de Ulloa, i. 341. Torquem. lib. xv. c 23 lib. xvi. c. 23. Gage, 171.

worship catch the eye, please and interest them; but when their instructers attempt to explain the articles of faith with which those external observances are connected, though the Indians may listen with patience, they so little conceive the meaning of what they hear, that their acquiescence does not merit the name of belief. Their indifference is still greater than their incapacity. Attentive only to the present moment, and engrossed by the objects before them, the Indians so seldom reflect upon what is past, or take thought for what is to come, that neither the promises nor threats of religion make much impression upon them; and while their foresight rarely extends so far as the next day, it is almost impossible to inspire them with solicitude about the concerns of a future world. Astonished equally at their slowness of comprehension, and at their insensibility, some of the early missionaries pronounced them a race of men so brutish as to be incapable of understanding the first principles of religion. A council held at Lima decreed, that, on account of this incapacity, they ought to be excluded from the sacrament of the Eucharist.* Though Paul III., by his famous bull issued in the year 1537, declared them to be rational creatures entitled to all the privileges of Christians;† yet, after the lapse of two centuries, during which they have been members of the church, so imperfect are their attainments in knowledge that very few possess such a portion of spiritual discernment as to be deemed worthy of being admitted to the holy communion.‡ From this idea of their incapacity and imperfect knowledge of religion, when the zeal of Philip II. established the inquisition in America in the year 1570, the Indians were exempted from the jurisdiction of that severe tribunal,§ and still continue under the inspection of their diocesans. Even after the most perfect instruction, their faith is held to be feeble and dubious; and though some of them have been taught the learned languages, and have gone through the ordinary course of academic education with applause, their frailty is still so much suspected, that few Indians are either ordained priests, or received into any religious order‖ [184].

From this brief survey some idea may be formed of the interior state of the Spanish colonies. The various productions with which they supply and enrich the mother country, and the system of commercial intercourse between them, come next in order to be explained. If the dominions of Spain in the New World had been of such moderate extent as bore a due proportion to the parent state, the progress of her colonising might have been attended with the same benefit as that of other nations. But when, in less than half a century, her inconsiderate rapacity had seized on countries larger than all Europe, her inability to fill such vast regions with a number of inhabitants sufficient for the cultivation of them was so obvious, as to give a wrong direction to all the efforts of the colonists. They did not form compact settlements, where industry, circumscribed within proper limits, both in its views and operations, is conducted with that sober persevering spirit which gradually converts whatever is in its possession to a proper use, and derives thence the greatest advantage. Instead of this, the Spaniards, seduced by the boundless prospect which opened to them, divided their possessions in America into governments of great extent. As their number was too small to attempt the regular culture of the immense provinces which they occupied rather than peopled, they bent their attention to a few objects that allured them with hopes of sudden and exorbitant gain, and turned away with contempt from the humbler paths of industry, which lead more slowly, but with greater certainty, to wealth and increase of national strength.

Of all the methods by which riches may be acquired, that of searching

* Torquem. lib. xvi. c. 20. † Id. lib. xvi. c. 25. Garcia Origin 311. ‡ Voy. de Ulloa, i. 343. § Recop. lib. vi. tit. i. l. 35. ‖ Torquem. lib. xvii. c. 13.

for the precious metals is one of the most inviting to men who are either unaccustomed to the regular assiduity with which the culture of the earth and the operations of commerce must be carried on, or who are so enterprising and rapacious as not to be satisfied with the gradual returns of profit which they yield. Accordingly, as soon as the several countries in America were subjected to the dominion of Spain, this was almost the only method of acquiring wealth which occurred to the adventurers by whom they were conquered. Such provinces of the continent as did not allure them to settle, by the prospect of their affording gold and silver, were totally neglected. Those in which they met with a disappointment of the sanguine expectations they had formed, were abandoned. Even the value of the islands, the first fruits of their discoveries, and the first object of their attention, sunk so much in their estimation, when the mines which had been opened in them were exhausted, that they were deserted by many of the planters, and left to be occupied by more industrious possessors. All crowded to Mexico and Peru, where the quantities of gold and silver found among the natives, who searched for them with little industry and less skill, promised an unexhausted store, as the recompense of more intelligent and persevering efforts.

During several years, the ardour of their researches was kept up by hope rather than success. At length, the rich silver mines of Potosi in Peru were accidentally discovered in the year 1545* by an Indian, as he was clambering up the mountains in pursuit of a llama which had strayed from his flock. Soon after, the mines of Sacotecas in New Spain, little inferior to the other in value, were opened. From that time successive discoveries have been made in both colonies, and silver mines are now so numerous, that the working of them, and of some few mines of gold in the provinces of Tierra Firme, and the new kingdom of Granada, has become the capital occupation of the Spaniards, and is reduced into a system no less complicated than interesting. To describe the nature of the various ores, the mode of extracting them from the bowels of the earth, and to explain the several processes by which the metals are separated from the substances with which they are mingled, either by the action of fire, or the attractive powers of mercury, is the province of the natural philosopher or chymist, rather than of the historian.

The exuberant profusion with which the mountains of the New World poured forth their treasures astonished mankind, who had been accustomed hitherto to receive a penurious supply of the precious metals from the more scanty stores contained in the mines of the ancient hemisphere. According to principles of computation, which appear to be extremely moderate, the quantity of gold and silver that has been regularly entered in the ports of Spain, is equal in value to four millions sterling annually, reckoning from the year 1492, in which America was discovered, to the present time. This, in two hundred and eighty-three years, amounts to eleven hundred and thirty-two millions. Immense as this sum is, the Spanish writers contend, that as much more ought to be added to it in consideration of treasure which has been extracted from the mines, and imported fraudulently into Spain without paying duty to the King. By this account, Spain has drawn from the New World a supply of wealth amounting at least to two thousand millions of pounds sterling† [185].

The mines, which have yielded this amazing quantity of treasure, are not worked at the expense of the crown or of the public. In order to encourage private adventurers, the person who discovers and works a new vein is entitled to the property of it. Upon laying his claim to such a discovery before the governor of the province, a certain extent of land is

* Fernandez, p. l. lib. xi c. 11.

† Uztariz Theor. y Pract. de Commercia, c 3 Herrera, dec. viii. lib. xi. c. 15.

measured off, and a certain number of Indians allotted him, under the obligation of his opening the mine within a limited time, and of his paying the customary duty to the King for what it shall produce. Invited by the facility with which such grants are obtained, and encouraged by some striking examples of success in this line of adventure, not only the sanguine and the bold, but the timid and diffident, enter upon it with astonishing ardour. With vast objects always in view, fed continually with hope, and expecting every moment that fortune will unveil her secret stores, and give up the wealth which they contain to their wishes, they deem every other occupation insipid and uninteresting. The charms of this pursuit, like the rage for deep play, are so bewitching, and take such full possession of the mind, as even to give a new bent to the natural temper. Under its influence the cautious become enterprising, and the covetous profuse. Powerful as this charm naturally is, its force is augmented by the arts of an order of men known in Peru by the cant name of *searchers*. These are commonly persons of desperate fortune, who, availing themselves of some skill in mineralogy, accompanied with the insinuating manner and confident pretensions peculiar to projectors, address the wealthy and the credulous By plausible descriptions of the appearances which they have discovered of rich veins hitherto unexplored; by producing, when requisite, specimens of promising ore; by affirming, with an imposing assurance, that success is certain, and that the expense must be trifling, they seldom fail to persuade. An association is formed; a small sum is advanced by each copartner; the mine is opened; the *searcher* is intrusted with the sole direction of every operation: unforeseen difficulties occur; new demands of money are made; but, amidst a succession of disappointments and delays, hope is never extinguished, and the ardour of expectation hardly abates. For it is observed, that if any person once enters this seducing path, it is almost impossible to return; his ideas alter, he seems to be possessed with another spirit; visions of imaginary wealth are continually before his eyes, and he thinks, and speaks, and dreams of nothing else.*

Such is the spirit that must be formed, wherever the active exertions of any society are chiefly employed in working mines of gold and silver. No spirit is more adverse to such improvements in agriculture and commerce as render a nation really opulent. If the system of administration in the Spanish colonies had been founded upon principles of sound policy, the power and ingenuity of the legislator would have been exerted with as much ardour in restraining its subjects from such pernicious industry, as is now employed in alluring them towards it. "Projects of mining," says a good judge of the political conduct of nations, "instead of replacing the capital employed in them, together with the ordinary profit of stock, commonly absorb both capital and profit. They are the projects, therefore, to which, of all others, a prudent lawgiver, who desired to increase the capital of his nation, would least choose to give any extraordinary encouragement, or to turn towards them a greater share of that capital than would go to them of its own accord. Such, in reality, is the absurd confidence which all men have in their own good fortune, that wherever there is the least probability of success, too great a share of it is apt to go to them of its own accord."† But in the Spanish colonies, government is studious to cherish a spirit which it should have laboured to depress, and by the sanction of its approbation, augments that inconsiderate credulity which has turned the active industry of Mexico and Peru into such an improper channel. To this may be imputed the slender progress which Spanish America has made, during two centuries and a half, either in useful manufactures, or in those lucrative branches of cultivation which furnish

* Ulloa Entreten. p. 223. † Dr. Smith's Inquiry, &c. ii. 155.

the colonies of other nations with their staple commodities. In comparison with the precious metals every bounty of nature is so much despised, that this extravagant idea of their value has mingled with the idiom of language in America, and the Spaniards settled there, denominate a country *rich*, not from the fertility of its soil, the abundance of its crops, or the exuberance of its pastures, but on account of the minerals which its mountains contain In quest of these, they abandon the delightful plains of Peru and Mexico, and resort to barren and uncomfortable regions, where they have built some of the largest towns which they possess in the New World. As the activity and enterprise of the Spaniards originally took this direction, it is now so difficult to bend them a different way, that although, from various causes, the gain of working mines is much decreased, the fascination continues, and almost every person, who takes any active part in the commerce of New Spain or Peru, is still engaged in some adventure of this kind [186].

But though mines are the chief object of the Spaniards, and the precious metals which these yield form the principal article in their commerce with America; the fertile countries which they possess there abound with other commodities of such value, or scarcity, as to attract a considerable degree of attention. Cochineal is a production almost peculiar to New Spain, of such demand in commerce that the sale is always certain, and yet yields such profit as amply rewards the labour and care employed in rearing the curious insects of which this valuable drug is composed, and preparing it for the market. Quinquina, or Jesuits' Bark, the most salutary simple, perhaps, and of most restorative virtue, that Providence, in compassion to human infirmity, has made known unto man, is found only in Peru, to which it affords a lucrative branch of commerce. The Indigo ot Guatimala is superior in quality to that of any province in America, and cultivated to a considerable extant. Cacao, though not peculiar to the Spanish colonies, attains to its highest state of perfection there, and, from the great consumption of chocolate in Europe, as well as in America, is a valuable commodity. The Tobacco of Cuba, of more exquisite flavour than any brought from the New World; the Sugar raised in that island, in Hispaniola, and in New Spain, together with drugs of various kinds may be mentioned among the natural productions of America which enrich the Spanish commerce. To these must be added an article of no inconsiderable account, the exportation of hides; for which, as well as for many of those which I have enumerated, the Spaniards are more indebted to the wonderful fertility of the country, than to their own foresight and industry. The domestic animals of Europe, particularly horned cattle, have multiplied in the New World with a rapidity which almost exceeds belief. A few years after the Spaniards settled there, the herds of tame cattle became so numerous that their proprietors reckoned them by thousands.* Less attention being paid to them as they continued to increase, they were suffered to run wild; and spreading over a country of boundless extent, under a mild climate and covered with rich pasture, their number became immense. They range over the vast plains which extend from Buenos Ayres towards the Andes, in herds of thirty or forty thousand; and the unlucky traveller who once falls in among them, may proceed several days before he can disentangle himself from among the crowd that covers the face of the earth, and seems to have no end. They are hardly less numerous in New Spain, and in several other provinces: they are killed merely for the sake of their hides; and the slaughter at certain seasons is so great that the stench of the carcasses, which are left in the field, would infect the air, if large packs of wild dogs, and vast flocks of *gallinazos*, or

* Oviedo ap. Ramus. iii. 101. B. Hakluyt, iii. 466. 511.

American vultures, the most voracious of all the feathered kind, did not instantly devour them. The number of those hides exported in every fleet to Europe, is very great, and is a lucrative branch of commerce.*

Almost all these may be considered as staple commodities peculiar to America, and different, if we except that last mentioned, from the productions of the mother country.

When the importation into Spain of those various articles from her colonies first became active and considerable, her interior industry and manufactures were in a state so prosperous, that with the product of these she was able both to purchase the commodities of the New World, and to answer its growing demands. Under the reigns of Ferdinand and Isabella, and Charles V., Spain was one of the most industrious countries in Europe. Her manufactures in wool, and flax, and silk, were so extensive, as not only to furnish what was sufficient for her own consumption, but to afford a surplus for exportation. When a market for them, formerly unknown, and to which she alone had access, opened in America, she had recourse to her domestic store, and found there an abundant supply [187]. This new employment must naturally have added vivacity to the spirit of industry. Nourished and invigorated by it, the manufactures, the population, and wealth of Spain, might have gone on increasing in the same proportion with the growth of her colonies. Nor was the state of the Spanish marine at this period less flourishing than that of its manufactures. In the beginning of the sixteenth century, Spain is said to have possessed above a thousand merchant ships,† a number probably far superior to that of any nation in Europe in that age. By the aid which foreign trade and domestic industry give reciprocally to each other in their progress, the augmentation of both must have been rapid and extensive, and Spain might have received the same accession of opulence and vigour from her acquisitions in the New World that other powers have derived from their colonies there.

But various causes prevented this. The same thing happens to nations as to individuals. Wealth, which flows in gradually, and with moderate increase, feeds and nourishes that activity which is friendly to commerce, and calls it forth into vigorous and well conducted exertions; but when opulence pours in suddenly, and with too full a stream, it overturns all sober plans of industry, and brings along with it a taste for what is wild and extravagant and daring in business or in action. Such was the great and sudden augmentation of power and revenue that the possession of America brought into Spain; and some symptoms of its pernicious influence upon the political operations of that monarchy soon began to appear. For a considerable time, however, the supply of treasure from the New World was scanty and precarious; and the genius of Charles V. conducted public measures with such prudence, that the effects of this influence were little perceived. But when Philip II. ascended the Spanish throne, with talents far inferior to those of his father, and remittances from the colonies became a regular and considerable branch of revenue, the fatal operation of this rapid change in the state of the kingdom, both on the monarch and his people, was at once conspicuous. Philip, possessing that spirit of unceasing assiduity which often characterizes the ambition of men of moderate talents, entertained such a high opinion of his own resources that he thought nothing too arduous for him to undertake. Shut up himself in the solitude of the Escurial, he troubled and annoyed all the nations around him. He waged open war with the Dutch and English; he encouraged and aided a rebellious faction in France; he conquered Portugal, and maintained armies and garrisons in Italy, Africa, and both the Indies. By

* Acosta, lib. iii c. 33. Ovallo Hist. of Chili. Church. Collect. iii 47, sept Ibid v. p 680 692. Lettres Edif. xiii. 235. Feuille, i. 240 † Campomanes, ii. 140.

such a multiplicity of great and complicated operations, pursued with ardour during the course of a long reign, Spain was drained both of men and money. Under the weak administration of his successor, Philip III. [A. D. 1611], the vigour of the nation continued to decrease, and sunk into the lowest decline, when the inconsiderate bigotry of that monarch expelled at once near a million of his most industrious subjects, at the very time when the exhausted state of the kingdom required some extraordinary exertion of political wisdom to augment its numbers, and to revive its strength. Early in the seventeenth century, Spain felt such a diminution in the number of her people, that from inability to recruit her armies she was obliged to contract her operations. Her flourishing manufactures were fallen into decay. Her fleets, which had been the terror of all Europe, were ruined. Her extensive foreign commerce was lost. The trade between different parts of her own dominions was interrupted, and the ships which attempted to carry it on were taken and plundered by enemies whom she once despised. Even agriculture, the primary object of industry in every prosperous state, was neglected, and one of the most fertile countries in Europe hardly raised what was sufficient for the support of its own inhabitants.

In proportion as the population and manufactures of the parent state declined, the demands of her colonies continued to increase. The Spaniards, like their monarchs, intoxicated with the wealth which poured in annually upon them, deserted the paths of industry to which they had been accustomed, and repaired with eagerness to those regions from which this opulence issued. By this rage of emigration another drain was opened, and the strength of the colonies augmented by exhausting that of the mother country. All those emigrants, as well as the adventurers who had at first settled in America, depended absolutely upon Spain for almost every article of necessary consumption. Engaged in more alluring and lucrative pursuits, or prevented by restraints which government imposed, they could not turn their own attention towards establishing the manufactures requisite for comfortable subsistence. They received (as I have observed in another place) their clothing, their furniture, whatever ministers to the ease or luxury of life, and even their instruments of labour, from Europe. Spain, thinned of people and decreasing in industry, was unable to supply their growing demands. She had recourse to her neighbours. The manufactures of the Low Countries, of England, of France, and of Italy, which her wants called into existence or animated with new vivacity, furnished in abundance whatever she required. In vain did the fundamental law, concerning the exclusion of foreigners from trade with America, oppose this innovation. Necessity, more powerful than any statute, defeated its operation, and constrained the Spaniards themselves to concur in eluding it. The English, the French, and Dutch, relying on the fidelity and honour of Spanish merchants, who lend their names to cover the deceit, send out their manufactures to America, and receive the exorbitant price for which they are sold there, either in specie, or in the rich commodities of the New World. Neither the dread of danger, nor the allurement of profit ever induced a Spanish factor to betray or defraud the person who confided in him ;* and that probity, which is the pride and distinction of the nation, contributes to its ruin. In a short time, not above a twentieth part of the commodities exported to America, was of Spanish growth or fabric.† All the rest was the property of foreign merchants, though entered in the name of Spaniards. The treasure of the New World may be said henceforward not to have belonged to Spain. Before it reached Europe it was anticipated as the price of goods purchased from foreigners. That wealth which by an internal circulation, would have spread through each vein of industry, and have conveyed life and movement to every branch of manu-

* Zavala Representacion, p. 226. † Campomanes, ii. 138.

facture, flowed out of the kingdom with such a rapid course as neither enriched nor animated it. On the other hand, the artisans of rival nations, encouraged by this quick sale of their commodities, improved so much in skill and industry as to be able to afford them at a rate so low, that the manufactures of Spain, which could not vie with theirs either in quality or cheapness of work, were still further depressed. This destructive commerce drained off the riches of the nation faster and more completely than even the extravagant schemes of ambition carried on by its monarchs. Spain was so much astonished and distressed at beholding her American treasures vanish almost as soon as they were imported, that Philip III., unable to supply what was requisite in circulation, issued an edict, by which he endeavoured to raise copper money to a value in currency nearly equal to that of silver;* and the lord of the Peruvian and Mexican mines was reduced to a wretched expedient, which is the last resource of petty impoverished states.

Thus the possessions of Spain in America have not proved a source of population and of wealth to her in the same manner as those of other nations. In the countries of Europe, where the spirit of industry subsists in full vigour, every person settled in such colonies as are similar in their situation to those of Spain, is supposed to give employment to three or four at home in supplying his wants.† But wherever the mother country cannot afford this supply, every emigrant may be considered as a citizen lost to the community, and strangers must reap all the benefit of answering his demands.

Such has been the internal state of Spain from the close of the sixteenth century, and such her inability to supply the growing wants of her colonies. The fatal effects of this disproportion between their demands, and her capacity of answering them, have been much increased by the mode in which Spain has endeavoured to regulate the intercourse between the mother country and her colonies. It is from her idea of monopolising the trade with America, and debarring her subjects there from any communication with foreigners, that all her jealous and systematic arrangements have arisen. These are so singular in their nature and consequences as to merit a particular explanation. In order to secure the monopoly at which she aimed, Spain did not vest the trade with her colonies in an exclusive company, a plan which has been adopted by nations more commercial, and at a period when mercantile policy was an object of greater attention, and ought to have been better understood. The Dutch gave up the whole trade with their colonies, both in the East and West Indies, to exclusive companies. The English, the French, the Danes, have imitated their example with respect to the East Indian commerce; and the two former have laid a similar restraint upon some branches of their trade with the New World. The wit of man cannot, perhaps, devise a method for checking the progress of industry and population in a new colony more effectual than this. The interest of the colony, and of the exclusive company, must in every point be diametrically opposite; and as the latter possesses such advantages in this unequal contest, that it can prescribe at pleasure the terms of intercourse, the former must not only buy dear and sell cheap, but must suffer the mortification of having the increase of its surplus stock discouraged by those very persons to whom alone it can dispose of its productions.‡

Spain, it is probable, was preserved from falling into this error of policy by the high ideas which she early formed concerning the riches of the New World. Gold and silver were commodities of too high a value to vest a monopoly of them in private hands. The crown wished to retain the direction of a commerce so inviting; and, in order to secure that, ordained

* Uztarez, c. 104 † Child on Trade and Colonies. ‡ Smith's Inquiry, ii. 171.

the cargo of every ship fitted out for America to be inspected by the officers of the *Casa de Contratacion* in Seville before it could receive a license to make the voyage; and that, on its return, a report of the commodities which it brought should be made to the same board before it could be permitted to land them. In consequence of this regulation, all the trade of Spain with the New World centred originally in the port of Seville, and was gradually brought into a form, in which it has been conducted, with little variation, from the middle of the sixteenth century almost to our own times. For the greater security of the valuable cargoes sent to America, as well as for the more easy prevention of fraud, the commerce of Spain with its colonies is carried on by fleets which sail under strong convoys. These fleets, consisting of two squadrons, one distinguished by the name of the *Galeons*, the other by that of the *Flota*, are equipped annually. Formerly they took their departure from Seville; but as the port of Cadiz has been found more commodious, they have sailed from it since the year 1720.

The Galeons destined to supply Tierra Firme, and the kingdoms of Peru and Chili, with almost every article of luxury or necessary consumption, that an opulent people can demand, touch first at Carthagena, and then at Porto Bello. To the former, the merchants of Santa Martha, Caraccas, the New Kingdom of Granada, and several other provinces, resort. The latter is the great mart for the rich commerce of Peru and Chili. At the season when the Galeons are expected, the product of all the mines in these two kingdoms, together with their other valuable commodities, is transported by sea to Panama. From thence, as soon as the appearance of the fleet from Europe is announced, they are conveyed across the isthmus, partly on mules and partly down the river Chagre to Porto Bello. This paltry village, the climate of which, from the pernicious union of excessive heat, continual moisture, and the putrid exhalations arising from a rank soil, is more fatal to life than any perhaps in the known world, is immediately filled with people. From being the residence of a few Negroes and Mulattoes, and of a miserable garrison relieved every three months, Porto Bello assumes suddenly a very different aspect, and its streets are crowded with opulent merchants from every corner of Peru and the adjacent provinces. A fair is opened, the wealth of America is exchanged for the manufactures of Europe; and, during its prescribed term of forty days, the richest traffic on the face of the earth is begun and finished with that simplicity of transaction, and that unbounded confidence, which accompany extensive commerce [188]. The Flota holds its course to Vera Cruz. The treasures and commodities of New Spain, and the depending provinces, which were deposited at Puebla de los Angeles, in expectation of its arrival, are carried thither; and the commercial operations of Vera Cruz, conducted in the same manner with those of Porto Bello, are inferior to them only in importance and value. Both fleets, as soon as they have completed their cargoes from America, rendezvous at the Havana, and return in company to Europe.

The trade of Spain with her colonies, while thus fettered and restricted, came necessarily to be conducted with the same spirit, and upon the same principles as that of an exclusive company. Being confined to a single port, it was of course thrown into a few hands, and almost the whole of it was gradually engrossed by a small number of wealthy houses, formerly in Seville, and now in Cadiz. These by combinations, which they can easily form, may altogether prevent that competition which preserves commodities at their natural price; and by acting in concert, to which they are prompted by their mutual interest, they may raise or lower the value of them at pleasure. In consequence of this, the price of European goods in America is always high, and often exorbitant. A hundred, two hundred, and even three hundred per cent., are profits not uncommon in the commerce of Spain with her colonies.* From the same engrossing spirit it frequently happens that traders of the second order, whose warehouses do not contain a complete assortment of commodities for the American market, cannot purchase from the more opulent merchants such goods as they want at a lower price than that for which they are sold in the colonies. With the same vigilant jealousy that an exclusive company guards against the intrusion of the free trader, those overgrown monopolists endeavour to check the progress of every one whose encroachments they dread.† This restraint of the American commerce to one port not only affects its domestic state, but limits its foreign operations. A monopolist may acquire more, and certainly will hazard less, by a confined trade which yields exorbitant profit, than by an extensive commerce in which he receives only a moderate return of gain. It is often his interest not to enlarge, but to circumscribe the sphere of his activity; and instead of calling forth more vigorous exertions of commercial industry, it may be the object of his attention to check and set bounds to them. By some such maxim the mercantile policy of Spain seems to have regulated its intercourse with America. Instead of furnishing the colonies with European goods in such quantity as might render both the price and the profit moderate, the merchants of Seville and Cadiz seem to have supplied them with a sparing hand, that the eagerness of competition, among customers obliged to purchase in a scanty market, might enable the Spanish factors to dispose of their cargoes with exorbitant gain. About the middle of the last century, when the exclusive trade to America from Seville was in its most flourishing state, the burden of the two united squadrons of the Galeons and Flota did not exceed twenty-seven thousand five hundred tons.‡ The supply which such a fleet could carry must have been very inadequate to the demands of those populous and extensive colonies, which depended upon it for all the luxuries and many of the necessaries of life.

Spain early became sensible of her declension from her former prosperity; and many respectable and virtuous citizens employed their thoughts in devising methods for reviving the decaying industry and commerce of their country. From the violence of the remedies proposed, we may judge how desperate and fatal the malady appeared. Some, confounding a violation of police with criminality against the state, contended that, in order to check illicit commerce, every person convicted of carrying it on should be punished with death, and confiscation of all his effects.§ Others, forgetting the distinction between civil offences and acts of impiety, insisted that contraband trade should be ranked among the crimes reserved for the cognisance of the Inquisition; that such as were guilty of it might be tried and punished according to the secret and summary form in which that dreadful tribunal exercises its jurisdiction.‖ Others, uninstructed by observing the pernicious effects of monopolies in every country where they have been established, have proposed to vest the trade with America in exclusive companies, which interest would render the most vigilant guardians of the Spanish commerce against the encroachment of the interlopers.¶

Besides these wild projects, many schemes, better digested and more beneficial, were suggested. But under the feeble monarchs with whom the reign of the Austrian line in Spain closed, incapacity and indecision are conspicuous in every department of government. Instead of taking for their model the active administration of Charles V., they affected to imitate the cautious procrastinating wisdom of Philip II.; and destitute of his talents, they deliberated perpetually, but determined nothing. No remedy was applied to the evils under which the national commerce,

* B. Ulloa Fetabliss. part ii p. 191. † Smith's Inquiry, ii. 171. Campomanes, Educ. Popul, i. 43. ‡ Ibid. i. 435. ii. 140. § M. de Santa Cruz Commercia Suelto, p. 142. ‖ Moncada Restauracion politica de Espagna, p. 41. ¶ Zavalla y Augncn Representacion, &c. p. 190

domestic as well as foreign, languished. These evils continued to increase and Spain, with dominions more extensive and more opulent than any European state, possessed neither vigour, nor money [189], nor industry. At length, the violence of a great national convulsion roused the slumbering genius of Spain. The efforts of the two contending parties in the civil war kindled by the dispute concerning the succession of the crown at the beginning of this century, called forth, in some degree, the ancient spirit and vigour of the nation. While men were thus forming, capable of adopting sentiments more liberal than those which had influenced the councils of the monarchy during the course of a century, Spain derived from an unexpected source the means of availing itself of their talents. The various powers who favoured the pretensions either of the Austrian or Bourbon candidate for the Spanish throne, sent formidable fleets and armies to their support; France, England, and Holland remitted immense sums to Spain. These were spent in the provinces which became the theatre of war. Part of the American treasure, of which foreigners had drained the kingdom, flowed back thither. From this era one of the most intelligent Spanish authors dates the revival of the monarchy; and, however humiliating the truth may be, he acknowledges, that it is to her enemies his country is indebted for the acquisition of a fund of circulating specie in some measure adequate to the exigencies of the public.*

As soon as the Bourbons obtained quiet possession of the throne, they discerned this change in the spirit of the people and in the state of the nation, and took advantage of it; for although that family has not given monarchs to Spain remarkable for superiority of genius, they have all been beneficent princes, attentive to the happiness of their subjects, and solicitous to promote it. It was, accordingly, the first object of Philip V. to suppress an innovation which had crept in during the course of the war, and had overturned the whole system of the Spanish commerce with America. The English and Dutch, by their superiority in naval power, having acquired such command of the sea as to cut off all intercourse between Spain and her colonies, Spain, in order to furnish her subjects in America those necessaries of life without which they could not exist, and as the only means of receiving from thence any part of their treasure, departed so far from the usual rigour of its maxims as to open the trade with Peru to her allies the French. The merchants of St. Malo, to whom Louis XIV. granted the privilege of this lucrative commerce, engaged in it with vigour, and carried it on upon principles very different from those of the Spaniards. They supplied Peru with European commodities at a moderate price, and not in stinted quantity. The goods which they imported were conveyed to every province of Spanish America in such abundance as had never been known in any former period. If this intercourse had been continued, the exportation of European commodities from Spain must have ceased, and the dependence of the colonies on the mother country have been at an end. The most peremptory injunctions were therefore issued [1713], prohibiting the admission of foreign vessels into any port of Peru or Chili,† and a Spanish squadron was employed to clear the South Sea of intruders, whose aid was no longer necessary.

But though, on the cessation of the war which was terminated by the treaty of Utrecht, Spain obtained relief from one encroachment on her commercial system, she was exposed to another which she deemed hardly less pernicious. As an inducement that might prevail with Queen Anne to conclude a peace, which France and Spain desired with equal ardour, Philip V. not only conveyed to Great Britain the *Assiento*, or contract for supplying the Spanish colonies with Negroes, which had formerly been

* Campomanes, i. 420. † Frezier Voy. 256. B. Ulloa Retab. ii. 104, &c. Alcedo y Herrera, Aviso, &c. 236.

enjoyed by France, but granted it the more extraordinary privilege of sending annually to the fair of Porto Bello a ship of five hundred tons, laden with European commodities. In consequence of this, British factories were established at Carthagena, Panama, Vera Cruz, Buenos Ayres, and other Spanish settlements. The veil with which Spain had hitherto covered the state and transactions of her colonies was removed. The agents of a rival nation, residing in the towns of most extensive trade, and of chief resort, had the best opportunities of becoming acquainted with the interior condition of the American provinces, of observing their stated and occasional wants, and of knowing what commodities might be imported into them with the greatest advantage. In consequence of information so authentic and expeditious, the merchants of Jamaica and other English colonies who traded to the Spanish main were enabled to assort and proportion their cargoes so exactly to the demands of the market, that the contraband commerce was carried on with a facility and to an extent unknown in any former period. This, however, was not the most fatal consequence of the Assiento to the trade of Spain. The agents of the British South Sea Company, under cover of the importation which they were authorized to make by the ship sent annually to Porto Bello, poured in their commodities on the Spanish continent without limitation or restraint. Instead of a ship of five hundred tons, as stipulated in the treaty, they usually employed one which exceeded nine hundred tons in burthen. She was accompanied by two or three smaller vessels, which, mooring in some neighbouring creek, supplied her clandestinely with fresh bales of goods to replace such as were sold. The inspectors of the fair, and officers of the revenue, gained by exorbitant presents, connived at the fraud [190]. Thus, partly by the operations of the company, and partly by the activity of private interlopers, almost the whole trade of Spanish America was engrossed by foreigners. The immense commerce of the Galeons, formerly the pride of Spain, and the envy of other nations, sunk to nothing [1737]; and the squadron itself, reduced from fifteen thousand to two thousand tons,* served hardly any purpose but to fetch home the royal revenue arising from the fifth on silver.

While Spain observed those encroachments, and felt so sensibly their pernicious effects, it was impossible not to make some effort to restrain them. Her first expedient was to station ships of force, under the appellation of *guarda costas*, upon the coasts of those provinces to which interlopers most frequently resorted. As private interest concurred with the duty which they owed to the public, in rendering the officers who commanded those vessels vigilant and active, some check was given to the progress of the contraband trade, though in dominions so extensive and so accessible by sea, hardly any number of cruisers was sufficient to guard against its inroads in every quarter. This interruption of an intercourse which had been carried on with so much facility, that the merchants in the British colonies were accustomed to consider it almost as an allowed branch of commerce, excited murmurs and complaints. These, authorized in some measure, and rendered more interesting by several unjustifiable acts of violence committed by the captains of the Spanish guarda costas, precipitated Great Britain into a war with Spain [1739]; in consequence of which the latter obtained a final release from the Assiento, and was left at liberty to regulate the commerce of her colonies without being restrained by any engagement with a foreign power.

As the formidable encroachments of the English on their American trade, had discovered to the Spaniards the vast consumption of European goods in their colonies, and taught them the advantage of accommodating their importations to the occasional demand of the various provinces, they

* Alcedo y Herrera, p. 359. Campomanes, i. 436

perceived the necessity of devising some method of supplying their colonies, different from their ancient one of sending thither periodical fleets. That mode of communication had been found not only to be uncertain, as the departure of the Galeons and Flota was sometimes retarded by various accidents, and often prevented by the wars which raged in Europe; but long experience had shown it to be ill adapted to afford America a regular and timely supply of what it wanted. The scarcity of European goods in the Spanish settlements frequently became excessive; their price rose to an enormous height; the vigilant eye of mercantile attention did not fail to observe this favourable opportunity; an ample supply was poured in by interlopers from the English, the French, and Dutch islands; and when the Galeons at length arrived, they found the markets so glutted by this illicit commerce, that there was no demand for the commodities with which they were loaded. In order to remedy this, Spain has permitted a considerable part of her commerce with America to be carried on by *register ships*. These are fitted out during the intervals between the stated seasons when the Galeons and Flota sail, by merchants in Seville or Cadiz, upon obtaining a license from the council of the Indies, for which they pay a very high premium, and are destined for those ports in America where any extraordinary demand is foreseen or expected. By this expedient, such a regular supply of the commodities for which there is the greatest demand is conveyed to the American market, that the interloper is no longer allured by the same prospect of excessive gain, or the people in the colonies urged by the same necessity to engage in the hazardous adventures of contraband trade.

In proportion as experience manifested the advantages of carrying on trade in this mode, the number of register ships increased; and at length, in the year 1748, the Galeons, after having been employed upwards of two centuries, were finally laid aside. From that period there has been no intercourse with Chili and Peru but by single ships, despatched from time to time as occasion requires, and when the merchants expect a profitable market will open. These ships sail round Cape Horn, and convey directly to the ports in the South Sea the productions and manufactures of Europe, for which the people settled in those countries were formerly obliged to repair to Porto Bello or Panama. These towns, as has been formerly observed, must gradually decline, when deprived of that commerce to which they owed their prosperity. This disadvantage, however, is more than compensated by the beneficial effects of this new arrangement, as the whole continent of South America receives new supplies of European commodities with so much regularity, and in such abundance, as must not only contribute greatly to the happiness, but increase the population of all the colonies settled there. But as all the register ships destined for the South Seas must still take their departure from Cadiz, and are obliged to return thither,* this branch of the American commerce, even in its new and improved form, continues subject to the restraints of a species of monopoly, and feels those pernicious effects of it which I have already described.

Nor has the attention of Spain been confined to regulating the trade with its more flourishing colonies; it has extended likewise to the reviving commerce in those settlements where it was neglected, or had decayed. Among the new tastes which the people of Europe have acquired in consequence of importing the productions of those countries which they conquered in America, that for chocolate is one of the most universal. The use of this liquor, made with a paste formed of the nut or almond of the cacao tree compounded with various ingredients, the Spaniards first learned from the Mexicans; and it has appeared to them, and to the other

* Campomanes, i 434. 440

European nations, so palatable, so nourishing, and so wholesome, that it has become a commercial article of considerable importance. The cacao tree grows spontaneously in several parts of the torrid zone; but the nuts of the best quality, next to those of Guatimala on the South sea, are produced in the rich plains of Caraccas, a province of Tierra Firme. In consequence of this acknowledged superiority in the quality of cacao in that province, and its communication with the Atlantic, which facilitates the conveyance to Europe, the culture of the cacao there is more extensive than in any district of America. But the Dutch, by the vicinity of their settlements in the small islands of Curazoa and Buenos Ayres, to the coast of Caraccas, gradually engrossed the greatest part of the cacao trade. The traffic with the mother country for this valuable commodity ceased almost entirely; and such was the supine negligence of the Spaniards, or the defects of their commercial arrangements, that they were obliged to receive from the hands of foreigners this production of their own colonies at an exorbitant price. In order to remedy an evil no less disgraceful than pernicious to his subjects, Philip V., in the year 1728, granted to a body of merchants an exclusive right to the commerce with Caraccas and Cumana, on condition of their employing, at their own expense, a sufficient number of armed vessels to clear the coast of interlopers. This society, distinguished sometimes by the name of the Company of Guipuscoa, from the province of Spain in which it is established, and sometimes by that of the Company of Caraccas, from the district of America to which it trades, has carried on its operations with such vigour and success, that Spain has recovered an important branch of commerce which she had suffered to be wrested from her, and is plentifully supplied with an article of extensive consumption at a moderate price. Not only the parent state, but the colony of Caraccas, has derived great advantages from this institution; for although, at the first aspect, it may appear to be one of those monopolies whose tendency is to check the spirit of industry instead of calling it forth to new exertions, it has been prevented from operating in this manner by several salutary regulations framed upon foresight of such bad effects, and on purpose to obviate them. The planters in the Caraccas are not left to depend entirely on the company, either for the importation of European commodities or the sale of their own productions. The inhabitants of the Canary islands have the privilege of sending thither annually a register ship of considerable burden; and from Vera Cruz, in New Spain, a free trade is permitted in every port comprehended in the charter of the company. In consequence of this, there is such a competition, that both with respect to what the colonies purchase and what they sell, the price seems to be fixed at its natural and equitable rate. The company has not the power of raising the former, or of degrading the latter, at pleasure; and accordingly, since it was established, the increase of culture, of population, and of live stock, in the province of Caraccas, has been very considerable [191].

But as it is slowly that nations relinquish any system which time has rendered venerable, and as it is still more slowly that commerce can be diverted from the channel in which it has long been accustomed to flow, Philip V in his new regulations concerning the American trade, paid such deference to the ancient maxim of Spain, concerning the limitation of importation from the New World to one harbour, as to oblige both the register ships which returned from Peru, and those of the Guipuscoan Company from Caraccas, to deliver their cargoes in the port of Cadiz. Since his reign, sentiments more liberal and enlarged begin to spread in Spain. The spirit of philosophical inquiry, which it is the glory of the present age to have turned from frivolous or abstruse speculations to the business and affairs of men, has extended its influence beyond the Pyrenees. In the researches of ingenious authors concerning the police or commerce of nations, the errors and defects of the Spanish system with respect to both met every eye, and have not only been exposed with severity, but are held up as a warning to other states. The Spaniards, stung with the reproaches of these authors, or convinced by their arguments, and admonished by several enlightened writers of their own country, seem at length to have discovered the destructive tendency of those narrow maxims, which, by cramping commerce in all its operations, have so long retarded its progress. It is to the monarch now on the throne that Spain is indebted for the first public regulation formed in consequence of such enlarged ideas.

While Spain adhered with rigour to her ancient maxim concerning her commerce with America, she was so much afraid of opening any channel by which an illicit trade might find admission into the colonies, that she almost shut herself out from any intercourse with them but that which was carried on by her annual fleets. There was no establishment, for a regular communication of either public or private intelligence, between the mother country and its American settlements. From the want of this necessary institution, the operations of the state, as well as the business of individuals, were retarded, or conducted unskilfully, and Spain often received from foreigners her first information with respect to very interesting events in her own colonies. But though this defect in police was sensibly felt, and the remedy for it was obvious, that jealous spirit with which the Spanish monarchs guarded the exclusive trade, restrained them from applying it. At length Charles III. surmounted those considerations which had deterred his predecessors, and in the year 1764 appointed packet boats to be despatched on the first day of each month from Corugna to the Havanna or Porto Rico. From thence letters are conveyed in smaller vessels to Vera Cruz and Porto Bello, and transmitted by post through the kingdoms of Tierra Firme, Granada, Peru, and New Spain. With no less regularity packet boats sail once in two months to Rio de la Plata, for the accommodation of the provinces to the east of the Andes. Thus provision is made for a speedy and certain circulation of intelligence throughout the vast dominions of Spain, from which equal advantages must redound to the political and mercantile interest of the kingdom.* With this new arrangement a scheme of extending commerce has been more immediately connected. Each of the packet boats, which are vessels of some considerable burden, is allowed to take in half a loading of such commodities as are the product of Spain, and most in demand in the ports whither they are bound. In return for these, they may bring home to Corugna an equal quantity of American productions.† This may be considered as the first relaxation of those rigid laws, which confined the trade with the New World to a single port, and the first attempt to admit the rest of the kingdom to some share in it.

It was soon followed by one more decisive. In the year 1765, Charles III. laid open the trade to the windward islands, Cuba, Hispaniola, Porto Rico, Margarita, and Trinidad, to his subjects in every province of Spain. He permitted them to sail from certain ports in each province, which are specified in the edict, at any season, and with whatever cargo they deemed most proper, without any other warrant than a simple clearance from the custom-house of the place whence they took their departure. He released them from the numerous and oppressive duties imposed on goods exported to America, and in place of the whole substituted a moderate tax of six in the hundred on the commodities sent from Spain. He allowed them to return either to the same port, or to any other where they might hope for a more advantageous market, and there to enter the homeward cargo or payment of the usual duties. This ample privilege, which at once brok-

* Pontz Viage de Espagna, vi. Prol. p. 15

† Append. ii. a la Educ. Pop. p. 31.

through all the fences which the jealous policy of Spain had been labouring for two centuries and a half to throw round its commercial intercourse with the New World, was soon after extended to Louisiana, and to the provinces of Yucatan and Campeachy.*

The propriety of this innovation, which may be considered as the most liberal effort of Spanish legislation, has appeared from its effects. Prior to the edict in favour of the free trade, Spain derived hardly any benefit from its neglected colonies in Hispaniola, Porto Rico, Margarita, and Trinidad. Its commerce with Cuba was inconsiderable, and that of Yucatan and Campeachy was engrossed almost entirely by interlopers. But as soon as a general liberty of trade was permitted, the intercourse with those provinces revived, and has gone on with a rapidity of progression of which there are few examples in the history of nations. In less than ten years, the trade of Cuba has been more than tripled. Even in those settlements where, from the languishing state of industry, greater efforts were requisite to restore its activity, their commerce has been doubled. It is computed that such a number of ships is already employed in the free trade, that the tonnage of them far exceeds that of the Galeons and Flota at the most flourishing era of their commerce. The benefits of this arrangement are not confined to a few merchants established in a favourite port. They are diffused through every province of the kingdom; and, by opening a new market for their various productions and manufactures, must encourage and add vivacity to the industry of the farmer and artificer. Nor does the kingdom profit only by what it exports; it derives advantage likewise from what it receives in return, and has the prospect of being soon able to supply itself with several commodities of extensive consumption, for which it formerly depended on foreigners. The consumption of sugar in Spain is perhaps as great, in proportion to the number of its inhabitants, as that of any European kingdom. But though possessed of countries in the New World whose soil and climate are most proper for rearing the sugar-cane; though the domestic culture of that valuable plant in the kingdom of Granada was once considerable; such has been the fatal tendency of ill judged institutions in America, and such the pressure of improper taxes in Europe, that Spain has lost almost entirely this branch of industry, which has enriched other nations. This commodity, which has now become an article of primary necessity in Europe, the Spaniards were obliged to purchase of foreigners, and had the mortification to see their country drained annually of great sums on that account.† But, if that spirit which the permission of free trade has put in motion shall persevere in its efforts with the same vigour, the cultivation of sugar in Cuba and Porto Rico may increase so much, that in a few years it is probable that their growth of sugars may be equal to the demand of the kingdom.

Spain has been induced, by her experience of the beneficial consequences resulting from having relaxed somewhat of the rigour of her ancient laws, with respect to the commerce of the mother country with the colonies, to permit a more liberal intercourse of one colony with another. By one of the jealous maxims of the old system, all the provinces situated on the South seas were prohibited, under the most severe penalties, from holding any communication with one another. Though each of these yields peculiar productions, the reciprocal exchange of which might have added to the happiness of their respective inhabitants, or have facilitated their progress in industry, so solicitous was the Council of the Indies to prevent their receiving any supply of their wants but by the periodical fleets from Europe, that, in order to guard against this, it cruelly debarred the Spaniards in Peru, in the southern provinces of New Spain, in Guatimala, and the new kingdom of Granada, from such a correspondence with their fellow

* Append. ii. a la Educ. Pop. 37. 54. 91.

† Uztariz, c. 94.

subjects as tended manifestly to their mutual prosperity. Of all the numerous restrictions devised by Spain for securing the exclusive trade with her American settlements, none perhaps was more illiberal, none seems to have been more sensibly felt, or to have produced more hurtful effects. This grievance, coeval with the settlements of Spain in the countries situated on the Pacific Ocean, is at last redressed. In the year 1774, Charles III. published an edict, granting to the four great provinces which I have mentioned the privilege of a free trade with each other.* [192] What may be the effects of opening this communication between countries destined by their situation for reciprocal intercourse, cannot yet be determined by experience. They can hardly fail of being beneficial and extensive. The motives for granting this permission are manifestly no less laudable than the principle on which it is founded is liberal; and both discover the progress of a spirit in Spain, far elevated above the narrow prejudices and maxims on which her system for regulating the trade and conducting the government of her colonies was originally founded.

At the same time that Spain has been intent on introducing regulations, suggested by more enlarged views of policy, into her system of American commerce, she has not been inattentive to the interior government of her colonies. Here, too, there was much room for reformation and improvement; and Don Joseph Galvez, who has now the direction of the department of Indian affairs in Spain, has enjoyed the best opportunities, not only of observing the defects and corruption in the political frame of the colonies, but of discovering the sources of those evils. After being employed seven years in the New World on an extraordinary mission, and with very extensive powers, as inspector-general of New Spain; after visiting in person the remote provinces of Cinaloa, Sonora, and California, and making several important alterations in the state of the police and revenue; he began his ministry with a general reformation of the tribunals of justice in America. In consequence of the progress of population and wealth in the colonies, the business of the Courts of Audience has increased so much that the number of judges of which they were originally composed has been found inadequate to the growing labours and duties of the office, and the salaries settled upon them have been deemed inferior to the dignity of the station. As a remedy for both, he obtained a royal edict, establishing an additional number of judges in each Court of Audience, with higher titles, and more ample appointments.†

To the same intelligent minister Spain is indebted for a new distribution of government in its American provinces. Even since the establishment of a third viceroyalty in the new kingdom of Granada, so great is the extent of the Spanish dominions in the New World, that several places subject to the jurisdiction of each viceroy were at such an enormous distance from the capitals in which they resided, that neither their attention nor their authority could reach so far. Some provinces subordinate to the viceroy of New Spain lay above two thousand miles from Mexico. There were countries subject to the viceroy of Peru still further from Lima. The people in those remote districts could hardly be said to enjoy the benefit of civil government. The oppression and insolence of its inferior ministers they often feel, and rather submit to these in silence than involve themselves in the expense and trouble of resorting to the distant capital, where alone they can find redress. As a remedy for this, a fourth viceroyalty has been erected, [Aug. 1776] to the jurisdiction of which are subjected the provinces of Rio de la Plata, Buenos Ayres, Paraguay, Tucuman, Potosi, St. Cruz de la Sierra Charcas, and the towns of Mendoza and St. Juan. By this well judged arrangement two advantages are gained. All

* Real Cedula penes me. Pontz Viage de Espagna vi. Prologo, p. 2. † Gazeta de Madrid 19th March, 177

the inconveniences occasioned by the remote situation of those provinces, which had been long felt, and long complained of, are in a great measure removed. The countries most distant from Lima are separated from the viceroyalty of Peru, and united under a superior, whose seat of government at Buenos Ayres will be commodious and accessible. The contraband trade with the Portuguese, which was become so extensive as must have put a final stop to the exportation of commodities from Spain to her southern colonies, may be checked more thoroughly, and with greater facility, when the supreme magistrate, by his vicinity to the places in which it is carried on, can view its progress and effects with his own eyes Don Pedro Zevallos, who has been raised to this new dignity, with appointments equal to those of the other viceroys, is well acquainted both with the state and the interests of the countries over which he is to preside, having served in them long, and with distinction. By this dismemberment, succeeding that which took place at the erection of the viceroyalty of the new kingdom of Granada, almost two-third parts of the territories originally subject to the viceroys of Peru, are now lopped off from their jurisdiction.

The limits of the viceroyalty of New Spain have likewise been considerably circumscribed, and with no less propriety and discernment. Four of its most remote provinces, Sonora, Cinaloa, California, and New Navarre, have been formed into a separate government. The Chevalier de Croix, who is intrusted with this command, is not dignified with the title of viceroy, nor does he enjoy the appointments belonging to that rank; but his jurisdiction is altogether independent on the viceroyalty of New Spain. The erection of this last government seems to have been suggested not only by the consideration of the remote situation of those provinces from Mexico, but by attention to the late discoveries made there which I have mentioned.* Countries containing the richest mines of gold that have hitherto been discovered in the New World, and which probably may rise into greater importance, required the immediate inspection of a governor to whom they should be specially committed. As every consideration of duty, of interest, and of vanity, must concur in prompting those new governors to encourage such exertions as tend to diffuse opulence and prosperity through the provinces committed to their charge, the beneficial effects of this arrangement may be considerable. Many districts in America, long depressed by the languor and feebleness natural to provinces which compose the extremities of an overgrown empire, may be animated with vigour and activity when brought so near the seat of power as to feel its invigorating influence.

Such, since the accession of the princes of the house of Bourbon to the throne of Spain, has been the progress of their regulations, and the gradua expansion of their views with respect to the commerce and government of their American colonies. Nor has their attention been so entirely engrossed by what related to the more remote parts of their dominions, as to render them neglectful of what was still more important, the reformation of domestic errors and defects in policy. Fully sensible of the causes to which the declension of Spain from her former prosperity ought to be imputed, they have made it a great object of their policy to revive a spirit of industry among their subjects, and to give such extent and perfection to their manufactures as may enable them to supply the demands of America from their own stock, and to exclude foreigners from a branch of commerce which has been so fatal to the kingdom. This they have endeavoured to accomplish by a variety of edicts issued since the peace of Utrecht. They have granted bounties for the encouragement of some branches of industry; they have lowered the taxes on others; they have either entirely prohibited, or

* Book vii.

have loaded with additional duties, such foreign manufactures as come in competition with their own; they have instituted societies for the improvement of trade and agriculture; they have planted colonies of husbandmen in some uncultivated districts of Spain, and divided among them the waste fields; they have had recourse to every expedient devised by commercial wisdom or commercial jealousy, for reviving their own industry, and discountenancing that of other nations. These, however, it is not my province to explain, or to inquire into their propriety and effects. There is no effort of legislation more arduous, no experiment in policy more uncertain than an attempt to revive the spirit of industry where it has declined, or to introduce it where it is unknown. Nations, already possessed of extensive commerce, enter into competition with such advantages, derived from the large capitals and extensive credit of their merchants, the dexterity of their manufacturers, and the alertness acquired by habit in every department of business, that the state which aims at rivalling or supplanting them, must expect to struggle with many difficulties, and be content to advance slowly. If the quantity of productive industry, now in Spain, be compared with that of the kingdom under the last listless monarchs of the Austrian line, its progress must appear considerable, and is sufficient to alarm the jealousy, and to call forth the most vigorous efforts of the nations now in possession of the lucrative trade which the Spaniards aim at wresting from them. One circumstance may render those exertions of Spain an object of more serious attention to the other European powers. They are not to be ascribed wholly to the influence of the crown and its ministers. The sentiments and spirit of the people seem to second the provident care of their monarchs, and to give it greater effect. The nation has adopted more liberal ideas, not only with respect to commerce, but domestic policy. In all the later Spanish writers, defects in the arrangement of their country concerning both are acknowledged, and remedies proposed, which ignorance rendered their ancestors incapable of discerning, and pride would not have allowed them to confess [193]. But after all that the Spaniards have done, much remains to do. Many pernicious institutions and abuses, deeply incorporated with the system of internal policy and taxation, which has been long established in Spain, must be abolished before industry and manufactures can recover an extensive activity.

Still, however, the commercial regulations of Spain with respect to her colonies are too rigid and systematical to be carried into complete execution. The legislature that loads trade with impositions too heavy, or fetters it by restrictions too severe, defeats its own intention, and is only multiplying the inducements to violate its statutes, and proposing a high premium to encourage illicit traffic. The Spaniards, both in Europe and America, being circumscribed in their mutual intercourse, by the jealousy of the crown, or oppressed by its exactions, have their invention continually on the stretch how to elude its edicts. The vigilance and ingenuity of private interest discover means of effecting this, which public wisdom cannot foresee nor public authority prevent. This spirit, counteracting that of the laws, pervades the commerce of Spain with America in all its branches; and from the highest departments in government descends to the lowest. The very officers appointed to check contraband trade are often employed as instruments in carrying it on; and the boards instituted to restrain and punish it are the channels through which it flows. The King is supposed, by the most intelligent Spanish writers, to be defrauded, by various artifices, of more than one half of the revenue which he ought to receive from America;* and as long as it is the interest of so many persons to screen those artifices from detection, the knowledge of them will never reach the throne. "How many ordinances," says Corita, "how

* Solorz. de Ind. Jure, ii. lib. v.

many instructions, how many letters from our sovereign, are sent in order to correct abuses! and how little are they observed, and what small advantage is derived from them! To me the old observation appears just, that where there are many physicians and many medicines, there is a want of health; where there are many laws and many judges, there is want of justice. We have viceroys, presidents, governors, oydors, corrigidors, alcaldes; and thousands of alguazils abound every where; but notwithstanding all these, public abuses continue to multiply."* Time has increased the evils which he lamented as early as the reign of Philip II. A spirit of corruption has infected all the colonies of Spain in America. Men far removed from the seat of government; impatient to acquire wealth, that they may return speedily from what they are apt to consider as a state of exile in a remote unhealthful country; allured by opportunities too tempting to be resisted, and seduced by the example of those around them; find their sentiments of honour and of duty gradually relax. In private life they give themselves up to a dissolute luxury, while in their public conduct they become unmindful of what they owe to their sovereign and to their country.

Before I close this account of the Spanish trade in America there remains one detached but important branch of it to be mentioned. Soon after his accession to the throne, Philip II. formed a scheme of planting a colony in the Philippine islands which had been neglected since the time of their discovery; and he accomplished it by means of an armament fitted out from New Spain† [1564]. Manila, in the island of Luconia, was the station chosen for the capital of this new establishment. From it an active commercial intercourse began with the Chinese, and a considerable number of that industrious people, allured by the prospect of gain, settled in the Philippine islands under the Spanish protection. They supplied the colony so amply with all the valuable productions and manufactures of the East as enabled it to open a trade with America, by a course of navigation the longest from land to land on our globe. In the infancy of this trade, it was carried on with Callao, on the coast of Peru; but experience having discovered the impropriety of fixing upon that as the port of communication with Manila, the staple of the commerce between the East and West was removed from Callao to Acapulco, on the coast of New Spain.

After various arrangements it has been brought into a regular form. One or two ships depart annually from Acapulco, which are permitted to carry out silver to the amount of five hundred thousand pesos;‡ but they have hardly any thing else of value on board; in return for which they bring back spices, drugs, china, and japan wares, calicoes, chintz, muslins, silks, and every precious article with which the benignity of the climate, or the ingenuity of its people has enabled the East to supply the rest of the world. For some time the merchants of Peru were admitted to participate in this traffic, and might send annually a ship to Acapulco, to wait the arrival of the vessels from Manila, and receive a proportional share of the commodities which they imported. At length the Peruvians were excluded from this trade by most rigorous edicts, and all the commodities from the East reserved solely for the consumption of New Spain.

In consequence of this indulgence, the inhabitants of that country enjoy advantages unknown in the other Spanish colonies. The manufactures of the East are not only more suited to a warm climate, and more showy than those of Europe, but can be sold at a lower price; while, at the same time, the profits upon them are so considerable as to enrich all those who are employed either in bringing them from Manila or vending them in New Spain. As the interest both of the buyer and seller concurred in favouring this branch of commerce, it has continued to extend in spite of

* MS. penes me. † Torquem. i. lib. v. c. 14. ‡ Recop. lib. ix. c. 45. l. 6.

regulations concerted with the most anxious jealousy to circumscribe it. Under cover of what the laws permit to be imported, great quantities of India goods are poured into the markets of New Spain [194]; and when the Flota arrives at Vera Cruz from Europe, it often finds the wants of the people already supplied by cheaper and more acceptable commodities.

There is not, in the commercial arrangements of Spain, any circumstance more inexplicable than the permission of this trade between New Spain and the Philippines, or more repugnant to its fundamental maxim of holding the colonies in perpetual dependence on the mother country, by prohibiting any commercial intercourse that might suggest to them the idea of receiving a supply of their wants from any other quarter. This permission must appear still more extraordinary, from considering that Spain herself carries on no direct trade with her settlements in the Philippines, and grants a privilege to one of her American colonies which she denies to her subjects in Europe. It is probable that the colonists, who originally took possession of the Philippines, having been sent out from New Spain began this intercourse with a country which they considered, in some measure, as their parent state, before the court of Madrid was aware of its consequences, or could establish regulations in order to prevent it. Many remonstrances have been presented against this trade, as detrimental to Spain, by diverting into another channel a large portion of that treasure which ought to flow into the kingdom, as tending to give rise to a spirit of independence in the colonies, and to encourage innumerable frauds, against which it is impossible to guard, in transactions so far removed from the inspection of government. But as it requires no slight effort of political wisdom and vigour to abolish any practice which numbers are interested in supporting, and to which time has added the sanction of its authority, the commerce between New Spain and Manila seems to be as considerable as ever, and may be considered as one chief cause of the elegance and splendour conspicuous in this part of the Spanish dominions.

But notwithstanding this general corruption in the colonies of Spain, and the diminution of the income belonging to the public, occasioned by the illicit importations made by foreigners, as well as by the various frauds of which the colonists themselves are guilty in their commerce with the parent state, the Spanish monarchs receive a very considerable revenue from their American dominions. This arises from taxes of various kinds, which may be divided into three capital branches. The first contains what is paid to the King, as sovereign, or superior lord of the New World: to this class belongs the duty on the gold and silver raised from the mines, and the tribute exacted from the Indians; the former is termed by the Spaniards the *right of signiory*, the latter is the *duty of vassalage*. The second branch comprehends the numerous duties upon commerce which accompany and oppress it in every step of its progress, from the greatest transactions of the wholesale merchant to the petty traffic of the vender by retail. The third includes what accrues to the king, as head of the church, and administrator of ecclesiastical funds in the New World. In consequence of this he receives the first fruits, annates, spoils, and other spiritual revenues, levied by the apostolic chamber in Europe; and is entitled likewise to the profit arising from the sale of the bull of Cruzado. This bull, which is published every two years, contains an absolution from past offences by the Pope, and, among other immunities, a permission to eat several kinds of prohibited food during Lent, and on meagre days. The monks employed in dispersing those bulls extol their virtues with all the fervour of interested eloquence; the people, ignorant and credulous, listen with implicit assent; and every person in the Spanish colonies, of European, Creolian, or mixed race, purchases a bull, which is deemed essential to his salvation, at the rate set upon it by government [195]

What may be the amount of those various funds, it is almost impossible to determine with precision. The extent of the Spanish dominions in America, the jealousy of government, which renders them inaccessible to foreigners, the mysterious silence which the Spaniards are accustomed to observe with respect to the interior state of their colonies, combine in covering this subject with a veil which it is not easy to remove. But an account, apparently no less accurate than it is curious, has lately been published of the royal revenue in New Spain, from which we may form some idea with respect to what is collected in the other provinces. According to that account the crown does not receive from all the departments of taxation in New Spain above a million of our money, from which one half must be deducted as the expense of the provincial establishment [196]. Peru, it is probable, yields a sum not inferior to this; and if we suppose that all the other regions of America, including the islands, furnish a third share of equal value, we shall not perhaps be far wide from the truth if we conclude that the net public revenue of Spain, raised in America, does not exceed a million and a half sterling. This falls far short of the immense sums to which suppositions, founded upon conjecture, have raised the Spanish revenue in America [197]. It is remarkable, however, upon one account. Spain and Portugal are the only European powers who derive a direct revenue from their colonies. All the advantage that accrues to other nations from their American dominions arises from the exclusive enjoyment of their trade: but besides this, Spain has brought her colonies towards increasing the power of the state, and, in return for protection, to bear a proportional share of the common burden.

Accordingly, the sum which I have computed to be the amount of the Spanish revenue from America arises wholly from the taxes collected there, and is far from being the whole of what accrues to the king from his dominions in the New World. The heavy duties imposed on the commodities exported from Spain to America [198], as well as what is paid by those which she sends home in return; the tax upon the Negro slaves with which Africa supplies the New World, together with several smaller branches of finance, bring large sums into the treasury, the precise extent of which I cannot pretend to ascertain.

But if the revenue which Spain draws from America be great, the expense of administration in her colonies bears proportion to it. In every department, even of her domestic police and finances, Spain has adopted a system more complex, and more encumbered with a variety of tribunals and a multitude of officers, than that of any European nation in which the sovereign possesses such extensive power. From the jealous spirit with which Spain watches over her American settlements, and her endeavours to guard against fraud in provinces so remote from inspection, boards and officers have been multiplied there with still more anxious attention. In a country where the expense of living is great, the salaries allotted to every person in public office must be high, and must load the revenue with an immense burden. The parade of government greatly augments the weight of it. The viceroys of Mexico, Peru, and the new kingdom of Granada, as representatives of the king's person, among people fond of ostentation, maintain all the state and dignity of royalty. Their courts are formed upon the model of that at Madrid, with horse and foot guards, a household regularly established, numerous attendants, and ensigns of power, displaying such pomp as hardly retains the appearance of a delegated authority. All the expense incurred by supporting the external and permanent order of government is defrayed by the crown. The viceroys have, besides, peculiar appointments suited to their exalted station. The salaries fixed by law are indeed extremely moderate; that of the viceroy of Peru is only thirty thousand ducats; and that of the viceroy of Mexico twenty thousand ducats.* Of late they have been raised to forty thousand.

These salaries, however, constitute but a small part of the revenue enjoyed by the viceroys. The exercise of an absolute authority extending to every department of government, and the power of disposing of many lucrative offices, afford them many opportunities of accumulating wealth. To these, which may be considered as legal and allowed emoluments, large sums are often added by exactions, which, in countries so far removed from the seat of government, it is not easy to discover, and impossible to restrain. By monopolising some branches of commerce, by a lucrative concern in others, by conniving at the frauds of merchants, a viceroy may raise such an annual revenue as no subject of any European monarch enjoys [199]. From the single article of presents made to him on the anniversary of his *Name-day* (which is always observed as a high festival), I am informed that a viceroy has been known to receive sixty thousand pesos. According to a Spanish saying, the legal revenues of a viceroy are unknown, his real profits depend upon his opportunities and his conscience. Sensible of this, the kings of Spain, as I have formerly observed, grant a commission to their viceroys only for a few years. This circumstance, however, renders them often more rapacious, and adds to the ingenuity and ardour wherewith they labour to improve every moment of a power which they know is hastening fast to a period; and short as its duration is, it usually affords sufficient time for repairing a shattered fortune, or for creating a new one. But even in situations so trying to human frailty, there are instances of virtue that remains unseduced. In the year 1772, the Marquis de Croix finished the term of his viceroyalty in New Spain with unsuspected integrity; and, instead of bringing home exorbitant wealth, returned with the admiration and applause of a grateful people, whom his government had rendered happy.

* Recop. lib. iii. tit. iii. c. 72.

THE

# HISTORY OF AMERICA.

## BOOKS IX. AND X.

CONTAINING THE

## HISTORY OF VIRGINIA

TO THE YEAR 1688;

AND THE

## HISTORY OF NEW ENGLAND

TO THE YEAR 1652

# ADVERTISEMENT.

---

THE original plan of my father, the late Dr. Robertson, with respect to the history of America, comprehended not only an account of the discovery of that country, and of the conquests and colonies of the Spaniards, but embraced also the history of the British and Portuguese establishments in the New World, and of the settlements made by the several nations of Europe in the West India Islands. It was his intention not to have published any part of the Work until the whole was completed. In the Preface to his History of America, he has stated the reasons which induced him to depart from that resolution, and to publish the two volumes which contain an account of the discovery of the New World, and of the progress of the Spanish arms and colonies in that quarter of the globe. He says, "he had made some progress in the History of British America;" and he announces his intention to return to that part of his Work as soon as the ferment which at that time prevailed in the British colonies in America should subside, and regular government be re-established. Various causes concurred in preventing him from fulfilling his intention.

During the course of a tedious illness, which he early foresaw would have a fatal termination, Dr. Robertson at different times destroyed many of his papers. But after his death, I found that part of the History of British America which he had wrote many years before, and which is now offered to the Public. It is written with his own hand, as all his Works were; it is as carefully corrected as any part of his manuscripts which I have ever seen; and he had thought it worthy of being preserved, as it escaped the flames to which so many other papers had been committed. I read it with the utmost attention; but, before I came to any resolution about the publication, I put the MS. into the hands of some of those friends whom my father used to consult on such occasions, as it would have been rashness and presumption in me to have trusted to my own partial decision. It was perused by some other persons also, in whose taste and judgment I have the greatest confidence: by all of them I was encouraged to offer it to the Public, as a fragment curious and interesting in itself, and not inferior to any of my father's works.

When I determined to follow that advice, it was a circumstance of great weight with me, that as I never could think myself at liberty to destroy those papers which my father had thought worthy of being preserved, and as I could not know into whose hands they might hereafter fall, I considered it as certain that they would be published at some future period, when they might meet with an editor who, not being actuated by the same sacred regard for the reputation of the Author, which I feel, might make alterations and additions, and obtrude the whole on the public as a genuine and authentic work. The MS. is now published, such as it was left by the Author; nor have I presumed to make any addition, alteration, or correction whatever.

WM. ROBERTSON.

QUEEN-ST., EDINBURGH, April, 1796

THE

# HISTORY OF AMERICA.

## BOOK IX.

The dominions of Great Britain in America are next in extent to those of Spain. Its acquisitions there are a recompense due to those enterprising talents which prompted the English to enter early on the career of discovery, and to pursue it with persevering ardour. England was the second nation that ventured to visit the New World. The account of Columbus's successful voyage filled all Europe with astonishment and admiration. But in England it did something more; it excited a vehement desire of emulating the glory of Spain, and of aiming to obtain some share in those advantages which were expected in this new field opened to national activity. The attention of the English court had been turned towards the discovery of unknown countries by its negotiation with Bartholomew Columbus Henry VII. having listened to his propositions with a more favourable ear than could have been expected from a cautious, distrustful prince, averse by habit as well as by temper to new and hazardous projects, he was more easily induced to approve of a voyage for discovery, proposed by some of his own subjects soon after the return of Christopher Columbus.

But though the English had spirit to form the scheme, they had not at that period attained to such skill in navigation as qualified them for carrying it into execution. From the inconsiderate ambition of its monarchs, the nation had long wasted its genius and inactivity in pernicious and ineffectual efforts to conquer France. When this ill-directed ardour began to abate, the fatal contest between the houses of York and Lancaster turned the arms of one half of the kingdom against the other, and exhausted the vigour of both. During the course of two centuries, while industry and commerce were making gradual progress, both in the south and north of Europe, the English continued so blind to the advantages of their own situation that they hardly began to bend their thoughts towards those objects and pursuits to which they are indebted for their present opulence and power. While the trading vessels of Italy, Spain, and Portugal, as well as those of the Hans Towns, visited the most remote ports in Europe, and carried on an active intercourse with its various nations, the English did little more than creep along their own coasts, in small barks, which conveyed the productions of one country to another. Their commerce was almost wholly passive. Their wants were supplied by strangers; and whatever necessary or luxury of life their own country did not yield was imported in foreign bottoms. The cross of St. George was seldom displayed beyond the precincts of the narrow seas. Hardly any English ship traded with Spain or Portugal before the beginning of the fifteenth century; and half a century more elapsed before the English marines became so adventurous as to enter the Mediterranean.

In this infancy of navigation, Henry could not commit the conduct of an armament destined to explore unknown regions to his own subjects. He invested Giovanni Gaboto, a Venetian adventurer, who had settled in Bristol, with the chief command; and issued a commission to him and his three sons, empowering them to sail, under the banner of England, towards the east, nortn, or west, in order to discover countries unoccupied by any Christian state; to take possession of them in his name, and to carry on an exclusive trade with the inhabitants, under condition of paying a fifth part of the free profit on every voyage to the crown. This commission was granted on March 5th, 1495, in less than two years after the return of Columbus from America.* But Cabot (for that is the name he assumed in England, and by which he is best known) did not set out on his voyage for two years. He, together with his second son Sebastian, embarked at Bristol [May, 1497], on board a ship furnished by the king, and was accompanied by four small barks fitted out by the merchants of that city

As in that age the most eminent navigators, formed by the instructions of Columbus, or animated by his example, were guided by ideas derived from his superior knowledge and experience, Cabot had adopted the system of that great man concerning the probability of opening a new and shorter passage to the East Indies by holding a western course. The opinions which Columbus had formed with respect to the islands which he had discovered, were universally received. They were supposed to lie contiguous to the great continent of India, and to constitute a part of the vast countries comprehended under that general name. Cabot accordingly deemed it probable, that, by steering to the north-west, he might reach India by a shorter course than that which Columbus had taken, and hoped to fall in with the coast of Cathay, or China, of whose fertility and opu lence the descriptions of Marco Polo had excited high ideas. After sailing for some weeks due west, and nearly on the parallel of the port from which he took his departure, he discovered a large island, which he called *Prima Vista*, and his sailors *Newfoundland:* and in a few days he descried a smaller isle, to which he gave the name of St. John. He landed on both these [June 24], made some observations on their soil and productions, and brought off three of the natives. Continuing his course westward, he soon reached the continent of North America, and sailed along it from the fifty-sixth to the thirty-eighth degree of latitude, from the coast of Labrador to that of Virginia. As his chief object was to discover some inlet that might open a passage to the west, it does not appear that he landed any where during this extensive run; and he returned to England without attempting either settlement or conquest in any part of that continent.†

If it had been Henry's purpose to prosecute the object of the commission given by him to Cabot, and to take possession of the countries which he had discovered, the success of this voyage must have answered his most sanguine expectations. His subjects were undoubtedly the first Europeans who had visited that part of the American continent, and were entitled to whatever right of property prior discovery is supposed to confer. Countries which stretched in an uninterrupted course through such a large portion of the temperate zone, opened a prospect of settling to advantage under mild climates, and in a fertile soil. By the time that Cabot returned to England, he found both the state of affairs and the king's inclination unfavourable to any scheme the execution of which would have required tranquillity and leisure. Henry was involved in a war with Scotland, and

* Hakluyt, iii 4. † Monson's Naval Tracts, in Churchill's Collect iii. 211.

the kingdom was not yet fully composed after the commotion excited by a formidable insurrection of his own subjects in the west. An ambassador from Ferdinand of Arragon was then in London; and as Henry set a high value upon the friendship of that monarch, for whose character he professed much admiration, perhaps from its similarity to his own, and was endeavouring to strengthen their union by negotiating the marriage which afterwards took place between his eldest son and the Princess Catharine, he was cautious of giving any offence to a prince jealous to excess of all his rights. From the position of the islands and continent which Cabot had discovered, it was evident that they lay within the limits of the ample donative which the bounty of Alexander VI. had conferred upon Ferdinand and Isabella. No person in that age questioned the validity of a papal grant; and Ferdinand was not of a temper to relinquish any claim to which he had a shadow of title. Submission to the authority of the Pope, and deference for an ally whom he courted, seem to have concurred with Henry's own situation in determining him to abandon a scheme in which he had engaged with some degree of ardour and expectation. No attempt towards discovery was made in England during the remainder of his reign; and Sebastian Cabot, finding no encouragement for his active talents there, entered into the service of Spain.*

This is the most probable account of the sudden cessation of Henry's activity, after such success in his first essay as might have encouraged him to persevere. The advantages of commerce, as well as its nature, were so little understood in England about this period, that by an act of parliament in the year 1488, the taking of interest for the use of money was prohibited under severe penalties.† And by another law, the profit arising from dealing in bills of exchange was condemned as savouring of usury.‡ It is not surprising, then, that no great effort should be made to extend trade by a nation whose commercial ideas were still so crude and illiberal. But it is more difficult to discover what prevented this scheme of Henry VII. from being resumed during the reigns of his son and grandson; and to give any reason why no attempt was made, either to explore the northern continent of America more fully, or to settle in it. Henry VIII. was frequently at open enmity with Spain: the value of the Spanish acquisitions in America had become so well known, as might have excited his desire to obtain some footing in those opulent regions; and during a considerable part of his reign, the prohibitions in a papal bull would not have restrained him from making encroachment upon the Spanish dominions. But the reign of Henry was not favourable to the progress of discovery. During one period of it, the active part which he took in the affairs of the continent, and the vigour with which he engaged in the contest between the two mighty rivals, Charles V. and Francis I., gave full occupation to the enterprising spirit both of the king and his nobility. During another period of his administration, his famous controversy with the court of Rome kept the nation in perpetual agitation and suspense. Engrossed by those objects, neither the king nor the nobles had inclination or leisure to turn their attention to new pursuits; and without their patronage and aid, the commercial part of the nation was too inconsiderable to make any effort of consequence. Though England by its total separation from the church of Rome soon after the accession of Edward VI., disclaimed that authority which, by its presumptuous partition of the globe between two

* Some schemes of discovery seem to have been formed in England towards the beginning of the sixteenth century. But as there is no other memorial of them than what remains in a patent granted by the King to the adventurers, it is probable that they were feeble or abortive projects. If any attempt had been made in consequence of this patent, it would not have escaped the knowledge of a compiler so industrious and inquisitive as Hakluyt. In his patent, Henry restricts the adventurers from encroaching on the countries discovered by the kings of Portugal, or any other prince in confederacy with England. Rymer's Fœdera, vol. xiii. p. 37.

† 3 Hen. VII. c 5. ‡ 3 Hen. VII. c. 6.

favourite nations, circumscribed the activity of every other state within very narrow limits; yet a feeble minority, distracted with faction, was not a juncture for forming schemes of doubtful success and remote utility. The bigotry of Mary, and her marriage with Philip, disposed her to pay a sacred regard to that grant of the Holy See, which vested in a husband, on whom she doted, an exclusive right to every part of the New World. Thus, through a singular succession of various causes, sixty-one years elapsed from the time that the English discovered North America, during which their monarchs gave little attention to that country which was destined to be annexed to their crown, and to be a chief source of its opulence and power.

But though the public contributed little towards the progress of discovery, naval skill, knowledge of commerce, and a spirit of enterprise, began to spread among the English. During the reign of Henry VIII. several new channels of trade were opened, and private adventurers visited remote countries, with which England had formerly no intercourse. Some merchants of Bristol, having fitted out two ships for the southern regions of America, committed the conduct of them to Sebastian Cabot, who had quitted the service of Spain. He visited the coasts of Brazil, and touched at the islands of Hispaniola and Puerto Rico; and though this voyage seems not to have been beneficial to the adventurers, it extended the sphere of English navigation, and added to the national stock of nautical science.* Though disappointed in their expectations of profit in this first essay, the merchants were not discouraged. They sent, successively, several vessels from different ports towards the same quarter, and seem to have carried on an interloping trade in the Portuguese settlements with success.† Nor was it only towards the West, that the activity of the English was directed. Other merchants began to extend their commercial views to the East; and by establishing an intercourse with several islands in the Archipelago, and with some of the towns on the coast of Syria, they found a new market for woollen cloths (the only manufacture which the nation had begun to cultivate,) and supplied their countrymen with various productions of the East, formerly unknown, or received from the Venetians at an exorbitant price.‡

But the discovery of a shorter passage to the East Indies, by the north west, was still the favourite project of the nation, which beheld with envy the vast wealth that flowed into Portugal from its commerce with those regions. The scheme was accordingly twice resumed under the long administration of Henry VIII. [1527 and 1536]; first, with some slender aid from the king, and then by private merchants. Both voyages were disastrous and unsuccessful. In the former, one of the ships was lost. In the latter, the stock of provisions was so ill proportioned to the number of the crew, that, although they were but six months at sea, many perished with hunger, and the survivors were constrained to support life by feeding on the bodies of their dead companions.§

The vigour of a commercial spirit did not relax in the reign of Edward VI. The great fishery on the banks of Newfoundland became an object of attention; and from some regulations for the encouragement of that branch of trade, it seems to have been prosecuted with activity and success.‖ But the prospect of opening a communication with China and the Spice Islands, by some other route than round the Cape of Good Hope, still continued to allure the English more than any scheme of adventure. Cabot, whose opinion was deservedly of high authority in whatever related to naval enterprise, warmly urged the English to make another attempt to discover this passage. As it had been thrice searched for in vain, by steering towards the north-west, he proposed that a trial

* Hakluyt, iii 498. † Id. iii 700 ‡ Id. ii. 96, &c. § Id. i. 213, &c. iii. 129, 130 ‖ Id. iii 131.

should now be made by the north-east; and supported this advice by such plausible reasons and conjectures as excited sanguine expectations of success. Several noblemen and persons of rank, together with some principal merchants, having associated for this purpose, were incorporated by a charter from the King, under the title of The Company of Merchant Adventurers for the Discovery of Regions, Dominions, Islands, and Places unknown. Cabot, who was appointed governor of this company, soon fitted out two ships and a bark, furnished with instructions in his own hand, which discover the great extent both of his naval skill and mercantile sagacity.

Sir Hugh Willoughby, who was intrusted with the command, stood dir ctly northwards along the coast of Norway [May 10], and doubled the North Cape. But in that tempestuous ocean, his small squadron was separated in a violent storm. Willoughby's ship and bark took refuge in an obscure harbour in a desert part of Russian Lapland, where he and all his companions were frozen to death. Richard Chancelour, the captain of the other vessel, was more fortunate; he entered the White Sea, and wintered in safety at Archangel. Though no vessel of any foreign nation had ever visited that quarter of the globe before, the inhabitants received their new visiters with an hospitality which would have done honour to a more polished people. The English learned there, that this was a province of a vast empire, subject to the Great Duke or Czar of Muscovy, who resided in a great city twelve hundred miles from Archangel. Chancelour, with a spirit becoming an officer employed in an expedition for discovery, did not hesitate a moment about the part which he ought to take, and set out for that distant capital. On his arrival in Moscow, he was admitted to audience, and delivered a letter which the captain of each ship had received from Edward VI. for the sovereign of whatever country they should discover, to John Vasilowitz, who at that time filled the Russian throne. John, though he ruled over his subjects with the cruelty and caprice of a barbarous despot, was not destitute of political sagacity. He instantly perceived the happy consequences that might flow from opening an intercourse between his dominions and the western nations of Europe; and delighted with the fortunate event to which he was indebted for this unexpected benefit, he treated Chancelour with great respect; and, by a letter to the King of England [Feb. 1554], invited his subjects to trade in the Russian dominions, with ample promises of protection and favour.*

Chancelour, on his return, found Mary seated on the English throne. The success of this voyage, the discovery of a new course of navigation, the establishment of commerce with a vast empire, the name of which was then hardly known in the West, and the hope of arriving, in this direction, at those regions which had been so long the object of desire, excited a wonderful ardour to prosecute the design with greater vigour. Mary, implicitly guided by her husband in every act of administration, was not unwilling to turn the commercial activity of her subjects towards a quarter where it could not excite the jealousy of Spain by encroaching on its possessions in the New World. She wrote to John Vasilowitz in the most respectful terms, courting his friendship. She confirmed the charter of Edward VI., empowered Chancelour, and two agents appointed by the company, to negotiate with the Czar in her name; and, according to the spirit of that age, she granted an exclusive right of trade with Russia to the Corporation of Merchant Adventurers.† In virtue of this, they not only established an active and gainful commerce with Russia, but, in hopes of reaching China, they pushed their discoveries eastward to the coast of Nova Zembla, the Straits of Waigatz, and towards the mouth of the great river Oby. But in those frozen seas, which Nature seems not to have

* Hakluyt i. 226, &c. † Id. i. 258, &c

destined for navigation, they were exposed to innumerable disasters, and met with successive disappointments.

Nor were their attempts to open a communication with India made only in this channel. They appointed some of their factors to accompany the Russian caravans which travelled into Persia by the way of Astracan and the Caspian Sea, instructing them to penetrate as far as possible towards the east, and to endeavour not only to establish a trade with those countries, but to acquire every information that might afford any light towards the discovery of a passage to China by the north-east.* Notwithstanding a variety of dangers to which they were exposed in travelling through so many provinces inhabited by fierce and licentious nations, some of these factors reached Bokara in the province of Chorassan; and though prevented from advancing further by the civil wars which desolated the country, they returned to Europe with some hopes of extending the commerce of the Company into Persia, and with much intelligence concerning the state of those remote regions of the East.†

The successful progress of the Merchant Adventurers in discovery roused the emulation of their countrymen, and turned their activity into new channels. A commercial intercourse, hitherto unattempted by the English, having been opened with the coast of Barbary, the specimens which that afforded of the valuable productions of Africa invited some enterprising navigators to visit the more remote provinces of that quarter of the globe. They sailed along its western shore, traded in different ports on both sides of the Line, and, after acquiring considerable knowledge of those countries, returned with a cargo of gold dust, ivory, and other rich commodities little known at that time in England. This commerce with Africa seems to have been pursued with vigour, and was at that time no less innocent than lucrative; for, as the English had then no demand for slaves, they carried it on for many years without violating the rights of humanity. Thus far did the English advance during a period which may be considered as the infant state of their navigation and commerce; and feeble as its steps at that time may appear to us, we trace them with an interesting curiosity, and look back with satisfaction to the early essays of that spirit which we now behold in the full maturity of its strength. Even in those first efforts of the English, an intelligent observer will discern presages of their future improvement. As soon as the activity of the nation was put in motion, it took various directions, and exerted itself in each, with that steady, persevering industry which is the soul and guide of commerce. Neither discouraged by the hardships and dangers to which they were exposed in those northern seas which they first attempted to explore, nor afraid of venturing into the sultry climates of the torrid zone, the English, during the reigns of Henry VIII., Edward VI., and Mary, opened some of the most considerable sources of their commercial opulence, and gave a beginning to their trade with Turkey, with Africa, with Russia, and with Newfoundland.

By the progress which England had already made in navigation and commerce, it was now prepared for advancing further; and on the accession of Elizabeth to the throne, a period commenced extremely auspicious to this spirit which was rising in the nation. The domestic tranquillity of the kingdom, maintained, almost without interruption, during the course of a long and prosperous reign; the peace with foreign nations, that subsisted more than twenty years after Elizabeth was seated on the throne; the Queen's attentive economy, which exempted her subjects from the burden of taxes oppressive to trade; the popularity of her administration; were all favourable to commercial enterprise, and called it forth into vigorous exertion. The discerning eye of Elizabeth having early perceived that

* Hakluyt, i. 301 † Id. i. 310, &c.

the security of a kingdom environed by the sea depended on its naval force, she began her government with adding to the number and strength of the royal navy; which, during a factious minority, and a reign intent on no object but that of suppressing heresy, had been neglected, and suffered to decay. She filled her arsenals with naval stores; she built several ships of great force, according to the ideas of that age, and encouraged her subjects to imitate her example, that they might no longer depend on foreigners, from whom the English had hitherto purchased all vessels of any considerable burden.* By those efforts the skill of the English artificers was improved, the number of sailors increased, and the attention of the public turned to the navy, as the most important national object. Instead of abandoning any of the new channels of commerce which had been opened in the three preceding reigns, the English frequented them with greater assiduity, and the patronage of their sovereign added vigour to all their efforts. In order to secure to them the continuance of their exclusive trade with Russia, Elizabeth cultivated the connection with John Vasilowitz, which had been formed by her predecessor, and, by successive embassies gained his confidence so thoroughly, that the English enjoyed that lucrative privilege during his long reign. She encouraged the Company of Merchant Adventurers, whose monopoly of the Russian trade was confirmed by act of parliament,† to resume their design of penetrating into Persia by land. Their second attempt, conducted with greater prudence, or undertaken at a more favourable juncture than the first, was more successful. Their agents arrived in the Persian court, and obtained such protection and immunities from the Shah, that for a course of years they carried on a gainful commerce in his kingdom;‡ and by frequenting the various provinces of Persia, became so well acquainted with the vast riches of the East, as strengthened their design of opening a more direct intercourse with those fertile regions by sea.

But as every effort to accomplish this by the north-east had proved abortive, a scheme was formed, under the patronage of the Earl of Warwick, the head of the enterprising family of Dudley, to make a new attempt, by holding an opposite course by the north-west. The conduct of this enterprise was committed to Martin Frobisher, an officer of experience and reputation. In three successive voyages [1576, 1577, and 1578,] he explored the inhospitable coast of Labrador, and that of Greenland (to which Elizabeth gave the name of *Meta Incognita*), without discovering any probable appearance of that passage to India for which he sought. This new disappointment was sensibly felt, and might have damped the spirit of naval enterprise among the English, if it had not resumed fresh vigour, amidst the general exultation of the nation, upon the successful expedition of Francis Drake. That bold navigator, emulous of the glory which Magellan had acquired by sailing round the globe, formed a scheme of attempting a voyage, which all Europe had admired for sixty years, without venturing to follow the Portuguese discoverer in his adventurous course. Drake undertook this with a feeble squadron, in which the largest vessel did not exceed a hundred tons, and he accomplished it with no less credit to himself than honour to his country. Even in this voyage, conducted with other views, Drake seems not to have been inattentive to the favourite object of his countrymen, the discovery of a new route to India. Before he quitted the Pacific Ocean, in order to stretch towards the Philippine Islands, he ranged along the coast of California, as high as the latitude of forty-two degrees north, in hopes of discovering, on that side, the communication between the two seas, which had so often been searched for in vain on the other. But this was the only unsuccessful attempt of Drake. The excessive cold of the climate, intolerable to men

* Camd Annales, p. 70. edit. 1615; fol. † Hakluyt i. 369. ‡ Id. i. 344, &c.

who had long been accustomed to tropical heat, obliged him to stop short in his progress towards the north; and whether or not there be any passage from the Pacific to the Atlantic Ocean in that quarter is a point still unascertained.*

From this period, the English seem to have confided in their own abilities and courage, as equal to any naval enterprise. They had now visited every region to which navigation extended in that age, and had rivalled the nation of highest repute for naval skill in its most splendid exploit. But notwithstanding the knowledge which they had acquired of the different quarters of the globe, they had not hitherto attempted any settlement out of their own country. Their merchants had not yet acquired such a degree either of wealth or of political influence, as was requisite towards carrying a scheme of colonization into execution. Persons of noble birth were destitute of the ideas and information which might have disposed them to patronise such a design. The growing power of Spain, however, and the ascendant over the other nations of Europe to which it had attained under Charles V. and his son, naturally turned the attention of mankind towards the importance of those settlements in the New World, to which they were so much indebted for that pre-eminence. The intercourse between Spain and England, during the reign of Philip and Mary; the resort of the Spanish nobility to the English court, while Philip resided there; the study of the Spanish language, which became fashionable; and the translation of several histories of America into English, diffused gradually through the nation a more distinct knowledge of the policy of Spain in planting its colonies, and of the advantages which it derived from them. When hostilities commenced between Elizabeth and Philip, the prospect of annoying Spain by sea opened a new career to the enterprising spirit of the English nobility. Almost every eminent leader of the age aimed at distinguishing himself by naval exploits. That service, and the ideas connected with it, the discovery of unknown countries, the establishment of distant colonies, and the enriching of commerce by new commodities, became familiar to persons of rank.

In consequence of all those concurring causes, the English began seriously to form plans of settling colonies in those parts of America which hitherto they had only visited. The projectors and patrons of these plans were mostly persons of rank and influence. Among them, Sir Humphry Gilbert, of Compton in Devonshire, ought to be mentioned with the distinction due to the conductor of the first English colony to America. He had early rendered himself conspicuous by his military services both in France and Ireland; and having afterwards turned his attention to naval affairs, he published a discourse concerning the probability of a north-west passage, which discovered no inconsiderable portion both of learning and ingenuity, mingled with the enthusiasm, the credulity, and the sanguine expectations which incite men to new and hazardous undertakings.† With those talents he was deemed a proper person to be employed in establishing a new colony, and easily obtained from the Queen letters patent [June 11, 1578,] vesting in him sufficient powers for this purpose.

As this is the first charter to a colony granted by the crown of England, the articles in it merit particular attention, as they unfold the ideas of that age with respect to the nature of such settlements. Elizabeth authorizes him to discover and take possession of all remote and barbarous lands, unoccupied by any Christian prince or people. She vests in him, his heirs and assigns for ever, the full right of property in the soil of those countries whereof he shall take possession. She permits such of her subjects as were willing to accompany Gilbert in his voyage, to go and settle in the countries which he shall plant. She empowers him, his heirs and assigns,

* Hakluyt, iii. 440. Camd. Annal. 301, &c.

† Hakluyt, iii. 11.

to dispose of whatever portion of those lands he shall judge meet, to persons settled there, in fee simple, according to the laws of England. She ordains, that all the lands granted to Gilbert shall hold of the crown of England by homage, on payment of the fifth part of the gold or silver ore found there. She confers upon him, his heirs and assigns, the complete jurisdictions and royalties, as well marine as other, within the said lands and seas thereunto adjoining; and as their common safety and interest would render good government necessary in their new settlements, she gave Gilbert, his heirs and assigns, full power to convict, punish, pardon, govern, and rule, by their good discretion and policy, as well in causes capital or criminal as civil, both marine and other, all persons who shall, from time to time, settle within the said countries, according to such statutes, laws, and ordinances, as shall be by him, his heirs and assigns, devised and established for their better government. She declared, that all who settled there should have and enjoy all the privileges of free denizens and natives of England, any law, custom, or usage to the contrary notwithstanding. And finally, she prohibited all persons from attempting to settle within two hundred leagues of any place which Sir Humphry Gilbert, or his associates, shall have occupied during the space of six years.*

With those extraordinary powers, suited to the high notions of authority and prerogative prevalent in England during the sixteenth century, but very repugnant to more recent ideas with respect to the rights of free men, who voluntarily unite to form a colony, Gilbert began to collect associates, and to prepare for embarkation. His own character, and the zealous efforts of his half brother Walter Ralegh, who even in his early youth displayed those splendid talents, and that undaunted spirit, which create admiration and confidence, soon procured him a sufficient number of followers. But his success was not suited either to the sanguine hopes of his countrymen, or to the expense of his preparations. Two expeditions, both of which he conducted in person, ended disastrously [1580]. In the last he himself perished, without having effected his intended settlement on the continent of America, or performing any thing more worthy of notice, than the empty formality of taking possession of the Island of Newfoundland in the name of his sovereign. The dissensions among his officers; the licentious and ungovernable spirit of some of his crew; his total ignorance of the countries which he purposed to occupy; his misfortune in approaching the continent too far towards the north, where the inhospitable coast of Cape Breton did not invite them to settle; the shipwreck of his largest vessel; and, above all, the scanty provision which the funds of a private man could make of what was requisite for establishing a new colony, were the true causes to which the failure of the enterprise must be imputed, not to any deficiency of abilities or resolution in its leader.†

But the miscarriage of a scheme, in which Gilbert had wasted his fortune, did not discourage Ralegh. He adopted all his brother's ideas; and applying to the Queen, in whose favour he stood high at that time, he procured a patent [March 26, 1584], with jurisdiction and prerogatives as ample as had been granted unto Gilbert.‡ Ralegh, no less eager to execute than to undertake the scheme, instantly despatched two small vessels [April 27], under the command of Amadas and Barlow, two officers of trust, to visit the countries which he intended to settle, and to acquire some previous knowledge of their coasts, their soil, and productions. In order to avoid Gilbert's error, in holding too far north, they took their course by the Canaries and the West India islands, and approached the North American continent by the Gulf of Florida. Unfortunately, their chief researches were made in that part of the country now known by the name of North Carolina, that province in America most destitute of commodious

* Hakluyt, iii. 135. † Ibid. iii. 243, &c. ‡ Ibid. iii. 243.

harbours. They touched first at an island, which they call Wokocon (probably Ocakoke,) situated on the inlet into Pamplicoe sound, and then at Roanoke, near the mouth of Albermarle sound. In both they had some intercourse with the natives, whom they found to be savages with all the characteristic qualities of uncivilized life, bravery, aversion to labour, hospitality, a propensity to admire, and a willingness to exchange their rude productions for English commodities, especially for iron, or any of the useful metals of which they were destitute. After spending a few weeks in this traffic, and in visiting some parts of the adjacent continent, Amadas and Barlow returned to England [Sept. 15], with two of the natives, and gave such splendid descriptions of the beauty of the country, the fertility of the soil, and the mildness of the climate, that Elizabeth, delighted with the idea of occupying a territory superior, so far, to the barren regions towards the north hitherto visited by her subjects, bestowed on it the name of Virginia; as a memorial that this happy discovery had been made under a virgin queen.*

Their report encouraged Ralegh to hasten his preparations for taking possession of such an inviting property. He fitted out a squadron of seven small ships, under the command of Sir Richard Greenville, a man of honourable birth, and of courage so undaunted as to be conspicuous even in that gallant age. But the spirit of that predatory war which the English carried on against Spain, mingled with this scheme of settlement; and on this account, as well as from unacquaintance with a more direct and shorter course to North America, Greenville sailed by the West India islands. He spent some time in cruising among these, and in taking prizes; so that it was towards the close of June before he arrived on the coast of North America. He touched at both the islands where Amadas and Barlow had landed, and made some excursions into different parts of the continent round Pamplicoe and Albermarle sounds. But as, unfortunately, he did not advance far enough towards the north, to discover the noble bay of Chesapeak, he established the colony [Aug. 25], which he left on the island of Roanoke, an incommodious station, without any safe harbour, and almost uninhabited.†

This colony consisted only of one hundred and eighty persons, under the command of Captain Lane, assisted by some men of note, the most distinguished of whom was Hariot, an eminent mathematician. Their chief employment, during a residence of nine months, was to obtain a more extensive knowledge of the country; and their researches were carried on with greater spirit, and reached further than could have been expected from a colony so feeble, and in a station so disadvantageous. But from the same impatience of indigent adventurers to acquire sudden wealth which gave a wrong direction to the industry of the Spaniards in their settlements, the greater part of the English seem to have considered nothing as worthy of attention but mines of gold and silver. These they sought for wherever they came: these they inquired after with unwearied eagerness. The savages soon discovered the favourite objects which allured them, and artfully amused them with so many tales concerning pearl fisheries, and rich mines of various metals, that Lane and his companions wasted their time and activity in the chimerical pursuit of these, instead of labouring to raise provisions for their own subsistence. On discovering the deceit of the Indians, they were so much exasperated, that from expostulations and reproaches they proceeded to open hostility [1586]. The supplies of provision which they had been accustomed to receive from the natives were of course withdrawn. Through their own negligence no other precaution had been taken for their support. Ralegh, having engaged in a scheme too expensive for his narrow funds, had not been able to send them that

* Hakluyt, iii. 246

† Id. iii. 251

recruit of stores with which Greenville had promised to furnish them early in the spring. The colony, reduced to the utmost distress, and on the point of perishing with famine, was preparing to disperse into different districts of the country in quest of food, when Sir Francis Drake appeared with his fleet [June 1], returning from a successful expedition against the Spaniards in the West Indies. A scheme which he formed, of furnishing Lane and his associates with such supplies as might enable them to remain with comfort in their station, was disappointed by a sudden storm, in which a small vessel that he destined for their service was dashed to pieces, and as he could not supply them with another, at their joint request, as they were worn out with fatigue and famine, he carried them home to England* [June 19].

Such was the inauspicious beginning of the English settlements in the New World; and, after exciting high expectations, this first attempt produced no effect but that of affording a more complete knowledge of the country; as it enabled Hariot, a man of science and observation, to describe its soil, climate, productions, and the manners of its inhabitants, with a degree of accuracy which merits no inconsiderable praise, when compared with the childish and marvellous tales published by several of the early visitants of the New World. There is another consequence of this abortive colony important enough to entitle it to a place in history. Lane and his associates, by their constant intercourse with the Indians, had acquired a relish for their favourite enjoyment of smoking tobacco; to the use of which, the credulity of that people not only ascribed a thousand imaginary virtues, but their superstition considered the plant itself as a gracious gift of the gods, for the solace of human kind, and the most acceptable offering which man can present to heaven.† They brought with them a specimen of this new commodity to England, and taught their countrymen the method of using it; which Ralegh and some young men of fashion fondly adopted. From imitation of them, from love of novelty, and from the favourable opinion of its salutary qualities entertained by several physicians, the practice spread among the English. The Spaniards and Portuguese had, previous to this, introduced it into other parts of Europe. This habit of taking tobacco gradually extended from the extremities of the north to those of the south, and in one form or other seems to be equally grateful to the inhabitants of every climate; and by a singular caprice of the human species, no less inexplicable than unexampled (so bewitching is the acquired taste for a weed of no manifest utility, and at first not only unpleasant but nauseous), that it has become almost as universal as the demands of those appetites originally implanted in our nature. Smoking was the first mode of taking tobacco in England; and we learn from the comic writers towards the close of the sixteenth century and the beginning of the seventeenth, that this was deemed one of the accomplishments of a man of fashion and spirit.

A few days after Drake departed from Roanoke, a small bark, despatched by Ralegh with a supply of stores for the colony, landed at the place where the English had settled; but on finding it deserted by their countrymen they returned to England. The bark was hardly gone, when Sir Richard Greenville appeared with three ships. After searching in vain for the colony which he had planted, without being able to learn what had befallen it, he left fifteen of his crew to keep possession of the island. This handful of men was soon overpowered and cut in pieces by the savages.‡

Though all Ralegh's efforts to establish a colony in Virginia had hitherto proved abortive, and had been defeated by a succession of disasters and

* Hakluyt, ii. 255. Camd. Annal. 387. † Hariot ap. Hakluyt, iii. 271. De Bry. America, pars i.
‡ Hakluyt, iii. 265. 283.

disappointments, neither his hopes nor resources were exhausted. Early in the following year [1587], he fitted out three ships, under the command of Captain John White, who carried thither a colony more numerous than that which had been settled under Lane. On their arrival in Virginia, after viewing the face of the country covered with one continued forest, which to them appeared an uninhabited wild, as it was occupied only by a few scattered tribes of savages, they discovered that they were destitute of many things which they deemed essentially necessary towards their subsistence in such an uncomfortable situation; and with one voice, requested White, their commander, to return to England, as the person among them most likely to solicit, with efficacy, the supply on which depended the existence of the colony. White landed in his native country at a most unfavourable season for the negotiation which he had undertaken. He found the nation in universal alarm at the formidable preparations of Philip II. to invade England, and collecting all its force to oppose the fleet to which he had arrogantly given the name of the Invincible Armada. Ralegh, Greenville, and all the most zealous patrons of the new settlement, were called to act a distinguished part in the operations of a year [1588], equally interesting and glorious to England. Amidst danger so imminent, and during a contest for the honour of their sovereign and the independence of their country, it was impossible to attend to a less important and remote object. The unfortunate colony in Roanoke received no supply, and perished miserably by famine, or by the unrelenting cruelty of those barbarians by whom they were surrounded.

During the remainder of Elizabeth's reign, the scheme of establishing a colony in Virginia was not resumed. Ralegh, with a most aspiring mind and extraordinary talents, enlightened by knowledge no less uncommon, had the spirit and the defects of a projector. Allured by new objects, and always giving the preference to such as were most splendid and arduous, he was apt to engage in undertakings so vast and so various as to be far beyond his power of accomplishing. He was now intent on peopling and improving a large district of country in Ireland, of which he had obtained a grant from the Queen. He was a deep adventurer in the scheme of fitting out a powerful armament against Spain, in order to establish Don Antonio on the throne of Portugal. He had begun to form his favourite but visionary plan, of penetrating into the province of Guiana, where he fondly dreamed of taking possession of inexhaustible wealth flowing from the richest mines in the New World. Amidst this multiplicity of projects, of such promising appearance, and recommended by novelty, he naturally became cold towards his ancient and hitherto unprofitable scheme of settling a colony in Virginia, and was easily induced to assign his right of property in that country, which he had never visited, together with all the privileges contained in his patent, to Sir Thomas Smith and a company of merchants in London [March, 1596]. This company, satisfied with a paltry traffic carried on by a few small barks, made no attempt to take possession of the country. Thus, after a period of a hundred and six years from the time that Cabot discovered North America in the name of Henry VII., and of twenty years from the time that Ralegh planted the first colony, there was not a single Englishman settled there at the demise of Queen Elizabeth, in the year one thousand six hundred and three.

I have already explained the cause of this during the period previous to the accession of Elizabeth. Other causes produced the same effect under her administration. Though for one half of her reign England was engaged in no foreign war, and commerce enjoyed that perfect security which is friendly to its progress; though the glory of her later years gave the highest tone of elevation and vigour to the national spirit; the Queen herself, from her extreme parsimony, and her aversion to demand extraordinary supplies of her subjects, was more apt to restrain than to second the ardent genius of her people. Several of the most splendid enterprises in her reign were concerted and executed by private adventurers. All the schemes for colonization were carried on by the funds of individuals, without any public aid. Even the felicity of her government was averse to the establishment of remote colonies. So powerful is the attraction of our native soil, and such our fortunate partiality to the laws and manners of our own country, that men seldom choose to abandon it, unless they be driven away by oppression, or allured by vast prospects of sudden wealth. But the provinces of America, in which the English attempted to settle, did not, like those occupied by Spain, invite them thither by any appearance of silver or gold mines. All their hopes of gain were distant; and they saw that nothing could be earned but by persevering exertions of industry. The maxims of Elizabeth's administration were, in their general tenor, so popular, as did not force her subjects to emigrate in order to escape from the heavy or vexatious hand of power. It seems to have been with difficulty that these slender bands of planters were collected, on which the writers of that age bestow the name of the first and second Virginian colonies. The fulness of time for English colonization was not yet arrived.

But the succession of the Scottish line to the crown of England [1603] hastened its approach. James was hardly seated on the throne before he discovered his pacific intentions, and he soon terminated the long war which had been carried on between Spain and England, by an amicable treaty. From that period, uninterrupted tranquillity continued during his reign. Many persons of high rank, and of ardent ambition, to whom the war with Spain had afforded constant employment, and presented alluring prospects not only of fame but of wealth, soon became so impatient of languishing at home without occupation or object, that their invention was on the stretch to find some exercise for their activity and talents. To both these North America seemed to open a new field, and schemes of carrying colonies thither became more general and more popular.

A voyage undertaken by Bartholomew Gosnold, in the last year of the Queen, facilitated as well as encouraged the execution of these schemes. He sailed from Falmouth in a small bark with thirty-two men. Instead of following former navigators in their unnecessary circuit by the West India isles and the Gulf of Florida, Gosnold steered due west as nearly as the winds would permit, and was the first English commander who reached America by this shorter and more direct course. That part of the continent which he first descried was a promontory in the province now called Massachusets Bay, to which he gave the name of Cape Cod. Holding along the coast as it stretched towards the south-west, he touched at two islands, one of which he called Martha's Vineyard, the other Elizabeth's Island; and visited the adjoining continent, and traded with its inhabitants. He and his companions were so much delighted every where with the inviting aspect of the country, that notwithstanding the smallness of their number, a part of them consented to remain there. But when they had leisure to reflect upon the fate of former settlers in America, they retracted a resolution formed in the first warmth of their admiration; and Gosnold returned to England in less than four months from the time of his departure.*

This voyage however inconsiderable it may appear, had important effects. The English now discovered the aspect of the American continent to be extremely inviting far to the north of the place where they had formerly attempted to settle. The coast of a vast country, stretching through the most desirable climates, lay before them. The richness of its virgin

* Purchas, iv. p. 1647

soil promised a certain recompense to their industry. In its interior provinces unexpected sources of wealth might open, and unknown objects of commerce might be found. Its distance from England was diminished almost a third part by the new course which Gosnold had pointed out. Plans for establishing colonies began to be formed in different parts of the kingdom; and before these were ripe for execution, one small vessel was sent out by the merchants of Bristol, another by the Earl of Southampton and Lord Arundel of Wardour, in order to learn whether Gosnold's account of the country was to be considered as a just representation of its state, or as the exaggerated description of a fond discoverer. Both returned with a full confirmation of his veracity, and with the addition of so many new circumstances in favour of the country, acquired by a more extensive view of it, as greatly increased the desire of planting it.

The most active and efficacious promoter of this was Richard Hakluyt, prebendary of Westminster, to whom England is more indebted for its American possessions than to any man of that age. Formed under a kinsman of the same name, eminent for naval and commercial knowledge, he imbibed a similar taste, and applied early to the study of geography and navigation. These favourite sciences engrossed his attention, and to diffuse a relish for them was the great object of his life. In order to excite his countrymen to naval enterprise, by flattering their national vanity, he published, in the year one thousand five hundred and eighty-nine, his valuable collection of voyages and discoveries made by Englishmen. In order to supply them with what information might be derived from the experience of the most successful foreign navigators, he translated some of the best accounts of the progress of the Spaniards and Portuguese in their voyages both to the East and West Indies, into the English tongue. He was consulted with respect to many of the attempts towards discovery or colonization during the latter part of Elizabeth's reign. He corresponded with the officers who conducted them, directed their researches to proper objects, and published the history of their exploits. By the zealous endeavours of a person equally respected by men of rank and men of business, many of both orders formed an association to establish colonies in America, and petitioned the king for the sanction of his authority to warrant the execution of their plans.

James, who prided himself on his profound skill in the science of government, and who had turned his attention to consider the advantages which might be derived from colonies, at a time when he patronized his scheme for planting them in some of the ruder provinces of his ancient kingdom, with a view of introducing industry and civilization there,* was now no less fond of directing the active genius of his English subjects towards occupations not repugnant to his own pacific maxims, and listened with a favourable ear to their application. But as the extent as well as value of the American continent began now to be better known, a grant of the whole of such a vast region to any one body of men, however respectable, appeared to him an act of impolitic and profuse liberality. For this reason he divided that portion of North America, which stretches from the thirty-fourth to the fifty-fifth degree of latitude, into two districts nearly equal; the one called the first or south colony of Virginia, the other, the second or north colony [April 10, 1616]. He authorized Sir Thomas Gates, Sir George Summers, Richard Hakluyt, and their associates, mostly resident in London, to settle any part of the former which they should choose, and vested in them a right of property to the land extending along the coast fifty miles on each side of the place of their first habitation, and reaching into the interior country a hundred miles. The latter district he allotted, as the place of settlement to sundry knights, gentlemen, and mer-

* Hist. of Scotland, vol. ii.

chants of Bristol, Plymouth, and other parts in the west of England, with a similar grant of territory. Neither the monarch who issued this charter, nor his subjects who received it, had any conception that they were proceeding to lay the foundation of mighty and opulent states. What James granted was nothing more than a simple charter of corporation to a trading company, empowering the members of it to have a common seal, and to act as a body politic. But as the object for which they associated was new, the plan established for the administration of their affairs was uncommon. Instead of the power usually granted to corporations, of electing officers and framing by-laws for the conduct of their own operations, the supreme government of the colonies to be settled was vested in a council resident in England, to be named by the king, according to such laws and ordinances as should be given under his sign manual; and the subordinate jurisdiction was committed to a council resident in America, which was likewise to be nominated by the king, and to act conformably to his instructions. To this important clause, which regulated the form of their constitution, was added the concession of several immunities to encourage persons to settle in the intended colonies. Some of those were the same which had been granted to Gilbert and Ralegh; such as the securing to the emigrants and their descendants all the rights of denizens, in the same manner as if they had remained or had been born in England; and granting them the privilege of holding their lands in America by the freest and least burdensome tenure. Others were more favourable than those granted by Elizabeth. He permitted whatever was necessary for the sustenance or commerce of the new colonies to be exported from England, during the space of seven years, without paying any duty; and, as a further incitement to industry, he granted them liberty of trade with other nations, and appropriated the duty to be levied on foreign commodities, for twenty-one years, as a fund for the benefit of the colony.*

In this singular charter, the contents of which have been little attended to by the historians of America, some articles are as unfavourable to the rights of the colonists as others are to the interest of the parent state. By placing the legislative and executive powers in a council nominated by the crown, and guided by its instructions, every person settling in America seems to be bereaved of the noblest privilege of a free man; by the unlimited permission of trade with foreigners, the parent state is deprived of that exclusive commerce which has been deemed the chief advantage resulting from the establishment of colonies. But in the infancy of colonization, and without the guidance of observation or experience, the ideas of men, with respect to the mode of forming new settlements, were not fully unfolded or properly arranged. At a period when they could not foresee the future grandeur and importance of the communities which they were about to call into existence, they were ill qualified to concert the best plan for governing them. Besides, the English of that age, accustomed tc the high prerogative and arbitrary rule of their monarchs, were not animated with such liberal sentiments, either concerning their own personal or political rights, as have become familiar in the more mature and improved state of their constitution.

Without hesitation or reluctance the proprietors of both colonies prepared to execute their respective plans; and under the authority of a charter, which would now be rejected with disdain as a violent invasion of the sacred and inalienable rights of liberty, the first permanent settlements of the English in America were established. From this period, the progress of the two provinces of Virginia and New England forms a regular and connected story. The former in the south, and the latter in the north, may be considered as the original and parent colonies; in imitation of which,

* Stith. Hist. of Virginia, p. 35 Append. p. 1. Purchas, v. 1683.

and under whose shelter, all the others have been successively planted and reared.

The first attempts to occupy Virginia and New England were made by very feeble bodies of emigrants. As these settled under great disadvantages, among tribes of savages, and in an uncultivated desert; as they attained gradually, after long struggles and many disasters, to that maturity of strength, and order of policy, which entitle them to be considered as respectable states, the history of their persevering efforts merits particular attention. It will exhibit a spectacle no less striking than instructive, and presents an opportunity which rarely occurs, of contemplating a society in the first moment of its political existence, and of observing how its spirit forms in its infant state, how its principles begin to unfold as it advances, and how those characteristic qualities which distinguish its maturer age are successively acquired. The account of the establishment of the other English colonies, undertaken at periods when the importance of such possessions was better understood, and effected by more direct and vigorous exertions of the parent state, is less interesting. I shall therefore relate the history of the two original colonies in detail. With respect to the subsequent settlements, some more general observations concerning the time, the motives, and circumstances of their establishment will be sufficient. I begin with the history of Virginia, the most ancient and most valuable of the British colonies in North America.

Though many persons of distinction became proprietors in the company which undertook to plant a colony in Virginia, its funds seem not to have been considerable, and its first effort was certainly extremely feeble. A small vessel of a hundred tons, and two barks, under the command of Captain Newport, sailed [Dec. 19] with a hundred and five men destined to remain in the country. Some of these were of respectable families, particularly a brother of the Earl of Northumberland, and several officers who had served with reputation in the reign of Elizabeth. Newport, I know not for what reason, followed the ancient course by the West Indies, and did not reach the coast of North America for four months [April 26, 1607]. But he approached it with better fortune than any former navigator; for, having been driven, by the violence of a storm, to the northward of Roanoke, the place of his destination, the first land he discovered was a promontory which he called Cape Henry, the southern boundary of the Bay of Chesapeak. The English stood directly into that spacious inlet, which seemed to invite them to enter; and as they advanced, contemplated, with a mixture of delight and admiration, that grand reservoir, into which are poured the waters of all the vast rivers, which not only diffuse fertility through that district of America, but open the interior parts of the country to navigation, and render a commercial intercourse more extensive and commodious than in any other region of the globe. Newport, keeping along the southern shore, sailed up a river which the natives called Powhatan, and to which he gave the name of James River. After viewing its banks, during a run of above forty miles from its mouth, they all concluded that a country, where safe and convenient harbours seemed to be numerous, would be a more suitable station for a trading colony than the shoaly and dangerous coast to the south, on which their countrymen had formerly settled. Here then they determined to abide; and having chosen a proper spot for their residence, they gave this infant settlement the name of James Town, which it still retains; and though it has never become either populous or opulent, it can boast of being the most ancient habitation of the English in the New World. But however well chosen the situation might be, the members of the colony were far from availing themselves of its advantages. Violent animosities had broke out among some of their leaders, during their voyage to Virginia. These did not subside on their arrival there The first deed of the council, which assumed the government in virtue of a commission brought from England under the seal of the company, and opened on the day after they landed, was an act of injustice. Captain Smith, who had been appointed a member of the council, was excluded from his seat at the board, by the mean jealousy of his colleagues, and not only reduced to the condition of a private man, but of one suspected and watched by his superiors. This diminution of his influence, and restraint on his activity, was an essential injury to the colony, which at that juncture stood in need of the aid of both. For soon after they began to settle, the English were involved in a war with the natives, partly by their own indiscretion, and partly by the suspicion and ferocity of those barbarians. And although the Indians, scattered over the countries adjacent to James River, were divided into independent tribes, so extremely feeble that hardly one of them could muster above two hundred warriors,* they teased and annoyed an infant colony by their incessant hostilities. To this was added a calamity still more dreadful; the stock of provisions left for their subsistence, on the departure of their ships for England [June 15], was so scanty and of such bad quality, that a scarcity, approaching almost to absolute famine, soon followed. Such poor unwholesome fare brought on diseases, the violence of which was so much increased by the sultry heat of the climate, and the moisture of a country covered with wood, that before the beginning of September one half of their number died, and most of the survivors were sickly and dejected. In such trying extremities, the comparative powers of every individual are discovered and called forth, and each naturally takes that station, and assumes that ascendant, to which he is entitled by his talents and force of mind. Every eye was now turned towards Smith, and all willingly devolved on him that authority of which they had formerly deprived him. His undaunted temper, deeply tinctured with the wild romantic spirit characteristic of military adventurers in that age, was peculiarly suited to such a situation. The vigour of his constitution continued fortunately still unimpaired by disease, and his mind was never appalled by danger. He instantly adopted the only plan that could save them from destruction. He began by surrounding James Town with such rude fortifications as were a sufficient defence against the assaults of savages. He then marched, at the head of a small detachment, in quest of their enemies. Some tribes he gained by caresses and presents, and procured from them a supply of provisions. Others he attacked with open force; and defeating them on every occasion, whatever their superiority in numbers might be, compelled them to impart to him some portion of their winter stores. As the recompense of all his toils and dangers, he saw abundance and contentment re-established in the colony, and hoped that he should be able to maintain them in that happy state, until the arrival of ships from England in the spring; but in one of his excursions he was surprised by a numerous body of Indians, and in making his escape from them, after a gallant defence, he sunk to the neck in a swamp, and was obliged to surrender. Though he knew well what a dreadful fate awaits the prisoners of savages, his presence of mind did not forsake him. He showed those who had taken him captive a mariner's compass, and amused them with so many wonderful accounts of its virtues as filled them with astonishment and veneration, which began to operate very powerfully in his favour. They led him, however, in triumph through various parts of the country, and conducted him at last to Powhatan, the most considerable Sachim in that part of Virginia. There the doom of death being pronounced, he was led to the place of execution, and his head already bowed down to receive the fatal blow, when that fond attachment of the American women to their Euro-

* Purchas, vol. iv. 1692. Smith's Travels, p. 23.

pean invaders, the beneficial effects of which the Spaniards often experienced, interposed in his behalf. The favourite daughter of Powhatan rushed in between him and the executioner, and by her entreaties and tears prevailed on her father to spare his life. The beneficence of his deliverer, whom the early English writers dignify with the title of the Princess Pocahuntas, did not terminate here; she soon after procured his liberty, and sent from time to time seasonable presents of provisions.*

Smith, on his return to James Town, found the colony reduced to thirty-eight persons, who, in despair were preparing to abandon a country which did not seem destined to be the habitation of Englishmen. He employed caresses, threats, and even violence, in order to prevent them from executing this fatal resolution. With difficulty he prevailed on them to defer it so long, that the succour anxiously expected from England arrived. Plenty was instantly restored; a hundred new planters were added to their number; and an ample stock of whatever was requisite for clearing and sowing the ground was delivered to them. But an unlucky incident turned their attention from that species of industry which alone could render their situation comfortable. In a small stream of water that issued from a bank of sand near James Town, a sediment of some shining mineral substance, which had some resemblance of gold, was discovered. At a time when the precious metals were conceived to be the peculiar and only valuable productions of the New World, when every mountain was supposed to contain a treasure, and every rivulet was searched for its golden sands, this appearance was fondly considered as an infallible indication of a mine. Every hand was eager to dig; large quantities of this glittering dust were amassed. From some assay of its nature, made by an artist as unskilful as his companions were credulous, it was pronounced to be extremely rich. "There was now," says Smith, "no talk, no hope, no work, but dig gold, wash gold, refine gold."† With this imaginary wealth the first vessel returning to England was loaded, while the culture of the land and every useful occupation were totally neglected.

The effects of this fatal delusion were soon felt. Notwithstanding all the provident activity of Smith, in procuring corn from the natives by traffic or by force, the colony began to suffer as much as formerly from scarcity of food, and was wasted by the same distempers. In hopes of obtaining some relief, Smith proposed, as they had not hitherto extended their researches beyond the countries contiguous to James River, to open an intercourse with the more remote tribes, and to examine into the state of culture and population among them. The execution of this arduous design he undertook himself, in a small open boat, with a feeble crew, and a very scanty stock of provisions. He began his survey at Cape Charles, and in two different excursions, which continued above four months, he advanced as far as the river Susquehannah, which flows into the bottom of the bay. He visited all the countries both on the east and west shores; he entered most of the considerable creeks; he sailed up many of the great rivers as far as their falls. He traded with some tribes; he fought with others; he observed the nature of the territory which they occupied, their mode of subsistence, the peculiarities in their manners; and left among all a wonderful admiration either of the beneficence or valour of the English. After sailing above three thousand miles in a paltry vessel, ill fitted for such an extensive navigation, during which the hardships to which he was exposed, as well as the patience with which he endured, and the fortitude with which he surmounted them, equal whatever is related of the celebrated Spanish discoverers in their most daring enterprises, he returned to James Town; he brought with him an account of that large portion of the

* Smith's Travels, p. 44, &c. Purchas, iv. 1704. Stith, p. 45, &c. † Smith's Travels, p. 53

American continent now comprehended in the two provinces of Virginia and Maryland,* so full and exact, that after the progress of information and research for a century and a half, his map exhibits no inaccurate view of both countries, and is the original upon which all subsequent delineations and descriptions have been formed.†

But whatever pleasing prospect of future benefit might open upon this complete discovery of a country formed by nature to be the seat of an exclusive commerce, it afforded but little relief for their present wants. The colony still depended for subsistence chiefly on supplies from the natives; as, after all the efforts of their own industry, hardly thirty acres of ground were yet cleared so as to be capable of culture.‡ By Smith's attention, however, the stores of the English were so regularly filled that for some time they felt no considerable distress; and at this juncture a change was made in the constitution of the company, which seemed to promise an increase of their security and happiness. That supreme direction of all the company's operations, which the King by his charter had reserved to himself, discouraged persons of rank or property from becoming members of a society so dependent on the arbitrary will of the crown. Upon a representation of this to James, he granted them a new charter [May 23, 1609], with more ample privileges. He enlarged the boundaries of the colony; he rendered the powers of the company, as a corporation, more explicit and complete; he abolished the jurisdiction of the council resident in Virginia; he vested the government entirely in a council residing in London; he granted to the proprietors of the company the right of electing the persons who were to compose this council, by a majority of voices; he authorized this council to establish such laws, orders, and forms of government and magistracy, for the colony and plantation, as they in their discretion should think to be fittest for the good of the adventurers and inhabitants there; he empowered them to nominate a governor to have the administration of affairs in the colony; and to carry their orders into execution.§ In consequence of these concessions, the company having acquired the power of regulating all its own transactions, the number of proprietors increased, and among them we find the most respectable names in the nation.

The first deed of the new council was to appoint Lord Delaware governor and captain-general of their colony in Virginia. To a person of his rank those high sounding titles could be no allurement; and by his thorough acquaintance with the progress and state of the settlement, he knew enough of the labour and difficulty with which an infant colony is reared, to expect any thing but anxiety and care in discharging the duties of that delicate office. But, from zeal to promote an establishment which he expected to prove so highly beneficial to his country, he was willing to relinquish all the comforts of an honourable station, to undertake a long voyage to settle in an uncultivated region, destitute of every accommodation to which he had been accustomed, and where he foresaw that toil, and trouble, and danger awaited him. But as he could not immediately leave England, the council despatched Sir Thomas Gates and Sir George Summers, the former of whom had been appointed lieutenant-general and the latter admiral, with nine ships and five hundred planters. They carried with them commissions by which they were empowered to supersede the jurisdiction of the former council, to proclaim Lord Delaware governor, and until he should arrive, to take the administration of affairs into their own hands. A violent hurricane separated the vessel in which Gates and Summers had embarked from the rest of the fleet, and stranded it on the coast of Bermudas [Aug. 11]. The other ships arrived safely at James Town. But the fate of their commanders was unknown. Their

* Smith's Travels, p. 65. &c † Stith, p. 83 ‡ Ibid p 97. § Ibid. Append. 8.

commission for new modelling the government, and all other public papers, were supposed to be lost together with them. The present form of government, however, was held to be abolished. No legal warrant could be produced for establishing any other. Smith was not in a condition at this juncture to assert his own rights, or to act with his wonted vigour. By an accidental explosion of gunpowder, he had been so miserably scorched and mangled that he was incapable of moving, and under the necessity of committing himself to the guidance of his friends, who carried him aboard one of the ships returning to England, in hopes that he might recover by more skilful treatment than he could meet with in Virginia.*

After his departure, every thing tended fast to the wildest anarchy. Faction and discontent had often risen so high among the old settlers that they could hardly be kept within bounds. The spirit of the new comers was too ungovernable to bear any restraint. Several among them of better rank were such dissipated hopeless young men, as their friends were glad to send out in quest of whatever fortune might betide them in a foreign land. Of the lower order many were so profligate, or desperate, that their country was happy to throw them out as nuisances in society. Such persons were little capable of the regular subordination, the strict economy, and persevering industry, which their situation required. The Indians observing their misconduct, and that every precaution for sustenance or safety was neglected, not only withheld the supplies of provisions which they were accustomed to furnish, but harassed them with continual hostilities. All their subsistence was derived from the stores which they had brought from England; these were soon consumed; then the domestic animals sent out to breed in the country were devoured; and by this inconsiderate waste, they were reduced to such extremity of famine, as no only to eat the most nauseous and unwholesome roots and berries, but to feed on the bodies of the Indians whom they slew, and even on those of their companions who sunk under the oppression of such complicated distress. In less than six months, of five hundred persons whom Smith left in Virginia, only sixty remained; and these so feeble and dejected that they could not have survived for ten days, if succour had not arrived from a quarter whence they did not expect it.†

When Gates and Summers were thrown ashore on Bermudas, fortunately not a single person on board their ship perished. A considerable part of their provisions and stores too, was saved, and in that delightful spot, Nature, with spontaneous bounty, presented to them such a variety of her productions, that a hundred and fifty people subsisted in affluence for ten months on an uninhabited island. Impatient, however, to escape from a place where they were cut off from all intercourse with mankind, they set about building two barks with such tools and materials as they had, and by amazing efforts of perseverance and ingenuity they finished them. In these they embarked, and steered directly towards Virginia, in hopes of finding an ample consolation for all their toils and dangers in the embraces of their companions, and amidst the comforts of a flourishing colony. After a more prosperous navigation than they could have expected in their ill constructed vessels, they landed at James Town [May 23]. But instead of that joyful interview for which they fondly looked, a spectacle presented itself which struck them with horror. They beheld the miserable remainder of their countrymen emaciated with famine and sickness, sunk in despair, and in their figure and looks rather resembling spectres than human beings. As Gates and Summers, in full confidence of finding plenty of provisions in Virginia, had brought with them no larger stock than was

* Purchas, iv. 1734, &c. Smith's Travels, p. 89. Stith, p. 102, &c. Purchas, iv. 1748

† Stith, p. 116

deemed necessary for their own support during the voyage, their inability to afford relief to their countrymen added to the anguish with which they viewed this unexpected scene of distress. Nothing now remained but instantly to abandon a country where it was impossible to subsist any longer; and though all that could be found in the stores of the colony when added to what remained of the stock brought from Bermudas, did not amount to more than what was sufficient to support them for sixteen days, at the most scanty allowance, they set sail, in hopes of being able to reach Newfoundland, where they expected to be relieved by their countrymen employed at that season in the fishery there.*

But it was not the will of Heaven that all the labour of the English, in planting this colony, as well as all their hopes of benefit from its future prosperity, should be for ever lost. Before Gates and the melancholy companions of his voyage had reached the mouth of James River, they were met by Lord Delaware with three ships, that brought a large recruit of provisions, a considerable number of new settlers, and every thing requisite for defence or cultivation. By persuasion and authority he prevailed on them to return to James Town, where they found their fort, their magazines, and houses entire, which Sir Thomas Gates, by some happy chance, had preserved from being set on fire at the time of their departure. A society so feeble and disordered in its frame required a tender and skilful hand to cherish it, and restore its vigour. This it found in Lord Delaware: he searched into the causes of their misfortunes, as far as he could discover them, amidst the violence of their mutual accusations; but instead of exerting his power in punishing crimes that were past, he employed his prudence in healing their dissensions, and in guarding against a repetition of the same fatal errors. By unwearied assiduities, by the respect due to an amiable and beneficent character, by knowing how to mingle severity with indulgence, and when to assume the dignity of his office, as well as when to display the gentleness natural to his own temper, he gradually reconciled men corrupted by anarchy to subordination and discipline, he turned the attention of the idle and profligate to industry, and taught the Indians again to reverence and dread the English name. Under such an administration, the colony began once more to assume a promising appearance; when unhappily for it, a complication of diseases brought on by the climate obliged Lord Delaware to quit the country† [March 28, 1611]; the government of which he committed to Mr. Percy.

He was soon superseded by the arrival [May 10] of Sir Thomas Dale; in whom the company had vested more absolute authority than in any of his predecessors, empowering him to rule by martial law; a short code of which, founded on the practice of the armies in the Low Countries, the most rigid military school at that time in Europe, they sent out with him. This system of government is so violent and arbitrary, that even the Spaniards themselves had not ventured to introduce it into their settlements; for among them, as soon as a plantation began, and the arts of peace succeeded to the operations of war, the jurisdiction of the civil magistrate was uniformly established. But however unconstitutional or oppressive this may appear, it was adopted by the advice of Sir Francis Bacon, the most enlightened philosopher, and one of the most eminent lawyers of the age.‡ The company, well acquainted with the inefficacy of every method which they had hitherto employed for restraining the unruly mutinous spirits which they had to govern, eagerly adopted a plan that had the sanction of such high authority to recommend it. Happily for the colony, Sir Thomas Dale, who was intrusted with this dangerous power, exercised

* A minute and curious account of the shipwreck of Gates and Summers, and of their adventures in Bermudas, was composed by Strachy, a gentleman who accompanied them, and was published by Purchas, iv. 1734.

† Stith, p. 117. Purchas, iv. 1764.

‡ Bacon, Essay on Plantations, p. 3.

it with prudence and moderation. By the vigour which the summary mode of military punishment gave to his administration, he introduced into the colony more perfect order than had ever been established there; and at the same time he tempered his vigour with so much discretion, that no alarm seems to have been given by this formidable innovation.*

The regular form which the colony now began to assume induced the king to issue a new charter for the encouragement of the adventurers [March 12, 1612], by which he not only confirmed all their former privileges, and prolonged the term of exemption from payment of duties on the commodities exported by them, but granted them more extensive property, as well as more ample jurisdiction. All the islands lying within three hundred leagues of the coast were annexed to the province of Virginia. In consequence of this, the company took possession of Bermudas and the other small islands discovered by Gates and Summers, and at the same time prepared to send out a considerable reinforcement to the colony at James Town. The expense of those extraordinary efforts was defrayed by the profits of a lottery, which amounted nearly to thirty thousand pounds. This expedient they were authorized to employ by their new charter;† and it is remarkable, as the first instance in the English history of any public countenance given to this pernicious seducing mode of levying money. But the House of Commons, which towards the close of this reign began to observe every measure of government with jealous attention, having remonstrated against the institution, as unconstitutional and impolitic, James recalled the license under the sanction of which it had been established.‡

By the severe discipline of martial law, the activity of the colonists was forced into a proper direction, and exerted itself in useful industry. This, aided by a fertile soil and favourable climate, soon enabled them to raise such a large stock of provisions, that they were no longer obliged to trust for subsistence to the precarious supplies which they obtained or extorted from the Indians. In proportion as the English became more independent, the natives courted their friendship upon more equal terms. The happy effects of this were quickly felt. Sir Thomas Dale concluded a treaty with one of their most powerful and warlike tribes, situated on the river Chickahominy, in which they consented to acknowledge themselves subjects to the King of Great Britain, to assume henceforth the name of Englishmen, to send a body of their warriors to the assistance of the English as often as they took the field against any enemy, and to deposite annually a stipulated quantity of Indian corn in the storehouses of the colony.§ An event, which the early historians of Virginia relate with peculiar satisfaction, prepared the way for this union. Pocahuntas, the favourite daughter of the great Chief Powhatan, to whose intercession Captain Smith was indebted for his life, persevered in her partial attachment to the English; and as she frequently visited their settlements, where she was always received with respectful hospitality, her admiration of their arts and manners continued to increase. During this intercourse, her beauty, which is represented as far superior to that of her countrywomen, made such impression on the heart of Mr. Rolfe, a young man of rank in the colony, that he warmly solicited her to accept of him as a husband. Where manners are simple, courtship is not tedious. Neither artifice prevents, nor ceremony forbids, the heart from declaring its sentiments Pocahuntas readily gave her consent; Dale encouraged the alliance, and Powhatan did not disapprove it. The marriage was celebrated with extraordinary pomp; and from that period a friendly correspondence subsisted between the colony and all the tribes subject to Powhatan, or that stood in awe of his power. Rolfe and his princess (for by that name the

* Stith, p. 112. † Ib. p. 191. Appendix, 23, &c. ‡ Chalmers' Annals, i. 32.
§ Hamer Solida Narratio, ap. de Bry, pars x. p. 33. Stith, p. 130.

writers of the last age always distinguish her,) set out for England, where she was received by James and his Queen with the respect suited to her birth. Being carefully instructed in the principles of the Christian faith, she was publicly baptized, but died a few years after, on her return to America, leaving one son, from whom are sprung some of the most respectable families in Virginia, who boast of their descent from the race of the ancient rulers of their country.* But notwithstanding the visible good effects of that alliance, none of Rolfe's countrymen seem to have imitated the example which he set them, of intermarrying with the natives. Of all the Europeans who have settled in America, the English have availed themselves the least of this obvious method of conciliating the affection of its original inhabitants; and, either from the shyness conspicuous in their national character, or from the want of that pliant facility of manners which accommodates itself to every situation, they have been more averse than the French and Portuguese, or even the Spaniards, from incorporating with the native Americans. The Indians, courting such a union, offered their daughters in marriage to their new guests: and when they did not accept of the proffered alliance, they naturally imputed it to pride, and to their contempt of them as an inferior order of beings.†

During the interval of tranquillity procured by the alliance with Powhatan, an important change was made in the state of the colony. Hitherto no right of private property in land had been established. The fields that were cleared had been cultivated by the joint labour of the colonists; their product was carried to the common storehouses, and distributed weekly to every family, according to its number and exigencies. A society, destitute of the first advantages resulting from social union, was not formed to prosper. Industry, when not excited by the idea of property in what was acquired by its own efforts, made no vigorous exertion. The head had no inducement to contrive, nor the hand to labour. The idle and improvident trusted entirely to what was issued from the common store; the assiduity even of the sober and attentive relaxed, when they perceived that others were to reap the fruit of their toil; and it was computed, that the united industry of the colony did not accomplish as much work in a week as might have been performed in a day, if each individual had laboured on his own account. In order to remedy this, Sir Thomas Dale divided a considerable portion of the land into small lots, and granted one of these to each individual in full property. From the moment that industry had the certain prospect of a recompense, it advanced with rapid progress. The articles of primary necessity were cultivated with so much attention as secured the means of subsistence; and such schemes of improvement were formed as prepared the way for the introduction of opulence into the colony.‡

The industrious spirit which began to rise among the planters was soon directed towards a new object; and they applied to it for some time with such inconsiderate ardour as was productive of fatal consequences. The culture of tobacco, which has since become the staple of Virginia, and the source of its prosperity, was introduced about this time [1616], into the colony. As the taste for that weed continued to increase in England, notwithstanding the zealous declamations of James against it, the tobacco imported from Virginia came to a ready market; and though it was so much inferior in quality or in estimation to that raised by the Spaniards in the West Indian islands, that a pound of the latter sold for eighteen shillings and of the former for no more than three shillings, it yielded a considerable profit. Allured by the prospect of such a certain and quick return, every other species of industry was neglected. The land which ought to have been reserved for raising provisions, and even the streets of James Town,

* Hamer Solida Narratio, ap. de Bry, pars x. p. 23. Stith, p. 129. 146. Smith's Travels, p. 113. 121. † Beverley's Hist. of Virg. p. 25. ‡ Smith's Travels, p. 114. Stith, p. 131.

were planted with tobacco. Various regulations were framed to restrain this ill directed activity. But, from eagerness for present gain, the planters disregarded every admonition. The means of subsistence became so scanty, as forced them to renew their demands upon the Indians, who seeing no end of those exactions, their antipathy to the English name revived with additional rancour, and they began to form schemes of vengeance, with a secrecy and silence peculiar to Americans.*

Meanwhile the colony, notwithstanding this error in its operations, and the cloud that was gathering over its head, continued to wear an aspect of prosperity. Its numbers increased by successive migrations; the quantity of tobacco exported became every year more considerable, and several of the planters were not only in an easy situation, but advancing fast to opulence;† and by two events, which happened nearly at the same time, both population and industry were greatly promoted. As few women had hitherto ventured to encounter the hardships which were unavoidable in an unknown and uncultivated country, most of the colonists, constrained to live single, considered themselves as no more than sojourners in a land to which they were not attached by the tender ties of a family and children. In order to induce them to settle there, the company took advantage of the apparent tranquillity in the country, to send out a considerable number of young women of humble birth indeed, but of unexceptionable character, and encouraged the planters, by premiums and immunities, to marry them.‡ These new companions were received with such fondness, and many of them so comfortably established, as invited others to follow their example; and by degrees thoughtless adventurers, assuming the sentiments of virtuous citizens and of provident fathers of families, became solicitous about the prosperity of a country which they now considered as their own. As the colonists began to form more extensive plans of industry, they were unexpectedly furnished with means of executing them with greater facility. A Dutch ship from the coast of Guinea, having sailed up James River, sold a part of her cargo of Negroes to the planters;§ and as that hardy race was found more capable of enduring fatigue under a sultry climate than Europeans, their number has been increased by continual importation; their aid seems now to be essential to the existence of the colony, and the greater part of field labour in Virginia is performed by servile hands.

But as the condition of the colony improved, the spirits of its members became more independent. To Englishmen the summary and severe decisions of martial law, however tempered by the mildness of their governors, appeared intolerably oppressive; and they longed to recover the privileges to which they had been accustomed under the liberal form of government in their native country. In compliance with this spirit, Sir George Yeardly, in the year 1619 [June], called the first general assembly that was ever held in Virginia; and the numbers of the people were now so increased, and their settlements so dispersed, that eleven corporations appeared by their representatives in this convention, where they were permitted to assume legislative power, and to exercise the noblest functions of free men. The laws enacted in it seem neither to have been many nor of great importance; but the meeting was highly acceptable to the people, as they now beheld among themselves an image of the English constitution, which they reverenced as the most perfect model of free government. In order to render this resemblance more complete, and the rights of the planters more certain, the company issued a charter of ordinance [July 24], which gave a legal and permanent form to the government of the colony. The supreme legislative authority in Virginia, in imitation of that in Great Britain, was divided and lodged partly in the governor, who held the

* Stith, p. 140. 147. 164. 168. Smith, p. 130. Purchas, iv 1787. † Smith, p. 139
‡ Stith, p. 166. 197. § Beverley, p. 37.

place of the sovereign; partly in a council of state named by the company, which possessed some of the distinctions, and exercised some of the functions belonging to the peerage; partly in a general council or assembly composed of the representatives of the people, in which were vested powers and privileges similar to those of the House of Commons. In both these councils all questions were to be determined by the majority of voices, and a negative was reserved to the governor; but no law or ordinance, though approved of by all the three members of the legislature, was to be of force until it was ratified in England by a general court of the company, and returned under its seal.* Thus the constitution of the colony was fixed, and the members of it are henceforth to be considered, not merely as servants of a commercial company dependent on the will and orders of their superior, but as free men and citizens.

The natural effect of that happy change in their condition was an increase of their industry. The product of tobacco in Virginia was now equal, not only to the consumption of it in Great Britain,† but could furnish some quantity for a foreign market. The company opened a trade for it with Holland, and established warehouses for it in Middelburg and Flushing. James and his privy council, alarmed at seeing the commerce of a commodity, for which the demand was daily increasing, turned into a channel that tended to the diminution of the revenue, by depriving it of a considerable duty imposed on the importation of tobacco, interposed with vigour to check this innovation. Some expedient was found, by which the matter was adjusted for the present; but it is remarkable as the first instance of a difference in sentiment between the parent state and the colony, concerning their respective rights. The former concluded, that the trade of the colony should be confined to England, and all its productions be landed there. The latter claimed, not only the general privilege of Englishmen to carry their commodities to the best market, but pleaded the particular concessions in their charter, by which an unlimited freedom of commerce seemed to be granted to them.‡ The time for a more full discussion of this important question was not yet arrived.

But while the colony continued to increase so fast that settlements were scattered, not only along the banks of James and York rivers, but began to extend to the Rapahannock, and even to the Potowmack, the English, relying on their own numbers, and deceived by this appearance of prosperity, lived in full security. They neither attended to the movements of the Indians, nor suspected their machinations; and though surrounded by a people whom they might have known from experience to be both artful and vindictive, they neglected every precaution for their own safety that was requisite in such a situation. Like the peaceful inhabitants of a society completely established, they were no longer soldiers but citizens, and were so intent on what was subservient to the comfort or embellishment of civil life that every martial exercise began to be laid aside as unnecessary. The Indians, whom they commonly employed as hunters, were furnished with fire arms, and taught to use them with dexterity. They were permitted to frequent the habitations of the English at all hours, and received as innocent visitants whom there was no reason to dread. This inconsiderate security enabled the Indians to prepare for the execution of

* Stith, Appendix, p. 32, &c.

† It is a matter of some curiosity to trace the progress of the consumption of this unnecessary commodity. The use of tobacco seems to have been first introduced into England about the year 1586. Possibly a few seafaring persons may have acquired a relish for it by their intercourse with the Spaniards previous to that period; but the use of it cannot be denominated a national habit sooner than the time I have mentioned. Upon an average of the seven years immediately preceding the year 1622, the whole import of tobacco into England amounted to a hundred and forty-two thousand and eighty-five pounds weight. Stith, p. 246. From this it appears, that the taste had spread with a rapidity which is remarkable. But how inconsiderable is that quantity to what is now consumed in Great Britain!

‡ Stith, p. 200, &c.

that plan of vengeance, which they meditated with all the deliberate forethought which is agreeable to their temper. Nor did they want a leader capable of conducting their schemes with address. On the death of Powhatan, in the year 1618, Opechancanough succeeded him, not only as wirowanee, or chief of his own tribe, but in that extensive influence over all the Indian nations of Virginia, which induced the English writers to distinguish him by the name of Emperor. According to the Indian tradition, he was not a native of Virginia, but came from a distant country to the south-west, possibly from some province of the Mexican empire.* But as he was conspicuous for all the qualities of highest estimation among savages, a fearless courage, great strength and agility of body, and crafty policy, he quickly rose to eminence and power.—Soon after his elevation to the supreme command, a general massacre of the English seems to have been resolved upon; and during four years, the means of perpetrating it with the greatest facility and success were concerted with amazing secrecy All the tribes contiguous to the English settlements were successively gained, except those on the eastern shore, from whom, on account of their peculiar attachment to their new neighbours, every circumstance that might discover what they intended was carefully concealed. To each tribe its station was allotted, and the part it was to act prescribed. On the morning of the day consecrated to vengeance [March 22], each was at the place of rendezvous appointed, while the English were so little aware of the impending destruction that they received with unsuspicious hospitality several persons sent by Opechancanough, under pretext of delivering presents of venison and fruits, but in reality to observe their motions. Finding them perfectly secure, at midday, the moment that was previously fixed for this deed of horror, the Indians rushed at once upon them in all their different settlements, and murdered men, women, and children, with undistinguishing rage, and that rancorous cruelty with which savages treat their enemies. In one hour nearly a fourth part of the whole colony was cut off, almost without knowing by whose hands they fell. The slaughter would have been universal, if compassion, or a sense of duty, had not moved a converted Indian, to whom the secret was communicated the night before the massacre, to reveal it to his master in such time as to save James Town and some adjacent settlements; and if the English in other districts had not run to their arms with resolution prompted by despair, and defended themselves so bravely as to repulse their assailants, who, in the execution of their plan, did not discover courage equal to the sagacity and art with which they had concerted it.†

But though the blow was thus prevented from descending with its full effect, it proved very grievous to an infant colony. In some settlements not a single Englishman escaped. Many persons of prime note in the colony, and among these several members of the council, were slain. The survivors, overwhelmed with grief, astonishment, and terror, abandoned all their remote settlements, and, crowding together for safety to James Town, did not occupy a territory of greater extent than had been planted soon after the arrival of their countrymen in Virginia. Confined within those narrow boundaries, they were less intent on schemes of industry than on thoughts of revenge. Every man took arms. A bloody war against the Indians commenced; and, bent on exterminating the whole race, neither old nor young were spared. The conduct of the Spaniards in the southern regions of America was openly proposed as the most proper model to imitate;‡ and regardless, like them, of those principles of faith, honour, and humanity, which regulate hostility among civilized nations and set bounds to its rage, the English deemed every thing allowable that tended to accomplish their design. They hunted the Indians like wild

* Beverley, p. 51. † Stith, p. 208, &c. Purchas, iv. 1788, &c ‡ Stith, p. 233.

beasts rather than enemies; and as the pursuit of them to their places of retreat in the woods, which covered their country, was both difficult and dangerous, they endeavoured to allure them from their inaccessible fastness by offers of peace and promises of oblivion, made with such an artful appearance of sincerity as deceived their crafty leader, and induced them to return to their former settlements, and resume their usual peaceful occupations [1623]. The behaviour of the two people seemed now to be perfectly reversed. The Indians, like men acquainted with the principles of integrity and good faith, on which the intercourse between nations is founded, confided in the reconciliation, and lived in absolute security without suspicion of danger; while the English, with perfidious craft, were preparing to imitate savages in their revenge and cruelty. On the approach of harvest, when they knew a hostile attack would be most formidable and fatal, they fell suddenly upon all the Indian plantations, murdered every person on whom they could lay hold, and drove the rest to the woods, where so many perished with hunger, that some of the tribes nearest to the English were totally extirpated. This atrocious deed, which the perpetrators laboured to represent as a necessary act of retaliation, was followed by some happy effects. It delivered the colony so entirely from any dread of the Indians, that its settlements began again to extend, and its industry to revive.

But unfortunately at this juncture the state of the company in England, in which the property of Virginia and the government of the colony settled there were vested, prevented it from seconding the efforts of the planters, by such a reinforcement of men, and such a supply of necessaries, as were requisite to replace what they had lost. The company was originally composed of many adventurers, and increased so fast by the junction of new members, allured by the prospect of gain, or the desire of promoting a scheme of public utility, that its general courts formed a numerous assembly.* The operation of every political principle and passion, that spread through the kingdom, was felt in those popular meetings, and influenced their decisions. As towards the close of James's reign more just and enlarged sentiments with respect to constitutional liberty were diffused among the people, they came to understand their rights better and to assert them with greater boldness; a distinction formerly little known, but now familiar in English policy, began to be established between the court and country parties, and the leaders of each endeavoured to derive power and consequence from every quarter. Both exerted themselves with emulation, in order to obtain the direction of a body so numerous and respectable as the company of Virginian adventurers. In consequence of this, business had been conducted in every general court for some years, not with the temperate spirit of merchants deliberating concerning their mutual interest, but with the animosity and violence natural to numerous assemblies, by which rival factions contend for superiority.†

As the king did not often assemble the great council of the nation in parliament, the general courts of the company became a theatre on which popular orators displayed their talents; the proclamations of the crown, and acts of the privy council, with respect to the commerce and police of the colony, were canvassed there with freedom, and censured with severity, ill suited to the lofty ideas which James entertained of his own wisdom, and the extent of his prerogative. In order to check this growing spirit of discussion, the ministers employed all their address and influence to gain as many members of the company as might give them the direction of their deliberations. But so unsuccessful were they in this attempt, that every measure proposed by them was reprobated by a vast majority,

* Stith, p. 272. 276. † Ibid. p. 229, &c. Chalmers, p. 59.

and sometimes without any reason but because they were the proposers of it. James, little favourable to the power of any popular assembly, and weary of contending with one over which he had laboured in vain to obtain an ascendant, began to entertain thoughts of dissolving the company, and new modelling its constitution. Pretexts, neither unplausible nor destitute of some foundation, seemed to justify this measure. The slow progress of the colony, the large sums of money expended, and great number of men who had perished in attempting to plant it, the late massacre by the Indians, and every disaster that had befallen the English from their first migration to America, were imputed solely to the inability of a numerous company to conduct an enterprise so complex and arduous. The nation felt sensibly its disappointment in a scheme in which it had engaged with sanguine expectations of advantage, and wished impatiently for such an impartial scrutiny into former proceedings as might suggest more salutary measures in the future administration of the colony. The present state of its affairs, as well as the wishes of the people, seemed to call for the interposition of the crown; and James, eager to display the superiority of his royal wisdom, in correcting those errors into which the company had been betrayed by inexperience in the arts of government, boldly undertook the work of reformation [May 9, 1623]. Without regarding the rights conveyed to the company by their charter, and without the formality of any judicial proceeding for annulling it, he, by virtue of his prerogative, issued a commission, empowering some of the judges, and other persons of note, to examine into all the transactions of the company from its first establishment, and to lay the result of their inquiries, together with their opinion concerning the most effectual means of rendering the colony more prosperous,* before the privy council. At the same time, by a strain of authority still higher, he ordered all the records and papers of the company to be seized, and two of its principal officers to be arrested. Violent and arbitrary as these acts of authority may now appear, the commissioners carried on their inquiry without any obstruction, but what arose from some feeble and ineffectual remonstrances of the company. The commissioners, though they conducted their scrutiny with much activity and vigour,† did not communicate any of their proceedings to the company; but their report, with respect to its operations, seems to have been very unfavourable, as the king, in consequence of it, signified to the company [Oct. 8], his intention of vesting the supreme government of the company in a governor and twelve assistants, to be resident in England, and the executive power in a council of twelve, which should reside in Virginia. The governor and assistants were to be originally appointed by the king. Future vacancies were to be supplied by the governor and his assistants, but their nomination was not to take effect until it should be ratified by the privy council. The twelve counsellors in Virginia were to be chosen by the governor and assistants; and this choice was likewise subjected to the review of the privy council. With an intention to quiet the minds of the colonists, it was declared that private property should be deemed sacred; and for the more effectual security of it, all grants of lands from the former company were to be confirmed by the new one. In order to facilitate the execution of this plan, the king required the company instantly to surrender its charter into his hands.‡

But here James and his ministers encountered a spirit of which they seem not to have been aware. They found the members of the company unwilling tamely to relinquish rights of franchises, conveyed to them with such legal formality, that upon faith in their validity they had expended considerable sums;§ and still more averse to the abolition of a popular form of government, in which every proprietor had a voice, in order to

* Stith, p. 288. † Smith's Travels, p. 165, &c. ‡ Stith, p 293, &c. § Chalmers, p. 61.

subject a colony, in which they were deeply interested, to the dominion of a small junto absolutely dependent on the crown. Neither promises nor threats could induce them to depart from these sentiments; and in a general court [Oct. 20], the king's proposal was almost unanimously rejected, and a resolution taken to defend to the utmost their chartered rights, if these should be called in question in any court of justice. James, highly offended at their presumption in daring to oppose his will, directed [Nov. 10] a writ of *quo warranto* to be issued against the company, that the validity of its charter might be tried in the Court of King's Bench; and in order to aggravate the charge, by collecting additional proofs of mal-administration, he appointed some persons in whom he could confide, to repair to Virginia to inspect the state of the colony, and inquire into the conduct of the company, and of its officers there.

The lawsuit in the King's Bench did not hang long in suspense. It terminated, as was usual in that reign, in a decision perfectly consonant to the wishes of the monarch. The charter was forfeited, the company was dissolved [June, 1624], and all the rights and privileges conferred upon it returned to the King, from whom they flowed.*

Some writers, particularly Stith, the most intelligent and best informed historian of Virginia, mention the dissolution of the company as a most disastrous event to the colony. Animated with liberal sentiments, imbibed in an age when the principles of liberty were more fully unfolded than under the reign of James, they viewed his violent and arbitrary proceedings on this occasion with such indignation that their abhorrence of the means which he employed to accomplish his designs, seems to have rendered them incapable of contemplating its effects with discernment and candour. There is not perhaps any mode of governing an infant colony less friendly to its liberty than the dominion of an exclusive corporation possessed of all the powers which James had conferred upon the company of adventurers in Virginia. During several years the colonists can hardly be considered in any other light than as servants to the company, nourished out of its stores, bound implicitly to obey its orders, and subjected to the most rigorous of all forms of government, that of martial law. Even after the native spirit of Englishmen began to rouse under oppression, and had extorted from their superiors the right of enacting laws for the government of that community of which they were members, as no act, though approved of by all the branches of the provincial legislature, was held to be of legal force until it was ratified by a general court in England, the company still retained the paramount authority in its own hands. Nor was the power of the company more favourable to the prosperity of the colony than to its freedom. A numerous body of merchants, as long as its operations are purely commercial, may carry them on with discernment and success. But the mercantile spirit seems ill adapted to conduct an enlarged and liberal plan of civil policy, and colonies have seldom grown up to maturity and vigour under its narrow and interested regulations. To the unavoidable effects in administration which this occasioned, were added errors arising from inexperience. The English merchants of that age had not those extensive views which a general commerce opens to such as have the direction of it. When they first began to venture out of the beaten track, they groped their way with timidity and hesitation. Unacquainted with the climate and soil of America, and ignorant of the productions best suited to them, they seem to have had no settled plan of improvement, and their schemes were continually varying. Their system of government was equally fluctuating. In the course of eighteen years ten different persons presided over the province as chief governors. No wonder that, under such administration, all the efforts to give vigour and stability to the

* Rymer, vol. xvii. p. 618, &c. Chalmers, p. 62.

colony should prove abortive, or produce only slender effects. These efforts, however, when estimated according to the ideas of that age, either with respect to commerce or to policy, were very considerable, and conducted with astonishing perseverance.

Above a hundred and fifty thousand pounds were expended in this first attempt to plant an English colony in America;* and more than nine thousand persons were sent out from the mother country to people this new settlement. At the dissolution of the company, the nation, in return for this waste of treasure and of people, did not receive from Virginia an annual importation of commodities exceeding twenty thousand pounds in value; and the colony was so far from having added strength to the state by an increase of population, that in the year one thousand six hundred and twenty-four, scarcely two thousand persons survived;† a wretched remnant of the numerous emigrants who had flocked thither with sanguine expectations of a very different fate.

The company, like all unprosperous societies, fell unpitied. The violent hand with which prerogative had invaded its rights was forgotten, and new prospects of success opened, under a form of government exempt from all the defects to which past disasters were imputed. The King and the nation concurred with equal ardour in resolving to encourage the colony. Soon after the final judgment in the Court of King's Bench against the company, James appointed a council of twelve persons [Aug. 26], to take the temporary direction of affairs in Virginia that he might have leisure to frame with deliberate consideration proper regulations for the permanent government of the colony.‡ Pleased with such an opportunity of exercising his talents as a legislator, he began to turn his attention towards the subject; but death prevented him from completing his plan.

Charles I., on his accession to the throne [March 27, 1625], adopted all his father's maxims with respect to the colony in Virginia. He declared it to be a part of the empire annexed to the crown, and immediately subordinate to its jurisdiction: he conferred the title of Governor on Sir George Yardely, and appointed him, in conjunction with a council of twelve, and a secretary, to exercise supreme authority there, and enjoined them to conform, in every point, to such instructions as from time to time they might receive from him.§ From the tenor of the king's commission, as well as from the known spirit of his policy, it is apparent that he intended to invest every power of government, both legislative and executive, in the governor and council, without recourse to the representatives of the people, as possessing a right to enact laws for the community, or to impose taxes upon it.—Yardely and his council, who seem to have been fit instruments for carrying this system of arbitrary rule into execution, did not fail to put such a construction on the words of their commission as was most favourable to their own jurisdiction. During a great part of Charles's reign, Virginia knew no other law than the will of the Sovereign. Statutes were published and taxes imposed, without once calling the representatives of the people to authorize them by their sanction. At the same time that the colonists were bereaved of their political rights, which they deemed essential to freemen and citizens, their private property was violently invaded. A proclamation was issued, by which, under pretexts equally absurd and frivolous, they were prohibited from selling tobacco to any person but certain commissioners appointed by the king to purchase it on his account;‖ and they had the cruel mortification to behold the sovereign, who should have afforded them protection, engross all the profits of their industry, by seizing the only valuable commodity which they had to vend, and retaining the monopoly of it in his own hands. While the staple of the colony

* Smith's Travels, p. 42. 167. † Chalmers' Annals, p. 69. ‡ Rymer, xvii 618, &c
§ Ibid. xviii. 72. 311. ‖ Ibid. xviii. 19.

in Virginia sunk in value under the oppression and restraints of a monopoly, property in land was rendered insecure by various grants of it, which Charles inconsiderately bestowed upon his favourites. These were not only of such exorbitant extent as to be unfavourable to the progress of cultivation, but from inattention, or imperfect acquaintance with the geography of the country, their boundaries were so inaccurately defined, that large tracts already occupied and planted were often included in them.

The murmurs and complaints which such a system of administration excited, were augmented by the rigour with which Sir John Harvey, who succeeded Yardely in the government of the colony,* enforced every act of power [1627]. Rapacious, unfeeling, and haughty, he added insolence to oppression, and neither regarded the sentiments nor listened to the remonstrances of the people under his command. The colonists, far from the seat of government, and overawed by authority derived from a royal commission, submitted long to his tyranny and exactions. Their patience was at last exhausted; and in a transport of popular rage and indignation, they seized their governor, and sent him a prisoner to England, accompanied by two of their number, whom they deputed to prefer their accusations against him to the king. But this attempt to redress their own wrongs, by a proceeding so summary and violent as is hardly consistent with any idea of regular government, and can be justified only in cases of such urgent necessity as rarely occur in civil society, was altogether repugnant to every notion which Charles entertained with respect to the obedience due by subjects to their sovereign. To him the conduct of the colonists appeared to be not only a usurpation of his right to judge and to punish one of his own officers, by an open and audacious act of rebellion against his authority. Without deigning to admit their deputies into his presence, or to hear one article of their charge against Harvey, the king instantly sent him back to his former station, with an ample renewal of all the powers belonging to it. But though Charles deemed this vigorous step necessary in order to assert his own authority, and to testify his displeasure with those who had presumed to offer such an insult to it, he seems to have been so sensible of the grievances under which the colonists groaned, and of the chief source from which they flowed, that soon after [1639] he not only removed a governor so justly odious to them, but named as a successor Sir William Berkeley, a person far superior to Harvey in rank and abilities, and still more distinguished, by possessing all the popular virtues to which the other was a stranger.†

Under his government the colony in Virginia remained, with some short intervals of interruption, almost forty years; and to his mild and prudent administration its increase and prosperity are in a great measure to be ascribed. It was indebted, however, to the king himself for such a reform of its constitution and policy, as gave a different aspect to the colony, and animated all its operations with new spirit. Though the tenor of Sir William Berkeley's commission was the same with that of his predecessor, he received instructions under the great seal, by which he was empowered to declare, that in all its concerns, civil as well as ecclesiastical, the colony was to be governed according to the laws of England: he was directed to issue writs for electing representatives of the people, who, in conjunction with the governor and council, were to form a general assembly, and to possess supreme legislative authority in the community: he was ordered to establish courts of justice, in which all questions, whether civil or criminal, were to be decided agreeably to the forms of judicial procedure in the mother country. It is not easy to discover what were the motives which induced a monarch, tenacious in adhering to any opinion or system which

* Rymer, xviii. 980. † Beverley's Hist. of Virg. p. 50. Chalmers's Annals, p. 118, &c

he had once adopted, jealous to excess of his own rights, and adverse on every occasion to any extension of the privileges claimed by his people, to relinquish his original plan of administration in the colony, and to grant such immunities to his subjects settled there. From the historians of Virginia, no less superficial than ill informed, no light can be derived with respect to this point. It is most probable, the dread of the spirit then rising in Great Britain, extorted from Charles concessions so favourable to Virginia. After an intermission of almost twelve years, the state of his affairs compelled him to have recourse to the great council of the nation. There his subjects would find a jurisdiction independent of the crown, and able to control its authority. There they hoped for legal redress of all their grievances. As the colonists in Virginia had applied for relief to a former parliament, it might be expected with certainty that they would lay their case before the first meeting of an assembly in which they were secure of a favourable audience. Charles knew that, if the spirit of his administration in Virginia were to be tried by the maxims of the English constitution, it must be severely reprehended. He was aware that many measures of greater moment in his government would be brought under a strict review in parliament; and, unwilling to give malecontents the advantage of adding a charge of oppression in the remote parts of his dominions to a catalogue of domestic grievances, he artfully endeavoured to take the merit of having granted voluntarily to his people in Virginia such privileges as he foresaw would be extorted from him.

But though Charles established the internal government of Virginia on a model similar to that of the English constitution, and conferred on his subjects there all the rights of freemen and citizens, he was extremely solicitous to maintain its connexion with the parent state. With this view he instructed Sir William Berkeley strictly to prohibit any commerce of the colony with foreign nations; and in order more certainly to secure exclusive possession of all the advantages arising from the sale of its productions, he was required to take a bond from the master of each vessel that sailed from Virginia, to land his cargo in some part of the King's dominions in Europe.* Even under this restraint, such is the kindly influence of free government on society, the colony advanced so rapidly in industry and population that at the beginning of the civil war the English settled in it exceeded twenty thousand.†

Gratitude towards a monarch from whose hands they had received immunities which they had long wished but hardly expected to enjoy, the influence and example of a popular governor passionately devoted to the interests of his master, concurred in preserving inviolated loyalty among the colonists. Even after monarchy was abolished, after one King had been beheaded, and another driven into exile, the authority of the crown continued to be acknowledged and revered in Virginia [1650]. Irritated at this open defiance of its power, the parliament issued an ordinance, declaring, that as the settlement in Virginia had been made at the cost and by the people of England, it ought to be subordinate to and dependent upon the English commonwealth, and subject to such laws and regulations as are or shall be made in parliament; that, instead of this dutiful submission, the colonists had disclaimed the authority of the state, and audaciously rebelled against it; that on this account they were denounced notorious traitors, and not only all vessels belonging to natives of England, but those of foreign nations, were prohibited to enter their ports, or carry on any commerce with them.

It was not the mode of that age to wage a war of words alone. The efforts of a high spirited government in asserting its own dignity were prompt and vigorous. A powerful squadron, with a considerable body of

* Chalmers's Annals, p. 219. 232. † Ibid. p. 125.

land forces, was despatched to reduce the Virginians to obedience. After compelling the colonies in Barbadoes and the other islands to submit to the commonwealth, the squadron entered the Bay of Chesapeak [1651]. Berkeley, with more courage than prudence, took arms to oppose this formidable armament; but he could not long maintain such an unequal contest. His gallant resistance, however, procured favourable terms to the people under his government. A general indemnity for all past offences was granted; they acknowledged the authority of the commonwealth, and were admitted to a participation of all the rights enjoyed by citizens.* Berkeley, firm to his principles of loyalty, disdained to make any stipulation for himself; and, choosing to pass his days far removed from the seat of a government which he detested, continued to reside in Virginia as a private man, beloved and respected by all over whom he had formerly presided.

Not satisfied with taking measures to subject the colonies, the commonwealth turned its attention towards the most effectual mode of retaining them in dependence on the parent state, and of securing to it the benefit of their increasing commerce. With this view the parliament framed two laws, one of which expressly prohibited all mercantile intercourse between the colonies and foreign states, and the other ordained that no production of Asia, Africa, or America, should be imported into the dominions of the commonwealth but in vessels belonging to English owners, or to the people of the colonies settled there, and navigated by an English commander,† and by crews of which the greater part must be Englishmen. But while the wisdom of the commonwealth prescribed the channel in which the trade of the colonies was to be carried on, it was solicitous to encourage the cultivation of the staple commodity of Virginia, by an act of parliament [1652], which gave legal force to all the injunctions of James and Charles against planting tobacco in England.‡

Under governors appointed by the commonwealth, or by Cromwell when he usurped the supreme power, Virginia remained almost nine years in perfect tranquillity. During that period, many adherents to the royal party, and among these some gentlemen of good families, in order to avoid danger and oppression, to which they were exposed in England, or in hopes of repairing their ruined fortunes, resorted thither. Warmly attached to the cause for which they had fought and suffered, and animated with all the passions natural to men recently engaged in a fierce and long protracted civil war, they, by their intercourse with the colonists, confirmed them in principles of loyalty, and added to their impatience and indignation under the restraints imposed on their commerce by their new masters. On the death of Matthews, the last governor named by Cromwell, the sentiments and inclination of the people, no longer under the control of authority, burst out with violence. They forced Sir William Berkeley to quit his retirement; they unanimously elected him governor of the colony: and as he refused to act under a usurped authority, they boldly erected the royal standard, and acknowledging Charles II. to be their lawful sovereign, proclaimed him with all his titles; and the Virginians long boasted, that as they were the last of the king's subjects who renounced their allegiance, they were the first who returned to their duty.§

Happily for the people of Virginia, a revolution in England, no less sudden than unexpected, seated Charles on the throne of his ancestors, and saved them from the severe chastisement to which their premature declaration in his favour must have exposed them. On receiving the first account of this event, the joy and exultation of the colony were universal and unbounded. These, however, were not of long continuance. Gracious

* Thurlow's State Papers, i. 197. Chalmers' Annals, p. 122. Beverley's Hist. p. 53. † Scobel's Acts, p. 132. 167. ‡ Ib. p. 117. § Beverley, p. 55. Chalmers, p. 124

but unproductive professions of esteem and good will were the only return made by Charles to loyalty and services which in their own estimation were so distinguished that no recompense was beyond what they might claim. If the king's neglect and ingratitude disappointed all the sanguine hopes which their vanity had founded on the merit of their past conduct, the spirit which influenced parliament in its commercial deliberations opened a prospect that alarmed them with respect to their future situation. In framing regulations for the encouragement of trade, which, during the convulsions of civil war, and amidst continual fluctuations in government, had met with such obstruction that it declined in every quarter; the House of Commons, instead of granting the colonies that relief which they expected from the restraints in their commerce imposed by the commonwealth and Cromwell, not only adopted all their ideas concerning this branch of legislation, but extended them further. This produced the *act of navigation*, the most important and memorable of any in the statute-book with respect to the history of English commerce. By it, besides several momentous articles foreign to the subject of this work, it was enacted, that no commodities should be imported into any settlement in Asia, Africa, or America, or exported from them, but in vessels of English or plantation built, whereof the master and three-fourths of the mariners shall be English subjects, under pain of forfeiting ship and goods; that none but natural born subjects, or such as have been naturalized, shall exercise the occupation of merchant or factor in any English settlement, under pain of forfeiting their goods and chattels; that no sugar, tobacco, cotton, wool, indigo, ginger, or woods used in dyeing, of the growth or manufacture of th colonies, shall be shipped from them to any other country but England; and in order to secure the performance of this, a sufficient bond, with one surety, shall be given before sailing by the owners, for a specific sum proportional to the rate of the vessel employed by them.* The productions subjected to this restriction are distinguished, in the language of commerce and finance, by the name of *enumerated commodities;* and as industry in its progress furnished new articles of value, these have been successively added to the roll, and subjected to the same restraint. Soon after [1663], the act of navigation was extended, and additional restraints were imposed, by a new law, which prohibited the importation of any European commodity into the colonies, but what was laden in England in vessels navigated and manned as the act of navigation required. More effectual provision was made by this law for exacting the penalties to which the transgressors of the act of navigation were subjected; and the principles of policy, on which the various regulations contained in both statutes are founded, were openly avowed in a declaration, that as the plantations beyond seas are inhabited and peopled by subjects of England, they may be kept in a firmer dependence upon it, and rendered yet more beneficial and advantageous unto it, in the further employment and increase of English shipping and seamen, as well as in the vent of English woollen and other manufactures and commodities; and in making England a staple, not only of the commodities of those plantations, but also of the commodities of other countries and places, for the supplying of them; and it being the usage of other nations to keep the trade of their plantations to themselves.† In prosecution of those favourite maxims, the English legislature proceeded a step further. As the act of navigation had left the people of the colonies at liberty to export the enumerated commodities from one plantation to another without paying any duty [1672], it subjected them to a tax equivalent to what was paid by the consumers of these commodities in England.‡

By these successive regulations, the plan of securing to England a mo

* Car. II c 18. † 15 Car. II. c. 7. ‡ 25 Car. II. c. 7

nopoly of the commerce with its colonies, and of shutting up every other channel into which it might be diverted, was perfected, and reduced into complete system. On one side of the Atlantic these regulations have been extolled as an extraordinary effort of political sagacity, and have been considered as the great charter of national commerce, to which the parent state is indebted for all its opulence and power. On the other, they have been execrated as a code of oppression, more suited to the illiberality of mercantile ideas than to extensive views of legislative wisdom. Which of these opinions is best founded, I shall examine at large in another part of this work. But in writing the history of the English settlements in America, it was necessary to trace the progress of those restraining laws with accuracy, as in every subsequent transaction we may observe a perpetual exertion, on the part of the mother country, to enforce and extend them; and on the part of the colonies, endeavours no less unremitting to elude or to obstruct their operation.

Hardly was the act of navigation known in Virginia, and its effects begun to be felt, when the colony remonstrated against it as a grievance, and petitioned earnestly for relief. But the commercial ideas of Charles and his ministers coincided so perfectly with those of parliament, that, instead of listening with a favourable ear to their applications, they laboured assiduously to carry the act into strict execution. For this purpose, instructions were issued to the governor, forts were built on the banks of the principal rivers, and small vessels appointed to cruise on the coast. The Virginians, seeing no prospect of obtaining exemption from the act, set themselves to evade it; and found means, notwithstanding the vigilance with which they were watched, of carrying on a considerable clandestine trade with foreigners, particularly with the Dutch settled on Hudson's River. Emboldened by observing disaffection spread through the colony, some veteran soldiers who had served under Cromwell, and had been banished to Virginia, formed a design of rendering themselves masters of the country, and of asserting its independence on England. This rash project was discovered by one of their associates, and disconcerted by the vigorous exertions of Sir William Berkeley. But the spirit of discontent, though repressed, was not extinguished. Every day something occurred to revive and to nourish it. As it is with extreme difficulty that commerce can be turned into a new channel, tobacco, the staple of the colony, sunk prodigiously in value when they were compelled to send it all to one market. It was some time before England could furnish them regularly full assortments of those necessary articles, without which the industry of the colony could not be carried on, or its prosperity secured. Encouraged by the symptoms of general languor and despondency which this declining state of the colony occasioned, the Indians seated towards the heads of the rivers ventured first to attack the remote settlements, and then to make incursions into the interior parts of the country. Unexpected as these hostilities were, from a people who during a long period had lived in friendship with the English, a measure taken by the king seems to have excited still greater terror among the most opulent people of the colony. Charles had imprudently imitated the example of his father, by granting such large tracts of lands in Virginia to several of his courtiers, as tended to unsettle the distribution of property in the country, and to render the title of the most ancient planters to their estates precarious and questionable. From those various causes, which in a greater or less degree affected every individual in the colony, the indignation of the people became general, and was worked up to such a pitch, that nothing was wanting to precipitate them into the most desperate acts but some leader qualified to unite and to direct their operations.*

* Chalmers's Annals. ch. 10. 13, 14, passim. Beverley's Hist. of Virg. p. 58, &c.

Such a leader they found in Nathaniel Bacon, a colonel of militia, who, though he had been settled in Virginia only three years, had acquired, by popular manners, an insinuating address, and the consideration derived from having been regularly trained in England to the profession of law, such general esteem that he had been admitted into the council, and was regarded as one of the most respectable persons in the colony. Bacon was ambitious, eloquent, daring, and, prompted either by honest zeal to redress the public wrongs, or allured by hopes of raising himself to distinction and power, he mingled with the malecontents; and by his bold harangues and confident promises of removing all their grievances, he inflamed them almost to madness. As the devastations committed by the Indians was the calamity most sensibly felt by the people, he accused the governor of having neglected the proper measures for repelling the invasions of the savages, and exhorted them to take arms in their own defence, and to exterminate that odious race. Great numbers assembled, and chose Bacon to be their general. He applied to the governor for a commission, confirming this election of the people, and offering to march instantly against the common enemy. Berkeley, accustomed by long possession of supreme command to high ideas of the respect due to his station, considered this tumultuary armament as an open insult to his authority, and suspected that, under specious appearances, Bacon concealed most dangerous designs. Unwilling, however, to give farther provocation to an incensed multitude by a direct refusal of what they demanded, he thought it prudent to negotiate in order to gain time; and it was not until he found all endeavours to soothe them ineffectual, that he issued a proclamation, requiring them in the king's name, under the pain of being denounced rebels, to disperse.

But Bacon, sensible that he had now advanced so far as rendered it impossible to recede with honour or safety, instantly took the only resolution that remained in his situation. At the head of a chosen body of his followers, he marched rapidly to James Town, and surrounding the house where the governor and council were assembled, demanded the commission for which he had formerly applied. Berkeley, with the proud indignant spirit of a cavalier, disdaining the requisitions of a rebel, peremptorily refused to comply, and calmly presented his naked breast to the weapons which were pointed against it. The council, however, foreseeing the fatal consequences of driving an enraged multitude, in whose power they were, to the last extremities of violence, prepared a commission constituting Bacon general of all the forces in Virginia, and by their entreaties prevailed on the governor to sign it. Bacon with his troops retired in triumph. Hardly was the council delivered by his departure from the dread of present danger, when, by a transition not unusual in feeble minds, presumptuous boldness succeeded to excessive fear. The commission granted to Bacon was declared to be null, having been extorted by force; he was proclaimed a rebel, his followers were required to abandon his standard, and the militia ordered to arm, and to join the governor.

Enraged at conduct which he branded with the name of base and treacherous, Bacon, instead of continuing his march towards the Indian country, instantly wheeled about, and advanced with all his forces to James Town. The governor, unable to resist such a numerous body, made his escape, and fled across the bay to Acomack on the eastern shore. Some of the counsellors accompanied him thither, others retired to their own plantations. Upon the flight of Sir William Berkeley, and dispersion of the council, the frame of civil government in the colony seemed to be dissolved, and Bacon became possessed of supreme and uncontrolled power. But as he was sensible that his countrymen would not long submit with patience to authority acquired and held merely by force of arms, he endeavoured to found it on a more constitutional basis, by obtaining the sanction of the people's approbation. With this view he called together the most considerable gentlemen in the colony, and having prevailed on them to bind themselves by oath to maintain his authority, and to resist every enemy that should oppose it, he from that time considered his jurisdiction as legally established.

Berkeley, meanwhile, having collected some forces, made inroads into different parts of the colony where Bacon's authority was recognised. Several sharp conflicts happened with various success. James Town was reduced to ashes, and the best cultivated districts in the province were laid waste, sometimes by one party and sometimes by the other. But it was not by his own exertions that the governor hoped to terminate the contest. He had early transmitted an account of the transactions in Virginia to the king, and demanded such a body of soldiers as would enable him to quell the insurgents' whom he represented as so exasperated by the restraint imposed on their trade, that they were impatient to shake off all dependence on the parent state. Charles, alarmed at a commotion no less dangerous than unexpected, and solicitous to maintain his authority over a colony the value of which was daily increasing and more fully understood, speedily despatched a small squadron with such a number of regular troops as Berkeley had required. Bacon and his followers received information of this armament, but were not intimidated at its approach. They boldly determined to oppose it with open force, and declared it to be consistent with their duty and allegiance, to treat all who should aid Sir William Berkeley as enemies, until they should have an opportunity of laying their grievances before their sovereign.*

But while both parties prepared, with equal animosity, to involve their country in the horrors of civil war [1677], an event happened, which quieted the commotion almost as suddenly as it had been excited. Bacon, when ready to take the field, sickened and died. None of his followers possessed such talents, or were so much objects of the people's confidence, as entitled them to aspire to the supreme command. Destitute of a leader to conduct and animate them, their sanguine hopes of success subsided; mutual distrust accompanied this universal despondency; all began to wish for an accommodation; and after a short negotiation with Sir William Berkeley, they laid down their arms, and submitted to his government, on obtaining a promise of general pardon.

Thus terminated an insurrection, which, in the annals of Virginia, is distinguished by the name of *Bacon's rebellion.* During seven months this daring leader was master of the colony, while the royal governor was shut up in a remote and ill-peopled corner of it. What were the real motives that prompted him to take arms, and to what length he intended to carry his plans of reformation, either in commerce or government, it is not easy to discover, in the scanty materials from which we derive our information with respect to this transaction. It is probable, that his conduct, like that of other adventurers in faction, would have been regulated chiefly by events; and accordingly as these proved favourable or adverse, his views and requisitions would have been extended or circumscribed.

Sir William Berkeley, as soon as he was reinstated in his office, called together the representatives of the people, that by their advice and authority public tranquillity and order might be perfectly established. Though this assembly met a few weeks after the death of Bacon, while the memory of reciprocal injuries was still recent, and when the passions excited by such a fierce contest had but little time to subside, its proceedings were conducted with a moderation seldom exercised by the successful party in a civil war. No man suffered capitally; a small number were subjected to fines; others were declared incapable of holding any office of trust; and with those exceptions the promise of general idemnity was confirmed

* Beverley's Hist. p. 75, 76

by law. Soon after Berkeley was recalled, and Colonel Jeffreys was appointed his successor.

From that period to the Revolution in 1688, there is scarcely any memorable occurrence in the history of Virginia. A peace was concluded with the Indians. Under several successive governors, administration was carried on in the colony with the same arbitrary spirit that distinguished the latter years of Charles II. and the precipitate councils of James II. The Virginians, with a constitution which in form resembled that of England, enjoyed hardly any portion of the liberty which that admirable system of policy is framed to secure. They were deprived even of the last consolation of the oppressed, the power of complaining, by a law which, under severe penalties, prohibited them from speaking disrespectfully of the governor, or defaming, either by words or writing, the administration of the colony.* Still, however, the laws restraining their commerce were felt as an intolerable grievance, and they nourished in secret a spirit of discontent, which, from the necessity of concealing it, acquired a greater degree of acrimony. But notwithstanding those unfavourable circumstances, the colony continued to increase. The use of tobacco was now become general in Europe; and though it had fallen considerably in price, the extent of demand compensated that diminution, and by giving constant employment to the industry of the planters diffused wealth among them. At the Revolution the number of inhabitants in the colony exceeded sixty thousand,† and in the course of twenty-eight years its population had been more than doubled.‡

---

# BOOK X.

When James I., in the year one thousand six hundred and six, made that magnificent partition, which has been mentioned, of a vast region in North America, extending from the thirty-fourth to the forty-fifth degree of latitude, between two trading companies of his subjects, he established the residence of the one in London, and of the other in Plymouth. The former was authorized to settle in the southern, and the latter in the northern part of this territory, then distinguished by the general name of Virginia. This arrangement seems to have been formed upon the idea of some speculative refiner, who aimed at diffusing the spirit of industry, by fixing the seat of one branch of the trade that was now to be opened, on the east coast of the island, and the other on the west. But London possesses such advantages of situation, that the commercial wealth and activity of England have always centered in the capital. At the beginning of the last century, the superiority of the metropolis in both these respects was so great, that though the powers and privileges conferred by the king on the two trading companies were precisely the same, the adventurers settled in Plymouth fell far short of those in London in the vigour and success of their efforts towards accomplishing the purpose of their institution. Though the operations of the Plymouth company were animated by the public-spirited zeal of Sir John Popham, chief justice of England, Sir Ferdinando Gorges, and some other gentlemen of the west, all its exertions were feeble and unfortunate.

The first vessel fitted out by the company was taken by the Spaniards [1606]. In the year one thousand six hundred and seven, a feeble settlement was made at Sagahadoc; but, on account of the rigour of the climate,

* Beverley, p. 81. Chalmers p 341. ‡ Chalmers's Annals, p. 356. ‡ Ibid. p. 125.

was soon relinquished, and for some time nothing further was attempted than a few fishing voyages to Cape Cod, or a pitiful traffic with the natives for skins and oil. One of the vessels equipped for this purpose [1614] was commanded by Captain Smith, whose name has been so often mentioned with distinction in the History of Virginia. The adventure was prosperous and lucrative. But his ardent enterprising mind could not confine its attention to objects so unequal to it as the petty details of a trading voyage. He employed a part of his time in exploring the coast, and in delineating its bays and harbours. On his return, he laid a map of it before Prince Charles, and, with the usual exaggeration of discoverers, painted the beauty and excellence of the country in such glowing colours, that the young prince, in the warmth of admiration, declared, that it should be called New England;* a name which effaced that of Virginia, and by which it is still distinguished.

The favourable accounts of the country by Smith, as well as the success of his voyage, seem to have encouraged private adventurers to prosecute the trade on the coast of New England with greater briskness; but did not inspire the languishing company of Plymouth with such vigour as to make any new attempt towards establishing a permanent colony there. Something more than the prospect of distant gain to themselves, or of future advantages to their country, was requisite in order to induce men to abandon the place of their nativity, to migrate to another quarter of the globe, and endure innumerable hardships under an untried climate, and in an uncultivated land, covered with woods, or occupied by fierce and hostile tribes of savages. But what mere attention to private emolument or to national utility could not effect, was accomplished by the operation of a higher principle. Religion had gradually excited among a great body of the people a spirit that fitted them remarkably for encountering the dangers, and surmounting the obstacles, which had hitherto rendered abortive the schemes of colonization in that part of America allotted to the company of Plymouth. As the various settlements in New England are indebted for their origin to this spirit, as in the course of our narrative we shall discern its influence mingling in all their transactions, and giving a peculiar tincture to the character of the people, as well as to their institutions both civil and ecclesiastical, it becomes necessary to trace its rise and progress with attention and accuracy.

When the superstitions and corruptions of the Romish church prompted different nations of Europe to throw off its yoke, and to withdraw from its communion, the mode as well as degree of their separation was various. Wherever reformation was sudden, and carried on by the people without authority from their rulers, or in opposition to it, the rupture was violent and total. Every part of the ancient fabric was overturned, and a different system, not only with respect to doctrine, but to church government, and the external rites of worship, was established. Calvin, who, by his abilities, learning, and austerity of manners, had acquired high reputation and authority in the Protestant churches, was a zealous advocate for this plan of thorough reformation. He exhibited a model of that pure form of ecclesiastical policy which he approved in the constitution of the church of Geneva. The simplicity of its institutions, and still more their repugnancy to those of the Popish church, were so much admired by all the stricter reformers, that it was copied, with some small variations, in Scotland, in the republic of the United Provinces, in the dominions of the House of Brandenburgh, in those of the Elector Palatine, and in the churches of the Hugonots in France.

But in those countries where the steps of departure from the church of Rome were taken with greater deliberation, and regulated by the wisdom

* Smith's Trav. book vi. p. 203, &c. Purchas, iv. p. 1837.

or policy of the supreme magistrate, the separation was not so wide. Of all the reformed churches, that of England has deviated least from the ancient institutions. The violent but capricious spirit of Henry VIII., who, though he disclaimed the supremacy, revered the tenets of the Papal see, checked innovations in doctrine or worship during his reign. When his son ascended the throne, and the Protestant religion was established by law, the cautious prudence of Archbishop Cranmer moderated the zeal of those who had espoused the new opinions. Though the articles to be recognised as the system of national faith were framed conformably to the doctrines of Calvin, his notions with respect to church government and the mode of worship were not adopted. As the hierarchy in England was incorporated with the civil policy of the kingdom, and constituted a member of the legislature, archbishops, and bishops, with all the subordinate ranks of ecclesiastics subject to them, were continued according to ancient form, and with the same dignity and jurisdiction. The peculiar vestments in which the clergy performed their sacred functions, bowing at the name of Jesus, kneeling at receiving the Sacrament of the Lord's Supper, the sign of the Cross in baptism, the use of the Ring in marriage, with several other rights to which long usage had accustomed the people, and which time had rendered venerable, were still retained. But though Parliament enjoined the observance of these ceremonies under very severe penalties,* several of the more zealous clergy entertained scruples with respect to the lawfulness of complying with this injunction: and the vigilance and authority of Cranmer and Ridley, with difficulty saved their infant church from the disgrace of a schism on this account.

On the accession of Mary, the furious zeal with which she persecuted all who had adopted the tenets of the reformers forced many eminent protestants, laymen as well as ecclesiastics, to seek an asylum on the continent. Francfort, Geneva, Basil, and Strasburgh received them with affectionate hospitality as sufferers in the cause of truth, and the magistrates permitted them to assemble by themselves for religious worship. The exiles who took up their residence in the two former cities, modelled their little congregations according to the ideas of Calvin, and with a spirit natural to men in their situation, eagerly adopted institutions which appeared to be further removed from the superstitions of Popery than those of their own church. They returned to England as soon as Elizabeth re-established the protestant religion, not only with more violent antipathy to the opinions and practices of that church by which they had been oppressed, but with a strong attachment to that mode of worship to which they had been for some years accustomed. As they were received by their countrymen with the veneration due to confessors, they exerted all the influence derived from that opinion in order to obtain such a reformation in the English ritual as might bring it nearer to the standard of purity in foreign churches. Some of the Queen's most confidential ministers were warmly disposed to co-operate with them in this measure. But Elizabeth paid little regard to the inclinations of the one or the sentiments of the other. Fond of pomp and ceremony, accustomed, according to the mode of that age, to study religious controversy, and possessing, like her father, such confidence in her own understanding, that she never doubted her capacity to judge and decide with respect to every point in dispute between contending sects,†

* 2 and 3 Edw. VI. c. 1.

† Of the high idea which Elizabeth entertained with respect to her own superior skill in theology, as well as the haughty tone in which she dictated to her subjects what they ought to believe, we have a striking picture in her speech at the close of the parliament, A. D. 1585.—"One thing I may not overskip—Religion, the ground on which all other matters ought to take root; and, being corrupted, may mar all the tree. And that there be some fault-finders with the order of the clergy, which so may make a slander to myself, and to the church, whose overruler God hath made me, whose negligence cannot be excused, if any schisms or errors heretical were suffered. Thus much I must say, that some faults and negligences must grow and be, as in all other great charges it happeneth; and what vocation without? All which, if you, my lords of the clergy, do not amend,

she chose to act according to her own ideas, which led her rather to approach nearer to the church of Rome, in the parade of external worship, than to widen the breach by abolishing any rite already established.* An act of parliament, in the first year of her reign, not only required an exact conformity to the mode of worship prescribed in the service book, under most rigorous penalties, but empowered the Queen to enjoin the observance of such additional ceremonies as might tend, in her opinion, to render the public exercises of devotion more decent and edifying.†

The advocates for a further reformation, notwithstanding this cruel disappointment of the sanguine hopes with which they returned to their native country, did not relinquish their design. They disseminated their opinions with great industry among the people. They extolled the purity of foreign churches, and inveighed against the superstitious practices with which religion was defiled in their own church. In vain did the defenders of the established system represent that these forms and ceremonies were in themselves things perfectly indifferent, which, from long usage, were viewed with reverence; and by their impression upon the senses and imagination, tended not only to fix the attention, but to affect the heart, and to warm it with devout and worthy sentiments. The Puritans (for by that name such as scrupled to comply with what was enjoined by the Act of Uniformity were distinguished) maintained that the rites in question were inventions of men, superadded to the simple and reasonable services required in the word of God; that from the excessive solicitude with which conformity to them was exacted, the multitude must conceive such a high opinion of their value and importance as might induce them to rest satisfied with the mere form and shadow of religion, and to imagine that external observances may compensate for the want of inward sanctity; that ceremonies which had been long employed by a society manifestly corrupt, to veil its own defects, and to seduce and fascinate mankind, ought now to be rejected as relics of superstition unworthy of a place in a church which gloried in the name of *Reformed*.

The people, to whom in every religious controversy the final appeal is made, listened to the arguments of the contending parties; and it is obvious to which of them, men who had lately beheld the superstitious spirit of popery, and felt its persecuting rage, would lend the most favourable ear. The desire of a further separation from the church of Rome spread wide through the nation. The preachers who contended for this, and who refused to wear the surplice, and other vestments peculiar to their order, or to observe the ceremonies enjoined by law, were followed and admired, while the ministry of the zealous advocates for conformity was deserted, and their persons often exposed to insult. For some time the nonconformists were connived at; but as their number and boldness increased, the interposition both of spiritual and civil authority was deemed necessary in order to check their progress. To the disgrace of Christians, the sacred rights of conscience and private judgment, as well as the charity and mutual forbearance suitable to the mild spirit of the religion which they professed, were in that age little understood. Not only the idea of toleration, but even the word itself in the sense now affixed to it, was then unknown. Every church claimed a right to employ the hand of power for the protection of truth and the extirpation of error. The laws of her

I mean to depose you. Look ye, therefore, well to your charges. This may be amended without needless or open exclamations. I am supposed to have many studies, but most philosophical. I must yield this to be true, that I suppose few (that be not professors) have read more. And I need not tell you, that I am not so simple that I understand not, nor so forgetful that I remember not; and yet amidst my many volumes, I hope God's book hath not been my seldomest lectures, in which we find that by which reason all ought to believe. I see many over-bold with God Almighty, making too many subtle scannings of his blessed will. The presumption is so great that I may not suffer it," &c. D'Ewes's Journal, p. 328.

* Neal's Hist. of the Puritans, i. 138. 176.

† 1 Eliz. c. 2.

kingdom armed Elizabeth with ample authority for this purpose, and she was abundantly disposed to exercise it with full vigour. Many of the most eminent among the puritan clergy were deprived of their benefices, others were imprisoned, several were fined, and some put to death. But persecution, as usually happens, instead of extinguishing, inflamed their zeal to such a height, that the jurisdiction of the ordinary courts of law was deemed insufficient to suppress it, and a new tribunal was established under the title of the *High Commission for Ecclesiastical Affairs*, whose powers and mode of procedure were hardly less odious or less hostile to the principles of justice than those of the Spanish Inquisition. Several attempts were made in the House of Commons to check these arbitrary proceedings, and to moderate the rage of persecution; but the Queen always imposed silence upon those who presumed to deliver any opinion with respect to a matter appertaining solely to her prerogative, in a tone as imperious and arrogant as was ever used by Henry VIII. in addressing his parliaments; and so tamely obsequious were the guardians of the people's rights that they not only obeyed those unconstitutional commands, but consented to an act, by which every person who should absent himself from church during a month was subjected to punishment by fine and imprisonment; and if after conviction he did not within three months renounce his erroneous opinions and conform to the laws, he was then obliged to abjure the realm; but if he either refused to comply with this condition, or returned from banishment, he should be put to death as a felon without benefit of clergy.*

By this iniquitous statute, equally repugnant to ideas of civil and of religious liberty, the puritans were cut off from any hope of obtaining either reformation in the church or indulgence to themselves. Exasperated by this rigorous treatment, their antipathy to the established religion increased, and with the progress natural to violent passions, carried them far beyond what was their original aim. The first puritans did not entertain any scruples with respect to the lawfulness of episcopal government, and seem to have been very unwilling to withdraw from communion with the church of which they were members. But when they were thrown out of her bosom, and constrained to hold separate assemblies for the worship of God, their followers no longer viewed a society by which they were oppressed, with reverence or affection. Her government, her discipline, her ritual, were examined with minute attention. Every error was pointed out, and every defect magnified. The more boldly any preacher inveighed against the corruptions of the church, he was listened to with greater approbation; and the further he urged his disciples to depart from such an impure community, the more eagerly did they follow him. By degrees, ideas of ecclesiastical policy, altogether repugnant to those of the established church, gained footing in the nation. The more sober and learned puritans inclined to that form which is known by the name of Presbyterian. Such as were more thoroughly possessed with the spirit of innovation, however much they might approve the equality of pastors which that system establishes, reprobated the authority which it vests in various judicatories, descending from one to another in regular subordination, as inconsistent with Christian liberty.

These wild notions floated for some time in the minds of the people, and amused them with many ideal schemes of ecclesiastial policy. At length Robert Brown [1580], a popular declaimer in high estimation, reduced them to a system, on which he modelled his own congregation. He taught that the church of England was corrupt and antichristian, its ministers not lawfully ordained, its ordinances and sacraments invalid; and therefore he prohibited his people to hold communion with it in any religious func-

* 35 Eliz. c. 1.

tion. He maintained, that a society of Christians, uniting together to worship God, constituted a church possessed of complete jurisdiction in the conduct of its own affairs, independent of any other society, and unaccountable to any superior; that the priesthood was neither a distinct order in the church, nor conferred an indelible character; but that every man qualified to teach might be set apart for that office by the election of the brethren, and by imposition of their hands; in like manner, by their authority, he might be discharged from that function, and reduced to the rank of a private Christian; that every person when admitted a member of a church, ought to make a public confession of his faith, and give evidence of his being in a state of favour with God; and that all the affairs of a church were to be regulated by the decision of the majority of its members.

This democratical form of government, which abolished all distinction of ranks in the church, and conferred an equal portion of power on every individual, accorded so perfectly with the levelling genius of fanaticism, that it was fondly adopted by many as a complete model of Christian policy. From their founder they were denominated Brownists; and as their tenets were more hostile to the established religion than those of other separatists, the fiercest storm of persecution fell upon their heads. Many of them were fined or imprisoned, and some put to death; and though Brown, with a levity of which there are few examples among enthusiasts whose vanity has been soothed by being recognised as heads of a party, abandoned his disciples, conformed to the established religion, and accepted of a benefice in the church, the sect not only subsisted, but continued to spread, especially among persons in the middle and lower ranks of life. But as all their motions were carefully watched, both by the ecclesiastical and civil courts, which, as often as they were detected, punished them with the utmost rigour, a body of them, weary of living in a state of continual danger and alarm, fled to Holland, and settled in Leyden, under the care of Mr. John Robinson their pastor. There they resided for several years unmolested and obscure. But many of their aged members dying, and some of the younger marrying into Dutch families, while their church received no increase, either by recruits from England or by proselytes gained in the country, they began to be afraid that all their high attainments in spiritual knowledge would be lost, and that perfect fabric of policy which they had erected would be dissolved, and consigned to oblivion, if they remained longer in a strange land.

Deeply affected with the prospect of an event which to them appeared fatal to the interests of truth, they thought themselves called, in order to prevent it, to remove to some other place, where they might profess and propagate their opinions with greater success. America, in which their countrymen were at that time intent on planting colonies, presented itself to their thoughts. They flattered themselves with hopes of being permitted, in that remote region, to follow their own ideas in religion without disturbance. The dangers and hardships to which all former emigrants to America had been exposed did not deter them. "They were well weaned (according to their own description,) from the delicate milk of their mother country, and inured to the difficulties of a strange land. They were knit together in a strict and sacred band, by virtue of which they held themselves obliged to take care of the good of each other, and of the whole. It was not with them, as with other men, whom small things could discourage, or small discontents cause to wish themselves at home again."* The first object of their solicitude was to secure the free exercise of their religion. For this purpose they applied to the king; and, though James refused to give them any explicit assurance of toleration, they seem to have obtained from him some promise of his connivance, as long as they con-

* Hutchinson's Hist. of Massach. p. 4.

tinued to demean themselves quietly. So eager were they to accomplish their favourite scheme, that, relying on this precarious security, they began to negotiate with the Virginian company for a tract of land within the limits of their patent. This they easily procured from a society desirous of encouraging migration to a vast country, of which they had hitherto occupied only a few spots.

After the utmost efforts, their preparations fell far short of what was requisite for beginning the settlement of a new colony. A hundred and twenty persons sailed from England [Sept. 6, 1620], in a single ship on this arducus undertaking. The place of their destination was Hudson's River, where they intended to settle; but their captain having been bribed, as is said, by the Dutch, who had then formed a scheme, which they afterwards accomplished, of planting a colony there, carried them so far towards the north, that the first land in America which they made [Nov. 11], was Cape Cod. They were now not only beyond the precincts of the territory which had been granted to them, but beyond those of the company from which they derived their right. The season, however, was so far advanced, and sickness raged so violently among men unaccustomed to the hardships of a long voyage, that it became necessary to take up their abode there. After exploring the coast, they chose for their situation a place now belonging to the province of Massachusetts Bay, to which they gave the name of New Plymouth, probably out of respect to that company within whose jurisdiction they now found themselves situated.*

No season could be more unfavourable to settlement than that in which the colony landed. The winter, which, from the predominance of cold in America, is rigorous to a degree unknown in parallel latitudes of our hemisphere, was already set in; and they were slenderly provided with what was requisite for comfortable subsistence, under a climate considerably more severe than that for which they had made preparation. Above one half of them was cut off before the return of spring, by diseases, or by famine: the survivors, instead of having leisure to attend to the supply of their own wants, were compelled to take arms against the savages in their neighbourhood. Happily for the English, a pestilence which raged in America the year before they landed, had swept off so great a number of the natives that they were quickly repulsed and humbled. The privilege of professing their own opinions, and of being governed by laws of their own framing, afforded consolation to the colonists amidst all their dangers and hardships. The constitution of their church was the same with that which they had established in Holland. Their system of civil government was founded on those ideas of the natural equality among men, to which their ecclesiastical policy had accustomed them. Every free man, who was a member of the church, was admitted into the supreme legislative body. The laws of England were adopted as the basis of their jurisprudence, though with some diversity in the punishments inflicted upon crimes, borrowed from the Mosaic institutions. The executive power was vested in a governor and some assistants, who were elected annually by the members of the legislative assembly.† So far their institutions appear to be founded on the ordinary maxims of human prudence. But it was a favourite opinion with all the enthusiasts of that age, that the Scriptures contained a complete system not only of spiritual instruction, but of civil wisdom and polity; and without attending to the peculiar circumstances or situation of the people whose history is there recorded, they often deduced general rules for their own conduct from what happened among men in a very different state. Under the influence of this wild

* Hubard's Pres. State, p. 3. Cotton's Magnalia, p. 7. Hutchinson's Hist. p. 3 &c.
† Chalmers's Annals, p. 87.

notion, the colonists of New Plymouth, in imitation of the primitive Christians, threw all their property into a common stock, and, like members of one family, carried on every work of industry by their joint labour for public behoof.* But, however this resolution might evidence the sincerity of their faith, it retarded the progress of their colony. The same fatal effects flowed from this community of goods, and of labour, which had formerly been experienced in Virginia; and it soon became necessary to relinquish what was too refined to be capable of being accommodated to the affairs of men. But though they built a small town, and surrounded it with such a fence as afforded sufficient security against the assaults of Indians, the soil around it was so poor, their religious principles were so unsocial, and the supply sent them by their friends so scanty, that at the end of ten years the number of people belonging to the settlement did not exceed three hundred.† During some years they appear not to have acquired right by any legal conveyance to the territory which they had occupied. At length [1630], they obtained a grant of property from the council of the New Plymouth Company, but were never incorporated as a body politic by royal charter.‡ Unlike all the other settlements in America, this colony must be considered merely as a voluntary association, held together by the tacit consent of its members to recognise the authority of laws, and submit to the jurisdiction of magistrates, framed and chosen by themselves. In this state it remained an independent but feeble community, until it was united to its more powerful neighbour, the colony of Massachusetts Bay, the origin and progress of which I now proceed to relate.

The original company of Plymouth having done nothing effectual towards establishing any permanent settlement in America, James I., in the year one thousand six hundred and twenty, issued a new charter to the Duke of Lenox, the Marquis of Buckingham, and several other persons of distinction in his court, by which he conveyed to them a right to a territory in America, still more extensive than what had been granted to the former patentees, incorporating them as a body politic, in order to plant colonies there, with powers and jurisdictions similar to those contained in his charters to the companies of South and North Virginia. This society was distinguished by the name of the Grand Council of Plymouth for planting and governing New England. What considerations of public utility could induce the king to commit such an undertaking to persons apparently so ill qualified for conducting it, or what prospect of private advantage prompted them to engage in it, the information we receive from contemporary writers does not enable us to determine. Certain it is, that the expectations of both were disappointed; and after many schemes and arrangements, all the attempts of the new associates towards colonization proved unsuccessful.

New England must have remained unoccupied, if the same causes which occasioned the emigration of the Brownists had not continued to operate. Notwithstanding the violent persecution to which puritans of every denomination were still exposed, their number and zeal daily increased. As they now despaired of obtaining in their own country any relaxation of the penal statutes enacted against their sect, many began to turn their eyes towards some other place of retreat, where they might profess their own opinions with impunity. From the tranquillity which their brethren had hitherto enjoyed in New Plymouth, they hoped to find this desired asylum in New England; and by the activity of Mr. White, a nonconformist minister at Dorchester, an association was formed by several gentlemen who had imbibed puritanical notions, in order to conduct a

* Chalmers's Annals, p. 89. Douglas's Summary, i. p. 370. † Chalmers's Annals, p 97
‡ Ibid. p. 97. 107.

colony thither. They purchased from the council of Plymouth [March 19, 1627], all the territory, extending in length from three miles north of the river Merrimack, to three miles south of Charles River, and in breadth, from the Atlantic to the Southern Ocean. Zealous as these proprietors were to accomplish their favourite purpose, they quickly perceived their own inability to attempt the population of such an immense region, and deemed it necessary to call in the aid of more opulent copartners.*

Of these they found without difficulty, a sufficient number, chiefly in the capital, and among persons in the commercial and other industrious walks of life, who had openly joined the sect of the puritans, or secretly favoured their opinions. These new adventurers, with the caution natural to men conversant in business, entertained doubts concerning the propriety of founding a colony on the basis of a grant from a private company of patentees, who might convey a right of property in the soil, but could not confer jurisdiction, or the privilege of governing that society which they had in contemplation to establish. As it was only from royal authority that such powers could be derived, they applied for these; and Charles granted their request, with a facility which appears astonishing, when we consider the principles and views of the men who were suitors for the favour.

Time has been considered as the parent of political wisdom, but its instructions are communicated slowly. Although the experience of above twenty years might have taught the English the impropriety of committing the government of settlements in America to exclusive corporations resident in Europe, neither the king nor his subjects had profited so much by what passed before their eyes as to have extended their ideas beyond those adopted by James in his first attempts towards colonization. The charter of Charles I. to the adventurers associated for planting the province of Massachusetts Bay, was perfectly similar to those granted by his father to the two Virginian companies and to the council of Plymouth. The new adventurers were incorporated as a body politic, and their right to the territory, which they had purchased from the council at Plymouth, being confirmed by the king, they were empowered to dispose of lands, and to govern the people who should settle upon them. The first governor of the company and his assistants were named by the crown; the right of electing their successors was vested in the members of the corporation. The executive power was committed to the governor and assistants; that of legislation to the body of proprietors, who might make statutes and orders for the good of the community, not inconsistent with the laws of England, and enforce the observance of them, according to the course of other corporations within the realm. Their lands were to be held by the same liberal tenure with those granted to the Virginian company. They obtained the same temporary exemption from internal taxes, and from duties on goods exported or imported; and notwithstanding their migration to America, they and their descendants were declared to be entitled to all the rights of natural born subjects.†

The manifest object of this charter was to confer on the adventurers who undertook to people the territory on Massachusetts Bay, all the corporate rights possessed by the council of Plymouth, from which they had purchased it, and to form them into a public body, resembling other great trading companies, which the spirit of monarchy had at that time multiplied in the kingdom. The king seems not to have foreseen, or to have suspected the secret intentions of those who projected the measure; for so far was he from alluring emigrants, by any hopes of indulgence with respect to their religious scruples, or from promising any relaxation from the rigour of the penal statutes against nonconformists, that he expressly pro-

* Neal's Hist. of New England, i. p. 122. † Hutchinson's Collect. of Original Papers, p. 1, &c.

vides for having the oath of supremacy administered to every person who shall pass to the colony, or inhabit there.*

But whatever were the intentions of the king, the adventurers kept their own object steadily in view. Soon after their powers to establish a colony were rendered complete by the royal charter [1629], they fitted out five ships for New England; on board of which embarked upwards of three hundred passengers, with a view of settling there. These were most zealous puritans, whose chief inducement to relinquish their native land was the hope of enjoying religious liberty in a country far removed from the seat of government and the oppression of ecclesiastical courts. Some eminent nonconformist ministers accompanied them as their spiritual instructers. On their arrival in New England, they found the wretched remainder of a small body of emigrants, who had left England [June 29], the preceding year, under the conduct of Endicott, a deep enthusiast, whom, prior to their incorporation by the royal charter, the associates had appointed deputy governor. They were settled at a place called by the Indians Naunekeag, and to which Endicott, with the fond affectation of fanatics of that age to employ the language and appellations of Scripture in the affairs of common life, had given the name of Salem.

The emigrants under Endicott, and such as now joined them, coincided perfectly in religious principles. They were puritans of the strictest form; and to men of this character the institution of a church was naturally of such interesting concern as to take place of every other object. In this first transaction, they displayed at once the extent of the reformation at which they aimed. Without regard to the sentiments of that monarch under the sanction of whose authority they settled in America, and from whom they derived right to act as a body politic, and in contempt of the laws of England, with which the charter required that none of their acts or ordinances should be inconsistent, they adopted in their infant church that form of policy which has since been distinguished by the name of Independent. They united together in religious society [Aug. 6], by a solemn covenant with God and with one another, and in strict conformity, as they imagined, to the rules of Scripture. They elected a pastor, a teacher, and an elder, whom they set apart for their respective offices, by imposition of the hands of the brethren. All who were that day admitted members of the church signified their assent to a confession of faith drawn up by their teacher, and gave an account of the foundation of their own hopes as Christians; and it was declared that no person should hereafter be received into communion until he gave satisfaction to the church with respect to his faith and sanctity. The form of public worship which they instituted was without a liturgy, disencumbered of every superfluous ceremony, and reduced to the lowest standard of Calvinistic simplicity.†

It was with the utmost complacence that men passionately attached to their own notions, and who had long been restrained from avowing them, employed themselves in framing this model of a pure church. But in the first moment that they began to taste of Christian liberty themselves, they forgot that other men had an equal title to enjoy it. Some of their number, retaining a high veneration for the ritual of the English church, were so much offended at the total abolition of it, that they withdrew from com-

* Hutchinson's Collect. of Orig. Papers, p. 18.—It is surprising that Mr. Neal, an industrious and generally well informed writer, should affirm, that "free liberty of conscience was granted by this charter to all who should settle in those parts, to worship God in their own way." Hist. of New Engl. i. 124. This he repeats in his History of the Puritans, ii. 210; and subsequent historians have copied him implicitly. No permission of this kind, however, is contained in the charter; and such an indulgence would have been inconsistent with all the maxims of Charles and his ministers during the course of his reign. At the time when Charles issued the charter, the influence of Laud over his counsels was at its height, the puritans were prosecuted with the greatest severity, and the kingdom was ruled entirely by prerogative. This is not an era in which one can expect to meet with concessions in favour of nonconformists, from a prince of Charles's character and principles.

† Math. Magnal, p. 18. Neal's Hist. of N. Engl. i. 126. Chalmers, p. 143.

munion with the newly instituted church, and assembled separately for the worship of God. With an inconsistency of which there are such flagrant instances among Christians of every denomination that it cannot be imputed as a reproach peculiar to any sect, the very men who had themselves fled from persecution became persecutors; and had recourse, in order to enforce their own opinions, to the same unhallowed weapons, against the employment of which they had lately remonstrated with so much violence. Endicott called the two chief malecontents before him; and though they were men of note, and among the number of original patentees, he expelled them from the society, and sent them home in the ships which were returning to England.* The colonists were now united in sentiments; but, on the approach of winter, they suffered so much from diseases, which carried off almost one half of their number, that they made little progress in occupying the country.

Meanwhile the directors of the company in England exerted their utmost endeavours in order to reinforce the colony with a numerous body of new settlers; and as the intolerant spirit of Laud exacted conformity to all the injunctions of the church with greater rigour than ever, the condition of such as had any scruples with respect to this became so intolerable that many accepted of their invitation to a secure retreat in New England. Several of these were persons of greater opulence and of better condition than any who had hitherto migrated to that country. But as they intended to employ their fortunes, as well as to hazard their persons in establishing a permanent colony there, and foresaw many inconveniences from their subjection to laws made without their own consent, and framed by a society which must always be imperfectly acquainted with their situation, they insisted that the corporate powers of the company should be transferred from England to America, and the government of the colony be vested entirely in those who, by settling in the latter country, became members of it.† The company had already expended considerable sums in prosecuting the design of their institution, without having received almost any return, and had no prospect of gain, or even of reimbursement, but what was too remote and uncertain to be suitable to the ideas of merchants, the most numerous class of its members. They hesitated, however, with respect to the legality of granting the demand of the intended emigrants. But such was their eagerness to be disengaged from an unpromising adventure, that, "by general consent it was determined, that the charter should be transferred, and the government be settled in New England."‡ To the members of the corporation who chose to remain at home was reserved a share in the trading stock and profits of the company during seven years.

In this singular transaction, to which there is nothing similar in the history of English colonization, two circumstances merit particular attention: one is the power of the company to make this transference; the other is the silent acquiescence with which the king permitted it to take place. If the validity of this determination of the company be tried by the charter which constituted it a body politic, and conveyed to it all the corporate powers with which it was invested, it is evident that it could neither exercise those powers in any mode different from what the charter prescribed, nor alienate them in such a manner as to convert the jurisdiction of a trading corporation in England into a provincial government in America. But from the first institution of the company of Massachusetts Bay, its members seem to have been animated with a spirit of innovation in civil policy, as well as in religion; and by the habit of rejecting established usages in the one, they were prepared for deviating from them in the other.

* Mather, p. 19. Neal, p. 129. † Hutchinson's Coll. of Papers, p. 25. ‡ Mather, p. 20. Hutchinson's Hist. p. 12. Chalmers, p. 150.

They had applied for a royal charter, in order to give legal effect to their operations in England, as acts of a body politic; but the persons whom they sent out to America, as soon as they landed there, considered themselves as individuals united together by voluntary association, possessing the natural right of men who form a society, to adopt what mode of government, and to enact what laws they deemed most conducive to general felicity. Upon this principle of being entitled to judge and to decide for themselves, they established their church in Salem, without regard to the institutions of the church of England, of which the charter supposed them to be members, and bound of consequence to conformity with its ritual. Suitable to the same ideas, we shall observe them framing all their future plans of civil and ecclesiastical policy. The king, though abundantly vigilant in observing and checking slighter encroachments on his prerogative, was either so much occupied at that time with other cares, occasioned by his fatal breach with his parliament, that he could not attend to the proceedings of the company; or he was so much pleased with the prospect of removing a body of turbulent subjects to a distant country, where they might be useful, and could not prove dangerous, that he was disposed to connive at the irregularity of a measure which facilitated their departure.

Without interruption from the crown, the adventurers proceeded to carry their scheme into execution. In a general court, John Winthrop was appointed governor, and Thomas Dudley deputy governor, and eighteen assistants were chosen; in whom, together with the body of freemen who should settle in New England, were vested all the corporate rights of the company. With such zeal and activity did they prepare for emigration, that in the course of the ensuing year seventeen ships sailed for New England, and aboard these above fifteen hundred persons, among whom were several of respectable families, and in easy circumstances. On their arrival in New England, many were so ill satisfied with the situation of Salem, that they explored the country in quest of some better station; and settling in different places around the Bay, according to their various fancies, laid the foundations of Boston, Charles Town, Dorchester, Roxborough, and other towns, which have since become considerable in the province. In each of these a church was established on the same model with that of Salem. This, together with the care of making provision for their subsistence during winter, occupied them entirely during some months. But in the first general court [Oct. 19], their disposition to consider themselves as members of an independent society, unconfined by the regulations of their charter, began to appear. The election of the governor and deputy governor, the appointment of all other officers, and even the power of making laws, all which were granted by the charter to the freemen, were taken from them, and vested in the council of assistants. But the aristocratical spirit of this resolution did not accord with the ideas of equality prevalent among the people, who had been surprised into an approbation of it. Next year [1631] the freemen, whose numbers had been greatly augmented by the admission of new members, resumed their former rights

But, at the same time, they ventured to deviate from the charter in a matter of greater moment, which deeply affected all the future operations of the colony, and contributed greatly to form that peculiar character by which the people of New England have been distinguished. A law was passed, declaring that none shall hereafter be admitted freemen, or be entitled to any share in the government, or be capable of being chosen magistrates, or even of serving as jurymen, but such as have been received into the church as members.* By this resolution, every person who did not hold the favourite opinions concerning the doctrines of religion, the discipline of the church, or the rites of worship, was at once cast out of the

* Hutchinson, p. 26. Chalmers, p. 153

society, and stripped of all the privileges of a citizen. An uncontrolled power of approving or rejecting the claims of those who applied for admission into communion with the church being vested in the ministers and leading men of each congregation, the most valuable of all civil rights was made to depend on their decision with respect to qualifications purely ecclesiastical. As in examining into these they proceeded not by any known or established rules, but exercised a discretionary judgment, the clergy rose gradually to a degree of influence and authority, from which the levelling spirit of the independent church policy was calculated to exclude them. As by their determination the political condition of every citizen was fixed, all paid court to men possessed of such an important power, by assuming those austere and sanctimonious manners which were known to be the most certain recommendations to their favour. In consequence of this ascendant, which was acquired chiefly by the wildest enthusiasts among the clergy, their notions became a standard to which all studied to conform, and the singularities characteristic of the puritans in that age increased, of which many remakable instances will occur in the course of our narrative.

Though a considerable number of planters was cut off by the diseases prevalent in a country so imperfectly cultivated by its original inhabitants as to be still almost one continued forest, and several, discouraged by the hardships to which they were exposed, returned to England, recruits sufficient to replace them arrived. At the same time the small-pox, a distemper fatal to the people of the New World, swept away such multitudes of the natives, that some whole tribes disappeared ; and Heaven, by thus evacuating a country in which the English might settle without molestation, was supposed to declare its intention that they should occupy it

As several of the vacant Indian stations were well chosen, such was the eagerness of the English to take possession of them, that their settlements became more numerous and more widely dispersed than suited the condition of an infant colony. This led to an innovation which totally altered the nature and constitution of the government. When a general court was to he held in the year one thousand six hundred and thirty-four, the freemen instead of attending it in person, as the charter prescribed, elected representatives in their different districts, authorizing them to appear in their name, with full power to deliberate and decide concerning every point that fell under the cognizance of the general court. Whether this measure was suggested by some designing leaders, or whether they found it prudent to soothe the people by complying with their inclination, is uncertain. The representatives were admitted, and considered themselves, in conjunction with the governor and assistants, as the supreme legislative assembly of the colony. In assertion of their own rights, they enacted that no law should be passed, no tax should be imposed, and no public officer should be appointed, but in the general assembly. The pretexts for making this new arrangement were plausible. The number of freemen was greatly increased ; many resided at a distance from the places where the supreme courts were held ; personal attendance became inconvenient ; the form of government in their own country had rendered familiar the idea of delegating their rights, and committing the guardianship of their liberties to representatives of their own choice, and the experience of ages had taught them that this important trust might with safety be lodged in their hands. Thus did the company of Massachusetts Bay, in less than six years from its incorporation by the king, mature and perfect a scheme which, I have already observed, some of its more artful and aspiring leaders seem to have had in view, when the association for peopling New England was first formed. The colony must henceforward be considered, not as a corporation whose powers were defined, and its mode of procedure regulated by its charter, but as a society, which, having acquired or assumed political liberty, had, by its own voluntary deed, adopted a constitution or government framed on the model of that in England.

But however liberal their system of civil policy might be, as their religious opinions were no longer under any restraint of authority, the spirit of fanaticism continued to spread, and became every day wilder and more extravagant. Williams, a minister of Salem, in high estimation, having conceived an antipathy to the cross of St. George in the standard of England, declaimed against it with so much vehemence, as a relic of superstition and idolatry which ought not to be retained among a people so pure and sanctified, that Endicott, one of the members of the court of assistants, in a transport of zeal, publicly cut out the cross from the ensign displayed before the governor's gate. This frivolous matter interested and divided the colony. Some of the militia scrupled to follow colours in which there was a cross, lest they should do honour to an idol; others refused to serve under a mutilated banner, lest they should be suspected of having renounced their allegiance to the crown of England. After a long controversy, carried on by both parties with that heat and zeal which in trivial disputes supply the want of argument, the contest was terminated by a compromise. The cross was retained in the ensigns of forts and ships, but erased from the colours of the militia. Williams, on account of this, as well as of some other doctrines deemed unsound, was banished out of the colony.*

The prosperous state of New England was now so highly extolled, and the simple frame of its ecclesiastic policy so much admired by all whose affections were estranged from the church of England, that crowds of new settlers flocked thither [1635]. Among these were two persons, whose names have been rendered memorable by the appearance which they afterwards made on a more conspicuous theatre; one was Hugh Peters, the enthusiastic and intriguing chaplain of Oliver Cromwell: the other Mr. Henry Vane, son of Sir Henry Vane, a privy counsellor, high in office, and of great credit with the king; a young man of a noble family, animated with such zeal for pure religion and such love of liberty as induced him to relinquish all his hopes in England, and to settle in a colony hitherto no further advanced in improvement than barely to afford subsistence to its members, was received with the fondest admiration. His mortified appearance, his demure look and rigid manners, carried even beyond the standard of preciseness in that society which he joined, seemed to indicate a man of high spiritual attainments, while his abilities and address in business pointed him out as worthy of the highest station in the community. With universal consent, and high expectations of advantage from his administration, he was elected governor in the year subsequent to his arrival [1636]. But as the affairs of an infant colony afforded not objects adequate to the talents of Vane, his busy pragmatical spirit occupied itself with theological subtilties and speculations unworthy of his attention. These were excited by a woman, whose reveries produced such effects both within the colony and beyond its precincts, that frivolous as they may now appear, they must be mentioned as an occurrence of importance in its history.

It was the custom at that time in New England, among the chief men in every congregation, to meet once a week in order to repeat the sermons which they had heard, and to hold religious conference with respect to the doctrine contained in them. Mrs. Hutchinson, whose husband was among the most respectable members of the colony, regretting that persons of her sex were excluded from the benefit of those meetings, assembled statedly in her house a number of women, who employed themselves in pious exercises

* Neal's Hist. of N Eng. p. 140, &c. Hutchinson, p. 37. Chalmers, p. 156.

similar to those of the men. At first she satisfied herself with repeating what she could recollect of the discourses delivered by their teachers. She began afterwards to add illustrations, and at length proceeded to censure some of the clergy as unsound, and to vent opinions and fancies of her own. These were all founded on the system which is denominated Antinomian by divines, and tinged with the deepest enthusiasm. She taught, that sanctity of life is no evidence of justification, or of a state of favour with God; and that such as inculcated the necessity of manifesting the reality of our faith by obedience preached only a covenant of works; she contended that the Spirit of God dwelt personally in good men, and by inward revelations and impressions they received the fullest discoveries of the divine will. The fluency and confidence with which she delivered these notions gained her many admirers and proselytes, not only among the vulgar but among the principal inhabitants. The whole colony was interested and agitated. Vane, whose sagacity and acuteness seemed to forsake him whenever they were turned towards religion, espoused and defended her wildest tenets. Many conferences were held, days of fasting and humiliation were appointed, a general synod was called; and, after dissensions so violent as threatened the dissolution of the colony, Mrs. Hutchinson's opinions were condemned as erroneous, and she herself banished [1637]. Several of her disciples withdrew from the province of their own accord. Vane quitted America in disgust, unlamented even by those who had lately admired him; some of whom now regarded him as a mere visionary, and others as one of those dark turbulent spirits doomed to embroil every society into which they enter.*

However much these theological contests might disquiet the colony of Massachusetts Bay, they contributed to the more speedy population of America. When Williams was banished from Salem in the year one thousand six hundred and thirty-four, such was the attachment of his hearers to a pastor whose piety they revered, that a good number of them voluntarily accompanied him in his exile. They directed their march towards the south; and having purchased from the natives a considerable tract of land, to which Williams gave the name of Providence, they settled there. They were joined soon after by some of those to whom the proceedings against Mrs. Hutchinson gave disgust; and by a transaction with the Indians they obtained a right to a fertile island in Narraganset Bay, which acquired the name of Rhode Island. Williams remained among them upwards of forty years, respected as the father and the guide of the colony which he had planted. His spirit differed from that of the puritans in Massachusetts; it was mild and tolerating; and having ventured himself to reject established opinions, he endeavoured to secure the same liberty to other men, by maintaining that the exercise of private judgment was a natural and sacred right; that the civil magistrate has no compulsive jurisdiction in the concerns of religion; that the punishment of any person on account of his opinions was an encroachment on conscience, and an act of persecution.† These humane principles he instilled into his followers; and all who felt or dreaded oppression in other settlements resorted to a community in which universal toleration was known to be a fundamental maxim. In the plantations of Providence and Rhode Island, political union was established by voluntary association, and the equality of condition among the members, as well as their religious opinions; their form of government was purely democratical, the supreme power being lodged in the freemen personally assembled. In this state they remained until they were incorporated by charter.‡

* Mather, book vii. c. 3. Hutchinson, p. 53. 74. Neal, p. 1. 144. 165, &c. Chalmers, p. 163.

† Neal's Hist. of N. Eng. p. 141. ‡ Hutchinson, p. 38. Neal, ii. 142. Dougl. Sum. ii. p. 76, &c. Chalmers, ch. ii.

To similar causes the colony of Connecticut is indebted for its origin. The rivalship between Mr. Cotton and Mr. Hooker, two favourite ministers in the settlement of Massachusetts Bay, disposed the latter, who was least successful in this contest for fame and power, to wish for some settlement at a distance from a competitor by whom his reputation was eclipsed. A good number of those who had imbibed Mrs. Hutchinson's notions, and were offended at such as combated them, offered to accompany him. Having employed proper persons to explore the country, they pitched upon the west side of the great river Connecticut as the most inviting station; and in the year one thousand six hundred and thirty-six, about a hundred persons, with their wives and families, after a fatiguing march of many days through woods and swamps, arrived there, and laid the foundation of the towns of Hartford, Springfield, and Weathersfield. This settlement was attended with peculiar irregularities. Part of the district now occupied lay beyond the limits of the territory granted to the colony of Massachusetts Bay, and yet the emigrants took a commission from the governor and court of assistants, empowering them to exercise jurisdiction in that country. The Dutch from Manhados or New York, having discovered the river Connecticut, and established some trading houses upon it, had acquired all the right that prior possession confers. Lord Say and Sele and Lord Brook, the heads of two illustrious families, were so much alarmed at the arbitrary measures of Charles I., both in his civil and ecclesiastical administration, that they took a resolution, not unbecoming young men of noble birth and liberal sentiments, of retiring to the New World, in order to enjoy such a form of religion as they approved of, and those liberties which they deemed essential to the well being of society. They, too, fixed on the banks of the Connecticut as their place of settlement, and had taken possession, by building a fort at the mouth of the river, which from their united names was called Say Brook. The emigrants from Massachusetts, without regarding either the defects in their own right or the pretensions of other claimants, kept possession, and proceeded with vigour to clear and cultivate the country. By degrees they got rid of every competitor. The Dutch, recently settled in America, and too feeble to engage in a war, peaceably withdrew from Connecticut. Lord Say and Sele and Lord Brook made over to the colony whatever title they might have to any lands in that region. Society was established by a voluntary compact of the freemen; and though they soon disclaimed all dependence on the colony of Massachusetts Bay, they retained such veneration for its legislative wisdom as to adopt a form of government nearly resembling its institutions, with respect both to civil and ecclesiastical policy. At a subsequent period, the colony of Connecticut was likewise incorporated by royal charter.*

The history of the first attempts to people the provinces of New Hampshire and Maine, which form the fourth and most extensive division in New England, is obscured and perplexed, by the interfering claims of various proprietors. The company of Plymouth had inconsiderately parcelled out the northern part of the territory contained in its grant among different persons: of these only Sir Ferdinando Gorges and Captain Mason seem to have had any serious intention to occupy the lands allotted to them. Their efforts to accomplish this were meritorious and persevering, but unsuccessful. The expense of settling colonies in an uncultivated country must necessarily be great and immediate; the prospect of a return is often uncertain, and always remote. The funds of two private adventurers were not adequate to such an undertaking. Nor did the planters whom they sent out possess that principle of enthusiasm, which animated their neighbours of Massachusetts with vigour to struggle through all the hardships and

* Hutchinson, p. 44, &c Neal, i. 147. Douglas, ii. 158, &c. Chalmers's Annals, ch. xii.

dangers to which society in its infancy is exposed in a savage land. Gorges and Mason, it is probable, must have abandoned their design, if, from the same motives that settlements had been made in Rhode Island and Connecticut, colonists had not unexpectedly migrated into New Hampshire and Maine. Mr. Wheelwright, a minister of some note, nearly related to Mrs. Hutchinson, and one of her most fervent admirers and partisans, had on this account been banished from the province of Massachusetts Bay.* In quest of a new station, he took a course opposite to the other exiles, and advancing towards the north, founded the town of Exeter on a small river flowing into Piscataqua Bay. His followers, few in number, but firmly united, were of such rigid principles, that even the churches of Massachusetts did not appear to them sufficiently pure. From time to time they received some recruits, whom love of novelty, or dissatisfaction with the ecclesiastical institutions of the other colonies prompted to join them. Their plantations were widely dispersed, but the country was thinly peopled, and its political state extremely unsettled. The colony of Massachusetts Bay claimed jurisdiction over them, as occupying lands situated within the limits of their grant. Gorges and Mason asserted the rights conveyed to them as proprietors by their charter. In several districts the planters, without regarding the pretensions of either party, governed themselves by maxims and laws copied from those of their brethren in the adjacent colonies.† The first reduction of the political constitution in the provinces of New Hampshire and Maine into a regular and permanent form, was subsequent to the Revolution.

By extending their settlements, the English became exposed to new danger. The tribes of Indians around Massachusetts Bay were feeble and unwarlike; yet from regard to justice, as well as motives of prudence, the first colonists were studious to obtain the consent of the natives before they ventured to occupy any of their lands; and though in such transactions the consideration given was often very inadequate to the value of the territory acquired, it was sufficient to satisfy the demands of the proprietors. The English took quiet possession of the lands thus conveyed to them, and no open hostility broke out between them and the ancient possessors. But the colonies of Providence and Connecticut soon found that they were surrounded by more powerful and martial nations. Among these the most considerable were the Narragansets and Pequods; the former seated on the bay which bears their name, and the latter occupying the territory which stretches from the river Pequods along the banks of the Connecticut. The Pequods were a formidable people, who could bring into the field a thousand warriors not inferior in courage to any in the New World. They foresaw, not only that the extermination of the Indian race must be the consequence of permitting the English to spread over the continent of America, but that, if measures were not speedily concerted to prevent it, the calamity would be unavoidable. With this view they applied to the Narragansets, requesting them to forget ancient animosities for a moment, and to co-operate with them in expelling a common enemy who threatened both with destruction. They represented that, when those strangers first landed, the object of their visit was not suspected, and no proper precautions were taken to check their progress; that now, by sending out colonies in one year towards three different quarters, their intentions were manifest, and the people of America must abandon their native seats to make way for unjust intruders.

But the Narragansets and Pequods, like most of the contiguous tribes in America, were rivals, and there subsisted between them an hereditary and implacable enmity. Revenge is the darling passion of savages; in order

* Hutchinson, p. 70. † Ibid. p. 103, &c. 176. Douglas's Sum. ii. 22, &c. Chalmers's Annals, ch. xvii.

to secure the indulgence of which there is no present advantage that they will not sacrifice, and no future consequence which they do not totally disregard. The Narragansets, instead of closing with the prudent proposal of their neighbours, discovered their hostile intentions to the governor of Massachusetts Bay: and, eager to lay hold on such a favourable opportunity of wreaking their vengeance on their ancient foes, entered into an alliance with the English against them. The Pequods, more exasperated than discouraged by the imprudence and treachery of their countrymen, took the field, and carried on the war in the usual mode of Americans. They surprised stragglers, and scalped them; they plundered and burnt remote settlements; they attacked Fort Say Brook without success, though garrisoned only by twenty men; and when the English began to act offensively, they retired to fastnesses which they deemed inaccessible. The different colonies had agreed to unite against the common enemy, each furnishing a quota of men in proportion to its numbers. The troops of Connecticut, which lay most exposed to danger, were soon assembled. The march of those from Mussachusetts, which formed the most considerable body, was retarded by the most singular cause that ever influenced the operations of a military force. When they were mustered previous to their departure, it was found that some of the officers, as well as of the private soldiers, were still under a covenant of works; and that the blessing of God could not be implored or expected to crown the arms of such unhallowed men with success. The alarm was general, and many arrangements necessary in order to cast out the unclean, and to render this little band sufficiently pure to fight the battles of a people who entertained high ideas of their own sanctity.*

Meanwhile the Connecticut troops, reinforced by a small detachment from Say Brook, found it necessary to advance towards the enemy. They were posted on a rising ground, in the middle of a swamp towards the head of the river Mistick, which they had surrounded with palisadoes, the best defence that their slender skill in the art of fortification had discovered. Though they knew that the English were in motion, yet, with the usual improvidence and security of savages, they took no measures either to observe their progress, or to guard against being surprised themselves. The enemy, unperceived, reached the palisadoes [May 20]; and if a dog had not given the alarm by barking, the Indians must have been massacred without resistance. In a moment, however, they started to arms, and, raising the war cry, prepared to repel the assailants. But at that early period of their intercourse with the Europeans, the Americans were little acquainted with the use of gunpowder, and dreaded its effects extremely. While some of the English galled them with an incessant fire through the intervals between the palisadoes, others forced their way by the entries into the fort, filled only with branches of trees; and setting fire to the huts which were covered with reeds, the confusion and terror quickly became general. Many of the women and children perished in the flames; and the warriors, in endeavouring to escape, were either slain by the English, or, falling into the hands of their Indian allies, who surrounded the fort at a distance, were reserved for a more cruel fate. After the junction of the troops from Massachusetts, the English resolved to pursue their victory; and hunting the Indians from one place of retreat to another, some subsequent encounters were hardly less fatal to them than the action on the Mistick. In less than three months the tribe of Pequods were extirpated: a few miserable fugitives, who took refuge among the neighbouring Indians, being incorporated by them, lost their name as a distinct people. In this first essay of their arms, the colonists of New England seem to have been conducted by skilful and enterprising officers, and dis-

* Neal, i. 168.

played both courage and perseverance as soldiers. But they stained their laurels by the use which they made of victory. Instead of treating the Pequods as an independent people, who made a gallant effort to defend the property, the rights, and the freedom of their nation, they retaliated upon them all the barbarities of American war. Some they massacred in cold blood, others they gave up to be tortured by their Indian allies, a considerable number they sold as slaves in Bermudas, the rest were reduced to servitude among themselves.*

But reprehensible as this conduct of the English must be deemed, their vigorous efforts in this decisive campaign filled all the surrounding tribes of Indians with such a high opinion of their valour as secured a long tranquillity to all their settlements. At the same time the violence of administration in England continued to increase their population and strength, by forcing many respectable subjects to tear themselves from all the tender connections that bind men to their native country, and to fly for refuge to a region of the New World, which hitherto presented to them nothing that could allure them thither but exemption from oppression. The number of those emigrants drew the attention of government, and appeared so formidable that a proclamation was issued, prohibiting masters of ships from carrying passengers to New England without special permission. On many occasions this injunction was eluded or disregarded. Fatally for the king, it operated with full effect in one instance. Sir Arthur Haslerig, John Hampden, Oliver Cromwell, and some other persons whose principles and views coincided with theirs, impatient to enjoy those civil and religious liberties which they struggled in vain to obtain in Great Britain, hired some ships to carry them and their attendants to New England. By order of council, an embargo was laid on these when on the point of sailing; and Charles, far from suspecting that the future revolutions in his kingdoms were to be excited and directed by persons in such an humble sphere of life, forcibly detained the men destined to overturn his throne, and to terminate his days by a violent death.†

But, in spite of all the efforts of government to check this spirit of migration, the measures of the king and his ministers were considered by a great body of the people as so hostile to those rights which they deemed most valuable, that in the course of the year one thousand six hundred and thirty-eight, about three thousand persons embarked for New England, choosing rather to expose themselves to all the consequences of disregarding the royal proclamation than to remain longer under oppression. Exasperated at this contempt of his authority, Charles had recourse to a violent but effectual mode of accomplishing what he had in view. A writ of *quo warranto* was issued against the corporation of Massachusetts Bay. The colonists had conformed so little to the terms of their charter that judgment was given against them without difficulty. They were found to have forfeited all their rights as a corporation, which of course returned to the crown, and Charles began to take measures for new modelling the political frame of the colony, and vesting the administration of its affairs in other hands. But his plans were never carried into execution. In every corner of his dominions the storm now began to gather, which soon burst out with such fatal violence, that Charles, during the remainder of his unfortunate reign, occupied with domestic and more interesting cares, had not leisure to bestow any attention upon a remote and inconsiderable province.‡

On the meeting of the Long Parliament, such a revolution took place in England that all the motives for migrating to the New World ceased.

* Hutchinson, p. 58. 76, &c. Mather, Magnalia, b. vii. ch. 6. Hubbard's State of N. Eng. p. 5. 116, &c. † Mather, Magnalia, b. i. ch. 5. p. 23. Neal's Hist. of N. Eng. i. 151. Chalmers' Annals, i. 155. 160, &c. ‡ Hutchinson, p. 86. 502, &c. Chalmers's Annals, i. 161.

The maxims of the puritans with respect to the government both of church and state became predominant in the nation, and were enforced by the hand of power. Their oppressors were humbled; that perfect system of reformed polity, which had long been the object of their admiration and desire, was established by law; and amidst the intrigues and conflicts of an obstinate civil war, turbulent and aspiring spirits found such full occupation that they had no inducement to quit a busy theatre, on which they had risen to act a most conspicuous part. From the year one thousand six hundred and twenty, when the first feeble colony was conducted to New England by the Brownists, to the year one thousand six hundred and forty, it has been computed that twenty-one thousand two hundred British subjects had settled there. The money expended by various adventurers during that period, in fitting out ships, in purchasing stock, and transporting settlers, amounted on a moderate calculation, nearly to two hundred thousand pounds:* a vast sum in that age, and which no principles, inferior in force to those wherewith the puritans were animated, could have persuaded men to lay out on the uncertain prospect of obtaining an establishment in a remote uncultivated region, which, from its situation and climate, could allure them with no hope but that of finding subsistence and enjoying freedom. For some years, even subsistence was procured with difficulty; and it was towards the close of the period to which our narrative is arrived, before the product of the settlement yielded the planters any return for their stock. About that time they began to export corn in small quantities to the West Indies, and made some feeble attempts to extend the fishery, and to open the trade in lumber, which have since proved the staple articles of commerce in the colony.† Since the year one thousand six hundred and forty, the number of people with which New England has recruited the population of the parent state, is supposed at least to equal what may have been drained from it by occasional migrations thither.

But though the sudden change of system in Great Britain stopped entirely the influx of settlers into New England, the principles of the colonists coincided so perfectly with those of the popular leaders in parliament that they were soon distinguished by peculiar marks of their brotherly affection. By a vote of the House of Commons in the year one thousand six hundred and forty-two, the people in all the different plantations of New England were exempted from payment of any duties, either upon goods exported thither, or upon those which they imported into the mother country, until the House shall take further order to the contrary. This was afterwards confirmed [1646] by the authority of both Houses. Encouraged by such an extraordinary privilege, industry made rapid progress in all the districts of New England, and population increased along with it. In return for those favours, the colonists applauded the measures of parliament, celebrated its generous efforts to vindicate the rights and liberties of the nation, prayed for the success of its arms, and framed regulations in order to prevent any exertion in favour of the king on the other side of the Atlantic.‡

Relying on the indulgent partiality with which all their proceedings were viewed by men thus closely united with them in sentiment and wishes, the people of New England ventured on a measure which not only increased their security and power, but may be regarded as a considerable step towards independence. Under the impression or pretext of the danger to which they were exposed from the surrounding tribes of Indians, the four colonies of Massachusetts, Plymouth, Connecticut, and New Haven, entered into a league of perpetual confederacy, offensive and defensive [May 19, 1643]; an idea familiar to several leading men in the

* Mather, b. i ch 4. p. 17. ch. 5. p. 23. Hutchinson, p. 193. Chalmers's Annals, p. 165.
† Hutchinson, p. 91, 92. ‡ Ibid. p. 114. App. 517. Chalmers's Annals, i. 174. 176.

colonies, as it was framed in imitation of the famous bond of union among the Dutch provinces, in whose dominions the Brownists had long resided. It was stipulated that the confederates should henceforth be distinguished by the name of the United Colonies of New England; that each colony should remain separate and distinct, and have exclusive jurisdiction within its own territory; and that in every war, offensive or defensive, each of the confederates shall furnish his quota of men, provisions, and money, at a rate to be fixed from time to time, in proportion to the number of people in each settlement; that an assembly composed of two commissioners from each colony shall be held annually, with power to deliberate and decide in all points of common concern to the confederacy; and every determination, in which six of their number concur, shall be binding on the whole.* In this transaction the Colonies of New England seem to have considered themselves as independent societies, possessing all the rights of sovereignty, and free from the control of any superior power. The governing party in England, occupied with affairs of more urgent concern, and nowise disposed to observe the conduct of their brethren in America with any jealous attention, suffered the measure to pass without animadversion.

Emboldened by this connivance, the spirit of independence gathered strength, and soon displayed itself more openly; some persons of note in the colony of Massachusetts, averse to the system of ecclesiastical polity established there, and preferring to it the government and discipline of the churches of England or Scotland, having remonstrated to the general court against the injustice of depriving them of their rights as freemen, and of their privileges as Christians [1646], because they could not join as members with any of the congregational churches, petitioned that they might no longer be bound to obey laws to which they had not assented, nor be subjected to taxes imposed by an assembly in which they were not represented. Their demands were not only rejected, but they were imprisoned and fined as disturbers of the public peace; and when they appointed some of their number to lay their grievances before parliament, the annual court, in order to prevent this appeal to the supreme power, attempted first to seize their papers, and to obstruct their embarkation for England. But though neither of these could be accomplished, such was the address and influence of the Colony's agents in England, that no inquiry seems to have been made into this transaction.† This was followed by an indication, still less ambiguous, of the aspiring spirit prevalent among the people of Massachusetts. Under every form of government the right of coining money has been considered as a prerogative peculiar to sovereignty, and which no subordinate member in any state is entitled to claim. Regardless of this established maxim, the general court ordered a coinage of silver money at Boston [1652], stamped with the name of the colony, and a tree as an apt symbol of its progressive vigour.‡ Even this usurpation escaped without notice. The Independents, having now humbled all rival sects, engrossed the whole direction of affairs in Great Britain, and long accustomed to admire the government of New England, framed agreeably to those principles which they had adopted as the most perfect model of civil and ecclesiastical polity, they were unwilling to stain its reputation by censuring any part of its conduct.

When Cromwell usurped the supreme power, the colonies of New England continued to stand as high in his estimation. As he had deeply imbibed all the fanatical notions of the Independents, and was perpetually surrounded by the most eminent and artful teachers of that sect, he kept a constant correspondence with the leading men in the American settle-

* Neal's Hist. of N, Eng. i. 202, &c. Hutchinson p. 124. Chalmers's Annals, p. 177. † Neal's Hist. of N. Eng. i. 121. Hutchinson's Hist. 145, &c Collect. 188, &c. Chalm. Ann. 179. Mather, Magnal. b. iii. ch. i. p 30. ‡ Hutchinson's Hist. 177, 178. Chalmers's Annals, p. 181

ments, who seem to have looked up to him as a zealous patron.* He in return considered them as his most devoted adherents, attached to him no less by affection than by principle. He soon gave a striking proof of this. On the conquest of Jamaica, he formed a scheme for the security and improvement of the acquisition made by his victorious arms, suited to the ardour of an impetuous spirit that delighted in accomplishing its ends by extraordinary means. He proposed to transport the people of New England to that island, and employed every argument calculated to make impression upon them, in order to obtain their consent. He endeavoured to rouse their religious zeal by representing what a fatal blow it would be to the man of sin, if a colony of the faithful were settled in the midst of his territories in the New World. He allured them with prospects of immense wealth in a fertile region, which would reward the industry of those who cultivated it with all the precious productions of the torrid zone, and expressed his fervent wish that they might take possession of it, in order to fulfil God's promise of making his people the head and not the tail. He assured them of being supported by the whole force of his authority, and of vesting all the powers of government entirely in their hands. But by this time the colonists were attached to a country in which they had resided for many years, and where, though they did not attain opulence, they enjoyed the comforts of life in great abundance ; and they dreaded so much the noxious climate of the West Indies, which had proved fatal to a great number of the English who first settled in Jamaica, that they declined, though in the most respectful terms, closing with the Protector's proposition.†

* Hutchinson, App. 520, &c. Collect. p. 233

† Hutchinson, p. 190, &c. Chalmers, p 188

# NOTES AND ILLUSTRATIONS.

### NOTE [1]. PAGE 10.

TYRE was situated at such a distance from the Arabian Gulf, or Red Sea, as made it impracticable to convey commodities from thence to that city by land carriage. This induced the Phœnicians to render themselves masters of *Rhinocrura* or *Rhinocolura*, the nearest port in the Mediterranean to the Red Sea. They landed the cargoes which they purchased in Arabia, Ethiopia, and India, at Elath, the safest harbour in the Red Sea towards the North. Thence they were carried by land to Rhinocolura, the distance not being very considerable; and, being re-shipped in that port were transported to Tyre, and distributed over the world. Strabon. Geogr. edit. Casaub. lib. xvi. p. 1128. Diodor. Sicul. Biblioth. Histor. edit. Wesselingii, lib. i. p. 70.

### NOTE [2]. PAGE 21.

THE Periplus Hannonis is the only authentic monument of the Carthaginian skill in naval affairs, and one of the most curious fragments transmitted to us by antiquity. The learned and industrious Mr. Dodwell, in a dissertation prefixed to the Periplus of Hanno, in the edition of the Minor Geographers published at Oxford, endeavours to prove that this is a spurious work, the composition of some Greek, who assumed Hanno's name. But M. de Montesquieu, in his l'Esprit des Loix, lib. xxi. c. 8. and M. de Bougainville, in a dissertation published tom. xxvi. of the Mémoires de l'Académie des Inscriptions, &c. have established its authenticity by arguments which to me appear unanswerable. Ramusio has accompanied his translation of this curious voyage with a dissertation tending to illustrate it. Racolte de Viaggi, vol. i. p. 112. M. de Bougainville has, with great learning and ability, treated the same subject. It appears that Hanno, according to the mode of ancient navigation, undertook this voyage in small vessels so constructed that he could keep close in with the coast. He sailed from Gedes to the island of Cerne in twelve days. This is probably what is known to the moderns by the name of the Isle of Arguim. It became the chief station of the Carthaginians on that coast; and M. de Bougainville contends, that the cisterns found there are monuments of the Carthaginian power and ingenuity. Proceeding from Cerne, and still following the winding of the coast, he arrived in seventeen days, at a promontory which he called *The West Horn*, probably Cape Palmas. From this he advanced to another promontory, which he named *The South Horn*, and which is manifestly Cape de Tres Puntas, about five degrees north of the line. All the circumstances contained in the short abstract of his journal, which is handed down to us, concerning the appearance and state of the countries on the coast of Africa, are confirmed and illustrated by a comparison with the accounts of modern navigators. Even those circumstances which, from their seeming improbability, have been produced to invalidate the credibility of his relation, tend to confirm it. He observes, that in the country to the south of Cerne, a profound silence reigned through the day; but during the night innumerable fires were kindled along the banks of the rivers, and the air resounded with the noise of pipes and drums and cries of joy. The same thing, as Ramusio observes, still takes place. The excessive heat obliges the Negroes to take shelter in the woods, or in their houses, during the day. As soon as the sun sets, they sally out, and by torchlight enjoy the pleasure of music and dancing, in which they spend the night. Ramus. i. 113. F. In another place, he mentions the sea as burning with torrents of fire. What occurred to M. Adanson, on the same coast, may explain this: "As soon," says he, "as the sun dipped beneath the horizon, and night overspread the earth with darkness, the sea lent us its friendly light. While the prow of our vessel ploughed the foaming surges, it seemed to set them all on fire. Thus we sailed in a luminous inclosure, which surrounded us like a large circle of rays, from whence darted in the wake of the ship a long stream of a light." Voy. to Senegal, p. 176. This appearance of the sea, observed by Hunter, has been mentioned as an argument against the authenticity of the Periplus. It is, however, a phenomenon very common in warm climates. Captain Cook's second voyage, vol. i. p. 15. The Periplus of Hanno has been translated, and every point with respect to it has been illustrated with much learning and ingenuity, in a work published by Don Pedr. Rodrig. Campomanes, entitled, Antiguedad maritima de Cartago, con el Periplo de su General Hannon traducido e illustrado. Mad. 1756. 4to.

### Note [3]. Page 21

Long after the navigation of the Phœnicians and of Eudoxus round Africa, Polybius, the most intelligent and best informed historian of antiquity, and particularly distinguished by his attention to geographical researches, affirms, that it was not known, in his time, whether Africa was a continued continent stretching to the south, or whether it was encompassed by the sea. Polybii Hist. lib. iii. Pliny the naturalist asserts, that there can be no communication between the southern and northern temperate zones. Plinii Hist. Natur. edit. in usum. Delph. 4to. lib. ii. c. 68. If they had given full credit to the accounts of those voyages, the former could not have entertained such a doubt, the latter could not have delivered such an opinion. Strabo mentions the voyage of Eudoxus, but treats it as a fabulous tale, lib. ii. p. 155; and, according to his account of it, no other judgment can be formed with respect to it. Strabo seems not to have known any thing with certainty concerning the form and state of the southern parts of Africa. Geogr. lib. xvii. p. 1180. Ptolemy, the most inquisitive and learned of all the ancient geographers, was equally unacquainted with any parts of Africa situated a few degrees beyond the equinoctial line; for he supposes that this great continent was not surrounded by the sea, but that it stretched, without interruption, towards the south pole; and he so far mistakes its true figure that he describes the continent as becoming broader and broader as it advanced towards the south. Ptolemæi Geogr. lib. iv. c. 9. Brietii Parallela Geogr. veteris et novæ, p. 86.

### Note [4]. Page 24.

A fact recorded by Strabo affords a very strong and singular proof of the ignorance of the ancients with respect to the situation of the various parts of the earth. When Alexander marched along the banks of the Hydaspes and Acesine, two of the rivers which fall into the Indus, he observed that there were many crocodiles in those rivers, and that the country produced beans of the same species with those which were common in Egypt. From these circumstances he concluded that he had discovered the source of the Nile, and prepared a fleet to sail down the Hydaspes to Egypt. Strab. Geogr. lib. xv. p. 1020. This amazing error did not arise from any ignorance of geography peculiar to that monarch; for we are informed by Strabo, that Alexander applied with particular attention in order to acquire the knowledge of this science, and had accurate maps or descriptions of the countries through which he marched. Lib. ii. p. 120. But in his age the knowledge of the Greeks did not extend beyond the limits of the Mediterranean.

### Note [5]. Page 24.

As the flux and reflux of the sea is remarkably great at the mouth of the river Indus, this would render the phenomenon more formidable to the Greeks. Varen Geogr. vol. i. p. 251.

### Note [6]. Page 25

It is probable that the ancients were seldom induced to advance so far as the mouth of the Ganges, either by motives of curiosity or views of commercial advantage. In consequence of this, their idea concerning the position of that great river was very erroneous. Ptolemy places that branch of the Ganges, which he distinguishes by the name of the Great Mouth, in the hundred and forty-sixth degree of longitude from his first meridian in the Fortunate Islands. But its true longitude, computed from that meridian, is now determined, by astronomical observations, to be only a hundred and five degrees. A geographer so eminent must have been betrayed into an error of this magnitude by the imperfection of the information which he had received concerning those distant regions; and this affords a striking proof of the intercourse with them being extremely rare. With respect to the countries of India beyond the Ganges, his intelligence was still more defective, and his errors more enormous. I shall have occasion to observe, in another place, that he has placed the country of the Seres, or China, no less than sixty degrees further east than its true position. M. d'Anville, one of the most learned and intelligent of the modern geographers, has set this matter in a clear light, in two dissertations published in Mem. de l'Académ. des Inscript. &c. tom. xxxii. p. 573. 604.

### Note [7]. Page 25.

It is remarkable, that the discoveries of the ancients were made chiefly by land; those of the moderns are carried on chiefly by sea. The progress of conquest led to the former, that of commerce to the latter. It is a judicious observation of Strabo, that the conquests of Alexander the Great made known the East, those of the Romans opened the West, and those of Mithridates King of Pontus the North. Lib. i. p. 26. When discovery is carried on by land alone, its progress must be slow and its operations confined. When it is carried on only by sea, its sphere may be more extensive, and its advances more rapid; but it labours under peculiar defects. Though it may make known the position of different countries, and ascertain their boundaries as far as these are determined by the ocean, it leaves us in ignorance with respect to their interior state. Above two centuries and a half have elapsed since the Europeans sailed round the southern promontory of Africa, and have traded in most of its ports; but, in a considerable part of that great continent, they have done little more than survey its coasts, and mark its capes and harbours. Its interior regions are in a great measure unknown. The ancients, who had a very imperfect knowledge of its coasts, except where they are washed by the Mediterranean or Red Sea, were accustomed to penetrate into its inland provinces, and, if we may rely on the testimony of Herodotus and Diodorus Siculus, had explored many parts of it now altogether unknown. Unless both modes of discovery be united, the geographical knowledge of the earth must remain incomplete and inaccurate.

### Note [8]. Page 27.

The notion of the ancients concerning such an excessive degree of heat in the torrid zone as rendered it uninhabitable, and their persisting in this error long after they began to have some commercial intercourse with several parts of India lying within the tropics, must appear so singular and absurd, that it may not be unacceptable to some of my readers to produce evidence of their holding this opinion, and to account for the apparent inconsistence of their theory with their experience. Cicero, who had bestowed attention upon every part of philosophy known to the ancients, seems to have believed that the torrid zone was uninhabitable, and, of consequence, that there could be no intercourse between the northern and southern temperate zones. He introduces Africanus thus addressing the younger Scipio: "You see this earth encompassed, and as it were bound in by certain zones, of which two, at the greatest distance from each other, and sustaining the opposite poles of heaven, are frozen with perpetual cold; the middle one, and the largest of all, is burnt with the heat of the sun; two are habitable; the people in the southern one are antipodes to us, with whom we have no connection." *Somnium Scipionis*, c. 6. Geminus, a Greek philosopher, contemporary with Cicero, delivers the same doctrine, not in a popular work, but in his Εισαγωγη εις Φαινομενα, a treatise purely scientific. "When we speak," says he, "of the southern temperate zone and its inhabitants, and concerning those who are called antipodes, it must be always understood, that we have no certain knowledge or information concerning the southern temperate zone, whether it be inhabited or not. But from the spherical figure of the earth, and the course which the sun holds between the tropics, we conclude that there is another zone situated to the south, which enjoys the same degree of temperature with the northern one which we inhabit." Cap. xiii. p. 31. ap. Petavii Opus de Doctr. Tempor. in quo Uranologium sive Systemata var. Auctorum. Amst. 1705. vol. 3. The opinion of Pliny the naturalist, with respect to both these points, was the same: "There are five divisions of the earth, which are called zones. All that portion which lies near to the two opposite poles is oppressed with vehement cold and eternal frost. There, unblessed with the aspect of milder stars, perpetual darkness reigns, or at the utmost, a feeble light reflected from surrounding snows. The middle of the earth, in which is the orbit of the sun, is scorched and burnt up with flames and fiery vapour. Between these torrid and frozen districts lie two other portions of the earth, which are temperate; but, on account of the burning region interposed, there can be no communication between them. Thus Heaven has deprived us of three parts of the earth." Lib. ii. c. 68. Strabo delivers his opinion to the same effect, in terms no less explicit: "The portion of the earth which lies near the equator, in the torrid zone, is rendered uninhabitable by heat." Lib. ii. p. 154. To these I might add the authority of many other respectable philosophers and historians of antiquity.

In order to explain the sense in which this doctrine was generally received, we may observe, that Parmenides, as we are informed by Strabo, was the first who divided the earth into five zones, and extended the limits of the zone which he supposed to be uninhabitable on account of heat beyond the tropics. Aristotle, as we learn likewise from Strabo, fixed the boundaries of the different zones in the same manner as they are defined by modern geographers. But the progress of discovery having gradually demonstrated that several regions of the earth which lay within the tropics were not only habitable, but populous and fertile, this induced later geographers to circumscribe the limits of the torrid zone. It is not easy to ascertain with precision the boundaries which they allotted it. From a passage in Strabo, who, as far as I know, is the only author of antiquity from whom we receive any hint concerning this subject, I should conjecture, that those who calculated according to the measurement of the earth by Eratosthenes, supposed the torrid zone to comprehend near sixteen degrees, about eight on each side of the equator; whereas such as followed the computation of Posidonius allotted about twenty-four degrees, or somewhat more than twelve degrees on each side of the equator to the torrid zone. Strabo, lib. ii. p. 151. According to the former opinion, about two-thirds of that portion of the earth which lies between the tropics was considered as habitable; according to the latter, about one-half of it. With this restriction, the doctrine of the ancients concerning the torrid zone appears less absurd; and we can conceive the reason of their asserting this zone to be uninhabitable, even after they had opened a communication with several places within the tropics. When men of science spoke of the torrid zone, they considered it as it was limited by the definition of geographers to sixteen, or at the utmost to twenty-four degrees; and as they knew almost nothing of the countries nearer to the equator, they might still suppose them to be uninhabitable. In loose and popular discourse, the name of the torrid zone continued to be given to all that portion of the earth which lies within the tropics. Cicero seems to have been unacquainted with those ideas of the later geographers; and, adhering to the division of

Parmenides, describes the torrid zone as the largest of the five. Some of the ancients rejected the notion concerning the intolerable heat of the torrid zone as a popular error. This we are told by Plutarch was the sentiment of Pythagoras; and we learn from Strabo, that Eratosthenes and Polybius had adopted the same opinion, lib. ii. p. 154. Ptolemy seems to have paid no regard to the ancient doctrine and opinions concerning the torrid zone.

### Note [9]. Page 35.

The court of Inquisition, which effectually checks a spirit of liberal inquiry, and of literary improvement, wherever it is established, was unknown in Portugal in the fifteenth century, when the people of that kingdom began their voyages of discovery. More than a century elapsed before it was introduced by John III., whose reign commenced A. D. 1521.

### Note [10]. Page 38.

An instance of this is related by Hakluyt, upon the authority of the Portuguese historian Garcia de Resende. Some English merchants having resolved to open a trade with the coast of Guinea, John II. of Portugal despatched ambassadors to Edward IV., in order to lay before him the right which he had acquired by the Pope's bull to the dominion of that country, and to request of him to prohibit his subjects to prosecute their intended voyage. Edward was so much satisfied with the exclusive title of the Portuguese, that he issued his orders in the terms which they desired. Hakluyt, Navigations, Voyages, and Traffics of the English, vol. ii. part ii. p. 2.

### Note [11]. Page 42.

The time of Columbus's death may be nearly ascertained by the following circumstances. It appears from the fragment of a letter addressed by him to Ferdinand and Isabella, A. D. 1501, that he had at that time been engaged forty years in a seafaring life. In another letter he informs them that he went to sea at the age of fourteen : from those facts it follows, that he was born A. D. 1447. Life of Christa. Columbus, by his son Don Ferdinand. Churchill's Collection of Voyages, vol. ii. p. 484, 485.

### Note [12]. Page 44.

The spherical figure of the earth was known to the ancient geographers. They invented the method, still in use, of computing the longitude and latitude of different places. According to their doctrine, the equator, or imaginary line which encompasses the earth, contained three hundred and sixty degrees ; these they divided into twenty-four parts, or hours, each equal to fifteen degrees. The country of the *Seres* or *Sinæ*, being the furthest part of India known to the ancients, was supposed by Marinus Tyrius, the most eminent of the ancient geographers before Ptolemy, to be fifteen hours, or two hundred and twenty-five degrees to the east of the first meridian, passing through the Fortunate Islands. Ptolemæi Geogr. lib. i. c. 11. If this supposition was well founded, the country of the Seres, or China, was only nine hours, or one hundred and thirty-five degrees west from the Fortunate or Canary Islands ; and the navigation in that direction was much shorter than by the course which the Portuguese were pursuing. Marco Polo, in his travels, had described countries, particularly the island of Cipango or Zipangri, supposed to be Japan, considerably to the east of any part of Asia known to the ancients. Marcus Paulus de Region. Oriental. lib. ii. c. 70. lib. iii. c. 2. Of course, this country, as it extended further to the east, was still nearer to the Canary Islands. The conclusions of Columbus, though drawn from inaccurate observations, were just. If the suppositions of Marinus had been well founded, and if the countries which Marco Polo visited, had been situated to the east of those whose longitude Marinus had ascertained, the proper and nearest course to the East Indies must have been to steer directly west. Herrera, dec. 1. lib. i. c. 2. A more extensive knowledge of the globe has now discovered the great error of Marinus, in supposing China to be fifteen hours, or two hundred and twenty-five degrees east from the Canary Islands; and that even Ptolemy was mistaken, when he reduced the longitude of China to twelve hours, or one hundred and eighty degrees. The longitude of the western frontier of that vast empire is seven hours, or one hundred and fifteen degrees from the meridian of the Canary Islands. But Columbus followed the light which his age afforded, and relied upon the authority of writers, who were at that time regarded as the instructers and guides of mankind in the science of geography.

### NOTE [13]. PAGE 53.

As the Portuguese, in making their discoveries, did not depart far from the coast of Africa, they concluded that birds, whose flight they observed with great attention, did not venture to any considerable distance from land. In the infancy of navigation it was not known that birds often stretched their flight to an immense distance from any shore. In sailing towards the West Indian Islands, birds are often seen at the distance of two hundred leagues from the nearest coast. Sloane's Nat. Hist. of Jamaica, vol. i. p. 30. Catesby saw an owl at sea when the ship was six hundred leagues distant from land. Nat. Hist. of Carolina, pref. p. 7. Hist. Naturelle de M. Buffon, tom. xvi. p. 32. From which it appears, that this indication of land, on which Columbus seems to have relied with some confidence, was extremely uncertain. This observation is confirmed by Capt. Cook, the most extensive and experienced navigator of any age or nation. "No one yet knows (says he) to what distance any of the oceanic birds go to sea; for my own part, I do not believe that there is one in the whole tribe that can be relied on in pointing out the vicinity of land" Voyage towards the South Pole, vol. i. p. 275.

### NOTE [14]. PAGE 58.

IN a letter of the Admiral's to Ferdinand and Isabella, he describes one of the harbours in Cuba with all the enthusiastic admiration of a discoverer.—"I discovered a river which a galley might easily enter: the beauty of it induced me to sound, and I found from five to eight fathoms of water. Having proceeded a considerable way up the river, every thing invited me to settle there. The beauty of the river, the clearness of the water through which I could see the sandy bottom, the multitude of palm trees of different kinds, the tallest and finest I had seen, and an infinite number of other large and flourishing trees, the birds, and the verdure of the plains are so wonderfully beautiful, that this country excels all others as far as the day surpasses the night in brightness and splendour, so that I often said, that it would be in vain for me to attempt to give your Highnesses a full account of it, for neither my tongue nor my pen could come up to the truth; and indeed I am so much amazed at the sight of such beauty, that I know not how to describe it." Life of Columb. c. 30

### NOTE [15]. PAGE 59.

THE account which Columbus gives of the humanity and orderly behaviour of the natives on this occasion is very striking. "The king (says he in a letter to Ferdinand and Isabella) having been informed of our misfortune, expressed great grief for our loss, and immediately sent aboard all the people in the place in many large canoes; we soon unloaded the ship of every thing that was upon deck, as the king gave us great assistance: he himself, with his brothers and relations, took all possible care that every thing should be properly done, both aboard and on shore. And, from time to time, he sent some of his relations weeping, to beg of me not to be dejected, for he would give me all that he had. I can assure your Highnesses, that so much care could not have been taken in securing our effects in any part of Spain, as all our property was put together in one place near his palace, until the houses which he wanted to prepare for the custody of it were emptied. He immediately placed a guard of armed men, who watched during the whole night, and those on shore lamented as if they had been much interested in our loss. The people are so affectionate, so tractable, and so peaceable, that I swear to your Highnesses, that there is not a better race of men, nor a better country in the world. They love their neighbour as themselves; their conversation is the sweetest and mildest in the world, cheerful and always accompanied with a smile. And although it is true that they go naked, yet your Highnesses may be assured that they have many very commendable customs; the king is served with great state, and his behaviour is so decent that it is pleasant to see him, as it is likewise to observe the wonderful memory which these people have, and their desire of knowing every thing, which leads them to inquire into its causes and effects." Life of Columbus, c. 32. It is probable that the Spaniards were indebted for this officious attention to the opinion which the Indians entertained of them as a superior order of beings.

### Note [16]. Page 62.

Every monument of such a man as Columbus is valuable. A letter which he wrote to Ferdinand and Isabella, describing what passed on this occasion, exhibits a most striking picture of his intrepidity, his humanity, his prudence, his public spirit, and courtly address. "I would have been less concerned for this misfortune had I alone been in danger, both because my life is a debt that I owe to the Supreme Creator, and because I have at other times been exposed to the most imminent hazard. But what gave me infinite grief and vexation was, that after it had pleased our Lord to give me faith to undertake this enterprise, in which I had now been so successful, that my opponents would have been convinced, and the glory of your Highnesses, and the extent of your territory, increased by me; it should please the Divine Majesty to stop all by my death. All this would have been more tolerable had it not been attended with the loss of those men whom I had carried with me, upon promise of the greatest prosperity, who, seeing themselves in such distress, cursed not only their coming along with me, but that fear and awe of me which prevented them from returning, as they often had resolved to have done. But besides all this, my sorrow was greatly increased by recollecting that I had left my two sons at school at Cordova, destitute of friends, in a foreign country, when it could not in all probability be known that I had done such services as might induce Your Highnesses to remember them. And though I comforted myself with the faith that our Lord would not permit that which tended so much to the glory of his Church, and which I had brought about with so much trouble, to remain imperfect, yet I considered, that, on account of my sins, it was his will to deprive me of that glory which I might have attained in this world. While in this confused state, I thought on the good fortune which accompanies Your Highnesses, and imagined that although I should perish, and the vessel be lost, it was possible that you might somehow come to the knowledge of my voyage, and the success with which it was attended. For that reason I wrote upon parchment with the brevity which the situation required, that I had discovered the lands which I promised, in how many days I had done it, and what course I had followed. I mentioned the goodness of the country, the character of the inhabitants, and that Your Highnesses' subjects were left in possession of all that I had discovered. Having sealed this writing, I addressed it to Your Highnesses, and promised a thousand ducats to any person who should deliver it sealed, so that if any foreigner found it, the promised reward might prevail on them not to give the information to another. I then caused a great cask to be brought to me, and wrapping up the parchment in an oiled cloth, and afterwards in a cake of wax, I put it into the cask, and having stopped it well, I cast it into the sea. All the men believed that it was some act of devotion. Imagining that this might never chance to be taken up, as the ships approached nearer to Spain, I made another packet like the first, and placed it at the top of the poop, so that, if the ship sunk, the cask remaining above water might be committed to the guidance of fortune."

### Note [17]. Page 64.

Some Spanish authors, with the meanness of national jealousy, have endeavoured to detract from the glory of Columbus, by insinuating that he was led to the discovery of the New World, not by his own inventive or enterprising genius, but by information which he had received. According to their account a vessel having been driven from its course by easterly winds, was carried before them far to the west, and landed on the coast of an unknown country, from which it returned with difficulty; the pilot and three sailors being the only persons who survived the distresses which the crew suffered from want of provisions and fatigue in this long voyage. In a few days after their arrival, all the four died; but the pilot having been received into the house of Columbus, his intimate friend disclosed to him before his death, the secret of the discovery which he had accidentally made, and left him his papers containing a journal of the voyage, which served as a guide to Columbus in his undertaking. Gomara, as far as I know, is the first author who published this story. Hist. c. 13. Every circumstance is destitute of evidence to support it. Neither the name of the vessel nor its destination is known. Some pretend that it belonged to one of the seaport towns in Andalusia, and was sailing either to the Canaries or to Madeira; others, that it was a Biscayner in its way to England; others, a Portuguese ship trading on the coast of Guinea. The name of the pilot is alike unknown, as well as that of the port in which he landed on his return. According to some, it was in Portugal; according to others, in Madeira, or the Azores. The year in which this voyage was made is no less uncertain. Monson's Nav. Tracts. Churchill, iii. 371. No mention is made of this pilot, or his discoveries, by And. Bernaldes, or Pet. Martyr, the contemporaries of Columbus. Herrera, with his usual judgment, passes over it in silence. Oviedo takes notice of this report, but considers it as a tale fit only to amuse the vulgar. Hist. lib. ii. c. 2. As Columbus held his course directly west from the Canaries, and never varied it, some later authors have supposed that this uniformity is a proof of his being guided by some previous information. But they do not recollect the principles on which he founded all his hopes of success, that by holding a westerly course he must certainly arrive at those regions of the east described by the ancients. His firm belief of his own system led him to take that course, and to pursue it without deviation.

The Spaniards are not the only people who have called in question Columbus's claim to the honour of having discovered America. Some German authors ascribed this honour to Martin Behaim their countryman. He was of the noble family of the Behaims of Schwartzbach, citizens of the first rank in the Imperial town of Nuremberg. Having studied under the celebrated John Muller, better known by the name of Regiomontanus, he acquired such knowledge of cosmography as excited a desire of exploring those regions, the situation and qualities of which he had been accustomed, under that able master, to investigate and describe. Under the patronage of the Dutchess of Burgundy he repaired to Lisbon, whither the fame of the Portuguese discoveries invited all the adventurous spirits of the age. There, as we learn from Herman Schedel, of whose *Chronicon Mundi*, a German translation was printed at Nuremberg, A. D. 1493, his merit as a cosmographer raised him, in conjunction with Diego Cano, to the command of a squadron fitted out for discovery in the year 1483. In that voyage he is said to have discovered the kingdom of Congo. He settled in the island of Fayal, one of the Azores, and was a particular friend of Columbus. Herrera, dec. 1. lib. i. c. 2. Magellan had a terrestrial globe made by Behaim, on which he demonstrated the course that he proposed to hold in search of the communication with the South Sea, which he afterwards discovered. Gomara Hist. c. 19. Herrera, dec. 11. lib. ii. c. 19. In the year 1492, Behaim visited his relations in Nuremberg, and left with them a map drawn with his own hand, which is still preserved among the archives of the family. Thus far the story of Martin Behaim seems to be well authenticated; but the account of his having discovered any part of the New World appears to be merely conjectural.

In the first edition, as I had at that time hardly any knowledge of Behaim but what I derived from a frivolous dissertation 'De vero Novi Orbis Inventore,' published at Frankfort, A. D. 1714, by Jo. Frid. Stuvenius, I was induced, by the authority of Herrera, to suppose that Behaim was not a native of Germany; but from more full and accurate information, communicated to me by the learned Dr. John Reinhold Forster, I am now satisfied that I was mistaken.

Dr. Forster has been likewise so good as to favour me with a copy of Behaim's map, as published by Doppelmayer in his account of the Mathematicians and Artists of Nuremberg. From this map the imperfection of cosmographical knowledge at that period is manifest. Hardly one place is laid down in its true situation. Nor can I discover from it any reason to suppose that Behaim had the least knowledge of any region in America. He delineates, indeed, an island to which he gives the name of St. Brandon. This, it is imagined, may be some part of Guiana, supposed at first to be an island. He places it in the same latitude with the Cape Verd isles, and I suspect it to be an imaginary island which has been admitted into some ancient maps on no better authority than the legend of the Irish St. Brandon or Brendan, whose story is so childishly fabulous as to be unworthy of any notice. Girald. Cambrensis ap. Missingham Florilegium Sanctorum, p. 427.

The pretensions of the Welsh to the discovery of America seem not to rest on a foundation much more solid. In the twelfth century, according to Powell, a dispute having arisen among the sons of Owen Guyneth, King of North Wales, concerning the succession to his crown, Madoc, one of their number, weary of this contention, betook himself to sea in quest of a more quiet settlement. He steered due west, leaving Ireland to the north, and arrived in an unknown country, which appeared to him so desirable, that he returned to Wales and carried thither several of his adherents and companions. This is said to have happened about the year 1170, and after that, he and his colony were heard of no more. But it is to be observed, that Powell, on whose testimony the authenticity of this story rests, published his history above four centuries from the date of the event which he relates. Among a people as rude and as illiterate as the Welsh at that period, the memory of a transaction so remote must have been very imperfectly preserved, and would require to be confirmed by some author of greater credit, and nearer to the era of Madoc's voyage than Powell. Later antiquaries have indeed appealed to the testimony of Meredith ap Rees, a Welsh bard, who died A. D. 1477. But he too lived at such a distance of time from the event, that he cannot be considered as a witness of much more credit than Powell. Besides, his verses, published by Hakluyt, vol. iii. p. 1., convey no information, but that Madoc, dissatisfied with his domestic situation, employed himself in searching the ocean for new possessions. But even if we admit the authenticity of Powell's story, it does not follow that the unknown country which Madoc discovered by steering west, in such a course as to leave Ireland to the north, was any part of America. The naval skill of the Welsh in the twelfth century was hardly equal to such a voyage. If he made any discovery at all, it is more probable that it was Madeira, or some other of the western isles. The affinity of the Welsh language with some dialects spoken in America, has been mentioned as a circumstance which confirms the truth of Madoc's voyage. But that affinity has been observed in so few instances, and in some of these is so obscure, or so fanciful, that no conclusion can be drawn from the casual resemblance of a small number of words. There is a bird, which, as far as is yet known, is found only on the coasts of South America, from Port Desire to the Straits of Magellan. It is distinguished by the name of *Penguin.* This word in the Welsh language signifies *White-head.* Almost all the authors who favour the pretensions of the Welsh to the discovery of America, mention this as an irrefragable proof of the affinity of the Welsh language with that spoken in this region of America. But Mr. Pennant, who has given a scientific description of the Penguin, observes that all the birds of this genus have black heads, "so that we must resign every hope (adds he) founded on this hypothesis of retrieving the Cambrian race in the New World." Philos. Transact. vol. lviii. p. 91, &c. Besides this, if the Welsh, towards the close of the twelfth century, had settled in any part of America, some remains of the Christian doctrine and rites must have been found among their descendants, when they were discovered about three hundred years posterior to their migration; a period so short that, in the course of it, we cannot well suppose that all European ideas and arts would be totally forgotten. Lord Lyttleton, in his notes to the fifth book of his History of Henry II., p. 371, has examined what Powell relates concerning the discoveries made by Madoc, and invalidates the truth of his story by other arguments of great weight

The pretensions of the Norwegians to the discovery of America seem to be better founded than those of the Germans or Welsh. The inhabitants of Scandinavia were remarkable in the middle ages for the boldness and extent of their maritime excursions. In 874, the Norwegians discovered and planted a colony in Iceland. In 982, they discovered Greenland, and established settlements there. From that, some of their navigators proceeded towards the west, and discovered a country more inviting than those horrid regions with which they were acquainted. According to their representation, this country was sandy on the coasts, but in the interior parts level and covered with wood, on which account they gave it the name of *Helle-land*, and *Mark-land*, and having afterwards found some plants of the vine which bore grapes, they called it *Win-land*. The credit of this story rests, as far as I know, on the authority of the *saga*, or chronicle of King Olaus, composed by Snorro Sturlonides, or *Sturlusons*, published by Perinskiold, at Stockholm, A. D. 1697. As Snorro was born in the year 1179, his chronicle might be compiled about two centuries after the event which he relates. His account of the navigation and discoveries of *Biorn*, and his companion *Lief*, is a very rude confused tale, p. 104. 110. 326. It is impossible to discover from him what part of America it was in which the Norwegians landed. According to his account of the length of the days and nights, it must have been as far north as the fifty-eighth degree of latitude, on some part of the coast of Labradore, approaching near to the entry of Hudson's Straits. Grapes certainly are not the production of that country. Torfeus supposes that there is an error in the text, by rectifying of which the place where the Norwegians landed may be supposed to be situated in latitude 49°. But neither is that the region of the vine in America. From perusing Snorro's tale, I should think that the situation of Newfoundland corresponds best with that of the country discovered by the Norwegians. Grapes, however, are not the production of that barren island. Other conjectures are mentioned by M. Mallet, Introd. à l'Hist. de Dannem. 175, &c. I am not sufficiently acquainted with the literature of the north to examine them. It seems manifest, that if the Norwegians did discover any part of America at that period, their attempt to plant colonies proved unsuccessful, and all knowledge of it was soon lost.

### Note [18]. Page 64.

Peter Martyr, ab Angleria, a Milanese gentleman, residing at that time in the court of Spain, whose letters contain an account of the transactions of that period, in the order wherein they occurred, describes the sentiments with which he himself and his learned correspondents were affected in very striking terms. "Præ lætitia prosiluisse te, vixque a lachrymis præ gaudio temperasse, quando literas adspexisti meas quibus, de antipodum orbe latenti hactenus, te certiorem feci, mi suavissime Pomponi, insinuasti. Ex tuis ipse literis colligo, quid senseris. Sensisti autem, tantique rem fecisti, quanti virum summa doctrina insignitum decuit. Quis namque cibus sublimibus præstari potest ingeniis, isto suavior? quod condimentum gratius? A me facio conjecturam. Beati sentio spiritus meos, quando accitos alloquor prudentes aliquos ex his qui ab ea redeunt provincia. Implicent animos pecuniarum cumulis augendis miseri avari, libidinibus obscœni; nostras nos mentes, postquam Deo pleni aliquando fuerimus, contemplando, hujuscemodi rerum notitia demulciamus." Epist. 152, Pomponio Læto.

### Note [19]. Page 69.

So firmly were men of science, in that age, persuaded that the countries which Columbus had discovered were connected with the East Indies, that Benaldes, the Cura de los Palacios, who seems to have been no inconsiderable proficient in the knowledge of cosmography, contends that Cuba was not an island, but a part of the continent, and united to the dominions of the Great Khan. This he delivered as his opinion to Columbus himself, who was his guest for some time on his return from his second voyage; and he supports it by several arguments, mostly founded on the authority of Sir John Mandeville.

MS. *penes me*. Antonio Gallo, who was secretary to the magistracy of Genoa towards the close of the fifteenth century, published a short account of the navigations and discoveries of his countryman Columbus, annexed to his Opuscula Historica de Rebus Populi Genuensis: in which he informs us, from letters of Columbus which he himself had seen, that it was his opinion, founded upon nautical observations, that one of the islands he had discovered was distant only two hours or thirty degrees from Cattigara, which, in the charts of the geographers of that age, was laid down, upon the authority of Ptolemy, lib. vii. c. 3, as the most easterly place in Asia. From this he concluded, that if some unknown continent did not obstruct the navigation, there must be a short and easy access, by holding a westerly course, to this extreme region of the East. Muratori Scriptores Rer. Italicarum, vol. xxiii. p. 304.

### Note [20]. Page 71.

Bernaldes, the *Cura* or Rector de los Palacios, a contemporary writer, says, that five hundred of these captives were sent to Spain, and sold publicly in Seville as slaves; but that, by the change of climate and their inability to bear the fatigue of labour, they all died in a short time. MS. *penes me*.

### Note [21]. Page 76.

Columbus seems to have formed some very singular opinions concerning the countries which he had now discovered. The violent swell and agitation of the waters on the coast of Trinidad led him to conclude this to be the highest part of the terraqueous globe, and he imagined that various circumstances concurred in proving that the sea was here visibly elevated. Having adopted this erroneous principle, the apparent beauty of the country induced him to fall in with a notion of Sir John Mandeville, c. 102, that the terrestrial paradise was the highest land in the earth; and he believed that he had been so fortunate as to discover this happy abode. Nor ought we to think it strange that a person of so much sagacity should be influenced by the opinion or reports of such a fabulous author as Mandeville. Columbus and the other discoverers were obliged to follow such guides as they could find; and it appears from several passages in the manuscript of Andr. Bernaldes, the friend of Columbus, that no inconsiderable degree of credit was given to the testimony of Mandeville in that age. Bernaldes frequently quotes him, and always with respect.

### Note [22]. Page 81.

It is remarkable that neither Gomara nor Oviedo, the most ancient Spanish historians of America, nor Herrera, consider Ojeda, or his companion Vespucci, as the first discoverers of the continent of America. They uniformly ascribe this honour to Columbus. Some have supposed that national resentment against Vespucci, for deserting the service of Spain, and entering into that of Portugal, may have prompted these writers to conceal the actions which he performed. But Martyr and Benzoni, both Italians, could not be warped by the same prejudice. Martyr was a contemporary author; he resided in the court of Spain, and had the best opportunity to be exactly informed with respect to all public transactions; and yet neither in his Decads, the first general history published of the New World, nor in his Epistles, which contain an account of all the remarkable events of his time, does he ascribe to Vespucci the honour of having first discovered the continent. Benzoni went as an adventurer to America in the year 1541, and resided there a considerable time. He appears to have been animated with a warm zeal for the honour of Italy, his native country, and yet does not mention the exploits and discoveries of Vespucci. Herrera, who compiled his general history of America from the most authentic records, not only follows those early writers, but accuses Vespucci of falsifying the dates of both the voyages which he made to the New World, and of confounding the one with the other, in order that he might arrogate to himself the glory of having discovered the continent. Her. dec. 1. lib. iv. c. 2. He asserts, that in a judicial inquiry into this matter by the royal fiscal, it was proved by the testimony of Ojeda himself, that he touched at Hispaniola when returning to Spain from his first voyage; whereas Vespucci gave out that they returned directly to Cadiz from the coast of Paria, and touched at Hispaniola only in their second voyage; and that he had finished the voyage in five months; whereas, according to Vespucci's account, he had employed seventeen months in performing it. Viaggio primo de Am. Vespucci, p. 36. Viag. secundo, p. 45 Herrera gives a more full account of this inquest in another part of his Decads, and to the same effect. Her. dec. 1. lib. vii. c. 5. Columbus was in Hispaniola when Ojeda arrived there, and had by that time come to an agreement with Roldan, who opposed Ojeda's attempt to excite a new insurrection, and, of consequence, his voyage must have been posterior to that of the admiral. Life of Columbus, c. 84. According to Vespucci's account, he set out on his first voyage May 10th, 1497. Viag. primo, p. 6. At that time Columbus was in the court of Spain preparing for his voyage, and seems to have enjoyed a considerable degree of favour. The affairs of the New World were at this juncture under the direction of Antonio Torres, a friend of Columbus. It is not probable that, at that period, a commission would be granted to another person to anticipate the admiral by undertaking a voyage which he himself intended to perform. Fonseca, who patronized Ojeda, and granted the license for his voyage, was not recalled to court, and reinstated in the direction of Indian affairs, until the death of Prince John, which happened September, 1497, (P. Martyr, Ep. 182,) several months posterior to the time at which Vespucci pretends to have set out upon his voyage. A life of Vespucci was published at Florence by the Abate Bandini, A. D. 1745, 4to. It is a work of no merit, written with little judgment, and less candour. He contends for his countryman's title to the discovery of the continent with all the blind zeal of national partiality, but produces no new evidence to support it. We learn from him that Vespucci's account of his voyage was published as early as the year 1510, and probably sooner. Vita di Am. Vesp. p. 52. At what time the name of AMERICA came to be first given to the New World is not certain.

### NOTE [23]. PAGE 99.

THE form employed on this occasion served as a model to the Spaniards in all their subsequent conquests in America. It is so extraordinary in its nature, and gives us such an idea of the proceedings of the Spaniards, and the principles upon which they founded their right to the extensive dominions which they acquired in the New World, that it well merits the attention of the reader. "I Alonso de Ojeda, servant of the most high and powerful kings of Castile and Leon, the conquerors of barbarous nations, their messenger and captain, notify to you, and declare in as ample form as I am capable, that God our Lord, who is one and eternal, created the heaven and the earth, and one man and one woman, of whom you and we, and all the men who have been or shall be in the world, are descended. But as it has come to pass through the number of generations during more than five thousand years, that they have been dispersed into different parts of the world, and are divided into various kingdoms and provinces, because one country was not able to contain them, nor could they have found in one the means of subsistence and preservation: therefore God our Lord gave the charge of all those people to one man named St. Peter, whom he constituted the lord and head of all the human race, that all men, in whatever place they are born, or in whatever faith or place they are educated, might yield obedience unto him. He hath subjected the whole world to his jurisdiction, and commanded him to establish his residence in Rome, as the most proper place for the government of the world. He likewise promised and gave him power to establish his authority in every other part of the world, and to judge and govern all Christians, Moors, Jews, Gentiles, and all other people of whatever sect or faith they may be. To him is given the name of *Pope*, which signifies admirable, great father and guardian, because he is the father and governor of all men. Those who lived in the time of this holy father obeyed and acknowledged him as their Lord and King, and the superior of the universe. The same has been observed with respect to them who, since his time, have been chosen to the pontificate. Thus it now continues, and will continue to the end of the world.

"One of these Pontiffs, as lord of the world, hath made a grant of these islands, and of the Tierra Firmè of the ocean sea, to the Catholic Kings of Castile, Don Ferdinand and Donna Isabella, of glorious memory, and their successors, our sovereigns, with all they contain, as is more fully expressed in certain deeds passed upon that occasion, which you may see if you desire it. Thus His Majesty is King and lord of these islands, and of the continent, in virtue of this donation; and, as King and lord aforesaid, most of the islands to which his title hath been notified, have recognised His Majesty, and now yield obedience and subjection to him as their lord, voluntarily and without resistance; and instantly, as soon as they received information, they obeyed the religious men sent by the King to preach to them, and to instruct them in our holy faith; and all these, of their own free will, without any recompense or gratuity, became Christians, and continue to be so; and His Majesty having received them graciously under his protection, has commanded that they should be treated in the same manner as his other subjects and vassals. You are bound and obliged to act in the same manner. Therefore I now entreat and require you to consider attentively what I have declared to you; and that you may more perfectly comprehend it, that you take such time as is reasonable in order that you may acknowledge the Church as the superior and guide of the universe, and likewise the holy father called the Pope, in his own right, and his Majesty, by his appointment, as King and sovereign lord of these Islands, and of the Tierra Firmè; and that you consent that the aforesaid holy fathers shall declare and preach to you the doctrines above mentioned. If you do this, you act well, and perform that to which you are bound and obliged; and His Majesty, and I in his name, will receive you with love and kindness, and will leave you, your wives and children, free and exempt from servitude, and in the enjoyment of all you possess, in the same manner as the inhabitants of the islands. Besides this, His Majesty will bestow upon you many privileges, exemptions, and rewards. But if you will not comply, or maliciously delay to obey my injunction, then, with the help of God, I will enter your country by force, I will carry on war against you with the utmost violence, I will subject you to the yoke of obedience to the Church and King, I will take your wives and children, and will make them slaves, and sell or dispose of them according to His Majesty's pleasure; I will seize your goods, and do you all the mischief in my power, as rebellious subjects, who will not acknowledge or submit to their lawful sovereign. And I protest, that all the bloodshed and calamities which shall follow are to be imputed to you, and not to His Majesty, or to me, or the gentlemen who serve under me; and as I have now made this declaration and requisition unto you, I require the notary here present to grant me a certificate of this, subscribed in proper form." Herrera, dec. 1. lib. vii. c. 14.

### Note [24]. Page 105.

Balboa, in his letter to the king, observes that of the hundred and ninety men whom he took with him, there were never above eighty fit for service at one time. So much did they suffer from hunger, fatigue, and sickness. Herrera, dec. 1. lib. x. c. 16. P. Mart. decad. 226.

### Note [25]. Page 110.

Fonseca, Bishop of Palencia, the principal director of American Affairs, had eight hundred Indians in property; the commendator Lope de Conchillos, his chief associate in that department, eleven hundred; and other favourites had considerable numbers. They sent overseers to the islands, and hired out those slaves to the planters. Herrera, dec. 1. lib. ix. c. 14. p. 325.

### Note [26]. Page 119.

Though America is more plentifully supplied with water than the other regions of the globe, there is no river or stream of water in Yucatan. This peninsula projects from the continent a hundred leagues, but, where broadest, does not extend above twenty-five leagues. It is an extensive plain, not only without mountains, but almost without any inequality of ground. The inhabitants are supplied with water from pits, and, wherever they dig them, find it in abundance. It is probable, from all those circumstances, that this country was formerly covered by the sea. Herreræ Descriptio Indiæ Occidentalis, p. 14. Histoire Naturelle, par M. de Buffon, tom. i. p. 593.

### Note [27]. Page 120.

M. Clavigero censures me for having represented the Spaniards who sailed with Cordova and Grijalva, as fancying in the warmth of their imagination, that they saw cities on the coast of Yucatan adorned with towers and *cupolas.* I know not what translation of my history he has consulted (for his quotation from it is not taken from the original), but I never imagined that any building erected by Americans could suggest the idea of a cupola or dome, a structure which their utmost skill in architecture was incapable of rearing. My words are, that they fancied the villages which they saw from their ships "to be cities adorned with towers and pinnacles." By *pinnacles* I meant some elevation above the rest of the building; and the passage is translated almost literally from Herrera, dec. 2. lib. iii. c. 1. In almost all the accounts of new countries given by the Spanish discoverers in that age, this warmth of admiration is conspicuous; and led them to describe these new objects in the most splendid terms. When Cordova and his companions first beheld an Indian village of greater magnitude than any they had beheld in the islands, they dignified it by the name of *Grand Cairo.* B. Diaz, c. 2. From the same cause Grijalva and his associates thought the country, along the coast of which they held their course, entitled to the name of New Spain.

### Note [28]. Page 123.

The height of the most elevated point in the Pyrenees is, according to M. Cassini, six thousand six hundred and forty-six feet. The height of the mountain Gemmi, in the canton of Berne, is ten thousand one hundred and ten feet. The height of the Peak of Teneriffe, according to the measurement of P. Feuillé, is thirteen thousand one hundred and seventy-eight feet. The height of Chimborazo, the most elevated point of the Andes, is twenty thousand two hundred and eighty feet; no less than seven thousand one hundred and two feet above the highest mountain in the ancient continent. Voyage de D. Juan Ulloa, Observations Astron. et Physiq. tom. ii. p. 114. The line of congelation on Chimborazo, or that part of the mountain which is covered perpetually with snow, is no less than two thousand four hundred feet from its summit. Prevot Hist. Génér. des Voyages, vol. xiii. p. 636.

### Note [29]. Page 123.

As a particular description makes a stronger impression than general assertions, I shall give one of Rio de la Plata by an eye-witness, P. Cattanco, a Modenese Jesuit, who landed at Buenos Ayres in 1749, and thus represents what he felt when such new objects were first presented to his view. "While I resided in Europe, and read in books of history or geography, that the mouth of the river de la Plata was a hundred and fifty miles in breadth, I considered it as an exaggeration, because in this hemisphere we have no example of such vast rivers. When I approached its mouth, I had the most vehement desire to ascertain the truth with my own eyes; and I found the matter to be exactly as it was represented. This I deduce particularly from one circumstance: When we took our departure from Monte Video, a fort situated more than a hundred miles from the mouth of the river, and where its breadth is considerably diminished, we sailed a complete day before we discovered the land on the opposite bank of the river; and when we were in the middle of the channel, we could not discern land on either side, and saw nothing but the sky and water as if we had been in some great ocean. Indeed we should have taken it to be sea, if the fresh water of the river, which was turbid like the Po, had not satisfied us that it was a river. Moreover, at Buenos Ayres, another hundred miles up the river, and where it is still much narrower, it is not only impossible to discern the opposite coast, which is indeed very low, but perceive the houses or the tops of the steeples in the Portuguese settlement at Colonia on the other side of the river." Lettera prima, published by Muratori, Il Christianesimo Felicè, &c. i. p. 257.

### Note [30]. Page 124.

Newfoundland, part of Nova Scotia, and Canada, are the countries which lie in the same parallel of latitude with the Kingdom of France; and in every part of these the water of the rivers is frozen during winter to the thickness of several feet; the earth is covered with snow as deep; almost all the birds fly during that season from a climate where they could not live. The country of the Eskimaux, part of Labrador, and the countries on the south of Hudson's Bay, are in the same parallel with Great Britain; and yet in all these the cold is so intense that even the industry of Europeans has not attempted cultivation.

### Note [31]. Page 125.

Acosta is the first philosopher, as far as I know, who endeavoured to account for the different degrees of heat in the old and new continents, by the agency of the winds which blow in each. Histoire Moral. &c. lib. ii. and iii. M. de Buffon adopts this theory, and has not only improved it by new observations, but has employed his amazing powers of descriptive eloquence in embellishing and placing it in the most striking light. Some remarks may be added, which tend to illustrate more fully a doctrine of much importance in every inquiry concerning the temperature of various climates.

When a cold wind blows over land, it must in its passage rob the surface of some of its heat. By means of this the coldness of the wind is abated. But if it continue to blow in the same direction, it will come, by degrees, to pass over a surface already cooled, and will suffer no longer any abatement of its own keenness. Thus, as it advances over a large tract of land, it brings on all the severity of intense frost.

Let the same wind blow over an extensive and deep sea; the superficial water must be immediately cooled to a certain degree, and the wind proportionally warmed. But the superficial and colder water, becoming specifically heavier than the warmer water below it, descends; what is warmer supplies its place, which, as it comes to be cooled in its turn, continues to warm the air which passes over it, or to diminish its cold. This change of the superficial water and successive ascent of that which is warmer, and the consequent successive abatement of coldness in the air, is aided by the agitation caused in the sea by the mechanical action of the wind, and also by the motion of the tides. This will go on, and the rigour of the wind will continue to diminish until the whole water is so far cooled, that the water on the surface is no longer removed from the action of the wind fast enough to hinder it from being arrested by frost. Whenever the surface freezes, the wind is no longer warmed by the water from below, and it goes on with undiminished cold.

From those principles may be explained the severity of winter frosts in extensive continents; their mildness in small islands; and the superior rigour of winter in those parts of North America with which we are best acquainted. In the north-west parts of Europe, the severity of winter is mitigated by the west winds, which usually blow in the months of November, December, and part of January.

On the other hand, when a warm wind blows over land, it heats the surface, which must therefore cease to abate the fervour of the wind. But the same wind blowing over water, agitates it, brings up the colder water from below, and thus is continually losing somewhat of its own heat.

But the great power of the sea to mitigate the heat of the wind or air passing over it, proceeds from the following circumstance:—that on account of the transparency of the sea, its surface cannot be heated to a great degree by the sun's rays; whereas the ground, subjected to their influence, very soon acquires great heat. When, therefore, the wind blows over a torrid continent, it is soon raised to a heat almost intolerable; but during its passage over an extensive ocean, it is gradually cooled; so that on its arrival at the furthest shore it is again fit for respiration.

Those principles will account for the sultry heats of large continents in the torrid zone: for the mild climate of islands in the same latitude; and for the superior warmth in summer which large continents, situated in the temperate or colder zones of the earth, enjoy when compared with that of islands. The heat of a climate depends not only upon the immediate effect of the sun's rays, but on their continued operation, on the effect which they have formerly produced, and which remains for some time in the ground. This is the reason why the day is warmest about two in the afternoon, the summer warmest about the middle of July, and the winter coldest about the middle of January.

The forests which cover America, and hinder the sunbaems from heating the ground, are a great cause of the temperate climate in the equatorial parts. The ground, not being heated, cannot heat the air; and the leaves, which receive the rays intercepted from the ground, have not a mass of matter sufficient to absorb heat enough for this purpose. Besides, it is a known fact, that the vegetative power of a plant occasions a perspiration from the leaves in proportion to the heat to which they are exposed: and, from the nature of evaporation, this perspiration produces a cold in the leaf proportional to the perspiration. Thus the effect of the leaf in heating the air in contact with it is prodigiously diminished. For those observations, which throw much additional light on this curious subject, I am indebted to my ingenious friend, Mr. Robison, professor of natural philosophy in the university of Edinburgh.

### NOTE [32]. PAGE 125.

THE climate of Brazil has been described by two eminent naturalists, Piso and Margrave, who observed it with a philosophical accuracy for which we search in vain in the accounts of many other provinces in America. Both represent it as temperate and mild when compared with the climate of Africa. They ascribe this chiefly to the refreshing wind which blows continually from the sea. The air is not only cool, but chilly through the night, insomuch that the natives kindle fires every evening in their huts. Piso de Medicina Brasiliensi, lib. i. p. 1, &c. Margravius Histor. Rerum Natural. Brasiliæ, lib. viii. c. 3. p. 264. Nieuhoff. who resided long in Brazil, confirms their description. Churchill's Collection, vol. ii. p. 26. Gumilla, who was a missionary many years among the Indians upon the river Oronoco, gives a similar description of the temperature of the climate there. Hist. de l'Oronoque, tom. i. p. 26. P. Acugna felt a very considerable degree of cold in the countries on the banks of the river Amazons. Relat. vol. ii. p. 56. M. Biet, who lived a considerable time in Cayenne, gives a similar account of the temperature of that climate, and ascribes it to the same cause. Voyage de la France, Equinox, p. 330. Nothing can be more different from these descriptions than that of the burning heat of the African coast given by M. Adanson. Voyage to Senegal, passim.

### NOTE [33]. PAGE 126.

Two French frigates were sent upon a voyage of discovery in the year 1739. In latitude 44° south, they began to feel a considerable degree of cold. In latitude 48°, they met with Islands of floating ice. Histoire des Navigations aux Terres Australes, tom. ii. p. 256, &c. Dr. Halley fell in with ice in latitude 59°. Id. tom. i. p. 47. Commodore Byron, when on the coast of Patagonia, latitude 50° 33′ south, on the fifteenth of December, which is midsummer in that part of the globe, the twenty-first of December being the longest day there, compares the climate to that of England in the middle of winter. Voyages by Hawkesworth, i. 25. Mr. Banks having landed on Terra del Fuego, in the Bay of Good Success, latitude 55°, on the sixteenth of January, which corresponds to the month of July in our hemisphere, two of his attendants died in one night of extreme cold, and all the party were in the most imminent danger of perishing. Id. ii. 51, 52. By the fourteenth of March, corresponding to September in our hemisphere, winter was set in with rigour, and the mountains were covered with snow. Ibid. 72. Captain Cook, in his voyage towards the South Pole, furnishes new and striking instances of the extraordinary predominance of cold in this region of the globe. "Who would have thought (says he) that an island of no greater extent than seventy leagues in circuit, situated between the latitude of 54° and 55°, should in the very height of summer be, in a manner, wholly covered, many fathoms deep, with frozen snow; but more especially the S. W. coast? The very summits of the lofty mountains were cased with snow and ice; but the quantity that lay in the valleys is incredible; and at the bottom of the bays, the coast was terminated by a wall of ice of considerable height." Vol. ii. p. 217.

In some places of the ancient continent, an extraordinary degree of cold prevails in very low latitudes. Mr. Bogle, in his embassy to the court of the Delai Lama, passed the winter of the year 1774, at Chamnanning, in latitude 31° 39′ N. He often found the thermometer in his room twenty-nine degrees under the freezing point by Fahrenheit's scale: and in the middle of April the standing waters were all frozen, and heavy showers of snow frequently fell. The extraordinary elevation of the country seems to be the cause of this excessive cold. In travelling from Indostan to Thibet, the ascent to the summit of the Boutan Mountains is very great, but the descent on the other side is not in equal proportion. The kingdom of Thibet is an elevated region, extremely bare and desolate. Account of Thibet, by Mr. Stewart, read in the Royal Society, p. 7. The extraordinary cold in low latitudes in America cannot be accounted for by the same cause. Those regions are not remarkable for elevation. Some of them are countries depressed and level.

The most obvious and probable cause of the superior degree of cold towards the southern extremity of America, seems to be the form of the continent there. Its breadth gradually decreases as it stretches from St. Antonio southwards, and from the bay of St. Julian to the Straits of Magellan its dimensions are much contracted. On the east and west sides it is washed by the Atlantic and Pacific Oceans. From its southern point it is probable that a great extent of sea, without any considerable tract of land, reaches to the Antarctic pole. In whichever of these directions the wind blows, it is cooled before it approaches the Magellanic regions, by passing over a vast body of water; nor is the land there of such extent, that it can recover any considerable degree of heat in its progress over it. These circumstances concur in rendering the temperature of the air in this district of America more similar to that of an insular, than to that of a continental climate, and hinder it from acquiring the same degree of summer heat with places in Europe and Asia in a correspondent northern latitude. The north wind is the only one that reaches this part of America, after blowing over a great continent. But from an attentive survey of its position, this will be found to have a tendency rather to diminish than augment the degree of heat. The southern extremity of America is properly the termination of the immense ridge of the Andes, which stretches nearly in a direct line from north to south, through the whole extent of the continent. The most sultry regions in South America, Guiana, Brazil, Paraguay, and Tucuman, lie many degrees to the east of the Magellanic regions. The level country of Peru, which enjoys the tropical heats, is situated considerably to the west of them. The north wind then, though it blows over land, does not bring to the southern extremity of America an increase of heat collected in its passage over torrid regions; but before it arrives there, it must have swept along the summits of the Andes, and becomes impregnated with the cold of that frozen region.

Though it be now demonstrated that there is no southern continent in that region of the globe which it was supposed to occupy, it appears to be certain from Captain Cook's discoveries, that there is a large tract of land near the south pole, which is the source of most of the ice spread over the vast southern ocean. Vol. ii. p. 230. 239, &c. Whether the influence of this remote frozen continent may reach the southern extremity of America, and affect its climate, is an inquiry not unworthy of attention.

## NOTE [34]. PAGE 127.

M. CONDAMINE is one of the latest and most accurate observers of the interior state of South America. "After descending from the Andes (says he,) one beholds a vast and uniform prospect of water and verdure, and nothing more. One treads upon the earth, but does not see it; as it is so entirely covered with luxuriant plants, weeds, and shrubs, that it would require a considerable degree of labour to clear it for the space of a foot." Relation abrégée d'un Voyage, &c. p. 48. One of the singularities in the forests is a sort of osiers, or withes, called *bejucos* by the Spaniards, *lianes* by the French, and *nibbes* by the Indians, which are usually employed as ropes in America. This is one of the parasitical plants, which twists about the trees it meets with, and rising above their highest branches, its tendrils descend perpendicularly, strike into the ground, take root, rise up around another tree, and thus mount and descend alternately. Other tendrils are carried obliquely by the wind, or some accident, and form a confusion of interwoven cordage, which resembles the rigging of a ship. Bancroft, Nat. Hist. of Guiana, 99. These withes are often as thick as the arm of a man. Id. p. 75. M. Boguer's account of the forests in Peru perfectly resembles this description. Voyages au Peru, p. 16. Oviedo gives a similar description of the forests in other parts of America. Hist. lib. ix. p. 144. D. The country of the Moxos is so much overflowed, that they are obliged to reside on the summit of some rising ground during some part of the year, and have no communication with their countrymen at any distance. Lettres Edifiantes, tom. x. p. 187. Garcia gives a full and just description of the rivers, lakes, woods, and marshes in those countries of America which lie between the tropics. Origen de los Indios, lib. ii. c. 5. § 4, 5. The incredible hardships to which Gonzalez Pizarro was exposed in attempting to march into the country to the east of the Andes, convey a very striking idea of that part of America in its original uncultivated state. Garcil. de la Vega, Royal Comment. of Peru, part ii. book iii. c. 2—5.

## NOTE [35]. PAGE 128.

THE animals of America seem not to have been always of a size inferior to those in other quarters of the globe. From antlers of the moose-deer which have been found in America, it appears to have been an animal of great size. Near the banks of the Ohio, a considerable number of bones of an immense magnitude have been found. The place where this discovery has been made lies about one hundred and ninety miles below the junction of the river Scioto with the Ohio. It is about four miles distant from the banks of the latter, on the side of the marsh called the Salt lick. The bones lie in vast quantities about five or six feet under ground, and the stratum is visible in the bank on the edge of the Lick. *Journal of Colonel George Croglan, MS. penes me.* This spot seems to be accurately laid down by Evans in his map. These bones must have belonged to animals of enormous bulk; but naturalists being acquainted with no living creature of such size, were at first inclined to think that they were mineral substances. Upon receiving a greater number of specimens, and after inspecting them more narrowly, they are now allowed to be the bones of an animal. As the elephant is the largest known quadruped, and the tusks which were found, nearly resembled, both in form and quality, the tusks of an elephant, it was concluded that the carcasses deposited on the Ohio were of that species. But Dr. Hunter, one of the persons of our age best qualified to decide with respect to this point, having accurately examined several parcels of tusks, and grinders, and jaw-bones, sent from the Ohio to London, gives it as his opinion that they did not belong to an elephant, but to some huge carnivorous animal of an unknown species. Phil. Transact. vol. lviii. p. 34. Bones of the same kind, and as remarkable for their size, have been found near the mouths of the great rivers Oby, Jeniseia, and Lena in Siberia. *Strahlenberg, Descript. of North and East Parts of Europe and Asia,* p. 402, &c. The elephant seems to be confined in his range to the torrid zone, and never multiplies beyond it. In such cold regions as those bordering on the frozen sea, he could not live. The existence of such large animals in America might open a wide field for conjecture. The more we contemplate the face of nature, and consider the variety of her productions, the more we must be satisfied that astonishing changes have been made in the terraqueous globe by convulsions and revolutions, of which no account is preserved in history.

### Note [36]. Page 128.

This degeneracy of the domestic European animals in America may be imputed to some of these causes. In the Spanish settlements, which are situated either within the torrid zone, or in countries bordering upon it, the increase of heat and diversity of food prevent sheep and horned cattle from attaining the same size as in Europe. They seldom become so fat, and their flesh is not so juicy, or of such delicate flavour. In North America, where the climate is more favourable, and similar to that of Europe, the quality of the grasses which spring up naturally in their pasture grounds is not good. Mitchell, p. 151. Agriculture is still so much in its infancy, that artificial food for cattle is not raised in any quantity. During a winter, long in many provinces, and rigorous in all, no proper care is taken of their cattle. The general treatment of their horses and horned cattle is injudicious and harsh in all the English colonies. These circumstances contribute more, perhaps, than any thing peculiar in the quality of the climate, to the degeneracy of breed in the horses, cows, and sheep of many of the North American provinces.

### te [37]. Page 128.

In the year 1518, the island of Hispaniola was afflicted with a dreadful visitation of those destructive insects, the particulars of which Herrera describes, and mentions a singular instance of the superstition of the Spanish planters. After trying various methods of exterminating the ants, they resolved to implore protection of the saints ; but as the calamity was new, they were at a loss to find out the saint who could give them the most effectual aid. They cast lots in order to discover the patron whom they should invoke. The lots decided in favour of St. Saturninus. They celebrated his festival with great solemnity, and immediately, adds the historian, the calamity began to abate. Herrera, dec. 2. lib. iii. c. 15. p. 107.

### Note [38]. Page 129.

The author of Recherches Philosophiques sur les Americains supposes this difference in heat to be equal to twelve degrees, and that a place thirty degrees from the equator in the old continent is as warm as one situated eighteen degrees from it in America, tom. i. p. 11. Dr. Mitchell, after observations carried on during thirty years, contends that the difference is equal to fourteen or fifteen degrees of latitude. Present State, &c. p. 257.

### Note [39]. Page 129.

January 3d, 1765, Mr. Bertram, near the head of St. John's river, in East Florida, observed a frost so intense that in one night the ground was frozen an inch thick upon the banks of the river. The limes, citrons, and banana trees, at St. Augustin, were destroyed. Bertram's Journal, p. 20. Other instances of the extraordinary operations of cold in the southern provinces of North America are collected by Dr. Mitchell. Present State, p. 206, &c. February 7th, 1747, the frost at Charleston was so intense, that a person having carried two quart bottles of hot water to bed, in the morning they were split to pieces, and the water converted into solid lumps of ice. In a kitchen where there was a fire, the water in a jar in which there was a live large eel, was frozen to the bottom. Almost all the orange and olive trees were destroyed. Description of South Carolina, 8vo. Lond. 1761.

NOTE [40]. PAGE 129.

A REMARKABLE instance of this occurs in Dutch Guiana, a country every where level, and so low, that during the rainy seasons it is usually covered with water near two feet in height. This renders the soil so rich, that on the surface, for twelve inches in depth, it is a stratum of perfect manure, and as such has been transported to Barbadoes. On the banks of the Essequibo, thirty crops of ratan canes have been raised successively; whereas in the West Indian islands not more than two is ever expected from the richest land. The expedients by which the planters endeavour to diminish this excessive fertility of soil are various. Bancroft, Nat. Hist. of Guiana, p. 10, &c.

NOTE [41]. PAGE 134.

MULLER seems to have believed, without sufficient evidence, that the Cape had been doubled, tom. i. p. 11, &c.; and the imperial academy of St. Petersburgh give some countenance to it by the manner in which *Tschukotskoi-noss* is laid down in their charts. But I am assured, from undoubted authority, that no Russian vessel has ever sailed round that cape; and as the country of *Tshutki* is not subject to the Russian empire, it is very imperfectly known.

NOTE [42]. PAGE 135.

WERE this the place for entering into a long and intricate geographical disquisition, many curious observations might arise from comparing the accounts of the two Russian voyages and the charts of their respective navigations. One remark is applicable to both. We cannot rely with absolute certainty on the position which they assign to several of the places which they visited. The weather was so extremely foggy, that they seldom saw the sun or stars; and the position of the islands and supposed continents was commonly determined by reckoning, not by observation. Behring and Tschirikow proceeded much further towards the east than Krenitzin. The land discovered by Behring, which he imagined to be part of the American continent, is in the 236th degree of longitude from the first meridian in the isle of Ferro, and in 58° 28′ of latitude. Tschirikow came upon the same coast in longitude 241°, latitude 56°. Muller, i. 248, 249. The former must have advanced 60 degrees from the port of Petropawlowski, from which he took his departure, and the latter 65 degrees. But from the chart of Krenitzen's voyage, it appears that he did not sail further towards the east than to the 208th degree, and only 32 degrees from Petropawlowski. In 1741, Behring and Tschirikow, both in going and returning, held a course which was mostly to the south of that chain of islands, which they discovered; and observing the mountainous and rugged aspect of the headlands which they descried towards the north, they supposed them to be promontories belonging to some part of the American continent, which, as they fancied, stretched as far south as the latitude 56. In this manner they are laid down in the chart published by Muller, and likewise in a manuscript chart drawn by a mate of Behring's ship, communicated to me by Mr. Professor Robison. But in 1769, Krenitzin, after wintering in the island Alaxa, stood so far towards the north in his return, that his course lay through the middle of what Behring and Tschirikow had supposed to be a continent, which he found to be an open sea, and that they had mistaken rocky isles for the headlands of a continent. It is probable, that the countries discovered in 1741, towards the east, do not belong to the American continent, but are only a continuation of the chain of islands. The number of volcanos in this region of the globe is remarkable. There are several in Kamtchatka, and not one of the islands, great or small, as far as the Russian navigation extends, is without them. Many are actually burning, and the mountains in all bear marks of having been once in a state of eruption. Were I disposed to admit such conjectures as have found place in other inquiries concerning the peopling of America, I might suppose that this part of the earth, having manifestly suffered violent convulsions from earthquakes and volcanos, an isthmus, which may have formerly united Asia to America, has been broken, and formed into a cluster of islands by the shock.

It is singular, that at the very time the Russian navigators were attempting to make discoveries in the north-west of America, the Spaniards were prosecuting the same design from another quarter. In 1769, two small vessels sailed from Loretto in California to explore the coasts of the country to the north of that peninsula. They advanced no further than the port of Monte-Rey, in latitude 36. But, in several successive expeditions fitted out from the port of St. Blas in New Galicia, the Spaniards have advanced as far as the latitude 58. *Gazeta de Madrid*, March 19, and May 14, 1776. But as the journals of those voyages have not yet been published, I cannot compare their progress with that of the Russians, or show how near the navigators of the two nations have approached to each other. It is to be hoped that the enlightened minister who has now the direction of American affairs in Spain, will not withhold this information from the public.

### Note [43]. Page 136.

Our knowledge of the vicinity of the two continents of Asia and America, which was very imperfect when I published the History of America in the year 1777, is now complete. Mr. Coxe's account of the Russian Discoveries between Asia and America, printed in the year 1780, contains many curious and important facts with respect to the various attempts of the Russians to open a communication with the New World. The history of the great voyage of Discovery, begun by Captain Cook in 1776, and completed by Captains Clerk and Gore, published in the year 1780, communicates all the information that the curiosity of mankind could desire with regard to this subject.

At my request, my friend, Mr. Playfair, Professor of Mathematics in the University of Edinburgh, has compared the narrative and charts of those illustrious navigators with the more imperfect relations and maps of the Russians. The result of this comparison I communicate in his own words, with much greater confidence in his scientific accuracy, than I could have ventured to place in any observations which I myself might have made upon the subject.

"The discoveries of Captain Cook in his last voyage have confirmed the conclusions which Dr. Robertson had drawn, and have connected together the facts from which they were deduced. They have now rendered it certain that Behring and Tschirikow touched on the coast of America in 1741. The former discovered land in latitude 58°, 28′, and about 236° east from Ferro. He has given such a description of the Bay in which he anchored, and the high mountain to the westward of it which he calls St. Elias, that though the account of his voyage is much abridged in the English translation, Captain Cook recognised the place as he sailed along the western coast of America in the year 1778. The isle of St. Hermogenes, near the mouth of Cook's river, Schumagins isles on the coast of Alashka, and Foggy Isle, retain in Captain Cook's chart the names which they had received from the Russian navigator. Cook's Voy. vol. ii. p. 347.

"Tschirikow came upon the same coast about 2° 30′ farther south than Behring, near the Mount Edgecumbe of Captain Cook.

"With regard to Krenitzin, we learn from Coxe's Account of the Russian Discoveries, that he sailed from the mouth of the Kamtchatka river with two ships in the year 1768. With his own ship he reached the island of Oonolashka, in which there had been a Russian settlement since the year 1762, where he wintered probably in the same harbour or bay where Captain Cook afterwards anchored. The other ship wintered at Alashka, which was supposed to be an island, though it be in fact a part of the American continent. Krenitzin accordingly returned without knowing that either of his ships had been on the coast of America; and this is the more surprising, because Captain Cook has informed us that Alashka is understood to be a great continent, both by the Russians and the natives at Oonolashka.

"According to Krenitzin, the ship which had wintered at Alashka had hardly sailed 30° to the eastward of the harbour of St. Peter and St. Paul in Kamtchatka; but, according to the more accurate charts of Captain Cook, it had sailed no less than 37° 17′ to the eastward of that harbour. There is nearly the same mistake of 5° in the longitude which Krenitzin assigns to Oonolashka. It is remarkable enough, that in the chart of those seas, put into the hand of Captain Cook by the Russians on that island, there was an error of the same kind, and very nearly of the same extent.

"But what is of most consequence to be remarked on the subject is, that the discoveries of Captain Cook have fully verified Dr. Robertson's conjecture 'that it is probable that future navigators in those seas, by steering farther to the north than Behring and Tschirikow or Krenitzin had done, may find that the continent of America approaches still nearer to that of Asia.' See p. 134. It has accordingly been found that these two continents, which, in the parallel of 55°, or that of the southern extremity of Alashka, are about four hundred leagues asunder, approach continually to one another as they stretch together toward the north, until, within less than a degree from the polar circle, they are terminated by two capes only thirteen leagues distant. The east cape of Asia is in latitude 66° 6′ and in longitude 190° 22′ east from Greenwich; the western extremity of America, or Prince of Wales' Cape, is in latitude 65° 46′, and in longitude 191° 45′. Nearly in the middle of the narrow strait (Behring's Strait) which separates these capes, are the two islands of St. Diomede, from which both continents may be seen. Captain King informs us, that as he was sailing through this strait, July 5, 1779, the fog having cleared away, he enjoyed the pleasure of seeing from the ship the continents of Asia and America at the same moment, together with the islands of St. Diomede lying between them. Cook's Voy. vol. iii. p. 244.

"Beyond this point the strait opens towards the Arctic Sea, and the coasts of Asia and America diverge so fast from one another, that in the parallel of 69° they are more than one hundred leagues asunder. Ib. p. 277. To the south of the strait there are a number of islands, Clerk's, King's, Anderson's, &c., which, as well as those of St. Diomede, may have facilitated the migrations of the natives from the one continent to the other. Captain Cook, however, on the authority of the Russians at Oonolashka, and for other good reasons, has diminished the number of islands which had been inserted in former charts of the northern Archipelago. He has also placed Alashka, or the promontory which stretches from the continent of America S. W. towards Kamtchatka, at the distance of five degrees of longitude farther from the coast of Asia than it was reckoned by the Russian navigators.

"The geography of the Old and New World is therefore equally indebted to the discoveries made in this memorable voyage; and as many errors have been corrected, and many deficiencies supplied, by means of these discoveries, so the accuracy of some former observations has been established. The basis of the map of the Russian empire, as far as regarded Kamtchatka, and the country of the Tschutzki, was the position of four places, Yakutsh, Ochotz, Bolcheresk, and Petropawlowski, which had been determined by the astronomer Krassilnicow in the year 1744. Nov. Comment. Petrop. vol. iii. p. 465, &c. But the accuracy of his observations was contested by M. Engel, and M. Robert de Vaugondy; Coxe, Append. i. No. 2. p. 267. 272. and the former of these geographers ventured to take away no less than 28 degrees from the longitude, which, on the faith of Krassilnicow's observations, was assigned to the eastern boundary of the Russian empire. With how little reason this was done, will appear from considering that our British navigators, having determined the position of Petropawlowski by a great number of very accurate observations, found the longitude of that port 158° 43′ E. from Greenwich, and its latitude 53° 1′; agreeing, the first to less than seven minutes, and the second to less than half a minute, with the calculations of the Russian astronomer: a coincidence which, in the situation of so remote a place, does not leave an uncertainty of more than four English miles, and which, for the credit of science, deserves to be particularly remarked. The chief error in the Russian maps has been in not extending the boundaries of that empire sufficiently towards the east. For as there was nothing to connect the land of the Tschutzki and the north-east point of Asia with those places whereof the position had been carefully ascertained, except the imperfect accounts of Behring's and Synd's voyages, considerable errors could not fail to be introduced, and that point was laid down as not more than 23° 2′ east of the meridian of Petropawlowski. Coxe, App. i. No. 2. By the observations of Captain King, the difference of longitude between Petropawlowski and the East Cape is 31° 9′; that is 8° 7′ greater than it was supposed to be by the Russian geographers."--It appears from Cook's and King's Voy. iii. p. 272, that the continents of Asia and America are usually joined together by ice during winter. Mr. Samwell confirms this account of his superior officer. "At this place, viz. near the latitude of 66° N. the two coasts are only thirteen leagues asunder, and about midway between them lie two islands, the distance from each to either shore is short of twenty miles. At this place the natives of Asia could find no difficulty in passing over to the opposite coast, which is in sight of their own. That in a course of years such an event would happen either through design or accident, cannot admit of a doubt. The canoes which we saw among the Tschutzki were capable of performing a much longer voyage; and, however rude they may have been at some distant period, we can scarcely suppose them unequal to a passage of six or seven leagues. People might have been carried over by accident on floating pieces of ice. They might also have travelled across on sledges or on foot; for we have reason to believe that the strait is entirely frozen over in the winter; so that, during that season, the continents, with respect to the communication between them, may be considered as one land." Letter from Mr. Samwell, Scot's Magazine for 1788, p. 604. It is probable that this interesting portion of geographical knowledge will, in the course of a few years, receive farther improvement. Soon after the publication of Captain Cook's last voyage, the great and enlightened Sovereign of Russia, attentive to every thing that may contribute to extend the bounds of science, or to render it more accurate, formed the plan of a new voyage of discovery, in order to explore those parts of the ocean lying between Asia and America, which Captain Cook did not visit, to examine more accurately the islands which stretch from one continent almost to the other, to survey the north-east coast of the Russian empire, from the mouth of the Kovyma, or Kolyma, to the North Cape, and to settle, by astronomical observations, the position of each place worth notice. The conduct of this important enterprise is committed to Captain Billings, an English officer in the Russian service, of whose abilities for that station it will be deemed the best evidence, that he accompanied Captain Cook in his last voyage. To render the expedition more extensively useful, an eminent naturalist is appointed to attend Captain Billings. Six years will be requisite for accomplishing the purposes of the voyage. Coxe's Supplement to Russian Discoveries, p. 27, &c.

### NOTE [44]. PAGE 141.

FEW travellers have had such opportunity of observing the natives of America, in its various districts, as Don Antonio Ulloa. In a work lately published by him, he thus describes the characteristical features of the race: "A very small forehead, covered with hair towards its extremities, as far as the middle of the eye-brows; little eyes; a thin nose, small and bending towards the upper lip; the countenance broad; the ears large; the hair very black, lank, and coarse; the limbs well turned, the feet small, the body of just proportion; and altogether smooth and free from hair, until old age, when they acquire some beard, but never on the cheeks." Noticias Americanas, &c. p. 307. M. le Chevalier de Pinto, who resided several years in a part of America which Ulloa never visited, gives a sketch of the general aspect of the Indians there. "They are all of copper colour with some diversity of shade, not in proportion to their distance from the equator, but according to the degree of elevation of the territory which they inhabit. Those who live in a high country are fairer than those in the marshy low lands, on the coast. Their face is round, further removed, perhaps, than that of any people from an oval shape. Their forehead is small, the extremity of their ears far from the face, their lips thick, their nose flat, their eyes black, or of a chesnut colour, small, but capable of discerning objects at a great distance. Their hair is always thick and sleek, and without any tendency to curl. They have no hair on any part of their body but the head. At the first aspect a southern American appears to be mild and innocent, but on a more attentive view, one discovers in his countenance something wild, distrustful, and sullen." MS. *penes me.* The two portraits drawn by hands very different from those of common travellers, have a near resemblance.

### NOTE [45]. PAGE 141.

AMAZING accounts are given of the persevering speed of the Americans. Adair relates the adventures of a Chikkasah warrior, who ran through woods and over mountains, three hundred computed miles, in a day and a half and two nights. Hist. of Amer. Ind. 396.

### NOTE [46]. PAGE 143

M. GODIN LE JEUNE, who resided fifteen years among the Indians of Peru and Quito, and twenty years in the French colony of Cayenne, in which there is a constant intercourse with the Galibis and other tribes on the Oronoco, observes, that the vigour of constitution among the Americans is exactly in proportion to their habits of labour. The Indians in warm climates, such as those on the coasts of the South Sea, on the river of Amazons, and the river Orinoco, are not to be compared for strength with those in cold countries; and yet, says he, boats daily set out from Para, a Portuguese settlement on the river of Amazons, to ascend that river against the rapidity of the stream, and with the same crew they proceed to San Pablo, which is eight hundred leagues distant. No crew of white people, or even of Negroes, would be found equal to a task of such persevering fatigue, as the Portuguese have experienced; and yet the Indians being accustomed to this labour from their infancy, perform it. MS. *penes me.*

### NOTE [47]. PAGE 145.

DON ANTONIA ULLOA, who visited a great part of Peru and Chili, the kingdom of New Granada, and several of the provinces bordering on the Mexican Gulf, while employed in the same service with the French Mathematicians during the space of ten years, and who afterwards had an opportunity of viewing the North Americans, asserts "that if we have seen one American, we may be said to have seen them all, their colour and make are so nearly the same." Notic. Americanas, p. 328. A more early observer, Pedro de Cieca de Leon, one of the conquerors of Peru, who had likewise traversed many provinces of America, affirms that the people, men and women, although there is such a multitude of tribes or nations as to be almost innumerable, and such diversity of climates, appear nevertheless like the children of one father and mother. Chronica del' Peru, parte i. c. 19. There is, no doubt, a certain combination of features, and peculiarity of aspect, which forms what may be called a European or Asiatic countenance. There must likewise be one that may be denominated American, common to the whole race. This may be supposed to strike the traveller at first sight, while not only the various shades, which distinguish people of different regions, but the peculiar features which discriminate individuals, escape the notice of a transient observer. But when persons who had resided so long among the Americans concur in bearing testimony to the similarity of their appearance in every climate, we may conclude that it is more remarkable than that of any other race. See likewise Garcia Origen de los Indies, p. 54. 242. Torquemada Monarch. Indiana, ii. 571.

### NOTE [48]. PAGE 146.

M. LE CHEVALIER DE PINTO observes, that in the interior parts of Brazil, he had been informed that some persons resembling the white people of Darien had been found; but that the breed did not continue, and their children became like other Americans. This race, however, is very imperfectly known. MS *penes me.*

NOTE [49]. PAGE 147.

THE testimonies of different travellers, concerning the Patagonians, have been collected and stated with a considerable degree of accuracy by the author of Recherches Philosophiques, &c. tom. i. 281, &c. iii. 181, &c. Since the publication of his work, several navigators have visited the Magellanic regions, and like their predecessors, differ very widely in their accounts of its inhabitants. By Commodore Byron and his crew, who sailed through the Straits in 1764, the common size of the Patagonians was estimated to be eight feet, and many of them much taller. Phil. Transact. vol. lvii. p. 78. By Captains Wallis and Carteret, who actually measured them in 1766, they were found to be from six feet to six feet five and seven inches in height. Phil. Trans. vol. lx. p. 22. These, however, seem to have been the very people whose size had been rated so high in the year 1764; for several of them had beads and red baize of the same kind with what had been put on board Captain Wallis's ship, and he naturally concluded that they had got these from Mr. Byron. Hawkesw. i. In 1767 they were again measured by M. Bougainville, whose account differs little from that of Captain Wallis. Voy. 129. To these I shall add a testimony of great weight. In the year 1762, Don Bernardo Ibegnez de Echavarri accompanied the Marquis de Valdelirios to Buenos Ayres, and resided there several years. He is a very intelligent author, and his reputation for veracity unimpeached among his countrymen. In speaking of the country towards the southern extremity of America, " By what Indians," says he, " is it possessed? Not certainly by the fabulous Patagonians who are supposed to occupy this district. I have from many eye-witnesses, who have lived among those Indians, and traded much with them, a true and accurate description of their persons. They are of the same stature with the Spaniards. I never saw one who rose in height two *varas* and two or three inches," *i. e.* about 80 or 81·332 inches English, if Echavarri makes his computation according to the *vara* of Madrid. This agrees nearly with the measurement of Captain Wallis. Reyno Jesuitico, 238. Mr. Falkner, who resided as a missionary forty years in the southern parts of America, says that " the Patagonians, or Puelches, are a large bodied people; but I never heard of that gigantic race which others have mentioned, though I have seen persons of all the different tribes of southern Indians." Introd. p. 26. M. Dobrizhoffer, a Jesuit, who resided eighteen years in Paraguay, and who had seen great numbers of the various tribes which inhabit the countries situated upon the Straits of Magellan, confirms, in every point, the testimony of his brother missionary Falkner. Dobrizhoffer enters into some detail with respect to the opinions of several authors concerning the stature of the Patagonians. Having mentioned the reports of some early travellers with regard to the extraordinary size of some bones found on that coast which were supposed to be human; and having endeavoured to show that these bones belonged to some large marine or land animal, he concludes, " de hisce ossibus crede quicquid libuerit, dummodo, me suasore, Patagones pro gigantibus desinas habere." Hist. de Abissonibus, vol. ii. p. 19, &c.

NOTE [50]. PAGE 149

ANTONIO SANCHES RIBEIRO, a learned and ingenious physician, published a dissertation in the year 1765, in which he endeavours to prove that this disease was not introduced from America, but took its rise in Europe, and was brought on by an epidemical and malignant disorder. Did I choose to enter into a disquisition on this subject, which I should not have mentioned if it had not been intimately connected with this part of my inquiries, it would not be difficult to point out some mistakes with respect to the facts upon which he founds, as well as some errors in the consequences which he draws from them. The rapid communication of this disease from Spain over Europe, seems however to resemble the progress of an epidemic, rather than that of a disease transmitted by infection. The first mention of it is in the year 1493, and before the year 1497, it had made its appearance in most countries of Europe, with such alarming symptoms as rendered it necessary for the civil magistrate to interpose, in order to check its career.—Since the publication of this work, a second edition of Dr. Sanchez's Dissertation has been communicated to me. It contains several additional facts in confirmation of his opinion, which is supported with such plausible arguments, as render it a subject of inquiry well deserving the attention of learned physicians.

### NOTE [51]. PAGE 150.

THE people of Otaheite have no denomination for any number above two hundred, which is sufficient for their transactions. Voyages by Hawkesworth, ii. 228.

### NOTE [52]. PAGE 152.

As the view which I have given of rude nations is extremely different from that exhibited by very respectable authors, it may be proper to produce some of the many authorities on which I found my description. The manners of the savage tribes in America have never been viewed by persons more capable of observing them with discernment, than the philosophers employed by France and Spain, in the year 1735, to determine the figure of the earth. M. Bouguer, D. Antonio d'Ulloa, and D. Jorge Juan, resided long among the natives of the least civilized provinces in Peru. M. de la Condamine had not only the same advantages with them for observation, but, in his voyage down the Maragnon, he had an opportunity of inspecting the state of the various nations seated on its banks, in its vast course across the continent of South America. There is a wonderful resemblance in their representation of the character of the Americans. "They are all extremely indolent," says M Bouguer, "they are stupid; they pass whole days sitting in the same place, without moving, or speaking a single word. It is not easy to describe the degree of their indifference for wealth, and all its advantages. One does not well know what motive to propose to them, when one would persuade them to perform any service. It is vain to offer them money; they answer, that they are not hungry." Voyage au Perou, p. 102. "If one considers them as men, the narrowness of their understanding seems to be incompatible with the excellence of the soul. Their imbecility is so visible that one can hardly form an idea of them different from what one has of the brutes. Nothing disturbs the tranquillity of their souls, equally insensible to disasters and to prosperity. Though half naked, they are as contented as a monarch in his most splendid array. Riches do not attract them in the smallest degree, and the authority of dignities to which they may aspire are so little the objects of their ambition, that an Indian will receive with the same indifference the office of a judge (Alcade) or that of a hangman, if deprived of the former and appointed to the latter. Nothing can move or change them. Interest has no power over them, and they often refuse to perform a small service, though certain of a great recompense. Fear makes no impression upon them, and respect as little. Their disposition is so singular that there is no method of influencing them, no means of rousing them from that indifference which is proof against all the endeavours of the wisest persons; no expedient which can induce them to abandon that gross ignorance, or lay aside that careless negligence which disconcert the prudence and disappoint the care of such as are attentive to their welfare." Voyage d'Ulloa, tom. i. 335. 356. Of those singular qualities he produces many extraordinary instances, p. 336—347. "Insensibility," says M. de la Condamine, "is the basis of the American character. I leave others to determine, whether this should be dignified with the name of apathy, or disgraced with that of stupidity. It arises, without doubt, from the small number of their ideas, which do not extend beyond their wants. Gluttons even to voracity, when they have wherewithal to satisfy their appetite. Temperate, when necessity obliges them, to such a degree, that they can endure want without seeming to desire any thing. Pusillanimous and cowardly to excess, unless when they are rendered desperate by drunkenness. Averse to labour, indifferent to every motive of glory, honour, or gratitude; occupied entirely by the object that is present, and always de termined by it alone, without any solicitude about futurity; incapable of foresight or of reflection; abandoning themselves when under no restraint, to a puerile joy, which they express by frisking about and immoderate fits of laughter; without object or design, they pass their life without thinking, and grow old without advancing beyond childhood, of which they retain all the defects. If this description were applicable only to the Indians in some provinces of Peru, who are slaves in every respect but the name, one might believe, that this degree of degeneracy was occasioned by the servile dependence to which they are reduced; the example of the modern Greeks being proof how far servitude may degrade the human species. But the Indians in the missions of the Jesuits, and the savages who still enjoy unimpaired liberty, being as limited in their faculties, not to say as stupid, as the other, one cannot observe without humiliation, that man, when abandoned to simple nature, and deprived of the advantages resulting from education and society, differs but little from the brute creation." Voyage de la Riv. de Amaz. 52, 53. M. de Chanvalon, an intelligent and philosophical observer, who visited Martinico in 1751, and resided there six years, gives the following description of the Caraibs: "It is not the ed colour of their complexion, it is not the singularity of their features, which constitutes the chief difference between them and us. It is their excessive simplicity: it is the limited degree of their faculties. Their reason is not more enlightened or more provident than the instinct of brutes. The reason of the most gross peasants, that of the negroes brought up in the parts of Africa most remote from intercourse with Europeans, is such, that we discover appearances of intelligence, which, though imperfect, is capable of increase. But of this the understanding of the Caraibs seems to be hardly susceptible. If sound philosophy and religion did not afford us their light, if we were to decide according to the first impression which the view of that people makes upon the mind, we should be disposed to believe that they do not belong to the same species with us. Their stupid eyes are the true mirror of their souls; it appears to be without functions. Their indolence is extreme; they have never the least solicitude about the moment which is to succeed that which is present." Voyage à la Martinique, p. 44, 45. 51. M. de la Borde, Tertre, and Rochefort, confirm this description. "The characteristics of the Californians," says P. Venegas, "as well as of all other Indians, are stupidity and insensibility; want of knowledge and reflection; inconstancy, impetuosity, and blindness of appetite; an excessive sloth, and abhorrence of all labour and fatigue; an excessive love of pleasure and amusement of every kind, however trifling or brutal; pusillanimity; and, in fine, a most wretched want of every thing which constitutes the real man, and renders him rational, inventive, tractable, and useful to himself and society. It is not easy for Europeans, who never were out of their own country, to conceive an adequate idea of those people; for, even in the least frequented corners of the globe, there is not a nation so stupid, of such contracted ideas, and so weak both in body and mind, as the unhappy Californians. Their understanding comprehends little more than what they see; abstract ideas, and much less a chain of reasoning, being far beyond their power; so that they scarce ever improve their first ideas, and these are in general false, or at least inadequate. It is in vain to represent to them any future advantages which will result to them from doing or abstaining from this or that particular immediately present; the relation of means and ends being beyond the stretch of their faculties. Nor have they the least notion of pursuing such intentions as will procure themselves some future good, or guard them against future evils. Their will is proportional to their faculties, and all their passions move in a very narrow sphere. Ambition they have none, and are more desirous of being accounted strong than valiant. The objects of ambition with us, honour, fame, reputation, titles, posts, and distinctions of superiority, are unknown among them; so that this powerful spring of action, the cause of so much seeming good and real evil in the world, has no power here. This disposition of mind, as it gives them up to an amazing languor and lassitude, their lives fleeting away in a perpetual inactivity and detestation of labour, so it likewise induces them to be attracted by the first object which their own fancy, or the persuasion of another, places before them; and at the same time renders them as prone to alter their resolutions with the same facility.

They look with indifference upon any kindness done them; nor is even the bare remembrance of it to be expected from them. In a word, the unhappy mortals may be compared to children, in whom the developement of reason is not completed. They may indeed be called a nation who never arrive at manhood." Hist. of California, English Transl. i. 64. 67. Mr. Ellis gives a similar account of the want of foresight and inconsiderate disposition of the people adjacent to Hudson's Bay. Voyage, p. 194, 195.

The incapacity of the Americans is so remarkable, that negroes from all the different provinces of Africa are observed to be more capable of improving by instruction. They acquire the knowledge of several particulars which the Americans cannot comprehend. Hence the negroes, though slaves, value themselves as a superior order of beings, and look down upon the Americans with contempt, as void of capacity and of rational discernment. Ulloa Notic. Americ. 322, 323.

## Note [53]. Page 155.

Dobrizhoffer, the last traveller I know who has resided among any tribe of the ruder Americans, has explained so fully the various reasons which have induced their women to suckle their children long, and never to undertake rearing such as were feeble or distorted, and even to destroy a considerable number of their offspring, as to throw great light on the observations I have made, p. 144. 154. Hist. de Abissonibus, vol. ii. p. 107. 221. So deeply were these ideas imprinted in the minds of the Americans, that the Peruvians, a civilized people when compared with the barbarous tribes whose manners I am describing, retained them; and even their intercourse with the Spaniards has not been able to root them out. When twins are born in any family, it is still considered as an ominous event, and the parents have recourse to rigorous acts of mortification, in order to avert the calamities with which they are threatened. When a child is born with any deformity, they will not, if they can possibly avoid it, bring it to be baptised, and it is with difficulty they can be brought to rear it. Arriaga Extirpac. de la Idolat. del Peru, p. 32, 33.

## Note [54]. Page 156.

The number of the fish in the rivers of South America is so extraordinary as to merit particular notice. "In the Maragnon (says P. Acugna,) fish are so plentiful, that, without any art, they may take them with the hands." p. 138. "In the Orinoco (says P. Gumilla,) besides an infinite variety of other fish, tortoise or turtle abound in such numbers, that I cannot find words to express it. I doubt not but that such as read my account will accuse me of exaggeration: but I can affirm that it is as difficult to count them as to count the sands on the banks of that river. One may judge of their number by the amazing consumption of them; for all the nations contiguous to the river, and even many who are at a distance, flock thither at the season of breeding, and not only find sustenance during that time, but carry off great numbers both of the turtles and of their eggs," &c. Hist. de l'Orenoque, ii. c. 22. p. 59. M. de la Condamine confirms their accounts, p. 159.

## Note [55]. Page 156.

Piso describes two of these plants, the *Cururuape* and the *Guajana-Timbo.* It is remarkable, that though they have this fatal effect upon fishes, they are so far from being noxious to the human species, that they are used in medicine with success. Piso, lib. iv. c. 88. Bancroft mentions another, the *Hiarree*, a small quantity of which is sufficient to inebriate all the fish to a considerable distance, so that in a few minutes they float motionless on the surface of the water, and are taken with ease. Nat. Hist. of Guiana, p. 106.

## Note [56]. Page 157.

Remarkable instances occur of the calamities which rude nations suffer by famine. Alvar Nugnez Cabeca de Vaca, one of the most gallant and virtuous of the Spanish adventurers, resided almost nine years among the savages of Florida. They were unacquainted with every species of agriculture. Their subsistence was poor and precarious. "They live chiefly (says he) upon roots of different plants, which they procure with great difficulty, wandering from place to place in search of them. Sometimes they kill game, sometimes they catch fish, but in such small quantities, that their hunger is so extreme as compels them to eat spiders, the eggs of ants, worms, lizards, serpents, a kind of unctuous earth, and, I am persuaded, that if in this country there were stones, they would swallow these. They preserve the bones of fishes and serpents, which they grind into powder and eat. The only season when they do not suffer much from famine, is when a certain fruit, which he calls *Tunas*, is ripe. This is the same with the *Opuntia*, or prickly pear, of a reddish and yellow colour, with a sweet insipid taste. They are sometimes obliged to travel far from their usual place of residence in order to find them. Naufragios, c. xviii. p. 20, 21, 22. In another place he observes, that they are frequently reduced to pass two or three days without food, c. xxiv. p. 27.

### NOTE [57]. PAGE 158.

M. FERMIN has given an accurate description of the two species of manioc, with an account of its culture, to which he has added some experiments, in order to ascertain the poisonous qualities of the juice extracted from that species which he calls the bitter cassava. Among the Spaniards it is known by the name of *Yuca brava*. Descr. de Surin. tom. i. p. 66.

### NOTE [58]. PAGE 158.

THE plantain is found in Asia and Africa, as well as in America. Oviedo contends, that it is not an indigenous plant of the New World, but was introduced into the Island of Hispaniola, in the year 1516, by Father Thomas de Berlanga, and that he transplanted it from the Canary Islands, whither the original slips had been brought from the East Indies. Oviedo, lib. viii. c. 1. But the opinion of Acosta and other naturalists, who reckon it an American plant, seems to be better founded. Acosta Hist. Nat. lib. iv. 21. It was cultivated by rude tribes in America, who had little intercourse with the Spaniards, and who were destitute of that ingenuity which disposes men to borrow what is useful from foreign nations. Gumil. iii. 186. Wafer's Voyage, p. 87.

### NOTE [59]. PAGE 159.

IT IS remarkable that Acosta, one of the most accurate and best informed writers concerning the West Indies, affirms that maize, though cultivated in the continent, was not known in the islands, the inhabitants of which had none but cassada bread. Hist. Nat. lib. iv. c. 16. But P. Martyr, in the first book of his first Decad, which was written in the year 1493, upon the return of Columbus from his first voyage, expressly mentions maize as a plant which the islanders cultivated, and of which they made bread, p. 7. Gomara likewise asserts that they were acquainted with the culture of maize. Histor. Gener. cap. 28. Oviedo describes maize without any intimation of its being a plant that was not natural to Hispaniola. Lib. vii. c. 1.

### NOTE [60]. PAGE 161.

NEW Holland, a country which formerly was only known, has lately been visited by intelligent observers. It lies in a region of the globe where it must enjoy a very favourable climate, as it stretches from the 10th to the 38th degree of southern latitude. It is of great extent, and from its square form must be much more than equal to all Europe. The people who inhabit the various parts of it appear to be of one race. They are evidently ruder than most of the Americans, and have made still less progress in improvement and the arts of life. There is not the least appearance of cultivation in any part of this vast region. The inhabitants are extremely few, so that the country appears almost desolate. Their tribes are still more inconsiderable than those of America. They depend for subsistence almost entirely on fishing. They do not settle in one place, but roam about in quest of food. Both sexes go stark naked. Their habitations, utensils, &c. are more simple and rude than those of the Americans. Voyages, by Hawkesworth, iii. 622, &c. This, perhaps, is the country where man has been discovered in the earliest stage of his progress, and exhibits a miserable specimen of his condition and powers in that uncultivated state. If this country shall be more fully explored by future navigators, the comparison of the manners of its inhabitants with those of the Americans will prove an instructive article in the history of the human species.

## Note [61]. Page 161.

P. Gabriel Marest, who travelled from his station among the Illinois to Michilimackinac, thus describes the face of the country:—"We have marched twelve days without meeting a single human creature. Sometimes we found ourselves in vast meadows, of which we could not see the boundaries, through which there flowed many brooks and rivers, but without any path to conduct us. Sometimes we were obliged to open a passage across thick forests, through bushes, and underwood filled with briars and thorns. Sometimes we had to pass through deep marshes, in which we sunk up to the middle. After being fatigued through the day, we had the earth for our bed, or a few leaves, exposed to the wind, the rain, and all the injuries of the air." Lettr. Edifiantes, ii. 360. Dr. Bicknell, in an excursion from North Carolina towards the mountains, A. D. 1730, travelled fifteen days without meeting with a human creature. Nat. Hist. of North Carolina, 389. Diego de Ordas, in attempting to make a settlement in South America, A. D. 1532, marched fifty days through a country without one inhabitant. Herrera, dec. 5. lib. i. c. 11.

## Note [62]. Page 162.

I strongly suspect that a community of goods, and an undivided store, are known only among the rudest tribes of hunters; and that as soon as any species of agriculture or regular industry is known, the idea of an exclusive right of property to the fruits of them is introduced. I am confirmed in this opinion by accounts which I have received concerning the state of property among the Indians in very different regions of America. "The idea of the natives of Brazil concerning property is, that if any person cultivate a field, he alone ought to enjoy the produce of it, and no other has a title to pretend to it. If an individual or family go a hunting or fishing, what is caught belongs to the individual or to the family, and they communicate no part of it to any but to their cazique, or to such of their kindred as happen to be indisposed. If any person in the village come to their hut, he may sit down freely, and eat without asking liberty. But this is the consequence of their general principle of hospitality; for I never observed any partition of the increase of their fields, or the produce of the chase, which I could consider as the result of any idea concerning a community of goods. On the contrary, they are so much attached to what they deem to be their property, that it would be extremely dangerous to encroach upon it. As far as I can see or can learn, there is not one tribe of Indians in South America among whom the community of goods which has been so highly extolled is known. The circumstance in the government of the Jesuits, most irksome to the Indians of Paraguay, was the community of goods which those fathers introduced. This was repugnant to the original ideas of the Indians. They were acquainted with the rights of private exclusive property, and they submitted with impatience to regulations which destroyed them." M. le Cheval, de Pinto, MS. *penes me*. "Actual possession (says a missionary who resided several years among the Indians of the five nations) gives a right to the soil; but, whenever a possessor sees fit to quit it, another has as good right to take it as he who left it. This law, or custom, respects not only the particular spot on which he erects his house, but also his planting-ground. If a man has prepared a particular spot of ground on which he designs in future to build or plant, no man has a right to incommode him, much less to the fruit of his labours, until it appears that he voluntarily gives up his views. But I never heard of any formal conveyance from one Indian to another in their natural state. The limit of every canton is circumscribed; that is, they are allowed to hunt as far as such a river on this hand, and such a mountain on the other. This area is occupied and improved by individuals and their families: individuals, not the community, have the use and profit of their own labours, or success in hunting." MS. of Mr. Gideon Hawley, *penes me.*

### Note [63]. Page 162.

This difference of temper between the Americans and Negroes is so remarkable, that it is a proverbial saying in the French islands, "Regarder un sauvage de travers, c'est le battre; le battre, c'est le tuer; battre un Negre, c'est le nourrir." Tertre, ii. 490.

### Note [64]. Page 163.

The description of the political state of the people of Cinaloa perfectly resembles that of the inhabitants of North America. "They have neither laws nor kings (says a missionary who resided long among them) to punish any crime. Nor is there among them any species of authority, or political government, to restrain them in any part of their conduct. It is true that they acknowledge certain caziques, who are heads of their families or villages; but their authority appears chiefly in war, and the expeditions against their enemies. This authority the caziques obtain not by hereditary right, but by their valour in war, or by the power and number of their families and relations. Sometimes they owe their pre-eminence to their eloquence in displaying their own exploits." Ribas Histor. de las Triumph, &c. p. 11. The state of the Chiquitos in South America is nearly the same. "They have no regular form of government or civil life, but in matters of public concern they listen to the advice of their old men, and usually follow it. The dignity of Cazique is not hereditary, but conferred according to merit, as the reward of valour in war. The union among them is imperfect. Their society resembles a republic without any head, in which every man is master of himself, and, upon the least disgust, separates from those with whom he seemed to be connected." Relacion Historical de las Missiones de los Chiquitos, por P. Juan, Patr. Fernandez, p. 32, 33. Thus, under very different climates, when nations are in a similar state of society, their institutions and civil government assume the same form.

### Note [65]. Page 168.

"I have known the Indians (says a person well acquainted with their mode of life) to go a thousand miles for the purpose of revenge, in pathless woods, over hills and mountains, through huge cane swamps, exposed to the extremities of heat and cold, the vicissitude of seasons, to hunger and thirst. Such is their overboiling revengeful temper, that they utterly contemn all those things as imaginary trifles, if they are so happy as to get the scalp of the murderer, or enemy, to satisfy the craving ghosts of their deceased relations." Adair's Hist. of Amer. Indians, p. 150.

### Note [66]. Page 168.

In the account of the great war between the Algonquins and Iroquois, the achievements of Piskaret, a famous chief of the Algonquins, performed mostly by himself alone, or with one or two companions, make a capital figure. De la Potherie, i. 297, &c. Colden's Hist. of Five Nations, 125, &c.

### Note [67]. Page 169.

The life of an unfortunate leader is often in danger, and he is always degraded from the rank which he had acquired by his former exploits. Adair, p. 388.

### Note [68]. Page 169.

As the ideas of the North Americans, with respect to the mode of carrying on war, are generally known, I have founded my observations chiefly upon the testimony of the authors who describe them. But the same maxims took place among other nations in the New World. A judicious missionary has given a view of the military operations of the people in Gran Chaco, in South America, perfectly similar to those of the Iroquois. "They are much addicted to war (says he), which they carry on frequently among themselves, but perpetually against the Spaniards. But they may rather be called thieves than soldiers, for they never make head against the Spaniards, unless when they can assault them by stealth, or have guarded against any mischance by spies, who may be called indefatigable; they will watch the settlements of the Spaniards for one, two, or three years, observing by night every thing that passes with the utmost solicitude, whether they may expect resistance or not, and until they are perfectly secure of the event, they will not venture upon an attack; so that, when they do give the assault, they are certain of success, and free from all danger. These spies, in order that they may not be observed, will creep on all four like cats in the night; but if they are discovered, make their escape with much dexterity. But, although they never choose to face the Spaniards, if they be surrounded in any place whence they cannot escape, they will fight with desperate valour, and sell their lives very dear." Lozano Descript. del Gran Chaco, p. 78.

### Note [69]. Page 170.

Lery, who was an eye-witness of the proceedings of the *Toupinambos*, a Brasilian tribe, in a war against a powerful nation of their enemies, describes their courage and ferocity in very striking terms. Ego cum Gallo altero, paulo curiosius, magno nostro periculo (si enim ab hostibus capti aut lesi fuissemus, devorationi fuissemus devoti), barbaros nostros in militiam ountes comitari volui. Hi, numero 4000 capita, cum hostibus ad littus decertârunt, tanta ferocitate, ut vel rabidos et furiosos quosque superarent. Cum primum hostes conspexere, in magnos atque editos ululatus perruperunt. Hæc gens adeo fera est et truculenta, ut tantisper dum virium vel tantillum restat, continuo dimicent, fugamque nunquam capessant. Quod a natura illis inditum esse reor. Testor interea me, qui non semel, tum peditum tum equitum copias ingentes, in aciem instructas hic conspexi, tanta nunquam voluptate videndis peditum legionibus armis fulgentibus, quanta tum pugnantibus istis percussum fuisse. Lery Hist. Navigat. in Brasil. ap. de Bry, iii. 207, 208, 209.

### Note [70]. Page 170.

It was originally the practice of the Americans, as well as of other savage nations, to cut off the heads of the enemies whom they slew, and to carry them away as trophies. But, as they found these cumbersome in their retreat, which they always make very rapidly, and often through a vast extent of country, they became satisfied with tearing off their scalps. This custom, though most prevalent in North America, was not unknown among the Southern tribes Lozano, p. 79.

### Note [71]. Page 172.

The terms of the war song seem to be dictated by the same fierce spirit of revenge. "I go to war to revenge the death of my brothers; I shall kill; I shall exterminate; I shall burn my enemies; I shall bring away slaves; I shall devour their heart, dry their flesh, drink their blood; I shall tear off their scalps, and make cups of their skulls." Bossu's Travels through Louisiana, vol. i. p. 102. I am informed, by persons on whose testimony I can rely, that as the number of people in the Indian tribes has decreased so much, almost none of their prisoners are now put to death. It is considered as better policy to spare and to adopt them. Those dreadful scenes which I have described occur now so rarely, that missionaries and traders who have resided long among the Indians, never were witnesses to them.

### NOTE [72]. PAGE 172.

ALL the travellers who have visited the most uncivilized of the American tribes, agree in this. It is confirmed by two remarkable circumstances, which occurred in the conquest of different provinces. In the expedition of Narvaez into Florida in the year 1528, the Spaniards were reduced to such extreme distress by famine, that, in order to preserve their own lives, they ate such of their companions as happened to die. This appeared so shocking to the natives, who were accustomed to devour none but prisoners, that it filled them with horror and indignation against the Spaniards. Torquemada Monarch. Ind. ii. p. 584. Naufragios de Alv. Nugnes Cabeca de Vaca, c. xiv. p. 15. During the siege of Mexico, though the Mexicans devoured with greediness the Spaniards and Tlascalans whom they took prisoners, the utmost rigour of the famine which they suffered could not induce them to touch the dead bodies of their own countrymen. Bern. Diaz del Castillo Conquist. de la N. Espagna, p. 156.

### NOTE [73]. PAGE 172.

MANY singular circumstances concerning the treatment of prisoners among the people of Brasil, are contained in the narrative of Stadius, a German officer in the service of the Portuguese, published in the year 1556. He was taken prisoner by the *Toupinambos*, and remained in captivity nine years. He was often present at those horrid festivals which he describes, and was destined himself to the same cruel fate with other prisoners. But he saved his life by his extraordinary efforts of courage and address. De Bry, iii. p. 34, &c. M. de Lery, who accompanied M. de Villagagnon in his expedition to Brasil in the year 1556, and who resided some time in that country, agrees with Stadius in every circumstance of importance. He was frequently an eye-witness of the manner in which the Brasilians treated their prisoners. De Bry, iii. 210. Several striking particulars omitted by them, are mentioned by a Portuguese author. Purch. Pilgr. iv. 1294, &c.

### NOTE [74]. PAGE 174.

THOUGH I have followed that opinion concerning the apathy of the Americans, which appeared to me most rational, and supported by the authority of the most respectable authors, other theories have been formed with regard to it, by writers of great eminence. D. Ant. Ulloa, in a late work, contends that the texture of the skin and bodily habit of the Americans is such, that they are less sensible of pain than the rest of mankind. He produces several proofs of this, from the manner in which they endure the most cruel chirurgical operations, &c. Noticias Americanas, p. 313, 314. The same observation has been made by surgeons in Brasil. An Indian, they say, never complains under pain, and will bear the amputation of a leg or an arm without uttering a single groan. MS. *penes me.*

### NOTE [75]. PAGE 174.

THIS is an idea natural to all rude nations. Among the Romans, in the early periods of their commonwealth, it was a maxim that a prisoner "tum decessisse videtur cum captus est." Digest. lib. xlix. tit. 15. c. 18. And afterwards, when the progress of refinement rendered them more indulgent with respect to this article, they were obliged to employ two fictions of law to secure the property, and permit the return of a captive; the one by the Lex Cornelia, and the other by the Jus Postliminii. Heinec. Elem. Jur. Civ. sec. ord. Pand. ii. p. 294. Among the Negroes the same ideas prevail. No ransom was ever accepted for a prisoner As soon as one is taken in war, he is reputed to be dead; and he is so in effect to his country and his family. Voy. du Cheval. des Marchais, i. p. 369.

NOTE [76]. PAGE 175.

THE people of Chili, the most gallant and high-spirited of all the Americans, are the only exception to this observation. They attack their enemies in the open field; their troops are ranged in regular order; their battalions advance to the charge not only with courage, but with discipline. The North Americans, though many of them have substituted the European fire-arms in place of their own bows and arrows, still adhere to their ancient maxims of war, and carry it on according to their own peculiar system. But the Chilese nearly resemble the warlike nations of Europe and Asia in their military operations. Ovalle's Relation of Chili. Church. Coll. iii. p. 71. Lozano's Hist. Parag. i. 144, 145.

NOTE [77]. PAGE 176.

HERRERA gives a remarkable proof of this. In Yucatan, the men are so solicitous about their dress, that they carry about with them mirrors, probably made of stone, like those of the Mexicans, Dec. iv. lib. iii. c. 8, in which they delight to view themselves; but the women never use them. Dec. iv. lib. x. c. 3. He takes notice that among the fierce tribe of the *Panches*, in the new kingdom of Granada, none but distinguished warriors were permitted either to pierce their lips and to wear green stones in them, or to adorn their heads with plumes of feathers. Dec. vii. lib. ix. c. 4. In some provinces of Peru, though that empire had made considerable progress in civilization, the state of women was little improved. All the toil of cultivation and domestic work was devolved upon them, and they were not permitted to wear bracelets, or other ornaments, with which the men were fond of decking themselves. Zarate Hist. de Peru, i. p. 15, 16.

NOTE [78]. PAGE 176.

I HAVE ventured to call this mode of anointing and painting their bodies, the *dress* of the Americans. This is agreeable to their own idiom. As they never stir abroad if they are not completely anointed; they excuse themselves when in this situation, by saying that they cannot appear because they are naked Gumilla, Hist. de l'Orenoque, i. 191.

NOTE [79]. PAGE 177.

SOME tribes in the province of Cinaloa, on the gulf of California, seem to be among the rudest people of America united in the social state. They neither cultivate nor sow; they have no houses in which they reside. Those in the inland country subsist by hunting; those on the seacoast chiefly by fishing. Both depend upon the spontaneous productions of the earth, fruits, plants, and roots of various kinds. In the rainy season, as they have no habitations to afford them shelter, they gather bundles of reeds, or strong grass; and binding them together at one end, they open them at the other, and fitting them to their heads, they are covered as with a large cap, which, like a penthouse throws off the rain, and will keep them dry for several hours. During the warm season, they form a shed with the branches of trees, which protects them from the sultry rays of the sun. When exposed to cold they make large fires, round which they sleep in the open air. Historia de los Triomphos de Nuestra Santa Fe entre Gentres las mas Barbaras, &c. por P. And. Perez de Ribas, p. 7, &c.

NOTE [80]. PAGE 177.

THESE houses resemble barns. "We have measured some which were a hundred and fifty paces long, and twenty paces broad. Above a hundred persons resided in some of them." Wilson's Account of Guiana. Purch. Pilgr. vol. iv. p. 1263. Ibid. 1291. "The Indian houses," says Mr. Barrere, "have a most wretched appearance, and are a striking image of the rudeness of early times. Their huts are commonly built on some rising ground, or on the banks of a river, huddled sometimes together, sometimes straggling, and always without any order. Their aspect is melancholy and disagreeable. One sees nothing but what is hideous and savage. The uncultivated fields have no gayety. The silence which reigns there, unless when interrupted by the disagreeable notes of birds, or cries of wild beasts, is extremely dismal." Relat. de la France Equin. p. 146.

### Note [81]. Page 178.

Some tribes in South America can send their arrows to a great distance, and with considerable force, without the aid of the bow. They make use of a hollow reed, about nine feet long and an inch thick, which is called a *Sarbacane.* In it they lodge a small arrow, with some unspun cotton wound about its great end; this confines the air, so that they can blow it with astonishing rapidity, and a sure aim, to the distance of above a hundred paces. These small arrows are always poisoned. Fermin. Descr. de Surin. i. 55. Bancroft's Hist. of Guiana, p. 281, &c. The Sarbacane is much used in some parts of the East Indies.

### Note [82]. Page 178.

I might produce many instances of this, but shall satisfy myself with one taken from the Eskimaux. "Their greatest ingenuity (says Mr. Ellis) is shown in the structure of their bows, made commonly of three pieces of wood, each making part of the same arch, very nicely and exactly joined together. They are commonly of fir or larch; and as this wants strength and elasticity, they supply both by bracing the back of the bow with a kind of thread, or line, made of the sinews of their deer, and the bowstring of the same materials. To make them draw more stiffly, they dip them into water, which causes both the back of the bow and the string to contract, and consequently gives it the greater force; and as they practise from their youth, they shoot with very great dexterity." Voyage to Hudson's Bay, p. 138.

### Note [83]. Page 178.

Necessity is the great prompter and guide of mankind in their inventions. There is, however, such inequality in some parts of their progress, and some nations get so far the start of others in circumstances nearly similar, that we must ascribe this to some events in their story, or to some peculiarity in their situation, with which we are unacquainted. The people in the island of Otaheite, lately discovered in the South Sea, far excel most of the Americans in the knowledge and practice of the arts of ingenuity, and yet they had not invented any method of boiling water; and having no vessel that could bear the fire, they had no more idea that water could be made hot, than that it could be made solid. Voyages by Hawkesworth, i. 466. 484.

### Note [84]. Page 178.

One of these boats, which could carry nine men, weighed only sixty pounds. Gosnol. Relat. des Voy. à la Virgin. Rec. de Voy. au Nord, tom. v. p. 403.

### Note [85]. Page 179.

A remarkable proof of this is produced by Ulloa. In weaving hammocks, coverlets, and other coarse cloths which they are accustomed to manufacture, their industry has discovered no more expeditious method than to take up thread after thread, and, after counting and sorting them each time, to pass the woof between them, so that in finishing a small piece of those stuffs they frequently spend more than two years. Voyage, i. 336. Bancroft gives the same description of the Indians of Guiana, p. 255. According to Adair, the ingenuity and despatch of the North American Indians are not greater, p. 422. From one of the engravings of the Mexican paintings in Purchas, vol. iii. p. 1106, I think it probable that the people of Mexico were unacquainted with any better or more expeditious mode of weaving. A loom was an invention beyond the ingenuity of the most improved Americans. In all their works they advance so slowly, that one of their artists is two months at a tobacco-pipe with his knife before he finishes it. Adair, p. 423.

### Note [86]. Page 180.

The article of religion in P. Lafitau's Mœurs des Sauvages extends to 347 tedious pages in quarto.

### Note [87]. Page 181.

I have referred the reader to several of the authors who describe the most uncivilized nations in America. Their testimony is uniform. That of P. Ribas concerning the people of Cinaloa coincides with the rest. "I was extremely attentive (says he), during the years I resided among them, to ascertain whether they were to be considered as idolaters; and it may be affirmed with the most perfect exactness, that though among some of them there may be traces of idolatry, yet others have not the least knowledge of God, or even of any false deity, nor pay any formal adoration to the Supreme Being who exercises dominion over the world; nor have they any conception of the providence of a Creator, or Governor, from whom they expect in the next life the reward of their good or the punishment of their evil deeds. Neither do they publicly join in any act of divine worship." Ribas Triumphos, &c. p. 16.

### Note [88]. Page 181.

The people of Brasil were so much affrighted by thunder, which is frequent and awful in their country, as well as in other parts of the torrid zone, that it was not only the object of religious reverence, but the most expressive name in their language for the Deity was *Toupan*, the same by which they distinguished thunder. Piso de Medec. Brasil, p. 8. Nieuhoff. Church. Coll. ii. p. 132

### Note [89]. Page 184.

By the account which M. Dumont, an eye-witness, gives of the funeral of the great chief of the Natchez, it appears that the feelings of the persons who suffered on that occasion were very different. Some solicited the honour with eagerness; others laboured to avoid their doom, and several saved their lives by flying to the woods. As the Indian Brahmins give an intoxicating draught to the women who are to be burned together with the bodies of their husbands, which renders them insensible of their approaching fate, the Natchez obliged their victims to swallow several large pills of tobacco, which produces a similar effect. Mém de Louis. i. 227.

### Note [90]. Page 187.

On some occasions, particularly in dances instituted for the recovery of persons who are indisposed, they are extremely licentious and indecent. De la Potherie Hist. &c. ii. p. 42. Charlev. N. Fr. iii. p. 319. But the nature of their dances is commonly such as I have described.

### Note [91]. Page 187.

The *Othomacoas*, a tribe seated on the banks of the Orinoco, employ for the same purpose a composition which they call *Yupa*. It is formed of the seeds of an unknown plant reduced to powder, and certain shells burned and pulverized. The effects of this when drawn up into the nostrils are so violent that they resemble madness rather than intoxication. Gumilla, i. 286.

### NOTE [92]. PAGE 188.

THOUGH this observation holds true among the greater part of the southern tribes, there are some in which the intemperance of the women is as excessive as that of the men. Bancroft's Nat. Hist. of Guiana, p. 275.

### NOTE [93]. PAGE 190.

EVEN in the most intelligent writers concerning the manners of the Americans, one meets with inconsistent and inexplicable circumstances. The Jesuit Charlevoix, who, in consequence of the controversy between his order and that of the Franciscans, with respect to the talents and abilities of the North Americans, is disposed to represent their intellectual as well as moral qualities in the most favourable light, asserts, that they are engaged in continual negotiations with their neighbours, and conduct these with the most refined address. At the same time he adds, "that it behooves their envoys or plenipotentiaries to exert their abilities and eloquence, for, if the terms which they offer are not accepted, they had need to stand on their guard. It frequently happens, that a blow with the hatchet is the only return given to their propositions. The envoy is not out of danger, even if he is so fortunate as to avoid the stroke; he may expect to be pursued, and, if taken, to be burnt." Hist. N. Fr. iii. 251. What occurs, p. 147, concerning the manner in which the Tlascalans treated the ambassadors from Zempoalla, corresponds with the fact related by Charlevoix. Men capable of such acts of violence seem to be unacquainted with the first principles upon which the intercourse between nations is founded; and instead of the perpetual negotiations which Charlevoix mentions, it seems almost impossible that there should be any correspondence whatever among them.

### NOTE [94]. PAGE 191.

IT is a remark of Tacitus concerning the Germans, "Gaudent muneribus, sed nec data imputant, nec acceptis obligantur." C. 21. An author who had a good opportunity of observing the principle which leads savages neither to express gratitude for favours which they had received, nor to expect any return for such as they bestowed, thus explains their ideas: "If (say they) you give me this, it is because you have no need of it yourself; and as for me, I never part with that which I think necessary to me." Mémoire sur le Galibis; Hist. des Plantes de la Guiane Françoise par M. Aublet, tom ii. p. 110.

### NOTE [95]. PAGE 196.

AND Bernaldes, the contemporary and friend of Columbus, has preserved some circumstances concerning the bravery of the Caribbees, which are not mentioned by Don Ferdinand Columbus, or the other historians of that period whose works have been published. A Caribbean canoe, with four men, two women, and a boy, fell in unexpectedly with the fleet of Columbus in his second voyage, as it was steering through their islands. At first they were struck almost stupid with astonishment at such a strange spectacle, and hardly moved from the spot for above an hour. A Spanish bark, with twenty-five men, advanced towards them, and the fleet gradually surrounded them, so as to cut off their communication with the shore. "When they saw that it was impossible to escape (says the historian), they seized their arms with undaunted resolution, and began the attack. I use the expression *with undaunted resolution*, for they were few, and beheld a vast number ready to assault them. They wounded several of the Spaniards, although they had targets, as well as other defensive armour; and even after their canoe was overset, it was with no little difficulty and danger that part of them were taken, as they continued to defend themselves, and to use their bows with great dexterity while swimming in the sea." Hist. de D. Fern. y Ysab. MS. c. 119.

### Note [96]. Page 196.

A probable conjecture may be formed with respect to the cause of the distinction in character between the Caribbees and the inhabitants of the larger islands. The former appear manifestly to be a separate race. Their language is totally different from that of their neighbours in the large islands. They themselves have a tradition, that their ancestors came originally from some part of the continent, and, having conquered and exterminated the ancient inhabitants, took possession of their lands, and of their women. Rochefort, 384. Tertre, 360. Hence they call themselves *Banaree*, which signifies a man come from beyond sea. Labat, vi. 131. Accordingly, the Caribbees still use two distinct languages, one peculiar to the men, and the other to the women. Tertre, 361. The language of the men has nothing common with that spoken in the large islands. The dialect of the women considerably resembles it. Labat, 129. This strongly confirms the tradition which I have mentioned. The Caribbees themselves imagine that they were a colony from the *Galabis*, a powerful nation of Guiana in South America. Tertre, 361. Rochefort, 348. But as their fierce manners approach nearer to those of the people in the northern continent, than to those of the natives of South America; and as their language has likewise some affinity to that spoken in Florida, their origin should be deduced rather from the former than from the latter. Labat, 128, &c. Herrera, dec. i. lib. ix. c. 4. In their wars, they still observe their ancient practice of destroying all the males, and preserving the women either for servitude or for breeding.

### Note [97]. Page 197.

Our knowledge of the events which happened in the conquest of New Spain, is derived from sources of information more original and authentic than that of any transaction in the history of America. The letters of Cortes to the Emperor Charles V. are an historical monument, not only first in order of time, but of the greatest authenticity and value. As Cortes early assumed a command independent of Velasquez, it became necessary to convey such an account of his operations to Madrid, as might procure him the approbation of his sovereign.

The first of his despatches has never been made public. It was sent from Vera Cruz, July 16th, 1519. As I imagined that it might not reach the Emperor until he arrived in Germany, for which he set out early in the year 1520, in order to receive the Imperial crown; I made diligent search for a copy of this despatch, both in Spain and in Germany, but without success. This, however, is of less consequence, as it could not contain any thing very material, being written so soon after Cortes arrived in New Spain. But, in searching for the letter from Cortes, a copy of one from the colony of Vera Cruz to the Emperor has been discovered in the Imperial library at Vienna. Of this I have given some account in its proper place, see p. 210. The second despatch, dated October 30th, 1520, was published at Seville A. D. 1522, and the third and fourth soon after they were received. A Latin translation of them appeared in Germany A. D. 1532. Ramusio soon after made them more generally known, by inserting them in his valuable collection. They contain a regular and minute history of the expedition, with many curious particulars concerning the policy and manners of the Mexicans. The work does honour to Cortes; the style is simple and perspicuous; but as it was manifestly his interest to represent his own actions in the fairest light, his victories are probably exaggerated, his losses diminished, and his acts of rigour and violence softened.

The next in order is the Chronica de la Nueva Espagna, by Francisco Lopez de Gomara, published A. D. 1554. Gomara's historical merit is considerable. His mode of narration is clear, flowing, always agreeable, and sometimes elegant. But he is frequently inaccurate and credulous; and as he was the domestic chaplain of Cortes after his return from New Spain, and probably composed his work at his desire, it is manifest that he labours to magnify the merit of his hero, and to conceal or extenuate such transactions as were unfavourable to his character. Of this, Herrera accuses him in one instance, Dec. ii. lib. iii. c. 2, and it is not once only that this is conspicuous. He writes, however, with so much freedom concerning several measures of the Spanish Court, that the copies both of his Historia de las Indias, and of his Chronica, were called in by a decree of the Council of the Indies, and they were long considered as prohibited books in Spain; it is only of late that license to print them has been granted. Pinelo Biblioth. 589.

The Chronicle of Gomara induced Bernal Diaz del Castillo to compose his Historia Verdadera de la Conquista de la Nueva Espagna. He had been an adventurer in each of the expeditions to New Spain, and was the companion of Cortes in all his battles and perils. When he found that neither he himself, nor many of his fellow-soldiers, were once mentioned by Gomara, but that the fame of all their exploits was ascribed to Cortes, the gallant veteran laid hold of his pen with indignation, and composed his true history. It contains a prolix, minute, confused narrative of all Cortes's operations, in such a rude vulgar style as might be expected from an illiterate soldier. But as he relates transactions of which he was witness, and in which he performed a considerable part, his account bears all the marks of authenticity, and is accompanied with such a pleasant *naviete*, with such interesting details, with such amusing vanity, and yet so pardonable in an old soldier who had been (as he boasts) in a hundred and nineteen battles, as renders his book one of the most singular that is to be found in any language.

Pet. Martyr ab Angleria, in a treatise De Insulis nuper inventis, added to his Decades de Rebus Oceanicis et Novo Orbe, gives some account of Cortes's expedition. But he proceeds no further than to relate what happened after his first landing. This work, which is brief and slight, seems to contain the information transmitted by Cortes in his first despatches, embellished with several particulars communicated to the author by the officers who brought the letters from Cortes.

But the book to which the greater part of modern historians have had recourse for information concerning the conquest of New Spain, is Historia do la Conquista de Mexico, por D. Antonio de Solis, first published A D. 1684. I know no author in any language whose literary fame has risen so far beyond his real merit. De Solis is reckoned by his countrymen one of the purest writers in the Castilian tongue; and if a foreigner may venture to give his opinion concerning a matter of which Spaniards alone are qualified to judge, he is entitled to that praise. But though his language be correct, his taste in composition is far from being just. His periods are so much laboured as to be often stiff, and sometimes tumid; the figures which he employs by way of ornament are frequently trite or improper, and his observations superficial. These blemishes, however, might easily be overlooked, if he were not defective with respect to all the great qualities of an historian. Destitute of that patient industry in research which conducts to the knowledge of truth; a stranger to that impartiality which weighs evidence with cool attention; and ever eager to establish his favourite system of exalting the character of Cortes into that of a perfect hero, exempt from error, and adorned with every virtue; he is less solicitous to discover what was true than to relate what might appear splendid. When he attempts any critical discussion, his reasonings are fallacious, and founded upon an imperfect view of facts. Though he sometimes quotes the *despatches* of Cortes, he seems not to have consulted them; and though he sets out with some censure on Gomara, he frequently prefers his authority, the most doubtful of any, to that of the other contemporary historians.

But of all the Spanish writers, Herrera furnishes the fullest and most accurate information concerning the conquest of Mexico, as well as every other transaction of America. The industry and attention with which he consulted not only the books, but the original papers and public records, which tended to throw any light upon the subject of his inquiries, were so great, and he usually judges of the evidence before him with so much impartiality and candour, that his Decads may be ranked among the most judicious and useful historical collections. If, by attempting to relate the various occurrences in the New World in a strict chronological order, the arrangement of events in his work had not been rendered so perplexed, disconnected, and obscure, that it is an unpleasant task to collect from different parts of his book, and piece together the detached shreds of a story, he might justly have been ranked among the most eminent historians of his country. He gives an account of the materials from which he composed his work, Dec. vi. lib. iii. c. 19.

### Note [98]. Page 198.

Cortes purposed to have gone in the train of Ovando when he set out for his government in the year 1502, but was detained by an accident. As he was attempting in a dark night to scramble up to the window of a lady's bedchamber, with whom he carried on an intrigue, an old wall, on the top of which he had mounted, gave way, and he was so much bruised by the fall as to be unfit for the voyage. Gomara, Cronica de la Nueva Espagna, cap. 1

### Note [99]. Page 198.

Cortes had two thousand pesos in the hands of Andrew Duero, and he borrowed four thousand. Those sums are about equal in value to fifteen hundred pounds sterling ; but as the price of every thing was extremely high in America, they made but a scanty stock when applied towards the equipment of a military expedition. Herrera, dec. ii. lib. iii. c. 2. B. Diaz, c. 20.

### Note [100]. Page 200.

The names of those gallant officers, which will often occur in the subsequent story, were Juan Velasquez de Leon, Alonso Hernandez Portocarrero, Francisco de Montejo, Christoval de Olid, Juan de Escalante, Francisco de Morla, Pedro de Alvarado, Francisco de Salceda, Juan de Escobar, Gines de Nortes. Cortes himself commanded the Capitana, or Admiral. Francisco de Orozco, an officer formed in the wars of Italy, had the command of the artillery. The experienced Alaminos acted as chief pilot.

### Note [101]. Page 201.

In those different conflicts, the Spaniards lost only two men, but had a considerable number wounded. Though there be no occasion for recourse to any supernatural cause to account either for the greatness of their victories, or the smallness of their loss, the Spanish historians fail not to ascribe both to the patronage of St. Jago, the tutelar saint of their country, who, as they relate, fought at the head of their countrymen, and by his prowess gave a turn to the fate of the battle. Gomara is the first who mentions this apparition of St. James. It is amusing to observe the embarrassment of B. Diaz del Castillo, occasioned by the struggle between his superstition and his veracity. The former disposed him to believe this miracle, the latter restrained him from attesting it. "I acknowledge," says he, "that all our exploits and victories are owing to our Lord Jesus Christ, and that in this battle there was such a number of Indians to every one of us, that if each had thrown a handful of earth they might have buried us, if by the great mercy of God we had not been protected. It may be that the person whom Gomara mentions as having appeared on a mottled gray horse, was the glorious apostle Signor San Jago or Signor San Pedro, and that I, as being a sinner, was not worthy to see him. This I know, that I saw Francisco de Morla, on such a horse, but as an unworthy transgressor, did not deserve to see any of the holy apostles. It may have been the will of God, that it was so as Gomara relates, but until I read his Chronicle I never heard among any of the conquerors that such a thing had happened." Cap. 34.

### Note [102]. Page 203.

Several Spanish historians relate this occurrence in such terms as if they wished it should be believed, that the Indians, loaded with the presents, had carried them from the capital, in the same short space of time that the couriers performed that journey. This is incredible, and Gomara mentions a circumstance which shows that nothing extraordinary happened on this occasion. This rich present had been prepared for Grijalva, when he touched at the same place some months before, and was now ready to be delivered, as soon as Montezuma sent orders for that purpose. Gomara Cron. c. xxvii. p. 28.

According to B. Diaz del Castillo, the value of the silver plate representing the moon was alone above twenty thousand pesos, above five thousand pounds sterling.

### Note [103]. Page 206.

This private traffic was directly contrary to the instructions of Velasquez, who enjoined, that whatever was acquired by trade should be thrown into the common stock. But it appears that the soldiers had each a private assortment of toys and other goods proper for the Indian trade, and Cortes gained their favour by encouraging this underhand barter. B. Diaz, c. 41.

### Note [104]. Page 211.

Gomara has published a catalogue of the various articles of which this present consisted. Cron. c. 49. P. Martyr ab Angleria, who saw them after they were brought to Spain, and who seems to have examined them with great attention, gives a description of each, which is curious, as it conveys some idea of the progress which the Mexicans had made in several arts of elegance. De Insulis nuper inventis Liber, p. 354, &c.

### Note [105]. Page 213.

There is no circumstance in the history of the conquest of America which is more questionable than the account of the numerous armies brought into the field against the Spaniards. As the war with the republic of Tlascala, though of short duration, was one of the most considerable which the Spaniards waged in America, the account given of the Tlascalan armies merits some attention. The only authentic information concerning this is derived from three authors. Cortes in his second despatch to the Emperor, dated at Segura de la Frontera, Oct. 30, 1520, thus estimates the number of their troops; in the first battle 6000; in the second battle 100,000; in the third battle 150,000. Relat. ap. Ramus. iii. 228. Bernal Diaz del Castillo, who was an eye witness, and engaged in all the actions of this war, thus reckons their numbers: in the first battle, 3000, p. 43; in the second battle 6000, ibid.; in the third battle 50,000, p. 45. Gomara, who was Cortes's chaplain after his return to Spain, and published his *Cronica* in 1552, follows the computation of Cortes, except in the second battle, where he reckons the Tlascalans, at 80,000, p. 49. It was manifestly the interest of Cortes to magnify his own dangers and exploits. For it was only by the merit of extraordinary services that he could hope to atone for his irregular conduct in assuming an independent command. Bern. Diaz, though abundantly disposed to place his own prowess, and that of his fellow-conquerors, in the most advantageous point of light, had not the same temptation to exaggerate; and it is probable that his account of the numbers approaches nearer to the truth. The assembling of an army of 150,000 men requires many previous arrangements, and such provisions for their subsistence as seems to be beyond the foresight of Americans. The degree of cultivation in Tlascala does not seem to have been so great as to have furnished such a vast army with provisions. Though this province was so much better cultivated than other regions of New Spain that it was called the *country of bread;* yet the Spaniards in their march suffered such want, that they were obliged to subsist upon *Tunas*, a species of fruit which grows wild in the fields. Herrera, dec. ii. lib. vi. c. 5. p. 182.

NOTE [106]. PAGE 215

THESE unhappy victims are said to be persons of distinction. It seems improbable that so great a number as fifty should be employed as spies. So many prisoners had been taken and dismissed, and the Tlascalans had sent so many messages to the Spanish quarters, that there appears to be no reason for hazarding the lives of so many considerable people in order to procure information about the position and state of their camp. The barbarous manner in which Cortes treated a people unacquainted with the laws of war established among polished nations, appears so shocking to the later Spanish writers, that they diminish the number of those whom he punished so cruelly. Herrera says, that he cut off the hands of seven, and the thumbs of some more. Dec. ii. lib. ii. c. 8. De Solis relates, that the hands of fourteen or fifteen were cut off, and the thumbs of all the rest. Lib. ii. c. 20. But Cortes himself, Relat. p. 228. b. and after him Gomara, c. 48, affirm, that the hands of all the fifty were cut off.

NOTE [107]. PAGE 216.

THE horses were objects of the greatest astonishment to all the people of New Spain. At first they imagined the horse and his rider, like the Centaurs of the ancients, to be some monstrous animal of a terrible form; and supposing that their food was the same as that of men, brought flesh and bread to nourish them. Even after they discovered their mistake, they believed the horses devoured men in battle, and when they neighed, thought that they were demanding their prey. It was not the interest of the Spaniards to undeceive them. Herrera, dec. ii. lib. vi. c. 11.

NOTE [108]. PAGE 218.

ACCORDING to Bart. de las Casas, there was no reason for this massacre, and it was an act of wanton cruelty, perpetrated merely to strike terror into the people of New Spain. Relac. de la Destruyc. p. 17, &c. But the zeal of Las Casas often leads him to exaggerate. In opposition to him, Bern. Diaz, c. 83, asserts, that the first missionaries sent into New Spain by the Emperor made a judicial inquiry into this transaction; and having examined the priests and elders of Cholula, found that there was a real conspiracy to cut off the Spaniards, and that the account given by Cortes was exactly true. As it was the object of Cortes at that time, and manifestly his interest, to gain the good will of Montezuma, it is improbable that he should have taken a step which tended so visibly to alienate him from the Spaniards, if he had not believed it to be necessary for his own preservation. At the same time the Spaniards who served in America had such contempt for the natives, and thought them so little entitled to the common rights of men, that Cortes might hold the Cholulans to be guilty upon slight and imperfect evidence. The severity of the punishment was certainly excessive and atrocious.

NOTE [109]. PAGE 218.

THIS description is taken almost literally from Bernal Diaz del Castillo, who was so unacquainted with the art of composition as to be incapable of embellishing his narrative. He relates in a simple and rude style what passed in his own mind and that of his fellow-soldiers on that occasion: "and let it not be thought strange," says he, "that I should write in this manner of what then happened, for it ought to be considered, that it is one thing to relate, another to have beheld things that were never before seen, or heard, or spoken of among men." Cap. 86. p. 64. b.

NOTE [110]. PAGE 223.

B. DIAZ DEL CASTILLO gives us some idea of the fatigue and hardships they underwent in performing this and other parts of duty. During the nine months that they remained in Mexico, every man, without any distinction between officers and soldiers, slept on his arms in his quilted jacket and gorget. They lay on mats, or straw spread on the floor, and each was obliged to hold himself as alert as if he had been on guard. "This," adds he, "became so habitual to me, that even now, in my advanced age, I always sleep in my clothes, and never in any bed. When I visit my *Encomienda*, I reckon it suitable to my rank to have a bed carried along with my other baggage, but I never go into it; but according to custom, I lie in my clothes, and walk frequently during the night into the open air to view the stars, as I was wont when in service." Cap. 108.

### Note [111]. Page 224.

Cortes himself, in his second despatch to the Emperor, does not explain the motives which induced him either to condemn Qualpopoca to the flames, or to put Montezuma in irons. Ramus. iii. 236. B. Diaz is silent with respect to his reasons for the former; and the only cause he assigns for the latter was, that he might meet with no interruption in executing the sentence pronounced against Qualpopoca, c. xcv. p. 75. But as Montezuma was his prisoner, and absolutely in his power, he had no reason to dread him, and the insult offered to that monarch could have no effect but to irritate him unnecessarily. Gomara supposes that Cortes had no other object than to occupy Montezuma with his own distress and sufferings, that he might give less attention to what befell Qualpopoca. Cron. c. 89. Herrera adopts the same opinion. Dec. ii. lib. viii. c. 9. But it seems an odd expedient, in order to make a person bear one injury, to load him with another that is greater. De Solis imagines, that Cortes had nothing else in view than to intimidate Montezuma, so that he might make no attempt to rescue the victims from their fate; but the spirit of that monarch was so submissive, and he had so tamely given up the prisoners to the disposal of Cortes, that he had no cause to apprehend any opposition from him. If the explanation which I have attempted to give of Cortes's proceedings on this occasion be not admitted, it appears to me, that they must be reckoned among the wanton and barbarous acts of oppression which occur too often in the history of the conquest of America.

### Note [112]. Page 226.

De Solis asserts, lib. iv. c. 3, that the proposition of doing homage to the King of Spain came from Montezuma himself, and was made in order to induce the Spaniards to depart out of his dominions. He describes his conduct on this occasion as if it had been founded upon a scheme of profound policy, and executed with such a refined address as to deceive Cortes himself. But there is no hint or circumstance in the contemporary historians, Cortes, Diaz, or Gomara, to justify this theory. Montezuma, on other occasions, discovered no such extent of art and abilities. The anguish which he felt in performing this humbling ceremony is natural, if we suppose it to have been involuntary. But, according to the theory of De Solis, which supposes that Montezuma was executing what he himself had proposed, to have assumed an appearance of sorrow would have been preposterous, and inconsistent with his own design of deceiving the Spaniards.

### Note [113]. Page 227.

In several of the provinces, the Spaniards, with all their industry and influence, could collect no gold. In others, they procured only a few trinkets of small value. Montezuma assured Cortes, that the present which he offered to the king of Castile, after doing homage, consisted of all the treasure amassed by his father: and told him, that he had already distributed the rest of his gold and jewels among the Spaniards. B. Diaz. c. 104. Gomara relates, that all the silver collected amounted to 500 marks. Cron. c. 93. This agrees with the account given by Cortes, that the royal fifth of silver was 100 marks. Relat. 239. B. So that the sum total of silver was only 4000 ounces, at the rate of eight ounces a mark, which demonstrates the proportion of silver to gold to have been exceedingly small.

### Note [114]. Page 227

De Solis, lib. iv. c. 1. calls in question the truth of this transaction, from no better reason than that it was inconsistent with that prudence which distinguishes the character of Cortes. But he ought to have recollected the impetuosity of his zeal at Tlascala, which was no less imprudent. He asserts, that the evidence for it rests upon the testimony of B. Diaz del Castillo, of Gomara, and of Herrera. They all concur, indeed, in mentioning this inconsiderate step which Cortes took; and they had good reason to do so, for Cortes himself relates this exploit in his second despatch to the Emperor, and seems to glory in it. Cort. Relat. Ramus. iii. 140. D. This is one instance, among many, of De Solis's having consulted with little attention the letters of Cortes to Charles V. from which the most authentic information with respect to his operations must be derived.

### Note [115]. Page 229.

Herrera and De Solis suppose that Velasques was encouraged to equip this armament against Cortes by the account which he received from Spain concerning the reception of the agents sent by the colony of Vera Cruz, and the warmth with which Fonseca Bishop of Burgos had espoused his interest, and condemned the proceedings of Cortes. Herrera, dec. ii. lib. ix. c. 18. De Solis, lib. iv. c. 5. But the chronological order of events refutes this supposition. Portocarrero and Montejo sailed from Vera Cruz, July 26, 1519. Herrera, dec. ii. lib. v. c. 4. They landed at St. Lucar in October, according to Herrera, ibid. But P. Martyr, who attended the court at that time, and communicated every occurrence of moment to his correspondents day by day, mentions the arrival of these agents for the first time in December, and speaks of it as a recent event. Epist. 650. All the historians agree that the agents of Cortes had their first audience of the Emperor at Tordesillas, when he went to that town to visit his mother in his way to St. Jago de Compostella. Herrera, dec. ii. lib. v. c. 4. De Solis, lib. iv. c. 5. But the Emperor set out from Valladolid for Tordesillas on the 11th of March, 1520; and P. Martyr mentions his having seen at that time the presents made to Charles. Epist. 1665. The armament under Narvaez sailed from Cuba in April 1520. It is manifest then that Velasquez could not receive any account of what passed in this interview at Tordesillas previous to his hostile preparations against Cortes. His real motives seem to be those which I have mentioned. The patent appointing him *Adelantado* of New Spain, with such extensive powers, bears date November 13, 1519. Herrera, dec. ii. lib. iii. c. 11. He might receive it about the beginning of January. Gomara takes notice, that as soon as this patent was delivered to him, he began to equip a fleet and levy forces. Cron. c. 96.

### Note [116]. Page 230.

De Solis contends, that as Narvaez had no interpreters, he could hold no intercourse with the people of the provinces, nor converse with them in any way but by signs, that it was equally impossible for him to carry on any communication with Montezuma. Liv. iv. c. 7. But it is upon the authority of Cortes himself that I relate all the particulars of Narvaez's correspondence both with Montezuma and with his subjects in the maritime provinces. Relat. Ramus. iii. 244. A. C. Cortes affirms that there was a mode of intercourse between Narvaez and the Mexicans, but does not explain how it was carried on. Bernal Diaz supplies this defect, and informs us that the three deserters who joined Narvaez acted as interpreters, having acquired a competent knowledge of the language, c. 110. With his usual minuteness, he mentions their names and characters, and relates, in chapter 122, how they were punished for their perfidy. The Spaniards had now resided above a year among the Mexicans; and it is not surprising that several among them should have made some pro ficiency in speaking their language. This seems to have been the case. Herrera, dec. 2. lib. x. c. 1. Both B. Diaz, who was present, and Herrera, the most accurate and best informed of all the Spanish writers, agree with Cortes in his account of the secret correspondence carried on with Montezuma. Dec. 2. lib. x. c. 18, 19. De Solis seems to consider it as a discredit to Cortes, his hero, that Montezuma should have been ready to engage in a correspondence with Narvaez. He supposes that monarch to have contracted such a wonderful affection for the Spaniards, that he was not solicitous to be delivered from them. After the indignity with which he had been treated, such an affection is incredible; and even De Solis is obliged to acknowledge, that it must be looked upon as one of the miracles which God had wrought to facilitate the conquest, lib. iv. c. 7. The truth is, Montezuma, however much overawed by his dread of the Spaniards, was extremely impatient to recover his liberty.

### Note [117]. Page 236.

These words I have borrowed from the anonymous Account of the European Settlements in America, published by Dodsley, in two volumes 8vo.; a work of so much merit, that I should think there is hardly any writer in the age who ought to be ashamed of acknowledging himself to be the author of it.

### Note [118]. Page 238.

The contemporary historians differ considerably with respect to the loss of the Spaniards on this occasion. Cortes in his second despatch to the Emperor, makes the number only 150. Relat. ap. Ramus. iii. p. 249. A. But it was manifestly his interest, at that juncture, to conceal from the court of Spain the full extent of the loss which he had sustained. De Solis, always studious to diminish every misfortune that befell his countrymen, rates their loss at about two hundred men. Lib. iv. c. 19. B. Diaz affirms that they lost 870 men, and that only 440 escaped from Mexico, c. 128. p. 108. B. Palafox, Bishop of Los Angeles, who seems to have inquired into the early transactions of his countrymen in New Spain with great attention, confirms the account of B. Diaz with respect to the extent of their loss. Virtudes del Indio, p. 22. Gomara states their loss at 450 men. Cron. c. 109. Some months afterwards, when Cortes had received several reinforcements, he mustered his troops, and found them to be only 590. Relat. ap. Ramus. iii. p. 255. E. Now, as Narvaez brought 880 men into New Spain, and about 400 of Cortes's soldiers were then alive, it is evident that his loss, in the retreat from Mexico, must have been much more considerable than what he mentions. B. Diaz, solicitous to magnify the dangers and sufferings to which he and his fellow-conquerors were exposed, may have exaggerated their loss; but, in my opinion, it cannot well be estimated at less than 600 men.

### Note [119]. Page 246.

Some remains of this great work are still visible, and the spot where the brigantines were built and launched is still pointed out to strangers. Torquemada viewed them. Monarq. Indiana, vol. i. p. 531.

### Note [120]. Page 249.

The station of Alvarado on the causeway of Tacuba was the nearest to the city. Cortes observes, that there they could distinctly observe what passed when their countrymen were sacrificed. Relat. ap. Ramus. iii. p. 273. E. B. Diaz, who belonged to Alvarado's division, relates what he beheld with his own eyes. C. 151. p. 148. b. 149. a. Like a man whose courage was so clear as to be above suspicion, he describes with his usual simplicity the impression which this spectacle made upon him. "Before (says he) I saw the breasts of my companions opened, their hearts yet fluttering, offered to an accursed idol, and their flesh devoured by their exulting enemies; I was accustomed to enter a battle not only without fear, but with high spirit. But from that time I never advanced to fight with the Mexicans without a secret horror and anxiety; my heart trembled at the thoughts of the death which I had seen them suffer." He takes care to add, that as soon as the combat began, his terror went off; and indeed, his adventurous bravery on every occasion is full evidence of this B. Diaz, c. 156. p. 157. a.

### Note [121]. Page 252.

One circumstance in this siege merits particular notice. The account which the Spanish writers give of the numerous armies employed in the attack or defence of Mexico seems to be incredible. According to Cortes himself, he had at one time 150,000 auxiliary Indians in his service. Relat. Ramus. iii. 275. E. Gomara asserts that they were above 200,000. Cron. c. 136. Herrera, an author of higher authority, says they were about 200,000. Dec. iii. lib. i. c. 19. None of the contemporary writers ascertain explicitly the number of persons in Mexico during the siege. But Cortes on several occasions mentions the number of Mexicans who were slain, or who perished for want of food; and, if we may rely on those circumstances, it is probable that above two hundred thousand must have been shut up in the town. But the quantity of provisions necessary for the subsistence of such vast multitudes assembled in one place, during three months, is so great, that it requires so much foresight and arrangement to collect these, and lay them up in magazines, so as to be certain of a regular supply, that one can hardly believe that this could be accomplished in a country where agriculture was so imperfect as in the Mexican empire, where there were no tame animals, and by a people naturally so improvident, and so incapable of executing a complicated plan, as the most improved Americans. The Spaniards, with all their care and attention, fared very poorly, and were often reduced to extreme distress for want of provisions. B. Diaz, p. 142. Cortes Relat. 271. D. Cortes on one occasion mentions slightly the subsistence of his army; and, after acknowledging that they were often in great want, adds, that they received supplies from the people of the country, of fish, and of some fruit, which he calls the cherries of the country. Ibid. B. Diaz says that they had cakes of maize, and serasas de la tierra; and when the season of these was over, another fruit, which he calls *Tunas;* but their most comfortable subsistence was a root which the Indians use as food, to which he gives the name of *Quilites*, p. 142. The Indian auxiliaries had one means of subsistence more than the Spaniards. They fed upon the bodies of the Mexicans whom they killed in battle. Cortes Relat. 176. C. B. Diaz confirms his relation, and adds, that when the Indians returned from Mexico to their own country, they carried with them large quantities of flesh of the Mexicans salted or dried, as a most acceptable present to their friends, that they might have the pleasure of feeding upon the bodies of their enemies in their festivals, p. 157. De Solis, who seems to consider it as an imputation of discredit to his countrymen, that they should act in concert with auxiliaries who fed upon human flesh, is solicitous to prove that the Spaniards endeavoured to prevent their associates from eating the bodies of the Mexicans, lib. v. c. 24. But he has no authority for this from the original historians. Neither Cortes himself nor B. Diaz seems to have had any such scruple; and on many occasions they mention the Indian repasts, which were become familiar to them, without any mark of abhorrence. Even with this additional stock of food for the Indians, it was hardly possible to procure subsistence for armies amounting to such numbers as we find in the Spanish writers. Perhaps the best solution of the difficulty is, to adopt the opinion of B. Diaz del Castillo, the most artless of all the *Historiadores primitivos.* "When Gomara (says he) on some occasions relates, that there were so many thousand Indians our auxiliaries, and on others, that there were so many thousand houses in this or that town, no regard is to be paid to his enumeration, as he has no authority for it, the numbers not being in reality the fifth of what he relates. If we add together the different numbers which he mentions, that country would contain more millions than there are in Castile." C. 129. But though some considerable deduction should certainly be made from the Spanish accounts of the Mexican forces, they must have been very numerous; for nothing but an immense superiority in number could have enabled them to withstand a body of nine hundred Spaniards, conducted by a leader of such abilities as Cortes.

### NOTE [122]. PAGE 257.

IN relating the oppressive and cruel proceedings of the conquerors of New Spain, I have not followed B. de las Casas as my guide. His account of them, Relat. de la Destruyc. p. 18, &c. is manifestly exaggerated. It is from the testimony of Cortes himself, and of Gomara who wrote under his eye, that I have taken my account of the punishment of the Panucans, and they relate it without any disapprobation. B. Diaz, contrary to his usual custom, mentions it only in general terms, c. 162. Herrera, solicitous to extenuate this barbarous action of his countrymen, though he mentions 63 caziques, and 400 men of note, as being condemned to the flames, asserts that 30 only were burnt, and the rest pardoned. Dec. 3. lib. v. c. 7. But this is contrary to the testimony of the original historians, particularly of Gomara, whom it appears he had consulted, as he adopts several of his expressions in this passage. The punishment of Guatimozin is related by the most authentic of the Spanish writers. Torquemada has extracted from a history of Tezeuco, composed in the Mexican tongue, an account of this transaction, more favourable to Guatimozin than that of the Spanish authors. Mon. Indiana, i. 575. According to the Mexican account, Cortes had scarcely a shadow of evidence to justify such a wanton act of cruelty. B. Diaz affirms, that Guatimozin and his fellow-sufferers asserted their innocence with their last breath, and that many of the Spanish soldiers condemned this action of Cortes as equally unnecessary and unjust, p. 200. b. 201. a.

### NOTE [123]. PAGE 259.

THE motive for undertaking this expedition was, to punish Christoval de Olid, one of his officers who had revolted against him, and aimed at establishing an independent jurisdiction. Cortes regarded this insurrection as of such dangerous example, and dreaded so much the abilities and popularity of its author, that in person he led the body of troops destined to suppress it. He marched, according to Gomara, three thousand miles, through a country abounding with thick forests, rugged mountains, deep rivers, thinly inhabited, and cultivated only in a few places. What he suffered from famine, from the hostility of the natives, from the climate, and from hardships of every species, has nothing in history parallel to it, but what occurs in the adventures of the other discoverers and conquerors of the New World. Cortes was employed in this dreadful service above two years; and though it was not distinguished by any splendid event, he exhibited, during the course of it, greater personal courage, more fortitude of mind, more perseverance and patience than in any other period or scene in his life. Herrera, dec. 3. lib. vi. vii. viii. ix. Gomara, Cron. c. 163—177. B. Diaz, 174—190. Cortes, MS. *penes me*. Were one to write a life of Cortes, the account of this expedition should occupy a splendid place in it. In a general history of America, as the expedition was productive of no great event, the mention of it is sufficient.

### NOTE [124]. PAGE 259.

ACCORDING to Herrera, the treasure which Cortes brought with him, consisted of fifteen hundred marks of wrought plate, two hundred thousand pesos of fine gold, and ten thousand of inferior standard, many rich jewels, one in particular worth forty thousand pesos, and several trinkets and ornaments of value. Dec. 4. lib. iii. c. 8. lib. iv. c. 1. He afterwards engaged to give a portion with his daughter of a hundred thousand pesos. Gomara Cron. c. 237. The fortune which he left his sons was very considerable. But, as we have before related, the sum divided among the conquerors, on the first reduction of Mexico, was very small. There appears, then, to be some reason for suspecting that the accusations of Cortes's enemies were not altogether destitute of foundation. They charged him with having applied to his own use a disproportionate share of the Mexican spoils; with having concealed the royal treasures of Montezuma and Guatimozin; with defrauding the king of his fifth; and robbing his followers of what was due to them. Herrera, dec. 3. lib. viii. c. 15. dec. 4. lib. iii. c. 8. Some of the conquerors themselves entertained suspicions of the same kind with respect to this part of his conduct. B. Diaz, c. 157.

### Note [125]. Page 261.

In tracing the progress of the Spanish arms in New Spain, we have followed Cortes himself as our most certain guide. His despatches to the Emperor contain a minute account of his operations. But the unlettered conqueror of Peru was incapable of relating his own exploits. Our information with respect to them, and other transactions in Peru, is derived, however, from contemporary and respectable authors.

The most early account of Pizarro's transactions in Peru was published by Francisco de Xerez, his secretary. It is a simple, unadorned narrative, carried down no further than the death of Atahualpa, in 1533; for the author returned to Spain in 1534, and, soon after he landed, printed at Seville his short History of the Conquest of Peru, addressed to the Emperor.

Don Pedro Sancho, an officer who served under Pizarro, drew up an account of his expedition, which was translated into Italian by Ramusio, and inserted in his valuable collection, but has never been published in its original language. Sancho returned to Spain at the same time with Xerez. Great credit is due to what both these authors relate concerning the progress and operations of Pizarro; but the residence of the Spaniards in Peru had been so short, at the time when they left it, and their intercourse with the natives are so slender, that their knowledge of the Peruvian manners and customs is very imperfect.

The next contemporary historian is Pedro Cieza de Leon, who published his Cronica del Peru at Seville in 1553. If he had finished all that he purposes in the general division of his work, it would have been the most complete history which had been published of any region in the New World. He was well qualified to execute it, having served during seventeen years in America, and having visited in person most of the provinces concerning which he had occasion to write. But only the first part of his chronicle has been printed. It contains a description of Peru, and several of the adjacent provinces, with an account of the institutions and customs of the natives, and is written with so little art, and such an apparent regard for truth, that one must regret the loss of the other parts of his work.

This loss is amply supplied by Don Augustine Zarate, who published, in 1555, his Historia del Descubrimiento y Conquesta de la Provincia del Peru. Zarate was a man of rank and education, and employed in Peru as comptroller-general of the public revenue. His history, whether we attend to its matter or composition, is a book of considerable merit: as he had an opportunity to be well informed, and seems to have been inquisitive with respect to the manners and transactions of the Peruvians, great credit is due to his testimony.

Don Diego Fernandez published his Historia del Peru in 1571. His sole object is to relate the dissensions and civil wars of the Spaniards in that empire. As he served in a public station in Peru, and was well acquainted both with the country and with the principal actors in those singular scenes which he describes, as he possessed sound understanding and great impartiality, his work may be ranked among those of the historians most distinguished for their industry in research, or their capacity in judging with respect to the events which they relate.

The last author who can be reckoned among the contemporary historians of the conquest of Peru is Garcilasso de la Vega, Inca. For though the first part of his work, entitled *Commentarios Reales del Origin de los Incas Reies del Peru*, was not published sooner than the year 1609, seventy-six years after the death of Atahualpa the last Emperor, yet as he was born in Peru, and was the son of an officer of distinction among the Spanish conquerors, by a *Coya*, or lady of the royal race, on account of which he always took the name of Inca; as he was master of the language spoken by the Incas, and acquainted with the traditions of his countrymen, his authority is rated very high, and often placed above that of all the other historians. His work, however, is little more than a commentary upon the Spanish writers of the Peruvian story, and composed of quotations taken from the authors whom I have mentioned. This is the idea which he himself gives of it, lib. i. c. 10. Nor is it in the account of facts only that he follows them servilely. Even in explaining the institutions and rites of his ancestors, his information seems not to be more perfect than theirs. His explanation of the Quipos is almost the same with that of Acosta. He produces no specimen of Peruvian poetry, but that wretched one which he borrows from Blas Valera, an early missionary, whose memoirs have never been published. Lib. ii. c. 15. As for composition, arrangement, or a capacity of distinguishing between what is fabulous, what is probable, and what is true, one searches for them in vain in the commentaries of the Inca. His work, however, notwithstanding its great defects, is not altogether destitute of use. Some traditions which he received from his countrymen are preserved in it. His knowledge of the Peruvian language has enabled him to correct some errors of the Spanish writers, and he has inserted in it some curious facts taken from authors whose works were never published, and are now lost.

### Note [126]. Page 263.

One may form an idea both of the hardships which they endured, and of the unhealthy climate in the regions which they visited, from the extraordinary mortality that prevailed among them. Pizarro carried out 112 men, Almagro 70. In less than nine months 130 of these died. Few fell by the sword; most of them were cut off by diseases. Xeres, p. 180.

### Note [127]. Page 264.

This island, says Herrera, is rendered so uncomfortable by the unwholesomeness of its climate, its impenetrable woods, its rugged mountains, and the multitude of insects and reptiles, that it is seldom any softer epithet than that of *infernal* is employed in describing it. The sun is almost never seen there, and throughout the year it hardly ever ceases to rain. Dec. iii. lib. x. c. 3. Dampier touched at this island in the year 1685; and his account of the climate is not more favourable. Vol. i. p. 172. He, during his cruise on the coast, visited most of the places where Pizarro landed, and his description of them throws light on the narrations of the early Spanish historians.

### Note [128]. Page 270.

By this time horses had multiplied greatly in the Spanish settlements on the continent. When Cortes began his expedition in the year 1518, though his armament was more considerable than that of Pizarro, and composed of persons superior in rank to those who invaded Peru, he could procure no more than sixteen horses.

### Note [129]. Page 271.

In the year 1740, D. Ant. Ulloa and D. George Juan travelled from Guayaquil to Motupe by the same route which Pizarro took. From the description of their journey, one may form an idea of the difficulty of his march. The sandy plains between St. Michael de Pieura and Motupe extend 90 miles, without water, without a tree, a plant, or any green thing, on a dreary stretch of burning sand. Voyage, tom. i. p. 399, &c.

### Note [130]. Page 273.

This extravagant and unseasonable discourse of Valverde has been censured by all historians, and with justice. But though he seems to have been an illiterate and bigotted monk, nowise resembling the good Olmedo, who accompanied Cortes; the absurdity of his address to Atahualpa must not be charged wholly upon him. His harangue is evidently a translation or paraphrase of that form, concerted by a junto of Spanish divines and lawyers in the year 1509, for explaining the right of their king to the sovereignty of the New World, and for directing the officers employed in America how they should take possession of any new country. See Note 23. The sentiments contained in Valverde's harangue must not then be imputed to the bigotted imbecility of a particular man, but to that of the age. But Gomara and Benzoni relate one circumstance concerning Valverde, which, if authentic, renders him an object not of contempt only but of horror. They assert, that during the whole action Valverde continued to excite the soldiers to slaughter, calling to them to strike the enemy not with the edge but with the points of their swords. Gom. Cron. c. 113. Benz. Histor. Nov. Orbis, lib. iii. c. 3. Such behaviour was very different from that of the Roman Catholic clergy in other parts of America, where they uniformly exerted their influence to protect the Indians, and to moderate the ferocity of their countrymen.

### Note [131]. Page 273.

Two different systems have been formed concerning the conduct of Atahualpa. The Spanish writers, in order to justify the violence of their countrymen, contend that all the Inca's professions of friendship were feigned; and that his intention in agreeing to an interview with Pizarro at Caxamalca, was to cut off him and his followers at one blow; that for this purpose he advanced with such a numerous body of attendants, who had arms concealed under their garments to execute this scheme. This is the account given by Xeres and Zarate, and adopted by Herrera. But if it had been the plan of the Inca to destroy the Spaniards, one can hardly imagine that he would have permitted them to march through the desert of Motupe, or have neglected to defend the passes in the mountains, where they might have been attacked with so much advantage. If the Peruvians marched to Caxamalca with an intention to fall upon the Spaniards, it is inconceivable that of so great a body of men, prepared for action, not one should attempt to make resistance, but all tamely suffer themselves to be butchered by an enemy whom they were armed to attack. Atahualpa's mode of advancing to the interview has the aspect of a peaceable procession, not of a military enterprise. He himself and his followers were in their habits of ceremony, preceded, as on days of solemnity, by unarmed harbingers. Though rude nations are frequently cunning and false; yet if a scheme of deception and treachery must be imputed either to a monarch that had no great reason to be alarmed at a visit from strangers who solicited admission into his presence as friends, or to an adventurer so daring and so little scrupulous as Pizarro, one cannot hesitate in determining where to fix the presumption of guilt. Even amidst the endeavours of the Spanish writers to palliate the proceedings of Pizarro, one plainly perceives that it was his intention, as well as his interest, to seize the Inca, and that he had taken measures for that purpose previous to any suspicion of that monarch's designs.

Garcilasso de la Vega, extremely solicitous to vindicate his countrymen, the Peruvians, from the crime of having concerted the destruction of Pizarro and his followers, and no less afraid to charge the Spaniards with improper conduct towards the Inca, has framed another system. He relates, that a man of majestic form, with a long beard, and garments reaching to the ground, having appeared in a vision to Viracocha, the eighth Inca, and declared that he was a child of the Sun, that monarch built a temple in honour of this person, and erected an image of him, resembling as nearly as possible the singular form in which he had exhibited himself to his view. In this temple divine honours were paid to him, by the name of Viracocha. P. i. lib. iv. c. 21. lib. v. c. 22. When the Spaniards first appeared in Peru, the length of their beards, and the dress they wore, struck every person so much with their likeness to the image of Viracocha, that they supposed them to be children of the Sun, who had descended from heaven to earth. All concluded that the fatal period of the Peruvian empire was now approaching, and that the throne would be occupied by new possessors. Atahualpa himself, considering the Spaniards as messengers from heaven, was so far from entertaining any thoughts of resisting them, that he determined to yield implicit obedience to their commands. From these sentiments flowed his professions of love and respect. To those were owing the cordial reception of Soto and Ferdinand Pizarro in his camp, and the submissive reverence with which he himself advanced to visit the Spanish general in his quarters; but from the gross ignorance of Philipillo, the interpreter, the declaration of the Spaniards, and his answer to it, were so ill explained, that by their mutual inability to comprehend each other's intentions, the fatal rencontre at Caxamalca, with all its dreadful consequences, was occasioned.

It is remarkable, that no traces of this superstitious veneration of the Peruvians for the Spaniards are to be found either in Xeres, or Sancho, or Zarate, previous to the interview at Caxamalca; and yet the two former served under Pizarro at that time, and the latter visited Peru soon after the conquest. If either the Inca himself, or his messengers, had addressed the Spaniards in the words which Garcilasso puts in their mouths, they must have been struck with such submissive declarations; and they would certainly have availed themselves of them to accomplish their own designs with greater facility. Garcilasso himself, though his narrative of the intercourse between the Inca and Spaniards, preceding the rencontre at Caxamalca, is founded on the supposition of his believing them to be Viracochas, or divine beings, P. ii. lib. i. c. 17, &c., yet, with his usual inattention and inaccuracy, he admits in another place that the Peruvians did not recollect the resemblance between them and the god Viracocha, until the fatal disasters subsequent to the defeat at Caxamalca, and then only began to call them Viracochas. P. i. lib. v. c. 21. This is confirmed by Herrera, dec. v. lib. ii. c. 12. In many different parts of America, if we may believe the Spanish writers, their countrymen were considered as divine beings who had descended from heaven. But in this instance, as in many which occur in the intercourse between nations whose progress in refinement is very unequal, the ideas of those who used the expression were different from the ideas of those who heard it. For such is the idiom of the Indian languages, or such is the simplicity of those who speak them, that when they see any thing with which they were formerly unacquainted, and of which they do not know the origin, they say that it came down from heaven. Nugnez. Ram. iii. 327. C.

The account which I have given of the sentiments and proceedings of the Peruvians, appears to be more natural and consistent than either of the two preceding, and is better supported by the facts related by the contemporary historians.

According to Xeres, p. 200, two thousand Peruvians were killed. Sancho makes the number of the slain six or seven thousand. Ram. iii. 274. D. By Garcilasso's account, five thousand were massacred. P. ii. lib. i. c. 25. The number which I have mentioned, being the medium between the extremes, may probably be nearest the truth.

### Note [132]. Page 274.

Nothing can be a more striking proof of this, than that three Spaniards travelled from Caxamalca to Cuzco. The distance between them is six hundred miles. In every place throughout this great extent of county, they were treated with all the honours which the Peruvians paid to their sovereigns, and even to their divinities. Under pretext of amassing what was wanting for the ransom of the Inca, they demanded the plates of gold with which the walls of the Temple of the Sun in Cuzco were adorned; and though the priests were unwilling to alienate those sacred ornaments, and the people refused to violate the shrine of their God, the three Spaniards, with their own hands, robbed the Temple of part of this valuable treasure; and such was the reverence of the natives for their persons, that though they beheld this act of sacrilege with astonishment, they did not attempt to prevent or disturb the commission of it Zarate, lib. ii. c. 6. Sancho ap. Ramus. iii. 375. D.

### Note [133]. Page 278.

According to Herrera, the spoil of Cuzco, after setting apart the King's *fifth*, was divided among 480 persons. Each received 4000 pesos. This amounts to 1,920,000 pesos. Dec. v. lib. vi. c. 3. But as the general and other officers were entitled to a share far greater than that of the private men, the sum total must have risen much beyond what I have mentioned. Gomara, c. 123, and Zarate, lib. ii. c. 8, satisfy themselves with asserting in general, that the plunder of Cuzco was of greater value than the ransom of Atahualpa.

### Note [134]. Page 279.

No expedition in the New World was conducted with more persevering courage than that of Alvarado, and in none were greater hardships endured. Many of the persons engaged in it were, like their leader, veterans who had served under Cortes, inured to all the rigour of American war. Such of my readers as have not an opportunity of perusing the striking description of their sufferings by Zarate, or Herrera, may form some idea of the nature of their march from the sea-coast to Quito, by consulting the account which D. Ant. Ulloa gives of his own journey in 1736, nearly in the same route. Voy. tom. i. p. 178, &c., or that of M. Bouguer, who proceeded from Puerto Viejo to Quito by the same road which Alvarado took. He compares his own journey with that of the Spanish leader, and by the comparison gives a most striking idea of the boldness and patience of Alvarado in forcing his way through so many obstacles. Voyage de Perou, p. 28, &c.

### Note [135]. Page 279.

According to Herrera, there was entered on account of the king in gold 155,300 pesos, and 5,400 marks (each 8 ounces) of silver, besides several vessels and ornaments, some of gold, and others of silver; on account of private persons, in gold 499,000 pesos, and 54,000 marks of silver. Dec. 5. lib. vi. c. 13.

### Note [136]. Page 283.

The Peruvians not only imitated the military arts of the Spaniards, but had recourse to devices of their own. As the cavalry were the chief objects of their terror, they endeavoured to render them incapable of acting by means of a long thong with a stone fastened to each end. This, when thrown by a skilful hand, twisted about the horse and its rider, and entangled them so as to obstruct their motions. Herrera mentions this as an invention of their own. Dec. 5. lib. viii. c. 4. But as I have observed, p. 178, this weapon is common among several barbarous tribes towards the extremity of South America; and it is more probable that the Peruvians had observed the dexterity with which they used it in hunting, and on this occasion adopted it themselves. The Spaniards were considerably annoyed by it. Herrera, ibid. Another instance of the ingenuity of the Peruvians deserves mention. By turning a river out of its channel, they overflowed a valley, in which a body of the enemy was posted, so suddenly, that it was with the utmost difficulty the Spaniards made their escape. Herrera, dec. 5. lib. viii. c. 5.

### Note [137]. Page 290.

Herrera's account of Orellana's voyage is the most minute and apparently the most accurate. It was probably taken from the journal of Orellana himself. But the dates are not distinctly marked. His navigation down the Coca, or Napo, began early in February, 1541; and he arrived at the mouth of the river on the 26th of August, having spent near seven months in the voyage. M. de la Condamine, in the year 1743, sailed from Cuenca to Para, a settlement of the Portuguese at the mouth of the river, a navigation much longer than that of Orellana, in less than four months. Voyage, p. 179. But the two adventurers were very differently provided for the voyage. This hazardous undertaking to which ambition prompted Orellana, and to which the love of science led M. de la Condamine, was undertaken in the year 1769, by Madame Godin des Odonais from conjugal affection. The narrative of the hardships which she suffered, of the dangers to which she was exposed, and of the dis asters which befell her, is one of the most singular and affecting stories in any language, exhibiting in her conduct a striking picture of the fortitude which distinguishes the one sex, mingled with the sensibility and tenderness peculiar to the other. Lettre de M. Godin à M. de la Condamine.

### NOTE [138]. PAGE 291.

HERRERA gives a striking picture of their indigence. Twelve gentlemen, who had been officers of distinction under Almagro, lodged in the same house, and having but one cloak among them, it was worn alternately by him who had occasion to appear in public, while the rest, from the want of a decent dress, were obliged to keep within doors. Their former friends and companions were so much afraid of giving offence to Pizarro, that they durst not entertain or even converse with them. One may conceive what was the condition, and what the indignation of men once accustomed to power and opulence, when they felt themselves poor and despised, without a roof under which to shelter their heads, while they beheld others, whose merits and services were not equal to theirs, living in splendour in sumptuous edifices. Dec. 6 lib viii. c. 6.

### NOTE [139]. PAGE 296.

HERRERA, whose accuracy entitles him to great credit, asserts, that Gonzalo Pizarro possessed domains in the neighbourhood of Chuquesaca de la Plata, which yielded him an annual revenue greater than that of the Archbishop of Toledo, the best endowed see in Europe. Dec. 7. lib. vi. c. 3.

### NOTE [140]. PAGE 301.

ALL the Spanish writers describe his march, and the distresses of both parties, very minutely. Zarate observes, that hardly any parallel to it occurs in history, either with respect to the length of the retreat, or the ardour of the pursuit. Pizarro, according to his computation, followed the viceroy upwards of three thousand miles. Lib. v. c. 16. 26.

### NOTE [141]. PAGE 307.

IT amounted, according to Fernandez, the best informed historian of that period, to one million four hundred thousand pesos. Lib. ii. c. 79.

### NOTE [142]. PAGE 308.

CARVAJAL, from the beginning, had been an advocate for an accommodation with Gasca. Finding Pizarro incapable of holding that bold course which he originally suggested, he recommended to him a timely submission to his sovereign as the safest measure. When the president's offers were first communicated to Carvajal, "By our Lady (says he in that strain of buffoonery which was familiar to him), the priest issues gracious bulls. He gives them both good and cheap; let us not only accept them, but wear them as reliques about our necks." Fernandez, lib. ii. c. 63.

### NOTE [143]. PAGE 310.

DURING the rebellion of Gonzalo Pizarro, seven hundred men were killed in battle, and three hundred and eighty were hanged or beheaded. Herrera, dec. 8. lib. iv. c. 4. Above three hundred of these were cut off by Carvajal. Fernandez, lib. ii. c. 91. Zarate makes the number of those put to a violent death five hundred. Lib. vii. c. 1.

### NOTE [144]. PAGE 313.

IN my inquiries concerning the manners and policy of the Mexicans, I have received much information from a large manuscript of Don Alonso de Corita one of the judges in the Court of Audience at Mexico. In the year 1553, Philip II., in order to discover the mode of levying tribute from his Indian subjects, that would be most beneficial to the crown, and least oppressive to them, addressed a mandate to all the Courts of Audience in America, enjoining them to answer certain queries which he proposed to them concerning the ancient form of government established among the various nations of Indians, and the mode in which they had been accustomed to pay taxes to their kings or chiefs. In obedience to this mandate, Corita, who had resided nineteen years in America, fourteen of which he passed in New Spain, composed the work of which I have a copy. He acquaints his sovereign, that he had made it an object, during his residence in America, and in all its provinces which he had visited, to inquire diligently into the manners and customs of the natives; that he had conversed for this purpose with many aged and intelligent Indians, and consulted several of the Spanish Ecclesiastics, who understood the Indian language most perfectly, particularly some of those who landed in New Spain soon after the conquest. Corita appears to be a man of some learning, and to have carried on his inquiries with the diligence and accuracy to which he pretends. Greater credit is due to his testimony from one circumstance. His work was not composed with a view to publication, or in support of any particular theory, but contains simple though full answers to queries proposed to him officially. Though Herrera does not mention him among the authors whom he had followed as guides in his history, I should suppose, from several facts of which he takes notice, as well as from several expressions which he uses, that this memorial of Corita was not unknown to him.

## Note [145]. Page 317.

The early Spanish writers were so hasty and inaccurate in estimating the numbers of people in the provinces and towns in America, that it is impossible to ascertain that of Mexico itself with any degree of precision. Cortes describes the extent and populousness of Mexico in general terms, which imply that it was not inferior to the greatest cities in Europe. Gomara is more explicit, and affirms, that there were 60,000 houses or families in Mexico. Cron. c. 78. Herrera adopts his opinion, Dec. 2. lib. vii. c. 13; and the generality of writers follow them implicitly without inquiry or scruple. According to this account, the inhabitants of Mexico must have been about 300,000. Torquemada, with his usual propensity to the marvellous, asserts, that there were 120,000 houses or families in Mexico, and consequently about 600,000 inhabitants. Lib. iii. c. 23. But in a very judicious account of the Mexican empire, by one of Cortes's officers, the population is fixed at 60,000 people. Ramusio, iii. 309. A. Even by this account, which probably is much nearer the truth than any of the foregoing, Mexico was a great city.

## Note [146]. Page 318.

It is to P. Torribio de Benavente that I am indebted for this curious observation. Palafox, Bishop of Ciudad de la Puebla Los Angeles, confirms and illustrates it more fully. The Mexican (says he) is the only language in which a termination indicating respect, *silavas reverentiales y de cortesia*, may be affixed to every word. By adding the final syllable *zin* or *azin* to any word, it becomes a proper expression of veneration in the mouth of an inferior. If, in speaking to an equal, the word Father is to be used, it is *Tatl*, but an inferior says *Tatzin*. One priest speaking to another, calls him *Teopixque*; a person of inferior rank calls him *Teopixcatzin*. The name of the emperor who reigned when Cortes invaded Mexico, was *Montezuma*; but his vassals, from reverence, pronounced it *Montezumazin*. Torribio, MS. Palaf. Virtudes del Indio, p. 65. The Mexicans had not only reverential nouns, but reverential verbs. The manner in which these are formed from the verbs in common use is explained by D. Jos. Aug. Aldama y Guevara in his Mexican Grammar, No. 188.

### Note [147]. Page 320.

From comparing several passages in Corita and Herrera, we may collect, with some degree of accuracy, the various modes in which the Mexicans contributed towards the support of government. Some persons of the first order seem to have been exempted from the payment of any tribute, and as their only duty to the public, were bound to personal service in war, and to follow the banner of their sovereign with their vassals. 2. The immediate vassals of the crown were bound not only to personal military service, but paid a certain proportion of the produce of their lands in kind. 3. Those who held offices of honour or trust paid a certain share of what they received in consequence of holding these. 4. Each *Capullæ*, or association, cultivated some part of the common field allotted to it, for the behoof of the crown, and deposited the produce in the royal granaries. 5. Some part of whatever was brought to the public markets, whether fruits of the earth, or the various productions of their artists and manufacturers, was demanded for the public use, and the merchants who paid this were exempted from every other tax. 6. The *Mayeques*, or *adscripti glebæ*, were bound to cultivate certain districts in every province, which may be considered as *crown lands*, and brought the increase into public storehouses. Thus the sovereign received some part of whatever was useful or valuable in the country, whether it was the natural production of the soil, or acquired by the industry of the people. What each contributed towards the support of government seems to have been inconsiderable. Corita, in answer to one of the queries put to the Audience of Mexico by Philip II., endeavours to estimate in money the value of what each citizen might be supposed to pay, and does not reckon it at more than three or four *reals*, about eighteen pence or two shillings a head.

### Note [148]. Page 321.

Cortes, who seems to have been as much astonished with this, as with any instance of Mexican ingenuity, gives a particular description of it. Along one of the causeways, says he, by which they enter the city, are conducted two conduits, composed of clay tempered with mortar, about two paces in breadth, and raised about six feet. In one of them is conveyed a stream of excellent water, as large as the body of a man, into the centre of the city, and supplies all the inhabitants plentifully. The other is empty, that when it is necessary to clean or repair the former, the stream of water may be turned into it. As this conduit passes along two of the bridges, where there are breaches in the causeway, through which the salt water of the lake flows, it is conveyed over them in pipes as large as the body of an ox, then carried from the conduit to the remote quarters of the city in canoes, and sold to the inhabitants. Relat ap. Ramus. 241. A.

### Note [149]. Page 32

In the armoury of the royal palace of Madrid are shown suits of armour, which are called Montezuma's. They are composed of thin lacquered copper-plates. In the opinion of very intelligent judges, they are evidently eastern. The forms of the silver ornaments upon them, representing dragons, &c. may be considered a confirmation of this. They are infinitely superior, in point of workmanship, to any effort of American art. The Spaniards probably received them from the Philippine islands. The only unquestionable specimen of Mexican art, that I know of in Great Britain, is a cup of very fine gold, which is said to have belonged to Montezuma. It weighs 5oz. 12dwt. Three drawings of it were exhibited to the Society of Antiquaries, June 10, 1765. A man's head is represented on this cup. On one side the full face, on the other the profile, on the third the back parts of the head. The relievo is said to have been produced by punching the inside of the cup, so as to make the representation of a face on the outside. The features are gross, but represented with some degree of art, and certainly too rude for Spanish workmanship. This cup was purchased by Edward Earl of Orford, while he lay in the harbour of Cadiz with the fleet under his command, and is now in the possession of his grandson, Lord Archer. I am indebted for this information to my respectable and ingenious friend Mr. Barrington. In the sixth volume of the Archæologia, p. 107, is published an account of some masks of Terra Cotta, brought from a burying-ground on the American continent, about seventy miles from the British settlement on the Mosquito shore. They are said to be likenesses of chiefs, or other eminent persons. From the descriptions and engravings of them, we have an additional proof of the imperfect state of arts among the Americans.

## Note [150]. Page 323

The learned reader will perceive how much I have been indebted, in this part of my work, to the guidance of the Bishop of Gloucester, who has traced the successive steps by which the human mind advanced in this line of its progress, with much erudition, and greater ingenuity. He is the first, as far as I know, who formed a rational and consistent theory concerning the various modes of writing practised by nations, according to the various degrees of their improvement. Div. Legation of Moses, iii. 69, &c. Some important observations have been added by M. le President de Brosses, the learned and intelligent author of the Traite de la Formation Mecanique des Langues, tom. i. 295, &c.

As the Mexican paintings are the most curious monuments extant of the earliest mode of writing, it will not be improper to give some account of the means by which they were preserved from the general wreck of every work of art in America, and communicated to the public. For the most early and complete collection of these published by Purchas, we are indebted to the attention of that curious inquirer, Hakluyt. Don Antonio Mendoza, viceroy of New Spain, having deemed those paintings a proper present for Charles V., the ship in which they were sent to Spain was taken by a French cruiser, and they came into the possession of Thevet, the King's geographer, who, having travelled himself into the New World, and described one of its provinces, was a curious observer of whatever tended to illustrate the manners of the Americans. On his death, they were purchased by Hakluyt, at that time chaplain of the English ambassador to the French court; and, being left by him to Purchas, were published at the desire of the learned antiquary, Sir Henry Spelman. Purchas, iii. 1065. They were translated from English into French by Melchizedeck Thevenot, and published in his collection of voyages, A. D. 1683.

The second specimen of Mexican picture-writing was published by Dr. Francis Gemelli Carreri, in two copper-plates. The first is a map, or representation of the progress of the ancient Mexicans on their first arrival in the country, and of the various stations in which they settled, before they founded the capital of their empire in the lake of Mexico. The second is a Chronological Wheel, or Circle, representing the manner in which they computed and marked their cycle of fifty-two years. He received both from Don Carlos de Siguenza y Congorra, a diligent collector of ancient Mexican Documents. But as it seems now to be a received opinion (founded, as far as I know, on no good evidence), that Carreri was never out of Italy, and that his famous *Giro del Mundo* is an account of a fictitious voyage, I have not mentioned these paintings in the text. They have, however, manifestly the appearance of being Mexican productions, and are allowed to be so by Boturini, who was well qualified to determine whether they were genuine or supposititious. M. Clavigero likewise admits them to be genuine paintings of the ancient Mexicans. To me they always appeared to be so, though from my desire to rest no part of my narrative upon questionable authority, I did not refer to them. The style of painting in the former is considerably more perfect than any other specimen of Mexican design; but as the original is said to have been much defaced by time, I suspect that it has been improved by some touches from the hand of a European artist. Carreri, Churchill, iv. p. 487. The Chronological Wheel is a just delineation of the Mexican mode of computing time, as described by Acosta, lib. vi. c. 2. It seems to resemble one which that learned Jesuit had seen; and if it be admitted as a genuine monument, it proves that the Mexicans had artificial or arbitrary characters, which represented several things besides numbers. Each month is there represented by a symbol expressive of some work or rite peculiar to it.

The third specimen of Mexican painting was discovered by another Italian. In 1736, Lorenzo Boturini Benaduci set out for New Spain, and was led by several incidents to study the language of the Mexicans, and to collect the remains of their historical monuments. He persisted nine years in his researches, with the enthusiasm of a projector, and the patience of an antiquary In 1746, he published at Madrid, *Idea de una Nueva Historia General de la America Septentrional*, containing an account of the result of his inquiries; and he added to it a catalogue of his American Historical Museum, arranged under thirty-six different heads. His idea of a New History appears to me the work of a whimsical credulous man. But his catalogue of Mexican maps, paintings, tribute-rolls, calendars, &c. is much larger than one could have expected. Unfortunately a ship, in which he had sent a considerable part of them to Europe, was taken by an English privateer during the war between Great Britain and Spain, which commenced in the year 1739; and it is probable that they perished by falling into the hands of ignorant captors. Boturini himself incurred the displeasure of the Spanish court, and died in an hospital at Madrid. The history of which the *Idea*, &c. was only a *prospectus*, was never published. The remainder of his Museum seems to have been dispersed. Some part of it came into the possession of the present Archbishop of Toledo, when he was primate of New Spain: and he published from it that curious tribute-roll which I have mentioned.

The only other collection of Mexican paintings, as far as I can learn, is in the Imperial Library at Vienna. By order of their Imperial Majestics I have obtained such a specimen of these as I desired, in eight paintings made with so much fidelity, that I am informed the copies could hardly be distinguished from the originals. According to a note in this *Codex Mexicanus*, it appears to have been a present from Emmanuel, King of Portugal, to Pope Clement VII. who died A. D. 1533. After passing through the hands of several illustrious proprietors, it fell into those of the Cardinal of Saxe-Eisenach, who presented it to the Emperor Leopold. These paintings are manifestly Mexican, but they are in a style very different from any of the former. An engraving has been made of one of them, in order to gratify such of my readers as may deem this an object worthy of their attention. Were it an object of sufficient importance, it might perhaps be possible, by recourse to the plates of Purchas, and the Archbishop of Toledo, as a key, to form plausible conjectures concerning the meaning of this picture. Many of the figures are evidently similar. A. A. are targets and darts, almost in the same form with those published by Purchas, p. 1070, 1071, &c. B. B. are figures of temples, nearly resembling those in Purchas, p. 1109 and 1113, and in Lorenzana. Plate II. C. is a bale of mantles, or cotton cloths, the figure of which occurs in almost every plate of Purchas and Lorenzana. E. E. E. seem to be Mexican captains in their war dress, the fantastic ornaments of which resemble the figures in Purchas, p. 1110, 1111. 2113. I should suppose this picture to be a tribute-roll, as their mode of noting numbers occurs frequently. D. D. D., &c. According to Boturini, the mode of computation by the number of knots was known to the Mexicans as well as to the Peruvians, p. 85, and the manner in which the number of units is represented in the Mexican paintings in my possession seems to confirm this opinion. They plainly resemble a string of knots on a cord or slender rope.

Since I published the former edition, Mr. Waddilove, who is still pleased to continue his friendly attention to procure me information, has discovered, in the Library of the Escurial, a volume in folio, consisting of forty sheets of a kind of pasteboard, each the size of a common sheet of writing paper, with great variety of uncouth and whimsical figures of Mexican painting, in very fresh colours, and with an explanation in Spanish to most of them. The first twenty-two sheets are the signs of the months, days, &c. About the middle of each sheet are two or more large figures for the month, surrounded by the signs of the days. The last eighteen sheets are not so filled with figures. They seem to be signs of Deities, and images of various objects. According to this Calendar in the Escurial, the Mexican year contained 286 days, divided into 22 months of 13 days. Each day is represented by a different sign, taken from some natural object, a serpent, a dog, a lizard, a reed, a house, &c. The signs of days in the Calendar of the Escurial are precisely the same with those mentioned by Boturini, Idea, &c. p. 45. But, if we may give credit to that author, the Mexican year contained 360 days, divided into 18 months of 20 days. The order of days in every month was computed, according to him, first by what he calls a *tridecennary* progression of days from one to thirteen, in the same manner as in the Calendar of the Escurial, and then by a *septenary* progression of days from one to seven, making in all twenty. In this Calendar, not only the signs which distinguish each day, but the qualities supposed to be peculiar to each month are marked. There are certain weaknesses which seem to accompany the human mind through every stage of its progress in observation and science. Slender as was the knowledge of the Mexicans in astronomy, it appears to have been already connected with judicial astrology. The fortune and character of persons born in each month are supposed to be decided by some superior influence predominant at the time of nativity. Hence it is foretold in the Calendar, that all who are born in one month will be rich, in another warlike, in a third luxurious, &c. The pasteboard, or whatever substance it may be on which the Calendar in the Escurial is painted, seems, by Mr. Waddilove's description of it, to resemble nearly that in the Imperial Library at Vienna. In several particulars the figures bear some likeness to those in the plate which I have published. The figures marked D, which induced me to conjecture that this painting might be a tribute-roll similar to those published by Purchas and the Archbishop of Toledo, Mr. Waddilove supposes to be signs of days: and I have such confidence in the accuracy of his observations, as to conclude his opinion to be well founded. It appears, from the characters in which the explanations of the figures are written, that this curious monument of Mexican art has been obtained soon after the conquest of the Empire. It is singular that it should never have been mentioned by any Spanish author.

### Note [151]. Page 324.

The first was called the Prince of the Deathful Lance; the second the Divider of Men; the third the Shedder of Blood; the fourth the Lord of the Dark-house. Acosta, lib. vi. c. 25.

### Note [152]. Page 327.

The temple of Cholula, which was deemed more holy than any in New Spain, was likewise the most considerable. But it was nothing more than a mount of solid earth. According to Torquemada, it was above a quarter of a league in circuit at the base, and rose to the height of forty fathoms. Mon. Ind. lib. iii. c. 19. Even M. Clavigero acknowledges that all the Mexican temples were solid structures, or earthen mounts, and of consequence cannot be considered as any evidence of their having made any considerable progress in the art of building. Clavig. ii. 207.

From inspecting various figures of temples in the paintings engraved by Purchas, there seems to be some reason for suspecting that all their temples were constructed in the same manner. See vol. iii. p. 1109, 1110, 1113.

### Note [153]. Page 327.

Not only in Tlascala and Tepeaca, but even in Mexico itself, the houses of the people were mere huts built with turf or mud, or the branches of trees. They were extremely low and slight, and without any furniture but a few earthen vessels. Like the rudest Indians, several families resided under the same roof, without having any separate apartments. Herrera, dec. 2 lib. vii. c. 13. lib. x. c. 22. dec. 3. lib. iv. c. 17. Torquem. lib. iii. c. 23.

## NOTE [154]. PAGE 327.

I AM informed by a person who resided long in New Spain, and visited almost every province of it, that there is not, in all the extent of that vast empire, any monument or vestige of any building more ancient than the conquest, nor of any bridge or highway, except some remains of the causeway from Guadaloupe to that gate of Mexico by which Cortes entered the city. MS. *penes me.* The author of another account in manuscript observes, "That at this day there does not remain even the smallest vestige of the existence of any ancient Indian building, public or private, either in Mexico or in any province of New Spain. I have travelled, says he, through all the countries adjacent to them, viz. New Galicia, New Biscay, New Mexico, Sonora, Cinaloa, the New Kingdom of Leon, and New Santandero, without having observed any monument worth notice, except some ruins near an ancient village in the valley *de Casas Grandes*, in lat. N. 3°. 46'. long. 258°. 24'. from the island of Teneriffe, or 460 leagues N. N. W. from Mexico." He describes these ruins minutely, and they appear to be the remains of a paltry building of turf and stone, plastered over with white earth or lime. A missionary informed that gentleman, that he had discovered the ruins of another edifice similar to the former, about a hundred leagues towards N. W. on the banks of the river St. Pedro. MS. *penes me.*

These testimonies derive great credit from one circumstance, that they were not given in support of any particular system or theory, but as simple answers to queries which I had proposed. It is probable, however, that when these gentlemen assert that no ruins or monuments of any ancient work whatever are now to be discovered in the Mexican empire, they meant that there were no such ruins or monuments as conveyed any idea of grandeur or magnificence in the works of its ancient inhabitants. For it appears from the testimony of several Spanish authors, that in Otumba, Tlascala, Cholula, &c. some vestiges of ancient buildings are still visible. Villa Segnor Theatro Amer. p. 143. 308. 353. D. Fran. Ant. Lorenzana, formerly Archbishop of Mexico, and now of Toledo, in his introduction to that edition of the Cartas de Relacion of Cortes, which he published at Mexico, mentions some ruins which are still visible in several of the towns through which Cortes passed in his way to the capital, p. 4, &c. But neither of these authors gives any description of them, and they seem to be so very inconsiderable, as to show only that some buildings had once been there. The large mount of earth at Cholula, which the Spaniards dignified with the name of temple, still remains, but without any steps by which to ascend, or any facing of stone. It appears now like a natural mount, covered with grass and shrubs, and possibly it was never any thing more. Torquem. lib. iii. c. 19. I have received a minute description of the remains of a temple near Cuernavaca, on the road from Mexico to Acapulco. It is composed of large stones, fitted to each other as nicely as those in the buildings of the Peruvians, which are hereafter mentioned. At the foundation it forms a square of twenty-five yards; but as it rises in height it diminishes in extent, not gradually, but by being contracted suddenly at regular distances, so that it must have resembled the figure B. in the plate. It terminated, it is said, in a spire.

## NOTE [155]. PAGE 329.

THE exaggeration of the Spanish historians, with respect to the number of human victims sacrificed in Mexico, appears to be very great. According to Gomara, there was no year in which twenty thousand human victims were not offered to the Mexican Divinities, and in some years they amounted to fifty thousand. Cron. c. 229. The skulls of those unhappy persons were ranged in order in a building erected for that purpose, and two of Cortes's officers, who had counted them, informed Gomara that their number was a hundred and thirty-six thousand. Ibid. c. 82. Herrera's account is still more incredible, that the number of victims was so great, that five thousand have been sacrificed in one day, nay, on some occasions, no less than twenty thousand. Dec. iii. lib. ii. c. 16. Torquemada goes beyond both in extravagance; for he asserts that twenty thousand children, exclusive of other victims, were slaughtered annually. Mon. Ind. lib. vii. c. 21. The most respectable authority in favour of such high numbers is that of Zumurraga, the first Bishop of Mexico, who, in a letter to the chapter-general of his order, A. D. 1631, asserts, that the Mexicans sacrificed annually twenty thousand victims. Davila. Teatro Eccles. 126. In opposition to all these accounts, B. de las Casas observes, that if there had been such an annual waste of the human species, the country could never have arrived at that degree of populousness for which it was remarkable when the Spaniards first landed there. This reasoning is just. If the number of victims in all the provinces of New Spain had been so great, not only must population have been prevented from increasing, but the human race must have been exterminated in a short time. For besides the waste of the species by such numerous sacrifices, it is observable that wherever the fate of captives taken in war is either certain death or perpetual slavery, as men can gain nothing by submitting speedily to an enemy, they always resist to the uttermost, and war becomes bloody and destructive to the last degree. Las Casas positively asserts, that the Mexicans never sacrificed more than fifty or a hundred persons in a year. See his dispute with Sepulveda, subjoined to his Brevissima Relacion, p. 105. Cortes does not specify what number of victims was sacrificed annually; but B. Diaz del Castillo relates that, an inquiry having been made with respect to this by the Franciscan monks who were sent into New Spain immediately after the conquest, it was found that about two thousand five hundred were sacrificed every year in Mexico. C. 207.

## Note [156]. Page 330.

It is hardly necessary to observe, that the Peruvian Chronology is not only obscure, but repugnant to conclusions deduced from the most accurate and extensive observations, concerning the time that elapses during each reign, in any given succession of Princes. The medium has been found not to exceed twenty years. According to Acosta and Garcilasso de la Vega, Huana Capac, who died about the year 1527, was the twelfth Inca. According to this rule of computing, the duration of the Peruvian monarchy ought not to have been reckoned above two hundred and forty years; but they affirm that it had subsisted four hundred years. Acosta, lib. vi. c. 19. Vega, lib. i. c. 9. By this account each reign is extended at a medium to thirty-three years, instead of twenty, the number ascertained by Sir Isaac Newton's observations; but so imperfect were the Peruvian traditions, that though the total is boldly marked, the number of years in each reign is unknown.

## Note [157]. Page 332.

Many of the earliest Spanish writers assert that the Peruvians offered human sacrifices. Xeres, p. 190. Zarate, lib. i. c. 11. Acosta, lib. v. c. 19. But Garcilasso de la Vega contends, that though this barbarous practice prevailed among their uncivilized ancestors, it was totally abolished by the Incas, and that no human victim was ever offered in any temple of the Sun. This assertion, and the plausible reasons with which he confirms it, are sufficient to refute the Spanish writers, whose accounts seem to be founded entirely upon report, not upon what they themselves had observed. Vega, lib. ii. c. 4. In one of their festivals, the Peruvians offered cakes of bread moistened with blood drawn from the arms, the eyebrows, and noses of their children. Id. lib. vii. c. 6. This rite may have been derived from their ancient practice, in their uncivilized state, of sacrificing human victims.

## Note [158]. Page 334.

The Spaniards have adopted both those customs of the ancient Peruvians. They have preserved some of the aqueducts or canals, made in the days of the Incas, and have made new ones, by which they water every field that they cultivate. Ulloa Voyage, tom. i. 422. 477. They likewise continue to use *guano*, or the dung of sea-fowls, as manure. Ulloa gives a description of the almost incredible quantity of it in the small islands near the coast. Ibid. 481.

### Note [159]. Page 335.

The temple of Cayambo, the palace of the Inca at Callo in the plain of Lacatunga, and that of Atun-Cannar, are described by Ulloa, tom. i. 286, &c. who inspected them with great care. M. de Condamine published a curious memoir concerning the ruins of Atun-Cannar. Mém. de l'Academie de Berlin, A. D. 1746, p. 435. Acosta describes the ruins of Cuzco, which he had examined. Lib. vi. c. 14. Garcilasso, in his usual style, gives pompous and confused descriptions of several temples and other public edifices. Lib. iii. c. 1. c. 21. lib. vi. c. 4. Don. —— Zapata, in a large treatise concerning Peru, which has not hitherto been published, communicates some information with respect to several monuments of the ancient Peruvians, which have not been mentioned by other authors. MS. *penes me*, Articulo xx. Ulloa describes some of the ancient Peruvian fortifications, which were likewise works of great extent and solidity. Tom. i. 391. Three circumstances struck all those observers: the vast size of the stones which the Peruvians employed in some of their buildings. Acosta measured one, which was thirty feet long, eighteen broad, and six in thickness; and yet, he adds, that in the fortress at Cuzco there were stones considerably larger. It is difficult to conceive how the Peruvians could move these, and raise them to the height even of twelve feet. The second circumstance is, the imperfection of the Peruvian art, when applied to working in timber. By the patience and perseverance natural to Americans, stones may be formed into any shape, merely by rubbing one against another, or by the use of hatchets or other instruments made of stone; but with such rude tools little progress can be made in carpentry. The Peruvians could not mortise two beams together, or give any degree of union or stability to any work composed of timber. As they could not form a centre, they were totally unacquainted with the use of arches in building; nor can the Spanish authors conceive how they were able to frame a roof for those ample structures which they raised.

The third circumstance is a striking proof, which all the monuments of the Peruvians furnish, of their want of ingenuity and invention, accompanied with patience no less astonishing. None of the stones employed in those works were formed into any particular or uniform shape, which could render them fit for being compacted together in building. The Indians took them as they fell from the mountains, or were raised out of the quarries. Some were square, some triangular, some convex, some concave. Their art and industry were employed in joining them together, by forming such hollows in the one as perfectly corresponded to the projections or risings in the other. This tedious operation, which might have been so easily abridged by adapting the surface of the stones to each other, either by rubbing, or by their hatchets of copper, would be deemed incredible, if it were not put beyond doubt by inspecting the remains of those buildings. It gives them a very singular appearance to a European eye. There is no regular layer or stratum of building, and no one stone resembles another in dimensions or form. At the same time, by the persevering but ill-directed industry of the Indians, they are all joined with that minute nicety which I have mentioned. Ulloa made this observation concerning the form of the stones in the fortress of Atun-Cannar. Voy. i. p. 387. Penito gives a similar description of the fortress of Cuzco, the most perfect of all the Peruvian works. Zapata MS. *penes me*. According to M. de Condamine, there were regular strata of building in some parts of Atun-Cannar, which he remarks as singular, and as a proof of some progress in improvement.

### Note [160]. Page 337.

The appearance of those bridges which bend with their own weight, wave with the wind, and are considerably agitated by the motion of every person who passes along them, is very frightful at first. But the Spaniards have found them to be the easiest mode of passing the torrents in Peru, over which it would be difficult to throw more solid structures either of stone or timber. They form those hanging bridges so strong and broad, that loaded mules pass along them. All the trade of Cuzco is carried on by means of such a bridge over the river Apurimac. Ulloa, tom. i. p. 358. A more simple contrivance was employed in passing smaller streams: A basket, in which the traveller was placed, being suspended from a strong rope stretched across the stream, it was pushed or drawn from one side to the other. Ibid.

### Note [161]. Page 341.

My information with respect to those events is taken from *Noticia breve* de la expedicion militar de Sinora y Cinaloa, su exito feliz, y vantojoso estado, en que por consecuentia de ello, se han puesto ambas provincias, published at Mexico, June 17th, 1771, in order to satisfy the curiosity of the merchants, who had furnished the viceroy with money for defraying the expense of the armament. The copies of this *Noticia* are very rare in Madrid; but I have obtained one, which has enabled me to communicate these curious facts to the public. According to this account, there was found in the mine Yecorato in Cinaloa a grain of gold of twenty-two carats, which weighed sixteen marks four ounces four ochavas; this was sent to Spain as a present fit for the king, and is now deposited in the royal cabinet at Madrid.

### Note [162]. Page 341.

The uncertainty of geographers with respect to this point is remarkable, for Cortes seems to have surveyed its coasts with great accuracy. The Archbishop of Toledo has published, from the original in the possession of the Marquis del Valle, the descendant of Cortes, a map drawn in 1541, by the pilot Domingo Castillo, in which California is laid down as a peninsula, stretching out nearly in the same direction which is now given to it in the best maps; and the point where Rio Colorada enters the gulf is marked with precision. Hist. de Nueva Espagna, 327.

### Note [163]. Page 342.

I am indebted for this fact to M. L'Abbé Raynal, tom. iii. 103; and upon consulting an intelligent person, long settled on the Mosquito shore, and who has been engaged in the logwood trade, I find that ingenious author has been well informed. The logwood cut near the town of St. Francis of Campeachy is of much better quality than that on the other side of Yucatan; and the English trade in the Bay of Honduras is almost at an end.

### Note [164]. Page 348.

P. Torribio de Benevente, or Motolinea, has enumerated ten causes of the rapid depopulation of Mexico, to which he gives the name of the Ten Plagues. Many of these are not peculiar to that province. 1. The introduction of the small pox. This disease was first brought into New Spain in the year 1520, by a Negro-slave, who attended Narvaez in his expedition against Cortes. Torribio affirms, that one half of the people in the provinces visited with this distemper died. To this mortality, occasioned by the small pox, Torquemada adds the destructive effects of two contagious distempers which raged in the year 1545 and 1576. In the former 800,000, in the latter above two millions perished, according to an exact account taken by order of the viceroys. Mon. Ind. i. 642. The small pox was not introduced into Peru for several years after the invasion of the Spaniards; but there, too, that distemper proved very fatal to the natives. Garcia Origin, p. 88. 2. The numbers who were killed or died of famine in their war with the Spaniards, particularly during the siege of Mexico. 3. The great famine that followed after the reduction of Mexico, as all the people engaged, either on one side or other, had neglected the cultivation of their lands. Something similar to this happened in all the other countries conquered by the Spaniards. 4. The grievous tasks imposed by the Spaniards upon the people belonging to their Repartimientos. 5. The oppressive burden of taxes which they were unable to pay, and from which they could hope for no exemption. 6. The numbers employed in collecting the gold carried down by the torrents from the mountains, who were forced from their own habitations, without any provision made for their subsistence, and subjected to all the rigour of cold in those elevated regions. 7. The immense labour of rebuilding Mexico, which Cortes urged on with such precipitate ardour as destroyed an incredible number of people. 8. The number of people condemned to servitude, under various pretexts, and employed in working the silver mines. These, marked by each proprietor with a hot iron, like his cattle, were driven in herds to the mountains. 9. The nature of the labour to which they were subjected there, the noxious vapours of the mines, the coldness of the climate, and scarcity were so fatal, that Torribio affirms the country round several of those mines, particularly near Guaxago, was covered with dead bodies, the air corrupted with their stench, and so many vultures and other voracious birds hovered about for their prey, that the sun was darkened with their flight. 10. The Spaniards, in the different expeditions which they undertook, and by the civil wars which they carried on, destroyed many of the natives whom they compelled to serve them as *Tamemes*, or carriers of burdens. This last mode of oppression was particularly ruinous to the Peruvians. From the number of Indians who perished in Gonzalo Pizarro's expedition into the countries to the east of the Andes, one may form some idea of what they suffered in similar services, and how fast they were wasted by them. Torribio, MS. Corita, in his Breve y Summaria Relacion, illustrates and confirms several of Torribio's observations, to which he refers. MS. *penes me.*

### Note [165]. Page 348.

Even Montesquieu has adopted this idea, lib. viii. c. 18. But the passion of that great man for system sometimes rendered him inattentive to research; and from his capacity to refine, he was apt, in some instances, to overlook obvious and just causes.

### Note [166]. Page 349.

A strong proof of this occurs in the testament of Isabella, where she discovers the most tender concern for the humane and mild usage of the Indians. Those laudable sentiments of the queen have been adopted in the public law of Spain, and serve as the introduction to the regulations contained under the title *Of the good treatment of the Indians.* Recopil. lib. vi. tit. x.

### Note [167]. Page 350.

In the seventh *Title* of the first book of the *Recopilacion*, which contains the laws concerning the powers and functions of archbishops and bishops, almost a third part of them relates to what is incumbent upon them as guardians of the Indians, and points out the various methods in which it is their duty to interpose, in order to defend them from oppression either with respect to their persons or property. Not only do the laws commit to them this honourable and humane office, but the ecclesiastics of America actually exercise it.

Innumerable proofs of this might be produced from Spanish authors. But I rather refer to Gage, as he was not disposed to ascribe any merit to the popish clergy to which they were not fully entitled. Survey, p. 142. 192, &c. Henry Hawks, an English merchant, who resided five years in New Spain previous to the year 1572, gives the same favourable account of the popish clergy. Hakluyt, iii. 466. By a law of Charles V. not only bishops, but other ecclesiastics, are empowered to inform and admonish the civil magistrates, if any Indian is deprived of his just liberty and rights; Recopilac. lib. vi. tit. vi. ley 14: and thus were constituted legal protectors of the Indians. Some of the

Spanish ecclesiastics refused to grant absolution to such of their countrymen as possessed *Encomiendas*, and considered the Indians as slaves, or employed them in working their mines. Gonz. Davil. Teatro Eccles. i. 157.

### Note [168]. Page 350.

According to Gage, Chiapa dos Indos contains 4000 families; and he mentions it only as one of the largest Indian towns in America, p. 104.

### Note [169]. Page 350.

It is very difficult to obtain an accurate account of the state of population in those kingdoms of Europe where the police is most perfect, and where science has made the greatest progress. In Spanish America, where knowledge is still in its infancy, and few men have leisure to engage in researches merely speculative, little attention has been paid to this curious inquiry. But in the year 1741, Philip V. enjoined the viceroys and governors of the several provinces in America, to make an actual survey of the people under their jurisdiction, and to transmit a report concerning their number and occupations. In consequence of this order, the Conde de Fuen-Clara, Viceroy of New Spain, appointed D. Jos. Antonio de Villa Segnor y Sanchez to execute that commission in New Spain. From the reports of the magistrates in the several districts, as well as from his own observations and long acquaintance with most of the provinces, Villa Segnor published the result of his inquiries in his *Teatro Americano*. His report, however, is imperfect. Of the nine dioceses, into which the Mexican empire has been divided, he has published an account of five only, viz. the archbishopric of Mexico, the bishoprics of Pueblo de los Angeles, Mechoacan, Oaxaca, and Nova Galicia. The bishoprics of Yucatan, Verapaz, Chiapa, and Guatimala, are entirely omitted, though the two latter comprehend countries in which the Indian race is more numerous than in any part of New Spain. In his survey of the extensive diocess of Nova Galicia, the situation of the different Indian villages is described, but he specifies the number of people only in a small part of it. The Indians of that extensive province, in which the Spanish dominion is imperfectly established, are not registered with the same accuracy as in other parts of New Spain. According to Villa Segnor, the actual state of population in the five diocesses above mentioned is of Spaniards, negroes, mulattoes, and mestizos, in the diocesses of

| | Families. |
|---|---|
| Mexico | 105,202 |
| Los Angeles | 30,600 |
| Mechoacan | 30,840 |
| Oaxaca | 7,296 |
| Nova Galicia | 16,770 |
| | 190,708 |

| | |
|---|---|
| At the rate of five to a family, the total number is | 953,540 |

| | |
|---|---|
| Indian families in the diocess of Mexico | 119,511 |
| Los Angeles | 88,240 |
| Mechoacan | 36,196 |
| Oaxaca | 44,222 |
| Nova Galicia | 6,222 |
| | 294,391 |

At the rate of five to a family, the total number is 1,471,955. We may rely with great certainty on this computation of the number of Indians, as it is taken from the *Matricula*, or register, according to which the tribute paid by them is collected. As four diocesses of nine are totally omitted, and in that of Nova Galicia the numbers are imperfectly recorded, we may conclude that the number of Indians in the Mexican empire exceeds two millions.

The account of the number of Spaniards, &c. seems not to be equally complete. Of many places, Villa Segnor observes in general terms, that several Spaniards, negroes, and people of mixed race, reside there, without specifying their number. If, therefore, we make allowance for these, and for all who reside in the four dioceses omitted, the number of Spaniards, and of those of a mixed race, may probably amount to a million and a half. In some places Villa Segnor distinguishes between Spaniards and the three inferior races of negroes, mulattoes, and mestizos, and marks their number separately. But he generally blends them together. But from the proportion observable in those places, where the number of each is marked, as well as from the account of the state of population in New Spain by other authors, it is manifest that the number of negroes and persons of a mixed race far exceeds that of Spaniards. Perhaps the latter ought not to be reckoned above 500,000 to a million of the former.

Defective as this account may be, I have not been able to procure such intelligence concerning the number of people in Peru, as might enable me to form any conjecture equally satisfying with respect to the degree of its population. I have been informed that in the year 1761, the protector of the Indians in the viceroyalty of Peru computed that 612,780 paid tribute to the king. As all females, and persons under age, are exempted from this tax in Peru, the total number of Indians ought by that account to be 2,449,120. MS. *penes me.*

I shall mention another mode by which one may compute, or at least form a guess concerning the state of population in New Spain and Peru. According to an account which I have reason to consider as accurate, the number of copies of the bull of Cruzada exported to Peru on each new publication, is, 1,171,953; to New Spain, 2,649,326. I am informed that but few Indians purchase bulls, and that they are sold chiefly to the Spanish inhabitants, and those of mixed race; so that the number of Spaniards, and people of a mixed race, will amount, by this mode of computation, to at least three millions.

The number of inhabitants in many of the towns in Spanish America may give us some idea of the extent of population, and correct the inaccurate but popular notion entertained in Great Britain concerning the weak and desolate state of their colonies. The city of Mexico contains at least 150,000 people. It is remarkable that Torquemada, who wrote his *Monarquia Indiana* about the year 1612, reckons the inhabitants of Mexico at that time to be only 7000 Spaniards and 8000 Indians. Lib. iii. c. 26. Puebla de los Angeles contains above 60,000 Spaniards, and people of a mixed race. Villa Segnor, p. 247 Guadalaxara contains above 30,000 exclusive of Indians. Ibid. ii. 206. Lima contains 54,000. De Cosme Bueno Descr. de Peru, 1764. Carthagena contains 25,000. Potosi contains 25,000. Bueno, 1767. Popayan contains above 20,000. Ulloa, i. 287. Towns of a second class are still more numerous. The cities in the most thriving settlements of other European nations in America cannot be compared with these.

Such are the detached accounts of the number of people in several towns, which I found scattered in authors whom I thought worthy of credit. But I have obtained an enumeration of the inhabitants of the towns in the province of Quito, on the accuracy of which I can rely; and I communicate it to the public, both to gratify curiosity, and to rectify the mistaken notion which I have mentioned. St. Francisco de Quito contains between 50 and 60,000 people of all the different races. Besides the city, there are in the *Corregimento* twenty-nine *curas* or parishes established in the principal villages, each of which has smaller hamlets depending upon it. The inhabitants of these are mostly Indians and mestizos. St. Juan de Pasto has between 6 and 8000 inhabitants, besides twenty-seven dependent villages. St. Miguel de Ibarra, 7000 citizens, and ten villages. The district of Havalla, between 18 and 20,000 people. The district of Tacuna, between 10 and 12,000. The district of Ambato, between 8 and 10,000, besides sixteen depending villages. The city of Riobamba, between 16 and 20,000 inhabitants, and nine depending villages. The district of Chimbo, between 6 and 8000. The city of Guayaquil, from 16 to 20,000 inhabitants, and fourteen depending villages. The district of Atuasi, between 5 and 6000 inhabitants, and four depending villages. The city of Cuenza, between 25 and 30,000 inhabitants, and nine populous depending villages. The town of Laxa, from 8 to 10,000 inhabitants, and fourteen depending villages. This degree of population, though slender if we consider the vast extent of the country, is far beyond what is commonly supposed. I have omitted to mention, in its proper place, that Quito is the only province in Spanish America that can be denominated a manufacturing country; hats, cotton stuffs, and coarse woollen cloths are made there in such quantities as to be sufficient not only for the consumption of the province, but to furnish a considerable article for exportation into other parts of Spanish America. I know not whether the uncommon industry of this province should be considered as the cause or the effect of its populousness. But among the ostentatious inhabitants of the New World, the passion for every thing that comes from Europe is so violent, that I am informed the manufactures of Quito are so much undervalued as to be on the decline.

### Note [170]. Page 352.

These are established at the following places:—St. Domingo in the island of Hispaniola, Mexico in New Spain, Lima in Peru, Panama in Tierra Firmè, Santiago in Guatimala, Guadalaxara in New Galicia, Santa Fé in the New Kingdom of Granada, La Plata in the country of Los Charcas, St. Francisco de Quito, St. Jago de Chili, Buenos Ayres. To each of these are subjected several large provinces, and some so far removed from the cities where the courts are fixed, that they can derive little benefit from their jurisdiction. The Spanish writers commonly reckon up twelve Courts of Audience, but they include that of Manilla, in the Philippine islands.

### Note [171]. Page 354.

On account of the distance of Peru and Chili from Spain, and the difficulty of carrying commodities of such bulk as wine and oil across the isthmus of Panama, the Spaniards in those provinces have been permitted to plant vines and olives: but they are strictly prohibited from exporting wine or oil to any of the provinces on the Pacific Ocean, which are in such a situation as to receive them from Spain. Recop. lib. i. tit. xvii. 1. 15—18.

### Note [172]. Page 355.

This computation was made by Benzoni, A. D. 1550, fifty-eight years after the discovery of America. Hist. Novi Orbis, lib. iii. c. 21. But as Benzoni wrote with the spirit of a malecontent, disposed to detract from the Spaniards in every particular, it is probable that his calculation is considerably too low.

### Note [173]. Page 355.

My information with respect to the division and transmission of property in the Spanish colonies is imperfect. The Spanish authors do not explain this fully, and have not perhaps attended sufficiently to the effects of their own institutions and laws. Solorzano de Jure Ind. (vol. ii. lib. ii. 1. 16.) explains in some measure the introduction of the tenure of *Mayorasgo*, and mentions some of its effects. Villa Segnor takes notice of a singular consequence of it. He observes, that in some of the best situations in the city of Mexico, a good deal of ground is unoccupied, or covered only with the ruins of the houses once erected upon it; and adds, that as this ground is held by right of *Mayorasgo*, and cannot be alienated, that desolation and those ruins become perpetual. Teatr. Amer. vol. i. p. 34.

### Note [174]. Page 356.

There is no law that excludes Creoles from offices either civil or ecclesiastic. On the contrary, there are many *Cedulas*, which recommend the conferring places of trust indiscriminately on the natives of Spain and America. Betan court y Figueroa Derecho, &c. p. 5, 6. But, notwithstanding such repeated recommendations, preferment in almost every line is conferred on native Spaniards. A remarkable proof of this is produced by the author last quoted. From the discovery of America to the year 1637, three hundred and sixty-nine bishops, or archbishops, have been appointed to the different dioceses in that country, and of all that number only twelve were Creoles, p. 40. This predilection for Europeans seems still to continue. By a royal mandate, issued in 1776, the chapter of the cathedral of Mexico is directed to nominate European ecclesiastics of known merit and abilities, that the King may appoint them to supply vacant benefices. MS. *penes me.*

NOTE [175]. PAGE 358.

MODERATE as this tribute may appear, such is the extreme poverty of the Indians in many provinces of America, that the exacting of it is intolerably oppressive. Pegna Itiner. par Paroches de Indios, p. 192.

NOTE [176]. PAGE 358.

IN New Spain, on account of the extraordinary merit and services of the first conquerors, as well as the small revenue arising from the country previous to the discovery of the mines of Sacatecas, the *encomiendas* were granted for three, and sometimes for four lives. Recopil. lib. vi. tit. ii. c. 14, &c.

NOTE [177]. PAGE 359.

D. ANT. ULLOA contends, that working in mines is not noxious, and as a proof of this informs us, that many Mestizos and Indians, who do not belong to any Repartimiento, voluntarily hire themselves as miners; and several of the Indians, when the legal term of their service expires, continue to work in the mines of choice. *Entreten.* p. 265. But his opinion concerning the wholesomeness of this occupation is contrary to the experience of all ages; and wherever men are allured by high wages, they will engage in any species of labour, however fatiguing or pernicious it may be. D. Hern. Carillo Altamirano relates a curious fact incompatible with this opinion. Wherever mines are wrought, says he, the number of Indians decreases; but in the province of Campeachy, where there are no mines, the number of Indians has increased more than a third since the conquest of America, though neither the soil nor climate be so favourable as in Peru or Mexico. Colbert Collect. In another memorial presented to Philip III. in the year 1609, Captain Juan Gonzales de Azevedo asserts, that in every district of Peru where the Indians are compelled to labour in the mines, their numbers were reduced to the half, and in some places to the third, of what it was under the viceroyalty of Don Fran. Toledo in 1581. Colb. Collect.

NOTE [178]. PAGE 359.

As labour of this kind cannot be prescribed with legal accuracy, the tasks seem to be in a great measure arbitrary, and, like the services exacted by feudal superiors *in vinea prato, aut messe*, from their vassals, are extremely burdensome, and often wantonly oppressive. Pegna Itiner. par Paroches de Indios

NOTE [179]. PAGE 359.

THE turn of service known in Peru by the name of *Mita* is called *Tanda* in New Spain. There it continues no longer than a week at a time. No person is called to serve at a greater distance from his habitation than 24 miles. This arrangement is less oppressive to the Indians than that established in Peru. Memorial of Hern. Carillo Altamirano. Colbert Collect.

### Note [180]. Page 360.

The strongest proof of this may be deduced from the laws themselves. By the multitude and variety of regulations to prevent abuses, we may form an idea of the number of abuses that prevail. Though the laws have wisely provided that no Indian shall be obliged to serve in any mine at a greater distance from his place of residence than thirty miles; we are informed, in a memorial of D. Hernan Carillo Altamirano presented to the king, that the Indians of Peru are often compelled to serve in mines at the distance of a hundred, a hundred and fifty, and even two hundred leagues from their habitation. Colbert Collect. Many mines are situated in parts of the country so barren and so distant from the ordinary habitations of the Indians, that the necessity of procuring labourers to work there has obliged the Spanish monarchs to dispense with their own regulations in several instances, and to permit the viceroys to compel the people of more remote provinces to resort to those mines. Escalona Gazophyl. Perub. lib. i. c. 16. But, in justice to them, it should be observed that they have been studious to alleviate this oppression as much as possible, by enjoining the viceroys to employ every method in order to induce the Indians to settle in some part of the country adjacent to the mines. Id. ibid.

### Note [181]. Page 362.

Torquemada, after a long enumeration which has the appearance of accuracy, concludes the number of monasteries in New Spain to be four hundred. Mon. Ind. lib. xix. c. 32. The number of Monasteries in the city of Mexico alone was, in the year 1745, fifty-five. Villa Segnor Theat. Amer. i. 34. Ulloa reckons up forty convents in Lima; and mentioning those for nuns, he says that a small town might be peopled out of them, the number of persons shut up there is so great. Voy. i. 429. Philip III., in a letter to the Viceroy of Peru, A. D. 1620, observes, that the number of convents in Lima was so great, that they covered more ground than all the rest of the city. Solorz. lib. iii. c. 23. n. 57. Lib. iii. c. 16. Torquem. lib. xv. c. 3. The first monastery in New Spain was founded A. D. 1525, four years only after the conquest. Torq. lib. xv. c. 16.

According to Gil Gonzalez Davila, the complete establishment of the American church in all the Spanish settlements was, in the year 1649, 1 patriarch, 6 archbishops, 32 bishops, 346 prebends, 2 abbots, 5 royal chaplains, 840 convents. Teatro Ecclesiastico de las Ind. Occident. Vol. i. Pref. When the order of Jesuits was expelled from all the Spanish dominions, the colleges, *professed* houses, and residences which it possessed in the province of New Spain were thirty, in Quito sixteen, in the New Kingdom of Granada thirteen, in Peru seventeen, in Chili eighteen, in Paraguay eighteen; in all, a hundred and twelve. Collection General de Providencias hasta aqui tomadas sobre estranamento, &c. de la Compagnia, part i. p. 19. The number of Jesuits, priests, and novices in all these amounted to 2245. MS. *penes me.*

In the year 1644 the city of Mexico presented a petition to the king, praying that no new monastery might be founded, and that the revenues of those already established might be circumscribed, otherwise the religious houses would soon acquire the property of the whole country. The petitioners request likewise, that the bishops might be laid under restrictions in conferring holy orders, as there were at that time in New Spain above six thousand clergymen without any living. Ibid. p. 16. These abuses must have been enormous indeed, when the superstition of American Spaniards was shocked, and induced to remonstrate against them.

### Note [182]. Page 363.

This description of the manners of the Spanish clergy I should not have ventured to give upon the testimony of Protestant authors alone, as they may be suspected of prejudice or exaggeration. Gage, in particular, who had a better opportunity than any Protestant to view the interior state of Spanish

America, describes the corruption of the church which he had forsaken with so much of the acrimony of a new convert, that I should have distrusted his evidence, though it communicates some very curious and striking facts. But Benzoni mentions the profligacy of ecclesiastics in America at a very early period after their settlement there. Hist. lib. ii. c. 19, 20. M. Frezier, an intelligent observer, and zealous for his own religion, paints the dissolute manners of the Spanish ecclesiastics in Peru, particularly the regulars, in stronger colours than I have employed. Voy. p. 51. 215, &c. M. Gentil confirms this account. Voy. i. 34. Correal concurs with both, and adds many remarkable circumstances. Voy. i. 61. 155. 161. I have good reason to believe that the manners of the regular clergy, particularly in Peru, are still extremely indecent. Acosta himself acknowledges that great corruption of manners had been the consequence of permitting monks to forsake the retirement and discipline of the cloister, and to mingle again with the world, by undertaking the charge of the Indian parishes. De Procur. Ind. Salute, lib. iv. c. 13, &c. He mentions particularly those vices of which I have taken notice, and considers the temptations to them as so formidable, that he leans to the opinion of those who hold that the regular clergy should not be employed as parish priests. Lib. v. c. 20. Even the advocates of the regulars admit, that many and great enormities abounded among the monks of different orders, when set free from the restraint of monastic discipline; and from the tone of their defence, one may conclude that the charge brought against them was not destitute of truth. In the French colonies the state of the regular clergy is nearly the same as in the Spanish settlements, and the same consequences have followed. M. Biet, superior of the secular priests in Cayenne, inquires, with no less appearance of piety than of candour, into the causes of this corruption, and imputes it chiefly to the exemption of regulars from the jurisdiction and censures of their diocessans; to the temptations to which they are exposed; and to their engaging in commerce. Voy. p. 320. It is remarkable, that all the authors who censure the licentiousness of the Spanish regulars with the greatest severity, concur in vindicating the conduct of the Jesuits. Formed under a discipline more perfect than that of the other monastic orders, or animated by that concern for the honour of the society which takes such full possession of every member of the order, the Jesuits, both in Mexico and Peru, it is allowed, maintain a most irreproachable decency of manners. Frezier, 223. Gentil. i. 34. The same praise is likewise due to the bishops and most of the dignified clergy. Frez. Ibid.

A volume of the Gazette de Mexico for the years 1728, 1729, 1730, having been communicated to me, I find there a striking confirmation of what I have advanced concerning the spirit of low illiberal superstition prevalent in Spanish America. From the newspapers of any nation one may learn what are the objects which chiefly engross its attention, and which appear to it most interesting. The Gazette of Mexico is filled almost entirely with accounts of religious functions, with descriptions of processions, consecrations of churches, beatifications of saints, festivals, autos de fe, &c. Civil or commercial affairs, and even the transactions of Europe, occupy but a small corner in this magazine of monthly intelligence. From the titles of new books, which are regularly inserted in this Gazette, it appears that two-thirds of them are treatises of scholastic theology, or of monkish devotion.

### Note [183]. Page 363.

Solorzano, after mentioning the corrupt morals of some of the regular clergy, with that cautious reserve which became a Spanish layman in touching on a subject so delicate, gives his opinion very explicitly, and with much firmness, against committing parochial charges to monks. He produces the testimony of several respectable authors of his country, both divines and lawyers, in confirmation of his opinion. De Jure Ind. ii. lib. iii. c. 16. A striking proof of the alarm excited by the attempt of the Prince d'Esquilachè to exclude the regulars from parochial cures, is contained in the Colbert collection of papers. Several memorials were presented to the king by the procurators for the monastic orders, and replies were made to these in name of the secular clergy

An eager and even rancorous spirit is manifest on both sides in the conduct of this dispute.

### Note [184]. Page 365.

Not only the native Indians, but the *Mestizos*, or children of a Spaniard and Indian, were originally excluded from the priesthood, and refused admission into any religious order. But by a law issued Sept. 28th, 1588, Philip 1 required the prelates of America to ordain such mestizos born in lawful wed lock, as they should find to be properly qualified, and to permit them to take the vows in any monastery where they had gone through a regular noviciate. Recopil. lib. i. tit. vij. l. 7. Some regard seems to have been paid to this law in New Spain; but none in Peru. Upon a representation of this to Charles II. in the year 1697, he issued a new edict, enforcing the observation of it, and professing his desire to have all his subjects, Indians and mestizos as well sa Spaniards, admitted to the enjoyment of the same privileges. Such, how ever, was the aversion of the Spaniards in America to the Indians and their race, that this seems to have produced little effect; for in the year 1725 Philip V. was obliged to renew the injunction in a more peremptory tone. But so unsurmountable are hatred and contempt of the Indians among the Peruvian Spaniards, that the present king has been constrained to enforce the former edicts anew, by a law published September 11, 1774. Real Cedula, MS. *penes me.*

M. Clavigero has contradicted what I have related concerning the ecclesiastical state of the Indians, particularly their exclusion from the sacrament o the eucharist, and from holy orders, either as seculars or regulars, in such a manner as cannot fail to make a deep impression. He, from his own knowledge, asserts, "that in New Spain not only are Indians permitted to partake of the sacrament of the altar, but that Indian priests are so numerous that they may be counted by hundreds; and among these have been many hundreds of rectors, canons, and doctors, and, as report goes, even a very learned bishop. At present there are many priests, and not a few rectors, among whom there have been three or four our own pupils." Vol. II. 348, &c. I owe it, therefore, as a duty to the public as well as to myself, to consider each of these points with care, and to explain the reasons which induced me to adopt the opinion which I have published.

I knew that in the Christian church there is no distinction of persons, but that men of every nation, who embrace the religion of Jesus, are equally entitled to every Christian privilege which they are qualified to receive. I knew likewise that an opinion prevailed, not only among most of the Spanish laity settled in America, but among "many ecclesiastics (I use the words of Herrera, dec. ii. lib. ii. c. 15), that the Indians were not perfect or rational men, and were not possessed of such capacity as qualified them to partake of the sacrament of the altar, or of any other benefit of our religion." It was against this opinion that Las Casas contended with the laudable zeal which I have described in Books III. and VI. But as the Bishop of Darien, doctor Sepulvida, and other respectable ecclesiastics, vigorously supported the common opinion concerning the incapacity of the Indians, it became necessary, in order to determine the point, that the authority of the Holy See should be interposed; and accordingly Paul III. issued a bull, A. D. 1537, in which, after condemning the opinion of those who held that the Indians, as being on a level with brute beasts, should be reduced to servitude, he declares that they were really men, and as such were capable of embracing the Christian religion, and participating of all its blessings. My account of this bull, notwithstanding the cavils of M. Clavigero, must appear just to every person who takes the trouble of perusing it; and my account is the same with that adopted by Torquemada, lib. xvi. c. 25, and by Garcia, Orig. p. 311. But even after this decision, so low did the Spaniards residing in America rate the capacity of the natives, that the first council of Lima (I call it by that name on the authority of the best Spanish authors) discountenanced the admission of Indians to the holy communion. Torquem. lib. xvi. c. 20. In New Spain the exclusion of Indians from the sacrament was still more explicit. Ibid. After two centuries have elapsed, and notwithstanding all the improvement that the Indians may be supposed to have derived from their intercourse with the Spaniards during that period, we are informed by D. Ant. Ulloa, that in Peru, where, as will appear in the sequel of this note, they are supposed to be better instructed than in New Spain, their ignorance is so prodigious that very few are permitted to communicate, as being altogether destitute of the requisite capacity. Voy. i. 341, &c. Solorz. Polit. Ind. i. 203.

With respect to the exclusion of Indians from the priesthood, either as seculars or regulars, we may observe that while it continued to be the common opinion that the natives of America, on account of their incapacity, should not be permitted to partake of the holy sacrament, we cannot suppose that they would be clothed with that sacred character which entitled them to consecrate and to dispense it. When Torquemada composed his *Monarquia Indiana* it was almost a century after the conquest of New Spain ; and yet in his time it was still the general practice to exclude Indians from holy orders. Of this we have the most satisfying evidence. Torquemada having celebrated the virtues and graces of the Indians at great length, and with all the complacency of a missionary, he starts as an objection to what he had asserted, "If the Indians really possess all the excellent qualities which you have described, why are they not permitted to assume the religious habit? Why are they not ordained priests and bishops, as the Jewish and Gentile converts were in the primitive church, especially as they might be employed with such superior advantage to other persons in the instruction of their countrymen?" Lib. xvii. c. 13.

In answer to this objection, which establishes, in the most unequivocal manner, what was the general practice at that period, Torquemada observes, that although by their natual dispositions the Indians are well fitted for a subordinate situation, they are destitute of all the qualities requisite in any station of dignity and authority; and that they are in general so addicted to drunkenness, that upon the slightest temptation one cannot promise on their behaving with the decency suitable to the clerical character. The propriety of excluding them from it, on these accounts, was, he observed, so well justified by experience, that when a foreigner of great erudition, who came from Spain, condemned the practice of the Mexican church, he was convinced of his mistake in a public disputation with the learned and most religious Father D. Juan de Gaona, and his retraction is still extant. Torquemada indeed acknowledges, as M. Clavigero observes with a degree of exultation, that in his name some Indians had been admitted into monasteries ; but, with the art of a disputant, he forgets to mention that Torquemada specifies only two examples of this, and takes notice that in both instances those Indians had been admitted by mistake. Relying upon the authority of Torquemada with regard to New Spain, and of Ulloa with regard to Peru, and considering the humiliating depression of the Indians in all the Spanish settlements, I concluded that they were not admitted into the ecclesiastical order, which is held in the highest veneration all over the New World.

But when M. Clavigero, upon his own knowledge asserted facts so repugnant to the conclusion I had formed, I began to distrust it, and to wish for further information. In order to obtain this, I applied to a Spanish nobleman, high in office, and eminent for his abilities, who, on different occasions, has permitted me to have the honour and benefit of corresponding with him. I have been favoured with the following answer: "What you have written concerning the admission of Indians into holy orders, or into monasteries, in Book VIII., especially as it is explained and limited in Note LXXXVIII. of the quarto edition, is in general accurate, and conformable to the authorities which you quote. And although the congregation of the council resolved and declared, Feb. 13, A. D. 1682, that the circumstance of being an Indian, or mulatto, or mestizo, did not disqualify any person from being admitted into holy orders, if he was possessed of what is required by the canons to entitle him to that privilege; this only proves such ordinations to be legal and valid (of which Solorzano and the Spanish lawyers and historians quoted by him, Pol. Ind. lib. ii. c. 29, were persuaded), but it neither proves the propriety of admitting Indians into holy orders, nor what was then the common practice with respect to this ; but, on the contrary, it shows that there was some doubt concerning the ordaining of Indians, and some repugnance to it.

"Since that time there have been some examples of admitting Indians into holy orders. We have now at Madrid an aged priest, a native of Tlascala. His name is D. Juan Cerilo de Castilla Aquihual Catehuttle, descended of a cazique converted to Christianity soon after the conquest. He studied the ecclesiastical sciences in a seminary of Puebla de los Angeles. He was a candidate, nevertheless, for ten years, and it required much interest before Bishop Abren would consent to ordain him. This ecclesiastic was a man of unexceptionable character, modest, self-denied, and with a competent knowledge of what relates to his clerical functions. He came to Madrid above thirty-four years ago with the sole view of soliciting admission for the Indians into the colleges and seminaries in New Spain, that if, after being well instructed and tried, they should find an inclination to enter into the ecclesiastical state, they might embrace it, and perform its functions with the greatest benefit to their countrymen, whom they could address in their native tongue. He has obtained various regulations favourable to his scheme, particularly that the first college which became vacant in consequence of the exclusion of the Jesuits should be set apart for this purpose. But neither these regulations, nor any similar ones inserted in the laws of the Indies, have produced any effect, on account of objections and representations from the greater part of persons of chief consideration employed in New Spain. Whether their opposition be well founded or not is a problem difficult to resolve, and towards the solution of which several distinctions and modifications are requisite.

"According to the accounts of this ecclesiastic, and the information of other persons who have resided in the Spanish dominions in America, you may rest assured, that in the kingdom of Tierra Firmè no such thing is known as either an Indian secular priest or monk; and that in New Spain there are very few ecclesiastics of Indian race. In Peru, perhaps, the number may be greater, as in that country there are more Indians who possess the means of acquiring such a learned education as is necessary for persons who aspire to the clerical character."

### Note [185]. Page 366.

Uztariz, an accurate and cautious calculator, seems to admit, that the quantity of silver which does not pay duty, may be stated thus high. According to Herrera there was not above a third of what was extracted from Potosi that paid the king's fifth. Dec. 8. lib. ii. c. 15. Solorzano asserts likewise, that the quantity of silver which is fraudulently circulated, is far greater than that which is regularly stamped, after paying the fifth. De Ind. Jure, vol. ii. lib v. p. 846.

### Note [186]. Page 368.

When the mines of Potosi were discovered in the year 1545, the veins were so near the surface, that the ore was easily extracted, and so rich that it was refined with little trouble and at a small expense, merely by the action of fire. The simple mode of refining by fusion alone continued until the year 1574, when the use of mercury in refining silver, as well as gold, was discovered Those mines having been wrought without interruption for two centuries, the veins are now sunk so deep, that the expense of extracting the ore is greatly increased. Besides this, the richness of the ore, contrary to what happens in most other mines, has become less as the vein continued to dip. The vein has likewise diminished to such a degree, that one is amazed that the Spaniards should persist in working it. Other rich mines have been successively discovered; but in general the value of the ores has decreased so much, while the expense of extracting them has augmented, that the court of Spain in the year 1736 reduced the duty payable to the king from a *fifth* to a *tenth*. All the quicksilver used in Peru is extracted from the famous mine of Guancabelica, discovered in the year 1563. The crown has reserved the property of this mine to itself; and the persons who purchase the quicksilver pay not only the price of it, but likewise a *fifth*, as a duty to the king. But in the year 1761 this duty on quicksilver was abolished, on account of the increase of expense in working mines. Ulloa, Entretenimientos, xii—xv. Voyage, i. p. 505. 523. In consequence of this abolition of the *fifth*, and some subsequent abatements of price, which became necessary on account of the increasing expense of working mines, quicksilver, which was formerly sold at eighty pesos the quintal, is now delivered by the king at the rate of sixty pesos. Campomanes, Educ. Popul. ii. 132, note. The duty on gold is reduced to a *twentieth*, or five per cent. Any of my readers who are desirous of being acquainted with the mode in which the Spaniards conduct the working of their mines, and the refinement of the ore, will find an accurate description of the ancient method by Acosta, lib. iv. c. 1—13, and of their more recent improvements in the metallurgic art, by Gamboa Comment. a las ordenanz. de Minas, c. 22.

### Note [187]. Page 369.

Many remarkable proofs occur of the advanced state of industry in Spain at the beginning of the sixteenth century. The number of cities in Spain was considerable, and they were peopled far beyond the proportion that was common in other parts of Europe. The causes of this I have explained. Hist. of Cha. V. p. 68. Wherever cities are populous, that species of industry which is peculiar to them increases: artificers and manufacturers abound. The effect of the American trade in giving activity to these is manifest from a singular fact. In the year 1545, while Spain continued to depend on its own industry for the supply of its colonies, so much work was bespoke from the manufacturers, that it was supposed they could hardly finish it in less than six years. Campom. i. 406. Such a demand must have put much industry in motion, and have excited extraordinary efforts. Accordingly, we are informed, that in the beginning of Philip II.'s reign, the city of Seville alone, where the trade with America centred, gave employment to no fewer than 16,000 looms in silk or woollen work, and that above 130,000 persons had occupation in carrying on these manufactures. Campom. ii. 472. But so rapid and pernicious was the operation of the causes which I shall enumerate, that before Philip III. ended his reign the looms in Seville were reduced to 400. Uztariz, c. 7.

Since the publication of the first edition, I have the satisfaction to find my ideas concerning the early commercial intercourse between Spain and her colonies confirmed and illustrated by D. Bernardo Ward, of the Junto de Comercio at Madrid, in his *Proyicto Economico*, part ii. c. i. "Under the reigns of Charles V. and Philip. II." says he, "the manufactures of Spain and of the Low-Countries subject to her dominion were in a most flourishing state. Those of France and England were in their infancy. The republic of the United Provinces did not then exist. No European power but Spain had colonies of any value in the New World. Spain could supply her settlements there with the productions of her own soil, the fabrics wrought by the hands of her own artisans, and all she received in return for these belonged to herself alone. Then the exclusion of foreign manufactures was proper, because it might be rendered effectual. Then Spain might lay heavy duties upon goods exported to America, or imported from it, and might impose what restraints she deemed proper upon a commerce entirely in her own hands. But when time and successive revolutions had occasioned an alteration in all those circumstances, when the manufactures of Spain began to decline, and the demands of America were supplied by foreign fabrics, the original maxims and regulations of Spain should have been accommodated to the change in her situation. The policy that was wise at one period became absurd in the other."

### Note [188]. Page 372.

No bale of goods is ever opened, no chest of treasure is examined. Both are received on the credit of the persons to whom they belong; and only one instance of fraud is recorded, during the long period in which trade was carried on with this liberal confidence. All the coined silver that was brought from

Peru to Porto-bello in the year 1654 was found to be adulterated, and to be mingled with a fifth part of base metal. The Spanish merchants, with sentiments suitable to their usual integrity, sustained the whole loss, and indemnified the foreigners by whom they were employed. The fraud was detected, and the treasurer of the revenue in Peru, the author of it, was publicly burnt. B. Ulloa. Retablis. de Manuf., &c. liv. ii. p. 102.

NOTE [189]. PAGE 374.

MANY striking proofs occur of the scarcity of money in Spain. Of all the immense sums which have been imported from America, the amount of which I shall afterwards have occasion to mention, Moncada asserts, that there did not remain in Spain, in 1619, above two hundred millions of *pesos*, one half in coined money, the other in plate and jewels. Restaur. de Espagna, disc. iii. c. 1. Uztariz, who published his valuable work in 1724, contends, that in money, plate, and jewels, there did not remain a hundred million. Theor., &c. c. 3. Campomanes, on the authority of a remonstance from the community of merchants in Toledo to Philip III., relates, as a certain proof how scarce cash had become, that persons who lent money received a third of the sum which they advanced as interest and premium. Educ. Popul. i. 417.

NOTE [190]. PAGE 375.

THE account of the mode in which the factors of the South Sea company conducted the trade in the fair of Porto-bello, which was opened to them by the Assiento, I have taken from Don Dion. Alcedo y Herrera, president of the Court of Audience in Quito, and governor of that province. Don Dionysio was a person of such respectable character for probity and discernment, that his testimony in any point would be of much weight; but greater credit is due to it in this case, as he was an eye-witness of the transactions which he relates, and was often employed in detecting and authenticating the frauds which he describes. It is probable, however, that his representation, being composed at the commencement of the war which broke out between Great Britain and Spain, in the year 1739, may, in some instances, discover a portion of the acrimonious spirit natural at that juncture. His detail of facts is curious; and even English authors confirm it in some degree, by admitting both that various frauds were practised in the transactions of the annual ship, and that the contraband trade from Jamaica, and other British colonies, was become enormously great. But for the credit of the English nation it may be observed, that those fraudulent operations are not to be considered as deeds of the company, but as the dishonourable arts of their factors and agents. The company itself sustained a considerable loss by the Assiento trade. Many of its servants acquired immense fortunes. Anderson Chronol. deduct. ii. 388.

NOTE [191]. PAGE 377.

SEVERAL facts with respect to the institution, the progress, and the effects of this company, are curious, and but little known to English readers. Though the province of Venezuela, or Caraccas, extends four-hundred miles along the coast, and is one of the most fertile in America, it was so much neglected by the Spaniards, that during the twenty years prior to the establishment of the company, only five ships sailed from Spain to that province; and, during sixteen years, from 1706 to 1722, not a single ship arrived from the Caraccas in Spain. Noticias de Real Campania de Caraccas, p. 28. During this period Spain must have been supplied almost entirely with a large quantity of cacao, which it consumes, by foreigners. Before the erection of the company, neither tobacco nor hides were imported from Caraccas into Spain. Ibid. p. 117. Since the commercial operations of the company, begun in the year 1731, the importation of cacao into Spain has increased amazingly. During thirty years subsequent to 1701, the number of *fanegas* of cacao (each a hundred and ten pounds) imported from Caraccas was 643,215. During eighteen years subsequent to 1731, the number of *fanegas* imported was 869,247; and if we suppose the importation to be continued in the same proportion during the remainder of thirty years, it will amount to 1,448,746 *fanegas*, which is an increase of 805,531 *fanegas*. Id. p. 148. During eight years subsequent to 1756, there have been imported into Spain by the company 88,482 *arrobas* (each twenty-five pounds) of tobacco; and hides to the number of 177,354. Id. 161. Since the publication of the Noticias de Campania, in 1765, its trade seems to be on the increase. During five years subsequent to 1769, it has imported 179,156 *fanegas* of cacao into Spain, 36,208 *arrobas* of tobacco, 75,496 hides, and 221,432 pesos in specie. Campomanes, ii. 162. The last article is a proof of the growing wealth of the colony. It receives cash from Mexico in return for the cacao, with which it supplies that province, and this it remits to Spain, or lays out in purchasing European goods. But, besides this, the most explicit evidence is produced, that the quantity of Cacao raised in the province is double to what it yielded in 1731; the number of its live stock is more than treble, and its inhabitants much augmented. The revenue of the bishop, which arises wholly from tithes, has increased from eight to twenty thousand pesos. Notic. p. 69. In consequence of the augmentation of the quantity of cacao imported into Spain, its price has decreased from eighty pesos for the *fanega* to forty. Ibid. 61. Since the publication of the first edition, I have learned that Guyana, including all the extensive provinces situated on the banks of the Orinoco, the Islands of Trinidad and Margarita are added to the countries with which the company of Caraccas had liberty of trade by their former charters. Real Cedula, Nov. 19, 1776. But I have likewise been informed, that the institution of this company has not been attended with all the beneficial effects which I have ascribed to it. In many of its operations the illiberal and oppressive spirit of monopoly is still conspicuous. But in order to explain this, it would be necessary to enter into minute details, which are not suited to the nature of this work.

### Note [192]. Page 380.

This first experiment made by Spain of opening a free trade with any o. her colonies, has produced effects so remarkable, as to merit some further illustration. The towns to which this liberty has been granted, are Cadiz and Seville, for the province of Andalusia: Alicant and Carthagena, for Valencia and Murcia; Barcelona, for Catalonia and Aragon; Santander, for Castile; Corugna, for Galicia; and Gijon, for Asturias. Append. ii. à la Educ. Popul. p. 41. These are either the ports of chief trade in their respective districts, or those most conveniently situated for the exportation of their respective productions. The following facts give a view of the increase of trade in the settlements to which the new regulations extend. Prior to the allowance of free trade, the duties collected in the custom house at the Havanna were computed to be 104,208 pesos annually. During the five years preceding 1774, they rose at a medium to 308,000 pesos a year. In Yucatan the duties have arisen from 8000 to 15,000. In Hispaniola, from 2500 to 5600. In Porto Rico, from 1200 to 7000. The total value of goods imported from Cuba into Spain was reckoned, in 1774, to be 1,500,000 pesos. Educ. Popul. i. 450, &c.

### Note [193]. Page 382.

The two treatises of Don Pedro Rodriguez Campomanes, *Fiscal del real Consejo y Supremo* (an officer in rank and power nearly similar to that of Attorney-General in England), and Director of the Royal Academy of History, the one entitled Discurso sobre el Fomento de la Industria Popular; the other, Discurso sobre la Education Popular de los Artesanos y su Fomento; the former published in 1774, and the latter in 1775, afford a striking proof of this. Almost every point of importance with respect to interior police, taxation, agriculture, manufactures, and trade, domestic as well as foreign, is examined in the course of these works; and there are not many authors, even in the nations most eminent for commercial knowledge, who have carried on their inquiries with a more thorough knowledge of those various subjects, and a more perfect freedom from vulgar and national prejudices, or who have united more happily the calm researches of philosophy with the ardent zeal of a public spirited citizen. These books are in high estimation among the Spaniards; and it is a decisive evidence of the progress of their own ideas, that they are capable of relishing an author whose sentiments are so liberal.

### Note [194]. Page 384.

The galeon employed in that trade, instead of the six hundred tons to which it is limited by law, Recop. lib. xlv. l. 15, is commonly from twelve hundred to two thousand tons burden. The ship from Acapulco, taken by Lord Anson, instead of the 500,000 pesos permitted by law, had on board 1,313,843 pesos, besides uncoined silver equal in value to 43,611 pesos more. Anson's Voy. 384

### Note [195]. Page 384.

The price paid for the bull varies according to the rank of different persons. Those in the lowest order who are servants or slaves, pay two reals of plate, or one shilling; other Spaniards pay eight reals, and those in public office, or who hold encomiendas, sixteen reals. Solorz. de Jure Ind. vol. ii. lib. iii. c. 25. According to Chilton, an English merchant who resided long in the Spanish settlements, the bull of Cruzado bore a higher price in the year 1570, being then sold for four reals at the lowest. Hakluyt, iii. 461. The price seems to have varied at different periods. That exacted for the bulls issued in the last *Predicacion* will appear from the ensuing table, which will give some idea of the proportional numbers of the different classes of citizens in New Spain and Peru.

There were issued for New Spain—

| | |
|---|---|
| Bulls at 10 pesos each | 4 |
| at 2 pesos each | 22,601 |
| at 1 peso each | 164,220 |
| at 2 reals each | 2,462,500 |
| | 2,649,325 |

For Peru—

| | |
|---|---|
| at 16 pesos 4½ reals each | 3 |
| at 3 pesos 3 reals each | 14,202 |
| at 1 peso 5½ reals each | 78,822 |
| at 4 reals each | 410,325 |
| at 3 reals each | 668,601 |
| | 1,171,953 |

### Note [196]. Page 385.

As Villa Segnor, to whom we are indebted for this information contained in his Theatro Americano, published in Mexico A. D. 1746, was accomptant-general in one of the most considerable departments of the royal revenue, and by that means had access to proper information, his testimony with respect to this point merits great credit. No such accurate detail of the Spanish revenues in any part of America has hitherto been published in the English language; and the particulars of it may appear curious and interesting to some of my readers.

| | |
|---|---|
| From the bull of Cruzado, published every two years, there arises an annual revenue in pesos | 150,000 |
| From the duty on silver | 700,000 |
| | 850,000 |

| | |
|---|---|
| *Brought forward* | 850,000 |
| From the duty on gold | 60,000 |
| From tax on cards | 70,000 |
| From tax on pulque, a drink used by the Indians | 161,000 |
| From tax on stamped paper | 41,000 |
| From ditto on ice | 15,522 |
| From ditto on leather | 2,500 |
| From ditto on gunpowder | 71,550 |
| From ditto on salt | 32,000 |
| From ditto on copper of Mechoachan | 1,000 |
| From ditto on alum | 6,500 |
| From ditto on Juego de los gallos | 21,100 |
| From the half of ecclesiastical annats | 49,000 |
| From royal ninths of bishoprics, &c. | 68,800 |
| From the tribute of Indians | 650,000 |
| From Alcavala, or duty on sale of goods | 721,875 |
| From the Almajorifasgo, custom house | 373,333 |
| From the mint | 357,500 |
| | 3,552,680 |

This sum amounts to 819,161 sterling*l.*; and if we add to it the profit accruing from the sale of 5000 quintals of quicksilver, imported from the mines of Almaden, in Spain, on the King's account, and what accrues from the *Averia*, and some other taxes which Villa Segnor does not estimate, the public revenue in new Spain may well be reckoned above a million pounds sterling money. Theat. Mex. vol. i. p. 38, &c. According to Villa Segnor, the total produce of the Mexican mines amounts at a medium to eight millions of Pesos in silver annually, and to 5912 marks of gold. Ibid. p. 44. Several branches of the revenue have been explained in the course of the history; some of which there was no occasion of mentioning, require a particular illustration. The right to the *tithes* in the New World is vested in the crown of Spain, by a bull of Alexander VI. Charles V. appointed them to be applied in the following manner: One fourth is allotted to the bishop of the diocess, another fourth to the dean and chapter, and other officers of the cathedral. The remaining half is divided into nine equal parts. Two of these, under the denomination of *los dos Novenos reales*, are paid to the crown, and constitute a branch of the royal revenue. The other seven parts are applied to the maintenance of the parochial clergy, the building and support of churches, and other pious uses. Recopil. lib. i. tit. xvi. Ley, 23, &c. Avendano Thesaur. Indic. vol. i. p. 184.

The *Alcavala* is a duty levied by an excise on the sale of goods. In Spain it amounts to ten per cent. In America to four per cent. Solorzano, Polit. Indiana, lib. vi. c. 8. Avendano, vol. i. 186.

The *Almajorifasco*, or custom paid in America on goods imported and exported, may amount on an average to fifteen per cent. Recopil. lib. viii. tit. xiv. Ley, i. Avendano, vol. i. p. 188.

The *Averia*, or tax paid on account of convoys to guard the ships sailing to and from America, was first imposed when Sir Francis Drake filled the New World with terror by his expedition to the South Sea. It amounts to two per cent. on the value of goods. Avendano, vol. i. p. 189. Recopil. lib. ix. tit. ix. Ley, 43, 44.

I have not been able to procure any accurate detail of the several branches of revenue in Peru later than the year 1614. From a curious manuscript containing a state of that viceroyalty in all its departments, presented to the Marquis of Montes-Claros by Fran. Lopez Caravantes, accomptant-general in the tribunal of Lima, it appears that the public revenue, as nearly as I can compute the value of the money in which Caravantes states his accounts, amounted in ducats at 4s. 11d. to 2,372,768

| | |
|---|---|
| Expenses of government | 1,242,992 |
| Net free revenue | 1,129,776 |

| | |
|---|---|
| The total in sterling money - - - - - - - - - | £583,303 |
| Expenses of government - - - - - - - - - | 305,568 |
| Net free revenue | 277,735 |

But several articles appear to be omitted in this computation, such as the duty on stamped paper, leather, ecclesiastical annats, &c. so that the revenue of Peru may be well supposed equal to that of Mexico.

In computing the expense of government in New Spain, I may take that of Peru as a standard. There the annual establishment for defraying the charge of administration exceeds one half of the revenue collected, and there is no reason for supposing it to be less in New Spain.

I have obtained a calculation of the total amount of the public revenue of Spain from America and the Philippines, which, as the reader will perceive from the two last articles, is more recent than any of the former.

| | |
|---|---|
| Alcavalas (Excise) and Aduanas (Customs), &c. in pesos fuertes - | 2,500,000 |
| Duties on Gold and silver - - - - - - - - - | 3,000,000 |
| Bull of Cruzado - - - - - - - - - - - | 1,000,000 |
| Tribute of the Indians - - - - - - - - - - | 2,000,000 |
| By sale of quicksilver - - - - - - - - - - | 300,000 |
| Paper exported on the king's account, and sold in the royal ware-houses - - - - - - - - - - - - - | 300,000 |
| Stamped paper, tobacco, and other small duties - - - - | 1,000,000 |
| Duty on coinage of, at the rate of one real de la Plata for each mark | 300,000 |
| From the trade of Acapulco, and the coasting trade from province to province - - - - - - - - - - - - - | 500,000 |
| Assiento of Negroes - - - - - - - - - - | 200,000 |
| From the trade of *Mathe*, or herb of Paraguay, formerly monopolized by the Jesuits - - - - - - - - - - - - | 500,000 |
| From other revenues formerly belonging to that order - - - - | 400,000 |
| Total | 12,000,000 |
| Total in sterling money | £2,700,000 |
| Deduct half, as the expense of administration, and there remains net free revenue - - - - - - - - - - - - | £1,350,000 |

## Note [197]. Page 385.

An author long conversant in commercial speculation has computed, that from the mines of New Spain alone the king receives annually, as his fifth, the sum of two millions of our money. Harris, Collect. of Voy. ii. p. 164. According to this calculation, the total produce of the mines must be ten millions sterling; a sum so exorbitant, and so little corresponding with all accounts of the annual importation from America, that the information on which it is founded must evidently be erroneous. According to Campomanes, the total product of the American mines may be computed at thirty millions of pesos, which, at four shillings and sixpence a peso, amounts to 7,425,000*l.* sterling, the king's fifth of which (if that were regularly paid) would be 1,485,000*l.* But from this sum must be deducted what is lost by a fraudulent withholding of the fifth due to the crown, as well as the sum necessary for defraying the expense of administration. Educ. Popular. vol. ii. p. 131. note. Both these sums are considerable.

## Note [198]. Page 385.

According to Bern. de Ulloa, all foreign goods exported from Spain to America pay duties of various kinds, amounting in all to more than 25 per cent. As most of the goods with which Spain supplies her colonies are foreign, such a tax upon a trade so extensive must yield a considerable revenue

Retablis. de Manuf. et du Commerce d'Esp. p. 150. He computes the value of goods exported annually from Spain to America to be about two millions and a half sterling. p. 97.

NOTE [199]. PAGE 386.

THE Marquis de Serralvo, according to Gage, by a monopoly of salt, and by embarking deeply in the Manilla trade, as well as in that to Spain, gained annually a million of ducats. In one year he remitted a million of ducats to Spain, in order to purchase from the Conde Olivares, and his creatures, a prolongation of his government, p. 61. He was successful in his suit, and continued in office from 1624 to 1635, double the usual time.

# INDEX.

# QUESTIONS

FOR THE

# EXAMINATION OF STUDENTS.

BY JOHN FROST, A.M.

# QUESTIONS

FOR

# EXAMINATION OF STUDENTS

IN

## ROBERTSON'S HISTORY OF AMERICA.

*N.B.—The figures prefixed to each paragraph refer to the pages of Harper's stereotype edition of Robertson's History of America.*

### BOOK I.

Page 17.

Was the earth rapidly peopled?—What occasioned the first dispersion of the human race?—How were the early migrations made?—Were navigation and ship-building rapidly perfected?—How is their early imperfection proved?—From what era must we date the origin of commerce?

Page 18.

What is the first species of commerce?—Give some account of its progress.—What besides conquest became a motive for long voyages?—Of what did trade become a great source?—Did navigation advance as rapidly as commerce?—Before the discovery of the mariner's compass how far were voyages extended?—Were voyages longer than at present?—At what season were they undertaken?

Page 19.

Where did the Egyptians open a commerce?—What seas were crossed in these voyages?—By what route were their commodities brought from India to Egypt?—What change took place in the character of the Egyptians?—Where is Egypt?—What other ancient nation was devoted to commerce?—Where was ancient Phœnicia?—What were its commercial cities?—Which way is it from Tyre to Egypt?—At what did the Phœnicians aim?—What places did their ships visit?—Where are the Straits of Gades?—What is the modern name?—Did the Phœnicians plant colonies?—Where did they acquire commodious harbours?—With what countries did they establish a regular intercourse?—Under what kings did the Jews direct their attention to commerce?—How did they obtain a share of the Phœnician commerce?

Page 20.

Where is Idumea?—Where is Palestine?—Which way from Phœnicia?—Which way are Tyre and Sidon from Jerusalem?—Whither did Solomon send fleets?—Where were probably the places called Ophir and Tarshish?—Did the Jews long continue commerce?—Did they improve navigation or extend discovery?—Who were the descendants of the Phœnicians?—Where was ancient Carthage?—Did the Carthaginians inherit the commercial spirit?—What countries did their voyagers visit in the north-west?—What countries in the south?—How far south did they sail?—What islands did they discover?—Did they undertake voyages of discovery?—Under what leaders?—Describe the voyage of Hanno.—Of Himlico.

Page 21.

Describe the voyage said to have been accomplished by a Phœnician fleet fitted out by Necho.—Who else is said to have accomplished the same?—Are these accounts well authenticated?—Why did the Phœnician and Carthaginian voyagers conceal their discoveries?—When did the memorials of their naval skill perish?—Did the Greeks and Romans learn navigation and commerce from the Phœnicians and Carthaginians?—What was the first object among the early Grecian voyagers?—What was the extent of the famous expedition of the Argonauts?—What is the modern name of the Euxine Sea?—Had navigation advanced much in Homer's time?

Page 22.

Describe the ships of the early Greeks.—To what rank among maritime nations did th ancient Greeks afterward arrive?—What sort of vessels were used in the Persian war?—How far did the ancient Grecian commerce extend?—With whom was their chief inter course?—What places did they occasionally visit?—Which way from Greece is Asia Mino or Lesser Asia?—Italy?—Sicily?—The Euxine?—The Hellespont?—What example of the ignorance of the Greeks is quoted?—How far did the geographical knowledge of the Greeks extend?—Of what facts were they ignorant

Page 23.

What expedition enlarged the geographical knowledge of the Greeks?—What commercial republic was among the conquests of Alex ander?—After reducing Tyre and Egypt what plan did he form?—What city did he found—Where?—With what design?—What was the consequence of its situation?—Whither did he conduct his army by land?—How far into India did he advance?—What did he resolve to examine?—By what communication did he design to furnish his Asiatic dominions with the commodities of the East?—How did he design to distribute them to the rest of the world?—Whom did he send to survey the Persian Gulf?—Was this justly considered a grea undertaking?

Page 24.

In executing it, what surprising discovery was made?—How was it regarded?—How long did the voyage last?—Was the navigation to India by this course continued?—Who were a ·ched afterward by the Indian trade of

Alexandria?—What progress did the Romans make in navigation and discovery?—Why was this?—What made them first aim at maritime power?—For what purpose was this power used?—Did the Romans ever become a commercial people?—In whose hands did their commerce remain?—Was it well protected and profitable?—What improved under it?

Page 25.

What fact was observed in the Indian Ocean?—What use was made of this observation?—What was the utmost limit of the Roman navigation?—How far did travellers probably penetrate by land?—What amount of money was drawn annually from Rome by the Indian trade?—What number of ships annually sailed from the Arabian Gulf to India?—How was the knowledge of remote countries obtained in ancient times?—What countries of Europe were conquered by the Romans?

Page 26.

In Africa?—In Asia?—Of what countries in Europe were the ancient Romans ignorant?—In Africa?—In Asia?—What did the ancients believe concerning the Zones?—By what class of people was this theory held?—What consequences follow from this theory?

Page 27.

What other extravagant theory did the ancients believe?—What does this theory prove?—Who brought geography to its highest point among the ancients?—When did he flourish, and what did he publish?—Did geographical knowledge decline after Ptolemy's time?—What city became first in point of commerce?—What was the consequence of the fall of the Roman empire?—What was the first effect of the settlement of the barbarous nations in the south of Europe?

Page 28.

Did geographical science nearly perish in the wreck of the Roman empire?—Did commerce?—What prevented commerce from ceasing altogether?—How far did the trade of Constantinople extend?—After the conquest of Egypt by the Arabians, how were commodities conveyed from India to Constantinople?—How did the Arabians acquire a fondness for geographical science?—Did they advance the science?—Where is Arabia?—Which way from Egypt?

Page 29.

What country first began to recover from the desolation and barbarism occasioned by the fall of the Roman empire?—What happened to the Italian cities?—What was the consequence?—What foreign city became the chief mart of the Italians?—At what other cities did they purchase the commodities of the East?—Where is Aleppo?—Tripoli?—Syria?—How were the goods conveyed from India to these ports?—To what port of Egypt did the Italian merchants resort?—What were the chief commercial cities of Italy?—To what countries beyond the Mediterranean did their merchants resort?—What event gave a new impulse to commerce?—Who furnished transports and provisions to the crusaders?—Were the Italians enriched by the crusades?

Page 30.

Did the other countries of Europe participate in the benefits of the crusades?—Give an account of the travels of Benjamin of Tudela.—Give an account of the mission of Carpini and Ascolino.

Page 31.

What induced St. Louis to send a mission to Tartary?—Who were sent?—What was the result?—Who was Marco Polo?—When did he flourish?—Under whose protection did he travel?—How long?—What countries before unknown did he visit?—What Englishman visited the same countries?—When?—Where is Pekin?—Japan?

Page 32.

What was the character of the narratives of these travellers?—What was their effect on the public?—What important discovery was made at this time?—What use did navigators make of it?—Who was the author of the discovery?—What injustice did he suffer?—Why was not the discovery immediately used for the purpose of making distant discoveries?

Page 33.

How long time elapsed before it was used for discovery?—For what purposes did the Spaniards first visit the Canaries?—Where are they?—To whom did Clement VI. give them?—By what right?—Who conquered them?—How far had navigation advanced at the beginning of the fifteenth century?—What kingdom first roused that spirit of curiosity and enterprise which led to the discovery of the New World?—Who was trained in this school?

Page 34.

What had raised the military spirit and enterprise of the Portuguese? -When did John I. become king of Portugal?—What was his character?—For what did he equip a fleet and armament?—Whither did he send ships for discovering new regions?—What may we date from this?—What had been the former boundary of the Portuguese voyagers?

Page 35.

What was the literary character of the Portuguese in the fifteenth century?—How far did their discoverers go in the first voyage?—What was the character of Henry duke of Viseo?—Where did he fix his residence?—For what purpose?—To what sources of information did he apply?—Whom did he engage in his service?

Page 36.

Describe his first effort?—What island did Zarco and Vaz discover?—What was done next year?—Describe the settlement of Madeira and its consequences?—Who first doubled Cape Bojador?—When?

Page 37.

What further discoveries did the Portuguese make towards the south of Africa?—Where is the river Senegal?—In what latitude?—In what latitude is Cape Blanco?—Cape Verd?—What sort of inhabitants did the Portuguese find south of the Senegal?—What objections were made to prince Henry's schemes?—Was he deterred by them?—Who supported him in his designs?—What did he request of the pope?

Page 38.

What grant was obtained from the pope?—What advantage arose from it?—What was the effect of the Portuguese discoveries on the public mind?—What new adventurers entered their service?—What new discoveries were made by them?—Where are the Azores?—The Cape Verd Isles?—What does the discovery of these clusters prove?—When did prince Henry die?—How far south had the Portuguese discoveries then extended?—What extent of the west coast of Africa was explored?

Page 39.

What prevented Alphonso king of Portugal from prosecuting the African discoveries with ardour?—To whom did he commit them?—What was the consequence?—When did the Portuguese cross the equinoctial?—What then surprised them?—When did John II. succeed Alphonso?—What did his voyagers find to be the character of the country north of the Senegal?—What, south?—What ensued?—When did king John fit out a new fleet?—What kingdoms were discovered?—Where did he build forts and settle colonies?—Where is Benin?—Congo?—Guinea?

Page 40.

What country did the Portuguese expect to arrive at by going round Africa to the south?—To whom did the king of Portugal send an embassy?—Was Prester John a real personage?—What was the origin of his name?—Who were the ambassadors sent in quest of Prester John's dominions by the king of Portugal?—What other expedition did king John project?—To whom was it intrusted?—When?—What was the length of the voyage?—What discoveries did he make?

Page 41.

What cape was the limit of his voyage?—Why was it so called?—How far did Covillam and Payva travel together?—What countries did they respectively visit after separating?—What important conclusion was conveyed in Covillam's despatches?—What design did the king of Portugal now entertain?—Who were alarmed at it?—Why?—What news was received before the expedition sailed?

BOOK II.

Page 42.

Of what country was Christopher Columbus a subject?—How was he educated?—When did he first go to sea?—What places did he visit in 1467?—Whose service did he next enter?—Relate an adventure of his off the coast of Portugal.—Whither did he go?—What happened to him there?

Page 43.

Who was his wife?—What effect did the perusal of Perestrello's papers have on Columbus?—With what places did he trade?—What did he acquire by these voyages?—What was the great object of voyagers at this time?—Why?—What was the only route to India which had ever been thought of before Columbus's time?—What route did he propose to take?

Page 44.

On what arguments, drawn from the figure and structure of the earth, did Columbus found his belief of a continent in the west?—What facts led to the same conclusion?—What led Columbus to believe that this western continent was connected with India?—Did Columbus suppose that the western continent was near the Western Isles?

Page 45.

To whom did Columbus communicate his opinions?—Did Paul encourage him?—To what design did Columbus's opinions lead him?—What was the first step towards prosecuting this design?—To whom did he first submit his project?—How was it received?—To whom next?

Page 46.

How did the king receive the proposal?—To whom did he refer it?—What was the result?—To whom did Columbus next apply?—When did he land in Spain?—To whom did he send his brother?—What circumstances were unfavourable to Columbus's success in Spain?—How was his character suited to please the Spanish?

Page 47.

What did he gain by it?—To whom did Ferdinand and Isabella remit the consideration of Columbus's project?—What remarks did the Spanish philosophers make on Columbus's project?—How long did Columbus urge his project before obtaining a report from Tala vera?—What was the answer of Ferdinand and Isabella founded on this report?—To what Spanish subjects did Columbus next apply?—With what success?

Page 48.

What had befallen Bartholomew Columbus?—Who prevented Columbus from leaving Spain, and going to England?—What was the character of Perez?—To whom did Perez apply on behalf of Columbus?—What did Isabella do?—What was the first effect of the interview?—What new friends did Columbus acquire?—How did Ferdinand regard Columbus's plot?

Page 49.

What demands did Columbus make?—How did the commissioners proceed?—What was the result of the negotiation?—What did Columbus then do?—What great event happened about this time?—What advantage did Quintanilla and Santangel take of it?—What arguments did they offer to the queen?

Page 50.

What was the effect?—What generous offer did Isabella make?—How did Santangel receive it?—When was the treaty of negotiation signed?—What was the first article?—The second?—Third?—Fourth?—Fifth?—How did Ferdinand behave?

Page 51.

Who defrayed the expense?—What precaution was taken with respect to the Portuguese?—Where was the expedition fitted?—Where is Palos?—Who assisted and accompanied Columbus?—Of what did the armament consist?—Who were the several commanders, and what were their vessels' names?—What was the number of men?—What was the whole sum employed in fitting out the squadron?—What circumstances rendered the undertaking a very bold one?

Page 52.

What religious act preceded the embarkation?—When did the squadron sail?—Where did they arrive August 13th?—Where are these islands?—What accident happened to the Pinta?—Whence and when did Columbus next take his departure?—What disposition did the sailors manifest?—How were the effects of it prevented?—What character and qualifications did Columbus now exhibit?

Page 53.

What did he endeavour to conceal?—What

new phenomenon respecting the compass alarmed them?—How did Columbus dissipate he fears occasioned by this appearance?—What wind did he fall in with?—What new appearance alarmed the sailors 400 leagues west of the Canaries?—How did Columbus reconcile them to this?—How far had they advanced, October 1st?—How far did Columbus pretend that they had advanced?

Page 54.

What did the sailors now resolve to do?—How did Columbus prevent them from open mutiny?—By what did he next steer his course?—Did he make the land in this direction?—What was the consequence?

Page 55.

By what means did he overcome this new difficulty?—What signs of land appeared?—What orders did Columbus give?—What did Columbus discover at 10 o'clock, P. M.?—From which ship was the cry of *land* first heard?—What was discovered in the morning?—What religious act was performed?—How did the crews behave towards Columbus?—What was done at sunrise?—What was discovered on shore?

Page 56.

How did the voyagers behave on landing?—For whom did they take possession of the country?—How did the natives regard the Spaniards and their ships?—Of this newly discovered island, what was the appearance of the soil?—Climate?—Trees?—Inhabitants?—What sort of trade was carried on between the Spaniards and natives?—What were the boats of the natives called?—What title and authority did Columbus assume?—What did he call the island?—Where is it?—Was it as rich as had been expected?

Page 57.

What induced Columbus to sail towards the south?—Whom did he take along with him?—To what other islands did he give names?—What did he next discover?—Whom did he send into the interior?—Give the particulars of their discoveries in the interior.—What is maize?—Does it appear by the narrative that this is an original production of Cuba?—Where did the natives tell Columbus that they found their gold?—What did he infer from this?—What part of the coast of Cuba did he explore?—Where is Porto del Principe?

Page 58.

To what island did the natives direct Columbus in quest of gold?—Where is Hayti?—What captain deserted the squadron?—When did Columbus reach Hayti?—What did he call the port?—The country?—What port did he next visit?—How did he here contrive to open a communication with the natives?—How did they behave?—Did they possess more gold than the natives of Cuba?—By whom was Columbus here visited?—How did this person behave?—What led Columbus to suppose that he had arrived at Japan?

Page 59.

Whither did he now direct his course?—What harbour did he put into?—What cazique governed the district?—What present did he make to Columbus?—When did Columbus set sail to visit Guacanahari?—Give an account of his shipwreck.—How did the natives behave?—How did Guacanahari?—What were now Columbus's circumstances?

Page 60.

Did Columbus determine to return to Spain?—What means did he adopt of prosecuting discoveries in Hayti?—How was an opportunity presented of colonizing the country?—Did the cazique accept his offer?—Give an account of the settlement.—How did Columbus strike terror into the natives?

Page 61.

What was the effect of firing the cannon?—How many men did Columbus leave?—Under whom?—What advice did he give?—When did he sail?—Whom did he overtake?—Did he excuse Pinzon?—What had Pinzon done in his absence?—What did Columbus now determine to do?—What preparations did he make?—How far and how long did he sail prosperously?

Page 62.

What now befell Columbus?—How were the sailors affected?—What did Columbus do to preserve a record of his voyage?—What land was discovered on the 15th?—Where are the Azores?—What disquieted Columbus here?—Whither was he driven by a second storm?—How was he treated there?

Page 63.

What satisfaction did Columbus enjoy?—How long did he remain in Lisbon?—When did he arrive in Palos?—After how long a voyage?—How was he received?—When did the Pinta arrive?—Where were the sovereigns?—What did they order?—Describe Columbus's journey.—His entrance into the city.—How was he received by Ferdinand and Isabella? How was he honoured?

Page 64.

How rewarded?—What was he commanded to do?—How was Columbus's discovery regarded in Europe?—To what opinion did Columbus adhere?—By what was it confirmed?—Was Columbus's opinion generally adopted?—What name was given to the country discovered by Columbus?—After the country was found not to be India, what was it called?—What were the natives called?

Page 65.

What number of ships were provided for the second expedition?—Of men?—What did they carry with them?—Did Ferdinand enter into the spirit of his subjects?—Who was pope at this time?—What grant did he make to Ferdinand and Isabella?—Where was the celebrated line drawn which was to separate the Spanish from the Portuguese possessions?—What preparations were made for converting the Indians?

Page 66.

When did Columbus sail on his second voyage?—Where did he touch?—How did he vary his course?—When did he make the land?—What did he call it?—What islands did he afterward visit?—Where is Dominica?—Martinica?—Marigalante?—Guadaloupe?—Antigua?—Porto Rico?—What people inhabited these islands?—Were they cannibals?—When did he arrive at Navidad?—What had happened there?—What account did the cazique's brother give of the colony?

Page 67.

What colony did Columbus now found?—What was the character of Columbus's colonists?—Were they suitable persons for colonizing a new country?—To what did their discontent lead?—How did Columbus treat those who conspired against him?—How many ships were sent home?—What did he request from Spain?

Page 68.

Whom did Columbus send to explore Cibao? —How did he proceed?—What were the Indian opinions concerning the horses?—How did they find the gold?—Why did Columbus call the port St. Thomas?—What distresses came upon the colonists?—Did these lead to discontents?

Page 69.

Who joined in them?—Was their discontent removed?—Whom did Columbus leave to govern the colony while he should make further discoveries?—What island did he discover?—What happened to him on the south coast of Cuba?—Whom did he meet on his return to Hispaniola?—Give an account of Bartholomew's adventures.

Page 70.

What had been the conduct of the soldiers under Margarita?—What were the habits of the Indians with respect to food?—What did they resolve to do?

Page 71.

What did Columbus determine to do?—What was the number of the Indians?—What king remained faithful to the Spaniards?—How was the attack managed?—What was the result? —How did Columbus then employ himself?—What tax did he impose?—Why did Columbus tax the Indians?

Page 72.

Who was Columbus's enemy at court?—What was his only means of counteracting the machinations of his enemies at court?—Why was the tribute peculiarly oppressive to the Indians?—What expedient did they devise for freeing themselves?—What was its effect on the Spaniards?—On the Indians?—What proportion of the inhabitants of Hayti perished?—What complaints were made of Columbus?—What was the consequence?—What person was appointed a commissioner to examine into Columbus's conduct?

Page 73.

How did Aguado behave in his new office?—What resolution did Columbus take?—To whom did he commit the administration of affairs?—What was he called?—Who was appointed chief justice?—What mistake did Columbus make in directing his course home? —What was the consequence?—How did he behave in this extremity?—How was he received at court?

Page 74.

What had he done for Spain?—What did he promise?—What was the effect on the king and queen?—What plan was now formed?—What sort of labourers were to go out?—How were they to be supported?—What improper persons did Columbus propose to take out?

Page 75.

What hindrances to Columbus's enterprise existed?—How long was he delayed by them? —How many ships were prepared?—What course did he resolve to steer?—When did he sail?—Where did he touch?—From the Canaries, how many ships were sent to Hispaniola? · What befell him near the equinoctial?

Page 76.

How did he alter his course?—What island was discovered, August 1st?—Where is it?—Near what river?—Describe the river.—How was Columbus's squadron endangered by it? —What did he call it?—What inference did he draw from its size and violence?—Was it confirmed?—What part of the continent of America did Columbus first visit?—What sort of people did he there find?—What animals? —What did the admiral imagine concerning it?—What compelled him to go to Hayti?—What islands did he discover on his way?—What did they become remarkable for?—What was Columbus's condition on his arrival?—What happened in his absence?

Page 77.

What city had the adelantado Bartholomew founded in Hayti?—Where is it?—How did he there employ the Spaniards?—Who rebelled against Bartholomew?—Who saved the fort at St. Domingo from the mutineers?—Whither did they retire?—What did they do?—What had befallen the ships sent by Columbus from the Canaries?—Who had gained a large part of the crews of these ships?—What was their character?

Page 78.

When did these ships arrive at St. Domingo?—Why was Columbus reluctant to fight the rebels?—How did he recover them to obedience?—How did he gain Roldan?—Did these negotiations occupy much time?—What new regulation concerning the Indians was introduced?—What did this regulation introduce? —What were the repartimientos?—What effect did they have?—What prevented Columbus from prosecuting his discoveries?—What did he send to Spain?—What complaints did Roldan make?—What did Columbus?

Page 79.

Which gained most credit?—For what purpose did Emanuel of Portugal send out a fleet? —To whom did he give the command?—What was his character?—Whence did he sail?—How long was he in passing the Cape of Good Hope?—Why?—Which way did he steer?—Where did he anchor?—What sort of people had he found on the east coast of Africa?—How did they change as he advanced north?—Whither did he go from Melinda?—Where is Melinda?—Calecut?—What sort of country and people did he find?—What is observed of the voyage?

Page 80.

When did he land at Lisbon, and after how long a voyage?—Give a summary of the discoveries of the fifteenth century.—What private adventurer set out for the new world?—With how many ships?—How did Fonseca, bishop of Badajos, assist him?—Give an account of his voyage.

Page 81.

Who accompanied him?—What was the consequence of Amerigo's account of the voyage?—What other private adventurers went to the new world?—Describe the voyage.—Describe Pinzon's voyage.—What did the king of Portugal undertake?—To whom did he give the command of the expedition?

Page 82.

Which way did Cabral steer, in order to avoid the coast of Africa?—What country did he accidentally discover?—For whom did he take possession of it?—Where is Brazil?—

Does it appear by this that America would have been discovered without Columbus's voyage?—What was the state of things in Hispaniola?—What was taking place in Spain to Columbus's disadvantage?

Page 83.

What was the effect of the accusations on the minds of the sovereigns?—What person was sent out to try and to supersede Columbus?—How did he proceed on his arrival?—What did Columbus do?—How was he treated?—How did he bear it?

Page 84.

How did Bovadilla render himself popular and Columbus unpopular?—How did he accumulate charges against Columbus?—How did the captain treat Columbus?—What was Columbus's answer to the captain's offer to take off his chains?—How were Ferdinand and Isabella affected on hearing of Columbus's arrival in chains?—What orders did they give?—How did he behave at the interview with the sovereigns?—Did they degrade Bovadilla?—Why did they not restore Columbus?

Page 85.

Whom did they appoint governor of Hispaniola?—How did Columbus manifest his feelings at this indignity?—What private adventurers fitted out two ships for America in January, 1501?—What coast did they discover?—What is that country now called?—What other adventurers visited the same coast?—For what was a fleet equipped at the public expense?—How was Bovadilla proceeding in Hispaniola?—How did he govern the Spanish colonists?—How did he treat the Indians?

Page 86.

What was the effect of this oppression on the Indians?—How many ships were there in Ovando's armament?—How many settlers?—How did the new governor, on his arrival, treat Bovadilla?—Roldan?—The Indians?—The Spaniards?—Who was Bovadilla?—Roldan?—What regulation was introduced respecting the gold?—What did Columbus demand of the sovereigns?—Why was it not granted?—How long was he urging his claim at court?—What opinion did Columbus adopt concerning a passage to the East Indies?

Page 87.

What did he ask of the sovereigns?—For what purpose?—What reasons disposed them to grant his request?—What had been the result of the Portuguese voyages to the East Indies?—What sort of fleet was allowed Columbus to find his passage to the East Indies?—Who accompanied him?—When did he sail?—Where did he touch?—What occasioned his going to Hispaniola?—What found he there?—What request did he make of Ovando?—Who was Ovando?—What advice did Columbus give him?—How were Columbus's request and his counsel treated?—What was the consequence?—Did Columbus suffer by the storm?

Page 88.

How many ships of Ovando's fleet were lost?—What men perished?—What amount of money was lost?—Were Columbus's effects saved?—What is remarked concerning this event by historians?—What construction did the people of that age put upon it?—When did Columbus leave Hispaniola?—What island did he discover?—What sort of inhabitants did he find?—What information did they give him?—Did Columbus go to the west?—What kingdom would he have found there?—Which way did he go?—What did he discover?—Describe the situation of these countries on the map.—Where is Cape Gracias a Dios?—Porto Bello?—Where did he attempt to fix a colony?—What was the result?

Page 89.

What misfortunes now befell Columbus?—Where was he wrecked?—When?—Who undertook to carry intelligence of his situation to Hispaniola?—In what sort of vessel?—Describe the voyage.—How were they treated on their arrival?—How long did they solicit assistance?—In the mean time, what happened to Columbus and his companions in Jamaica?—What did the seamen do?

Page 90.

How did the natives behave?—Relate Columbus's expedient for striking awe into the minds of the Indians?—What was the effect?—Meantime what had the mutineers done?—How did Ovando, the governor of Hispaniola, insult Columbus?

Page 91.

How did Columbus explain this cruel proceeding to his followers?—How did the mutineers proceed?—Who marched against them?—Describe the battle and its results.—What happened after tranquillity was restored?—How long had they remained on the island?—What island was it?—Which way is it from Hispaniola?—How far distant?—How did Ovando treat Columbus on his arrival at St. Domingo?—How did he treat the captain of the mutineers?—How the faithful men who had adhered to Columbus?—When did he sail for Spain?—What befell him on his voyage?—Where did he arrive?—Where is St. Lucar?—What event did he hear of on his arrival?—Why was this news afflictive to him?

Page 92.

What did Columbus demand of Ferdinand?—How were his claims treated?—What was the result?—When and where did he die?—How?

BOOK III.

What was the effect of Isabella's regulations in favour of the Indians of Hispaniola?—What was the effect of the king's claiming half the gold?—How did Ovando modify these regulations?

Page 93.

Were these acts of Ovando approved?—What was the effect of this new oppression of the Indians?—How did the Spaniards regard the Indians?—How did they treat them?—What occasioned the war against the cazique of Higuey?—How was it terminated?—Who was cazique of Xaragua?—How had she treated the Spaniards?

Page 94.

What exasperated the adherents of Roldan against her?—Of what did they accuse her?—With what force did Ovando march into her country?—Under what pretence?—Relate the manner in which he betrayed her and her people.—What was her fate?—What was the effect of this cruel treatment on the Indians?—How was Isabella's death a misfortune to the Indians?—How much of the revenues of the New World belonged to Ferdinand?—To whom did he confer grants?—How did the courtiers profit by these grants?—What was the effect in Hispaniola?

Page 95.

What amount of money was annually received from Hispaniola?—How did Ovando govern the Spaniards?—What new source of wealth did he open?—What was the effect?—Who seconded Ovando in promoting the welfare of the colony?—What court did he erect?—Where did it assemble?—Where is Seville?—How did he regulate the ecclesiastical government of America?—What did he prohibit?

Page 96.

How many inhabitants were there in Hispaniola when Columbus discovered it?—To what number were they reduced in fifteen years?—To what causes does the historian attribute this waste of human life?—What was its effect on the Spanish improvements?—What remedy did Ovando propose?—Under what pretence were the inhabitants of the Lucayo islands removed to Hispaniola?—How many were removed?—What urged the Spaniards to new discoveries?

Page 97.

Who was Juan Ponce de Leon?—What island did he settle?—Which way is it from Hispaniola?—Is it larger or smaller than Hispaniola?—What became of the original inhabitants of that island?—What two adventurers made a voyage to the continent?—What country did they discover?—How is it situated?—Between what bays?—What important discovery did Sebastian de Ocampo make?—What claim did Don Diego Columbus prefer against king Ferdinand?—How much time did he waste in fruitless importunity?—Before what council did he then bring his celebrated lawsuit with the king?—What was the decision?—How did Don Diego strengthen his influence at court?—At the instance of the duke of Alva and his family, what did king Ferdinand then do?

Page 98.

Who accompanied the new governor to Hispaniola?—How did he there live?—Who are descended from the persons who accompanied Don Diego Columbus?—How were the Indians treated by Don Diego?—For what purpose was Cubagua settled?—Who were employed to dive for pearls?—What was the effect?—How far south did Solis and Pinzon go in their second voyage?—Did they leave a colony?—What adventurers went out to colonize the north coast of South America?—Under whose patronage?—What part of the coast did Ferdinand give to Ojeda?—What part to Nicuessa?—Point these out on the map, and show to what governments they now belong.

Page 99.

Describe the manner in which the Spanish lawyers and priests directed these adventurers to take possession of South America.—Did the natives assent to the doctrines?—What did Ojeda and Nicuessa then do?—What was the character of the natives?—How were they armed?—What was the consequence?—What other disasters befell the Spaniards?

Page 100.

How many reinforcements did the colony receive from Hispaniola?—What befell the greatest part of the colony?—Where did the remnant settle?—Under whom?—What two other great Spanish leaders were originally engaged in this expedition?—Why did Cortes stay at Hispaniola?—What roused the spirit of adventure among the Spaniards?—What made them leave Hispaniola?—What island did Don Diego Columbus propose to conquer?—When?—Who was sent for that purpose?—With how many men?—What is the length of Cuba?

Page 101.

What was the character of the people of Cuba?—Did they prepare for defence?—Who opposed the Spaniards?—How was he treated?—Give an account of his conference with the Franciscan friar.—What was the effect of Velasquez's cruelty to Hatuey?—How many ships did Juan Ponce de Leon fit out?—Towards what islands did he sail?—Where did he touch?—What country did he discover?—Why did he call it Florida?—Where is it?—To whom does it now belong?—How did the natives behave?—Through what channel did he return to Porto Rico?—What curious tradition led Ponce de Leon to the Lucayos?

Page 102.

How is the Spanish belief of this tradition accounted for?—Where was Balboa's colony?—How did he try to gain from the crown a confirmation of his election as governor?—Relate the incident which happened in one of his excursions.—To what country did the cazique refer in this conversation?—What did Balboa suppose?

Page 103.

What preparations did Balboa make for his expedition?—Describe the isthmus of Darien—Was it easy to cross it?—What was Balboa's character?—What was the number of his men?—Of Indians who accompanied him?—For what purpose did he take dogs with him?—What difficulties did he encounter?—

Page 104.

How did he reassure his men?—How was he opposed?—What ensued?—How many days had they spent?—Relate the manner of Balboa's discovering the Pacific Ocean.—In what manner did he take possession of it?—What part of the Pacific did he discover?—Where is it?—What wealth did he obtain?—How?—What information did he receive concerning Peru?—What country did he suppose it to be near?

Page 105.

What did Balboa determine to do?—To what place did he return?—After how long an absence?—What officer distinguished himself in this expedition?—What was Balboa's first care?—What was the effect of this intelligence?—Who was Balboa's enemy at court?—Who was appointed governor of Darien instead of Balboa?—How many vessels and soldiers were sent out?—How many people embarked in the fleet?—How did he find Balboa engaged?—How was he received by him?

Page 106.

How did Balboa behave?—How was he treated?—What misfortunes befell the colony?—How did the forces of Pedrarias treat the surrounding Indians?—What country was desolated by him?—What is this country now called?—What accounts were sent to Spain by Balboa?—By Pedrarias?—What did king

Ferdinand do?—What did he order Pedrarias to do?

Page 107.

How did Pedrarias treat Balboa?—Who effected a reconciliation between them?—What was the consequence of it?—What was the first effect of their concord?—For what did he begin to prepare?—With what number of ships and men did he furnish himself?—How did Pedrarias regard this?—What did he order Balboa to do?—Relate the manner of his arrest, trial, and death.—Why did not the king punish Pedrarias for this arbitrary act?—Whither did he remove the colony?—Of what use was this removal?—Where is Santa Maria?—On what ocean Panama?

Page 108.

For what purpose did king Ferdinand fit out two ships?—Under whose command did he place them?—What river did he enter January 1st, 1516?—Where is Rio de Janeiro?—What mistake did he make concerning the Rio de la Plata?—What put a stop to their discoveries and sent the ships home?—How did the Spaniards still regard Hispaniola?—How did king Ferdinand retrench the authority of Don Diego Columbus in Hispaniola?—What did Don Diego do?—Who was appointed to the office of distributing the Indians?—How did he execute it?—How many Indians did he find of the 60,000 who had escaped their former oppressions?—What was the effect of his causing them to be sold at auction?

Page 109.

What was the occasion of a controversy between the Dominican and Franciscan friars?—Which party befriended the Indians?—To whom did they apply to decide the dispute?—To whom did Ferdinand refer it?—What was the decision?—Did it abolish the *repartimientos*?—What did the Dominicans then do?—What was the substance of the decree by which Ferdinand silenced them?

Page 110.

What grants did Ferdinand make?—What edict did he publish?—How did the Dominicans then proceed?—What new advocate for the Indians did the oppression of Albuquerque call forth?—What was his history and character?—How did he now attempt to serve the cause of the Indians?—How was he received by the king?—What did Ferdinand promise?

Page 111.

What prevented him from fulfiling his promise?—Who succeeded him?—How was Las Casas prevented from visiting Charles in the Low Countries?—How did Cardinal Ximenes settle the affair?—Why did he confide the office of superintendents to monks of St. Jerome?—What lawyer was joined with them?—What title did he give to Las Casas?—Who opposed this measure of Ximenes?—How did he treat them?—Did they issue the necessary despatches?—How did these new-made officers proceed on their arrival in Hispaniola?—What was the effect on the colonists?—What conclusion did the fathers of St. Jerome afterward arrive at?

Page 112.

What were the habits of the Indians?—What did the superintendents find necessary?—What did they endeavour to secure?—How?—What did Zuazo do?—Who was Zuazo?—How were the Spanish settlers pleased with Zuazo and the superintendents?—To whom did they give the credit of the whole?—Give an account of Las Casas's behaviour.—Where did he take shelter?—With what determination did he set sail for Europe?—In what state did he find Cardinal Ximenes?—Who took the government?—Who were Charles's counsellors?

Page 113.

How did Las Casas ingratiate himself with Charles's Flemish ministers?—What scheme did he censure?—Who joined in his censures?—Who were recalled?—Who superseded them?—What was he instructed to do?—What was the objection to treating the Indians as free subjects?—What remedy did Las Casas propose for this?—Had this trade been abolished?—When had slaves been imported into America?—By whose permission?—For what reasons were they preferred to the Indians?—Had Cardinal Ximenes encouraged this traffic?—Why did Las Casas?

Page 114.

Was his plan adopted?—What patent did Charles grant?—To whom?—To whom did he sell it?—What did they do?—What limited the effects of their trade?—What other expedient did Las Casas have recourse to?—Who defeated it?—What did he next attempt?—Of what country did he solicit a grant?—How, and with what sort of people did he propose to colonize it?

Page 115.

What objections did the bishop of Burgos and the Council of the Indies make to this scheme?—To whom did he then have recourse?—To whom did Charles refer his petition?—What country did they grant Las Casas?—Who censured this determination?—What was the effect?—For what did the emperor Charles V. himself discover an inclination?—How was an opportunity afforded?—Where was the court then held?—Where is Barcelona?—For what purpose did Charles resolve to confront Las Casas and the bishop of Darien?—Where was the solemn audience held?

Page 116.

Who attended?—What observations did the bishop of Darien make?—What reply did Las Casas make?—What patent did Charles grant?—What hindered Las Casas from procuring settlers?—How many did he obtain?—Did he set sail with these?—Where did he touch?—What news did he hear there?—Owing to the high price of negroes, whither had the Spaniards lately resorted for slaves?

Page 117.

How did they obtain them?—How were the Indians of Cumana affected by these atrocities?—Whom did they murder?—How did the people of Hispaniola resolve to revenge this?—What number of ships and men were placed under the command of Ocampo?—For what purpose?—Where did Las Casas meet this armament?—What did he perceive to be the effect of this movement?—Whither did he go?—How was he received there?—What had rendered him unpopular there?—What experiment had Figueroa there made?—What inference was drawn from the result of this experiment?—What did Las Casas obtain in Hispaniola?

Page 118

What did he find on returning to Porto Rico?—What did he do with the remnant of his colonists ?—What rendered their situation dangerous ?—What did he call the place where he established his colony ?—Did the troops remain with him ?—Whither did he go in search of protection for his colony ?—What happened to them in his absence ?—Whither did he retreat after the complete failure of all his schemes ?—What comment does the historian make on Las Casas's system ?—When did Diego Velasquez conquer Cuba ?—What had been the state of the island under his administration ?—How is Cuba situated ?—Had the sea west of it been explored ?—Was this sea considered the est field for discoveries ;

Page 119.

What officers were desirous to attempt discoveries in that quarter ?—Whom did they persuade to join them ?—Who approved and assisted in the design ?—How many men embarked ?—When ?—From what port ?—Where is this port situated ?—Who was pilot ?—Why did they sail due west ?—When did they make land ?—What did it prove to be ?—Where is this cape ?—Where is Yucatan ?—How were they received ?—By what sort of people ?—On landing, what befell them ?—Which way did he sail when he left this place ?—What place did he come to next ?—Where is this place ?—Which way from Cape Catouche ?—What surprised the Spaniards ?—Where did they find a river ?—Which way is this place from Campeachy ?—What befell the watering party which Cordova landed ?—What befell the Spaniards on their way back to Cuba ?

Page 120.

What befell Cordova on his return ?—Did the result of this expedition damp the ardour of discovery ?—Why did Velasquez encourage a new expedition ?—How many embarked in the new enterprise ?—Under whose command ?—Whence and when did it sail ?—Who was pilot ?—What was the first land they made ?—Where is this island ?—Why did they not stay there ?—Where did they next land ?—What transpired there ?—Which way did they sail from Potonchan ?—What did they observe on the coast ?—What country did one of the soldiers say it resembled ?—What name did Grijalva, in consequence, give the country ?—Was this name retained ?—Where did they next land ?—Where is the river Tabasco ?

Page 121.

How were they here received ?—At what place did they next touch ?—Where is the province of Guaxaca ?—How were the Spaniards there received ?—What amount of gold did they obtain for their toys in trade with the natives ?—Who did the natives say was their king ?—Where did Grijalva behold the horrid effects of the Indian superstitions ?—Whom did he despatch to Valasquez ?—With what information ?—From what place ?—To what river did he then proceed ?—What did Grijalva's officers wish him to do ?—Why did he not comply with their wishes ?—To what port of Cuba did he return?—When ?—After how long a voyage ?—What had the Spaniards discovered in this imortant voyage ?

Page 122.

In what direction had they pursued their course ?—How far ?—For what purposes did Velasquez send a confidential messenger to Spain ?—What preparations did he make before Grijalva's return ?

*Note.*—The editor has omitted the Fourth Book in his set of Questions, as it interrupts the narrative with a disquisition concerning the aborigines of America, which may be considered as superseded by the works of writers of later date and better means of information on that particular subject.

## BOOK V.

Page 197.

What did Grijalva find on his return to Cuba ?—Who was the author of this expedition ?—Did he defray a considerable part of the expense ?—What sort of commander did Velasquez seek ?—Could he find one courageous and servile too ?—Who was recommended to him by Lares and Ducro ?—Where and when was Cortes born ?—Where is Estremadura ?—To what university was Cortes sent ?—Did he finish his studies there ?—Why did his father send him abroad ?

Page 198.

What were then the two great fields of military enterprise for the Spanish youth ?—What prevented Cortes from going to Italy ?—Under whose patronage did he seek his fortune in America ?—How was he employed in Hispaniola ?—With whom did he go to Cuba ?—When ?—How did Velasquez reward his services there ?—What was now his character ?—What did Velasquez expect from him ?—How did he proceed on receiving his commission ?—How were his zeal and activity misrepresented to Velasquez ?

Page 199.

Was Velasquez suspicious of him ?—Why was his departure hastened ?—When did he sail ?—From what port ?—Where did he touch for stores and recruits ?—What did Velasquez do after his departure ?—Whom did he empower to deprive Cortes of his commission ?—How did Cortes prevent this ?—For what port did Cortes next sail ?—What did Velasquez then do ?—How did Cortes hear of Velasquez's intentions ?

Page 200.

How did Cortes remove Diego de Ordaz ?—Why ?—What information did Cortes then give his troops ?—What request did they make ?—What ensued ?—Were great efforts made in fitting out this expedition ?—What was the number and size of the vessels ?—Of men ?—How were the soldiers divided and commanded ?—How many of them had muskets ?—How many were crossbow-men ?—How were the rest armed ?—What sort of defensive armour did they wear ?—How many horses, field-pieces, and falconets had they ?—When did they sail ?—What sign and superscription was on their banners ?

Page 201.

Were they confident of success ?—Where did Cortes first touch ?—What important acquisition did he make there ?—Where did he next touch ?—How was the disposition of the Indians here altered since Grijalva's visit ?—Did Cortes make war on them ?—With what success ?—Where did Cortes next land ?—How was he here received ?—What embarrassed him in his intercourse with these Indians ?—How was he relieved ?—Give an account of Donna Marina.

Page 202.

Who had sent two persons to Cortes ?—For what purpose had they been sent ?—What answer did he give ?—What did he do next morning ?—Who entered the camp next morning ?

—How did Cortes receive them?—What did he tell them?—How did they receive the information?—How did they attempt to conciliate him?—Of what did this present consist?—What was its effect?—On what did Cortes insist?—During the interview, how were some of the Mexican attendants employed?—How did Cortes take advantage of this?

Page 203.

What exhibitions of power and skill did he make?—How were the Indians affected by it?—What information and presents were now sent to Montezuma?—What refinement in police had the Mexican monarchs introduced?—How far was the capital from St. Juan de Ulua?—How soon were the presents transported and the answer returned?—How did the Mexican ambassadors renew the negotiation?—Of what did these presents consist?—How did Cortes receive them?—With what message were they accompanied?

Page 204.

What reply did Cortes make?—What did the astonished Mexicans prevail on him to do?—What was the state of the Mexican empire at this time?—How long had it existed?—What was its length and breadth?—The character of the people?—The situation of the monarch?—What would have been the result, if Montezuma had brought his forces at once to act against the Spanish intruders?—What was Montezuma's general character?—What symptoms had he discovered since the appearance of the Spaniards?—What seems to have been the remote source of his indecision and fear?

Page 205.

Does this tradition account in part for the alarm of Montezuma and his subjects?—What was the effect on Montezuma of Cortes's refusal to depart?—What did his counsellors advise?—With what was their positive injunction to Cortes to depart accompanied?—What two parties existed in the Spanish camp?—Had Cortes become popular among the soldiers?

Page 206.

During the intrigues in the camp, who arrived from the Mexican court?—With what?—When Cortes refused to depart, how did Teutile behave?—What happened next morning?—How did the adherents of Velasquez take advantage of this?—Whom did they send to remonstrate with Cortes?—What request did they make through Ordaz?—What orders did Cortes then issue?—What ensued?—Had Cortes foreseen this?—Did he affect surprise at it?—What did he declare?—What did he say had been his own private opinion?

Page 207.

What did he offer to do?—How was the offer received?—Were the malecontents obliged to join in the enthusiastic applause expressed by the other soldiers?—What did Cortes set about?—What officers of the colony were elected by his contrivance?—What sort of persons were chosen?—Did they acknowledge dependence on Velasquez?—What name did they give the settlement?—What is this in Spanish?—What is the place now called?—How is St. Juan de Ulua situated with respect to Vera Cruz?—What did Cortes do at the first meeting of the council?—What was the substance of his harangue?—What did he do after having finished his discourse?

Page 208.

Was his resignation accepted?—To what offices was he then elected?—Who ratified the choice?—On accepting his new commission, how did Cortes proceed?—What did the adherents of Velasquez do?—Who of them were arrested by Cortes?—How were they treated?—What was the effect on their dependants?—How did Cortes conciliate these three leaders?—Did they always afterward remain faithful to him?—What was the chief instrument of Cortes's intrigue?—What caziques offered friendship to Cortes?—Why?—What did Cortes infer from this offer?

Page 209.

How did he receive the Zempoallans?—What place had been fixed on for a settlement?—How far from Vera Cruz?—Which way?—In marching thither whom did Cortes visit?—What did he learn from the cazique?—To what place did Cortes continue his march?—Relate the manner of building and fortifying this town.—Who assisted the Spaniards in their labours?—How did Cortes gain the caziques of Zempoalla and Quiabislan to his interest while the town was built?—What insult did they offer to the Mexican power?

Page 210.

Who saved the deputies of Montezuma from being sacrificed?—How did the two caziques now complete their union with the Spaniards?—What did they offer?—How long had Cortes been in Mexico?—What had he reason to apprehend?—Why?—Before he began his march towards the capital of Mexico, what did he persuade the magistrates of Vera Cruz to do?—In this letter, what did they say concerning Velasquez?—Concerning Cortes and his officers?—What request did they make?—What did they say concerning the country?—Did Cortes write?

Page 211.

What did he prevail on his soldiers to do?—Who were sent with the letters and present?—With what instructions?—What alarming event occurred while the vessel was preparing for their departure?—How was the conspiracy betrayed?—What appearances did Cortes now observe in his army?—What did he apprehend?—What did he resolve to do?—How did he prevail on his soldiers to destroy the ships?—How was the project executed?—What remark does the historian make on this transaction?

Page 212.

What act of Cortes at this time gave great offence to the Zempoallans?—How were the consequences of it avoided?—When did Cortes march from Zempoalla?—With what forces and equipments?—Where and with whom did he leave a garrison?—With what did the cazique of Zempoalla supply him?—Where is Flascala?—Which way from Vera Cruz?—What was the character of the people of Flascala?—How did Cortes hope to gain their alliance?

Page 213.

Whom did Cortes send to the Flascalans?—How were they treated?—Why?—When did Cortes advance into the Flascalan territories?—What loss did he sustain in the first battle with the Flascalans?—What precaution did he then take?—How long did he suffer assaults from them?—Did they make any impression on the Spaniards?—What peculiar practice was a hindrance to them?

Page 214.

What were their weapons?—Were they of

much use against the Spaniards?—What examples of generosity did the Flascalans exhibit?—When repulsed, to whom did they have recourse?—What answer did the priests give?—What did they do in consequence of the priests' opinion?—Did their night-attack succeed?—To what did they then incline?

Page 215.

What made the Flascalans suppose the Spaniards to be benevolent?—What circumstance favoured the opposite opinion?—What curious address did their deputies make?—On what terms was peace concluded?—What sufferings had the Spaniards endured?—What caused them to forget these sufferings?—How long did Cortes remain at Flascala?—For what purpose?—What information did he there acquire?

Page 216.

How did the Flascalans regard the Spaniards?—What did they offer?—How did the Spaniards all consider themselves?—Did Cortes attempt to convert the Flascalans to Christianity?—Did they acknowledge the truth of what he taught?—What did they claim of him and the other Europeans?—What did Cortes demand?—When refused, what was he about to do?—Who prevented him?—By what arguments?

Page 217.

When leaving the Flascalans in the exercise of their own rites, what did Cortes require?—What warning did the Flascalans give Cortes on his leaving the country for Mexico?—How many Flascalans accompanied him?—Towards what place did they march?—Where is Cholula?—Had Montezuma consented to their going thither?—How was the place considered by the Mexicans?—What offerings were there made?—Why did Montezuma invite the Spaniards thither?—What signs of treachery did two Flascalans discover?—What information did Marina obtain?—How did Cortes prepare to revenge this treachery?—Describe the massacre.

Page 218.

How long did it last?—How many Cholulans fell?—How many Spaniards?—What did Cortes then order?—Was he obeyed?—Towards what city did Cortes next advance?—Which way is Mexico from Cholula?—In his march, what dispositions did he observe among the Mexicans towards Montezuma's government?—Where did the Spaniards first behold the plain of Mexico?—Describe the appearance of the plain.—The situation of the city of Mexico.—What messages did Cortes receive from Montezuma?—What persuasion seems to have preserved the Spaniards from any attack?

Page 219.

Over what did they continue their march?—Who met them as they drew near the city?—Whose approach did they announce?—Who preceded Montezuma?—How was he attended?—Describe the pageant.—How did Cortes receive him?—Describe the ceremonial.—What did the Spaniards hear among the crowd of Mexicans?—What did Montezuma say at parting?—Describe the place allotted for the Spaniards.—How did Cortes strengthen it?—What happened in the evening?

Page 220.

What tradition did Montezuma communicate to Cortes?—What reply did Cortes make?—What happened next morning?—How were the three succeeding days employed?—How is Mexico situated?—How watered?—What is the size of the two largest lakes?—On what is the city of Mexico built?—By what was the access to the city?—What was the length of these causeways?—How were they constructed?—Describe the buildings.—How large w the great square for the market?

Page 221.

What was now the situation of the Spaniards?—What circumstances rendered it very perilous?—What had Cortes heard before leaving Cholula?—Of what did he become sensible on his arrival in the city of Mexico?—On what did his success depend?

Page 222.

What bold resolution did he form?—How did his officers at first receive it?—Did they afterward accede to it?—How did he prepare to execute it?—Who accompanied him?—How was Cortes received?—How did he address Montezuma?—How did Montezuma behave?—What orders did he give?—What reason did Cortes then offer for Montezuma's repairing to his quarters?—What did he promise?—How was the proposition received?—What was the reply?—How long did the interview last?

Page 223.

What exclamation did Velasquez de Leon utter?—What was the effect?—How were the officers and people of Montezuma affected by his surrender?—How did Montezuma hush the tumult?—What remark is made concerning this transaction?—How was Montezuma received and treated in the Spanish quarters?—Who were brought prisoners to Mexico?—By whose order?—For what act?—How were they tried?—What was their sentence?—What part had these men acted?—Of what was the pile composed on which they suffered death?

Page 224.

How was Montezuma treated?—How did this treatment affect him and his attendants?—What happened on the return of Cortes from the execution?—What motive of policy seems to have actuated Cortes in these atrocious acts of cruelty to the officers, and contumely towards the sovereign?—Did they produce the desired effect?—How long did Montezuma remain tranquilly in the Spanish quarters?—How were the affairs of the empire conducted?

Page 225.

How was Montezuma guarded when hunting beyond the lake?—Is this management of Cortes considered an extraordinary refinement in policy?—For what purpose did he send Spaniards into the interior?—While they were thus employed, what did Cortes do?—What was still wanting to complete his security?—How was this attained?—What did he next urge Montezuma to do?—Did he comply?

Page 226.

In what manner was Montezuma affected on making his submission to the Spanish government?—How did his princes receive the proposal?—How did Cortes reconcile them to it?—With what was Montezuma's submission accompanied?—To what did the amount of treasure received from the Mexicans amount?—How much was set apart for the king?—For Cortes?—How was the rest divided?—How much did each soldier's share amount to?—Were they satisfied?

Page 227.

Why was the amount of gold collected in so rich a country so small?—Did the Mexicans use it as money?—For what purposes did they use it?—Did they work the mines of their country?—How did they obtain gold?—On what point was Montezuma inflexible?—What was the effect of his firmness on Cortes?—How was Cortes deterred from throwing down all the idols?—With what did he content himself?—What did the Mexicans now resolve?—How did they propose to effect it?—What did Montezuma observe to Cortes?

Page 228.

What threat did he add to this declaration?—What answer did Cortes give?—What preparations did he make?—How long had his messengers to Spain been gone?—What was his situation?—What news was brought by a Mexican courier?—What by Sandoval's courier?—How had Velasquez learned the situation of Cortes?—How was he affected by the intelligence?

Page 229.

How had Velasquez's messenger been received at the Spanish court?—What appointment had Velasquez received?—What did he determine to do?—What number of ships, men, and cannon composed his armament?—Under what commander?—What were his instructions?—When and where did he land?—How did he obtain interpreters and information of Cortes's movements?—How did these soldiers misrepresent Cortes's situation?—What message did he send to Sandoval, the governor of Vera Cruz?—How were his messenger and suite treated by Sandoval?—How by Cortes?—What was the benefit which Cortes derived from this?—What information did they give concerning Narvaez?

Page 230.

What representations had Narvaez secretly conveyed to Montezuma?—What was their effect on the Mexicans?—On Montezuma?—What did Cortes resolve to do?—Whom did he send to Narvaez?—How did he receive Olmedo?—How was Olmedo received by Narvaez's men?—What was the effect of Cortes's presents on Narvaez's soldiers?

Page 231.

What course did Narvaez take?—What did Cortes determine to do?—Whom did he leave in charge of Montezuma and the capital?—With how many men?—When reinforced by Sandoval, what was his force?—How did he arm his soldiers against Narvaez's cavalry?—Towards what place did he advance?—What prevented an accommodation between Cortes and Narvaez?—How did Cortes take advantage of the intercourse between the two armies?—How were nearly all Narvaez's officers and men inclined?—What was the effect of this on Narvaez?

Page 232.

Which leader offered battle?—Was the offer accepted?—What compelled Narvaez's soldiers to retreat to Zempoalla?—What did Cortes now resolve?—What part of the undertaking did he intrust to Sandoval?—To Olid?—What did he reserve for himself?—Describe the action.

Page 233.

What befell Narvaez?—What was the result of the action?—What was the loss of Cortes?—Of Narvaez?—How were the vanquished party treated?—What was the effect of this treatment? How many soldiers had Cortes now?—To what should these events be ascribed?—What news came from Mexico?

Page 234.

What had occasioned the revolt in the city of Mexico?—What was its extent?—What did Cortes do on hearing the news of this revolt?—What number of Flascalans joined him?—What did he learn on entering the Mexican territories?—What precautions did the Mexicans neglect to take?—What was the consequence?—When did Cortes enter the city?—How did Alvarado and his soldiers receive him?—Of what imprudence was Cortes guilty?

Page 235.

Who reported the contemptuous expressions of Cortes?—What was their effect?—Where was the first attack made?—What discovery was made by the Mexicans on this occasion?—What happened next day?—What was the effect of this determined attack on Cortes?—How did it affect the soldiers who had come with Narvaez?—What was the cause of the Mexicans ceasing from hostilities at night?—What did Cortes do next day?—What animated the courage of the Mexicans?—What enabled the Spaniards to cut through the Mexicans wherever they met?—What disadvantages did they suffer from fighting among houses?

Page 236.

Did the Spaniards effect any thing decisive on the second day of battle?—What loss did they suffer?—What happened to Cortes in the next sally?—What expedient was now resorted to?—What was the effect of Montezuma's appearance?—What did he advise?—How was his harangue received?—When Montezuma fell, how did his subjects behave?—How did Montezuma treat Cortes's attempt to console him?—In what manner did he die?—For what did Cortes now prepare?—What new motion of the Mexicans engaged him in new conflicts?—Who was commissioned to dislodge them from the tower?—How often was he repulsed?

Page 237.

What did Cortes then do?—What extraordinary instance of self-devotion in two Mexicans is recorded?—When possessed of the tower, how did the Spaniards dispose of it?—What rendered a retreat absolutely necessary?—How did the Spaniards attempt to effect their escape?—Who commanded the van?—The rear?—The centre?—What relations of Montezuma were carried with them?—How did the Mexicans interrupt their retreat?—Describe the attack.

Page 238.

What happened when the Spaniards began to give way?—Which general first passed the causeway, and reached the mainland?—With how many men?—What did they hear?—Where did those who escaped from the city to the mainland assemble?—What number?—What trait of feeling was observed in Cortes?—What distinguished officer fell in the action?—What supplies were lost?—What number of Flascalans?—What injury was occasioned by the gold in possession of the Spaniards?

Page 239.

Where did the Spaniards take shelter?—Which side of the lake were they on?—On which side was Flascala?—Which end of the lake were they obliged to go round?—Under whose guidance?—To what distresses were they exposed in their retreat towards Flascala?—What circumstance animated them?—Where did they arrive on the sixth day?—What exclamation did they hear from the Mexicans as they approached towards it?—How was its meaning explained?—What was the effect of this sight on the Spaniards?—What did Cortes do?

Page 240.

How did Cortes effect the dispersion of this great army?—What treasure did he get?—Where did they arrive next day?—How were they received by the Flascalans?—What losses did Cortes now hear of?—Was he discouraged from his undertaking by this intelligence?

Page 241.

What colony of the Spaniards in New Spain remained unmolested?—How did Cortes secure the Flascalan chiefs?—What did he bring from Vera Cruz?—For what did he send to Hispaniola and Jamaica?—What did he prepare to build?—What portion of his army was discontented?—What was the effect of their discontent?—What was the utmost which Cortes could effect with them?—What expedition did he employ them in?

Page 242.

What was its success?—How did he afterward employ his troops?—How did Cortes gain the soldiers sent by Velasquez to reinforce Narvaez?—What other reinforcement did Cortes receive?—What occasioned their joining him?—What reinforcement did he receive from Spain?—What was now the amount of his army?

Page 243.

Whom did Cortes now dismiss?—What number of soldiers and guns did he then muster?—Of Flascalans and other friendly Indians?—When did he begin his march towards Mexico?—Who had succeeded Montezuma?—How had he shown his courage and capacity?—What preparations had he made for resisting the renewed attack of the Spaniards?—Had he succeeded in gaining the Flascalans?—What happened in the midst of his preparations?—Who succeeded Quetlavaca?

Page 244.

Of what city did Cortes take possession?—Where was it situated?—How did Cortes secure his possession of this place?—Was he ready to attack the city?—How did he employ his troops?—What was the condition of most of the cities adjacent to the city of Mexico?—How did Cortes prevail on several of them to acknowledge the king of Castile as their sovereign?—Did Guatimozin attempt to prevent this?

Page 245.

What soldiers formed a conspiracy in the Spanish camp?—Who headed it?—How far had it proceeded?—How was it betrayed?—How suppressed?—By what stroke of policy did Cortes retain the allegiance of all the surviving conspirators?

Page 246.

Whom did Cortes send to bring down the materials for the brigantines to the lake?—With what force?—What did these materials consist of?—In what manner were they conveyed?—By how many Tamenes?—What were the Tamenes?—How did they carry these heavy articles?—How far did the company extend when most scattered?—Did they arrive safe at Tezeuco?—What number of men, horses, and cannon arrived at Vera Cruz from Hispaniola?—How long was the canal through which the brigantines were conveyed from the building-place to the lake?—When were they launched?—With what ceremonies?

Page 247.

How did Cortes determine to attack the city?—To what officers did he assign the three points of attack?—What did he reserve for himself?—How did Alvarado and Olid distress the inhabitants of the city?—In what condition did they find the towns which they were sent to occupy on the borders of the lake?—How did Guatimozin attempt to destroy the Spanish brigantines?—Describe the attack, and its result.—Of what advantage did Cortes find the possession of the lake?—Did Cortes conduct the siege in a regular manner?—What was done each morning?

Page 248.

What rendered this mode of warfare necessary?—How long did Cortes adhere to it?—How did he then attempt to take the city?—What officer was charged to secure a retreat?—How?—How did he discharge the duty?—How did Guatimozin take advantage of his neglect?

Page 249.

How did he inspirit his men?—Describe the consequences of this movement of Guatimozin.—How many Spaniards were lost?—What did the Spaniards observe in the city at night?—How did Cortes bear his misfortune?—What proclamation did the Mexicans send into the country?

Page 250.

How did Cortes defeat this stratagem?—When the eight days expired, how did the Indians proceed?—How many of them joined Cortes?—How did Cortes now proceed in the siege?—What weapons did his men use?—How did Cortes deprive the besieged Mexicans of supplies?—What were the consequences?—How did Guatimozin behave?

Page 251.

How much of the city was laid in ruins?—What did the Mexicans now design?—How did they endeavour to conceal this design?—Who was ordered to watch their movements on the lake?—Relate the capture of Guatimozin.—What was his address to Cortes?—What was the effect of his capture?—How long had the siege lasted?—By whose aid did Cortes effect the reduction of Mexico?

Page 252.

In what were the Spaniards disappointed?—What had Guatimozin done with his treasures?—By what deed did Cortes sully the glory of his conquest?—Relate the behaviour of Guatimozin under the torture.—What was the consequence of the fate of the capital?—How far did the Spaniards penetrate?—What new discovery did Cortes now meditate?

Page 253.

Who was Ferdinand Magellan?—Where had he served?—Whither did he go, on quitting the service under Albuquerque?—What offer did he make to the king of Portugal?—Why was his suit refused?—How did Magellan manifest his indignation at this treatment?—Where did he next offer his project?—To wha.

minister did he apply?—What monarch ordered an expedition to be equipped under Magellan?—What titles were given him?—When did he sail?—From what port?—With how many ships and men?

Page 254.

Where did he search for a passage to India? —What river did he reach January 12th, 1520? —What led him to suppose that this was the long-sought passage?—What made him renounce the idea?—Where did he winter?—In what latitude?—What events transpired there? —In what latitude did he discover the strait? —How long was he in passing through it to the great Southern Ocean?—What name did he give to the strait?—How long did he sail northwest without discovering land?—What did the crews suffer?—Why did they call the ocean Pacific?—What islands did he discover March 6th?—What others?—What happened at one of them?—At what place did the expedition arrive November 8th?

Page 255.

What surprised the Portuguese there?—What sort of cargo was put on board the Victory?—Under whose command did the expedition return to Spain?—By what route?—After how long a voyage?—Was this the first voyage round the world?—To whom belongs the honour of these great discoveries?—What merit now belonged to Spain?—For what did their men of science contend?—In what trade did their merchants engage?—For what sum did Charles V. give up the rich commerce of the Spice Islands to the Portuguese?—Was it ever recovered by Spain?—What important commercial effects resulted to Spain from the voyage of Magellan?

Page 256.

While effecting the conquest of Mexico, of what was Cortes destitute?—Who was sent to supersede him?—By whose influence? —When and where did Tapia land?—What was his character?—How did Cortes prevail upon him to abandon the province?—With what did he send deputies to Spain?—What request were they ordered to urge?—At what juncture did they arrive in Spain?—How was their account received?—What appointment did the emperor give to Cortes?—What authority had Cortes already exercised?

Page 257.

Where did he determine to establish the seat of government?—Did he attend to the mines and to the agricultural interests of the country?—What did he grant his officers?—Did the Mexicans submit to their conquerors without resistance?—How did the several rebellions end?—How were the common people treated?—The chiefs?—How many were burnt at once in Panuco?—By whose command?—With the advice of Cortes?—What circumstance heightened the cruelty of the scene?—What other horrible example of severity was Cortes guilty of?—What was the effect of these examples on the inferior Spanish officers?

Page 258.

Who distinguished himself by acts of cruelty?—What circumstance probably saved the Mexicans from extermination?—When were the rich mines of Mexico discovered?—What was then the state of the colony?—Were the conquerors of Mexico enabled to live in ease and splendour?—What arrangement did Charles V. make?—What was the character of these commissioners?—What representations did they make concerning Cortes?—What effect did these have on the ministers?

Page 259.

Did they infuse the same suspicions into Charles's mind?—What did he order?—What prevented the execution of Ponce de Leon's commission?—What was its effect on the mind of Cortes?—Were his actions still misrepresented to his sovereign?—What was the consequence?—What did the followers of Cortes advise?—What did Cortes do?—How did he appear in Spain?—What did he take with him? —Who attended him?—How was he received? —What honours and rewards did he receive? —How was he treated by the emperor himself?—Was he reinstated in his office?—What department was committed to him?

Page 260.

To whom was the supreme direction of civil affairs in Mexico given?—Who was afterward made viceroy?—What effect did this arrangement have on Cortes?—What did he now engage in?—What befell the squadrons sent out by him to make discoveries?—What did he then do?—What country did he discover?—When did he return once more to Spain?—What sort of reception did he meet with?—How did the emperor treat him?—How was the rest of his life passed?—When did he die? —In what particulars did his fate resemble that of all the other persons who had distinguished themselves in the discovery or conquest of the New World?

## BOOK VI.

Page 261.

Who discovered the Pacific Ocean?—What was the effect of this discovery on the adventurers of the 16th century?—For what purpose were several armaments fitted out?—Under what sort of leaders?—What opinion resulted from their failure?—What three persons resolved to execute Balboa's scheme?—Who was Pizarro?—What was his character? —Where did he first serve?—Where afterward?—With what success?

Page 262.

Who was Almagro?—What was his character?—Who was Luque?—Who authorized their confederacy?—What did Pizarro engage to do?—What did Almagro?—Luque?—How was the confederacy confirmed?—Whence did Pizarro sail?—With what force?—What retarded his progress?—Where did he touch?—What difficulties did he encounter?

Page 263.

Whither did he retire?—Describe Almagro's adventures.—What wound did he receive?—After joining Pizarro, whither did he repair?—For what purpose?—How many men did he raise?—What bay did he and Pizarro reach? —Where is it?—What sort of country did they find?—What prevented their invading it?—Whither did Pizarro retire?—Whither did Almagro go?—For what purpose?—What prevented his succeeding?—What did the governor of Panama do?—What advice did Almagro and Luque send to Pizarro?

Page 264.

What was Pizarro's resolution?—How many of his men adhered to him?—Where did they stay?—How long was it before the governor sent a vessel to their relief?—What did Pizarro induce the crew of the vessel and his followers o do?—What coast did they discover?—Where did they land?—Where is Tumbez?—What did they find there?—What chiefly attracted their notice?

Page 265.

After exploring the country, what did Pizarro take with him?—Whither did he then sail?—After how long an absence?—What is observed of Pizarro?—Did the governor of Panama still discourage Pizarro's scheme?—Why?—To whom did the three associates now esolve to apply?—What stations did they repectively resolve to apply for?—Who went o Spain to urge their suit?—How did Pizarro conduct at court?—How was his scheme regarded by the emperor Charles V. and his ministers?—What did he obtain for Luque?—For Almagro?

Page 266.

What did Pizarro secure to himself?—What was the extent of his territory?—Of his power with respect to his appointments?—Was he to be independent of the governor of Panama?—What did he engage to do in return for these concessions?—From what port did he sail?—In what manner?—Why secretly?—Who supplied him with money?—Where did he land?—Whither did he march?—What were the names of the four brothers who accompanied him?—What was their character?—Why was Almagro offended with Pizarro?—How was he pacified?—On what terms was the confederacy renewed?—What was their force?—When did Pizarro sail?

Page 267.

For what purpose was Almagro left at Panama?—How long was the voyage?—Where did Pizarro land his troops?—Which way did they march?—What difficulties did they encounter?—What amount of booty did they gain in Coaque?—What was the effect of this success?—Whither did Pizarro despatch ships?—Did he use force, or did he use policy in reducing the natives?—How long was he occupied in subjecting Puna?—Where is this island?—How long was he detained at Tumbez?—By what cause?—What reinforcements did he receive?—Under what commanders?—Where did he establish the first Spanish colony in Peru?—Under what name?

Page 268.

What was the extent of Peru at the time of the Spanish invasion?—What was the character of its early inhabitants?—Who, according to their tradition, appeared on the banks of the Titiaca lake?—From whom did they claim descent?—For what did they say they had been sent?—What city did they found?—What were their names?—What did Manco Capac teach?—What did Mama Ocollo?—What did Manco Capac introduce, after teaching the arts of civilized life?—What was thus founded?—What was at first the extent of the empire?—What was the nature of Manco's authority?

Page 269.

How were the incas regarded?—Were the royal family forbidden to ally themselves with their subjects?—Was their despotic power abused?—What was the character of twelve of their monarchs in succession?—Who was their monarch when the Spaniards first visited Peru?—What was his character?—What kingdom did he subject?—How did he violate the ancient laws?—When did he die?—How did he divide his empire?—What did Huascar require his brother to do?—How did Atahualpa proceed?—Which brother conquered?—What use did he make of his victory?—Why did he spare Huascar?

Page 270.

What was the state of the empire when Pizarro visited Peru the second time?—What prevented the Peruvians from resisting his encroachments?—Who sent to solicit his aid?—What did he determine to do?—Where did he leave a garrison?—With what force did he march?—Towards what place?—Who was there?—Who met him on his march?—What assurances did Pizarro send to Atahualpa?

Page 271.

What opinions did the Peruvians form concerning the Spaniards?—What sort of reception did the inca resolve to give them?—Did he, in consequence of this resolution, neglect good opportunities to cut them off?—Where did Pizarro take his station on entering Caxamalca?—Whom did he send to Atahualpa?—For what purpose?—How were they received?—What did they observe?—On their return, what did Pizarro resolve to do?

Page 272.

How did he prepare for seizing the inca?—In what style did the inca appear when he came to Pizarro's quarters?—What part did Father Valverde perform in this transaction?—Describe his proceedings.—What did he require of Atahualpa?—Was his harangue understood?—What was the inca's reply?

Page 273.

How did he exasperate the priest?—What did the priest say?—What did Pizarro do?—Describe the massacre of the people and the capture of the inca.—How many Peruvians fell?—How many Spaniards?—How were the Spaniards affected by their victory?—How was the inca affected by his misfortune?—Did Pizarro attempt to console him?—What discovery did the inca make?—What offer?—Was it accepted?

Page 274.

How was the gold collected, the inca being a prisoner?—Why was not his rescue attempted?—Did all the Spaniards remain at Caxamalca?—What news did Pizarro hear?—What number of soldiers did Almagro bring?—How was the inca affected with the intelligence of this reinforcement?—What news did he hear from his brother?—Why did this alarm him?—How did he dispose of Huascar?—Did the Spaniards wait for the reception of all the promised treasure before dividing it?—How much was set apart for the crown of Spain?—How much for Almagro's men?—How much remained for Pizarro and his men?

Page 275.

With what ceremonies was it divided?—How much did each soldier receive?—Is there any parallel for this in history?—Why did Pizarro allow sixty of his followers to go to Spain?—Did he now grant Atahualpa his liberty?—What is observed of this transaction?—Was the possession of Atahualpa's person of as great advantage to Pizarro as Montezuma's capture was to Cortes?—Why not?—What part of Pizarro's army was dissatisfied?—Why?

Page 276.

What did they insist on?—What alarmed

Pizarro?—Who increased his apprehensions? —Who was this miscreant?—Why did he wish to cut off Atahualpa?—How did Atahualpa hasten his own fate?—How did Pizarro seek to cover the guilt of Atahualpa's murder? —Who were his judges?—What crimes was he charged with?

Page 277.

How did Philippillo conduct during the trial? —What was Atahualpa's sentence?—How was he affected by it?—What did Valverde offer him for embracing the Christian faith?—How was he put to death?—Whom did Pizarro now invest with the ensigns of royalty? —Whom did the people of Cuzco acknowledge as inca?—What was the state of the country?

Page 278.

How did the people behave after Atahualpa's death?—How did the general who commanded for Atahualpa in Quito behave?—Were the Spaniards pleased with these appearances?—Towards what city did Pizarro march?—What had been the effect of the return of some of his followers with their gold to Panama?—How many men had he now?—Was he opposed?—What was the result?—Did he take Cuzco?—What treasures were found there?—When did Atahualpa's son die?—Who was then acknowledged as inca?—What general set out to reduce Quito?

Page 279.

What difficulties did he encounter?—Did he take the city?—What disappointment did he meet there?—What other general advanced to attack Quito?—With how many men?—Where did he land?—What route did he take?—What hardships did he suffer?—How many men did he lose?—On arriving at the plain of Quito, whom did he find opposed to him?—On what terms did Alvarado agree to return to Guatimala?—What did most of his followers do?—When did Ferdinand Pizarro land in Spain?—What was the effect of his wealth?—How was he received by the emperor?

Page 280.

How were his brother's services recompensed?—How was Almagro rewarded?—How was Ferdinand?—Did he set out again for Peru?—When Almagro heard of his promotion, what did he do?—Who opposed him? What was the effect of Francis Pizarro's arrival?—What were the terms of their reconciliation?—To what part of the country did Pizarro now march?—How did he employ himself?

Page 281.

Where did he establish the capital of the empire?—Where is Lima?—Cuzco?—Quito? —Callao?—Whither did Almagro march?—With what force?—What route did he take? —What was the consequence?—What sort of people did they find in Chili?—Were the Spaniards completely victorious and successful in Chili?

Page 282.

What recalled them from Chili to Peru?—How did Pizarro find occupation for the numerous adventurers who flocked to Peru?—How did Manco Capac take advantage of their dispersion into different parts of the empire? —How did he contrive to raise troops while he was himself a prisoner?—How did he make his escape?—How many men did he raise?—What city did he attack?—Who defended it? —With how many men?—What other city did the Peruvians invest?—What did the men of these besieged cities suppose concerning each other?—How long was Cuzco invested?—Who commanded there?

Page 283.

How did the Peruvians imitate the Spaniards?—How much of the city did they recover from the Spaniards?—What officer fell in the siege?—What Spaniard appeared in the neighbourhood of Cuzco?—What had he received from Spain?—How did he interpret it? —What was his object in coming to Cuzco? —Who endeavoured to gain his friendship?

Page 284.

Failing of this, how did the inca proceed?—Did he gain his object?—How did Almagro gain possession of the city?—Was his jurisdiction over Cuzco acknowledged?—Whom did Francisco Pizarro send to Cuzco to relieve his brothers?—With how many men?—On what river were they opposed by Almagro?—How did Almagro attempt to gain these men and their leader?—When he did not succeed in this, how did he contrive to surprise Alvarado's camp and take him?—What advice did Orgognez give Almagro?—What prevented his taking his advice?

Page 285.

What did Almagro do?—Was Pizarro acquainted with the late events at Cuzco?—What events did he hear of at one time?—What was his situation?—How did he contrive to gain time?—Who escaped from Almagro?—With how many men?—What proposal did Pizarro then make to Almagro?—Did Almagro accede to it?—When Ferdinand Pizarro was released, how did Francisco proceed?—What city did he design to attack?—How many men did he muster?—Who had command of them?

Page 286.

By what route did they approach Cuzco?—Why did not Almagro cut them off in the defiles of the Andes?—On what plain did the two factions meet?—Who were assembled to witness the battle?—Who led Almagro's army?—Why did not he lead it himself?—What is observed of the respective forces?—Of the battle?—What forces decided the fate of the day?—Who was dangerously wounded?—Who were massacred?—How many men fell?

Page 287.

What befell Almagro?—How did the Indians behave?—What city was pillaged?—By whom? —Was much plunder obtained?—Were the new adventurers of Ferdinand Pizarro's army satisfied with this plunder?—How did he employ them?—For what did the conquerors impeach and try Almagro?—What was his sentence?—Did he attempt to avert his fate?—How?—How did he die?—At what age?—How many children did he leave?

Page 288.

Who first carried the news of the dissensions in Peru to Spain?—Who arrived in Spain afterward?—What did he endeavour to do?—Who was sent out to settle the disputes of the Spaniards in Peru?—What were his instructions?—How was Ferdinand Pizarro treated? —How was Francisco Pizarro proceeding in Peru?—How did he proceed in parcelling out the territory?

Page 289.

To whom did he assign the best portions of the country?—What was the effect of this partiality?—How did Pizarro's officers employ themselves?—Who invaded Chili?—What city did he found?—Who succeeded to the government of Quito?—In whose stead?—What was Gonzalo instructed to attempt?—Why?—With how many soldiers did he set out from Quito?—How many Indians?—What did they suffer?

Page 290.

What river did they reach?—Into what does it empty?—Where is the Maragnon?—Into what does it empty?—What ocean borders on Peru?—What did they construct on their arrival at the banks of the Napo?—Who took command of it?—With how many men?—What scheme did Orellana now form?—What is said of it?—How far had he to sail?—By what rivers did he reach the ocean?—How did he obtain provisions on his way?—To what island did he at last arrive?—Whither did he then go?—What marvellous stories did he tell there?—What was the fabulous region described by him called?—Have reason and observation at last exploded Orellana's fables?—Of what extensive countries was he the first discoverer?—How was Gonzalo Pizarro affected on not finding Orellana at the junction of the Napo and Maragnon?

Page 291.

How far did he advance on the Maragnon in search of him?—How did he hear of Orellana's treachery?—What was the effect of this news on his men?—Did Pizarro consent to return?—How far were they from Quito?—To what extremities of famine were they reduced on their return?—How many Spaniards and Indians perished in this expedition?—How many returned to Quito?—In what condition?—Who composed the discontented party in Peru?—Who headed them?—What was his character?—What did they plot?—Was Pizarro warned of it?—Did he regard the warning?

Page 292.

Who was Almagro's tutor?—What part did he take?—Relate the story of Pizarro's assassination.—After the assassination, how many conspirators joined the nineteen assassins?—Whom did they proclaim governor?—What dwellings were pillaged?

Page 293.

How many men did Almagro muster?—Whom did he appoint to act as general?—Why?—Did all the Spanish officers join Almagro?—Why not?—At what city was the royal standard erected?—While this opposition to Almagro was acquiring vigour, who arrived in Popayan?—To what city did he march?—On learning Pizarro's death, what did he do?—What two commanders acknowledged his jurisdiction?—What talents did Vaca de Castro discover?—How did he gain followers?—For what place did Almagro set out?—Who commanded there?—Whom did he lose on the march?

Page 294.

Did Holguin escape from Almagro?—Whom did he join?—Who entered their camp and took the supreme command?—By what right?—Where did he meet the followers of Almagro?—How far from Cuzco?—What distinguished veteran fought on Vaca de Castro's side?—Which side prevailed?—How many fought on both sides?—How many fell?—What did Vaca de Castro do after the battle?—What was Almagro's fate?

Page 295.

Was the expense of the expeditions to Peru paid by the Spanish crown?—By whom then?—How long were the Spaniards occupied in acquiring their possessions in America?—Was the crown entitled to claim much from the conquerors?—Why not?—What was reserved for the crown?—What was the great object of the conquerors?—Had they any thing like well-regulated government?—What evil in particular required a remedy?—Were the emperor Charles V. and his ministers anxious to prevent the extinction of the Indian race?—Who was at Madrid then?

Page 296.

What representations did he make to the emperor?—What treatise did he compose?—How was Charles affected?—Were his views confined merely to the relief of the Indians?—How did he regard the conquerors of Peru?—What did he prepare?—What provisions of his code of laws were approved?—What regulations were disapproved?

Page 297.

Who remonstrated against these regulations?—What did they say?—Did Charles persist?—Whom did he send to Mexico?—In what capacity?—To Peru?—With what title?—How was the entry of Sandoval into Mexico viewed?—Did the inhabitants submit to the new laws?—Why?—Did Mendoza and Sandoval agree to remonstrate against the new laws?—Did Charles relax the rigour of the laws?

Page 298.

Were the laws as well received in Peru?—Why not?—What did the colonists say concerning the new laws?—For what were they ready?—How were they diverted from their design?—What had now become necessary?

Page 299.

What was the character of the viceroy?—How did he proceed on landing at Tumbez?—How was he received?—What did he declare on entering Lima?—How did he behave there?—How did he treat the persons of rank in Lima?—How Vaca de Castro?—To whom did the colonists look for relief?—What was his character?—What considerations prompted him to rebel?—What restrained him?—What induced him to repair to Cuzco?

Page 300.

How was he received?—To what office did the people elect him?—What did they empower him to do?—What measures did he take under the sanction of this nomination?—Who resorted to his standard?—Who deserted from the viceroy to him?—What had happened at Lima?—Who had quarrelled with the viceroy?—Which prevailed?—What did they do with the viceroy?—What did the judges then do?—With what intention?—Who corresponded with Pizarro?—What adviser had Pizarro?—What did he wish Pizarro to aim at?—What did Pizarro demand?

Page 301.

When the judges hesitated to comply with this command, what did Carvajal do?—What did the court of audience do next morning?—Was Pizarro's government firmly and quietly settled?—Relate the circumstances of Nugnez Vela's embarkation, sailing for Spain, and return to Tumbez.—What did he do on landing at Tumbez?—Who joined him?—Who put the lieutenant-governor of Charcas to death, and declared for the viceroy?—Against whom did Pizarro march?—Whither did Vela retreat?—

Who pursued him?—Whither did he fly from Quito?—Who now pursued him?—To what place did Pizarro return?

Page 302.

Whither did he send Carvajal?—How many men did the viceroy raise in Popayan?—By whose assistance?—Whither did he march?—When did he and Pizarro meet?—What was the result of the battle?—Who fell?—What city did Pizarro enter in triumph?—Who defeated Centeno?—Where did Centeno conceal himself?—What was now the extent of Pizarro's command?—Where did he place a garrison?—Where is Nombre de Dios?—How did Pizarro's followers behave?—What was the substance of Carvajal's letter to Pizarro?

Page 303.

Who seconded these exhortations?—What did he attempt to demonstrate?—To what did Pizarro confine his views?—For what did he send a person to Spain?—How was Charles V. occupied during these troubles in Peru?—To whom did he leave the care of providing a remedy for them?—What were the chief obstacles to the employment of force in quelling the rebels in Peru?

Page 304.

What were the different routes for arriving at Peru?—Were they practicable at that time for an army?—What remained for the ministers to do?—Whom did the ministers choose for an envoy to Peru?—What was his character?—What did the emperor do?—Did Gasca accept the appointment?—What did he refuse?—What title did he accept?—What instances of self-denial did he exhibit?—What sort of authority did he require to be invested with?

Page 305.

Enumerate some of the powers which he demanded for himself?—Who refused them?—Who granted them?—In what style did he set out for the purpose of quelling a rebellion?—Who received him at Nombre de Dios?—How?—Why?—Who received him at Panama?—How?—What did he declare in both places?—Who were gained over to his interest?—What exasperated Pizarro?—What did he resolve to do?—For what purpose did he send a deputation to Spain?—What did these persons require of Gasca?

Page 306.

What instructions did they carry to Hinojosa?—What circumstances pushed Pizarro to these wild measures?—To what did he trust for continuance in power?—Was he aware of the disaffection spreading among his followers?—What did Hinojosa and his officers do?—What did the deputies?—What news did Pizarro hear?—For what did he prepare?—For what did he order Gasca to be tried?—Who acted as judge and condemned him?—What was the object and effect of this proceeding?—Had Pizarro the power of executing the sentence at this time?—Why not?—How many men did he raise?—From what places did Gasca raise troops?—When did he detach a squadron of his fleet to the coast of Peru?—Did they land?—How did they do more effectual service?—What was the effect of the offers of pardon?

Page 307.

Who emerged from his cave, and took Cuzco with a few men?—What was the number of soldiers there?—What did most of them do?—Whom did Pizarro set out to oppose?—What happened on the march?—How many soldiers had he on arriving in sight of Huarina?—Where is Huarina?—Where is the lake of Titiaca?—What was the character of Pizarro's remaining troops?—When did he attack Centeno?—What was Centeno's force?—What was the result of the battle?—What counterbalanced this victory?—Who took possession of Lima?—Who landed at Tumbez?—With how many men?—What territory was now in Pizarro's possession?—What was in Gasca's?—Which way did Gasca march?—How did he behave?—Where did he stop?—For what purpose?

Page 308.

How many men had Pizarro?—Did he listen to Gasca's offers of pardon?—Who advised him to do so?—Towards what city did Gasca march?—With how many men?—Why did not Pizarro advance to meet him?—How near did Gasca approach to Cuzco?—When Pizarro had marched out to meet him, who chose the ground?—What was there unusual in the appearance of Pizarro's army?—Of Gasca's?—Who deserted Pizarro when both armies were ready to engage?—What was the effect of this defection?—What did Pizarro and Carvajal do?—How soon was their army dispersed?—What did Pizarro say to his officers?—What answer did they make?—What did he do?—What befell Carvajal?—How did Gasca use his victory?—When was Pizarro beheaded?—How did he die?—How did Carvajal die?

Page 309.

What befell Cepeda?—Were the adventurers to Peru hired soldiers?—What did each of them expect to do for himself?—Were the troops raised at a great expense?—Did the chiefs make expensive presents to their officers?—What did Gonzalo Pizarro expend in raising a thousand soldiers?—What did Gasca expend in raising his army?—What did Cepeda receive?—For what?—What did Hinojosa receive?—For what?—What was the effect of this wealth on the soldiers?

Page 310.

What was the character of the conquerors of Peru?—What was their leading passion?—Give examples of their rapacity.—Of their treachery and inconstancy.—What was the effect of Pizarro's death?—What two objects now occupied the president's attention?—How was the *former* of these accomplished?

Page 311.

What was the amount of *repartimientos* to be distributed in consequence of Pizarro's death?—Did Gasca reserve any of it for himself?—Whither did he retire to make the distribution?—With whom?—How did he avoid the effects of his impartiality in the distribution?—What was the effect of publishing the decree of partition?—Of what was Gasca accused?—How was this mutinous spirit checked?—How did Gasca labour to sooth the malecontents?—How did he endeavour to strengthen the hands of his successors?—What improvements did he make?—To whom did he commit the government of Peru?—When did he sail for Spain?—How much of the public money did he carry with him?

Page 312.

How was he received in Spain?—Give a summary account of his services.—How did the emperor receive him?—To what office was he promoted?—How did he pass the remainder of his days?—Did tranquillity continue long in Peru after Gasca's departure?—What desolated the country for several years?—What were the ultimate effects of these commotions?—To what state was Peru finally brought?—Where is Peru?—How is it bounded?—What are its chief cities?—Ports?—Mountains?—Does it now belong to Spain?

## BOOK VII.

### Page 313.

How did Mexico and Peru differ from the other parts of the New World?—How did they compare with Europe?—Were the people of these countries acquainted with the useful metals?—What animals had the Mexicans reared?—What had the Peruvians tamed?—For what were the lamas useful?—What are considered very important steps in the progress of civilization?

### Page 314.

What effect had the ignorance of these on the Mexicans and Peruvians?—Which empire was first subjected to the Spanish crown?—Were Cortes and his followers well qualified to examine the government and policy of Mexico?—Why not?—How was the memory of past events preserved?—Why did the early missionaries destroy these records?—What was the effect of this piece of fanaticism?—Can tradition be depended upon for a history of past events?—On what writers must we depend for the particulars of the Mexican history?

### Page 315.

Was the Mexican empire of long duration?—How was their country originally peopled?—When did certain tribes from the north and north-west enter New Spain?—When did the Mexicans take possession of the plain of Mexico?—What town did they found fifty years afterward?—How were they for a long time governed?—How afterward?—Who was their ninth monarch?—According to *this account*, what was the age of the Mexican nation?—Of the monarchy?

### Page 316.

Was the right of private property understood in Mexico?—Was the distinction between real and personal estate established?—Did any part of the citizens hold land so as to transmit it to their heirs?—What was the second mode of tenure?—To what classes of citizens did these modes of tenure appertain?—How was land divided among the great body of the people?—What other striking circumstance distinguishes Mexico from other nations in America?

### Page 317.

Which were the principal cities?—Did Cortes and his followers exaggerate the importance of these cities?—How many inhabitants had the city of Mexico?—What is the next-mentioned symptom of improvement?—Does it exist among savages?—Did it exist to any considerable extent in Mexico?—What is the next circumstance that merits attention?—Were the savage tribes of America *distinguished* by this characteristic?

### Page 318

Did it exist in Mexico?—Who were the *Mayeques*?—Describe their situation.—How were the freemen treated?—How were the nobles divided?—Were their titles and lands hereditary?—What mark of distinction between the nobles and the people existed?—What marks of homage did the nobles pay the king?—What is observed of the Mexican tongue?—Have the Spaniards described the Mexican government and laws accurately?—What inconsistency appears in their accounts?

### Page 319.

From what has it arisen?—What was Montezuma's object?—How did he pursue it?—How was Cortes benefited by these proceedings of Montezuma?—Where can we discover the original form and genius of the Mexican policy?—Who composed the most respectable order of the state?—Were they all of equal rank?—How many inhabitants were there in the territories of each of the first thirty nobles?—How many inferior nobles were there?—What nobles levied taxes from their vassals?—Did they all pay military service and tribute to the emperor?—What policy is found in this view of the Mexican state?—What are the three distinguishing features of the feudal system?—Did the system operate here as in Europe?—Who possessed the real and effective power in Mexico?—What constitutional restraints had the nobles imposed on the emperor?—How was the crown disposed of?—Who at first were electors?—Who afterward?—Where did the choice generally fall?

### Page 320.

What was the character of the Mexican princes?—At what particular appearances in Montezuma's court were the Spaniards surprised?—How was justice administered in the different parts of the empire?—How was the government supported?—How were the taxes paid?—Where was the produce of the taxes collected?—What use was made of them?—How did people of inferior condition and without property pay their taxes?—What evidence of civilization is found in the Mexican police and public works?

### Page 321.

What improvements of polished life existed in the city of Mexico?—What is considered as the most decisive proof of Mexican refinement?—Give examples.—Are the Spanish accounts of these manufactures probably exaggerated?—Are they contradicted by the existing remains of Mexican art?

### Page 322.

In what view are these rude pictures important and interesting?—For what were the first essays of this art probably first used?—What is this sort of record called?—Where do we find traces of it?—For what did the Indian chiefs use it?—Are the Mexican pictures superior to these Indian records?—What could the Mexicans represent in their pictures?—Who has published the best series of them?—What does the first part contain?—The second?—The third?—Who has published another specimen?

### Page 323.

What do these pictures represent?—Do they address the eye or the understanding?—What may they be considered?—Are they very defective records?—To what might the Mexicans have eventually arrived?—By what steps?—Were they approaching towards writing?—How did they indicate a town?—How did they distinguish one town from another?—Did they sometimes indicate a particular town by the emblem without the house?—How did they represent a king who had made conquests?—In what notation did they attempt to exhibit ideas without any corporeal form?—How di they represent a unit?—How small numbers?—How large numbers?—To what amount?—What prevented a further improvement?—Are their records any thing more than picture-writing?—How did the Mexicans divide their year?—How did they make out the complete year?—What did they call these five days?

Page 324.

How did they employ them?—Were the Mexicans a warlike people?—What was usually their object in war?—How were their captives treated?—How was the emperor's funeral celebrated?—Were the Mexicans a hardy, laborious people?—To what was their weakness attributed?

Page 325.

Did Montezuma rule over the whole of what is now called Mexico?—Who possessed the provinces towards the north and west?—What other provinces were independent of the emperor?—Was there much intercourse between the different parts of the empire?—What proofs of this are given?

Page 326.

Had the Mexicans any money?—Is this a strong proof of barbarism?—Was money an early invention in the Old World?—How was commercial intercourse carried on in Mexico?—What sort of nuts had acquired a standard value like that of money?—What is said of the Mexican cities?—How is Tlascala described?—What sort of a structure was the great temple of Mexico?

Page 327.

Did the other temples resemble this?—Do the Spaniards describe the emperor's house and those of the nobility as being magnificent?—What reason is there to doubt their statements?—From this enumeration of facts, what is evident?—What is no less manifest?

Page 328.

Are the Spanish accounts of the Mexican government and policy to be considered substantially true?—If Cortes had made false statements to the emperor, would his enemies have contradicted them?—What institution of the Mexicans is mentioned which had no parallel in Europe at that time?

Page 329.

In what respect were the Mexicans represented as more barbarous than they really were?—What was the character of the Mexican religion?—What were the ornaments of their temples?—What means were employed to appease the wrath of their gods?—What sacrifices were deemed most acceptable?—What was the effect of this religion on the feelings and character of the people?—How long had Peru subsisted as an empire before the conquest?—Under how many monarchs?

Page 330.

What were the quipos?—For what were they used?—Were they still more imperfect records than the Mexican pictures?—How were most of them lost?—Who attempted to throw light on the Peruvian history by means of the quipos?—Did he succeed?—Is much credit due to the traditional stories of the early Peruvian monarchs?

Page 331.

Is there any satisfactory statement concerning the real origin of Manco Capac and Mama Ocollo?—Who did they pretend to be?—How far did Manco's successors extend their dominion?—On what was the whole system of policy in Peru founded?—How were the children of the sun regarded?—Was it a part of the people's religion to reverence the royal family?—What consequences resulted from these ideas?—What was the badge of an executive officer of the emperor?

Page 332.

How were all crimes punished in Peru?—Why?—Did these severe laws render crimes rare?—What were the principal objects of worship among the Peruvians?—Is this sort of superstition milder than the worship of imaginary divinities?—Where have we examples of the two kinds?—What were offered to the sun?—Did the incas offer human sacrifices?—What was the national character of the Peruvians compared with that of the Mexicans?

Page 333.

Was the mixture of religion in the Peruvian system of policy favourable to the character of both kings and people?—Were rebellious subjects and tyrannical rulers equally rare?—For what did the incas conquer?—How were prisoners treated?—How were the lands divided in Peru?—How was the product of the first share employed?—The second?—The third?—How often was the land divided?—How was it cultivated?—What was the effect of this arrangement on the character of the people?

Page 334.

Was the distinction of ranks established in Peru?—Who were the *Yanaconas?*—Were they numerous?—Who were the next class?—Who were the *Orejones?*—Who were the head of all?—To what was this form of society favourable?—Were the arts more advanced in Peru than in Mexico?—What is observed of agriculture in Peru?—How did the Peruvians provide for times of scarcity?—Is Peru well watered?—How did the Peruvians water their fields?

Page 335.

Did they use the plough?—How did they turn up the earth?—How were the houses built on the coast?—In the mountainous regions?—Do any of their buildings remain?—What is observed of their temples and palaces?—What was the extent of the temple of Pachacamac?—Describe it.—What was the greatest work of the incas?

Page 336.

What was the extent of these roads?—Describe their construction.—Did the Spaniards keep this work in repair?—In what respect did the Peruvian policy resemble the Roman?—Were the roads of the incas superior to any work of public utility then existing in Europe?—Describe the rope bridges of the Peruvians.

Page 337.

What advances had the Peruvians made in navigation?—How did the Peruvians obtain gold?—How did they obtain silver?—How did they supply the want of bellows?—What is said of their vessels and trinkets?—What were the *guacas?*—What articles were found in them?—Did they use copper?

Page 338.

What was the only city, properly so called, of ancient Peru?—Are cities necessary to the progress of refinement in arts and manners?

Was the separation of professions so complete in Peru as in Mexico?—What was the only separate order of artists?—What other consequence followed from the want of cities in Peru?—Explain the connexion between commerce and agriculture.—What was the difference between Mexico and Peru with respect to commerce?—What was the most fatal defect in the Peruvian character?

Page 339.

How did they differ from the other Americans in this respect?—Does the same pacific character still appear in the native Peruvians?—What cruel custom existed in Peru?—What was their reason for it?—How many were sacrificed on the death of Huana Capac?—In what particular were the Peruvians more barbarous than the most rude tribes?—Were Peru and Mexico the only possessions of Spain in the New World?—When were the others conquered?—By whom?—What provinces of New Spain were never subject to the dominion of the Mexicans?

Page 340.

What is said of their soil and productions?—What circumstance is favourable to the increase of their population?—What happened in the provinces of Cinaloa and Sonora in 1765?—To whom did the Spanish inhabitants apply for aid?—Why was he at first unable to give it?—How did he raise money for the war?—How long did it last?—How did it terminate?—What discoveries were made during the war?—What was discovered at Cineguilla?

Page 341.

Who discovered California?—When?—Where is it situated?—What religious order acquired dominion over it?—Why did they represent it as barren and unwholesome?—On the expulsion of the Jesuits from the Spanish dominions, who was sent to California?—What discoveries did he make?—What provinces are east of Mexico?—What is their extent?—What do they produce in abundance?—After conquering Jamaica, what was the first object of the English?

Page 342.

Where did they make their first attempt?—Where did they afterward establish their principal station?—How did the Spaniards endeavour to stop this encroachment on their territories?—Have they been compelled to consent to it?—What method did they devise for rendering it of little consequence?—Where are Costa Rica and Veragua?—What is said of them?—Where is Chili?—Who attempted its conquest?—Did Almagro succeed?—What was the fate of Valdivia?—Who saved the remnant of his army?—What part of Chili was conquered by the Spaniards?—What part is possessed by the Indians?—What is the extent of Chili?—What is observed of its soil and climate?

Page 343.

What is said of its animals?—Its mines?—Was it neglected by the Spaniards?—Through what ports was its commerce long carried on with Spain?—Has a direct intercourse been since opened?—What are now the chief ports of Chili?—Is it a Spanish province at the present time?—What provinces are east of Chili?—What mountains separate them from Chili?—On what viceroyalty were they formerly dependent?—What is their extent?—How is this region divided?—What country is north of Rio de la Plata?

Page 344.

Where are Tucuman and Buenos Ayres?—What is the chief settlement?—What is the most remarkable feature of the province of Tucuman?—By what European animals have these plains been filled?—What article of commerce do they furnish?—What sort of trade was carried on through the Rio de la Plata and Brazil with Peru?—Where is Terra Firma?—What is it now called?—Where is New Granada?—What lies east of Veragua?

Page 345.

What are its harbours?—Which is on the east side?—What were they called?—Was another communication to the Pacific opened afterward?—Where are Carthagena and St. Martha?—Who conquered these provinces?—When?—What does the country produce?—What is the chief port?—What enriched this place?—What Spaniard first visited Santa Martha?—Why was Venezuela so called?—Upon whom did Charles V. bestow the province of Venezuela?—For what?

Page 346.

On what condition?—To whom did they commit the execution of their plan?—How did they proceed?—What was the consequence?—To whom did the province revert?—What were the other Spanish provinces on the north coast of South America?—Where are they situated?—Who conquered New Granada?—When?—What rendered its conquest difficult?—What renders the climate of New Granada temperate?—How is gold obtained there?—Who are employed in finding it?—Why are the negroes unfit for mining?

Page 347.

What facts are mentioned illustrating the wealth of New Granada?—To what country does New Granada now belong?—Is it now a Spanish province?

## BOOK VIII.

To what objects does the historian now direct our attention?—What was the first consequence of the establishment of the Spaniards in America?—What was the first cause of depopulation?—Where was it first experienced?—What was there besides war to cause the depopulation of these countries?—How were many of the natives destroyed in Mexico?—In Peru?

Page 348.

What was more destructive than war to the natives of Mexico and Peru?—What was the chief object of the conquerors of these countries?—For this, what did they neglect?—Where were the mines situated?—Who were employed to work them?—From whence were they brought?—What was the consequence?—What disease increased the evil?—What false charge is brought against the Spaniards?—Is such a design necessary to account for the depopulation of Spanish America?

Page 349.

Did the Spanish government try to prevent the destruction of lives among the Indians?—Why could it not be prevented by the government?—To whom should the desolation of the New World be attributed?—To what other cause is the depopulation of Spanish America unjustly attributed?—What reasons are opposed to this?

Page 350.

Whom did the Indians consider as their natural guardians and protectors?—Are many of the Indians still left in Mexico and Peru?—In what other provinces are they numerous?—How many were there in New Spain in Robertson's time?—What nations were most easily civilized?—Were the Spaniards successful in civilizing the most savage tribes?—What was the condition of the government of Spain when Spanish America was settled?—What peculiarity distinguishes the Spanish from other European colonies?

Page 351.

What was the fundamental maxim of the Spanish colonial policy?—What was their great charter?—Was the power of the Spanish crown over the colonies absolute?—How was Spanish America at first divided?—How far did the jurisdiction of the first division extend?—The second?—What inconveniences attended this arrangement?—Where was a third viceroyalty established?—How far did its jurisdiction extend?—What power did the viceroys possess?—What pomp of state did they exhibit?

Page 352.

In whom was the administration of justice in Spanish America vested?—What is the characteristic of the most despotic governments?—How were the Spanish viceroys restrained from intermeddling with the administration of justice?—On whom did the government devolve in case of the viceroy's death?

Page 353.

What was vested in the council of the Indies?—What laws originate in this council?—What offices are conferred by it?—Who were accountable to it?—What has been the object of the Spanish monarchs?—Where did the council meet?—For what was the Casa de la Contratacion instituted?—Where and when?—What commerce was at first confined to Seville?—On what river is Seville?—What are the powers of the house of trade?—What was the first object of the Spanish monarchs?

Page 354.

Why did they dread the intrusion of strangers?—What two kinds of colonies existed in ancient times?—Give examples of each.—Which kind speedily became independent?—What did the Spanish monarchs do in America?—How did they secure the dependence of the colonies on the parent state?—What were the colonies principally employed about?—Whence were they supplied with manufactured articles and a part of their provisions?—What was severely prohibited in the Spanish colonies?—Why?—What did the colonies give in exchange for clothes, furniture, luxuries, &c. imported from Spain?—What vessels monopolized all the commerce between Spain and her colonies?

Page 355.

What restrictions were laid respecting all foreigners?—What was the effect of this policy on the colonies?—Was the progress of the colonies slow?—How many Spaniards were there in all the provinces sixty years after their settlement?—What is necessary in order to promote a rapid increase of people in any new settlement?—Did the Spaniards regard this?—What were the *encomiendas?*—The *mayorasgos?*—How did they descend?—Were the evil effects of these extensive entails severely felt?

Page 356.

What other severe burthen did the Spanish colonies bear?—What articles paid tithes?—Were the colonists liberal towards the churches?—Who were the *chapetones?*—What offices were confined to them?—What was meant by old Christians?—What was the character of the chapetones?—Who were the *creoles?*—What was their character in Robertson's time?

Page 357.

Who conducted the internal commerce of the colonies?—With what were the creoles satisfied?—How did the chapetones and creoles regard each other?—Did the Spanish court encourage this hostility?—Why?—Were the *mestizos* and *mulattoes* numerous?—What were carried on by them?—How were the negroes mostly employed?—Were they favourites of the Spaniards?

Page 358.

Whom did they hate?—Why did the Spaniards encourage this hostility?—Which was the most depressed order of men in the Spanish colonies?—Who freed them from slavery?—When?—What tax was imposed on them?—Of whom was every Indian in Spanish America a vassal?—To whom was three-fourths of the tax paid?—To whom was the country parcelled out when first conquered?—For how long a time?—To whom did the grant then revert?—Was this a constant source of patronage and power to the crown?

Page 359.

Were the Indians compelled to work?—Were they paid?—In what different occupations were they required to work?—What were the *mitas?*—What portion of the people of a district might be called out at once in Peru?—In New Spain, how many could be called out in a district?—How long was each mita kept in a mine in Peru?—At what wages?—How were the Indians in the principal towns governed?—How in their own villages?—Was the office of cazique hereditary?—What was the duty of the officer called protector of the Indians?

Page 360.

How was the tribute raised from the Indians applied?—Have the laws enacted by the council of the Indies proved effectual remedies of the evils they were intended to prevent?—Why have they not?—What wrongs did the Indians suffer in defiance of these laws?—Where did these wrongs most abound?—For what did Ferdinand solicit Alexander VI.?—On what condition did he obtain it?—What did Julius II. confer on the kings of Spain?

Page 361.

What was the consequence of these grants?—In what did all authority in Spanish America centre?—What council must approve of all papal bulls relating to Spanish America?—What was the effect of this limitation of the papal power in Spanish America?—Were there archbishops, bishops, &c. in Spanish America?—How were the inferior clergy divided?—What were the *curas?*—The *doctrineros?*—The *missioneros?*—Are the revenues of the church large?—How is the wealth of the church displayed?—Have the effects of the monasteries been favourable to the country?

Page 362.

Are the ecclesiastics of Spanish America distinguished for their literary attainments?—Whom did the popes permit to assume parochial charges in America?—Did this increase the number of missionaries?—What honours did many of them gain?

Page 363.

What useful history was written by the Jesuit Acosta?—Were many of the missionaries from the European convents to America of a bad character?—What prince opposed the regulars?—Did he succeed?—What edict did Ferdinand VI. issue?

Page 364.

Have the priests been successful in converting the Indians?—What imprudent course did the first missionaries take?—How many Mexicans did one clergyman baptize in a day?—How many Mexicans were baptized in a few years?—What was the effect of this measure?—What is the greatest obstacle to the progress of Christianity among the Indians?

Page 365.

What did the early missionaries say concerning the Indians?—What did the council of Lima decree?—Why had the inquisition no jurisdiction over the Indians?—Were the Spanish colonies too large for Spain to people?

Page 366.

What was the chief object of the Spanish colonists?—Why did they abandon many of their islands?—To what countries did they crowd?—When were the mines of Potosi discovered?—In what other provinces were rich mines discovered?—What amount of gold and silver was annually brought to Spain from her colonies?—Were the mines worked at the expense of the crown?—Who was entitled to own a mine?—On what condition?

Page 367.

Who were the *searchers?*—How did they proceed?—What was the effect of the rage for mining on commerce and agriculture?—What ought to have been the policy of the Spanish government?

Page 368.

Are the countries colonized by Spain in America rich in other productions besides gold and silver?—Where is cochineal produced?—What is it?—Where is the jesuits' bark found?—Indigo?—Cacao?—The best tobacco?—Sugar?—Hides?

Page 369.

Under what sovereigns was Spain an industrious country?—What manufactures did the Spaniards engage in?—What market had they for them?—How many merchant-ships had Spain at the beginning of the sixteenth century?—Was the sudden increase of wealth unfavourable to the Spanish character?—What was its effect on Philip II.?—What nations did he annoy with hostile operations?

Page 370.

What was the effect of his wars?—In what manner did Philip III. weaken his empire?—Describe the state of Spain in the 17th century.—What occasioned a still further drain of population from Spain?—Could Spain supply her colonies with articles of necessary consumption?—From what countries were they smuggled?—Where did the wealth of the New World then go?

Page 371.

To what expedient was Philip III. driven?—Has the possession of her colonies proved a source of wealth to Spain in the same proportion as the colonies of other countries?—Was Spain anxious to monopolize the trade of her colonies?—How have the Dutch, English, French, and Danes monopolized the trade of their East Indian colonies?—What prevented Spain from adopting this policy?

Page 372.

What regulation was adopted?—What was the consequence?—What were the fleets to America called?—Whence did they sail at first?—Whence after 1720?—What countries did the galeons supply?—Where did they touch?—Who went to Santa Martha to trade with them?—Of what kingdoms was Porto Bello the mart?—Describe the fairs of Porto Bello.—To what port did the flota go?—What province did it supply?—Where did the fleets rendezvous?—Whence did they proceed from Havana?—Where is Santa Martha?—Carthagena?—Vera Cruz?—Havana?—Was the whole commerce of Spain with her colonies confined to these two fleets?—What was the effect of this absurd arrangement?—What profits did the monopolists of Seville and Cadiz charge on their goods?

Page 373.

Is it always the interest of a monopolist to check commerce?—Why?—What was the amount of tonnage of the two fleets?—What violent punishments for smuggling were proposed?—Was any remedy applied to the evils under which the commerce of Spain laboured?

Page 374.

What roused the energies of Spain?—What nations engaged in the war, and sent armies, fleets, and treasure to Spain?—What was the consequence?—Who gained quiet possession of the throne of Spain?—What privilege did Philip V. grant to the French merchants?—How did they use it?—To what provinces were they limited?—Did their commodities find their way to all the other provinces?—What would have been the consequence if this had continued?—Was it prohibited, and the French merchants again excluded from all Spanish America?—What grants did Philip V. make to Great Britain?

Page 375.

Where were British factories established?—What did their agents learn?—How did the English merchants profit by this?—How did they abuse the grant concerning the ship of 500 tons?—By whom was nearly all the commerce of South America engrossed?—How did this affect the galeons?—How did Spain attempt to check this illicit commerce?—What led to a war with England?—What was the consequence?—What did the smuggling of the English teach the Spaniards?

Page 376.

What inconveniences attended the use of the *galeons* and *flota* for supplying the Spanish colonies?—How did Spain remedy these inconveniences?—What was the effect of this arrangement?—When were the galeons laid aside?—How was the commerce with Peru and Chili then carried on?—What course did the single ships take?—Was this favourable to Peru and Chili?—What ports declined in consequence of it?—To what port did all the register ships return?—How is chocolate made?

Page 377.

Is it an article of much commercial importance?—Where is the cacao raised?—What nation engrossed much of the trade in it?—Did they supply Spain with it?—How did Philip V. remedy this?—Who have profited by this institution?—Where were the register ships of this company obliged to deliver their home cargo?

Page 378.

Who exposed the defects of the Spanish colonial system?—What was the effect of their writings?—How did Charles III. open a regular communication between Spain and the colonies?—What places did the packet-boats visit?—What cargo were they allowed to carry?—What did Charles III. do in 1765?

Page 379.

What were the effects of this measure?—How much did it increase the trade of Cuba?—Did its benefits extend to Spain?—What was its effect on the sugar trade?—What regulation existed with respect to the intercourse of the colonies with each other?—Was this good policy?

Page 380.

What were its effects?—How was this grievance redressed?—By whom?—What reforms did Don Joseph Galvez effect?—What inconveniences resulted from the great extent of the three Spanish viceroyalties?—Where did Galvez establish a fourth?—What did it include?—What two advantages resulted from this?

Page 381.

Who was the fourth viceroy?—What part of the former territories of Peru were under his jurisdiction?—What change was made in New Spain?—Who was intrusted with the new government?—What was the object of the Bourbons in Spain?—How did they attempt to effect this?

Page 382.

Did the Spanish people learn the defects of their own commercial policy?—What did their writers notice?—What has been the effect of the rigid commercial regulations of Spain?—What conduct of the revenue officers is noticed?—To what extent was the king defrauded?

Page 383.

Where is Manilla?—Which way from Acapulco?—What ocean lies between them?—When did Philip II. establish a colony at Manilla?—With whom did this colony commence an intercourse?—With what country did this colony afterward open a trade?—To what port?—To what port was it afterward removed?—What amount of money did the ships take out to Manilla?—What did they take back to Acapulco?—How was Peru allowed to participate in the traffic?—Were the Peruvians afterward excluded from it?—Describe the effects of this trade.

Page 384.

Is this trade inconsistent with the usual policy of Spain?—What was the first kind of taxes paid by the Spanish colonies to the government of Spain?—What was meant by *right of signiory*?—What by *duty of vassalage*?—What does the second branch of taxes comprehend?—The thi[illegible]?—What was meant by *bull of cruzado*?

Page 385.

What was the amount of annual revenue of Spain raised in America?—What domestic sources of revenue on exports, &c. are to be added to this?—Was the government of the Spanish colonies expensive?—How did the viceroys augment it?—What was the salary of the viceroy of Peru?

Page 386.

Of Mexico?—To what were they raised?—How did the viceroys add to their income?—What amount did a viceroy sometimes receive in presents on *name-day*?—What officer administered his government without corruption?—What is observed of him?

## BOOK IX.

Page 389.

Whose dominions in America were next in extent to those of Spain?—What was the effect of Columbus's discoveries on the English?—Under what king was a voyage to America first proposed?—Were the English qualified to undertake it?—Why not?—What was then their commercial character?

Page 390.

When did the English first trade with Spain and Portugal?—When did they enter the Mediterranean?—To whom did Henry VII. commit the command of their first voyage of discovery?—With what powers?—When?—When did Cabot embark?—With how many ships and barks?—What country did they expect to reach?—What island was their first discovery?—What did they bring away?—What part of the coast did he pass?—Did he return without landing on the continent?—What advantages did England gain by this voyage?

Page 391.

What circumstances prevented Henry VII. from prosecuting his scheme?—What service did Cabot enter?—What laws unfriendly to commerce existed in England?—What prevented Henry VIII. from prosecuting discoveries in America?

Page 392.

What prevented Mary?—How long was the scheme neglected?—Who now employed Cabot?—What places did he visit?—With what places in the east was a trade opened by English merchants?—What was the favourite project of the nation?—What attempts were made in it?—With what success?—What fishery became an object of attention in the reign of Edward VI.?—What did Cabot propose?

Page 393.

What company was formed?—For what purpose?—Who was made governor of it?—What did he fit out?—Who took the command of the fleet?—What befell Willoughby?—Who escaped the storm, and arrived at Archangel?—Where is Archangel?—How does one sail from England thither?—Relate Chancelour's adventures in Russia.—What did he receive from the czar?—Who was queen when he returned to England?—To whom did she write?—What did she empower Chancelour to do?—To whom did she grant the exclusive right of trade?—Whither did they push their discoveries?

Page 394.

By what other channel did they attempt to

open a communication with the east?—How far did their factors go?—Where is Chorassan?—What part of Africa did the English visit?—What did they trade in?—With what countries did the English open a trade in the reigns of Henry VIII., Edward VI., and Mary? —Who succeeded Mary?—Did she encourage commerce?—The navy?

Page 395.

With what sovereign did she cultivate commercial relations?—What company did she encourage?—What empire did their agents visit?—What did they effect?—What scheme did the earl of Warwick set on foot?—Who took command of the expedition?—What coast did he explore?—What did Sir Francis Drake undertake?—What coast did he explore?—What did he expect to find there?—Was he the first Englishman who sailed round the world?

Page 396.

Had the English hitherto attempted to settle a colony?—What circumstances directed their attention to the formation of colonies?—Who was conductor of the first English colony to America?—Under whose auspices?—What were the terms of his charter?

Page 397.

Who joined Gilbert?—What was the fate of his expeditions?—Of himself?—What island did he take possession of?—For whom?—Did this failure discourage Raleigh?—When did he procure a patent?—Whom did he send out? —What course did they take?—In what part of the country did they make researches?

Page 398.

What island did they take?—Where is it?—With whom did they trade?—What accounts did they give on their return?—What did Elizabeth call the country?—Whom did Raleigh next send out?—With how many ships?—Whither did he go?—Where did he make excursions?—Where did he establish a colony? —Was it a suitable place?—How many men were there in the colony?—Under whose command?—Who was Hariot?—What did he effect?—What was the object of the colonists? —How did the Indians deceive them?—How were they punished?—What did the colony now suffer?

Page 399.

Who relieved them, and took them home to England?—What sort of account did Hariot give of the country?—What fashion did Lane and his people learn of the Indians?—Who adopted it in England?—What has been the consequence?—What happened a few days after Drake's departure?—Who came with three ships, and left another colony at Roanoke?—What was its fate?

Page 400.

What person did Raleigh send out next year?—With how many ships?—For what purpose did White return?—What prevented his success?—What was the fate of the colony?—What diverted Raleigh's attention from Virginia?—To whom did he assign the country and his patent?—Did they settle the country?—When did Queen Elizabeth die?—Were there any English colonies in America then?—How long was this after Cabot's discovery of North America?—Was Elizabeth favourable to colonization?—Why not?

Page 401.

Who succeeded her?—What was now the state of things?—Who was Gosnold?—What places did he discover and name?—How long was his voyage?—What were its effects?—Where is Elizabeth Island?—Nantucket?—Martha's Vineyard?—Cape Cod?

Page 402.

Who sent out a small vessel?—For what purpose?—What account did their messengers bring back?—Who was Richard Hakluyt?—What did he publish?—What were the effects of his efforts?—How did James I. divide the country?—For what reason?—What grant did he make to Gates, Summers, and Hakluyt?—To whom did he give the south colony?

Page 403.

What sort of government did he establish for the colony?—What privileges with respect to duties and trade did he grant the colonists? —What articles of this charter were inconsistent with freedom?—What articles were contrary to the usual colonial policy of all nations?—Which were the two original parent colonies of North America?

Page 404.

Who sailed for Virginia, December 19th?—With how many vessels and men?—What persons of distinction were with him?—What land did he first discover?—What bay did he enter?—What river?—How far?—What town did the colonists found?—What is said of it? —What troubles ensued?

Page 405.

What act of injustice was done?—Who annoyed the colony?—What other circumstance distressed them?—Who was chosen their leader?—What measures did he take?—What was their effect?—What befell him?—Whither was he carried?—What was his sentence?—By whom was it pronounced?

Page 406.

Who saved his life?—How?—What did she afterward do?—How many colonists did Smith find on his return to Jamestown?—What unlucky incident now happened?—What was its effect?—What remedy did Smith propose?—How was it executed?—What discoveries did he make?—How far did he sail in his boat?

Page 407.

What is said of his account and map of the country?—On what did the colony depend for subsistence?—What changes did King James make in the government of the colony?—What was the consequence?—Who was made governor of Virginia?—What was his character? —Who was sent out from England?—With what offices?—What befell them?—Who arrived at Jamestown?

Page 408.

What was now the state of affairs in the colony?—What had disabled Smith?—Whither did he go?—What ensued?—What did the colony suffer from the Indians?—To what extremities were they reduced by famine?—What loss of lives ensued?—What were the circumstances of Gates and Summers's shipwreck on Bermudas?—How did they proceed?—Where did they land May 23d?—What did they there find?

Page 409.

For what place did they set sail?—What prevented their voyage to Newfoundland?—Did they return with Lord Delaware?—How did Lord Delaware proceed on his arrival at Jamestown?—What were the effects of his administration?—What caused his return to England?—Who succeeded him?—Who superseded Mr. Percy?—What sort of law did he introduce?

Page 410.

How did he exercise his power?—What new privileges were granted in the new charter of 1612?—What territories were added to Virginia?—How was the expense defrayed?—Was the lottery afterward abolished?—By whose interference?—What was the effect of martial law in Dale's hands?—With whom did he make a treaty?—To whom was Pocahuntas married?—Whither did they go?

Page 411.

Where did she die?—Who are descended from her?—Was Rolfe's example generally followed?—What had been the state of landed property in Virginia?—What was the effect of this?—How did Dale remedy it?—What ensued?—What did the Virginians now begin to cultivate?—Was it profitable?—To what extent was it cultivated?

Page 412.

What evil effect resulted from this?—What was now the state of the colony?—What circumstance attached the colonists more firmly to the country?—What incident furnished them with a new kind of workmen?—Who called the first general assembly that ever was held in Virginia?—When?—How many corporations were represented in it?—What powers did they assume?—What made it acceptable to the people?—What was issued by the company, July 24th?—Where was the supreme legislative power in Virginia vested?

Page 413.

How were questions determined?—By whom could laws be negatived?—By whom were they ratified?—How were the members of the colony after this time considered?—What was the effect of this change?—With whom was a trade in tobacco opened?—To what did this lead?—What did the parent state require?—What did the colony claim?—To what rivers did the settlements extend?—What conspiracy was now formed?

Page 414.

Who was the Indian leader?—What was his character?—What tribes united?—What day was fixed for the massacre?—How did the Indians proceed?—How many English were cut off in one hour?—What saved Jamestown and the adjacent settlements?—Where did the colonists assemble?—What now occupied their thoughts?

Page 415.

How did they execute their purposes?—What was the effect of this war on the Indians?—On the colony?—What disturbed the general courts of the company?—What were discussed in the general courts?—How did James I. regard these proceedings?—What did his ministers attempt?—Did they succeed?

Page 416.

What did James now design?—What pretexts had he for dissolving the company?—What sort of commission did he issue?—What did he order?—What sort of report did the commissioners make to the king?—What intention did he signify, 8th October?—What was declared, to quiet the minds of the colonists?—What did the king require to be surrendered?

Page 417.

Did the company submit to these orders?—What was done in general court, October 20th?—What did James then direct?—Whom did he send to Virginia?—For what purpose?—How was the lawsuit decided?—What does Stith say concerning this measure?

Page 418.

How much had been expended on the Virginia colony?—What were the annual receipts from it?—How many of the colonists survived?—Who resolved to encourage the colony?—To whom did James commit the government of the colony?—What prevented his making a new set of regulations?—Who succeeded James I.?—What did he declare?—Whom did he appoint governor?—What did he intend?—How was Virginia governed during most of Charles's reign?—What proclamation was issued?—What was the effect of this?

Page 419.

How was the value of land diminished?—Who succeeded Yardely?—What was his character?—How did he behave?—How was he treated?—How were the deputies of the colonies treated by Charles?—Whom did he appoint to succeed Harvey?—What was Berkeley's character?—How long was he governor?—What were the effects of his administration?—For what was the colony indebted to the king?—What directions did he give Berkeley?

Page 420.

What reasons are assigned for Charles's liberal treatment of the Virginia colony?—For what was he solicitous?—What instructions did he give Berkeley for this purpose?—To what number did the colonists increase?—What instances of attachment to the king were given by the Virginia colonists?—What ordinance did the parliament issue?—What measure was taken to enforce obedience?

Page 421.

What colonies did they compel to submit?—Whither did the squadron then go?—Who opposed them?—What terms were gained in consequence of his resistance?—How did Berkeley then behave?—What two laws did the parliament make?—What did they prohibit in England?—How long did the colony remain quiet under Cromwell's governors?—What persons came out from England?—What was the consequence?—What was done after Governor Matthews's decease?—What boast did the Virginians make?—How was the news of the restoration of Charles II. received in Virginia?

Page 422.

How did Charles II. treat the Virginians?—What did the *acts of navigation* provide?—What did a subsequent law provide?—What tax was laid?

Page 423.

How were these statutes regarded in England?—How in Virginia?—Did the colonists remonstrate against them?—Were they successful?—What measures were taken to enforce obedience?—Did the Virginians elude the laws?—With whom did they trade?—What design did some old soldiers of Cromwell form?—Who disconcerted their project?—What was the cause of the reduction in the value of tobacco?—What was its effect?—Who annoyed the remote settlements?—What act of Charles caused discontent?—What was the effect of all these grievances on the colonists?

Page 424.

Who was Nathaniel Bacon?—What was his character?—How did he behave?—To what office was he chosen?—Who refused him a commission?—What proclamation did Berkeley issue?—To what place did Bacon march?—What did he demand?—Was it granted?—What did the council prevail on Berkeley to do?—How did they proceed when Bacon had retired?—Whither did Bacon march on hearing of the proceedings of the council?—Whither did Berkeley flee?—Whither the council?—Who now had supreme power?

Page 425.

How did he endeavour to confirm it?—How did Berkeley proceed?—What town was burnt in the contest?—To whom had Berkeley applied for aid?—What aid did Charles send?—What did Bacon and his party resolve to do?—What event now happened?—What was the consequence?—What is this insurrection called?—How long did it last?—Whom did Berkeley call together?—How did they proceed?

Page 426.

Who succeeded Berkeley?—To what time is the history brought down?—With whom was peace concluded?—In what spirit was the government *administered*?—What oppressive law was enacted?—Did the colony still increase?—What diffused wealth among the colonists?—What was the number of the colonists at the period when the Revolution in England took place in 1688?

## BOOK X.

In what ports of England did James I. establish two trading companies?—For what purpose?—Which was the more flourishing?—What gentlemen belonged to the Plymouth company?—Where was a settlement made in 1607?

Page 427.

Was it continued?—Who went out on a trading voyage?—How did he employ a part of his time?—To whom did he communicate his discoveries?—What did Prince Charles call the country?—What cause now began to operate in favour of emigration?—What was the consequence of the Reformation?—Of what was Calvin an advocate?—What did he exhibit?—Where was it copied?

Page 428.

What prevented the English from adopting it?—Did the English articles of religion conform to Calvin's doctrines?—In what respects did the English church differ from Calvin?—Was the church and the state policy connected in England?—What rites of the Catholic church did the English church retain?—How did Queen Mary treat her Protestant subjects?—What was the effect of her persecution?—Where did those who fled from it take refuge?—When did they return?—With what feelings?—To what mode of worship were they attached?—What did they endeavour to reform?—Who were disposed to co-operate with them?—Who opposed them?—Why?

Page 429.

What act of parliament was passed?—Did the advocates of a further reformation relinquish their design?—What did they do?—What name did they acquire?—Did they acquire influence among the people?—What do you understand by *conformists* and *nonconformists*?—Was toleration understood at this period of history?

Page 430.

How were the puritan clergy treated by the queen?—What new court was established?—Who attempted to check the arbitrary proceedings of the queen?—Did she silence them?—To what oppressive act did she compel them to assent?—What was its effect on the puritans?—How did they retaliate the wrongs they suffered from the queen?—Did the people follow them?—To what form of church government did the more learned and sober puritans incline?—Who was Robert Brown?—What did he teach?

Page 431.

What sort of government does the historian call that of Brown?—What were his followers called?—How were they treated?—How did he end his career?—Did his sect become extinct?—Whither did a body of them fly?—Who was their pastor?—What directed their attention towards America as an asylum?—For what did they apply to the king?

Page 432.

From whom did the Brownists obtain a grant of land?—How many of them sailed from England?—When?—Where did they design to land?—How did their captain deceive them?—What land did they first make?—When?—What did they suffer on the voyage?—Where did they settle?—At what season?—How many died before spring?—Who attacked them?—Were they repulsed?—What consolation had they?—What church government had they?—What system of civil government?—On what did they attempt to found their system of civil government chiefly?

Page 433.

In what did they imitate the primitive Christians?—What was the effect of this?—Was it relinquished?—To what number did they increase in ten years?—What did they obtain in 1630?—How must this colony be considered?—To what was it afterward united?—To whom did James I. grant a new charter in 1620?—With what powers?—What was this society called?—Was it successful in colonization?—What was the situation of the puritans in England?—Whither did they wish to emigrate?—Who formed an association of puritanical gentlemen?

Page 434.

What did they purchase?—When?—Where did they seek and find new copartners?—Did these new proprietors consider the grant which had been obtained from the council of Plymouth a sufficient basis for the government of a colony?—To whom did they apply for full powers of government?—Did they succeed?—To what was this charter similar?—Who named the first governor?—Who had the right of electing his successors?—Who had the executive power?—Who the legislative?—What exemption did they obtain?—What was the object of the charter?—Did Charles see the real motives of the puritans?

Page 435.

What did he expressly provide for?—How many ships and men were sent out to New England?—Who accompanied them as spiritual teachers?—What did they find on their arrival?—Who was Endicott?—Where were he and his followers settled?—What form of policy did the new colony adopt?—What did they elect?—Who seceded from them?

Page 436.

What inconsistency were the puritans now guilty of?—What did Endicott do?—What part of the colonists died in the winter?—Who were now compelled by Laud's persecutions to migrate to New-England?—On what did these new emigrants insist?—Did they gain their point?—Does the historian think that the company had any right to transfer the governm nt of the colony from England to America?

Page 437.

What does he suppose to have been the king's motive for permitting this transfer?—Who were appointed governor and deputy-governor?—How many ships and people sailed from England for New-England?—In what places did they settle?—What disposition appeared in their first general court?—What rights did they take from the freemen?—In whom were they vested?—When did the freemen resume their rights?—What singular law was passed?

Page 438.

What were its effects?—What destroyed many of the Indians?—How was this event regarded by the colonists?—What innovation was introduced in consequence of the great spread and increase of the colony?—What were the pretexts for it?—How must the colony henceforward be considered?

Page 439.

Who was Williams?—What did he raise a controversy about?—How was he punished?—Who now emigrated to New-England?—What was Vane's character?—To what office was he elected?—To what did he direct his attention?—For what purpose were religious meetings held?—Who was Mrs. Hutchinson?—What did she establish?

Page 440.

What did she teach?—Who embraced her opinions?—What was the consequence?—How was Mrs. Hutchinson treated?—Whither did Vane go?—What was the effect of these dissensions?—Where did Williams settle?—What island did his followers buy of the Indians?—What did Williams teach?—What was a fundamental maxim of his community?—What was the form of government?

Page 441.

What caused Mr. Hooker to emigrate from Massachusetts?—How many persons went with him?—When?—What towns did they found?—On which side of Connecticut river are Hartford and Weathersfield?—On which side is Springfield?—In what state are Hartford and Weathersfield?—In what state is Springfield?—Where had the Dutch formed a settlement?—Where had Lord Say and Sele and Lord Brook formed a settlement?—Where is Saybrook?—Did the emigrants from Massachusetts get rid of all these competitors?—Did they become independent of Massachusetts and gain a royal charter?—What provinces are next considered?—What two gentlemen wer the first settlers of these provinces?

Page 442.

Who was Mr. Wheelwright?—Where did he found a town?—What was it called?—What colony claimed jurisdiction over them?—What new danger attended the colonists?—How did the people of Massachusetts acquire their lands?—What warlike tribes surrounded the settlers of Providence and Connecticut?—What did the Pequods ask of the Narragansets?

Page 443.

What prevented their uniting against the common enemy?—What did the Narragansets do?—How did the Pequods proceed?—Where were they repulsed?—What colony first mustered troops?—What hindered the advance of the Massachusetts people?—What troops advanced to attack the Indians?—Where were the Indians posted?—What prevented their being completely surprised and massacred?—What gave the English a great advantage?—Describe the action.—What was its result?—What was done after the arrival of the troops from Massachusetts?—In how long a time were the Pequods extirpated?—What was the character of the English officers in this first New-England war?

Page 444.

What was the true character of the war?—What was its effect on the other tribes?—What was the effect of the persecution in England?—What was done to prevent emigration?—What individuals were prevented from embarking for New-England?—What remark is made on this important event?—How many persons embarked in 1638?—How did Charles resent this contempt of his proclamation?—What prevented Charles from punishing the colonists?—What happened on the meeting of the Long Parliament?

Page 445.

How many persons had gone from England to New-England between 1620 and 1640?—How much money had been expended on the colony?—What beginnings of commerce appeared about the latter part of this period?—Who distinguished the colony with peculiar marks of favour?—What vote did the house of commons pass?—What was its effect?—What return did the colonists make for these favours?—What step did the colonies take towards independence?

Page 446.

What stipulations did the contract contain?—Was this measure censured in England?—Why not?—What act of intolerance and oppression was perpetrated by the general court of Massachusetts?—What other act of usurpation did they commit?—Did the English government censure these proceedings?—Why not?—Did Oliver Cromwell favour the colonies of New-England?

Page 447.

What striking proof of his attachment did he give?—What reasons did he offer in support of his scheme?—Why did the colonists decline to comply with his wishes?

www.ingramcontent.com/pod-product-compliance
Lightning Source LLC
LaVergne TN
LVHW021218110826
845150LV00002B/193
*9781425565008*